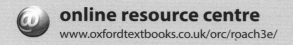
online resource centre

www.oxfordtextbooks.co.uk/orc/roach3e/

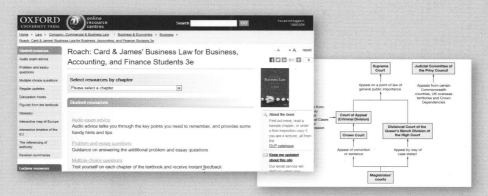

Wherever you see this icon 🌐 remember to visit the accompanying
Online Resource Centre where you will find a wealth of resources which
will help further your study of business law, including:

Self-assessment exercises:

- Problem and essay questions with
  answer guidance
- Multiple choice questions

Revision aids:

- Revision summaries
- Legal updates and news via the
  author's Twitter account

For lecturers:

- Topic PowerPoint presentations

Additional materials:

- Bonus chapters on business ethics,
  corporate governance, credit
  transactions, and sale of goods
- Discussion boxes
- Glossary of the key terms
- Figures from the textbook
- EU timeline—delineating the
  development of the European Union
- Map of Europe—providing useful
  details on each country, and its
  legal standing

> **!** Remember to check the Online Resource Centre regularly for
> updates and news in the area of business law or follow the
> author's business law Twitter feed @UKBusinessLaw

D1342482

To Tom and Sandra Roach

Card & James'
BUSINESS
LAW

3rd Edition

Lee Roach LLB, PhD, FHEA

Senior Lecturer in Law,
School of Law,
University of Portsmouth

OXFORD
UNIVERSITY PRESS

OXFORD

UNIVERSITY PRESS

Great Clarendon Street, Oxford, OX2 6DP,
United Kingdom

Oxford University Press is a department of the University of Oxford.
It furthers the University's objective of excellence in research, scholarship,
and education by publishing worldwide. Oxford is a registered trade mark of
Oxford University Press in the UK and in certain other countries

© Lee Roach 2014

The moral rights of the author have been asserted

First edition 2009
Second edition 2012
Impression: 1

All rights reserved. No part of this publication may be reproduced, stored in
a retrieval system, or transmitted, in any form or by any means, without the
prior permission in writing of Oxford University Press, or as expressly permitted
by law, by licence or under terms agreed with the appropriate reprographics
rights organization. Enquiries concerning reproduction outside the scope of the
above should be sent to the Rights Department, Oxford University Press, at the
address above

You must not circulate this work in any other form
and you must impose this same condition on any acquirer

Public sector information reproduced under Open Government Licence v1.0
(http://www.nationalarchives.gov.uk/doc/open-government-licence/open-government-licence.htm)

Crown Copyright material reproduced with the permission of the
Controller, HMSO (under the terms of the Click Use licence)

Published in the United States of America by Oxford University Press
198 Madison Avenue, New York, NY 10016, United States of America

British Library Cataloguing in Publication Data

Data available

Library of Congress Control Number: 2013956030
ISBN 978–0–19–870412–6

Printed in Great Britain by
Ashford Colour Press Ltd, Gosport, Hampshire

Links to third party websites are provided by Oxford in good faith and
for information only. Oxford disclaims any responsibility for the materials
contained in any third party website referenced in this work.

preface

In the three years between the publication of the first and second editions of *Card & James' Business Law*, there has been a steady stream of legal developments. Since the second edition was published, this stream has turned into a torrent (as is evidenced by the 'new to this edition' page), with 2012–14 being noteworthy for the sheer amount of legal developments, many of which have fundamentally altered certain aspects of the law. Indeed, there are several developments that are still ongoing that will soon render parts of this text out of date (although upcoming changes have been noted where appropriate). Developments in the law are always of interest to a lawyer, but it can be frustrating for an author to witness parts of their book becoming outdated due to legal developments.[1] In an attempt to combat this, this third edition of *Card & James'* has been published a year earlier than originally planned, and future editions will be published every two years.

The law will continue to develop between editions and, accordingly, it is vital that students remain up to date with legal developments. To that end, this text is accompanied by two Twitter accounts that will provide details of legal updates shortly after they occur. General business law updates can be obtained by following **@UKBusinessLaw**, and company law/corporate governance updates can be obtained by following **@UKCompanyLaw**.

Section 6 of the Interpretation Act 1978 provides that, in relation to statutory interpretation, unless otherwise stated, the masculine shall also indicate the feminine. This text follows the same rule and, accordingly, 'he', 'him', and 'his' shall, unless otherwise indicated, also be taken to mean 'she', 'her', and 'hers', respectively.

I offer my thanks to the publishing team at OUP, especially John Carroll, Sarah Stephenson, and Deborah Hey. I would also like to thank the anonymous reviewers for their comments and feedback regarding the second edition of the text. Finally, my thanks go to my family, my friends, and my colleagues for their tolerance, help, and support.

I have attempted to state the law as at March 2014. With the kind indulgence of the publisher, minor amendments have been made to accommodate subsequent changes in the law.

LRR
Portsmouth
January 2014

---

1. For example, and much to the author's frustration, the enactment of the Equality Act 2010 resulted in one chapter of the first edition of *Card & James' Business Law* becoming partially out of date very shortly after the book's publication.

approach of the book

🔗 More details on OSCOLA can be found on the Online Resource Centre where a document entitled 'The Referencing of Authority' provides guidance on when and how to cite authority.

Referencing: Most business, finance, and accounting degrees will use a referencing system called Harvard APA. However, the predominant referencing system in law (and a referencing system your lecturer may require you to use) is called OSCOLA (the Oxford Standard for the Citation of Legal Authorities). Accordingly, to enable you to become comfortable with this referencing system, this textbook references sources in accordance with the 4th edition of OSCOLA. The full OSCOLA document can be found at <http://www.law.ox.ac.uk/publications/oscola.php>.

Footnotes: Whereas Harvard APA cites sources in-text, law textbooks and journal articles use footnotes, and OSCOLA also states that footnotes must be used. Accordingly, in this textbook, authority is cited using footnotes.

new to this edition

Every chapter has been fully updated and revised to provide an up-to-date account of the law. Key revisions in the 3rd edition include:

- Reorganization of the book into a clearer five-part structure.
- Updated coverage of devolved legislative powers.
- Coverage of updates to the Civil Procedure Rules.
- Updated coverage on the enlargement of the EU and progress towards the EU's accession to the European Convention on Human Rights.
- Coverage of the Draft Consumer Rights Bill.
- Coverage of new rules relating to exemptions from an audit.
- Coverage of the new rules relating to the registration of company charges.
- Coverage of changes to the composition and fee systems of employment tribunals and the Employment Appeal Tribunal.
- Coverage of changes to the Transfer of Undertakings (Protection of Employees) Regulations 2006.
- Coverage of the reduction of employment rights of employee shareholders.
- Coverage of new legislation, including:
  - Children and Families Act 2014
  - Crime and Courts Act 2013
  - Defamation Act 2013
  - Enterprise and Regulatory Reform Act 2013
  - European Union Act 2011
  - Growth and Infrastructure Act 2013
  - Protection of Freedoms Act 2012

- Notable case law developments including:
  - *Berg v Blackburn Rovers Football Club & Athletic plc* [2013] (penalty clauses)
  - *Bowen v National Trust* [2011] (occupiers' liability)
  - *Chandler v Cape plc* [2012] (duty of care owed by parent company)
  - *Church v MGN Ltd* [2012] (defamation)
  - *Eweida and Others v United Kingdom* (2013) (religious discrimination)
  - *JGE v Portsmouth Roman Catholic Diocesan Trust* [2012] (vicarious liability)
  - *Kudos Catering (UK) Ltd v Manchester Central Convention Complex Ltd* [2013] (exclusion clauses)
  - *Lord McAlpine of West Green v Bercow* [2013] (defamation)
  - *Macdonald v Costello* [2011] (payment of a *quantum meruit*)
  - *Petrodel Resources Ltd v Prest* [2013] (piercing of the corporate veil)
  - *Pulse Healthcare Ltd v Carewatch Care Services Ltd* [2012] (zero hours contracts)
  - *Rainy Sky SA v Kookmin Bank* [2011] (interpretation of terms)
  - *Rolf v De Guerin* [2011] (unreasonable refusal of mediation)
  - *Sienkiewicz v Grief (UK) Ltd* [2011] (causation in tort)
  - *Simmons v Castle* [2012] (damages)
  - *Stannard (t/a Wyvern Tyres) v Gore* [2012] (the tort of *Rylands v Fletcher*)
  - *USDAW v Ethel Austin Ltd and Others* [2013] (consultation upon redundancy)
  - *VTB Capital plc v Nutritek International Corp* [2013] (corporate personality)
  - *Various Claimants v Institute of the Brothers of Christian Schools* [2012] (vicarious liability)
  - *Vivendi SA v Richards* [2013] (duties of a shadow director)
  - *Yam Seng Pte Ltd v International Trade Corp Ltd* [2013] (implication of term of good faith)

guide to the book

This guide outlines the features that have been devised to make the learning experience easier and more enjoyable for you. This brief overview explains the features and how to make the most of them for effective study of the law.

Features to aid learning

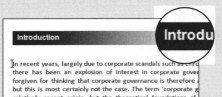

Introductions at the start of each chapter explain why that area of law is particularly relevant and how it will relate to you as a business, accounting, or finance student.

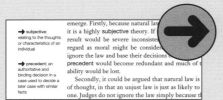

Definition boxes highlight and explain all of the new terms that you will come across within the text. They are also collated on the Online Resource Centre in a searchable glossary.

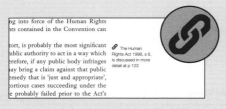

Cross references direct you to other areas of the textbook with page references to highlight fundamental connections across the chapters, thereby aiding your understanding of the overarching themes.

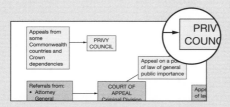

Diagrams summarize the more complex areas of the law to provide a clear and concise visual overview.

FACTS: In 1964, the claimant was crossing the road when th
him over in his car, thereby causing injury to the claimant's left leg and reduci
capacity. The claimant sued the defendant, but, in 1967, before the case r
the claimant was shot in his left leg during an armed robbery. The leg had to b
The defendant argued that his liability only extended up until the time of the
is, between 1964 and 1967). After that time, the original injury no longer exi
the claimant's leg was removed, and so the defendant contended that he a

Key cases integral to an effective understanding of the law are clearly explained and discussed to emphasise their relevance.

---

cathing and undisguised attack levelled at the
House of Lords. At various points, the notion
s described as 'anathema in any country which
at to the life of the nation',⁹⁸ and 'the stuff of
passed the Prevention of Terrorism Act 2005,
ders' that could be levelled at any suspected
rther, these orders will last for a maximum
enewed if the Secretary of State considers it

★ See DM Dwyer,
'Rights Brought
Home?' (2005) 121
LQR 359

Case analysis boxes provides links to articles in which academics discuss and debate the landmark cases in detail. Be sure to follow these links to journal articles for a more detailed discussion of the case.

Eg **The Wills Act 1837, s 9**

Originally, the Wills Act 1837, s 9, stated that in order for a will to be
signature must appear 'at the foot or end' of the will. At first glance, this
relatively straightforward—but closer scrutiny reveals a significant ambigu
word 'end' could mean, among other things:

1. that the signature must appear at the end of the content of the will, but th
   the will can be inserted at a later date; or

Example boxes help to explain the sometimes complex and unfamiliar aspects of the law by contextualising the theory via an everyday example.

⟨⟩ Key points summary

- Currently, the European Union (EU) and European Conven
  are completely independent of each other, with separate courts ar
  Membership of one is not dependent upon being a signatory of the c
  versa.

- The EU currently has twenty-seven member States, whereas forty
  (including the twenty-seven EU member states) have signed up to the EC

Key point summaries at the end of each chapter highlight the essential areas of the law. These also help you to focus your study, not to mention making great revision aids!

Self-test questions

1. Explain the relationship between the EU and the E
   the creation of the EU and the ECHR.

2. Explain the composition and functions of:
   (a) the Council of the European Union;
   (b) the European Council;
   (c) the European Commission;

Self-test questions are provided at the end of each chapter to help you to check your understanding of the chapter and assess your progress.

Further reading

Gillespie, A, *The English Legal System* (OUP, Oxford, 200
*Provides a clear and lucid account of what is the 'English legal system
meaning of the words 'English', 'legal', and 'system'*
Jones, TH, Turnbull, JH, and Williams, JM, 'The Law of Wales and the L
and Wales?' (2005) 23 Stat LR 135
Discusses how statutes that apply only to Wales can be reconciled with the

Further reading references conclude each chapter. Annotated, they point you in the direction of articles, textbooks, reports, and websites which develop the issues discussed in the chapter.

guide to the Online Resource Centre

This book is accompanied by a fully integrated Online Resource Centre which provides a whole host of additional resources to support you in your studies, and advance your understanding of the topics.

General guidance on answering essay and problem questions

The two main types of questions you will encounter in the study of law are essay questions and problem questions. This section of the ORC will provide you with a number of essay questions and problem questions and guidance as to how they should best be answered. This document will discuss what skills these types of questions aim to assess and offer some general hints and tips on how best to approach these questions and what pitfalls should be avoided.

This guidance is meant to accompany the practice questions and model answers found on the ORC. It should be noted that, as regards the model answers, footnotes are used to cite relevant sources. In an exam situation, you would not be expected to cite sources in this way. The footnotes are included in the model answers simply to make you aware of the sources discussed.

Essay questions

Problem and essay questions with answer guidance

Try the further problem and essay questions for each chapter to practice the technique of answering problem questions, then check the author's answer guidance.

Question 1

Who of the following was NOT a proponent of natural law?

- a) Aristotle
- b) Jeremy Bentham
- c) St Augustine
- d) St Thomas Aquinas

Question 2

The term 'common law' has three different meanings. Which of the following is NOT a meaning of the term 'common law'?

- a) The body of law as made by judges through the determination of cases.

Multiple-choice questions

Test yourself with the multiple-choice questions written for each chapter. Feedback for each question and page references to the textbook are provided to direct you back to the content.

BUSINESS LAW

Lee Roach
@UKBusinessLaw

Official Twitter account accompanying the 2nd edition of Card & James' Business Law, published by Oxford University Press. Provides legal updates and commentary
oup.com/uk/orc/bin/978

TWEETS   FOLLOWING   FOLLOWERS

Follow

Regular updates

Keep up to date with the latest news and developments in business law by following the author's own business law Twitter feed @ UKBusinessLaw.

Revision Summary Chapter 1

What is Law?

- Natural law theories concentrate on the relationship between law and morality.
- Legal positivists are not concerned with morality or values that cannot be scientifically evaluated. Validly created laws are laws, irrespective of their content.
- The term 'common law' has three meanings:
  1. a legal system that is based on the system existing in England;
  2. the body of law created by the judges via case law; and
  3. the body of law that operates alongside the system of equity.
- The term 'civil law' has two meanings:
  1. the body of law that regulates the rights and obligations existing between

Revision summaries

Use these summaries of the key points to test yourself when revising the topics, and as useful key points to remember.

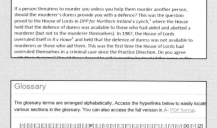

Discussion boxes

Discussion boxes on areas of the law which have incited debate – use these boxes to pause and reflect on the legal provisions.

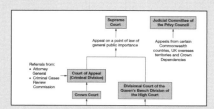

Glossary

Over 600 legal terms from the textbook are collated in this searchable glossary as a complete reference for all the terms you will need to be familiar with.

Diagrams

Selected diagrams used in this book are freely available for download.

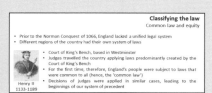

Bonus chapters

Bonus chapters on business ethics, corporate governance, credit transactions, and sale of goods help you gain a more holistic appreciation of law, especially for those studying for CIMA or ACCA.

These chapters are available free of charge to all readers of the book. To access them please follow the instructions below:

1. Go to: www.oxfordtextbooks.co.uk/orc/roach3e/
2. Click on the 'Bonus chapters' link
3. Enter the login details opposite (case sensitive)

Username: Roach3e
Password: businesslaw

For lecturers

The following resources are password-protected and only available for lecturers who have adopted the textbook to assist their teaching. Registering is easy: click on 'Lecturer resources' on the Online Resource Centre and complete a simple registration form which allows you to use your own username and login.

Classifying the law
Common law and equity

- Prior to the Norman Conquest of 1066, England lacked a unified legal system
- Different regions of the country had their own system of laws

- Court of King's Bench, based in Westminster
- Judges travelled the country applying laws predominantly created by the Court of King's Bench
- For the first time, therefore, England's people were subject to laws that were common to all (hence, the 'common law')
- Decisions of judges were applied in similar cases, leading to the beginnings of our system of precedent

Henry II
1133-1189

PowerPoint presentations

Each chapter of the book has an accompanying PowerPoint presentation which can be downloaded and customized for your lectures.

contents in brief

detailed contents

PART V: Employment Law

Visit the **Online Resource Centre** that accompanies this book to access these chapters and other useful materials: <http://www.oxfordtextbooks.co.uk/orc/roach3e>

list of abbreviations

The following is a list of abbreviations used in this text, including the abbreviations of law reports and journals.

AC or App Cas	Appeal Cases
ACAS	Advisory, Conciliation and Arbitration Service
ADR	alternative dispute resolution
AG	Attorney General
AGM	annual general meeting
All ER	All England Law Reports
All ER (Comm)	All England Law Reports (Commercial Cases)
All ER Rep	All England Law Reports Reprint
AML	additional maternity leave
APL	additional paternity leave
art/Art	article (domestic)/Article (supranational)
Atk	Atkyns Law Reports
B & Ald	Barnewell & Adolphus Law Reports
B & CR	Bankruptcy and Companies Winding Up
BCC	British Company Cases
BCLC	Butterworths' Company Law Cases
Beav	Beavan Law Reports
BERR	Department for Business, Enterprise and Regulatory Reform
Bing	Bingham Law Reports
BLR	Building Law Reports
BPMMR 2008	Business Protection from Misleading Marketing Regulations 2008
CA	Court of Appeal
CA 1985	Companies Act 1985
CA 2006	Companies Act 2006
CARICOM	Caribbean Community
CAT	Competition Appeal Tribunal
CC	Competition Commission
CCRC	Criminal Cases Review Commission
CDDA 1986	Company Directors Disqualification Act 1986
CDO	Competition Disqualification Order
CEO	chief executive officer
CFI	Court of First Instance
CFSP	Common Foreign and Security Policy
Ch	Chancery Division of the High Court
ch	chapter
Ch App	Chancery Appeal Law Reports
Ch or Ch D	Chancery Division Law Reports
CIC	interest company
CILEx	Chartered Institute of Legal Executives
CIO	charitable incorporated organization

CJQ	Civil Justice Quarterly
cl	clause
CLJ	Cambridge Law Journal
CML	compulsory maternity leave
CMLR	Common Market Law Reports
CoJ	Court of Justice
Co Law	Company Lawyer
Colum LR	Columbia Law Review
Comm	Commercial Court
Cowp	Cowper Law Reports
Cox CC	Cox Criminal Cases
CPA 1987	Consumer Protection Act 1987
CPC	Community protection cooperation
CPS	Crown Prosecution Service
CPUTR 2008	Consumer Protection from Unfair Trading Regulations 2008
CRTPA 1999	Contracts (Rights of Third Parties) Act 1999
CVA	company voluntary arrangement
DDA 1995	Disability Discrimination Act 1995
DEFRA	Department for Environment, Food and Rural Affairs
DGFT	Director General of the Office of Fair Trading
DPP	Director of Public Prosecutions
DTI	Department of Trade and Industry
EAT	Employment Appeal Tribunal
EC	European Community
ECHR	European Convention on Human Rights
ECJ	European Court of Justice
ECR	European Court Reports
ECSC	European Coal and Steel Community
ECtHR	European Court of Human Rights
EEA	European Economic Area
EEAR 2006	Employment Equality (Age) Regulations 2006
EEC	European Economic Community
EERBR 2003	Employment Equality (Religion or Belief) Regulations 2003
EESOR 2003	Employment Equality (Sexual Orientation) Regulations 2003
EG, or Est Gaz	Estates Gazette
EHRC	Equality and Human Rights Commission
EHRR	European Human Rights Reports
EMLR	Entertainment and Media Law Reports
ENE	early neutral evaluation
EPA 1970	Equal Pay Act 1970
ERA 1996	Employment Rights Act 1996
ET	employment tribunal
EU	European Union
EWC	expected week of childbirth
EWCA Civ	Civil Division of the Court of Appeal (England and Wales)
EWCA Crim	Criminal Division of the Court of Appeal (England and Wales)
EWHC	High Court (England and Wales)

Ex	Court of Exchequer
ex p	*ex parte*
Fam	Family Division of the High Court
FTER 2002	Fixed-Term Employees (Prevention of Less Favourable Treatment) Regulations 2002
Harv LR	Harvard Law Review
HL	Appellate Committee of the House of Lords
HL	Cas House of Lords Cases
HMRC	Her Majesty's Revenue and Customs
HMSO	Her Majesty's Stationery Office
HSE	Health and Safety Executive
HSWA 1974	Health and Safety at Work etc. Act 1974
IA 1986	Insolvency Act 1986
ICR	Industrial Cases Reports
IPCC	Intergovernmental Panel on Climate Change
IRLR	Industrial Relations Law Reports
IT	industrial tribunal
J/JJ	Mr/Mrs Justice(s)
JAC	Judicial Appointments Commission
JHA	Co-operation in Justice and Home Affairs
JP	Justice of the Peace
KB	King's Bench Division of the High Court
LC	Lord Chancellor
LCJ	Lord Chief Justice
LJ/LJJ	Lord/Lady Justice(s)
LLA	liability limitation agreement
Lloyd's Rep	Lloyd's List Law Reports
LLP	limited liability partnership
LLPA 2000	Limited Liability Partnerships Act 2000
LMCLQ	Lloyd's Maritime and Commercial Law Quarterly
LQR	Law Quarterly Review
LR CP	Law Reports: Common Pleas
LR Eq	Law Reports: Equity
LR Ex	Law Reports: Exchequer
LR HL	Law Reports: English and Irish Appeals
LR QB	Law Reports: Queen's Bench
LSB	Legal Services Board
LT	Law Times
MEP	member of the European Parliament
MLR	Modern Law Review
MP	member of Parliament
MR	Master of the Rolls
NI	National Insurance
NIRC	National Industrial Relations Court
NLJ	New Law Journal
NMWA 1998	National Minimum Wage Act 1998
NPC	New Property Cases
OFT	Office of Fair Trading
OLA 1957	Occupiers' Liability Act 1957

OLA 1984	Occupiers' Liability Act 1984
OLC	Office for Legal Complaints
OML	ordinary maternity leave
OPL	ordinary paternity leave
P	Probate (Law Reports)
P & CR	Property, Planning and Compensation Reports
PCP	provision, condition, or practice
p/pp	page(s)
PA 1890	Partnership Act 1890
PC	Judicial Committee of the Privy Council
PJC	Police and Judicial Co-operation in Criminal Matters
PMB	private member's Bill
Pt	Part
PTWR 2000	Part-Time Workers (Prevention of Less Favourable Treatment) Regulations 2000
QB, or QBD	Queen's Bench Division of the High Court or Queen's Bench Law Reports
QC	Queen's Counsel
r/rr	rule(s)
R	Regina (Queen) or Rex (King)
reg	regulation
RESA 2008	Regulatory Enforcement and Sanctions Act 2008
RRA 1976	Race Relations Act 1976
s/ss	section(s)
Sch	Schedule
SDA 1975	Sex Discrimination Act 1975
SE	Societas Europaea
SGA 1979	Sale of Goods Act 1979
SGITA 1973	Supply of Goods (Implied Terms) Act 1973
SI	statutory instrument
SJ or Sol Jo	Solicitors' Journal and Reporter
SMP	Statutory Maternity Pay
Stat LR	Statute Law Review
TLR	Times Law Reports
TUPE 2006	Transfer of Undertakings (Protection of Employment) Regulations 2006
UCPD	Unfair Commercial Practices Directive
UCTA 1977	Unfair Contract Terms Act 1977
UKHL	House of Lords (UK)
UKPC	Judicial Committee of the Privy Council
UTCCR 1999	Unfair Terms in Consumer Contracts Regulations 1999
VAT	value-added tax
WLR	Weekly Law Reports
WTR 1998	Working Time Regulations 1998

PART I

the English legal system

1 What is law?

- Theoretical conceptualizations of law
- Classifying the law
- Defining the 'English legal system'

INTRODUCTION

An ordered society is premised upon the adherence to rules. Rules exist in many forms, whether social rules (for example, hats should not be worn in church), scientific rules (for example, $E = MC^2$), sporting rules (for example, in basketball, players may not run with the ball), or legal rules (for example, it is a crime to steal the property of others). Whilst it could be said that all laws are rules, it is certainly not the case that all rules are laws. So why are some rules elevated to legal status and others not? How are the various legal rules categorized? What is the geographical limit of English law? These issues will be explored in this opening chapter.

The purpose of this chapter is to provide students with a rounded conception of what law is. Whilst much of what is discussed is not of crucial importance in the context of how businesses operate, it will aid the students in developing a more thorough appreciation of the theories that underpin English law, as well as in understanding the various ways in which English law can be classified and the parameters of English law. Much of the terminology used in this discussion is embedded in our legal system and will be of considerable aid in subsequent chapters, when we discuss the law as it applies specifically to businesses.

Theoretical conceptualizations of law

For several millennia, legal philosophers have struggled to find answers to the questions stated above. Given the scope of the arguments involved, a detailed discussion will be beyond the scope of this text. A brief discussion of the principal schools of thought will, however, be of significant aid to any student who is interested in exploring the question of 'what is law'. It may be considered that such theories offer little to a person seeking to understand how the law applies to businesses, but it should not be thought that business law operates in a vacuum. The legal theories that underpin the law apply to all laws, whether they are applicable to natural persons or businesses. Further, an appreciation of the theory behind the law will result in a more rounded understanding of the operation of the law. Oliver Wendell Holmes Jr, a Justice of the US Supreme Court from 1902 to 1932 and one of the most highly regarded jurists ever, stated that:

> If a man goes into law it pays to be a master of it, and to be a master of it means to look straight through all the dramatic incidents and to discern the true basis for prophecy. Therefore, it is well to have an accurate notion of what you mean by law.[1]

Natural law

In terms of chronology, the earliest identifiable theory discussing the issue of what is law concerns the role of 'natural law'. The first major natural law writings can be traced back to the works of Plato (427–347 BCE) and his pupil, Aristotle (384–322 BCE), but the theory gained prominence during the Judaeo-Christian period with the works of St Augustine (354–430 CE) and St Thomas Aquinas (1225–74 CE). Augustine was the Bishop of Hippo and in his 5th-century text *De Civitate Dei* ('The City of God'), he postulated the existence of the *lex aeterna* (eternal law), an unchanging form of law that derived directly from the will of God. The *lex aeterna* was the highest form of law and, in *De Libero Arbitrio* ('On Free Will'), Augustine infamously stated '*lex iniusta non est lex*' ('an unjust law is no law at all'), meaning that any man-made laws that conflicted or failed to uphold the *lex aeterna* were unjust and need not be obeyed. A similar viewpoint was expressed by St Thomas Aquinas when he stated '*lex tyrannica cum non sit secundum rationem non est simpliciter lex sed magis est quadam perversitas legis*' ('a tyrannical law made contrary to reason is not straightforwardly a law, but rather a perversion of true law'). Therefore, for a natural lawyer, when discussing the issue of what is law, the relationship between law and morality is the crucial factor.

In time, the influence of natural law waned as a number of weaknesses began to emerge. First, because natural law places great emphasis on the morality of the law, it is a highly **subjective** theory. If our legal system were to embrace natural law, the result would be severe inconsistency in decisions, because what one judge would regard as moral might be considered immoral by another. If judges were free to base their decisions on their own sense of morality, the doctrine of **precedent** would become redundant and much of the law's consistency and predictability would be lost.

➔ **subjective:** relating to the thoughts or characteristics of an individual

➔ **precedent:** an authoritative and binding decision in a case used to decide a later case with broadly similar facts

Second, it could be argued that natural law is not a particularly realistic school of thought, in that an unjust law is just as likely to be applied by the courts as a just one. Judges do not ignore the law simply because they view it as unjust or immoral.

One should not, however, conclude that natural law has no role to play in the English legal system. Judges may not be free to ignore the law if they consider it immoral (although, as we shall see, they do have ways in which to avoid precedent and considerable discretion in the interpretation of statutes), but there does exist a group of persons who can—namely, juries. As shall be seen in Chapter 2, there are numerous examples of cases in which juries have blatantly and unashamedly delivered a verdict contrary to the law on the basis that an application of the law would

---

1. Oliver Wendell-Holmes Jr, 'The Path of the Law' (1896–97) 10 Harv LR 457, 475.

produce an unjust result. Further, although judges cannot act overtly on the basis of what is considered moral, the system of law known as 'equity' (see 'Common law and equity' at p 12) is concerned with notions of fairness, equality, and justice—notions that lie at the heart of classic natural law theory.

Ultimately, however, natural law theories do not help us to understand what the law is, but rather what the law should aspire to be. A number of legal philosophers became disenchanted with natural law due to its inherent subjectivity, and sought to propound a theory that was more **objective** and which better defined what the law actually was. This resulted in the birth of 'legal positivism'.

➡️ objective: unbiased, impartial, and detached; not affected by personal feelings or opinions

Legal positivism

From a philosophical standpoint, positivism is a school of thought that states that true knowledge can only derive from the perception of our senses—notably, observation. Only that which can be observed and empirically evaluated can be regarded as proven. Accordingly, judgements based on values, morals, or perceptions of good and evil are irrelevant, because they cannot be measured scientifically. From a legal point of view, the fathers of legal positivism were Jeremy Bentham (1748–1832) and John Austin (1790–1859). Bentham objected to the predominant naturalistic legal philosophy of the day and, in a prophetic passage written thirteen years before the events of the French Revolution, Bentham stated 'the natural tendency of such [naturalist] doctrine is to impel a [person]..., by the force of conscience, to rise up in arms against any law whatever that he happens not to like'.[2]

Bentham and Austin's answer was to devise the 'command theory of law'. According to this theory, a law can be viewed as a command issued by an unfettered sovereign that is backed up by the imposition of a sanction. The views of Bentham and Austin have come to be doubted by modern legal positivists who argue that:

- not all laws are in the form of commands;
- the command theory is based upon an unfettered sovereign, but in many modern countries the 'rule of law' is dependent upon the state's powers being limited; and
- only breaches of criminal law are backed with sanctions.

Accordingly, the command theory fell out of favour and more modern positivist theories have emerged, the most prominent of which derived from HLA Hart's 1961 text, *The Concept of Law*.[3] Hart chose to base his definition of law on rules, as opposed to commands, and he argued that rules were of two types. Primary rules set out the basic rights of obligations of citizens (that is, what they should and should not do). Hart recognized, however, that a body of primary rules would be ineffective in itself, in that there would be no mechanism for their interpretation, alteration, and enforcement. Accordingly, there also had to exist secondary rules, which would establish how the primary rules should be administered, enforced, and reformed.

Just as Hart rejected 'commands' in favour of rules, so, in turn, have recent theories rejected 'rules' in favour of 'rights'. Notably, Ronald Dworkin[4] has argued against legal positivism, partly on the ground that it is too preoccupied with rules.

---

2. Jeremy Bentham, *A Fragment on Government* (Basil Blackwell 1967) [19].
3. HLA Hart, *The Concept of Law* (2nd edn, OUP 1997).
4. Ronald Dworkin, *Law's Empire* (Harvard University Press 1986).

Dworkin argued that a legal system is not only made up of rules, but also of rights, principles, and policies, and that very often, these rights, principles, and policies are more important than the rules. As an example, Dworkin cites the case of a man who murders his grandfather in order to claim his inheritance early.[5] According to the strict letter of the law, the murderer would be entitled to the inheritance, but the courts denied his claim, applying the public policy principle that a person should not be allowed to profit from his own crime. Accordingly, policies and principles often determine the operation of the law.

Classifying the law

Criminal law and civil law

Perhaps the most fundamental legal distinction is that between criminal law and civil law. Understanding whether a particular act constitutes a crime or a civil wrong (or both) is fundamental in determining where the case will be tried, what the parties will need to establish, what procedural rules apply, and what the potential outcome may be. Fortunately, distinguishing between civil and criminal acts is usually straightforward, because civil and criminal law cases are tried in different courts, and have different procedures, outcomes, and terminology. Table 1.1 clearly outlines the fundamental differences between criminal and civil law cases.

TABLE 1.1 Distinguishing criminal law and civil law

	Criminal law	Civil law
Purpose of the law	To preserve social order by punishing wrongdoers and deterring others from committing crimes	To compensate a person who has suffered loss or injury due to the acts or omissions of another
Parties in the case	The state (*R—Regina* ('Queen') or *Rex* ('King')) prosecutes the defendant (for example, *R v James*)	The claimant (the person who has suffered loss) initiates a claim against the defendant (the person alleged to have caused the loss) (for example, *Card v James*)
Outcome of the case	If innocent, the defendant is acquitted. If guilty, the defendant is convicted and a sentence (for example, imprisonment, fine, community service) is imposed	The claimant either wins the case and is awarded a remedy, or loses and is not awarded a remedy
Courts involved	First heard in either a magistrates' court or the Crown Court	First heard in either a county court or the High Court (although some civil cases can be heard in a magistrates' court)
Burden/ standard of proof	The prosecution must prove the guilt of the defendant beyond a reasonable doubt	The claimant must prove his case on a balance of probabilities
Examples	Murder; manslaughter; theft; sexual offences; offences involving the misuse of drugs; terrorist offences	Breach of contract; negligence; slander; employment law disputes; cases involving the sale of good

5. The case in question, *Riggs v Palmer* 115 NY 506 (1889), was a US case, but the English case of *R v National Insurance Commissioner, ex p Connor* [1981] QB 758 (DC) has almost identical facts and came to the same conclusion.

Based on Table 1.1, it can be deduced that the most effective way in which to determine if an act is a crime or a civil wrong is not to focus on the act itself, but rather to focus on the consequences of the act. For example, if the legal consequence of an act is the prosecution and punishment of the perpetrator, then the act will constitute a crime. If a person is seeking compensation, the case is likely (although not necessarily) to be a civil one.

It should, however, be noted that the criminal/civil distinction is not mutually exclusive (that is, that an act can result in both criminal and civil liability), as the following example demonstrates.

Eg Crimes and civil wrongs

Joanne leaves her coat in a nightclub cloakroom. Andrew, the cloakroom attendant, searches through Joanne's coat and steals her mobile phone, which is secreted in one of the pockets. In such a case, Andrew would be guilty of the crime of theft. He would also have committed several civil wrongs—namely, the tort of **conversion** and breach of contract (his actions would breach the contract between him and his employer).

➡ conversion: interfering with goods in a manner that is consistent with another's right to possession (see p 427)

The distinction between criminal law and civil law is further blurred by the existence of 'hybrid' offences that combine criminal and civil legal proceedings. For example, the Protection from Harassment Act 1997 provides that it is a criminal offence to act in a manner that causes another person to fear, on at least two occasions, that violence will be used against him.[6] Section 3 goes on to provide a civil remedy for victims of harassment that can result in the payment of damages or the imposition of a restraining order. Although such an order is a civil remedy, its breach will result in the commission of a criminal offence.[7]

Public law and private law

This textbook is concerned primarily with private law topics—but in order to understand what we mean by 'private law', it is important to explain how it differs from public law. At its simplest level, public law concerns laws that regulate the relationship between the state and its citizens (this would include legal persons, as well as natural persons). Examples of public law topics would therefore include criminal law (the state prosecutes and punishes persons who commit crimes), human rights (persons may initiate proceedings against the state if their human rights have been breached), and administrative law, which deals with disputes between persons and government agencies.

Conversely, private law concerns laws that regulate the relationships between persons. In private law cases, the role of the state is limited to providing a forum within which to remedy disputes and the subsequent enforcement of that forum's decision. Examples of private law topics include family law (laws regulating disputes between spouses, children, etc), contract law (laws governing the rights and obligations of contracting parties), and company law (laws governing the rights and responsibilities of directors, shareholders, etc). Table 1.2 illustrates the principal differences between public law and private law.

In recent years, however, the line between public law and private law has become blurred, because the state has become increasingly involved in traditional private law

---

6. Protection from Harassment Act 1997, ss 1 and 4(1).   7. ibid s 3(6).

TABLE 1.2 Distinguishing between public law and private law

	Public law	Private law
Regulates the relationship between	The state and persons (both natural and legal)	Persons (both natural and legal)
Purpose	Focuses on conduct that the state wishes to discourage	Focuses on enforcing the rights and obligations of persons
Case usually initiated by	The state	The person alleging wrongdoing
Role of the state	Undertakes responsibility for detection, prosecution, and (if relevant) punishment.Also provides a forum for dispute resolution and mechanisms to enforce the forum's decisions	Limited to providing a forum for dispute resolution and enforcement of that forum's decision
Examples	Criminal law; human rights breaches; constitutional law; administrative law	Contract law; the law of torts; company law; property law; the law of trusts

disputes. For example, historically, contract law has been a quintessentially private law topic, with little, to no, state involvement. However, as consumer protection has become an increasing priority for governments, the state's role in contract law has grown considerably—notably, through statutory measures, such as the imposition of **implied terms** in consumer contracts. For example, s 14(2) of the Sale of Goods Act 1979 implies a term into sale of goods contracts that goods will be of 'satisfactory quality'.

➡ **implied terms:** terms added to the contract by the law, which usually serve to protect consumers (discussed at p 173)

Common law and civil law

To understand fully the operation of the English legal system and its place within the legal systems of the world, it is necessary to understand the various meanings of the term 'common law'. Matters are complicated, however, by the fact that the phrase has three different meanings. At its broadest level, it refers to those countries around the world that have based their legal system on that of England—namely, the Commonwealth countries (notably, Australia, New Zealand, and Canada) and the USA (at both federal and state level).[8]

Juxtaposed with common law systems are civil law systems. Just as the phrase 'common law' has several different meanings, so too does the term 'civil law'. It has already been noted that it can refer to laws that are not criminal in nature. A second meaning refers to those legal systems that are based largely on Roman law.

The civil law system is undoubtedly the most widespread legal system in the world and is especially dominant in Continental Europe. In fact, the only common law systems in Europe belong to the UK and the Republic of Ireland. Civil law systems are characterized by a codified written body of laws that will attempt to set out the entire law in a certain area (for example, all of the crimes that can be committed may be found in a single Code).[9] Such Codes tend to be less specific and more

---

8. Except the state of Louisiana, which, being a former French and Spanish colony, has a civil law system.
9. It should, however, be noted that common law systems may also have certain areas of the law codified.

abstract than legislation in common law systems. The reason for this is that, in civil law systems, the judiciary and the legislature appear to cooperate more harmoniously than in common law systems. Civil law judges view their role as simply interpreting the various Codes in line with the intention of the legislature and do not seek to create law. Conversely, the role of judges in common law countries tends to go beyond interpretation into law creation, and when common law judges do interpret legislation, it has not always been consistent with the legislature's intentions. As judges in civil law countries cooperate more closely with the legislature, there is no pressing need for a system of binding precedent, although the decisions of 'higher' judges do tend to be followed.

The role of the judiciary when interpreting legislation is discussed in 'Statutory interpretation' at p 53

Table 1.3 sets out the main differences between common law and civil law systems.

TABLE 1.3 Distinguishing between common law and civil law legal systems

	Common law systems	Civil law systems
Origins	Originated during the Norman Conquest in 1066, but it was during the reign of Henry II that the foundations of the modern common law system were established	Originated in Roman law—notably, the *Corpus Juris Civilis ('Body of Civil Law')* created by Emperor Justinian during the period 529–34 Ce
Source of laws	The bulk of the law is usually found in case law (deriving from the courts), but statute (deriving from Parliament) is playing an increasing role	All laws tend to be set out in a number of written documents known as 'Codes'
Role of the judiciary	Judges in common law systems both create and interpret law	To interpret the law in line with the legislature's intentions and not to create law
Role of precedent	Common law systems have a well-established system of binding precedent	Civil law systems tend not to have a doctrine of binding precedent, but, in practice, the decisions of 'higher' judges are usually followed
Authority of academic writings	Rarely cited and of little weight, although there is evidence that this is changing	Not a source of law, but accorded significant weight—often greater weight than previous judicial decisions
Recruitment of judiciary	Normally recruited from the ranks of legal practitioners	Civil law systems tend to have a career judiciary, who are trained to be judges straight from university

Common law and statute law

The second meaning of the term 'common law' refers to the body of law dures created by the judiciary and applied via the doctrine of precedent statute law concerns laws created by Parliament in the form of legislat century has witnessed a substantial increase in the amount of legislati Parliament, due largely to the increasing role played by the state in This legislation needs to be interpreted and applied, and Parliament re judiciary to interpret legislation in a manner that is consistent with the Parliament.

Common law and equity

The third meaning of the term 'common law' relates to the system of law that emerged following the Norman Conquest in 1066. Prior to this, England lacked a unified legal system; instead, different regions of the country had their own system of laws, based on a mixture of custom and the incorporation of laws imposed by invading forces. For example, Viking invaders who had settled in northern England during the ninth century caused the northern counties of England to have a system of laws that was based heavily on Danish law.

The Norman Conquest brought about a legal revolution that paved the way for the system in place today. Although William the Conqueror is often credited with commencing the process that led to the establishment of the common law, it was actually a century later, during the reign of Henry II, that we find the genesis of our modern legal system. When Henry took the throne in 1154, there were only eighteen judges in England.[10] Five of those judges remained in Westminster and established the Court of King's Bench. The remaining judges travelled the country[11]—but applying what laws? It is generally believed that the most appropriate customs of the counties of England were selected to form the basis of a unified, national body of laws. In reality, the travelling judges applied laws that were created predominantly by the King's Bench and many local customs were replaced by a body of laws deriving from Westminster that were soon being applied throughout the country. For the first time in England's history, its people were subject to a body of laws that were common to all (hence the 'common law'). The decisions of the judges were recorded and applied in similar cases throughout the country, thereby creating the beginnings of our system of precedent. However, as the system grew, a number of problems began to emerge.

→ **damages:** an award of money designed to compensate loss

- Initially, the only remedy at common law was an award of **damages**—but damages are not always an appropriate remedy. For example, an award of damages would be of little use to a landowner who is plagued by ramblers who unlawfully enter his land. He would prefer a court order prohibiting the ramblers from entering his land, but such a remedy was not available under the common law.

→ **writ:** a written command from the court requiring either the performance of, or the abstention from, an act

- To commence an action in the common law courts, the claimant needed to obtain a **writ**, with different writs existing based upon the different types of case. The claimant would need to demonstrate that his case fell within the parameters of an existing writ. If it did not, he would be unable to proceed with his claim. Further, during the reign of Henry III, the passing of the Provisions of Oxford meant that new forms of writ could not be created, thereby hampering the expansion of the common law. Even if the claimant could obtain a writ, the slightest defect in the writ's wording would defeat the claim.

- Whilst the broad-brush approach of the common law made the law certain, it also made it inflexible and, in cases involving unusual or unforeseeable circumstances, following previous decisions could often lead to an unjust result.

The result was that many persons with legitimate grievances could not obtain justice. The response was to permit persons to petition the King directly for a remedy.

---

10. Today, there are over 9,100 judges (including Tribunal judges), and just over 23,000 magistrates.
11. This system, whereby a core group of judges remained in London and the remaining judges travelled the country, was to continue for over 800 years. It was finally abolished in 1971.

As the number of such petitions grew, they were delegated to the Lord Chancellor and a specific court created to hear them—the Court of Chancery. The important point to note is that these cases were not based upon obtaining writs, or following strict procedures and precedents; rather, these cases were decided based upon fairness, morality, and natural justice. For this reason, this supplementary system of law became known as 'equity'.

In time, equity developed new remedies (notably, **injunctions** and **specific performance**) for situations in which damages were inappropriate. However, unlike at common law, winning a case did not guarantee a remedy. As equity is based upon fairness, the claimant would only be granted a remedy if he had acted fairly. The famous equitable maxims were developed, chief among them being 'He who comes to Equity must come with clean hands', meaning that a claimant seeking an equitable remedy must himself behave equitably. To ensure that the principles of equity could not be defeated by the rigidity of the common law, the courts held that where equity and the common law conflicted, equity would prevail.[12]

➡ **injunction:** a court order restraining an act, or requiring an act to be performed

➡ **specific performance:** a court order requiring performance of an act, normally to fulfil a contract

Although equity was never intended to be a rival system to the common law, in time, it came to be regarded as such. As the common law was based upon consistency and predictability, and equity was based upon morality and flexibility, it was inevitable that conflict would arise. Further, the administrative and procedural rigidity that plagued the common law courts soon came to affect the Court of Chancery too, and equity cases soon gained a reputation for being lengthy and expensive. The problems largely derived from having the two systems of law being based in separate courts. Therefore, the Supreme Court of Judicature Acts of 1873 and 1875 merged the courts to create the modern court structure that we have today. The administration of the common law and equity was fused, but the systems of law themselves continued to exist separately. Any court could apply common law or equitable principles and, if a claimant had a cause of action in common law and equity, he could bring his case in a single action, as opposed to two.

Equity as a supplementary system of law remains of crucial importance. In fact, equity's continuing importance is demonstrated in that the rule providing that equity prevails over the common law has now been **codified**.[13] As time progressed, new equitable remedies were developed, but it is still a fundamental principle that they are discretionary and the courts will not hesitate in denying a remedy to a person with a valid claim/defence if his conduct does not meet with equitable principles, as the following case demonstrates.

➡ **codified:** the placing of law into statute

🔑 *D&C Builders Ltd v Rees* [1965] 3 All ER 837 (CA)

FACTS: Rees owed £482 to D&C Builders Ltd. Knowing that the company was in financial difficulty, Rees's wife offered it £300 in settlement of the debt, adding that if it refused, it would receive nothing. The company accepted, but later sued for the remaining £182. Rees's wife attempted to rely on the doctrine of promissory estoppel.

HELD: The Court of Appeal did not permit Rees to rely on the equitable doctrine of promissory estoppel, because his wife's conduct had been improper (that is, she had not come to equity with clean hands).

🔗 Promissory estoppel is discussed at p 157

---

12. *Earl of Oxford's Case* (1615) 1 Rep Ch 1.   13. Senior Courts Act 1981, s 49(1).

Table 1.4 clarifies the main differences between equity and the common law.

TABLE 1.4 Distinguishing the common law from equity

	Common law	Equity
Origin	Derived from the body of precedent created by circuit judges following the Norman Conquest in 1066	Derived from decisions of monarchs and, later, of Lords Chancellor sitting in the Court of Chancery
Status	A complete system of law	A supplementary system of law created to remedy the harshness of the common law, but which could not exist without the common law
Availability of a remedy	The claimant acquires a remedy as of right upon winning the case	Remedies are granted at the discretion of the court, and subject to maxims, including: • 'He who comes into Equity must come with clean hands' • 'Delay defeats equity' • 'Equity regards that as done which ought to be done'
Examples of remedies	Damages	Injunctions; specific performance; estoppel; rectification; rescission

Defining the 'English legal system'

Laws have geographical limitations. A person resident in England would not usually be subject to the laws of France whilst he is present in England—he is subject to the laws of what judges, academics, and practitioners universally refer to as the 'English legal system'. Those not familiar with the historical, political, and cultural factors that led to the creation of the United Kingdom could be forgiven for thinking that the laws of the English legal system apply only to those within England, but the truth is somewhat more complex, leading to the term 'English legal system' being somewhat inaccurate. Having discussed what law is and how it may be classified, it is equally important to understand to whom the laws of the English legal system apply.

Geographically, the United Kingdom[14] consists of four countries (Wales,[15] England, Scotland,[16] and Northern Ireland). From a legal point of view, however, the United Kingdom is anything but united, with three separate legal systems existing within the UK, namely:

1. the legal system of England and Wales;
2. Scots law; and
3. the legal system of Northern Ireland.

---

14. Or, to give it its full title, the 'United Kingdom of Great Britain and Northern Ireland'.
15. There is debate as to whether Wales is a country or is still regarded as a principality (that is, a state ruled by a prince). Current weight of opinion would appear to lean towards it being a country.
16. It is worth noting that a referendum is due to take place in Scotland on the 18 September 2014, which will determine whether or not Scotland remains part of the United Kingdom.

England and Wales

Although England and Wales may constitute two separate countries, they essentially constitute one legal system. The Law in Wales Acts of 1535 and 1542 provided that the laws of England would also apply fully in Wales, thereby legally annexing Wales to England. Therefore, when we refer to the 'English legal system', we are actually discussing the laws that apply usually to both England and Wales (so, technically, we should refer to the legal system of England and Wales).

Recent developments have complicated matters. Although the move towards **devolution** in Wales has not been as pronounced as that in Scotland and Northern Ireland, significant steps have still been taken. The Government of Wales Act 1998 created the National Assembly for Wales, but did not grant it legislative competence. This was redressed in part by the Government of Wales Act 2006, which allowed the Assembly to pass **delegated legislation** in relation to specified devolved areas.[17] Potentially more significant is the fact that the 2006 Act provided that, upon the passing of a referendum in Wales, the Assembly would gain the ability to pass **primary legislation**, thereby bringing the Welsh Assembly onto a footing similar to that of the Scottish Parliament. In March 2011, such a referendum was passed, thereby allowing the Welsh Assembly to create primary legislation in the form of Acts of the National Assembly for Wales.[18] To date, the Assembly has passed twelve Acts, some of which have introduced extremely significant reforms (e.g. the Human Transplantation (Wales) Act 2013, which aims to increase the number of donor organs available by introducing an opt-out system).

Despite the considerable law-making powers of the National Assembly, in relation to areas that are not devolved (for example, defence and immigration), the UK Parliament will still make laws for Wales and so the phrase 'English legal system' will continue to refer to the system in England and Wales,[19] and it will be some years before the general legal systems of the two countries differ.

→ **devolution:** the transfer of power to a lower level (for example, from central government to local government)

→ **delegated legislation:** legislation made by those authorized by Parliament to create legislation (see 'Types of legislation' at p 46)

→ **primary legislation:** legislation passed by Parliament in the form of an Act (see 'Acts of Parliament' at p 46)

Scotland

Unlike Wales, which gained its own Assembly relatively recently, Scotland can trace the existence of its own Parliament back to the mid-thirteenth century. Prior to the Acts of Union 1707, England and Scotland had their own Parliaments creating and administering their own laws. The 1707 Acts joined the kingdoms of Scotland and England to form the 'United Kingdom of Great Britain'. The Acts also dissolved the Parliaments of England and Scotland, and replaced them with the UK Parliament, based in Westminster. Crucially, whilst the 1707 Acts dissolved the Scottish Parliament, they preserved Scots law, with the result that, to this day, Scotland has its own legal system and set of laws. Following a referendum in Scotland in 1997, a new Scottish Parliament was created (under the Scotland Act 1998), which has the power to create legislation in certain devolved areas. Note however, that the Parliament at Westminster remains the supreme legislature in Scotland, and can pass laws that apply to Scotland with the same force of law as in England and Wales. However,

---

17. Government of Wales Act 2006, Pt 3. The list of devolved matters can be found in Sch 5.

18. ibid s 107. The ability to pass primary legislation is limited to twenty devolved areas—see Sch 7.

19. Compare Timothy Jones, John Turnbull, and Jane Williams, 'The Law of Wales and the Law of England and Wales?' (2005) 23 Stat LR 135, 145, arguing that it may be time to recognize formally the 'law of Wales'.

following the move towards devolution, the convention is that an Act of Parliament will only apply to Scotland (and Northern Ireland, discussed next) if it expressly states as much.

Northern Ireland

In 1801, the United Kingdom of Great Britain became the 'United Kingdom of Great Britain and Ireland' when the Acts of Union 1800 were passed. As with Scotland, Ireland retained its own legal system and laws, but dissatisfaction soon grew with the union and there were increasing calls for Irish independence. Following numerous failures to achieve Home Rule, the Government of Ireland Act 1920 was eventually passed, which split Ireland into two distinct regions: six predominantly Protestant counties became Northern Ireland, and the remaining twenty-six predominantly Catholic counties became Southern Ireland. Whilst Northern Ireland became a fully functioning region with its own Parliament and executive, in Southern Ireland, no government was ever established and its Parliament never passed any laws, with the result that whilst Southern Ireland may have existed *de jure*, it never really existed *de facto*.

➡ **Home Rule:** the granting of independence or self-government to a constituent part of a state or country

➡ *de jure:* 'in law'

➡ *de facto:* 'in fact'

The passing of the Anglo-Irish Treaty 1921 created an independent Irish republic, although the Parliament of Northern Ireland exercised its treaty right to opt out of the republic and remain part of the UK, thereby creating the current United Kingdom of Great Britain and Northern Ireland.

The Government of Ireland Act 1920 was eventually repealed by the Northern Ireland Act 1998, which provided for a process of devolution in Northern Ireland similar to that in Scotland. The Northern Ireland Assembly, like the Welsh Assembly and the Scottish Parliament, has the power to legislate in certain devolved areas. As in Scotland, convention states that an Act of Parliament will only apply to Northern Ireland if the Act expressly states so.

Chapter conclusion

A sound understanding of what is law is fundamental to understanding the legal topics that will be discussed throughout this text. It may be thought that much that was discussed in this chapter is of limited relevance to those seeking to understand the laws that regulate businesses, but this is not the case. For example, in an era dominated by increasing globalization and the prevalence of multinational corporations, many businesses will operate in, or import or export goods to, countries all around the world. In such cases, understanding the geographical limitations of a country's legal system is crucial.

Having discussed in this chapter what law is, how it is classified, and its geographical extent, the next chapter moves on to discuss the practical issue of how the law is administered, by discussing those persons and bodies that are responsible for applying, interpreting, and debating what the law is, and how their decisions are put into practice.

Key points summary

- Natural law theories concentrate on the relationship between law and morality.

- Legal positivists are not concerned with morality or values that cannot be scientifically evaluated. Validly created laws are laws, irrespective of their content.

- The term 'common law' has three meanings:
  1. a legal system that is based on the system existing in England;
  2. the body of law created by the judges via case law; and
  3. the body of law that operates alongside the system of equity.

- The term 'civil law' has two meanings:
  1. the body of law that regulates the rights and obligations existing between persons;
  2. a system of law based upon Roman law and characterized by a codified set of laws.

- Equity is a supplementary system of law designed to mitigate against the potential harshness of the common law.

- The phrase 'English legal system' refers to the legal system of England and Wales.

- Wales, Scotland, and Northern Ireland all have their own bodies with various legislative powers, but the Parliament at Westminster retains legislative supremacy.

Self-test questions

1. Define the following:
   (a) positivism;
   (b) common law;
   (c) civil law;
   (d) equity;
   (e) public law;
   (f) private law;
   (g) devolution.

2. Explain and critically evaluate natural law theory. Does legal positivism provide a more attractive definition of what law is and, if so, why?

3. Parliament passes the (fictional) Punishment of Terrorists Act 2014. Section 10 of the Act allows suspected members of Al Qaeda to be detained, questioned, and executed without charge or trial. How would a natural lawyer and a legal positivist view the Act?

4. What are the three domestic legal systems operating in the UK?

Further reading

Andrew Gillespie, *The English Legal System* (4th edn, OUP 2013) ch 1
Provides a clear and lucid account of what is the 'English legal system', focusing on the meaning of the words 'English', 'legal', and 'system'

Timothy Jones, John Turnbull, and Jane Williams, 'The Law of Wales and the Law of England and Wales?' (2005) 23 Stat LR 135
Discusses how statutes that apply only to Wales can be reconciled with the notion that England and Wales comprise a unified legal system and contends that the time may be right to recognize the 'law of Wales'

Ian Mcleod, *Legal Theory* (6th edn, Palgrave 2012) chs 3 and 4
Provides a clear and well-structured discussion regarding the basics of natural law and legal positivism

Gary Slapper and David Kelly, *The English Legal System* (12th edn, Routledge 2011) ch 1
Contains a particularly clear discussion of how the law is classified

Websites

<http://assemblywales.org>
The website of the National Assembly for Wales

<http://www.niassembly.gov.uk>
The website of the Northern Ireland Assembly

<http://www.scottish.parliament.uk>
The website of the Scottish Parliament

 Remember to visit the **Online Resource Centre** at **<http://www. oxfordtextbooks.co.uk/orc/roach3e>** to access the following resources for Chapter 1, 'What is law?': more **practice questions** and answers; a **glossary** of key terms; **multiple-choice questions**; and **revision summaries**. Updates to the law can be found on Twitter by following **@UKBusinessLaw**.

2 The administration of the law

- The courts
- Tribunals
- Alternative dispute resolution
- The judiciary, the law officers, and the legal profession

INTRODUCTION

Laws can only be as effective as the mechanisms and personnel put in place to administer them. In the previous chapter, it was noted that Hart argued that an effective legal system needs primary rules and secondary rules but, in reality, it could be argued that much more is required. Courts are required to adjudicate on disputes that arise, but what should the jurisdiction and function of these courts be? Where should these courts be located? The decisions of lower courts may need to be re-examined, thereby requiring that a robust appeals process exists. A system of legal representation must be established. It can therefore be seen that the administration of the law is an extremely complex issue. This chapter will aim to clarify how, and by whom, the law is administered.

The courts

An understanding of the functions, jurisdiction, and composition of the various courts is vital in order to appreciate the operation of the English legal system (especially in relation to the doctrine of precedent, which is discussed in the next chapter). Some courts hear only civil cases; others hear only criminal cases; some will hear both. Certain courts are largely courts of **first instance**, whereas others will only hear **appeals**. It is crucial to understand which types of case the various courts will hear and how a case can proceed through the court hierarchy. Figures 2.1 (which focuses on criminal cases) and 2.2 (which focuses on civil cases) help to explain the court hierarchy and the appeal routes through the courts.

➡ **first instance:** cases tried for the first time are said to be heard 'at first instance'

➡ **appeals:** the process whereby a losing party, seeking to reverse or modify a first-instance decision, may apply to have the case reheard on certain grounds

Magistrates' courts

The 240 magistrates' courts throughout England and Wales are predominantly courts of first instance, and have both a criminal and civil jurisdiction.

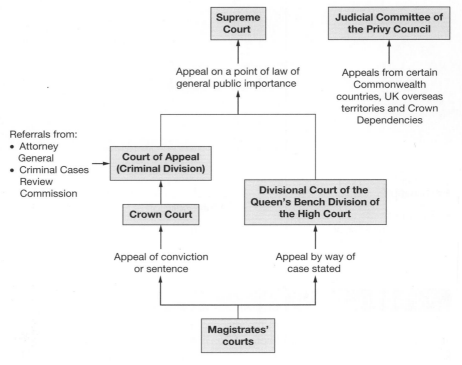

FIGURE 2.1 The structure of the criminal courts

Criminal jurisdiction

The vast majority of cases heard by magistrates are criminal cases—in fact, over 95 per cent of all criminal cases commence in magistrates' courts and, in 2012, 1.66 million defendants were proceeded against.[1] All criminal cases can be divided into one of three types:

1. **Summary offences** Ninety-eight per cent of all criminal cases relate to summary offences that must be tried in a magistrates' court. Summary offences tend to be the more minor criminal offences and this is reflected in the magistrates' limited sentencing powers. Currently, the magistrates' sentencing powers are limited to six months for one offence, and twelve months for two or more offences to be served consecutively (providing those offences are either way offences).[2] The maximum fine that can be imposed in a magistrates' court is a Level 5 fine (currently £5,000),[3] although in the case of certain offences committed by businesses, the maximum fine is £20,000.

2. **Offences triable on indictment only** These offences are more serious and cannot be heard in a magistrates' court. In such cases, the case may still commence in a magistrates' court, but the magistrates will have no option but to send the case to the Crown Court for trial.

3. **Offences triable either way** These are offences that are triable either summarily in a magistrates' court or on indictment in the Crown Court. A strict

➡ **indictment:** a formal document setting out charges against the defendant

---

1. Ministry of Justice, *Court Statistics Quarterly: June to March 2013* (2013) 31.

2. The Criminal Justice Act 2003, ss 154–155, increased the sentencing powers of magistrates to 51 weeks for one offence and 65 weeks for two or more offences, to be served consecutively. These sections are yet to come into force and have been suspended indefinitely.   3. Criminal Justice Act 1982, s 37.

An exception to this occurs where the appeal raises important points of principle or practice, or there is some compelling reason why it should be heard by the Court of Appeal: in such cases, decisions of a county court can be appealed directly to the Civil Division of the Court of Appeal.[34] Permission to appeal is normally required.[35]

The Crown Court

The Courts Act 1971 introduced the Crown Court system to replace the inefficient system of assize courts and quarter sessions. It is often stated that there are a number of crown courts around the country, but this is not strictly true. There is only one Crown Court—but its business may be conducted anywhere in England and Wales.[36] Currently, the Crown Court sits in 77 locations across England and Wales, and, in 2012, around 133,371 cases were sent to the Crown Court.[37] The Crown Court is a court of almost exclusive criminal jurisdiction, holding trials for all indictable offences[38] and those either way offences that have been sent to the Crown Court for trial. The Crown Court will also deal with either way cases that have been determined in a magistrates' court, but then sent for sentence to the Crown Court. The Crown Court also hears appeals from those summarily convicted in a magistrates' court. These appeals involve a complete rehearing of the case, and, if the appeal is dismissed, the judge may impose any sentence that the magistrates could have imposed, in addition to a harsher sentence than the one originally imposed.

Cases in the Crown Court normally take place in front of a single judge and a jury of twelve—but a jury is not used where the defendant pleads guilty, in appeal cases, or where the case has been sent to the Crown Court for sentence. In addition, the Criminal Justice Act 2003 allows the prosecution to apply to the court for the trial to be conducted without a jury in certain fraud cases,[39] and in cases where there is a danger of jury tampering.[40]

The judge involved will depend upon the class of the crime, as illustrated in Table 2.1.[41]

A decision of the Crown Court heard on appeal from a magistrates' court can be appealed to the High Court. Appeals against conviction/sentence of the Crown Court are made to the Criminal Division of the Court of Appeal. The right of appeal is not automatic: leave to appeal is required and this can either be obtained from the trial judge or from the Court of Appeal itself.[42] Clearly, it would be odd for a trial judge to declare a case fit for appeal as soon as it has been decided. Accordingly, the Court of Appeal has stated that leave to appeal should only be granted by the trial judge in exceptional circumstances.[43]

---

34. Civil Procedure Rules, r 52.14(1).

35. ibid r 52.3(1) and (2).

36. Senior Courts Act 1981, s 78(1).

37. Statistics derived from the website of the Ministry of Justice.

38. Senior Courts Act 1981, s 46.   39. Criminal Justice Act 2003, s 43 (not yet in force).

40. ibid s 44. The 2010 case of *R v Twomey and Others* was the first Crown Court trial on indictment in England and Wales to be heard without a jury, and arose due to a s 44 application.

41. The full list of crimes and their corresponding classes can be found in Part III.21 of the *Consolidated Criminal Practice Direction.*   42. Criminal Appeal Act 1968, s 1(2).

43. *R v Bansal* [1999] Crim LR 484 (CA).

TABLE 2.1 The classification and allocation of cases

Class of offence	Examples	Heard by
Class 1	• Genocide • Treason • Murder, manslaughter • Torture, hostage-taking • Mutiny, piracy • Infanticide, child destruction	Almost always heard by a High Court judge, but can also be released to a circuit judge who has been authorized by the Lord Chief Justice to hear Class 1 cases
Class 2	• Rape • Rape/sexual intercourse/ incest with a girl/child under the age of 13 • Inducement to procure sexual activity with a mentally disordered person	Usually heard by a High Court judge, but can also be released to a circuit judge who has been authorized by the Lord Chief Justice to hear Class 2 cases
Class 3	• All other offences not listed in Classes 1 or 2	Will be tried by a circuit judge, recorder, or assistant recorder (High Court judges can act in Class 3 cases, but this is rare)

Trial by jury

In practice, the role of the jury forms a minor part of the English legal system. As noted, 95 per cent of criminal trials are heard in magistrates' courts and, of the remaining 5 per cent that are heard in the Crown Court, the majority of defendants will plead guilty and no jury will be required. The result is that juries decide less than 1 per cent of criminal cases. Despite this, the jury is still regarded by many as symbolically fundamental. Lord Devlin famously described jury service as 'the lamp that shows freedom lives'[44] and Lord Denning stated that jury service gives 'ordinary folk their finest lesson in citizenship'.[45]

It is argued that juries add certainty to the law—their decisions are not open to dispute, because they provide no reasons for the verdict that they deliver:[46] they simply find the accused 'guilty' or 'not guilty'.[47] It follows that, because juries do not have to justify their verdict, they are in practice free to decide a case based on any factors they wish, including their own personal beliefs or the dictates of their conscience. They may even ignore the law completely and deliver a verdict contrary to that required by the law.

The extent to which this ability to depart from the law and base a verdict on conscience is beneficial or detrimental has been a matter of substantial academic debate. Some regard the ability of the jury to depart from the law as a fundamental ingredient in the pursuit of justice.[48] Others argue that it demonstrates a lack of

---

44. Lord Devlin, *Trial by Jury* (Stevens & Sons 1956) 164.

45. Lord Denning, *What Next in the Law?* (Butterworths 1982) 33.

46. In fact, jurors who disclose their reasoning will be held in contempt of court (Contempt of Court Act 1981, s 8), as will any newspaper that publishes such disclosures (*Attorney General v Associated Newspapers* [1994] 2 WLR 227 (HL)).

47. It could be legitimately argued that convicting a defendant without justifying the decision is a breach of the defendant's right to a fair trial under Art 6 of the European Convention on Human Rights. To date, this issue has not arisen before the courts.

48. See Lord Devlin, *Trial by Jury* (Stevens & Sons 1956) 160, who argues that the ability to act on conscience ensures 'that the criminal law will conform to the ordinary man's idea of what is fair and just'.

competence[49] on the part of the jury and constitutes a 'blatant affront to the legal process'.[50]

Below are several cases in which the jury clearly decided the case based upon its conscience; whether their verdicts could be regarded as just or perverse is very much a matter of personal opinion. Would you have decided differently to the jury?

 R v Owen, The Times 12 December 1991

FACTS: Owen's son was run over and killed by a drink-driver. The driver had prior convictions for drink-driving and had never taken a driving test. At the trial, he showed no remorse for his actions, and was duly convicted of drink-driving and sentenced to eighteen months' imprisonment. Upon his release, he continued to drive unlawfully. Feeling that justice had not been done, Owen located the driver and shot him with a shotgun, severely injuring him.

HELD: Despite the substantial amount of evidence against him, the jury acquitted Owen of attempted murder.

 R v Ponting [1985] Crim LR 318

FACTS: Ponting was a senior civil servant at the Ministry of Defence. He passed two confidential documents to a Member of Parliament (MP) in contravention of s 2 of the Official Secrets Act 1911. The MP, in turn, passed them on to a national newspaper and they were published. The documents indicated that the government had lied to the public in relation to the sinking of the ship *ARA General Belgrano* during the Falklands War.[51] Ponting admitted handing over the documents, but argued that his actions were in the public interest.

HELD: Despite a direction from the judge indicating that the government was to decide what was in the public interest, the jury acquitted Ponting.

The growth of the Internet (especially social network sites, such as Facebook and Twitter) has also had a detrimental impact upon the effectiveness of the jury. A 2010 survey revealed that a small, but notable, proportion of jurors consulted the Internet to seek information about their trial, despite being warned not to by the judge.[52] More recently, the competence of jurors was once again called into question when a £6 million drugs trial collapsed following the discovery that, during the trial, a juror had been in contact with one of the eight defendants via Facebook. Such discussions

---

49. An often-cited case backing up this contention is *R v Young* [1995] QB 324 (CA), in which a murder case had to be retried following revelations that the jury based its decision to convict on answers that it received from the deceased via the use of a Ouija board. On retrial, the defendant was convicted.

50. Lord Justice Auld, *Review of the Criminal Courts of England and Wales* (HMSO 2001) [105].

51. The Argentine warship *ARA General Belgrano* was sunk in 1982 by the British submarine *HMS Conqueror*, with the loss of 323 lives. A 200-mile exclusion zone had been established and any Argentine ship found within it would be attacked. The *Belgrano* was not within the exclusion zone, but the then Prime Minister Margaret Thatcher authorized the attack on the ground that the ship was sailing towards the Royal Navy taskforce, presumably intending to attack. The documents leaked by Ponting revealed that the *Belgrano* was actually moving away from the taskforce when it was attacked and sunk.

52. Cheryl Thomas, *Are Juries Fair?* (Ministry of Justice 2010) 43. See also Billy Kenber and Frances Gibb, 'Trial by Facebook as Jurors Seek a Verdict From Their Online Friends' *The Times* (London, 13 June 2011).

are prohibited by s 8 of the Contempt of Court Act 1981. Accordingly, in June 2011, in the first case of its kind, both the defendant in question and the juror were held in contempt of court for communicating via Facebook, with the juror being sentenced to eight months' imprisonment and the defendant receiving a custodial sentence of two months suspended for two years.[53]

The High Court of Justice

The High Court was created by the Supreme Court of Judicature Act 1873 and consists of three divisions—namely, the Chancery Division, the Queen's Bench Division, and the Family Division.[54] Each division has a substantial first-instance jurisdiction, as well as an appellate role via two judges (or, in some cases, a single judge) sitting as a Divisional Court. The three divisions also house a number of specialist courts. The High Court has a virtually unlimited civil jurisdiction, and the Queen's Bench Division also has an important criminal jurisdiction and supervisory jurisdiction. Cases in the High Court are normally heard by a single Justice of the High Court (usually known as 'puisne' (pronounced 'puny', meaning 'lesser') judges).

The High Court is based at the Royal Courts of Justice in London, but sittings can take place anywhere in England and Wales.[55]

The Chancery Division

The senior division of the High Court is the Chancery Division, which currently consists of the Chancellor of the High Court[56] and a number of puisne judges.[57] The Chancery Division hears cases not only in London, but also in eight designated provincial High Court centres around the country. Like all divisions of the High Court, the jurisdiction of the Chancery Division can be found in Sch 1 of the Senior Courts Act 1981 and includes:

- the sale, exchange, or partition of land, or the raising of charges on land;
- the redemption or foreclosure of mortgages;
- the execution of trusts;
- the administration of the estates of deceased persons; and
- the dissolution of partnerships.

In addition, there is a specialist Patents Court that settles disputes relating to patents, designs and trademarks, and a Bankruptcy and Companies Court that deals with certain insolvency law and company law cases.

Judges sitting as the Chancery Divisional Court can hear appeals from circuit judges in county courts on certain matters (for example, bankruptcy), and will hear appeals from Her Majesty's Commissioners of Revenue and Customs (HMRC) on income tax disputes.

---

53. *Attorney General v Fraill & Sewart* [2011] EWHC 1629 (Admin), [2011] 2 Cr App R 21.
54. Senior Courts Act 1981, s 5(1).   55. ibid s 71(1).
56. The Chancellor of the High Court was formerly known as the 'Vice-Chancellor', but following the passing of the Constitutional Reform Act 2005 and the removal of the Lord Chancellor as head of the Chancery Division, the office of Vice-Chancellor had to be replaced.
57. Senior Courts Act 1981, s 5(1)(a).

The Queen's Bench Division

The largest division of the High Court is the Queen's Bench Division (QBD, which becomes the King's Bench Division, or KBD, when a male is monarch) and consists of the Lord Chief Justice, the President of the QBD,[58] the Vice-President of the QBD, and a number of puisne judges.[59] Its jurisdiction can be divided into four sections, as follows.

1. **First-instance civil jurisdiction** The QBD hears a large number of first-instance common law civil claims, predominantly in contract and tort. The Commercial Court—a specialist court that exists within the QBD, which is discussed in more detail below—will hear commercial cases. Disputes involving ships and aircraft will be heard by the Admiralty Court, and complex disputes involving engineering, construction, and information technology, will be heard by the Technology and Construction Court.

2. **Appellate civil jurisdiction** The QBD will hear appeals from the decisions of circuit judges in the county courts.

3. **Appellate criminal jurisdiction** The Queen's Bench Divisional Court will hear appeals on points of law or jurisdiction by way of case stated from magistrates' courts. It will also hear appeals on points of law or jurisdiction from decisions of the Crown Court, except in relation to cases tried on indictment.

4. **Judicial review** Judges sitting as an Administrative Court can hear cases relating to alleged *ultra vires* acts committed by magistrates' courts, the Crown Court (except in relation to matters concerning trial on indictment), county courts, public bodies (for example, local authorities), and individuals such as police officers and government ministers.

As noted, several specialist courts exist within the QBD, of which particular mention should be made of the Commercial Court. The Commercial Court was formed in 1970,[60] although its origins can be traced back to a Commercial List that was established in 1895. The Commercial Court currently consists of around fifteen nominated judges, and hears cases relating to both national and international business disputes, with specific emphasis on cases involving international trade, banking, and arbitration disputes. The procedures[61] of the Commercial Court tend to be more flexible than those of the High Court generally (for example, many of the rules relating to case management in the High Court do not apply to the Commercial Court). The work of the Commercial Court is often extremely complex, with around 80 per cent of cases involving a claimant or defendant that derives from outside the jurisdiction of the Court.[62] That many parties choose to resolve their disputes in the Commercial Court is a testament to how highly the Court is regarded worldwide. Accordingly, it is inundated with work, which provides another reason why it is granted its own more flexible rules of procedure.

The Family Division

The Family Division was created by the Administration of Justice Act 1970 and consists of the President of the Family Division and a number of puisne judges,[63] who

---

58. Like the Chancellor of the High Court, the post of 'President of the Queen's Bench' was also created by the Constitutional Reform Act 2005.   59. Senior Courts Act 1981, s 5(1)(b).
60. Administration of Justice Act 1970, s 3(1).
61. These procedural rules can be found in the Civil Procedure Rules, Pt 58.
62. Judiciary of England and Wales, *Report of the Commercial Court and Admiralty Court 2005–06* (2006) 2.
63. Senior Courts Act 1981, s 5(1)(c).

are assisted by a number of district judges. Its jurisdiction is entirely civil, and will hear first-instance cases involving matrimonial matters, cases involving the legitimacy, custody, and maintenance of children, adoption cases, and cases concerning the exclusion of a violent spouse. In addition, the Divisional Court (or, in some cases, a single judge) will hear appeals from magistrates' courts and from circuit judges in county courts on family issues.

Jury trial in civil cases

The decline of trial by jury is evidenced starkly in relation to civil cases, where jury trial has been abolished in all but a handful of case types. Historically, virtually all civil trials would have been conducted in front of a jury, but the Common Law Procedure Act 1854 began a lengthy process that has all but eradicated the use of juries in civil trials. Today, the role of the jury in civil trials taking place in the QBD is governed by s 69 of the Senior Courts Act 1981, which establishes a presumption that cases concerning fraud, malicious prosecution, and false imprisonment will be tried by jury.[64] However, it is subject to a limitation—namely, that the court will not order a jury trial where the case involves 'a prolonged examination of documents or accounts or any scientific or local examination which cannot conveniently be made with a jury'.[65] In practice, the only substantial use of juries in civil cases was in relation to **defamation** cases but, as noted, the presumption that such cases would be heard by a jury has now been removed.

→ **defamation:** a statement that lowers the claimant in the estimation of right-thinking members of society generally, or which would tend to make them shun or avoid him (see p 446)

In cases not covered by s 69, there is a presumption against trial by jury, but the court has discretion to grant a jury trial.[66] Whilst this discretion might once have been unlimited,[67] today, it is heavily restricted and is used exceptionally. For example, in *Ward v James*,[68] the Court of Appeal stated that, unless special circumstances were present, juries should not be used in personal injury cases. The Court's advice has been followed—for example, since *Ward*, only one reported personal injury case has involved a jury.[69]

The final point to note is that juries in civil trials not only determine the victor, but also the level of damages to be awarded. This has proved to be extremely controversial, especially in defamation cases where juries have been accused of awarding excessive damages. For example, in 1990, a jury awarded £600,000 in damages to the defamed wife of Peter Sutcliffe, the serial killer known as the 'Yorkshire Ripper'.[70] The wife eventually settled for £60,000 after the Court of Appeal indicated that it would reduce the award. In another case,[71] the award of damages was so high (£1.5 million) that it was held to amount to a breach of the defendant's rights under Art 10 of the European Convention on Human Rights. Section 8 of the Courts and Legal Services Act 1990 aims to remedy this problem by providing that where a jury awards damages that are excessive or inadequate, the Court of Appeal may grant a new trial, or substitute the sum awarded with a sum that the Court thinks proper.

---

64. Libel and slander (collectively known as defamation) were also part of this list, but were removed by s 11(1) of the Defamation Act 2013.   65. Senior Courts Act 1981, s 69(1).   66. ibid s 69(3).
67. *Hope v Great Western Rly Co* [1937] 2 KB 130 (CA).   68. [1966] 1 QB 273 (CA).
69. *Hodges v Harland & Wolff Ltd* [1965] 1 WLR 523 (CA).
70. *Sutcliffe v Pressdram Ltd* [1991] 1 QB 153 (CA).
71. *Tolstoy Miloslavsky v UK* (1995) 20 EHRR 442.

Appeals

In relation to civil cases, decisions of the High Court may be appealed to the Civil Division of the Court of Appeal. It is possible, however, to appeal directly to the Supreme Court via what is known as the 'leapfrog' procedure. For this to occur, the trial judge must grant a certificate indicating that the various conditions have been met—namely, that the case involves a point of law of general public importance that either involves the interpretation of a statute, or is one that derives from the House of Lords, Supreme Court or Court of Appeal and would bind the High Court.[72] In addition, all of the parties involved in the case will need to agree to the case proceeding directly to the Supreme Court.

Regarding criminal cases, before 1960, there was no further right to appeal the decision of a single judge or Divisional Court of the QBD. The Administration of Justice Act 1960 altered this and now provides that decisions of a single judge or Divisional Court of the QBD may be appealed to the Supreme Court, provided that the appeal is based on a point of law of general public importance and that leave to appeal has been obtained from either the single judge or the Divisional Court that heard the appeal, or the Supreme Court.[73]

The Court of Appeal

The Criminal Appeal Act 1966 split the Court of Appeal into the two divisions that exist today—namely, the Civil Division and the Criminal Division. The Court consists of a number of *ex officio* judges and up to thirty-eight Lord/Lady Justices of Appeal.[74] In addition, any High Court judge or circuit judge may be required to sit in the Court of Appeal, although circuit judges may only sit in the Criminal Division.[75] The Court's jurisdiction is entirely appellate.

The Court of Appeal is, like the High Court, based at the Royal Courts of Justice in London (with an increasing number of regional sittings), which can hear up to twelve cases at any one time. A panel of three judges normally hears cases, with cases of particular importance occasionally being heard by a panel of five. In order to reduce waiting times, since 1982 it has been possible to hear cases with a panel of two judges. As a result of the above measures, the Court of Appeal hears considerably more cases than the Supreme Court: in 2012, the Supreme Court disposed of 82 appeals, compared with 8,793 disposed of by the Court of Appeal.[76]

The Civil Division

The Civil Division hears appeals from the High Court and can also hear appeals directly from a county court if the appeal raises important points of principle or practice, or if there is some compelling reason why the Court of Appeal should hear it.[77] The Civil Division also has the power to reopen any case if it feels that it is necessary to do so to avoid a real injustice, that the circumstances are exceptional, and that there is no alternative effective remedy.[78] The Civil Division will also

---

72. Administration of Justice Act 1969, s 12.   73. Administration of Justice Act 1960, ss 1 and 2.
74. Senior Courts Act 1981, s 2. *Ex officio* judges include the Master of the Rolls (who is President of the Civil Division), the Lord Chief Justice (who is President of the Criminal Division), the heads of the three divisions of the High Court, and the Justices of the Supreme Court.   75. ibid s 9.
76. Statistics derived from the website of the Ministry of Justice.   77. Civil Procedure Rules, r 52.14
78. ibid r 52.17(1).

hear appeals on points of law from various tribunals (for example, the Employment Appeal Tribunal).

Decisions of the Civil Division may be appealed to the Supreme Court, provided that leave to appeal is obtained from either the Court of Appeal or Supreme Court. The appeal need not raise a point of general public importance, although the majority do so.

The Criminal Division

The Criminal Division hears cases from a number of different sources, as follows.

- **The Crown Court** Defendants convicted of an offence on indictment in the Crown Court may appeal to the Criminal Division against their conviction or against sentence.[79] A defendant who appeals against conviction will either have his conviction quashed or his appeal will be dismissed. Defendants who appeal against sentence may have their sentences confirmed or reduced, but not increased.[80] In both cases, permission to appeal is required, either from the trial judge or the Criminal Division.

- **The Criminal Cases Review Commission** The Home Secretary used to have the power to refer cases to the Criminal Division,[81] but this power proved to be extremely controversial and so, in 1995, the power was transferred to a newly created independent body called the Criminal Cases Review Commission (CCRC).[82] The CCRC can refer convictions on indictment[83] to the Criminal Division, provided that the CCRC believes that there is 'a real possibility that the conviction, verdict, finding or sentence would not be upheld were the reference to be made'.[84] As of January 2013, the CCRC had received 17,356 applications and referred 546 to the Criminal Division, of which 353 resulted in the conviction being quashed.

- **Appeals against acquittal** It is a cardinal principle of the UK's criminal justice system that no one should be tried twice for the same offence (known as the 'double jeopardy' rule). The murder of Stephen Lawrence in 1993 provided a catalyst for a reappraisal of the rule that eventually resulted in Pt 10 of the Criminal Justice Act 2003, which permits prosecutors to apply to the Criminal Division for an order quashing the acquittal and ordering a retrial, where new and compelling evidence comes to light. The acquittal will need to be in relation to a 'qualifying offence'[85] and the prosecutor will need to obtain the written permission of the Director of Public Prosecutions, who will need to satisfy himself that new evidence is available, that it is in the public interest to rehear the case, and that the trial will not break the European Union's equivalent of the double jeopardy rule.[86]

- **Attorney General's references** In two instances, the Attorney General has the power to refer a case to the Court of Appeal. First, he may, in relation to certain offences, refer a point of law to the Court of Appeal that arose in a case in which the defendant was acquitted.[87] Second, where he considers that a defendant

---

79. Criminal Appeal Act 1968, s 1. A defendant cannot appeal against a sentence fixed by law (Criminal Appeal Act 1968, s 9(1)), such as murder.   80. ibid s 11(3).   81. ibid s 17 (repealed).
82. Criminal Appeal Act 1995, Pt II.
83. The CCRC can refer summary convictions to the Crown Court.
84. Criminal Appeal Act 1995, s 13(1).
85. The list of qualifying offences can be found in the Criminal Justice Act 2003, Sch 5, and are all extremely serious, including murder, rape, manslaughter, kidnapping, importing Class A drugs, arson, and genocide.   86. Criminal Justice Act 2003, s 76(4).
87. Criminal Justice Act 1972, s 36. It should be noted that the reference will have no effect upon the original acquittal.

has been sentenced leniently, he may, with the leave of the Court of Appeal, refer the case to the Criminal Division, which may impose a more severe sentence.[88] The aim of both procedures is to remedy quickly a mistake made at trial by providing a more authoritative Court of Appeal ruling.

Either the prosecution or defence may appeal the decision of the Criminal Division to the Supreme Court, provided that the case involves a point of law of general public importance, and that permission to appeal has been granted by either the Court of Appeal or the Supreme Court.

The Supreme Court of the United Kingdom

For over 600 years, the House of Lords was the highest court in the United Kingdom in relation to cases of a purely domestic nature. Originally, appeals would be heard by the whole House, but the Appellate Jurisdiction Act 1876 changed this by providing that appeals would be heard by a new group of life peers called 'Lords of Appeal in Ordinary' (usually known as the 'Law Lords'). The bombing of the Palace of Westminster in 1941 led to the Law Lords being reorganized to form the Appellate Committee of the House of Lords.

In October 2009, the Appellate Committee of the House of Lords was replaced by the Supreme Court of the United Kingdom. The announcement in 2003 of the Appellate Committee's abolition came as something of a surprise, because it was not preceded by a consultation document; instead, the consultation document[89] was published *after* the decision to abolish the Appellate Committee was announced. This was extremely unusual, especially given the constitutional importance of the decision, and understandably led to significant judicial criticism, especially from six of the twelve Lords of Appeal in Ordinary, who believed that the reform was 'unnecessary' and 'harmful'.[90] The consultation document emphasizes that the catalyst for the reform was the need to comply with the doctrine of separation of powers.[91]

Jurisdiction and composition

The Supreme Court hears both criminal and civil cases, and, whilst it does have an extremely limited first-instance jurisdiction,[92] it is predominantly an appellate court, hearing cases from the Court of Appeal, the High Court (using the 'leapfrog' procedure), the Court of Session (the final civil court in Scotland),[93] and the Northern Irish Court of Appeal and High Court of Justice.

---

88. Criminal Justice Act 1988, s 36.

89. Department for Constitutional Affairs, *Constitutional Reform: A Supreme Court for the United Kingdom* (CP 11/03, HMSO 2003).

90. House of Lords, *The Law Lords' Response to the Government Consultation Paper on Constitutional Reform: A Supreme Court for the United Kingdom* (CP 11/03, 2003) [1].

91. Department for Constitutional Affairs, *Constitutional Reform: A Supreme Court for the United Kingdom* (CP 11/03, HMSO 2003) [10]–[11].

92. For example, the Supreme Court will hear first-instance cases relating to impeachment (the commission of a crime against the state, usually by a public official, who is removed from office upon conviction)—but the last time that this function was exercised was in 1806, when Viscount Melville was charged (but acquitted) with the misappropriation of public funds.

93. No appeal will lie to the Supreme Court from the High Court of Justiciary (the final criminal court in Scotland): see Supreme Court Practice Direction 1 [1.2.10].

The jurisdiction of the Supreme Court differs slightly from that of the Appellate Committee of the House of Lords. Its appellate jurisdiction remains the same,[94] but it has taken over devolution cases that were previously dealt with by the Judicial Committee of the Privy Council.[95] An appeal to the Supreme Court is dependent upon two conditions being satisfied. First, the lower court or Supreme Court must grant leave to appeal to the Supreme Court and second, the point of law involved in the appeal must be of general public importance.

The Supreme Court consists of a President, a Deputy President, and ten Justices of the Supreme Court. The 2005 Act provides that the twelve Lords of Appeal in Ordinary would become the first Justices of the Supreme Court, with the Senior Law Lord becoming the President and the second senior becoming the Deputy President.[96] The first appointees remained members of the Upper Chamber of Parliament (although they cannot sit or vote in the Upper Chamber), but future appointees will not.[97] Therefore, the ties between the judiciary and the legislature are not yet fully severed. The monarch will appoint future Justices, following a recommendation by the Prime Minister.[98] The Prime Minister's recommendation is based upon the selection made by the Lord Chancellor, which will in turn be based upon recommendations made by the Judicial Appointments Commission. As the Supreme Court is the final appeal court in cases from the Scottish Court of Session and the Northern Irish Court of Appeal and High Court, it is customary that one or two judges are appointed from Scotland, and one from Northern Ireland.

The Judicial Committee of the Privy Council

The Judicial Committee of the Privy Council (hereinafter referred to as the 'Privy Council') was formally created by the Judicial Committee Act 1833 to better deal with appeals arising from cases in British colonies and Crown dependencies. Today, the Privy Council still acts as the final appeal court for a number of Crown dependencies (for example, the Isle of Man and Jersey), UK overseas territories (for example, Bermuda and Gibraltar), and Commonwealth countries[99] (for example, the Bahamas and Jamaica). It will also hear appeals from certain domestic disciplinary bodies (for example, the Royal College of Veterinary Surgeons) and specialist courts (for example, the ecclesiastical courts). In 2012, the Privy Council heard 39 cases.[100]

Only Privy Councillors who hold (or have held) 'high judicial office'[101] may sit on the Privy Council. Further, due to the court's overseas appellate jurisdiction, judges from Commonwealth countries have also been eligible to sit.[102] Privy Council judges do not hand down individual judgments; instead one judgment will be handed down

---

94. Constitutional Reform Act 2005, s 40.   95. ibid s 40(4)(b).   96. ibid s 24.
97. ibid s 137.   98. ibid ss 23(2) and 26(2).
99. Initially, all Commonwealth countries could appeal to the Privy Council. But as time progressed, many of these countries abolished the right to appeal and created their own final appeal courts. Examples include (year of abolition follows): Canada (1949); Malaysia (1985); Australia (1986); Singapore (1994); Hong Kong (1997); and New Zealand (2003).
100. Statistics derived from the website of the Ministry of Justice.
101. Judicial Committee Act 1833, s 1. The Constitutional Reform Act 2005, s 60 states that this includes judges of the Supreme Court, the Court of Appeal, the High Court, the Court of Session in Scotland, and the Northern Irish High Court and Court of Appeal.
102. Judicial Committee Amendment Act 1895, s 1 and Sch 1.

for unanimous decisions, while for split decisions, one judgment is handed down for the majority and one for each dissenting judge.

Tribunals

Although tribunals have existed for over 200 years,[103] it is only within the last century that they have experienced a dramatic increase in importance. The importance of tribunals has increased so much that Carnwath LJ, the former Senior President of Tribunals, has stated that 'more people bring a case before a tribunal than go to any other part of the justice system'.[104] Tribunals usually consist of a panel of three: a legally trained chairperson and two laypersons with expertise in the area in question.

A major review of tribunals, known as the Franks Report, was carried out in 1957,[105] but no further review of the system was carried out until 2001,[106] by which time a number of problems had emerged. Key among these was the fact that the number of tribunals had grown considerably since the previous review, and that each tribunal had developed its own set of complex rules and procedures. This lack of a coherent framework had made the tribunal system inaccessible, incoherent, and needlessly complex. Further, a significant number of tribunals were set up by the very government departments that they were established to regulate; of such tribunals, the Legatt Review states that 'plainly, they are not independent'.[107] The Review's main recommendation was to transfer responsibility for the administration of all tribunals to a single body, thereby ensuring that the tribunals were independent of the bodies they were regulating. This body was known as the Tribunals Service and it was established on 1 April 2006 as an executive agency of the Ministry of Justice. On 1 April 2011, the Tribunals Service was merged with Her Majesty's Courts Service to create Her Majesty's Courts and Tribunals Service—a single body that supports the administration of justice in courts and tribunals.

The Tribunals, Courts and Enforcement Act 2007

The establishment of the Tribunals Service was one part of the Legatt Review's aim of creating a simplified tribunals administration. Other significant reforms were also introduced with the passing of the Tribunals, Courts and Enforcement Act 2007, of which the most notable was the reorganization of the majority of tribunals into a unified structure. Section 3 of the 2007 Act created two new tribunals: (i) the First-tier Tribunal, and (ii) the Upper Tribunal. Within these new tribunals were established 'chambers' that grouped together many existing tribunals. Figure 2.3 sets out the current chamber structure.

As can be seen, First-tier Tribunal decisions can be appealed to the Upper Tribunal, whose decisions can in turn be appealed on a point of law to the Civil

---

103. The first identifiable tribunal, the General Commissioners of Income Tax Tribunal, was established in 1799.

104. Quoted in Trevor Buck, 'Precedent in Tribunals and the Development of Principle' (2006) 25 CJQ 458, 459.

105. *Report of the Committee on Administrative Tribunals and Enquiries* (Cmnd 218, HMSO 1957).

106. Sir Andrew Legatt, *Tribunals for Users: One System, One Service* (HMSO 2001).   107. ibid [1.19].

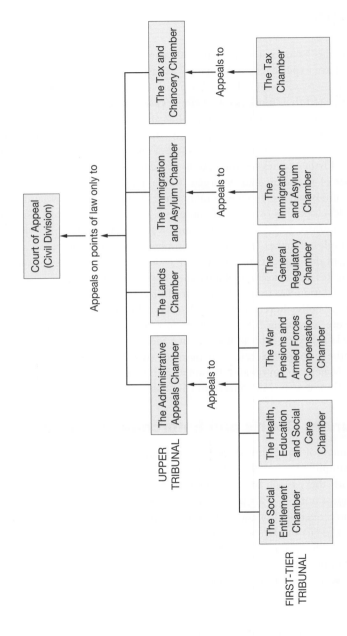

FIGURE 2.3 The Tribunals structure

Division of the Court of Appeal.[108] As a result, tribunals are now a firm part of the UK's legal system—a fact reflected in that legally qualified members of tribunals are to have the title of 'judge'.[109]

The First-tier Tribunal and Upper Tribunal tend to hear applications from citizens against state bodies. Tribunals that hear applications based on disputes between private parties (for example, employment tribunals) are not part of the above framework, although certain provisions of the 2007 Act will apply to them.[110]

Alternative dispute resolution

In practice, the vast majority of disputes are resolved 'out of court' by a number of differing methods that are collectively known as 'alternative dispute resolution' (ADR). Before discussing the various forms of ADR, it is worth briefly identifying several reasons why parties may wish to avoid formal legal proceedings.

- **Cost** Taking a dispute to court can still be extremely costly. Further, the cost-saving reforms introduced by the Woolf Report do not yet appear to have had a significant impact.
- **Time** The Woolf reforms have reduced the time that it takes for a case to reach court and the length of trial, but cases can still be protracted.
- **Salvaging the relationship** Taking another person to court will almost certainly destroy any chance of being able to transact with him again in the future. The use of ADR is more likely to result in disputing parties working together again once the dispute is resolved, especially if a mutually acceptable solution is reached.
- **Publicity** For large, well-known businesses, becoming involved in a bitter and public legal battle may result in adverse publicity, causing a loss of reputation, a drop in sales, or a reduction in share price. Further, confidential details of the business and its practices may be revealed to competitors.

Accordingly, in 1998, the government stated that 'in civil matters, for most people, most of the time, going to court is, and should be, the last resort'.[111] The courts themselves recognize this and will strongly encourage (but cannot compel)[112] parties to use ADR before resorting to legal proceedings. This is codified in the Civil Procedure Rules, which state that effective case management is to include 'encouraging the parties to use an [ADR] procedure if the court considers that appropriate'.[113] The court's encouragement can be 'in the strongest terms'[114] and parties who

---

108. Tribunals, Courts and Enforcement Act 2007, ss 11 and 13.   109. ibid ss 4–5.

110. For example, s 4(3)(d) of the 2007 Act provides that chairmen of employment tribunals are judges of the First-tier Tribunal.

111. Lord Chancellor, *Modernising Justice: The Government's Plans for Reforming Legal Services and the Courts* (Cm 4155, HMSO 1998) [1.10].

112. In *Halsey v Milton Keynes General NHS Trust* [2004] EWCA Civ 576, [2004] 1 WLR 3002, the Court held that to compel a person to use ADR would be the denial of the right to a fair trial, as provided for by Art 6 of the European Convention on Human Rights.

113. Civil Procedure Rules, r 1.4(2)(e). The courts can even refuse to award costs to a successful litigant who unreasonably refuses to use ADR (see e.g. *Rolf v De Guerin* [2011] EWCA Civ 78, [2011] CP Rep 24).

114. *Halsey v Milton Keynes General NHS Trust* [2004] EWCA Civ 576, [2004] 1 WLR 3002 [9] (Dyson LJ).

unreasonably refuse ADR may find that costs applications are not awarded in their favour.[115] Numerous court-related ADR procedures have been established—for example, HM Courts and Tribunals Service operates the Small Claims Mediation Service, a service that offers free mediation to parties involved in small claims disputes.

Parties who wish to avoid the adverse consequences of litigation would do well to consider ADR, but it is important that parties understand which type of ADR is most suitable for their particular dispute. The principal types of ADR are as follows.

Arbitration

Arbitration is the oldest and one of the most formal types of ADR and aims 'to obtain the fair resolution of disputes by an impartial tribunal without necessary delay or expense'.[116] To this end, instead of commencing legal proceedings, the parties involved will let their case be decided by an independent third party, known as an 'arbitrator'. An arbitrator need not be legally qualified, but he will usually be an expert in the area in question.

In several respects, arbitration is similar to litigation:

- the rules of procedure may be similar to rules in court;
- lawyers will act in almost the same way that they would in court;
- the decision of the arbitrator is legally binding and may be enforced by a court order;[117] and
- the arbitrator's decision may be appealed to the courts, but on limited grounds— namely, that the arbitrator lacked jurisdiction to decide the case, there was a procedural irregularity, or there was contention on a point of law.[118]

The upshot of this is that, whilst the case may be decided more quickly and with more privacy, it is unlikely to be significantly cheaper than resolving the issue through the courts.

Arbitration is used most commonly in commercial cases—notably, where a contract contains an arbitration clause (commonly known as a '*Scott v Avery*[119] clause'). The aim of such a clause is to ensure that, in the event of a dispute, the parties refer the matter to arbitration before commencing legal proceedings. The courts have long held that such clauses are perfectly valid and will not be defeated easily.[120] Where a party breaches such a clause by initiating legal proceedings, the other party may apply to the court for an order staying those proceedings.[121]

Mediation

Arbitration can be extremely useful, but, like a decision of the court, it still involves the imposition of a decision upon the parties. Alternatively, the parties could employ a mediator, whose function is to help the parties reach a mutually acceptable

---

115. See e.g. *Dunnet v Railtrack plc* [2002] EWCA Civ 302, [2002] 2 All ER 850.
116. Arbitration Act 1996, s 1(a).   117. ibid s 66.   118. ibid ss 67–69.
119. (1856) 5 HL Cas 811.
120. See, e.g., *Cable & Wireless plc v IBM United Kingdom Ltd* [2002] EWHC 2059, [2002] 2 All ER (Comm) 1041.   121. Arbitration Act 1996, s 9(1).

agreement. The mediator's function is not to impose a resolution, but to facilitate the negotiation between the parties so that they can resolve the matter themselves. If no resolution is reached, the parties may resort to legal proceedings. Mediation is therefore a less certain form of ADR than arbitration, in which a resolution is guaranteed. To combat this, a hybrid form of ADR entitled 'mediation-arbitration' ('med-arb') has been introduced that involves the parties undertaking mediation, but moving on to arbitration if mediation fails.

Because mediation is less confrontational than litigation or arbitration, it is much more suitable for resolving disputes between parties who need, or desire, to maintain a legal relationship once the issue is resolved. Obvious examples include divorcing couples who will need to remain in contact due to custody issues, or employment cases in which the parties involved will continue to work together.

Conciliation

Conciliation is similar to mediation, except that the conciliator will take a much more proactive role and will actually suggest solutions to the dispute. A notable form of conciliation is that provided by the Advisory Conciliation and Arbitration Service (ACAS). Before an employment case is heard by the courts or employment tribunal, an ACAS member will attempt to resolve the case via conciliation. In 93 per cent of cases, the conciliation is successful and litigation is avoided.[122]

Expert involvement

There are two other forms of ADR that involve appointing certain experts, as follows.

1. **Expert determination** The parties jointly appoint an independent expert to rule on their dispute and agree to be bound by his decision.
2. **Early neutral evaluation** This is similar to expert determination, except that the parties are not bound by the decision of the expert. The Commercial Court offers such a service, with a judge providing his opinion. If litigation ensues, the judge will be barred from taking part in the case.

Ombudsmen

Ombudsmen operate to resolve disputes arising between citizens and public bodies. The Parliamentary Commissioner Act 1967 established the first ombudsman, the Parliamentary Commissioner for Administration, whose function is to investigate alleged maladministration in governmental departments. Since then, the ombudsman scheme has been extended beyond governmental activities to include, *inter alia*, the provision of legal services (the Legal Services Ombudsman), complaints against the judiciary (the Judicial Appointments and Conduct Ombudsman), the provision of financial services (the Financial Ombudsman Service), and complaints regarding pensions (the Pensions Ombudsman).

---

122. ACAS, *Annual Report and Accounts 2012/13* (TSO 2013) 12.

The judiciary, the law officers, and the legal profession

Having discussed the institutions that administer the law, the next section moves on to discuss the persons who work within these institutions, starting with the judiciary.

The judiciary

Central to the effective administration of the law is the judiciary. The composition of the courts and the general judicial offices have been briefly mentioned already. The interpretive and law-making functions of the judiciary are discussed in the next chapter. Here, the judicial hierarchy will be set out, but first, it is important to understand the role of certain specific judicial (and former judicial) posts, as follows.

- **The Lord Chancellor** Historically, the Lord Chancellor was head of the judiciary, the head of the High Court's Chancery Division and presided over the Appellate Committee of the House of Lords. He was also a senior member of the cabinet and the Speaker of the House of Lords. Following the Constitutional Reform Act 2005, the Lord Chancellor is not eligible to sit in any court and will not be *ex officio* Speaker of the Lords. As the Lord Chancellor will also be the Secretary of State for Justice, he will remain a cabinet minister.
- **The Lord Chief Justice** The Lord Chief Justice is the President of the Criminal Division of the Court of Appeal and, following the passing of the Constitutional Reform Act 2005, is also the President of the Courts of England and Wales,[123] the Head of Criminal Justice, and the UK's most senior judge.
- **The President/Deputy President of the Supreme Court** The President and Deputy President exercise administrative responsibilities over the running of the Supreme Court, including allocating Justices to appropriate cases. The President is the joint second-ranking highest member of the judiciary.
- **The Master of the Rolls** The Master of the Rolls is the President of the Civil Division of the Court of Appeal, the Head of Civil Justice and, along with the President of the Supreme Court, the joint second-ranking highest member of the judiciary.
- **The Chancellor of the High Court** The Chancellor is the Head of the Chancery Division of the High Court.
- **The President of the QBD**
- **The President of the Family Division**

Outside of these specific posts, the general judicial hierarchy is shown in Figure 2.4.

The law officers and the Director of Public Prosecutions

An independent judiciary is vital to the rule of law, but it does not follow that all figures involved in the administration of the law are independent. The law officers and the Director of Public Prosecutions occupy central roles within the administration of the law, but are appointed by the government (or by those who are appointed by the government), and so cannot be regarded as independent.

---

123. Constitutional Reform Act 2005, s 7(1).

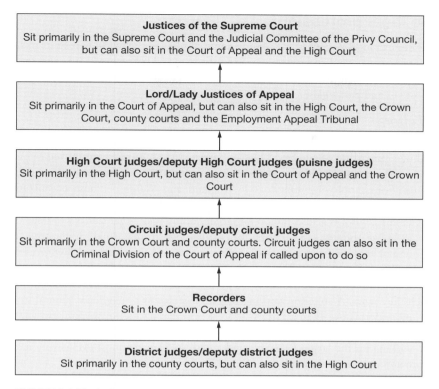

FIGURE 2.4 The judicial hierarchy

The 'law officers', namely the Attorney General and the Solicitor General, are the government's chief legal advisers. They are both Ministers of the Crown (but do not sit in the Cabinet) with overall responsibility for the work of several prosecuting departments such as the Crown Prosecution Service (CPS), and the Serious Fraud Office. The Attorney General represents the government in particularly important or serious litigation, and can also institute proceedings for contempt of court in cases where media exposure jeopardizes a trial.[124] Although the Solicitor General is the Attorney General's deputy, he can exercise any function of the Attorney General.[125] Mention should also be made of the Director of Public Prosecutions (DPP). Although not a law officer, the DPP is appointed by the Attorney General[126] and occupies a vital role within the criminal justice system as head of the Crown Prosecution Service. In addition, the prosecution of certain offences can only occur with the consent of the DPP.[127]

124. For example, in *Her Majesty's Attorney General v MGN Ltd and News Group Newspapers Ltd* [2011] EWHC 2074 (Admin), *The Daily Mirror* and *The Sun* were held in contempt over their portrayal of Christopher Jeffries (who was arrested for the murder of Joanna Yeates, but was later found not to have committed the crime). The defendants were, between them, fined £68,000.   125. Law Officers Act 1997, s 1(1). 126. Prosecution of Offences Act 1985, s 2(1).
127. A current and controversial example of this can be found in the Suicide Act 1961, s 2(4) which provides that no one may be prosecuted for the crime of assisted suicide without the consent of the DPP.

The legal profession

The English legal system is one of only a few systems in the world that splits its legal profession into two distinct occupations: solicitors and barristers.[128] It is also important to consider the role of other persons within the legal profession—namely, legal executives and paralegals.

Solicitors

As of July 2012, there were 150,128 solicitors in England and Wales, with 128,778 holding a practising certificate.[129] Unlike barristers, solicitors are permitted to incorporate or form partnerships, and the most recent statistics indicate there are 10,102 organizations employing solicitors in England and Wales.[130] These organizations may be firms of solicitors (usually in the form of a partnership or limited liability partnership), but it is also common for larger commercial organizations to have their own in-house solicitors. Solicitors' firms can range from a small, high-street firm with one or two solicitors in a single office, to massive multinational law firms with offices all over the world and thousands of practising solicitors.[131]

The type of work undertaken by a solicitor depends on the nature of the firm for which they work. A solicitor working in a high-street firm may have general expertise and undertake work in a variety of areas, whereas a solicitor working for a larger firm will be much more likely to specialize in a particular field (for example, solicitors working for the larger firms in London will specialize almost exclusively in corporate and commercial matters).

Solicitors are usually the first point of contact for anyone with a legal issue. A solicitor may have to refer certain clients to a barrister because the solicitor lacks expertise in a particular area, or because the case may need to be heard in a court in which the solicitor is not qualified to advocate. A solicitor has a right to **litigate** in any court,[132] but his right to advocate in higher courts is limited (the courts in which a member of the legal profession may advocate are known as his rights of audience). Upon qualification, solicitors only have rights of audience in magistrates' courts and county courts, and highly limited rights in the Crown Court. Since the passing of the Courts and Legal Services Act 1990, solicitors who wish to acquire rights of audience to higher courts can do so by qualifying as solicitor-advocates.

The Law Society is the professional body for solicitors. Previously, it both represented the interests of solicitors and regulated their professional activity. But it was decided that these two functions could not stand with each other and so, in 2005, the Law Society ceased to be the regulatory body for solicitors—this function being handed over to the Solicitors Regulation Authority.

Barristers

The majority of barristers (around 81 per cent) in the UK are self-employed. Bar Council rules prohibit barristers from incorporating or forming partnerships, but instead they can coalesce into loose organizations known as 'chambers'. As of

litigate: pursue or defend a legal action

---

128. Other systems that have a split legal profession include Scotland, the Republic of Ireland, Hong Kong, and the Australian states of Queensland and New South Wales.
129. Law Society, *Trends in the Solicitors' Profession: Annual Statistical Report 2012: Summary Figures* (The Law Society 2013) 2.   130. ibid.
131. For example, Baker & McKenzie has 75 offices in 47 countries and over 4,000 legal advisers.
132. Courts and Legal Services Act 1990, s 119.

November 2012, there are 12,674 self-employed barristers practising in 768 chambers.[133] There are, however, a significant number (2,907) of barristers who are not self-employed and who are instead employed in companies, local government, or the CPS.

The functions of a barrister are several, as follows.

- **Advocacy** Representing clients in court is a major function of a barrister, with all qualified barristers having rights of audience in any court.[134]

- **Writing opinions** Prior to trial, barristers will provide a written opinion advising the client and the instructing solicitor on the significant points of law, the evidential requirements, the likelihood of success, and the potential liability of the client. Alternatively, written opinions may also be provided where litigation is not intended.

- **Drafting documents** These can include general legal documents such as contracts and wills, as well as specific claim litigation documents such as claim forms.

Traditionally, a barrister could only receive instructions from a solicitor; clients could not approach barristers directly. Further, via what is known as the 'cab rank' rule, barristers must (with some exceptions) take any case referred to them. Whilst the 'cab rank' rule still exists, the rules regarding the receipt of instructions were relaxed in 2004 and barristers may now receive instructions directly from professional clients and the public.

All newly qualified barristers are known as 'juniors' and will remain so, unless they become QCs (a process known as 'taking silk' due to the silk robes worn by QCs). There are around 1,500 QCs in England and Wales, and, in 2012–13, 84 barristers took silk. Historically, only barristers could become QCs, but this was changed in 1996 to permit solicitors also to take silk, although the majority of QCs are still barristers (of the 84 new QCs appointed in 2012–13, only one was a solicitor).

The Bar Council is the professional body for barristers. Like the Law Society, the Bar Council used to represent and regulate its members, but it has split these functions in the same manner as the Law Society has. The Bar Council continues to represent the interests of barristers, but its regulatory responsibility has been transferred to the Bar Standards Board.

Legal executives and paralegals

Increasingly, persons who are not qualified solicitors or barristers are undertaking legal work. Specific mention must be made of legal executives and paralegals.

There are currently around 22,000 trainee and practising chartered legal executives in the UK. Legal executives are legally authorized to engage in 'reserved legal activities' that are very similar to the activities of solicitors, including:

- exercising a right of audience;
- conducting litigation;
- engaging in probate activities;
- notarial activities; and
- the administration of oaths.[135]

---

133. The General Council of the Bar, *Bar Barometer: Trends in the Profile of the Bar* (2012) 6.
134. Courts and Legal Services Act 1990, s 31(1).   135. Legal Services Act 2007, s 12(1).

Legal executives will often specialize in a certain field and, to that end, legal executives may engage in much of the same work as a qualified solicitor. Like solicitors, they can be fee-earners, and legal executives are now eligible to be appointed as judges.[136] The Chartered Institute of Legal Executives (CILEx) is the professional body for legal executives, and the ILEx Professional Standards Ltd acts as regulator.

The Institute of Paralegals defines a paralegal as 'someone who does legal work even though they have not qualified as a solicitor or barrister',[137] (legal executives should also be added). The Institute estimates that there are around 500,000 persons engaged in paralegal work (meaning that paralegals form the largest group within the legal profession), but only 50,000 of those work in law firms or in-house legal departments. The remainder work in companies, trade unions, governmental departments, local council and finance, and the insurance sectors.

Paralegals have yet to acquire the recognition afforded to other members of the legal profession. Unlike a solicitor, barrister, or legal executive, anyone can call themselves a 'paralegal' and there are no formal qualifications needed. A professional qualification is offered by the Institute of Paralegals whereby persons can become 'qualified paralegals'.

The Legal Services Act 2007

In 2004, Sir David Clementi carried out a review of the provision of legal services. The final report highlighted three significant problems:

1. the regulatory framework of the legal profession was outdated, rigid, overly complex, and lacked transparency;
2. the complaints procedure was inefficient and unsatisfactory; and
3. the business structures used by the legal profession were unduly restrictive.[138]

The review recommended a number of reforms, many of which were eventually implemented by the Legal Services Act 2007. The three major criticisms noted will hopefully be remedied via the three principal reforms, all of which are now in place.

1. Instead of barristers and solicitors being regulated by different bodies, a new body, called the Legal Services Board (LSB), was established to regulate all legal services.[139] The Solicitors Regulation Authority, the Bar Standards Board, and ILEx Professional Standards Ltd will, however, continue to act as 'Approved Regulators', with the LSB supervising their regulation. The LSB became fully operational on 1 January 2010.
2. Any complaints relating to the provision of legal services are now handled by a newly established Office for Legal Complaints, now known as the Legal Ombudsman.[140] The Legal Ombudsman became fully operational on 6 October 2010 and, in 2012/13, it was contacted by 71,000 people, with 7,630 of these complaints being accepted for investigation and resolved.[141]

---

136. Tribunals, Courts and Enforcement Act 2007, s 50(2). At the time of writing, the highest judicial post available to a legal executive is that of district judge.
137. See <http://www.theiop.org>.
138. Sir David Clementi, *Review of the Regulatory Framework for Legal Services in England and Wales: Final Report* (2004) 1–3.
139. Legal Services Act 2007, s 2 and Sch 1. See <http://www.legalservicesboard.org.uk>.
140. ibid s 114 and Sch 15. See <http://www.legalombudsman.org.uk>.
141. The Office for Legal Complaints, *Annual Report and Accounts* (TSO 2013) 9.

3. The most significant part of the 2007 Act is undoubtedly Pt 5, which allows legal services to be provided through 'alternative business structures' (ABS). These structures could consist solely of lawyers (for example, a single ABS could contain a mixture of solicitors and barristers); alternatively, it could consist of lawyers and non-lawyers (for example, lawyers could work with accountants or bankers). Even bodies with no history of providing legal services (for example, supermarkets)[142] are able to offer legal services. In October 2011, Premier Property Lawyers became the first firm to register as an ABS.

Chapter conclusion

Laws would be ineffective without a system in place that provides for their application. As we have seen, the court system in England and Wales is relatively complex, but one can only begin to understand the legal system (and the system of precedent) if one has an understanding of the court system.

The cost of taking a dispute to court may, however, be prohibitively expensive. Increasingly, therefore, parties are looking for more informal, non-legal mechanisms with which to resolve their disputes. Parties not wishing to take their dispute to court have a number of other options, which, in many circumstances, may produce a more acceptable compromise than if the dispute was litigated in court. In recent years, the use of tribunals and ADR has grown considerably and many businesses will make wise use of ADR before taking their dispute to court. Of course, ADR will not always work and, in such cases, resort to the courts may be unavoidable. In such a case, the parties involved will usually wish to avail themselves of the services of a member of the legal profession.

Having discussed how the law is administered, the next two chapters discuss the various sources of law, beginning with domestic sources of law.

‹ › Key points summary

- Civil cases will usually commence in either a county court or the High Court. All criminal cases will commence in a magistrates' court.

- In civil cases, county court decisions can be appealed to the High Court. High Court decisions can be appealed to the Civil Division of the Court of Appeal.

- In criminal cases, magistrates' court decisions can be appealed to the Crown Court. Crown Court convictions or sentences can be appealed to the Criminal Division of the Court of Appeal.

- The Supreme Court is the highest court in the UK.

- Tribunals exist to resolve disputes in certain specialist areas (for example, employment disputes, tax disputes, etc).

- Alternative Dispute Resolution (ADR) tends to be cheaper, quicker, and more private than litigation. It is also more likely to preserve the relationship between the parties.

---

142. At the time of writing, The Co-op has established a group known as 'The Co-operative Legal Services'. Tesco has indicated that it has plans to offer conveyancing services to the public, leading to the term 'Tesco law' becoming a popular synonym for the services offered by ABS.

- The legal profession in the UK is rare in that it is split into two branches: solicitors and barristers.

- Increasingly, legal executives are undertaking much of the work that was formerly carried out by solicitors.

- Paralegals are persons who engage in legal work, but who are not solicitors, barristers, or legal executives.

Self-test questions

1. Define the following:
   (a) magistrate;
   (b) first instance;
   (c) appeal;
   (d) judicial review;
   (e) separation of powers;
   (f) alternative dispute resolution;
   (g) rights of audience.

2. Explain the distinction between offences: (i) heard summarily; (ii) tried on indictment only; and (iii) triable either way.

3. Answer the following.
   (a) Tom has been arrested for the suspected murder of his wife, Helen. In which court will Tom's case be heard? If he is convicted, to which court could he appeal the decision?
   (b) Pablo has been convicted of theft in a magistrates' court, but he feels that the magistrates have made a mistake regarding the law. What options does Pablo have?

4. Explain the operation of the track system as regards the allocation of civil cases.

5. Explain the distinction between: (i) arbitration; (ii) mediation; and (iii) conciliation.

Further reading

Sir David Clementi, *Review of the Regulatory Framework for Legal Services in England and Wales: Final Report* (Department for Constitutional Affairs 2004)
Discusses several problems relating to the regulation of the legal profession and suggests reforms, now implemented by the Legal Services Act 2007

Andrew Gillespie, *The English Legal System* (4th edn, OUP 2013) ch 18
Provides an accessible and interesting account of the function and operation of tribunals

Sir Andrew Leggatt, *Tribunals for Users: One System, One Service* (Department for Constitutional Affairs 2001)
Provides a review of the use of tribunals in the UK and suggests a number of reforms that were implemented by the Tribunals, Courts and Enforcement Act 2007

Gary Slapper and David Kelly, *The English Legal System* (14th edn, Routledge 2013) chs 4-9, 11-13
Provides a detailed, yet accessible, account of the administration of justice, including the courts and tribunals system, the role of the judiciary, and the effectiveness of juries

Websites

<http://www.barcouncil.org.uk>
The website of the Bar Council, the body that represents the interests of barristers

<http://www.cilex.org.uk>
The website of the Institute of Legal Executives. Provides useful information on the role of legal executives, including how to qualify as one

<http://www.judiciary.gov.uk>
The website of the judiciary of England and Wales; provides an impressive amount of information concerning the role and composition of the judiciary

<http://www.justice.gov.uk/about/hmcts>
The Ministry of Justice's website of Her Majesty's Courts and Tribunals Service; provides a substantial amount of accessible information concerning the court and tribunal system and the various forms of legal proceedings

<http://www.lawsociety.org.uk>
The website of the Law Society, the body that represents the interests of solicitors

<http://www.supremecourt.uk>
The website of the Supreme Court. Provides detailed information on the Court and its Justices. Additionally, Supreme Court hearings are available to watch live at <http://news. sky.com/info/supreme-court>

 Remember to visit the **Online Resource Centre** at **<http://www. oxfordtextbooks.co.uk/orc/roach3e>** to access the following resources on Chapter 2, 'The administration of the law': more **practice questions** and answers; a **glossary** of key terms; **multiple-choice questions**; **revision summaries**; **diagrams** in pdf. Updates to the law can be found on Twitter by following **@UKBusinessLaw**.

3 Domestic sources of law

- Legislation
- Case law
- Custom

INTRODUCTION

Having discussed in Chapter 1 what law is, this chapter moves on to discuss the various types of law and their sources. Understanding the sources of law and the complex relationships that exist between them is crucial in understanding the operation of the English legal system. In this chapter, the three principal domestic sources of law will be discussed, namely legislation, case law, and custom.

Legislation

Legislation is the primary domestic source of law in the UK, taking priority over other sources of domestic law. This section of the chapter will look at how legislation is made and how it is applied in practice, but first, it is important to understand the different types of legislation that exist under the English legal system.

Types of legislation

Legislation comes in three forms:

1. Acts of Parliament;
2. subordinate legislation; and
3. legal acts deriving from the European Union.

European Union legal acts are discussed in Chapter 4. Accordingly, this section will concentrate on domestic legislation, beginning with the primary form of domestic legislation, namely Acts of Parliament.

Acts of Parliament

Acts of Parliament (also known as 'primary legislation' or 'statute law') constitute the supreme source of domestic law in the English legal system, and cannot be overruled or modified by the courts. Parliament is the supreme law-making body within the

UK and, according to the doctrine of parliamentary sovereignty, can create any law that it wishes (except laws that would bind future Parliaments). An Act of Parliament will consist of sections and subsections, with technical details coming in the form of Schedules at the end of the Act. Acts can range from minor pieces of legislation containing a few short sections, to massive statutes, such as the Companies Act 2006, which contains 1,300 sections and sixteen Schedules, and a combined total of over 305,000 words. Acts establish laws that remain in force until such time as they are repealed, and there are many Acts in force today that are centuries old (for example, the Distress Act 1267). With some exceptions, only Parliament has the power to repeal or amend an Act.

Table 3.1 demonstrates the various types of Act, in terms of their function.

TABLE 3.1 The functions of Acts of Parliament

Type of Act	Function	Examples
Original Act	Creates completely new law	• Human Rights Act 1998 • Hunting Act 2004
Codifying Act	Takes all existing statute law and case law in a particular area and sets it out anew in a single Act	• Partnership Act 1890 • Marine Insurance Act 1906
Consolidating Act	Brings together into one Act provisions that were previously contained in several Acts. Such Acts usually simplify the law, rather than substantially amend it	• Sale of Goods Act 1979 • Income and Corporation Taxes Act 1988
Amending Act	Merely alters existing legislation	• Parliament Act 1949 • Consumer Credit Act 2006

Subordinate legislation

Acts of Parliament may be the primary form of legislation in the UK, but, numerically, the volume of subordinate legislation (also known as 'secondary legislation')[1] passed each year greatly exceeds the number of Acts that make it onto the statute book. In 2013, thirty-three public Acts and seven private Acts were passed, compared to 3,266 statutory instruments. Creating an Act of Parliament can be a time-consuming process and the parliamentary timetable is so crowded that not all of the laws that require passing can be passed as Acts of Parliament. Instead, Parliament may pass an 'enabling' Act setting out the broad principles and aims of the legislation, but delegating the specifics to another person (for example, a government minister) or body (for example, governmental departments, local authorities, the Crown, companies, or devolved bodies). Thus, Parliament can delegate its law-making function to other persons/bodies that are better qualified to legislate the technical detail.

Subordinate legislation has the same force as primary legislation, and comes in various forms, as follows.

- **Statutory instruments** The vast majority of subordinate legislation comes in the form of statutory instruments (SIs). Most SIs permit governmental ministers

---

1. Very often, it is contended that subordinate legislation is also known as 'delegated legislation', but there is a difference, in that not all subordinate legislation is delegated. For example, Orders in Council made under the royal prerogative do not always derive their authority from an enabling Act. Accordingly, such orders may be subordinate, but not delegated.

to make legislation in areas specified by the enabling Act, but can also, controversially, allow ministers to amend or even repeal primary legislation in order to remove certain burdens (for example, financial burdens or obstacles to efficiency).[2]

- **Orders in Council** Technically, a form of SI, these are made by the monarch upon advice from the Privy Council,[3] and tend to be used in times of emergency to create legislation and to provide **direct effect** to EU provisions that lack direct effect.

- **Byelaws** These are, subject to approval from a government minister, legally binding laws created by local authorities, and certain public and nationalized bodies. The majority of byelaws relate to local issues of relatively minor importance. Breaching a byelaw is a criminal offence.

➡ **direct effect:** an EU provision has direct effect if it can be relied on in a domestic court (see 'Treaties and legal acts of the EU' at p 87)

The advantages of subordinate legislation are well known, but what is not prominent is that these advantages often come hand in hand with some notable disadvantages.

- **Convenience v constitutionality** Parliament's ability to delegate its law-making function is crucial. However, the fact is that, via the use of subordinate legislation, the majority of legislation created in the UK is not created by the democratically elected Parliament. One could question whether this is constitutionally correct, especially amidst a growing belief that recent governments have used subordinate legislation to implement policy.

- **Speed v scrutiny** Subordinate legislation can be introduced, created, and altered quickly, enabling it to respond to changes much more effectively and speedily than primary legislation. However, it is also important that legislation is effectively scrutinized. Unfortunately, given the sheer bulk of subordinate legislation, and the fact that it may be highly detailed and technical, it is unlikely that the vast majority of subordinate legislation receives any significant parliamentary scrutiny.

- **Expertise v bias** As legislative power is delegated to specialist experts, subordinate legislation should be more effective and cost-efficient than primary legislation created by MPs who lack the requisite expertise. However, there is always the danger that the person/body will create legislation that best serves itself or those persons that it should be regulating. Such a danger is more likely given the aforementioned lack of scrutiny.

Concern has also been expressed at the breadth of subordinate legislation that has been passed in recent years and, in particular, the amount of power that is placed in the hands of government ministers. A former Parliamentary Counsel has stated that, in certain areas, a minister can now, through the use of subordinate legislation, 'almost entirely bypass Parliament and legislate in a form as powerful as an Act but with much less scrutiny.'[4] In a worrying passage, he then goes on to state that:

> if an anti-democratic and dictatorial regime were to acquire significant political power in the United Kingdom, it would be able to bypass Parliament and legislate in an extreme and controlling way on a troublingly wide range of subjects, all through reliance on powers that have been duly granted by Parliament.[5]

---

2. Legislative and Regulatory Reform Act 2006, s 1.

3. A body consisting primarily of all members of the Cabinet (past and present), but also includes ambassadors, members of the royal family, senior judges, archbishops, and other notable figures. In practice, the advice given to the monarch derives directly from Cabinet ministers.

4. Daniel Greenberg, *Laying Down the Law* (Sweet & Maxwell 2011) 213.   5. ibid 214–15.

Creating legislation

The origins of a piece of legislation

A piece of legislation may originate from a number of sources for a number of reasons, including:

- The political party with the highest number of seats in the House of Commons will form the government,[6] and will seek to implement its policies and election manifesto pledges via the passing of legislation.
- Legislation may need to be enacted to respond to[7] or remedy[8] a judicial decision.
- Legislation may need to be enacted in order to give effect to, or implement, European treaties and legislation.

The majority of legislative proposals derive from government and, since 1965, it has been assisted hugely by the Law Commission—an independent body with a statutory duty to:

> review all the law…with a view to its systematic development and reform, including in particular the codification of such law, the elimination of anomalies, the repeal of obsolete and unnecessary enactments, the reduction of the number of separate enactments and generally the simplification and modernisation of the law.[9]

As of March 2014, the Law Commission had published 340 reports, more than two-thirds of which have, in some form, been implemented by Parliament.

Often, the government will announce its intention to legislate by publishing a consultation document or Green Paper, in which it invites suggestions in relation to the specific legislative proposal. These are often followed up with a White Paper, which will contain specific and more finalized proposals, and may even contain a draft Bill. A Bill is simply a draft piece of legislation, and Bills come in three principal forms, as follows.

1. **Public Bills** The most common type of Bill are Public Bills, which deal with matters of public interest that usually affect the general population. Public Bills come in one of two forms:

   - government Bills, which are introduced by a minister of the government and which, accordingly, almost always pass through Parliament; and

   - Private Member's Bills, which are introduced by a single non-ministerial MP of any political party. The majority of Private Member's Bills fail, largely due to lack of governmental support or a lack of time, but a number of notable Acts began life as Private Member's Bills, including the Murder (Abolition of Death Penalty) Act 1965, and the Abortion Act 1967.

---

6. Unless, as is the case at the time of writing, no single party obtains the requisite number of seats, in which case a coalition government may be formed.

7. For example, the Theft (Amendment) Act 1996 was passed in response to the case of *R v Preddy* [1996] AC 815 (HL).

8. For example, the Police (Bail and Detention) Act 2011 was passed in a matter of days in order to remedy the unfortunate effects of the case of *R (Chief Constable of Greater Manchester Police) v Salford Magistrates' Court and Paul Hookway* [2011] EWHC 1578 (Admin).   9. Law Commission Act 1965, s 3(1).

2. **Private Bills** Not to be confused with Private Member's Bills, these affect specific individuals, groups of individuals, companies, or localities. The individual or group desiring the Bill will present it to Parliament. Historically, Private Bills were common during the nineteenth century and were used to grant construction rights to companies to build roads, railways, canals, etc. Today, Private Bills are largely sought by local authorities and large companies.

3. **Hybrid Bills** As their name suggests, Hybrid Bills mix the qualities of Public and Private Bills. They usually relate to works that affect the general population, but are likely to have more significant impacts upon specific persons, groups or localities. For example, the Channel Tunnel Act 1987, which authorized construction of the Channel Tunnel, was of clear importance to the UK in general, but particularly affected the south-east of England via specific provisions permitting extensive building works in that region.

The legislative process

To become an Act of Parliament, a Bill must pass through Parliament, which comprises the House of Commons, the House of Lords, and the monarch. Most Bills are introduced in the House of Commons, but any Bill (except **Money Bills**) may also be introduced in the House of Lords. In each House, it will go through the same five stages (albeit with some procedural differences, which are highlighted below). As the majority of Bills that become law are Public Bills, the following discussion will focus on the passage of a Public Bill through Parliament.

➡ **Money Bills:** Bills that concern national taxation, public money or loans, and their management

1. **First reading** This is a purely formal stage at which the Bill is introduced, its title read out, and an order for the Bill to be printed is made. The purpose of the first reading is simply to inform the MPs/Lords that a Bill is coming up for discussion. There is no debate and no vote, so all Bills automatically pass through this stage and onto the second reading.

2. **Second reading** This is the first crucial stage of the Bill, and usually takes place no sooner than two weekends following the first reading. The purpose of the Bill is stated to the House and its main principles debated, although no amendments may be made. To save parliamentary time, certain Bills will not be debated by the full House, but will instead be referred to a standing second reading committee, which will report to the House on whether the Bill should receive a second reading or not. The House will vote on whether the Bill should proceed to the next stage. Unsurprisingly, the vast majority of government Bills pass their second reading[10] and pass onto the Committee stage.

3. **Committee stage** In the Commons, the Bill is passed onto a Public Bill Committee of between sixteen and fifty MPs, who scrutinize the Bill clause by clause. The reason for this delegation is that a smaller group of MPs can have a more productive debate than the entire House of 650 MPs. The entire Commons may, however, debate controversial Bills or Bills of constitutional importance.[11] In the Lords, the entire House will be involved in scrutinizing the Bill. For the first time, amendments may be proposed. Once the desired amendments are made, the amended Bill then progresses onto the report stage.

4. **Report stage** The Public Bill Committee reports back to the full House, highlighting any amendments made during the committee stage. MPs/Lords who

---

10. In fact, since 1905, only three government Bills have been voted down at their second reading—the last being in 1986, when the Shops Bill (which aimed to relax the laws relating to Sunday trading) was defeated.

11. For example, the European Union (Amendment) Act 2008, which ratified the Treaty of Lisbon, was debated by a committee of the whole House of Commons.

were not involved in the committee stage will have the opportunity to propose their own amendments. Alternatively, the House may reject or replace amendments made during the committee stage. Once the desired amendments are made, the Bill passes onto its third reading.

5. **Third reading** The third reading usually happens immediately after the report stage. Further debate may occur, but, in practice, will usually be very short. In the Commons, no further amendments can be made, but amendments can be made in the Lords. The final Bill is voted on and, if successful, progresses on to the next House.

Once the first House has passed the Bill, it is passed on to the second House, where it will pass through the exact same stages, albeit with some differences in procedure as stated above. Both Houses must agree the text of the Bill. Therefore, if one House proposes any amendments, the Bill is referred back to the other House for its approval. If the amendments are accepted, the Bill can progress to the final stage—namely, Royal Assent. But if a House rejects the amendments or proposes new ones, the Bill will once again be referred to the other House for further consideration. A Bill may travel between the two Houses several times (a process known as 'ping pong') before one of a possible number of outcomes is reached:

- agreement is reached between the two Houses and the Bill may progress to the monarch to receive Royal Assent;

- Public Bills must normally be passed within their current **parliamentary session** (although Private and Hybrid Bills may carry over into another). Accordingly, if agreement cannot be reached before the end of a session, the Bill will lapse and will need to pass through the entire legislative process again when Parliament reconvenes. A process now exists, however, whereby Public Bills can be carried over by agreement.[12]

➡ **parliamentary session:** the period between the State Opening of Parliament (usually November) and Parliament's prorogation (closing) (again, usually in November)

Special provision has been made to deal with the case in which the two Houses cannot reach an agreement and the House of Lords remains opposed to a Bill passed by the House of Commons. In such a case, the Bill will not lapse at the end of the parliamentary session and will be passed in the next session without the consent of the House of Lords.[13] This ability to pass a Bill without the Lords' consent was first granted to the Commons by the Parliament Act 1911, which was passed following the Lords' initial refusal to pass the 'People's Budget' of 1909.[14] The 1911 Act removed the Lords' power of veto and replaced it with the power to delay a Bill by up to two years. The power of delay was reduced further to one year by the Parliament Act 1949, but the Parliament Act 1949 itself was passed without the consent of the Lords using the 1911 Act procedure (the importance of this will be seen when the case of *R (Jackson) v Attorney General*[15] is discussed later in this chapter).

---

12. HC Standing Order No 80A. Notable Acts that were passed using this process include the Financial Services and Markets Act 2000, the Constitutional Reform Act 2005, and the Corporate Manslaughter and Corporate Homicide Act 2007.   13. Parliament Act 1911, s 2(1).

14. The 1909 Budget aimed to introduce a radical programme of welfare reform by increasing the top rate of income tax and imposing a land tax, which would have hit large landowners hardest. Unsurprisingly, the Conservative-dominated House of Lords (which included some of the largest landowners in the country) was violently opposed to the Budget and vetoed it—the first time that it had done so since the seventeenth century.

15. [2005] UKHL 56, [2006] 1 AC 262.

It should be noted that four types of Bill are not subject to the Parliament Acts, namely:

1. Private Bills;
2. Bills that were introduced in the House of Lords;
3. Bills that seek to extend the length of a Parliament beyond five years; and
4. Bills sent to the Lords less than a month before the end of a parliamentary session.

Since 1949, only four Acts have been passed without the consent of the Lords—the most recent being the Hunting Act 2004,[16] which resulted in an attack on the legality of the Parliament Acts themselves.

 ### R (Jackson) v HM Attorney General [2005] UKHL 56

FACTS: The Hunting Act 2004 banned the hunting of animals (notably, foxes) with dogs. The Bill was rejected by the House of Lords and so was passed without its consent using the Parliament Acts. The Countryside Alliance challenged the validity of the 2004 Act by challenging the validity of the Act that allowed it to be passed—namely, the Parliament Act 1949. The Alliance argued that using the 1911 Act to pass the 1949 Act was invalid, because the 1949 Act amended the 1911 Act: in effect, the 1911 Act was used to amend itself, which was improper. Accordingly, the 1949 amendments were invalid, which consequently invalidated the Hunting Act 2004, because it was not passed in accordance with the unamended 1911 Act.

HELD: The High Court, the Court of Appeal, and a nine-strong bench in the House of Lords all unanimously rejected the Countryside Alliance's claims, and upheld the validity of the Parliament Act 1949. The key issue was what were the limits of the 1911 Act—specifically, could it be used to amend itself? The House held that it could be used for such a purpose (although there were limitations on this power, which did not arise in this case).

COMMENT: Whilst the House's decision might have been unanimous, there was disagreement, especially in relation to whether limitations on the use of the Parliament Acts could be implied by the courts. On this issue, the House appeared divided, with four judges[17] stating that no further limitations could be implied, whilst another four[18] contended that further future limitations might be possible. In a key passage, Lord Steyn stated:

> the supremacy of Parliament is still the *general* principle of our constitution. It is a construct of the common law. The judges created this principle. If that is so, it is not unthinkable that circumstances could arise where the courts may have to qualify a principle established on a different hypothesis of constitutionalism.[19]

★ See Robin Cooke, 'A Constitutional Retreat' (2006) 122 LQR 224

Once a Bill passes through both Houses, the Bill is submitted to the monarch for Royal Assent. Although the monarch can personally grant Assent,[20] today, it is granted either by Lord Commissioners in the presence of both Houses, or (as is more common) via simple notification to each House that the Bill has been Assented.[21]

---

16. The other three were the War Crimes Act 1991, the European Parliamentary Elections Act 1999, and the Sexual Offences (Amendment) Act 2000.
17. Lords Bingham, Nicholls, and Steyn, and Baroness Hale.
18. Lords Hope, Walker, Carswell, and Brown.   19. [2005] UKHL 56, [2006] 1 AC 262, [102].
20. The last monarch to Assent a Bill personally was Queen Victoria in 1854.
21. Royal Assent Act 1967, s 1(1)(b).

Constitutionally, there is no rule that states that the monarch must grant Assent to a Bill, but today, Assent is regarded as an automatic process and no monarch would dare refuse it for fear of jeopardizing the position of the monarchy.[22] Upon Assent, the Bill becomes an Act of Parliament and, unless otherwise stated, comes into force at the beginning of the day that Assent was granted.[23] Many Acts, however, do not come into force upon their Assent and are brought into effect months, or even years,[24] after Assent, via the passing of a commencement order, which may bring the entire Act into effect, or via multiple commencement orders, with each one bringing specific sections of the Act into effect.[25]

Figure 3.1 demonstrates the legislative process of a public Bill.

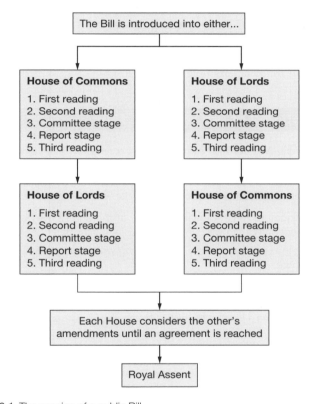

FIGURE 3.1 The passing of a public Bill

Statutory interpretation

Whilst Royal Assent may mark the conclusion of the legislative process, in practical terms, it merely commences the infancy of a statute that may remain on the statute book for years, decades, or possibly even centuries. The effectiveness of a statute is

---

22. The last monarch to refuse Assent was Queen Anne, who refused to Assent the Scottish Militia Bill 1707.   23. Interpretation Act 1978, s 4.

24. The Easter Act 1928, which aimed to establish a fixed date for Easter, has yet to come into force.

25. An extreme example of this is the Town and Country Planning Act 1971, which had 75 separate commencement orders.

dependent upon how it is interpreted and applied. Constitutionally, the role of the judges is simply to interpret statute and apply it to the case before them. Unlike judges in countries with written constitutions (notably, the US Supreme Court Justices), judges in the English legal system have no power to strike down legislation as unconstitutional. One would therefore assume that the judges have little influence over the application of a statute, but through their interpretive function, judges play a significant role in the application of a statute. This interpretative role becomes more important the higher up the court hierarchy a case progresses.

The limitations of language

The problem (or opportunity, depending on your viewpoint) facing judges is that, despite the highly skilled nature of statutory draftsmen,[26] they are still limited to using words as a means of communicating the law. The English language, despite being the most descriptive language in the world, is still something of an imprecise tool with the consequence that the precise meaning of a statute may be unclear or ambiguous, as the following example demonstrates.

> **Eg   Section 9 of the Wills Act 1837**
>
> Originally, s 9 of the Wills Act 1837 stated that in order for a will to be validly executed, the signature must appear 'at the foot or end' of the will. At first glance, this appears to be relatively straightforward—but closer scrutiny reveals a significant ambiguity in that the word 'end' could mean, among other things:
>
> 1. that the signature must appear physically at the end of the content of the will, but that sections of the will can be inserted at a later date; or
> 2. that the signature is temporally the last thing written on the will, but can be written anywhere.
>
> Judges were unable to interpret the phrase consistently, leading some judges to permit signatures anywhere on the will, while other judges required the signature to be physically at the end of the will. As a result of the ambiguity, the phrase was removed and replaced in 1852.

A statute may contain clear and unambiguous wording that is subsequently rendered unclear by developments that could not have been foreseen when the statute was enacted. In such a case, the judges will be required to interpret and apply statute to novel cases that the statute was never designed to cover.

> **_R v Ireland (Burstow)_ [1998] AC 147 (HL)**
>
> **FACTS:** The Offences Against the Person Act 1861 was enacted to deal with all instances of physical attack, except murder, including the well-known crimes of 'actual bodily harm' and 'grievous bodily harm'. The defendant made repeated telephone calls to a number of women, but remained silent when they answered. The effect of the calls was eventually to

---

26. For an account of the problems faced by draftsmen when drafting statutes, see FAR Bennion, _Bennion on Statute Law_ (3rd edn, Longman 1990).

cause the women to suffer psychological damage and the court had to determine whether this constituted 'bodily harm'.

HELD: Although 'psychiatry was in its infancy in 1861'[27] and therefore the 1861 Act was not passed with psychiatric harm in mind, it nevertheless was within the definition of 'bodily harm'. Lord Steyn stated that, in some cases, judges should interpret legislation as 'if one were interpreting it the day after it was passed'.[28] In many cases, however, a statute 'should be deemed to be always speaking'[29] and therefore the courts must be 'free to apply the current meaning of the statute to present day conditions'.[30]

COMMENT: Lord Steyn was not particularly clear on when the court should apply an historical interpretation and when it should apply a current interpretation. Subsequent courts have aimed to clarify matters and have limited Lord Steyn's 'always speaking' rule by emphasizing that, before a court applies a new interpretation to a statute, it 'must be very clear that the new situation falls within the Parliamentary intention'.[31]

★ See Simon Gardner, 'Stalking' (1998) 114 LQR 33

Aids to interpretation

The interpretive function of the judges is rendered slightly easier by the presence of certain interpretive aids, of which there are three principal types:

- presumptions;
- intrinsic aids; and
- extrinsic aids.

In certain unclear cases, the court may apply certain presumptions in order to ascertain what Parliament intended the provision in question to mean. Note, however, that they are presumptions only and may be rebutted by the statute itself.

It is impossible to list all of the presumptions, because they may be 'modified or even abandoned with the passage of time, and with the modification of the social values which they embody'.[32] Below, therefore, is a selection of the principal presumptions. Note, however, that they are in no particular order and that the lack of a hierarchy can create problems where multiple presumptions conflict.

- Parliament is presumed to know the common law and not to intend to change it, unless the wording of the statute clearly and unmistakably indicates that the common law is to be changed.[33]

- It is presumed that statute will not affect factual situations and cases that arose before the statute was passed, unless it indicates the contrary.[34] This presumption is especially strong in relation to the creation of criminal offences—indeed, today, the creation of retrospective criminal offences would breach Art 7 of the European Convention on Human Rights.

---

27. [1998] AC 147 (HL) 150 (Lord Steyn).   28. ibid 158.   29. ibid.   30. ibid.

31. *Victor Chandler International Ltd v Customs and Excise Commissioners* [2000] 1 WLR 1296 (CA) 1304 (Sir Richard Scott V-C).

32. Law Commission, *Interpretation of Statutes: Report by the Two Commissions* (Law Com No 21, HMSO 1969) [34].

33. *Black-Clawson International Ltd v Papierwerke Waldhof-Aschaffenburg AG* [1975] AC 591 (HL).

34. *L'Office Cherifien des Phosphates v Yamashita-Shinnihon Steamship Co Ltd* [1994] 1 AC 486 (HL). Legislation that does have specific retrospective effect includes the Police (Detention and Bail) Act 2011, the War Damage Act 1965, and the War Crimes Act 1991.

- The courts tend to act in a hostile manner towards any statute that seeks to oust their jurisdiction. The courts tend to interpret such statutes narrowly, or to find ways in which to evade them altogether.
- It is presumed that statutes do not apply to the Crown unless expressly stated,[35] or if it is necessary to imply that the Crown is bound. Note that 'the Crown' here refers not only to the monarch personally, but also to certain employees and agents of the Crown.

Intrinsic aids refer to aids contained within the statute itself. A fundamental principle of statutory interpretation is that the statute should be read as a whole.[36] Therefore, judges may look at any part of a statute in order to interpret a difficult section. This may involve an analysis of any or all of the following.

- **The Preamble** Older statutes used to contain a Preamble, which would set out, often at length, the purposes for which the statute was enacted. Judges may use the Preamble to interpret any section in the Act, but it may not be used to defeat the clear wording of a provision. In more modern statutes (except Private Acts), the Preamble has been replaced by the long title.
- **The long title** Statutes are almost always known by their short title, but all statutes also have a long title that explains in more detail the purposes of the Act. For example, the long title of the Companies Act 2006 is 'An Act to reform company law and restate the greater part of the enactments relating to companies; to make other provision relating to companies and other forms of business organisation; to make provision about directors' disqualification, business names, auditors and actuaries; to amend Part 9 of the Enterprise Act 2002; and for connected purposes'. Judges are free to use the long title to interpret unclear provisions,[37] but it may not be used to defeat the clear wording of a provision.
- **Punctuation, side notes, and headings** Although these are not voted on by Parliament and may be altered any time before Royal Assent, they may still be used to aid interpretation. Punctuation and side notes carry little weight, but headings can, in theory, be useful in determining the scope of a section.
- **Interpretive sections** Many statutes will provide their own interpretation of key words and phrases, usually via a dedicated section(s). For example, s 61 of the Sale of Goods Act 1979 defines twenty-seven words and phrases that appear throughout the Act.

Unlike courts in Continental Europe, English and Welsh courts historically have been unable to examine material outside the confines of the Act itself. In certain circumstances, however, the courts do have access to a range of extrinsic material to aid interpretation, as follows.

- **The Interpretation Act 1978** This Act defines terms that commonly appear in statute and imposes these definitions on all statutes, unless the Act in question states that an alternative definition is to be used.[38] The Act also states that, unless otherwise stated, 'he' will also mean 'she' (and vice versa), and terms in the singular tense will also include the plural (and vice versa).[39]
- **Dictionaries and academic texts** The courts regularly use dictionaries to define words that have a non-legal meaning. Academic texts are increasingly being used, although their use is still not as common as in civil law systems.

---

35. For example, the Crown Proceedings Act 1947 provided, for the first time, that the Crown could be subject to a civil action.
36. *Attorney General v Prince Ernest Augustus of Hanover* [1957] AC 436 (HL).
37. *Fielding v Morley Corporation* [1900] AC 133 (HL).   38. Interpretation Act 1978, s 5 and Sch 1.
39. ibid s 6.

- **Official reports** For the purpose of ascertaining the 'mischief' that an Act was meant to remedy, judges may examine certain official reports (for example, Law Commission reports, reports of Royal Commissions, government White Papers)—but because Parliament may not have accepted the findings of these reports, they cannot be used to ascertain the intention of Parliament.[40]

- **Explanatory Notes** Since November 1998, Explanatory Notes must accompany all Bills and Acts, and may be used to aid interpretation, even if there is no ambiguity.[41]

- **Parliamentary materials** As noted, a Bill may be debated in Parliament several times before it becomes an Act. These debates are recorded and reported in the official record of parliamentary debates (known as **Hansard**).[42] Historically, the courts have held that they may not refer to parliamentary materials when interpreting statutes.[43] As time progressed, the rule was relaxed and judges were permitted to utilize certain parliamentary materials. Using Hansard was, however, still prohibited on the grounds that to permit recourse to it would lead to a significant increase in the length and cost of litigation, and also because Hansard does not necessarily indicate the intention of Parliament, but rather the views of the MPs who took part in the debate. The prohibition was lifted in the following seminal and controversial case.

➡️ **Hansard:** the official report of parliamentary debates

 ## *Pepper (Inspector of Taxes) v Hart* [1993] AC 593 (HL)

FACTS: The facts of the case are not directly relevant.

HELD: The House of Lords held that if a provision is ambiguous or unclear, or if applying a literal meaning would lead to absurdity, then the courts may have recourse to Hansard if:

1. Hansard discloses the mischief that the provision was meant to remedy, or the legislative intention behind the provision in question;
2. the statements relied on were made by a minister or other promoter of the Bill; and
3. such statements are clear.

COMMENT: The above conditions indicate that Hansard was never intended to be referred to routinely and, in the vast majority of cases, Hansard will provide little, if any, clarification.[44] Despite this, *Pepper v Hart* remains an extremely controversial decision—especially the second condition stated by the House. Reference to Hansard should be used to ascertain the intention of Parliament—why therefore is such reference limited to statements of ministers and promoters of the Bill? The voice of a minister is not the voice of Parliament, and it could be argued that the second condition provides an unfair preference for the views of the government that could ultimately result in 'a real danger of the courts becoming too close to the executive's intentions'.[45] A growing consensus also seems to be that permitting

---

40. *Eastman Photographic Materials Co Ltd v Comptroller General of Patents* [1898] AC 571 (HL).

41. *R (on the Application of Westminster City Council) v National Asylum Support Service* [2002] UKHL 38, [2002] 1 WLR 2956.

42. Named after Thomas Hansard, who purchased the rights to print parliamentary debates in the early nineteenth century.   43. *Davis v Johnson* [1979] AC 264 (HL).

44. The House in *Pepper v Hart* itself admitted this: see [1993] AC 593 (HL) 634, in which Lord Browne-Wilkinson stated that '[i]n many…cases reference to Parliamentary material will not throw any light on the matter' and would be unlikely to yield a 'crock of gold'.

45. David Miers, 'Taxing Perks and Interpreting Statutes: *Pepper v Hart*' (1993) 56 MLR 695, 708.

⭐ See BJ Davenport, 'Perfection—But at What Cost?' (1993) 109 LQR 149

reference to Hansard has increased the costs of litigation,[46] leading one commentator to conclude that 'the *pragmatic* reasons for overruling or restricting *Pepper v Hart* are now very strong'.[47]

In addition to presumptions, intrinsic and extrinsic aids, the courts have also developed several contextual linguistic rules to aid interpretation, of which three need be noted. The first is expressed by the Latin maxim *expressio unius est exclusio alterius* ('to express one thing is to exclude another'), and applies where a statutory provision lists certain items. This effect of the rule is to presume that only those items listed will be within the scope of the provision, as demonstrated in the following case.

 R v The Inhabitants of Sedgely (1831) 2 B & Ald 65

 poor rate: a form of tax levied on certain persons, the proceeds of which were used to help the poor

FACTS: Section 1 of the Poor Relief Act 1601 provided that a **poor rate** be levied on the occupiers of 'lands, houses, tithes and coal mines'. The limestone mine of the Earl of Dudley was charged the poor rate and he applied to the court, arguing that his mine was not within the definition contained in s 1 and so he was not liable to pay the poor rate.

HELD: Whilst coal mines were listed in s 1, limestone mines were not. The *expressio unius* rule provided that only those items listed were within the scope of the provision and so the limestone mine was not rateable under the 1601 Act.

It is common, however, for a statute to provide a list of specific items and then follow it with a general phrase (for example, 'this Act will apply to *X, Y, Z*, and any other relevant items'). The addition of the general phrase means that the *expressio unius* rule cannot be used and so a second rule is used, which is known as the *ejusdem generis* ('of the same class') rule. This simply means that the general phrase will relate only to things of the same class or type as the specific items, as is demonstrated by the following case.

Powell v Kempton Park Racecourse Co Ltd [1899] AC 143 (HL)

FACTS: The Betting Act 1853 made it an offence to use a 'house, office, room or other place for betting' ('house, office and room' constituted the specific items, and 'other place' constituted the general phrase). The defendant, who operated Tatersall's Ring, an outdoor enclosure in which betting took place, was charged with breach of the 1853 Act.

---

46. See Lord Steyn, '*Pepper v Hart*: A Re-examination' (2001) 21 OJLS 59, 64, where he stated: 'It remains my view that *Pepper v Hart* has substantially increased the cost of litigation to very little advantage. Many appellate judges share this view.'
47. SH Bailey, JPL Ching, and NW Taylor, *The Modern English Legal System* (5th edn, Sweet & Maxwell 2007) 454.

HELD: The House of Lords held that no contravention of the 1853 Act had occurred. The specific items listed were all indoor locations and, accordingly, the phrase 'other place' could only include locations of the same class. As Tatersalls' Ring was outside, it was not an 'other place' for the purposes of the 1853 Act.

The third rule to be discussed is represented by the maxim *noscitur a sociis* ('it is known from its associates'). This rule provides that the words of a statute should be interpreted in the context of the words surrounding them and the neighbouring provisions. The application of this rule can be seen in the following case.

 Pengelley v Bell Punch Co Ltd **[1964] 1 WLR 1055 (CA)**

FACTS: Section 28 of the Factories Act 1961 provided that 'floors, steps, stairs, passageways and gangways' should be kept clear of obstruction. The defendant used a section of the factory floor to store reels of paper. The claimant injured himself whilst reaching over these reels and alleged that the defendant had breached s 28.

HELD: The Court of Appeal held that s 28 had not been breached. The word 'floor' in s 28 should be interpreted in context with the words around it. The words around it clearly indicated that 'floor' was being used in the sense of a passageway; the floor on which the reels were stored was not a passageway, but was used for storage. Accordingly, it did not fall within the definition of 'floor' contained in s 28.

Presumptions, intrinsic and extrinsic aids, and linguistic rules may be useful in specific cases, but their general usefulness is limited. It has therefore been largely left to the judges themselves to determine the most appropriate methods of interpreting legislation. Over time, the judiciary formed what are known as the 'canons of interpretation'—three rules that are designed to provide the judiciary with the flexibility to interpret legislation effectively and in line with the intention of Parliament:

1. the literal rule;
2. the golden rule; and
3. the mischief rule.

Unfortunately, the precise relationship between the three rules has never been clarified and they can produce vastly different outcomes. The general belief appears to be that the rules are hierarchical (that is, that the court will use the literal rule first, and, if that produces an unacceptable result, it will move onto the golden rule, etc)—but there is no conclusive evidence to indicate that such a belief is justified and it is actually more accurate to state that:

> a court invokes whichever of the rules produces a result that satisfies its sense of justice in the case before it. Although the literal rule is the one most frequently referred to in express terms, the courts treat all three as valid and refer to them as occasion demands.[48]

---

48. John Willis, 'Statute Interpretation in a Nutshell' (1938) 16 Can Bar Rev 1, 6.

The literal rule

Under the literal rule, the words of a statute are given their literal, normal, every-day meaning, irrespective of the result that such an interpretation produces. So, for example, in *Whitely v Chapell*,[49] s 3 of the Poor Law Amendment Act 1851 made it an offence to personate at an election 'any person entitled to vote'. The defendant was found 'not guilty' after he personated a dead voter, because a dead person is not entitled to vote.

The literal rule is the most constitutionally acceptable rule, because it focuses on the actual words that Parliament used and if Parliament chooses words that produce unacceptable results, it is for Parliament to rectify the law, not the judges. As Lord Esher stated: 'If the words of an Act are clear, you must follow them, even though they lead to a manifest absurdity. The court has nothing to do with the question of whether the legislature has committed an absurdity.'[50] Whilst such an approach may respect the principle of parliamentary sovereignty, that will provide little comfort to the litigant who loses his case due to a literal, but absurd, interpretation. In criminal law cases, the results of an overly literal interpretation can be even more severe, as the following case demonstrates.

 R v Maginnis [1987] 1 All ER 907 (HL)[51]

FACTS: The police had discovered a package containing cannabis resin in Maginnis' car. He claimed that the package was not his, but was left in his car by a friend, who intended to collect it later. Despite this, Maginnis was charged under s 5(3) of the Misuse of Drugs Act 1971, which makes it a criminal offence for 'a person to have a controlled drug in his possession, whether lawfully or not, with intent to supply it to another'.

HELD: The key words were 'intent to supply'. Applying their literal meaning, a four- to-one majority (Lord Goff dissenting) in the House of Lords upheld Maginnis' conviction. He intended to give the drugs back to his friend; ergo he intended to supply them.

COMMENT: This case demonstrates a fundamental flaw of the literal rule—namely, the presumption that all words have a single, literal, normal meaning. In reality, few words will have a single everyday meaning; they will usually have several. None of the judges involved in *Maginnis* could agree on what was the literal definition of the word 'supply': both the majority and Lord Goff were able to point to dictionary definitions that upheld their respective viewpoints. This case also demonstrates that a literal interpretation can actually run counter to the intention of Parliament. There is little doubt that the offence contained in s 5(3) was aimed at drug dealers (a point made by Lord Goff), as opposed to drug users, who were subject to a less serious offence under s 5(1)—namely, being in possession of a controlled drug. By convicting Maginnis of the more serious offence, there is little doubt that the courts had applied the Act in a way that Parliament had not intended.

As time progressed, criticisms of the literal rule began to emerge. In 1969, the Law Commission stated:

---

49. (1869) 4 QB 147.   50. *R v Judge of the City of London Court* [1892] 1 QB 273 (CA) 290.
51. Another case universally regarded as producing an absurd result is *London and North Eastern Railway v Berriman* [1946] AC 278 (HL).

> To place undue emphasis on the literal meaning of the words of a provision is to assume an unattainable perfection in draftsmanship…Such an approach ignores the limitations of language, which is not infrequently demonstrated even at the level of the House of Lords when Law Lords differ as to the so-called 'plain meaning' of words.[52]

Clearly, the literal rule could not be the sole governing rule for the interpretation of statutes. A rule was needed that could be used where the literal interpretation was insufficient, and such a rule was created in 1857—namely, the golden rule.

The golden rule

The golden rule was first advanced by Lord Wensleydale when he stated 'the grammatical and ordinary sense of the words is to be adhered to, unless that would lead to some absurdity…in which case the grammatical and ordinary sense of words may be modified, so as to avoid that absurdity…but no farther'.[53] Based on this, it could validly be argued that the golden rule is nothing more than an evolution of the literal rule. The courts have since categorically stated that the literal rule will not be used where it would produce an absurd result;[54] instead, the courts will use an alternative meaning of the relevant words that 'though less proper, is one which the Court thinks the words will bear'.[55] The use of the golden rule to avoid an absurd result can be seen in the following case.

 ### R v Allen (1872) 1 CCR 367

FACTS: Allen had married another woman whilst his existing wife was still alive. He was charged with the crime of bigamy under s 57 of the Offences Against the Person Act 1861, which states: 'Whosoever being married shall marry any other person during the life of the former husband or wife…shall be guilty of bigamy.' Allen argued that, because he was already married, it was technically impossible to marry someone else: he may take part in a marriage ceremony, but he would not be lawfully marrying the second 'wife'; ergo he was not guilty under the 1861 Act.

HELD: Allen's defence failed and he was convicted. From a literal point of view, he was correct—but a literal interpretation of s 57 would have rendered it useless. Therefore, the court held that the words 'shall marry' would be interpreted to mean shall 'go through the form and ceremony of marriage with another person'.[56]

It should be noted that the court cannot abandon the literal rule in favour of the golden rule whenever it wishes. The golden rule can be used only where the literal rule would produce 'an inconsistency, or an absurdity or inconvenience so great as to convince the Court that the intention could not have been to use [the words of the statute] in their ordinary signification'.[57] This limitation can lead to situations in which a court is bound to adopt a literal interpretation when it would desperately

---

52. Law Commission, *Interpretation of Statutes: Report by the Two Commissions* (Law Com No 21, HMSO 1969) [30].   53. *Grey v Pearson* (1857) 6 HL Cas 61, 106.
54. *McMonagle v Westminster City Council* [1990] 2 AC 716 (HL).
55. *River Wear Commissioners v Adamson* (1877) 2 App Cas 743 (HL) 765 (Lord Blackburn).
56. (1872) 1 CCR 367, 375 (Cockburn CJ).
57. ibid 764–5 (Lord Blackburn).

wish not to. This occurred in the decision of the High Court in *R v Human Fertilisation and Embryology Authority, ex p Blood*,[58] in which Diane Blood wished to be inseminated with sperm taken from her husband before he died. Unfortunately for her, Sch 3(1) of the Human Fertilisation and Embryology Act 1990 provided that the donor would need to provide written consent, which was obviously impossible. In dismissing her appeal against the decision of the Human Fertilisation and Embryology Authority's decision not to allow her to be inseminated, Sir Stephen Brown described the case as 'most anxious and moving [and that his] heart went out to this applicant who wishes to preserve an essential part of her late beloved husband'.[59] The requirement for written consent was, however, clear and, as a matter of statutory construction, the Court had no option but to dismiss her appeal.[60]

Whilst an application of the golden rule may be preferable to the literal rule in certain cases, this does not mean that the golden rule is without problems. The Law Commission noted that the application of the golden rule is based upon the literal rule producing an 'absurdity, inconsistency or inconvenience, but provides no clear means to test the existence of these characteristics or to measure their quality or extent'.[61] Often, the justification behind an application of the golden rule is to apply a rule of public policy,[62] with such rules being notoriously vague and amorphous. The golden rule would appear to provide a measure of flexibility to statutory interpretation, but at the cost of reducing certainty.

The mischief rule and the purposive approach

The final rule to be examined was actually the first to be established. The mischief rule was laid down in 1584 in *Heydon's Case*[63] and basically states that, where a statute was enacted to remedy a problem (mischief), the court will, if possible, adopt an interpretation of the statute that corrects that mischief. More specifically, the court in *Heydon's Case* stated that four factors needed to be considered.

1. What was the common law before the enactment of the Act?
2. What was the defect (mischief) that the common law failed to remedy?
3. What remedy had Parliament implemented to cure the mischief?
4. What was the true reason for the adoption of the remedy?

The following case demonstrates the mischief rule in action.

 Royal College of Nursing v DHSS [1981] AC 800 (HL)

FACTS: Section 1(1) of the Abortion Act 1967 provides that no criminal offence is committed 'when a pregnancy is terminated by a registered medical practitioner'. When the Act was passed, abortions were carried out surgically by doctors, but in 1972, chemical abortions

---

58. [1996] 3 WLR 1176 (QB).   59. ibid 1191.

60. Fortunately for Diane Blood, whilst the Court of Appeal agreed with the interpretation of the trial judge, it reversed his decision ([1999] Fam 151) on the ground that the EC Treaty provided Mrs Blood with the right to receive medical treatment in another Member State. Accordingly, she was permitted to receive IVF treatment in Belgium using her dead husband's sperm. She subsequently gave birth to two sons (on separate occasions) and won another legal battle to have Mr Blood legally recognized as the boys' father.

61. Law Commission, *Interpretation of Statutes: Report by the Two Commissions* (Law Com No 21, HMSO 1969) [32].   62. See e.g. *Re Sigsworth* [1935] Ch 89 (Ch).   63. (1584) 3 Co Rep 7a.

were introduced, which involved a doctor inserting a catheter and a nurse pumping a chemical into the womb. The introduction of the chemical was carried out while the doctor was on call, but not actually present. The Royal College of Nursing sought a declaration from the court that the new procedure was in breach of s 1(1).

HELD: The House of Lords, by a majority of three to two, held that the new procedure was lawful. Lord Diplock focused on the mischief behind the 1967 Act, which was to clarify and remedy the uncertain nature of the law prior to 1967, and to render unlawful the 'back-street abortions' that many women undertook due to the law's lack of clarity. The 1967 Act achieved this by broadening the grounds upon which a lawful abortion may be obtained and ensuring that the abortion is carried out in hygienic conditions with the requisite skill. Given this, a nurse in a hospital administering a chemical under the instruction of a doctor is clearly not what s 1(1) was enacted to prevent.

COMMENT: Clearly, in order to reach their verdict, the majority had to reject a literal interpretation of s 1(1). Much of the confusion in this case could be seen to be the result of the drafting of s 1(1), which was described as 'far from elegant'.[64] But is the poor drafting of a provision reason enough to reject a literal interpretation? The two dissenting judges (Lords Wilberforce and Edmund-Davies) thought not. Both judges adopted a literal interpretation and found the procedure to be unlawful because the pregnancy was clearly not terminated by a 'registered medical practitioner', but by a nurse. Lord Edmund-Davies was particularly critical of the majority, arguing that they had engaged in 'redrafting with a vengeance'.[65] It is interesting to note that, of the nine judges who were involved in this case in the various courts, only four believed the new procedure to be lawful.

Whilst the mischief rule may be the preferred rule of the Law Commission, it still acknowledges that the legal environment today has changed hugely since *Heydon's Case*.[66] When the rule was conceived, parliamentary sovereignty was not yet fully established and statute was a much less important source of law than it is today. Accordingly, a rule that, in essence, allows the judges to rectify the meaning of a statute to allow it to remedy the mischief that it was intended to was appropriate. Today, with parliamentary sovereignty well established and statute a primary source of law, allowing judges such a quasi-legislative role is less constitutionally justifiable. Further, when the rule was conceived, judges played a prominent role in the drafting of statutes; they were therefore well placed to identify the mischief that a statute was meant to remedy. Today, skilled parliamentary draftsmen draft statutes and the judges may not be as well placed to identify the mischief that an Act was designed to remedy.

Much modern legislation is not concerned with remedying a particular mischief, but rather with achieving some other, more general, purpose. For this reason, in recent decades, the 'pendulum has swung towards purposive methods of construction',[67] whereby the courts will interpret the statute by reference to its context and purpose, as the following case demonstrates.

---

64. [1981] AC 800 (HL) 827 (Lord Diplock).   65. ibid 831.
66. Law Commission, *Interpretation of Statutes: Report by the Two Commissions* (Law Com No 21, HMSO 1969) [33].
67. *R (Quintavalle) v Secretary of State for Health* [2003] 2 AC 687 (HL) 700 (Lord Steyn).

> ### R (Quintavalle) v Secretary of State for Health [2003] UKHL 13
>
> **FACTS:** The Human Fertilisation and Embryology Act 1990 was passed to regulate the creation of human embryos outside the body, with an embryo being originally defined by s 1(1)(a) as 'a live human embryo where fertilisation is complete'.[68] After the Act was passed, scientists developed a new technique (called cell nuclear replacement (CNR)) by which an embryo was created by introducing a nucleus to an unfertilized egg. The claimant, on behalf of the Pro-Life Alliance, contended that, as fertilization does not take place, this new technique did not fall within the definition of embryo and, accordingly, the Human Fertilisation and Embryology Authority (HFEA) could not lawfully license CNR research. The government disagreed and stated that CNR did fall within the regulatory remit of the HFEA. The claimant sought a court declaration that CNR was not within the scope of s 1(1)(a).
>
> **HELD:** The House of Lords held that CNR was within the scope of s 1(a)(a) and therefore fell within the regulatory remit of the HFEA. Lord Bingham stated
>
>> The basic task of the court is to ascertain and give effect to the true meaning of what Parliament has said in the enactment to be construed. But that is not to say that attention should be confined and a literal interpretation given to the particular provisions which give rise to difficulty... The court's task, within the permissible bounds of interpretation, is to give effect to Parliament's purpose.[69]
>
> He went on to state that an embryo created through fertilization and one created through CNR were 'very similar organisms' and that Parliament could not possibly have intended that CNR embryos should fall outside the scope of the 1990 Act's regulation.

★ See Kathy Liddell, 'Purposive Interpretation and the March of Genetic Technology' (2003) 62 CLJ 563

This purposive approach is widely accepted and judges will frequently refer to their interpretation of a statute being 'purposive'. This approach is wider than the golden rule, because it does not depend on the literal approach producing an absurd result, or a result that Parliament could not have intended. It is also wider than the mischief rule, because it does not focus on a particular mischief, but rather the broad aims and purposes of the statute.

The courts' reliance on the purposive approach is demonstrated in that the courts have held that a statute that fails to fulfil its purpose due to a drafting error can be rectified by the courts by adding, removing, or substituting words. However, before the court remedies a drafting error, it must be sure:[70]

- of the intended purpose of the statute or provision;
- that the draftsmen and Parliament have, inadvertently, failed to give effect to that purpose; and
- of the substance (although not the precise working) of the provision that Parliament would have enacted, had it noticed the error.

These three rules impose clear limits on the courts' ability to remedy a statute using the purposive approach. Where a case involves a *casus omissus* (that is, something for which statute should provide, but which it does not), the court cannot fill the gap in the statute; to do so would attribute an intention that Parliament clearly did not have

---

68. Note that this definition has subsequently been altered.

69. [2003] UKHL 13, [2003] 2 AC 687 [8].

70. *Inco Europe Ltd v First Choice Distribution* [2000] 1 WLR 586 (HL) 592 (Lord Nicholls).

and would constitute 'naked usurpation of the legislative function under the thin disguise of interpretation'.[71] Where statute does contain a gap, it is for Parliament to fill it by passing an amending Act.

Case law

Although the amount of legislation passed by Parliament has increased in recent years, the bulk of law within the English legal system is still largely derived from cases and the English legal system is still very much a common law system. 'Case law' refers to the body of law that is created and developed via the decisions of judges.

The doctrine of precedent

Central to our common law system is what is known as the doctrine of 'precedent'. The *Oxford English Dictionary* defines 'precedent' as '[a] previous instance taken as an example or rule by which to be guided in similar cases or circumstances'.[72] In legal terms, it simply refers to the process whereby cases are decided based upon previous judicial decisions.

There are three principal levels of precedent, as explained in Table 3.2 below.

TABLE 3.2 The levels of precedent

Level	Strength of precedent	Examples
No precedent value	Does not establish a precedent and need not be followed	Decisions of magistrates' courts and county courts
Persuasive authority	Need not be followed, but are persuasive, with varying levels of persuasiveness existing. For example, decisions of the Judicial Committee of the Privy Council are extremely persuasive	• Decisions of the Judicial Committee of the Privy Council and the Crown Court • *Obiter dicta* • Decisions of Irish, Scottish, Commonwealth and US courts
Binding precedent	Establish binding precedents that must be followed by later courts, unless the court is not bound by the precedent, or the precedent can be distinguished	• Cases of higher courts are binding on lower courts • Some courts (e.g. Court of Appeal) bind themselves

Having established that cases may be binding on later courts, two questions need to be answered: (i) when is a case binding, and (ii) exactly what aspect of a case binds later courts?

---

71. *Magor and St Mellons Rural District Council v Newport Corporation* [1952] AC 189 (HL) 191 (Lord Simonds).
72. Definition derived from Oxford English Dictionary Online <http://www.oed.com>.

The court hierarchy

The extent to which a court is bound by precedent (and can bind other courts) is dependent upon where it sits in the court hierarchy. The UK court system is made up of seven main courts (eight, if the Divisional Courts are regarded as distinct from the High Court). The general rule is that higher courts bind lower courts, but, as is discussed later, there are exceptions to this, and one court, the Judicial Committee of the Privy Council, does not sit easily within the hierarchy.

Table 3.3 demonstrates in brief the court hierarchy in relation to the doctrine of precedent.

TABLE 3.3 Precedent and the court hierarchy

Court	Bound by	Binds
Supreme Court/ House of Lords	• Judicial Committee of the Privy Council, but only in relation to appeals from specialist courts	• Every court below, except the Judicial Committee of the Privy Council in relation to common law issues, and appeals from certain specialist courts
Court of Appeal	• Supreme Court/House of Lords • Court of Appeal (subject to exceptions)	• Court of Appeal (subject to exceptions) • Every court below it in the court hierarchy
Divisional Courts	• Supreme Court/House of Lords • Court of Appeal • Divisional Courts (subject to exceptions)	• Divisional Courts (subject to exceptions) • Every court below it in the court hierarchy (including the High Court)
High Court	• Supreme Court/House of Lords • Court of Appeal • Divisional Courts	• Every court below it in the court hierarchy
County courts, Crown Courts, magistrates' courts	• Supreme Court/House of Lords • Court of Appeal • High Court	• No court—these cannot create binding precedent, but Crown Court decisions constitute persuasive authority
Judicial Committee of the Privy Council	• Supreme Court/House of Lords, in relation to non-common law issues	• Every other court (except itself) in relation to appeals from specialist courts (for example, the ecclesiastical courts)

The Supreme Court/House of Lords

The highest domestic court in the United Kingdom is the Supreme Court (as noted, prior to October 2009, the highest court was the Appellate Committee of the House of Lords). Decisions of the Supreme Court/House of Lords are binding on all other UK courts in civil matters, and on all other courts in England, Wales, and Northern Ireland in criminal matters. It used to be the case that the House of Lords was also bound by its own decisions,[73] but the unfortunate effect of this was to make House

---

73. *London Tramways v London County Council* [1898] AC 375 (HL).

of Lords' decisions unalterable, except by statute. Recognizing that 'too rigid adherence to precedent may lead to injustice in a particular case and…unduly restrict the proper development of the law',[74] the House of Lords issued a Practice Statement indicating that it was no longer bound by its own decisions and would depart from them 'when it appears right to do so'.[75] The Supreme Court is accordingly free to overrule its own decisions and those of the Appellate Committee, although it does so rarely.

It is well established that the Supreme Court will not overrule a previous decision simply because it is 'wrong'.[76] So when will the Supreme Court overrule itself? Should it only be allowed to overrule itself in specific circumstances, or should it have full discretion? Pre-Supreme Court authority exists for both positions. In *Vestey v Inland Revenue Commissioners*,[77] Lord Wilberforce stated that the House of Lords' power to overrule itself should be 'governed by stated principles'.[78] Conversely, in *The Hannah Blumenthal*,[79] Lord Roskill stated that instances in which the House of Lords can overrule itself 'cannot be categorized'.[80] Currently, there are no set criteria in place establishing when the Supreme Court will exercise the power granted to it by the Practice Statement, but it has been argued[81] that an analysis of the cases in which the power has been used reveals that the Supreme Court should not overrule a previous decision:

- where no new reasons or arguments are advanced;
- where 'a class of the citizenry'[82] has justifiably relied upon the previous decision and ordered its affairs based upon it;
- where Parliament has enacted legislation based upon the assumption that the previous decision is the law; and
- where, in criminal cases, the issue is moot (that is, having no practical significance).

In addition, the Supreme Court must be of the opinion that '[t]he present law, all things considered, would be improved'[83] by overruling a previous decision.

The Court of Appeal

It is necessary to consider the two divisions of the Court of Appeal separately. Decisions of the Civil Division of the Court of Appeal bind all lower civil courts (namely, the High Court (including Divisional Courts), county courts, and, in respect of their civil jurisdiction, magistrates' courts). The Civil Division is bound by its own decisions, as well as those of the Supreme Court/House of Lords—but the ability of the Civil Division to bind itself is subject to a number of exceptions, as laid down in the following case.

---

74. *Practice Statement (Judicial Precedent)* [1966] 3 All ER 77 (HL).   75. ibid.
76. *R v National Insurance Commissioner, ex p Hudson* [1972] AC 944 (HL) 966.
77. [1980] AC 1148 (HL).   78. ibid 1150.   79. [1983] 1 AC 845 (HL).   80. ibid 922.
81. See Sir Rupert Cross and JW Harris, *Precedent in English Law* (4th edn, OUP 1991) 135–43.
82. ibid 169.
83. JW Harris, 'Towards Principles of Overruling: When Should a Final Court of Appeal Second Guess?' (1990) 10 OJLS 135, 149.

Young v Bristol Aeroplane Co Ltd [1944] KB 718 (CA)

FACTS: The facts of the case are not directly relevant.

HELD: The Court of Appeal reiterated that it is usually bound by its own decisions, but stated that three exceptions exist to this principle, as follows.

1. If two previous Court of Appeal decisions conflict, the Court must choose which case to follow. The other case is automatically overruled.
2. The Court of Appeal may ignore its own previous decision, which 'although not expressly overruled, cannot stand with a subsequent decision of the [Supreme Court or] House of Lords'.[84]
3. If a Court of Appeal decision is *per incuriam* ('through want of care'), it need not be followed. An example of a decision being *per incuriam* is where a key case or statute was overlooked and, had the Court known of this case or statute, it would have reached a contrary decision.

Since *Young*, a number of other exceptions have been established, including:

- Court of Appeal judgments in relation to the granting of permission to appeal are not binding;[85]
- the decision of a two-judge Court of Appeal in relation to an interlocutory appeal will not bind a future three-judge Court of Appeal;[86]
- if a Court of Appeal decision is appealed to the Supreme Court and the Justices decide the appeal on different grounds from those argued in the Court of Appeal, then the Court of Appeal decision will not be binding on itself;[87]
- there is authority indicating that a Court of Appeal decision may not be binding on itself (or, indeed, on a first-instance judge)[88] if it is inconsistent with a decision of the Privy Council,[89] although this issue is far from settled;[90]
- although not overtly established, it is highly probable that a Court of Appeal decision will not be binding on itself if it is inconsistent with a decision of the Court of Justice of the EU. This is because s 3(1) of the European Communities Act 1972 imposes a duty upon all domestic courts either to refer cases involving European law to the Court of Justice, or, if a referral is not made, to determine the case in accordance with principles and decisions of the Court of Justice.

Decisions of the Criminal Division of the Court of Appeal bind all lower criminal courts (namely, the Queen's Bench Division of the High Court, the Crown Court, and magistrates' courts). The Criminal Division is bound by its own decisions, as well as by those of the Supreme Court/House of Lords. The above exceptions that apply to the Civil Division also apply to the Criminal Division, except that relating to an inconsistent decision of the Privy Council.[91] As criminal cases involve the potential to deprive defendants of their liberty, precedent is not followed as strictly as it is in the Civil Division and the discretion of the Criminal Division to ignore its

---

84. [1944] KB 718 (CA) 722 (Lord Greene MR).
85. *Clark v University of Lincolnshire and Humberside* [2000] 3 All ER 752 (CA).
86. *Boys v Chaplin* [1968] 2 QB 1 (CA).
87. *Al-Mehdawi v Secretary of State for the Home Department* [1990] 1 AC 876 (CA).
88. See *Daraydan Holdings Ltd v Solland International Ltd* [2004] EWHC 622, [2005] Ch 119.
89. *Doughty v Turner Manufacturing Co Ltd* [1964] 1 QB 518 (CA).
90. See e.g. *Davis v Johnson* [1979] AC 264 (CA).   91. *R v Campbell* [1997] Cr App R 199 (CA).

own decisions is wider. So, for example, the Criminal Division may ignore an earlier case if it believes that the earlier case 'misapplied or misunderstood'[92] the law.

The Divisional Courts

Judges in each of the three divisions of the High Court may also sit as a Divisional Court. Decisions of a Divisional Court bind other Divisional Courts and all lower courts, including the standard High Court, if a judge sits alone. The Divisional Courts are bound by the decisions of the Supreme Court/House of Lords, the Court of Appeal,[93] and themselves. In civil cases, however, the *Young v Bristol Aeroplane Co Ltd* exceptions outlined above apply to a Divisional Court.[94] In criminal cases and cases involving judicial review, the Court may depart from previous decisions where it feels that 'the previous decision was plainly wrong'.[95]

The High Court

High Court decisions are binding upon all lower courts (namely the Crown Court, county courts, and magistrates' courts). The High Court is bound by decisions of the Supreme Court/House of Lords, the Court of Appeal, and its Divisional Courts. The High Court is not bound by itself, although decisions by other High Court judges are considered extremely persuasive and are departed from reluctantly. It has been argued that a High Court judge should only depart from a previous High Court decision if he is convinced that it was incorrect,[96] and that deputy High Court judges should follow the decisions of High Court judges.[97] If two High Court decisions conflict, the practice is to follow the later decision, provided that the later decision fully considered the earlier decision.[98]

The Crown Court

Although legal rulings of the Crown Court are not binding, they do constitute persuasive authority, especially if the judge sitting is a High Court judge. The Crown Court is bound by decisions of the Supreme Court/House of Lords, Court of Appeal, and the High Court. It was held in *R v Colyer*[99] that the Crown Court is not bound by decisions of a Divisional Court, but given that the High Court and Divisional Courts themselves are bound by decisions of a Divisional Court, such an assertion is unlikely ever to be accepted.

The inferior courts

County courts and magistrates' courts are referred to collectively as the 'inferior courts', and their decisions do not establish binding precedent or constitute persuasive authority. Consequently, decisions of these courts bind no one, including themselves. These courts are all bound by decisions of the Supreme Court/House of Lords, Court of Appeal, and High Court (including Divisional Courts).

---

92. *R v Gould* [1968] 2 QB 65 (CA) 69 (Diplock LJ).

93. Unless the Court of Appeal decision was *per incuriam* and the missing authority was a Supreme Court/House of Lords' decision (*R v Northumberland Compensation Appeal Tribunal, ex p Shaw* [1952] 1 KB 338 (CA)).   94. *Huddersfield Police Authority v Watson* [1947] KB 842 (DC).

95. *Hornigold v Chief Constable of Lancashire* [1986] Crim LR 792 (DC).

96. *Re Hillas-Drake, National Provincial Bank v Liddell* [1944] Ch 235.

97. *R v Hertsmere Borough Council, ex p Woolgar* (1996) HLR 703 (QB).

98. *Colchester Estates (Cardiff) v Carlton Industries plc* [1986] Ch 80.   99. [1974] Crim LR 243.

The Judicial Committee of the Privy Council

One court that does not fit neatly into the court hierarchy is the Judicial Committee of the Privy Council. As a general rule, its decisions are not binding on any court, except in relation to appeals from certain specialist courts.[100] Even when not binding, Privy Council decisions are regarded as extremely persuasive, largely due to the fact that it comprises principally of Justices of the Supreme Court. In fact, in one extremely controversial decision,[101] it was decided that, in extremely exceptional (if not unique) circumstances,[102] a ruling of the Privy Council can take precedence over a previous decision of the Supreme Court/House of Lords, and that the Court of Appeal and courts below will be bound to follow the ruling of the Privy Council. Furthermore, in relation to common law issues, the Privy Council is not bound by decisions of the Supreme Court/House of Lords,[103] although such decisions will be extremely persuasive. The reason for this is that the Privy Council acts as a final appeal court for numerous other countries and such countries may require the law to develop in a manner different from that of the UK.

Stare decisis and ratio decidendi

Once it has been established that the decisions of one court bind another, it then needs to be determined exactly which aspect of a case is binding. The UK system of binding precedent is based upon the Latin maxim *stare decisis*. This is, however, a shortened version of the full maxim and its abbreviation is unfortunate, because the full phrase is descriptively more accurate. The full maxim *stare rationibus decidendis* indicates that it is the *reasoning* behind the court's decision that is binding upon later courts, not the actual decision itself, nor the specific facts of the case. By making the reasoning binding, the case can be applied to other cases with a wide range of facts. This reasoning is known as the *ratio decidendi*, but, unfortunately, identifying the *ratio* of a case can, in practice, be extremely difficult, especially because judges will never expressly identify the *ratio*. To make matters more complicated, a case may have more than one *ratio* (known as *rationes*).

The following example demonstrates that, whilst the *ratio* differs from the facts, it is still influenced by them.

→ **stare decisis:** 'keep to what has been decided previously'

→ **stare rationibus decidendis:** 'keep to the reasoning of what has been decided previously'

→ **ratio decidendi:** 'reason for deciding'

> **Eg** **Identifying the *ratio***
>
> Andrew is driving down the road in his black BMW. He takes his eyes off the road in order to tune in the car's radio. He does not notice that Ceri is trying to cross the road at a zebra crossing and he runs her over, injuring her severely and damaging the laptop she was carrying. Ceri sues Andrew in negligence and is successful. Possible *rationes* could be any of the following.

---

100. This would include the Ecclesiastical Court, which hears disputes relating to religious matters, and the Prize Court, which hears cases on whether ships have been lawfully captured in times of war.
101. *R v James* [2006] EWCA Crim 14, [2006] QB 588.
102. Namely that the Privy Council decision that was followed was decided by a bench of nine Law Lords. Over half of them were Law Lords at the time that the case was decided and, had the case been appealed to the House of Lords, the result would have been a foregone conclusion.
103. See e.g. *Australian Consolidated Press Ltd v Uren* [1969] 1 AC 590 (PC).

1. **Men who drive black BMWs and who run over women at zebra crossings are liable in negligence** This *ratio* is far too narrow and could only be applied in cases with identical facts to our case. Do the genders of the driver and victim matter? Do the colour and make of car matter? The answer to both of these questions is 'no'.

2. **Drivers of cars are liable if they negligently run over a person at a zebra crossing** This *ratio* is better, but is still too narrow. Why are only drivers of cars liable? What if I negligently run over someone by mounting the pavement instead of at a zebra crossing?

3. **Drivers of motor vehicles who drive without due care and attention may be liable in negligence for injuries caused to another as a result of such negligence** This seems like a much more sensible *ratio*, but it is still be too narrow, in that it would not help claimants, like Ceri, who also sustained damage to their property. What if Andrew ran over Ceri on a bicycle? This *ratio* would not cover this situation.

4. **Drivers of vehicles who operate their vehicle without due care and attention may be liable in negligence for losses sustained as a result of such negligence** This is an effective *ratio* that could be used to cover cases with wide-ranging facts, including all of the hypothetical situations mentioned above.

The *ratio* of a case may be the only aspect of a case that provides binding authority, but persuasive authority may derive from what are known as **obiter dicta**. *Obiter dicta* are statements of law that do not form part of the *ratio* and can arise in several ways, as follows.

➡ *obiter dicta*: 'statements said by the way'

- The judge may apply the law to a hypothetical case with facts that differ from those of the case before him.

- The judge may state a legal principle that is wider than necessary to deal with the current case. In such a situation, the *ratio* will be limited to the part of the principle that applies to the facts. The remainder of the principle will be *obiter dictum*.[104]

- Statements of law in dissenting judgments constitute *obiter dicta*.

The application of precedent

Once a binding precedent is established, there are a number of possible ways in which it can be applied and used by later courts, as illustrated by Table 3.4.

TABLE 3.4 The application of precedent

Application	Meaning
Followed (or applied)	Provided that the facts of the current case sufficiently resemble those of the precedent, the *ratio* of the precedent will be applied to the current case
Overruled	If the court is not bound by the precedent, it may overrule it, in which case, the old precedent ceases to be good law and a new precedent is created
Distinguished	If the court feels that the facts of the current case differ materially from the facts of the case that established the precedent, it can distinguish the precedent and will not need to follow it. The judge will need to justify why he is distinguishing the precedent and an insufficient justification is likely to lead to the case being criticized or reversed

104. *Cassidy v Ministry of Health* [1951] 2 KB 343 (CA).

Advantages and disadvantages of precedent

The doctrine of precedent is something of a paradox, in that it can produce, simultaneously, an advantage and its opposing disadvantage. For example, perhaps the most touted advantage of precedent is that, by applying like cases in a consistent manner, the law becomes more certain. There is no doubt that the doctrine of precedent does promote certainty, but the UK system of precedent can also result in uncertainty. The ability of judges to distinguish cases, often based upon minute and illogical distinctions of fact, can render the law increasingly uncertain.

Other potential combinations of advantages and disadvantages include the following.

- **(Un)predictability** It is argued that the fact that the law is rendered more certain by the existence of an established precedent makes the law more predictable. This is certainly true—but there is also a strong element of chance and unpredictability, in that case law can only be reformed by cases actually reaching court (unless Parliament decides to legislate in the area in question). There are numerous examples of areas of the law that require a definitive Supreme Court ruling, but have not received one, because a relevant case has not reached the Supreme Court.

- **(In)efficiency** As the law is rendered more predictable, people can discover the relevant precedents and organize their affairs so as not to breach the law, thereby reducing the number of cases and making the legal system more efficient. Furthermore, if a person does intend to initiate proceedings, he can locate the precedent to use it to gauge the likelihood of success, further reducing the number of weak cases being brought. However, the sheer bulk of case law and precedent significantly affects the efficiency of the system. A person seeking a definitive statement of law on his legal position may have to wade through hundreds of cases. These cases may often run to hundreds of pages and, as previously stated, the *ratio* is never clearly stated.

- **(In)flexibility** Case law can continually adapt to meet the changing needs of society, thereby keeping the law up to date. An ineffective precedent can be overruled and replaced. But the doctrine of precedent can also make the law rigid and inflexible: lower courts cannot overrule higher courts and will be forced to apply a precedent, even if it produces a manifestly unacceptable decision. Further, as noted, precedent can only evolve if cases reach the appropriate court. There are numerous examples of anachronistic House of Lords precedents remaining good law because a similar case took a long time to reach the Lords—the classic example being the perpetuation of the marital rape exemption that was eventually abolished in *R v R*[105] (discussed below).

One final criticism can be made regarding the doctrine of precedent, namely that it can be retrospective. As noted, in virtually all cases, legislation changes the law only from the date on which it comes into effect. Conversely, case law can act in a retrospective manner, as the following controversial case demonstrates.

 ***R v R* [1992] 1 AC 599 (HL)**

FACTS: The defendant assaulted and attempted to have sexual intercourse with his wife against her will after the couple had been separated for three weeks. The husband contended that, at the time that he forced sex upon his wife, the law still stated that (with

---

105. [1992] 1 AC 599 (HL).

some limited exceptions) marriage granted perpetual consent to sexual intercourse and that therefore a husband who forced sex upon his wife had not committed rape (this was known as the 'marital exemption'). At first instance, he was convicted and the Court of Appeal upheld the conviction.

HELD: The House of Lords abolished the marital exemption and upheld the husband's conviction for rape.

COMMENT: Irrespective of how contemptible the acts of the husband were, the simple fact is that, at the time that he forced sex upon his wife, the marital exemption still existed and marriage was deemed to provide perpetual consent to sexual intercourse. At the time that the forced sex was committed, it was not technically rape—yet the courts retrospectively deemed it so. Article 7(1) of the European Convention on Human Rights prohibits imposing criminal liability upon a person when the act in question did not constitute a crime when it was committed. The European Court of Human Rights held that Art 7 was not breached in R's case,[106] stating that a development in the law would not breach Art 7 provided that it was reasonably foreseeable. As the marital exemption had been eroded over time, it was foreseeable that it could be abolished.

⭐ See M Giles, 'Judicial Lawmaking in the Criminal Courts: The Case of Marital Rape' (1992) Crim LR 407

Do judges make law?

The final issue to be discussed is the extent to which judges make law. Blackstone's declaratory theory of law states that judges are 'not delegated to pronounce a new law, but to maintain and expound the old one'.[107] In other words, the role of the judges is to interpret and apply the law, not to create it, because judges lack the constitutional legitimacy of Parliament and therefore the right to create law. Although the judiciary has reiterated the declaratory theory of law on countless occasions, it is universally accepted that judges do, in fact, make law. A principal reason for this is historical: historically, statute law was not a major source of law and it was therefore left to the judges, via the common law, to create much of the law of the English legal system. Even today, a court may be faced with a situation in which there is no legislative guidance. In such a case, the court cannot wait for Parliament to legislate on the issue; it must make a decision.

 Airedale NHS Trust v Bland [1993] AC 789 (HL)

FACTS: As a result of injuries sustained during the Hillsborough disaster, Anthony Bland had remained in a persistent vegetative state for three years. All medical practitioners involved in the case agreed that there was no hope of improvement or recovery. Accordingly, the Hospital Trust, with the full backing of Bland's parents, sought a declaration from the court that it could lawfully discontinue Bland's treatment, thereby allowing him to die. The Official Solicitor of the Senior Courts, acting as Bland's **guardian *ad litem***, opposed the Trust's application, arguing that such discontinuance of treatment would amount to murder.

➡️ **guardian *ad litem*:** a person who protects the rights and property of a person who lacks capacity, or who is incapable of managing his own affairs

---

106. *SW v UK* (1996) 21 EHRR 363.
107. See Sir William Blackstone, *Commentaries on the Laws on England: Volume 1* (University of Chicago Press, 1979) 69–70.

> **HELD:** During the course of their judgments, all of the judges involved in this case stressed repeatedly that this case raised entirely new moral and ethical issues that should not be addressed by the courts, but by Parliament. Despite this, the House of Lords was obliged to rule on the case and held that the treatment could be lawfully discontinued. The purpose of medical care was to benefit the patient, but the treatment being administered to Bland conferred no benefit at all. The duty placed upon the doctors to treat had come to an end and, consequently, they could lawfully end the treatment of the patient. Given the importance of the issue, and the need to protect both doctors and patients, however, the House stated that, before discontinuing treatment, an application should be made to the Family Division of the High Court. Several judges also urged that the issue required urgent consideration by Parliament.

⭐ See John Keown, 'Doctors and Patients: Hard Case, Bad Law, "New" Ethics' (1993) 52 CLJ 209

Even where statute does dominate, the law-making ability of the judiciary is not curtailed completely. As noted earlier, legislation needs to be interpreted and applied, and, given the aforementioned imperfections of the English language, this legislation may very well contain provisions that are ambiguous or vague. A court faced with an ambiguous or vague provision cannot ask Parliament for guidance, or wait until Parliament reforms the Act in question; the court has to make a decision.

Therefore, as time progressed, it became universally accepted that judges do make law, and even the judges themselves have started to admit this—albeit with some reluctance, with Lord Radcliffe stating that judges 'will serve the public interest better if they keep quiet about their legislative function'.[108] The next step in the issue was stated forcefully by Lord Reid: 'We do not believe in fairy tales any more. So we must accept the fact that for better or worse judges do make law, and tackle the question how do they approach their task and how they should approach it.'[109] The House of Lords attempted to answer this question in *C (a Minor) v DPP*,[110] in which, having examined the relevant authorities, Lord Lowry established five propositions.[111]

1. If the solution is doubtful, the judges should beware of imposing their own remedy.
2. Caution should prevail if Parliament has rejected opportunities of clearing up a known difficulty or has legislated, while leaving the difficulty untouched.
3. Disputed matters of social policy are less suitable areas for judicial intervention than purely legal problems.
4. Fundamental legal doctrines should not be lightly set aside.
5. Judges should not make a change unless they can achieve finality and certainty.

The above list would indicate the adoption of a cautious approach by the courts that pays due respect to the principle of parliamentary sovereignty. In practice, however, judges have, on occasions, not followed the above rules too closely and have been a touch zealous in the exercise of their law-making function, with one commentator referring to a 'growing appetite of some judges for changing the law themselves, rather than waiting for Parliament to do it'.[112] The case of *R v R*[113]

---

108. Lord Radcliffe, *Not in Feather Beds* (Hamilton 1968) 271
109. Lord Reid, 'The Judge as Lawmaker' (1972) 12 JSPTL 22, 22.   110. [1996] AC 1 (HL).
111. ibid 28.
112. Francis AR Bennion, 'A Naked Usurpation?' (1999) 149 NLJ 421, 421.
113. [1992] 1 AC 599 (HL).

(discussed above) provides a classic example of this. At the time of the case, rape was defined in statute as 'unlawful sexual intercourse with a woman who at the time of the intercourse does not consent to it'.[114] It had been long accepted by both the courts[115] and academics[116] that Parliament had included the word 'unlawful' specifically to preserve the marital exemption. When the 1976 Act was being debated in Parliament, there existed a clause in the Bill that would have abolished the marital exemption, but Parliament rejected it. Despite this, the House of Lords held that the word 'unlawful' was mere **surplusage**, even though it was well established by the courts that 'it was the duty of the court to give a meaning to every word in the section'.[117] The case has been summed up well by Glanville Williams, who describes it as 'high-handed judicial action taken for a praiseworthy purpose',[118] but goes on to question 'whether the praiseworthiness redeemed the high-handedness'.[119] It is contended that, despite the honourable motives of the House, it ultimately stepped over its constitutional boundaries and adopted a quasi-legislative role. If the word 'unlawful' and its consequent preservation of the marital exemption were regarded as inappropriate, it was for Parliament, and not the courts, to remove it.

➡ **surplusage:** in law, a word or phrase that is superfluous or useless to the case in question

Custom

The third—and, today, the least important—source of domestic law is custom. In Anglo-Saxon times, custom (that is, patterns of behaviour recognized and enforced by the courts) was the principal source of law. Today, custom, as a source of law that can apply throughout the land, is largely non-existent, save for those customs that have been absorbed into statute or the common law. Local customs still, however, have a role to play, and it is not unheard of for the courts to give legal effect to a particular local custom, even if it conflicts with the common law. However, in order for a local custom to be recognized by the courts, it will need to comply with a number of strict conditions, as follows.

* The local custom must have existed since 'time immemorial'. This rather vague phrase has, for historical reasons, been fixed by statute[120] as the 6 July 1189.[121] Initially, it would appear almost impossible to prove this, but provided that it can be shown that the custom has existed in the locality for a substantial time, the court will presume that it has existed since time immemorial,[122] provided that the custom was possible in 1189.

---

114. Sexual Offences (Amendment) Act 1976, s 1(1).

115. *R v Chapman* [1959] 1 QB 100 (CA).

116. See Glanville Williams, 'Rape is Rape' (1992) 142 NLJ 11, 11, who states that '[e]very criminal lawyer knew in 1976, when the relevant statute was passed, that this phrase meant fornication, coition outside marriage, which was the meaning intended in the Act'.

117. *R v Williams* [1953] 1 QB 660 (CA) 663 (Goddard CJ).

118. Glanville Williams, 'Rape is Rape' (1992) 142 NLJ 11, 11.   119. ibid.

120. Statute of Westminster I 1275.

121. This was the date of the accession to the throne of Richard I (Richard the Lionheart).

122. *Mercer v Denne* [1905] 2 Ch 538 (CA). In order to prove the existence of the custom for a substantial time, the court will sometimes call as a witness the locality's oldest living inhabitant.

- The custom must have existed continuously since that date. This does not mean that the custom has not been exercised,[123] but that the ability to exercise it has not been interrupted.
- The custom must not be unreasonable,[124] it must be certain in nature and scope, and must be specific to a defined locality.
- The custom must be compulsory (for example, if the custom grants someone a discretion to do something, it will not be compulsory), and must not conflict with a statutory provision.

Chapter conclusion

It is impossible to have a thorough understanding of the law applicable to businesses without also having an understanding of the sources of such laws and the relationships between the different sources. Hopefully, after reading this chapter, you will have a sound understanding of the principal domestic sources of law.

Domestic law cannot, however, be fully appreciated without an understanding of how it is affected by laws that derive from outside the UK. In particular, European Union law and the European Convention on Human Rights have had a huge impact upon domestic law. Both of these sources of European law, and the extent to which they affect domestic law, are discussed in the next chapter.

 Key points summary

- Domestic legislation comes in two principal forms, namely (i) Acts of Parliament and (ii) subordinate legislation.

- Acts of Parliament (also known as 'primary legislation', or 'statute law') are the highest form of UK law. Subordinate legislation is legislation created by bodies authorized by Parliament to legislate. It is also known as 'secondary legislation'.

- The three 'canons of statutory interpretation' are the literal rule, the golden rule, and the mischief rule. In more recent times, the purposive approach has come to be used more by the courts.

- The doctrine of precedent states that the reasoning behind decisions of higher courts is binding upon lower courts. This is based on the principle of *stare decisis* ('keep to what has been decided previously').

- Only the reasoning behind a court's decision (the *ratio decidendi*) is binding upon lower courts. Cases may have multiple *rationes*.

- Although, from a constitutional point of view, the role of judges should be limited to interpreting and applying the law (known as the 'declaratory theory of law'), it is universally acknowledged that judges do, in fact, make law.

---

123. In *New Windsor Corporation v Mellor* [1975] Ch 380 (CA) the Court recognized a custom even though it had not been exercised for a hundred years.
124. *Wolstanton Ltd v Newcastle-Under-Lyme Borough Council* [1940] AC 860 (HL).

Self-test questions

1. Define the following:
   (a) subordinate legislation;
   (b) Hansard;
   (c) *stare decisis*;
   (d) *ratio decidendi*;
   (e) *obiter dicta*.

2. Explain the distinction between:
   (a) a Public Bill, a Private Bill, and a Private Member's Bill;
   (b) binding precedent and persuasive precedent;
   (c) primary legislation and subordinate legislation.

3. Explain the process by which a Bill becomes an Act.

4. Explain the difference between an Act of Parliament that is: (i) original; (ii) consolidating; (iii) codifying; and (iv) amending.

5. Explain the rules of statutory interpretation. For each rule, provide a case that demonstrates the use of that rule in practice.

6. In relation to precedent, explain what is meant by: (i) following a decision; (ii) overruling a decision; (iii) reversing a decision; and (iv) distinguishing a case.

7. Explain how the doctrine of precedent would operate in the following situations.
   (a) The Court of Appeal is hearing an appeal. There are two previous Court of Appeal decisions on the issue and they were both decided on the same day—but their decisions conflict. Which decision should the Court of Appeal follow? What happens to the decision that was not followed?
   (b) An either-way offence is being heard summarily in a magistrates' court. There is a decision of the Crown Court that involves similar facts. Are the magistrates obliged to follow the decision of the Crown Court?

8. Do you think that judges should have the ability to make law? Provide reasons for your answer.

Further reading

Francis AR Bennion, *Statutory Interpretation* (5th edn, Butterworths 2008)
The definitive text on statutory interpretation

Emily Finch and Stefan Fafinski, *Legal Skills* (4th edn, OUP 2013) chs 3 and 6
Provides a practical account of how best to use domestic sources of law, including how to interpret statutes and how to find the ratio of a case

Andrew Gillespie, *The English Legal System* (4th edn, OUP 2013) chs 2 and 3
Provides a clear account of domestic sources of law, backed up with a number of extremely interesting examples

Websites

<http://www.supremecourt.uk>
The official website of the Supreme Court. Provides detailed information on the Court and its Justices. Additionally, Supreme Court hearings are available to watch live at <http://news. sky.com/info/supreme-court>

<http://www.parliament.uk/business/bills-and-legislation>
Parliament's official Bills and legislation page; provides the text and progress of all Bills before Parliament

<http://www.publications.parliament.uk/pa/cm/cmhansrd.htm>
The official website of the House of Commons debates (Hansard)

 Remember to visit the **Online Resource Centre at <http://www.oxfordtextbooks.co.uk/orc/roach3e>** to access the following resources on Chapter 3, 'Domestic sources of law': more **practice questions and answers**; a **glossary** of key terms; **multiple-choice questions**; and **revision summaries**. Updates to the law can be found on Twitter by following **@UKBusinessLaw**

4 Europe and the English legal system

- The relationship between EU law and the European Convention on Human Rights
- The European Union and EU law

- The European Convention on Human Rights and the Human Rights Act 1998

INTRODUCTION

In the previous chapter, the principal domestic sources of law were discussed. Increasingly, however, laws that derive from outside the UK are having a greater effect on the operation of the English legal system. Since 1973, European Union law (hereafter referred to as 'EU law') has taken precedence over domestic law to such an extent that Acts of Parliament that fail to comply with EU law can be suspended by the courts. Since 1953, the UK has had to ensure that its domestic laws do not breach the rights protected by the European Convention on Human Rights, although UK citizens have only been able to enforce these rights in the European Court of Human Rights since 1966, and in domestic courts since October 2000. Accordingly, in order to obtain a full appreciation and understanding of the operation of the English legal system, it is essential that students understand the full impact of European law upon domestic law. This will involve a discussion of the various aspects of EU law and the impact of the European Convention on Human Rights, but, first, it is important that the relationship between these two sources of European law is understood.

The relationship between EU law and the European Convention on Human Rights

Students often fail to understand the relationship between EU law and the European Convention on Human Rights (ECHR) by assuming that membership of the EU automatically brings about ratification of the ECHR, or vice versa. However, this is not the case: the EU is not currently a party to the ECHR (although, as is discussed later, this will change) and has no administrative role as regards the European Court of Human Rights (ECtHR). This is borne out by the fact that the EU currently comprises twenty-eight Member States,[1] whereas the ECHR has forty-seven signatories (including all twenty-eight EU Member States).

Even though the EU and ECHR are currently completely separate, a strong relationship does exist between them in three ways. First, accession to the EU is dependent upon satisfying what are known as the 'Copenhagen criteria', with one criterion being that countries must have achieved 'stability of institutions guaranteeing democracy, the rule of law, human rights and respect for and protection of minorities'. Whilst being a signatory of the ECHR is not currently a mandatory requirement of EU membership, becoming a signatory will be compelling evidence that a candidate country does have the requisite respect for human rights. Second, fundamental rights contained within the ECHR constitute general principles of the EU's law.[2] Third, prior to the Treaty of Lisbon of 2007, Art 6(2) of the Treaty of Rome stated that '[t]he Union shall respect fundamental rights, as guaranteed by the European Convention for the Protection of Human Rights and Fundamental Freedoms'. There is no doubt that the Court of Justice of the EU has been heavily influenced by decisions of the ECtHR, especially where there is no EU law on a topic, but EU human rights law and the ECHR differ, leading to situations in which similar facts produce different outcomes in the different courts. Further, it has long been regarded as anomalous that, whilst acts of EU Member States are subject to the ECHR, acts of the EU itself are not.

To remedy such inconsistencies, as far back as 1979,[3] it was contended that the EU should formally accede to the ECHR. The first major step in achieving this took place in 2004, when Protocol 14 to the ECHR inserted Art 59(2) into the ECHR, which states 'The European Union may accede to this Convention'. Article 6(2) of the Treaty of Lisbon committed the EU to accession by stating that '[t]he Union shall accede to the European Convention for the Protection of Human Rights and Fundamental Freedoms'. It should be noted that the EU will, like any other state, have to apply to become a signatory of the ECHR and, given the complexities and formalities involved, it is likely to take several years for the EU to become the ECHR's forty-eighth signatory. At the time of writing, the EU and the Council of Europe have agreed a draft accession agreement and this agreement is currently being examined by the Court of Justice. When the EU does accede, it will have to comply with the ECHR and the judgments of the ECtHR, with the ECtHR also being able to review the acts of the various EU institutions. Within the EU, the ECtHR will become the highest and final court in relation to human rights issues.

The European Union and EU law

In 1950, the French Foreign Minister Robert Schuman put forward a proposal that was to form the foundations of the current European Union, and which was designed to ensure that the events of World Wars I and II could never happen again. As the

---

1. Five countries are currently candidates for accession to the EU—namely the Former Yugoslav Republic of Macedonia, Iceland, Montenegro, Serbia, and Turkey. Albania, Bosnia and Herzegovina, and Kosovo have been identified by the EU as potential candidates.

2. Treaty on European Union, Art 6(3).

3. European Commission, *Accession of the Communities to the European Convention on Human Rights* (EC Bull, Supp 2/79).

waging of war was heavily dependent upon heavy industry (notably, coal and steel), Schuman proposed that the production of coal and steel should be placed under the control of a single supranational organization. A year later, Schuman's vision became a reality, with six countries[4] signing the Treaty of Paris,[5] which established the 'European Coal and Steel Community'. In 1957, the same six countries signed the Treaty of Rome (or the Treaty on the Functioning of the European Union (TFEU) as it is now known), thereby establishing the 'European Economic Community' (EEC). The UK joined in 1973, following the passing of the European Communities Act 1972. As time progressed, further measures were passed that were designed to increase European cooperation and integration. The Single European Act 1986 (which is a European treaty and not a UK Act of Parliament) indicated the Member States' commitment to the creation of an internal (or single) market by the end of 1992. The Maastricht Treaty (or the Treaty on European Union (TEU)) was signed in 1992 and created the European Union, and further advanced the cause of monetary and economic union, via the establishment of a single European currency (the euro (€)). The 1997 Treaty of Amsterdam[6] renumbered[7] and simplified the Treaty of Rome, introduced a number of provisions aimed at benefiting citizens, and, for the first time, made reference to the ECHR. The 2000 Treaty of Nice[8] paved the way for the enlargement of the EU from fifteen Member States to twenty-seven. Finally, in 2007, the Treaty of Lisbon[9] was signed and provides for a number of institutional reforms designed to improve the workings of the EU and its institutions. Crucially, it also incorporates the EU's Charter for Fundamental Freedoms into EU law (although this Charter will not apply fully to the UK because it secured an opt-out), and provides for the EU's compulsory accession to the ECHR.

To understand the operation of the EU and its effect upon the English legal system, we need to discuss the various institutions of the EU, the differing types of EU laws and their effects on national law, and the operation of the Court of Justice of the EU.

Institutions of the EU

Article 13 of the TEU states that seven bodies, the functions of which can be categorized as financial, legal, or political, shall carry out the functions of the EU. The financial bodies, namely the Court of Auditors and the European Central Bank, are outside the scope of this text and will not be discussed. This section will focus on the four 'political' institutions (namely (i) the European Parliament; (ii) the European Council; (iii) the Council; and (iv) the European Commission) and the EU's legal institution, namely the Court of Justice of the European Union.

---

4. Belgium, France, Italy, Luxembourg, the Netherlands, and West Germany.

5. Treaty Establishing the European Coal and Steel Community (1951).

6. Treaty of Amsterdam Amending the Treaty on European Union, the Treaties Establishing the European Communities and Related Acts (1997).

7. It should be noted that the Treaty of Rome has been renumbered twice. In this text, the most recent numbering will be used.

8. Treaty of Nice Amending the Treaty on European Union, the Treaties Establishing the European Communities and Certain Related Acts (2000).

9. Treaty of Lisbon Amending the Treaty on European Union and the Treaty Establishing the European Community (2007).

The European Parliament

Of all the EU institutions, the European Parliament has undergone the most change. Created in 1952, it began life as the relatively powerless Assembly, but as time progressed, its power has grown to reflect its democratic nature and, today, it is one of the most powerful EU bodies. The European Parliament is the only democratically elected body in the EU, and currently consists of 766 Members of the European Parliament (MEPs), who are directly elected by the citizens of their Member States every five years. The number of MEPs that each Member State has is roughly in proportion to the size of its population (the UK currently has 73 MEPs). MEPs do not sit in Parliament according to their nationality, but rather according to their membership of one of the eight political groupings.

The various roles of the European Parliament include the following.

- In relation to the creation of legislation, Parliament's role was consultative only, but today, its role is much more significant, with virtually all legislative proposals requiring Parliament's involvement or approval. Parliament cannot initiate legislation, but it can request that the Commission proposes legislation.

- The European Parliament can, by passing a vote of censure, force the European Commission to resign.[10] In 1999, such a vote took place, but the requisite two-thirds majority was not obtained. However, following independent reports of fraud and nepotism, the entire Commission resigned shortly thereafter.

- The European Parliament elects the President of the Commission, and has the right of approval over other members of the Commission.[11]

- The European Parliament can appoint an ombudsman to investigate complaints made by EU citizens in relation to maladministration of any EU institution (except the Court of Justice, when acting in its judicial role).[12]

- The European Parliament shares joint responsibility with the Council in approving the EU's budget.

There is little doubt that the powers of the European Parliament have increased significantly. Initially, it had very little real power, but it soon came to be viewed as incongruous that the only democratically elected EU institution was the least powerful—this became known as the 'democratic deficit'. To reduce this democratic deficit, each new treaty has increased the power of the European Parliament significantly to reflect its democratic status.

The European Council

The European Council[13] has existed informally since 1974, but has only been a formal institution of the EU since the passing of the Treaty of Lisbon in 2007. The European Council consists of the Heads of State or Government of each Member State, along with the President of the European Council and the President of the Commission.[14] As such, it is the highest decision-making body in the EU and will 'provide the Union with the necessary impetus for its development and shall define the general political directions and priorities thereof'.[15]

---

10. TFEU, Art 234. 11. TEU, Art 17(7). 12. TFEU, Art 228.
13. Not to be confused with the Council (which is discussed next), or the Council of Europe, which is a body that also works towards European integration, but which is not part of the EU. The Council of Europe oversees the ECHR and the ECtHR.
14. TEU, Art 15(2). 15. ibid, Art 15(1).

The Council

Formerly known as the 'Council of Ministers', the Council (or Council of the EU) is the principal decision-making body of the EU, responsible, along with the European Parliament, for passing legislation and approving the EU's budget.[16] The Council does not have a fixed membership, but instead consists of a ministerial representative from each Member State,[17] with the minister in question depending on the 'configuration' of the Council in question. So, for example, if the Council is discussing matters of justice, the Council will consist of the twenty-eight Member States' Ministers of Justice, and the meeting will be known as the 'Justice and Home Affairs Council'. Presidency of the Council rotates amongst Member States, with each state holding the Presidency for six months. The position of the President has assumed increased importance in recent years, because the President has substantial control over the setting of meetings and the agenda of Council activity during his Presidency.

As the Council consists of national ministers, it strongly represents national interests, as opposed to the interests of the EU. To ensure that the advocacy of national interests does not bog down discussion, the Council has a robust decision-making process in place. Certain simple administrative decisions can be passed by a simple majority, whereas matters of special importance may require unanimity. The majority of decisions are, however, passed based upon attaining a 'qualified majority'. Under this system, a total of 352 votes are allocated to the twenty-eight Member States, with countries with larger populations having more votes. In order to pass a qualified majority vote, two conditions need to be met:

1. 260 out of 352 votes are required; and
2. a majority of Member States (that is, fifteen) must approve.[18]

In addition, if a decision is adopted by qualified majority, a Member State may ask for confirmation that the votes in favour represent at least 62 per cent of the total population of the EU. If this is not the case, then the decision will not be adopted.

The European Commission

Along with the European Council, the European Commission forms the executive of the EU and it shall 'promote the general interest of the Union and take appropriate initiatives to that end'.[19] In addition, as 'guardian of the treaties', it is responsible for ensuring that treaty obligations are met and that EU law is enforced. To further that aim, the Commission is granted extensive powers to investigate and punish breaches of EU law committed by Member States, companies, and individuals. These powers exist in all areas of EU law, but one area in which the Commission has been especially active is in relation to breaches of competition law, with Arts 101 and 102 of the TFEU granting the Commission extensive powers to investigate and punish those who engage in anti-competitive activities.

Competition law is discussed further in the Online Resource Centre in the chapter entitled Unfair Commercial Practices

---

16. ibid Art 16(1).   17. ibid Art 16(2).
18. It is anticipated that this system will change in November 2014 (see TEU, Art 16(4)).
19. TEU, Art 17(1).

***Intel* (Case COMP/ 37.990) Commission Decision 2009/C227/07**

FACTS: Intel held the dominant position in the worldwide central processing unit (CPU) market. Following a series of complaints from Intel's chief competitor, AMD, the Commission discovered that Intel had given hidden rebates to computer manufacturers on the condition that they bought their CPUs from Intel only, and had made a direct payment to a major retailer on the condition that it stock only those computers with Intel CPUs. Intel also made direct payments to computer manufacturers on the condition that they halted or delayed launching products containing CPUs manufactured by Intel's competitors.

HELD: The Commission found that the above practices constituted abuses of Intel's dominant position in the CPU market, and prevented customers from choosing alternative products. The then Competition Commissioner, Neelie Kroes, stated that 'Intel has harmed millions of European consumers by deliberately acting to keep competitors out of the market for computer chips for many years. Such a serious and sustained violation of the EU's antitrust rules cannot be tolerated.'[20] The Commission fined Intel a record €1.06 billion (around £854 million) and ordered it to cease any anti-competitive practices that were still ongoing.

Perhaps the most important role of the Commission is in relation to the creation of legislation. Unless the treaties state otherwise, only the Commission can propose legislation,[21] making the Commission a key driver of policy and leading to it being branded as the EU's 'motor of integration'. The Commission is based in Brussels and comprises twenty-eight Commissioners (one from each Member State),[22] who are appointed for renewable terms of five years and tend to be senior politicians.

The Court of Justice of the European Union

The European Court of Justice (ECJ) was set up as part of the Treaty of Paris in 1952. Due to an increasing caseload, in 1974, the ECJ requested the establishment of a secondary court to deal with less important cases. Nothing was done, however, until the passing of the Single European Act, which amended the Treaty of Rome to allow for the creation of a Court of First Instance (CFI), which was eventually established in 1989. Following the Treaty of Lisbon, the ECJ was renamed as the Court of Justice (CoJ) and the CFI was renamed as the General Court. Both courts are known collectively as the Court of Justice of the European Union.

The CoJ currently consists of twenty-eight judges (one for each Member State)[23] and eight Advocates General, each being appointed for a renewable term of six years. The role of an Advocate General is 'with complete impartiality and independence, to make, in open court, reasoned submissions on cases which…require his involvement'.[24] The judges are free to disregard the opinions of their Advocates General, but, in practice, they are usually followed.[25] Cases in the CoJ are heard either before

---

20. EU Press Release, IP/09/745, 13 May 2009.
21. TEU, Art 17(2). Although both the European Parliament and the Council can request that the Commission propose legislation in a particular area.
22. From November 2014, this will cease and the number of Commissioners will correspond to two-thirds of the number of Member States (TEU, Art 17(5)).   23. TEU, Art 19(2).
24. TFEU, Art 252.
25. A Dashwood, 'The Advocate General in the Court of Justice of the European Communities' (1982) 2 LS 202, 212, contends that judges follow the opinion of the Advocate General in about 70 per cent of cases.

a chamber (comprising three or five judges), a Grand Chamber (comprising fifteen judges), or as a full Court (comprising all twenty-eight judges). Unlike UK courts, there are no majority and minority opinions, and each judge does not provide an individual judgment; rather, one judgment is issued for the entire Court, and if there are any dissenters, this will be indicated within the language of the judgment. The CoJ has jurisdiction in a number of areas, including:

- If a Member State has failed to fulfil its obligations under EU law, proceedings in the CoJ may be initiated by the Commission or another Member State.[26] If the CoJ finds that the Member State has failed to uphold its obligations, then the Member State will be required to undertake the necessary measures to comply with the CoJ's judgment.[27]

- Articles 263 and 265 of the TFEU provide that the CoJ will review the legality of the acts (or omissions) of the various EU institutions. Applications may be made by Member States, other EU institutions, and, in some cases, by persons. Where an action is upheld, the CoJ has considerable remedial power, and can:

  - annul acts of the Council, Commission or European Central Bank;[28]

  - declare that, contrary to the Treaties, an institution has failed to act;[29]

  - require the institution to take the necessary measures to comply with the CoJ's judgment.[30]

- The CoJ has jurisdiction to hear disputes between the EU and any of its employees.[31]

- Decisions of the General Court can be appealed to the CoJ, provided that the appeal is on a point of law.[32]

The General Court consists of at least one judge per Member State[33] and judges are appointed for a (renewable) term of six years. Decisions of the General Court may be appealed to the CoJ. The General Court has jurisdiction to hear a wide range of cases, including:

- direct actions brought by natural or legal persons against acts of EU institutions (addressed to them or directly concerning them as individuals),[34] or against a failure to act on the part of those institutions;[35]

- actions seeking compensation for damage caused by EU institutions or their staff.[36]

Perhaps the principal function of the Court of Justice of the EU is ensuring the consistent application of EU law throughout the EU. To this end, Art 267 of the TFEU permits any domestic court or tribunal to apply to the Court for a preliminary ruling in relation to (i) the interpretation of the treaties, or (ii) the validity and interpretation of legal acts of EU institutions, bodies, offices, or agencies. It should be noted that an Art 267 ruling is not an appeal, because the decision to refer belongs to the domestic court and not the parties. Further, the possibility of a preliminary ruling only arises where the case involves EU law. The stages of a preliminary ruling are as follows.

---

26. ibid Arts 258 and 263. Actions brought by Member States tend to be rare.
27. ibid Art 260(1).   28. ibid Art 264.   29. ibid Art 266.   30. ibid.
31. ibid Art 270.   32. ibid Art 256(1).   33. TEU, Art 19(2).   34. TFEU, Art 263.
35. ibid Art 265.   36. ibid Arts 268 and 340.

1. Any court or tribunal *may* request a preliminary ruling, but courts or tribunals 'against whose decisions there is no judicial remedy under national law' *must* apply for a ruling if a point of EU law is involved (except in certain circumstances).[37] In the UK, this would appear to be referring only to the Supreme Court, but the issue is more complex. For example, in some cases, decisions of the Court of Appeal cannot be appealed to the Supreme Court—in such cases, the Court of Appeal is the final appeal court and is therefore subject to the mandatory requirement to refer.[38] The key issue to be determined is whether the court's decision is subject to appeal *in the particular case*.[39]

2. The Court will decide whether or not to accept the request for a ruling. The Court has reserved the right to reject a request where the questions raised are not articulated clearly,[40] where the questions raised are not substantially relevant to the action in the domestic court[41] or are hypothetical,[42] and where the facts of the case lack clarity.[43]

3. If the Court accepts the request for a ruling, proceedings are suspended in the domestic court until the Court completes the ruling. Given that, in 2010, the average ruling took 15.7 months to complete,[44] this can be problematic for the parties involved.

4. The Court will interpret the relevant legislation. Note that it will not apply the legislation: that is still the function of the domestic court (although, in practice, the distinction between interpretation and application can be extremely thin). Once the Court has interpreted a provision, that interpretation is binding on all courts within the EU.

5. Once the Court has provided a ruling, it will refer the case back to the domestic court. The ruling does not compel the domestic court to decide the case in a certain way; the decision is still a matter for the domestic court. In practice, however, the ruling of the Court is always followed, unless the Court oversteps its authority under Art 267.[45] If the ruling indicates that domestic legislation conflicts with EU law, the domestic legislation is usually changed, as the following case demonstrates.

Case C-152/84 *Marshall v Southampton and South West Hampshire Area Health Authority* [1986] ECR 723

FACTS: The local area authority that employed the claimant required employees to retire when social security pensions became payable. For men, this was at the age of 65, and for women, this was at the age of 60. As the claimant was 62 years old, she was dismissed.

---

37. Namely (i) where the question of EU law is not relevant; (ii) where the relevant provision has already been interpreted by the Court of Justice of the EU; and (iii) where the interpretation is so obvious as to leave no room for reasonable doubt.

38. *Chiron Corporation v Murex Diagnostics Ltd (No 8)* [1995] All ER (EC) 88 (CA).

39. C-99/00 *Criminal Proceedings Against Lyckescog* [2002] ECR I-4839.

40. Case C-88/99 *Roquette Frères SA v Direction des Services Fiscaux du Pas-de-Calais* [2000] ECR I-10465.

41. Case C-83/91 *Wienland Meilicke v ADV/ORGA FA Meyer AG* [1992] ECR I-4871.

42. Case C-467/04 *Criminal Proceedings Against Gasparini and Ors* [2006] ECR I-9199.

43. Case C-320–322/90 *Telemarsicabruzzo SpA v Circostel, Ministero delle Poste e Telecommunicazioni and Ministerio della Difesa* [1993] ECR I-393.

44. Court of Justice of the EU, *Annual Report 2012* (EU 2013) 10. This delay is one reason why the General Court was granted the power to provide Art 267 rulings in specified areas (see TFEU, Art 256(3)).

45. *Arsenal Football Club plc v Reed* [2003] EWCA Civ 696, [2003] 3 All ER 865.

She argued that this amounted to sex discrimination under the Sex Discrimination Act 1975 and the Equal Treatment Directive,[46] because a man would have been able to continue working until the age of 65. The Court of Appeal dismissed her claim under the 1975 Act, because that Act specifically did not apply to cases concerning retirement. In relation to the Directive, the Court sought a preliminary ruling.

HELD: The ECJ held that the claimant had been discriminated against under the Directive, and that s 6(2)(b) of the Sex Discrimination Act 1975 (which excluded discrimination relating to retirement) was in conflict with the provisions of the Equal Treatment Directive.

COMMENT: Following this case, the Sex Discrimination Act 1986 was passed, which amended the 1975 Act to require employers to set a retirement age that did not discriminate on grounds of sex. Several years later, Marshall was once again in the ECJ, successfully arguing that the statutory limit on compensation recoverable for sex discrimination under the 1975 Act was in breach of EU law.[47] The limits were subsequently removed.

★ See Susan Atkins, 'Equal Treatment and Retirement Age' (1986) 49 MLR 508

Treaties and legal acts of the EU

As noted, the European Commission, the European Parliament, and the Council all play a strong role in the creation of legislation. Article 288 of the TFEU provides that there are five types of EU legislation (or 'legal acts' as they are known), namely regulations, directives, decisions, recommendations, and opinions.[48] In addition, the role of treaty provisions needs to be understood. However, before these legal acts can be discussed, it is important to explain how they affect UK law and in order to do that, the concepts of direct applicability and direct effect need to be understood.

- **Direct applicability** Normally, in order for any piece of international law to become part of the UK law, it will need to be incorporated into UK law (normally via the passing of legislation)—but EU legal acts that are directly applicable are automatically incorporated into domestic law as soon as they are passed. This does not mean, however, that persons will be able to enforce the act in a domestic court: in order for them to do that, the act will need to have direct effect, and not all directly applicable legislation will be directly effective.

- **Direct effect** Legal acts that can be relied on in a domestic court are said to have 'direct effect'. In order for an act to be directly effective, the case of *van Gend en Loos*[49] established that a number of conditions must be met: the obligations laid down by it must be clear; it must be unconditional (that is, subject to no limitations);[50] and it must not require the implementation of domestic legislation. There are two types of direct effect.

  1. *Vertical direct effect* A provision will have vertical direct effect if it imposes legal obligations upon Member States that can be enforced by persons.

---

46. Council Directive EEC 76/207 [1976] OJ L039/40.

47. Case C-271/91 *Marshall v Southampton and South West Hampshire Area Health Authority* [1993] ECR I-4367.

48. TFEU, Art 288 provides that recommendations and opinions have no binding force and so will not be discussed.

49. Case C-26/62 *NV Algemene Transporten Expeditie Onderneming van Gend en Loos v Nederlandse Administratie der Belastigen* [1963] ECR 1.

50. This requirement has since been relaxed and the court is more willing to accept justifiable limitations: see Case C-41/74 *Van Duyn v Home Office* [1974] ECR 1337.

2. *Horizontal direct effect* A provision will have horizontal direct effect if it imposes legal obligations upon persons that can be enforced by other persons.

Treaty provisions

Treaty provisions (notably the TFEU and the TEU) form the primary source of EU law and are directly applicable and, provided that they meet the conditions discussed earlier,[51] will also be directly effective. Many treaty provisions do not satisfy the criteria for direct effect, because they provide only broad and vague statements of intent. Numerous key treaty provisions do have direct effect, however, an obvious example being Art 157 of the TFEU, which states: 'Each Member State shall ensure that the principle of equal pay for male and female workers for equal work or work of equal value is applied.' This obligation is clear, unconditional, and is not dependent upon domestic implementation. Accordingly, in *Macarthys Ltd v Smith*,[52] a female worker who was paid less than her male predecessor was able to enforce Art 157, even though domestic legislation at the time provided her with no right to equal pay.[53]

Treaty provisions that meet the criteria for direct effect usually have both vertical and horizontal direct effect, but the wording of a provision may indicate otherwise. For example, Art 34 of the TFEU states: 'Quantitative restrictions on imports and all measures having equivalent effect shall be prohibited between Member States.' As this obligation is imposed only upon Member States (and not persons), it follows that Art 34 has vertical direct effect only.

Regulations

Article 288 of the TFEU specifically states that regulations are directly applicable and therefore become binding in their entirety and form part of UK law as soon as they come into force. Provided that the conditions for direct effect are met, regulations can also have both vertical and horizontal direct effect. Regulations are used in order to provide uniformity across the laws of Member States and, accordingly, must be enforced by a domestic court, even if the regulation conflicts with domestic law.[54]

Directives

Whilst regulations are extremely useful for securing uniformity of the law, they ignore the fact that the Member States have vastly differing legal systems, and a regulation that is simple to enforce in one state, may produce massive legal difficulties in another. In such a case, it may be preferable to use a directive. Article 288 of the TFEU states that a directive 'shall be binding, as to the result to be achieved, upon each Member State to which it is addressed, but shall leave to the national

---

51. Case C-26/62 *NV Algemene Transporten Expeditie Onderneming van Gend en Loos v Nederlandse Administratie der Belastigen* [1963] ECR 1.　　52. Case C-129/79 [1980] ECR 1275.
53. At the time, the Equal Pay Act 1970 required equality only as between men and women working together contemporaneously; it did not apply in the case of successive employment.
54. Case C-93/71 *Leonesio v Ministero dell'Agricoltura e Foreste* [1972] ECR 287.

authorities the choice of form and methods'. Directives, therefore, are a much more flexible form of legal act than regulations.

Once a directive is passed, the Member State will be given a period of time to implement it. As directives are dependent upon implementation, they are not directly applicable, but are they directly effective? As directives permit Member States to decide the best method of implementation, it follows that they will not have direct effect during the implementation period. If, however, a Member State fails to implement a directive by the implementation date, it will become directly effective, and may be relied on in a domestic court[55] (provided that they comply with the *van Gend en Loos* conditions).[56] Thus, in *Marshall v Southampton and South West Hampshire Area Health Authority*,[57] the claimant alleged discrimination under the Sex Discrimination Act 1975 and the Equal Treatment Directive. Unfortunately, the 1975 Act did not apply in her particular case. Further, the UK had not implemented the Directive and the implementation date had passed. The European Court of Justice (ECJ) held that, once the implementation date had passed, the Directive became directly effective; ergo the claimant could rely on it. However, the Court imposed a limitation: because directives impose obligations upon Member States (and not persons), they would have only vertical direct effect, which means that they would provide rights only to persons to be enforced against the state. Thus, when Westminster Council attempted to rely on a directive[58] to challenge the introduction of the congestion charge, its claim failed, because the directive did not confer rights upon emanations of the state.[59]

The Marshall case is discussed in more detail at p 86

It should be noted that directives not only have direct effect, but also have indirect effect.[60] This means that national courts are required, as far as is possible, to interpret national law in light of the wording and purpose of directives.[61] This obligation usually arises in relation to implementing legislation, but it also applies to legislation unrelated to implementation.[62]

Decisions

A decision is an instrument of law created by one of the EU institutions. Unlike regulations and directives, which are addressed to all Member States, decisions may be addressed to a single Member State, company, or individual. Article 288 of the TFEU states that a decision 'which specifies those to whom it is addressed shall be binding only on them'. It follows from this that decisions are not directly applicable, but, providing that a decision satisfies the *van Gend en Loos* conditions, it will be directly effective against its addressee.[63]

Table 4.1 sets out the general effect of EU legislation.

55. Case C-148/78 *Pubblico Ministero v Tullio Ratti* [1980] 1 CMLR 96.

56. Case C-41/74 *Van Duyn v Home Office* [1975] 1 CMLR 1.   57. Case C-152/84 [1986] ECR 723.

58. Council Directive 85/337 EEC on the assessment of the effects of certain public and private projects on the environment [1985] OJ L175/40.

59. *R (on the Application of Westminster City Council) v Mayor of London* [2002] EWHC 2440 (Admin), [2003] BLGR 611.

60. It should be noted that other legal acts (e.g. recommendations) are also capable of having indirect effect.   61. Case C-14/83 *Von Colsen v Land Nordrhein-Westfalen* [1984] ECR 1891.

62. Case C-106/89 *Marleasing SA v La Comercial Internacional de Alimentación* [1990] ECR I-4135.

63. Case C-9/70 *Franz Grad v Finanzamt Traunstein* [1970] ECR 825.

TABLE 4.1 The general effect of EU legislation

Legislation	Direct applicability	Direct effect (provided that conditions are met)	
		Vertical	Horizontal
Treaty provisions	Yes	Yes (if wording permits)	Yes (if wording permits)
Regulations	Yes	Yes	Yes
Directives	No	Yes (once implementation date has passed)	No
Decisions	No	Yes (only upon addressee)	No

The supremacy of EU law

The doctrine of parliamentary sovereignty states that Acts of Parliament constitute the highest form of law, and that Parliament is free to legislate in any manner[64] that it wishes and its legislation cannot be called into question by the courts. As one commentator stated, the doctrine of parliamentary sovereignty provides the principle 'upon which the whole system of legislation hangs'.[65] The question is to what extent has this principle been affected by the UK's membership of the EU.

Prior to 1973, the UK was in no way bound by EU law. Further, the TFEU did not state that EU law was to take precedence over domestic law. The issue was therefore left to the ECJ, which stated that 'the EEC Treaty has created its own legal system which, on the entry into force of the Treaty, became an integral part of the legal systems of the Member States and which their courts are bound to apply'.[66] This, in turn, brought about 'a permanent limitation of their sovereign rights'.[67] The reason for this is one of practicality: if the Member States were free to ignore EU law, the EU would become entirely impotent. Accordingly, by the time that the UK joined the EC in 1973, the supremacy of EU law was well established, and this was reflected in s 2(1) of the European Communities Act 1972, which states:

> All such rights, powers, liabilities, obligations and restrictions…created or arising by or under the Treaties, and all such remedies and procedures…provided for by or under the Treaties, as in accordance with the Treaties are without further enactment to be given legal effect or used in the United Kingdom shall be recognised and available in law, and be enforced, allowed and followed accordingly.

Therefore, directly applicable or effective EU law is to take precedence over domestic law, and domestic laws that were incompatible with EU law would have to be changed, as the following case demonstrates.

R v Secretary of State for Employment, ex p Equal Opportunities Commission [1995] 1 AC 1 (HL)

FACTS: The Employment Protection (Consolidation) Act 1978 provided full-time employees with the right to receive redundancy pay, and the right not to be unfairly dismissed, but excluded these rights from certain part-time employees. The Equal Opportunities

---

64. The only exception to this is that Parliament cannot pass legislation that binds future Parliaments.
65. HWR Wade, 'The Basis of Legal Sovereignty' [1955] CLJ 172, 188.
66. Case C-14/64 *Costa v ENEL* [1964] ECR 585, 593.   67. ibid.

Commission alleged that, as the majority of part-time workers were women, the 1978 Act was discriminatory and incompatible with Art 119 of the EC Treaty (now Art 157 of the TFEU, which provides for equal pay between men and women).

HELD: The House of Lords held that the 1978 Act did indeed indirectly discriminate against women and was therefore incompatible with Art 119.

Following this case, Parliament amended the 1978 Act to provide greater rights to part-time employees. However, what should the court do if faced with a piece of legislation that is incompatible with directly applicable or effective EU law? Can the court ignore the incompatible domestic law, or is it bound to apply it, but indicate the incompatibility to Parliament? The answer came in the following seminal case.

 R v Secretary of State for Transport, ex p Factortame (No 2) [1991] 1 AC 603 (HL)

FACTS: EC fishing policy subjected each Member State to fishing quotas. Factortame, a Spanish fishing firm, attempted to avoid these quotas by registering its vessels in the UK and fishing in UK waters (thereby contributing to the UK quota). In response, Parliament passed the Merchant Shipping Act 1988, which stated that, in order to register as a British vessel, legal title to the vessel had to be vested wholly in a British citizen or company, and a company would only be classified as British if 75 per cent of its directors and shareholders were British citizens.[68] Ninety-five Spanish vessels could not meet these requirements, and so they challenged the 1988 Act, arguing that it breached treaty provisions relating to the prohibition of discrimination and the freedom of establishment. The High Court had referred the case to the ECJ and granted the claimants an interim injunction restraining the government from enforcing the 1988 Act until the ECJ had provided a ruling. The House of Lords rescinded this injunction, but referred the case to the ECJ, asking whether interim relief should be available. The ECJ held that it was a requirement of the EC Treaty that domestic courts enforce any provision that has direct effect, and, if a national law constituted an obstacle to this, the national law should be set aside and subsequently amended by the Member State's legislature.

HELD: The House of Lords renewed the injunction suspending the operation of the Merchant Shipping Act 1988. Subsequently, the Spanish fishermen were able to sue and obtain damages from the government for their loss.[69] The offending sections of the 1988 Act were removed.

COMMENT: It could be argued that this decision severely emasculates the principle of parliamentary sovereignty for two reasons: first, the House acknowledged that EU law was supreme to domestic law; second, it permitted an English court to overrule an Act of Parliament. The case has, unsurprisingly, attracted criticism—Lord Denning stated '[n]o longer is European law an incoming tide flowing up the estuaries of England. It is now like a tidal wave bringing down our sea walls and flowing inland over our fields and houses—to the dismay of all'.[70] The House of Lords, however, did not regard this case as weakening the sovereignty of Parliament. Lord Bridge stated that the supremacy of EU law was established

---

68. Merchant Shipping Act 1988, s 14 (now repealed).

69. *R v Secretary of State for Transport, ex p Factortame (No 5)* [2000] 1 AC 524 (HL).

70. Lord Denning, *Introduction to the European Court of Justice: Judges or Policy Makers?* (Bruges Group 1990) 8.

★ See HWR Wade, 'Sovereignty: Revolution or Evolution?' (1996) 112 LQR 568

by Parliament itself via the 'entirely voluntary'[71] passing of the European Communities Act 1972. Indeed, this argument has been placed on a statutory footing via s 18 of the European Union Act 2011,[72] which states that directly applicable or directly effective EU law is only recognized in the UK by virtue of s 2(1) of the 1972 Act. Accordingly, Parliament retains ultimate supremacy in that it could repeal the 1972 Act whenever it wished. Whilst this may be accurate from a legal standpoint, in political and economic terms, it is highly questionable that the UK would ever wish to leave the EU.

The supremacy of EU law can also be seen in relation to the interpretation of EU law in domestic courts. Whereas domestic legislation tends to be drafted in a very specific, detailed manner, EU law tends to be drafted in a much more open manner, focusing on general principles, with the detailed application left to the European courts. Accordingly, when domestic courts interpret EU law, the domestic canons of interpretation may not be suitable and domestic courts should use a method of interpretation that is consistent with that of the European courts. European courts (and the courts of most civil law systems) adopt what is known as the 'teleological approach' when interpreting legislation, whereby the courts will seek to give effect to the 'spirit' of the legislation, taking into account any relevant social, cultural, or economic considerations. The supremacy of EU law requires that domestic courts adopt a similar approach when interpreting EU law.

The European Convention on Human Rights and the Human Rights Act 1998

Many countries throughout the world protect the rights of their citizens via a specific physical document, the most obvious example being the US Constitution. It is often stated that the English legal system has no equivalent document, but this is not strictly true. The UK may not have a single, codified constitution, but there are documents that serve to protect the rights of citizens, as follows.

➜ **Magna Carta:** 'Great Charter'

- **Magna Carta 1215** Arguably the first statute ever,[73] the 1297 version of which remains in force today, albeit with most of its provisions repealed. It aimed to reduce the power of the monarch, as well as to provide citizens with certain fundamental rights, the most significant of which—the writ of ***habeas corpus***—is still in force today.

➜ ***habeas corpus:*** 'you have the body'; a writ whereby an individual can challenge the lawfulness of his detention

- **The Bill of Rights 1689** Passed following the tyrannical reign of James II, the Bill of Rights lays down a collection of rights, largely in relation to abuses of power by the monarch and Parliament. It remains in force today and is regarded as a significant influence on the US Constitution and Bill of Rights.

---

71. [1991] AC 603 (HL) 658.

72. Mention should also be made of the primary purpose of the 2011 Act, which is to provide that any treaty amendments that expand the competencies of the EU must be approved by an Act of Parliament and a national referendum (in some cases, just an Act of Parliament is required).

73. It should be stated that Magna Carta would not be regarded as a statute based on the modern definition of the term (that is, an Act of Parliament), because Parliament did not exist in 1215.

Of course, neither of these documents can be regarded as indicative of modern human rights, but they do still contain important (albeit limited) rights that are occasionally relied upon today. The modern source of human rights protection can be found in the ECHR[74] and accompanying Protocols.

The European Convention on Human Rights

Keen to ensure that the horrific events of World War II could not happen again, Winston Churchill proposed in 1946 that a Council of Europe be created to further the cause of European integration. In 1949, his proposal became a reality and the Statute of the Council of Europe (known as the 'Treaty of London') came into force and was signed by ten countries.[75] Article 3 stated that '[e]very member of the Council of Europe must accept the principles of the rule of law and of the enjoyment by all persons within its jurisdiction of human rights and fundamental freedoms' and to fulfil this aim, in 1950, the ECHR was adopted by the Council of Europe. It was ratified by the UK in 1951, and came into force in 1953.

The ECHR itself currently consists of fifty-nine Articles, of which Arts 2–14 are the most important, because they contain the various human rights upon which citizens of the signatory countries may rely. They include rights such as the right to life (Art 2), prohibition of torture (Art 3), prohibition of slavery and forced labour (Art 4), the right to liberty and security (Art 5), the right to a fair trial (Art 6), the right to respect of private and family life (Art 8), freedom of expression (Art 10), and the prohibition of discrimination (Art 14). Additional human rights have been created via the passing of Protocols (for example, the First Protocol provides for, *inter alia*, the right to education and the right to free elections). It should be noted, however, that the protection offered by the ECHR is not always absolute: certain human rights can be limited or qualified, as Table 4.2 demonstrates.

TABLE 4.2 Absolute, limited, and qualified rights

Right	Meaning	Examples
Absolute	Cannot be limited or withheld by the state	• Art 3 (prohibition of torture) • Art 4 (prohibition of slavery and forced labour)
Limited	Can be limited by the state in finite and express circumstances. Such limitations are usually found in the Article itself, but can also be found in a derogation	• Art 5 (right to liberty and security of the person) • Art 6 (right to a fair trial) • Art 12 (right to marry) • Art 14 (prohibition on discrimination)
Qualified	Rights of citizens which must be balanced with the rights of other parties, or the state. The qualification must be used for a legitimate purpose	• Art 8 (right to respect for private and family life) • Art 9 (freedom of thought, conscience and religion) • Art 10 (freedom of expression)

74. Or to give it its full title, the 'European Convention on Human Rights and Fundamental Freedoms'.
75. They were Belgium, Denmark, France, Ireland, Italy, Luxembourg, Netherlands, Norway, Sweden, and the UK. Today, the Council of Europe's membership stands at forty-seven full members, with six other countries having 'observer' status.

A significant number of Convention rights are therefore not absolute and may either be subject to derogations (which disapply rights completely) or reservations (which limits a right). The UK government has made a reservation only once, whereas derogations have been used more often—especially in relation to the prevention of terrorism.

The ECHR and businesses

The title of the ECHR is somewhat inaccurate. The use of the word 'human' indicates that the protection afforded is limited to natural persons, thereby excluding businesses. This is most certainly not the case and, unlike other human rights regimes,[76] the text of the ECHR makes it clear that the rights embodied can apply to legal persons (for example, companies), as well as natural persons. Sometimes, the ECHR states this overtly, as is the case with Art 1 of the First Protocol, which states: 'Every natural or legal person is entitled to the peaceful enjoyment of his possessions.' Other provisions do not overtly include legal persons, but state that the protection is afforded to 'everyone'. Article 34, which identifies which parties can petition the European Court of Human Rights (ECtHR), provides that '[t]he Court may receive applications from any person, non-governmental organisation or group of individuals claiming to be the victim of a violation...of the rights set forth in the Convention or the protocols thereto'. There is no doubt that, for the purposes of Art 34, businesses qualify as non-governmental organizations[77] and therefore can freely petition the ECtHR. But it was not until 1980 that the first business petitioned the ECtHR[78] and, even today, claims deriving from individuals far outweigh those from businesses. Between 1998 and 2003, the ECtHR delivered 3,307 judgments—only 126 of which related to claims filed by companies.[79]

Not all of the rights contained in the ECHR will apply to businesses. For example, Art 3 (which prohibits torture) clearly cannot apply to a business. In practice, human rights cases involving businesses tend to concentrate around a few key provisions of the ECHR, as follows.

- **Article 6 (right to a fair trial)** Businesses are entitled to the right to a fair trial, including the right to bring a case in the first place. Depriving a business of access to the court may constitute a breach of Art 6, as occurred in the late 1980s and early 1990s when Belgium attempted to deny a group of shipowners access to the Belgian courts.[80]

- **Article 10 (freedom of expression)** Article 10 cases involving businesses have almost universally focused on businesses involved in the media industry, which contend that certain acts of censorship or other state-imposed restrictions breach their Art 10 right to free expression. Alternatively, Art 10 is often pleaded as a defence in cases where the claimant contends that publication or disclosure has breached his right to privacy under Art 8. For example, when the now-defunct *News of the World* published stories accusing Max Mosley (former

---

76. The United Nations' International Bill of Human Rights applies only to natural persons, as does the US Convention on Human Rights.

77. Businesses would qualify as persons, were it not for the fact that the authentic French text of the ECHR refers to a *personne physique* ('physical person'). Accordingly, under the ECHR, businesses do not qualify as persons and must be categorized as non-governmental organizations.

78. *Sunday Times v UK* (1980) 2 EHRR 245.

79. Marius Emberland, *The Human Rights of Companies: Exploring the Structure of ECHR Protection* (OUP 2006) 14–15.

80. *Pressos Compania Naviera SA v Belgium* (1996) 21 EHRR 301.

president of the Formula 1 governing body) of engaging in Nazi-themed activities with a number of prostitutes, the newspaper's publisher sought (unsuccessfully) to justify publication under Art 10.[81]

• **Article 1 of the First Protocol (protection of property)** This provides, *inter alia*, that everyone is entitled to peaceful enjoyment of their property and that the state will not deprive persons of their property, unless it is in the public interest.

The European Court of Human Rights

The European Court of Human Rights (ECtHR), based in Strasbourg, was created in 1959. Initially, due to the relatively low number of cases, the Court only sat part-time. As time progressed, new states acceded to the ECHR and the number of cases increased substantially, with the result that the Court was unable to cope with the caseload. Therefore, in 1998, the Eleventh Protocol was passed, which replaced the old administration with a new, full-time Court. The reform was well timed, because the number of cases immediately exploded. In 1998, the Court had disposed of 5,979 applications; in 2001, it dealt with 13,858—a rise of 130 per cent.[82] In 2012/13, the ECtHR disposed of 93,397 applications.[83]

The ECtHR currently consists of forty-seven judges (equal to the number of signatory states),[84] a registrar, and a deputy registrar. Depending on importance, cases can be heard by (i) a single judge; (ii) in Committees of three judges; (iii) in chambers of seven judges; or (iv) in a Grand Chamber consisting of seventeen judges.[85] The role of the ECtHR is to interpret and apply the ECHR, and its decisions form a significant source of law in relation to human rights. The ECHR itself is relatively brief, so the judges of the ECtHR have considerable discretion. Unlike UK judges who, due to the doctrine of precedent, have a reputation for being conservative and favouring the status quo, judges in the ECtHR have to be flexible enough to adapt to changes in society and a consequent change in the nature of human rights. Such flexibility often produces an impetus for UK law to change when, normally, it would be slow to respond, as the following example demonstrates.

 The right to marry

Developments in relationship types have forced the court to reconsider which relationships attract the protection of the ECHR. In the case of *Rees v UK*,[86] the ECtHR limited the protection provided by Art 12 (the right to marry) to different-sex heterosexual couples and upheld s 11(c) of the Matrimonial Causes Act 1973, which prohibited post-operative transsexuals from marrying by rendering ***void ab initio*** any marriage not between a male and a female. Sixteen years later, in *Goodwin v UK*,[87] the ECtHR reversed its previous position and stated that prohibiting transsexuals to marry constituted a breach of Art 12.

→ ***void ab initio:*** 'invalid from the beginning'

---

81. *Mosley v News Group Newspapers Ltd* [2008] EWHC 1777 (QB), [2008] EMLR 20.

82. Statistics derived from the ECtHR website <http://www.echr.coe.int>.

83. European Court of Human Rights, *Annual Report 2013: Provisional Version* (Registry of the European Court of Human Rights 2014) 193.

84. Although it is not a requirement that each signatory state appoints one judge from its own state (e.g. the judge currently occupying San Marino's seat was born in New York, USA).

85. ECHR, Art 26(1).

86. (1986) 9 EHRR 56.   87. [2002] 35 EHRR 18.

> The Court cited 'major social changes in the institution of marriage' and 'dramatic changes brought about by developments in medicine and science in the field of transsexuality'[88] as compelling reasons for the recognition of the transsexual's right to marry. Less than a year later, in the case of *Bellinger v Bellinger*,[89] the House of Lords held that s 11(c), was incompatible with Art 12.
>
> UK law was subsequently amended and s 9(1) of the Gender Recognition Act 2004 now allows transsexuals to live permanently according to their acquired gender and, consequently, to marry. The requirement that a marriage must be between a male and female was not removed, however, meaning that same-sex marriages were, at the time, not possible in the UK, although same-sex couples could form a civil partnership under the Civil Partnership Act 2004. However, in July 2013, Parliament passed the Marriage (Same Sex Couples) Act 2013, s 1(1) of which states that '[m]arriage of same sex couples is lawful'.[90]

In the above example, the decision of the ECtHR provided the catalyst for legislative reform. It should be noted, however, that whilst domestic courts are required to take into account decisions of the ECtHR,[91] they are not required to follow them. Despite this, the Supreme Court has stated that, where there is a clear and constant line of ECtHR decisions, and those decisions are not inconsistent with, or have not overlooked, some fundamental aspect of UK law, then the court should follow that line of decisions.[92]

The Human Rights Act 1998

Although the ECHR came into force in 1953, it was not until 1966 that UK citizens could take their case to the ECtHR. The process was, however, notoriously difficult: petitioners first had to exhaust all domestic rights of appeal[93] (an extremely expensive and time-consuming process in itself) before being allowed to petition the ECtHR directly. Unlike other signatory states, the UK did not incorporate the ECHR into domestic law, nor are Convention rights directly applicable or effective in the way that EU law can be. The result was that there was no mechanism to enforce the ECHR in a UK court. A governmental White Paper discovered that, on average, it took five years for a case to reach the ECtHR, by which time costs would have, on average, reached £30,000.[94] Accordingly, the Labour government indicated its intention to allow claimants to enforce Convention rights in a domestic court.

The Human Rights Act 1998, which came into force on October 2000, consists of only twenty-two sections and four short Schedules, but its importance cannot be overstated. The immediate effect of the Act was, to use the language of the White Paper that led to the 1998 Act, to 'bring rights home'[95] by allowing certain

---

88. ibid [100].

89. [2003] UKHL 21, [2003] 2 AC 467.

90. Section 1(1) came into force on 13 March 2014, but other provisions are not yet in force. It is anticipated that the Act will be fully in force by 2015 at the latest. In December 2013, the Government announced that the first same-sex marriages will take place from the 29 March 2014.

91. Human Rights Act 1998, s 2(1)(a).

92. *Manchester City Council v Pinnock* [2010] UKSC 45, [2010] 3 WLR 1441.

93. ECHR, Art 35(1). This condition still applies to litigants who wish to take their case to the ECtHR.

94. Secretary of State for the Home Department, *Bringing Rights Home: The Human Rights Bill* (Cm 3782, HMSO 1997) [1.14].   95. ibid.

Convention rights to be enforced in a domestic court,[96] but, as is discussed later, the full effects of the Act are much wider.

Enforcing the ECHR in a domestic court

The principal effect of the Human Rights Act 1998 is to permit persons to enforce the ECHR in a domestic court. It is important to note, however, that not all of the rights contained within the Convention can be enforced; only those rights contained in Arts 2–12 and 14, Arts 1–3 of the First Protocol, and Art 1 of the Thirteenth Protocol.[97] The person bringing the claim will need to demonstrate that he is a 'victim' within the meaning of Art 34,[98] but, unfortunately, Art 34 does not provide a definition of 'victim', other than to state it can include 'any person, non-governmental organisation or group of individuals claiming to be the victim of a violation' by the state. The exact definition has therefore been left to the judges, who have established that a victim is someone who has been 'directly or indirectly affected by the alleged infringement of the Convention…[or]…those who are potentially at risk of an infringement of their rights'.[99] Proceedings must be brought within one year of the date on which the alleged infringement took place, although the court may permit a longer period if it considers it equitable to do so.[100] Finally, if a person can establish that his Convention rights have been breached, the court 'may grant such relief or remedy, or make such order, within its powers as it considers just and appropriate'.[101]

Mention should be made to the 'margin of appreciation'—a concept that has long been recognized by the ECtHR, but which is increasingly being taken into account in domestic cases involving human rights. As the ECHR is an international convention, it will be applied amongst states with vastly differing cultures and legal systems. Accordingly, the ECtHR has been careful not to enforce certain rights too rigidly and will give signatory states a margin of appreciation to take into account the state's idiosyncrasies. Thus, when a particular book was prohibited from being sold in England for breaching the Obscene Publications Acts 1959 and 1964, but could be purchased in many other countries in Europe, the ECtHR held that the prohibition in England did not breach the publisher's right to freedom of expression, because each country is better placed to determine what is obscene based on its own culture and traditions.[102] Domestic recognition of the margin of appreciation arrived prior to the 1998 Act coming into force when Lord Hope stated that:

> difficult choices may have to be made by the executive or the legislature between the rights of the individual and the needs of society. In some circumstances it will be appropriate for the courts to recognise that there is an area of judgment within which the judiciary will defer, on democratic grounds, to the considered opinion of the elected body or person whose act or decision is said to be incompatible with the Convention.[103]

---

96. Human Rights Act 1998, s 7.   97. ibid s 1.   98. ibid s 7(7).

99. Richard Stone, *Textbook on Civil Liberties and Human Rights* (8th edn, OUP 2010) 41.

100. Human Rights Act 1998, s 7(5).   101. ibid s 8(1).

102. *Handyside v UK* (1979–80) 1 EHRR 737.

103. *R v DPP, ex p Kebilene* [2000] 2 AC 326 (HL) 381.

Human rights and statutory interpretation

In Chapter 3, the various rules created by the judges to aid in the interpretation of statutes were discussed. With the passing of the Human Rights Act 1998, a new rule[104] was created and can be found in s 3(1), which states: 'So far as it is possible to do so, primary legislation and subordinate legislation must be read and given effect in a way which is compatible with the Convention rights.' The effect of this section is significant for two reasons:

1. Although the 1998 Act came into force in October 2000, s 3 also applies to all legislation passed before that date[105] (that is, it has retrospective effect). In relation to legislation passed after that date, s 19 states that the minister responsible for a Bill must, before the second reading, make a statement indicating to what extent the Bill is compatible with the ECHR.

2. The statutory rule in s 3 outranks the doctrine of precedent. Therefore an inferior court may validly refuse to follow a precedent established by a higher court if it feels that the precedent is incompatible with a Convention right. This could be regarded as a potentially substantial erosion of the doctrine of precedent.

Section 3 requires the judiciary to walk an extremely thin line between legislative interpretation and legislative amendment. In the majority of cases, the courts have been able to interpret legislation in a way that complies with the Convention, yet still pays respect to Parliament's intentions. For example, in *Ghaiden v Godin-Mendoza*,[106] the House of Lords was able to extend the protection offered under the Rent Act 1977 to same-sex couples by interpreting the phrase 'as his or her wife or husband' to mean 'as if they were his or her wife or husband'. In several cases, however, the courts have strayed from this line and have interpreted a statute in a way that Parliament clearly did not intend in order to ensure that it complies with Convention rights.

 R v A (No 2) [2001] UKHL 25

FACTS: A common tactic of defence lawyers in rape cases is to attempt to discredit the alleged victim by cross-examining her about her past sexual experiences. The public exposure of such intimate, but often evidentially worthless, details could be extremely harrowing, and so the Youth Justice and Criminal Evidence Act 1999 was passed, with s 41 providing for a so-called 'rape shield', which prohibited the asking of questions or provision of evidence concerning the victim's previous sexual history, except for in a number of very narrow and exhaustive instances. The defendant argued that by making such evidence inadmissible, he was denied the right to a full defence and, consequently, a fair trial, as provided for by Art 6 of the ECHR.

HELD: To avoid s 41 compromising the defendant's Art 6 rights, the House of Lords held that s 41 should be 'subject to the implied provision that evidence or questioning which is required to ensure a fair trial under article 6 of the Convention should not be treated as inadmissible'.[107] Lord Steyn went on to state that 'the interpretive obligation under s 3 . . . is a

---

104. The rule cannot be regarded as an extension of the literal rule, because it permits the court to reject a literal interpretation if it is incompatible with the ECHR. Further, it cannot be regarded as an extension of the golden or mischief rules, because they are concerned with the intention of Parliament at the time that the legislation was passed, which may have been many years before the Human Rights Act 1998 came into effect.   105. Human Rights Act 1998, s 3(2)(a).

106. [2004] UKHL 30, [2004] 2 AC 557.

107. [2001] UKHL 25, [2002] 1 AC 45 [45] (Lord Steyn).

next step being the creation of a Bill of Rights. This proposal received support from a joint committee of the House of Commons and House of Lords.[136] Upon coming into power in May 2010, the coalition government announced that it would establish a Commission to 'investigate the creation of a Bill of Rights that incorporates and builds upon all our obligations under the [ECHR]'.[137] The Commission was established in March 2011 and published its first consultation paper in August 2011.[138] In April 2011, to the annoyance of the government, the ECtHR rejected the government's request to appeal the case of *Greens and MT v UK*,[139] in which the ECtHR held that that s 3 of the Representation of the People Act 1973 (which imposed a blanket ban on prisoners' voting rights) was a breach of Art 3 of the First Protocol (the right to free elections).

In December 2012, the Commission on the Bill of Rights published its final report and, concluded that the creation of a Bill of Rights 'is an idea of potential value which deserves further exploration at an appropriate time and in an appropriate way'.[140] The Commission is now disbanded and no further progress has been made. However, in 2013, a number of Conservative ministers has expressed dissatisfaction with the ECHR and indicated that repealing the HRA 1998 and withdrawing from the ECHR may be a possible course of action.

Chapter conclusion

The impact that EU membership has had upon the English legal system cannot be overstated. The creation of the EU resulted in a new legal order that takes priority over domestic laws. From a business perspective, the creation of a Europe-wide system of law can be seen as extremely beneficial. A system of laws that applies uniformly throughout the EU will be of considerable benefit to businesses that operate in several EU countries. Such a business would previously have needed to be aware of the laws of every country within which they operated or with which they had commercial dealings. In cases involving directly applicable law, such laws will apply uniformly throughout the EU, thereby reducing the need to understand fully the laws of numerous countries.

Similarly, ratifying the ECHR has had an appreciable and often unpredictable effect upon the operation of businesses in the UK, especially since the enactment of the Human Rights Act 1998, which permits much of the ECHR to be enforced in a domestic court. The extension of many human rights to cover legal persons is accepted without dispute, but determining the exact scope and application of human rights principles to businesses has proved to be an extremely controversial and problematic issue. The effect of the 1998 Act in relation to the interpretation and application of statutes has already been felt, and will continue to do so for some time as the judges reinterpret statutes in light of the obligations imposed by the 1998 Act. As discussed, however, the long-term future of the Act may be in doubt, especially if the Conservative Party manages to secure an overall majority in the 2015 election.

---

136. Joint Committee on Human Rights, *A Bill of Rights for the UK?* (HMSO 2008).
137. HM Government, *The Coalition: Our Programme for Government* (Cabinet Office 2010) 11.
138. Commission on a Bill of Rights, *Do We Need a UK Bill of Rights?* (2011).
139. App Nos 60041/08 and 60054/08 (ECtHR, 23 November 2010).
140. Commission on a Bill of Rights, *A UK Bill of Rights? The Choice Before Us: Vol 1* (2012) Overview, [67].

Key points summary

- There are seven EU institutions:
  1. the European Parliament;
  2. the European Council;
  3. the Council;
  4. the European Commission;
  5. the Court of Justice of the EU;
  6. the European Central Bank; and
  7. the Court of Auditors.

- The Court of Justice of the EU will provide preliminary rulings, hear actions against Member States that breach EU law, hear actions against EU institutions, and hear cases involving disputes between EU institutions and their employees.

- A preliminary ruling is the referral of a case to the Court for an authoritative and conclusive interpretation of a point of EU law. The Court will not apply the law to the case; that is still the responsibility of the domestic court.

- The principal forms of EU legislation are treaty provisions, regulations, directives, and decisions.

- EU legislation that is directly applicable automatically forms part of domestic law, without the need for further implementation. Treaty provisions and regulations are directly applicable.

- EU legislation capable of having direct effect can be enforced in a domestic court, provided that it is clear and unconditional, and does not require further implementation.

- EU legislation that has vertical direct effect can be enforced by individuals only against the state, or an emanation of the state. Legislation that has horizontal direct effect can be enforced between individuals.

- Almost all of the rights provided for by the ECHR can be enforced in a UK domestic court following the implementation of the Human Rights Act 1998 in October 2000.

- Section 3 of the Human Rights Act 1998 places a duty upon domestic courts to interpret domestic legislation, as far as possible, in line with the ECHR. If the court feels that it cannot do this, however, it may issue a declaration of incompatibility.

- Declarations of incompatibility have no effect upon Acts of Parliament, so the court will still have to apply the incompatible provision.

Self-test questions

1. Explain the relationship between EU law and the ECHR. Explain the reasons behind the creation of the EU and the ECHR.

2. Explain the composition and functions of:
   (a) the Council;
   (b) the European Council;
   (c) the European Commission;
   (d) the European Parliament;
   (e) the Court of Justice of the European Union.

3. Explain the difference between 'direct applicability' and 'direct effect'. How does vertical direct effect differ from horizontal direct effect?

4. Do all directly applicable provisions also have direct effect?

5. How do directives differ from regulations?

6. In August 2013, the (fictional) Employee Records Directive is passed. It provides that 'all employees have a right to see their personnel records, subject to this right being excluded by the employee's contract of employment'. Peter requests to see his personnel record, but his employer refuses, arguing that Peter's employment contract contains a term stating that he does not have the right to see his personnel record. Advise Peter.

7. How has the enactment of the Human Rights Act 1998 affected: (i) the enforcement of the ECHR; and (ii) the way in which legislation is interpreted?

Further reading

Paul Craig and Gráinne De Búrca, *EU Law: Text, Cases and Materials* (5th edn, OUP 2011) chs 1–3
Provides an in-depth, but easy-to-understand, account of the development and institutions of the European Union, as well as a well-chosen selection of relevant materials

Marius Emberland, *The Human Rights of Companies* (OUP 2006)
Provides a detailed analysis of the protection offered to companies by the European Convention on Human Rights and the Human Rights Act 1998

Richard Stone, *Textbook on Civil Liberties and Human Rights* (9th edn, OUP 2012) chs 1 and 2
Provides a clear and accessible account of the ECHR and the Human Rights Act 1998

Websites

<http://curia.europa.eu>
The official website of the Court of Justice of the European Union; contains extensive and up-to-date information on the working of both courts, as well as providing access to court decisions

<http://eur-lex.europa.eu>
Provides full access to EU treaties, legislation, and case law

<http://europa.eu>
The official website of the EU; contains a massive amount of accessible and up-to-date information on all of the workings of the EU, including detailed information on the workings of all of its institutions

<http://www.echr.coe.int>
The official website of the European Court of Human Rights; contains up-to-date information on the ECHR and the ECtHR, as well as providing access to decisions of the ECtHR

Remember to visit the **Online Resource Centre** at <**http://www. oxfordtextbooks.co.uk/orc/roach3e**> to access the following resources on Chapter 4, 'Europe and the English legal system': more **practice questions** and answers; a **glossary** of key terms; **multiple-choice questions**; **revision summaries**; and **diagrams** in pdf. Updates to the law can be found on Twitter by following **@UKBusinessLaw**

PART II
the law of contract

5 An introduction to the law of contract

- Why are contracts enforced?
- Formalities
- The capacity to contract
- Privity of contract and third-party rights

INTRODUCTION

We are all aware of the importance of a contract when we buy a house or a car and we have to 'sign on the dotted line', but apart from such obvious instances, we tend not to think about the role that contracts play. Put simply, contracts dominate our ability to transact: whenever you purchase goods from a shop, watch a film in a cinema, take a ride on a bus, or pay another to perform a service for you, you are entering into a contract. For businesses, the importance of contract is even more pronounced, as virtually every transaction will be governed by contract. When all goes well, our ignorance of the contractual relationships into which we enter is not a problem—but when things do not go well and one party fails to deliver what it has promised, the dispute can only be resolved by reference to the contract that has been created. It is therefore of paramount importance that we know what a contract actually is.

Unfortunately, in English law, there is no legally accepted, formal definition of the word 'contract'. In the absence of a legal definition, the issue has been left largely to academics and, whilst individual definitions differ, the majority of definitions broadly cover the same ground. Perhaps the most straightforward and well-known definition is that provided by Treitel, who defines a contract as 'an agreement giving rise to obligations which are enforced or recognized by law'.[1] Whilst such a definition provides an adequate understanding of what a contract is, it does not explain why the law enforces such agreements, or the role of contract law. At its most basic level, the role of contract law is to determine which contractual obligations can be enforced and which cannot. It is therefore important to understand the theoretical justifications behind why contracts are enforced.

Why are contracts enforced?

For centuries, contract theorists have argued and debated the theoretical justifications behind why some promises are legally enforceable and others are not. A detailed account of these theories is beyond the scope of this text, but it is worth

---

1. Edwin Peel, *Treitel on the Law of Contract* (13th edn, Sweet & Maxwell 2011) 1.

briefly explaining the theoretical and practical justifications behind the enforcement of certain agreements.

- **The moral argument** On a moral level, enforcing contracts simply ensures that we keep our promises.[2] In this sense, the law is not imposing obligations upon us; rather, it is giving effect to obligations that we voluntarily undertook.

- **The efficiency argument** Enforcing contractual promises maximizes efficiency in that, when negotiating, persons will attempt to reach a conclusion that maximizes their own benefit. A freely negotiated contract produces an outcome that maximizes the benefit of all parties to the contract. If all parties act this way, societal wealth will be maximized.

- **The reliance argument** Numerous academics[3] have contended that the principal modern theory for enforcing contractual obligations is based upon the notion of 'reliance'. According to this theory, it is not the making of the promise that justifies enforcement, but the other party's reliance on it.

- **The relationship argument** Some have argued that the role of contract law is to better encourage and protect the forming of valuable relationships.[4]

Having highlighted the theoretical justifications for enforcing contracts, we will now examine three practical issues relating to the enforcement of contracts, beginning with the issue of formality.

Formalities

It is a common belief amongst laypersons that a contract must be in writing and both parties must 'sign on the dotted line'. In reality, however, this is a misconception and, in the majority of cases, the law imposes no requirements regarding the form that a contract takes, although there are clear advantages to putting a contract into writing—namely, that it will render less likely the possibility of the parties subsequently disagreeing over what was agreed. Generally, a contract made orally is just as valid in law as a written contract signed by both parties.

Whilst it could legitimately be argued that, from an evidential perspective, it would be desirable that all contracts were in writing, one could also argue that, from a practical viewpoint, imposing formality requirements could be unworkable for several reasons:

- given the number of contracts entered into daily, the task of determining which contracts should be subject to formality would be an unduly burdensome task;

- ensuring that the text and form of a contract complies with formality can be a time-consuming task;

- requiring strict adhesion to a set of formalities could be regarded as out of touch in an era increasingly dominated by electronic commerce.

Accordingly, the general rule that contracts require no particular formalities is one of efficiency and convenience, and the law will only impose requirements as to

---

2. Charles Fried, *Contract As Promise: A Theory of Contractual Obligation* (Harvard University Press 1981) 14–17.
3. See e.g. Grant Gilmore, *The Death of Contract* (Ohio State University Press 1974); PS Atiyah, *The Rise and Fall of the Freedom of Contract* (Clarendon Press 1979).
4. Joseph Raz, 'Promises in Morality and Law' (1982) 95 Harv LR 916.

formality when 'there is some good reason for doing so'.[5] For example, in some contracts (for example, consumer contracts), there is considerable inequality of bargaining power between the parties, and the setting of certain formalities helps to protect the weaker party against the stronger party abusing its dominant position.

Three principal forms of formality can be identified:

1. contracts required to be made by deed;
2. contracts required to be in writing; and
3. contracts required to be evidenced in writing.

Figure 5.1 summarizes the principal forms of formality and provides examples of contracts requiring such formalities.

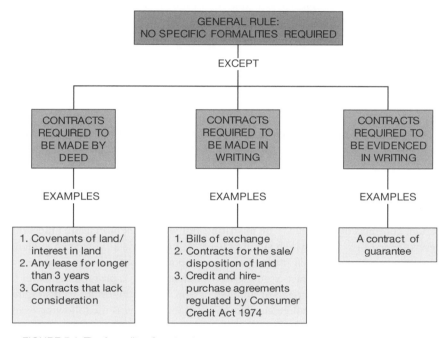

FIGURE 5.1 The formality of contracts

Contracts required to be made by deed

Certain contracts must be made in the form of a **deed**. It is often said the deeds must be 'signed, sealed and delivered', but the requirement that a deed be sealed was abolished in 1989.[6] Today, the validity of a deed is dependent upon it indicating that it is a deed (although the word 'deed' need not be used),[7] and that the deed is signed in the presence of a witness and then delivered.[8] If one of the parties to a deed is a company, the formalities are different. Corporate deeds can be signed by affixing the company's seal, if it has retained one. Failing that, it will need to be signed by two

➡ **deed:** a legal document that is used to create a right; similar to a contract, except it is subject to stricter formalities

---

5. Hein Kotz, *European Contract Law Volume 1: Formation, Validity and Content of Contracts—Contract and Third Parties* (OUP 1997) 80.

6. Law of Property (Miscellaneous Provisions) Act 1989, s 1.

7. ibid s 1(2).   8. ibid s 1(3).

'authorized signatories' (defined as either a director or company secretary), or signed by one director in the presence of a witness.[9]

Examples of contracts that must be made by deed include:

➜ **void *ab initio*:** 'invalid from the beginning'

🔗 The law relating to consideration is discussed at p 149

- A lease for more than three years will be **void *ab initio*** for the purpose of creating a lease if not made by deed.[10]
- An agreement that lacks consideration will not normally constitute a binding contract, unless it is made by deed.[11]

Contracts required to be made in writing

In order to be valid, certain types of contract must be made in writing, including the following.

- A bill of exchange must be in writing and signed.[12] A bill of exchange is simply a written instruction from one person to pay a specified sum of money to another.

🔗 Visit the **Online Resource Centre** for more on the law relating to consumer credit agreements in the chapter entitled 'Consumer credit'

- Most contracts for the sale or disposition of an interest in land must be made in writing and all of the terms agreed by the parties must be in one document.[13]
- Regulated consumer credit and hire-purchase agreements must be in writing and must contain certain information, or they will be unenforceable unless a court order is obtained.[14]

Contracts required to be evidenced in writing

Certain contracts do not need to be in writing, but will be unenforceable unless they are evidenced in writing, which simply means that there must be written evidence that the agreement has been made. The most important contract that must be evidenced in writing is a contract of guarantee, which is simply 'a promise to answer for the debt, default or miscarriage of another person'.[15] It is important to distinguish between a contract of guarantee and a contract of indemnity, as the following example demonstrates.

Eg Guarantees and indemnities

Tom and Dave enter a BMW showroom. Tom enters into a contract with BMW to purchase a car. Dave enters into an agreement with BMW, stating that he will pay for the car if Tom fails to do so. The contract between Tom and BMW is a normal contract, and so would require no formality. The contract between Dave and BMW is a contract of guarantee, and so would need to be evidenced in writing. This evidence would need to identify the parties,[16] describe

---

9. Companies Act 2006, s 44.

10. Law of Property Act 1925, ss 52 and 54(2).   11. *Rann v Hughes* (1778) 7 Term Rep 350n (HL).

12. Bills of Exchange Act 1882, ss 3(1) and 17(2).

13. Law of Property (Miscellaneous Provisions) Act 1989, s 2(1).

14. Consumer Credit Act 1974, s 60; Consumer Credit (Agreements) Regulations 1983, SI 1983/1553, regs 2 and 3.   15. Statute of Frauds 1677, s 4.   16. *William v Jordan* (1877) 6 Ch D 517.

the subject matter of the contract,[17] contain the material terms of the contract,[18] and be signed by the person giving the guarantee (Dave), or his agent.[19] Failure to evidence the contract would not render it void or voidable, but would render it unenforceable.

Note that if Tom were to enter into the contract with BMW, but Dave agreed to pay for the car, the contract between Dave and BMW would not be a contract of guarantee—it would be a contract of indemnity—and the agreement would not need to be evidenced in writing. A guarantee is a promise by *A* to pay for another (*B*), if *B* fails to pay, whereas an indemnity is simply the promise, by *A*, to pay for another (*B*), irrespective of *B*'s liability (that is, *A* is liable in any event).

Formalities and e-commerce

The advent of e-commerce has created problems regarding the formality of contract. For example, how can one sign an electronic document? Will printing off a contract satisfy the requirement that it be in writing? Article 9(1) of the Electronic Commerce Directive[20] required the UK to confront these problems by stating that:

> Member States shall ensure that their legal system allows contracts to be concluded by electronic means. Member States shall in particular ensure that the legal requirements applicable to the contractual process neither create obstacles for the use of electronic contracts nor result in such contracts being deprived of legal effectiveness and validity on account of their being made by electronic means.

As a result, three major reforms have been introduced in order to ensure that UK laws relating to formalities do not fall foul of Art 9(1), as follows.

1. The Electronic Commerce (EC Directive) Regulations 2002[21] were made in order to implement the Electronic Commerce Directive.
2. Section 7 of the Electronic Communications Act 2000 recognizes the validity of 'electronic signatures' and provides that they will fulfil the same function as a handwritten signature, provided that they meet the test of authenticity in s 15(2).
3. Section 8 of the Electronic Communications Act 2000 empowers the Secretary of State to amend legislation 'for the purpose of authorising or facilitating the use of electronic communications or electronic storage'.

The Law Commission has contended that s 8 will only need to be used in 'very rare cases',[22] because, in the majority of cases, existing legislation will comply with Art 9(1). Further, where the legislation is vague, it can be interpreted in such a way as to permit the use of e-commerce, thereby avoiding the need to amend it. Thus, in *Pereira Fernandes SA v Mehta*,[23] the court held that a contractual offer sent by email satisfied the requirement of being in 'writing' for the purposes of the Statute of Frauds 1677, and that by including his name in the email text, the sender had successfully 'signed' the document.

---

17. *Burgess v Cox* [1951] Ch 383 (Ch).   18. *Cook v Taylor* [1942] Ch 349 (Ch).
19. Statute of Frauds 1677, s 4.
20. European Parliament Directive (EC) 2000/31 OJ L178/1.   21. SI 2002/2013.
22. Law Commission, *Electronic Commerce: Formal Requirements in Commercial Transactions* (2001), [3.49].
23. [2006] EWHC 813 (Ch), [2006] 1 WLR 1543.

The capacity to contract

➜ *Prima facie*: 'at first glance'; initially

An individual who has the ability to enter into a binding contract is said to have 'contractual capacity'. *Prima facie* the law assumes that all living, sober adults of sound mind have contractual capacity. It follows that individuals who do not fall within this description may lack the ability to enter into binding contracts. The determination of contractual capacity can be a delicate one, because the law is required to balance two justifiable aims:

1. the need to protect vulnerable or incapacitated individuals; and
2. the need to protect those who fairly enter into contracts with persons who may lack capacity.

Note that the following is concerned with the ability of natural persons to contract; the contractual capacity of bodies corporate is examined at pp 542 and 556.

Minors

Any person below the age of 18 is legally regarded as a minor[24] and will lack the capacity to makes many types of contract. Where a minor lacks capacity, however, this does not mean that the contract is void *ab initio*. Generally, whilst the party contracting with the minor will be unable to enforce the contract, nor can he escape the contract by relying on the minor's lack of capacity, the minor can enforce the contract should he wish to do so. However, there are a number of situations where a minor can create a binding contract, or may be able to escape a contract on the ground of it being voidable.

Binding contracts

In two situations, a minor will acquire full contractual capacity to enter into binding contracts. The first situation concerns contracts for necessaries, which are held to be binding 'not for the benefit of the tradesman who may trust the infant, but for the benefit of the infant himself'.[25] A minor will acquire full contractual capacity when purchasing goods or hiring services that are 'necessary' to maintain him, given his circumstances. In relation to goods, the Sale of Goods Act 1979 states that 'necessaries' include 'goods suitable to the condition in life of the minor and to his actual requirements at the time of the sale and delivery' and that a minor will be required to pay a reasonable price for such goods.[26] Clearly, goods such as food, drink, and clothing will be regarded as necessaries, but it is important to note that, in determining what is necessary, the court will have regard to characteristics of the minor in question.[27] This has resulted in the term 'necessaries' receiving a somewhat wide definition and has been held to include a selection of rings, breast pins, and watch chains for the child of a rich MP,[28] and a uniform for a minor's servant.[29] Clearly, the word 'necessaries' is not to have the same meaning as the word 'necessities', although the courts have stated that 'mere luxuries' will not constitute necessaries.[30] This principle also applies to services, and will include the provision of education,[31] legal

---

24. Family Law Reform Act 1969, s 1.
25. *Ryder v Wombwell* (1868) LS 4 EX 32, 38.   26. Sale of Goods Act 1979, s 3(2) and (3).
27. *Chapple v Cooper* (1844) 13 M & W 253 (Ex).   28. *Peters v Fleming* (1840) 6 M & W 42 (Ex).
29. *Hands v Slaney* (1800) 8 TR 578.   30. *Peters v Fleming* (1840) 6 M & W 42 (Ex).
31. *Walter v Everard* [1891] 2 QB 369 (CA).

advice,[32] and medical services.[33] Where a contract for the supply of necessary goods or services contains harsh or onerous terms that operate against the minor, then the contract will be void.[34]

The second situation in which a minor acquires full contractual capacity is in relation to contracts for service—namely, employment or apprenticeship. The rationale behind holding such contracts valid is that the law should not prevent a minor from pursuing an occupation. Such contracts will be binding where they are for the minor's benefit as a whole, and a contract that benefits the minor overall will not be called into question simply because one or two terms are disadvantageous.[35] However, if the disadvantageous terms outweigh the benefits of the contract, the contract will be unenforceable.

 De Francesco v Barnum (1890) 45 Ch D 430 (Ch)

FACTS: A contract provided that a minor would, for a period of seven years, learn to dance under the tutelage of Signor De Francesco. During this period, he was not obliged to maintain her or provide employment for her, and she could not marry or obtain any professional work without obtaining permission from De Francesco. Finally, De Francesco had the right to terminate the contract without notice at any time.

HELD: The contract was unenforceable. The terms of the contract were unduly harsh and unreasonable, and, overall, were not for the minor's benefit.

Voidable contracts

In several situations, a minor can create a voidable contract, meaning that it will bind both parties, but that the minor is free to repudiate the contract at any time before he reaches the age of 18, or within a reasonable time afterwards.[36] The other party cannot repudiate the contract.[37] Examples of voidable contracts that can be created by a minor include:

repudiate: to refuse to honour or fulfil a contract

1. Contracts concerning land, including contracts to rent property,[38] or contracts to purchase or sell land.[39]
2. A minor who purchases or subscribes for shares is liable to pay for them, unless he repudiates.[40]
3. A minor may become a partner, but will not be made liable for the partnership's debts whilst he remains a minor.[41]

The effect of repudiation is to free the minor from all future obligations—but obligations may have accrued prior to repudiation (e.g. rent payments may be due on a lease of property) and whether the minor is bound by such obligations is unclear. The weight of authority appears to favour the view that the repudiation rescinds the contract and, because repudiation is retrospective, the minor will not be bound by any obligations that have accrued.[42] Authority also exists, however, for the view that

---

32. *Helps v Clayton* (1864) 29 JP 263.
33. *Huggins v Wiseman* (1690) Carth 110.   34. *Fawcett v Smethurst* (1914) 84 LJKB 473.
35. *Clements v London and North Western Railway Company* [1894] 2 QB 482 (CA).
36. *Edwards v Carter* [1893] AC 360 (HL).   37. *Clayton v Ashdown* (1714) 2 Eq Ca Arb 516.
38. *Keteley's Case* (1613) 1 Brownl 1.   39. *Whittingham v Murdy* (1889) 60 LT 956 (QB).
40. *Steinberg v Scala (Leeds) Ltd* [1923] 2 Ch 452 (CA).
41. *Lovell and Christmas v Beauchamp* [1894] AC 607 (HL).
42. See e.g. *North Western Rly Co v McMichael* (1850) 5 Exch 114.

minors are bound by obligations that accrue prior to repudiation.[43] A definitive decision on the matter is required.

Ratification and restitution

Even if a contract does not come within one of the above instances, a minor may still be bound if, upon reaching the age of 18, he expressly or impliedly **ratifies** it.[44] Prior to ratification, however, the contract would not be binding on the minor, but the minor may choose to enforce it, and may have received a benefit from it. The court has the discretion to require the minor to return any property gained where it is 'just and equitable' to do so;[45] this will usually be used where the minor has acquired property without paying for it. If a minor has expended money in relation to a contract that he later repudiates, he will only be permitted to claim back the money if there has been a total failure of consideration.[46]

ratifies: approves or sanctions

Mental incapacity

The law presumes that a person has mental capacity unless the contrary is established.[47] Section 2(1) of the Mental Capacity Act 2005 states that a person will lack capacity in relation to a matter if 'at the material time he is unable to make a decision for himself in relation to a matter because of an impairment of, or a disturbance of the functioning of, the mind or brain'.[48] Despite this, a contract with a person who lacks capacity under s 2(1) will normally be binding, except:

- when the other party knew of the mental incapacity, in which case, the contract is voidable at the option of the mentally incapacitated party.[49]
- when the mentally incapacitated person's affairs are subject to the control of the **Court of Protection**, any contract that interferes with the court's control of said property will not bind the incapacitated individual,[50] although it will bind the other party.

Court of Protection: a court set up to deal with the affairs of adults (and some children) who lack capacity

A mentally incapacitated person who enters into a contract for 'necessaries' will be liable for the full contract price if (i) the other person is not aware of the incapacity, and (ii) the incapacitated person's affairs are not under the control of the Court of Protection.[51] If these two conditions are not met, the action is limited to recovery of a reasonable price.[52]

Intoxication

If, at the time of making a contract, a party is intoxicated (through drink or drugs) to such an extent that he is unable to understand the transaction and the other party knows this, the contract is voidable at the intoxicated party's discretion.[53] If, however, he does not avoid the contract, he must pay a reasonable price for any necessary goods (not services) delivered under the contract.[54]

Figure 5.2 clarifies the rules relating to a person's contractual capacity.

43. See e.g. *Blake v Concannon* (1870) IR 4 CL 323.   44. *Williams v Moor* (1843) 11 M & W 256.
45. Minors' Contracts Act 1987, s 3(1).   46. *Corpe v Overton* (1833) 10 Bing 252.
47. Mental Capacity Act 2005, s 1(2).
48. The impairment can be temporary or permanent (Mental Capacity Act 2005, s 2(2)).
49. *Molton v Camroux* (1849) 4 Ex 17.   50. *Re Walker* [1905] 1 Ch 160 (CA).
51. *Baxter v Portsmouth* (1826) 5 B & C 170.   52. Mental Capacity Act 2005, s 7(1).
53. *Gore v Gibson* (1843) 13 M & W 623, as qualified by *Matthews v Baxter* (1873) LR 8 Exch 132.
54. Sale of Goods Act 1979, s 3(2).

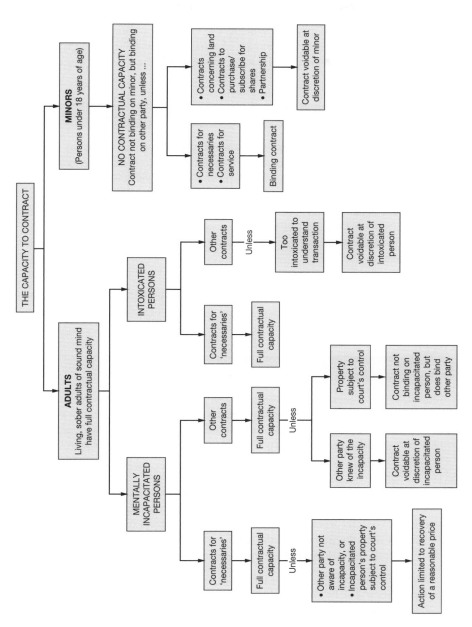

FIGURE 5.2 Contractual capacity

Privity of contract and third-party rights

Privity of contract is a long-established doctrine in contract law that consists of two rules. The first rule provides that only the parties to a contract may enforce the contract. Third parties have no right to enforce the contracts of others or to sue if the contract is breached, even if they have an interest in the contract, as can be seen in the following case.

 Tweddle v Atkinson (1831) 1 B & S 393

FACTS: John Tweddle's son (the claimant) was marrying William Guy's daughter. Tweddle and Guy contracted with each other to pay the claimant a sum of money (Tweddle would pay £100 and Guy would pay £200). Guy died without paying the £200 promised and the claimant sued Guy's personal representatives for the money.

HELD: The claimant's action failed. He was not a party to the contract and so could not enforce it. Tweddle would be able to sue Guy's representatives for the failure to pay, but because Tweddle had not actually suffered any loss, he would only be able to recover nominal damages.

The second rule provides that a contract only imposes obligations on the parties to it. Contracts do not impose obligations on third parties, as the following example demonstrates.

 Privity of contract

Rhian, Ceri, and Steve are shareholders of Bastion plc. Rhian and Ceri enter into a contract with each other, which provides that either Rhian or Ceri can require Steve to sell them half of his shares. This obligation on Steve will be unenforceable, and neither Rhian nor Ceri will be able to compel Steve to sell his shares, because he is not a party to the contract.

As time progressed, the doctrine became subject to criticism from judges,[55] the Law Commission,[56] and academics[57]—namely, that preventing third parties with an interest in a contract from being able to enforce it defeats the entire purpose of a contract that both the parties and the third party would wish to see enforced. As far back as 1937, the Law Revision Committee recommended that:

> Where a contract by its express terms purports to confer a benefit directly on a third party it shall be enforceable by a third party in his own name subject to any defence that would have been valid between the contracting parties.[58]

---

55. For example, *Woodar Investment Development Ltd v Wimpey Construction UK Ltd* [1980] 1 WLR 277 (HL) 291 (Lord Salmon).
56. Law Commission, *Contracts for the Benefit of Third Parties* (Law Com No 3329, HMSO 1996) [3.2].
57. For example, MP Furmston, 'Return to *Dunlop v Selfridge*?' (1960) 23 MLR 373.
58. Law Revision Committee, *Sixth Interim Report* (Cmnd 5449, HMSO 1937) [48].

This recommendation was not taken any further until 1996, when the Law Commission published a report[59] that contained a draft Bill, which would implement the Law Revision Committee's recommendation. The Bill was, with some amendments, enacted as the Contracts (Rights of Third Parties) Act 1999.

The Contracts (Rights of Third Parties) Act 1999

Section 1(1) of the Contracts (Rights of Third Parties) Act 1999 (CRTPA 1999) provides an important exception to the first rule of the privity doctrine, but this exception applies only to those contracts covered by the Act, with the Act itself specifying a number of contracts that are excluded from its operation:

- Contracts containing a bill of exchange, promissory note, or any other negotiable instruments confer no rights on third parties.[60]

- The contract between a company and its members by virtue of the constitution confers no rights on third parties.[61] The same would apply to an incorporation document of a limited liability partnership.[62]

- A third party cannot enforce any term in a contract of employment against an employee or worker.[63]

Section 1(1) states that, subject to the provisions of the Act, a third party may enforce a term of the contract if (i) the contract expressly provides that he may; or (ii) the term purports to confer a benefit on him. As a result of s 1(1), had *Tweddle v Atkinson* been decided today, the claimant would have been able to recover the £200 from Guy's estate. However, the exception contained in s 1(1)(b) will not operate where, on a proper construction of the contract, it appears that the parties did not intend the term to be enforceable by a third party.[64] Accordingly, the default position (or, as the Law Commission termed it, a 'rebuttable presumption')[65] is that third parties may enforce terms that confer a benefit upon them, unless the contract indicates otherwise.

The exception contained in s 1(1) does not provide that all third parties can enforce the contract; only third parties expressly[66] identified in the contract by name, as a member of a class (for example, 'employees' of a certain business), or by reference to a description (for example, the party of a particular sale of goods contract) may enforce the term.[67] Such persons will be able to obtain any remedy that would be available for breach of contract had they actually been a party to the contract[68] (for example, damages, injunction, or specific performance). Further, a third party can also rely on an exclusion or limitation clause that is contained in the contract[69]— but where the exclusion clause could not be relied on even by a party to the contract (for example, because it contravened the Unfair Contract Terms Act 1977), then the third party will also be unable to rely on the clause.[70]

The constitution of the company is discussed at p 555 and the contract created by the constitution is discussed at p 559

The Unfair Contract Terms Act 1977 is discussed at p 224

---

59. Law Commission, *Contracts for the Benefit of Third Parties* (Law Com No 3329, HMSO 1996).
60. CRTPA 1999, s 6(1).
61. ibid s 6(2). This contract exists by virtue of the Companies Act 2006, s 33(1).   62. ibid s 6(2A).
63. ibid s 6(3).   64. ibid, s 1(2).
65. Law Commission, *Contracts for the Benefit of Third Parties* (Law Com No 3329, HMSO 1996) [7.5].
66. The CRTPA 1999 does not require express identification, but in *Avraamides v Colwill* [2006] EWCA Civ 1533, [2007] BLR 76, the Court held that implied identification would not suffice.
67. CRTPA 1999, s 1(3). Provided that the third party is identified, he does not need to exist at the time that the contract was entered into. Therefore, unborn children and companies awaiting incorporation are also able to enforce the term.   68. ibid s 1(5).   69. ibid s 1(6).   70. ibid s 3(6).

Discharge and variation

The third party's right to enforce the contractual term would be worthless if the original parties to the contract were able simply to discharge the contract or to vary it to remove the third party's rights. Conversely, the third party acquiring the right to enforce a term should not unduly restrict the original parties' rights to discharge or vary the contract. Section 2(1) aims to strike this balance by providing that the contracting parties' right to discharge or vary the contract remains intact, except where such discharge or variation would extinguish the third party's rights under the term and:

(a) the third party has communicated his assent to the term to the promisor;

(b) the promisor is aware that the third party has relied on the term; or

(c) the promisor can reasonably be expected to have foreseen that the third party would rely on the term and the third party has in fact relied on it.

However, this limitation on the contracting parties' right to discharge or vary the contract will not apply where the contract expressly provides that the parties may vary or discharge the contract without the third party's consent, or where the consent of the third party is required in circumstances that are different from those stated in s 2(1).[71]

The defences available to the promisor

Where a third party acquires the right to enforce a term under s 1(1), then the promisor (that is, the party against whom the term is being enforced) has available any defences or set-offs that arise from or in connection with the contract, and would have been available to him had the proceedings been brought by the promisee.[72] Accordingly, the third party does not acquire any more rights than the promisee would have and if the promisor has a defence that would render the contract void, discharged, or unenforceable, then this defence will work against the third party, as well as the promisee.

However, whilst the third party is no better off than the promisee, there is one notable situation in which the third party is worse off than the promisee, namely where the promisor is protected by a clause that excludes or limits liability for acts of negligence. In such a case, the promisee can challenge such a clause by arguing that it is unreasonable,[73] but the third party cannot challenge the clause on this ground,[74] meaning that, against third parties, a promisor can enforce an unreasonable exclusion or limitation clause.

Other exceptions

In addition to the 'general and wide-ranging'[75] exception contained in s 1(1) of the 1999 Act, a number of other common law and statutory exceptions exist, which are unaffected by s 1(1) of the 1999 Act.[76]

Statute

As the privity rule is a common law creation, it follows that it can be excluded by statute. For example, s 148(7) of the Road Traffic Act 1988 provides that a third party

---

71. ibid s 2(3).   72. ibid s 3(2).

73. Unfair Contract Terms Act 1977, s 2(2).   74. CRTPA 1999, s 7(2).

75. Law Commission, *Contracts for the Benefit of Third Parties* (Law Com No 3329, HMSO 1996) [5.16].

76. CRTPA 1999, s 7(1).

who is injured in a road traffic accident can enforce the driver's insurance policy against the insurance company.

Agency

A relationship of agency occurs where one party (the principal) instructs another (the agent) to carry out some task on his behalf. An agent has the power to bind his principal contractually to a third party, provided that the agent acts within his authority, as the following example demonstrates.

 The law of agency is discussed in more depth in Chapter 8

Eg   Privity and agency

John (the principal) instructs Elen (the agent) to locate a 1956 Rolls Royce Phantom and to purchase it for him, provided that it costs no more than £100,000. Ricardo has such a car and offers to sell it for £95,000. She accepts. Although Elen and Ricardo created the contract, it will be binding between John and Ricardo, because Elen was acting as John's agent and was acting within her authority.

Collateral contracts

A collateral contract is not really an exception to the privity rule, but is rather a means of avoiding the privity rule. The effect of a collateral contract is to create a contract between the promisor and a third party, as the following case demonstrates.

⚷   *Shanklin Pier Ltd v Detel Products Ltd* [1951] 2 KB 854 (KB)

FACTS: The claimant (the third party) employed a contractor to paint a pier. The claimant required that the contractor use a special type of paint manufactured by the defendant (the promisor) who promised that this paint would last for seven to ten years. The contractor purchased the paint from the defendant and applied it to the pier, but it lasted only three months. The claimant sued, and the defendant argued that, because the contract was between itself and the contractor, the claimant could not sue.

HELD: The High Court held that whilst the claimant could not sue on the contract of sale (because it was between the contractor and the defendant), a collateral contract existed between the claimant and the defendant, which arose due to the defendant's promise that the paint would last for seven to ten years.

Actions in tort

A third party prevented from bringing a claim in contract due to the privity rule may have a claim in tort if one of the parties to the contract owes a duty of care to the third party. The following example provides a situation in which such a duty may occur.

 The concept of the duty of care is discussed at p 364

Privity and tort

Spartan plc engages Price & Young LLP to audit its financial accounts, stating that a copy of the audit report should be sent to Emily, a local billionaire, who is considering purchasing a large number of shares in Spartan. The audit report indicates that Spartan is very profitable and so Emily purchases a 10 per cent stake in the company. It transpires that the audit was conducted negligently and that Spartan is actually close to insolvency. Emily could not sue Price & Young in contract, because she was not party to the audit contract, but it may be the case that Price & Young owed Emily a duty of care, which it breached in conducting the audit in a negligent manner.

Assignment

Assignment simply refers to a situation in which one party transfers his contractual rights to another. Therefore, if a party to a contract assigns his rights to a third party, that third party will acquire the right to sue on the contract.

 The assignment of contractual rights

Under an existing contract, Gus owes Damon £1,000. Damon owes £1,000 to Marcus. Damon could therefore assign to Marcus the contractual right to the £1,000 owed by Gus in full satisfaction of his debt to Marcus. If Gus agrees to the assignment, Damon will have no right to recover the debt from Gus, because it will be owed to Marcus, who will have the contractual right to enforce it.

At common law, contractual rights cannot be assigned, but both equity[77] and statute[78] have recognized that assignment can occur, subject to certain limitations (for example, the right to the salary of a public officer cannot be assigned)[79] and compliance with certain formalities (for example, see the four requirements for statutory assignment as set out in s 136(1) of the Law of Property Act 1925).

Chapter conclusion

This chapter has focused on a number of preliminary pre-contractual issues. Although most contracts require no formalities in order to be binding, a number of important types of contract do impose requirements as to form. A failure to comply with the required formalities will render the contract unenforceable. Similarly, a contract entered into with a person who lacks capacity may not be enforceable against that person. Businesses that contract with those who lack capacity should be aware of the precarious nature of such contracts. Finally, parties to contracts need to be aware that whilst the general rule is that they are the only parties that can enforce the contract, in certain situations, third parties may also acquire the right to enforce the contract—especially where the contract confers some form of benefit on a third party.

---

77. *Crouch v Martin* (1707) 2 Vern 595.   78. Law of Property Act 1925, s 136(1).
79. *Grenfell v Dean and Canons of Westminster* (1840) 2 Beav 544.

Compliance with formality and having contractual capacity is not enough to bring a contract into existence. In order for a legally binding contract to be created, a number of ingredients must be present. It is these ingredients that are examined in detail in the next chapter.

Key points summary

- As a general rule, contracts require no special formalities in order to be valid and binding.

- Certain contracts are subject to formalities, namely:
    - contracts required to be made by deed;
    - contracts required to be in writing; and
    - contracts required to be evidenced in writing.

- The legal ability to enter into a contract is known as 'capacity' and, as a general rule, all living, sober adults of sound mind have the capacity to enter into contracts.

- Privity of contract consists of two rules:
    - only parties to a contract may enforce the contract; and
    - contracts do not impose obligations on third parties.

- A third party may enforce a contractual term where the contract expressly states that he can or where the term confers a benefit on him.

Self-test questions

1. Define the following:
   (a) capacity
   (b) void *ab initio*;
   (c) voidable;
   (d) repudiate;
   (e) ratification;
   (f) privity of contract.

2. Why should the law enforce contractual obligations?

3. Hamish offers to sell his car to Ross for £5,000, with payment to be made by the end of the month. Ross agrees, but nothing is put into writing. The end of the month arrives and Ross is refusing to accept or pay for the car. Advise Hamish.

4. Louise decides to leave school at the age of 16, once she hears that a friend is looking for an apprentice for his carpentry firm. Louise enters into a contract that states that she shall be an apprentice of the firm. A week before she is due to start, she changes her mind and decides to complete her A levels. Does the carpenter have a right of action against Louise?

5. 'Third parties should never be allowed to enforce the contracts of others and the Contracts (Rights of Third Parties) Act 1999 should therefore be repealed.' Do you agree?

6. 'The law relating to contractual capacity is confusing and in dire need of reform.' Discuss.

Further reading

Mindy Chen-Wishart, *Contract Law* (4th edn, OUP 2012) ch 1
An excellent discussion of the theoretical underpinnings behind contract law

Laurence Koffman and Elizabeth Macdonald, *The Law of Contract* (7th edn, OUP 2010)
  ch 17
*A clear and straightforward account of the various persons who normally lack full contractual
  capacity*

Law Commission, *Contracts for the Benefit of Third Parties* (Law Com No 3329,
  HMSO 1996)
Provides a clear account of the law of privity and criticisms of the pre-1999 law

Jill Poole, *Textbook on Contract Law* (11th edn, OUP 2012) 171–80
A clear account of the law relating to contractual formalities

Robert Stevens, 'The Contracts (Rights of Third Parties) Act 1999' (2004) 120
  LQR 292
*Discusses the reasons behind, and the effectiveness of, the Contracts (Rights of Third
  Parties) Act 1999*

Remember to visit the **Online Resource Centre** at <**http://www.
oxfordtextbooks.co.uk/orc/roach3e**> to access the following resources
for Chapter 5, 'An introduction to the law of contract': more **practice
questions** and answers; a **glossary** of key terms; **multiple-choice
questions; revision summaries**; and **diagrams** in pdf. Updates to the
law can be found on Twitter by following **@UKBusinessLaw**

6 The formation of the contract

- The objective nature of agreement
- Bilateral and unilateral contracts
- Offer

- Acceptance
- Certainty
- Consideration
- Intention to create legal relations

INTRODUCTION

Having discussed what a contract is, our attention now turns to what ingredients are required in order to create a legally binding contract. The law needs to be able to distinguish between those promises that may be enforced in a court of law and those that cannot. For businesses, the importance of this distinction is even more important, because virtually every transaction in which a business engages will be via contract. Businesses need to know that the parties with whom they enter into agreements will fulfil their obligations and that, if these obligations are not fulfilled, the court will grant the business a legal remedy. Accordingly, businesses will wish to ensure that the agreements into which they enter have contractual force.

A contract consists of five ingredients that, if present, will create legally enforceable obligations. The previous chapter discussed certain preliminary ingredients, such as formality and capacity. To use a sporting metaphor, these preliminary ingredients can be thought of as entry requirements that allow a party onto the starting line. To complete the race and create a binding contract, five further ingredients are needed:

1. offer;
2. acceptance;
3. certainty;
4. consideration; and
5. intention to create legal relations.

The first two requirements (offer and acceptance) are collectively known as 'agreement', and once agreement is reached, a valid contract usually comes into existence. Accordingly, the determination of agreement is crucial. Therefore, before examining the individual requirements in detail, the court's approach to determining whether agreement is present or not must be discussed.

The objective nature of agreement

In many cases, determining whether or not agreement is present will be straight-forward, as both parties will have signed a written document. But this is not always the case and situations occur in which one party contends that an agreement was reached, whereas the other party denies that agreement was reached. In such a case, the law will have to determine whether agreement was present. It used to be said that, in order for agreement to arise, the law would require *consensus ad idem* ('agreement as to the same thing', but more loosely translated as 'a meeting of the minds'). This would seem to require that the parties actually and subjectively agree on the terms of the contract, but this is not the case. The law is more concerned with the objective appearance of agreement, based upon the available evidence, than with the actual intentions of the parties. As Lord Denning MR stated:

> In contracts you do not look into the actual intent in a man's mind. You look at what he said and did. A contract is formed, when there is, to all outward appearances, a contract. A man cannot get out of a contract by saying: 'I did not intend to contract,' if by his words he has done so.[1]

The reason for a rejection of subjective agreement is because, evidentially, it is almost impossible to know what a person is thinking or intending. Accordingly, agreement is determined not on the basis of what the parties actually intended, but on what their words or actions objectively inferred. This could result in a court finding that an agreement has been concluded on terms that one of the parties clearly did not intend, as the following case demonstrates.

 ### *Centrovincial Estates plc v Merchant Investors Assurance Co Ltd* [1983] Comm LR 158 (CA)

FACTS: A landlord wrote to a prospective tenant offering to rent commercial property to it for £65,000 per annum. The tenant wrote back accepting, but the landlord then wrote back stating that a mistake had been made and that the true figure was £126,000 per annum.

HELD: The Court of Appeal held that there was a valid contract for £65,000. The words and conduct of the landlord and tenant objectively indicated that they had reached agreement, even though the landlord clearly did not intend to rent the property for so low a sum.

Therefore, 'the judicial task is not to discover the actual intentions of each party; it is to decide what each was reasonably entitled to conclude from the attitude of the other'.[2]

---

1. *Storer v Manchester City Council* [1974] 1 WLR 1403 (CA) 1408.
2. WM Gloag, *Gloag on Contract* (2nd edn, W Green 1929) 7, approved by Lord Reid in *McCutcheon v David Macbrayne Ltd* [1964] 1 WLR 125 (HL) 128.

Bilateral and unilateral contracts

Before discussing the five ingredients of a binding contract, it is important to distinguish between bilateral and unilateral contracts. The importance of the distinction lies in that some of the general rules that apply to bilateral contracts do not apply, or are modified, in the case of unilateral contracts.

The distinction is relatively simple and can be deduced from the contract's names. A bilateral contract is a contract in which both parties are legally bound to perform their side of the agreement (that is, both parties exchange promises). Conversely, in a unilateral contract, only one party is obliged to perform (that is, one party makes a promise in exchange for the performance by the other party of an act, but the other party does not promise to perform that act). Put simply, bilateral contracts consist of two promises, whereas unilateral contracts consist of one, as the following example demonstrates.

 Bilateral and unilateral contracts

Bilateral contract

Adam enters his local BMW showroom, and enters into negotiations to buy a new car. A contract is presented to Adam, which states that the car will cost £25,000 and will be delivered before the end of the month, with full payment due within ten working days of signing the contract. Adam signs the contract. This is a bilateral contract, because both parties have made promises—Adam must pay the purchase price within ten working days of signing the contract and BMW must deliver the car to Adam before the end of the month. If either party fails to perform, it will constitute breach of contract.

Unilateral contract

Adam purchases the car but, a few days later, it is stolen. Adam puts an advertisement in his local newspaper stating that he will pay £100 to anyone who locates the car. This is a unilateral offer: only Adam is bound, because only he has made a promise. No one is legally obliged to search for the car and no one can be sued for failing to find the car. If somebody does locate the car or provides information leading to its recovery, Adam is legally obliged to pay that person the £100 reward and if he fails to do so, he will be in breach of contract.

The five ingredients of a valid contract will now be discussed.

Offer

Treitel defines an offer as 'an expression of willingness to contract on specified terms, made with the intention that it is to become binding as soon as it is accepted by the person to whom it is addressed'.[3] The person making an offer is known as the 'offeror' and the person to whom an offer is addressed is known as the 'offeree'. An

---

3. Edwin Peel, *Treitel on the Law of Contract* (13th edn, Sweet & Maxwell 2011) 8.

offer may be made in writing, orally, or may be inferred through conduct. An offer may be made to a specific person, a group of persons, or to the entire world.[4] An offer made to a specific person cannot be accepted by anyone other than that person.[5] An offer will only be valid if it is communicated to the intended offeree.[6] This is a logical requirement: how can an offeree accept an offer about which he knows nothing?

As noted, the courts adopt an objective approach when determining the existence of agreement. Accordingly, the courts may hold that a valid offer was made, when, in fact, the offeror had no intention of making an offer, but had acted in such a way as to make a reasonable person believe that an offer was being made.

Moran v University College Salford (No 2), The Times 23 November 1993 (CA)

FACTS: Moran applied to gain entry onto a physiotherapy course. His application was rejected, but he was mistakenly sent an unconditional offer by the college, which he accepted. Moran phoned the college to make enquiries about the course, but was told that his application was rejected and a place on the course was not available for him.

HELD: The Court of Appeal held that a binding agreement existed between Moran and the college to enrol him on the course, because, despite the college's error, the unconditional offer was capable of acceptance by him.

Offers and invitations to treat

In the course of negotiations, the parties may make a number of preliminary statements, and it is important to be able to identify which statements amount to an offer and which do not. For example, if Pat asks Charlotte, 'at what price would you be prepared to sell your car?', to which Charlotte replies '£5,000', has Charlotte made an offer to Pat to sell her car for £5,000? The answer is 'no'. Charlotte is not making an offer; rather, she is inviting Pat to make an offer. These invitations to negotiate, or to make an offer, are known as 'invitations to treat'.

Distinguishing between an offer and an invitation to treat can sometimes be difficult, as the distinction is often based upon the parties' intentions; the issue to objectively determine is whether one of the parties has indicated a willingness to be bound. Use of the word 'offer' by one of the parties may indicate such a willingness, but it is not conclusive.[7] In order to identify whether a particular statement amounts to an offer or an invitation to treat, the courts have created a number of presumptions in relation to certain commonly occurring transactions.

Advertisements

The general presumption is that advertisements are regarded as invitations to treat, as the following case demonstrates.

---

4. *Carlill v Carbolic Smoke Ball Co* [1893] 1 QB 256 (CA).
5. *Cundy v Lindsay* (1877–78) LR 3 App Cas 459 (HL).   6. *Taylor v Laird* (1856) 25 LJ Ex 329.
7. *Spencer v Harding* (1869–70) LR 5 CP 561.

Partridge v Crittenden [1968] 1 WLR 1204 (QB)

FACTS: The defendant placed an advertisement in a magazine, which stated 'bramblefinch cocks, bramblefinch hens, 25s each'. Bramblefinches were a protected species and it was a criminal offence to 'offer to sell' a protected species of bird.[8] Therefore, the court had to determine whether or not the advertisement amounted to an offer.

HELD: The High Court held that the advertisement was merely an invitation to treat. Accordingly, the defendant was not guilty of the offence under the 1954 Act.

COMMENT: Chapter 1 discussed the distinction between civil law and criminal law, and noted that the two are not mutually exclusive. *Partridge* is an excellent example of this: in order to determine whether a crime had been committed, the court had to discuss a point of civil law.

★ See 'Offers for Sale' (1968) 32 J Crim L 223

The rationale behind this general presumption is based upon two practical considerations.

1. If advertisements were regarded as offers, sellers of goods would be in breach of contract if they could not supply the advertised goods to anyone who wanted them, even if they had a legitimate reason (for example, the goods were out of stock).[9] Sellers will often state that any claims made in the advertisement will only apply 'while stocks last', but such protective statements are not actually necessary.

2. Prices and conditions stated in advertisements may not be final and further bargaining may be envisaged. For example, a company that places an advertisement indicating that goods purchased on credit will attract 0 per cent finance will still want to carry out credit checks on potential customers to determine the likelihood of repayment.

This principle is, however, only a presumption and can be rebutted if the facts indicate a willingness to be bound. Specifically, the presumption only tends to apply in the case of bilateral contracts. In cases involving unilateral contracts, as further bargaining is not envisaged (or even possible), the presumption is reversed and an advertisement will be presumed to constitute an offer, as the following case demonstrates.

 Carlill v Carbolic Smoke Ball Co [1893] 1 QB 256 (CA)

FACTS: Carbolic Smoke Ball Co (the defendant) manufactured the 'Carbolic Smoke Ball'. It placed an advertisement in the *Pall Mall Gazette*, stating that it would pay £100 to anyone who correctly used the smoke ball, but still contracted influenza. To demonstrate its sincerity, it deposited £1,000 into a bank. Mrs Carlill (the claimant) purchased a smoke ball, used it correctly, and still caught influenza. Accordingly, she sought the £100, but Carbolic refused to pay on the grounds that the advertisement was a 'mere puff' that was not meant to be taken seriously or intended to be binding, and that it was impossible to make a contract with the entire world.

---

8. Protection of Birds Act 1954, s 6(1).

9. The House acknowledged such a rationale in *Grainger & Son v Gough* [1896] AC 325 (HL) 334 (Lord Herschell).

HELD: The Court of Appeal found in favour of Mrs Carlill. The £1,000 deposit indicated that the advertisement was not a mere puff and demonstrated that Carbolic intended to be bound. Further, offers made to the whole world were perfectly valid. Accordingly, the advertisement constituted an offer, which Mrs Carlill accepted by purchasing and using the smoke ball, and she was therefore entitled to the £100.

Displays of goods

Displays of goods (for example, within shops or shop windows) constitute the most common form of invitation to treat. The rationale for classifying displays of goods as invitations to treat was stated in the following case.

 Pharmaceutical Society of Great Britain v Boots Cash Chemists (Southern) Ltd [1953] 1 QB 401 (CA)

FACTS: Boots had opened one of the first 'self-service' shops in the country. The goods were displayed on shelves and customers would choose which goods they wanted, before taking them to a cashier near the exit. A registered pharmacist was adjacent to the cashier. Boots was prosecuted under s 18 of the Pharmacy and Poisons Act 1933, which made it an offence to sell certain drugs unless a registered pharmacist supervised the sale. The Pharmaceutical Society argued that, as the display of goods amounted to an offer, which was accepted by placing the goods in the basket, the sale took place when the customer put the goods in the basket and not at the cash desk under the supervision of the pharmacist.

HELD: The Court of Appeal held that the display of goods constituted an invitation to treat. The customer made the offer by presenting the goods to the cashier and the cashier accepted the offer by taking the customer's money. As the pharmacist was present at the cash desk, the transaction was supervised, and s 18 was not contravened.

COMMENT: The Court justified its decision by stating that if displays of goods were to amount to an offer, the customer would accept the goods by placing them in his basket. At this point, a binding contract would exist, so that if the customer then changed his mind and put the goods back, he would technically be in breach of contract.[10] Clearly, this would negate the whole purpose of a self-service store.

★ See J Unger, 'Self-Service Shops and the Law of Contract' (1959) 16 MLR 369

Transactions effected through machines

Particular problems can arise when transactions are effected through machines (for example, vending machines or 'pay and go' petrol pumps). The traditional view that displays of goods amount only to invitations to treat would mean that the customer would make the offer by proffering payment. But this throws up difficult questions, such as how does the machine accept, and when exactly would the contract be formed. At a self-service store, if a customer changes his mind, he can put the goods back on the shelf; this cannot be done with goods obtained from a machine. Further, there is no possibility of negotiations taking place with a machine. Therefore, in relation to sales effected through a machine, the courts are likely to state that the machine makes the offer.

---

10. [1953] 1 QB 401 (CA) 406 (Somervell LJ).

🔑 *Thornton v Shoe Lane Parking Ltd*
[1971] 2 QB 163 (CA)

FACTS: The claimant drove his car into an automatic car park. A sign at the car park entrance stated the cost of parking and that all cars were 'parked at owner's risk'. The claimant drove up to a machine, took the offered ticket, and parked his car. Upon returning, there was an accident and he was injured. The defendant argued that it was not liable due to the exclusion clause at the car park's entrance. The validity of the clause depended upon when the contract was concluded—that is, on who made the offer and who accepted. **HELD:** In the Court of Appeal, Lord Denning MR stated:

> The customer pays his money and gets a ticket. He cannot refuse it. He cannot get his money back...He is committed beyond recall. He was committed at the very moment when he put his money into the machine. The contract was concluded at that time. It can be translated into offer and acceptance in this way: the offer is made when the proprietor of the machine holds it out as being ready to receive the money. The acceptance takes place when the customer puts his money into the slot.[11]

⭐ See Roger Brownsword, 'Incorporating Exemption Causes' (1972) 35 MLR 179

Accordingly, the machine makes the offer, which the customer accepts by committing himself fully. In the case of a vending machine, this would occur when the customer puts the money into the machine. At a petrol pump, this would occur when the customer puts the petrol into his car.[12]

E-commerce

Today, purchasing goods online is as natural as purchasing goods from a high-street shop. From a contractual point of view, however, e-commerce can be problematic. EU legislation exists that aims to harmonize and facilitate e-commerce,[13] but this legislation does not indicate at what point a contract is created, nor does it indicate the legal status of goods displayed on websites. The issue can be problematic, as evidenced by a significant number of recent cases concerning websites displaying incorrect prices. For example, in January 2012, Next's website mistakenly priced a pair of sofas for offer at £98, when the correct price was £1,198. The uncorrected price remained on the website for over six months and, unsurprisingly, numerous customers attempted to take advantage of the pricing error.

The question is whether, when such pricing mistakes occur, online retailers are acting in breach when they inevitably refuse to sell the goods at the incorrect price (as occurred in the Next example above).[14] To answer this question, it is necessary to determine the identities of the offeror and offeree. A number of arguments would operate in the online retailer's favour, as follow.

- Websites are simply virtual shops and the goods displayed would almost certainly be regarded the same as displays of goods in an actual store (that is, as invitations to treat). Instead of examining goods on a shelf, the customer

---

11. [1971] 2 QB 163 (CA) 169.   12. *Re Charge Card Services* [1989] Ch 497 (CA).

13. The Electronic Commerce (EC Directive) Regulations 2002, SI 2002/2013, implementing Council Directive (EC) 2000/31 on electronic commerce.

14. It is worth noting that, very rarely, retailers have agreed to sell the goods at the erroneous price, as occurred in January 2012 when Marks & Spencer agreed (following the setting up of an online petition by disgruntled customers) to honour sales of a 50 inch plasma TV worth £1,099 that its website mistakenly advertised for sale at £199.

examines the goods on a computer screen. Instead of putting goods into a physical basket, goods are added to a virtual basket. Irrespective of whether the goods are bought physically or online, the goods are paid for at the 'checkout'. Given this, online retailers would be free to reject the customer's offers.

- In many cases, online retailers emailed the customers 'accepting' their order. But it is highly likely that this will not constitute legal acceptance and will simply constitute a confirmation of the customer's order.

- The courts have made clear that they will not assist a purchaser who is aware that a pricing mistake has been made and is attempting to obtain a bargain.[15] The situation is less clear if the pricing mistake made was modest.

The conclusion is that, in the absence of a definitive higher court ruling or a statutory clarification, displays of goods on websites are likely to constitute invitations to treat. Many online retailers now make this absolutely clear by indicating to the customer at exactly what point the customer becomes bound, with such clarification now required under reg 9(1) of the Electronic Commerce (EC Directive) Regulations 2002.[16]

Auctions

The general rule is that when an auctioneer calls for bids, he is not making an offer to sell the goods to the highest bidder; he is merely making an invitation to treat.[17] Bidders make the offer, which the auctioneer is free to accept or reject,[18] with the making of a higher bid destroying a previous offer. Items may be sold at auction advertised as 'with reserve'—meaning that the item will not be sold unless it reaches a minimum price. If the bidding fails to reach that price, or if the auctioneer mistakenly accepts a bid lower than the reserve price,[19] no contract will be formed. Where an item reaches the reserve price, the auctioneer is still not bound to sell, because bids above the reserve price still amount only to invitations to treat. The seller of the goods may therefore withdraw the goods from auction at any time before the fall of the auctioneer's hammer.

Where an auction is advertised as 'without reserve' (that is, where there is no minimum price), the situation is more complex. Three parties are involved: (i) the seller of the goods; (ii) the bidder; and (iii) the auctioneer. If the auctioneer fails to accept the highest bid, no contract of sale will exist between the seller and the highest bidder. There will, however, be a collateral contract between the highest bidder and the auctioneer. The rationale behind this is that, in advertising the sale as 'without reserve', the auctioneer is making an offer to accept the bid of the highest bidder, which is then accepted by the highest bidder.[20]

 Barry v Davies (t/a Heathcote Ball & Co) [2000] 1 WLR 1962 (CA)

FACTS: The defendant auctioneer auctioned without reserve two engine analysers, each one costing £14,251 new. The highest bid of £400 for both machines derived from the claimant. Unable to secure a higher price, the auctioneer withdrew the machines from the

---

15. *Hartog v Colin & Shields* [1939] 3 All ER 566 (KB).   16. SI 2002/2013.

17. *Payne v Cave* [1775] All ER Rep 492.

18. Sale of Goods Act 1979, s 57(2), indicates that the offer is accepted by the auctioneer on the 'fall of the hammer, or in any other customary manner'.   19. *McManus v Fortescue* [1907] 2 KB 1 (CA).

20. *Warlow v Harrison* (1859) 1 El & El 309.

auction. The claimant sued the auctioneer, arguing that the auctioneer legally had to accept the highest bid.

HELD: The Court of Appeal stated that there was no contract between the claimant and the owner of the machines. There did, however, exist a collateral contract between the claimant and the defendant, which the defendant breached by withdrawing the goods. Accordingly, the claimant was awarded £27,600 damages.

COMMENT: One initial reaction may be to think that the claimant received something of a windfall, but, as will be seen when the calculation of damages for non-delivery in sale of goods cases is discussed, this is not the case.

> ★ See Frank Meisel, 'What Price Auctions Without Reserve?' (2001) 64 MLR 468

Tenders

Tenders are a common mechanism in larger commercial and construction contracts, whereby a company that is seeking to purchase an expensive item, or requires the performance of a substantial service, will invite tenders from interested parties. As inviting tenders does not generally constitute an offer,[21] but will form an invitation to treat only, there is no obligation to accept the most competitive tender. It follows that the parties submitting the tenders are the offerors, and the party who invited the tenders is free to accept or reject any tender made based on any considerations that it deems relevant. However, this rule is subject to two qualifications:

1. If the party inviting the tenders indicates that it will accept the most competitive tender, this will amount to a unilateral offer whereby the party inviting the tenders promises to accept the most competitive tender. This offer will be accepted by the party that submits the most competitive tender, and the person seeking the tender will then be contractually obliged to accept that tender.[22]

2. When an invitation to tender is made to only a small, selected group of persons and is accompanied by conditions (for example, tenders must be in writing, or submitted by a certain date), it will be held to be accompanied by an offer to consider all tenders that comply with the conditions. Parties accept the offer by submitting a tender that complies with the conditions and the party seeking the tenders will thereby commit a breach of contract if it fails to consider conforming tenders.[23]

Termination of an offer

An offer may be terminated in a number of different ways, and once an offer has been effectively terminated, it cannot subsequently be accepted, because it no longer exists.

Rejection of an offer

An offer will be terminated if the offeree rejects it.[24] If the offeree purports to accept the offer, but based on new or differing terms to the offer, this will serve to reject the original offer and will constitute a counter-offer.[25]

> 🔗 Counter-offers are discussed at p 138

---

21. *Spencer v Harding* (1870) LR 5 CP 561.

22. *Harvela Investments Ltd v Royal Trust Co of Canada* [1986] AC 207 (HL).

23. *Blackpool and Fylde Aero Club Ltd v Blackpool Borough Council* [1990] 1 WLR 1195 (CA).

24. *Tinn v Hoffman & Co* (1873) 29 LT 271.   25. *Hyde v Wrench* (1840) 3 Beav 334.

🔗 The postal rule is discussed at p 142

Although there is no settled law on the point, it appears to be the case that a rejection is only effective once it is communicated to the offeror. Further, it would appear (but again, there is no established authority) that the postal rule (the rule providing that acceptance by post occurs as soon as the letter is posted) would not apply to rejection by post, so that a postal rejection seems to take effect only when received by the offeror. Assuming that this is the law, it has been contended that if an offeree rejects an offer by post, but before the letter reaches the offeror, the offeree accepts the offer (for example, by phoning the offeror or visiting him), the acceptance will be effective and the rejection letter will have no effect.[26]

Lapse of time

Offerors are perfectly free to stipulate that if the offer is not accepted by a certain time or date, then it will cease to exist. In the majority of cases, offers do not normally have an expiry date, but this does not mean that offers last forever. As the following case shows, an offer that does not have an expiry date will still lapse after a reasonable time.

Ramsgate Victoria Hotel Co Ltd v Montefiore (1866) LR 1 Ex 109

FACTS: The two defendants offered to purchase shares in the claimant company on 8 June. Hearing nothing from the claimant, one of the defendants withdrew his offer on 8 November. The other defendant did not withdraw his offer. On 23 November, the claimant allotted shares to both defendants and requested that the balance be paid. Both defendants refused to pay and the claimant commenced proceedings.

HELD: The defendants were justified in refusing the shares. Once the defendants had made the offer, acceptance (the allotment of the shares) should have occurred within a reasonable time. As it had not, the defendants' offers had lapsed and so they were not bound to accept the shares.

What is reasonable will depend upon the facts of the case and, in particular, the subject matter of the contract. If the quality of the subject matter of the contract is in some way time-sensitive (for example, perishable goods), then a shorter period of time will be regarded as reasonable. Thus, if a person was offering to sell a consignment of apples and was also separately offering to sell his car, the offer to sell the apples would lapse long before the offer to sell the car.

Death of offeror or offeree

🔗 The doctrine of frustration is discussed in 'Discharge by frustration' at p 305

The effect of the death of the offeror or offeree on an offer is unclear. What is clear is that once an offer has been accepted, the death of either party will not terminate the offer, although it may lead to the contract being frustrated. It is less clear what the effect would be if a party were to die after the offer has been made, but before it has been accepted. It is contended that the death of either party does not automatically terminate the offer, but termination may be justified depending upon the nature of the contract.

---

26. Edwin Peel, *Treitel on the Law of Contract* (13th edn, Sweet & Maxwell 2011) 44.

It is likely that the death of the offeror will result in the termination of the offer if the contract is one of personal service. For example, if an opera singer were to offer to perform at an opera house, but then die, the offer would lapse regardless of whether the offeree knew of the death. If, however, the contract is not one for personal service, the effect of the offeror's death is less clear. It has been argued that, in such a case, the offer is terminated automatically,[27] but the more accepted view appears to be that, if the offeree knows of the offeror's death, then acceptance will not be effective.[28] However, if the offeree is ignorant of the offeror's death, then acceptance will be effective, and the contract will have to be performed by the deceased offeror's personal representatives.[29]

> **personal representatives:** an administrator or executor whose function it is to settle the affairs of deceased persons

There is no conclusive law on the effect of the death of the offeree, but uncontradicted *dicta* favour the view that the offeree's death will cause the offer to lapse.[30] It has, however, been contended that the same rule should apply as regards the offeror's death (that is, that the offer would stand, provided that it was not for the supply of a personal service and could therefore be accepted by the offeree's personal representatives).[31]

Failure of a condition precedent

The offeror may stipulate that the offer will only exist based on other considerations, and such stipulations are known as **conditions precedent**. It may be the case that the offeror stipulates that, upon the occurrence of some event, the offer will lapse and, in such a case, it will no longer be capable of acceptance.

> **conditions precedent:** conditions that must be complied with before an offer can be accepted, or before a contract becomes operational

 Offers and conditions precedent

Cathy offers to purchase a car from Melissa, but states that the offer will only exist while the car is roadworthy. A day later, before Melissa has accepted the offer, she is involved in a minor accident and the car requires repairs in order for it to function. This would constitute a breach of the condition precedent and so Cathy's offer would lapse.

It should be noted that conditions precedent need not be express; they may also be implied (for example, an offer to sell life insurance to a person cannot be accepted after that person is seriously injured by falling off a cliff).[32]

Revocation

As acceptance of an offer will usually bring about a binding contract, it follows that the revocation of an offer post-acceptance can constitute a breach of contract. However, before acceptance has occurred, the offeror is perfectly free to revoke any offer made.[33] Once revoked, the offer is destroyed and acceptance is impossible. This applies even where the offeror has indicated that an offer will remain open for a

---

27. *Dickinson v Dodds* (1876) 2 Ch D 463 (CA) 475 (Mellish LJ).
28. *Coulthart v Clementson* (1870) 5 QBD 42.   29. *Bradbury v Morgan* (1862) 1 H & C 249.
30. See e.g. *Reynolds v Atherton* (1921) 125 LT 690; *Kennedy v Thomassen* [1929] 1 Ch 426.
31. See e.g. Edwin Peel, *Treitel on the Law of Contract* (13th edn, Sweet & Maxwell 2011) 46; Jill Poole, *Textbook on Contract Law* (11th edn, OUP 2012) 68.
32. *Canning v Farquhar* (1885) 16 QBD 722 (CA).
33. *Payne v Cave* (1789) 3 Term Rep 148.

certain time. For example, in *Routledge v Grant,*[34] the defendant offered to purchase the claimant's house and stated that the offer was to last for six weeks. The defendant revoked the offer after only three weeks and the court held that he was perfectly free to do this.

In order for revocation to be valid, it must be communicated to the offeree, as the following case demonstrates.

 Byrne & Co v Van Tienhoven & Co (1880) 5 CPD 344

FACTS: The defendant offered to sell goods to the claimant. The offer was made by letter on 1 October. On 8 October, the defendant revoked the offer by post. The claimant received the letter making the offer on 11 October and accepted by telegram on the same day. It also posted a letter of acceptance on 15 October. On the 20 October, the claimant received the letter revoking the offer. The defendant refused to supply the goods on the ground that the offer had been revoked before it was accepted. The claimant brought an action.

HELD: The claimant accepted the offer on 11 October and this was when a valid contract came into being. The claimant did not receive the defendant's revocation of the offer until 20 October. As acceptance had already occurred, the revocation was invalid and the defendant was therefore in breach of contract.

It should, however, be noted that whilst notice of revocation must be communicated to the offeree, it does not follow that the notice must come from the offeror. Provided that acceptance has not taken place, an offeree who hears about the revocation of the offer from a reliable third party and thereby knows beyond all question of the revocation will then be unable to accept that offer.[35]

In relation to unilateral contracts, the above rules are problematic, as the following example demonstrates.

 Eg **Revocation of a unilateral offer**

Roger says to James: 'If you climb to the summit of Mount Everest, I will pay you £10,000.' This is clearly a unilateral offer, because James is under no obligation to climb the mountain, but if he does, Roger is under an obligation to pay. James indicates that he will climb the mountain, and spends £1,000 on climbing gear and mountain-climbing tuition. James begins to climb the mountain. When he is 10 metres short of the summit, Roger phones James on his mobile phone and states that he is revoking the offer.

Historically, the law stated that an offeree accepts a unilateral offer by fully performing the act in question (that is, by climbing Mount Everest). According to this logic, Roger is free to revoke when he did, because James has not fully accepted Roger's offer.

🔗 On the rules relating to acceptance of offers of a unilateral contract, see p 145

In the above example, an application of the standard revocation rule would be extremely harsh on James. Accordingly, in cases involving unilateral offers, the courts distinguish between commencement of the specified act and completion of the specified act. As soon as the offeree commences performance of the specified act,

---

34. (1828) 4 Bing 653.   35. *Dickinson v Dodds* (1876) 2 Ch D 463 (CA).

the offeror cannot withdraw the unilateral offer, but the offeror will only be required to perform his side of the contract once the act is fully performed.

 Errington v Errington & Woods [1952] 1 KB 290 (CA)

FACTS: A father purchased a house in his own name, but his son and daughter-in-law occupied it. The father stated that, provided that the couple continued to pay the mortgage instalments, once the mortgage was paid off, he would transfer title of the house to them. Subsequently, the father died, and the son and daughter-in-law split up, but the daughter-in-law continued to live in the house and pay the mortgage instalments. The father's widow wished to evict the daughter-in-law and claim possession of the house.

HELD: The Court of Appeal held that the father's promise could not be revoked. Denning LJ stated:

> The father's promise was a unilateral contract—a promise of the house in return for their act of paying the instalments. It could not be revoked by him once the couple entered on performance of the act, but it would cease to bind him if they left it incomplete and unperformed, which they have not done. If that was the position during the father's lifetime, so it must be after his death.... They have acted on the promise, and neither the father nor his widow...can eject them in disregard of it.[36]

One final problem to note regarding the revocation of unilateral offers is that such offers are often made to the whole world (for example, the offer of a reward). As noted, revocation of an offer is normally effective only upon its communication to the offeree, but clearly this rule cannot be applied to offers made to the whole world. Although there is no English authority on the issue, the consensus is that we would follow the approach taken in the USA, whereby the revocation of a unilateral offer would be valid if the revocation were communicated in the same manner as the offer was made[37] (for example, if the offer was made in a newspaper, the revocation should be made in the same newspaper).

Acceptance

In order for agreement to exist and a binding contract to be formed, the offeree must accept the offer. There appears to be no judicially accepted definition of 'acceptance', but Treitel's formulation is generally regarded as authoritative. He defined acceptance as 'a final and unqualified expression of assent to the terms of an offer'.[38] From this simple definition, a number of consequences flow.

- As the offeree must 'assent' to the terms of the offer, it follows that he must know of the offer in the first place. Acceptance will not be valid where the offeree accepted an offer the he did not know existed. Thus, a person who discovers the offeror's lost dog cannot claim an offered reward if he did not know of the reward at the time that he found the dog.[39]

---

36. [1952] 1 KB 290 (CA) 295, 300.   37. *Shuey v US* 92 US 73 (1875).
38. Edwin Peel, *Treitel on the Law of Contract* (13th edn, Sweet & Maxwell 2011) 17.
39. *R v Clarke* (1927) 40 CLR 227 (High Court of Australia).

The communication of acceptance is discussed at p 141

- The phrase 'expression of assent' indicates that, generally, the offeree's acceptance must be communicated to the offeror in order to be valid.
- The words 'final' and 'unqualified' mean that the acceptance must match precisely the terms of the offer. Any variation will not amount to valid acceptance and may even constitute a counter-offer. This is a result of what is known as the 'mirror image' rule, which is discussed next.

The 'mirror image' rule and counter-offers

The 'mirror image' rule basically states that the acceptance must precisely and unequivocally mirror the terms of the offer. It follows that if, in accepting the offer, the offeree adds a new term or varies an existing term, this will not constitute valid acceptance and will be regarded as a counter-offer. A counter-offer has two effects:

1. A new offer is created by the former offeree, who now becomes the offeror, and the original offeror now becomes the offeree.
2. The original offer is destroyed, so that the former offeree cannot subsequently accept it.

 Hyde v Wrench (1840) 3 Beav 334

FACTS: Wrench (the defendant) offered to sell a farm to Hyde (the claimant) for £1,000. Hyde sent a letter, indicating that he would pay £950, but Wrench was not willing to sell at this price and did not reply to the letter. Subsequently, Hyde attempted to accept the original offer of £1,000 and the court had to determine whether this was valid acceptance.

HELD: The court held that the acceptance was invalid. Hyde's letter amounted to a counter-offer, which destroyed Wrench's original offer, meaning that Hyde could not subsequently accept it.

Care must be taken when determining the status of an offeree's reply to an offer. In certain cases, what may initially appear to be a counter-offer may actually be a mere request for information.

Distinguishing counter-offers from requests for information

It is important to distinguish counter-offers from requests for information, because the former will destroy the original offer and create a new offer capable of acceptance, whereas the latter will have no effect upon the original offer and will not create a new offer.

 Stevenson, Jacques & Co v McLean (1880) LR 5 QBD 346 (QB)

FACTS: The defendant offered to sell a consignment of iron at a price of 40 shillings per tonne. The claimant sent a telegram, asking whether the defendant would accept payment of the 40 shillings over a two-month period. The claimant received no reply and purported to accept the original offer, but the defendant had already sold the iron to a third party. The claimant sued for non-delivery. The defendant argued that the claimant's telegram amounted to a counter-offer, which it was free to reject.

HELD: The High Court held that the telegram did not constitute a counter-offer: it was merely an inquiry. As the original offer was still open for the claimant to accept, it could therefore recover damages for non-delivery.

'Battle of the forms'

Determining if and when acceptance has occurred has been complicated by the commercial prevalence of standard terms (or 'standard-form contracts'), which are terms that are drafted specifically to cater for the particular needs of a business. The advantages of using such terms are obvious. Standard terms obviate the need for lengthy and expensive negotiations, and, because they are drafted to meet the particular needs of a business, such terms will strongly favour that business. However, problems arise when two businesses wish to contract with each other and each has its own set of standard terms. Which set of terms will form the basis of the contract?

This has come to be known as the 'battle of the forms' and it has resulted in a major problem. Imagine that *A* offers to sell goods to *B* and accompanies the offer with a copy of his standard terms. *B* purports to accept the offer, but includes a set of his standard terms. Both parties perform the contract, mistakenly believing that their terms are governing the contract. If both parties perform as planned, no problem arises, but should a dispute occur, the court would seek to resolve the dispute by looking to the contract. However, under the mirror image rule, no contract would exist, because it cannot be established objectively that there has been an offer on a party's standard terms that has been accepted by the other. Despite this unfortunate outcome, the courts have tended to stick to the orthodox position, as the following case demonstrates.

 ***Butler Machine Tool Co Ltd v Ex-Cell-O Corporation (England) Ltd* [1979] 1 WLR 401 (CA)**

FACTS: The seller offered to sell a piece of machinery to the buyer on its standard terms and conditions, which were to 'prevail over any terms and conditions in the buyer's order'. The seller's terms contained a price-variation clause, which allowed the seller to increase the price quoted if its costs had increased at the date of delivery. The buyer placed an order for the machine using its own order form, which did not contain a price-variation clause. This order form was sent to the seller. At the bottom of the order form was a tear-off slip, which was to be signed by the seller and returned to the buyer. This slip stated that the seller accepted the order 'on the terms and conditions stated therein'—that is, on the buyer's terms. The seller signed and returned the slip to the buyer. Upon delivery of the machine, the seller exercised the price-variation clause and charged an extra £2,892. The buyer argued that the contract was based on its own terms and so the seller was not entitled to the extra £2,892. Both sets of terms claimed primacy over the other. Which terms were to prevail?

HELD: The Court of Appeal unanimously agreed that the buyer's terms prevailed. When the seller signed and returned the tear-off slip, it accepted the terms of the buyer's offer. The buyer had got in the 'last shot'. As the buyer's terms contained no price-variation clause, the seller had no contractual right to claim the extra £2,892.

COMMENT: Lawton and Bridge LJJ decided the case based upon the mirror image rule—namely, that whichever party gets in the 'last shot' will win the battle of the forms, provided that the other party acknowledges the terms of the last shot and unequivocally accepts them. Whilst such an approach promotes certainty, if the last shot is not unequivocally accepted, there will be no contract. To avoid this, Denning MR argued that, where the principal terms do not materially differ, the court should reconcile those terms that do differ to create a harmonious compromise contract. If the terms cannot be reconciled, the court should scrap those terms and replace them with terms of 'reasonable implication'.[40] Such a commercially flexible approach will avoid the finding that no contract exists between the parties, but it lacks the certainty of the last-shot approach. Further, the judiciary might not relish the interventionist role that Lord Denning's approach envisages. For these reasons, recent cases[41] have confirmed that the mirror image rule remains dominant.

 See Rick Rawlings, 'The Battle of the Forms' (1979) MLR 715

It would appear that the key determinant of the battle of the forms is the drafting of the standard terms. As Treitel notes, 'it is possible by careful draftsmanship to avoid losing the battle of the forms, but not (if the other party is equally careful) to win it'.[42] Where both parties have well-drafted standard terms, the result would appear to be a stalemate and the mirror image rule would seem to dictate that the judge rule that no contract exists.

Acceptance by conduct

In many cases, acceptance will be express and communicated orally or in writing. But it is also possible to accept an offer by conduct. This most commonly occurs in contracts for the sale of goods in which the offeree accepts the offer by dispatching the ordered goods.[43] In order for acceptance by conduct to be valid, however, it must be objectively established that the offeree knew of the offer, and performed and acted in reliance on it.[44] The following case demonstrates these principles.

Brogden v Metropolitan Railway Company (1877) 2 App Cas 666 (HL)

FACTS: Brogden (the defendant) had, for many years, supplied the Metropolitan Railway Company (the claimant) with coal—but no formal agreement had ever been created. They finally decided to formalize their relationship. The claimant drafted a contract, but left certain areas blank for Brogden to fill in (for example, the identity of the arbitrator). Brogden completed the blank areas, signed it, and wrote 'approved' at the end of the contract, before returning it to the claimant. The claimant received the contract and its manager placed it in his desk. The parties continued trading on the basis of the contract, but a dispute subsequently arose and Brogden refused to supply any more coal, claiming that there was no contract between them. The claimant sued.

HELD: The House of Lords held that a contract had come into existence either when the claimant had ordered the first supply of coal, or when the defendant supplied it. Sending

---

40. [1979] 1 WLR 401 (CA) 405.

41. See e.g. *Tekdata Interconnections Ltd v Amphenol Ltd* [2009] EWCA Civ 1209, [2010] 1 Lloyd's Rep 357.

42. Edwin Peel, *Treitel on the Law of Contract* (13th edn, Sweet & Maxwell 2011) 22.

43. *Harvey v Johnston* (1848) 6 CB 295.   44. *Taylor v Allon* [1966] 1 QB 304 (DC).

the draft contract to Brogden amounted to an offer. Because Brogden added a term (by adding the arbitrator's name), the return of the contract constituted a counter-offer. The issue was whether the claimant accepted Brogden's offer. The claimant's conduct (that is, not objecting to Brogden's choice of arbitrator and continuing to transact on the basis of the contract) amounted to acceptance of Brogden's counter-offer.

Communication of acceptance

It is a general rule that, in order for acceptance to be effective, it must be communicated to the offeror. The rationale behind this general principle is that if acceptance could be valid without being communicated to the offeror, this would place the offeror in an extremely difficult position, because he would not able to determine whether or not he could make offers to others. It follows that the communication of acceptance need not come from the offeree,[45] but can be made by a third party authorized by the offeree (for example, his agent).

As a general rule, the communication of acceptance must actually be brought to the offeror's attention. Attempted communication will be insufficient, even where the reasons for failure are not attributable to the offeree (for example, the telephone line goes dead as he is communicating acceptance).[46] The contract will be concluded at the time and place of the receipt of communication of acceptance. In the case of cross-border contracts, determining the exact time and place that a contract came into being can often be crucial in determining which legal system has jurisdiction.

Entores Ltd v Miles Far East Corporation [1955] 2 QB 327 (CA)

FACTS: The claimant was based in London. It telexed (the forerunner to email) the defendant, which was based the Netherlands, and offered to purchase a quantity of copper cathodes. The defendant replied by telex, accepting the claimant's offer. Later, a dispute arose and the claimant initiated an action for breach of contract in an English court. The defendant argued that the contract was concluded in the Netherlands and that the English courts therefore lacked the jurisdiction to decide the case.

HELD: The Court of Appeal held that acceptance may have taken place in the Netherlands, but it only became valid once it was communicated to the offeror. As this took place in England, that was where the contract was concluded and so the English courts had jurisdiction.

⭐ See EH Scamell, 'Offer and Acceptance by Teleprinter' (1956) 19 MLR 89

The rule that communication of acceptance must be received by the offeror is not, however, absolute. As we shall see in the following sections, in some cases, the rule is modified; in other cases, it is reversed.

Prescribed methods of acceptance

If the offeror is concerned that he may be bound by a contract before he has notice of acceptance, it is always open for him to prescribe a specific form of acceptance.

---

45. *Bloxham's Case* (1864) 33 Beav 529.
46. *Entores Ltd v Miles Far East Corporation* [1955] 2 QB 327 (CA) 332 (Denning LJ).

For example, the offeror could require the offeree to deliver acceptance personally, in writing, thereby removing all doubt as to where and when acceptance took place. The general rule is that if the offeror states that acceptance may *only* occur via the prescribed means, then acceptance will only be effective if it complies with the offeror's specifications. Accordingly, if the offeror requires acceptance in writing to be sent to a particular place and it is sent elsewhere, he will not be bound.[47] The offeror may, however, indicate that a form of acceptance should be used, but not prescribe that it is the only way in which acceptance can occur. In such a case, an alternative method of acceptance will be effective, provided that it is no less advantageous to the offeror than the prescribed method,[48] as the following example demonstrates.

 Prescribed methods of acceptance

Paul offers to sell a consignment of goods to Marc, stating that acceptance should be 'by return of mail'. In many cases, 'return of mail' does not literally mean that acceptance should only be sent in the post; it merely indicates that acceptance should be communicated quickly. Accordingly, if Marc were to accept Paul's offer via email, it could be argued that Marc would have complied with Paul's intention.

The 'postal rule'

A common form of acceptance is by post, and postal acceptance constitutes perhaps the most important exception to the rule that acceptance is not valid until it is communicated to the offeror. The 'postal rule' states that, where it applies, acceptance takes place as soon as the letter is posted, not when the offeror receives it.

 Adams v Lindsell (1818) 1 B & Ald 681

FACTS: On 2 September, the defendant posted a letter offering to sell wool to the claimant, requesting a reply 'in the course of post'. Due to the letter being misdirected, it was delivered to the claimant two days later than expected, on the evening of 5 September. The claimant posted his acceptance on the same day and it was delivered to the defendant on 9 September. Had the defendant's original letter of offer not been misdirected, he would have expected to receive acceptance on 7 September. As he did not, he sold the wool to someone else. The claimant alleged that there existed a binding contract, which the defendant breached by selling the wool to another party.

HELD: The court held that as soon as the claimant posted his acceptance on 5 September, a binding contract was created and the defendant was therefore in breach.

COMMENT: It is apparent that the postal rule can be extremely harsh upon the offeror. Suppose that the acceptance letter is lost in the post. The offeror may sell the goods to a third party, completely unaware that he is party to a binding contract for the goods with the offeree. The offeror would have acted completely honestly and innocently, yet would be in breach of contract.[49]

47. *Frank v Knight* (1937) OQPD 113. Similarly, if he states that acceptance must be in writing, but it is delivered orally, he will not be bound (*Financings Ltd v Stimson* [1962] 1 WLR 1184 (CA)).
48. *Tinn v Hoffmann* (1873) 29 LT 271.
49. *Household Fire and Carriage Accident Insurance Co v Grant* (1879) 4 Ex D 216 (CA).

Clearly, the postal rule favours the offeree at the expense of the offeror. Several justifications have been advanced for why this should be so:

- If the offeror expressly or impliedly (for example, by making the offer by post) indicates that postal acceptance is acceptable, he should bear the risks associated with the postal system.
- The postal rule prevents an offeree from taking advantage of the market (for example, by posting a letter of acceptance and then, if the market changes, retracting the acceptance—perhaps by email—before the letter reaches the offeror, and then contracting based on the new favourable market conditions).
- The postal rule facilitates the provision of evidence, because it is easier to prove that a letter has been posted than it is to prove that it has been received.

In two situations, the postal rule will not apply. First, the postal rule can be completely disapplied by a prudent offeror, by simply specifying that post may not be used or that, if post is used, acceptance will not be effective until the offeror actually receives the offeree's letter of acceptance.[50] Second, the postal rule will not apply where acceptance by post would give rise to a manifest inconvenience or absurdity,[51] or where it is unreasonable to use the post to accept.[52]

Electronic forms of communication

The advent of electronic forms of communication has necessitated the application of the acceptance rules to novel and developing situations. In many cases, this poses no problems. In the case of instantaneous forms of electronic communication, the standard rule that acceptance must be communicated to the offeror will continue to apply, because, although the parties might be thousands of miles apart, the fact that communication is instantaneous means that it is *as if* they were in each other's presence. Accordingly, the standard rules of acceptance normally apply to contracts created by telephone,[53] telex,[54] and fax[55] (see Figure 6.1).

However, due to technological difficulties, instantaneous forms of communication may not prove so instantaneous in practice (for example, a fax machine might malfunction, or a mobile phone may lose a signal). What is the outcome in such situations? The answer came from Denning LJ in *Entores v Miles Far East Corporation.*[56]

- Where the offeree knows that his acceptance has not been received (for example, if his phone goes dead, or his fax machine malfunctions whilst midway through sending a message), there will be no contract. The offeree will need to repeat acceptance.
- Where the offeree believes that his acceptance has been communicated, but, in fact, it has not (for example, the offeror's fax malfunctions and does not receive the offeree's acceptance), then unless the offeror asks for the message to be repeated, a contract will exist. This is because the offeror is at fault for his failure to receive the acceptance.
- If no party is at fault and neither party is aware of the communication problem, then there will be no contract.

---

50. *Holwell Securities v Hughes* [1974] 1 WLR 155 (CA).   51. ibid.
52. *Henthorn v Fraser* [1892] 2 Ch 27 (CA).
53. *Entores v Miles Far East Corporation* [1955] 2 QB 327 (CA).   54. ibid.
55. *JSC Zestafoni Nikoladze Ferroalloy Plant v Ronly Holdings Ltd* [2004] EWHC 245 (Comm), [2004] 2 Lloyd's Rep 335.
56. [1955] 2 QB 327 (CA).

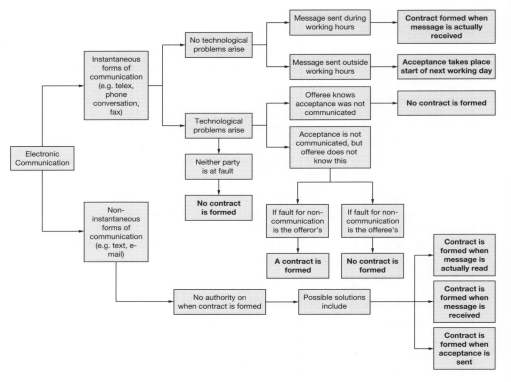

FIGURE 6.1 Electronic communication of acceptance

Aside from technological malfunctions, there is another reason to believe that instantaneous forms of communication may not be received instantly—namely, that businesses may work within set office hours.

- If communication of acceptance is received during office hours, acceptance will occur when the acceptance was received on the machine, not when it was actually read.[57] During office hours, fax machines, etc should be regularly monitored and therefore offerors who do not monitor such machines should not be able to rely on the standard communication of acceptance rule.

- If acceptance is received outside office hours, then acceptance will be deemed to have taken place at the start of the next working day.[58]

The above rules do not apply to all situations of electronic communication. In particular, there has been much discussion and deliberation on how the rules of acceptance should apply to contracts created via email. Although email is invariably quicker than postal mail, it is not an instantaneous form of communication, because the email is stored on a server before being sent to the recipient. This may lead us to believe that the standard rules should not apply and that emails should be treated as postal mails—that is, that acceptance occurs when the 'send' button is clicked. But most commentators prefer acceptance to occur when the email is received, with the dominant view being that an email is received when it is delivered to the recipient's inbox.[59] Until the issue is definitively determined by statute or the courts, uncertainty will remain.

57. *Brinkibon v Stahag Stahl und Stahlwarenhandelsgesellschaft GmbH* [1983] 2 AC 34 (HL).
58. *Mondial Shipping and Chartering BV v Astarte Shipping Ltd* [1995] 2 Lloyd's Rep 249 (QB).
59. See e.g. Deveral Capps, 'Electronic Mail and the Postal Rule' (2004) 15 ICCLR 207, 212.

Acceptance through silence

As an offeror can specify the method of communication of acceptance, does it follow that he can choose to waive the requirement of communication of acceptance if he so wishes? The general answer appears to be 'no'.

 Felthouse v Bindley (1862) 11 CB NS 869

FACTS: The claimant sent a letter to his nephew, offering to buy a horse from him. The letter stated: 'If I hear no more about him, I will consider the horse mine.' The horse was due to be sold at auction, but the nephew, apparently happy with the claimant's offer, instructed the auctioneer (the defendant) to withdraw the horse from auction. Mistakenly, the horse was not withdrawn and was sold to a third party. The claimant argued that the horse belonged to him when the auctioneer sold it and so sued under the tort of **conversion**.

HELD: The claim failed. The court held that silence could not constitute valid acceptance. Therefore, the nephew never accepted the claimant's offer and no contract came into being. Accordingly, when the horse was sold, it still belonged to the nephew.

COMMENT: It could be argued that this was not a case of acceptance by silence, but rather acceptance by conduct. The claimant could have validly contended that, by removing the horse from auction, the nephew's conduct indicated acceptance. But the counter-argument to this would be that the nephew never informed the claimant that he was withdrawing the horse from the auction and so the conduct was not communicated to the offeror.

➡ **conversion:** the act of interfering with goods in a manner inconsistent with another's right of possession (see p 427)

Accordingly, the general rule is that silence cannot constitute valid acceptance. There is, however, a growing belief that this rule is not absolute. In *Vitol SA v NorElf Ltd*,[60] Lord Steyn stated that silence could constitute valid acceptance in 'exceptional cases',[61] although he did not elaborate on this. Poole has argued that silence can constitute acceptance in several different circumstances (e.g. where there has been a course of dealing between the offeror and offeree under which the offeree has taken the benefit of services offered).[62]

Unilateral contracts

Precisely why the general rules relating to contractual offers needed to be modified, or even disapplied, in the case of unilateral contracts has already been discussed. The same is true in relation to the rules of acceptance, as the following example demonstrates.

 Acceptance and unilateral contracts

Kirsty places an advertisement in her local newspaper stating that she will pay £100 to any person who finds her lost dog and returns it to her. This is clearly a unilateral offer, because no one is compelled to search for the dog, but if anyone does comply with the advertisement, Kirsty will be bound to pay the £100.

---

60. [1996] AC 800 (HL).   61. ibid 812.
62. Jill Poole, *Textbook on Contract Law* (11th edn, OUP 2012) 57–9.

Two issues arise, as follows.

1. How is such an offer accepted? Although there has been academic debate on the subject, it is still the accepted view that unilateral offers are accepted by fully performing the stipulated act.[63] Accordingly, someone finding her dog and returning it to her would accept Kirsty's offer. The rationale behind this is that, at any time, the offeree is free to give up searching for Kirsty's dog without fear of penalty. If offerees are free to abandon performance at any time, then the offeror should be similarly free to retract the offer at any time prior to full performance being completed. As we have seen previously, however, the courts have significantly limited the offeror's ability to revoke a unilateral offer once performance has commenced.

2. Is communication of acceptance required? It is settled law that, in the case of unilateral offers, the offeree does not have to communicate acceptance of the offer.[64] The reason for this is one of practicality. As unilateral offers may be made to the entire world, it would be impractical to require every person who decided to look for Kirsty's dog first to contact her and inform her that they were going to search for the dog.

Certainty

Even where agreement is present, there will not be a binding contract if the agreement lacks sufficient certainty. An agreement that lacks certainty will not be rewritten by the courts and will instead be declared invalid. Where possible, however, the courts prefer to uphold the validity of contracts (especially where performance has commenced), rather than be perceived as 'the destroyer of bargains'.[65] Uncertain contracts can fall into one of two categories, although there is significant potential for overlap.

Vague agreements

Where the words of a contract are vague, the court will attempt to uphold the contract by divining the intention of the parties. Where the intention cannot be divined, the court will deny the existence of a legally binding contract.

 G Scammell and Nephew Ltd v Ouston [1941] AC 251 (HL)

FACTS: The defendant wrote to the claimant offering to sell it a van for £286 and also offering to take its Bedford van for £100 in part-exchange. The agreement provided that 'this order is given on the understanding that the balance of purchase price can be had on hire-purchase terms over a period of two years'. The relationship deteriorated when the defendant refused to accept the Bedford van, due to its poor condition. The claimant sued for breach of contract.

---

63. *Daulia Ltd v Four Millbank Nominees Ltd* [1978] Ch 231 (CA).
64. *Carlill v Carbolic Smoke Ball Co* [1893] 1 QB 256 (CA).
65. *Hillas & Co Ltd v Arcos Ltd* (1932) 43 Ll L Rep 359 (HL) 364 (Lord Tomlin).

HELD: The claim failed. The House of Lords held that there was no contract between the parties, because the phrase 'on hire-purchase terms' was so vague and had so many possible interpretations that it was impossible to determine which interpretation the parties had intended.

It may, however, be the case that whilst the terms of the contract are vague, the contract itself might provide some implied mechanism through which to clarify the vague terms. In such a case, the courts will apply the maxim *id certum est quod certum reddi potest* ('that is certain which may be rendered certain')—that is, if the courts can make the contract certain, then it will become certain.

 Hillas & Co Ltd v Arcos Ltd (1932) 43 Ll L Rep 359 (HL)

FACTS: The claimant had entered into an agreement with the defendant whereby it would, in the 1930 season, purchase 22,000 standards of timber 'of fair specification'. The contract also provided the claimant with the option to purchase another 100,000 standards of timber in 1931, but did not provide details relating to the timber's size and quality. Come 1931, the claimant decided to exercise this option, but the defendant had already sold all of its timber. The claimant sued for breach of contract. The defendant contended that the agreement was so vague that it did not give rise to a contract.

HELD: The claimant succeeded. The House of Lords held that, even though the option did not specify the size and quality of the timber, this information could be implied by reference to the previous season's dealing and by reference to the normal practices of the timber trade.

Where a particular term is vague, it may also be possible for the court to sever that term and enforce the remaining agreement.

 Nicolene Ltd v Simmonds [1953] 1 QB 543 (CA)

FACTS: The claimant ordered 3,000 tonnes of reinforced steel bars from the defendant. The agreement was subject to 'the usual conditions of acceptance', but no usual conditions existed. The defendant failed to deliver the goods and the claimant sued. The defendant argued that, because there were no usual conditions of acceptance, the contract was too vague to be enforced.

HELD: The Court of Appeal held that the clause was meaningless and could be severed from the contract. The remaining agreement was certain and complete, and could be enforced. Denning LJ was quick to draw a distinction between:

> a clause which is meaningless and a clause which is yet to be agreed. A clause which is meaningless can often be ignored, whilst still leaving the contract good; whereas a clause which has yet to be agreed may mean that there is no contract at all, because the parties have not agreed on all the essential terms.[66]

---

66. [1953] 1 QB 543 (CA) 551.

Where the parties have wholly or partially performed their obligations under the contract (known as 'executed performance'), it will be:

> difficult to submit that the contract is void for vagueness or uncertainty. Specifically, the fact that the transaction is executed makes it easier to imply a term resolving any uncertainty, or alternatively, it may be possible to treat a matter not finalised in negotiations as inessential.[67]

Incomplete agreements

The parties may agree on broad terms, but may wish to leave certain matters for future negotiation. Provided that the essential terms of the contract have been agreed upon and that the parties agree to be bound immediately, the fact that further terms require negotiation will not prevent the court from finding a concluded agreement, as the following case demonstrates.

Bear Stearns Bank plc v Forum Global Equity Ltd [2007] EWHC 1576 (Comm)

FACTS: The defendant wished to purchase from the claimant loan notes in respect of companies within the Parmalat group. The parties entered into negotiations and reached an agreement on price, but several minor terms were not agreed on. It was decided that the parties' lawyers would negotiate the remaining terms but, believing that an agreement had been made, the claimant agreed to sell the loan notes to the defendant. Before the lawyers had finalized terms, the defendant decided not to proceed with the purchase. The claimant sued for breach of contract and the defendant argued that no agreement was ever made.

HELD: The Commercial Court held that a contract existed, which the defendant had breached. The essential term of the contract—namely, price—had been agreed. Andrew Smith J stated:

> If parties have shown an intention to be contractually committed, albeit while deferring discussion of some aspect or aspects of the deal, then the court will recognise a contract unless what remains outstanding is not merely important but essential in the sense that without it the contract is too uncertain or incomplete to be enforced.[68]

 See Paul Nicholls, 'My Word is My Bond' (2008) 158 NLJ 122

This case indicates the courts' commitment to give effect to business dealings wherever possible. But the courts will only go so far. Where essential terms are missing, or are yet to be agreed upon by the parties, there will be no contract; there will be merely an 'agreement to agree'.

May and Butcher Ltd v R [1934] 2 KB 17 (HL)

FACTS: The claimant entered into an agreement with the defendant to purchase surplus war equipment. The agreement stated that the price to be paid and the date of payment

---

67. *G Percy Trentham Ltd v Archital Luxfer Ltd* [1993] 1 Lloyd's Rep 25 (CA) 27 (Steyn LJ).
68. [2007] EWHC 1576 (Comm) [155].

would be decided 'from time to time'. The relationship between the parties broke down and the claimant sought to enforce the agreement at a 'reasonable price'.

HELD: The House of Lords held that there was no contract. As an essential term was left open for future negotiation, the contract was therefore too incomplete to enforce.

As with uncertain agreements, the presence of certain factors will make the court more willing to conclude that a contract exists, namely that performance has already begun, or that the contract provides for some effective form of mechanism to resolve the lack of agreement. Both of these factors were present in the following case.

 Foley v Classique Coaches Ltd [1934] 2 KB 1 (CA)

FACTS: The claimant sold a piece of land to the defendant. It was a term of the sale agreement that the defendant enter into a second agreement with the claimant, whereby it agreed to purchase all of its petrol from the claimant at a price to be agreed from 'time to time'. The second agreement also provided that, in the event of a lack of agreement, the parties would aim to resolve their dispute through arbitration. For three years, the agreement continued, until the defendant decided to repudiate the second agreement. The claimant sued and the defendant argued that there was no contract due to the uncertain price clause.

HELD: The Court of Appeal held that the second agreement was binding and enforceable. The Court implied a term that the petrol should be sold to the defendant at a reasonable price.

COMMENT: Initially, this case appears very similar to *May and Butcher*, discussed earlier, but there are two crucial differences:

1. The parties had acted on the agreement for three years—which was not the case in *May and Butcher*.
2. The contract provided that, in the absence of agreement, the issue was to be determined by arbitration.

Consideration

A promise in a contract must, unless executed by deed, be supported by consideration from the person to whom the promise is made. It follows that (unless made by deed) **gratuitous promises** cannot be enforced.[69] For example, if I promise to donate £100 to charity and then change my mind, the charity cannot sue me to recover the donation, because the charity has not provided any consideration for my promise.

→ **gratuitous promises:** promises for which consideration is not given

Various attempts have been made to define 'consideration'. Historically, consideration was viewed in terms of benefit and detriment, as the following definition indicates:

> A valuable consideration in the sense of the law may consist either in some right, interest, profit or benefit accruing to one party, or some forbearance, detriment, loss or responsibility given, suffered or undertaken by the other.[70]

The following example demonstrates the principal weakness of this definition.

---

69. *Re Hudson* (1885) 54 LJ Ch 811.   70. *Currie v Misa* (1875) LR 10 Ex 153 (Lush J) 162.

Eg   Benefit and detriment

Martin purchases goods worth £100 online from Expensivestuff.co.uk. Martin will suffer a detriment (payment of the £100) and the seller will gain a benefit (receipt of the £100). At the same time, Martin will gain a benefit (receipt of the goods) and the seller will suffer a detriment (loss of the goods).

The problem with this approach is that, at the time that the contract is concluded, neither party has gained or lost anything: the above benefits and detriments will take place in the future, once both parties have performed their obligations. Therefore, in normal bilateral contracts, defining consideration purely in terms of benefit and detriment is descriptively inaccurate.

For this reason, the House of Lords[71] has approved the more modern definition of Sir Frederick Pollock (1845–1937), an eminent academic, who defined consideration as '[a]n act of forbearance of one party, or the promise thereof, is the price for which the promise of the other is bought, and the promise thus given for value is enforceable'.[72]

Forms of consideration

Consideration can be classified into one of three forms:

1. executed;
2. executory; and
3. past.

As a general rule, executed and executory consideration constitute valid consideration, whereas past consideration does not.

Executory and executed consideration

Executory consideration is consideration that is yet to be provided, whereas executed consideration is consideration that has already been provided. The following examples demonstrate the distinction.

Executory and executed consideration

Executory consideration

Heavy Construction plc contracts to purchase 2,000 tonnes of steel girders from Steel Smelting Ltd at a price of £250,000. At the time the contract is drawn up, neither party has performed its obligations—but this does not mean that they have not provided consideration, because their promises to perform constitute valid consideration. As each party has yet to perform (execute) its obligations, their consideration is executory.

Executed consideration

Gareth loses his Rolex watch at the gym. He puts up posters at the gym indicating that he will pay £100 to anyone who finds the watch and returns it to him. Melanie finds the watch and returns it to Gareth. By finding the watch and returning it to Gareth, Melanie has performed (executed) her obligation. Accordingly, Melanie's consideration for Gareth's promise is executed.

---

71. *Dunlop Pneumatic Tyre Co Ltd v Selfridge Ltd* [1915] AC 847 (HL) 855 (Lord Dunedin).
72. Sir Percy Winfield, *Pollock's Principles of Contract* (13th edn, Stevens 1950) 133.

Past consideration

Normally, the parties will each make a promise and then carry out the promised act. In this case, the promise constitutes consideration and, because it occurs before performance of the act, it will be valid. Conversely, where a party performs an act that is then followed by a promise, that act will normally constitute past consideration, which generally does not provide good consideration for a promise, as the following case demonstrates.

 Re McArdle [1951] Ch 669 (CA)

FACTS: A father died and his will provided that his five children would inherit his house upon the death of their mother. The mother lived in the house, along with her son and his wife (the claimant). The claimant carried out alterations to the house worth £488, although she had not been asked to do this. A year later, all five children agreed to reimburse her, out of the estate, for the work done. The mother died and the house was sold. The claimant sued when the children refused to pay her the £488 promised.

HELD: The Court of Appeal held that the agreement was unenforceable. The work that the claimant undertook pre-dated the promise to reimburse. Accordingly, she had provided no consideration for the £488.

★ See OM Stone, 'Assignment and Consideration in Action' (1951) 14 MLR 330

Past consideration will, however, be regarded as good consideration if the following three-part test is satisfied:

> The act must have been done at the promisors' request: the parties must have understood that the act was to be remunerated either by a payment or the conferment of some other benefit: and payment, or the conferment of a benefit, must have been legally enforceable had it been promised in advance.[73]

The following case demonstrates this test in practice.

 Lampleigh v Braithwait (1615) Hob 105[74]

FACTS: Braithwait had killed a man and requested that Lampleigh petition the King for a pardon. At considerable effort and expense, Lampleigh secured the pardon, and Braithwait then promised to pay Lampleigh £100 for his efforts. Braithwait subsequently refused to pay the £100, so Lampleigh sued.

HELD: Lampleigh could recover the £100. The court held that Braithwait's request to obtain a pardon and his subsequent promise were so closely connected as to form essentially part of the same transaction. Further, given the obvious time and expense through which Lampleigh would have to go to obtain a pardon, the court held that there was an implied promise to pay Lampleigh a reward for his efforts.

---

73. *Pao On v Lau Yiu Long* [1980] AC 614 (PC) 630.
74. See also *Re Casey's Patents* [1892] 1 Ch 104 (CA).

Sufficiency of consideration

The general rule is that consideration for another's promise must be sufficient, but need not be adequate. The word 'adequate' is being used in a legal sense to refer to consideration being equal in value. Accordingly, the consideration of both parties need not be equal in value, provided that it is legally sufficient.

 Mountford v Scott [1975] Ch 258 (CA)

FACTS: The defendant granted the claimant a six-month option to purchase his house for £10,000, in return for which the claimant provided £1. The defendant purported to withdraw the offer, but two months later, the claimant exercised the option. The defendant argued that no binding agreement existed, because the claimant had not provided sufficient consideration.

HELD: Despite the obvious inequality of the bargain, the £1 had value in the eyes of the law and so the Court of Appeal held that it constituted good consideration.

In determining what constitutes sufficient consideration, the court generally refuses to recognize the sufficiency of certain promises. These promises can be classified into two groups:

The rules relating to part-payment are discussed at p 156

1. promises to perform, or performance of, an existing duty; and
2. promises to pay in part, or part-payment of, a debt.

To clarify discussion, this section will focus on the former—namely, a promise to perform an existing legal duty—which can arise where:

- the party performs, or promises to perform, an existing legal duty;
- the party performs, or promises to perform, an existing contractual duty that is owed to the other party; and
- the party performs, or promises to perform, an existing contractual duty owed to a third party.

Performance of an existing legal duty

The performance (actual or promised) of an existing legal duty does not generally provide sufficient consideration for the promise of another, as the following case demonstrates.

 Collins v Godefroy (1831) 1 B & Ad 950

subpoena: a writ compelling a person to attend a trial as a witness (now known as a 'witness summons')

FACTS: The defendant issued a **subpoena**, requiring the claimant to attend a civil trial and give evidence. The claimant attended court for six days, but was not required to give any evidence. After the trial, the defendant agreed to pay the claimant a fee of one guinea (£1.05) per day. The defendant never paid this fee and the claimant sued.

HELD: The claim failed. Once subpoenaed, the claimant was legally obliged to attend court and give evidence if required. As he was doing no more than was required by the law, he had not provided consideration for the six guineas.

However, where a party has done more than is required by the law, this will constitute good consideration for the other party's promise.

Glasbrook Bros v Glamorgan County Council [1925] AC 270 (HL)[75]

FACTS: The owner of a colliery feared that striking employees might cause violence and property damage. He therefore requested extra protection from the police, adding that the colliery could only be protected properly if the police were actually billeted on the premises. The police did not think that this was necessary, because regular police patrols would be adequate. Nevertheless, the police agreed to billet a number of police officers at the colliery, provided that the owner agreed to pay for this, which he did. After the strike had ended, the police presented the colliery owner with a bill for £2,300. He refused to pay, contending that the police had a legal duty to protect his premises and that therefore they had not provided sufficient consideration for the £2,300.

HELD: The House of Lords ordered the colliery owner to pay the £2,300. The police were free to choose which method of protection was most effective. Because, at the insistence of the colliery owner, they had provided more protection than was deemed necessary, they had gone beyond the obligations imposed upon them and had therefore provided good consideration for the £2,300.

The case of *Williams v Roffey Bros & Nicholls (Contractors) Ltd*[76] (discussed later) established that performance of an existing contractual duty can provide good consideration if it provides the other party with a practical benefit, or avoidance of a disbenefit. It is now clear that this principle also applies to cases in which a duty is imposed by the law.[77] Therefore, the performance of a legal duty can constitute good consideration if it provides a practical benefit, or avoids a disbenefit, to the other party.

Performance of a contractual duty owed to the other party

The following example demonstrates the type of situation that we will discuss in this section.

Existing contractual duty owed to the other party

Keith is a sculptor who has agreed to provide, for a fee of £50,000, a sculpture to be placed in the lobby of the new corporate headquarters of Covenant plc. One month later, Keith informs the board of Covenant that he cannot complete the sculpture at the contracted price and will require an extra £10,000. Covenant promises to pay Keith the extra £10,000.

Has Keith provided consideration for the extra £10,000? In other words, does the performance of his existing contractual duty provide sufficient consideration for the

---

75. This case can be contrasted with *Chief Constable of Greater Manchester v Wigan Athletic AFC Ltd* [2008] EWCA Civ 1449, in which the police were unable to obtain extra payment.

76. [1991] 1 QB 1 (CA). 77. *Re Selectmove Ltd* [1995] 1 WLR 474 (CA).

extra sum? Traditionally, the answer has been 'no'. The mere performance, or promise of performance, of an existing contractual duty will not provide sufficient consideration for a new promise by the person to whom the contractual duty is owed.

 Stilk v Myrick (1809) 2 Camp 317

FACTS: The claimant was a crewman aboard a ship chartered to transport goods from London to the Baltic and back. During the voyage, two crewmen deserted, leaving the ship short-handed. The captain of the ship promised that if the remaining crew got the ship back to London, he would divide the deserting crewmen's wages amongst them. Upon returning to London, the captain refused to pay the crewmen extra.

HELD: The claimant (and the other crewmen) had not done any more than they were already contractually obliged to do. Accordingly, they had provided no consideration for the extra wages and so the claim failed.

COMMENT: This case can be contrasted with *Hartley v Ponsonby*,[78] which had almost identical facts to *Stilk*, except that seventeen crewmen out of thirty-six deserted. Given that the remaining crew would have to undertake considerably more work than they were contractually obliged to do, their claim for the extra £40 promised was upheld.

The principle in *Stilk v Myrick* promotes certainty and prevents a party placing undue pressure on the other once performance has commenced. Certainly, in cases similar to *Stilk*, to permit recovery of the extra wages would invite crewmen to hold their captains to ransom when far from home. The problem with the rule is that it is out of line with commercial reality, in so much as it is reasonably common to make new promises in order to secure timely performance. Perhaps for this reason, a limitation to the principle in *Stilk* was created in the following case.

 Williams v Roffey Bros & Nicholls (Contractors) Ltd [1991] 1 QB 1 (CA)

FACTS: The defendant was contracted to refurbish a block of flats. It subcontracted the carpentry work to the claimant, who would be paid £20,000 in a series of instalments. The claimant commenced performance, but realized soon afterwards that he could not complete the work for £20,000. As the defendant was subject to a substantial time penalty clause if the flats were not completed on time, the defendant agreed to pay the claimant a further £10,300, payable at the rate of £575 per flat completed. The claimant completed a number of flats, but did not receive the extra payment, and so commenced proceedings.

HELD: The Court of Appeal held that the claimant could recover the extra payment as he had provided consideration for the extra money, this consideration coming in the form of 'practical benefits'[79] (or avoidance of disbenefits) that the defendant obtained by paying the extra amount. These benefits were the avoidance of the penalty clause and the avoidance of having to engage substitute carpenters. The Court did, however, state that had the extra money been secured via duress or fraud, the 'practical benefit' principle would not apply.

---

78. (1857) 7 E & B 872.   79. [1991] 1 QB 1 (CA) 11 (Glidewell LJ).

> **COMMENT:** Given that a new promise will rarely be made unless some form of 'practical benefit' is derived, it could be argued that, in practical terms, the principle established in *Williams* obliterates the principle in *Stilk*. Soon after *Williams* was decided, it was argued that the principle in *Stilk* now existed in name only.[80] The Court in *Williams* denied that it was overruling the principle in *Stilk*, with Purchas LJ describing *Stilk* as 'a pillar stone of the law of contract'.[81] Glidewell LJ stated that the principle established in *Williams* is designed to 'refine and limit'[82] the principle in *Stilk*. With all due respect to their Lordships, it is contended that the decision in *Williams* goes far beyond mere refinement.

★ See Roger Halson, 'Sailors, Subcontractors and Consideration' (1990) 106 LQR 183

In *Re Selectmove Ltd*,[83] the Court of Appeal indicated a restrictive approach to its decision in *Williams*, saying that it did not apply where the existing obligation was one to pay money. Other cases have gone further and have openly criticized the decision in *Williams*. In *South Caribbean Trading v Trafalgar Beheer BV*,[84] Coleman J stated *obiter* that '[b]ut for the fact that *Williams v Roffey Bros* was a decision of the Court of Appeal, I would not have followed it'.[85]

Although *Williams* has proven to be controversial, there is a significant body of opinion that contends that, in terms of commercial reality, the result is beneficial. The Court in *Williams* demonstrated a willingness to give effect to commercial reality—namely, that once contracts are concluded, subsequent renegotiation may be beneficial. The decision 'signals that the courts, in deciding whether or not to enforce a promise, may be guided less by technical questions of consideration than by questions of fairness, reasonableness and commercial utility'.[86]

Performance of a contractual duty owed to a third party

It is accepted that a party to a contract may provide sufficient consideration for the promise of the other party by fulfilling a contractual duty owed to a third party, or by promising to fulfil it. This would occur where *A* makes a promise to *B* and, in return, *B* promises to do an act that he is already contractually obliged to perform for *C* (the third party). *B* will have provided sufficient consideration for *A*'s promise, by performing his contractual obligation towards *C*, as the following case demonstrates.

 Scotson v Pegg (1861) 6 H & N 295[87]

FACTS: The claimant entered into a contract with *X* to deliver coal to *X*, or to a party of *X*'s choice. *X* required the coal to be delivered to the defendant. The defendant then promised to the claimant that, if he delivered to coal to him, he would unload it at the rate of 49 tonnes per day. The claimant delivered the coal to the defendant, but the defendant failed to unload

---

80. Norma J Hird and Ann Blair, 'Minding Your Own Business: *Williams v Roffey* Re-visited—Consideration Reconsidered' [1996] JBL 254, 255.　　81. [1991] 1 QB 1 (CA) 20.　　82. ibid 16.
83. [1995] 1 WLR 474 (CA).　　84. [2004] EWHC 2676 (Comm), [2005] 1 Lloyd's Rep 128.
85. ibid [108].
86. John N Adams and Roger Brownsword, 'Contract, Consideration and the Critical Path' (1990) 53 MLR 536, 537.
87. *Scotson* was a first-instance decision, but it has since been upheld by the Privy Council in *New Zealand Shipping Co Ltd v AM Satterthwaite & Co Ltd (The Eurymedon)* [1975] AC 154 (PC).

it at the promised rate. When the claimant sued, the defendant argued that the claimant had not provided good consideration for the promise, because he was already obliged to deliver the coal under the contract with *X*.

HELD: The claimant succeeded. The claimant had provided good consideration for the defendant's promise, by carrying out the obligation that he already owed to *X*.

Therefore, it can be seen that the principle in *Stilk v Myrick* discussed earlier only applies to existing contractual obligations of the other party; it does not apply to existing contractual obligations owed to third parties.

Part-payment of a debt

The following example provides the factual circumstances in which part-payment will occur.

 Part-payment of debt

Black Horse Bank plc lends £2 million to Welsh Petroleum Ltd—but Welsh Petroleum Ltd soon suffers significant financial difficulties. It informs Black Horse Bank plc that it will be unable to repay the loan in full when it is due. It will, however, be able to pay back £1.5 million, provided that Black Horse Bank plc promises to forgo the remainder of the loan.

The question with which we are concerned here is this: if Black Horse Bank plc does promise to forgo the remainder of the loan, will that promise be legally binding, or can it accept the £1.5 million and then sue for the remainder? In other words, does part-payment of a debt provide sufficient consideration for Black Horse Bank plc's promise to accept the lesser sum?

Common law

Generally, part-payment of a debt does not provide sufficient consideration and a creditor is not bound by any promise to accept a lower sum. This rule was established in 1602 in *Pinnel's Case*,[88] in which the court stated: 'Payment of a lesser sum on the day in satisfaction of a greater sum cannot be any satisfaction for the whole.' The House of Lords approved this rule in the following case.

 ***Foakes v Beer* (1884) 9 App Cas 605 (HL)**

FACTS: In a previous legal action, Dr Foakes had been ordered to pay Mrs Beer £2,090. Beer was entitled to this money immediately and, for every day it remained unpaid, she was also entitled to interest. Foakes was unable to pay and asked Beer for more time. She replied that if he were to paid £500 immediately, he could pay the balance in instalments and she would 'not take any proceedings whatever on the said judgment'. In accordance with this agreement, Foakes paid the £2,090, but Beer then sued Foakes for £360 interest.

88. (1602) 5 Co Rep 117a.

> Foakes argued that she had promised not to sue, provided that he paid the instalments, which he did.
>
> **HELD:** As Foakes had only paid the £2,090 judgment debt and not the accompanying interest (to which Beer was entitled), he had not provided sufficient consideration for Beer's promise not to sue. Accordingly, Beer could recover the £360 interest.

The common law provides for a number of exceptions to this principle. First, part-payment of a debt will constitute sufficient consideration if it is accompanied by something else requested by the creditor. In *Pinnel's Case*, Lord Coke referred to 'the gift of a horse, hawk or robe', but more modern examples would include early payment in part of the debt, payment in kind, or part-payment in a different location. It is important to note that the creditor, not the debtor, must request the new element.[89] This is to ensure that financially vulnerable creditors cannot be bullied by debtors who are aware of the creditor's financial difficulties (although, today, such creditors would be protected by the doctrine of economic duress).

Economic duress is discussed at p 271

The second exception occurs where a debtor has multiple creditors and he enters into an arrangement (known as a 'composition agreement') with them, whereby he promises to pay them all a percentage of what they are owed. In this case, the percentage paid will satisfy the full debt and no creditor can recover more than that percentage.[90]

The third exception is that where the debtor's debt is paid in part by a third party, the creditor cannot recover the balance from the debtor.[91]

The strict rule laid down in *Pinnel's Case* and evidenced in *Foakes v Beer* can been criticized on two grounds;

1. It is arguably unfair to permit a creditor to recover full payment when he has freely promised to accept part-payment (as was the case in *Foakes v Beer*).
2. The rule appears to be commercially unrealistic. Businesses will often accept part-payment of a debt in full satisfaction, provided that payment is made early. They regard certain part-payment now to be preferable to possible part-payment later.

To mitigate the harshness of the common law rule in *Pinnel's Case*, equity has provided a means to evade the part-payment rule where it appeared just to do so—namely, the doctrine of promissory estoppel. As will be seen, however, promissory estoppel is a second-best solution, because it merely suspends the creditor's rights, whereas a finding of sufficient consideration extinguishes the creditor's rights completely.

Promissory estoppel

Chapter 1 noted that equity exists as supplementary system of law to mitigate the harshness of common law rules. This is evident in relation to the part-payment of debt, where the equitable doctrine of promissory estoppel has significantly mitigated the harshness of the rule in *Pinnel's Case*. Promissory estoppel applies where *A* promises not to enforce his strict legal rights, and *B* relies on this promise. If *A* goes back

The relationship between the common law and equity is discussed at p 10

89. *D & C Builders Ltd v Rees* [1966] 2 QB 617 (CA). 90. *Good v Cheesman* (1831) 2 B & Ad 328.
91. *Welby v Drake* (1825) 1 C & P 557; *Hirachand Punamchand v Temple* [1911] 2 KB 330 (CA).

on his promise and tries to enforce his strict legal rights against *B*, he will be estopped (prevented) from doing so, although normally *A* can revert to his strict legal rights after a period of reasonable notice has elapsed.

The application of promissory estoppel to the part-payment of debt was first established in the following case.

Central London Property Trust Ltd v High Trees House Ltd [1947] KB 130 (KB)

FACTS: In September 1937, the claimant let a block of flats to the defendant for ninety-nine years at a ground rent of £2,500 per year. The defendant would generate a profit by subletting the flats to others, which it was able to do for several years. But by January 1940, due to wartime conditions, many of the flats were empty and the defendant could not afford the ground rent. The claimant agreed to halve the ground rent to £1,250, but no time limit was established for this arrangement. Come September 1945, the flats were once again full. In 1946, the claimant initiated friendly proceedings to recover full rent from September 1945 onwards.

HELD: The High Court held that the reduced rent arrangement was meant to apply only when wartime conditions rendered the flats empty. Once this ended, the claimant was once again entitled to full rent. Accordingly, the claim succeeded. It was clear, however, that this was merely a test claim and that the claimant intended to attempt to recover the full rent for the period 1940–45, which, under the rule in *Pinnel's Case*, it would be entitled to do. Denning J, relying on the already existing doctrine of equitable estoppel, pre-empted this by stating *obiter* that the doctrine of promissory estoppel would prevent the claimant from claiming full rent for that period. It is this *dictum*, and not the actual decision, that forms the most important and most controversial element of this case.

It could be argued that Denning J's *dictum* was inconsistent with *Foakes v Beer*. Denning circumvented this criticism (not entirely successfully) by stating that the House in *Foakes v Beer* had not considered applying the doctrine of equitable estoppel and, had it done so, the case might have been decided differently. The problem with this reasoning is that *Hughes v Metropolitan Railway Company* was decided only seven years before *Foakes*, and Lords Selborne and Blackburn sat on both cases. Therefore, it would seem more likely that the House of Lords simply did not consider equitable estoppel to be relevant.

In *High Trees*, Denning J's account of promissory estoppel lacked accuracy. Subsequent cases have established that, in order for promissory estoppel to arise, four conditions must be satisfied:

1. There must be a clear and unequivocal promise, by words or conduct, that strict legal rights will not be enforced.[92] In *High Trees*, the claimant was entitled to £2,500 rent per year under the contract, but he clearly promised to accept £1,250. The promise must be clear and precise, but need not be express. A promise may be implied if sufficiently clear,[93] but silence or inaction will usually not suffice, because these are equivocal acts.[94]

---

92. *Woodhouse Israel Cocoa Ltd v Nigerian Produce Marketing Co Ltd* [1972] AC 741 (HL).
93. *Hughes v Metropolitan Railway Company* (1877) 2 App Cas 439 (HL).
94. *Allied Marine Transport Ltd v Vale do Rio Doce Navegacao SA (The Leonidas D)* [1985] 1 WLR 925 (CA).

- **Agreements 'subject to contract'** Very often, agreements will be entered into 'subject to contract', meaning that the agreement is simply an 'agreement to agree', pending the creation of the formal contract. As such, the inclusion of the phrase will normally rebut the presumption and no contract will exist.

Finally, an exception to this presumption must be discussed, namely collective bargaining agreements. A collective bargaining agreement is an agreement between employers and trade unions, and usually relates to working conditions, rates of pay, etc. The common law provided that, even though such agreements are clearly commercial in nature, they are not intended to be *prima facie* binding,[105] on the ground that such agreements are often mere expressions of aspirations, and are usually written in extremely general and imprecise language. Section 179 of the Trade Union and Labour Relations (Consolidation) Act 1992 now states that such agreements are 'conclusively presumed' not to be binding, unless expressly stated otherwise in writing. The incorporation of a collective bargaining agreement into an employee's employment contract will, however, be presumed to be binding.[106]

Chapter conclusion

Business is conducted through a series of voluntary exchanges and transactions entered into with other parties. Accordingly, what constitutes a contract and exactly when a contract comes into existence are crucial to the running of a business. Ultimately, a contract is little more than a series of ingredients, which, if present, create binding rights and obligations that can be enforced in court. To ensure that a business has the right to hold others to account for a failure to provide it with what was agreed, it will wish to ensure that the transactions into which it enters have legally binding status. This, in turn, will require those who run businesses to have a thorough appreciation of what ingredients are needed to create binding obligations. In most cases, should one of the five ingredients discussed be lacking, a contract will fail to exist and businesses will be unable to enforce the terms of the agreement. This could prove extremely costly—especially where obtaining goods and services from others is central to the operation of the business, and these goods and services are not supplied.

Key points summary

- An offer is a willingness to contract on specified terms that will become binding once accepted by the person to whom it is addressed.

- Treitel defined acceptance as 'a final and unqualified expression of assent to the terms of the offer'.[107] It can be spoken, in writing, or by conduct.

- As soon as the offer is accepted and (generally) communicated, a contract is created. The requirement of communication of acceptance does not apply to unilateral contracts.

- Acceptance that varies a term of the offer or adds a new term will amount to a counter-offer. A counter-offer destroys the original offer and creates a new offer capable of acceptance by the former offeror.

---

105. *Ford Motor Co Ltd v Amalgamated Union of Engineering and Foundry Workers* [1969] 2 QB 303 (QB).
106. *Robertson v British Gas Corporation* [1983] ICR 351 (CA).
107. Edwin Peel, *Treitel on the Law of Contract* (13th edn, Sweet & Maxwell 2011) 17.

- A contract will only be binding if it is sufficiently certain.

- If the terms of a contract are vague, the court will generally attempt to hold the contract valid by divining the intentions of the parties.

- Consideration can be simply defined as the price for which the promise of the other is bought.

- Both parties are required to provide consideration in order to create a binding contract (unless the contract is made by deed).

- Consideration must be sufficient (that is, of value in the eyes of the law), but it need not be adequate (that is, of equal value).

- A contract will only be valid if both parties have an objective intention to create legal relations.

- Where the agreement is social or domestic, there is a rebuttable presumption that there is no intention to create legal relations.

- Where the agreement is commercial, there is a very strong rebuttable presumption that the agreement was intended to create legal relations.

Self-test questions

1. Define the following:
   (a) offer;
   (b) acceptance;
   (c) consideration;
   (d) promissory estoppel.

2. Explain the distinction between a bilateral and a unilateral contract.

3. Expensive Gadgets Ltd operates a website (ExpensiveGadgets.co.uk) specializing in selling new mobile phones. The website offers customers the opportunity to order a new iPhone, but due to a mistake by the web designer, the phone is advertised for £9.99, instead of £199.99. Thousands of customers order the phone and receive an email confirming their order. A day later, customers receive another email, informing them that the stated price was incorrect and that the phone actually costs £199.99. It also confirms that their order has been cancelled and that they will need to re-order at the correct price. Can the customers hold Expensive Gadgets Ltd to the £9.99 price?

4. Steel Smelting Ltd offers to sell 1,000 tonnes of reinforced steel girders to Rees Construction Ltd. Rees Construction Ltd accepts the offer by letter, the letter also informing Steel Smelting where the girders should be delivered. The letter is lost in the post and Steel Smelting Ltd sells the girders to a third party. Has acceptance occurred in this situation and, if so, when did it occur?

5. Read the case of *Williams v Roffey Bros & Nicholls (Contractors) Ltd*[108] and answer the following.
   (a) What effect do you think this case has had on the principle in *Stilk v Myrick*?
   (b) Could the Court have reached the same decision using the doctrine of promissory estoppel? If so, why did it not do so?
   (c) Do you think the 'practical benefit' approach should apply to cases involving part-payment of a debt? Why has it not done so to date?

---

108. [1991] 1 QB 1 (CA).

6. Every year, Tom, Helen, and Dave (who are friends) each contribute £100 and place a £300 bet on a horse in the Grand National, with any winnings being split equally three ways. Dave is at the betting shop, and Tom and Helen send him a text message stating that if he puts in their £100, they will pay him back later. Dave places a £300 bet on a horse at five to one. The horse wins and Dave collects £1,500 from the betting shop — but he refuses to share the winnings with Tom and Helen, and is refusing to accept the £100 that they claim to owe him. Does a binding contract exist in this situation?

7. Will an agreement that has terms missing always be held not to be a contract on the grounds of uncertainty?

Further reading

Sir Jack Beatson, Andrew Burrows, and John Cartwright, *Anson's Law of Contract* (29th edn, OUP 2010) ch 4
Provides a detailed but accessible account of the law relating to consideration and promissory estoppel

Deveral Capps, 'Electronic Mail and the Postal Rule' (2004) 15 ICCLR 207
Discusses when acceptance occurs in relation to contracts by email and argues that the postal rule should not apply to such contracts

Bob Hepple, 'Intention to Create Legal Relations' [1970] CLJ 122
Discusses the purpose and effect of the requirement of an intention to create legal relations

William Howarth, 'The Meaning of Objectivity in Contract' (1984) 100 MLR 265
Discusses what is meant by 'objectivity' in contract, and rejects promisor and promisee objectivity in favour of an entirely objective approach

Laurence Koffman and Elizabeth Macdonald, *The Law of Contract* (7th edn, OUP 2010) ch 2
A clear and accessible account of the law relating to offer and acceptance

Janet O'Sullivan, 'In Defence of Foakes v Beer' (1996) 55 CLJ 219
Provides an excellent analytical discussion of Williams v Roffey Bros, and argues that the law relating to existing contractual performance and part-payment should be harmonized by reverting to the strict rule in Foakes v Beer

Jill Poole, *Textbook on Contract Law* (11th edn, OUP 2012) ch 5
Discusses how the law determines the existence of an intention to create legal relations

 Remember to visit the **Online Resource Centre** at <**http://www. oxfordtextbooks.co.uk/orc/roach3e**> to access the following resources on Chapter 6, 'The formation of the contract': more **practice questions** and answers; a **glossary** of key terms; **multiple-choice questions**; **revision summaries**; and **diagrams** in pdf. Updates to the law can be found on Twitter by following **@UKBusinessLaw**.

7 The terms of the contract

- Express terms
- Implied terms

- The interpretation of contractual terms

INTRODUCTION

The previous two chapters focused on the pre-contractual process—namely, who has the ability to contract, what formalities are required, and what are the necessary ingredients for a valid contract. This chapter moves on to discuss the actual content of a contract. Contracts are made up of terms that set out the rights and obligations of all of the parties involved, and come in a number of different forms and derive from a number of different sources. The parties may expressly agree terms, but other terms may be imposed upon the parties by statute, the courts, or through custom. Because businesses conduct virtually all transactions through contract, it is vital that they appreciate all of the sources from which terms can potentially derive.

Terms can be classified in a number of different ways, but from the point of view of determining the origin and extent of a contract's terms, the crucial classification that needs to be understood is the distinction between express and implied terms.[1] It is also important to understand how the terms of a contract are interpreted by the courts should a dispute arise.

Express terms

Terms that the parties have specifically negotiated should form part of the contract are known as 'express terms', because they are included at the express wishes of the parties. Where a contract is in writing, identifying the express terms poses little problem and, in the event of a dispute, all that the court is required to do is to interpret and apply the terms as written. Problems arise, however, when a contract is made orally, based upon the negotiations of the parties. Not every promise made during negotiations will amount to a term: certain oral statements will be 'mere puffs' that will have no legal standing and will never provide any form of remedy. Many advertisements

---

1. In relation to the consequences of breaching terms, the crucial classification is between conditions, warranties and innominate terms. As this classification is more relevant to breach of contract, it is discussed in 'Defective performance' at p 298.

contain statements that are clearly not meant to be taken seriously (for example, washing powders that clean 'whiter than white'); clearly, such statements are not meant to be taken literally and relied upon, and so will not be actionable. But other statements may amount to either a term or a mere **representation**, which can be actionable. The ability to distinguish between terms and mere representations is fundamental in determining the extent of the rights and obligations imposed under a contract.

➡ **representation:** a pre-contractual statement concerning some fact or belief that is designed to induce a party into entering a contract

Terms and mere representations

Terms are contractual undertakings that set out the rights and obligations of the parties, which, if not complied with, can result in an action for breach of contract. Conversely, mere representations are simple statements made to induce the other party to contract, but which are not intended to form part of the contract and which will not give rise to an action for breach of contract (although, as is discussed in Chapter 10, they may result in the contract being set aside on the ground of **misrepresentation**).

The remedies for breach of contract and misrepresentation differ, so it is vital to determine whether a statement is a term or a mere representation, as the following example demonstrates.

➡ **misrepresentation:** a false statement that induces a party to enter into a contract

---

 Terms and representations

Tom visits Dave to inspect a car that Dave wishes to sell. During the inspection, Dave says: 'That is an excellent car. 20,000 miles on the clock, has never broken down, and has never been involved in an accident. It's yours for £5,000.' Upon completing the inspection, Tom accepts Dave's offer. Tom later discovers that the car's odometer has actually been once around the clock and has therefore done 120,000 miles, and that three years previously, it was involved in a serious accident. Two weeks after Tom purchases the car, it starts to develop serious mechanical faults. Tom wishes to return the car and recover his money, but Dave refuses.

There is little doubt that Dave's offer is a valid term, as is Tom's acceptance, but because Tom has paid the £5,000 and Dave has delivered the car, neither term has been breached. The issue is whether the statements made by Dave regarding the quality of the car are terms or mere representations. If they are terms, Tom will have a valid claim for breach of contract. If they are mere representations, Tom will have to base his claim in misrepresentation.

The courts, when determining whether a particular statement is a term or a representation, will look objectively at the words and conduct of the parties in order to determine whether the parties intended the representation to amount to a term or not.[2] As the test is objective, not subjective, the courts are not concerned with the actual intentions of the parties, but rather their intentions as evidenced by their words and conduct. As Denning LJ stated that the status of a representation 'depends on the conduct of the parties, on their words and behaviour, rather than on their thoughts'.[3] The reason for this is that, in the majority of cases, the parties will not have an intention concerning the legal status of a particular statement and so a subjective intention will not exist.[4] This objectivity of the test can be seen in the following case.

---

2. *Heilbut, Symons & Co v Buckleton* [1913] AC 30 (HL).
3. See *Oscar Chess Ltd v Williams* [1957] 1 WLR 370 (CA) 375.
4. Stephen Smith, *Atiyah's Introduction to the Law of Contract* (6th edn, Clarendon Press 2005) 134.

Thake v Maurice [1986] QB 644 (CA)

FACTS: Mr and Mrs Thake (the claimants) did not wish to conceive any more children, and approached the defendant surgeon to enquire about Mr Thake having a vasectomy. The surgeon explained that the procedure was irreversible, but failed to inform the Thakes that, in a small number of cases, the vasectomy might reverse itself naturally. The operation was performed and, believing it to be a success, the Thakes had unprotected sex. The procedure naturally reversed itself and, by the time that Mrs Thake realized she was pregnant, it was too late to abort the pregnancy. The Thakes sued, alleging that it was a term of the contract that the procedure would render Mr Thake sterile and that, because he was not, the surgeon had breached the contract.

HELD: The Thakes believed that the statements made by the surgeon would guarantee Mr Thake's sterility, whereas, from the surgeon's point of view, no such promise was made. Accordingly, a subjective test was of no use. Applying an objective test, the Court held that a reasonable person would know that 'the results of medical treatment are to some extent unpredictable [and] would not have left thinking that the defendant had given a guarantee that Mr Thake would be absolutely sterile'.[5] Accordingly, the claim for breach of contract failed, but, by failing to warn the Thakes of the risk of natural reversal, the surgeon had acted negligently, and so the Court awarded the Thakes £11,177.

★ See Andrew Grubb, 'Failed Sterilisation: Is a Claim in Contract or Negligence a Guarantee of Success?' (1986) 45 CLJ 197

To ensure consistency, the courts have identified a number of factors that can be taken into account, but it should be noted that these factors:

> cannot be said to furnish decisive tests, because it cannot be said as a matter of law that the presence or absence of those features is conclusive of the intention of the parties. The intention of the parties can only be deduced from the totality of the evidence, and no secondary principles of such a kind can be universally true.[6]

Timing

As a general rule, the longer the time between the making of the statement and the entering into of the contract, the less likely it will be that the statement was intended to be a term.

 Bannerman v White (1861) 10 CBNS 844

FACTS: Two parties were negotiating for the sale of hops. During negotiations, White (the defendant) indicated that he would not purchase hops that had been treated with sulphur and Bannerman (the claimant) assured White that sulphur had not been used. A short time later, a contract was concluded. It transpired that 5 of the 300 acres had been treated with sulphur. White argued that a term had been breached, thereby allowing him to terminate the contract and not pay the agreed price. Bannerman argued that, because the issue of sulphur had arisen in negotiations immediately prior to the contract being entered into, it did not constitute a term. Bannerman sued for the contract price.

HELD: The importance of the statement, and the short period of time between its making and the contract being concluded, indicated that both parties objectively intended it to amount to a term. Accordingly, White was entitled to repudiate the contract.

---

5. [1986] QB 644 (CA) 685 (Neill LJ).
6. *Heilbut, Symons & Co v Buckleton* [1913] AC 30 (HL) 50, 51 (Lord Moulton).

This principle is not absolute, however, and cases exist where the courts have found a statement to be a term, even though a protracted period existed between the statement and the contract's conclusion.[7] Similarly, the courts have found a statement to be a mere representation, even though it was only made one day before the contract was entered into.[8] Clearly, each case must be decided on its own facts.

The importance of the statement

The more important a statement is to one of the parties, the more likely it is to be a term. If a statement is of such importance that the **representee** would not have entered into the contract had the statement not been made, then the statement will almost certainly amount to a term.

→ **representee:** the party hearing the statement

 J Evans & Son (Portsmouth) Ltd v Andrea Merzario Ltd [1976] 1 WLR 1078 (CA)

FACTS: The claimant, an English company, had purchased some machinery from Italy. It engaged the defendant to arrange transport, because they had had previous dealings. As the machinery was prone to rusting, it was always stowed in crates below deck. The defendant changed its standard terms to indicate that items would be shipped in containers, not crates. The claimant agreed to the change in terms, provided that the containers were held below deck, and the defendant's representative gave oral assurances that this would be the case— but this assurance was never included in any subsequent written agreement. It transpired that the containers containing the claimant's goods were stored on deck and, owing to rough seas, two containers fell overboard and were lost. The defendant argued that it had not breached the contract, because the oral assurance never amounted to a term.

HELD: The claimant only agreed to contract with the defendant on the basis that the containers were shipped below deck. Given the importance attached to the representative's oral assurance, it was held by the Court of Appeal to be a term of the contract, and the claimant could therefore recover damages for breach of contract.

★ See JN Adams, 'Exemption Clauses Overboard! Oral Assurance and Written Exemptions: Which Wins?' (1977) 40 MLR 223

The knowledge of the parties

In many contracts (especially consumer contracts), one party will rely considerably on the knowledge of the other. Parties with specialist knowledge are much more likely to be able to ascertain the truth of a statement than a party with no knowledge. Accordingly, statements made by parties with specialist knowledge are more likely to be regarded as terms, and statements made by those without specialist knowledge are more likely to amount to mere representations, as the following case demonstrates.

 Oscar Chess Ltd v Williams [1957] 1 WLR 370 (CA)[9]

FACTS: The defendant purchased a car from the claimant car dealer and traded in his old car in part-exchange. The registration book of the old car indicated that it was a Morris 10, first registered in 1948. Based on this, the claimant offer £290 part-exchange, which

---

7. See e.g. *Schawel v Reade* [1913] 2 IR 64 (HL).   8. *Hopkins v Tanqueray* (1854) 15 CB 130.
9. See also *Dick Bentley (Productions) Ltd v Harold Smith (Motors) Ltd* [1965] 1 WLR 623 (CA), where a statement made by a car dealer regarding a car's mileage was held to be a term.

★ See O
Daly, 'Innocent
Misrepresentation or
Term of the Contract?'
(1957) 20 MLR 410

was accepted by the defendant. It transpired that the car was made in 1939 (there was no evidence that the defendant knew this) and so would have been worth only £175. The claimant sued for breach of contract to recover the £115 difference.

HELD: The Court of Appeal held that the statement indicating the car's age was a mere representation. The claimant had specialist knowledge, whereas the defendant did not, and so it was the claimant who was better placed to discover the true age of the car.

Statements of opinion

As is discussed in Chapter 10, the general rule is that statements of opinion do not even amount to representations,[10] although they may do so where the court is of the opinion that a reasonable man possessing all of the knowledge of the **representor** could not have honestly held such an opinion.[11] In limited cases, however, it would appear that a statement of opinion can amount to a term—namely, where the opinion states a fact that is difficult to verify.[12]

representor:
the party making a
statement

 The legal status of
statements of opinion
is discussed at p 240

Statements inviting verification

If the representor invites the other party to verify a statement's validity, it is highly unlikely that the statement will be regarded as a term.

Ecay v Godfrey (1947) 80 Ll L Rep 286 (KB)

FACTS: The seller of a boat assured the buyer that it was seaworthy, but advised a survey nonetheless. The buyer bought the boat and a survey subsequently discovered that it was not seaworthy.

HELD: The seller's statement advising the buyer to verify the seaworthiness of the boat negatived any intention that he might have that such statement was to be a term. Accordingly, the statement amounted to a representation.

If, however, the representor specifically states that his statement can be relied upon and that no verification is required, the court will be likely to regard such a statement as a term.

Schawel v Reade [1913] 2 IR 64 (HL)

FACTS: The claimant required a horse for stud purposes. Whilst inspecting the defendant's horse, the defendant said: 'You need not look for anything; the horse is perfectly sound. If there was anything the matter with the horse I would tell you.' Satisfied by this, the claimant purchased the horse. The horse turned out to be violent and unsuitable as a stud, and the claimant sought his money back, alleging breach of contract.

HELD: As the defendant's statement was designed to prevent the claimant from discovering the truth, the House of Lords held it to be a term and the claimant's action succeeded.

---

10. *Bisset v Wilkinson* [1927] AC 177 (PC).
11. *Smith v Land and House Property Corporation* (1884) 2 Ch D 7 (CA).
12. *Power v Barham* (1836) 4 A & E 473; cf *Jendwine v Slade* (1797) 2 Esp 571.

The parol evidence rule

As noted, where a contract is wholly in writing, identifying the express terms will be simple, but a party may still argue that it does not contain all of the terms and that additional terms were intended to be included. In order to establish this, the party will need to provide evidence indicating that additional terms were intended to form part of the contract. The ability to adduce such evidence is determined by what is known as the '**parol** evidence' rule, which provides that 'evidence cannot be admitted to add to, vary or contradict a deed or other written document'.[13] It has been correctly pointed out that to describe this as a 'rule' is somewhat misleading, because in reality, it merely establishes a presumption that a written contractual document contains all of the terms of the contract[14]—albeit a very strong one.[15] Accordingly, the presumption that a written document contains all of the terms can be rebutted if one party can show that other terms were intended to form part of the contract.

➤ **parol:** oral; not to be confused with 'parole', which means the early release of a prisoner

The rationale behind the rule is clearly to promote contractual certainty, by imposing a presumption that the only terms that can be relied on are those contained within the written document. But the rigid adherence to such a rule could result in injustice, and so the courts have established a substantial number of exceptions; so many, in fact, that the Law Commission stated that 'the exceptions were so numerous and so extensive that it might be wondered whether the rule itself had not been largely destroyed'.[16] The number of exceptions initially caused the Law Commission to recommend abolition of the rule.[17] Following consultation, however, the Law Commission altered its position and recommended its retention—but noted, correctly, that the rule 'no longer has either the width or effect once attributed to it'.[18] Exceptions or qualifications to the rule include the following.

- **Incompleteness** If the court is of the opinion that the written document was not intended to represent the full extent of the agreement between the parties, then it will permit extrinsic evidence to be adduced.[19]

- **Implied terms** The parol evidence rule applies only in the case of express terms. It does not exclude evidence being adduced that indicates that the contract contains an implied term.[20]

- **Invalidity** The rule does not apply to any evidence that casts doubt upon the validity of the written contract (for example, lack of consideration or intention,[21] incapacity, misrepresentation, or mistake).[22]

- **Rectification** The written document may have failed to reflect the true intentions of the parties. In such a case, evidence can be adduced to indicate the party's true intentions[23] and, if accepted, the court will rectify the contract accordingly.

➤ **rectification:** the correction by the court of an error in a written document

---

13. *Jacobs v Batavia and General Plantations Trust Ltd* [1924] 1 Ch 287 (CA) 295 (Lawrence J).

14. Laurence Koffman and Elizabeth Macdonald, *The Law of Contract* (7th edn, OUP 2010) 120–1.

15. *Gillespie Bros & Co v Cheney, Eggar & Co* [1896] 2 QB 59 (QB).

16. Law Commission, *Law of Contract: The Parol Evidence Rule* (Law Com No 154, Cmnd 9700, HMSO 1986) [1.3].

17. See Law Commission, *Law of Contract: The Parol Evidence Rule* (Working Paper No 70, HMSO 1976).

18. Law Commission, *Law of Contract: The Parol Evidence Rule* (Law Com No 154, Cmnd 9700, HMSO 1986) [1.7].   19. *J Evans & Son (Portsmouth) Ltd v Andrea Merzario Ltd* [1976] 1 WLR 1078 (CA).

20. *Gillespie Bros & Co v Cheney Eggar & Co* [1896] 2 QB 59 (QB).

21. *Kleinwort Benson Ltd v Malaysia Mining Corporation Berhad* [1989] 1 WLR 379 (CA).

22. *Campbell Discount Co v Gall* [1961] 1 QB 431 (CA).   23. *Murray v Parker* (1854) 19 Beav 305.

Two qualifications to the parol evidence rule deserve more detailed discussion—namely, the finding of a collateral contract and the use of 'entire agreement' clauses.

Collateral contracts

If a party cannot establish that a particular statement is a term of the contract, the court may hold that the statement actually creates a second contract, known as a 'collateral contract'. Breach of a term in a collateral contract is just as actionable as a breach of the main contract.[24]

 collateral: parallel; running side by side

> ### Birch v Paramount Estates (Liverpool) Ltd (1956) 167 EG 396 (CA)
>
> **FACTS:** The defendant housing estate developers offered a house to the claimant, claiming that it would be of the same quality as the show home. Accordingly, the claimant entered into an agreement, but the contract made no mention of the developer's statement. The house was not of the same quality as the show home and the claimant initiated proceedings
>
> **HELD:** The Court of Appeal held that the oral statement created a collateral contract, alongside the contract of sale, and accordingly awarded the claimant damages.

The use of the collateral contract has been described as 'a fudge, a cheat…[and an]…escape route'.[25] There is little doubt that they have been used effectively by the courts to avoid certain inconvenient principles of law—notably, the parol evidence rule,[26] with one commentator stating that '[i]t could be argued that the collateral contract device largely destroys the parol evidence rule'.[27]

The House of Lords has held that courts should not be too quick to find that a collateral contract exists and that such contracts 'must from their very nature be rare'.[28] There must be evidence adduced that objectively indicates an intention that the statement should form a collateral contract and not a mere representation. Failure to take a strict approach would have 'the effect of lessening the authority of written contracts by making it possible to vary them by suggesting the existence of verbal collateral agreements relating to the same subject-matter'.[29]

'Entire agreement' clauses

Parties who wish to ensure that oral statements do not become terms may attempt to do so by inserting an 'entire agreement' clause, which will normally state that the written document contains the entire terms of the contract and that no further terms can be added. An effectively drafted clause should prevent parol evidence being adduced and should also prevent any oral statements from forming the basis of a collateral contract.[30]

---

24. This is so even if the terms of the collateral contract conflict with those of the main contract (*City and Westminster Properties (1934) Ltd v Mudd* [1959] Ch 129 (Ch)).
25. Richard Taylor and Damian Taylor, *Contract Law: Directions* (4th edn, OUP 2013) 99.
26. See Lord Wedderburn, 'Collateral Contracts' [1959] CLJ 58, 69, who states that the collateral contract 'eases the consciences of those who believe that the parol evidence rule is a strict and meaningful prohibition'.   27. Edwin Peel, *Treitel on the Law of Contract* (13th edn, Sweet & Maxwell 2011) 221.
28. *Heilbut, Symons & Co v Buckleton* [1913] AC 30 (HL) 47 (Lord Moulton).   29. ibid.
30. *Inntrepreneur Pub Co v East Crown Ltd* [2000] 2 Lloyd's Rep 611 (Ch).

Implied terms

The majority of terms in a contract will usually be express, but the ability of the parties to foresee and plan for eventualities and contingencies is limited. Accordingly, even carefully drafted contracts will contain gaps of some kind. If the gaps are too large, the contract will be unenforceable on the ground of uncertainty; if the gaps are not unacceptably substantial, they may be filled by implying terms into the contract.

The implication of terms arguably runs counter to classical contract theory, which strongly advocates the exclusive right of the parties to determine the content of a contract. Accordingly, if classical theory is to be departed from, the courts will require a strong justification. The chosen justification of the court for its ability to imply terms into contracts has been 'necessity', but it can be argued that, in a number of the cases that will be examined, the implication of a term was by no means necessary. Consequently, a number of prominent commentators have argued that the rationale behind the implication of terms is not necessity, but rather the need to protect the reasonable expectations of the parties (or the courts' view of what the parties' reasonable expectations should be).[31]

Principally, implied terms fall under one of two headings, namely (i) terms implied in law; and (ii) terms implied in fact. The distinction between the two was set out neatly by Lord Denning, who began by stating that terms implied by law concern:

> all those relationships which are of common occurrence. Such as the relationship of seller and buyer, owner and hirer, master and servant, landlord and tenant…and so forth. In all those relationships the courts have imposed obligations on one party or the other, saying they are 'implied terms'. These obligations are not founded on the intention of the parties, actual or presumed, but on more general considerations…In such relationships the problem is not to be solved by asking what did the parties intend?…It is to be solved by asking: has the law already defined the obligation or the extent of it? If so, let it be followed. If not, look to see what would be reasonable in the general run of such cases.
>
> [Implied terms in fact concern] those cases which are not within the first category. These are cases—not of common occurrence—in which from the particular circumstances a term is to be implied. In these cases the implication is based on an intention imputed to the parties from their actual circumstances…Such an imputation is only to be made when it is necessary to imply a term to give efficacy to the contract and make it a workable agreement in such manner as the parties would clearly have done if they had applied their mind to the contingency which has arisen…In such cases a term is not to be implied on the ground that it would be reasonable: but only when it is necessary and can be formulated with a sufficient degree of precision.[32]

From a theoretical perspective, the implication of terms by law is problematic. As noted, classical contract law theory is based upon the notion that the terms of a contract are to be determined by the parties and not by the courts, but terms implied by the law may be completely at odds with the intentions of the parties and therefore appear to be theoretically irreconcilable with classical theory. In effect, the implication of terms in law involves the judges actually making a contract for the parties.[33]

---

31. See Lord Steyn, 'Contract Law: Fulfilling the Reasonable Expectations of Honest Men' (1997) 113 LQR 433, 441. 32. *Shell UK Ltd v Lostock Garage Ltd* [1976] 1 WLR 1187 (CA) 1196, 1197.
33. Stephen A Smith, *Contract Theory* (OUP 2004) 280.

Terms implied in fact

The court may be of the opinion that the facts of a particular case merit the implication of a term. In such a case, the court will imply a term on the basis that the parties meant to include the term, but for some reason did not. Therefore, the implication of terms in fact is the court giving recognition to the unexpressed intentions of the parties and, accordingly, can be reconciled with classical contract theory.

Over the years, the courts have established a number of tests to determine whether to imply a term in fact, with the two principal tests being the 'business efficacy' test and the 'officious bystander' test, which were established respectively in the following two cases.

 The Moorcock (1889) LR 14 PD 64 (CA)

FACTS: The defendant owned a wharf and contracted with the claimant permitting him to dock his ship at a jetty, so that goods could be loaded and unloaded. The jetty extended into the Thames and, at low tide, the ship would touch the river bed—a fact known to both parties. At low tide, the ship was grounded on a ridge of hard ground and was damaged. The defendant denied liability on the ground that there was no term in the contract guaranteeing the safety of the claimant's ship.

HELD: The Court implied a term into the contract providing that the defendant would take 'reasonable care to find out that the bottom of the river is reasonably fit for the purpose for which they agree that their jetty should be used'.[34] However, the Court stated that a term should only be implied where it is necessary to 'give such business efficacy to the transaction as must have been intended at all events by both parties who are business men'.[35]

 Shirlaw v Southern Foundries (1926) Ltd [1939] 2 KB 206 (CA)

FACTS: In 1933, Shirlaw (the claimant) entered into a contract with Southern Foundries (the defendant), which provided that he would be managing director for ten years. In 1936, Southern Foundries was taken over by another company, which changed Southern Foundries' articles of association to allow it to remove Shirlaw from the company, which it did.

HELD: The Court of Appeal implied a term that Shirlaw would not be removed in this manner before the ten-year period had expired. MacKinnon LJ stated that the court will only imply a term if it is:

> something so obvious that it goes without saying; so that, if, while the parties were making their bargain, an officious bystander were to suggest some express provision for it in their agreement, they would testily suppress him with a common 'Oh, of course!'.[36]

Unfortunately, the courts have not been consistent when explaining the relationship between the two tests. In some cases, the courts have stated that they are 'distinct tests with the result that a term may sometimes be implied on the basis of

---

34. (1889) LR 14 PD 64 (CA) 67 (Escher MR).   35. ibid 68 (Bowen LJ).
36. [1939] 2 KB 206 (CA) 227.

one but not of the other',[37] but in other cases, the courts have stated that both tests needed to be satisfied in order to imply a term.[38] Fortunately, in *Attorney General of Belize v Belize Telecom Ltd*,[39] Lord Hoffmann provided a pleasingly clear restatement of the court's approach to implying terms, stating that the court:

> is concerned only to discover what the instrument means…It follows that in every case in which it is said that some provision ought to be implied in an instrument, the question for the court is whether such a provision would spell out in express words what the instrument, read against the relevant background, would reasonably be understood to mean.[40]

Lord Hoffmann is stating that the implication of terms in fact[41] is simply part of the court's quest to interpret the terms of the contract, and that tests, such as the business efficacy and officious bystander tests, 'are best regarded, not as a series of independent tests, which must each be surmounted, but rather as a collection of different ways in which judges have tried to express the central idea that the proposed implied term must spell out what the contract actually means.'[42] Lord Hoffmann also stated that the 'question of implication arises when the instrument does not expressly provide for what is to happen when some event occurs. The most usual inference in such a case is that nothing is to happen…the loss lies where it falls.'[43] From this, it is clear that the courts will not quickly imply a term into a contract, and Lord Hoffmann's statement was not intended to relax the rules relating to implication. As Lord Clarke stated, Lord Hoffmann 'is emphasising that the process of implication is part of the process of construction, he is not in any way resiling from the often stated proposition that it must be necessary to imply the proposed term'.[44] From this strict approach, it follows that:

- A term will not be implied if it would conflict with an express term of the contract,[45] or if one party is ignorant of the facts on which the implied term would have been based.[46]
- The court is unlikely to imply a term where 'the parties have entered into a carefully drafted written contract containing detailed terms agreed between them',[47] or where it is unclear whether or not both parties would have agreed to the term, at the time that the contract was made.[48]
- The court is reluctant to imply a term in order to resolve a 'bitter and contentious' dispute.[49]

A question that has long concerned UK courts and academics is whether UK law should recognize a general requirement to act in good faith in relation to contractual

---

37. *Ashmore v Corporation of Lloyd's (No 2)* [1992] 2 Lloyd's Rep 620 (QB) 627 (Gatehouse J).

38. See e.g. *Association of British Travel Agents v British Airways plc* [2000] 1 Lloyd's Rep 169 (CA).

39. [2009] UKPC 10, [2009] 1 WLR 1988.

40. ibid [16] and [21].

41. Lord Hoffmann did not actually specify that his statements are confined to the implication of terms in fact, but this is undoubtedly the case.   42. [2009] UKPC 10, [2009] 1 WLR 1988 [27].

43. ibid [17].

44. *Mediterranean Salvage & Towage Ltd v Seamar Trading & Commerce Inc (The Reborn)* [2009] EWCA Civ 531, [2009] 2 Lloyd's Rep 639 [15].   45. *Duke of Westminster v Guild* [1985] QB 688 (CA).

46. *Spring v National Amalgamated Stevedores and Dockers Society* [1956] 1 WLR 585 (Ch).

47. *Shell UK Ltd v Lostock Garages Ltd* [1976] 1 WLR 1187 (CA) 1200 (Ormrod LJ).

48. *Luxor (Eastbourne) Ltd v Cooper* [1941] AC 108 (HL).

49. *Nicholson v Markham* (1998) 75 P & CR 428 (CA) 433 (Otton LJ).

dealings. Such a concept is common to many civil law legal systems, but English law has, to date, not recognized the existence of a general concept of good faith. However, contract law does utilize the concept of good faith in specific areas (e.g. in relation to unfair terms covered by the Unfair Terms in Consumer Contracts Regulations 1999, discussed in Chapter 9). Recent cases have also indicated a willingness to imply a duty of good faith into certain commercial contracts, with the following case being especially noteworthy.

Yam Seng Pte Ltd v International Trade Corp Ltd [2013] EWHC 111 (QB)

FACTS: In January 2009, the defendant (an English company) contacted the claimant (a company based in Singapore) with an offer to be part of a distribution agreement for certain Manchester United branded toiletries that it had 'recently signed' a licence to distribute. In fact, the defendant did not obtain the licence until May 2009, which was around the same time that the claimant signed the distribution agreement. The agreement granted the claimant the exclusive right to distribute the toiletries in certain markets for a 30-month period. Fifteen months later, the claimant terminated the contract following a series of alleged breaches by the defendant, including failing to provide the toiletries on time, providing false information, and denying the claimant the right to sell the product in certain markets covered by the agreement. The claimant then discovered the falsity of the defendant's original January 2009 statement. The claimant sued for damages for breach of contract and misrepresentation. The defendant counterclaimed that the claimant did not have the right to terminate the contract.

HELD: The claimant was awarded damages for the defendant's misrepresentation. As to the issue of termination, the court held that the defendant had breached a number of express terms that permitted the claimant to terminate the contract. However, Leggatt J also stated, *obiter*, that the defendant had breached an implied duty to act in good faith. He acknowledged that 'the general view among commentators appears to be that in English contract law there is no legal principle of good faith of general application'[50] but added that he saw 'no difficulty . . . in implying such a duty into ordinary commercial contracts based on the presumed intentions of the parties'.[51]

COMMENT: Leggatt J's *dictum*[52] that such a term is implied based on the presumed intention of the parties clearly indicates that the duty is implied in fact, and not in law. Indeed, he expressly stated that 'I doubt that English law has reached the stage . . . where it is ready to recognise a requirement of good faith as a duty implied by law, even as a default rule, into all commercial contracts.'[53] Accordingly, whether such a term will be implied will be decided on a case-by-case basis. Despite this, the case indicates the increasing role that good faith has to play across certain areas of contract law, and is an example of what Bingham LJ termed our contract law's practice of utilizing good faith to develop 'piecemeal solutions in response to demonstrated problems of unfairness.'[54]

⭐ See Simon Whittaker, 'Good Faith, Implied Terms and Commercial Contracts' (2013) 129 LQR 463.

---

50. [2013] EWHC 111 (QB), [2013] 1 All ER (Comm) 1321 [121].   51. ibid [131].
52. Support for Leggatt J's *dictum* can be found in the Court of Appeal decision in *Mid Essex Hospital Services NHS Trust v Compass Group UK and Ireland Ltd* [2013] EWCA Civ 200, [2013] BLR 265 [105] and [150].   53. [2013] EWHC 111 (QB), [2013] 1 All ER (Comm) 1321 [131].
54. *Interfoto Picture Library Ltd v Stiletto Visual Programmes Ltd* [1989] 1 QB 433 (CA) 439.

Terms implied in law

Terms implied in law can be split into two types, namely (i) terms implied by the courts; and (ii) terms implied by statute.

Terms implied by the courts

In addition to implying terms in fact, the court can also imply terms in law, which leads us to question the difference between the two. Two main differences can be advanced.

1. When courts imply terms in fact, they do so on the basis of the idiosyncratic facts of the case. Accordingly, the term is what Atiyah called an 'individualized implied term',[55] meaning that it is a 'one-off' and does not establish a precedent that such terms should be implied in all contracts of that type in the future. Conversely, a term implied by law will establish a precedent that such a term should be implied in all similar contracts in the future (what Atiyah termed a 'standardized implied term'),[56] unless the term is validly excluded by, or is inconsistent with, the contract.[57]

2. Terms implied in fact are implied based upon the unexpressed intentions of the parties. Terms implied in law are not based upon the intentions of the parties, but are obligations that are imposed upon certain commonly arising contracts as necessary incidents of them (for example, employment contracts, sale of goods contracts, etc).

These two points are evidenced in the following case.

 ### *Liverpool City Council v Irwin* [1977] AC 239 (HL)

FACTS: Liverpool City Council (the claimant) owned a dilapidated block of flats, within which Mr Irwin (the defendant) and his wife lived. The tenancy agreement imposed a number of obligations on the Irwins, but none on the Council. The lifts were inoperative, vandalism was rife, stair lighting was inadequate, and the rubbish chutes were often blocked. The Irwins therefore withheld their rent as a protest, on the ground that the Council had breached an implied term of the contract—namely, to maintain adequately the common areas of the building.

HELD: The House of Lords agreed with the Irwins and implied a duty on the Council 'to take reasonable care to keep in reasonable repair and usability'[58] the communal areas of the building. On the facts, however, the House did not believe that the term had been breached.

COMMENT: It is clear that this was a term implied in law and not a term implied in fact for two reasons.

1. Terms implied in fact are only implied in the case in question, whereas in *Liverpool*, the House stated that such a term was to be implied into all contracts involving local authority and private lettings.

2. Terms implied in fact are based upon the imputed intentions of the parties, yet it was clear that the Council did not intend such a term to be implied.

⭐ See D McIntyre, 'Implied Obligations of Landlords: High-rise Blocks' (1976) 35 CLJ 25

---

55. Stephen Smith, *Atiyah's Introduction to the Law of Contract* (6th edn, Clarendon Press 2005) 157.
56. ibid 159.   57. *Lynch v Thorne* [1956] 1 WLR 303 (CA).
58. [1977] AC 239 (HL) 256 (Lord Wilberforce).

Whilst the House may have unanimously agreed that a term should be implied, it could not agree on when such a term should be implied. Lord Cross stated that a term should be implied in law where 'in the general run of such cases the term in question would be one which it would be reasonable to insert'.[59] But Lords Edmund-Davies, Salmon, and Wilberforce were of the opinion that the 'touchstone is always necessity and not merely reasonableness'.[60] Subsequent authority has indicted that the test of necessity has prevailed, and it is now clear that two requirements must be fulfilled before the court will imply a term in law: '[T]he first requirement is that the contract in question should be a contract of a defined type…The second requirement is that the implication of the term should be necessary.'[61]

'Contracts of a defined type' refers to certain commonly occurring contracts (for example, employment contracts, contracts involving the sale of goods, contracts between landlord and tenant, etc) that are usually easy to identify. The test of 'necessity' is slightly more complex. What is clear is that the test of necessity in relation to terms implied in law is less strict than the necessity test in relation to terms implied in fact:

> [Concerning] terms implied in fact, the criterion of necessity is a truly narrow one, having regard to the specific position of the contracting parties themselves. Where terms implied in law are concerned, however, the criterion of necessity is a much broader one: the presence (or absence) of necessity is ascertained by reference to not only the category of contract concerned but also to broader policy factors.[62]

However, it is not clear exactly what these 'broader policy factors' are. Accordingly, it has been argued that, to better differentiate implied terms in law and implied terms in fact, the court should adopt a reasonableness test when implying terms in law,[63] and there is evidence that the courts may be starting to acknowledge this. In *Crossley v Faithful & Gould*,[64] Dyson LJ stated:

> rather than focus on the elusive concept of necessity, it is better to recognise that, to some extent at least, the existence and scope of standardised implied terms raise questions of reasonableness, fairness and the balancing of competing policy considerations.[65]

Perhaps the current position has been summed up best by Atiyah who, referring to *Irwin*, stated that '[i]t is obviously not strictly or literally *necessary* to have lifts in blocks of flats ten storeys high, though it would no doubt be exceedingly inconvenient not to have them. So "necessary" really seems to mean "reasonably necessary", and that must mean "reasonably necessary having regard to the context and the price".'[66]

*✐ Visit the **Online Resource Centre** for more on the implied terms contained in the Sale of Goods Act 1979 in the chapter entitled 'The sale of goods'*

Terms implied by statute

Terms that have been implied into contracts by the court may eventually be placed on a statutory footing (for example, the terms implied by ss 12–15 of the Sale of Goods Act 1979).

---

59. ibid 258.
60. ibid 266 (Lord Edmund-Davies).
61. *El Awadi v Bank of Credit and Commerce International SA* [1990] 1 QB 606 (QB) 624 (Hutchison J).
62. Andrew Phang, 'Implied Terms in English Law: Some Recent Developments' [1993] JBL 242, 246.
63. ibid 245.   64. [2004] EWCA Civ 293, [2004] ICR 1615.   65. ibid [36].
66. Stephen Smith, *Atiyah's Introduction to the Law of Contract* (6th edn, OUP 2006) 161.

The number of statutorily implied terms is too numerous to discuss in depth, but notable examples include:

- Section 13 of the Supply of Goods and Services Act 1982 implies a term into contracts for the supply of services that services provided in the course of a business will be carried out with reasonable skill and care.
- The Partnership Act 1890 implies a number of terms into the partnership agreement that are aimed at regulating the relationship between the partners.

 The terms implied by the Partnership Act 1890 are discussed in 'The relationship between the partners' at p 510

It is common for statutes implying terms to set out detailed rules regarding which contracts will qualify and which will not. Certain terms will only be implied into contracts between certain parties (for example, businesses and consumers). Some implied terms may be avoided by inserting an exclusion clause, but other implied terms are incapable of exclusion. A term will only be imposed within the confines and requirements of the statute that implies it.

Terms implied by trade usage, previous dealings, or local custom

Although terms implied in fact and terms implied in law constitute the two principal sources of implied terms, there are three other notable instances where the courts will imply a term into a contract. First, a term may be implied because it is customary within a particular trade or profession, as the following case demonstrates.

 British Crane Hire Corporation Ltd v Ipswich Plant Hire Ltd [1975] QB 303 (CA)

FACTS: The defendant hired a crane from the claimant. After the contract was concluded, the claimant sent out a document containing the terms (which were based on model terms of the relevant trade association), but the defendant never signed this document. One of the terms stated that the defendant would be responsible for recovering the crane if it were to sink on soft ground, which was what happened. The claimant sought to recover the cost of recovering the crane from the defendant. The defendant argued that, because it had not agreed to the relevant term, it was not binding upon it.

HELD: The Court held that, because the terms sent out were customary within the trade, it was implied into the contract and the claimant could obtain damages covering the cost of recovery.

Second, the court may imply terms based on the parties' previous dealings, providing that such dealings are consistent,[67] as occurred in the following case.

 Motours Ltd v Euroball (West Kent) Ltd [2003] EWHC 614 (QB)

FACTS: The claimant and defendant had contracted with each other fourteen times over an eighteen-month period, based on the defendant's standard terms—but the claimant had never read the terms. Accordingly, the claimant was unaware of a clause excluding the

---

67. It follows that, where the parties' dealings change from one course of dealing to the next, no term will be implied (*McCutcheon v David Macbrayne Ltd* [1964] 1 WLR 125 (HL)).

> defendant of all liability for consequential loss caused by breach of contract or negligence. When problems arose, the claimant initiated a claim and the defendant sought to rely on the exclusion clause.
>
> **HELD:** The High Court held that, after eighteen months, the defendant was entitled to believe that the claimant knew of the clause, and so it was implied into the contract.[68]

Third, a term may be customary within a certain geographical area, as the following case demonstrates.

 Hutton v Warren (1836) 1 M & W 466

FACTS: A tenant of a Lincolnshire farm was given notice to quit by his landlord. Given that the landlord would benefit from the produce planted by the tenant, the tenant argued that he should be compensated for the money spent on purchasing seeds and also for the hours of labour that he had invested in the farm.

HELD: Although such a term was not in the contract, it was regarded as a local custom, and so the court implied a term requiring the landlord to pay an allowance to the tenant.

The rationale behind the above implications is that, if both parties are aware of a term that is commonly included through trade usage, etc, they must have intended it to be a term of the contract. However, it should be noted that, for three reasons, establishing that such terms should be implied can be difficult:

1. A term based on trade usage, etc will not be implied if it conflicts with the express wording of the contract.[69]
2. A well-drafted entire agreements clause will prevent the implication of terms based on trade usage, etc.[70]
3. The trade usage, etc must be certain, notorious, and reasonable.[71]

The requirement of notoriety appears especially difficult to establish, because it will require 'evidence of a universal and acknowledged practice of the market'.[72]

The interpretation of contractual terms

Once the terms of the contract have been identified, they will need to be interpreted. The aim of the courts when interpreting contracts is to ascertain and put into

---

68. However, the clause could not be relied upon by the defendant, because it was deemed unreasonable under the Unfair Contract Terms Act 1977.
69. *Les Affréteurs Réunis Société Anonyme v Walford* [1919] AC 801 (HL).
70. *Exxonmobil Sales and Supply Corporation v Texaco Limited (The Helene Knutsen)* [2003] EWHC 1964 (Comm), [2003] 2 Lloyd's Rep 686.
71. *Cunliffe-Owen v Teather & Greenwood* [1967] 1 WLR 1421 (Ch).
72. *Baker v Black Sea and Baltic General Insurance Ltd* [1998] 2 All ER 833 (HL).

practice the intentions of the parties. Historically, as a result of the parol evidence rule, the courts adopted a largely literal approach, whereby courts would ascertain the parties' intentions by reference to the contract itself, giving the words used their everyday, grammatical meaning[73] and deeming extrinsic evidence inadmissible. As with statutory interpretation, however, the courts acknowledged that a literal approach was not always appropriate or helpful, and, in certain situations, the court could look outside the contract itself and take into account extrinsic factors.

This original approach was therefore principally literal, with a more purposive secondary approach in evidence where a literal approach was inappropriate or would produce an absurdity. In the case of *Investors Compensation Scheme Ltd v West Bromwich Building Society*,[74] however, Lord Hoffmann restated the principles by which contracts are to be interpreted and advocated a much more purposive approach. Lord Hoffmann's restatement consists of five principles. Before discussing these principles, we should be wary of allowing them too much weight: how a contract is interpreted is heavily dependent on the facts of the particular case, so much so that Lord Goff (who sat in the House of Lords in *Investors Compensation Scheme*) has stated extrajudicially that when interpreting contracts, examining previous case law would provide little help.[75]

Lord Hoffmann's restatement

Lord Hoffmann's first principle states that:

> Interpretation is the ascertainment of the meaning which the document would convey to a reasonable person having all the background knowledge which would reasonably have been available to the parties in the situation in which they were at the time of the contract.[76]

This principle indicates that the courts should take an objective approach to interpreting contracts. What the parties actually intended or understood is irrelevant; what is important is what a reasonable person would have understood the words to mean.

More importantly, the reasonable person can take into account 'background knowledge' and Lord Hoffmann's second principle demonstrates the breadth of such knowledge, stating that:

> Subject to the requirement that [the background knowledge] should have been reasonably available to the parties and to the exception to be mentioned next, it includes absolutely anything which would have affected the way in which the language of the document would have been understood by a reasonable man.[77]

Lord Hoffmann defines 'background knowledge' extremely widely. In fact, it could be argued that his definition is too wide and he subsequently sought to place a limit on his second principle, stating that when he restated the principles of interpretation, he 'did not think it necessary to emphasise that [he] meant anything which a reasonable man would have regarded as *relevant*'[78] and that he 'was certainly not encouraging a trawl through "background" which could not have made a reasonable person think that the parties must have departed from conventional usage'.[79]

---

73. *Lovell and Christmas Ltd v Wall* (1911) 104 LT 85 (CA).   74. [1998] 1 WLR 896 (HL).
75. Lord Goff, 'Commercial Contracts and the Commercial Court' [1984] LMCLQ 382, 385.
76. *Investors Compensation Scheme Ltd v West Bromwich Building Society* [1998] 1 WLR 896 (HL) 912.
77. ibid 912–13.   78. *BCCI v Ali* [2001] UKHL 8, [2001] 1 AC 251, [39].   79. ibid.

A further limit on what constitutes background information is found in Lord Hoffmann's third principle, which states that '[t]he law excludes from the admissible background the previous negotiations of the parties and their declarations of subjective intent'.[80] Given the objective nature of the interpretive role, this limitation is unsurprising, but excluding evidence regarding negotiations has proven extremely divisive, with both judges[81] and academics[82] arguing that there are instances in which such evidence can be extremely valuable.

Lord Hoffmann's first three principles indicate that the courts are no longer confined to examining only the contract itself and that taking into account wider background knowledge forms an essential part of their interpretive role. This would indicate that the courts are no longer limited to a literal approach and can instead interpret the words of the contract in line with relevant background information—a point emphasized by the fourth principle:

> The meaning which a document (or any other utterance) would convey to a reasonable man is not the same thing as the meaning of its words. The meaning of words is a matter of dictionaries and grammars; the meaning of the document is what the parties using those words against the relevant background would reasonably have been understood to mean. The background may not merely enable the reasonable man to choose between the possible meanings of words which are ambiguous but even…to conclude that the parties must, for whatever reason, have used the wrong words or syntax.[83]

This principle makes absolutely clear that 'contextualism is now king and is to be preferred to literalism'[84]—a sentiment that has been echoed by the judges themselves, who have stated that '[t]he tendency should therefore generally speaking be against literalism'.[85] The Supreme Court has stated that where a term is ambiguous and is capable of several different interpretations, the courts should 'adopt the interpretation which is most consistent with business common sense.'[86]

Principle 4 does not, however, mean that a literal interpretation of the words used should be abandoned, because, as Lord Hoffmann's fifth and final principle states:

> The 'rule' that words should be given their 'natural and ordinary meaning' reflects the common sense proposition that we do not easily accept that people have made linguistic mistakes, particularly in formal documents. On the other hand, if one would nevertheless conclude from the background that something must have gone wrong with the language, the law does not require judges to attribute to the parties an intention which they plainly could not have had.[87]

This principle provides that establishing the grammatical and ordinary meaning of the words used is the first step in determining the objective intentions of the parties. The courts should then take into account the relevant background information

---

80. *Investors Compensation Scheme Ltd v West Bromwich Building Society* [1998] 1 WLR 896 (HL) 913.
81. Lord Nicholls, 'My Kingdom for a Horse: The Meaning of Words' (2005) 121 LQR 577.
82. Gerard McMeel, 'Prior Negotiations and Subsequent Conduct: The Next Step Forward for Contractual Interpretation?' (2003) 119 LQR 272.
83. *Investors Compensation Scheme Ltd v West Bromwich Building Society* [1998] 1 WLR 896 (HL) 913.
84. Michael Furmston, *Cheshire, Fifoot & Furmston's Law of Contract* (16th edn, OUP 2012) 166.
85. *Sirius International Insurance Co (Publ) v FAI General Insurance Ltd* [2004] UKHL 54, [2004] WLR 3251 [19] (Lord Steyn).
86. *Rainy Sky SA v Kookmin Bank* [2011] UKSC 50, [2011] 1 WLR 2900 [30] (Lord Clarke).
87. *Investors Compensation Scheme Ltd v West Bromwich Building Society* [1998] 1 WLR 896 (HL) 913.

to determine whether this information would convey to a reasonable man a different meaning from that provided by a literal approach. Lord Hoffmann's restatement is clearly more focused on the commercial realities of a situation, as opposed to the literal wording used by the parties. That this was the role of the judiciary when interpreting contracts was recognized long before Lord Hoffmann's restatement, when, in 1984, Lord Goff stated that '[w]e are there to help businessmen, not to hinder them: we are there to give effect to their transactions, not to frustrate them: we are there to oil the wheels of commerce, not to put a spanner in the works, or even grit in the oil'.[88]

Chapter conclusion

The layperson's conception of a contract is a written document that contains the totality of the terms affecting the parties. This chapter has demonstrated that the truth is very different and that a contract can consist of more than express terms. A spoken statement of a party can become a term of a contract and additional terms can be implied into the contract from a number of different sources. It is vital that businesses are aware that they may have rights, obligations, and duties outside those specifically negotiated with the other party. Many implied terms or terms implied through trade usage, etc can be excluded via an express provision, and businesses would do well to have a thorough understanding of such terms, so that they can exclude them if they so desire.

 Key points summary

- Express terms are those terms that have been specifically agreed upon by the parties.

- When distinguishing between terms and representations, the courts will try to ascertain the parties' objective intentions. Relevant factors include the timing of the statement, the importance of the statement, the respective knowledge of the parties, and whether the representor invited the representee to verify the statement.

- The parol evidence rule states that evidence cannot be submitted that would seek to add to, or vary, the terms of a contract, but this rule only establishes a presumption that can be rebutted, and the courts have established a number of exceptions and qualifications.

- Terms may be implied into a contract by the court, statute, or by custom.

- The courts will imply terms in fact to give effect to the unexpressed intention of the parties. Implied terms in law are not based on the party's intentions.

- The courts will only apply a term in law if the contract in question falls within a number of commonly occurring contracts, and the implication of the term is 'necessary'. The courts have, however, taken a generous view regarding what is necessary.

- Terms may be implied based on customs that occur within a particular trade or profession, locality, or between customs that have arisen between the parties.

- The courts take an objective approach when interpreting contracts and interpret words based on how a reasonable person would understand them, taking into account relevant background information.

---

88. Lord Goff, 'Commercial Contracts and the Commercial Court' [1984] LMCLQ 382, 391.

Self-test questions

1. Define the following:
   (a) representation;
   (b) the parol evidence rule;
   (c) collateral contract;
   (d) entire agreement clause.

2. Dean is an antique dealer specializing in ancient Greek manuscripts. He acquires a painting that he is told is a genuine Constable. Matthew, a renowned expert in Constable paintings, walks into Dean's antique shop. Although Dean has little knowledge of Constable paintings, he states to Matthew: 'This is a genuine Constable painting and one of his finest.' Matthew purchases the painting for £3 million. It transpires that the painting is a forgery. Is Dean in breach of contract? What is the legal status of Dean's statement?

3. Why do you think the courts regard the collateral contract as such a useful device? Back up your answer with examples from case law.

4. 'The exceptions to the parol evidence rule are now so numerous that the rule should be abandoned.' Do you agree with this assertion?

5. Explain the distinction between:
   (a) express terms and implied terms;
   (b) terms and representations;
   (c) terms implied in fact and terms implied in law.

Further reading

Law Commission, *Law of Contract: The Parol Evidence Rule* (Law Com No 154, Cmnd 9700, HMSO 1986)
A clear, yet in-depth, examination of the parol evidence rule; over twenty years old, so may not reference more modern cases or include all of the exceptions

Lord Nicholls, 'My Kingdom for a Horse: The Meaning of Words' (2005) 121 LQR 577
Discusses the law's approach to the interpretation of contracts; provides arguments for and against allowing evidence of prior negotiations to be adduced, and argues that such evidence can be useful

Kelvin FK Low and Kelry CF Loi, 'The Many "Tests" for Implied Terms in Fact: Welcome Clarity' (2009) 125 LQR 561
Discusses the case of Attorney General of Belize v Belize Telecom Ltd, *and contends that this 'remarkable little gem of a judgment' provides much-needed clarity to this area of the law*

Ewan McKendrick, *Contract Law: Text, Cases and Materials* (5th edn, OUP 2012) chs 8-10
A very clear and lucid account of the law relating to express and implied terms

Andrew Phang, 'Implied Terms, Business Efficacy and the Officious Bystander: A Modern History' [1998] JBL 1

This article explores the 'business efficiency' and 'officious bystander' tests, and examines the relationship between them

Andrew Phang, 'Implied Terms in English Law: Some Recent Developments' [1993] JBL 242

Discusses the distinction between terms implied in fact and terms implied in law

 Remember to visit the **Online Resource Centre** at **<http://www. oxfordtextbooks.co.uk/orc/roach3e>** to access the following resources on Chapter 7, 'The terms of the contract': more **practice questions** and answers; a **glossary** of key terms; **multiple-choice questions; and revision summaries**. Updates to the law can be found on Twitter by following **@UKBusinessLaw.**

8 The law of agency

- What is 'agency'?
- The creation of the agency relationship
- The authority of an agent
- Contracts effected through agency
- The duties of an agent
- The rights of an agent
- The termination of agency

INTRODUCTION

Various chapters of this text have referred to the concept of 'agency' and to persons known as 'agents'. The words 'agency' and 'agent' are common words that have a very specific and important legal meaning, and the law of agency is a free-standing topic in itself. It is discussed here within the section of the text that looks at contract law because, in many cases, agency is a mechanism that helps to facilitate the process of contracting and has thus become a fundamental component of commercial dealing. Without agency, those who run and manage businesses would be required to enter personally into contracts with each and every person with whom they had dealings. The inefficiency in terms of time and cost is obvious. Agency allows those who run businesses to authorize others to enter into contracts on their behalf, thereby greatly facilitating the contractual process which, in turn, reduces costs and time spent in contractual negotiations. However, it should be noted that the role of an agent can be much wider than simply entering into contracts on the principal's behalf. Further, as will be discussed, a relationship of agency need not be contractual at all.

The first step in examining this fundamental topic is to define exactly what 'agency' is.

What is 'agency'?

Agency is a specific form of legal relationship between two persons (who may be natural or legal) whereby one person (known as the 'principal') appoints[1] another person (known as the 'agent') to act on his behalf, which will usually involve negotiating

---

1. Although, as we shall see, one type of agency (namely, agency by necessity) can arise without the need for appointment.

and entering into contracts with third parties on behalf of the principal. Once the agent's task is complete, he usually 'drops out' of the transaction, leaving a binding contract between the principal and a third party. Therefore, a typical agency transaction usually involves three persons:

1. the principal;
2. the agent; and
3. a third party.

The classic everyday example of an agency situation is that of an auction.

 Eg   The auctioneer as an agent

Jeremy (the principal) decides to sell an antique oak cabinet at auction and instructs the auctioneer, Richard (the agent), to sell it for him, but not to sell it for less than £1,000. The highest bid is made by James (the third party) and is for £1,300. The hammer falls and the sale is made. Richard, after obtaining his commission from the sale, then drops out, leaving a binding contract between Jeremy and James.

Central to the concept of agency is the agent's authority, which is discussed later. The point that should be noted here is that it is normal for the agent's authority to bind the principal to be limited in some way (in the example above, Richard's authority was limited by the imposition of a reserve price). Generally, the agent can only bind his principal where he acts within his authority. Where the agent acts outside his authority, the principal may not be bound and the agent may be contractually liable to the third party. Accordingly, had Richard sold the oak cabinet for £900, Jeremy might not have been bound to James, but Richard could be liable to James for breach of warranty of authority.

Breach of warranty of authority is discussed at p 201

Commercial agents

Historically, the law did not distinguish between different forms of agent, but due to a perceived fear that self-employed agents were vulnerable to exploitation by their principals, the Commercial Agents (Council Directive) Regulations 1993[2] were passed, which provide additional rights to 'commercial agents', who are defined as:

> a self-employed intermediary who has continuing authority to negotiate the sale or purchase of goods on behalf of another person (the 'principal'), or to negotiate and conclude the sale or purchase of goods on behalf of and in the name of that principal[3]

This definition restricts the application of the Regulations in four ways:

1. As the Regulations apply only to self-employed agents, agents who are agents by virtue of their employment will not be classified as commercial agents.
2. The phrase 'continuing authority' envisages a long-term relationship, so agents engaged for a short period of time, or to perform a single transaction, are unlikely to be classified as commercial agents.

---

2. SI 1993/3053.   3. ibid reg 2(1).

3. Only agents involved in contracts for the sale and purchase of goods will qualify—agents involved in contracts for the provision of services will not qualify.

4. The phrase 'negotiate and conclude' means that an agent who has no power to negotiate on the principal's behalf will not be a commercial agent.[4]

The various rights of commercial agents will be discussed as and when they arise in relation to a normal agency relationship.

The creation of the agency relationship

A relationship of agency can be created by express or implied agreement between principal and agent, but it can also be created without the consent of the parties. Before looking at how a relationship of agency can be created, it is important to understand how the parties' contractual capacity can affect the agency relationship.

Capacity

⌗ General contractual capacity is discussed in 'The Capacity to contract' at p 114. The contractual capacity of bodies corporate is discussed in 'Extent of a registered company's contractual capacity' at p 556

It is important to discuss whether or not the principal has contractual capacity to appoint an agent, and whether the person purporting to act as an agent has the capacity to do so. Where there is a lack of capacity, a relationship of agency can still arise, but the relationship may not be contractual.

Capacity of the principal

An agent can be appointed to enter into any transaction for which the principal has capacity.[5] Where the principal has full contractual capacity, no problems arise, but where the principal has no, or limited, capacity, the issue is more complex. As discussed in Chapter 5, the two main groups of persons who can lack full capacity are minors and mentally disordered persons.

A minor can appoint an agent to buy necessaries or make a beneficial contract of employment[6] for him, but a minor cannot enter into trading contracts merely by the interposition of an adult agent.[7] A mentally disordered person can appoint an agent to purchase or obtain necessaries, and an agent who incurs expense on behalf of a mentally disordered principal is entitled to reimbursement.

Capacity of the agent

Anyone not suffering from a mental disorder can act as an agent. A minor can act as agent in a transaction into which he would not have capacity to enter on his own behalf. For example, a father could appoint his 17-year-old son to purchase non-necessary goods on his behalf even though the son, being a minor, could not make a binding contract for non-necessary goods on his own behalf. However, an

---

4. *Parks v Esso Petroleum Co Ltd* [2000] ECC 45 (CA).

5. An exception to this is where the principal is a company, because the Companies Act 2006, s 39(1), provides that 'the validity of an act done by a company shall not be called into question on the ground of lack of capacity'.   6. *Doyle v White City Stadium* [1935] 1 KB 110 (CA).

7. *G (A) v G (T)* [1970] 2 QB 643 (CA).

agent who lacks full contractual capacity can only be made personally liable on those contracts that he would have had capacity to make on his own behalf[8] and may well not be liable on the contract of agency.

Having discussed the capacity of the parties, this part of the chapter, will move on to discuss the various methods by which a relationship of agency can be created, namely:

- agency by agreement;
- agency by ratification;
- agency by operation of law; and
- agency arising due to estoppel.

Agency by agreement

The vast majority of agency relationships are created through an agreement between the principal and agent (i.e. both parties consent to an agency relationship coming into existence). In many cases (especially in commercial agencies), the agreement will be established contractually, either orally, in writing or via the execution of a deed. However, there is no requirement that a relationship of agency be contractual, and where no contract of agency exists or where a contract does exist but lacks valid-ity,[9] then the agency is said to be 'gratuitous.' Agency by agreement is founded upon consent, not on the existence of a contract.

Most agency agreements will be express, but the courts might also find an agreement can be implied based upon the conduct of the parties.

Express agreement

A person may be appointed as an agent by express agreement with the principal. This agreement is usually, but not necessarily, a contract and the usual rules for the formation of contracts apply. For example, an agent who acts without payment will not be acting under a contract, because the principal has provided no consideration for the agent's actions.[10] The appointment can normally be made informally, even if the agent is to transact contracts that must be made, or evidenced, in writing.[11] All that is necessary is a desire to appoint *A* as agent and *A*'s consent to act as such. Where an agent is appointed as a commercial agent, he is entitled to receive, on request, a signed, written contract setting out the terms of the agency agreement and any terms subsequently agreed.[12]

The agreement that appoints an agent will usually specify the authority (that is, powers) that the principal bestows on him, but this may be extended based on the relationship between the parties or their conduct.

Implied agreement

If the parties have not expressly agreed to become principal and agent, it may be possible to find an implied agreement based on their words, conduct or relationship.

---

8. *Smally v Smally* (1700) 1 Eq Cas Abr 6.

9. For example, because sufficient consideration is not present, or because one/both of the parties lack the requisite contractual capacity.

10. *Chaudhry v Prabhakar* [1989] 1 WLR 29 (CA). A contract for gratuitous agency can exist if executed by deed.   11. *Heard v Pilley* (1869) LR 4 Ch 548.

12. Commercial Agents (Council Directive) Regulations 1993, reg 13(1). The principal has a similar right against the agent.

The key requirement is mutual consent—one party (*A*) acts in such a way towards another party (*B*), that it is reasonable for *B* to infer that *A* consents to an agency relationship arising between them. This could occur in numerous ways, including:

- The principal (*A*) might appoint the agent (*B*) to a position which would usually result in *B* having the authority to act on *A*'s behalf.[13] By being appointed to that position, *B* reasonably infers that he has *A*'s consent to act on *A*'s behalf.

- The principal may acquiesce to another person acting as his agent. However, it should be noted that there will need to be an indication that the principal has acquiesced and acquiescence will not be presumed merely because the principal remained silent.[14]

The agent (*B*) may act on behalf of the principal (*A*).[15] From this, *A* might reasonably infer that *B* has consented to act as his agent. However, it should be noted that merely carrying out the principal's instructions will not, in itself, result in the implication of an agency relationship, and that there must be some indication present that *B* was acting on *A*'s behalf.[16]

Agency by ratification

Normally, a relationship of agency is created before the agent engages in any acts on behalf of the principal. An agency relationship can, however, be created retrospectively by ratification. The following example demonstrates the typical way in which agency by ratification can come about.

> **Eg   Agency by ratification**
>
> Brian purports to act as Freddie's agent. In fact, Brian is not Freddie's agent and has no authority to act on his behalf. Brian enters into an agreement with John on Freddie's behalf. Normally, Freddie would not be bound, because Brian has no actual authority and, because Freddie has not made a representation indicating that Brian has authority, Brian does not have apparent authority. However, if Freddie chooses to do so, he can ratify Brian's act. In such a case, Freddie's ratification will retrospectively grant Brian actual authority to enter into the contract with John.[17] The contract will therefore be binding on Freddie if he ratifies Brian's actions.

The idea that an agent is granted retrospective authority is, of course, a 'wholesome and convenient fiction',[18] but it is a fiction that gives effect to the common wishes of the parties involved and is therefore justified. However, the ability to contractually bind others without having the requisite authority could, if not monitored closely, have an adverse effect upon the doctrine of privity of contract. Accordingly, agency by ratification is subject to a number of restrictions and conditions:

🔗 Privity of contract is discussed at p 118

1. The principal must exist at the time that the agent purported to act as an agent. Ratification will not occur where a purported agent enters into a contract on behalf

---

13. *Pole v Leask* (1863) 33 LJ Ch 155.
14. *Burnside v Dayrell* (1849) 3 Ex 224.   15. *Roberts v Ogilby* (1821) 9 Price 269.
16. *Kennedy v De Trafford* [1897] AC 180 (HL).
17. *Bolton Partners v Lambert* (1889) 41 Ch D 295 (CA).
18. *Keighley, Maxsted & Co v Durant* [1901] AC 240 (HL) 247 (Lord Macnaghten).

of a principal who will exist in the future and who will ratify his actions. Thus, where a purported agent enters into a contract on behalf of a company that has not yet been incorporated, subsequent ratification by the company will be ineffective[19] and the purported agent will be personally liable on the pre-incorporation contract, unless personal liability has been excluded by the agreement.[20] The company will need to create a new contract to take the benefit of it.[21]

2. The agent must purport to act as an agent for a disclosed principal. Ratification will not occur where an agent has not revealed that he is acting as an agent (that is, he has not disclosed that he has a principal).[22]

3. Only the principal can ratify the actions of the purported agent.[23] Where the ratification is by conduct, the principal must be aware of all of the material facts,[24] or intend to ratify irrespective of such facts.[25]

4. In order to ratify, the principal must have had contractual capacity to enter into the contract on the date on which the agent entered into the contract[26] and at the time at which ratification takes place.[27]

5. The principal must have a choice whether or not to ratify. Where the principal has no choice but to accept the benefit conferred by the acts of the purported agent, this will not constitute ratification. For example, where an agent has had unauthorized repairs done on a ship, merely retaking the ship with these repairs is not ratification by the principal.[28]

6. An act that is void in law or an act contrary to statute cannot be ratified.[29]

7. Ratification must take place within a reasonable time.[30] What is reasonable is a question of fact in every case, but if the time for performance of a contract has passed, ratification is impossible.[31]

8. Ratification will not be permitted where it would defeat the vested property right of a third party,[32] or unfairly prejudice him in some manner.[33]

Method and effect of ratification

The easiest form of ratification is express affirmation of the purported agent's unauthorized acts by the principal.[34] Ratification need not take any special form, except where the agent executed a deed. In such a case, ratification must also be by deed.[35] Ratification can also occur by conduct, but it would appear that passive acceptance or acquiescence may be insufficient.[36]

Where ratification takes place, the ratified act is regarded as authorized at the time the agent performed it and the agent is regarded as having actual authority to

---

19. *Kelner v Baxter* (1866) LR 2 CP 174.   20. Companies Act 2006, s 51(1).

21. *Howard v Patent Ivory Manufacturing Co* (1888) 38 Ch D 156 (Ch).

22. *Keighley, Maxsted & Co v Durant* [1901] AC 240 (HL) 247.

23. *Wilson v Tumman* (1843) 6 Man & G 236.   24. *The Bonita; The Charlotte* (1861) 1 Lush 252.

25. *Marsh v Joseph* [1897] 1 Ch 213 (CA).

26. *Boston Deep Sea Fishing and Ice Co Ltd v Farnham* [1957] 1 WLR 1051 (Ch).

27. *Grover & Grover Ltd v Mathews* [1910] 2 KB 401 (KB).

28. *Forman & Co Pty Ltd v The Liddesdale* [1900] AC 190 (PC).

29. *Re Tiedemann and Ledermann Frères* [1899] 2 QB 66 (QB).

30. *Re Portuguese Consolidated Copper Mines Ltd, ex p Bosanquet* (1890) 45 Ch D 16 (CA).

31. *Metropolitan Asylums Board of Managers v Kingham & Sons* (1890) 6 TLR 217.

32. *Bird v Brown* (1850) 4 Ex 786.

33. *Smith v Henniker-Major* [2002] EWCA Civ 762, [2003] Ch 182.

34. *Soames v Spencer* (1822) 1 Dow & Ry KB 32.   35. *Hunter v Parker* (1840) 7 M & W 322.

36. *Hughes v Hughes* (1971) 221 Estates Gazette 145 (CA).

perform such an act.[37] Ratification only affects past acts of the agent—it does not provide him with authority to repeat such acts in the future,[38] although repeated ratification may provide the agent with implied or apparent authority to engage in the ratified acts.[39] Since the acts of the agent are retrospectively validated, the agent cannot be liable to a third party for breach of warranty of authority, nor can he be liable to the principal for acting outside the scope of his authority,[40] and he can claim commission and an indemnity.[41]

Agency by operation of law

In several cases, an agency relationship may be imposed upon the parties by the operation of law. In such cases, the fact that the parties do not intend or wish for an agency relationship to arise is irrelevant. It does not follow, however, that the agency relationship is not consensual, as the law will deem that the parties consented, even if, in fact, they did not do so.

Agency of necessity

Agency of necessity arises where there is some pressing need for action to safeguard the interests of another. In such a case, the courts might be willing to deem that the person acted as an agent to safeguard the interests of a principal, as the following example demonstrates.

 Agency of necessity

FoodCorp plc charters a ship to transport a cargo of wheat from the UK to India. En route, the ship becomes stranded on a reef, and the shipmaster enters into a salvage agreement with CargoSave Ltd. CargoSave manages to salvage 15,000 tonnes of wheat and, to protect the wheat from deterioration, it arranges for it to be stored at its own expense. CargoSave then bills FoodCorp for the salvage costs and the storage costs. FoodCorp refuses to pay the storage costs. In such a case, the court would be likely to find that a relationship of agency exists by virtue of necessity, thereby requiring FoodCorp to pay the storage costs too.

Agency by necessity will only arise where four criteria are met,[42] namely:

1. the agent's actions must be necessary;
2. it is not reasonably practicable for the agent to communicate with the principal to seek instructions (given the technological advances in mobile communications, this requirement may be difficult to satisfy);
3. the agent's actions should be performed bona fide in the principal's interests;
4. the agent's actions must be reasonable and prudent.

---

37. *Bolton Partners v Lambert* (1889) 41 Ch D 295 (CA).
38. *Irvine v Union Bank of Australia* (1877) 2 App Cas 366 (PC).
39. *Midland Bank Ltd v Reckitt* [1933] AC 1 (HL).   40. *Smith v Cologan* (1788) 2 Term Rep 188n.
41. *Hartas v Ribbons* (1889) 2 QBD 254 (CA).
42. *Industrie Chimiche Italia Centrale and Cerealfin SA v Alexander G Tsavliris & Sons Maritime Co (The Choko Star)* [1990] 1 Lloyd's Rep 516 (CA) 525 (Slade LJ).

Agency imposed by statute or the courts

An agency relationship may be imposed upon certain parties by statute. Examples include:

- Every partner in an ordinary partnership is an agent of the firm and of his fellow partners for the purposes of the business of the partnership.[43] Similarly, every member of a limited liability partnership is an agent of the limited liability partnership.[44]

- The administrator of a company is an agent of the company,[45] as is a receiver[46] and an administrative receiver.[47]

- In certain regulated consumer credit agreements, the person negotiating with the debtor will be deemed to be acting as an agent for the creditor.[48]

A relationship of agency may also, based upon the particular facts of the case, be imposed upon certain parties by the courts. For example, it is well established that while the directors of a company are agents of the company, they are not normally agents of the company's members.[49] However, in limited situations (e.g. where the directors act for the members in selling their shares),[50] the courts have held that the directors can be acting as agents of the members.

Agency arising due to estoppel

An agent may be imbued with authority where his principal represents to a third party that the agent has authority to act in a particular way. In such a case, the agent may be imbued with apparent authority, and the principal may be estopped from denying that an agency relationship exists. The use of estoppel as the theoretical basis of apparent authority has been described as 'shaky'[51] and 'artificial',[52] principally on the ground that many cases of apparent authority do not fully satisfy the requirements for estoppel. Despite this, it is now generally accepted that estoppel does form the basis of apparent authority, albeit a form of estoppel 'with weak requirements, special to agency'.[53] Apparent authority and its basis in estoppel are discussed later in this chapter. All that need be noted here is that estoppel can serve to extend an agent's authority or to create a relationship of agency where none previously existed.

The authority of an agent

Repeated mention has been made of an agent's ability to enter into legally binding agreements on behalf of his principal. The general rationale behind holding such agreements as binding is that the principal has consented to the agent acting in such

---

43. Partnership Act 1890, s 5.

44. Limited Liability Partnerships Act 2000, s 6(1).   45. Insolvency Act 1986, Sch B1, para 69.

46. ibid s 57(1). The receiver will only be an agent in relation to the property that is attached to the floating charge by which he was appointed.

47. ibid s 44(1)(a). Note that an administrative receiver will not be an agent of the company if the company is in liquidation.   48. Consumer Credit Act 1974, s 56(2).

49. *Gramophone and Typewriter Ltd v Stanley* [1908] 2 KB 89 (CA).

50. *Allen v Hyatt* (1914) 30 TLR 444 (PC).

51. Roderick Munday, *Agency: Law and Principles* (OUP 2010) 61.

52. Peter G Watts, *Bowstead & Reynolds on Agency* (19th edn, Sweet & Maxwell 2010) [8-029].

53. ibid [2-100].

a way by bestowing authority upon the agent to act on his behalf. It follows that the authority of an agent is a central concept of the law of agency, with two principal types of authority being identifiable, namely actual authority and apparent authority. There is a third form of authority, known as usual authority, but, as will be seen, the reasoning behind the cases that established this form of authority is highly suspect.

Actual authority

The classic definition of actual authority was provided by Diplock LJ who stated that:

> An actual authority is a legal relationship between the principal and agent created by a consensual agreement to which they alone are parties. Its scope is to be ascertained by applying ordinary principles of construction of contracts, including any proper implications from the express words used, the usages of the trade, or the course of business between the parties.[54]

This definition indicates that there are two types of actual authority:

1. Express actual authority, which refers to the authority that the principal has expressly bestowed upon the agent, either orally or in writing.
2. Implied actual authority, which refers to authority that the law deems to have been bestowed by the principal upon the agent as a result of their dealings, circumstances, or relationship.

Both forms of actual authority will now be discussed.

Express actual authority

The simplest form of authority is express actual authority, whereby the agency agreement expressly delineates the authority of the agent. The extent of an agent's express actual authority is a matter of construction of the agency agreement, but the courts will not require every possible transaction to be expressly provided for in order for express authority to exist.[55] Where express authority is ambiguous and has several meanings, the agent may be deemed to have express authority if he acts on a bona fide interpretation.[56] However, where the agent is capable of contacting the principal to clarify the meaning of the ambiguous provision, a failure to do so may very well place the act outside the scope of the agent's express authority.[57]

Implied actual authority

The actual authority of the agent can also be implied based on the relationship between the principal and agent, or based on their conduct.

 Hely-Hutchinson v Brayhead Ltd [1968] 1 QB 549 (CA)

FACTS: Richards (the agent) was chairman of the defendant company (the principal) and, although he was not formally appointed as the company's managing director, he acted in this role with the board's acquiescence. Richards, on the defendant's behalf, agreed to indemnify the claimant (the third party) for any loss in relation to a number of loans made by the claimant

---

54. *Freeman & Lockyer v Buckhurst Park Properties (Mangal) Ltd* [1964] 2 QB 480 (CA) 503.
55. *SMC Electronics Ltd v Akhter Computers Ltd* [2001] 1 BCLC 433 (CA).
56. *Ireland v Livingstone* (1872) LR 5 HL 395 (HL).
57. *European Asian Bank AG v Punjab and Sind Bank (No 2)* [1983] 1 WLR 642 (CA) 656 (Goff LJ).

Relationships between the principal and third party

Where the agent has authority to contract with a third party on behalf of his principal, the resulting contract is known as an 'authorized contract'. An authorized contract is deemed to be between the principal and the third party—the agent drops out of the picture once he has effected the contract. Therefore, only the principal and third party can generally enforce the contract, but there are instances in which the agent can sue and be sued on the contract. It will depend primarily on whether or not the principal is disclosed or undisclosed.

The disclosed principal

A disclosed principal is one whose existence, although not necessarily his identity, is known to the third party at the time that the agent makes the contract. In other words, where the third party knows that he is dealing with an agent, the principal will be disclosed.[79] Where the principal is disclosed, a contract is formed between the principal and the third party, on which either party can sue and be sued. There are, however, two exceptions to this rule:

1. Where the agent contracts by deed **inter partes**, the principal will not be a party to it unless it is executed in his name and he is described as being party to it.[80]

   ➔ *inter partes*: 'between the parties'

2. A principal cannot be made liable for any **negotiable instrument** that he has not signed.[81]

   ➔ **negotiable instrument**: a transferable document that promises to pay the bearer a sum of money at a future date (for example, a cheque)

As the principal is disclosed, the doctrine of privity will normally prevent the third party from suing the agent or vice versa, but, as shall be seen, there are several situations in which an agent can enforce the contract against, or is jointly liable with his disclosed principal towards, a third party.

The undisclosed principal

Where the third party does not know the principal exists (that is, he is not aware that he is dealing with an agent), the principal is said to be 'undisclosed'. In such a situation, it would be assumed that no contract would be created between the third party and the undisclosed principal, and that neither party could commence enforcement proceedings against the other, but this is not the case. Where an agent enters into a contract on behalf of an undisclosed principal, a contract is formed between the undisclosed principal and the third party, which both can enforce.[82] As the third party believed that he was dealing with the agent, allowing the principal to sue and be sued on the contract appears contrary to privity of contract. How does the law justify a rule that 'is inconsistent with the elementary doctrines of the law of contract'?[83]

Although several reasons have been advanced, the accepted view appears to be the simplest—namely, that the rule relating to an undisclosed principal constitutes an exception to the privity rule created as a matter of 'commercial convenience'.[84]

---

79. *Langton v Waite* (1868) LR 6 Eq 165.

80. *Re International Contract Co v Pickering's* (1871) LR 6 Ch App 525.

81. Bills of Exchange Act 1882, s 23.

82. *Montgomerie v United Kingdom Mutual Steamship Association* [1891] 1 QB 370 (QB).

83. Sir Frederick Pollock (1887) 3 LQR 358, 359.

84. *Siu Yin Kwan v Eastern Insurance Co Ltd* [1994] 2 AC 199 (PC) 207 (Lord Lloyd).

Given that the rule relating to the undisclosed principal existed before the doctrine of privity was fully established, this seems justified. However, because this rule can result in a third party being contractually bound to a principal that he did not know existed, or with which he would not have wished to contract, the rule is subject to a number of conditions and restrictions:

- the principal cannot enforce the contract where it expressly[85] or impliedly[86] prohibits his intervention;
- the principal cannot enforce the contract where he lacked capacity or, in the case of a body corporate, where it did not exist at the time that the agent contracted;
- the principal cannot enforce the contract if the third party can establish that he wanted to contract personally with the agent (for example, because the agent has a certain skill or reputation);[87]
- the principal cannot enforce the contract where his intervention would materially worsen the legal position of the third party;[88]
- the principal cannot enforce the contract against a third party where the third party has a defence against the agent;[89]
- the principal cannot enforce the contract where the third party can demonstrate some good reason for not wanting to contract with the undisclosed principal, or where the principal knows that the third party would not wish to deal with him, as occurred in the following case.

 Said v Butt [1920] 3 KB 497 (KB)

FACTS: The claimant (the undisclosed principal) was a theatre critic, who wished to see the first-night performance of a play in a theatre managed by the defendant. However, the claimant had previously made serious and unfounded allegations against members of the theatre staff, and so knew that his application for a ticket would be refused. He therefore asked a friend (the agent) to purchase a ticket for him, but not to disclose whom it was for. When the claimant attended the opening night of the play, the defendant refused him admission. The claimant alleged that, in refusing entry, the defendant had maliciously procured the proprietors of the theatre (the third party) to breach their contract with the claimant.

HELD: There was no contract between the claimant and the proprietors of the theatre. The identity of the undisclosed principal was a material factor and a ticket would not have been sold to him had his identity been disclosed.

Where the principal is undisclosed, the result is largely the same as where he is disclosed (that is, a contract exists between himself and the third party, which can usually be enforced by either party). There is, however, a notable difference, namely that where the principal is undisclosed, the agent is also personally liable on the contract, and can sue and be sued on it.[90] This is entirely justifiable, because the third

---

85. *United Kingdom Mutual Steamship Assurance Association v Nevill* (1887) 19 QBD 110 (CA).
86. *Humble v Hunter* (1848) 12 QB 310.
87. *Collins v Associated Greyhounds Racecourses Ltd* [1930] 1 Ch 1 (CA). 88. ibid.
89. *Isaac Cook & Sons v Eshelby* (1887) 12 App Cas 271 (HL).
90. *Siu Yin Kwan v Eastern Insurance Co Ltd* [1994] 2 AC 199 (PC).

party believed that it was the agent that he was contracting with. The third party may elect to sue either the undisclosed principal or the agent.[91]

Relationships between the agent and third party

As discussed, where the principal is disclosed, the agent is not party to the contract and cannot generally be sued on it. This is, however, subject to exceptions and there are several instances in which an agent is liable under, and can enforce, a contract either alone or jointly with his disclosed principal, including:

- An agent can be liable on a contract where the contract expressly or impliedly indicates this to be the intention of the parties. In some cases, statute will imply such an intention. For example, s 5 of the Partnership Act 1890 provides that a partner who contracts on behalf of the partnership is jointly liable on that contract along with the other partners.

  Section 5 of the Partnership Act 1890 is discussed in more detail at p 519

- Where a contract is executed by deed, an agent will be liable on it, even where the third party knows that the agent is acting as an agent.[92] As discussed earlier, the principal will not be liable on such a contract unless it was executed in his name and it provides that he shall be a party to it.

- An agent will be liable on a contract where a trade or local custom provides that the agent should be liable,[93] unless the custom is inconsistent with the contract.

- There may be instances in which an agent is acting for himself and not for his principal, even though he may purport to be acting for an unnamed principal. In such a case, the agent is liable on the contract.[94]

- Where the agent acts for a principal who does not yet exist, the agent is liable if he intended to assume personal liability.[95] Where the non-existent principal is a company that has yet to be incorporated, the agent will be liable on the contract unless he can establish an agreement to the contrary[96] and, as noted, the company cannot ratify the contract on incorporation.

Breach of warranty of authority

In addition to a right to sue on the contract, the third party might also be able to sue the agent for breach of warranty of authority. Such a breach occurs where a person, knowing that he has no actual authority, represents to a third party that he has authority[97] and the third party, in reliance on that representation, sustains a loss.[98] The rule is a strict one and, as the following case demonstrates, an agent will be in breach even where he honestly, but mistakenly, believes that he has authority.

 Yonge v Toynbee [1910] 1 KB 215 (CA)

FACTS: The defendant (the principal) had been threatened with legal proceedings alleging that he had defamed the claimant (the third party). The defendant engaged a firm of solicitors (the agent) to defend the action. Before the action commenced, and unknown to

---

91. *Paterson v Gandasequi* (1812) 15 East 62.
92. *Schack v Anthony* (1813) 1 M & S 573.
93. *Barrow & Bros v Dyster, Nalder & Co* (1884) 13 QBD 635 (DC).
94. *Bickerton v Burrell* (1816) 5 M & S 383.   95. *Kelner v Baxter* (1886) LR 2 CP 174.
96. Companies Act 2006, s 51(1).
97. Simply acting as an agent will constitute such a representation.
98. *Collen v Wright* (1857) 8 E & B 647.

→ **interlocutory**
proceedings:
proceedings that are
incidental to the main
object of the cause of
action

the solicitors, the defendant was certified as insane. The action proceeded and the solicitors delivered a defence in **interlocutory proceedings**. The solicitors and the claimant then discovered that the defendant had been certified insane. The claimant argued that the solicitors should personally pay his costs to date on the ground that they had acted without authority.

HELD: The solicitors were required to pay the claimant's costs. The defendant's certification of insanity had terminated their authority and they had accordingly breached their warranty of authority. The fact that they did not know their authority was terminated was irrelevant.

The harshness of the decision in *Yonge* is mitigated by several factors:

- no breach will lie where the third party knew, or ought to have known, that the agent lacked authority;[99]
- no breach will be committed where the principal ratifies the agent's act;
- the representation must be one of fact, not law[100]—although, given the abolition of the distinction in other areas of contract law (that is, misrepresentation and mistake), it remains to be seen whether this limitation will be upheld in the future.

Where a breach does occur, the third party will be entitled to damages, calculated by reference to the amount required to put the third party in the position in which he would have been had the representation been true.[101] Normally, damages are assessed on the date of the breach, but the courts will abandon this rule if it is appropriate to do so, as occurred in the following case.

Habton Farms v Nimmo [2003] EWCA Civ 68

FACTS: The defendant (the agent) was a bloodstock agent (that is, someone who purchases and sells horses on behalf of others). He purchased a horse from the claimant (the third party) for £70,000, claiming that the purchase was on behalf of a racehorse owner named Williamson (the principal). The agent lacked the authority to purchase horses on Williamson's behalf and Williamson refused to accept the horse. The claimant refused to sell the horse to anyone else and continued to press for payment. Around four weeks later, after the delivery date, the horse contracted peritonitis and died. The claimant sued for recovery of the £70,000. The defendant argued that, at the time of his breach of warranty of authority, the horse was still worth £70,000, so the claimant had lost nothing and damages should therefore be nil.

HELD: The claimant was awarded the full £70,000. Auld LJ stated that '[i]f the contract had proceeded, [the claimant] would have divested himself of the ownership, possession and risk of harm to the horse in return for the price some four weeks before the horse had to be put down'.[102]

★ See CA Hopkins,
'Damages for Breach
of Warranty of
Authority' (2003) 62
CLJ 559

COMMENT: In *Habton Farms*, the claimant refused to accept the principal's termination and therefore the normal rule of assessing damages at the date of breach was not appropriate. Conversely, where the claimant accepts the termination, assessing damages at the date of breach is likely to be more appropriate.

---

99. *Halbot v Lens* [1901] 1 Ch 344 (Ch).   100. *Rashdall v Ford* (1866) LR 2 Eq 750.
101. *Simons v Patchett* (1857) 7 E & B 568.   102. [2003] EWCA Civ 68, [2004] QB 1 [127].

Tort

An agent may also be liable in tort to a third party (for example, for deceit or negligent misstatement), even where the principal is vicariously liable for the tortious act.

The duties of an agent

Irrespective of how a relationship of agency is created, an agent will be subject to a number of duties imposed upon him by the law (where agency is created by express agreement, the agency agreement is likely to contain further duties). Whilst the duties imposed by the law cannot conflict with the duties contained in an express agreement, they are nevertheless independent of such agreements and will apply even after a contract of agency has been terminated.[103] In the case of a commercial agent, the Commercial Agents (Council Directive) Regulations 1993 impose a number of duties, which cannot be excluded by the parties.

Failure to comply with a contractual duty or the general duties imposed by the law will normally disentitle the agent from any remuneration to which he would otherwise be entitled, and may also render him liable to pay damages for breach of contract (if there is an agency contract) or in tort.

Duty to act

A paid agent is under a duty to do any act required by the contract of agency, other than an act that is illegal or void,[104] and any loss suffered by the principal because of failure to fulfil this duty (either through non-performance or defective performance) is recoverable from the agent by the principal. Thus, where an agent was engaged to insure the principal's ship and he failed to do so, the principal could sue the agent for breach of contract when the uninsured ship was lost.[105]

Where the agent is a commercial agent, he is under a duty to 'make proper efforts to negotiate and, where appropriate, conclude the transactions he is instructed to take care of'.[106]

A gratuitous agent is not subject to the duty to act, but if he chooses to act and does so in a negligent manner, he will be liable in tort.[107]

Duty to perform personally

Related to the duty to act is the general requirement that the agent must perform the act personally and not delegate it to another, unless (i) such delegation is expressly authorized by the principal;[108] (ii) where such a power can be implied; (iii) where the act required is one of skill that requires the services of another; or (iv) where delegation becomes necessary.

Even where an agent is authorized to appoint a subagent to carry out his instructions, it is presumed that the person appointed is merely an agent of the agent. He

---

103. *Kelly v Cooper* [1993] AC 205 (PC).   104. *Cohen v Kittell* (1889) 22 QBD 680 (QB).
105. *Turpin v Bilton* (1843) 5 Man & G 455.
106. Commercial Agents (Council Directive) Regulations 1993, reg 3(2)(a).
107. *Wilkinson v Coverdale* (1793) 1 Esp 74.   108. *De Bussche v Alt* (1878) 8 Ch D 286 (CA).

does not, unless clear evidence indicates otherwise, become an agent of the principal.[109] Consequently, the subagent has no claim against the principal for remuneration or indemnity, nor does he owe the principal any duty to act or to obey instructions. It seems that a subagent who knew both of the existence and of the identity of the principal could owe the principal a duty of care under the normal principles of negligence,[110] and might owe the principal fiduciary duties.[111]

Duty to obey instructions

The primary obligation imposed on an agent is to act strictly in accordance with the instructions of his principal in so far as they are lawful and reasonable. Where the agent is a commercial agent, he is under a duty to 'comply with reasonable instructions given by his principal'.[112] An agent has no discretion to disobey his principal's instructions, even if he honestly and reasonably believes disobedience to be his principal's best interests.[113] When an agent carries out his instructions, he cannot be liable for loss suffered by the principal because the instructions were at fault.[114] If the principal's instructions are not complied with, the agent will be responsible to his principal for any loss thereby suffered, even if the loss is not occasioned by any fault on his part.[115] If the instructions are ambiguous, however, the agent will not breach this duty if he makes a reasonable, but incorrect, interpretation of them.[116] If the instructions confer a discretion on an agent, he will not be liable for failure to obey them if he exercises that discretion reasonably.[117]

Duty to exercise care and skill

A paid agent is required to display reasonable care in carrying out his instructions and also, where appropriate, such skill as may reasonably be expected from a member of his profession.[118] Should he fail to do so, he will be liable for any consequential loss that his principal suffers.

The standard of care that can be expected from a gratuitous agent is similar, namely to exercise such care and skill as could reasonably be expected in the circumstances.

 ### Chaudhry v Prabhakar [1989] 1 WLR 29 (CA)

FACTS: The claimant (the principal), who had just passed her driving test, asked the defendant (the gratuitous agent), a friend of hers, to locate for her a second-hand car, stipulating that the car should not have been involved in an accident. The defendant was

---

109. *Calico Printers' Association Ltd v Barclays Bank Ltd* (1931) 145 LT 51 (CA).

110. *Henderson v Merrett Syndicates Ltd* [1995] 2 AC 145 (HL).

111. *Powell and Thomas v Evan Jones & Co* [1905] 1 KB 11 (CA); cf *New Zealand and Australian Land Co v Watson* (1881) 7 QBD 374 (CA).

112. Commercial Agents (Council Directive) Regulations 1993, reg 3(2)(c).

113. *Bertram, Armstrong & Co v Godfray* (1830) 1 Knapp 381 (PC).

114. *Overend, Gurney & Co v Gibb* (1872) LR 5 HL 480.   115. *Lilley v Doubleday* (1881) 7 QBD 510.

116. *Weigall & Co v Runciman & Co* (1916) 85 LJ KB 1187 (CA).

117. *Boden v French* (1851) 10 CB 886.

118. The Supply of Goods and Services Act 1982, s 13, makes the exercise of reasonable care and skill an implied term of all contracts of agency, provided that the agent is acting in the course of a business.

not a mechanic, but was a keen amateur enthusiast. He located a car and recognized that the bonnet had been straightened or repaired, but did not enquire as to whether the car had been involved in an accident. He recommended the car to the claimant, who purchased it. Subsequently, it was discovered that the car had been involved in an accident and was a valueless insurance write-off.

HELD: In failing to question the vendor regarding the repaired bonnet, the defendant had failed to fulfil the duty to exercise reasonable care and skill that he owed as a gratuitous agent.

COMMENT: Counsel for the defendant had conceded that the defendant was acting as a gratuitous agent and owed such a duty to the claimant, but May LJ thought that such a concession should not be made in a social context. This implies that a duty will not be owed in all circumstances, but May LJ did not specify when a duty would not be owed. It could be argued that, in such a case, there is no need to establish a relationship of agency and the matter could be dealt with via the law of negligence.

Duty to provide information

Since the agent has the ability to effect contractual relations between his principal and a third party, it is important that the agent provides adequate information to the principal. A commercial agent is also under a duty to 'communicate to his principal all the necessary information available to him'.[119] This duty could even extend to providing the principal with a right to inspect the books and records of his agent.[120]

Fiduciary duties

Unless excluded by the agency agreement,[121] every agent owes fiduciary duties to his principal. This is a consequence of the trust and confidence that should exist between a principal and his agent, and because the agent has the power to affect the principal's legal position. Whereas the other duties are positive duties (that is, they tell an agent what he should do), fiduciary duties are negative (that is, they tell an agent what he should not do). It is important to note that an agent may breach his fiduciary duties, and be liable for such breach, even where he is acting completely innocently[122]—although, in some cases, an agent may be able to recover commission.

Conflict of interest

Lord Cairns, in *Parker v McKenna*,[123] stated: 'No man can in…acting as an agent, be allowed to put himself into a position in which his interest and his duty will be in conflict.' Where an agent's own interests come into conflict with those of his principal, he must make a full disclosure to the principal of all relevant facts, so that the principal may decide whether to continue with the transaction. It is this rule that prevents an agent, in the absence of disclosure, from selling his own property to

---

119. Commercial Agents (Council Directive) Regulations 1993, reg 3(2)(b).

120. *Yasuda Fire and Marine Insurance Co of Europe Ltd v Orion Marine Insurance Underwriting Agency Ltd* [1995] QB 174 (QB).

121. The requirement imposed upon commercial agents to look after the interests of their principals and act in good faith (found in the Commercial Agents (Council Directive) Regulations 1993, reg 3(1)) cannot be excluded by the agency agreement. 122. *Keppel v Wheeler* [1927] 1 KB 577 (CA).

123. (1874) LR 10 Ch 96, 118.

the principal,[124] purchasing the principal's property for himself,[125] acting as agent for both parties to a transaction,[126] or receiving commission from a third party.[127]

If the agent is in breach of this duty, the principal may have any resulting transaction set aside, claim any profit accruing to the agent, and refuse to pay commission.[128]

Secret profits and bribes

Where an agent, in the course of the agency, and without his principal's knowledge and consent, makes a profit for himself out of his position or his principal's property, or out of information with which he is entrusted by virtue of his agency, he must account for this profit to the principal.[129] Thus, an agent may not accept commission from both parties to a transaction,[130] nor keep for himself the benefit of a trade discount while charging his principal the full price,[131] without the principal's informed consent. It makes no difference that the agent has acted honestly throughout, nor even that his actions have conferred substantial benefits upon the principal.[132]

Where the secret profit takes the form of a payment from a third party, who is aware that he is dealing with an agent, it is called a 'bribe'—even if the payment is not made with any unmeritorious motive and even if the principal suffers no loss thereby.[133] Accordingly, acts of corporate hospitality could constitute bribes in this sense. The taking of a bribe entitles the principal to:

- dismiss the agent;[134]
- recover either the amount of the bribe or his actual loss (if greater) from the agent or third party;[135]
- refuse to pay commission;
- repudiate any transaction in respect of which the bribe was given (provided that he can return to any third party any contractual benefits that he has received);[136]
- where an agent has taken a bribe and used the money to good effect so that he has increased its value, to claim not only the amount of the bribe, but also any increase in its value.[137]

Duty to account

The agent is under a duty to keep his own property separate from that of his principal. Where the agent fails to do this, the principal will be entitled to all of the property, unless the agent can establish which property belongs to him. Related to

---

124. *Gillett v Peppercorne* (1840) 3 Beav 78.   125. *McPherson v Watt* (1877) 3 App Cas 254 (HL).
126. *Harrods Ltd v Lemon* [1931] 2 KB 157 (CA).
127. *Hurstanger Ltd v Wilson* [2007] EWCA Civ 299, [2007] 1 WLR 2351.
128. Note that in *Kelly v Cooper* [1993] AC 205 (PC), the court suggested, *obiter*, that an agent who committed an innocent breach of fiduciary duty could recover any commission otherwise payable. Whether this would be sufficient to disentitle a commercial agent to recover commission is uncertain.
129. *Regal (Hastings) Ltd v Gulliver* [1967] 2 AC 134n (HL).
130. *Andrews v Ramsay & Co* [1903] 2 KB 635 (KB).   131. *Hippisley v Knee Bros* [1905] 1 KB 1 (KB).
132. *Boardman v Phipps* [1967] 2 AC 46.
133. *Industries and General Mortgage Co Ltd v Lewis* [1949] 2 All ER 573 (KB).
134. *Boston Deep Sea Fishing and Ice Co v Ansell* (1888) 39 Ch D 339 (CA).
135. *Armagas Ltd v Mundogas SA* [1986] AC 717 (HL).
136. *Shipway v Broadwood* [1899] 1 QB 369 (CA).
137. *AG of Hong Kong v Reid* [1994] 1 AC 324 (PC).

this duty to account is a requirement that the agent maintains accurate records of his dealings and provides them to the principal upon request.[138] This duty will continue even after the agency has ended.

Duty of confidentiality

The agent is under a duty to keep confidential any information acquired whilst acting as an agent. This duty will continue even after the agency has ended.[139]

The rights of an agent

In addition to owing duties to a principal, an agent will also be granted a number of rights in relation to this principal. Compared to the duties owed by an agent, the rights an agent has under the common law are somewhat sparse, but the rights of commercial agents have been bolstered by statute—notably, a duty is imposed upon the principal to act dutifully and in good faith towards his agent.[140]

Payment

In the absence of an express agreement stating otherwise, commercial agents are entitled to be paid for their services.[141] Non-commercial agents have no common law right to be paid, but, in practice, most are. The right to be paid will only arise if there is an express or implied term to that effect, and the normal contractual rules regarding implication of terms will apply. The courts will not imply a term where it would conflict with an express term of the agreement.[142] Where the agent is a professional person, there is a very strong presumption that he will be paid for his services and the courts are likely to imply such a term where no express term provides otherwise.[143]

An agent employed under a contract of agency is entitled to be paid only if he has performed, precisely and completely, the obligations in the agency agreement, unless the contract otherwise provides. Consequently, when an agent does less than he is contractually required to do, he can recover nothing, unless the contract provides for payment for part-performance. The right of an agent to be paid depends upon the type of payment provided for, or implied into, in the agreement, with two types of payment identifiable—namely, remuneration and commission.

Remuneration

Payment by remuneration occurs where the agent is to be paid, irrespective of whether he enters into a transaction on behalf of the principal. Where such a term is express and provides the amount of remuneration, this is what the agent will receive. Where the agreement fails to provide the amount, the agent will be entitled to a reasonable amount.[144] Where no express term as to remuneration exists, the courts

---

138. *Yasuda Fire and Marine Insurance Co of Europe Ltd v Orion Marine Insurance Underwriting Agency Ltd* [1995] QB 174 (QB).   139. *Bolkiah v KPMG* [1999] 2 WLR 215 (HL).
140. Commercial Agents (Council Directive) Regulations 1993, reg 4(1).   141. ibid, reg 6(1).
142. *Kofi Sunkersette Obu v A Strauss & Co Ltd* [1951] AC 243 (PC).
143. *Miller v Beal* (1879) 27 WR 403.   144. *Way v Latilla* [1937] 3 All ER 759 (HL).

→ *quantum*
meruit: 'as much as
he has deserved'; a
reasonable sum based
on services provided

will imply such a term only where it was clearly the intention of the parties that the agent be remunerated.[145] Where no contract of agency exists, the agent may be entitled to a *quantum meruit*, provided that the agent has engaged in the acts required by the principal.[146]

Commission

Payment by commission occurs where the agent is to be paid only if he complies fully and precisely with the requirements of the agency agreement. Failure to comply fully and precisely will entitle the agent to nothing. Further, the agent will only be entitled to commission if he brought about the act in question, unless the contract provides otherwise.[147] No commission need be paid where the act occurs without the agent's involvement. A non-commercial agent will not usually be able to recover commission where he failed to perform the required act due to the hindrance of the principal, nor can he sue the principal unless the agency contract contains a term providing that the principal will not hinder the agent in his efforts to earn commission. Further, if there is no express term to this effect, the courts will be reluctant to imply such a term.[148] A principal who hinders a commercial agent will certainly breach the duty of good faith mentioned earlier. An agent who acts outside his actual authority,[149] breaches his duties,[150] or who enters into a transaction rendered void or illegal by statute normally forfeits the right to commission.

Reimbursement and indemnity

Unless the contract provides otherwise, an agent who has suffered loss (for example, incurred expenses) or incurred liabilities (for example, in tort) in the course of carrying out authorized actions for his principal is entitled to be reimbursed or indemnified by the principal.[151] This entitlement is destroyed where the agent acts outside his actual authority,[152] where the loss or liability is the result of his negligence, default, or breach of duty,[153] or where he engages in a transaction that is rendered void or illegal by statute.[154]

Lien

Where an agent is entitled to payment, reimbursement, or an indemnity, and his principal refuses to pay, reimburse, or indemnify the agent, the agent will have a lien over any goods belonging to the principal that are in the lawful possession of the agent. The agent can then retain possession of the goods until payment or the indemnity is received, but cannot dispose of them. No right to a lien will arise where it is inconsistent with, or is excluded by, the terms of the agency agreement.[155]

---

145. *Reeve v Reeve* (1858) 1 F & F 280. See also the Supply of Goods and Services Act 1982, s 15.
146. *Howard Houlder & Partners Ltd v Manx Isles Steamship Co Ltd* [1923] 1 KB 110 (KB).
147. *Millar, Son & Co v Radford* (1903) 19 TLR 575 (CA).
148. *Luxor (Eastbourne) Ltd v Cooper* [1941] AC 108 (HL).   149. *Mason v Clifton* (1863) F & F 899.
150. *Salomons v Pender* (1865) 3 H & C 639. The agent may, however, still be entitled to commission where the breach is technical and the agent acted honestly (*Keppel v Wheeler* [1927] 1 KB 577 (CA)).
151. *Hooper v Treffry* (1847) 1 Exch 17.   152. *Barron v Fitzgerald* (1840) 6 Bing NC 201.
153. *Lage v Siemens Bros & Co Ltd* (1932) 42 Ll L Rep 252 (KB).
154. *Capp v Topham* (1805) 6 East 392.
155. *Wolstenholm v Sheffield Union Banking Co* (1886) 54 LT 746.

Information

The common law has not formulated an obligation whereby a principal must provide his agent with relevant information, although a term to this effect might well be implied into an agency contract. If the agent is a commercial agent, then the principal must provide his agent with the necessary documentation relating to the goods concerned and the information necessary for the performance of the agency contract.[156]

The termination of agency

Like any other contract, a contract of agency may be terminated[157] by performance, agreement, repudiatory breach, or frustration. As has been discussed, even where the contract of agency is terminated, the ability of the agent contractually to bind his principal may continue. In addition, there are the following special rules applicable to the termination of agency, some of which relate only to commercial agents.

These grounds for termination are discussed in Chapter 11

Termination by one of the parties

Where both parties desire the agency relationship to end, it can be simply terminated by agreement. But what is the situation where only one party wishes to terminate the relationship? As an agency contract is one for personal services, the courts have indicated that they will not compel performance via an order for specific performance.[158] Consequently, either party may terminate the agency agreement at will, although such a termination is likely to amount to breach of contract (for example, where the agency agreement is for a fixed term, or where inadequate notice is given). In some cases, however, termination without notice will not amount to breach, including:

- where an agent accepts a bribe, his contract can be terminated without notice;
- the contract may expressly, or through its construction, allow one of the parties to terminate without notice;[159]
- where the agent acts in a manner inconsistent with the continuation of the agency, his contract can be terminated without notice.[160]

Dissolution

Where the principal is a partnership, limited liability partnership, or company and it is wound up or dissolved, or where a sole proprietor ceases to carry on business, the contract of agency will be terminated.[161] In order to recover damages, the agent will

---

156. Commercial Agents (Council Directive) Regulations 1993, reg 4(2).

157. Many cases and texts use the word 'determine' instead of the word 'terminate'. 'Determine' is being used in its legal sense to mean 'to bring to an end or extinguish'.

158. *Chinnock v Sainsbury* (1860) 30 LJ Ch 409

159. For example, *Atkinson v Cotesworth* (1825) 3 B & C 647.

160. *EP Nelson & Co v Rolfe* [1950] 1 KB 139 (CA).

161. *Pacific and General Insurance Co Ltd v Hazell* [1997] BCC 400 (QB).

need to prove that either the principal's action in dissolving the business amounts to breach of an express term, or the contract contained an implied term providing that the principal would not deprive the agent of the opportunity to earn his commission. The courts are extremely reluctant to imply such a term, as the following case demonstrates.

 Rhodes v Forwood (1876) LR 1 App Cas 256 (HL)

FACTS: The defendant colliery owner (the principal) appointed the claimant as the sole agent for the sale of coal from the defendant's colliery in Liverpool. The agreement provided that it would last for seven years, or as long as the defendant conducted business in Liverpool. After four years, the defendant sold the colliery and the agreement was terminated. The claimant sought damages for the loss of future commission, arguing that there was an implied term that the defendant would send coal to Liverpool to be sold by the claimant.

HELD: The claimant's action failed. The defendant had not contracted, expressly or impliedly, to keep the claimant supplied with coal and therefore he was not liable for breach of contract.

In the following case, however, the Court of Appeal distinguished *Rhodes* and held the principal liable to pay damages for breach of contract.

 Turner v Goldsmith [1891] 1 QB 544 (CA)

FACTS: The defendant shirt manufacturer (the principal) expressly agreed to employ a travelling salesman (the agent) for five years. After only two years, the defendant's factory was destroyed by fire and the business was not resumed. The agent commenced legal proceedings for loss of commission.

HELD: The Court distinguished *Rhodes* and awarded the claimant substantial damages. In failing to send the claimant a reasonable amount of clothing to sell, the defendant had breached the implied term not to deprive the claimant of the opportunity to earn commission.

COMMENT: On what basis was *Rhodes* distinguished? In *Rhodes*, it was a term of the contract that the claimant would be supplied with coal from the defendant's colliery. Conversely, in *Turner*, there was no term in the contract providing that the defendant would supply the claimant with clothing from the destroyed factory. The defendant in *Turner* might have had other sources with which to supply the claimant. Therefore, whether a term is implied will depend very much on the construction of the contract—but one could question whether or not the distinction is significant enough to sustain such a different approach.

Death

The death of either the principal or agent will terminate the agency relationship, irrespective of whether the surviving party has notice of the other's death.[162] Where the principal dies, the actual authority of the agent (and probably his apparent

---

162. *Blades v Free* (1829) 9 B & C 167.

authority too)[163] ceases, and any transactions entered into by the agent after the principal's death will contractually bind the agent and not the estate of the deceased principal, irrespective of whether the agent knows of the principal's death.[164]

Insanity

The agency relationship will be terminated where either party becomes insane. Where the principal becomes insane, however, the agent continues to have apparent authority and so he can contractually bind the principal to any third parties who were not aware of his insanity.[165]

Bankruptcy

The bankruptcy of the principal terminates the agency relationship.[166] The bankruptcy of the agent does not terminate the relationship, unless his bankruptcy prevents him acting as an agent, or renders him unfit to perform his duties.[167]

Effects of termination

The events described above will, in many cases, terminate the agency agreement, but it does not follow that the agent is robbed of his authority, or his ability to bind the principal. Termination of the agreement will terminate the agent's actual authority. Agents with apparent authority, or authority deriving from an agency of necessity, may, however, be able to continue contractually to bind the principal to a third party. To avoid being bound, the principal needs to inform the third party of the termination of the agency agreement.[168]

An agent is entitled to any commission or indemnity payments due prior to termination.[169] The agent loses his entitlement to commission or indemnity post-termination.[170]

Commercial agents

Additional rights are provided to commercial agents in relation to the termination of their agency by Pt IV of the Commercial Agents (Council Directive) Regulations 1993. These rights apply to all forms of termination by the principal, and can even apply to termination by the agent in limited circumstances. These rights do not apply where the agent was terminated without notice due to his failure to carry out all, or part, of his obligations, or due to exceptional circumstances[171] (although the Regulations provide no guidance as to what circumstances are regarded as 'exceptional').

---

163. *Watson v King* (1815) 4 Camp 272.
164. *Blades v Free* (1829) 9 B & C 167.   165. *Drew v Nunn* (1879) 4 QBD 661 (CA).
166. *Elliott v Turquand* (1881) 7 App Cas 79 (PC).
167. *McCall v Australian Meat Co Ltd* (1870) 19 WR 188.
168. *AMB Generali Holding AG v SEB Trygg Liv Holding Aktiebolag* [2005] EWCA Civ 1237, [2006] 1 WLR 2276.   169. *Chappell v Bray* (1860) 6 H & N 145.
170. *Farrow v Wilson* (1869) LR 4 CP 744.
171. Commercial Agents (Council Directive) Regulations 1993, reg 16.

Notice periods

Regulation 14 provides that an agency agreement for a fixed period, which continues beyond the expiry of that period, shall be converted into an agency agreement of indefinite duration. The significance of this is found in reg 15, which establishes minimum notice periods for agency agreements of indefinite duration, as follows:

- one month for the first year of the contract;
- two months for the second year of the contract;
- three months where the contract has lasted longer than two years.

Where an agreement of fixed duration is converted into an agreement of indefinite duration by reg 14, the fixed period shall also be taken into account when determining the minimum notice period.[172] Parties cannot agree shorter notice periods than those contained in reg 15, but they can agree longer notice periods, provided that the notice period to be observed by the principal is not shorter than that to be observed by the agent.[173]

The minimum notice periods will not apply where immediate termination could occur through frustration or repudiatory breach of the agency agreement.[174]

Compensation and indemnity

Regulations 17 and 18 provide the agent with the right to compensation or an indemnity upon termination of the agency agreement. The usual entitlement will be compensation, unless the agency agreement provides that an indemnity shall be paid instead.[175] The right to compensation or an indemnity cannot be excluded by the agency agreement,[176] but it will be lost in four situations:

1. Where the agent does not inform the principal, within one year following the date of termination, that he intends to pursue his entitlement.[177]
2. Where the principal has terminated the agency agreement for a reason that would justify immediate termination under reg 16 (that is, due to the agent's failure to carry out all, or part, of his obligations, or due to exceptional circumstances).[178]
3. Where the agent himself has terminated the agreement, unless such termination was justified due to circumstances attributable to the principal, or was due to age, infirmity, or illness of the agent.[179]
4. Where the agent, with the agreement of the principal, has assigned his rights to another person.[180]

Regulation 17 provides that an agent shall be entitled to compensation or an indemnity for the damage that he suffers as a result of the termination of his relations with his principal. According to normal compensatory principles, where no loss has been suffered, substantial compensation will not be awarded.

Regulation 17(7) provides two particular forms of damages for which reg 17(6) should provide compensation:

1. where the termination deprives the agent of commission that he would have obtained had the agency agreement continued; and

---

172. ibid reg 15(5).

173. ibid reg 15(3).

174. *Crane v Sky-in-Home Service Ltd* [2007] EWHC 66 (Ch), [2007] All ER (Comm) 599.

175. Commercial Agents (Council Directive) Regulations 1993, reg 17(2).   176. ibid reg 19.

177. ibid reg 17(9).   178. ibid reg 18(a).   179. ibid reg 18(b).

180. ibid reg 18(c).

2. where the termination has deprived the agent with the opportunity to **amortize** the costs and expenses that he has incurred on the advice of his principal.

→ **amortize:** reduce or recoup an amount or debt

The Regulations provide no guidance as to how compensation is to be assessed. The issue has therefore been left to the courts, but for a significant period, the courts could not articulate a consistent approach, until the House of Lords stated that a two-part approach should be adopted.[181] The first part was to ask for what the agent should be compensated. Regulation 17(6) answers this question, namely the damage suffered as a result of the termination of his relations with the principal. The second, and more difficult part is the question of how compensation should be assessed. Lord Hoffmann's answer was to assess compensation based on what a sale of the agency business would fetch on the open market. This would be determined by asking what a hypothetical purchaser would be willing to pay for the agency business at the time of termination, but also taking into account factors in the real world, such as whether the 'market for the product in which the agent dealt was rising or declining'.[182]

An agent will receive an indemnity instead of compensation where the agency contract provides so, and only then if two conditions imposed by reg 17(3) are met:

1. the agent has brought the principal new customers or has significantly increased the volume of business with existing customers,[183] and the principal continues to derive substantial benefits from the business with such customers; and

2. the payment of this indemnity is equitable, having regard to all of the circumstances and, in particular, the commission lost by the commercial agent on the business transacted with such customers.

Regulation 17(4) limits the amount of the indemnity to a figure equivalent to an indemnity for one year. This one-year figure is calculated by determining the agent's average annual remuneration over the previous five-year period. Where the agent has worked for less than five years, the average shall be calculated based on the period for which he has worked.

Irrevocable agencies

The law provides for a number of irrevocable agencies. Any attempts to terminate such agencies will not only amount to breach of contract, but will also be ineffective and the agent's authority will remain intact. Examples of irrevocable agencies include:

- where the agent's authority is granted by deed, or for some other valuable consideration, for the purpose of securing an interest of the agent that is independent of the agency[184] (the earning of commission will not suffice, because this interest is not independent of the agency);

- where the agent incurs personal liability through the exercise of his authority for which he must be indemnified by the principal.[185]

---

181. *Lonsdale v Howard & Hallam Ltd* [2007] UKHL 32, [2007] 1 WLR 2055.
182. ibid [13].
183. The agent need not be the sole cause of the increase in customers or business volume, but he must have played an active role in obtaining the increase (*Moore v Piretta PTA Ltd* [1999] 1 All ER 174 (QB)).
184. *Re Hannan's Empress Gold Mining and Development Company, ex p Carmichael* [1896] 2 Ch 643 (CA).
185. *Chappell v Bray* (1860) 6 H & N 145.

Chapter conclusion

Having discussed what agency is and the relationships that it creates, its importance cannot be underestimated. Large businesses will enter into thousands of contracts every day with customers, suppliers, consumers, employees, accountants, lawyers, manufacturers, and creditors. Only through the use of agents can this contractual volume be met. Without agency, the number of contracts into which businesses could enter would fall drastically. Given its importance, it is therefore of no surprise that agency has become a legal topic in its own right, with agents subject to their own rights and duties, and a complex body of centuries-old case law in place to help to determine how the relationships between the various parties should operate. In recent years, however, statute has intervened and provided extra protection for commercial agents who enter into contracts for the sale of goods.

 Key points summary

- Agency can be created (i) by agreement; (ii) by ratification; (iii) by the operation of law; and (iv) through estoppel.

- There are two principal types of authority, namely (i) actual authority; and (ii) apparent authority. Actual authority can be express or implied.

- Where a third party knows that a principal exists (although not necessarily who he is), that principal will be disclosed. An agent who contracts for a disclosed principal is not normally liable on any authorized contract into which he enters on the principal's behalf.

- Where the principal is undisclosed, both the principal and agent are liable on the contract, and the third party may elect which one to sue. The ability of the principal to enforce the contract is limited.

- An agent who acts outside his authority may be liable to the third party for breach of warranty of authority.

- Agents are subject to a number of duties, including a duty to perform personally any acts required by the agency agreement and a duty to obey the lawful instructions of the principal.

- Unless an agency is irrevocable, it can be terminated by one of the parties at any time, although such termination may amount to a breach of the agency agreement

Self-test questions

1. Define the following terms:
   (a) principal;
   (b) commercial agent;
   (c) gratuitous agent;
   (d) actual authority;
   (e) usual authority;
   (f) agency of necessity;
   (g) disclosed principal;
   (h) commission.

2. Explain the various ways in which a relationship of agency can be created.

3. John owns a 1951 Mercedes SL that he wishes to sell. He instructs Ross to sell the car and, in return, Ross will be paid £5,000 commission. Ross manages to find a buyer, Paul, and introduces Paul to John. But John decides not to proceed with the sale. Advise Ross.

4. Explain the distinction between:
    (a) implied actual authority and apparent authority;
    (b) remuneration and commission;
    (c) a disclosed principal and an undisclosed principal;
    (d) a secret profit and a bribe.

Further reading

Eric Baskind, Greg Osborne, and Lee Roach, *Commercial Law* (OUP 2013) chs 3–9
Provides an accessible, yet thorough, account of the law of agency topics discussed in this chapter

Ian Brown, 'The Agent's Apparent Authority: Paradigm or Paradox?' [1995] JBL 360
Discusses the theoretical basis of apparent authority and argues that the theoretical basis of apparent authority stated by the court is not always in line with modern commercial reality

FE Dowrick, 'The Relationship of Principal and Agent' (1954) 17 MLR 24
A seminal article discussing the distribution of power between, and the liability faced by, principals and their agents

Roderick Munday, *Agency: Law and Principles* (2nd edn, OUP, 2013)
An excellent text that provides a highly readable account of the law of agency

Peter G Watts, *Bowstead & Reynolds on Agency* (19th edn, Sweet & Maxwell, 2010)
The leading text on agency and regularly referred to by the courts in agency cases

Remember to visit the **Online Resource Centre** at **<http://www.oxfordtextbooks.co.uk/orc/roach3e>** to access the following resources on Chapter 8, 'The law of agency': more **practice questions** and answers; a **glossary** of key terms; **multiple-choice questions; and revision summaries**. Updates to the law can be found on Twitter by following **@UKBusinessLaw**.

9 Exclusion clauses and unfair terms

- Common law limitations
- The Unfair Contract Terms Act 1977
- The Unfair Terms in Consumer Contracts Regulations 1999
- The Draft Consumer Rights Bill

INTRODUCTION

As noted in Chapter 7, classical contract law theory was based on the notion that the parties should be free to determine the terms of their contracts. It was only a matter of time before parties began including terms that altered the nature of contractual liability itself in their favour as against the other party. This was the advent of the exclusion clause (also known as an 'exemption clause'). Exclusion clauses come in numerous different forms, but their basic effect is either to exclude completely liability for a legal wrong, or to restrict such liability (for example, by limiting the amount of compensation payable).

Initially, it may seem bizarre to allow a party to exclude liability for breaching a term by which it has freely agreed to be bound, but the following example demonstrates the rationale behind upholding the validity of exclusion clauses.

Eg   Exclusion clauses and contractual bargaining

MoneyCorp, a large bank, has been accused of fraud. Clifford & McKenzie, a large firm of solicitors, has agreed to defend the bank. Clifford & McKenzie wishes to insert a term into the proposed contract excluding its liability completely should it commit any acts of negligence in relation to the case. MoneyCorp will only permit such a term to be included if Clifford & McKenzie agrees to reduce its fee by 10 per cent. Clifford & McKenzie agree and a contract is drawn up.

In this case, both parties have equal bargaining power, and the negotiations are free and mutual. The exclusion clause was 'purchased' for a 10 per cent reduction in the fee charged. The risk of being unable to claim compensation for negligence has been offset by an immediate reduction in the fee. The negotiations have therefore led to a mutually beneficial outcome and an allocation of risk that is acceptable to both parties.

However, a significant number of contracts (notably, consumer contracts) demonstrate a stark inequality of bargaining power between the parties, which allows the stronger party to impose its own standard terms on the weaker party, and such terms could contain extremely wide-ranging or potentially unfair exclusion clauses. It therefore became necessary to begin regulating the use of exclusion clauses. Accordingly, the courts began imposing limitations upon the use of exclusion clauses and these common law limitations will be discussed first. Later, it will become clear that the principal source of regulation can now be found in statute.

Common law limitations

Common law limitations fall into two categories:

- limitations relating to incorporation; and
- limitations relating to construction and interpretation.

Incorporation

In order for the **proferens** to rely on an exclusion clause, he will need to demonstrate that the clause is part of the contract. Although the following rules relating to incorporation are discussed in relation to exclusion clauses,[1] they are of general application and can apply to the incorporation of other forms of terms.

➡ **proferens:** the party favoured by an exclusion clause

The effect of a signature

A person who signs a contract will generally be bound by the terms of that contract, irrespective of whether or not he has actually read them, as the following, somewhat harsh, decision demonstrates.

 L'Estrange v Graucob Ltd [1934] 2 KB 394 (KB)

FACTS: The claimant purchased from the defendant a vending machine and placed it in her cafe. She signed, but did not read, an order form, which was written in standard sized print and which also contained 'in regrettably small print'[2] a term excluding liability for breach of any implied terms. The vending machine did not work and the claimant sued for breach of the implied term as to fitness for purpose.

HELD: The High Court rejected the claim. She had signed the contract and was bound by its terms. That she had not read the contract and therefore did not know of the exclusion clause was irrelevant.

The rule in *L'Estrange* is not absolute and the courts have mitigated its harshness to an extent by providing for several exceptions. A plea of *non est factum* will, in very limited circumstances, allow a party who has signed a contract to escape that contract. More importantly, a person seeking to rely on an exclusion clause will be unable to do so if he misrepresented to the other person the effect of the exclusion clause.

🔗 *Non est factum* is discussed at p 268

---

1. Indeed, the bulk of of the case law relating to the incorporation of terms concerns the incorporation of exclusion clauses.
2. [1934] 2 KB 394 (KB) 405 (Maugham LJ).

Curtis v Chemical Cleaning and Dyeing Co Ltd [1951] 1 KB 805 (CA)

FACTS: The claimant took her wedding dress to the defendant's shop to be cleaned. The dress was trimmed with beads and sequins. The claimant was presented with a receipt and asked to sign it. When she inquired why her signature was required, the defendant replied that it was required in order to exclude the defendant from liability for damage to the beads and sequins. In fact, the receipt contained a clause excluding liability for any damage howsoever caused. The dress was returned to the claimant, but it was badly stained. The claimant brought an action and the defendant sought to rely on the exclusion clause.

HELD: The Court of Appeal held that the defendant was not protected by the exclusion clause, because it had misrepresented the effect of the clause.

Is the document contractual?

A signature will bind the signatory only if the document signed constitutes a contractual document. Even where a document is not signed, some or all of the terms printed on it may be incorporated if the document is deemed to be a contractual document.

Determining whether a document is contractual or not can be difficult. Where an exclusion clause is located within a written contractual document, there is no difficulty in determining its incorporation. However, very often, an exclusion clause will be contained in a separate document, such as a ticket or a receipt, or may be displayed on a sign or other notice. Such documents are unlikely to be signed, so the rule in *L'Estrange* has no application. The approach of the courts is that a document will be regarded as contractual if a reasonable person would assume it to contain contractual terms, as the following case demonstrates.

Chapelton v Barry UDC [1940] 1 KB 532 (CA)

FACTS: The defendant council hired deckchairs to the public. A notice near the deckchairs stated that members of the public hiring chairs should obtain a ticket from the deckchair attendant and keep it for inspection. The claimant hired two chairs and placed the tickets in his pocket without reading them. The tickets contained a clause excluding any liability for injury arising from the use of the chairs. The claimant's chair was defective and, when he sat on it, it collapsed, injuring him. The defendant sought to rely on the exclusion clause.

HELD: The Court of Appeal held that the exclusion clause was ineffective. The ticket was merely a voucher or receipt and no reasonable person would expect it to amount to more than this.

COMMENT: It is important to remember that the status of a document is highly dependent upon the facts of the case. Although, in *Chapelton*, a receipt was not deemed to constitute a contractual document, this does not mean that any document called a 'receipt' will fail to have contractual force and, based on the facts, terms located on a receipt could become incorporated into the contract.[3]

---

3. *Parker v South Eastern Rly Co* (1877) 2 CPD 416 (CA).

The requirement of notice

An exclusion clause will not be incorporated into the contract if it was not brought to the party's reasonable notice before or at the time that the contract was entered into. If the clause is brought to the party's notice after the contract is entered into, it will not become part of the contract.

 Olley v Marlborough Court Ltd [1949] 1 KB 532 (CA)

FACTS: The claimant and her husband arrived at the defendant's hotel, checked in, and paid for a week's stay in advance. They went up to their room, where a notice, displayed on a wall, stated that the defendant was not liable for any items lost or stolen. Due to the negligence of the hotel staff, property belonging to the claimant was stolen from the hotel room. The claimant sued and the defendant sought to rely on the exclusion clause.

HELD: As the contract was entered into at the checking-in desk, the notice was communicated to the claimant after the contract was entered into. Accordingly, the exclusion clause was ineffective.

The requirement of prior notice is subject to two exceptions. First, where there has been a consistent course of dealings between the parties on the basis of documents incorporating similar terms excluding liability, then, provided that those dealings have been of a consistent nature, the courts may imply the exclusion clause into a particular contract where express notice is given too late.[4]

 J Spurling Ltd v Bradshaw [1956] 1 WLR 461 (CA)

FACTS: The defendant had, for many years, dealt with the claimant warehouseman. The defendant delivered eight barrels of orange juice to the claimant to store, in return for which he received a document acknowledging receipt of the barrels and referring to a number of terms located on the rear of the document, one of which excluded the claimant from any liability caused by its negligence. The defendant did not read these terms. When the defendant came to collect the barrels, they were either empty or damaged to such an extent as to be useless. He refused to pay the storage charges. The claimant sued and the defendant counterclaimed for negligence.

HELD: The Court of Appeal held that the exclusion clause was effective and the claimant could recover the charges, and the defendant's counterclaim failed. Although the defendant never read the document, he had dealt with the claimant on such terms for many years.

COMMENT: The requirement of a consistent course of dealings means that incorporation through prior dealings is less likely to occur where a private party is involved, because such persons are unlikely to have had sufficient dealings for there to be a course of dealing. For example, in one case, the Court of Appeal held that three or four dealings over a five-year period did not establish a course of dealing.[5]

---

4. See also *McCutcheon v David MacBrayne Ltd* [1964] 1 WLR 125 (HL).
5. *Hollier v Rambler Motors (AMC) Ltd* [1972] 2 QB 71 (CA).

The second exception is where an exclusion clause is implied through trade usage or local custom. In such cases, prior notice of the clause will not be required and there is no need for parties within the particular trade or locality to have dealt with each other previously; all that matters is that the usage or custom existed when the contract was entered into and that it was used so frequently that the party affected must, as a reasonable person in that trade or locality, have known that it would be included in the contract.[6]

The requirement of notice does not require that the party actually knew of the existence of the clause prior to the contract being formed; all that is required is that the proferens did what was reasonable to bring the exclusion clause to the other party's attention.[7] This will depend upon the facts of the case, but the courts have held that the more onerous or unusual the clause, the higher the degree of notice required from the proferens. In one case, Denning LJ stated 'Some clauses I have seen would need to be printed in red ink on the face of the document with a red hand pointing to it before the notice could be held to be sufficient.'[8] The following case provides an example of a particularly onerous term (albeit not an exclusion clause).

Interfoto Picture Library Ltd v Stiletto Visual Programmes Ltd [1988] QB 433 (CA)

FACTS: The claimant ran a photographic transparency library. It loaned forty-seven transparencies to the defendant. The transparencies were accompanied by a delivery note containing nine conditions, one of which stated that the transparencies had to be returned within fourteen days of delivery and that failure to do so would result in a £5 penalty per transparency per day. The defendant had not contracted with the claimant before and did not read the conditions. It returned the transparencies some four weeks later, whereupon the claimant invoiced it for £3,783. The defendant refused to pay and the claimant commenced proceedings.

HELD: Given how onerous the penalty clause was, the claimant should have done more to bring it to the defendant's attention. Accordingly, the Court held that the claimant could not recover the £3,783, but could recover a *quantum meruit*.

★ See JA Holland and PA Chandler, 'Notice of Contractual Terms' (1988) 104 LQR 359

➜ *quantum meruit*: 'as much as he has deserved'; a reasonable sum based on services provided

Construction and interpretation

Once it is established that an exclusion clause is a term of the contract, it must be determined whether or not the clause covers the liability in question. In construing exclusion clauses, the courts take a restrictive approach,[9] but the current approach is less restrictive than in years past. It used to be the case that the courts would not allow the proferens to rely on an exclusion clause that excluded or limited liability for a fundamental breach of contract. Today, the doctrine of fundamental breach

---

6. *British Crane Hire Corporation Ltd v Ipswich Plant Hire Ltd* [1975] QB 303 (CA).

7. *Parker v South Eastern Rly Co* (1877) 2 CPD 416 (CA).

8. *J Spurling Ltd v Bradshaw* [1956] 1 WLR 461 (CA) 466.

9. It should be noted that the courts will take a more restrictive approach in relation to exclusion clauses than they will in relation to limitation clauses, for obvious reasons.

has been abolished and the approach adopted by the courts can be seen in the following case.

Photo Productions Ltd v Securicor Transport Ltd [1980] AC 827 (HL)

FACTS: The claimant employed the defendant to patrol its factories at night, and to guard against fire and theft. The contract excluded the liability of the defendant for any injurious acts of its employees, unless such acts could be foreseen and prevented by the defendant's due diligence. It further excluded the liability of the defendant for any loss caused by fire, except in so far as such loss was solely attributable to the negligence of the defendant's employees acting within the scope of their employment. One of the defendant's employees deliberately started a fire in one of the claimant's factories and his actions caused £615,000 worth of damage. The defendant sought to rely on the exclusion clause, but the claimant argued that it was invalid, because it excluded liability for a fundamental breach.

HELD: The doctrine of fundamental breach was no longer good law and the correct approach was to determine, based on the construction of the exclusion clause, whether or not it covered the liability in question. Applying this approach, the House held that the exclusion clause covered the liability in question and the defendant could therefore rely on it.

COMMENT: The effect of this decision was to permit the defendant to avoid liability, even though its employee's act destroyed the claimant's factory. It may be thought that this decision was a harsh one and that its application to consumer contracts containing imposed standard exclusion clauses would be highly detrimental, but it should be remembered that even where an exclusion clause covers the liability in question, it may still be subject to additional statutory safeguards—notably, the requirement of reasonableness imposed by the Unfair Contract Terms Act 1977. Accordingly, the relatively harsh approach evident in this case will tend to apply only to contracts between businesspersons, who should be capable of looking after their own interests.

Contra proferentem

The doctrine of fundamental breach might have been abolished, but the courts still construe and interpret exclusion clauses in a restrictive manner, and this is evidenced in what is known as the **contra proferentem** rule. The *contra proferentem* rule basically provides that where an exclusion clause contains an ambiguity, the courts will interpret it against the proferens.[10] Thus, where an exclusion clause's ambiguity produces two possible meanings, one of which brings the liability within the clause and the other takes the liability outside the scope of the clause, the courts should choose the latter.

➜*contra proferentem*: 'against a person who proffers a thing'; an ambiguous exclusion clause will be construed against the proferens

Although the rule is limited to cases involving an ambiguity, the courts have been creative in finding ambiguities, as the following case demonstrates.

---

10. In relation to consumer contracts, the *contra proferentem* rule is established in statute by virtue of reg 7(2) of the Unfair Terms in Consumer Contracts Regulations 1999, SI 1999/2083.

Houghton v Trafalgar Co Ltd [1954] 1 QB 247 (CA)

FACTS: The claimant was involved in a car accident and claimed on his insurance policy. The policy contained an exclusion clause stating that the defendant insurance company would not be liable to pay out where the damage was 'caused or arising whilst the car is conveying any load in excess of that for which it was constructed'. As the car was designed for five people and was carrying six at the time of the accident, the defendant relied on the clause and denied liability.

HELD: The Court of Appeal affirmed the trial judge's decision that the limitation imposed by the clause was based on excess weight, as opposed to an excess number of passengers. Accordingly, the exclusion clause did not apply.

Excluding liability for negligence

The restrictive approach of the *contra proferentem* rule is demonstrated clearly in relation to exclusion clauses that seek to exclude liability for negligence. The general approach is that the courts are reluctant to allow an exclusion clause to cover non-contractual liability (for example, liability in tort) unless the clause expressly provides that such liability is covered. The rationale behind this approach is the desire not to leave claimants without a remedy. The exact effect of this rule depends on the drafting of the exclusion clause and the type of obligation breached.

Where an exclusion clause expressly covers all forms of liability, or where the words used are wide enough to cover liability in contract and tort, effect must be given to it irrespective of the nature of liability[11] (subject to it satisfying the requirements of statute discussed later). However, many clauses do not provide such blanket coverage and the effect of such clauses depends upon the types of obligation imposed by the contract, as follows.

- Where the proferens breaches a contractual term that imposes a strict obligation (that is, a person who breaches the term is liable despite the absence of negligence or fault), then the exclusion clause is normally construed so that it will protect him against liability in contract, but will not extend to cover liability in tort for negligence.[12]
- Where liability can be based only in negligence (whether only in tort, or for breach of a contractual term requiring the exercise of reasonable care and skill), the clause will normally be interpreted to extend to cover that liability (that is, negligence), because, otherwise, the clause would lack a subject matter and would be redundant.[13]

The need for clear words

For an exclusion clause to cover a particular liability, the words used must clearly cover that liability. The courts will apply this rule more strictly to exclusion clauses than to limitation clauses.[14] The following case demonstrates the strictness of the courts' approach.[15]

---

11. *Canada Steamship Lines v The King* [1952] AC 192 (PC).
12. *White v John Warwick & Co Ltd* [1953] 1 WLR 1285 (CA).
13. *Alderslade v Hendon Laundry Ltd* [1945] KB 189 (CA).
14. *Ailsa Craig Fishing Co Ltd v Malvern Fishing Co Ltd* [1983] 1 WLR 964 (HL).
15. See also *Wallis, Son and Wells v Pratt and Haynes* [1911] AC 394 (HL).

Andrews Bros (Bournemouth) Ltd v Singer & Co Ltd [1934] 1 KB 17 (CA)

FACTS: The claimant entered into a contract to purchase a number of 'new Singer cars' from the defendant. The contract excluded the liability of the defendant for breach of all 'conditions, warranties and liabilities implied by common law, statute or otherwise'. One of the cars delivered had 550 miles on the odometer and the claimant brought an action for breach of contract, because the car was not new. The defendant sought to rely on the exclusion clause.

HELD: The Court of Appeal held that the clause did not protect the defendant, because it only excluded liability for breach of implied terms, whereas the requirement for the cars to be new was an express obligation.

A restrictive approach?

Recent cases have indicated that the courts are taking a more restrictive approach when interpreting exclusion clauses, even where the clause clearly and expressly covers the loss in question. In the following case, the Court of Appeal, principally in an effort to achieve justice, invalidated an exclusion clause that expressly and unequivocally covered the loss in question.

Kudos Catering (UK) Ltd v Manchester Central Convention Complex Ltd [2013] EWCA Civ 38

FACTS: The claimant and defendant entered into a five-year contract, under which the claimant would have the exclusive right to provide catering services to the defendant. The contract contained a clause (clause 18.6) found in many commercial contracts, which stated that the claimant agreed that the defendant would 'have no liability whatsoever in contract, tort (including negligence) or otherwise for any loss of goodwill, business, revenue or profits...' Three years into the contract, the defendant wrongfully repudiated the contract. The claimant accepted the defendant's repudiatory breach and sought £1.3 million in damages for the loss of profits it would have expected to obtain had the contract run its course. The defendant sought to rely on the exclusion clause. The High Court held that the clause was clear in its wording and so rejected the claimant's claim for damages.[16] The claimant appealed.

HELD: The appeal was allowed and the defendant was ordered to pay damages to the claimant. The Court stated that the clause did not cover the loss in question for several reasons. First, the Court stated that the clause only covered defective performance and not a refusal to perform. Second, the Court stated that the clause was very wide in scope and, if it were allowed to stand, it would defeat the whole purpose of the claimant entering into the contract (namely, to make a profit). Further, it would, if enforced, devoid the contract of content as there would be no sanction for non-performance by the defendant. Third, the Court stated that, if the clause were meant to cover all forms of liability for financial loss, then it should have been placed in a free-standing clause and not as a sub-clause of clause 18.

COMMENT: It is clear that the Court had to adopt some creative reasoning in order to hold that clause 18.6 did not apply. It is clear that the courts are not shy to invalidate or restrictively

---

16. *Kudos Catering (UK) Ltd v Manchester Central Convention Complex Ltd* [2012] EWHC 1192 (QB).

interpret exclusion clauses in an attempt to do justice in individual cases (especially where the effect of the clause will be to defeat a party's purpose in entering into the contract, or where it will deny a party the right to a suitable remedy). Parties seeking to rely on such clauses would do well to set out the commercial justification for the clause's existence, and ensure that the clause is not buried within the other terms of the contract.

The Unfair Contract Terms Act 1977

As discussed earlier, exclusion clauses were initially regulated by the common law alone, but, as time progressed, such clauses began to be subject to increasing levels of statutory regulation. At first, such regulation was piecemeal and applied only to specific contracts, but as time progressed, Parliament passed an Act that covered exclusion clauses in general. The Unfair Contract Terms Act 1977 (UCTA 1977), described by Furmston as 'the most important statute in the English contract law since the Statute of Frauds',[17] basically has two effects.

1. It renders certain exclusion/limitation clauses completely unenforceable.
2. It renders certain exclusion/limitation clauses unenforceable, unless they satisfy a requirement of reasonableness.

Before discussing the extent to which the UCTA 1977 affects the enforceability of exclusion clauses, it is important to understand the extent and scope of the Act.

Scope

The title of the 'Unfair Contract Terms Act 1977' is 'grossly misleading'[18] for two reasons. First, the Act does not apply solely to contractual terms, but can also apply to exclusions contained in non-contractual notices. Second, the Act does not seek to regulate unfair terms generally, but merely terms that limit or exclude 'business liability'[19] which is defined as liability for breach of obligations or duties arising from things done or to be done by a person in the course of a business;[20] or the occupation of premises used for business purposes of the occupier.[21]

From this, it is clear that the Act does not generally cover exclusion clauses in contracts between private individuals (but there are exceptions to this, as is discussed later). It is also apparent that the Act applies exclusively to contractual clauses and non-contractual notices that seek to exclude or limit liability. This will cover not only express exclusions of liability, but also clauses that aim to:

(i)   make liability or its enforcement subject to strict or onerous conditions;
(ii) exclude any right or remedy in relation to liability;

---

17. Michael Furmston, *Cheshire, Fifoot and Furmston's Law of Contract* (16th edn, OUP 2012) 255.
18. ibid 234.
19. Not all of the terms are limited to the exclusion of business liability (e.g. UCTA 1977, s 6(1), (3), and (4)).
20. Section 14 of the Act defines a business as 'a profession and the activities of any government department or local or public authority'.
21. UCTA 1977, s 1(3).

(iii) subject persons to prejudice who exercise such a right or remedy; and

(iv) exclude rules of evidence or procedure.

The Act applies to most forms of contract that contain a term seeking to exclude business liability, but several types of contract are excluded wholly or in part, including:

- certain contracts (for example, contracts of insurance, contracts relating to the constitution, rights, or obligations of a company's members) are excluded from the operation of ss 2–4 of the UCTA 1977;[22]
- contracts of employment are excluded from the operation of s 2 of the UCTA 1977, except where the clause operates in favour of the employee;[23]
- contracts for the sale of goods between parties whose places of business are in different states are wholly outside the operation of the Act.[24]

Excluding liability for negligence

Section 1(1) defines 'negligence' as the breach of:

- any obligation, arising from the express or implied terms of a contract, to take reasonable care or exercise reasonable skill in the performance of the contract;
- any common law duty to take reasonable care or exercise reasonable skill; and
- the common duty of care imposed by the Occupiers' Liability Act 1957

The Occupiers' Liability Act 1957 is discussed at p 429

Section 2(1) provides that a person cannot, by reference to an exclusion clause or notice, exclude or restrict his liability for death or personal injury (including any disease or impairment of physical or mental condition) resulting from negligence. Any clause purporting to do so will be ineffective. In relation to contract, the limitation contained in s 2(1) applies only to obligations to exercise reasonable care or skill (this is consequential upon the definition of negligence discussed earlier). Accordingly, liability for death and personal injury can be excluded where it is caused by breach of a strict obligation, provided that the clause or notice complies with s 3 (discussed later).

In relation to any other type of loss (for example, property damage or financial loss) caused by negligence, s 2(2) provides that such liability can be excluded, but 'only in so far as the term or notice satisfies the requirement of reasonableness'. The use of the phrase 'only in so far as' means that an unreasonable clause is not automatically unenforceable (although, in many cases, it will be); rather, the court may be able to keep part of the clause effective (the part of the clause that is reasonable) and hold ineffective the unreasonable part. As will be seen, this phrase is used several times throughout the Act.

The requirement of reasonableness is discussed at p 228

Excluding liability for breach of contract

Section 2 limits the ability to exclude liability for qualified contractual obligations (that is, those that require the exercise of reasonable care and skill) and tortious acts that amount to negligence, but it does not cover obligations that are not based on a duty to take reasonable care (that is, a strict obligation). An exclusion clause or

---

22. ibid Sch 1, para 1.

23. ibid Sch 1, para 4.   24. ibid s 26(1).

notice that excludes liability for a breach of a strict contractual obligation is primarily regulated by s 3 (although it will be regulated by ss 6 and 7 in some cases), which only applies where:

- one party to the contract deals as a consumer; or
- the contract is formed based on the other's written standard terms of business.[25]

Both of these limitations require further discussion.

'Deals as a consumer'

Under UCTA 1977, a 'consumer' is defined as someone who neither makes the contract in the course of a business, nor holds himself out as doing so, and the other party does make the contract in the course of a business.[26] This definition indicates that a business could never deal as a consumer, but this is not so, as the following case established.

 R & B Customs Brokers Co Ltd v United Dominions Trust Ltd [1988] 1 WLR 321 (CA)

FACTS: The claimant company was a freight forwarding and shipping agent. It purchased a car for one of its directors, which was used for both business and private purposes. The car was defective and the claimant alleged that the term implied by s 14(3) of the Sale of Goods Act 1979 (fitness for purpose) had been breached. The defendant sought to rely on a clause excluding liability for breach of s 14(3), but liability for breach of s 14(3) can only be validly excluded against a party not dealing as a consumer. The Court therefore had to determine whether or not the claimant company dealt as a consumer.

HELD: Dillon LJ stated:

> there are some transactions which are clearly integral parts of the businesses concerned, and these should be held to have been carried out in the course of those businesses…There are other transactions, however, such as the purchase of the car in the present case, which are at highest only incidental to the carrying on of the relevant business; here a degree of regularity is required before it can be said that they are an integral part of the business carried on, and so entered into in the course of that business.[27]

The purchase of the car was clearly not an integral part of the claimant's business, nor was it regular enough to be regarded as integral. Therefore, the claimant was regarded as a consumer and liability for breach of s 14(3) could not be excluded.

★ See Diane R Price, 'When Is a Consumer Not a Consumer?' (1989) 52 MLR 245

🔗 Visit the Online Resource Centre for more on *Stevenson v Rogers* in the chapter entitled 'The sale of goods'

Unsurprisingly, *R & B Customs Brokers* has proved controversial and has attracted considerable criticism. In the case of *Stevenson v Rogers*,[28] the Court of Appeal stated that, in the context of the law relating to contracts for the sale of goods, the test laid down in *R & B Customs Brokers* was not the correct test and that a sale would be in the course of business unless it was purely private. The Court distinguished *R & B Customs Brokers* and held that it applied solely to cases under UCTA 1977. Many believed the test laid down in *Stevenson* to be preferable to that established in

---

25. ibid s 3(2).   26. ibid s 12(1).   27. [1988] 1 WLR 321 (CA) 330-1.
28. [1999] QB 1028 (CA).

R & B,[29] and it was hoped that, when the issue was litigated again, the test in *Stevenson* would be the one adopted. However, when the Court of Appeal was invited to hold that the test in *Stevenson* was preferable to that in *R & B Customs Brokers*, it declined and applied the latter test.[30]

Subsequently, the Law Commission considered the issue and recommended that a new regime should be created that applied to 'consumer contracts'.[31] A consumer contract would be between an individual (the consumer) who enters into it wholly or mainly for purposes unrelated to a business of his, and a person (the business) who enters into it wholly or mainly for purposes related to his business.[32] Under this definition, only natural persons could become consumers and, in order to be such, the contract would have to be for a purpose wholly or mainly unrelated to the person's business. In 2006, the government indicated that it was ready to go forward with the Law Commission's recommendations, but no progress has been made.

'On the other's written standard terms of business'

Section 3 can apply where the consumer deals 'on the other's written standard terms of business'. It is crucial that the standard terms are those of the other party and not standard terms simply used by the other party, but drafted by someone else. For example, it is common for professional and trade associations to draft standard terms that are used by their members. These terms would not be regarded as the members' terms and so would not be subject to s 3,[33] which substantially limits the protection offered by s 3.

It is common for certain terms contained in a standard form contract to be amended following negotiation. To what extent can such standard terms be amended before s 3 no longer applies? This question was considered in a number of cases and the following principles are evident.

- Whether the terms are still standard is a question of fact, taking into account the degree of negotiation and amendment, and the equality of bargaining power between the parties.[34]

- Where the exclusion clause itself is subject to negotiation, the terms will no longer be regarded as standard and s 3 will not apply.[35]

It is clear that variation of the terms will reduce the chances of terms being regarded as standard terms, a view advanced by Edwards-Stuart J when he stated that the terms should be 'terms which the company…uses for all, or nearly all, of its contract of a particular type without alteration…In my view, it is the essence of such terms that they are not varied from transaction to transaction.'[36]

---

29. See e.g. Elizabeth Macdonald, '"In the Course of a Business": A Fresh Examination' [1999] 3 Web JLI.
30. *Feldaroll Foundry plc v Hermes Leasing (London) Ltd* [2004] EWCA Civ 747, (2004) 101 LSG 32.
31. Law Commission, *Unfair Terms in Contracts* (Law Com No 292, Cm 6464, HMSO, 2005) Pt 3.
32. Draft Unfair Contract Terms Bill, cl 26.
33. *British Fermentation Products Ltd v Compare Reavell Ltd* [1999] 2 All ER (Comm) 389 (QB).
34. *Salvage Association v CAP Financial Services Ltd* [1995] FSR 654 (QB).
35. *St Albans City and District Council v International Computers Ltd* [1996] 4 All ER 481 (CA).
36. *Yuanda (UK) Co Ltd v WW Gear Construction Ltd* [2010] EWHC 720 (TCC), [2011] Bus LR 360 [21]–[22].

The effect of s 3

Section 3(2) provides that, as against the party dealing as consumer or on the other's written standard terms of business, the other party cannot, by reference to any contract term, exclude or restrict his liability for breach of contract, or claim to be entitled:

(i) to render a contractual performance substantially different from that which was reasonably expected of him; or

(ii) in respect of the whole or any part of his contractual obligation, to render no performance at all except in so far as the contract term satisfies the requirement of reasonableness.

Unreasonable indemnity clauses

A contract may require one party to indemnify the other for any liability incurred in performance of the contract. The following example demonstrates how such a clause can operate in a manner identical to an exclusion clause.

 Indemnity clauses

Anna hires a car from QuickHire Ltd. The hire agreement provides that Anna is obliged to indemnify QuickHire for any damage caused whilst driving the hire car. As such, the liability for causing damage is transferred from QuickHire to Anna. The practical effect of this is that it allows QuickHire indirectly to exclude its liability.

As indemnity clauses can have the same practical effect as exclusion clauses, it is appropriate that they should be restricted by the UCTA 1977. Section 4 provides that a person dealing as consumer cannot, by reference to any contract term, be made to indemnify another person (whether a party to the contract or not) in respect of liability that may be incurred by the other for negligence or breach of contract, except in so far as the contract term satisfies the requirement of reasonableness. The definition of 'dealing as a consumer' is the same as that under s 3.

The requirement of reasonableness

It can be seen that many types of exclusion clause are of no effect, except in so far as they satisfy the requirement of reasonableness, with the person claiming that the term is reasonable bearing the burden of establishing reasonableness.[37] This requirement lies at the heart of the UCTA 1977, but by its very nature, it is inherently uncertain and it can be doubted that judges lack the expertise to determine what is reasonable in a business context. To aid the judges, the Act itself provides three sources of limited guidance. First, s 11(1) provides that a term will be reasonable if it is 'a fair and reasonable one to be included, having regard to the circumstances that were, or ought reasonably to have been, known to or in the contemplation of the parties when the contract was made'.

---

37. UCTA 1977, s 11(5).

That the courts should determine reasonableness based on the circumstances when the contract was made, not at the time when the case was heard, could, from an evidential perspective, cause problems, especially where there is a considerable period of time between the act complained of and the case being heard.

Second, s 11(2) provides that the court is to have regard in particular to those matters specified in Sch 2. The use of the words 'in particular' indicates that the list of matters in Sch 2 is not exhaustive. The matters listed in Sch 2 include:

- the strength of the bargaining positions of the parties relative to each other;
- whether the customer received an inducement to agree to the term, or, in accepting it, had an opportunity of entering into a similar contract with other persons, but without having to accept a similar term;
- whether the customer knew, or ought reasonably to have known, of the existence and extent of the term;
- where the term excludes or restricts any relevant liability if some condition is not complied with, whether it was reasonable at the time of the contract to expect that compliance with that condition would be practicable.

Strictly speaking, the matters identified in Sch 2 apply only to cases involving ss 6 and 7, but, in practice, these matters are deemed relevant for all cases under UCTA 1977. As Stuart-Smith LJ stated: 'Although Schedule 2 does not apply in the present case, the considerations there set out are usually regarded as being of general application to the question of reasonableness.'[38]

The third source of guidance can be found in s 11(4) and applies solely to clauses seeking to restrict liability to a specified sum of money (that is, s 11(4) does not apply to clauses that exclude liability). In such cases, the court should have regard in particular to:

- the resources that the party could expect to be available to him for the purpose of meeting the liability should it arise; and
- how far it was open to him to cover himself by insurance.

It cannot be overemphasized that, in all cases, it is the clause as a whole that must be reasonable in relation to the particular contract; the question is not whether its particular application in the particular case is reasonable. If a clause is drawn so widely as to be capable of applying in unreasonable circumstances, it will be deemed unreasonable, even though, in the actual situation that has arisen, its application is reasonable.[39] A clause may well have various parts to it, but, because the whole clause must be subjected to the test of reasonableness, it is not permissible to look only at that part of it on which the proferens relies.[40] A court will be particularly unwilling to find a clause reasonable if it purports to exclude all potential liability.[41]

Where a term is found to be unreasonable, it cannot be relied on to exclude or restrict the liability of the proferens. In other words, the contract continues as normal, but without reference to the unreasonable exclusion clause.

38. *Stewart Gill Ltd v Horatio Myer & Co Ltd* [1992] QB 600 (CA) 608.
39. *Walker v Boyle* [1982] 1 WLR 495 (Ch).
40. *Stewart Gill Ltd v Horatio Myer & Co Ltd* [1992] QB 600 (CA).
41. *Lease Management Services Ltd v Purnell Secretarial Services Ltd* [1994] CCLR 127 (CA).

The Unfair Terms in Consumer Contracts Regulations 1999

In an effort to harmonize the law relating to unfair contractual terms, in 1993, the EU Council adopted the Directive on Unfair Terms in Consumer Contracts.[42] The Directive was implemented by the Unfair Terms in Consumer Contracts Regulations 1994,[43] which have since been repealed and replaced by the Unfair Terms in Consumer Contracts Regulations 1999 (UTCCR 1999).[44]

Scope

Given the relatively short deadline for implementation, the Directive was implemented without taking into account the potential overlaps or inconsistencies that exist between the Directive's provisions and those of the UCTA 1977. The result is that there is a considerable overlap between UCTA 1977 and the UTCCR 1999, with parties often having a claim under both pieces of legislation. As we shall see, however, in some respects, the Regulations are wider in scope then the UCTA 1977, but in other respects, the Regulations are noticeably narrower. Also, the tests established are different, with the result that a term could comply fully with the Act, but contravene the Regulations, or vice versa. To combat the potential confusion that can arise from having exclusion clauses subject to two differing pieces of legislation, the Law Commission has recommended[45] that a unified legislative regime be created that merges key provisions of UCTA 1977 and UTCCR 1999, and has even produced a Draft Unfair Contract Terms Bill. To date, however, its recommendations have not been acted upon but the government has published a Draft Consumer Rights Bill, which is discussed later.

Consumer contracts

Regulation 4(1) provides that the Regulations apply 'in relation to unfair terms in contracts concluded between a seller or a supplier and a consumer'. Immediately, it is apparent that, in this respect, the Regulations are narrower than UCTA 1977, in that the 1977 Act is not limited to consumer contracts, whereas the Regulations apply only to consumer contracts.

A 'seller', or 'supplier', is defined as 'any natural or legal person who, in contracts covered by these Regulations, is acting for purposes relating to his trade, business or profession, whether publicly owned or privately owned'.[46] A 'consumer' is defined as 'any natural person who, in contracts covered by these Regulations, is acting for purposes which are outside his trade, business or profession'.[47] Accordingly, under the Regulations, legal persons, such as companies and limited liability partnerships, can never be classified as a consumer,[48] whereas under the 1977 Act, such an entity could constitute a consumer provided that the transaction was not integral to its business.

---

42. Council Directive No 93/13/EC.
43. SI 1994/3159.   44. SI 1999/2083.
45. Law Commission, *Unfair Terms in Contracts* (Law Com No 292, Cm 6464, HMSO 2005).
46. UTCCR 1999, reg 3(1).   47. ibid.
48. There is one exception to this—namely, where the term is an arbitration agreement (i.e. a term that requires disputes to be referred to arbitration before commencing legal proceedings), then a legal person can constitute a consumer: see the Arbitration Act 1996, s 90.

likely that the Bill will undergo notable amendments prior to its introduction into Parliament and, of course, may undergo substantial amendment as it progresses through Parliament.

Chapter conclusion

Exclusion and limitation clauses are a common tool in the business world, but they are not inviolate. They are strongly regulated by both statute and the common law, and any party who wishes to exclude or limit its liability via such a clause would be wise to have a sound knowledge of those clauses that the law prohibits, and those clauses that must be reasonable in order to remain effective. This strict regulation does not simply apply to exclusion clauses and, as discussed, any form of unfair term may be rendered unenforceable if it is deemed to be unfair under the Unfair Terms in Consumer Contracts Regulations 1999.

Having discussed situations in which exclusion clauses and unfair terms might be unenforceable, the Chapter 10 focuses on certain situations in which the entire contract can be rendered unenforceable.

 Key points summary

- An exclusion clause will only be effective if it is incorporated into a contract. An exclusion clause contained in a signed contract will usually be effective, irrespective of whether the signatory read it or not.

- An exclusion clause will usually only be effective if it was brought to the other party's attention prior to the contract being formed.

- The Unfair Contract Terms Act 1977 principally regulates exclusion clauses that exclude or restrict 'business liability'.

- The Act absolutely prohibits the exclusion or limitation of liability for death or personal injury caused by negligence. For other types of loss, an exclusion clause will only be effective insofar as it satisfies the requirement of reasonableness.

- Where standard terms exclude or restrict liability against a consumer for breach of contract, such terms will only be effective insofar as they satisfy the requirement of reasonableness.

- An indemnity clause will be ineffective, except insofar as it satisfies the requirement of reasonableness.

- The Unfair Terms in Consumer Contracts Regulations 1999 apply to any type of term that could potentially be unfair, provided that the term is not individually negotiated and is contained in a consumer contract.

- Unfair terms will be ineffective. A term will be unfair if, contrary to the requirement of good faith, it causes a significant imbalance in the parties' rights and obligations arising under the contract, to the detriment of the consumer.

- The Draft Consumer Rights Bill proposes to replace the UTCCR 1999 and limit the scope of the UCTA 1977.

Self-test questions

1. Define the following:
    (a) exclusion clause;
    (b) proferens;
    (c) *contra proferentem*;
    (d) notice;
    (e) strict obligation;
    (f) indemnity clause.

2. Do you believe that enacting the Law Commission's draft Unfair Contract Terms Bill would be a beneficial development? Provide reasons for enacting the Bill and for retaining the current position.

3. Discuss whether each of the following would be unenforceable under the common law, the 1977 Act, or the 1999 Regulations:
    (a) a contractual term that excludes liability for property damage caused by a negligent employee;
    (b) a term in an insurance contract that requires the policyholder to pay a voluntary excess of 95 per cent of the amount claimed for;
    (c) a term providing that, when winding up a company, the liquidator is not to be liable for any losses caused by his negligent conduct;
    (d) a term providing that a seller of goods can unilaterally alter the terms of a contract for the sale of goods;
    (e) a term that requires an employee to indemnify his employer if the employer is made vicariously liable for the employer's conduct;
    (f) a term that provides that a company is not liable to pay any compensation due to any breach of any express or implied term, or any statutory duty.

4. Explain in what respects the 1977 Act is wider in scope than the 1999 Regulations, and vice versa.

Further reading

Sir Jack Beatson, Andrew Burrows, and John Cartwright, *Anson's Law of Contract* (29th edn, OUP 2010) ch 6
Provides a clear, but detailed, account of the common law and statutory regulation of exclusion clauses and unfair terms

Roger Brownsword and John N Adams, 'The Unfair Contract Terms Act: A Decade of Discretion' (1988) 104 LQR 94
Discusses the operation of the Unfair Contract Terms Act 1977 and focuses on how the courts have applied the requirement of reasonableness

Law Commission, *Unfair Terms in Contracts* (Law Com No 292, Cm 6464, HMSO 2005)
Recommends that the UCTA 1977 and the Unfair Terms in Consumer Contracts Regulations 1999 should be unified, and provides a draft Unfair Contract Terms Bill

Elizabeth Macdonald, 'Unifying Unfair Terms Legislation' (2004) 67 MLR 69
Discusses the problems associated with having two pieces of legislation regulating unfair terms; analyses the Law Commission's draft Unfair Contract Terms Bill

Websites

<https://www.gov.uk/government/publications/draft-consumer-rights-bill>
The webpage of the Draft Consumer Rights Bill. Provides access to the Bill itself as well as detailed background information

 Remember to visit the **Online Resource Centre** at <**http://www. oxfordtextbooks.co.uk/orc/roach3e**> to access the following resources on Chapter 9, 'Exclusion clauses and unfair terms'*:* more **practice questions** and answers; a **glossary** of key terms; **multiple-choice questions**; and **revision summaries**. Updates to the law can be found on Twitter by following **@UKBusinessLaw**.

10 Vitiating factors

- Misrepresentation
- Mistake
- Duress

- Undue influence
- Unconscionable bargains
- Illegality and public policy

INTRODUCTION

The need for commercial certainty goes beyond the formation of a contract. Businesses need to be aware in what circumstances validly formed contracts may be set aside or removed from existence. Businesses may engage in activities prior to the contract being formed that can subsequently cause the contract to become unenforceable, resulting in the business sustaining a substantial loss, or the loss of reputation and future business. Businesses need to know what type of pre-contract activity should be avoided—whether it be the making of false statements, the infliction of improper pressure, or the taking advantage of another's weakness. However, there are instances in which a contract can be set aside even though no reprehensible conduct has taken place. Businesses need to be aware that innocent activities can render a contract void or voidable, so that measures can be taken to avoid such conduct.

➡ **vitiate:** to render incomplete, imperfect or faulty

Situations such as those mentioned above are said to 'vitiate' the contract. Certain vitiating factors (for example, mistake) will render a contract void, whereas others (for example, misrepresentation) will merely render the contract voidable. It is therefore important to understand the difference between a contract that has become 'void' and a contract that has become 'voidable'.

➡ **void *ab initio*:** 'invalid from the beginning'

- Void is an abbreviation of **void *ab initio***, and a contract held to be void is treated as if it never existed, with the parties having no discretion as to whether the contract should continue to exist.

➡ **voidable:** valid until set aside

- **Voidable** contracts are not wiped from existence, and will continue to be valid and enforceable until such time as the relevant party sets it aside.

Having established the difference between a void and voidable contract, we can now turn our attention to the various vitiating factors, beginning with misrepresentation.

Misrepresentation

As noted in Chapter 7, certain statements can become terms of the contract and, if untrue, can form the basis of a claim for breach of contract. Conversely, other statements will not be regarded as terms: they will amount to mere representations and cannot found a cause of action for breach. A false representation may, however, result in an action for misrepresentation, which will usually entitle the innocent party to **rescind** the contract and, depending upon the type of misrepresentation, also claim damages for misrepresentation. An action in misrepresentation can lie irrespective of whether a representation has become a term of the contract or not.

🔗 The distinction between terms and representations is discussed at p 167

➜ **rescind:** terminate a contract, either by an act of the parties or the court

For an action in misrepresentation to succeed, three conditions must be satisfied:

1. There must be a false statement of past or existing fact, or of law.
2. The false statement of fact or law must have been addressed to the person misled.
3. The statement must have induced the other person to enter into the contract.

A false statement of fact or law

Traditionally, only false statements of fact could normally constitute a misrepresentation, but it would now appear that false statements of law may also constitute misrepresentations. Although a statement will normally be made by words, it is possible for a statement to be made by conduct, as the following case demonstrates.

🔗 Statements of law are discussed at p 241

Spice Girls Ltd v Aprilia World Service BV [2002] EWCA Civ 151

FACTS: The Spice Girls' world tour was sponsored by the defendant, a motor scooter manufacturer. Prior to the contract being signed, all five members of the band engaged in advertising activities (for example, photo shoots, television commercials, etc) for the Spice Sonic scooter. At the time that they engaged in these activities, the band knew that Geri Halliwell would be leaving the group before the sponsorship agreement ended, but the defendant was not told of this. When she left the group, the defendant argued that it had paid for the right to use the image of all five members of the band. As a result, it withheld the next sponsorship fee instalment. The band sued.

HELD: The Court of Appeal held that, by appearing in the promotional material, the Spice Girls' conduct constituted a statement that the Spice Girls did not know or have reasonable grounds to believe that any of them intended to leave the group before the minimum term of the advertising contract. Because the band already knew that Geri would leave before the end of the transaction, that statement was false.[1]

Where a statement is ambiguous and has several meanings, some being true and others being false, then, provided that the representor's interpretation of the statement was reasonable, it will not be regarded as false.[2]

'Mere puffs'

Statements that constitute sales talk, or which are so vague as to be almost meaningless, will not be regarded as representations and will instead amount to 'mere puffs'. Thus, in *Dimmock v Hallet*,[3] an auctioneer described a piece of land as 'fertile and improvable', whereas, in fact, it was abandoned and useless. The Court of Appeal

---

1. See also *Crystal Palace Football Club (2000) Ltd v Dowie* [2007] EWHC 1392 (QB), [2007] IRLR 682.
2. *McInerny v Lloyd's Bank Ltd* [1974] 1 Lloyd's Rep 246 (CA).   3. (1867) 2 Ch App 21 (CA).

held that the statement did not amount to a representation, because it was 'a mere flourishing description by an auctioneer'.[4]

Statements of opinion

A statement of opinion does not, in itself, constitute a misrepresentation if the opinion turns out to be incorrect, because opinions are not facts.

 Bisset v Wilkinson [1927] AC 177 (PC)

FACTS: The seller of a farm told a prospective purchaser that, in his opinion, the farm could support 2,000 sheep. Based upon this, the representee purchased the farm and discovered that the farm could not support anywhere near 2,000 sheep. The representee alleged that the representor's statement amounted to a misrepresentation.

HELD: The Privy Council held that because the seller had never been a sheep farmer and the farm had never reared sheep, his statement was a mere statement of opinion aimed at providing an honest estimate. Accordingly, it was not a statement of fact and consequently did not amount to a misrepresentation.

However, in two situations, a statement of opinion can involve a misrepresentation of fact:

1. If the representor states an opinion that he knows that he does not believe in, this constitutes a misrepresentation of fact because he falsely represents the fact that he holds a particular opinion.[5]
2. If the representor represents an opinion for which he does not have reasonable grounds, and he impliedly represents that he has such grounds, this will constitute a misrepresentation of fact, as the following case demonstrates.

 Smith v Land and House Property Corporation (1884) 28 Ch D 7 (CA)

FACTS: The claimant wished to sell a hotel and he described the hotel as let to a 'Mr Frederick Fleck (a most desirable tenant)'. The defendant purchased the hotel, but discovered that Fleck had not paid rent for the last quarter and, shortly after the sale, the business that Fleck was running went into liquidation. The defendant refused to complete the sale and the claimant sought an order for specific performance. The defendant counterclaimed, alleging that the claimant's statement regarding Fleck amounted to a misrepresentation. The claimant argued that the statement was merely one of opinion and so was not actionable.

HELD: The Court of Appeal held that the claimant's statement involved a misrepresentation of fact, because the claimant had impliedly stated that it had reasonable grounds for the opinions expressed regarding Fleck. That the claimant actually knew of Fleck's financial difficulties meant that the statement amounted to a misrepresentation and the defendant was therefore entitled to rescind the contract.

---

4. ibid 21 (Turner LJ).   5. *Jendwine v Slade* (1797) 2 Esp 571.

Statements of intention or prediction

Statements concerning the future (the notable example being statements of intention) are generally not actionable, because such statements are not factual. However, a representor who makes a statement concerning a future state of affairs will have made a misrepresentation of fact if, *at the time that the statement was made*, he either knows or does not believe that the state of affairs will arise.

 Edgington v Fitzmaurice (1885) 29 Ch D 459 (CA)

FACTS: The directors of a company issued a **prospectus** in order to attract investment. The prospectus stated that any money raised would be used to expand and develop the company's business. In fact, the money was going to be used to pay off the company's debts. The claimant advanced money and then discovered the real reason behind the issuing of the prospectus.

HELD: The Court of Appeal held that the statement in the prospectus constituted a misrepresentation and the claimant could recover damages. Although it was a statement of intention, at the time that the statement was made, the defendant knew that it was not going to act in accordance with the statement.

➡ **prospectus:** a document providing information concerning a company, issued when that company wishes to attract investment

Statements of law

Traditionally, neither the common law[6] nor equity[7] would regard a false statement as to the state of the law as a misrepresentation, unless the representation related to foreign law.[8] But this traditional view needs elaboration. What is true is that pure or abstract statements of law (that is, statements of law that did not relate to the facts of the case) were not actionable, but that statements of law related to the facts of a particular case (known as a 'misrepresentation of private rights') may be regarded as statements of fact.[9]

The rule that pure statements of law cannot constitute misrepresentation needs to be reassessed in light of more recent cases. In *Kleinwort Benson Ltd v Lincoln City Council*,[10] the House of Lords abolished the rule that stated that monies could not be recovered where a *mistake* of law had been made. In *Pankhania v Hackney London Borough Council*,[11] the High Court stated that the rule preventing misstatements of law from being actionable 'has not survived the decision in Kleinwort Benson'.[12] This would appear to abolish the distinction between law and fact mentioned previously, but we should remain cautious. The decision in *Pankhania* was only a first-instance decision and it is still open to a higher court to affirm the traditional rule, although this is unlikely to occur: both Maurice Kay LJ and Bodey J in the Court of Appeal in *Brennan v Bolt Burdon*,[13] speaking *obiter*, expressed approval for the decision in *Pankhania*. However, in a subsequent case, Rix LJ stated *obiter* that in cases involving the tort of deceit,[14] a statement of fact is still required.[15] Rix LJ did not, however,

---

6. *Beattie v Lord Ebury* (1872) 7 Ch App 777.   7. *Rashdall v Ford* (1866) LR 2 Eq 750.
8. *André & Cie SA v Ets Michel Blanc & Fils* [1979] 2 Lloyd's Rep 427 (CA).
9. *Solle v Butcher* [1950] 1 KB 671 (CA).   10. [1999] 2 AC 349 (HL).
11. [2002] EWHC 2441 (Ch), [2002] NPC 123.   12. ibid [57] (Rex Tedd QC).
13. [2004] EWCA Civ 303, [2005] QB 303.
14. A claim for damages for fraudulent misrepresentation is brought under the tort of deceit, but that tort is not limited to a fraudulent misrepresentation resulting in a contract.
15. *AIC Ltd v ITS Testing Services (UK) Ltd* [2006] EWCA Civ 1601, [2007] 1 Lloyd's Rep 555, [255].

consider *Pankhania* or *Brennan*, so his *dictum* is of doubtful authority. Therefore, one can cautiously state that false statements of law are likely to be just as actionable as false statements of fact.

Can silence constitute a false statement?

The general rule is that silence cannot constitute a misrepresentation, because parties to a contract are generally not under a duty to disclose relevant facts to one another. A consequence of the principle of **caveat emptor** is that parties are free to profit from their superior knowledge.

 caveat emptor: 'let the buyer beware'

 Fletcher v Krell (1873) 42 LJ QB 55

FACTS: The defendant agreed to employ the claimant as a governess for three years. She had been described to the defendant as a spinster and, upon this basis, he employed her. In fact, she was a divorcee and, had the defendant known this, he would not have employed her. Upon discovering the truth, he rescinded her contract of employment, claiming that she had misrepresented her position. The claimant alleged breach of contract.

HELD: The claimant was under no obligation to reveal that she was divorced, nor had she been asked if she had been married before. Accordingly, there had been no misrepresentation, and the claimant could recover damages for the breach of contract resulting from the wrongful rescission.

This principle is not absolute, however, and silence can constitute a false statement in several situations. First, if a representation that is true when it is made subsequently becomes untrue to the representor's knowledge due to a change of circumstances, then the representor is under a duty to notify the representee of the change. A failure to do so may amount to a misrepresentation.

With v O'Flanagan [1936] Ch 575 (CA)

FACTS: A doctor, seeking to sell his medical practice, represented to a prospective buyer that the practice generated £2,000 per year, which was true. Five months later, the representee purchased the practice. By the time that the contract was signed, however, the income that the practice was generating had fallen to around £5 per week (due to the illness of the doctor) and the majority of the practice's patients had left. The claimant, upon discovering this, alleged misrepresentation.

HELD: The Court of Appeal held that representation inducing the other party into entering into a contract is to be regarded as continuing until the contract is signed. Accordingly, where a change of circumstances renders a previously true representation untrue, the representor should disclose the change to the representee and failure to do so may constitute a misrepresentation.

Second, where a statement is literally true, but fails to convey the whole truth by omitting certain facts (that is, it is a half-truth), the non-disclosure may amount to a misrepresentation.

Nottingham Patent Brick and Tile Co v Butler (1886) 16 QBD 778 (CA)

FACTS: The defendant contracted to sell a piece of land to claimant. The claimant's solicitor asked the defendant's solicitor whether the land was subject to any restrictive covenants. The defendant's solicitor stated that he was not aware of any covenants, but did not disclose that this was because he had not read the title deeds. It transpired that the land was subject to restrictive covenants. The claimant alleged misrepresentation.

HELD: Although the defendant's solicitor's statement was literally true, it omitted key facts that the claimant would wish to know. This omission changed the statement of fact into a misstatement of fact. Accordingly, the Court of Appeal held that the statement amounted to a misrepresentation.

Third, certain contracts are classified as *uberrimae fidei* and impose a duty upon the parties to disclose all material facts to one another. The classic example of an *uberrimae fidei* contract is a contract of insurance. Accordingly, a contract of insurance is voidable if a party fails to disclose a material fact before the contract was entered into and if that non-disclosure induced the making of the contract[16] (for example, failure to disclose motoring offences in a contract for motor insurance, or the failure to disclose a terminal medical condition in a life insurance contract). In relation to insurance contracts between consumers and businesses that are engaged in the provision of insurance, s 2(2) of the Consumer Insurance (Disclosure and Representations) Act 2012 places a duty on the consumer 'to take reasonable care not to make misrepresentations to the insurer'.

➡ *uberrimae fidei*: 'utmost good faith'

The third instance in which silence can constitute a misrepresentation is where the parties are in a fiduciary relationship. A fiduciary relationship is one of trust and confidence, which tends to arise only in certain professional relationships (for example, principal and agent, partner and partner, solicitor and client, etc). Where such a relationship exists, there is a duty to disclose all material facts and non-disclosure may therefore amount to a misrepresentation.

The statement must be addressed to the person misled

In order for misrepresentation to be founded, the statement must have been addressed to the person misled or his agent.[17] This does not mean, however, that a statement must be specifically addressed to a particular person, because statements can be made to the public. Further, it may be the case that the representor makes a statement that he intends or knows will be passed on to others. In such a case, provided that the person alleging misrepresentation falls within the class of persons on to whom the representor intends or knows the information could be passed, this requirement will be satisfied.[18]

---

16. *St Paul Fire and Marine Insurance Co (UK) Ltd v McConnell Dowell Constructors Ltd* [1995] 2 Lloyd's Rep 116 (CA).

17. *Peek v Gurney* (1873) LR 6 HL 377 (HL).   18. *Andrews v Mockford* [1896] 1 QB 372 (CA).

Inducement

Once the existence of an actionable statement has been established, the party misled will need to prove that the statement induced him[19] to enter the contract (that is, he relied and acted upon the statement). From this, it follows that misrepresentation will not be established where the representee:

- was unaware of the representor's false statement at the time the contract was entered into;[20] or
- knew that the statement was false;[21] or
- would have entered into the transaction, even if he knew the truth;[22] or
- relied upon his own information, as the following case demonstrates.

 Attwood v Small (1838) 6 Cl & F 232

FACTS: The defendant offered to sell a mine and made exaggerated statements about the mine's earning potential. The claimant agreed to purchase the mine on the condition that his agent could investigate the validity of the defendant's statements. The defendant agreed and the agent carried out an investigation. The agent failed to discover the falsity of the statement and verified the defendant's statement. The claimant purchased the mine and discovered the truth.

HELD: The contract could not be rescinded for misrepresentation, because the claimant was not induced into entering the contract by the defendant's statement, but by the statement of his own agent.

Whilst the representee's own investigation into the validity of the representor's statement might result in a failure to establish inducement, the mere fact that the representee could have discovered the truth, but failed to do so, will not cause his claim to fail.[23]

Materiality

In order for a statement to induce a party, it must be shown to be material.[24] A material statement has been defined as:

> one which would have affected the judgment of a reasonable person in deciding whether, or on what terms, to enter into the contract; or one which would induce him into entering the contract without making such enquiries as he would otherwise make.[25]

In practice, the requirement of materiality is usually a formality, simply existing in order to filter out trivial claims that, even if successful, would most likely only result in an award of nominal damages.

Figure 10.1 illustrates the actionability of a false statement.

---

19. Provided that the statement was a genuine inducement, it is irrelevant that other factors also induced the representee into entering the contract (*Edgington v Fitzmaurice* (1885) 29 Ch D 459 (CA)).

20. *Re Northumberland and Durham District Banking Co, ex p Biggs* (1858) 28 Ch 50.

21. *Begbie v Phosphate Sewage Co* (1875) LR 10 QB 491 (CA).

22. *JEB Fasteners Ltd v Marks Bloom & Co* [1983] 1 All ER 583 (CA).

23. *Redgrave v Hurd* (1881) 20 Ch D 1 (CA).   24. *McDowell v Fraser* (1779) 1 Dougl 247.

25. Edwin Peel, *Treitel on the Law of Contract* (13th edn, Sweet & Maxwell 2011) 367.

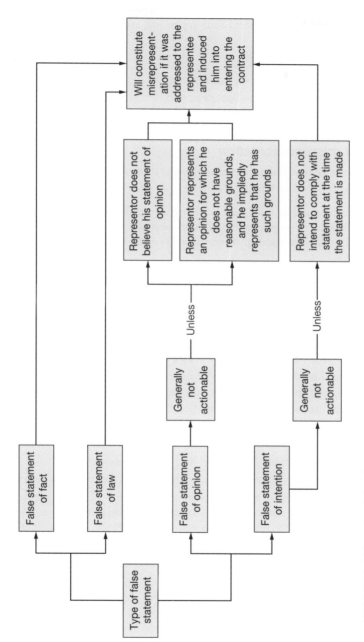

FIGURE 10.1 The actionability of a statement

Remedies for misrepresentation

Once the representee has established the existence of an actionable misrepresentation, the next step is to determine what remedy will be awarded. This will be largely dependent upon the type of misrepresentation that was committed. Misrepresentations come in one of four types and are determined by the state of mind of the representee:

1. fraudulent misrepresentation;
2. common law negligent misrepresentation;
3. statutory negligent misrepresentation; and
4. innocent misrepresentation.

Fraudulent misrepresentation

The classic definition of fraudulent misrepresentation was made in the case of *Derry v Peek*,[26] in which Lord Herschell stated that:

> there must be proof of fraud, and nothing short of that will suffice...[F]raud is proved when it is shown that a false representation has been made, (1) knowingly, or (2) without belief in its truth, or (3) recklessly, careless whether it be true or false.[27]

It follows that a statement will not be fraudulent if (i) the representor honestly believes it to be true, even if there are no reasonable grounds for such belief;[28] and (ii) the statement is merely negligent—even gross negligence will not suffice.[29] What is required is that the representor knew the statement to be untrue, or, if he did not know that it was untrue, that he had no grounds for believing it to be true. The motive of the representor is irrelevant; the lack of dishonesty or the intent to deceive or cause another loss does not need to be established.[30] However, provided that the representor believed the statement was true, an unreasonable interpretation will not be regarded as a fraudulent misrepresentation.[31]

If the representee can establish that a fraudulent misrepresentation has been made, he will have access to several remedies, as follows.

affirm: continue with a voidable contract, or continue with a contract that has been breached by the other party

- He will be able to **affirm** the contract and then recover damages.
- Alternatively, he may choose to rescind the contract and then recover damages.
- If the representee does rescind the contract, and the representor claims damages for breach of contract or tries to obtain specific performance, the representee may plead the representor's fraud as a defence, and counterclaim for damages.

Although misrepresentation is a contractual concept, an action for fraudulent misrepresentation is based in the tort of deceit. Accordingly, damages are assessed on a tortious basis (that is, the amount required to put the claimant in the position in which he would have been had the misrepresentation not been made). As the following case demonstrates, this provides a very wide measure of damages, because it

---

26. (1889) 14 App Cas 337 (HL).   27. ibid 374.
28. ibid.   29. *Angus v Clifford* [1891] 2 Ch 449 (CA).
30. *Bradford Third Equitable Benefit Building Society v Borders* [1941] 2 All ER 205 (HL).
31. *Akerhielm v De Mare* [1959] AC 789 (PC).

permits the representee to claim for all losses flowing directly from the misrepresentation, including losses that are not reasonably foreseeable.[32]

 ### Kinch v Rosling [2009] EWHC 286 (QB)

FACTS: Kinch (the claimant) was a successful businessman, who wished to finance a takeover of Leicester Football Club. To that end, he sold his existing business and used the capital to purchase shares in the football club, and to provide additional capital to the club. He also entered into negotiations with an organization that acted through its solicitor, Rosling (the first defendant). Rosling represented that funds were available, providing that Kinch first paid various fees in advance. These fees were paid, but it soon became apparent that the represented funds were not available. The claimant became liable for debts that he could not pay. The bid for the club fell through, and the club entered administration, thereby rendering the claimant's shares worthless. The claimant was declared bankrupt.

HELD: Rosling's representation was clearly fraudulent. The claimant was therefore awarded special damages of just under £2.3 million, which included the fees paid to Rosling, fees paid to various professional advisors, and the loss of the claimant's shareholding. Additionally, the claimant obtained £10,000 general damages in respect of the 'humiliation, distress and anxiety that he has suffered as a consequence of the bankruptcy'.[33]

Damages for fraudulent misrepresentation will not be reduced on the ground of contributory negligence (because this defence cannot be pleaded in actions in deceit),[34] and the rules relating to remoteness are relaxed. However, given that the claimant is alleging fraud, the standard of proof is likely to be higher than the usual civil standard of proof. Further, the rules relating to mitigation of loss will apply fully to a representee who has sustained loss due to a fraudulent misrepresentation.[35]

> Contributory negligence is discussed at p 332

> The rules relating to mitigation of loss are discussed at p 331

Common law negligent misrepresentation (negligent misstatement)

Prior to 1964, negligent misrepresentation did not exist and any misrepresentation that was not fraudulent was classified as innocent. The lack of a specific form of misrepresentation covering negligent statements was problematic, in so much as whilst the victim of an innocent misrepresentation could rescind the contract, he could not normally recover any damages. This changed following the case of *Hedley Byrne & Co Ltd v Heller & Partners Ltd*,[36] in which the House of Lords created a new category of misrepresentation to cover negligent misstatements. However, the House made clear that establishing the requirements of negligence would not be enough to establish the existence of a negligent misstatement. The usual requirements would need to be established (for example, existence of a duty of care, breach of duty, causation, and remoteness), but the representee would also need to show that a 'special relationship' existed between himself and the representor. The case of *Hedley Byrne* and what constitutes a special relationship is discussed in depth in Chapter 14; it will therefore not be repeated here.

> The case of *Hedley Byrne* is discussed in more detail at p 380

---

32. *Doyle v Olby (Ironmongers) Ltd* [1969] 2 QB 158 (CA).   33. [2009] EWHC 286 (QB) [18].
34. *Standard Chartered Bank v Pakistan National Shipping Corporation* [2001] QB 167 (CA).   35. ibid.
36. [1964] AC 465 (HL).

The remedies for common law negligent misrepresentation are largely the same as those for fraudulent misrepresentation, but with one crucial difference. Whilst damages are still measured on a tortious basis (because the action is based on negligent misstatement), only losses that are reasonably foreseeable can be recovered.

Statutory negligent misrepresentation

In 1962 (one year before *Hedley Byrne* established negligent misstatement), the Law Reform Committee published a report recommending the creation of a Misrepresentation Act, which would fill in the gap in the law by providing a remedy for those who sustain loss due to a negligent misrepresentation. With the creation of common law negligent misrepresentation in *Hedley Byrne*, one would suspect that the Law Reform Committee's proposals would become redundant. But in the years following *Hedley Byrne*, subsequent courts severely restricted the scope of negligent misstatement by placing an extremely strict interpretation upon the requirement of a 'special' relationship. Accordingly, the recommendations of the Law Reform Committee were implemented and the Misrepresentation Act 1967 was passed, of which s 2(1) states:

> Where a person has entered into a contract after a misrepresentation has been made to him by another party thereto and as a result thereof he has suffered loss, then, if the person making the misrepresentation would be liable to damages in respect thereof had the misrepresentation been made fraudulently, that person shall be so liable notwithstanding that the misrepresentation was not made fraudulently, unless he proves that he had reasonable ground to believe and did believe up to the time the contract was made the facts represented were true.

Four notable points can be made about s 2(1), as follows.

1. Establishing negligent misrepresentation under s 2(1) is not dependent upon the existence of a duty of care or a special relationship. The only requirement of 'proximity' is the existence of a contract between representor and representee.
2. Section 2(1) only applies where the other party to the contract is the representor. Accordingly, the three-party situation in *Hedley Byrne* (where the contract is entered into on the basis of a third party's representation) is outside the scope of s 2(1).
3. Section 2(1) only applies where a contract is formed. Where contractual negotiations do not result in a contract, but the representee suffers loss in reliance of a misrepresentation, the representee will have to rely on the common law to obtain a remedy.
4. The burden of proof is reversed. Accordingly, the representor is liable unless he had reasonable grounds to believe that his statement was true.

The Court of Appeal in *Royscot Trust Ltd v Rogerson*[37] held that damages under s 2(1) are calculated in exactly the same way as damages for fraudulent misrepresentation, even though the misrepresentation is not fraudulent (this has been labelled the 'fiction of fraud').[38] Unsurprisingly, the fiction of fraud has attracted considerable criticism on the ground that it is objectionable in principle to 'treat the foolish but honest man as if he were dishonest'.[39] There is increasing evidence of judicial dissatisfaction

---

37. [1991] 2 QB 297 (CA).
38. PS Atiyah and GH Treitel, 'Misrepresentation Act 1967' (1967) 30 MLR 369, 373.
39. Richard Hooley, 'Damages and Misrepresentation Act 1967' (1991) 107 LQR 547, 549.

with the fiction of fraud. For example, Lord Steyn has stated that 'it is a rational and defensible strategy to impose wider liability on an intentional wrongdoer',[40] arguing that such an approach 'serves a deterrent purpose in discouraging fraud'.[41] More recently, Hamblen J stated that, if *Royscot* were to come before a higher court, there was 'a real possibility of it being reversed.'[42] It is submitted that the fiction of fraud is yet another example of the Act's poor drafting and numerous academics have validly argued that the Act should be amended to remove the reference to fraud.

A representor who is ordered to pay damages under s 2(1) can plead the defence of contributory negligence, provided that he is also liable in tort for negligence.[43]

Innocent misrepresentation

With the creation of negligent misrepresentation, it now follows that innocent misrepresentations include only those that are wholly innocent (that is, those that include no fraud or negligence whatsoever).

As with other misrepresentations, the claimant may affirm or rescind the contract. Damages are not available as of right, but, as is discussed later, the court does have the power to award damages in lieu of rescission.[44] Where damages are not granted in lieu of rescission, the representee may be able to obtain an indemnity. An indemnity is an ancillary order[45] requiring the representor to reimburse the representee for any payments made arising from obligations necessarily created by the contract. An indemnity is much more limited than an award of damages, as the following case demonstrates.

 ### *Whittington v Seale-Hayne* (1900) 82 LT 49 (Ch)

FACTS: The defendant owned premises that the claimant wished to use for the purpose of breeding poultry. The defendant represented that the premises were completely sanitary and in a good state of repair. Relying on this, the claimant took up a lease on the premises. The lease required the claimant to execute such work as might be required by a local or public authority. Due to unsanitary conditions, the premises' water supply was poisoned, resulting in the farm manager becoming ill and a large number of poultry dying, with those that did survive rendered useless for the purposes of breeding. The premises were subsequently condemned by the local authority, which required the claimant to repair them. The claimant sought an indemnity for the loss of the dead birds, loss of profits on sales, recovery of rent payments, recovery of medical expenses in respect of the manager, and the cost of repairing any defects in the premises.

HELD: The High Court rescinded the lease—but it held that the claimant's action was in reality a claim for damages, not an indemnity. Accordingly, whilst the claimant could recover an indemnity for those expenses that were a necessary obligation created by the lease— namely, the rates and rent payments, and repair costs—the claimant could not recover an indemnity for the loss of stock, loss of profits, and medical expenses, because the lease did not oblige the claimant to carry on business as a poultry farm or to employ a manager.

---

40. *Smith New Court Securities Ltd v Citibank NA* [1997] AC 254 (CA) 279.   41. ibid.
42. *Cheltenham Borough Council v Laird* [2009] EWHC 1253 (QB), [2009] IRLR 621 [524].
43. *Gran Gelato Ltd v Richcliff (Group) Ltd* [1992] Ch 560 (Ch).
44. Misrepresentation Act 1967, s 2(2).
45. As an indemnity order will be ancillary to a rescission order, it follows that an indemnity cannot be recovered where rescission is barred.

As an award of damages will naturally cover the losses recoverable under an indemnity, it follows that an indemnity order is pointless where damages are awarded. For this reason, indemnity orders are usually made only where the misrepresentation is innocent and the court does not exercise the power to award damages in lieu of rescission.

Rescission

→ *restitutio in integrum*: 'restoration to the original position'

Misrepresentation renders a contract voidable,[46] which means that it will continue until such time as the representee sets it aside (this is known as 'rescission'). Rescission has the effect of setting aside the contract as if it had never been made. Accordingly, its principal aim is to return the parties to their pre-contract position (this is known as *restitutio in integrum*). The representee can rescind in one of two ways, as follows.

1. The representee can apply to the court for a rescission order. Where a formal document (for example, a lease) is to be rescinded, a rescission order might be necessary. A rescission order might also be necessary if one party fails to return what is due.

2. In many cases, a court order will not be necessary. The representee can rescind the contract simply by indicating to the representor that he is no longer bound by the contract. Whilst communication of rescission is normally required, where the misrepresentation is fraudulent and the representor has since absconded, communication of rescission is not required, provided that the representee performs some overt act that indicates his intention to rescind.[47]

Whilst rescission is normally available for all forms of misrepresentation, in a number of instances, the representee will be barred from exercising the right to rescind.

Affirmation

The representee may not wish the contract to come to an end, and can therefore waive his right to rescind (known as 'affirmation'). Once the representee has expressly or impliedly indicated affirmation, the right to rescind is lost, but affirmation will only be valid if the representee knew that the representor's statement was false and that he had the right to rescind.[48] Following the acquisition of this knowledge, the representee may find that his subsequent action or inaction is enough to indicate affirmation,[49] as the following example demonstrates.

Eg **Rescission and affirmation**

BioCorp Ltd issues a prospectus stating that any money raised through the selling of shares will be used to purchase new premises and expand the business. Relying on the prospectus, Richard purchases a large number of shares in BioCorp. Richard then discovers that the money raised from selling shares is to be used to pay off BioCorp's substantial debt. However, he takes no further action and continues to accept dividend payments. Some time later, when BioCorp's financial position worsens and insolvency looms, Richard decides that he wishes to rescind the contract.

---

46. *Clough v L & NW Rly* (1871) LR 7 Ex 26.
47. *Car and Universal Finance Co Ltd v Caldwell* [1965] 1 QB 525 (CA).
48. *Peyman v Lanjani* [1985] Ch 457 (CA).   49. See *Long v Lloyd* [1958] 1 WLR 753 (CA).

It is likely that Richard will be barred from rescinding. His failure to act (for example, by removing his name from the register of shareholders)[50] and his continued acceptance of dividend payments[51] would be likely to amount to affirmation. Depending on the length of time that passed between becoming aware of the truth and attempting to rescind, the court may also bar rescission on the basis that too much time has lapsed.

Lapse of time

Lapse of time provides evidence of affirmation in cases of inaction by the representee. In addition, the right to rescind will be lost if the falsity is not discovered within a reasonable time.

 Leaf v International Galleries [1950] 2 KB 86 (CA)

FACTS: The defendant innocently represented that a painting that it wished to sell was a genuine Constable. Relying on this, the claimant purchased the painting. Five years later, the claimant attempted to sell the painting, whereupon it was discovered that the painting was not by Constable. The claimant sought to rescind the contract based on the defendant's innocent misrepresentation.

HELD: The claimant had sought rescission promptly after discovering the falsity of the statement. Therefore, the lapse of time did not indicate that he had affirmed the contract. Despite this, the Court of Appeal held that the right to rescind was lost due to the fact that the claimant did not discover the falsity of the statement within a reasonable time.

⭐ See LCB Gower, 'Contract: Sale of Goods—Innocent Misrepresentations and Conditions' (1950) 13 MLR 362

When time starts running will depend upon the type of misrepresentation. Where the misrepresentation is fraudulent, then time will start running when the fraud was, or could reasonably have been, discovered. In all other cases, time starts running from the date of the contract (as in *Leaf* above).

Third-party rights

The right to rescind may be lost where an innocent third party (that is, one who does not know of the falsity of the statement) acquires, by purchase, rights in the subject matter of the contract. As misrepresentation renders a contract voidable only, this means that good title can be passed to an innocent third-party purchaser at any time before the representee rescinds the contract,[52] as the following case demonstrates.

 White v Garden (1851) 10 CB 919

FACTS: A rogue bought 50 tonnes of iron from Garden. The rogue paid for the iron using a fraudulent **bill of exchange**. The rogue then sold the iron to White, who was unaware of

➡ **bill of exchange:** a document that promises to pay the bearer a sum of money at a future date

50. *Re Scottish Petroleum Co (No 2)* (1883) 23 Ch D 413 (CA).
51. *Scholey v Central Railway Co of Venezuela* (1867) LR 9 Eq 266.
52. In the case of contracts involving the sale of goods, this rule is statutory: see Sale of Goods Act 1979, s 23.

→ **conversion:**
interfering with goods
in a manner that is
inconsistent with
another's rights (see
'Conversion' at p 427)

the rogue's prior fraudulent activities. When the bill of exchange was dishonoured, Garden removed some of the iron that had been delivered to White, alleging that he had the right to rescind the contract due to the rogue's misrepresentation. White alleged that, in removing the iron, Garden had committed the tort of **conversion**.

HELD: Garden was held liable for the tort of conversion. White had acquired good title to the goods, because he had no knowledge of the rogue's misrepresentation. Garden had therefore lost the right to rescind.

COMMENT: In this case, White acquired rights in the goods before Garden attempted to rescind. If rescission takes place before the third party acquires the rights, the rescission will be valid.[53]

Impossibility of restitutio in integrum

As noted, the principal aim of rescission is to place the claimant into his pre-contract position[54] (*restitutio in integrum*). This is usually achieved by each party giving back what was gained from the other party. It follows that if *restitutio in integrum* is impossible, the right to rescind will be lost.[55] However, because rescission is an equitable remedy, the courts will not strictly enforce this requirement if it would cause unfairness or injustice. Accordingly, rescission will not be barred:

* where *restitutio in integrum* becomes impossible due to a fraudulent representee's own dealings;[56]
* simply because one party has spent the money that he received;
* because precise *restitutio in integrum* is impossible. Provided that substantial *restitutio in integrum* is possible (for example, where the subject matter of the contract has deteriorated in some way or lessened in value),[57] this will suffice and rescission will not be barred.[58]

Awarding damages in lieu of rescission

→ **in lieu of:** instead
of, or in place of

The right to rescind will be lost if the court exercises its power under s 2(2) of the Misrepresentation Act 1967 by awarding damages in lieu of rescission. This power can only be exercised in relation to negligent and innocent misrepresentations, and is exercised where 'it would be equitable to do so, having regard to the nature of the misrepresentation and the loss that would be caused by it if the contract were upheld, as well as to the loss that rescission would cause to the other party'. The existence of this provision recognizes that rescission is a serious remedy and in cases in which the misrepresentation is trivial,[59] damages are a more appropriate remedy. The exercise of s 2(2) is not pleaded by the parties; its use is entirely at the court's discretion.

The following case demonstrates the court's approach to the use of s 2(2).

---

53. *Car and Universal Finance Co Ltd v Caldwell* [1965] 1 QB 525 (CA).
54. *Spence v Crawford* [1939] 3 All ER 271 (HL).   55. *Clarke v Dickson* (1858) EB & E 148.
56. *Spence v Crawford* [1939] 3 All ER 271 (HL).   57. *Armstrong v Jackson* [1917] 2 KB 822 (KB).
58. *Erlanger v New Sombrero Phosphate Co* (1873) 3 App Cas 1218 (HL).
59. The law never regards fraud as trivial, hence the reason why s 2(2) does not apply in cases of fraudulent misrepresentation.

> ### William Sindall plc v Cambridgeshire County Council [1994] 1 WLR 1016 (CA)
>
> **FACTS:** The claimant purchased a piece of land from the defendant, for the purposes of property development, for £5 million. It took eighteen months to obtain planning permission, by which time the value of the land had dropped to £2 million. When the builders began development of the land, they discovered a sewer running throughout the land. This sewer meant that the proposed development could not go ahead unless drainage work costing £18,000 was carried out. The claimant sought rescission on the ground that the defendant's failure to disclose the existence of the sewer amounted to a misrepresentation.
>
> **HELD:** The Court of Appeal held that there was no misrepresentation. Hoffmann LJ stated *obiter* that, if a misrepresentation were present, the Court would have exercised its power under s 2(2) to prevent rescission for two reasons. First, because remedying the problem would have cost a mere £18,000, this seems trivial in comparison to a sale involving £5 million. Second, had rescission been allowed, the defendant would have suffered enormously. It would have to return the purchase price with interest (around £8 million) and, in return, it would recover land worth less than £2 million.
>
> **COMMENT:** It was clear that the claimant was alleging misrepresentation in order to escape what turned out to be a bad bargain. Had the misrepresentation caused the bargain to be bad, then it is doubtless that rescission would be an appropriate remedy, but this was not the case here.

★ See Hugh Beale, 'Damages in Lieu of Rescission for Misrepresentation' (1995) 111 LQR 60

As s 2(2) applies where 'the representee...would be entitled to rescind', it would appear that, where the representee cannot rescind (that is, because rescission is barred), s 2(2) should have no application. The courts have struggled with this issue. Certain cases have followed a literal interpretation and denied the use of s 2(2) where rescission is barred.[60] This approach was branded 'unattractive' by one judge,[61] but in more recent cases, it is the literal approach that has been favoured.[62] The disparity of opinion is not a product of judicial indecisiveness, but is rather more indicative of the Act's poor drafting.

Representations that have become contractual terms

The above discussion has concerned those situations in which a statement amounts to a mere representation (that is, it does not become a term of the contract). If a misrepresentation has become a contractual term, then the claimant may initiate a claim for breach of contract. Alternatively, the claimant can make use of s 1(a) of the Misrepresentation Act 1967, which provides that where a person enters into a contract after a misrepresentation has been made to him, and the misrepresentation becomes a term of the contract, then that person can rescind the contract, subject to the bars to rescission discussed earlier. If that person does rescind, he cannot then recover damages for breach of contract, because rescission

---

60. For example, *Zanzibar v British Aerospace (Lancaster House) Ltd* [2000] 1 WLR 2333 (QB).
61. *Thomas Witter Ltd v TBP Industries Ltd* [1996] 2 All ER 573 (Ch) 590 (Jacob J).
62. *Pankhania v Hackney London Borough Council* [2002] EWHC 2441 (Ch), [2002] NPC 123.

sets aside not only the contract, but also any right to claim damages for its breach. The right to claim damages for misrepresentation may still exist, depending on the circumstances.

Excluding liability for misrepresentation

The ability to exclude liability for misrepresentation is regulated by both the common law and statute. In addition to the common law requirements relating to notice and incorporation, three pieces of legislation regulate the ability to exclude liability for misrepresentation contractually. The Unfair Contract Terms Act 1977 and the Unfair Terms in Consumer Contracts Regulations 1999[63] are examined in Chapter 9. Here, the discussion will focus on s 3 of the Misrepresentation Act 1967, which provides that any term in a contract that seeks to exclude or restrict liability or any remedy for misrepresentation will only be valid in so far as it satisfies the requirement of reasonableness, found in the Unfair Contract Terms Act 1977. As s 3 is subject to the test found in the 1977 Act, it follows that the 1977 Act is the controlling instrument, so that contracts not subject to the 1977 Act will also not be subject to s 3.[64]

⊘ The reasonableness test found in the 1977 Act is discussed at p 228

The courts have not been entirely consistent in their application of the reasonableness test. In particular, two issues have tested the courts. The first issue is whether an exclusion clause will be unreasonable because it could potentially exclude liability for unreasonable or fraudulent behaviour. In several cases, the courts have held that an exclusion clause that is capable of covering such behaviour is unreasonable.[65] Conversely, other cases have held that, because fraud cannot be excluded, any clause that could potentially exclude liability for fraud would not actually intend to exclude liability for fraud and, as such, could be reasonable.[66] What does appear clear is that the courts will not allow a person to exclude liability for his own fraudulent misrepresentation.[67]

The second issue concerns the applicability of s 3 to 'entire agreement clauses'. Entire agreement clauses provide that the entire agreement is contained in the contract and that the parties have not relied on any representations made prior to, or during, negotiations. The Court of Appeal has held that s 3 does not apply to such agreements, for the following reason:

> Liability in damages under the Misrepresentation Act 1967 can arise only where the party who has suffered the damage has relied on the misrepresentation. Where both parties to the contract have acknowledged, in the document itself, that they have not relied on any pre-contract representation, it would be bizarre…to attribute to them an intention to exclude a liability which they must have thought could never arise.[68]

The problem is that a very fine line exists between entire agreement clauses (to which s 3 will not apply) and clauses merely stating that statements made are not to be construed as assertions of fact, or are statements of opinion only (which will be subject

---

63. SI 1999/2083.
64. *Trident Turboprop (Dublin) Ltd v First Flight Couriers Ltd* [2009] EWCA Civ 290, [2010] QB 86 [19].
65. *Thomas Witter Ltd v TBP Industries Ltd* [1996] 2 All ER 573 (Ch).
66. *Zanzibar v British Aerospace (Lancaster House) Ltd* [2000] 1 WLR 2333 (QB) 2347 (Raymond Jack QC).
67. *S Pearson & Son Ltd v Dublin Corp* [1907] AC 351 (HL).
68. *Watford Electronics Ltd v Sanderson CFL Ltd* [2001] EWCA Civ 317, [2001] All ER (Comm) 696 [41] (Chadwick LJ).

to s 3).[69] In such cases, the application of s 3 may depend on technical constructions of the contract, but this will do little to aid predictability and a party to a contract may find that his exclusion clause is subject to regulation that he specifically wished to avoid.

Mistake

Chapter 6 notes that, in order for a valid and enforceable contract to exist, classical contract law required there to be a *consensus ad idem* ('agreement as to the same things'). It followed that where the parties have contracted based on some form of mistake, the required consensus would not be present and the courts would invalidate the contract.[70] Today, the courts are much more reluctant to invalidate a contract on the ground of mistake, for several reasons.

- The finding of mistake can result in the contract being declared void. Given that a principal aim of the English system of contract law is to uphold contracts where possible, the courts should not be quick to erase contracts from existence.
- If contracts were regularly declared void due to the discovery of a fact that was unknown to the parties when they contracted, commercial certainty would be considerably reduced. The contractual process could become burdensome, because parties would be forced to investigate every facet of the agreement to ensure that no mistakes existed.
- A party who had made a bad bargain could attempt to use the doctrine of mistake to avoid the adverse consequences of the bargain.

There are many different forms of mistake (see Table 10.1), but their classification is a matter of considerable debate, with different commentators taking different approaches. In this text, mistake is divided into the traditional three categories, as follows.

TABLE 10.1. Types of mistake

Type of mistake	Definition
Common mistake	Both parties have made the same mistake
Mutual mistake	Both parties have made a mistake, but they have made a different mistake
Unilateral mistake	Only one party is mistaken, and the other party knows, or can be taken to know, of the mistake

Common mistake

Common mistake occurs where both parties to a contract have made the same mistake. In many cases of common mistake, the law provides that the contract will be rendered void, but this only applies if the contract does not, expressly or impliedly, allocate the risk of a common mistake to one party or the other, or provide some other solution. In many cases, the contract will provide for this and the solution as specified in the contract will dictate the effect of a common mistake (that is, the

---

69. *Cremdean Properties Ltd v Nash* (1977) 244 EG 547 (CA).
70. See e.g. *Smith v Wheatcroft* (1878) 9 Ch D 223 (Ch).

doctrine of common mistake will be excluded).[71] The law discussed in this section can therefore be thought of as a fallback position for those situations in which the contract is silent on this issue.

Categories of common mistake include the following.

Mistake as to existence of the subject matter

This form of mistake occurs where:

* the subject matter of the contract may never have existed; or
* the subject matter of the contract did exist, but has subsequently ceased to exist (this is known as *res extincta*).

 res extincta: 'the thing has ceased to exist'

In cases involving a mistake regarding the existence of the subject matter, performance of the contract is impossible[72] and so the contract will be held void, as the following case demonstrates.

Couturier v Hastie (1856) 5 HL Cas 673

FACTS: The claimant sold a cargo of corn to the defendant. At the time that the contract was made, both parties believed the corn to be on board a ship on its way to London. Unknown to both parties, however, whilst in transit, the corn began to ferment and, shortly before the contract was made, it was sold by the ship's captain whilst in port at Tunis. The defendant argued that, as the corn had 'perished'[73] at the time of the contract, the contract was void and he was not required to pay the contract price. The claimant disagreed and argued that the contract was not a simple contract for the sale of goods, but was a contract for the entire 'adventure', which would include any risks faced by the shipment of the cargo.

HELD: The House of Lords held that, on the construction of the contract, it was a contract for the sale of goods and that, because the goods did not exist at the time that the contract was made, the contract was held void and the defendant was not required to pay the contract price.

In *Couturier*, Lord Cranworth LC stated: 'The whole question turns upon the construction of the contract',[74] which would indicate that the contract will not automatically be held void, but that the result will depend upon the contract's construction. However, in relation to contracts for the sale of goods, s 6 of the Sale of Goods Act 1979 appears to indicate the opposite, stating that:

> Where there is a contract for the sale of specific goods, and the goods without the knowledge of the seller have perished at the time the contract is made, the contract is void.

---

71. See e.g. *William Sindall plc v Cambridgeshire CC* [1994] 1 WLR 1016 (CA)

72. This is why *res extincta* is also known as 'initial impossibility'. Where the subject matter is destroyed after the contract has been formed, the contract will be frustrated on the ground of 'subsequent impossibility'.

73. In law, 'perishing' not only includes destruction of goods, but also includes situations in which they are so damaged that they cease to comply with their contractual description or purpose.

74. (1856) 5 HL Cas 673 (HL) 681.

Several commentators have argued, however, that s 6 merely establishes the *prima facie* position,[75] or that where one party expressly agrees to bear the risk that the goods may not exist, then s 6 should not serve to render the contract void.[76] Whilst such conclusions would result in a more commercially flexible position and some ingenious sophistry may be able to lead to such conclusions, the wording of s 6 does seem to clearly indicate that Parliament did not intend s 6 to be the *prima facie* position. Further, the fact that certain sections of the Sale of Goods Act 1979[77] can be expressly excluded by a contractual term would lead to the conclusion that, if Parliament had intended s 6 to be capable of exclusion, it would have expressly stated as much.

Mistake as to title

Mistake as to title is also known as *res sua*, which is an abbreviation of *nulli enim res sua servit jure servitutis* ('no one can have a servitude over his own property'). Mistake as to title typically occurs where a buyer purchases an item that he already owns, but neither he nor the seller are aware of this.[78] Both parties labour under the mistaken belief that the seller owns the goods (hence the mistake is common). Where there is a mistake as to title, the contract will be void,[79] but, if the contract provides, expressly or impliedly, that the seller has the right to sell the goods, then the rules regarding mistake as to title will not apply and the seller can be liable for breach of contract. Such a term is implied into sale of goods contracts by s 12 of the Sale of Goods Act 1979.

Mistake as to quality

In cases involving mistakes as to title or the existence of the subject matter, the nature of the mistake is so fundamental that it justifies rendering the contract void. Where the parties are mistaken regarding the quality of the subject matter of the contract, the issue is more complex, because the mistake as to quality can be of varying degrees. Before discussing the law in this area, it is important to note that, in many cases, the issue of mistake as to quality will not arise, because one party (normally the seller) will bear the risk of the subject matter lacking quality. For example, s 14(2) of the Sale of Goods Act 1979 implies a term into sale of goods contracts providing that goods sold will be of 'satisfactory quality' and that, should the goods not be of satisfactory quality, the buyer will normally have the right to reject the goods. Where the risk of a lack of quality is not contractually allocated, the starting point will be to examine the following leading case.

*Visit the **Online Resource Centre** for more on this implied term in the chapter entitled 'The sale of goods'*

Bell v Lever Bros Ltd [1932] AC 161 (HL)

FACTS: The defendants were employed by the claimant on a fixed-term contract. In 1926, the defendants' contracts were renewed for another five years, but in 1929, the claimant company merged with another and the defendants' services were no longer required. Accordingly, the claimant contractually agreed to pay the defendants £50,000 compensation

---

75. PS Atiyah, '*Couturier v Hastie* and the Sale of Non-Existent Goods' (1957) 73 LQR 340.
76. Edwin Peel, *Treitel on the Law of Contract* (13th edn, Sweet & Maxwell 2011) 316.
77. For example, the Sale of Goods Act 1979, s 55(1), provides that certain terms implied by law may be negatived or varied by express agreement.
78. See e.g. *Cooper v Phibbs* (1867) LR 2 HL 149 (HL).
79. *Bell v Lever Bros Ltd* [1932] AC 161 (HL).

for the early termination of their employment contracts. It was subsequently discovered that the defendants had acted in breach of their employment contracts, which would have allowed the claimant to terminate their contracts without paying any compensation. The claimant brought an action alleging that the contract providing for the payment of compensation was void on the ground of common mistake (that is, both parties mistakenly believed that the defendants were entitled to compensation) and that it could therefore recover the £50,000 paid.

HELD: The House of Lords, by a majority of three to two, held that the contract was valid and the defendants could keep the compensation paid. Lord Atkin stated that the mistake was not a fundamental one, but was rather one of quality, and mistakes as to quality will not affect the contract 'unless it is a mistake of both parties, and is as to the existence of some quality which makes the thing without the quality essentially different from the thing it was believed to be'.[80] Applying this test, the mistake had not rendered the contract essentially different from what it was believed to be. The contract was one to terminate early the employment of the defendants and that is exactly what the contract did. The fact that it could have been achieved without paying the defendants compensation did not render the contract 'essentially different'.

★ See C Macmillan, 'How Temptation Led to Mistake: An Explanation of *Bell v Lever Brothers Ltd*' (2003) 119 LQR 625

COMMENT: The test laid down by Lord Atkin is so strict that no case has ever satisfied it. If mistake as to quality was not established in *Bell*, it is difficult to see when it will ever be established. Some have gone further and argued that *Bell* is so stringent that it does not provide authority for the existence of mistake as to quality as a separate class of mistake.[81]

The result of *Bell* is that mistake as to quality will not normally render a contract void. In fact, it is still not clear that a mistake as to quality will ever render a contract void. Lord Atkin's test was merely *obiter*, and whilst a number of judges (for example, Steyn J in *Associated Japanese Bank*) have stated that a sufficiently fundamental mistake as to quality may render the contract void, these comments were *obiter* too.

🔑 Associated Japanese Bank (International) Ltd v Credit Du Nord SA [1989] 1 WLR 255 (QB)

FACTS: A fraudster, named Bennett, entered into a transaction with the claimant whereby the claimant would purchase four textile machines, which would then be leased to Bennett. Before entering into the agreement, the claimant required that Bennett obtain a guarantor (a party who would pay the rental payments should Bennett not pay). The defendant agreed to act as guarantor. Bennett was given just over £1 million to purchase the machines on the bank's behalf, but the machines did not exist. Bennett absconded with the £1 million and never paid any of the rental instalments. Bennett was subsequently caught and charged with fraud, but by this time, he was bankrupt. Accordingly, the claimant sought to enforce the guarantee against the defendant.

HELD: In the High Court, Steyn J held that, on the construction of the contract, the existence of the machines was a condition precedent and that, because the machines did not exist, the defendant was not liable to act as guarantor. But he then proceeded to discuss *obiter* whether the contract would have been void on the ground of common mistake. Echoing

---

80. [1932] AC 161 (HL) 256.
81. Michael Furmston, *Cheshire, Fifoot & Furmston's Law of Contract* (16th edn, OUP 2012) 302.

the words of Lord Atkin in *Bell*, Steyn J stated that the mistake as to quality must render the contract essentially different from that which the parties believed it to be, and that the current facts would pass this test and render the contract void.

COMMENT: It may be thought that this was a case of mistake as to the existence of the subject matter, but it was not. The subject matter of the contract was not the machines themselves, but Bennett's representations regarding his use of the machines and his obligations once they were purchased.

⭐ See GH Treitel, 'Mistake in Contract' (1988) 104 LQR 501

The following case demonstrates that, if mistake as to quality is an established category of common mistake, it will be extremely difficult to establish.

Great Peace Shipping Ltd v Tsavliris Salvage (International) Ltd (Great Peace) [2002] EWCA Civ 1407

FACTS: Whilst in the Indian Ocean, a ship, the *Cape Providence*, sustained structural damage and was in danger of sinking. The defendant offered to salvage the ship and the shipowners accepted. The defendant located a tug that could salvage the *Cape Providence*, but it was at least five days away, by which time it was feared that the *Cape Providence* would have sunk. The defendant therefore consulted with various parties to try to locate a ship that was closer to the *Cape Providence*. A ship, the *Great Peace*, was located that was believed to be only 35 miles away from the *Cape Providence*. Accordingly, the defendant contracted with the owners of the *Great Peace* (the claimant) to salvage the *Cape Providence*. At the time that the contract was formed, both parties believed that the *Great Peace* was 35 miles away from the *Cape Providence*; shortly after, it was discovered that the *Great Peace* was, in fact, 410 miles away and would take over three days to reach the *Cape Providence*. The defendant therefore cancelled the contract and located a closer ship to perform the salvage. The claimant sued to recover the hire price and the defendant argued that the contract was void at common law on the ground of common mistake.

HELD: The Court of Appeal held that there was no mistake at common law. Applying the test established by Lord Atkin in *Bell v Lever Bros*, the Court held that the contract was still one of salvage, and the mistake as to distance did not render the contract 'essentially different'. The *Great Peace* could still have performed the contract and, had the defendant not located a closer ship, the *Great Peace* probably would have performed the salvage. Accordingly, the claimant succeeded.

⭐ See FMB Reynolds, 'Reconsider the Contract Textbooks' (2003) 119 LQR 177

Common mistake as to a fundamental assumption

A contract is void if the parties have made their agreement on the basis of a particular assumption that turns out to be untrue, provided that the assumption was fundamental to the continued validity of the contract, or was a foundation essential to its existence.[82]

---

82. *Grains & Fourrages SA v Huyton* [1997] 1 Lloyd's Rep 628 (QB).

Common mistake as to possibility of performance

A contract is void if it is made under a common mistaken belief that it is possible to perform it, unless the risk of impossibility of performance is allocated to a party or the contract provides for some other solution. Thus, a contract whereby one party agreed to cut and process a certain tonnage of a particular crop on a specific piece of land was held to be void when it was discovered that the land could not yield the tonnage of the crop stated in the contract.[83]

Common mistake in equity

The above categories of common mistake were created by the common law. For a time, however, there also existed a separate doctrine of common mistake in equity, and there existed two notable differences between common mistake at common law and in equity, as follows.

1. Mistake in equity could be established in situations in which mistake at common law could not.
2. Common mistake at common law would render the contract void, whereas common mistake in equity merely rendered the contract voidable.

The doctrine of common mistake in equity appears to have been created by Lord Denning in the case of *Solle v Butcher*.[84] The decision in *Solle* was followed numerous times over the course of the next fifty years[85] and the existence of a doctrine of common mistake in equity was well accepted, although there were judges[86] who argued that *Solle* was incompatible with the House of Lords' decision in *Bell v Lever Bros Ltd*. In *Associated Japanese Bank (International) Ltd v Credit Du Nord SA* (discussed earlier), Steyn J took time to explain the relationship between the doctrines of common mistake at common law and in equity. He stated:

> Where common law mistake has been pleaded, the court must first consider this plea. If the contract is held to be void, no question of mistake in equity arises. But if the contract is held to be valid, a plea of mistake in equity may have to be considered.[87]

Despite this, there was always a tension and uncertainty regarding the relationship between common mistake at common law and in equity. Accordingly, in *Great Peace* (discussed earlier), the Court of Appeal, whilst expressing sympathy for Lord Denning's desire to mitigate the harshness of the approach in *Bell*, held that after 'full and mature consideration',[88] there was 'no way that *Solle v Butcher* can stand with *Bell v Lever Bros*'.[89]

The immediate effect of the decision in *Great Peace* was to abolish the doctrine of common mistake in equity. Whilst this will result in the law relating to common mistake (especially mistake as to quality) becoming considerably more certain, it also means that the flexibility evidenced in cases such as *Solle v Butcher* has been lost. The Court in *Great Peace* acknowledged this, with Lord Phillips stating that:

> An equitable jurisdiction to grant rescission on terms where a common fundamental mistake has induced a contract gives greater flexibility than a doctrine of common law which holds the contract void in such circumstances.[90]

---

83. *Sheikh Bros v Ochsner* [1957] AC 136 (PC).
84. [1950] 1 KB 671 (CA).
85. See e.g. *Grist v Bailey* [1967] Ch 532 (Ch); *Magee v Pennine Insurance Co Ltd* [1969] 2 QB 507 (CA).
86. See e.g. Winn LJ (dissenting) in *Magee v Pennine Insurance Co Ltd* [1969] 2 QB 507 (CA).
87. *Associated Japanese Bank (International) Ltd v Credit Du Nord SA* [1989] 1 WLR 255 (QB) 268.
88. [2002] EWCA Civ 1407, [2003] QB 679 [160].   89. ibid.   90. ibid [161].

He went on to state that there is 'scope for legislation to give greater flexibility to our law of mistake than the common law allows'.[91] Legislation might not even be required if a future Supreme Court is of the opinion that *Bell* should be overruled. For the time being, however, common mistake exists at common law only and the court will adopt an 'all or nothing approach', whereby if mistake is established, the contract will be void, and if no mistake exists, the contract will be valid.

Mutual mistake

Mutual mistake occurs where both parties are mistaken regarding the essence of the subject matter of the contract (as opposed to the quality of it), but they have made a different mistake (unlike common mistake, where both parties make the same mistake). Such a mistake can render a contract void.

 ## Scriven Bros & Co v Hindley & Co [1913] 2 KB 564 (KB)

FACTS: The claimant put up for auction a number of bales of hemp and of tow. All of the bales had the same shipping mark and the auction catalogue failed to mention that the bales were of differing commodities. The defendant inspected the hemp, but not the tow. It accordingly believed that all of the bales were of hemp and made a successful bid based on this. As hemp was more expensive than tow, the result was that the defendant paid well over the odds for the bales of tow. The defendant refused to pay for the tow, and the claimant commenced proceedings.

HELD: The High Court held that the contract was void, because there was no agreement.

When determining whether or not mutual mistake is present, the courts will require that the agreement between the parties contain an element of ambiguity. Whether this ambiguity is enough to warrant rendering the contract void is determined objectively. It will need to be established that a reasonable man could not have chosen between the view of the offeror or the offeree. If a reasonable man would have thought that the view of the offeror or offeree was intended to form the basis of the contract, then no mutual mistake will exist.

 ## Smith v Hughes (1871) LR 6 QB 597

FACTS: The defendant wished to purchase a quantity of oats to feed to his racehorses. The claimant demonstrated a sample of oats to the defendant, who agreed to purchase a larger quantity. When the oats were delivered, the defendant discovered that the oats were new oats, whereas he had wanted—and had thought that he was buying—old oats. The defendant rejected the oats and refused to pay. The claimant sued for price.

HELD: The claimant succeeded and recovered the contract price. The court held that the claimant had never described the oats as old and that there was no evidence to indicate that the age of the oats was a term of the contract. Accordingly, a reasonable man would have understood the contract in the way that the claimant understood it and so there was no mistake.

91. ibid.

Unilateral mistake

Common and mutual mistake occur where both parties are mistaken. Conversely, unilateral mistake occurs where only one party is mistaken and the other party is aware, or is taken to be aware, of the mistake. Unilateral mistake operates at common law to render a contract void within extremely narrow boundaries and tends to be found in mistakes involving the identity of the person, or the terms of the contract.

Mistake as to identity of the person

Mistake as to the identity of the person can be a somewhat complex issue and typically occurs in situations similar to that in the following example.

Eg **Mistake as to identity of the person**

Isaac owns a small high-street jewellery business. He is approached by an individual claiming to be Viscount Bill Sugar, a well-known entrepreneur. Being aware of Viscount Sugar's reputation, Isaac allows him to purchase on credit a number of necklaces and several expensive wristwatches. It transpires that the man is not Viscount Bill Sugar, but an impostor (these characters are known in such cases as 'rogues'). Consequently, the credit is dishonoured. The rogue sells the necklaces and watches to Vicki, an innocent purchaser, and then disappears with his ill-gotten money. Isaac, having discovered that the rogue was an impostor, discovers that his property was sold to Vicki. Isaac will obviously wish to recover his property from Vicki, usually via the tort of conversion. The problem is that both Isaac and Vicki are innocent parties—so who should bear the loss?

Isaac will need to establish that the contract between himself and the rogue was void on the ground of mistake as to identity. If established, it follows that the rogue did not acquire good title to the goods and so cannot lawfully pass good title onto Vicki, even though she bought them in good faith.[92] Vicki will therefore have to return the goods to Isaac. Conversely, Vicki would try to establish that the contract between Isaac and the rogue was valid. This would result in the rogue acquiring good title, which he could in turn pass onto Vicki, who could then keep the goods.[93]

As can be seen from this example, the question that the courts face is whether they should favour the innocent owner of the property (Isaac) or the innocent third party (Vicki). Either way, an innocent party will suffer, which is why this area of the law has become so controversial and it is generally regarded that the law in this area is unsatisfactory, and the validity of a contract depends on a number of complex, technical, and (arguably) artificial distinctions.

A crucial requirement of mistake as to identity is that the mistake should relate to the *identity* of the person, not merely to some *attribute* of the person. In practice, this distinction can be extremely difficult to discern. The following two cases demonstrate the distinction. In the first case, the mistake related to identity and so the contract was held void, whereas in the second case, the mistake related to the attributes of the rogue and so the contract was held not to be void.

---

92. Sale of Goods Act 1979, s 21(1). The common law also provides that *nemo dat quod non habet* ('no one gives who possesses not').
93. ibid s 23.

Cundy v Lindsay (1878) 3 App Cas 459 (HL)

FACTS: A rogue by the name of Alfred Blenkarn hired premises at 37 Wood Street. He placed an order with the claimant for a consignment of linen handkerchiefs. The rogue signed his name on the order so that it looked like 'Blenkiron & Co', which was a respectable business known to the claimant that was based at 123 Wood Street. Relying on the respectable reputation of Blenkiron & Co, the claimant sent the handkerchiefs to 37 Wood Street, with payment to follow at some point in the future. The payment was never made. The rogue then sold a number of handkerchiefs to the defendant and fled. The claimant sought the recovery of the handkerchiefs.

HELD: The House of Lords held that the contract between the claimant and the rogue was void. In this case, the identity of the person was crucial to the claimant. He intended to deal with a respectable businessman (Blenkiron), but instead had dealt with a rogue (Blenkarn). As the rogue knew this, there was clearly a unilateral mistake as to identity.

King's Norton Metal Co Ltd v Edridge, Merrett & Co Ltd (1897) 14 TLR 98 (CA)

FACTS: A rogue named Wallis set up a company called Hallam & Co, which sent a letter to the claimant ordering a quantity of brass rivet wire. The letterhead gave the impression that Hallam & Co was a large, successful factory, with multiple depots and agencies around Europe, which, of course, was not the case. Relying on the letterhead's description of the company, the claimant dispatched the goods on credit to Hallam & Co's (that is, Wallis') address. The goods were never paid for and Wallis sold the goods to the defendant, who knew nothing of the deception. The claimant sought to recover the goods.

HELD: The Court of Appeal held that the contract was not void for mistake, but was merely voidable for fraud. The identity of Hallam & Co was not important; what was important was its perceived attributes (for example, its size, success, and creditworthiness). In fact, because Wallis *was* Hallam & Co, subject to the principle of corporate personality, it was probably the case that no mistake of identity was present. Accordingly, the defendant was entitled to keep the goods.

🔗 Corporate personality is discussed at p 545

The above cases demonstrate that the distinction between identity and attributes can be extremely fine. This distinction can be even more difficult to discern when the parties contract face-to-face. In such cases, the courts tend to presume that the party intended to contract with the person in front of him (not the person that the rogue is claiming to be), so that any mistake will be as to that person's attributes as opposed to his identity.

Lewis v Averay [1972] 1 QB 198 (CA)

FACTS: The claimant placed an advertisement in a local newspaper stating that he wished to sell his car. The rogue introduced himself as the then famous actor Richard Green, and offered to purchase the car. The claimant agreed and the rogue wrote a cheque for the advertised price of £450. The rogue signed the cheque 'RA Green' and indicated that he wished to take the car immediately. Understandably, the claimant was cautious and asked the rogue if he had any proof of identification. The rogue produced a Pinewood Studios admission pass, which bore his photograph. The claimant therefore permitted the rogue to take the car before the cheque had cleared. The rogue was not Richard Green and the cheque failed to clear. The rogue sold the car to the innocent defendant, from whom the claimant sought recovery of the car.

HELD: The Court of Appeal held that the claimant had intended to contract with the person in front of him, irrespective of his identity. Accordingly, the Court held that the contract was not void for mistake; it was merely voidable for misrepresentation. As the contract had not been rescinded when the defendant acquired the car, his title was good and he could keep the car.

COMMENT: The distinction between identity and attributes was not wholly accepted in this case. Lord Denning stated that it was:

> a distinction without a difference. A man's very name is one of his attributes. It is also a key to his identity. If then, he gives a false name, is it a mistake as to his identity? Or a mistake as to his attributes? These fine distinctions do no good to the law.[94]

It is contended that Lord Denning's view is correct. The distinction creates considerable uncertainty and inconsistency in the law. The mistake in *Lewis* was extremely similar to the mistake in *Cunday v Lindsay*, yet in the latter case, the contract was held void, whereas in the former, it was merely voidable.

⭐ See CC Turpin, 'Mistake of Identity' (1972) 30 CLJ 19

It follows that, when parties deal face-to-face, mistake as to identity will only be established in exceptional cases—but the presumption that the party deals with the person in front of them can be rebutted, as occurred in the following case.

🔑 *Ingram v Little* [1961] 1 QB 31 (CA)

FACTS: The claimants, two elderly sisters and another lady, advertised their car for sale. A rogue approached the claimants and identified himself as 'Hutchinson'. He offered the asking price for the car, which the claimants accepted, but when the rogue produced a chequebook, one of the claimants stated that payment by cheque was not acceptable. The rogue stated that he was a businessman: 'PGM Hutchinson' of Stanstead House, Caterham. One of the sisters checked the telephone directory and discovered that such a person did, indeed, live at the stated address. On the strength of this, the claimants accepted the cheque. The rogue was not Hutchinson and the cheque was predictably dishonoured. By this time, the rogue had sold the car to the innocent defendant. The claimants sought recovery of the car.

HELD: The Court of Appeal held that the contract between the claimants and the rogue was void. Accordingly, the defendant had to return the car to the claimants. The checking of the telephone directory was evidence that they intended to deal with PGM Hutchinson.

COMMENT: This case has been severely criticized and subsequently doubted by the courts[95] to such an extent that it should now be regarded as wrongly decided. It has been argued that it is 'difficult to escape the conclusion that the court allowed its sympathy for the ladies to cloud its judgment of the issues'.[96]

---

94. [1972] 1 QB 198 (CA) 206.
95. See e.g. *Shogun Finance Ltd v Hudson* [2003] UKHL 62, [2004] 1 AC 919 [87] (Lord Millett).
96. Laurence Koffman and Elizabeth Macdonald, *The Law of Contract* (7th edn, OUP 2010) 290–1.

Where the parties do not deal face-to-face (for example, in contracts by corre-spondence), the presumption would appear to be that the party intends to contract with the person identified. Accordingly, the presumption is that identity is crucial and a mistake will render the contract void. The case of *Cunday v Lindsay* discussed earlier is a good example of this presumption in practice.

The above discussion indicates that the law relating to mistake as to identity was highly unsatisfactory, because it rested on a number of technical, complex, and arguably unjustifiable distinctions. Accordingly, when the opportunity arose for the House of Lords to re-examine the law relating to mistake as to identity, it was hoped that a measure of much-needed clarity would be introduced. Sadly, this did not occur.

Shogun Finance Ltd v Hudson [2003] UKHL 62

FACTS: A rogue visited a car dealer and indicated that he wished to purchase a vehicle on hire purchase. The rogue identified himself as Dulabh Patel and produced a driving licence bearing this name. The rogue had stolen the driving licence from the real Mr Patel. A price of £22,500 was agreed and the rogue signed the draft hire-purchase agreement using a signature that resembled that of the real Mr Patel. The car dealer then faxed a copy of the draft agreement and the driving licence to the claimant finance company[97] to run a credit check. Mr Patel's credit rating was good and so the claimant finance company entered into a hire-purchase agreement with the rogue, believing him to be Mr Patel. The rogue took immediate delivery of the vehicle and drove it away. Shortly thereafter, the rogue sold the vehicle to the innocent defendant for £17,000. The rogue disappeared and the claimant finance company brought an action to recover the vehicle from the defendant.

HELD: By a three to two majority, the House of Lords held that the hire-purchase agreement between the claimant finance company and the rogue was void on the ground of unilateral mistake as to identity. Accordingly, the defendant had to return the car and was left bearing the £17,000 loss.

COMMENT: Lords Phillips and Walker, in the majority, affirmed the view that different presumptions exist where contracts are made face-to-face, and where contracts are made at a distance. Lords Millett and Nicholls (dissenting) contended that the distinction between face-to-face contracting and distance contracting should be abandoned. Further, they argued that *Cunday v Lindsay* should be overruled and that the principle in *Lewis v Averay* should be followed—namely, that the innocent third-party purchaser should be protected, rather than the original owner.

⭐ See Andrew Phang, Pey-Woan Lee, and Pearlie Koh, 'Mistaken Identity in the House of Lords' (2004) 63 CLJ 24

It is contended that the approach of the minority is the more attractive one. In his dissenting judgment, Lord Millett stated:

It is surely fairer that the party who was actually swindled and who had an opportunity to uncover the fraud should bear the loss rather than a party who entered the picture only after the swindle had been carried out.[98]

---

97. In such contracts, the car dealer sells the vehicle to the finance company and the finance company will then sell or lease the car to the purchaser on its standard terms. This explains why the finance company, and not the car dealer, brought the claim.

98. [2003] UKHL 62, [2004] 1 AC 919 [82].

This is a powerful argument. In *Shogun Finance*, the defendant was left £17,000 out of pocket, whereas the claimant finance company, which clearly had not taken sufficient steps to verify the identity of the rogue, was permitted to recover the vehicle. Whilst the third-party purchaser might not always be more deserving of protection than the original owner, it is usually the case that 'the person selling to a fraudster is in a stronger position to check their credentials than the person who buys from a fraudster'.[99] The decision in *Shogun Finance*, rather than encouraging parties to check the identity of those with whom they deal, indicates that the law will protect parties whose lax efforts to identify others results in a mistake as to identity.

The minority were also extremely critical of the distinction between face-to-face contracts and contracts at a distance, with Lord Millett describing the distinction as 'the real objection to the present state of the law'.[100] Lord Nicholls agreed, stating that there is 'no magic attaching to a misrepresentation made in writing rather than by word of mouth'.[101] Certainly, it could be argued that the seemingly inconsistent decisions discussed previously are the result of the distinction (for example, *Cundy v Lindsay* and *Lewis v Averay*).

 The law relating to frustration is discussed at p 305

The result is that many commentators believe *Shogun Finance* to be 'a huge disappointment in terms of clarifying the applicable principles'.[102] It has been contended that the clear judicial divergence over the issues might warrant parliamentary intervention, in the same way that Parliament intervened to clarify the law relating to the effects of frustration. The comparison with the rules relating to frustration of a contract is a relevant one, because Devlin LJ has recommended that instead of placing the loss fully on either the original owner or third party, the law could apportion the loss between the two parties, as it does in cases involving frustration.[103] If such an approach could be devised, it would surely provide a more acceptable outcome than that evidenced in *Shogun Finance*.

Mistake as to the terms of the contract

Where one party is mistaken as to the terms of the contract and the other party is aware of this mistake, then the court may hold the contract void for unilateral mistake. It is important to note that a mistake as to the terms is required; a mistake as to quality is not sufficient to establish unilateral mistake.[104] Unlike other forms of mistake, however, there is no requirement that the mistake is fundamental.

> **Eg   *Hartog v Colin & Shields* [1939] 3 All ER 566 (KB)**
>
> **FACTS:** The contract involved the sale of 30,000 hare skins. The defendant offered to sell the hare skins to the claimant, but mistakenly stated the price at 'per pound', when he meant to state 'per piece'. Trade custom was to quote the price 'per piece' and negotiations had been conducted on this basis. The result of the mistake was that the price offered was about one-third of what the defendant intended. Unsurprisingly, the claimant accepted the offer. The defendant realized the mistake and refused to deliver the skins at that contract price. The claimant brought an action to enforce the contract.

---

99. Catherine Elliot, 'No Justice for Innocent Purchasers of Dishonestly Obtained Goods: *Shogun Finance v Hudson*' [2004] JBL 381, 386.   100. [2003] UKHL 62, [2004] 1 AC 91, [68].   101. ibid [24].
102. Jill Poole, *Textbook on Contract Law* (11th edn, OUP 2012) 108.
103. *Ingram v Little* [1961] 1 QB 31 (CA) 73, 74.   104. *Smith v Hughes* (1871) LR 6 QB 597.

HELD: Singleton J stated that:

> I am satisfied that it was a mistake on the part of the defendants or their servants which caused the offer to go forward in that way, and I am satisfied that anyone with any knowledge of the trade must have realised that there was a mistake.[105]

Accordingly, the High Court held that the contract was void for unilateral mistake.

Mistakes of law

When misrepresentation was discussed, it was noted that traditionally only false representations of fact could constitute misrepresentation, but that, recently, the courts had acknowledged that false representations of law could also constitute misrepresentation. The impetus for this extension was the recognition that mistakes of law could be actionable. Historically, only mistakes of fact were actionable and a mistake of law would only be actionable if it also amounted to a mistake of fact.[106] This limitation has now been removed[107] and a mistake of law can now render a contract void. The distinction between mistakes of fact and mistakes of law was not always easy to draw, so the decision to abolish the distinction is a welcome one.

Mistaken documents

Where a contract in writing contains a mistake, two additional remedies may be available—namely, rectification and a plea of *non est factum.*

Rectification

Where the parties have engaged in negotiations that result in a written contract, it may be that key terms may be omitted, or that the final contract is drafted incorrectly, so that it fails to reflect what the parties agreed. In such a case, the equitable remedy of rectification may be available, which will enable the court to rectify the contract so that it accurately reflects what the parties agreed.

 Craddock Brothers v Hunt [1923] 2 Ch 136 (CA)

FACTS: The claimant agreed to sell a piece of property to the defendant. Both parties orally agreed that an adjoining yard would not form part of the sale and would remain the property of the claimant—but the final written contract provided that this yard would also be sold to the defendant. The claimant alleged that the contract was void on the ground of common mistake.

HELD: The Court of Appeal rectified the contract to reflect the true agreement of the parties. The defendant would have to convey the adjoining yard back to the claimant.

---

105. [1939] 3 All ER 566 (KB) 568.   106. *Solle v Butcher* [1950] 1 KB 671 (CA).
107. *Brennan v Bolt Burdon* [2004] EWCA Civ 1017, [2005] QB 303.

🔗 The parol evidence rule is discussed at p 171

As rectification involves adducing oral evidence to amend a contract, it follows that it constitutes an exception to the parol evidence rule. In order for rectification to be ordered in cases of common mistake, three conditions must be satisfied:

1. The agreement for which rectification is being sought must fail to reflect accurately the agreement of both parties. It follows that if the agreement omits a term desired by one party, but not the other, then rectification will not be ordered.[108]

2. To prevent the courts imposing terms upon parties that they did not desire, the party seeking rectification will need to provide 'convincing proof'[109] that the agreement failed to reflect the parties' intentions.

3. It must be equitable to grant rectification.

Where the mistake is unilateral, then rectification will only be ordered:

- if one party (B) knew of[110] that mistake, but nevertheless failed to draw the mistake to the other party's (A's) notice and allowed the document to be executed,[111] or conducted himself as to divert A from discovering the mistake;[112] and

- the mistake would inequitably benefit B or be detrimental to A.[113]

Like rescission, rectification will be barred due to lapse of time[114] or where an innocent third party acquires rights to the subject matter of the contract.[115] The impossibility of achieving *restitutio in integrum* will not, however, bar rectification.[116]

Non est factum

➡ *non est factum:* 'it is not my deed'

The general rule is that a person who signs a contract is bound by that contract, irrespective of whether he reads it or understands it.[117] In the sixteenth century, when few people could read, the courts developed an exception to this general rule and provided that a contract would not be binding where it was incorrectly read to a person who could not read.[118] Such a person could plead *non est factum*. The rationale behind the doctrine was that there was no *consensus ad idem* in that the signer signed a contract that he did not intend to, or, to put it another way, that 'the mind of the signer did not accompany his signature'.[119]

Today, the doctrine of *non est factum* is not limited to those who cannot read, nor is it limited to contracts executed by deed. However, because a successful plea of *non est factum* results in the contract being held void, it follows that its use should be restricted, as the following case demonstrates.

---

108. *Riverlate Properties Ltd v Paul* [1975] Ch 133 (CA).

109. *Joscelyne v Nissen* [1970] 2 QB 86 (CA) 98 (Russell LJ).

110. Knowledge here includes wilfully shutting one's eyes to the obvious, or wilfully and recklessly failing to make reasonable enquiries (*Commission for the New Towns v Cooper (Great Britain) Ltd* [1995] Ch 259 (CA)).   111. *Thomas Bates & Son Ltd v Wyndham's (Lingerie) Ltd* [1981] 1 WLR 505 (CA).

112. *Commission for the New Towns v Cooper (Great Britain) Ltd* [1995] Ch 259 (CA).

113. *Thomas Bates & Son Ltd v Wyndham's (Lingerie) Ltd* [1981] 1 WLR 505 (CA).

114. *Bloomer v Spittle* (1872) LR 13 Eq 427.   115. *Smith v Jones* [1954] 1 WLR 1089 (Ch).

116. *Cook v Fearn* (1878) 48 LJ Ch 63.   117. *L'Estrange v Graucob* [1934] 2 KB 394 (KB).

118. *Thoroughgood's Case* (1584) 2 Co Rep 9a.

119. *Foster v Mackinnon* (1869) LR 4 CP 704, 711 (Byles J).

Saunders v Anglia Building Society [1970] AC 1004 (HL)[120]

FACTS: The claimant, Gallie, was a 78-year-old widow. She agreed to transfer the title of her house to her nephew, Parkin, to enable him to raise money by using the house as security. The claimant stated that she would only agree to the transfer if she could remain in the house until she died. Parkin and a business associate, Lee (the first defendant), asked the claimant to sign a document that, due to her glasses being broken, she was unable to read. Lee told her that the document would transfer title of the house to Parkin and, relying on this, she signed it. In fact, the document transferred the house to Lee for the price of £3,000, payable to Parkin. Lee failed to pay the £3,000 and mortgaged the house to the building society (the second defendant). The claimant sought to have the contract held void on the ground of *non est factum*. By the time that the case reached the House of Lords, the claimant had died and her action was continued by her **executrix**.

HELD: The House of Lords held that the claimant's plea of *non est factum* should fail and the contract remained valid. The House held that for *non est factum* to succeed, the mistake must render the contract radically, substantially, or fundamentally different from what the party seeking relief intended. In *Saunders*, the contract was designed to enable Parkin to raise money by transferring the house, and that is what the contract did. That it transferred the house to Lee and not Parkin did not render it sufficiently different enough to warrant being held void. Further, *non est factum* could only be pleaded in the absence of carelessness. The claimant had been careless in signing the contract without asking for it to be read to her, or without obtaining professional advice.

➡ **executrix:** a female executor—appointed by the testator (the person making a will) to administer the estate upon the testator's death

★ See CJ Miller, '*Non est Factum* and Mistaken Identity' (1969) 32 MLR 431

The above requirements place significant limitations upon the doctrine of *non est factum*. Further, Lord Reid stated that the doctrine would apply to:

> Those who are permanently or temporarily unable through no fault of their own to have without explanation any real understanding of the purport of a particular document, whether that be from defective education, illness or innate incapacity.[121]

It follows that persons of full capacity who can read will be unlikely to be able to plead *non est factum* successfully[122] unless they have been tricked in some way into signing the document.[123] As a result of these limitations, *non est factum* will only be successfully pleaded in a small number of cases.

Duress

As discussed in Chapter 6, classical contract law theory is based upon the notion of consent. It follows that if an individual is, in some way, pressured or forced into entering a contract, the law should provide some form of relief. This was recognized by both the common law (via the concept of duress) and equity (via the concept of undue influence). This section will focus on the law relating to duress. Undue influence will be examined later in the chapter.

🔗 Undue influence is discussed at p 273

---

120. This case is also sometimes known as *Gallie v Lee*.   121. [1970] AC 1004 (HL) 1016.
122. ibid.   123. ibid 1025.

Duress occurs where a party enters into a contract as a result of some form of illegitimate pressure or threat, and it is well established that a contract made under duress is voidable.[124] As the contract is voidable, it follows that the principal remedy is rescission, but it should be remembered that the bars to rescission discussed in misrepresentation cases also apply to cases involving duress.

🔗 The bars to rescission are discussed at p 250

Pressure or threats

Initially, the concept of duress only applied where physical violence was threatened against a person,[125] but, eventually, the common law also came to recognize that duress against goods and property could be just as illegitimate.[126] Consequently, the subject matter of the contract is no longer relevant; all that matters is the legitimacy of the pressure or threat, and whether the victim had no realistic alternative but to enter the contract.[127]

Duress against the person

There is no doubt that actual violence or the physical threat of violence will amount to illegitimate pressure, as will the threat of imprisonment.[128]

Barton v Armstrong [1976] AC 104 (PC)

FACTS: The claimant was the managing director of a company. The defendant was the chairman of the same company. Both were major shareholders. The defendant had threatened to kill the claimant unless he executed a deed selling his interest in the company to the defendant. The claimant sought relief on the ground of duress, but the defendant argued that, because the deed was in the commercial interests of the claimant, the claimant would have executed the deed even if the threat had not been made. The New South Wales Court of Appeal accepted this and dismissed the claim. The claimant appealed.

HELD: The Privy Council allowed the claimant's appeal. It was clear that the threat constituted illegitimate pressure and it was irrelevant that it was not the claimant's sole, or even dominant, reason for entering into the contract. Provided that the threat was *a* reason behind the choice to enter into the contract, it does not matter that it was not the sole reason or even a dominant one.

Duress against property

During the nineteenth century, the courts refused to extend the concept of duress beyond threatened or actual acts of physical violence. The result of this was that if *A* were to unlawfully seize goods belonging to *B* and then force *B* to enter into a contract promising to pay money in return for the goods, such an agreement would be

---

124. *Pao On v Lau Yiu Long* [1980] AC 614 (PC); *Universe Tankships Inc of Monrovia v International Transport Workers Federation (The Universe Sentinel)* [1983] 1 AC 366 (HL).
125. *Skeate v Beale* (1840) 11 A & E 983.
126. *Occidental Worldwide Investment Corp v Skibs A/S Avanti (The Siboen and The Sibotre)* [1976] 1 Lloyd's Rep 293 (QB).   127. *B&S Contracts & Design Ltd v Victor Green Publications Ltd* [1984] ICR 419 (CA).
128. *Williams v Bayley* (1886) LR 1 HL 200 (HL).

valid.[129] The common law eventually came to realize the harshness of this approach and, in *The Siboen and The Sibotre*,[130] the High Court stated *obiter* that a contract entered into due to threatened or actual violence against goods or unlawful seizure of goods could amount to duress.

Recognition that threats against property could constitute duress did not, however, completely fill the gaps in the doctrine. Pressure could be placed upon a party's economic interests without threatening his person or property (for example, by taking advantage of a person who is financially vulnerable). To accommodate such cases, the courts developed the concept of economic duress and, today, cases involving duress against property are likely to be regarded as a form of economic duress.[131]

Economic duress

Economic duress concerns those cases in which a party's economic or business interests are threatened. Usually, this will take the form of one party threatening not to perform its contractual obligations unless the other party agrees to forgo, vary, or reduce some benefit owed to them. A classic example of this would be a case that is discussed several times in previous chapters: *D & C Builders Ltd v Rees*.[132] That case, like many other early cases involving economic duress, was decided based upon a lack of consideration and did not establish economic duress as we know it today. It was in the following case that a formal doctrine of economic duress emerged.

Occidental Worldwide Investment Corp v Skibs A/S Avanti (The Siboen and The Sibotre) [1976] 1 Lloyd's Rep 293 (QB)

FACTS: The claimant chartered two of the defendant's ships. Subsequently, a worldwide recession caused the charter market to weaken, resulting in charter rates substantially lower than those being paid by the claimant. The claimant therefore attempted to renegotiate its charter rates by falsely informing the defendant that, unless the rates were lowered, it would be unable to pay and would become insolvent. The claimant also knew that, given the recession, the defendant was unlikely to find another party to charter the ships. Accordingly, the defendant amended the charter to reduce the rates payable by the claimant. The defendant subsequently withdrew the ships and chartered them to other parties (making large profits in the process). The claimant alleged that the ships were wrongfully withdrawn. The defendant argued that it had been subject to duress.

HELD: The High Court rejected the defendant's plea of duress, stating that duress would only be present where the behaviour complained of constituted 'a coercion of will so as to vitiate consent'.[133] On the facts, this was not present.

COMMENT: The defendant actually succeeded and the court declared the contract voidable—but not on the ground of duress; rather it was on the ground that the claimant had misrepresented its financial position.

129. *Skeate v Beale* (1840) 11 A & E 983.

130. *Occidental Worldwide Investment Corp v Skibs A/S Avanti (The Siboen and The Sibotre)* [1976] 1 Lloyd's Rep 293 (QB).

131. *Vantage Navigation Corp v Suhail & Saud Bahwan Building Materials (The Alev)* [1989] 1 Lloyd's Rep 138 (QB).   132. [1966] 2 QB 617 (CA).   133. [1976] 1 Lloyd's Rep 293 (QB) 336 (Kerr J).

This case provided a basis for the establishment of the doctrine of economic duress. In particular, subsequent courts have latched onto Kerr J's test. In *Pao On v Lau Yiu Long*,[134] Lord Scarman stated that, in order to establish economic duress, two requirements must be present:

1. coercion of the will that vitiates consent; and
2. illegitimate pressure or threat.

No realistic alternative

Early cases relating to economic duress used Kerr J's formulation as the first step in establishing the presence of economic duress. The problem that arose was that these cases stated that the requisite coercion of will would only be present where the victim's act was not voluntary (known as the 'overborne will' theory). The principal criticism of this approach was first stated by Atiyah,[135] who correctly noted that, in cases involving duress, victims voluntarily enter into or vary their contracts because an alternative course of action would cause greater damage, but this does not alter the fact that voluntary consent is present. Fortunately, more recent cases have doubted the utility of a test based upon coercion of will and, as a result, the coercion of will requirement has been replaced with a test based upon causation, as follows.

1. Did the illegitimate pressure or threat cause the victim to enter the contract? Such pressure does not need to be the sole cause, but it does need to be a 'significant cause'[136] or 'decisive or clinching'.[137]
2. Did the victim have 'no realistic alternative' but to enter the contract? The following case provides an example of a situation in which this was the case.

 B & S Contracts & Design Ltd v Victor Green Publications Ltd [1984] ICR 419 (CA)

FACTS: The defendant had let a number of exhibition stands to various exhibitors at a trade show. The stands were to be built by the claimant. The claimant's employees knew that they were to be made redundant following the building of the stands and so they refused to work unless they received £9,000 severance pay between them. The claimant offered their employees £4,500, but this was rejected. The claimant then stated that, unless the defendant paid the balance (£4,500), the workers would be allowed to strike. The defendant agreed to pay but, when the work was complete, the defendant deducted the £4,500 from the contract price. The claimant argued that it was entitled to the contract price and the £4,500.

HELD: The claimant's indication amounted to a veiled threat. The Court of Appeal therefore held that the defendant did not have to pay the £4,500, because it had acted under duress. It had no realistic alternative but to pay £4,500 up front. It could have refused payment and initiated a claim for breach of contract when the claimant did not build the stands on time—but this would have 'exposed [the defendant] to very heavy claims from the exhibitors'[138] for failing to provide the stands promised.

See NE Palmer and Louise Catchpole, 'Industrial Conflict, Breach of Contract and Duress' (1985) 48 MLR 102

---

134. [1980] AC 614 (PC).
135. PS Atiyah, 'Economic Duress and the "Overborne Will"' (1982) 98 LQR 197.
136. *Dimskal Shipping Co SA v International Transport Workers' Federation (The Evia Luck)* [1992] 2 AC 152 (HL) 165 (Lord Goff).
137. *Huyton SA v Peter Cremer GmbH & Co* [1999] 1 Lloyd's Rep 620 (QB) 636 (Mance J).
138. [1984] ICR 419 (CA) 426 (Griffiths LJ).

Illegitimate pressure or threat

The threat or pressure exerted must be illegitimate, but determining this is difficult as distinguishing illegitimate pressure from 'the rough and tumble of the pressures of normal commercial bargaining'[139] is not always straightforward. The following case provides an example of illegitimate pressure.

Universe Tankships Inc of Monrovia v International Transport Workers' Federation (The Universe Sentinel) [1983] 1 AC 36 (HL)

FACTS: The claimant owned a Liberian ship, which docked in Milford Haven. The defendant trade union considered that the claimant's crewmen were being paid too little and so they 'blacked' the ship. This meant that the tugs that towed the ship out of harbour would not be made available to the claimant unless the claimant paid US$80,000 back pay to the crewmen and US$6,480 to the defendant's welfare fund. The claimant paid the money, but subsequently sued the defendant for recovery of the US$6,480. The defendant argued that its acts were given immunity by statute.

HELD: The House of Lords held that the statute did not apply and therefore the defendant's actions amounted to illegitimate pressure.

⭐ See BW Napier, 'Economic Duress, Restitution and Industrial Conflict' (1983) 42 CLJ 43

Unsurprisingly, an unlawful act (for example, breach of contract or the commission of a crime) will almost certainly be regarded as illegitimate. The courts have confirmed that a lawful act can amount to duress, but that it would be extremely unlikely.[140]

Undue influence

As noted earlier, the common law originally would only find duress in cases involving threats or actual violence to the person. Conversely, equity provided relief in cases concerning wider forms of pressure via the creation of the concept of undue influence. Undue influence traditionally applies to cases in which the pressure exerted is less direct or subtler than in duress cases. Undue influence cases are divided into two classes:

1. actual undue influence; and
2. presumed undue influence.

Actual (or Class 1) undue influence

Actual undue influence overlaps considerably with the doctrine of duress. Actual undue influence is present where one party actually causes the other to enter into a

---

139. *DSND Subsea Ltd v Petroleum Geo Services ASA* [2000] BLR 530 (QB) [131] (Dyson J).
140. *CTN Cash & Carry Ltd v Gallaher Ltd* [1994] 4 All ER 714 (CA).

contract, or make a gift, via some form of improper pressure or inappropriate use of influence. Examples of such pressure and influence include:

- *A* threatening to prosecute *B*, or *B*'s family, unless payment is provided to *A*;[141]
- taking advantage of a person's religious beliefs;[142]
- husbands who place pressure on their wives to consent to using the matrimonial home as security for a loan.[143]

Actual undue influence is not dependent upon the existence of a particular relationship, or the transaction in question causing a disadvantage.[144] All that need be established is that the requisite level of influence existed and that it was exercised unduly. With the expansion in the scope of duress, the instances of actual undue influence have declined sharply in recent years.

Presumed (or Class 2) undue influence

Presumed undue influence arises where the relationship between the parties gives rise to a 'presumption of undue influence'.[145] Historically, presumed undue influence was divided into two types, namely Type 2A and Type 2B.[146]

Type 2A—special relationship

Certain types of relationship automatically give rise to a presumption that undue influence is present (the 'relationship presumption'). Examples of such relationships include:

- parent and child;[147]
- doctor and patient;[148]
- trustee and beneficiary;[149]
- solicitor and client,[150] including ex-clients;[151]
- guardian and ward.[152]

It is worth noting that two important relationships do not come within Type 2A—namely, husband and wife[153] and employer and employee.[154]

The presumption in Type 2A cases is limited. In *Royal Bank of Scotland v Etridge (No 2)*,[155] Lord Nicholls stated:

> It would be absurd for the law to presume that every gift by a child to a parent, or every transaction between a client and his solicitor or between a patient and his doctor, was brought about by undue influence unless the contrary is affirmatively proved. Such a presumption would be too far-reaching…So something more is needed before the law reverses the burden of proof, something which calls for an explanation.[156]

---

141. *Williams v Bayley* (1866) LR 1 HL 200 (HL).   142. *Morley v Loughnan* [1893] 1 Ch 736 (Ch).
143. *CIBC Mortgages v Pitt* [1994] 1 AC 200 (HL).   144. ibid.
145. *Barclays Bank plc v O'Brien* [1994] 1 AC 180 (HL) 189 (Lord Browne-Wilkinson).   146. ibid.
147. *Powell v Powell* [1900] 1 Ch 243 (Ch). The presumption will not arise, however, where the child is an adult (*Avon Finance Co Ltd v Bridger* [1985] 2 All ER 281 (CA)).
148. *Dent v Bennett* (1839) 4 My & Cr 269.   149. *Benningfield v Baxter* (1886) 12 App Cas 167 (PC).
150. *Wright v Carter* [1903] 1 Ch 27 (CA).   151. *McMaster v Byrne* [1952] 1 All ER 1362 (PC).
152. *Hylton v Hylton* (1754) 2 Ves Sen 547.
153. *Bank of Montreal v Stuart* [1911] AC 120 (PC).
154. *Matthew v Bobbins* (1980) 256 EG 603 (CA).   155. [2001] UKHL 44, [2002] 2 AC 773.
156. ibid [24].

What Lord Nicholls is saying is that the existence of a Type 2A relationship is not enough **per se** to establish a presumption of undue influence; the court will also need to examine the nature of the transaction between the two parties. Where the transaction is suspect to such a degree that it 'calls for an explanation' or is 'not readily explicable by the relationship of the parties',[157] then the 'evidential presumption' will be satisfied and undue influence will be presumed. The burden of proof will then be transferred to the other party, who will need to rebut the presumption. Obviously, only the evidential presumption need be rebutted; the relationship presumption is irrebuttable.

➡ **per se:** 'in itself'

Type 2B—no special relationship

Where a Type 2A relationship does not exist, it used to be the case that undue influence would be presumed where the relationship was one that involved such trust and confidence that one party could exert improper influence over the other (for example, husband and wife).[158] This presumption no longer exists, and the party claiming relief will need to establish that he placed sufficient trust and confidence in the other party. If this is established, he will then need also to establish the evidential presumption (that is, that the transaction is one that calls for an explanation). If this can also be shown, a *prima facie* case for undue influence will be established and the burden of proof will shift to the other party.

Transactions 'calling for explanation'

In cases of presumed undue influence, the party seeking relief will need to show that the transaction was one that called for an explanation. This used to be expressed in terms of requiring the party seeking relief to show that the transaction was one that caused him 'manifest disadvantage',[159] but, following *Etridge*, this term is no longer used. Whether a transaction calls for an explanation will very much depend on the individual facts of the case, with the following case providing an example of such a transaction.

🔵 *Hammond v Osborn* [2002] EWCA Civ 885

FACTS: Pritler was a frail 72-year-old man. He became friends with the defendant, who was a neighbour. Pritler was hospitalized following an accident and the defendant visited him regularly. Upon his discharge, the defendant continued to care for him as he became more infirm. The defendant claimed that Pritler told her to cash all of his investments and keep the proceeds (£297,500). This she did, leaving Pritler with hardly any savings. The consequences of this act were never discussed. Pritler died **intestate**, and one of his next of kin (the claimant) sought to have the agreement between Pritler and the defendant rescinded on the ground of undue influence.

➡ **intestate:** having not made a will (on death)

HELD: Ward LJ described Pritler's gift as 'an act of generosity wholly out of proportion to the kindness shown to him. Looking at the matter objectively, it was an irrational decision, not a good one'.[160] Evidence for this could be found in the consequences of the gift: the gift represented 91.6 per cent of his assets, and he became liable to pay tax amounting to £49,670. Accordingly, the transaction was clearly one that called for an explanation. As the defendant could not rebut the presumption, the Court of Appeal found that undue influence was present.

---

157. ibid [21].   158. *Howes v Bishop* [1909] 2 KB 390 (CA).
159. *National Westminster Bank plc v Morgan* [1985] AC 686 (HL).
160. [2002] EWCA Civ 885 [58].

> **COMMENT:** This decision has been described as 'cruel but correct'.[161] However deserving the actions of the defendant might have been, the simple fact is that Pritler's decision to gift his assets was not 'the product of full, free and independent volition'.[162]

Rescission

Transactions tainted by undue influence are voidable and may therefore be rescinded at the claimant's instance. Rescission may be barred on the same grounds as misrepresentation and duress (that is, affirmation,[163] third-party rights,[164] and impossibility of *restitutio in integrum*).[165] The sole exception to this is that lapse of time alone will not bar rescission in cases of undue influence,[166] but once the actual or presumed influence has been removed, the party seeking relief must do so within a reasonable time.[167] Although damages are not available to those unduly influenced, where rescission has been barred, the court may make an award of equitable compensation to compensate the victim for his loss.[168]

Unconscionable bargains

Whereas duress and undue influence are fully recognized doctrines that operate within reasonably well-defined borders, the law relating to unconscionable bargains is somewhat unclear.[169] That equity will provide relief to a party who has entered into an unconscionable bargain[170] is clear, but the cases themselves comprise a motley selection of idiosyncratic situations that do not fit neatly into either duress or undue influence. Further, attempts to draw these cases together into one coherent doctrine[171] (entitled either 'unconscionable bargains' or 'inequality of bargaining power') have been rejected by the House of Lords[172] on the ground that such cases are preferably decided under the doctrine of undue influence.

Establishing an unconscionable bargain does not depend upon the existence of a certain relationship (as is the case with undue influence), nor does it require any illegitimate pressure (as is the case under duress). Unconscionable bargain cases usually involve one party taking advantage of another party who has some form of weakness or deficiency. Examples of transactions set aside on the ground of unconscionability include:

- a poor man who sold, for 200 guineas (£210), a share in an estate worth £1,200;[173]

---

161. Peter Birks, 'Undue Influence as Wrongful Exploitation' (2004) 120 LQR 34, 37.

162. [2002] EWCA Civ 885 [60] (Ward LJ).   163. *Mitchell v Homfray* (1882) 8 QBD 587 (CA).

164. *Bainbrigge v Brown* (1881) 18 Ch D 188 (Ch).

165. *O'Sullivan v Management Agency & Music Ltd* [1985] QB 428 (CA).

166. *Re Pauling's Settlement Trusts* [1964] Ch 303 (CA).

167. *Allcard v Skinner* (1887) Ch D 145 (CA).   168. *Mahoney v Purnell* [1996] 3 All ER 61 (QB).

169. There are numerous statutory provisions that aim to protect consumers from unconscionable bargains—these are discussed in other chapters.

170. As we are dealing with unconscionable *bargains*, it follows that this doctrine does not apply to gifts. Conversely, both duress and undue influence can apply to gifts.

171. For example, *Lloyds Bank v Bundy* [1975] QB 326 (CA).

172. *National Westminster Bank v Morgan* [1985] AC 686 (HL).

173. *Evans v Llewellin* (1787) 1 Cox CC 333.

- an employee, of limited financial means, who guaranteed the £270,000 overdraft of her employer;[174]
- a senile 84-year-old widow who sold paintings worth £6,000–£7,000 for £40;[175]
- pilgrims, whose ship had sunk and who were trapped on a rock, agreeing to pay £4,000 to be rescued.[176]

It should be noted that the courts are not quick to grant relief in such cases. Relief will not be granted merely because the consideration is inadequate,[177] or simply because a transaction is improvident[178] or unfair.[179] 'The courts [will] only interfere in exceptional cases where as a matter of common fairness it was not right that the strong should be allowed to push the weak to the wall.'[180]

The following case laid down guidelines for establishing the existence of an unconscionable bargain.

 ***Boustany v Pigott* (1995) 69 P & CR 298 (PC)**

FACTS: Pigott leased a flat to the defendant. Pigott was ageing and 'quite slow', so her cousin (the claimant) dealt with her affairs. The defendant wished to renegotiate the lease with the claimant, but no action was taken. The defendant and her barrister went to see Pigott. They presented her with a new lease, to which she agreed, despite the fact that this new lease contained terms that were unfavourable to her—notably, that the lease was to last ten years, and that the rent payable was relatively low and was unreviewable. When the claimant discovered this, he sought to have the lease set aside.

HELD: The Privy Council viewed the lease as unconscionable and set it aside. Lord Templeman approved several submissions of counsel, as follows.

- Equity will not provide relief simply because the bargain is hard, unreasonable, or foolish. One of the parties must have imposed terms in a morally reprehensible manner.
- 'Unconscionable' relates not only to the terms of the agreement, but also to the stronger party's behaviour, which must demonstrate moral culpability or impropriety.
- Equity will usually not interfere solely because the parties' bargaining power is unequal, or because the terms are unreasonable.
- The party seeking relief will need to establish that the other party's conduct was unconscionable.
- The party seeking relief will need to establish that his weakness or disabling circumstances were taken advantage of by the other party.

Illegality and public policy

As Figure 10.2 indicates, the law places limits on an individual's ability to contract by branding certain contracts illegal or by declaring them contrary to public policy. The largely judge-made law in this area was branded as 'complex and technical'[181] by the

---

174. *Credit Lyonnais Bank Nederland NV v Burch* [1997] 1 All ER 144 (CA).

175. *Ayres v Hazelgrove*, unreported 9 February 1984.   176. *The Medina* (1876) 1 P 272.

177. *Collier v Brown* (1788) 1 Cox CC 428.

178. *Kalsep v X-Flow BV*, The Times (London, 3 May 2001).

179. *Alec Lobb (Garages) Ltd v Total Oil (Great Britain) Ltd* [1985] 1 WLR 173 (CA).

180. ibid 183 (Dillon LJ).

181. Law Commission, *Illegal Transactions: The Effect of Illegality on Contract and Trusts* (Law Com CP No 154, 1999) [9.1].

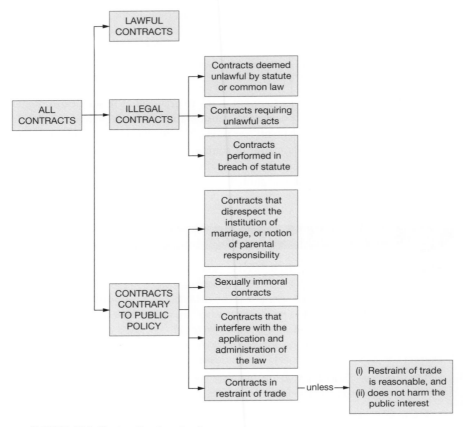

FIGURE 10.2 The legality of contracts

Law Commission who, in 1999, recommended that legislative reform was needed. However, in 2009, the Law Commission reversed its position and stated that 'in most cases, legislation is unnecessary. The courts could reach the desired outcome through development of the case law.'[182]

Illegal contracts

There are three principal forms of illegal contract:

1. Certain contracts may be regarded as illegal irrespective of their aims and motives.

2. A contract may be lawful per se, but become illegal by requiring the parties to perform unlawful acts.

3. Both the contract itself and the acts required may be lawful, but may be performed by the parties in an unlawful manner.

Each of these instances will be discussed, but it should be noted that this is not an exhaustive list and that there are other instances in which a contract may be deemed illegal.

---

182. Law Commission, *The Illegality Defence: A Consultative Report* (Law Com CP No 189, 2009) [1.5]. This was confirmed in the final report—*The Illegality Defence* (Law Com No 320, 2010) [3.41].

Contracts amounting to a legal wrong

Some contracts are unlawful simply by virtue of their existence; the mere making of such contracts is a legal wrong, irrespective of the lawfulness of the acts to be performed. Examples include:

- **Contracts for 'maintenance' and 'champerty'** 'Maintenance' refers to the situation in which a person supports the litigation of another, but has no legitimate interest in such litigation. 'Champerty' occurs if a person 'maintaining' another receives a share of the other's damages. Although civil and criminal liability for champertous acts has been abolished, the general rule is still that champerty is unlawful.[183]
- **Contracts to secure the misprision of an arrestable offence**[184] 'Misprision' is accepting a reward in return for not reporting a crime.
- **Contracts that seek to prevent, restrict, or distort competition**[185]
- **Contracts that involve commercial dealings with the enemy during wartime**[186] Trading with the enemy is also a statutory offence.[187]

Contracts requiring unlawful acts

A contract that requires the intentional commission of an unlawful act will clearly be unlawful and unenforceable by either party. Examples include:

- a contract requiring the commission of an assault;[188]
- a contract that aims to defraud the shareholders of a company;[189]
- any contract for the sale of bodily organs or human material for the purposes of transplantation;[190]
- a contract involving the publishing of libellous information.[191]

A contract that does not require the commission of an unlawful act, but which results in a person benefiting from the unlawful act, is similarly unlawful. Thus, in *Beresford v Royal Insurance Co Ltd*,[192] an individual took out an insurance policy that provided for a financial payout of £50,000 upon his committing suicide. Shortly afterwards, he shot himself. His next of kin claimed on the insurance policy, but the claim was rejected, because, at the time, suicide was illegal.

Contracts performed in breach of statute

A lawful contract may exist between the parties, but may be performed in a manner that is in breach of a statute. In such a case, the general rule is that a party who performs a contract unlawfully cannot enforce it,[193] but the innocent party can (providing that he did not know of the illegal performance).

---

183. Criminal Law Act 1967, s 14(2). An obvious exception to this would be the validity of conditional fee agreements under the Courts and Legal Services Act 1990, s 58.
184. Criminal Law Act 1967, s 5(1).
185. Competition Act 1998, s 2.
186. *Sovfracht (V/O) v Van Udens Scheepvaart en Agentuur Maatschppij (NV Gebr)* [1943] AC 203 (HL).
187. Trading with the Enemy Act 1939, s 1(1).   188. *Allen v Rescous* (1676) 2 Lev 174.
189. *Begbie v Phosphate Sewage Co Ltd* (1875) LR 10 QB 491.
190. Human Tissue Act 2004, s 32.
191. *Apthorp v Neville & Co* (1907) 23 TLR 575.   192. [1938] AC 586 (HL).
193. *Anderson Ltd v Daniel* [1924] 1 KB 138 (CA).

Archbolds (Freightage) Ltd v S Spanglett Ltd [1961] 1 QB 374 (CA)

FACTS: The claimant employed the defendant to transport a consignment of whisky from Leeds to London. The vans used to transport the whisky were only licensed to carry goods belonging to the defendant, however, not goods belonging to anyone else. Due to the defendant's negligence, the whisky was stolen en route. The claimant sued for breach of contract, but the defendant claimed that the contract was unenforceable on the ground of illegality—namely, the use of vans that were not licensed for the purpose of carrying other people's goods.

HELD: The Court of Appeal stated that the contract itself was clearly not an illegal one. The claimant had no knowledge of the unlawful performance, nor did it play a role in it. Accordingly, it was permitted to claim for the loss of the whisky.

This rule is not absolute, however, insomuch that, depending on the purpose of the law that was breached, a party who performed in an unlawful manner may still be able to enforce the contract. There does not appear to be a general principle in place and the courts appear to take a case-by-case approach, with the result heavily dependent upon the wording of the statute that was breached.

Shaw v Groom [1970] 2 QB 504 (CA)

FACTS: Section 4 of the Landlord and Tenant Act 1962 required that any person leasing a property should be provided with a rent book containing specified information and that failure to comply amounted to a criminal offence. The claimant gave the defendant a rent book, but it did not contain the prescribed information. Some time later, the claimant sued the defendant for unpaid rent amounting to £103. The defendant argued that, because the rent book was incomplete, the contract was unlawful and unenforceable.

HELD: The Court of Appeal allowed the claimant to recover the back rent. Where performance was unlawful, the enforceability test to be applied was whether Parliament intended to prevent the claimant from enforcing the contract. With regards to the 1962 Act, Parliament intended to punish those who breached the legislation, but it did not intend to prevent landlords from recovering unpaid rent.

The effects of illegality

It is impossible to generalize about the effects that illegality can have on a contract, because there are numerous degrees of unlawfulness. Two general principles can, however, be stated:

1. Any person who is aware of the illegality of a contract will not be permitted to enforce it.[194]
2. Money or property that has changed hands due to an illegal contract cannot be recovered and the defendant can therefore keep what he has obtained.

---

194. *Holman v Johnson* (1775) 1 Cowp 341.

Parkinson v College of Ambulance Ltd and Harrison [1925] 2 KB 1

FACTS: The defendant company was set up to teach first aid and ambulance work, and to administer aid to the poor. The president of the company was a member of the royal family. A representative of the company (Harrison, another defendant) informed the claimant, Colonel Parkinson, that if he were to donate a substantial sum of money to the company, the company could arrange for Parkinson to receive a knighthood. An agreement was entered into and Parkinson donated £3,000 to the company, but never received a knighthood. When questioned, the company stated that the money was donated as an act of charity and would not be returned. Parkinson sued.

HELD: A contract to purchase a knighthood is clearly illegal. Because the claimant knew this, he would be unable to enforce the contract. Accordingly, he could not recover the £3,000.

COMMENT: In response to this case, the Honours (Prevention of Abuses) Act 1925 was quickly passed, which makes it a criminal offence to contract for the purchase of an honour.

However, there are exceptions to the rule and, in several situations, the courts will permit money or property transferred under a illegal contract to be recovered, including:

- Where the parties are *not* equally at fault (for example, where one party is induced into the illegal contract by a misrepresentation),[195] the less culpable party may be able to recover money paid or property transferred.[196]
- A party to an illegal contract may be able to recover money or property if he repents and voluntarily withdraws from the contract before the unlawful purpose commences.[197] Note that the repentance must be genuine: recovery will not be permitted where withdrawal is the result of the contract being frustrated,[198] or where the illegality is discovered by the authorities.[199]

⚭ Frustration is discussed at p 305

- A party to an illegal contract who did not know of, or take part in, the illegality may be able to recover money or property if there is complete failure of consideration by the other party (that is, if the innocent party has gained no benefit from the contract).[200]

Contracts in breach of public policy

A contract that is not illegal may nevertheless be deemed unenforceable by the parties (or one of them) if it involves activity that the law regards as contrary to public policy. Instances in which the courts will declare a contract void on the grounds of public policy are many and the categories are not closed. Below is a selection of the most significant examples, with contracts in restraint of trade being perhaps the most important.

---

195. *Hughes v Liverpool Victoria Legal Friendly Society* [1916] 2 KB 482 (CA).
196. *Kiriri Cotton Ltd v Dewani* [1960] AC 192 (PC).
197. *Kearley v Thomson* (1890) 24 QBD 742 (CA).   198. *Bigos v Bousted* [1951] 1 All ER 92 (KB).
199. *Alexander v Rayson* [1936] 1 KB 169 (CA).
200. *Re Cavalier Insurance Co Ltd* [1989] 2 Lloyd's Rep 430 (Ch).

Family agreements

Contracts that serve to affect adversely the institution of marriage, or the status of the family or parental responsibility, will breach public policy. Examples of such contracts include the following.

- Contracts that unjustifiably restrict a person's ability to marry may be invalid (for example, a contract to promise only ever to marry a specific person).[201]
- A contract whereby a person promises to obtain a prospective husband or wife for another in return for payment (known as a 'marriage brokage contract') is unenforceable.[202]
- Contracts that require the performance of acts that are inconsistent with the responsibilities of a parent[203] will be invalid (for example, a parent with legal custody of a child contracting that custody away to another).[204]

Sexually immoral contracts

Historically, this principle was absolute and any contract that could be regarded as sexually immoral was regarded as unenforceable. Thus, a carriage owner who knew that a carriage that he had leased out was to be used for the purposes of prostitution was unable to claim when the prostitute refused to pay.[205] In recent years, however, the attitudes of the courts have undoubtedly started to relax.

Armhouse Lee Ltd v Chappell and Anor, The Times 7 August 1996 (CA)

FACTS: The defendant was a pornographer whose company ran a telephone sex line. The claimant was an advertising agency, which placed advertisements in magazines advertising the defendant's service. The defendant's business became unprofitable and he stopped paying the claimant for its advertising services. As a result, the claimant went into liquidation and eventually initiated proceedings against the defendant, who argued that the contract was unenforceable on the ground of public policy—namely, that the advertisements were obscene and could corrupt public morality.

HELD: The claimant could recover the monies owed. The Court of Appeal was scathing in its attack on the defendant, not for the activities it undertook, but in relation to its hypocrisy. The defendant requested and profited from the advertisements, and provided the very services that it claimed were immoral. The Court therefore, with confessed relief, rejected the claims of the defendant.

Contracts that oust the jurisdiction of the courts

Contracts that seek to indirectly avoid justice by ousting the jurisdiction of the courts are contrary to public policy and the offending parts of the contract will be held void.[206] But agreements that provide that the parties shall resort to alternative dispute resolution before commencing legal proceedings are perfectly valid.

---

201. *Lowe v Peers* (1768) 2 Burr 2225.   202. *Cole v Gibson* (1750) 1 Ves Sen 503.
203. 'Parental responsibility' is defined in the Children Act 1989, s 3.
204. *Vansittart v Vansittart* (1858) D & J 249 (Ch).
205. *Pearce v Brooks* (1866) LR 1 Ex 213 (Ex).   206. *Thompson v Charnock* (1799) 8 Term Rep 139.

Scott v Avery (1856) 5 HL Cas 811 (HL)

FACTS: An insurance contract provided that if the insured goods were damaged or lost, the question of the amount of compensation would be referred to a committee. If the committee's determination of loss differed from that of the insurance company, the issue could not be decided by the courts until the matter had been referred to arbitration and a decision reached. One party alleged that such a clause ousted the jurisdiction of the courts.

HELD: The House of Lords held that the clause was valid, because it did not oust the jurisdiction of the courts; rather, it imposed a condition that needed to be satisfied before the courts could exercise their jurisdiction.

Contracts in restraint of trade

Healthy competition in the marketplace can result in increased innovation, higher quality goods, and lower prices. Accordingly, contracts that purported to restrict a business or individual's ability to carry on trade were historically regarded as void.[207] As time progressed, however, the courts came to realize that there are actually very good practical reasons to restrain trade in certain circumstances:

> A master might be reluctant to employ and train apprentices if he could not to some extent restrain them from competing with him after the end of their apprenticeship. And a trader might be unable to sell the business he had built up if he could not bind himself not to compete with the purchaser.[208]

Therefore, the law started to regard contracts in restraint of trade as *prima facie* valid.[209]

Today, the position has reversed and the following case established that the general position is that contracts that restrain trade are *prima facie* void, but will be valid if they reasonably protect a legitimate interest and do not harm the public interest.

 Nordenfelt v Maxim Nordenfelt Guns and Ammunition Co [1894] AC 535 (HL)

FACTS: Nordenfelt was a manufacturer of guns and ammunition. He transferred all of the guns, ammunition, plant, and patents to another company (MNGA), for which he was paid £237,000 in cash and £50,000 in shares. He also covenanted not to manufacture guns or ammunition for any other company in the world for a period of twenty-five years. Soon thereafter, Nordenfelt began manufacturing guns and ammunition for competing companies. MNGA sought an injunction to enforce the covenant.

HELD: The House of Lords held that the covenant was valid and binding. In a key judgment, Lord Macnaghten stated:

> The public have an interest in every person's carrying on his trade freely: so has the individual. All interference with individual liberty of action in trading, and all restraints of trade of themselves, if there is nothing more, are contrary to public policy, and therefore

---

207. *Claygate v Batchelor* (1602) Owen 143 (KB).
208. Edwin Peel, *Treitel on the Law of Contract* (13th edn, Sweet & Maxwell 2011) 502.
209. *Mitchel v Reynolds* (1711) 1 P Wms 181.

> void...But there are exceptions: restraints of trade and interference with individual liberty of action may be justified by the special circumstances of a particular case. It is a sufficient justification, and indeed it is the only justification, if the restriction is reasonable—reasonable, that is, in reference to the interests of the parties concerned and reasonable in reference to the interests of the public, so framed and so guarded as to afford adequate protection to the party in whose favour it is imposed, while at the same time it is in no way injurious to the public.[210]

In practice, very few contracts are set aside on the ground that they are not in the public interest, leaving the test of 'reasonableness' as the dominant test to determine validity. When determining reasonableness, the courts will take into account a number of factors—notably, the duration of the restraint and the geographical extent of the restraint. Both of these issues are very much dependent upon the facts of the case.

Although the categories of contracts in relation to which restraint may be justified are open, the court has stated that, in two instances in particular, a legitimate interest may exist that warrants the imposition of a restraint, namely (i) contracts for the sale of a business; and (ii) contracts of employment.[211] Both will be discussed briefly.

A restraint of trade clause in a contract providing for the sale of a business is more likely to be valid than in other contracts, since the new owner has a legitimate interest in preventing the previous owner from setting up a new competing business. It should be emphasized, however, that imposing a restraint simply to prevent competition per se is not enough to rebut the general rule that restraint clauses are void.[212] When a business is purchased, the price paid does not only reflect the cost of the plant, materials, and tangible goods belonging to the company, it also reflects the cost of the company's reputation, its customer connections, and the potential increase in future customers via word-of-mouth recommendations.[213] Collectively, these intangible assets are known as 'goodwill' and it is this goodwill that must be protected by a restraint clause. In order for goodwill to be to be protected validly, two conditions must be present: first, the sale of goodwill must relate to an actual business in existence that is then sold;[214] second, the restraint must go no further than is reasonably necessary as between the parties and in the public interest to protect the business that has been bought. The following case provides an example of a restraint that went beyond what was reasonably necessary.

 British Reinforced Concrete Engineering Co Ltd v Schelff [1921] 2 Ch 563 (Ch)

FACTS: The defendant carried on a small local business selling (not manufacturing) 'Loop' road reinforcements. He sold this business to a larger company (the claimant) that manufactured and sold 'BRC' road reinforcements throughout the UK. He also covenanted not to compete with the company anywhere in the UK (either through setting up a business or joining a competitor) in relation to the manufacture or sale of road reinforcements.

210. [1894] AC 535 (HL) 565.
211. *Herbert Morris Ltd v Saxelby* [1916] AC 688 (HL) 713 (Lord Shaw).
212. *Vancouver Malt and Sake Brewing Co Ltd v Vancouver Breweries Ltd* [1934] AC 181 (PC).
213. *Allied Dunbar (Frank Weisinger) Ltd v Weisinger* [1988] IRLR 60.
214. *Vancouver Malt and Sake Brewing Co Ltd v Vancouver Breweries Ltd* [1934] AC 181 (PC).

Subsequent to the sale, the defendant was employed by a rival company and the claimant sued.

HELD: The High Court held that the covenant was invalid, because it was too wide. The defendant's business concerned only the sale of road reinforcements, yet the covenant prohibited him from engaging in the sale or *manufacture* of road reinforcements. Accordingly, the restraint sought not to protect the business sold, but rather to protect the claimant's own business.

The second type of contract in which a legitimate interest is more likely to be protected by a restraint clause is a contract of employment, wherein restraint of trade clauses may be express or implied. Certainly, during the lifetime of the employment, the employer is quite justified in restricting the actions of its employees (for example, by requiring them to not work for a rival firm). Problems arise when an employee is subject to a restraint clause after he has left an employer's business. In these cases, the clause will only be valid if it serves to protect a '**proprietary** interest' of the employer. Proprietary interests fall into three categories, as follows.

➡**proprietary:** relating to exclusive ownership, control or use

1. **Trade secrets** Trade secrets are clearly an asset of a company deserving of protection. In *Forster & Sons Ltd v Suggett*,[215] the claimant instructed the defendant in secret methods for the production of glass bottles. Upon leaving the claimant company, the defendant agreed not to work for a rival firm or be involved in glass bottle manufacturing for a period of five years, but he later sought to be released from the restraint. The court held that the restraint was valid and granted an injunction to enforce it. In practice, however, it may be the case that employees are prohibited from disclosing trade secrets at any time after their employment ends, even in the absence of a restraint clause.[216]

2. **Confidential information** The line between trade secrets and confidential information can be thin, but the distinction is important, because the courts appear to afford less protection to confidential information than to trade secrets. The Court of Appeal has indicated that, whilst the duty not to disclose trade secrets continues after employment ends, the duty not to disclose confidential information generally only lasts as long as the employment, unless there exists an express provision to the contrary.[217]

3. **Customer connections** In the absence of a restraint clause, the law will only prevent an employee from soliciting his employer's customers during the life of his employment.[218] Once employment has ended, the courts will permit an employer to protect his customer connections via a restraint clause.[219]

Although contractual restraints relating to the selling of a business and contracts of employment form the main bulk of cases in this area, a third form of restraint has become more common over the last few decades—namely, exclusive trading agreements (also known as 'solus' agreements, or 'vertical' agreements). These occur where a retailer agrees to sell the products of one manufacturer only and not those of its rivals. Such agreements are common between oil companies and petrol station proprietors, and the leading case involves such an arrangement.

---

215. (1918) 35 TLR 87.   216. *Faccenda Chicken Ltd v Fowler* [1987] Ch 117 (CA).   217. ibid.
218. *Wessex Dairies Ltd v Smith* [1935] 2 KB 60 (CA).   219. *Fitch v Dewes* [1021] 2 AC 158 (HL).

Esso Petroleum Co Ltd v Harper's Garage (Stourport) Ltd [1968] AC 269 (HL)

FACTS: The defendant owned two garages (G1 and G2). It entered into an agreement with the claimant, whereby both garages would sell only the claimant's petrol, in return for which the defendant would receive a discount on the price of petrol. The agreement with G1 was to last four years and five months. The claimant also lent the defendant £7,000 and secured the loan via a mortgage over G2. The mortgage agreement also contained the same restriction as in the contract with G1 and was to last for the duration of the mortgage repayments—namely, twenty-one years. The defendant started to sell a rival brand of petrol and the claimant sued. The defendant argued that the agreements were unreasonable.

HELD: The House of Lords noted that solus agreements were not invalid per se, because both parties often benefited from them. But because solus agreements sought to restrain trade, they were *prima facie* void unless the claimant could establish that they were reasonable.

1. The agreement with G1 was valid. The period involved was reasonable in order to protect the claimant's legitimate interest of securing continuity of sale outlets and ensuring stability of sales. In return, the defendant received cheaper petrol and the financial backing of a major oil company.
2. The agreement with G2 was held void. The period of twenty-one years was unreasonable, in so much as it went well beyond what was necessary in order to protect the claimant's legitimate interests.

⭐ See KL Koh, 'Contract: Doctrine of Restraint of Trade' [1967] CLJ 151

As with many cases involving restraint of trade, however, it should be noted that the validity of a clause will always be dependent upon the individual facts of the case.

The effects of a breach of public policy

Where a contract breaches public policy, it will be unenforceable, unless those terms that breach public policy can be severed, in which case the remainder of the contract may be valid and enforceable. However, the courts will only sever a term, or part of a term, as follows.

1. The court will not sever a term if the main consideration for the contract derived from the defendant's breach of public policy.[220]
2. An objectionable term will only be severed if it can be cut out of the contract and the rest of the contract remains capable of standing alone.[221] This is known as the 'blue pencil' test, because the court is, in effect, running an editing pencil through the offending words. The court will not sever terms where it would have to rearrange, add, or delete words in order to make the severed contract workable.
3. The court will not sever a term if to do so would alter the nature of the original contract.[222]

---

220. *Lound v Grimwade* (1888) 39 Ch D 605 (Ch). 221. *Goldsoll v Goldman* [1915] 1 Ch 292 (CA).
222. *Attwood v Lamont* [1920] 3 KB 571 (CA).

Chapter conclusion

Chapter 6 stated that a contract will be formed provided there is valid agreement and consideration, and an intention to create legal relations. As we have seen, however, in a number of situations, the courts will hold that, despite the validity of the contract's formation, the contract should not be enforceable. Given that the stability of commercial contracts is crucial for businesses, it is essential that those who run businesses are aware of those situations that can result in a contract being declared void or voidable, and take steps to avoid those situations arising.

This chapter has demonstrated that contracts, once formed, are not beyond challenge. In Chapter 11, this will be advanced to examine those instances in which a contract can become discharged.

 Key points summary

Misrepresentation

- Misrepresentation occurs where a party is induced into entering into a contract by another's false statement of fact or law.

- Statements of opinion and statements of intention will not usually constitute a misrepresentation, but there are exceptions.

- There are four types of misrepresentation: (i) fraudulent misrepresentation; (ii) common law negligent misrepresentation; (iii) statutory negligent misrepresentation; and (iv) innocent misrepresentation.

- Misrepresentation renders a contract voidable, but in certain circumstances, the representee will be barred from rescinding the contract. In cases of negligent and innocent misrepresentation, the court can award damages in lieu (instead) of rescission.

Mistake

- Mistakes may be common (both parties have made the same mistake), mutual (both parties have made a different mistake), or unilateral (only one party has made a mistake).

- At common law, mistake can render a contract void *ab initio*. There is no doctrine of common mistake in equity.

Duress

- Duress occurs where a party enters into a contract due to the presence of some form of illegitimate pressure or threat that causes him to have no realistic alternative other than to enter into the contract.

Undue influence

- Actual undue influence exists where one party causes another party to enter into a contract, or make a gift, via the use of some form of improper pressure or inappropriate use of influence.

- Presumed undue influence occurs where the relationship between the parties gives rise to a presumption that undue influence may be present. In order for the presumption to arise, the party seeking relief will need to establish that the transaction was one that calls for an explanation—but there is no need to establish that the transaction was 'manifestly disadvantageous'.

• Where a contract is tainted by undue influence, it will be voidable.

Unconscionable bargains

• Equity may provide relief to a party who has entered into an unconscionable bargain. An unconscionable bargain will usually be one in which a stronger party has taken advantage of some weakness or deficiency of a weaker party.

Illegality and public policy

• Illegal contracts include:
  – contracts that amount to a legal wrong;
  – contracts that require the commission of an unlawful act;
  – contracts that are performed in breach of statute.
• Contracts that offend public policy include:
  – contracts that disrespect the institution of marriage or parental responsibility;
  – contracts that promote sexually immoral behaviour;
  – contracts that interfere with the application or administration of justice;
  – contracts that restrain trade.

Self-test questions

1. Define the following legal words and phrases:
   (a) vitiate;
   (b) misrepresentation;
   (c) *uberrimae fidei*;
   (d) rescission;
   (e) duress;
   (f) undue influence;
   (g) affirmation.

2. Paul established and has built up a relatively successful, high-street accountancy firm. He is due to retire in six months, so decides to sell the firm. He is approached by Aled, who expresses interest in purchasing the firm and asks why the firm has been so successful. Paul replies that it is because: 'There are no other accountancy firms within 30 miles. This business will make you a fortune. I believe the annual level of profit is around £1.2 million.' Aled asks his accountant, Chloe, to verify Paul's stated level of profits. Chloe confirms Paul's statement, but, in fact, the firm only makes around £100,000 profit per year. Aled asks for a few weeks to think it over. Paul then discovers that Ernst & Waterhouse, a multinational accountancy firm, is due to open an office close to his firm. He does not inform Aled of this. Aled agrees to purchase the firm and subsequently discovers the true level of profit, as well as the opening of the rival office. Aled seeks your advice to his legal options.

3. Explain the distinction between:
   (a) fraudulent, negligent, and innocent misrepresentation;
   (b) actual and presumed undue influence;
   (c) common, mutual, and unilateral mistake;

(d)   initial impossibility and subsequent impossibility;

(e)   illegality and public policy.

4.   Alfonso works for a local firm of accountants based in Hampshire. For the last six months, he has been considering setting up his own firm and, to that end, he has been sounding out clients to see which ones would be keen on having their accounts audited by his new firm. He has also been collecting documents belonging to his current firm relating to new and potentially more efficient accounting systems. Alfonso resigns and his former employer draws his attention to a clause in his contract that prevents him from competing in any way with the firm anywhere in the UK for a period of five years. Despite this, Alfonso sets up a new business in London and acquires a number of his old firm's former clients. Alfonso's old firm is seeking an injunction to prevent Alfonso from accepting its prior clients. Discuss.

Further reading

Sir Jack Beatson, Andrew Burrows, and John Cartwright, *Anson's Law of Contract* (29th edn, OUP 2010) ch 8
A comprehensive, but straightforward account of the complex topic of mistake

Andrew Chandler, James Devenney, and Jill Poole, 'Common Mistake: Theoretical Justification and Remedial Inflexibility' [2004] JBL 34
Analyses the law relating to common mistake as to quality, focusing on the decision to abolish common mistake in equity; argues that whilst Great Peace has clarified the law, it has also made it unduly rigid

Laurence Koffman and Elizabeth Macdonald, *The Law of Contract* (7th edn, OUP 2010) ch 13
A clear and well-structured account of the law relating to misrepresentation; useful discussion of the advantages of claiming based on s 2(1) of the Misrepresentation Act 1967

Edwin Peel, *Treitel on the Law of Contract* (13th edn, Sweet & Maxwell 2011) ch 11
A detailed, but accessible and highly interesting, account of the law relating to illegality and public policy

Jill Poole, *Textbook on Contract Law* (11th edn, OUP 2012) ch 15
Provides an up-to-date and analytical account of the law relating to duress, undue influence, and unconscionable bargains

Remember to visit the Online **Resource Centre** at <**http://www. oxfordtextbooks.co.uk/orc/roach3e**> to access the following resources on Chapter 10, 'Vitiating factors': more **practice questions** and answers; a **glossary** of key terms; **multiple-choice questions**; **revision summaries**; and **diagrams** in pdf;. Updates to the law can be found on Twitter by following **@UKBusinessLaw**.

11 Discharge of the contract

- Discharge by performance
- Discharge by agreement

- Discharge by breach
- Discharge by frustration

INTRODUCTION

The importance of contract to the operation of businesses cannot be overemphasized. It is crucial that businesses know at what point a contract is created and what the terms of the contract are. It is equally important to know when the rights and obligations contained in a contract have come to an end. Chapter 10 noted that a contract might be rendered void or voidable due to the behaviour of the parties. This chapter will discuss in what situations a contract will become discharged. In some cases (for example, frustration), a contract will be automatically discharged with no possibility of continuance. In other cases (for example, breach), the actions of one party may result in the other party being entitled to terminate (discharge) the contract or may simply entitle him to recover damages only.

It is vital to understand when a contract will become discharged and what the effects of discharge will be. This will depend upon the method of discharge and four methods can be identified:

1. discharge by performance;
2. discharge by agreement;
3. discharge by breach; and
4. discharge by frustration.

Discharge by performance

Although much discussion of contract law revolves around situations in which something goes wrong, the simple fact is that the vast majority of contracts are performed straightforwardly, with both parties fulfilling their obligations under the contract. Once both parties have fulfilled their obligations, their liability under the contract ceases and the contract comes to a natural end. This is known as 'discharge by performance'. If only one party performs his side of the contract, he will be discharged from liability under the contract and will acquire a right of action against the other party for breach of contract.

What constitutes performance?

In order for a contract to be discharged by performance, the requisite standard of performance will need to be present. The general rule is that all of the obligations of the contract must be precisely and completely performed. This requirement is a strict one, and parties who depart from their precise obligations cannot claim that the contract is discharged by performance. Further, the other party may acquire the right to sue for damages, or may even be able to elect to terminate the contract on the ground of breach. These points are demonstrated in the following case.

Arcos Ltd v EA Ronaasen & Son [1933] AC 470 (HL)

FACTS: An English company contracted to purchase a number of timber staves to be used to make barrels. The contract stated that the staves should be half an inch thick. Upon the staves' delivery, it was discovered that many of the staves were nine-sixteenths of an inch thick. The one-sixteenth increase in thickness made no difference to the company's ability to use them to manufacture barrels, but the company rejected the staves anyway and terminated the contract.

HELD: Lord Atkin stated: 'A ton does not mean about a ton, or a yard about a yard.'[1] Accordingly, the terms of the contract had not been precisely complied with and, as the term breached was a condition, the termination of the contract was valid, even though the company suffered no actual loss.

COMMENT: The ability of non-consumers to reject goods for minor breaches of the contract is now heavily limited by s 15A of the Sale of Goods Act 1979, to such an extent that if this case were to be decided today, the company's termination would most likely amount to a breach.

> *Visit the **Online Resource Centre** for more on s 15A, in the chapter entitled 'The sale of goods'*

The de minimis rule

The rule that performance must comply precisely and completely with the terms of the contract is subject to an important exception that was stated in *Arcos* itself when Lord Atkin stated: 'No doubt there may be microscopic deviations which business men and therefore lawyers will ignore.'[2] This is known as the *de minimis* rule, because it based upon the maxim *de minimis non curat lex*. Thus, in *Shipton, Anderson & Co v Weil Bros & Co*,[3] a contract provided for the delivery of 4,950 tonnes of wheat. The seller delivered 55 lbs more than the contractual amount, but the court, applying the *de minimis* rule, held that this constituted performance of the contract by the seller.

> → *de minimis non curat lex*: 'the law does not concern itself with trifles'

Divisible obligations

Another important exception to the rule requiring precise and complete performance is in relation to divisible obligations. A divisible obligation is one that is due in intervals or instalments (for example, the monthly payment of an employee's wage). Where an obligation is divisible, a party who has performed the requisite part can recover the accompanying divisible payment, even though the contract as a whole has not been performed,[4] as the following example demonstrates.

---

1. [1933] AC 470 (HL) 479.   2. ibid.
3. [1912] 1 KB 574 (KB).   4. *Ritchie v Atkinson* (1808) 10 East 295.

> ### (Eg) Divisible obligations and performance
>
> Caroline is hired to work as part of the crew aboard *The Fearne*, a ship chartered to transport goods between ports in Europe. The charterparty is to last one year. Caroline's employment contract provides that she will work for the entire duration of the charter and will be paid £1,500 per month, but will not be paid until the charter is complete. Accordingly, after one year, she will receive £18,000.
>
> After six months, Caroline decides that she no longer wishes to work aboard *The Fearne* and leaves. Although she has not completed the contract, because the obligation to pay her is divisible (that is, a monthly rate of £1,500), she can recover her wages for the six months' work completed (£9,000), even though she was not due to be paid until the end of the charter. Of course, her failure to complete the charter period will amount to breach of contract, for which she may be required to pay damages.

Payment

In many contracts (for example, consumer contracts), the obligations of one party will amount to no more than to pay the price stipulated in the contract. Where this is the case, the payment of that sum will constitute performance of that party's obligations and discharge his liability. As a general rule, payment must be in legal tender (that is, bank notes and coins of certain denominations),[5] but an alternative method of payment will be acceptable where it is agreed upon by the parties.

A party who claims that he has discharged his obligations by the payment of a sum will need to provide proof of payment. In many cases, this proof will constitute a written receipt, but, contrary to popular belief, other forms of proof are acceptable. In fact, any form of evidence from which payment may be inferred can be valid.[6] In many cases, however, a receipt is the most usual and most easily obtainable form of proof—but a debtor has no legal entitlement to insist on being given a receipt and, even if one is provided, it only provides *prima facie* evidence of payment,[7] which can be rebutted by adducing evidence showing that payment was never made, or that the receipt was given mistakenly or obtained by fraud.

Time of performance

Where the contract does not provide that performance must be completed by a certain date, both the courts[8] and statute[9] state that the party's obligations must be performed within a reasonable time. Failure by a party to perform within a reasonable time will not constitute proper performance and that party will be in breach of contract. Where the contract requires the obligations to be performed by a certain date, the issue is slightly more complex and will depend on whether the time stipulation is 'of the essence of the contract'. Where a contract is not specifically enforceable (that is, where equity will not order performance via an order for **specific performance**),

➡ **specific performance:** a court order requiring performance of an act, normally to fulfil a contract

---

5. *Official Solicitor v Thomas* [1986] 2 EGLR 1 (CA). What constitutes legal currency can be found in the Currency and Bank Notes Act 1954, s 3, the Coinage Act 1971, s 2, and the Currency Act 1983, s 4.

6. *Eyles v Ellis* (1827) 4 Bing 112.

7. *Wilson v Keating* (1859) 27 Beav 121.   8. *Postlethwaite v Freeland* (1880) 5 App Cas 599 (HL).

9. For example, Sale of Goods Act 1979, s 29(3). Note that this Act only applies to contracts concerning the sale of goods.

whether or not time is of the essence will depend upon the express or implied intentions of the parties. In determining this, the law does put in place certain presumptions. For example, s 10(1) of the Sale of Goods Act 1979 provides that a term as to the time of payment for goods is deemed not to be of the essence of the contract, unless the contrary intention appears from the contract.

Where a contract is specifically enforceable, the common law and equity have historically taken different positions on whether or not time was of the essence. At common law, unless the parties agreed otherwise, the courts would regard a time stipulation as of the essence of the contract, with the result that if the obligation was not performed on time, the other party could terminate the contract and claim damages. Conversely, equity did not regard time stipulations as of the essence of the contract, and would decline to order specific performance against a party in breach of a time stipulation. When the Supreme Court of Judicature Acts 1873–75 merged the courts of equity and common law, they provided that, where there was a conflict, equity would prevail. Accordingly, s 41 of the Law of Property Act 1925 provides that:

> Stipulations in a contract, as to time or otherwise, which according to rules of equity are not deemed to be or to have become of the essence of the contract, are also construed and have effect at law in accordance with the same rules.

As s 41 preserves the rules of equity, it follows that any exceptions created under the rules of equity will also be preserved. Accordingly, in the following three instances, a time stipulation will be regarded as of the essence of the contract:

1. where the contract expressly states that time is of the essence;[10]
2. where the contract does not expressly provide that time is of the essence, but upon the passing of the stipulated or implied date, the party subject to the delay gives notice that time has become of the essence and fixes a reasonable time for performance;[11] or
3. where the subject matter of the contract, or the circumstances surrounding it, indicate that time should be regarded of the essence.

Where the court holds that time is of the essence, even the slightest delay will constitute failed performance and will entitle the other party to terminate. Thus, in *Union Eagle Ltd v Golden Achievement Ltd*,[12] a party's termination of the contract was valid when the other party performed its obligations ten minutes late. Where time is not of the essence, the failure to perform by the date stipulated in the contract will still constitute breach, but will entitle the innocent party to damages only.[13]

Contracts concluded over distance

In the case of contracts concluded over distance (for example, email, Internet, letter), reg 9(1) of the Consumer Protection (Distance Selling) Regulations 2000[14] provides that '[u]nless the parties agree otherwise, the supplier shall perform the contract within a maximum of 30 days beginning with the day after the day the consumer sent his order to the supplier'.

If the contract is not performed within this period, it is regarded as having not been made, save for any remedies the consumer would normally have for non-performance[15] (for example, the right to claim damages).

---

10. *Steedman v Drinkle* [1916] 1 AC 275 (PC).   11. *Stickney v Keeble* [1915] AC 386 (HL).
12. [1997] AC 514 (PC).   13. *Raineri v Miles* [1981] AC 1050 (HL).   14. SI 2000/2334.
15. ibid reg 19(5).

Discharge by agreement

As a contract is brought into existence upon the parties' agreement, it follows that it can also be brought to an end through the parties' agreement. In many cases, no formality is required: the parties can simply abandon performance and walk away. In order to prevent a party changing his mind and subsequently alleging breach of contract, however, it is desirable that some form of written discharge is obtained.

Consideration

 The distinction between executed and executory consideration is discussed at p 150

The requirement of consideration not only applies to the formation of a contract—it also applies to the discharge of a contract. Both parties will need to provide consideration for the other's agreement to discharge (unless the agreement to discharge is executed by deed). This is known as 'accord' and 'satisfaction'. 'Accord' refers to the agreement to discharge and 'satisfaction' refers to the need to provide consideration for the other's promise to agree to discharge. The form of this consideration will depend upon whether the contract is executed or executory, as the following example demonstrates.

> ### Eg Consideration and discharge by agreement
>
> **Executory consideration**
>
> Gareth wishes to sell a genuine Constable painting. Melanie wishes to purchase it. A contract is drawn up, stating that payment and delivery will take place within a month. Before payment or delivery occurs, Gareth decides that he wishes to keep the painting and Melanie discovers another Constable painting in better condition elsewhere. The parties therefore decide to discharge the contract. As the contract is executory (that is, neither party has performed their obligations), Gareth's promise to discharge Melanie's obligations will provide consideration for his own non-performance, and vice versa. There is both accord and satisfaction.
>
> **Executed consideration**
>
> Imagine that Gareth has delivered the painting (so his consideration is executed), but Melanie is yet to pay (so her consideration will be executory). If the parties then decide to discharge the contract, Melanie would not have provided any consideration for the painting or the agreement to discharge. There is accord, but no satisfaction. In order for the agreement to discharge to be valid, it will either need to be executed via a deed,[16] or Melanie will need to provide fresh consideration (satisfaction)[17] for Gareth's agreement to discharge. This fresh consideration could amount to the payment of a sum of money or some other benefit, but the fresh consideration cannot be less than what was due originally under the contract. This is because, as we have discussed, part-payment of a debt is not normally sufficient consideration.

 The rules relating to part-payment are discussed at p 156

Formalities

 The formalities of a contract are discussed at p 110

As discussed in Chapter 5, certain contracts require specific formalities in order to be created (for example, to be made in writing). The question arising is whether the discharge needs to comply with the same formalities as the creation. The common

---

16. *Foster v Dawber* (1851) 6 Exch 839.
17. *British Russian Gazette and Trade Outlook Ltd v Associated Newspapers Ltd* [1933] 2 KB 616 (CA).

law provides that a contract made under deed can only be discharged via a deed, but equity provides that a deed is not required. As equity prevails,[18] it follows that a contract executed by deed does not require any formality in order to be discharged.[19] The same rule applies to contracts required to be in, or evidenced in, writing.[20]

The parties may not wish the discharge to be total, and may instead merely desire to vary some of the terms within the original contract (subject to formalities). In this case, the agreement is to discharge certain terms and replace them with new terms. This is known as 'partial discharge' and will usually be ineffective unless it complies with the relevant formalities (for example, it must be in writing if the contract itself must be in writing). Thus, if the parties agree orally to vary the terms of a contract, the variation will be ineffective.

Discharge by breach

A party will be in breach of contract where, without a lawful excuse, he fails to perform his contractual obligations, or where he performs them in a defective manner. Subject to an effective exclusion clause to the contrary, breach of contract will entitle the non-breaching party to damages, and equitable remedies such as an injunction or specific performance may also be available. Additionally, the innocent party may be entitled to terminate the contract, depending upon the type of breach that has occurred. A breach that entitles the innocent party to terminate the contract is known as a 'repudiatory breach'. There are four types of breach:

1. renunciation;
2. incapacitation;
3. anticipatory breach; and
4. defective performance.

Renunciation

Renunciation occurs where one party demonstrates an intention not to perform his contractual obligations. Where a party expressly and unequivocally refuses to perform, establishing an intention not to perform is straightforward and the other party may freely terminate the contract, as the following example demonstrates.

> **Eg** **Renunciation and termination**
>
> Dominic is an employee of Keep Trucking Ltd, a haulage firm. His contract requires him to transport items to designated depots around the country. His manager, Marcus, instructs Dominic to transport a consignment of goods from London to Aberdeen. Not wishing to engage in such a long drive, Dominic refuses and tells Marcus to get one of the other drivers to transport the consignment.

18. Senior Courts Act 1981, s 49.   19. *Berry v Berry* [1929] 2 KB 316 (KB).
20. *Morris v Baron & Co* [1918] AC 1 (HL).

> As Dominic has expressly and unequivocally evinced an intention not to perform his contractual obligations, Keep Trucking Ltd can terminate his contract of employment and dismiss him.

More problematic are those cases in which an alleged intention not to perform is implied through the actions or conduct of a party. The difficulties can be seen in the following case.

Woodar Investment Development Ltd v Wimpey Construction UK Ltd [1980] 1 WLR 277 (HL)

FACTS: The defendant contracted to purchase a piece of land from the claimant. The defendant subsequently purported to terminate the contract on the basis of an honest, but mistaken, belief that the contract granted it such a right. The claimant alleged that the defendant's conduct (that is, the purported termination of the contract) demonstrated an intention not to perform and that the defendant had therefore renounced the contract, entitling the claimant to obtain damages.

HELD: The House of Lords dismissed the claimant's action. The House held that the defendant had not demonstrated an intention not to perform. In fact, the defendant had relied on the contract and invoked one of its provisions (albeit mistakenly and invalidly). Where an express intention is lacking, the crucial issue is whether 'a reasonable person in the position of the respondents would properly infer [from the circumstances and the party's words and conduct] an intention'[21] not to be bound by the contract.

★ See JW Carter, 'Regrettable Developments in the Law of Contract?' (1980) 39 CLJ 256

Before terminating a contract on the ground of the other party's renunciation, the innocent party should be confident that the other party has, in fact, renounced the contract. If *A* terminates a contract and claims damages on the belief that *B* has renounced it, but that belief is mistaken, *B* is likely to be able to claim damages from *A* for wrongful termination.

Incapacitation

A contract may be regarded as discharged where it is breached due to one party, through his own act or default,[22] incapacitating himself from performing his contractual obligations. Discharge will occur even where the breaching party still wishes to perform.

Universal Cargo Carriers Corporation v Citati [1957] 2 QB 401 (QB)

FACTS: The claimant chartered a ship to the defendant. The charterparty provided that the defendant would provide cargo and nominate a shipper by a certain date. Three days

---

21. [1980] 1 WLR 277 (HL) 296 (Lord Keith).
22. Where the incapacity is not due to the fault of either party, then the contract may be regarded as discharged by frustration (discussed later in this chapter).

before this date, the defendant had provided no cargo and no shipper had been nominated, meaning that, even if the defendant did nominate a shipper before the expiry date, the purpose of the charterparty had become frustrated. Accordingly, the claimant cancelled the charter and chartered the ship to someone else. It then claimed damages for breach of contract. The defendant counterclaimed for wrongful repudiation of the contract.

HELD: Although the defendant had not renounced the contract, the High Court held that his own failure to nominate a shipper meant that the purpose of the charterparty had become frustrated. The fact that the defendant still wished to perform did not matter. Devlin J (as he then was) stated: 'To say "I would like to but cannot" negatives intent to perform as much as "I will not".'[23]

The burden of proof is placed upon the innocent party to establish that the other party's conduct rendered performance impossible. It should be noted that the insolvency of one of the parties will not constitute incapacitation.[24]

Anticipatory breach

Although anticipatory breach is often considered as a type of breach in its own right, it is probably more accurate to regard it as a form of renunciation or incapacitation. So far, we have discussed actual breaches of contract (that is, breaches that occur at the time when performance is due)—but an anticipatory breach occurs where a party renounces the contract, or incapacitates himself from performing it, *before performance is due*. At this point, the non-breaching party has two options.

The first option is that the innocent party may accept the other party's breach and terminate the contract immediately[25] (it is not necessary to wait until the date of performance before terminating). The innocent party may also immediately bring a claim for damages, but the normal rules of mitigation of loss apply, so damages may be reduced if the non-breaching party fails to mitigate his loss. Once the innocent party exercises his right to terminate, the other party cannot tender performance, even if such performance is completed within the due date.[26] If, however, the innocent party has acquired the right to terminate but has yet to exercise it, performance can be validly tendered.[27]

⌐ The rules relating to mitigation of loss in contract cases are discussed at p 331

The second option available to the innocent party is slightly more complex. Instead of accepting the other party's breach, the non-breaching party might reject it and continue to insist on performance (that is, affirm the breach)—in which case, the contract remains in force and both parties are required to fulfil their obligations. As the innocent party has affirmed the anticipatory breach, he will lose his immediate right to terminate the contract and claim damages. These rights will resurrect if the other party fails to perform by the due date. The following case provides an example of this option.

23. [1957] 2 QB 401 (QB) 437.   24. *Re Agra Bank* (1867) LR 5 Eq 160.
25. *Hochster v De La Tour* (1853) 2 E & B 678.
26. *Xenos v Danube and Black Sea Rly Co* (1863) 13 CBNS 825.
27. *Norwest Holst Group Administration Ltd v Harrison* [1985] ICR 668 (CA).

White and Carter (Councils) Ltd v McGregor [1962] AC 413 (HL)

FACTS: The defendant entered into a contract with the claimant, whereby the claimant would advertise the defendant's business on litter bins for a period of three years. In return, the defendant would pay for the advertising space by instalments. On the same day that the contract was made, the defendant wrote to the claimant cancelling the contract. The claimant refused to accept this anticipatory breach and proceeded to advertise the defendant's business. The contract provided that, if the defendant were to fail to pay an instalment, the claimant could sue for the full amount due under the contract. Upon missing an instalment, the claimant brought an action for the agreed sum. The defendant argued that, because the claimant had not attempted to sell the advertising space to anyone else, it had failed to mitigate its loss.

HELD: The House of Lords allowed the claimant to perform the contract and recover the full contract price. Lord Keith stated that where a party affirms an anticipatory breach, the rules relating to mitigation would not apply (because this was an action for an agreed sum, the rules relating to mitigation did not apply anyway).

COMMENT: This case has been criticized on the ground that it requires the party in breach to 'engage in performance that is entirely pointless and wasteful'.[28] The House was fully aware of this criticism, with Lord Reid stating that the innocent party could only insist on performance where he had a 'legitimate interest' in doing so, which the claimant in *White* did. Subsequent courts have added a second limitation—namely, that the innocent party cannot insist on performance where the cooperation of the party in breach is required in order for performance to continue.[29] In *White*, the claimant clearly did not require the defendant's cooperation to perform.

The law relating to an action for an agreed sum is discussed at p 335

Defective performance

The most common form of breach is where one party has failed to perform his contractual obligations adequately. Where the performance is defective, it does not automatically follow that the non-breaching party will have the right to terminate the contract. The ability to terminate depends upon whether the term that was breached is classified as a condition, a warranty, or an innominate term.

It may be the case that the classification of the term will be determined by statute. For example, the majority of the implied terms contained in the Sale of Goods Act 1979 are classified as conditions.[30] The parties themselves are free to expressly classify the terms of the contract and whilst such a classification will usually be followed,[31] it will not provide a conclusive classification, as the following case demonstrates.

L Schuler AG v Wickman Machine Tool Sales Ltd [1974] AC 235 (HL)

FACTS: The defendant provided the claimant with the sole right to sell a certain piece of machinery for four-and-a-half years. The contract provided that it was a condition of the

---

28. *Stocznia Gdanska SA v Latvian Shipping Co* [2001] 1 Lloyd's Rep 537 (QB) 565 (Thomas J).
29. *Hounslow London Borough Council v Twickenham Garden Developments Ltd* [1971] Ch 233 (Ch).
30. See Sale of Goods Act 1979, ss 12(5A), 13(1A), 14(6), and 15(3).
31. *Lombard North Central plc v Butterworth* [1987] QB 527 (CA).

contract that the claimant shall send its representatives to visit the six largest UK motor manufacturers at least once a week to solicit orders (over the four-and-a-half-year period, this would amount of around 1,400 visits). The claimant failed to visit the six manufacturers every week and the defendant purported to terminate the contract for breach of the condition.

HELD: The House of Lords held that the term breached was not a condition. If it were a condition, missing a single visit could result in termination and the House did not believe that either party had intended such a consequence. Accordingly, it was held that the parties had used the word 'condition' in a non-legal sense merely to indicate that it was a term.

★ See Roger Brownsword, '*L Schuler AG v Wickman Machine Tool Sales Ltd:* A Tale of Two Principles' (1974) 37 MLR 104

In the absence of classification by statute, by a previous binding decision regarding the particular type of term, or by the parties, the courts will classify the term.

Conditions and warranties

Historically, the principal distinction has been between 'conditions' and 'warranties', as follows.

- **Conditions** are the most important terms that 'go to the root of the contract'. If a condition is breached, the innocent party may terminate the contract and claim damages.

- **Warranties** are less important terms. Whereas conditions relate to the main purpose of the contract, warranties tend to be 'collateral to the main purpose of . . . a contract'.[32] As warranties are less important and the consequences of their breach usually less severe, it follows that their breach can adequately be compensated by an award of damages and therefore the innocent party may not terminate the contract.

The practical distinction between conditions and warranties is extremely important from the perspective of the non-breaching party, as the following example demonstrates.

> **Eg** **Breach, conditions, and warranties**
>
> Glacius plc enters into a contract with Orchid Ltd. Orchid breaches a term of the contract. Two options exist.
>
> 1. If the term breached is a condition, Glacius can terminate the contract and/or claim damages from Orchid.
> 2. If the term breached is a warranty, Glacius can recover damages from Orchid, but it cannot terminate the contract.
>
> Glacius, believing the term to be a condition, terminates the contract, refuses to perform its obligations, and claims damages for breach. Orchid counterclaims for damages, contending that the term that it breached was merely a warranty and that Glacius's termination of the contract is improper, and therefore itself constitutes a repudiatory breach of contract because it amounts to a renunciation. Should the court agree with Orchid, Glacius will have wrongfully terminated and will be liable for breach.

---

32. *Dawsons Ltd v Bonnin* [1922] 2 AC 413 (HL) 422 (Lord Haldane).

This example demonstrates how important it can be that the classification of a term is known before the innocent party elects to terminate (although, as will be discussed, the advent of the innominate term has lessened this importance somewhat). The distinction between conditions and warranties can be seen in the following two cases with similar facts, which were decided in the same year.

 Poussard v Spiers (1876) 1 QB 410 (DC)

FACTS: Madame Poussard (the claimant) contracted to perform at the defendant's opera house for three months. A few days before opening night, she became ill and was unable to perform for the first four performances. A substitute was located, but would only perform for the full three-month contract. Given that the defendant did not know how long Poussard would be ill, he terminated her contract and took on the substitute. Poussard sued.

HELD: The High Court held that Poussard's inability to perform from the opening night onward went to the root of the contract and that therefore the defendant's termination of the contract was valid.

 Bettini v Gye (1876) 1 QB 183 (DC)

FACTS: Mr Bettini (the claimant) had agreed to perform in the defendant's opera for three-and-a-half months. It was a term of the contract that he arrive six days before the opening night to take part in rehearsals. Due to illness, he arrived three days before the opening night. The defendant refused to let him sing and obtained a replacement. Bettini sued.

HELD: The High Court held that the defendant was not entitled to terminate Bettini's contract. The term requiring six days' rehearsal time did not go to the root of the contract, and was a mere warranty. Accordingly, the defendant was not entitled to terminate Bettini's employment, and Bettini could therefore recover damages for wrongful termination.

The distinction between *Poussard* and *Bettini* is clear, but this is not always the case and it may be that a term is not so easy to classify. So how will the courts determine the term's status?

Where statute or a binding precedent does not classify the term, the courts will attempt to determine the status of a term by reference to the parties' intentions. In many cases, however, the parties may have given no thought to the legal status of the terms when negotiating them. Accordingly, the court will attempt to ascertain the intentions of the parties, based on the nature, purpose, and construction of the contract. If, based on the context of the whole contract, it is clear that that term is so important that it goes to 'the very root…of the contract'[33] and that an injured party would always want to be entitled to terminate for breach of the term, then it will be regarded as a condition. Thus, where a charterparty provided that a ship was 'now in the port of Amsterdam', when, in fact, it was elsewhere, the term was held to be a condition, because the location of the ship was commercially vital to the charterer.[34] Conversely, where a term of a charterparty provided that the ship

---

33. *Glaholm v Hays* (1841) 2 Man & G 257, 268.   34. *Behn v Burness* (1863) 3 B & S 751.

should be seaworthy, the court held it was not a condition, because the term could be breached in a number of ways, some of which the parties could not intend to result in termination.[35]

Innominate terms

Classifying terms as either conditions or warranties provides certainty insofar as it gave the parties clarity in relation to whether or not they could terminate if the other party were to commit a breach. However, the approach was also unjustifiably rigid in that, once a term was classified as a condition, the innocent party could escape the contract irrespective of the seriousness of the breach. The case of *Arcos Ltd v EA Ronaasen & Son* is a stark example of this. Further, this approach allowed parties to escape from a bad bargain by upholding their right to terminate based on a trivial breach of a condition. Accordingly, in the following case, the Court of Appeal established a third type of term—namely, the innominate term.

 Arcos is discussed at p 291

 Hong Kong Fir Shipping Co Ltd v Kawasaki Kisen Kaisha Ltd [1962] 2 QB 26 (CA)

FACTS: The claimant owned a ship, which it chartered to the defendant for a period of two years. The charterparty provided that the claimant would provide a ship that was 'in every way fitted for ordinary cargo service'. The ship was actually in a poor state of repair and the engine crew was incompetent. Consequently, on the ship's first voyage, significant repairs were needed, resulting in use of the ship being lost for twenty weeks whilst repairs were being made. Shortly before the ship was fully repaired, the defendant purported to terminate the charter for repudiatory breach. Subsequently, the ship was repaired (with seventeen months of the contract left to go) and was completely seaworthy. The claimant brought an action for wrongful termination.

HELD: There was no doubt that the claimant was in breach of contract, but was it a breach that entitled the defendant to terminate? Under the approach in *Arcos*, the answer would almost certainly have been 'yes'—but the Court of Appeal took a different approach, stating that there were:

> contractual undertakings of a more complex character which cannot be categorised as being 'conditions' or 'warranties' . . . Of such undertakings all that can be predicated is that some breaches will and others will not give rise to an event which will deprive the party not in default of substantially the whole benefit which it was intended that he should obtain from the contract; and the legal consequences of a breach of such an undertaking, unless provided for expressly in the contract, depend upon the nature of the event to which the breach gives rise and do not follow automatically from a prior classification of the undertaking as a 'condition' or a 'warranty'.[36]

These terms that cannot be categorized as conditions or warranties would be classed as innominate terms, breach of which would only give the innocent party the right to terminate if the breach were to deprive him of substantially the whole benefit of the contract. The term in the contract requiring seaworthiness was deemed to be such an innominate term and, as the ship had been fully repaired and the defendant still had seventeen months' potential use, it had not been deprived of substantially the whole benefit, and therefore the defendant's termination was wrongful.

---

35. *Hong Kong Fir Shipping Co Ltd v Kawasaki Kisen Kaisha Ltd* [1962] 2 QB 26 (CA).
36. ibid 70 (Diplock LJ).

★ See Michael P Furmston, 'The Classification of Contractual Terms' (1962) 25 MLR 584

> **COMMENT:** The introduction of the innominate term represents a stark departure from the approach evidenced in previous cases, with one commentator describing the decision as 'revolutionary'.[37] Under the previous approach, the seriousness and effects of the breach were largely inconsequential. Where an innominate term is breached, the seriousness and effects of the breach become all-important in determining the innocent party's right to terminate.

There is little doubt that the courts now rarely classify terms as warranties, given that a classification as an innominate term will provide the court with much more flexibility. The courts will only classify a term as a warranty where there is clear evidence that the parties did not intend a breach to result in the right to terminate, or where statute or a binding precedent classifies a term as such. Accordingly, since *Hong Kong Fir*, the crucial distinction is now between conditions and innominate terms. This has led one academic[38] to contend that there are now, in practice, only two types of contractual terms, namely conditions (breach of which will allow repudiation) and non-conditions (breach of which will only allow repudiation if the consequences of the breach are sufficiently serious).

The problem that has arisen is that the courts now have to balance two opposing objectives. The first objective is to uphold the validity of contracts where possible. The introduction of the innominate term is clearly evidence of this, because it restricts the innocent party's right to terminate. In the absence of clear agreement as to the term being a condition, the courts should 'lean in favour of construing'[39] the term as innominate. This is widely regarded as a beneficial development, because it prevents parties from avoiding contracts for technical or trivial breaches, or where they have simply made a bad bargain.

 ### Reardon-Smith Line Ltd v Yngvar Hansen Tangen [1976] 1 WLR 989 (HL)[40]

FACTS: To help finance the construction of a tanker, it was chartered before it had been constructed. The charterers subchartered the tanker to the claimant. As the tanker did not yet have a name, it was referred to in the charterparty by reference to the shipyard at which it was built—namely, 'Yard No. 354 at Osaka'. The ship was too large to be built at Osaka, so it was built at another shipyard in Oshima. Upon completion of the tanker, the charter market had fallen due to an oil crisis, meaning that such tankers could be chartered for much less than the claimant had agreed to pay in the contract. The claimant therefore terminated the contract, on the ground that the tanker was not built at the shipyard specified in the contract.

HELD: Lord Wilberforce described the traditional approach of classifying a term as either a condition or warranty as 'excessively technical and due for fresh consideration in this House'.[41] He stated that the court should have more regard to 'the nature and gravity of a breach or departure rather than in accepting rigid categories which do or do not automatically give a right to rescind'.[42] On this basis, the House of Lords held that the term breached was innominate, and that, because the effect of the breach was minor, the claimant had no right to terminate, and the termination was therefore invalid.

---

37. Tony Weir, 'Contracts: The Buyer's Right to Reject Defective Goods' [1976] CLJ 33, 35.
38. FMB Reynolds, 'Discharge of Contract by Breach' (1981) 97 LQR 541.
39. *Tradax Internacional SA v Goldschmidt SA* [1977] 2 Lloyd's Rep 604 (QB) 612 (Slynn J).
40. See also *Cehave NV v Bremer Hangelsgesellschaft mbH (The Hansa Nord)* [1976] QB 44 (CA).
41. [1976] 1 WLR 989 (HL) 998.   42. ibid.

The second objective is the need to provide commercial certainty to the parties' dealings, but the flexibility of the innominate term has resulted in increased uncertainty. Under the pre-*Hong Kong Fir* approach, all that the non-breaching party needed to know was whether the term breached was a condition or a warranty, and such information was usually discernable from the wording of the contract. Where a term is innominate, the ability to terminate depends not on the words of the contract, but on events, and these events 'may be in the China Sea rather than in the head office where decisions are taken, and one will probably have to wait for them, since consequences tend to occur after their causes'.[43] Accordingly, where the term is innominate, the non-breaching party cannot terminate with certainty; it will have to 'wait and see' whether the breach is of sufficient gravity to enable it to terminate. Parties who terminate before such knowledge is available risk being subject to a wrongful termination action should the consequences of the breach not be sufficiently serious.

The courts' concern over the uncertainty inherent in the use of the innominate term is evidenced in the following case.

Maredelanto Compania Naviera SA v Bergbau-Handel GmbH (The Mihalis Angelos) [1971] 1 QB 164 (CA)[44]

FACTS: The defendant chartered a ship from the claimant shipowner. Clause 1 of the charterparty provided that the ship would be expected to load cargo at Haiphong on about 1 July 1965. The claimant knew, however, that this expectation was unreasonable (because the ship was engaged elsewhere) and that the ship would not be at Haiphong until around 13–14 July. In the meantime, the defendant had discovered that it could not obtain any of the cargo that it had hoped to transport on the chartered ship. The defendant therefore terminated the charterparty and the claimant sued for damages. The claimant argued that clause 1 was an innominate term and that, because the defendant had not been deprived of substantially the whole benefit of the contract, it had no right to terminate.

HELD: The Court of Appeal declined to follow *Hong Kong Fir* and held the termination by the defendant to be valid, with Megaw LJ stating:

> [S]uch a term in a charterparty ought to be regarded as being a condition of the contract, in the old sense of the word 'condition'... One of the important elements of the law is predictability... [T]here are obvious and substantial advantages in having, where possible, a firm and definite rule for a particular class of legal relationship... It is surely much better... to be able to say categorically: 'If a breach is proved, then the charterer can put an end to the contract', rather than that they should be left to ponder whether or not the courts would be likely... to decide that in the particular circumstances the breach was or was not such as 'to go to the root of the contract'. Where justice does not require greater flexibility, there is everything to be said for, and nothing against, a degree of rigidity in legal principle.[45]

COMMENT: The decision does not reject the innominate term, but it does indicate that the Court's reasoning in *Hong Kong Fir* is not appropriate in all cases. In certain cases, the need for certainty may outweigh the need for flexibility.

★ See WVH Rogers, 'The Late Ship and the Non-existent Cargo' (1971) 34 MLR 190

---

43. Tony Weir, 'Contracts: The Buyer's Right to Reject Defective Goods' [1976] CLJ 33, 35.
44. See also *Bunge Corporation v Tradax Export SA* [1981] 1 WLR 711 (HL).
45. [1971] 1 QB 164 (CA) 205.

A measure of clarity has been provided by Waller LJ,[46] who expressed approval for the relevant passage in *Chitty on Contracts*, which stated that a term is likely to be regarded as innominate, unless it comes within one of the following situations, when it will likely be classed as a condition:

- if statute expressly classifies a term as a condition;
- if, subject to the rules of precedent, a previous judicial decision classifies a type of term as a condition;
- if the contract itself provides that the term is a condition, or that its breach can result in termination;
- if the nature or the subject matter or the circumstances of the case lead to the conclusion that the parties must have intended that the term's breach would entitle the innocent party to terminate.

These situations are relatively narrow and fit in with the widely held judicial belief that 'the courts should not be too ready to interpret contractual clauses as conditions'.[47] Accordingly, the law appears to have completely moved away from the traditional position, whereby the effect of the breach was not important, to a position in which, in the majority of cases, the effect of the breach becomes the determining factor.

Termination and affirmation

Unlike frustration, breach does not automatically discharge the contract. As discussed, subject to an effective exclusion clause to the contrary, the innocent party *may* have the right to terminate the contract and therefore discharge it, or he may simply have a right to recover damages only. Alternatively, a party that has the right to terminate may instead choose to affirm the contract. Termination and affirmation will now be examined.

Termination

A repudiatory breach does not automatically discharge the contract; rather, the non-breaching party may elect to terminate the contract. The party terminating need not comply with any formalities in order to terminate the contract, but the termination 'must be unequivocal and it must be communicated to the party in breach'[48] (for example, by refusing to accept the other party's performance or by refusing to perform himself). A valid election to terminate can result in a number of consequences, including:

- The party that terminated the contract is released from performing any obligations that remain to be performed. This could include accepting or paying for future performance,[49] paying any future instalments,[50] or adhering to a restrictive covenant contained in the contract.[51] Should the party in breach commence an action for non-performance, the innocent party can raise the termination as a defence.

---

46. *BS & N Ltd (BVI) v Micado Shipping Ltd (Malta) (The Seaflower)* [2001] 1 Lloyd's Rep 341 (CA) 348.
47. *Bunge Corporation v Tradax Export SA* [1981] 1 WLR 711 (HL) 715 (Lord Wilberforce).
48. *Sookraj v Samaroo* [2004] UKPC 50, [2005] 1 P & CR DG 11 [17] (Lord Scott).
49. *Photo Production Ltd v Securicor Transport Ltd* [1980] AC 827 (HL).
50. *SCI (Sales Curve Interactive) v Titus SARL* [2001] EWCA Civ 591, [2001] 2 All ER (Comm) 416.
51. *General Billposting Co Ltd v Atkinson* [1909] AC 118 (HL).

- Termination operates only in relation to future obligations. The obligations of both parties due at the time of termination remain in force and must be performed. For example, if the non-breaching party terminates a contract that requires it to pay for goods in instalments, any instalments unpaid at the time of discharge will still need to be paid, but future instalments need not be paid.

- The innocent party can recover any monies paid if there has been a total failure of consideration (that is, where the party in breach has not performed any part of its contractual duties in respect of which payment is due under the contract.)[52]

- If the innocent party has supplied goods or performed a service but, at the time that it exercised the right to terminate, has not been paid, it can sue for a *quantum meruit* (reasonable sum).

- A party that exercises the right to terminate a contract cannot subsequently change its mind, affirm the breach, and demand performance.[53]

- Termination does not necessarily discharge the whole contract. Certain terms may impose obligations post-termination (for example, a term requiring that any disputes be referred to arbitration before commencing legal proceedings) and these terms are likely to continue to be binding if it was the intention of the parties that this be so.[54]

Affirmation

The innocent party may not want to contract to end. Accordingly, it may elect to affirm the breach or it may simply decide not to exercise the right to terminate. In either event, several consequences will follow.

- The contract will remain in force and will continue to bind both parties.[55]

- Where the innocent party expressly and unequivocally elects to affirm the breach, his right to terminate is lost and he cannot subsequently change his mind.

- If the innocent party obtains an order for specific performance requiring the party in breach to fulfil its contractual obligations, this will amount to conditional affirmation only. If the party in breach fails to comply with the order or if performance becomes impossible, the non-breaching party may terminate the contract and recover damages.[56]

Discharge by frustration

Where a lack of proper contractual performance is caused by events outside the control of either party, it would be unfair to impose liability for breach. In such a case, the court is likely to hold that the contract has been frustrated, and the effect of frustration is to provide the breaching party with a lawful excuse for its breach of contract.

Frustrating events

Numerous events can bring about a contract's frustration. It should be noted that, in order for a contract to be frustrated, the event must occur after the contract was made. Where the event existed at the time that the contract was made, frustration

---

52. *Stocznia Gdanska SA v Latvian Shipping Co* [1998] 1 WLR 574 (HL).
53. *Johnson v Agnew* [1980] AC 367 (HL).   54. *Heyman v Darwins Ltd* [1942] AC 356 (HL).
55. *BMBF (No 12) v Harland & Wolff Shipbuilding & Heavy Industries Ltd* [2001] EWCA Civ 862, [2001] 2 Lloyd's Rep 227.   56. *Austins of East Ham Ltd v Macey* [1941] Ch 338 (CA).

will not apply and the relevant party will need to seek relief via the law relating to illegality or mistake. There are four principal categories of frustrating event, beginning with physical impossibility.

Physical impossibility

The most straightforward form of frustrating event is one that occurs after the contract was entered into which serves to render performance of the contract physically impossible. The obvious example of this would be where the subject matter of the contract has been destroyed.

 ### Taylor v Caldwell (1863) 3 B & S 826

FACTS: The defendant granted the claimant the use of a music hall in order to put on a series of concerts. Accidentally, and without any fault on the part of either party, the music hall was burnt down. As the music hall was unavailable, the defendant was in breach of contract and so the claimant sued.

HELD: The claimant's action failed. The contract had become frustrated and so the defendant was not liable to pay damages. Blackburn J justified this by imposing an implied term into the contract, which provided that liability would not be imposed where performance becomes impossible. It should be noted that this implied term theory is no longer accepted today.

COMMENT: Destruction of the contract's subject matter will not always result in the contract's frustration. Certain contracts (for example, sale of goods contracts) may be governed by rules, or may contain terms, that place the risk of destruction upon one of the parties before performance is completed. In such a case, if the risk has been imposed upon a party before the subject matter is destroyed, then the contract will not be frustrated.

The above principle will also apply where it is not the subject matter of the contract, but rather some other object essential to performance, that is destroyed.[57] Further examples of subsequent impossibility that could cause a contract to become frustrated include the following.

- Where the contract is a personal one and requires performance from a particular person (for example, employment, skilled service), the death of either party will frustrate the contract.[58] The same will apply to a party who is rendered incapable of performing the contract (for example, due to physical or mental disability).[59]

- Where the subject matter of the contract (or something essential to performance) is not destroyed, but becomes unavailable (for example, where a specified ship becomes unavailable to carry out the charterparty at the specified time due to strike activity),[60] the contract is likely to be frustrated. Unavailability is often regarded as a separate head of frustration, but it is contended that it is more appropriate to regard it as a subspecies of impossibility.

Frustration of a common purpose or basic assumption

Where performance is possible and lawful, a contract may still be frustrated where its common purpose, or the basic assumptions upon which it was made, are destroyed by subsequent events.

---

57. *Appleby v Myers* (1867) LR 2 CP 651. 58. *Stubbs v Holywell Railway Co* (1867) LR 2 Ex 311.
59. *Condor v The Barren Knights Ltd* [1966] 1 WLR 87.
60. *Pioneer Shipping Ltd v BTP Tioxide Ltd (The Nema) (No 2)* [1982] AC 724 (HL).

Krell v Henry [1903] 2 KB 740 (CA)

FACTS: The defendant hired a flat from the claimant in order to watch the coronation procession of Edward VII. The coronation was cancelled and the claimant claimed the balance of the contract price. The defendant refused to pay.

HELD: The Court of Appeal held the contract to be frustrated, because the fundamental assumption on which both parties contracted had been destroyed. Clearly, the defendant had hired the flat to watch the procession; the claimant had also let the flat for the purpose of watching the procession. This was not stated in the contract, but was inferred from the flat's advertisement, which stated that its windows faced the procession route.

It is essential that the purposes or assumptions of both parties must be destroyed; it is not enough that the purposes of one party in making the contract cannot be fulfilled, as the following case demonstrates.

 Herne Bay Steamboat Co v Hutton [1903] 2 KB 683 (CA)

FACTS: The defendant hired a steamship from the claimant for the express purpose of taking fare-paying passengers to observe the King's naval review and for taking a cruise around the fleet. The review was cancelled, but the fleet remained anchored. Hearing this, the claimant contacted the defendant for instructions, but received no reply. The claimant therefore used the steamship himself and made a profit. A day later, the defendant repudiated the contract and the claimant sued to recover the contract price, less the profits made. The defendant argued that the contract had become frustrated.

HELD: The Court of Appeal (in fact, the same three judges who decided *Krell v Henry*) held that the contract was not frustrated. The naval review was not the sole basis of the contract and, even if it was, it was not the claimant's sole basis. Accordingly, the common purpose was not destroyed and so the contract was not frustrated.

Fundamental change of circumstances

The general rule is that an event that causes performance of a contractual obligation to become impracticable, or more onerous or expensive, does not cause the contract to become frustrated.

 Davis Contractors Ltd v Fareham Urban UDC [1956] AC 696 (HL)

FACTS: The claimant agreed to build seventy-two houses in eight months, in return for which the defendant would pay it £94,000. Due to shortages in the availability of labour, the houses were not completed until twenty-two months later and had cost the claimant £115,000. The claimant alleged that the shortage of labour had caused the contract to become frustrated, thereby allowing it to claim a *quantum meruit* in excess of the agreed contractual price.

HELD: The House of Lords held that the contract was not frustrated. Lord Radcliffe stated:

> it is not hardship or inconvenience or material loss itself which calls the principle of frustration into play. There must be as well such a change in the significance of the obligation that the thing undertaken would, if performed, be a different thing from that contracted for.[61]

Lord Radcliffe's statement in *Davis* indicates that, although a contract could still be physically performed, where a fundamental change of circumstances occurs that results in a situation whereby, if the contract were performed, it would become something radically different from that contracted for, the court may be prepared to regard the contract as frustrated.

Metropolitan Water Board v Dick Kerr & Co Ltd [1918] AC 119 (HL)

FACTS: The defendant contracted to build a reservoir for the claimant water board within six years. The contract contained a term that stated that this time limit would be extended if the defendant were to encounter any difficulties, impediments, or obstructions. When World War I started, the Minister of Munitions, acting under the Defence of the Realm (Consolidation) Act 1914, required the defendant to cease work on the reservoir, and to remove and sell any plant there. The claimant alleged that the contract was still valid, but the defendant argued that the Minister's actions had frustrated the contract.

HELD: The effect of the Minister's prohibition was such that performance of the contract, if resumed at a later date, would be radically different from the contract originally made. Accordingly, the House of Lords held that the contract was frustrated.

Cases such as *Metropolitan Water Board* are rare. The courts are usually extremely reluctant to allow impracticability or financial hardship to result in frustration, as the following case demonstrates.

Tsakiroglou & Co Ltd v Noblee Thorl GmbH [1962] AC 93 (HL)

FACTS: The defendant had agreed to sell to the claimant 300 tonnes of groundnuts. The defendant would also transport the groundnuts from the Sudan to the claimant in Hamburg. This would normally involve passing through the Suez Canal (and, indeed, this is what both parties envisaged, although it was not a term of the contract)—a journey of 4,386 miles. The Canal was, however closed for several months, meaning that the only way to transport the groundnuts was to go around the Cape of Good Hope—a journey of 11,137 miles. The defendant therefore decided not to perform, on the ground that the Canal's closure had frustrated the contract.

HELD: The House of Lords held that the contract was not frustrated. There was no term in the contract indicating that the Canal should be used, nor could a term requiring the Canal

---

61. [1956] AC 696 (HL) 729.

be used be implied, because the route used made no difference to the claimant. Therefore, the contract was not physically impossible to perform. In addition, although the closure of the Canal involved a change in performance at considerable expense to the defendant, it did not render performance radically different from the contract as originally made.

★ See CJ Hamson, 'Contract: CIF—Frustration: Closure of Suez Canal' (1961) CLJ 150

Illegality

Where a contract is illegal at the time it is made, it will usually be void on the ground of illegality and frustration will therefore not apply. Where a contract entered into is lawful, but, subsequently, its performance becomes illegal, it will become frustrated.

 ### Denny, Mott and Dickson Ltd v James B Fraser & Co Ltd [1944] AC 265 (HL)

FACTS: The claimant timber merchant agreed to purchase all of its timber from the defendant and also that it would let a timber yard to the defendant, over which the defendant would have an option to purchase in the event of the contract being terminated. With the outbreak of World War II, increased timber was needed for the war effort. Legislation was passed prohibiting dealing in the timber being sold by the defendant. The defendant therefore terminated the contract and exercised the option to purchase. The claimant brought an action to determine the rights of the parties.

HELD: The House of Lords held that the contract was frustrated. Lord Macmillan stated: 'It is plain that a contract to do what it has become illegal to do cannot be legally enforceable.'[62] The defendant could not therefore exercise the option to purchase the timber yard, because the contract was not terminated; rather, it was frustrated by the prohibition in dealing in timber.

COMMENT: This case also demonstrates that frustration can occur where the illegality (or impossibility or unavailability) is only temporary. Once the war ended, the prohibition on timber trading was removed. In such cases, the courts will need to take into account the likely period that the contractual relations of the parties will be interrupted.[63] The longer the period (relative to the duration of the contract), the more likely it will be that the contract will be frustrated.

The limitations of frustration

Even if a frustrating event occurs, it does not automatically follow that the contract will be frustrated. In several situations, the court is likely to hold that a contract is not frustrated, even though an event capable of causing frustrating the contract has occurred.

Contractual provision

The principal purpose of the doctrine of frustration is to allocate risk fairly in the event of an unforeseen event that affects a party's ability to perform the contract. There is, however, nothing stopping the parties from expressly allocating this risk themselves by including a term in the contract (known as a '*force majeure* clause')

➡ *force majeure*: 'superior force,' referring to an event or cause that cannot be prevented

---

62. [1944] AC 265 (HL) 272.
63. *National Carriers Ltd v Panalpina (Northern) Ltd* [1981] AC 675 (HL).

that states what the outcome will be should a frustrating event occur (for example, one party bears the risk, the contract is suspended, etc). In effect, this will contractually exclude the doctrine of frustration and prevent the courts' intervention. There are, however, two limitations on the parties' ability to do this, as follows.

1. Where the contract is frustrated due to subsequent illegality, a contractual provision avoiding the effects of frustration will be ineffective.[64]

2. Such provisions are restrictively interpreted and, even though a provision may literally cover the frustrating event, the court will not allow its enforcement if it renders the contract radically different from what the parties contracted for (as was demonstrated in the *Metropolitan Water Board* case, discussed at p XXX)

Foreseeability

If the frustrating event was foreseen or was foreseeable by *one* of the parties, then the doctrine of frustration will not usually apply. The party who foresaw the event should have provided for it in some manner and his failure to do so (and consequent breach) will not be excused by the contract being frustrated.

 Walton Harvey Ltd v Walker & Homfrays Ltd [1931] 1 Ch 274 (CA)

FACTS: The defendant had leased a hotel. It granted the claimant advertising agency the right to display advertisements on top of the hotel for a period of seven years. Before the seven years had expired, the hotel was compulsorily purchased by the local authority and demolished. The claimant brought an action for damages against the defendant, who argued that the contract had been frustrated.

HELD: The Court of Appeal held that the contract was not frustrated and that the defendant was therefore liable to pay damages. The defendant knew that compulsory purchase of the hotel was a possibility, whereas the claimant did not. That the defendant chose not to provide contractually for the risk of compulsory purchase indicated that it undertook the risk of it occurring.

What degree of foreseeability is required to displace the doctrine of frustration? Given enough time and expense, every possible contingency could be planned for, but this would be an extremely inefficient use of the parties' resources. Hence, the law will require a reasonably high degree of foreseeability before frustration will cease to apply. Further, the following case demonstrates that the details of the event will also need to be foreseen or foreseeable.

 WJ Tatem Ltd v Gamboa [1939] 1 KB 132 (KB)

FACTS: The defendant chartered a ship from the claimant for a period of thirty days, in order to evacuate refugees of the Spanish Civil War. The rate of hire was £250 per day, payable until the ship was returned—but payment would cease if the ship were to go 'missing'. Two weeks after the ship was chartered, it was seized by Nationalist forces and not returned

---

64. *Ertel Bieber & Co v Rio Tinto Co Ltd* [1918] AC 260 (HL).

for two months. The claimant claimed the daily rate for the period of two months and two weeks.

HELD: The High Court held that the contract was frustrated. Whilst the seizure of the ship was foreseeable, it was not foreseeable that it would be held for so long after the charter period. Accordingly, the details of the seizure were not foreseeable enough to displace the doctrine of frustration.

If the frustrating event was foreseen or foreseeable by both parties, then their failure contractually to provide for such an event will ensure that the doctrine of frustration can apply.[65]

Fault

A party cannot rely on the doctrine of frustration if the event was caused by his fault. Otherwise, the law would allow parties to induce frustration themselves and then use it as an excuse for their breach of contract.

Maritime National Fish Ltd v Ocean Trawlers Ltd [1935] AC 524 (PC)

FACTS: The claimant owned a trawler that was fitted with an otter trawl. Such trawlers required a licence from the Minister of Fisheries. The claimant chartered this trawler to the defendant, which already owned four similar trawlers. The defendant accordingly applied for five licences, but was only granted three. The defendant decided to license its own trawlers and not those of the claimant. It claimed that the inability to obtain a licence for the claimant's trawler had frustrated the contract, so that it did not have to pay the claimant. The claimant sued for the contract price.

HELD: The contract was not frustrated. The inability to use the claimant's trawler was caused by the defendant's decision not to license it. Therefore, the supervening event was the defendant's fault, which remained liable for the charter price.

The courts take a very strict approach to self-induced frustration. Provided that a party makes a choice that results in the supervening event, the court will not regard the contract as frustrated, no matter how reasonable or commercially sensible the party's choice might appear.

J Lauritzen AS v Wijsmuller BV (The Super Servant Two) [1990] 1 Lloyd's Rep 1 (CA)

FACTS: The claimant owned an oil rig that it wished to transport from Japan to Rotterdam. The defendant agreed to transport the rig using one or other of two transportation units—namely, the *Super Servant One* or the *Super Servant Two*. The defendant chose to use the *Super Servant Two* to transport the rig and the *Super Servant One* was used to fulfil contracts with other parties. Before transportation of the rig commenced, the *Super Servant Two* sank. Given that the *Super Servant One* was engaged elsewhere, the defendant could not perform the contract and, to avoid being liable for breach, claimed that the contract had been frustrated.

HELD: As the inability to perform was the choice of the defendant, the contract was not frustrated. It could have performed the contract by using the *Super Servant One*; the fact that this would have resulted in the defendant breaching its contract with a third party was irrelevant.

COMMENT: Understandably, this case has proven controversial. The result is seen as harsh and many have questioned whether it was true to say that the defendant had a choice. It could be argued that the defendant did not have a real choice, because it would have ended up being in breach of contract to either the claimant or the third parties.

 See Ewan McKendrick, 'The Construction of *Force Majeure* Clauses and Self-induced Frustration' [1990] LMCLQ 153

The above cases were based on deliberate acts. It would also appear that a negligent act that renders contractual performance impossible or illegal will not cause the contract to become frustrated.[66] Therefore, if, in *Taylor v Caldwell*, the concert hall were to have burned down due to the owner's negligence, then the contract would not have been frustrated.

The effects of frustration

To appreciate the legal effects of frustration fully, it is necessary to examine the original position at common law, before discussing the current position under statute. It will be seen that the current position under statute is much more satisfactory.

Common law

At common law, the effects of frustration are as follows.

1. The contract is automatically discharged.[67] This is not the same as holding the contract void, voidable, or terminated, because the discharge is automatic at the point of frustration and the contract cannot survive at the discretion of the parties or the court.
2. Any rights or liabilities that arise after the frustrating event are discharged.[68]
3. Any rights or obligations that arose before the frustrating event remain enforceable.[69]

These three effects are demonstrated in the following case (like *Krell v Henry* discussed earlier, this was concerned with the cancellation of Edward VII's coronation procession).

Chandler v Webster [1904] 1 KB 493 (CA)

FACTS: The defendant let a room to the claimant for the purpose of watching the coronation procession. The contract price was £141 15s, payable immediately, but the defendant paid only £100. The coronation was cancelled before he had paid the remaining £41 15s and

---

66. *Joseph Constantine Steamship Line Ltd v Imperial Smelting Corp Ltd* [1942] AC 154 (HL).

67. Except those provisions intended by the parties to apply in the event of frustration: *Heyman v Darwins Ltd* [1942] AC 356 (HL). 68. *Chandler v Webster* [1904] 1 KB 493 (CA).

69. ibid.

the contract was accordingly frustrated. The claimant sought recovery of the £100 and the defendant counterclaimed for the remaining £41 15s.

HELD: The frustration automatically discharged the contract. As the obligation to pay the full contract price arose before the contract was frustrated, the Court of Appeal held that the claimant could not recover the £100 paid and remained liable for the remaining £41 15s.

⭐ See RG McElroy and Glanville Williams, 'The Coronation Cases' (1941) 4 MLR 241 and (1942) 5 MLR 1

The result in *Chandler v Webster* is clearly an extremely harsh one: the claimant received no benefit whatsoever, yet remained liable to pay the full amount. Fortunately, the harshness of *Chandler* was partially remedied in the following case.

 Fibrosa Spolka Akcyjna v Fairbairn Lawson Combe Barbour Ltd [1943] AC 32 (HL)

FACTS: The defendant (based in Leeds) agreed to sell certain machinery to the claimant, a company based in Poland. The contract price was £4,800, with £1,600 payable immediately, although only £1,000 was paid. Before the machinery could be manufactured, Germany invaded and occupied Poland, thereby frustrating the contract. The claimant requested that the £1,000 be returned. The defendant refused, arguing that, based on *Chandler*, it did not need to return the £1,000.

HELD: The House of Lords held that advance payments could be recovered where there had been a total failure of consideration (that is, where a party had not gained any benefit from the contract). Accordingly, the claimant could recover the £1,000, and Lord Atkin stated *obiter* that it did not need to pay the remainder of what was due at the time of frustration (that is, £600). Obviously, because the contract was discharged, the claimant would not have to pay the remaining contract price either (£3,200).

Whilst the decision in *Fibrosa* can be regarded as a step in the right direction, it still left the law in an unsatisfactory state for two reasons. First, a party could only recover an advance payment where there was a total failure of consideration. Where a party has gained any form of benefit, no matter how small, the advance payment would be irrecoverable.[70] Second, allowing a party to recover an advance payment fully might be harsh where the other party has incurred expenses in preparing to perform.

These two criticisms led to Parliament's intervention in the form of the Law Reform (Frustrated Contracts) Act 1943, which serves to remedy the deficiencies of the common law.

Statute

The Law Reform (Frustrated Contracts) Act 1943 deals solely with the consequences of frustration. As under the common law, an express contractual provision allocating risk can exclude the operation of the Act.[71] Section 1(2) establishes three crucial rules designed to overrule *Chandler v Webster* and to remove the limitation

---

70. *Whincup v Hughes* (1871) LR 6 CP 78.
71. Law Reform (Frustrated Contracts) Act 1943, s 2(3).

established in *Fibrosa*. In addition to the contract being discharged, s 1(2) provides as follows.

1. Any sums payable before the occurrence of the frustrating event cease to be payable, irrespective of whether or not there is a total failure of consideration. Thus, if *Chandler v Webster* were to be decided today, the defendant's counter-claim for the remaining £41 15s would fail.

2. Any sums paid before the frustrating event occurred are recoverable, irre-spective of whether or not there has been a total failure of consideration. This removes the limitation established in *Fibrosa* and would mean that the claimant in *Chandler* could recover the £100.

3. Where one party is seeking recovery of sums paid, however, and the other party has incurred expenditure before the contract is discharged, the court has a dis-cretion to set off any expenses incurred against the sum that can be recovered.

The following fictional example demonstrates these three rules in practice.

 The effect of frustration

DataCorp plc agrees to provide custom-built laptops that will be used by the Crimson Cow Formula One team. DataCorp will provide fifty such laptops, for which Crimson Cow will pay £1 million upon delivery. A term of the contract provides that £250,000 is payable immediately, and that this money must be used by DataCorp to commence research and development on the laptops—but Crimson Cow pays only £200,000. DataCorp spends £100,000 in research and development, but before production can go ahead, DataCorp's manufacturing facility is the victim of an arson attack and is completely destroyed. The contract is frustrated.

1. At the time of the frustrating event, Crimson Cow owed DataCorp £50,000 (the contract provided that £250,000 was payable immediately, but Crimson Cow paid only £200,000). Under the first rule identified above, Crimson Cow would not be liable to pay the £50,000.

2. Crimson Cow had already paid £200,000. Under the second rule, Crimson Cow could recover this money.

3. As DataCorp had already incurred expenditure of £100,000 preparing for the contract, the court has the discretion to offset this against any monies recoverable by Crimson Cow. Should the court exercise this discretion, Crimson Cow will not recover the full £200,000; it will recover only £100,000, or whatever sum the court deems reasonable.

However, what if the £100,000 spent by DataCorp in research and development were to result in some discovery or technological development that could be used outside of the contract with Crimson Cow? What is the position where a party to a frustrated contract gains some form of valuable benefit from something done by the other party in, or for the purpose of, performing the contract before it is frustrated? Under the common law, a party could not recover a sum for a valuable benefit gained before frustration,[72] but this has been altered by s 1(3) of the 1943 Act, which pro-vides that:

---

72. *Appleby v Myers* (1867) LR 2 CP 651.

Where any party to the contract has, by reason of anything done by any other party thereto in, or for the purpose of, the performance of the contract, obtained a valuable benefit…before the time of discharge, there shall be recoverable from him by the said other party such sum (if any), not exceeding the value of the said benefit to the party obtaining it, as the court considers just, having regard to all the circumstances of the case

The courts' approach to quantifying a sum under s 1(3) can be seen in the following case.

BP Exploration Co (Libya) Ltd v Hunt (No 2) [1979] 1 WLR 783 (QB)[73]

FACTS: The defendant, a wealthy US citizen, obtained a concession from the Libyan government to explore for, and exploit, any oil found. He lacked the resources to exploit the oil himself, so he entered into an agreement with BP (the claimant), whereby BP would pay for and conduct the exploratory work, in return for a half-share in the concession. The contract also allowed BP to recover its expenses at a certain rate. A large oil field was found but, following a revolution, the new Libyan government expropriated the concession, thereby frustrating the contract. BP had only recovered one-third of its expenses, so brought a claim against the defendant under s 1(3), arguing that the defendant had received a valuable benefit from it.

HELD: Goff J (as he then was) stated that the correct approach in s 1(3) cases was, first, to identify and value the benefit received at the date of frustration. As an award under s 1(3) cannot exceed the value of the benefit, this would constitute the maximum sum that could be recovered. In the case, the court valued the benefit received by the defendant at US$85 million.

Second, the court must decide what is a just sum. The court calculated this by reference to what the claimant had already expended in developing the concession (US$87 million) plus any monies paid to the defendant (US$10 million). From this, it deducted any monies already recovered from the defendant (US$62 million). Using this method, the claimant recovered US$35 million from the defendant.

Finally, it should be noted that the 1943 Act does not apply to all types of contract. Excluded contracts include:

- contracts in which the parties have included an express term providing what will occur in the event of a frustrating event;[74]
- those in which a part of a contract is severable (that is, it contains divisible obligations), in which case, that part will be treated as a separate contract that will not be frustrated—the Act will apply only to remainder of the contract;[75]

  Divisible obligations are discussed at p 291

- contracts of insurance,[76] in which case, generally, once the risk has attached, premiums are non-returnable.[77]

---

73. Affirmed by both the Court of Appeal ([1981] 1 WLR 232) and the House of Lords ([1983] 2 AC 352).
74. Law Reform (Frustrated Contracts) Act 1943, s 2(3). 75. ibid s 2(4). 76. ibid s 2(5)(b).
77. *Tyrie v Fletcher* (1777) 2 Cowp 666.

Chapter conclusion

As discharge causes liability under a contract to cease, it is important that the parties understand when a contract can become discharged. Where the parties fully perform their contractual obligations, the discharge of the contract is relatively straightforward to discern. Similarly, where the parties agree to end a contract, the discharge of the contract is a relatively straightforward affair, provided that the parties have provided consideration for the discharge.

Discharge due to frustration or breach is significantly more complex and the effects are wildly different. A frustrated contract is automatically discharged and cannot be continued or performed simply because the parties so desire. Conversely, breach of contract does not automatically discharge the contract—but, in some instances (that is, in cases of repudiatory breach), it normally provides the non-breaching party with the right to terminate the contract and thereby discharge it. Should the non-breaching party wish to continue to deal with a party in repudiatory breach, it can affirm the breach, in which case, the contract continues in force. Where a contract is frustrated, the law tries to apportion any monetary loss between the two parties in order to achieve a fair result. In cases of breach, the law normally achieves a satisfactory result via granting the non-breaching party a right to terminate in the case of a repudiatory breach and the ability to claim damages (in any event).

The purpose and scope of an award of contractual damages is considered in Chapter 12. Damages may not, however, always compensate the claimant for his loss; accordingly, a number of other remedies are also examined.

 Key points summary

- Where the parties precisely and completely perform their contractual obligations, the contract will be discharged by performance—but a discharge by performance may still occur where deviations in performance are 'microscopic' (the *de minimis* rule).

- A contract may be brought to an end by the mutual consent of the parties.

- Breach of contract occurs where a party to a contract, without lawful excuse, fails to perform its contractual obligations or performs them in a defective manner.

- If the breach is repudiatory, the non-breaching party is entitled to terminate the contract. Renunciation, incapacitation, and anticipatory breach are all repudiatory breaches.

- Breach of a condition allows the non-breaching party to terminate the contract and claim damages. Breach of warranty allows the recovery of damages only. Breach of an innominate term will provide a right to terminate where the breach deprives the non-breaching party of substantially the whole benefit of the contract.

- Instead of terminating the contract, the non-breaching party may affirm the breach and continue with the contract.

- Frustration provides the parties with a lawful excuse for breaching their contractual obligations where an event occurred that was outside of their control.

- Frustrating events include performance of the contract becoming physically impossible, where a common and fundamental assumption of the parties is destroyed, where performance becomes illegal, where something essential to performance becomes unavailable, and where performance becomes radically different from that for which the parties contracted.

- Frustration causes the contract to be discharged automatically. Any money payable ceases to be payable. Any money paid can be recovered, although this may be offset against any expenses incurred by the other party. Any party that gained some form or valuable benefit may have to pay a sum for such benefit.

Self-test questions

1. Define the following legal words and phrases:
   (a) *de minimis*;
   (b) breach of contract;
   (c) renunciation;
   (d) anticipatory breach;
   (e) innominate term;
   (f) repudiatory breach;
   (g) frustration.

2. A ship is chartered by BuildCorp Ltd to transport a cargo of 100 tonnes of steel girders from London to New York. The charterparty provides that the shipowner, TransShip plc, will receive £500 for each tonne that arrives in New York. The ship only transports 40 tonnes and, upon arrival, BuildCorp refuses to pay, because the complete cargo was not delivered. Advise TransShip.

3. Explain the differences between conditions, warranties, and innominate terms. What is the effect of breach of these terms?

4. Discuss how the effects of frustration under the Law Reform (Frustrated Contracts) Act 1943 provide a fairer and more satisfactory result than the effects of frustration under the common law. Provide case law examples to back up your arguments.

5. Woodhouse plc contracts Buildmore to build its new office complex for £1.2 million. Due to a worldwide timber shortage, the cost of building the office complex is increased by £20,000. On completion, Woodhouse plc refuses to pay more than the contracted £1.2 million. Advise Buildmore.

Further reading

Sir Jack Beatson, Andrew Burrows, and John Cartwright, *Anson's Law of Contract* (29th edn, OUP 2010) ch 14
A detailed and comprehensive, but very readable, account of the law relating to the frustration of contracts

Mindy Chen-Wishart, *Contract Law* (4th edn, OUP 2012) ch 12
An excellent and highly accessible account of the law relating to breach of contract and termination

Jill Poole, *Textbook on Contract Law* (11th edn, OUP 2012) 281–3
A simple and easy-to-understand account of the law relating to discharge by performance and discharge by agreement

A Stewart and JW Carter, 'Frustrated Contracts and Statutory Adjustment: The Case for a Reappraisal' [1992] CLJ 66
Provides an excellent analysis of the effects of frustration at common law and under statute, before discussing how other countries have legislated in this area; contends that none of these statutes have proved successful

GH Treitel, 'Affirmation After Repudiatory Breach' (1998) 114 LQR 22

Examines the role of affirmation in breach of contract cases, focusing specifically on the ability to revoke affirmation and discharge the contract

GH Treitel, *Frustration and Force Majeure* (2nd edn, Sweet & Maxwell 2004)
The leading text on the law of frustration; provides an extremely comprehensive account of the law and also a comparative analysis on the law of frustration in the US

 Remember to visit the **Online Resource Centre** at <**http://www. oxfordtextbooks.co.uk/orc/roach3e**> to access the following resources on Chapter 11, 'Discharge of the contract': more **practice questions** and answers; a **glossary** of key terms; **multiple-choice questions**; and **revision summaries**. Updates to the law can be found on Twitter by following **@UKBusinessLaw**.

12 Remedies for breach of contract

- Damages
- Action for the price or other agreed sum
- Restitutionary remedies

- Specific performance
- Injunctions
- Limitation periods

INTRODUCTION

Once the claimant has established the existence of a breach of contract, the final matter to be determined is the availability of a remedy. It may be the case that the claimant will have a self-help remedy that will avoid the need to initiate legal proceedings. In the absence of such a remedy, and provided that the claimant is not subject to an effective exclusion clause, the claimant may seek one or more of the remedies discussed in this chapter, providing that his claim was brought sufficiently promptly.

Damages

As damages are awarded to compensate the claimant for his actual loss,[1] it follows that:

1. The claimant cannot recover more than he actually lost. Therefore, if a breach of contract causes the claimant no loss, he will only receive **nominal damages**.

2. Contractual damages do not aim to punish the defendant for his behaviour[2] and will not be increased because the defendant behaved in a reprehensible manner (such damages are known as 'exemplary', or 'punitive', damages).

3. A claimant cannot normally recover damages for loss sustained to a third party,[3] although exceptions to this rule do exist.

4. Although damages are normally assessed at the date when the cause of action arose,[4] the courts have recently demonstrated flexibility and a willingness to assess damages at a later date if to do so would provide a more accurate compensatory award.[5]

➡ **nominal damages:** damages awarded when no loss has been sustained, which consequently tend to amount to around £2

🔗 Exemplary damages are recoverable in tort, as is discussed at p 490

---

1. *Tai Hing Cotton Mill Ltd v Kamsing Knitting Factory* [1979] AC 91 (PC).
2. *Addis v Gramophone Co Ltd* [1909] AC 488 (HL).
3. *Woodar Investment Ltd v Wimpey Construction Ltd* [1980] 1 WLR 277 (HL).
4. *Dodd Properties (Kent) v Canterbury City Council* [1980] AC 367 (CA).
5. *Golden Strait Corporation v Nippon Yusen Kubishika Kaisha (The Golden Victory)* [2007] UKHL 12, [2007] 2 AC 353.

Expectation loss

The general purpose of an award of damages is to put the claimant in the position in which he would have been had the breach not occurred[6] (that is, if the contract had been performed properly). Accordingly, the claimant is being compensated for his 'expectation loss', because the damages will compensate him for the benefits that he would have expected to gain had the breached not occurred. In many cases, this will involve a simple loss of profit, as the following example demonstrates.

 Loss of expected profit

Andrew runs a business selling luxury cars. Cathryn informs him that she is looking for a second-hand Rolls Royce Phantom in good condition, and that she is willing to pay £50,000 for such a car (which is in line with the market value). Unfortunately, Andrew does not have such a car in stock. Several days later, he discovers that Lawrence has a Phantom that matches Cathryn's specifications. Andrew enters into a contract with Lawrence to purchase the car for £30,000 and informs Cathryn that he has located a car for her. Cathryn is overjoyed. Lawrence then, in breach of contract, changes his mind and refuses to sell the car to Andrew. Andrew sues.

Had Lawrence performed his obligations, Andrew would have purchased the car for £30,000 and sold it for £50,000, thereby making an expected profit of £20,000. Accordingly, Lawrence will be ordered to pay Andrew £20,000 in damages.

This example involves an application of the 'difference in value' approach to quantifying expectation loss, under which damages are assessed based on the difference between the expected value and the actual value. Such an approach is preferable in cases involving sale of goods, but, in many cases, the claimant will enter into a contract, the purpose of which is not to make a profit (for example, employing a builder to install a swimming pool). In such cases, the difference in value measure is still often used, but an alternative approach exists, whereby the court may instead be prepared to quantify damages based on the 'cost of cure'.

Cost of cure

The parties to a contract may have subjective, non-financial motives for contracting (this is known as the 'consumer surplus'). For example, booking a holiday with a travel agent is a contract that, from the consumer's point of view, is entered into for non-financial reasons. Where a breach denies the innocent party these non-financial benefits, the court may be prepared to award damages based on the cost of securing substitute or remedial performance. This is known as the 'cost of cure', because damages are quantified based on how much it would cost to cure the defendant's breach, as the following case demonstrates.

---

6. *Robinson v Harman* (1848) 1 Ex 855 (Ex); *Addis v Gramophone Co Ltd* [1909] AC 488 (HL).

Radford v De Froberville [1977] 1 WLR 1262 (Ch)

FACTS: The claimant owned a piece of land that contained a plot suitable for the building of a house. After obtaining planning permission to build a house on this plot, the claimant sold the plot of land to the defendant, on the condition that, once she had built the house, she would also build a boundary wall to divide her land from the claimant's land. The defendant failed to build the wall. The court had to decide whether to quantify damages based on the difference in value (which would have resulted in nominal damages only, because the failure to build the wall resulted in no difference in value), or on the cost of cure (it would cost £3,000 to have the wall built).

HELD: The High Court awarded damages based on cost of cure. Oliver J stated:

> If [the claimant] contracts for the supply of that which he thinks serves his interests—
> be they commercial, aesthetic or merely eccentric—then if that which is contracted
> for is not supplied by the other contracting party, I do not see why...he should not be
> compensated by being provided with the cost of supplying it through someone else or
> in a different way.[7]

The courts have, however, been cautious in permitting the cost of cure, especially where the cost of curing the defendant's breach is completely out of proportion to the benefit that would be obtained. Accordingly, the court will only permit recovery of the cost of cure where it is reasonable to do so.

 Ruxley Electronics and Construction Ltd v Forsyth [1996] AC 344 (HL)

FACTS: The claimant entered into a contract with the defendant builder to build a swimming pool in his garden. The pool was to be 7 feet 6 inches deep at the diving point—a depth that would allow the claimant to dive safely into the pool. The pool was only 6 feet deep at the diving point, but evidence indicated that the pool was still perfectly safe to dive into. As it constituted a breach of contract, however, the claimant sued but, as the lack of depth caused no difference in value to the pool, the claimant sought cost of cure. To remedy the breach, the entire pool would have to be ripped out and a new pool installed at a cost of £21,560.

HELD: The House of Lords refused to award cost of cure and instead awarded £2,500 for loss of amenity. It would be wholly unreasonable to award cost of cure, because it would be completely out of proportion to the benefit obtained. Further, the courts should take into account whether, if the claimant were awarded cost of cure, the damages would actually be used to remedy the defect. In a case such as this, it was doubtful that the claimant would actually use the money to cure the defect.

See Janet O'Sullivan, 'Contract Damages for Failed Fun: Taking the Plunge' (1995) 54 CLJ 496

The current position regarding recovery of cost of cure is that, in cases involving defective construction or contracts to secure a non-financial benefit, the normal measure of damages is the cost of cure. Where the cost of cure is unreasonable, however, the difference in value measure shall instead be applied. If there is no difference in value, the claimant will receive nominal damages.

---

7. [1977] 1 WLR 1262 (Ch) 1270.

Reliance loss

In certain cases, expectation loss may be extremely difficult to assess because the extent of the expected benefit is uncertain or speculative. However, the courts will not refuse to award damages based on expectation loss simply because such damages are difficult to quantify.

 Chaplin v Hicks [1911] 2 KB 786 (CA)

FACTS: The defendant placed an advertisement in the *Daily Express*, stating that he was looking to employ twelve actresses. Aspiring actresses sent their photographs into the newspaper and three hundred were selected to be published. Readers of the newspaper then selected their favourite fifty and, from those, the defendant would choose the twelve to be employed based on an interview. The claimant was one of the fifty selected, but the defendant, in breach of contract, made an appointment for the interview at a time that was wholly unreasonable. As the claimant could not attend the interview, she lost her chance to gain employment as an actress, for which she claimed damages.

HELD: Although the damages were difficult to quantify, because they were based on the loss of a chance, this did not prevent the Court of Appeal from awarding the claimant £100 in damages. Provided that the chance is real and substantial (and not merely speculative), difficulty in quantifying the loss will not prevent a claim. As the claimant's chance of securing employment was real and substantial (around one in four), she was awarded damages.

In certain cases, however, the expectation loss may be too speculative to quantify, and so the claimant is likely to choose instead to seek to recover his reliance loss. This is based not on the expected benefit of the contract, but on monies already paid out in reliance of performance. As reliance loss is based on expenditure already paid and wasted as a result of the breach, it does not place the claimant in the position in which he would have been had the breach not occurred; rather, it places him in the position in which he would have been had the contract never been entered into, as the following case demonstrates.

 Anglia Television Ltd v Reed [1972] 1 QB 60 (CA)

FACTS: The defendant actor contracted with the claimant to star in a television film. Relying on this, the claimant spent money on hiring directors, support artists, stage managers, etc. Shortly after, in breach of contract, the defendant withdrew from the contract and, as it was too late to obtain a replacement actor, the film was never made. As there was no way of knowing how successful the film would have been, the claimant elected not to claim for expectation loss and instead sought to recover the wasted expenditure.

HELD: The claimant was entitled to recover the £2,750 that it had spent in pre-contractual expenditure, which was wasted as a result of the defendant's breach.

★ See Al Ogus, 'Damages for Pre-contract Expenditure' (1972) 35 MLR 423

Expectation loss and/or reliance loss?

The law does not fetter a claimant's ability to base his claim on whatever form of loss he chooses.[8] The court does, however, have the power to deny the claimant's claim for expectation loss and to award reliance loss instead if it considers it more appropriate, as the following Australian case demonstrates.

 McRae v Commonwealth Disposals Commission (1951) 84 CLR 377 (High Court of Australia)

FACTS: The defendant invited tenders for the salvage rights to a shipwrecked oil tanker. The claimant's tender was accepted and he incurred substantial expenditure in preparing the salvage expedition. When the claimant arrived at the location provided by the defendant, no tanker was found. It transpired that the tanker had never existed. The claimant sought to recover his expectation loss (that is, the amount of profit gained through selling the tanker and any oil within it).

HELD: The Court refused recovery of expectation loss. The defendant had no idea how big the tanker was, nor how much oil it contained. Instead, the Court allowed the claimant to recover the wasted expenditure (that is, his reliance loss).

In certain cases, the court will not allow a claimant to recover his reliance loss—namely, where the reliance loss exceeds the benefit that would be obtained had the contract been performed.

 C & P Haulage v Middleton [1983] 1 WLR 1461 (CA)

FACTS: The defendant garage owner contracted with the claimant to let it use his garage for a six-month period. The claimant purchased various pieces of machinery and installed them within the garage. A term of the contract provided that any machinery installed would become the property of the defendant once the claimant stopped using the garage. In breach of contract, the defendant terminated the contract ten weeks early. The claimant used its own garage for the remaining ten weeks. The claimant then initiated a claim to recover the expenditure on the machinery (that is, his reliance loss).

HELD: The Court of Appeal rejected the claim for reliance loss and the claimant recovered only nominal damages. Had the defendant not breached the contract, the machinery would still have become the defendant's property once the six months expired. To permit recovery of the reliance loss would therefore place the claimant in a better position than it would have been in had the contract been properly performed.

Double recovery

Can a claimant obtain damages for expectation loss *and* reliance loss? In *Anglia Television Ltd v Reed*,[9] Lord Denning MR stated: 'It seems to me that a [claimant] in

---

8. *CCC Films (London) v Impact Quadrant Films* [1985] QB 16 (QB).
9. [1972] 1 QB 60 (CA).

such a case has an election: he can either claim for his loss of profits; or for his wasted expenditure. But he must elect between them. He cannot claim both.'[10] Lord Denning was seeking to ensure that there was no possibility of double recovery in respect of the same loss. Double recovery is the situation in which the claimant is overcompensated by receiving the reliance loss twice. The following example demonstrates this, and also demonstrates why Lord Denning's prohibition is no longer absolute.

> **Eg** **Double recovery**
>
> John runs a business that specializes in locating rare books. Elen contracts with John to locate a book, stating that if he finds it, she will purchase it from him for £1 million. John locates the book and purchases it for £500,000. Elen decides that she no longer wishes to purchase the book. John's options are as follows.
>
> 1. **Claim the expectation loss** Had Elen performed the contract, John would have made £500,000 profit. As John is currently £500,000 out of pocket, his expectation loss is therefore £1 million.
> 2. **Claim the reliance loss** John may decide to simply claim the £500,000 spent in acquiring the book. Clearly, this will not yield as much compensation as claiming for the expectation loss and will result in John only breaking even.
> 3. **Claim both** Claiming both would amount to £1.5 million, and this is clearly more than John would have received had the contract been performed and would constitute double recovery. Accordingly, the courts will not allow John to recover this sum. This is because John's expectation loss of £1 million constitutes the **gross** amount, which includes the expected profit (£500,000) and the sum that John has already paid (£500,000). Accordingly, the reliance loss is already part of that sum. Therefore, to allow John to claim the gross expectation loss and his reliance loss would be to pay him his reliance loss twice. Deducting the cost of the book from the gross amount would provide the **net** expectation loss. Claiming the net expectation loss (£500,000) and the reliance loss (£500,000) is not objectionable, because it does not result in double recovery.

➡ **gross:** before deductions (for example, tax) are made

➡ **net:** following deductions

Accordingly, the courts have now recognized that recovery of both expectation loss and reliance loss is permissible, provided that expectation loss is calculated on a net basis.[11]

Non-pecuniary loss

To what extent are damages for non-pecuniary losses recoverable? The word 'pecuniary' simply means 'financial', and, as such, the availability of damages for physical inconvenience, disappointment, and loss of reputation will be discussed. It should be noted that the Court of Appeal has stated that, from 1 April 2013, general damages will be increased by 10 per cent in relation to the following non-pecuniary losses:

(i) pain and suffering;

(ii) loss of amenity;

(iii) physical inconvenience and discomfort;

(iv) social discredit; or

(v) mental distress.[12]

---

10. ibid 63–4.

11. *Western Web Offset Printers Ltd v Independent Media Ltd* [1996] CLC 77 (CA).

12. *Simmons v Castle* [2012] EWCA Civ 1288, [2013] 1 WLR 1239 [48] (Lord Judge LCJ).

Physical inconvenience

It is well established that damages are recoverable for a breach of contract that causes physical discomfort, injury, or inconvenience. Accordingly, in *Hobbs v London & South Western Railway*,[13] when a railway company, in breach of contract, transported a married couple to the wrong station, the couple could recover damages for the physical inconvenience caused by having to walk several miles in the rain to their home.

Mental distress and disappointment

Generally, contractual damages cannot be recovered for mental distress or disappointment.

 Addis v Gramophone Co [1909] AC 488 (HL)

FACTS: The claimant's contract of employment provided him with six months' notice of dismissal. His employer (the defendant) gave him notice of dismissal, but instead of allowing the claimant to work for six months, it immediately appointed his replacement and took steps to prevent the claimant from carrying out his functions. He claimed damages for breach of contract, including an additional amount for the injured feelings that he suffered as a result of the manner of his dismissal.

HELD: Although he could claim damages for his lost salary, he could not claim damages for the injured feelings caused by the harsh manner of his dismissal.

This rule still stands, but the courts have since held that damages for mental distress or disappointment are recoverable in two situations:[14]

1. where mental distress is directly consequential upon physical injury or inconvenience (for example, mental distress caused by living in a house that was represented as being in good condition, but was actually in poor condition);[15]

2. where the purpose of the contract is to provide enjoyment or to prevent distress, as in the following case.

 Jarvis v Swans Tours Ltd [1973] QB 233 (CA)

FACTS: The claimant booked a two-week holiday with the defendant tour operator. The defendant's brochure described the holiday as a 'house party', with excellent entertainment, including skiing, and afternoon tea and cakes. It also promised a friendly welcome from the owners of the hotel. For the first week of the holiday, there were thirteen people in the hotel and, in the second week, the claimant was alone. The hotel owners did not speak English, so he had no one to talk to during the second week. The cakes promised were wholly disappointing, and the skiing facilities were only available for two days. At first instance, the claimant obtained £31.72 in damages based on the difference in value measure. He appealed, claiming an extra amount for the distress and disappointment caused.

HELD: His appeal was allowed and he was awarded him a further £60 to compensate him for his disappointment.

---

13. (1875) LR 10 QB 11 (QB).   14. *Watts v Morrow* [1991] 1 WLR 1421 (CA).
15. *Perry v Sidney Phillips & Son* [1982] 1 WLR 1297 (CA).

Where the purpose of the contract is to provide enjoyment, not compensating the claimant for disappointment caused by breach will result in under-compensation. In such cases, damages for disappointment are justifiably awarded. It follows that such damages are normally not available in employment or commercial contracts, because providing enjoyment or peace of mind is not a normal purpose of such contracts.

Damages may also be recovered where the purpose of the contract is to prevent distress. For example, damages for mental distress were recoverable where a solicitor failed to take prompt measures against a stalker who was distressing his client.[16]

Loss of reputation

Generally, damages are not recoverable for a breach of contract that damages the claimant's reputation.[17] But where the breach of contract results in a loss of reputation, which in turn causes financial loss, then so-called 'stigma damages' may be recovered.

Malik (or Mahmud) v Bank of Credit and Commerce International SA [1998] AC 20 (HL)

FACTS: The claimants were senior employees of BCCI, a bank that collapsed amidst allegations of fraud and corruption. They claimed that, due to the stigma that was attached to former employees of BCCI, they were unable to obtain employment (the claimants were in no way involved with the events that led to BCCI's collapse). They claimed damages against BCCI for the damage that had been caused to their reputation.

HELD: BCCI had breached the implied obligation not, without reasonable excuse, to conduct its business in a way likely to destroy or damage the relationship of confidence between an employer and employee. If the claimants could prove that this breach had handicapped them in the labour market and thereby caused financial loss as a result of the injury done to the claimant's reputation, they would be entitled to damages for this.

★ See Michael Jefferson, '"Stigma" Damages Against Corrupt Companies' (1998) 19 Co Law 21

The House of Lords has since extended the principle in *Malik* to cover a loss of reputation caused by an unfair suspension,[18] but has refused to extend it to cases of unfair dismissal.[19]

Limitations on the recovery of damages

In *British Columbia Saw-Mill Co Ltd v Nettleship*,[20] Willes J clearly indicated why a claimant should not be free to claim damages for any loss caused by the defendant's breach of contract. He referred to an early seventeenth-century case in which the claimant was being transported to marry an heiress. On the journey, his horse lost a shoe, so he employed a blacksmith to forge a new one. The blacksmith's work was of such poor quality that the shoe rendered the horse lame, with the result that the claimant failed to arrive on time and the heiress married another. The blacksmith was held liable for the claimant's loss caused by the marriage not occurring.

---

16. *Heywood v Wellers* [1976] QB 446 (CA).   17. *Addis v Gramophone Co* [1909] AC 488 (HL).
18. *Eastwood v Magnox Electric plc* [2004] UKHL 35, [2005] 1 AC 503.
19. *Johnson v Unisys Ltd* [2001] UKHL 13, [2003] 1 AC 518.   20. (1868) LR 3 CP 499, 508.

Such a case indicates that there need to be limitations on the claimant's ability to claim damages and, here, we will discuss four such limitations, beginning with causation.

Causation

The recovery of damages is dependent upon the claimant establishing that the breach was the effective or dominant cause of the loss sustained.[21] In the majority of cases, determining causation will pose little difficulty. Problems begin to arise, however, when the occurrence of an intervening act threatens to break the causal link. This can occur in a number of ways:

- The defendant breaches the contract, but the claimant's loss is caused entirely by an intervening act or natural event—the latter being described as an 'act of God'. In such cases, the intervening act will constitute a *novus actus interveniens*, which serves to break the chain of causation, thereby rendering the defendant not liable for the claimant's loss. For example, a ship transporting cargo encounters a storm and the ensuing rough seas damage the cargo. If it were to transpire that the ship was in breach of contract because it failed to have proper medical facilities, this breach would not permit the cargo owner to claim damages for the damaged cargo, because this loss was entirely attributable to the storm.[22]

➜ *novus actus interveniens*: 'new intervening act' (discussed in more detail in a tortious capacity in 'Intervening acts or events' at p 408)

- If the claimant's loss is caused partly by the defendant's breach of contract and partly by an intervening act or natural event, then, provided that the two causes are cooperating and contributed equally to the loss, the defendant will still be liable for the loss. Thus, in a contract to transport goods by sea, if the claimant's cargo is damaged partly because of rough weather conditions, but also partly because the shipowner breached the contract and provided an unseaworthy vessel, the shipowner will be liable for the claimant's loss.[23]

- If the claimant's loss is caused partly by the defendant's breach of contract and partly by the intervening act of a third party, the defendant will only be liable for the claimant's loss if the act of the intervening third party was reasonably foreseeable. In *Stansbie v Troman*,[24] a painter breached his contract by leaving the claimant's house unlocked. Thieves gained easy access and stole a number of the claimant's items. The claimant commenced proceedings, alleging that the painter had breached his contractual duty to exercise reasonable care regarding the state of the premises if they were left during work or at its conclusion. It was reasonably foreseeable that leaving the house unlocked would be a security risk and so the painter was held liable for the claimant's loss.

- If the defendant breaches the contract, but the loss is caused by the claimant's own negligence, the claimant's negligence will constitute a *novus actus interveniens* and the defendant will not be liable. For example, if the defendant breaches the contract by providing a defective machine, but the claimant then repairs it inadequately and puts it back to use without testing the repairs, the defendant will not be liable for any loss caused by the machine exploding.[25]

---

21. *Galoo Ltd v Bright Grahame Murray* [1994] 1 WLR 1360 (CA).
22. *Monarch Steamship Co Ltd v Karlshamns Oljefabriker (A/B)* [1949] AC 196 (HL) 226 (Lord Wright).
23. *Smith, Hogg & Co Ltd v Black Sea & Baltic General Insurance Co Ltd* [1940] AC 997 (HL).
24. [1948] 2 KB 48 (CA).
25. *Beoco Ltd v Alfa Laval Co Ltd* [1994] 4 All ER 464 (CA).

Remoteness

The claimant may have established that the defendant's breach of contract caused his loss, but it does not follow that the defendant is liable for every loss that his breach causes. Certain losses will be regarded as too remote from the breach and irrecoverable, as the following case established.

 ### Hadley v Baxendale (1854) 9 Exch 341

FACTS: The claimant owned a mill. A mill shaft broke and the claimant had no spares, so the broken shaft was sent to an engineer in Greenwich to act as a template for the construction of a new shaft. The defendant was employed to transport the broken shaft to Greenwich and to bring the new shaft back to the claimant's mill. In breach of contract, the defendant failed to deliver the broken shaft to the engineer on time, resulting in the mill ceasing production for five extra days. The claimant sought damages for the loss of profits during this period.

HELD: Alderson B stated that the damages awarded:

> should be such as may fairly and reasonably be considered either arising naturally, that is, according to the usual course of things, from such breach of contract itself, or such as may reasonably be supposed to have been in the contemplation of both parties at the time they made the contract as the probable result of the breach.[26]

Applying this test to the facts, the claimant's action failed for two reasons: first, the loss did not arise naturally from the breach, because the mill owner might have had a spare mill shaft; second, the loss of profits was not within 'the contemplation of both parties at the time they made the contract', because the claimant did not tell the defendant that he had no spare shaft. Accordingly, the claimant could not claim for the loss of profits.

It can be seen that the test for remoteness established by Alderson B has two limbs. Accordingly, a loss will not be too remote if it comes within either of the following:

1. Losses that arise naturally (that is, according to the usual course of things), which are in the reasonable contemplation of both parties at the time they made the contract

2. Losses that do not arise naturally, but which are in the reasonable contemplation of both parties, based on facts known to both parties.

The application of the two limbs can be seen in the following case.

 ### Victoria Laundry (Windsor) Ltd v Newman Industries Ltd [1949] 2 KB 528 (CA)

FACTS: The claimant ran a laundry business. Hoping to expand its business, it bought a second-hand boiler from the defendant, which knew that the claimant wanted the boiler for immediate use. When dismantling the boiler to send to the claimant, the boiler was damaged, resulting in it being delivered some five months late. The claimant sought:

---

26. *Hadley v Baxendale* (1854) 9 Exch 341, 354.

1. £16 per week (which represented the profit that would have been made had the boiler arrived on time); and

2. £262 (which represented the cost of a particularly lucrative government contract it had acquired, but could not fulfil due to the boiler arriving late).

HELD: The Court of Appeal held that the claimant could claim the £16 per week under the first limb, because it was an inevitable loss. It could not, however, claim the £262, because it was not an inevitable loss, nor was it in the contemplation of both parties, because the claimant did not inform the defendant of the government contract.

COMMENT: Asquith LJ slightly reformulated the second limb of the *Hadley* test, stating that a claimant may recover 'such part of the loss actually resulting as was at the time of the contract reasonably foreseeable as liable to result from the breach'.[27] This test is almost identical to the test of remoteness in tort and is more generous than the test established in *Hadley*.

However, Asquith LJ's reformulation of the second limb was severely criticized in a later House of Lords case,[28] with Lord Reid stating that the test for remoteness in contract is not the same as that in tort and that Asquith LJ was wrong to apply such a test. The tortious test of 'reasonable foreseeability' is more generous than the contractual test of 'reasonable contemplation'. The tortious test could be satisfied by a 'slight possibility', whereas the contractual test requires 'a serious possibility'[29] or 'a real danger'[30] of loss. The test in contract must be stricter because the parties to a contract are able to protect themselves by informing the other party of the exceptional or special loss. Conversely, in tort cases, the two parties are often strangers.

In the next case to consider remoteness, it was held that, provided that the *type* of loss is not too remote, it does not matter that the *extent* of the loss was greater than could be reasonably contemplated, or that the loss occurred in a manner that could not be reasonably contemplated.

H Parsons Livestock Ltd v Uttley Ingham
[1978] QB 791 (CA)

FACTS: The claimant pig farmer required an animal feed hopper in which to store pig feed. He purchased, from the defendant, a hopper that was described as 'ventilated'. The hopper's ventilation hatch was closed during transit and, upon delivery, the defendant failed to open it. Consequently, the pig feed that was placed within it became mouldy and contaminated. Following a subsequent outbreak of E. coli, 254 of the claimant's pigs died. The claimant alleged that the defendant was liable for their deaths. The defendant argued that the extent of the loss was not foreseeable and so was too remote.

HELD: The type of loss (physical harm to the pigs caused by poor storage conditions) was reasonably contemplatable, even if the extent and manner of the loss were not. Accordingly, the loss was not too remote and the claimant was awarded damages.

COMMENT: The Court also discussed the remoteness test in contract and tort. Lord Denning MR argued that it was immaterial whether the action was brought in contract or tort; instead, the nature of the damage inflicted was the key factor. A case involving economic

27. [1949] 2 KB 528 (CA) 539.
28. *Koufos v Czarnikow Ltd (The Heron II)* [1969] 1 AC 350 (HL).
29. ibid 414–15.   30. ibid 425.

loss or loss or profits would be subject to the 'contractual' test of reasonable contemplation, whereas a case involving physical injury or property damage would be subject to the relaxed 'tortious' test of reasonable foreseeability. The other members of the majority rejected this distinction, although Lord Scarman expressed the view that the test of remoteness should not differ in contract and tort. Ultimately, this was a Court of Appeal decision, so the views of their Lordships in *The Heron II* will remain the most authoritative decision in the issue and the remoteness test in contract will continue to be stricter than the remoteness test in tort.

 See DH Hadjihambis, 'Remoteness of Damage in Contract' (1978) 41 MLR 464

The final case to discuss is the most recent, and must be regarded as the current leading case on the law of remoteness. Unfortunately, due to the divergent reasoning of the judges, it leaves the law in a rather unclear state.

Transfield Shipping Inc v Mercator Shipping Inc (The Achilleas) [2008] UKHL 48

FACTS: The claimant owned a vessel, which it chartered to the defendant, with redelivery due by 2 May. In April, market hire rates rose, and so the claimant arranged for the vessel to be chartered to another company (*X*) upon its redelivery, at a daily rate of $39,500 for a period of 191 days. This agreement also provided that *X* could terminate the agreement if the vessel was not available by 8 May. It became apparent that the defendant would not be able to return the vessel by 8 May but, by this time, the market hire rates had fallen. In order to secure *X*'s agreement to extend the cancellation date to 11 May (when the vessel would be redelivered), the claimant had to agree to a reduced rate of $31,500 per day. The claimant sought damages of $1,364,584 for the defendant's breach of contract (based on the $8,000 loss per day over the 191-day charter). The defendant contended that the claimant was only entitled to damages for the overrun period of nine days (which amounted to $158,301). The arbitrators, first instance judge, and the Court of Appeal agreed with the claimant. The defendant appealed to the House of Lords.

HELD: The appeal was allowed, and the claimant's damages were limited to $158,301. Lord Rodger and Baroness Hale came to this conclusion via an application of the traditional reasonable contemplation test discussed earlier. Lords Hope and Hoffmann, however, took an entirely different approach, with Lord Hoffmann asking whether the contractual test for remoteness of damages was:

> an external rule of law, imposed upon the parties to every contract in default of express provision to the contrary, or is it a prima facie assumption about what the parties may be taken to have intended, no doubt applicable in the great majority of cases but capable of rebuttal in cases in which the context, surrounding circumstances or general understanding in the relevant market shows that a party would not reasonably have been regarded as assuming responsibility for such losses?[31]

Lords Hope and Hoffman thought it was the latter, and that the basis of the law of remoteness was whether the defendant ought reasonably to be regarded to have assumed responsibility for the loss in question. Lords Hope and Hoffman did not think that the defendant assumed responsibility for the full loss.

COMMENT: *The Achilleas* has been strongly criticized for 'taking a sledge hammer to existing principles of remoteness'[32] with Lord Hoffmann's approach being described as 'of doubtful utility'.[33] Lord Hoffmann was keen to stress that departure from the standard

31. [2008] UKHL 48, [2009] 1 AC 61 [9].
32. Jill Poole, *Textbook on Contract Law* (10th edn, OUP 2010) 371.
33. Edwin Peel, 'Remoteness Re-visited' (2009) 125 LQR 6, 10.

foreseeability test would be unusual, so the impact of the decision might not be as profound as some expect. Lord Hoffmann's comments will not be confined to shipping cases and have already found support from the Court of Appeal.[34] However, the fact that their Lordships advocated two distinctly different approaches has certainly introduced an unwelcome measure of confusion. A definitive Supreme Court ruling would seem to be required.

★ Edwin Peel, 'Remoteness Re-visited' (2009) 125 LQR 6

The final point to note is that, irrespective of what the intellectual underpinning of the test of remoteness may be, what is relevant is the parties' knowledge at the time the contract was made, and not their knowledge at the time that breach occurred.[35]

Mitigation

A claimant who suffers loss due to a breach of contract cannot just sit back, initiate a claim, and recover compensation: the law expects the claimant to take reasonable steps to mitigate (minimize) his loss. It is often stated that the claimant is under a 'duty' to mitigate, but this is incorrect. Breach of any 'duty' will result in a cause of action, but a failure to mitigate results in no cause of action;[36] it simply results in a claimant being unable to recover those losses that he could have avoided by taking reasonable steps, as the following example demonstrates.

Eg The mitigation of loss

Tom is appointed as a company director. His service contract is to last for three years and he is to receive an annual salary of £120,000. After two years, the company terminates Tom's contract. Accordingly, Tom decides to sue the company for breach of contract and to claim damages of £120,000 (the wages that he would have gained had the contract lasted its final year). Dave hears that Tom's contract has been terminated and offers Tom an identical job at his company, except that the annual salary will be £110,000. Tom turns down Dave's offer, because he would rather claim the £120,000 and have a year off.

In such a case, the court is likely to hold that Tom taking the alternative job would be a reasonable step in mitigating his loss.[37] Had he done so, his loss of £120,000 would have been mitigated to a loss of only £10,000. Accordingly, if the court were to believe that the acceptance of the alternative job was a reasonable step, Tom would only be able to claim £10,000 in damages from his previous employer.

If mitigation is so successful that the claimant's losses are completely eradicated, then only nominal damages will be awarded.[38] It may be the case that the claimant's reasonable steps to mitigate actually increase his loss. In such a case, the claimant is entitled to claim the increased loss,[39] but any increased losses incurred due to unreasonable attempts at mitigation are not recoverable.[40]

---

34. See *Supershield Ltd v Siemens Building Technologies FE Ltd* [2010] EWCA Civ 7, [2010] 1 Lloyd's Rep 349 [40] (Toulson LJ).   35. *Jackson v Royal Bank of Scotland plc* [2005] UKHL 3, [2005] 1 WLR 377.
36. *Sotiros Shipping Inc v Sameiet Solholt (The Solholt)* [1983] 1 Lloyd's Rep 605 (CA) 608 (Donaldson MR).
37. *Brace v Calder* [1895] 2 QB 253 (CA).
38. *British Westinghouse Electric & Manufacturing Co Ltd v Underground Electric Railways Co of London Ltd (No 2)* [1912] AC 673 (HL).   39. *Banco de Portugal v Waterlow & Sons Ltd* [1932] AC 452 (HL).
40. *Compania Financiera Soleada SA v Hamoor Tanker Corp Inc (The Borag)* [1981] 1 WLR 287 (CA).

As the claimant is expected to take reasonable steps to mitigate his loss, the obvious question is what actions constitute 'reasonable steps'. This question is one of fact[41] and the burden of proof is placed upon the defendant to show that the claimant failed to mitigate.[42] As only reasonable steps are needed, the claimant will not be required to take steps immediately, nor will he be required to engage in extremely difficult, time-consuming, or expensive activities. Accepting some form of substitute performance is regarded as reasonable, provided that it is comparable to the original performance. Thus, in the example that we discussed earlier, Tom would not be expected to accept employment as a floor sweeper. Similarly, in a contract for sale of goods, the claimant would not be expected to accept goods of vastly inferior quality.

Contributory negligence

🔗 Contributory negligence in tort is discussed in more detail at p 484

A claimant may have his damages reduced because he actually contributed to the act that caused his loss—this is known as 'contributory negligence'. At common law, contributory negligence operates as a complete defence, thereby completely defeating the claimant's action, but as a general rule, it only applied in tort cases and not in contract.[43] It could, however, apply to cases in which a breach of contract also amounted to a tort.

Contributory negligence also exists in statute, and its effects are quite different from those under the common law. Section 1(1) of the Law Reform (Contributory Negligence) Act 1945 states:

> Where any person suffers damage as the result partly of his own fault and partly of the fault of any other person or persons, a claim in respect of that damage shall not be defeated by reason of the fault of the person suffering the damage, but the damages recoverable in respect thereof shall be reduced to such extent as the court thinks just and equitable having regard to the claimant's share in the responsibility for the damage.

The question arising is to what extent s 1(1) applies to liability for breach of contract. This is dependent upon the interpretation of the word 'fault', which is defined in s 4 as 'negligence, breach of statutory duty or other act or omission which gives rise to a liability in tort or would, apart from this Act, give rise to the defence of contributory negligence'. It is clear that s 4 was drafted with tortious acts in mind, and so applying it to cases involving breach of contract has proven to be a complex and controversial issue.

The extent to which breach of contract comes within s 4 was discussed in the case of *Forsikringsaktieselskapet Vesta v Butcher*,[44] in which the High Court applied s 4 to three classes of cases:

1. **Where the defendant commits a breach of a contractual term that imposes a strict obligation (that is, not dependent upon a failure to take reasonable care), but his conduct does not amount to a tort** As the breach does not give rise to liability in tort, it will not fall within the definition of 'fault' in s 4 and so the 1945 Act will not apply. Contractual terms normally

---

41. *Payzu Ltd v Saunders* [1919] 2 KB 581 (CA) 586.
42. *James Finlay & Co v NV Kwik Hoo Tong TM* [1928] 2 KB 604 (CA) 614.
43. *AB Marintrans v Comet Shipping Co Ltd (The Shinjitsu Maru No 5)* [1985] 1 WLR 1270 (QB).
44. [1986] 2 Lloyd's Rep 179 (QB).

impose strict obligations and so the 1945 Act will not apply to the majority of breaches.

2. **Where the defendant commits a breach of a contractual duty to take reasonable care (or equivalent), but no corresponding duty exists in tort** Again, because no liability arises in tort, the Act will not apply.

3. **Where the defendant's conduct has breached a contractual duty of care and is also an independent tort** In this case, the defendant is liable in tort, and so the Act will apply and the court may reduce damages in line with s 1(1).

Finally, it should be noted that, where the claimant's contribution to his loss is so great as to prevent the defendant's breach of contract being an effective or dominant cause of the claimant's loss, then the claimant will not be able to recover any damages at all on the ground of a lack of causation.[45] Moreover, if the defendant successfully brings a counterclaim to a successful claim by the claimant, the effect on the damages awarded to each party may be the same as if there were an apportionment of liability on grounds of contributory negligence.[46]

Liquidated damages and penalties

Thus far, the discussion has been limited to unliquidated damages. Given the complexity and unpredictability of the rules discussed, it is common for the parties themselves to insert a clause into the contract stating how the quantum of damages will be assessed in the event of breach. This might take one of two forms:

➡ **unliquidated damages:** unascertained damages that will be quantified by the courts

1. **The level of damages specified represents a genuine pre-estimate of the loss resulting from a breach** This is known as a 'liquidated damages clause' and such clauses will be upheld by the courts, even where the actual loss sustained is more or less than the amount estimated in the clause.

2. **The level of damages specified represents an excessive amount designed to intimidate the party into proper performance** This is known as a 'penalty clause' and such a clause will only be enforced to the extent that it is commensurate with the actual loss sustained.[47] Accordingly, if the actual loss sustained is less than the amount specified in the penalty clause, only the loss sustained can be claimed.[48] If the actual loss is greater than that specified, the court will ignore the penalty clause and award the greater amount.[49] A penalty clause in a consumer contract will be regulated by the Unfair Terms in Consumer Contracts Regulations 1999, and is very likely to be regarded as an unfair term and so will not be binding on the consumer.

🔗 The Unfair Terms in Consumer Contracts Regulations 1999 are discussed at p 230

Liquidated damages clauses are often found in contracts that have to be completed within a certain time. Thus contracts for building or civil engineering work normally provide for a specified sum to be paid for every day or week of delay. Similarly, most, if not all, voyage charterparties of ships contain a provision for a specified sum per day to be paid by the charterer to the shipowner if the ship is delayed due to the charterer's failure to load or unload within a stipulated period of time.

➡ **charterparty:** a written agreement whereby a person (known as the 'charterer') leases a ship for the purposes of transporting goods

---

45. *Marintrans AB v Comet Shipping Co Ltd* [1985] 1 WLR 1270 (QB).

46. See, e.g., *Tennant Radiant Heat Ltd v Warrington Development Corporation* [1988] 1 EGLR 41 (CA).

47. Note that this is not the same as saying that the courts will ignore the clause or that it is unenforceable, although, in most cases, the result will be the same.

48. *Jobson v Johnson* [1989] 1 WLR 1026 (CA).

49. *Cellulose Acetate Silk Co v Widnes Foundry (1925) Ltd* [1933] AC 20 (HL).

Distinguishing between liquidated damages and penalties clauses

A party may attempt to evade the restrictive rules relating to penalty clauses by labelling a clause as a 'liquidated damages clause'. The courts have indicated that such a label, whilst relevant, is not decisive.[50] The test used by the courts is based upon the party's intentions at the time that the contract was made. In the case of *Dunlop Pneumatic Tyre Co Ltd v New Garage and Motor Co Ltd*,[51] Lord Dunedin established four tests to help distinguish between a liquidated damages clause and a penalty clause:

1. If the stipulated amount is extravagant and unconscionable compared to the maximum loss that could conceivably arise following the breach, the clause will be a penalty clause.

2. If a contract requiring payment of a fixed sum of money stipulates that if that sum is not paid, a larger sum will become payable, the clause will be a penalty clause.

3. A clause is presumed to be a penalty if it provides for the payment of a single lump sum upon the occurrence of a number of different events, some of which are serious, some of which are trifling.

4. The fact that loss is difficult or impossible to pre-estimate will not automatically mean that the pre-estimate is not genuine.

In commercial cases (especially in cases involving complex commercial contracts), it appears that the courts will not lightly rule that a clause is a penalty clause. In *Philips Hong Kong Ltd v A-G of Hong Kong*,[52] Lord Woolf stated that 'what the parties have agreed should normally be upheld. Any other approach will lead to undesirable uncertainty especially in commercial contracts'. In *Meretz Investments NV v ACP Ltd*,[53] Lewison J stated: 'To characterise a clause as a penalty, with the consequence that the court will refuse to enforce it, is a blatant interference with freedom of contract, and should normally be reserved for cases of oppression.'[54]

One final point to note is that the above rules against penalty clauses apply only to sums payable upon breach of contract. A penalty payable upon any other event will not be called into question by the courts,[55] as the following case demonstrates.

 Berg v Blackburn Rovers Football Club & Athletic plc [2013] EWHC 1070 (Ch)

FACTS: Mr Berg was appointed as manager of Blackburn Rovers Football Club, on a contract lasting approximately three years. Clause 15.3 of the contract provided that Blackburn Rovers could, at any time, terminate the contract with immediate effect, providing that it paid Berg the salary for the unexpired period. Blackburn Rovers terminated the contract six months after it began, but did not pay Berg his salary for the unexpired period (which amounted to £2.25 million). Blackburn Rovers argued, *inter alia*, that Clause 15.3 was a penalty clause and so was unenforceable.

---

50. In *Kemble v Farren* (1829) 6 Bing 141, a clause labelled a 'liquidated damages clause' was held to be a penalty. In *Elphinstone v Monkland Iron & Coal Co Ltd* (1886) 11 App Cas 332 (HL), the opposite was true.
51. [1915] AC 79 (HL).   52. (1993) 61 BLR 41 (PC).
53. [2006] EWHC 74 (Ch), [2007] Ch 197.   54. ibid [349].
55. *Export Credit Guarantee Department v Universal Oil Products Co* [1983] 1 WLR 399 (HL).

HELD: Blackburn Rovers was ordered to pay Berg the £2.25 million it owed him. The High Court held that Clause 15.3 was not a penalty clause because '[a] sum of money payable under a contract on the occurrence of an event other than a breach of a contractual duty owed by the paying to the receiving party is not a penalty'.[56] Clause 15.3 did not operate upon breach of contract, but upon Blackburn Rovers exercising its right to terminate the contract at any time.

COMMENT: This is arguably unsatisfactory because it allows a stronger party to impose an excessive penalty clause on a weaker party, provided that the clause does not come into effect upon breach. It also leads to the illogical situation in which the weaker party would rather breach the contract than trigger the event that activates the penalty clause.

Action for the price or other agreed sum

The rules for calculating the quantum of damages can be complex, resulting in the claimant never being able to predict with certainty how much compensation he will obtain. Accordingly, in certain circumstances, it is preferable to bring an action for the price or some other agreed sum (hereinafter referred to as an 'action for the price'). Indeed, an action for the price is the most common action following a breach of contract.[57] The operation of, and advantages of such an action over an action in damages, can be seen in the following example.

 Eg   The action for price or other agreed sum

Greg agrees to sell Charles his car in return for £5,000. The car will be delivered to Charles by 12 October. Payment is to take place by 15 October. Greg delivers the car to Charles on 11 October. By the end of October, Charles has yet to pay the £5,000.

An action for damages

Greg would argue that Charles has breached the contract and must pay damages. Greg would need to establish that breach occurred and justify to the court why the amount that he is claiming is appropriate to compensate him for his loss. He would also need to establish that the loss suffered was caused by, and was not too remote from, the breach and that he had taken reasonable steps to mitigate his loss.

An action for the price

An action for the price would be much simpler. Greg would still need to establish breach, but would simply claim the exact amount specified in the contract (£5,000). Given the simplicity of the claim, it can be dealt with summarily,[58] thereby making the process quick and relatively cheap. Further, because Greg is simply claiming the fixed sum owed to him under the contract, the rules regarding quantum, causation, remoteness, and mitigation do not apply.[59] Greg is simply applying to the court for enforcement of Charles' primary obligation. As such, it is a form

---

56. [2013] EWHC 1070 (Ch), [2013] IRLR 537 [33] (Pelling J).
57. Hugh Beale, *Remedies for Breach of Contract* (Sweet & Maxwell 1980) 144.
58. Civil Procedure Rules, Pt 24.
59. *White and Carter (Councils) Ltd v McGregor* [1962] AC 413 (HL); cf Edwin Peel, *Treitel on the Law of Contract* (13th edn, Sweet & Maxwell 2011) 1096–8, who argues that, in certain circumstances, the rules on mitigation can apply to cases involving an action for price or other agreed sum.

> of specific performance, but because it involves only the recovery of money, it is not subject to the normal limitations of specific performance actions. Should any additional losses accrue as a result of Charles not paying on time, Greg can also seek damages for these additional losses.[60]

An action for the price will arise only once the duty to pay has arisen. An obvious example would be a contract for the sale of goods, in which the price is 'payable on a day certain irrespective of delivery'.[61] Once this date has passed, an action for price can commence, but not before. Where one party indicates that he has no intention of paying the price and the other party has yet to commence performance, then two possibilities exist:

1. The innocent party may continue to perform the contract, and commence an action for the price when the debt becomes due.
2. The innocent party may accept the other party's breach as discharging the contract, but he can only then recover damages and cannot succeed in an action for the price.

Restitutionary remedies

Restitution is often classified as a third measure of damages alongside expectation loss and reliance loss. But restitution has been specifically recognized by the House of Lords as a separate area of law[62] and so will be examined separately.

Restitution refers to those situations in which the defendant has been unjustly enriched at the claimant's expense. Restitutionary remedies fall into two broad categories.

1. **Unjust enrichment by subtraction** This occurs where the defendant has been unjustly enriched at the expense of causing the claimant actual loss.
2. **Recovery of profits** This occurs where the defendant has been unjustly enriched, but the claimant, whilst having a wrong committed against him, has suffered no actual loss.[63]

Unjust enrichment by subtraction

Total failure of consideration

A party (*A*) may make advance payments in anticipation of a contract coming into existence. It may then follow that, due to the other party's breach, *A* obtains no benefit whatsoever from the contract. This is known as a 'total failure of consideration'

---

60. *Overstone Ltd v Shipway* [1962] 1 WLR 117 (CA).   61. Sale of Goods Act 1979, s 49(2).
62. *Lipkin Gorman v Karpnale Ltd* [1991] 2 AC 548 (HL).
63. Chadwick LJ in *WWF-World-Wide Fund for Nature v World Wrestling Federation* [2007] EWCA Civ 286, [2008] 1 WLR 445 [59], opined that an award for recovery of profits might not be restitutionary at all, but might simply be a form of compensatory damages.

and, where this occurs, any monies paid out in anticipation of the contract can be recovered. However, if *A* receives even a small proportion of the consideration under the agreement (that is, the failure of consideration is partial), advance monies paid will not be recoverable.[64] If, however, the partial performance is such as to entitle *A* to terminate the contract and he elects to do so, it is possible to convert a partial failure into total failure by returning the partial benefit that he has obtained. He will then be able to reclaim any advance monies.[65]

Quantum meruit

A party to a contract (*A*) may have completed work under the contract, or supplied certain goods, but then the other party may unjustifiably have prevented performance and *A* may have terminated the contract for this repudiatory breach. In such a case, *A* may be able to obtain a *quantum meruit*.

 quantum meruit: 'as much as he has deserved', but more loosely translated to mean a 'reasonable sum'

> ### ⊙ *Planché v Colburn* (1831) 8 Bing 14
>
> **FACTS:** The claimant was engaged to write a book for a series of books being compiled by the defendant. Midway through writing the book, the series was cancelled. The defendant offered to publish the book separately, but the claimant refused and instead claimed a *quantum meruit*.
>
> **HELD:** The claimant was entitled to refuse the offer of separate publication and to terminate the contract for repudiatory breach. He was awarded a *quantum meruit* of 50 guineas (£52.50).

It should be noted that the court is more likely to award a *quantum meruit* in cases where a contract was expected to arise, but did in fact not. In cases where a contract does exist, the remedy awarded will be usually be based upon the terms of the contract.[66] However, in limited cases, the court will award a *quantum meruit* even where a contract exists (e.g. where a contract exists, but is silent on the issue of payment).

A *quantum meruit* is not an award of damages, and differs from an award of damages in two ways:

1. Damages are dependent upon the existence of a contract and that contract being breached. As restitution is not a part of contract law, but is an area of law in its own right, a *quantum meruit* can be claimed even where no contract exists (for example, where a party incurs expense or undertakes work in anticipation of a formal contract coming into existence in the future, but no such contract is entered into).[67]

2. Damages are compensatory and will aim to put the claimant in the position in which he would have been had the breach not occurred. Conversely, a *quantum meruit* aims to award the claimant an amount equal to the work that he has completed. Accordingly, an award of damages will normally be higher than a *quantum meruit*, but where the claimant has made a bad bargain, or where only nominal damages can be recovered, a *quantum meruit* may be preferable.

---

64. *Whincup v Hughes* (1871) LR 6 CP 78.
65. *Baldry v Marshall* [1925] 1 KB 260 (CA).
66. *Macdonald v Costello* [2011] EWCA Civ 930, [2011] 3 WLR 1341.
67. *British Steel Corporation v Cleveland Bridge and Engineering Co Ltd* [1984] 1 All ER 504 (QB).

If the defendant commits a repudiatory breach of the contract, the claimant may elect to discharge the contract and claim damages, or he may alternatively claim a *quantum meruit*.

Recovery of profits

Where the defendant has committed a breach of contract against the claimant for which he has been unjustly enriched, but the breach has not caused the claimant loss, can the claimant recover the benefit (or a proportion of it) unjustly gained by the defendant? In the following case, the High Court answered in the affirmative.

 Wrotham Park Estate Co Ltd v Parkside Homes Ltd [1974] 1 WLR 798 (Ch)

FACTS: The defendant purchased a piece of land that was subject to a restrictive covenant, which had been imposed for the benefit of the claimant, who owned land adjacent to the defendant's land. The covenant stated that houses could not be built on the land. The defendant breached the covenant and built houses on the newly acquired land. The claimant sought an injunction to prevent the houses being built and a further mandatory injunction to demolish the houses that had already been built.

HELD: The High Court refused to grant any injunction, but the claimant was awarded damages based on the profit that the defendant had made by breaching the covenant. These damages were based on the hypothetical sum that might have been gained had the defendant bargained with the claimant for the release of the covenant (even though the claimant had no intention of engaging in such bargaining). This has come to be known as the 'hypothetical release' approach.

⭐ See CT Emery, 'Restrictive Covenants: Annexation to the Whole or to All or Any Parts of the Land' (1974) 33 CLJ 214

In the following case, however, *Wrotham Park* was distinguished and the Court of Appeal held that the claimant can only recover damages for his actual loss.

 Surrey County Council v Bredero Homes Ltd [1993] 1 WLR 1361 (CA)

FACTS: The claimant sold a piece of land to the defendant, on the basis that the defendant would only develop the land in accordance with existing planning permission, which limited the number of houses that could be built on the land to seventy-two. After the sale of the land was completed, the defendant obtained new planning permission, which enabled it to build seventy-seven houses on the land, which it then did. The claimant sought damages based on the profits that the defendant made on the sale of the extra houses.

HELD: The Court of Appeal held that the claimant could only recover nominal damages, because it had not suffered any loss as a result of the breach. The Court distinguished *Wrotham Park*, stating that it was not an application of restitutionary principles, but was a case of awarding damages in lieu of injunction, as permitted by s 50 of the Senior Courts Act 1981.

⭐ See Peter Birks, 'Profits in Breach of Contract' (1993) 109 LQR 518

The next case to arise constituted a major common law development by allowing full recovery of unjustly acquired profit and was subsequently described as marking 'a new start in this area of the law'.[68]

 Attorney General v Blake [2001] 1 AC 268 (HL)

FACTS: George Blake (the defendant) was a British spy, who had become a double agent working for the Soviet Union. In 1961, he was convicted of treason and espionage and sentenced to forty-two years' imprisonment. He escaped from prison and fled to Moscow where, in 1989, he wrote his autobiography, *No Other Choice*. The Crown had no knowledge of the book until it was published, by which time Blake had received around £60,000 from the British publisher and could expect further payments totalling around £90,000. The Attorney General initiated a claim against Blake to recover the £60,000 and to prevent him receiving any further payments, on the ground that Blake's employment contract provided that he would not divulge official information in press or book form. Accordingly, there was no doubt that Blake was in breach of contract. The problem was that, by the time the book was published, the information that he divulged was no longer confidential. Accordingly, the Crown had not suffered any loss and, following *Bredero* (discussed earlier), the Court of Appeal held that the Crown could only recover nominal damages.

HELD: The House of Lords held that the Crown could recover the profits from Blake, but Lord Nicholls stated:

> An account of profits will be appropriate only in exceptional circumstances. Normally the remedies of damages, specific performance and injunction, coupled with the characterisation of some contractual obligations as fiduciary, will provide an adequate response to a breach of contract.[69]

COMMENT: In addition to allowing the recovery of profit, the House also indicated a preference for the approach evidenced in *Wrotham Park* over the approach evidenced in *Bredero*. Lord Nicholls (with whom the majority agreed) described *Bredero* as a 'difficult decision'[70] and commented that strict adherence to it could constitute a 'sorry reflection on the law'.[71] Conversely, he described *Wrotham Park* as:

> a solitary beacon, showing that in contract as well as tort damages are not always narrowly confined to recoupment of financial loss. In a suitable case damages for breach of contract may be measured by the benefit gained by the wrongdoer from the breach.[72]

★ See David Fox, 'Restitutionary Damages to Deter Breach of Contract' (2001) 60 CLJ 33

The obvious question is how future courts are to determine what constitutes an 'exceptional' case. The Court of Appeal in *Attorney General v Blake* established fixed situations in which profits would be recoverable, but the House of Lords rejected this approach, stating that fixed rules should be avoided and that '[e]xceptions to the general principle that there is no remedy for disgorgement of profits against a contract breaker are best hammered out on the anvil of concrete cases'.[73] The Court did not have to wait long for such a case.

---

68. *Experience Hendrix LLC v PPX Enterprises Inc* [2003] EWCA Civ 323, [2003] EMLR 25 [16] (Mance LJ).
69. [2001] 1 AC 268 (HL) 285.   70. ibid 283.   71. ibid.   72. ibid 283–4.
73. ibid 291 (Lord Steyn).

Experience Hendrix LLC v PPX Enterprises Inc [2003] EWCA Civ 323

FACTS: The defendant entered into an agreement, whereby it covenanted not to license certain music in which Jimi Hendrix appeared as a support guitarist. The defendant breached the agreement, and the claimant (the Hendrix estate) sought to recover the profits made from the breach and to restrain future breaches.

HELD: The Court of Appeal granted an injunction restraining future breaches of the agreement. As for the recovery of profits, the claimant had suffered no actual loss, so the Court had to determine whether the case was exceptional enough to allow the recovery of profits. The Court concluded that this case was not exceptional in the way that *Blake* was and so the recovery of profits was not allowed. The Court still awarded damages, however, based on the 'hypothetical release' approach evidenced in *Wrotham Park* (that is, damages were assessed based on the hypothetical sum that the defendant would pay the claimant to obtain release from the agreement).

 See Martin Graham, 'Restitutionary Damages: The Anvil Struck' (2004) 120 LQR 26

It has been argued that the decision in *Experience Hendrix* has 'fully resurrected *Wrotham Park*...a case which until *Blake*, was languishing in the shadow of *Surrey County Council v Bredero Homes Ltd*.[74] Shortly after the *Experience Hendrix* case, a string of cases occurred in which damages were awarded based on the 'hypothetical release' approach established in *Wrotham Park*.[75] Accordingly, it would appear that the full recovery of profits, as seen in *Blake*, will seldom be granted and will be limited to exceptional cases. In cases not deemed exceptional, damages may still be awarded to the claimant based on the 'hypothetical release' approach. It would therefore appear that this approach provides a middle ground between *Bredero* (no recovery of profits is permitted) and *Blake* (full recovery of profits is permitted).

Specific performance

In the majority of breach of contract cases, an award of damages can adequately compensate a claimant who has suffered loss. There will, however, be cases in which damages are an inadequate remedy, as the following example demonstrates.

Eg The inadequacy of damages

Mike is an avid car collector with a particular passion for rare cars. He enters into a contract with Anna to purchase the last remaining Model T Ford in existence. After the contract is made, however, Anna decides to keep the car and informs Mike that he cannot purchase it. In this case, an award of damages will not adequately compensate Mike for his loss: he will want Anna to fulfil her contractual obligations and sell him the car. In such a case, the court might be prepared to grant Mike the remedy of specific performance.

---

74. Martin Graham, 'Restitutionary Damages: The Anvil Struck' (2004) 120 LQR 26, 30.
75. For example, *Lane v O'Brien Homes Ltd* [2004] EWHC 303 (QB); *Wynn-Jones v Bickley* [2006] EWHC 1991 (Ch); *Lunn Poly Ltd v Liverpool & Lancashire Properties Ltd* [2007] L & TR 6 (CA).

Specific performance is simply a court order requiring a person to fulfil his contractual obligations. Failure to comply with an order for specific performance constitutes contempt of court, which can result in a fine and/or imprisonment.

Instances in which specific performance is not available

Unlike the common law remedy of damages, which claimants acquire as of right upon a successful claim, the remedy of specific performance is equitable, meaning that it is only granted at the court's discretion. It is granted sparingly and, over the years, the courts have created a number of rules dictating when specific performance may not be granted.

Where damages are adequate

Specific performance will not be granted where damages provide an adequate remedy.[76] The general test used by the courts to determine the adequacy of damages is whether, if damages were awarded, the claimant would be able to purchase substitute performance. If the claimant would be readily able to purchase a substitute, then clearly damages will be an adequate remedy. Accordingly, in the vast majority of sale of goods cases, specific performance will not be granted, because the claimant can easily obtain the goods elsewhere.

Where a substitute cannot be obtained, an order of specific performance may be granted. This could include goods that are rare or unique (for example, antiques or rare works of art),[77] or the purchase of shares that would determine the controlling interest in a company.[78] The courts view every plot of land as unique, with the result that contracts involving the sale or lease of land are always specifically enforceable.[79]

Where the contract is for personal services

Both statute[80] and the courts have confirmed that equity will not compel performance of a contract of personal service[81] (for example, a contract of employment), because forcing a person to work for another would be an unjustifiable restriction on personal liberty and contrary to public policy. For example, if an employment tribunal rules that an employee has been unfairly dismissed, it can order the employee to be reinstated, but if the employer chooses not to comply, the tribunal cannot order specific performance; it can only require the employer to pay compensation.[82]

---

76. *Harnett v Yielding* (1805) 2 Sch & Lef 549.
77. *Pusey v Pusey* (1684) 1 Vern 273.
78. *Harvela Investments Ltd v Royal Trust Co of Canada* [1986] AC 207 (HL).
79. Unless the claimant elects to claim damages (*Meng Leong Developments Pte Ltd v Jip Hong Trading Co Pte Ltd* [1985] AC 511 (PC)).
80. See, e.g., the Trade Union and Labour Relations (Consolidation) Act 1992, s 236.
81. *Johnson v Shrewsbury and Birmingham Rly* (1853) 3 DM & G 358.
82. Employment Rights Act 1996, s 117(1).

Where the contract would require constant court supervision

In contracts imposing continuous obligations, the court will not order specific performance if such performance would require constant supervision by the court, as the following case demonstrates.

Co-operative Insurance Society Ltd v Argyll Stores (Holdings) Ltd [1998] AC 1 (HL)

FACTS: The defendant took out a thirty-five-year lease on a unit in a shopping centre that belonged to the claimant, intending to use the unit as a supermarket. A term of the lease was that the defendant would keep the supermarket open during normal business hours. Unfortunately, the supermarket became unprofitable and the defendant closed it down. The claimant, believing that the closure of the supermarket would adversely affect trade in the shopping centre, offered the defendant a rent concession if it kept the supermarket open until someone else could be found to take over the lease. No reply was heard from the defendant and so the claimant sought specific performance to keep the supermarket open.

HELD: The House of Lords refused to grant specific performance as granting such an order would require the court's constant supervision, which was likely to be a very expensive and time-consuming undertaking. Conversely, a simple award of damages was likely to be much simpler and cheaper overall.

COMMENT: Lord Hoffmann, speaking *obiter*, distinguished between (i) contracts that require a person to continue an activity over a period of time; and (ii) contracts for results (for example, building contracts). In the former, specific performance would not be ordered, because it would require constant supervision. As regards the latter, however, constant supervision would not be required, because the court 'only has to examine the finished work'.[83] In a number of cases, the courts have ordered specific performance where the purpose of the business was to achieve a particular result.[84]

 See Hwee Ying Yeo, 'Specific Performance: Covenant to Keep Business Running' [1998] JBL 254

Where there is a lack of mutuality

The courts have a discretion to not award specific performance where there is a lack of mutuality (that is, where it would not be available to both parties), as the following example demonstrates.

Eg The requirement of mutuality

Roger enters into a contract with Mike. Mike indicates that he does not intend to fulfil his obligations and so Roger applies to the court for specific performance. The court has a discretion to only grant specific performance in favour of Roger, if it could similarly grant specific performance in favour of Mike. Therefore, if Roger was a minor and the contract was of a type not binding on him because of a lack of contractual capacity, the court could refuse to order specific performance against Mike, because Mike could not obtain it against Roger, due to Roger's lack of contractual capacity.[85]

---

83. [1998] AC 1 (HL) 13 (Lord Hoffmann).
84. See e.g. *Jeune v Queens Cross Properties Ltd* [1974] Ch 97 (Ch); *Rainbow Estates Ltd v Tokenhold Ltd* [1998] 2 All ER 860 (Ch).   85. *Flight v Bolland* (1828) 4 Russ 298.

The courts have clearly established that mutuality must exist at the time of the hearing, not when the contract was made.[86] Accordingly, applying this to our example above, if Roger was aged 17 when he entered into the contract, but had turned 18 years old by the time of the hearing, he would be able to obtain specific performance.[87]

The nature of the equitable discretion

Even if a claim does not come within the above categories, there is no guarantee that specific performance will be ordered, as it is a discretionary remedy. The court's discretion is not exercised arbitrarily, but is 'governed as far as possible by fixed rules and principles',[88] including the following.

- Specific performance may be denied where a contract was procured by unfair (although not invalid) means.[89] This is simply an application of the principle that 'He who comes to Equity must come with clean hands'.
- Specific performance is unlikely to be granted where it would cause severe hardship for the defendant,[90] or where the cost of performance is wholly out of proportion to any benefit.[91]
- The maxim 'Delay defeats Equity' means that specific performance may be denied where the claimant took so long to bring the claim for specific performance that, in the meantime, the defendant altered his position to such an extent that enforcing the contract would be unjust.[92]
- As 'Equity will not assist a volunteer', specific performance will not be ordered where a claimant has not provided any consideration.[93]

It should be noted that s 50 of the Senior Courts Act 1981 grants the courts the power to award damages in addition to, or in substitution of, an award of specific performance or an injunction.

Injunctions

Injunctions come in two types and the injunction sought by a claimant will depend upon the type of term that has been breached.

1. Where the term imposes a positive obligation (that is, to do something) and the defendant has not fulfilled that obligation, the claimant can seek an injunction requiring the claimant to perform the act in question. This is known as a 'mandatory injunction' and is clearly very similar to an order for specific performance. A mandatory injunction can also be used to order the remedying of a breach that has already occurred (that is, to restore the situation to what it would have been but for the breach). Mandatory injunctions are rare and will only be granted if the defendant has deliberately flouted the claimant's rights,[94] or if the claimant would be gravely prejudiced if the mandatory injunction were not granted.[95]

---

86. *Price v Strange* [1978] Ch 337 (CA).   87. *Clayton v Ashdown* (1714) 9 Vin Abr 393.

88. *Lamare v Dixon* (1873) LR 6 HL 414 (HL) 423 (Lord Chelmsford).

89. *Walters v Morgan* (1861) 3 DF & J 718.

90. *Denne v Light* (1857) 8 DM & G 774; *Patel v Ali* [1984] Ch 283 (Ch).

91. *Tito v Waddell (No 2)* [1977] Ch 106 (Ch).

92. *Stuart v London and North Western Rly Co* (1852) 1 De GM & G 721.

93. *Cannon v Hartley* [1949] Ch 213 (Ch).   94. *Luganda v Service Hotels* [1969] 2 Ch 209 (CA).

95. *Shepherd Homes v Sandham* [1971] Ch 340 (Ch).

2. Where the term imposes a negative obligation (that is, to refrain from doing something) and the defendant engages in the prohibited act, the claimant can seek an injunction preventing the defendant from carrying on the prohibited act. This is known as a 'prohibitory injunction'.

Breaching the terms of an injunction constitutes contempt of court. As injunctions constitute a discretionary equitable remedy, the equitable maxims applicable to orders for specific performance will also apply to injunctions.

The relationship between prohibitory injunctions and specific performance

The courts will not issue a prohibitory injunction if this would amount to an indirect form of specific performance. This issue has arisen most commonly in employment cases, especially where contracts contain a restraint of trade clause. The rule is that injunctions will not be used to compel a defendant to work for the claimant, but they can be used to prevent a defendant working for anyone other than the claimant. The distinction is a fine, but important, one.

 Lumley v Wagner (1852) 1 De GM & G 604

FACTS: Wagner contracted to sing at Lumley's theatre for a three-month period. The contract provided that she could not sing at any other theatre without Lumley's written consent. She abandoned the contract with Lumley and entered into a contract to sing at Gye's theatre. Lumley applied for an injunction to prevent her from singing at Gye's theatre.

HELD: The court granted Lumley the injunction restraining Wagner from singing for Gye.

COMMENT: Had the contract provided that Wagner could sing only for Lumley, the court would have not granted the injunction. But the contract did not say that she had to work for Lumley, only that she could not work for anyone else. Is this distinction justifiable? The contract may not have forced Wagner to sing for Lumley, but it did provide that she could not earn a living by singing for anyone else. From a practical viewpoint, it has be argued that such an injunction could place so much economic pressure on a defendant as to compel him to work for the claimant in order to earn a living.[96]

Given this criticism, more recent cases have indicated that where an injunction would, 'as a practical matter',[97] force the defendant to continue working for the claimant, then an injunction would not be granted. The question for the court is therefore whether the injunction would place undue pressure on the defendant to work for the claimant.

 Page One Records Ltd v Britton [1968] 1 WLR 157 (Ch)

FACTS: The defendants, a pop group named The Troggs, employed the first of two claimants as their manager. The agreement was to last five years and contained a term stating that, during this period, the defendants would not appoint anyone else as manager. Shortly after, the defendants sought to replace the claimants with another manager. The claimants could not obtain specific performance, because this was a contract for personal

---

96. CD Ashley, 'Specific Performance by Injunction' (1906) 6 Colum LR 82, 90.
97. *Page One Records Ltd v Britton* [1968] 1 WLR 157 (Ch) 166 (Stamp J).

service. Accordingly, they applied to the court for an injunction preventing the defendants from employing anyone else as their manager.

HELD: Stamp J stated:

> These groups, if they are to have any great success, must have managers. Indeed, it is the [claimant's] own case that The Troggs are simple persons, of no business experience, and could not survive without the services of a manager. As a practical matter on the evidence before me, I entertain no doubt that they would be compelled, if the injunction was granted…to continue to employ the first [claimant] as their manager and agent.[98]

As the defendants would have been compelled to continue to employ the claimants, this would have amounted to an order for specific performance. Accordingly, the High Court refused the application for an injunction.

Limitation periods

A claimant who has suffered loss due to a breach of contract does not obtain an immortal right to sue on that breach. The case must be brought within a certain timeframe, or it will be barred. The rationale behind this is that, as time passes, available evidence becomes more unreliable. Accordingly, the following limitations apply.

- Actions concerning a simple contract (that is, one not made by deed) cannot be brought after six years, beginning with the date on which the cause of action arose.[99] This date is normally the date of the breach and is never the date when the damage is suffered. If the action includes a claim for damages for personal injury, then the time limit is reduced to three years,[100] although it may be extended if it is equitable to do so.[101]
- Actions concerning a contract made by deed cannot be brought after twelve years, beginning with the date on which the action arose.[102] If the claim involves damages for personal injury, the period is reduced to three years.

Exceptions

Minors and the mentally incapacitated

If the claimant is under the age of 18 when the cause of action arises, the above time limits will not begin to run until the claimant reaches the age of 18, or dies. If the claimant lacks mental capacity to conduct legal proceedings when the cause of action arises, the time limit will not begin to run until he ceases to be mentally disabled, or dies.[103] If, however, the claimant is mentally sound when the limitation period commences, the countdown will not be suspended simply because the claimant then becomes mentally disabled.

The effect of fraud, concealment, or mistake

The general rule is that the limitation period will start to run irrespective of whether or not the claimant realizes that he has a cause of action. However, s 32 of the Limitation Act 1980 provides that this general rule will not apply where:

- the action is based upon the fraud of the defendant, or the defendant's agent;

---

98. ibid. 99. Limitation Act 1980, s 5. 100. ibid s 11(4).
101. ibid s 33. 102. ibid s 8(1). 103. ibid s 28(1).

- any fact relevant to the claimant's right of action has been deliberately concealed from him by the defendant, or the defendant's agent; or
- the action is for relief from the consequences of a mistake, whether of fact or law.

In such cases, the limitation period will not start running until the claimant has discovered (that is, he knows of, and not simply suspects)[104] the fraud, deliberate concealment, or mistake, or could, with reasonable diligence, have discovered it.[105]

Extending the limitation period

Section 29(5) of the Limitation Act 1980 provides that where the debtor acknowledges the debt, or provides part-payment of a debt or other liquidated (that is, agreed) pecuniary claim, the limitation period starts again from this date. The period will start afresh with each acknowledgement or part-payment, providing that the acknowledgement or part-payment occurs while the limitation period is still running; once the limit has expired, the right of action will become statute-barred and cannot be revived.[106]

Equitable relief

The limitation periods discussed earlier do not apply to certain claims for equitable relief;[107] instead, equitable remedies are subject to the doctrine of laches. The word 'laches' basically upholds the equitable maxim 'Delay defeats Equity', and refers to a situation in which an equitable remedy is denied to a party on the ground that there has been so substantial a delay between the cause of action accruing and the claimant initiating his claim that it is unconscionable for him to be permitted to assert his rights.[108]

Chapter conclusion

A business that sustains loss due to the other party's breach of contract has access to a number of potential remedies. In order to obtain the best possible result, those who run the business would be wise to be aware of the advantages, disadvantages, and limitations of the remedies available. In many cases, an award of damages will be adequate to compensate the claimant for the loss sustained, but it is important to determine correctly what type of damages to claim as the calculation of the various forms of damages can result in significantly differing amounts. In some cases, damages will not be an adequate remedy and the claimant will want either the other party to comply with its contractual obligations, or to cease engaging in an action that amounts to a breach. In such cases, seeking an order for specific performance or an injunction is likely to provide a more appropriate remedy than an award of damages. It should be remembered, however, that whereas damages are

---

104. *Barnstaple Boat Co Ltd v Jones* [2007] EWCA Civ 727, [2008] 1 All ER 1124.
105. Limitation Act 1980, s 32(1).
106. ibid s 29(7).   107. ibid s 36(1).
108. For example, *Frawley v Neill* [2000] CP Rep 20 (CA).

available as of right, specific performance and injunctions (being equitable remedies) are granted at the court's discretion.

This chapter concludes our discussion of the law of contract. In Chapter 13, another major area of civil liability will begin to be discussed—namely, the law of torts.

 Key points summary

- The basic aim of damages is to put the claimant in the position in which he would have been had the breach not occurred, thereby compensating the claimant for his 'expectation loss'.

- Alternatively, the claimant may elect to cover his 'reliance loss' (that is, monies already spent in anticipation of the defendant's proper performance).

- Damages that are a natural consequence of the breach can be claimed, provided they are in the reasonable contemplation of both parties. Damages that are not a natural consequence of the breach cannot be claimed, unless such loss is in the reasonable contemplation of both parties at the time that the contract was made.

- Restitutionary remedies arise where the defendant has been unjustly enriched by his breach of contract.

- A claimant may be able to claim a *quantum meruit* (reasonable sum) based on work already performed if he has terminated the contract for a repudiatory breach by the defendant.

- In exceptional cases, a claimant may be able to recover profits from a defendant who has benefited from a breach of contract, even though the claimant has suffered no loss.

- Specific performance is a discretionary order of the court requiring the defendant to fulfil his contractual obligations. Failure to comply with an order for specific performance constitutes contempt of court.

- Whereas the common law remedy of damages is available as of right, the equitable remedy of injunction is available at the court's discretion. Failure to comply with an injunction constitutes contempt of court.

- Injunctions may be mandatory (requiring the defendant to do something) or prohibitory (requiring the defendant to refrain from doing something).

- Actions concerning simple contracts (that is, those not made by deed) must be brought within six years, beginning with the date on which the action arose. Actions concerning contracts made by deed must be brought within twelve years, beginning with the date on which the action arose

Self-test questions

1. Defin.e the following:
   (a) double recovery;
   (b) pecuniary;
   (c) mitigation;
   (d) restitution;
   (e) *quantum meruit*;
   (f) specific performance.

2. Explain the distinction between expectation and reliance loss, and the circumstances in which a claimant would prefer to claim one over the other.

3. What course of action is there for a company that has cancelled a contract, but finds that the other party performs the contract despite the cancellation?

4. Explain the distinction between a liquidated damages clause and a penalty clause.

5. What advantages does an action for the price have over a claim for damages?

6. Johnny Cab is a comedian who agrees to perform at The Happy Club in Cardiff. The contract provides that he will perform three shows a week for one month and that he will not perform at any other venues in Wales for the duration of the contract. Johnny receives a lucrative offer to perform at the Millennium Centre in Cardiff. The owners of The Happy Club hear of this and seek an injunction to prevent Johnny from performing there. What would be the most appropriate remedy for the owners of The Happy Club to seek? Would your answer differ if the agreement between Johnny and The Happy Club were to state that he could only work for The Happy Club for the duration of the contract?

Further reading

John Cartwright, 'Remoteness of Damage in Contract and Tort: A Reconsideration' (1966) 55 CLJ 488
Analyses the rules relating to remoteness, focusing on the differences between the rules in contract and tort

Martin Graham, 'Restitutionary Damages: The Anvil Struck' (2004) 120 LQR 26
Discusses the Experience Hendrix case; argues that it has resulted in a full resurrection of the 'hypothetical release' approach of Wrotham Park

Laurence Koffman and Elizabeth Macdonald, *The Law of Contract* (7th edn, OUP 2010) ch 21
A clear account of the remedies available for breach of contract, especially in relation to the recovery of profits made through unjust enrichment

Andrew Phang, 'The Crumbling Edifice? The Award of Contractual Damages for Mental Distress' [2003] JBL 341
Discusses in depth the general prohibition of recovery of damages for non-pecuniary loss and the exceptions to the general prohibition

Jill Poole, *Textbook on Contract Law* (11th edn, OUP 2012) ch 10
A detailed, but accessible, analysis of actions for the price, and equitable and restitutionary remedies

 Remember to visit the **Online Resource Centre** at <**http://www. oxfordtextbooks.co.uk/orc/roach3e**> to access the following resources on Chapter 12, 'Remedies for breach of contract': more **practice questions** and answers; a **glossary** of key terms; **multiple-choice questions**; and **revision summaries**. Updates to the law can be found on Twitter by following **@UKBusinessLaw**.

PART III

the law of torts

13 An introduction to the law of torts

- What is a tort?
- The aims of the law of torts
- The tortious duty

- Breach of duty
- The claimant and defendant
- Tort and human rights

INTRODUCTION

In 2012–13, 1,048,309 individuals claimed nearly £133 million in compensation for accidents and diseases.[1] There were 16,006 cases of clinical negligence, 828,489 claims in relation to motor vehicle use, and 91,115 claims made against employers. In all of these cases, compensation was payable because these persons were victims of a civil wrong known as a 'tort'.

Along with contract law, tort law forms the backbone of the UK's civil justice system and is of immense importance to the business community. Businesses that commit acts that harm others can potentially be liable for significant sums. Businesses that negligently release harmful products onto the market may be liable for injuries caused. Every year, thousands of employees are injured due to the tortious acts of their employers, resulting in substantial compensation payments. Businesses that interfere in the business activities of others may find themselves liable under what are known as the 'economic torts'. Accordingly, tort represents a significant source of legal exposure for businesses and it is fundamental that they understand the duties placed upon them.

What is a tort?

Numerous definitions exist regarding what constitutes a tort, but these definitions have 'varying degrees of lack of success'[2] and no single definition can fully capture the nature of what a tort is. Understanding what constitutes a tort is best approached by examining the nature of liability imposed and the aims of the law of torts.[3]

---

1. Statistics derived from the Compensation Recovery Unit website, <http://www.dwp.gov.uk/other-specialists/compensation-recovery-unit/>.

2. WVH Rogers, *Winfield & Jolowicz on Tort* (18th edn, Sweet & Maxwell 2010) 1.

3. As there are numerous types of tort, it is more appropriate to refer to the law of torts, as opposed to the law of tort. It has been estimated that there may be as many as forty torts in the English legal system: see Nicholas J McBride and Roderick Bagshaw, *Tort Law* (2nd edn, Pearson 2005) 21.

The word itself derives from the Latin word *tortus* ('twisted' or 'wrong')—but this does not mean that all wrongful acts are tortious.

1. The law of torts relates only to civil wrongs—but this is not to say that tortious acts cannot result in criminal proceedings, because certain acts can result in both criminal and civil liability. For example, **battery** is a crime and a tort, which could result in the perpetrator being prosecuted and punished under the criminal law, and, in separate proceedings in a different court, being sued and ordered to pay the victim compensation under civil law.

2. Even though torts can result in civil liability, it does not follow that all civil liability results from torts. Tort is merely one type of civil liability, with other notable instances of civil liability being breach of contract and unjust enrichment. In fact, it has been argued that tort constitutes 'our residual category of civil liability',[4] meaning that liability is likely to result from a tort if breach of contract and unjust enrichment have been discounted. However, forms of civil liability are not mutually exclusive and parties in a contractual relationship may also owe tortious duties to each other. A significant overlap between contract and tort is relatively common, with numerous acts constituting simultaneously a tort and a breach of contract.

3. The law of torts protects only certain interests. Certain acts caused by another will be regarded as compensatable, whilst other acts may not. It is not always easy to understand why the law of torts protects certain interests but not others.

4. The mere fact that a party has harmed another is insufficient per se to result in the payment of compensation. A tortious remedy will only exist if the party causing the harm owed the victim a legal duty not to cause that harm and was in breach of this duty.

➡ **battery:** the direct application of unlawful violence to another

The aims of the law of torts

Compensation

The principal aim of the law of torts is to compensate those who have suffered harm via an award of damages (although compensation for certain torts can be recovered where no harm occurs). Theoretically, tort law shifts the loss from those who suffer harm to those who cause it; in reality, it can be argued that the imposition of damages does not shift the loss, but rather spreads the loss. In the majority of cases, **tortfeasors** are insured against liability (for example, motor insurance); therefore it is the insurance company that usually compensates the victim,[5] using its own funds derived from premiums paid by the tortfeasor and other customers. The loss is therefore not borne by the insurance company alone, but is spread throughout the insurance company's customers.

➡ **tortfeasor:** a person who commits a tort

The ability of the tort system to provide an efficient system for the payment of compensation has been doubted for several reasons. First, the system has, historically, been extremely expensive. In his review of civil litigation costs, Jackson LJ

---

4. Grant Gilmore, *The Death of Contract* (Ohio State University Press 1974) 87.

5. According to Tamara Goriely, Richard Moorhead, and Pamela Abrams, *More Civil Justice? The Impact of the Woolf Reforms on Pre-action Behaviour* (The Law Society and Civil Justice Council 2002) 90, 94% of compensation is paid out by insurance companies.

noted that, in certain personal injury cases, the costs paid to the claimants were, on average, 158 per cent of the damages paid to the claimants.[6] Such statistics support Lord Woolf's contention that 'the present system provides higher benefits to lawyers than to their clients'.[7]

Second, the civil system is regarded as slow, with tort cases proving the slowest. The Woolf reforms appear to have had a limited effect and cases can still take considerable time to reach court, as Table 13.1 demonstrates.

TABLE 13.1 The average time taken to reach a small claims hearing or trial

Year	Time between issue of case and start of hearing/trial (weeks)	
	Small claims	Fast- and multi-track
2006	27	53
2007	27	53
2008	29	52
2009	31	53
2010	31	54
2011	30	56

Source: Ministry Justice, *Judicial and Court Statistics 2011* (Ministry of Justice 2012) Table 1.11.

Deterrence

The law of torts is preventative, because it encourages potential defendants to alter their behaviour and comply with any duties of care to which they are subject, in order to avoid the payment of damages. The deterrent effect of tort law has, however, been doubted, largely due to the prevalence of insurance. Persons realize that certain types of harm caused to others will usually be covered by their insurance policy. Therefore, where the potential tortfeasor is insured, the deterrent value of an award of damages is emasculated, because he will realize that he may not bear the loss. It is no coincidence that the vast majority of tort cases occur in relation to road traffic accidents and accidents at work—two of the few areas in which insurance is compulsory.[8]

The protection of interests

Sustaining loss is not enough per se to establish a claim in tort; the claimant will also need to establish that the defendant breached a duty owed to him. Duties are arguably imposed upon persons to protect the rights or interests of others. In this sense, the law of torts provides a means whereby our interests are protected and, if

6. Lord Justice Jackson, *Review of Civil Litigation Costs: Final Report* (TSO 2009).

7. Lord Woolf, *Access to Justice: Final Report to the Lord Chancellor on the Civil Justice System in England and Wales* (HMSO 1996) [10].

8. Road Traffic Act 1988, s 143, makes it a criminal offence to drive on a road without insurance. Employers' Liability (Compulsory Insurance) Act 1969, s 1, provides that every employer must insure his employees against 'liability for bodily injury or disease'.

breached, a remedy provided. The right to enjoy property is protected by the torts of trespass and nuisance. The right to personal safety is protected by the torts of negligence and trespass to the person.

Certain interests are deemed so important that compensation may be recovered for their breach even where no actual harm is suffered. For example, the tort of battery (which seeks to protect our physical safety) can be actionable even though no physical harm has been sustained. However, the opposite is also true, with some interests deemed so important that no tortious liability will result even though they cause harm to others. For example, a business that cuts its prices in order to harm a competitor, or even to drive a competitor out of business, will not commit a tort (unless several businesses act in concert to force a competitor out of business, which could constitute the tort of conspiracy).

🔗 Visit the **Online Resource Centre** for more on the tort of conspiracy in the chapter entitled 'The economic torts'

The tortious duty

A remedy will lie only if there exists a tortious duty not to cause a particular harm. Liability in tort is similar to liability in contract, in that both are civil cases in which the usual remedy is an award of damages, but the source of the duty differs. Under a contract, parties choose to undertake contractual obligations and so the legal duty is usually self-imposed; conversely, tortious duties are imposed upon the parties by the law, although, in some cases, it will be possible for the parties to modify the duty owed (for example, via the use of exclusion clause or notice). Figure 13.1 illustrates the two sources of tortious duties and offers several examples.

As society evolves, new forms of harm may arise that require the imposition of new duties and the creation of new torts. It has been argued for some time that the UK requires the creation of a tort of privacy and, whilst it does not yet exist as a recognized tort, tentative steps have been taken by the judiciary to improve persons' rights to privacy by extending the scope of the equitable wrong of **breach of confidence**, and the judiciary's recent willingness to grant anonymized injunctions and superinjunctions.

➡ **breach of confidence:** the unauthorized disclosure and use of confidential information

Changes in society may also render certain torts out of date and in need of abolition. For example, in the nineteenth century, all men were placed under a duty not to commit adultery with another man's wife[9]—a duty imposed to reflect the notion that a man's 'wife was…regarded by the common law as the property of her husband'[10] and that adultery with a wife therefore constituted an unlawful violation of that property (the tort was quaintly termed 'criminal conversation'). As society came to realize that wives could not be regarded as the property of their husbands, the imposition of this duty became regarded as anachronistic and so the duty was abolished.[11]

Very often, both parties will have legitimate interests that are deserving of protection by the law, with the courts having to determine which interest is protected and which is not. A classic example of competing, legitimate interests is the media's right to freedom of expression (protected by Art 10 of the European Convention

---

9. Matrimonial Causes Act 1837, s 33.

10. *Butterworth v Butterworth and Englefield* [1920] P 126, 130 (McCardie J).

11. Law Reform (Miscellaneous Provisions) Act 1970, s 4, provides that damages may not be claimed on the ground of adultery.

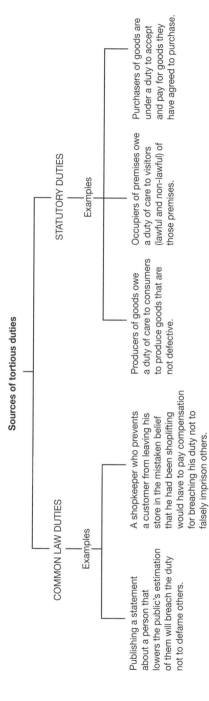

FIGURE 13.1 Examples of sources of tortious duties

on Human Rights) and the right to respect for private and family life (protected by Art 8). Reconciling these arguably irreconcilable interests has been the main reason for the reluctance of the UK to create a tort of privacy, but the following high-profile case indicates that the courts are willing to protect reasonable expectations of privacy.

CTB v News Group Newspapers Ltd and Imogen Thomas [2011] EWHC 1232 (QB)

FACTS: In April 2011, *The Sun* newspaper (which was published by the first defendant) ran a story alleging that Ms Thomas (the second defendant), a glamour model and former *Big Brother* contestant, had engaged in a sexual relationship with a married professional footballer, although the footballer was not named. Ms Thomas subsequently met with the footballer (the claimant) and informed him that *The Sun* was going to publish the details of their six-month affair. A day later, the claimant sought and obtained a temporary injunction[12] restraining the publication of the story and the revelation of his identity. Several weeks later, the court had to determine whether, if the case went to trial, the claimant would be granted a permanent injunction.

HELD: Eady J stated that the claimant was

> still entitled to a 'reasonable expectation of privacy' and no countervailing argument has been advanced to suggest that the Article 10 rights of the Defendants...should prevail. There is certainly no suggestion of any legitimate public interest in publishing such material.[13]

Accordingly, Eady J stated that, if the case went to trial, the claimant would be likely to obtain a permanent injunction.

COMMENT: Despite the fact that the footballer's identity (namely Ryan Giggs) was revealed on Facebook, Twitter, on numerous television and radio programmes, and in Parliament during an urgent Commons question on privacy orders, Eady J rejected several subsequent attempts to have the injunction lifted. The injunction was finally lifted in February 2012. Giggs' subsequent claim for damages against News Group Newspapers Ltd was struck out.[14]

★ See Edward Craven, 'CTB v News Group—Privacy Law and the Judiciary' (2011) 22 Ent LR 179

Historically, legitimate tortious duties have been denied on the ground of public policy—notably in cases against public authorities, which received blanket immunities from prosecution. With the passing of the Human Rights Act 1998, many of these blanket immunities have been removed, but even where the 1998 Act has no effect, policy reasons change constantly, resulting in new immunities being created and old immunities abolished. For example, it used to be the case that barristers owed no duty of care to their clients in negligence on public policy grounds.[15] Changes in

---

12. It is worth noting that, as the existence of the injunction is known, this is not an example of a so-called superinjunction, but an example of an anonymized injunction.

13. [2011] EWHC 1232 (QB) [37].

14. *Giggs v News Group Newspapers Ltd* [2012] EWHC 431 (QC), [2013] EMLR 5.

15. *Rondel v Worsely* [1969] 1 AC 191 (HL).

the laws relating to negligence and the administration of justice have resulted in this immunity being abolished.[16]

Breach of duty

Once the court has determined that a tortious duty exists, it must then determine whether that duty was breached, thereby causing the claimant harm. In relation to certain torts, establishing breach of duty may also require establishing a particular state of mind on the part of the defendant. The tort of trespass to land requires an intention to enter the land of another. The tort of malicious falsehood requires that a false statement be made with malice. No breach of duty will occur if the requisite mental element is absent.

Some torts impose 'strict liability', meaning that no mental element or proof of fault is required. There are numerous examples of statutes that impose strict liability in specific situations, such as the Nuclear Installations Act 1965[17] and the Animals Act 1971.[18] Similarly, the common law can impose strict liability: the tort of defamation is a strict liability tort because the defendant is not required to know that the statement is defamatory, nor is he required to have intended to refer to the claimant.[19]

The claimant and defendant

Who can sue?

Generally, any victim of a tort has a cause of action in respect of the harm caused to him. There are, however, several specific instances in which persons other than the victim may commence proceedings:

- In respect of harm suffered by a minor, the action will be brought by 'the next friend' (usually the child's parent or guardian).
- The death of a tort victim does not usually cause the claim to fail.[20] Further, if legal proceedings have not commenced upon the death of the deceased, his **personal representatives** have six years from the date of death in which to initiate a claim.[21]

➜ **personal representatives:** an administrator or executor whose function it is to settle the affairs of deceased persons

---

16. *Hall v Simons* [2002] 3 All ER 673 (HL). Interestingly, whilst solicitors and barristers may have had their immunity revoked, the Arbitration Act 1996, s 29, still provides arbitrators with a blanket immunity unless they have acted in bad faith.

17. Nuclear Installations Act 1965, s 7, imposes strict liability on licensees of nuclear installations for damage caused by nuclear matter or the escape of radiation.

18. Animals Act 1971, s 2(1), imposes strict liability for any damage on a keeper of an animal belonging to a dangerous species. 19. *Hulton & Co v Jones* [1910] AC 20 (HL).

20. Law Reform (Miscellaneous Provisions) Act 1934, s 1. There are exceptions to this (e.g. defamation cases).

21. Limitation Act 1980, s 2. Section 11(5) provides that where the victim's death is the result of personal injury, the limitation period is reduced to three years.

- The death of a family member can have serious financial implications for the deceased's dependants. Accordingly, s 1 of the Fatal Accidents Act 1976 allows the deceased's dependants to initiate a claim against the tortfeasor, provided that, had the deceased lived, he would have had a claim. Additionally, the spouse, civil partner, or parents may bring an additional claim for 'bereavement'.[22]

Special mention needs to be made regarding the role of insurance companies. In many cases, the victim's loss will be recovered by claiming on his insurance policy, leading one commentator to contend that liability insurance is the 'primary medium for the payment of compensation and tort law [is] a subsidiary part of the process'.[23] This will mean, however, that the victim's insurance provider is bearing the loss resulting from the tortfeasor's actions. Therefore, via a long-established[24] process known as **subrogation**, the victim's insurance provider is permitted to take over the legal rights of the policyholder in relation to the claim and initiate proceedings against the tortfeasor to recoup any monies paid out by it to the victim. Consequently, the claimants in many tort cases are not actually the victims of the tort, but their insurance companies seeking to recover monies paid out.

➡ **subrogation:** the ability to take on the legal rights of others

Who can be sued?

Generally, any tortfeasor is capable of being sued in tort, although there are exceptions. Further, except in the case of defamation, the tortfeasor's death does not prevent the continuance of the action. Problems arise where a claimant's loss is caused by two or more tortfeasors. In such a situation, there are a number of possible consequences, depending on the nature of the liability involved.

Joint tortfeasors

Two or more persons who commit a joint tort, or commit a tort whilst in pursuance of a common design, will be regarded as 'joint tortfeasors'. In *Brooke v Bool*,[25] Bool had leased a shop to Brooke, but retained the right to enter the premises to ensure that they were secure. Bool was informed by a lodger of the shop that he could smell gas. Whilst investigating, Bool told the lodger to light a match, which caused an explosion. The court held that the lodger and Bool were engaged in a concerted enterprise, and so were jointly liable.

In the case of joint tortfeasors, all tortfeasors are jointly and severally liable. This gives the claimant two options. First, he may elect to sue some (or all) of the tortfeasors in a joint action. Second, he may elect to claim the entire value of the loss from one tortfeasor (usually the tortfeasor with the most money, or the one who is covered by insurance), but s 1 of the Civil Liability (Contribution) Act 1978 allows that tortfeasor to obtain a contribution from his fellow tortfeasors in respect of the 'same damage'.[26] Section 2 provides that the amount of the contribution will be 'just and equitable having regard to the extent of that person's responsibility for the damage in question'.

---

22. Fatal Accidents Act 1976, s 1A(3). The amount claimable is currently fixed at £12,980.
23. Peter Cane, *Atiyah's Accidents, Compensation and the Law* (6th edn, Cambridge University Press 1999) 191.
24. In *Mason v Sainsbury* (1782) 3 Doug KB 61, 64, Lord Mansfield stated that '[e]very day the insurer is put into the shoes of the assured'.   25. [1928] 2 KB 578 (KB).
26. Section 1 can also apply to other civil wrongs (e.g. breach of contract).

Fitzgerald v Lane [1988] 2 All ER 961 (HL)

FACTS: The claimant stepped into traffic at a busy road. He was struck by a car being driven negligently by the first defendant, which knocked him into the path of a car being driven negligently by the second defendant.

HELD: The House of Lords held that the defendants were both liable and total damages were assessed at £596,553. The House held that the claimant was 50 per cent to blame by stepping into the traffic, leaving the two defendants jointly 50 per cent to blame. The House held that, as between the two defendants, both were equally to blame and ordered each of them to contribute £149,138 (25 per cent of the total loss).

Several concurrent tortfeasors

Two or more persons may inflict the same damage upon the claimant, but through independent actions. For example, two separate newspapers may publish a defamatory statement about an individual. Such tortfeasors will be known as 'several concurrent tortfeasors', and their liability is joint and several.

Separate or independent tortfeasors

Finally, two or more tortfeasors may independently cause different damage to the same claimant. In such a case, the tortfeasor's liability is limited to the damage caused by his own tortious act and liability is not joint.

Tort and human rights

The ability to enforce domestically rights found in the European Convention on Human Rights has had a significant effect upon the law of torts. Section 6 of the Human Rights Act 1998 (which, in relation to tort, is probably the most significant provision) provides that '[i]t is unlawful for a public authority to act in a way which is incompatible with a Convention right'. Therefore, if any public body infringes a person's human rights, that person may bring a claim against that public body and obtain, at the court's discretion, a remedy that is 'just and appropriate', including damages.[27] Already, the courts have seen tortious cases succeeding under s 6 of the 1998 Act that would have probably failed prior to the Act's commencement.

Section 6 of the Human Rights Act 1998 is discussed in 'Acts of public authorities' at p 100

 D v East Berkshire Community NHS Trust and Other Cases [2003] EWCA Civ 1151

FACTS: This case was actually three conjoined cases brought against three different NHS Trusts. In the first case, a paediatrican wrongfully accused the claimant of harming her child and attempting to cover it up as a medical condition. In the second case, a doctor wrongfully accused a father of sexually abusing his daughter, resulting in the father being unable to

27. Human Rights Act 1998, s 8(1).

live at home upon the daughter's release from hospital. In the third case, a paediatrician wrongfully accused two parents of abusing their child, leading to the child being placed in care for eight months. In all three cases, the claimants alleged that the actions of the NHS Trusts' employees had been negligent, which had resulted in them (and their children) suffering various forms of psychiatric injury. The court at first instance dismissed the claims, because there existed a House of Lords' case that held that the imposition of a duty of care on the NHS Trusts in these circumstances was not fair, just, and reasonable.[28] The claimants appealed.

HELD: The Court upheld the claims of the children and stated that the NHS Trusts did owe the children a duty of care, which had been breached. Article 8 of the Convention states that everyone has the 'right to respect for his private and family life' and the NHS Trusts had breached this right. Accordingly, Lord Phillips stated that the previous House of Lords case 'cannot survive the Human Rights Act [1998]'.[29] However, the Court dismissed the parents' claims and held that the NHS Trusts owed no duty to the parents. The Court stated that, in cases involving suspected child abuse, the interest of the child could result in the child having to be removed from its parents. In such cases, it is always in the parents' interests that the child should not be removed. This conflict between the interests of the child and parent led the Court to conclude that there were valid policy grounds to deny the existence of a duty to the parents.

⭐ See Paula Case, 'The Accused Strikes Back: The Negligence Action and Erroneous Allegations of Child Abuse' (2005) 21 PN 214

COMMENT: The parents unsuccessfully appealed to the House of Lords.[30] However, the European Court of Human Rights has since stated that the House of Lords, in refusing to recognize the existence of a duty towards the parents, had breached Art 13 of the Convention (right to an effective remedy for violation of Convention rights), which entitled the parents to damages.[31]

Chapter conclusion

The issues discussed in this chapter were designed simply to provide an introduction to a number of aims and concepts that occur throughout the law of torts. In subsequent chapters, much that is discussed in this chapter is expanded upon greatly. For example, when we discuss tortious remedies in Chapter 17, the aims of compensation and deterrence are very much in evidence.

In Chapter 14, the most important tort of all will be discussed—namely, the tort of negligence—in relation to which the concepts of duty of care and breach of duty, briefly discussed in this chapter, are of fundamental importance.

---

28. *X v Bedfordshire County Council* [1995] 2 AC 633 (HL).
29. [2003] EWCA Civ 1151, [2004] QB 558, [83].
30. *D v East Berkshire Community NHS Trust and Others* [2005] UKHL 23, [2005] 2 AC 373.
31. *RK and AK v United Kingdom* (2009) 48 EHRR 29; *AD v United Kingdom* (2010) 51 EHRR 8; *MAK v United Kingdom* (2010) 51 EHRR 14.

Key points summary

- A tort is a civil wrong, but not all civil wrongs are torts. Tortious acts can give rise to both civil and criminal consequences.

- The aims of tort law are (i) to compensate those who suffer harm; (ii) to deter conduct that causes harm; and (iii) to protect legitimate interests.

- In order to establish tortious liability, it is necessary to show that the defendant owed the claimant a duty of care and breached that duty.

- Once the claimant has established that the defendant owed him a duty of care, he will need to establish that the defendant breached that duty.

- Two persons who commit a joint tort, or commit a tort whilst engaged in a common design, are known as 'joint tortfeasors', and are jointly and severally liable. Where two persons are acting independently, but cause the same damage, they are known as 'concurrent tortfeasors', and are jointly and severally liable. Where different forms of damage are created by two or more tortfeasors, each is liable for the damage caused by his act.

Self-test questions

1. How do torts differ from other wrongful acts?

2. What are the aims of tort law?

3. In the following situations, identify whether the tortfeasors are joint, concurrent, or independent.
   (a) *The Daily Sun* publishes a story accusing a member of Parliament of taking cash from big businesses in return for proposing legislation favourable to big business. The same story is run by *The Daily Post*. The stories are defamatory.
   (b) The board of Microtech plc is about to launch a takeover bid for NanoCorp Ltd. The bid is being handled by Baker & Chance LLP (a firm of solicitors) and Cooper & Young (a firm of accountants). The documentation is drafted based on negligent input from both parties. Consequently, the documentation omits key information and, as a result, the bid cannot go ahead. NanoCorp ends up being taken over by another party.

4. In what circumstances can someone other than the victim make a tortious claim?

5. What does s 6 of the Human Rights Act 1998 state and why is it significant in the area of tort?

Further reading

Richard Buxton, 'The Human Rights Act and Private Law' (2000) 116 LQR 48
Examines the nature of the rights provided for under the Human Rights Act 1998 and argues that the Act does not provide rights that can be enforced against private individuals; also examines the controversial case of Osman v UK and argues that the Act does not create a tort of privacy

Kirsty Horsey and Erika Rackley, *Tort Law* (3rd edn, OUP 2013) ch 1
A clear and accessible account of what tort is and the operation of the tort system

Richard Lewis, 'Insurance and the Tort System' (2005) 25 LS 85
Examines the role of insurance law on the law of torts, and presents the views of judges and academics; argues that insurance is the 'lifeblood of the [tort] system'

Richard Lewis, Annette Morris and Ken Oliphant, 'Tort Personal Injury Claim Statistics: Is There a Compensation Culture in the UK?' (2006) 2 JPIL 87
Presents and analyses statistics relating to the number and costs of personal injury claims; refutes the claim that the UK has developed a damaging 'compensation culture'

WVH Rogers, *Winfield & Jolowicz on Tort* (18th edn, Sweet & Maxwell 2010) ch 1
A highly detailed, but readable, account on the nature and functions of the law of torts

Remember to visit the **Online Resource Centre** at **<http://www. oxfordtextbooks.co.uk/orc/roach3e**> to access the following resources for Chapter 13, 'An introduction to the law of torts': more **practice questions** and answers; a **glossary** of key terms; **multiple-choice questions**; **revision summaries**; and **diagrams** in pdf. Updates to the law can be found on Twitter by following **@UKBusinessLaw**.

14 The tort of negligence

- The duty of care
- Breach of duty
- Causation
- Remoteness

INTRODUCTION

Despite its importance, the tort of negligence is of relatively recent origin. Historically, any wrongs committed against a person or his property were regarded as examples of trespass, with negligence operating as a cause of action in specific and highly limited circumstances. The Industrial Revolution introduced widespread mechanization and a consequent increase in the number of persons injured by emerging inventions. The development of the railway network enabled persons to purchase products from manufacturers hundreds of miles away, thereby increasing the scope of damage that could be caused by defective products. The welfare state and insurance markets of today did not exist, so the only way for claimants to obtain redress for their losses was to commence legal proceedings, but there still did not exist a unified, generally recognized, tort of negligence. Then, in 1928, in a café just outside Glasgow, a woman found a snail in her bottle of ginger beer, and the resulting litigation[1] established the modern tort of negligence and radically altered the English system of tort law forever.

Since then, the tort of negligence has expanded rapidly to become the most important and frequently occurring tort in the English legal system. Negligence can be defined as 'a breach of a legal duty to take care which results in damage to the claimant'.[2] Within this simple definition exist the four requirements that must be proven by the claimant:

1. the defendant must owe the claimant a duty of care;
2. the defendant must have breached that duty;
3. the defendant's breach of duty must cause the claimant loss; and
4. the loss must not be too remote.

Each of these four requirements will now be discussed in detail.

---

1. *Donoghue v Stevenson* [1932] AC 562 (HL).
2. WVH Rogers, *Winfield & Jolowicz on Tort* (18th edn, Sweet & Maxwell 2010) 150.

The duty of care

If persons were to be liable to anyone who was affected by any act of carelessness they engaged in, this would impose an intolerable burden on our personal freedom, not to mention subjecting us to excessive and unpredictable liability. Accordingly, the law imposes a number of what Lunney and Oliphant term 'control devices',[3] which serve to limit the extent of our liability for negligence. The most important control device is the requirement that the claimant will need to establish that the defendant owed him a duty of care. A motorist will owe a duty of care to passing pedestrians, but he will not owe a duty of care to somebody working in the twenty-fifth floor of an office block that he happens to drive by. A duty of care is not owed to the world, but only to those classes of persons that the court deems to be deserving of protection.

In reality, the establishment of a duty of care is actually not needed in many cases, since once the court has determined that a duty of care exists in a particular relationship, a duty will be presumed to exist in all subsequent similar cases. Prominent duties established by the courts include:

- the duty of care that manufacturers of products owe to the ultimate users of their products;[4]
- the duty that employers have to take reasonable care of their employees' safety;[5]
- the duty of care that providers of a service (for example, carpenters, solicitors, accountants) owe to the recipient of that service to exercise reasonable skill and care in its performance.

The 'neighbour' test

The starting point for any discussion of the duty of care is the case that established the modern tort of negligence.

 Donoghue v Stevenson [1932] AC 562 (HL)

FACTS: The claimant and her friend entered a café, and the friend purchased a bottle of ginger beer. The claimant poured half of the bottle's contents into a glass and drank it. When she proceeded to pour the remaining ginger beer into the glass, the remains of a decomposed snail fell out. The claimant suffered from shock at the sight of the snail and gastroenteritis as a result of consuming the contaminated ginger beer. The claimant could not sue the café owner, because she had no contractual relationship with him (her friend bought the ginger beer). Accordingly, the claimant sued the manufacturers of the ginger beer.

HELD: A three to two majority of the House of Lords held that the defendant owed the claimant a duty of care. Manufacturers owed a duty of care to users of their products and this duty was breached. Lord Atkin stated:

> The rule that you are to love your neighbour becomes in law, you must not injure your neighbour; and the lawyer's question, Who is my neighbour? receives a restricted reply.

---

3. Mark Lunney and Ken Oliphant, *Tort Law: Text and Materials* (5th edn, OUP 2013) 121.
4. *Donoghue v Stevenson* [1932] AC 562 (HL).
5. Health and Safety at Work etc. Act 1974, s 2(1) and (2).

You must take reasonable care to avoid acts or omissions which you can reasonably foresee would be likely to injure your neighbour. Who, then, in law, is my neighbour? The answer seems to be persons who are so closely and directly affected by my act that I ought reasonably to have them in contemplation as being so affected when I am directing my mind to the acts or omissions which are called in question.[6]

The neighbour test was only the first part of a two-part test. The second part of the test required that there should be a close and direct relationship of proximity between the person causing the harm and the person who suffers injury. Again, quoting Lord Atkin:

I think that this sufficiently states the truth if proximity be not confined to mere physical proximity, but be used…to extend to such close and direct relations that the act complained of directly affects a person whom the person alleged to be bound to take care would know would be directly affected by his careless acts.[7]

Donoghue v Stevenson is a revolutionary decision for three reasons. First, it established the independence of tort from contract and created a tortious cause of action in situations in which the doctrine of privity of contract would bar a contractual action. The case also eliminated the 'privity fallacy', which stated that where a defendant was liable to the claimant for breach of contract, he could not be liable to a third party for any torts resulting from the breach.[8] Second, it established that manufacturers of goods owe a duty of care to the ultimate users of those goods. This is undoubtedly the *ratio* of the case, but because it is considerably narrower than Lord Atkin's neighbour test, it is known as the 'narrow rule' of *Donoghue v Stevenson*. Third, although attempts had been made prior to *Donoghue* to devise a general test for the determination of negligence liability, they were never fully accepted.[9] Whilst Lord Atkin's test can be criticized, there is little doubt that it provides the foundations for the modern law of negligence.

Privity of contract is discussed at p 118

The 'narrow rule' of *Donoghue v Stevenson* is discussed in 'Common law' at p 418

The neighbour test evolves

Lord Atkin's neighbour test, perhaps the most quoted judgment in *Donoghue*, was obviously far wider than was necessary for the purposes of determining the case and, as such, was only *obiter*. Given this, it may be the case that the greater reliance was placed upon the neighbour test than was intended by Lord Atkin and that 'it is probable that Lord Atkin never intended it to be an exact or comprehensive statement of law'.[10] Further, the test suffered from a number of problems, as follows.

- Lord Atkin's test refers to 'acts or omissions', yet it is generally recognized that the law of torts does not normally impose liability for negligent omissions, although, as will be discussed, there are exceptions to this rule.

- The test is somewhat vague. It does not indicate to what types of damage the test applied. For this reason, subsequent courts were extremely reluctant to apply it to situations in which a duty of care had been previously denied.

The law relating to omission is discussed at p 371

Given that it could be argued that Lord Atkin's test 'had been called upon to bear a weight…manifestly greater than it could support',[11] it therefore came as little surprise

6. [1932] AC 562 (HL) 580.   7. ibid 581.   8. *Winterbottom v Wright* (1842) 10 M & W 109.
9. The most notable example being Brett MR's formulation in *Heaven v Pender* (1883) 11 QBD 503 (CA) 509.   10. John Murphy and Christian Witting, *Street on Torts* (13th edn, OUP 2012) 27.
11. RVF Heuston, '*Donoghue v Stevenson* in Retrospect' (1957) 20 MLR 1, 23.

when subsequent courts attempted to reformulate the test. The most ambitious and optimistic reformulation came in the case of *Anns v Merton LBC*,[12] in which Lord Wilberforce established a new two-stage test to determine whether or not a duty of care existed:

> First one has to ask whether, as between the alleged wrongdoer and the person who has suffered damage there is a sufficient relationship of proximity or neighbourhood such that, in the reasonable contemplation of the former, carelessness on his part may be likely to cause damage to the latter—in which case a prima facie duty of care arises. Secondly, if the first question is answered affirmatively, it is necessary to consider whether there are any considerations which ought to negative, or to reduce or limit the scope of the duty or the class of person to whom it is owed or the damages to which a breach of it may give rise.[13]

Lord Wilberforce's test had three notable effects:

1. Lord Atkin's test, which previously applied in a number of specific areas, was expanded to have universal application. The result was that negligence liability expanded in unpredictable and uncontrollable ways.

2. The test abolished proximity as a separate requirement and made it part of the neighbour test. This arguably downplayed the importance of proximity and led to the court ignoring key policy considerations that would not have been ignored had proximity been retained as a separate requirement.[14]

3. Prior to *Anns*, policy reasons were used to justify an expansion of liability. Following *Anns*, liability could be expanded unless there was a policy reason for not doing so, but the courts were extremely reluctant to let policy restrict the scope of liability. As a result, Lord Wilberforce's test was much easier to satisfy than that of Lord Atkin.

The effect of *Anns* was to increase greatly the number of successful negligence actions and dramatically expand the scope of negligence liability. The neighbour test, which originally only applied to physical injury, was expanded to cover economic loss[15] and psychiatric injury.[16] The courts greatly expanded the categories of established duties and even created duties that previous courts had denied.

The modern duty of care

Come the mid-1980s, however, concerns were starting to be expressed regarding the breadth of the test in *Anns*, and the courts started to retreat from Lord Wilberforce's universal test and instead started advocating a more incremental approach. In *Caparo Industries plc v Dickman*,[17] the House of Lords overtly stated that Lord Wilberforce's test in *Anns* was no longer to be used and established a new approach, as stated by Lord Bridge:

> [I]n addition to the foreseeability of damage, necessary ingredients in any situation giving rise to a duty of care are that there should exist between the party owing the duty and the party to whom it is owed a relationship characterised by the law as one of 'proximity' or 'neighbourhood' and that the situation should be

---

12. [1978] AC 728 (HL).   13. ibid 752.

14. Richard Kidner, 'Resiling from the *Anns* Principle: The Variable Nature of Proximity in Negligence' (1987) 7 LS 319, 323, 324.   15. *Hedley Byrne & Co Ltd v Heller & Partners Ltd* [1964] AC 465 (HL).

16. *McLoughlin v O'Brian* [1983] 1 AC 410 (HL).   17. [1990] 2 AC 605 (HL).

one in which the court considers it fair, just and reasonable that the law should impose a duty of a given scope upon the one party for the benefit of the other. But it is implicit in the passages referred to that the concepts of proximity and fairness embodied in these additional ingredients are not susceptible of any such precise definition as would be necessary to give them utility as practical tests, but amount in effect to little more than convenient labels to attach to the features of different specific situations which, on a detailed examination of all the circumstances, the law recognises pragmatically as giving rise to a duty of care of a given scope.[18]

Initially, it would appear that the House in *Caparo* established a three-stage test, involving:

1. foreseeability of damage;
2. proximity; and
3. that the imposition of a duty must be fair, just, and reasonable.

A closer examination, however, reveals this not to be the case. First, Lord Bridge labelled the above elements as 'ingredients', not tests. Second, unlike in *Anns*, in which foreseeability was the prime requirement, the three ingredients in *Caparo* have equal status. Accordingly, proximity and policy are resurrected from the subsidiary role that they played under *Anns*. Third, the House re-emphasized the importance of an incremental approach, whereby cases are decided on a case-by-case basis, having regard to established duties. The law of negligence should evolve step by step, 'rather than allowing huge leaps into unknown territory',[19] as was the case under *Anns*.

Despite the above, it is almost universally, if incorrectly, believed by both judges and commentators that *Caparo* has established a three-stage test, and it is probably too late to reverse this belief. The three ingredients or tests will now be discussed.

Reasonable foreseeability

Lord Bridge stated that the damage suffered by the claimant must be foreseeable. In practice, this imposes two requirements, with the first being that a duty will only exist if it can be shown that the claimant was within a class of persons who could foreseeably be harmed by the defendant's negligence. The following case illustrates this requirement well.

 Haley v London Electricity Board [1965] AC 778 (HL)

FACTS: The defendant was carrying out electrical maintenance and had dug a 60-foot trench along a pavement. To warn passers-by, it had put up a sign and created a makeshift barrier using hammers, pickaxes, and shovels. The claimant, who was blind, could not see the makeshift barrier. He tripped over one of the tools and fell into the trench, suffering serious injuries that resulted in him becoming deaf. The defendant denied liability arguing

---

18. ibid 618.   19. Jenny Steele, *Tort Law: Text, Cases and Materials* (2nd edn, OUP 2010) 163.

that, given the low percentage of people who are blind, it was not foreseeable that a blind person would be walking along that street.

HELD: The House of Lords held that the defendant was under a duty to take reasonable care of the safety of all persons who used the pavement. This duty extends to blind persons if it was reasonably foreseeable that blind persons would use the pavement. The fact that blind people constitute a small percentage of the population does not make them unforeseeable. Accordingly, the claimant could recover damages for his injuries.

 See AGS Pollock, 'Negligence: Duty of Care to Blind' (1964) CLJ 189

The second requirement is that the type of damage suffered must be reasonably foreseeable.[20] A tortious act can result in several different types of loss. For example, a motorist negligently mounts the pavement and runs over a pedestrian. Obviously, the pedestrian's physical injuries are foreseeable, but other foreseeable injuries might include damage to any property that the defendant hit, psychiatric injury to those who witnessed the accident, and loss of earnings of those suffering injury. Losses that are not reasonably foreseeable are not recoverable, as the following case demonstrates.

Bourhill v Young [1943] AC 92 (HL)

FACTS: A motorcyclist negligently drove into a motorcar and was killed. The claimant, a pregnant lady standing about 45 feet away, heard the collision, but did not see it, although she did subsequently see a pool of blood on the road. Consequently, she suffered nervous shock and a back injury (a month later, her baby was delivered stillborn, but it could not be established that this was due to the back injury or the nervous shock). She claimed damages against the estate of the motorcyclist.

HELD: It was certainly foreseeable that the negligence of the motorcyclist would result in injury to some people, and a duty of care would be established to those persons. The claimant, however, was outside the foreseeable area of potential danger and so the House of Lords held that she could not recover damages.

Proximity

Under *Caparo*, proximity is once again a separate requirement and, in many cases, it is a decisive one. However, it cannot be denied that there is a strong connection between foreseeability and proximity and, in many cases, the establishment of one will establish the other. In *Bourhill v Young* (discussed above), the injuries sustained to the claimant were not foreseeable, because she was not within the potential area of danger—that is, she was not sufficiently proximate.

'Proximity', in a legal sense, does not simply refer to closeness in terms of distance or time. For example, in the following case, proximity referred to the nature of the relationship between the parties.

---

20. This is also a condition for establishing that the damage suffered was not too remote. The requirements of duty, breach, and causation often overlap this way.

Goodwill v British Pregnancy Advisory Service [1996] 1 WLR 1397 (CA)

FACTS: The defendant performed a vasectomy on MacKinlay. MacKinlay was told that the operation was successful and that he was permanently sterile. Three years later, he entered into a relationship with Goodwill (the claimant). Believing that MacKinlay was sterile, the couple did not use contraception. MacKinlay's vasectomy reversed itself and the claimant became pregnant, eventually giving birth to a healthy daughter. She claimed damages from the defendant for the costs of raising her daughter.

HELD: Her claim was struck out. The relationship between the defendant and the claimant was not sufficiently proximate to establish the existence of a duty of care. It was suggested, *obiter*, that had the claimant been MacKinlay's wife or partner at the time of the vasectomy and had the doctor known that the operation was to confer a benefit on both of them, then the result might have been different. The claimant was not his wife or partner; she was merely part of an indeterminate class of persons—namely, women with whom MacKinlay might have sex in the future.

COMMENT: This case also demonstrates that proximity may not exist even where foreseeability is present. Doctors are aware that vasectomies can spontaneously reverse themselves, so whilst such an event was unlikely, it was foreseeable.

In some cases, proximity will be a greater determining factor than in others. In cases in which the defendant negligently and directly inflicts physical injury on the claimant, proximity is not likely to be a major issue. Conversely, in other cases, proximity will be a central issue. For example, a professional who provides negligent advice could foreseeably cause economic damage to a wide number of people. In such a case, the courts are likely to use proximity to limit the number of potential claimants.

Yuen Kun Yeu v A-G of Hong Kong [1988] AC 175 (PC)

FACTS: The defendant was the Attorney General of Hong Kong, who was sued as representing the Commissioner of Deposit-taking Companies in Hong Kong. The Commissioner's role was to determine which companies should be registered on the register of deposit-taking companies. If a company was deemed unfit, he should refuse or revoke registration. The claimant had deposited money with a registered company, which went into liquidation, largely because it was run in a fraudulent manner. The claimant argued that, by registering the company, the Commissioner had represented that the company was fit to receive funds.

HELD: The Commissioner owed no duty of care to the claimant. The loss suffered might have been reasonably foreseeable, in that the Commissioner could foresee that the continued registration of an uncreditworthy company might lead to the loss of investors' money, but an unspecified group of potential investors could not be regarded as sufficiently proximate in the circumstances.

There is an extremely strong relationship between proximity and policy. In a number of cases, the courts have given effect to policy concerns by holding that a particular relationship is insufficiently proximate, as the following case demonstrates.

Hill v Chief Constable of West Yorkshire [1989] AC 53 (HL)

FACTS: The claimant's daughter was the final victim of Peter Sutcliffe—a serial killer known as the 'Yorkshire Ripper', who was convicted of murdering thirteen women between 1975 and 1980. The claimant argued that the police had been negligent in their investigations and that, had they not been, they would have apprehended Sutcliffe before he murdered their daughter.

HELD: The House of Lords struck out the claim. Although it was reasonably foreseeable that, if Sutcliffe were not caught, he would continue to murder women, there was nothing to indicate that the claimant's daughter was especially at risk. Accordingly, the relationship between her and the police lacked proximity. The House went on to state that, as a matter of public policy, imposing a duty on the police to catch criminals would be undesirable in so much as it could 'lead to the exercise of a function being carried on in a detrimentally defensive frame of mind'.[21] Therefore, the House stated that the police were immune from negligence actions when investigating or suppressing crime.

COMMENT: Subsequent cases extended the police's immunity to other functions, including the inspection of crime scenes[22] and the dispersal of violent protesters.[23] As is discussed later, however, such immunities came into question following the passing of the Human Rights Act 1998: in particular, claimants alleged that such immunities were not compatible with the right to a fair trial under Art 6 of the European Convention on Human Rights.

Fairness, justice, and reasonableness

The court will only impose a duty where it is fair, just, and reasonable to do so. Like the requirement of proximity, policy plays a significant role, but it appears that, in relation to the third requirement of the *Caparo* test, policy considerations are less established and more ad hoc. As Lunney and Oliphant state:

> Whereas the tendency is to use proximity as the heading for relatively well-settled rules limiting liability for certain types of loss,…the third stage of the *Caparo* approach can be regarded as the general repository for the miscellaneous set of policy arguments, undefined in nature and unlimited in number, which are invoked haphazardly and in an ad hoc fashion by the courts in determining whether a duty of care should arise.[24]

The requirement of fairness, justice, and reasonableness can be used by the courts to deny the existence of a duty of care (even where the claimant has established foreseeability and proximity), as the following case demonstrates.

Marc Rich & Co v Bishop Rock Marine Co Ltd (The Nicholas H) [1996] AC 211 (HL)

FACTS: The defendant was the owner of a ship transporting the claimant's cargo. En route, the ship's hull developed a crack, so the ship anchored in Puerto Rico. The ship's classification society, NKK, sent a surveyor to assess the damage. The surveyor allowed the ship to set off

---

21. [1989] AC 53 (HL) 63 (Lord Keith).   22. *Alexandrou v Oxford* [1993] 4 All ER 328 (CA).
23. *Hughes v National Union of Mineworkers* [1991] 4 All ER 278 (QB).
24. Mark Lunney and Ken Oliphant, *Tort Law: Text and Materials* (5th edn, OUP 2013) 140.

after making temporary repairs. A few days later, the ship sank and the claimant's cargo was lost. The claimant sued the shipowners and the case was settled for $500,000. However, the value of the cargo was over $6 million, so the claimant sued NKK for the remainder.

HELD: The claimant successfully established the requisite foreseeability and proximity. However, the House of Lords held that, in the interests of fairness and justice, a duty of care should not be imposed. Classification societies such as NKK are independent, non-profit-making organizations, whose sole purpose is to promote the collective welfare of ships and mariners. If a duty were to be imposed, the survival of these classification societies might be jeopardized, and without these societies' classifications, ships would be almost impossible to insure. Accordingly, NKK was not liable for the remaining damages.

★ See Michael Wood and David H Reisner, 'No Duty of Care Owed by Classification Societies' (1996) 4 Int ILR 30

The requirement of fairness, justice, and reasonableness can also be used to create a new duty, or extend an existing one.

 Arthur JS Hall & Co v Simons [2002] 1 AC 615 (HL)

FACTS: Three claimants were alleging negligence against their former solicitors. The claimants argued that a rule established in 1969,[25] which provided that advocates would enjoy immunity from negligence actions, should be overruled.

HELD: The House of Lords ruled that advocate immunity should be abolished in both civil and criminal cases, and advocates therefore owe their clients a duty of care. The House stated that the policy considerations that first justified the immunity were no longer present and that therefore, from a policy point of view, the immunity could not be justified. Lord Steyn argued that other professionals do not enjoy an immunity from negligence claims, so why should advocates?

Problematic areas

Now that the duty of care has been discussed in a general sense, the chapter will move on to examine a number of specific instances in which the courts have had difficulty in determining whether or not a duty of care should be imposed.

Omissions

The majority of negligence cases concern some form of negligent act, but is it possible to be liable in negligence for failing to perform an act (that is, an omission)? In *Donoghue v Stevenson*,[26] Lord Atkin stated: 'You must take reasonable care to avoid acts or omissions which you can reasonably foresee would be likely to injure your neighbour.'[27] Despite this, it generally regarded that 'the common law does not impose liability for what are called pure omissions'.[28] Accordingly, a witness to a car accident is not legally obliged to provide aid, nor is a person who witnesses someone being mugged. The general method of expressing this is that the law does not require

---

25. *Rondel v Worsley* [1969] 1 AC 191 (HL).
26. [1932] AC 562 (HL).   27. ibid 580.
28. *Smith v Littlewoods Organisation Ltd* [1987] 2 AC 241 (HL) 271 (Lord Goff).

people to be good Samaritans. Referring to the biblical parable, Lord Diplock stated that the priest and the Levite who walked on the other side would not incur civil liability under English law.[29] The question arising is why the law does not impose liability on those who fail to prevent harm.

In *Stovin v Wise*,[30] Lord Hoffmann stated that the justifications for the rule could be expressed in political, moral, and economic terms:

> In political terms it is less of an invasion of an individual's freedom for the law to require him to consider the safety of others in his actions than to impose upon him a duty to rescue or protect. A moral version of this point may be called the 'why pick on me?' argument. A duty to prevent harm to others or to render assistance to a person in danger or distress may apply to a large and indeterminate class of people who happen to be able to do something. Why should one be held liable rather than another? In economic terms, the efficient allocation of resources usually requires an activity should bear its own costs. If it benefits from being able to impose some of its costs on other people…the market is distorted because the activity appears cheaper than it really is.[31]

The following case provides an example of the general rule in practice.

 Sutradhar v National Environmental Research Council [2006] UKHL 33

FACTS: The British Geological Survey (BGS, a department of the defendant organization) was testing water samples in Bangladesh. The tests were designed to test for the presence of a number of toxic substances, but they would not detect the presence of arsenic. The report published based on the tests did not, however, state that arsenic was not tested for. The claimant drank water that had been tested and subsequently developed arsenic poisoning. He alleged that the BGS had breached its duty by failing to test for arsenic.

HELD: The House of Lords dismissed the claimant's action, with Lord Hoffmann describing it as 'hopeless'.[32] He further stated that the BGS 'can be liable only for the things they did and the statements they made, not for what they did not do'.[33]

In practice, distinguishing between acts and omissions is not always simple. Bankes LJ provides the example of a 'medical man who diagnoses a case of measles as a case of scarlet fever may be said to have omitted to make a correct diagnosis; he may equally well be said to have made an incorrect diagnosis'.[34] A useful distinction is advanced by Lunney and Oliphant, who contend that a negligent act 'makes things worse', whereas an omission 'fails to make things better'.[35]

The principle is not absolute, however, and in certain cases, the courts have established that a person has a duty to act and a failure to act can result in liability (although it should be noted that precise classification of such cases does not exist). The degree of control that a person exercises over another may result in the controlling party owing a duty to act towards the other, as occurred in the following case.

---

29. *Home Office v Dorset Yacht Co Ltd* [1970] AC 1004 (HL) 1060.   30. [1996] AC 923 (HL).
31. ibid 943–4.   32. [2006] UKHL 33, [2006] 4 All ER 490 [2].   33. ibid [27].
34. *Harnett v Bond* [1924] 2 KB 517 (HL) 541.
35. Mark Lunney and Ken Oliphant, *Tort Law: Text and Materials* (5th edn, OUP 2013) 456.

Reeves v Commissioner of Police for the Metropolis [2000] 1 AC 360 (HL)

FACTS: Mr Lynch had been arrested and was held in custody at a police station for which the defendant was responsible. The police officers had been told that Lynch represented a suicide risk (as he had tried to commit suicide whilst in police custody on two prior occasions), but a doctor who attended the police station following Lynch's arrest found him to be of sound mind. Nevertheless, the doctor advised the police to observe him frequently. An hour later, at 1.57 pm, a police officer checked up on Lynch and saw him lying on his bed. Shortly after, Lynch used his shirt as a noose and hanged himself. At 2.05 pm, he was found hanging in his cell and could not be revived. The administratrix of Lynch's estate commenced proceedings against the defendant, and the defendant argued that prior case law[36] established that, in such cases, a duty of care would only be owed if the prisoner was mentally ill.

HELD: The House of Lords held that the defendant was liable. Lord Hope stated that the police officers were under a duty to take reasonable care of Lynch whilst he was in their custody and that this duty was owed 'irrespective of whether he is mentally disordered or of sound mind'.[37] Lord Hoffmann stated that this duty arose 'from the complete control which the police or prison authorities have over the prisoner...'[38] Accordingly, the defendant was ordered to pay damages, but these were reduced by 50 per cent to reflect the fact that Lynch was also clearly partially responsible for his own death.

> ★ See Kay Wheat, 'The Law's Treatment of the Suicidal' (2000) 8 Med L Rev 182.

The relationship between the claimant and defendant may give rise to an undertaking or imposition of responsibility to prevent or rescue the claimant from a certain type of harm.

Costello v Chief Constable of Northumbria [1999] ICR 752 (CA)

FACTS: The claimant was a female police officer who was attacked by a female prisoner whilst escorting her to a cell at a police station. A police inspector was detailed to accompany the officer whilst the prisoner was being escorted but, despite the officer crying out for help, the inspector did not come to the officer's aid. The claimant commenced proceedings against the defendant for the injuries she suffered in the attack.

HELD: The Court held that the defendant was vicariously liable for the inspector's failure to act. The Court held that the inspector had assumed a responsibility towards the claimant which resulted in a duty to act. Liability could therefore be imposed where this duty arose and a 'failure to do so will expose a fellow officer to unnecessary risk of injury'.[39]

> ★ See John Hodgson, 'Public Policy Immunity and Competing Interests' (1999) 8 Nott LJ 45.

A person not normally under a duty to act may nevertheless acquire a duty to act if their actions create a situation that results in another person sustaining loss, as occurred in the following case.

---

36. Namely *Kirkham v Chief Constable of the Greater Manchester Police* [1990] 2 QB 283 (CA).

37. [2000] 1 AC 360 (HL) 380.   38. ibid 369.

39. [1999] ICR 752 (CA) 767 (May LJ).

Capital & Counties plc v Hampshire County Council [1997] QB 1004 (CA)

FACTS: This case was a consolidated appeal involving three cases. In the first case, the two claimants' premises were destroyed by fire after a fire brigade turned off the sprinkler system. In the second case, the claimant's premises where destroyed by fire that spread from adjacent premises—the fire brigade left after the fire at the adjacent premises was extinguished. In the third case, the claimant's chapel was destroyed after a fire brigade failed to extinguish it due to a lack of a proper supply of water. In all three cases, the claimants commenced proceedings against the bodies responsible for the various fire brigades.

HELD: The Court held that a fire brigade was not under a duty to answer calls to fires or to take care to do so, nor did it become subject to a duty to act simply because it attended a fire and fought it. Consequently, the claims in the second and third cases failed. Where, however, a fire brigade by their negligence cause the danger which caused the claimant's injury, then a duty would be owed. As the defendant in the first case created the danger by shutting down the sprinkler system, the Court held that this claim would succeed.

★ See John Hartshorne, ' "Caparo Under Fire": A Study Into the Effects Upon the Fire Service of Liability in Negligence' (2000) 63 MLR 502.

Acts of third parties

Linked closely to the issue of liability for omissions is the issue of whether a person can be liable for the acts of a third party. Generally, persons are not liable for the acts of third parties and are under no duty to prevent others from causing harm. As Toulson LJ stated:

> A defendant, D, is not ordinarily liable to a claimant, C, for personal injury or physical damage caused by the negligence of a third person, T, merely because D could have foreseen and prevented it. Something more is required to place on D a duty to protect C from the consequences of foreseeable negligence on the part of T.[40]

As this quote indicates, the rule is a general one only and, in certain cases, a person can be held liable for the acts of a third party (or parties).

The relationship between one person (*A*) and another (*B*) may justify the imposition upon *A* of a duty to prevent *B* from coming to harm due to the acts of third parties. For example, an occupier of land will owe a duty to lawful visitors to ensure that they are not harmed by the acts of third parties. An employer will owe a similar duty to his employees. Such a duty can arise, however, outside the scope of these established relationships, as the following case demonstrates.

Stansbie v Troman [1948] 2 KB 48 (CA)

FACTS: Stansbie, a decorator, was employed by Troman to carry out decoration work in his house. Troman's wife informed Stansbie that she had to go out, thereby leaving Stansbie alone in the house. Stansbie went to a nearby shop to purchase some wallpaper, but he failed to lock the door when he left. He had difficulty locating the wallpaper and did not return for two hours. Upon his return, he discovered that a thief had entered the house and stolen clothing and jewellery. Troman sued Stansbie for the cost of the stolen items.

40. *Glaister v Appleby-in-Westmorland Town Council* [2009] EWCA Civ 1325, [2010] PIQR P6 [45].

HELD: Troman's claim succeeded. Tucker LJ held that the contractual relationship between Troman and Stansbie imposed upon Stansbie 'a duty…to take reasonable care with regard to the state of the premises if he left them during the performance of his work'.[41]

A duty may arise based on the relationship between the defendant and a third party, especially where the defendant is responsible for, or has control over, the actions of the third party, as occurred in the following case.

 ### Home Office v Dorset Yacht Co Ltd [1970] AC 1004 (HL)

FACTS: Seven borstal boys were working on an island under the supervision of three wardens. At night, they escaped from custody and boarded a yacht in order to escape to the mainland. The yacht collided with, and damaged, the claimant's yacht, which the boys then boarded. The claimant commenced proceedings against the defendant, stating that it was vicariously liable for the negligence of the wardens. The defendant argued that neither it nor its servants owed the claimant a duty of care.

HELD: The claimant succeeded and obtained damages from the defendant. The wardens had breached their duty of care by allowing the boys to escape. The justification for this was provided by Lord Pearson who stated that 'the borstal boys were under the control of the Home Office's officers, and control imports responsibility'.[42]

A duty may also arise where the defendant creates, or permits to be created, a source of danger and it is reasonably foreseeable that third parties may interfere with that danger, thereby causing harm.

 ### Haynes v Harwood [1935] 1 KB 146 (CA)

FACTS: The claimant was a police officer who was on duty inside a police station on what was, at the time of the incident, a crowded street. An employee of the defendant left a two-horse-drawn van unattended on this street. The horses bolted (likely caused by a stone being thrown at them by a child) and the claimant rushed out of the police station, grabbed the horses' reins and managed to stop them. In doing so, one of the horses fell on top of the claimant, causing him serious personal injuries. The claimant sued the defendant for damages.

HELD: The claimant succeeded. Greer LJ stated that 'it would be a little surprising if a rational system of law in those circumstances denied any remedy to a brave man who had received his injuries through the original default of the defendants' servant'.[43] As for the reason for imposing liability, Greer LJ stated 'any one who invites or gives an opportunity to mischievous children to do a dangerous thing cannot escape liability on the ground that he did not do the wrong but that it was done by the mischievous children'.[44]

---

41. [1948] 2 KB 48 (CA) 50–1.   42. [1970] AC 1004 (HL) 1055.
43. [1935] 1 KB 146 (CA) 152.   44. ibid 154.

Psychiatric damage

The courts have long held that mental injury consequential upon physical injury is recoverable under the head of damage known as 'pain and suffering'. Historically, the courts have, however, been reluctant to impose a duty of care where the damage sustained has been purely psychiatric, for three reasons:

1. The courts did not regard psychiatric damage as serious as physical injury.
2. Whereas the extent of a physical injury was readily discernable, psychiatric damage was extremely difficult to diagnose and could be feigned.
3. The courts were concerned that establishing a duty of care to victims of psychiatric damage would flood the courts with claims.

Accordingly, up until the beginning of the twentieth century, the courts were relatively dismissive of such claims for 'nervous shock'.[45] As time progressed, however, the courts' prejudices regarding psychiatric damage began to fade, and they recognized that such damage was 'no less real and frequently no less painful and disabling'[46] than physical injury. Further, modern diagnostic techniques make it increasingly difficult to fake psychological conditions. However, the court was still wary and two limitations were introduced, both of which survive today. First, the claimant must suffer from a medically recognized psychiatric condition. Accordingly:

> Grief, sorrow, deprivation and the necessity for caring for loved ones who have suffered injury or misfortune must...be considered as ordinary and inevitable incidents of life which...must be sustained without compensation.[47]

Second, the psychological damage must be sustained due to a sudden event, or must arise in the immediate aftermath of a sudden event. Accordingly, parents who witness the slow death of their child, who has been injured due to the defendant's negligence, would be unable to obtain damages for any resultant psychological damage that they suffer.[48]

Initially, the courts would only establish a duty of care in relation to 'primary' victims, of which there were two types:

1. A person who sustains physical injury due to an incident caused by the defendant's negligence can recover damages for his physical injuries and for any psychiatric damage that he might have suffered.
2. Where a person is directly involved, as a participant, in an incident caused by the defendant's negligence and personal injury (whether physical or psychiatric) is foreseeable, then that person can recover damages for psychiatric damage sustained, even if he did not sustain any physical injuries.[49]

This restrictive approach meant that 'secondary' victims (that is, those who witnessed the defendant's negligence, or were told about it, but did not fear for their physical safety) were unable to claim. This rule was first relaxed when the court established that psychological damage caused to those who witnessed shocking events whilst attempting to rescue others was claimable.[50] In the following case, the House of

---

45. In *Attia v British Gas plc* [1988] QB 304 (CA) 318, Bingham LJ dubbed the phrase 'nervous shock' as a 'misleading and inaccurate expression', and instead recommended that the term 'psychiatric damage' be used.   46. *McLoughlin v O'Brian* [1983] AC 410 (HL) 433 (Lord Bridge).
47. *Alcock v Chief Constable of South Yorkshire Police* [1992] 1 AC 310 (HL) 416 (Lord Oliver).
48. *Sion v Hampstead Health Authority* [1994] 5 Med LR 170 (CA).
49. *Page v Smith* [1996] 1 AC 155 (HL).   50. *Chadwick v British Railways Board* [1967] 1 WLR 912 (QB).

Lords expanded the duty to cover those who had witnessed a shocking event, provided that there was a sufficiently proximate relationship both between the witness and the primary victim, and between the witness and the event in question, in terms of time and space.

 McLoughlin v O'Brian [1983] 1 AC 410 (HL)

FACTS: The claimant's husband and three children were involved in a car accident, due to the negligent driving of the defendant. At the time of the incident, the claimant was at home, some two miles away. Around two hours later, a neighbour told the claimant of the accident and she immediately drove to the local hospital. There, she learned that her youngest daughter had been killed, she saw her husband and another daughter covered in oil and dirt, and she heard her badly injured son screaming. She alleged that witnessing this caused her to become depressed and altered her personality, affecting her abilities as a wife and mother. Both at first instance and on appeal, it was held that, because she was not a primary victim, the defendant did not owe her a duty of care.

HELD: The House of Lords unanimously held that the defendant owed her a duty of care. The psychological damage suffered by the claimant was a reasonably foreseeable result of the injuries caused to her family by the defendant's negligence. In order to claim, however, the claimant would either need to witness the shocking event or come upon its 'immediate aftermath'. The House held that she had witnessed the immediate aftermath and so could recover damages for her psychiatric injuries.

The modern law on when a duty of care is imposed in relation to cases involving pure psychological damage was established in the following case, one of many to arise from the Hillsborough disaster.

 Alcock v Chief Constable of the South Yorkshire Police [1992] 1 AC 310 (HL)

FACTS: Hillsborough stadium in Sheffield was to be the venue for a FA Cup semi-final match between Liverpool FC and Nottingham Forest FC. The match was sold out, and received extensive television and radio coverage. Many stadia at the time had a wire fence separating the crowd from the pitch. After six minutes, the match was stopped when it became apparent that the police had admitted too many fans into the Liverpool end of the stadium. The weight of numbers resulted in fans being crushed against the wire fences. Ninety-six Liverpool fans died and over 400 were injured. A number of people who witnessed or heard about the disaster suffered psychological damage. A **test case** was brought to determine the extent of the duty of care owed by the negligent police force. Test claimants included witnesses who were present inside the stadium, those who witnessed the events on television, those who heard about the events on the radio, and one claimant who was outside the stadium, but later had to identify the body of a friend at a makeshift mortuary. The test claimants also covered numerous relationships (for example, parents of disaster victims, spouses, friends, etc). The defendant admitted negligence, but denied owing a duty of care to the test claimants.

➡ **test case:** a case that is brought and the result applied to similar cases that are not litigated

HELD: None of the test claimants were owed a duty of care by the police. The House of Lords laid down an extensive list of requirements that would all need to be met before a duty of care would exist. Most of these requirements revolve around establishing proximity:

- The claimant will need to establish sufficiently 'close ties of love and affection'[51] with the person injured or endangered. The House deliberately left open the types of relationship that would qualify, but certain relationships (for example, parent and child, husband and wife, engaged couples) would raise a rebuttable presumption of sufficient closeness. This would indicate that a duty is not owed to bystanders, but Lords Keith and Ackner thought that a duty could exist to bystanders who witnessed an accident that was 'particularly horrific'.[52] It has been noted that the problem with this is that 'it is not clear how any "scale of horrors" could be devised'.[53] If the Hillsborough disaster did not qualify, what would?
- The claimant will need to be sufficiently proximate in both time and space. Directly witnessing or hearing the event will be sufficient, as will coming upon the 'immediate aftermath' of an event,[54] but their Lordships refused to define exactly what this meant. In *Alcock*, identifying a body in a morgue nine hours after the disaster did not qualify.[55] Claimants who witnessed the disaster on television were also not sufficiently proximate.
- The event must have been communicated to the claimant in a sufficiently proximate way. Accordingly, a person who was informed of the event by a third party would lack proximity,[56] as would a person who saw the event on television or read about it in a newspaper.
- The claimant must establish that it was reasonably foreseeable that a person of normal or reasonable fortitude would have suffered psychiatric damage as a result of the event.
- The damage caused to the claimant must be caused by shock. A series of gradual events that eventually cause psychological damage will not suffice to establish a duty of care. However, the 'shock' need not derive from a single disastrous negligent act. For example, the courts held that psychological damage caused by the death of the claimant's son due to a series of negligent acts and medical misdiagnoses over a 36-hour period constituted sufficient shock.[57]
- The primary victim does not owe a duty of care to a secondary victim where the primary victim is injured through his own negligence.[58]

⭐ See Bernadette Lunch, 'A Victory for Pragmatism? Nervous Shock Reconsidered' (1992) 108 LQR 367

There is almost universal dissatisfaction with the current state of the law regarding psychological damage. Todd argues that 'it is not very controversial to assert that the law concerning liability for causing mental injury is in a dreadful mess'.[59] The judiciary seems to have given up on finding a series of workable rules: Lord Hoffmann, in *White v Chief Constable of South Yorkshire Police*,[60] conceded that '[i]t seems to me that in this area of the law, the search for principle was called off'.[61] Opinion regarding the way forward is divided. Some commentators have argued that the restrictive treatment of psychological damage should be abandoned and that it should be regarded as the

---

51. [1992] 1 AC 310 (HL) 397 (Lord Keith).
52. ibid.   53. Mark Lunney and Ken Oliphant, *Tort Law: Text and Materials* (5th edn, OUP 2013) 339.
54. See e.g. *Fenn v City of Peterborough* (1976) 73 DLR (3d) 177 (a duty was owed to a claimant who arrived home minutes after a gas explosion killed his children).
55. Contrast *Galli-Atkinson v Seghal* [2003] EWCA Civ 697, [2003] Lloyd's Rep Med 285, in which a duty was established where a father identified his daughter's body in a morgue several hours after a motor accident that caused her death.
56. *Ravenscroft v Rederiaktiebolaget Transatlantic* [1992] 2 All ER 470 (Note) (CA).
57. *North Glamorgan NHS Trust v Walters* [2002] EWCA Civ 1792, [2003] PIQR P16.
58. *Greatorex v Greatorex* [2000] 1 WLR 1970 (QB).
59. Stephen Todd, 'Psychiatric Injury and Rescuers' (1999) 115 LQR 345, 349.
60. [1999] 2 AC 455 (HL).   61. ibid 511.

same as physical injury.[62] Others have gone so far as to argue that the law relating to psychological damage should be abolished completely, on the ground that acceptable boundaries will never be found.[63] The Law Commission proposed a statutory duty of care[64] that could be viewed as a compromise between these two extremes, but it was never acted upon. A governmental Consultation Paper, published in May 2007, rejected the Law Commission's proposals and recommended that this area of the law continue to develop through the common law.[65] Based on the above, it appears that neither the courts themselves, nor commentators, share the government's confidence in the ability of the common law effectively to develop sound principles for the recovery of compensation for psychiatric damage.

'Pure' economic loss

Based on the discussion thus far, it can be seen that negligence is largely concerned with compensating victims of physical damage, whether to their person or property. Economic loss is recoverable if it is consequential upon physical damage (for example, loss of earnings due to physical injury). As a general rule, however, 'pure' economic loss (that is, financial loss unassociated with physical injury or property damage) is not recoverable and the courts enforce this principle by finding that a duty of care does not exist, as demonstrated clearly in the following case.

Spartan Steel & Alloys Ltd v Martin & Co Ltd [1973] QB 27 (CA)

FACTS: The defendant's employees were carrying out roadworks when they negligently cut a power cable. The cable was the direct supply of electricity to the claimant's factory, which was engaged in the smelting of steel alloys. As a result of the power cut, the claimant suffered three distinct types of damage:

(1) Molten metal could not be kept at the correct temperature and thus became damaged.
(2) The damage to the metal meant that it depreciated in value.
(3) As a result of the power cut, the claimant could not melt any further metal, resulting in a loss of profit.

HELD: The Court of Appeal held that the claimant could recover in relation to (1), because this constituted physical damage. It could also recover (2), because this loss was consequential upon the physical damage. It could not, however, recover (3), because this loss was purely economic and was not based upon damage to any property.

★ See JA Jolowicz, 'Negligence: Loss of Profits—Economic Loss' (1973) 32 CLJ 20

The obvious question to ask is why the law protects those who suffer consequential economic loss, but will not protect those who suffer pure economic loss. Numerous reasons have been advanced, including:

---

62. For example, Peter Handford, *Mullaney & Handford's Tort Liability for Psychiatric Damage* (2nd edn, Law Book Co 2006) [30.40].

63. For example, Jane Stapledon, 'In Restraint of Tort' in Peter Birks (ed), *The Frontiers of Liability, Vol 2* (OUP 1994).

64. Law Commission, *Liability for Psychiatric Illness* (Law Com No 249, HMSO 1998).

65. Department of Constitutional Affairs, *The Law on Damages* (CP 9/07, HMSO 2007) [94].

- 'The law should provide greater protection to personal safety and health than to purely economic interests.'[66] This argument is certainly true and physical injury should be afforded greater protection than pure economic loss, but that does not mean that pure economic loss should be completely irrecoverable.

- Permitting widespread recovery of pure economic loss would result in indeterminate liability. In *Spartan Steel*, discussed earlier, if the power cable had been connected to a wide geographical area, the extent of the loss would be unpredictable in terms of the number of claimants and the size of potential claims. Conversely, the extent of physical damage will normally be limited and relatively predictable.

- Persons concerned with potential pure economic losses should obtain protection via contract, either by contracting with the potential tortfeasors directly or by taking out insurance against economic loss.

- Perhaps the most-cited argument is that if pure economic loss were generally recoverable, it would open the 'floodgates', thereby exposing defendants to widespread liability and inundating the courts with claims. It is, however, highly unlikely that this would occur. As is discussed later in this chapter, there are extensive rules relating to causation and remoteness that, in many cases, would substantially limit the liability of a tortfeasor.

Like many legal principles, the rule that pure economic loss cannot be recovered is not absolute. There exists one major exception to the rule—namely, where the defendant has made a negligent misstatement that causes the claimant pure economic loss, this loss can be recovered.

Negligent misstatements

Historically, a claimant could only recover damages against a defendant who had committed a negligent act. Losses as a result of negligent statements were not recoverable for two reasons.

1. A negligent act will usually result in fairly limited and predictable damage. Conversely, negligent statements may be spoken to, or repeated to, many persons, thereby resulting in unpredictable and indeterminate liability.

2. Negligent statements do not tend to result in physical damage and, as discussed, the general rule is that damages can only be recovered for physical damage, or loss that is consequential upon physical damage.

The law did acknowledge that certain damaging statements were deserving of compensation (for example, the tort of deceit provided the claimant with a remedy in tort if the statement was fraudulent),[67] but damage caused by negligent statements was irrecoverable. This changed after the following seminal case.

Hedley Byrne & Co Ltd v Heller & Partners Ltd [1964] AC 465 (HL)

FACTS: The claimant advertising agent had concerns regarding the financial viability of a client company called Easipower, and so asked its bankers to inquire into Easipower's financial status. The claimant's bankers sought this information from the defendant's bankers,

---

66. Simon Deakin, Angus Johnston, and Basil Markesinis, *Markesinis and Deakin's Tort Law* (7th edn, OUP 2013) 141.
67. *Derry v Peek* (1889) LR 14 App Cas 337 (HL).

who replied that Easipower was a properly constituted company that could be considered good for its normal business engagements (this advice was subject to a disclaimer abdicating responsibility for the advice). Relying on this, the claimant procured advertising space on Easipower's behalf—but the nature of the contract meant that if Easipower failed to pay for the advertising, the claimant would be liable. Easipower subsequently became insolvent and the claimant became liable for Easipower's debt of £17,661. The claimant alleged that the defendant's advice had been negligent and sued accordingly. The defendant argued that, because the loss was purely economic, it did not owe the claimant a duty of care.

HELD: The House of Lords held that the defendant was not liable. The reason for this was that the disclaimer prevented a duty of care from arising. The House also stated *obiter* that the defendant owed the claimant a duty of care, notwithstanding that the loss was purely economic. The House was not, however, prepared to extend the general duty of care to cover negligent misstatements. The House instead established a test that was much narrower than Lord Atkin's 'neighbour' test: in addition to satisfying the requirement of reasonable foreseeability, the claimant also had to demonstrate that there was a 'special relationship' between himself and the defendant.

COMMENT: This case was decided prior to the passing of the Unfair Contract Terms Act 1977. If *Hedley Byrne* were to be decided today, it is possible that the disclaimer would be regarded as unreasonable and therefore invalid.[68]

★ See Robert Stevens, 'Hedley Byrne v Heller: Judicial Creativity and Doctrinal Possibility' (1964) 27 MLR 121

Unfortunately, there exists no unanimous or authoritative statement as to what constitutes a 'special relationship', leading the High Court of Australia to comment that '[s]ince the decision in *Hedley Byrne & Co Ltd v Heller & Partners Ltd*, confusion bordering on chaos has reigned in the law of negligence'.[69]

An analysis of the judgments in *Hedley Byrne* reveals that the judges involved could not precisely agree what was needed to establish a special relationship. Lord Morris stated:

> [I]t should now be regarded as settled that if someone possessed of a special skill undertakes, quite irrespective of contract, to apply that skill for the assistance of another person who relies upon such skill, a duty of care will arise.[70]

It can be seen that Lord Morris laid down two requirements: first, the defendant must possess a special skill; second, the claimant must reasonably rely upon that skill. But two other members of the House thought that a third requirement was needed—namely, that there must also be 'a voluntary undertaking to assume responsibility'[71] by the defendant. The problem that arises is that these three requirements have not been applied consistently, with some cases regarding the requirement of reliance as crucial, while others have completely ignored it. In one case in 1990, Lord Griffiths stated: 'I do not think that voluntary assumption of responsibility is a helpful or realistic test for liability.'[72] Conversely, in a 1995 case, Lord Goff stated: '[A]n assumption of responsibility coupled with reliance by the plaintiff which, in all the circumstances, makes it appropriate that a remedy in law should be available.'[73] More recently, Lord

---

68. See Unfair Contract Terms Act 1977, s 2, and *Smith v Eric S Bush* [1990] 1 AC 831 (HL).
69. *Woolcock Street Investments v CDG Pty Ltd* [2004] HCA 16 (High Court of Australia) [45] (McHugh J.)
70. *Hedley Byrne & Co Ltd v Heller & Partners Ltd* [1964] AC 465 (HL) 502–03.
71. ibid 529 (Lord Devlin). See also [1964] AC 465 (HL) 486 (Lord Reid).
72. *Smith v Eric S Bush* [1990] 1 AC 831 (HL) 862.
73. *Henderson v Merrett Syndicates Ltd* [1995] 2 AC 145 (HL) 186–7.

Bingham stated that 'it is correct to regard an assumption of responsibility as a sufficient but not a necessary condition of liability'.[74]

Given these inconsistencies, subsequent cases have attempted to specify more accurately what is required to establish a special relationship. The following case, which established the modern test for the establishment of a duty of care, also laid down specific guidance on what a claimant would need to establish in order to recover pure economic loss.

Caparo Industries plc v Dickman [1990] 2 AC 605 (HL)

FACTS: Caparo (the claimant) was considering initiating a takeover bid of a company called Fidelity plc. Before making the bid, Caparo scrutinized Fidelity's annual accounts, which had been prepared for Fidelity by the defendant firm of auditors, Touche Ross. The accounts indicated that Fidelity's pre-tax profits were £1.2 million, and, on this basis, Caparo purchased further shares and took the company over. Caparo then discovered that the accounts were inaccurate and that Fidelity was actually running at a loss of £400,000. It also appeared that a number of Fidelity's directors were engaging in fraudulent activities. Caparo sued Touche Ross, alleging that the auditors owed it a duty of care.

HELD: The House of Lords held that the auditors were not liable. Lord Oliver stated:

> the necessary relationship between the maker of a statement or giver of advice ('the adviser') and the recipient who acts in reliance upon it ('the advisee') may typically be held to exist where (1) the advice is required for a purpose, whether particularly specified or generally described, which is made known, either actually or inferentially, to the adviser at the time when the advice is given; (2) the adviser knows, either actually or inferentially, that his advice will be communicated to the advisee, either specifically or as a member of an ascertainable class, in order that it should be used by the advisee for that purpose; (3) it is known either actually or inferentially, that the advice so communicated is likely to be acted upon by the advisee for that purpose without independent inquiry; and (4) it is so acted upon by the advisee to his detriment.[75]

The annual accounts were prepared in order to enable Fidelity's shareholders to determine whether or not the company was being run effectively. Accordingly, it was clear that the auditors owed a duty to Fidelity. The House went on to say that the auditors did not prepare accounts in order to inform those who might wish to make investment decisions. Accordingly, no duty was owed to Caparo.

★ See Robyn Martyn, 'Categories of Negligence and Duties of Care: Caparo in the House of Lords' (1990) 53 MLR 824

It will be noted that Lord Oliver's formulation makes no reference to the 'voluntary assumption of responsibility' that certain judges in *Hedley Byrne* regarded as essential. It would appear, therefore, that Lord Oliver in *Caparo* 'fatally weakened'[76] the requirement of voluntary assumption—but this may not be the case. All of the above cases concerned the provision of negligent advice (although negligent misstatement need not only relate to advice) and, as noted, this constitutes the principal exception to the rule that pure economic loss is not recoverable. The possibility always existed

---

74. *Customs and Excise Commissioners v Barclays Bank plc* [2006] UKHL 28, [2007] 1 AC 181 [4].

75. [1990] 2 AC 605 (HL) 638.

76. Jenny Steele, *Tort Law: Text, Cases and Materials* (2nd edn, OUP 2010) 382.

that the *Hedley Byrne* principles would be extended beyond cases concerning the provision of advice. This possibility has now occurred and is generally known as 'extended' *Hedley Byrne* liability, and many cases involving this extended liability have confirmed the importance of the 'assumption of responsibility'.

'Extended' Hedley Byrne *liability*

Soon after *Hedley Byrne* was decided, a key issue arose—namely, whether the principles laid down in *Hedley Byrne* were confined to cases concerning the provision of advice. It is now clear that the answer is 'no' and the courts have extended the *Hedley Byrne* principle to other areas—notably to cases concerning the provision of services. This extension to services is a logical one. It would be incongruous if a professional could be liable in tort for negligent advice, but not for negligently providing a service. As Lunney and Oliphant state: 'It would be an odd result if a solicitor could be liable under *Hedley Byrne* for careless advice but not for carelessly drafting a document.'[77]

 White v Jones [1995] 2 AC 207 (HL)

FACTS: Barratt quarrelled with his two daughters (the claimants), and subsequently cut them both out of his will. A few months later, Barratt and his daughters were reconciled, and he instructed his solicitor, Jones (the defendant), to draft a new will restoring his daughter's legacies, which amounted to £9,000 each. The solicitor negligently delayed drafting the new will and Barratt died before the will was completed, with the result that Barratt's daughters did not receive their legacies. Barratt's daughters sued Jones. Jones argued that, because the loss was purely economic, he did not owe the daughters a duty of care.

HELD: The House of Lords held that Jones owed the daughters a duty of care. However, the reasoning of the majority differed. Lord Goff acknowledged that, although the defendant had, factually, not assumed responsibility towards the claimants, only to his client, if the claimants were not provided with a remedy, there would be 'a lacuna in the law'.[78] Accordingly, based on little more than an 'impulse to do practical justice',[79] Lord Goff held that 'the assumption of responsibility by the solicitor towards his client should be held *in law* to extend to the intended beneficiary'.[80] Conversely, Lord Browne-Wilkinson did not appear to believe that an assumption in law was needed, because he found that, factually, Jones had voluntarily assumed responsibility towards the claimants and that this assumption of responsibility created the *Hedley Byrne* 'special relationship' between the parties. Although subsequent courts have indicated that Lord Goff's judgment expresses the reasoning of the majority,[81] the divergent reasoning of the judges involved makes finding the *ratio* of this case extremely difficult.

⭐ See Tony Weir, 'A *Damnosa Hereditas?*' (1995) 111 LQR 357

It can be seen, from the above discussion relating to pure economic loss, negligent misstatement, and 'extended' *Hedley Byrne* liability, that the law in this area is far from

---

77. Mark Lunney and Ken Oliphant, *Tort Law: Text and Materials* (5th edn, OUP 2013) 423.
78. *White v Jones* [1995] 2 AC 207 (HL) 265.   79. ibid 259.   80. ibid 268 (emphasis added).
81. See e.g. *Carr-Glynn v Frearsons* [1999] Ch 326 (CA) 335, in which Chadwick LJ stated that the 'reasoning in Lord Goff's speech—and only that reasoning—that can be said to have received the support of the majority in the House of Lords'.

certain and principled. Numerous tests have been advocated, but the exact requirements for recovery of pure economic loss are far from certain, especially in relation to cases outside established duty situations. Accordingly, in the following case, the House of Lords considered the differing tests and attempted to provide guidance on their application.

Customs and Excise Commissioners v Barclays Bank plc [2006] UKHL 28

FACTS: The claimant sought to recover outstanding VAT payments from two companies. To this end, injunctions were obtained freezing the assets of the two companies involved. The companies involved held their bank accounts at the defendant bank. The defendant was informed of the injunctions, but it failed to prevent the companies from drawing on the accounts. The claimant sought damages from the defendant in respect of the sums paid out and it was necessary to determine if the defendant owed the claimant a duty of care.

HELD: The House of Lords held that the defendant did not owe the claimant a duty of care. As the bank was obliged to comply with the injunction and could be held in contempt of court if it did not, there was no voluntary assumption of responsibility so as to give rise to a duty of care. Their Lordships were all agreed that 'there is no single common denominator, even in cases of economic loss, by which liability may be determined'.[82] What then followed was a series of speeches indicating that the established tests provided 'no more than a helpful channelling for judicial thought'.[83] All five Law Lords involved provided a judgment, but Lord Walker's was largely in agreement with those of the others. The other four judgments all provided useful guidance as to when pure economic loss is recoverable. The key points from each judgment are set out as follows.

Lord Bingham

1. The assumption of responsibility test is 'a sufficient, but not necessary condition of liability, a first test which, if answered positively, may obviate the need for further enquiry. If answered negatively, further consideration is called for'.[84] This further consideration would appear to be an application of the three-stage *Caparo* test.
2. The assumption of responsibility test is to be applied objectively and is not concerned with what the defendant actually thought or intended.
3. The general three-stage duty of care test established in *Caparo* does not provide a straightforward answer in cases involving novel situations.
4. The incremental test is little use alone and it should be combined with other tests.
5. The outcomes of the leading cases were sensible and just, irrespective of what test was applied.

Lord Hoffmann

1. In cases involving economic loss, reasonable foreseeability is not enough to establish a duty of care.
2. The purpose of the assumption of responsibility test is to determine if the relationship between the parties was sufficiently proximate.

---

82. [2006] UKHL 28, [2007] 1 AC 181 [93] (Lord Mance).
83. Steven Gee, 'The Remedies Carried by a Freezing Injunction' (2006) 122 LQR 535, 536.
84. [2006] UKHL 28, [2007] 1 AC 181 [4].

Lord Rodger

1. Although some cases have indicated that the assumption of responsibility test is the 'touchstone' for establishing liability for pure economic loss, this is not the case.
2. In the absence of a single 'touchstone', the court should apply the three-stage test in *Caparo* to novel situations.

Lord Mance

1. The differing approaches often (although not invariably) lead to the same result.
2. 'Assumption of responsibility is on any view a core area of liability for economic loss.'[85]
3. '[T]here is no single common denominator, even in cases of economic loss, by which liability may be determined. In my view the threefold test of foreseeability, proximity and fairness, justice and reasonableness provides a convenient general framework although it operates at a high level of abstraction.'[86]

⭐ See Steven Gee, 'The Remedies Carried by a Freezing Injunction' (2006) 122 LQR 535

The effect of the Human Rights Act 1998

The final issue to discuss in relation to the duty of care is the effect of the Human Rights Act 1998. The most significant effect has been in relation to the duty of care, where, for a time, it appeared that the 1998 Act would seriously jeopardize the survival of the *Caparo* test. Article 6 of the European Convention on Human Rights provides for the right to a fair trial and any procedural rule or substantive law that interferes with a person's right to a fair trial may infringe Art 6.

As noted, the third part of the *Caparo* test (it must be fair, just, and reasonable to impose a duty) has, in a number of cases, resulted in certain groups receiving immunity from negligence claims via the courts' refusal to impose a duty of care. It was the imposition of such an immunity that the European Court of Human Rights found to be in breach of Art 6 in the following case.

 Osman v UK (2000) 29 EHRR 245

FACTS: Paget-Lewis, a teacher, had developed an infatuation with a pupil named Osman. Over the course of the next few months, Paget-Lewis harassed Osman and his family, including engaging in acts of property damage. The harassment was reported to the police and, after several interviews, they decided to arrest Paget-Lewis. Unfortunately, he had fled the area. Several months later, he returned and, using a stolen shotgun, killed Osman's father and seriously injured Osman. The claimants (Osman and his mother) argued that the police had been negligent in failing to capture Paget-Lewis. The Court of Appeal, applying *Hill v Chief Constable of West Yorkshire* (discussed earlier), held that no duty existed and struck out the claim.[87] The Osmans took their case to the European Court of Human Rights.

HELD: The European Court of Human Rights (ECtHR) held that the Osmans' Art 6 rights had been infringed. In applying a blanket immunity, the Court of Appeal had failed to balance the policy factors identified in *Hill* with any other factors existing in Osman's case that could merit the imposition of a duty (for example, the seriousness of the harm suffered and the extent of Paget-Lewis' wrongdoing). Therefore, the automatic imposition of a blanket immunity was a disproportionate measure.

⭐ See Giorgio Monti, '*Osman v UK*: Transforming English Negligence into French Administrative Law?' (1999) 48 ICLQ 757

---

85. ibid [83].   86. ibid [93].   87. *Osman v Ferguson* [1993] 4 All ER 344 (CA).

The effect of the ruling appears to be that the striking out of a claim based on the lack of a duty of care would infringe the claimant's Art 6 rights. Certainly, in the period following *Osman*, domestic courts were much more reluctant to strike out a negligence claim, especially based on the third part of the *Caparo* test. There is little doubt that, domestically, the decision was not popular. One commentator stated that there were 'few who were favourably disposed to the judgment'[88] and one judge branded the decision as 'extremely difficult to understand'.[89]

Fortunately, more recent decisions have indicated that the ECtHR has retreated from its openly hostile stance towards *Caparo* and there is now a recognition that the ECtHR in *Osman* failed to understand properly the nature of the *Caparo* test.

Z v UK (2002) 34 EHRR 3

FACTS: The claimants were four young siblings, who were neglected and poorly treated by their parents. Reports from a string of concerned parties detailed practices that included locking the children out of the house all day, that the children were poorly fed, and that there was a perceived risk of sexual abuse. Social services visited the house and, despite the blatantly poor conditions, the children were not placed on the child protection register. Five years later, during which time there were continued reports of abuse and neglect, the council eventually placed the children on the child protection register and the children found foster homes. The children sued the council on the basis that its failure to act more promptly affected their physical and emotional well-being. The House of Lords held that their negligence claim should fail on the ground that it would not be fair, just, and reasonable to impose a duty on the council.[90] The claimants took their claim to the ECtHR.

HELD: Retreating from *Osman*, the ECtHR held that 'the inability of the [claimants] to sue the local authority flowed not from an immunity but from the applicable principles governing the substantive right of action in domestic law'.[91] Accordingly, Art 6 was not infringed.

COMMENT: It would appear that the effect of this case is to confine Art 6 complaints to breaches of procedure, not complaints against substantive law. Accordingly, it would appear that a claimant would be unable to succeed on an argument based on Art 6 where the courts have used the third part of the *Caparo* test to refuse to impose a duty of care.

⭐ See ACL Davies, 'The European Convention and Negligence Actions: *Osman* "Reviewed" ' (2001) 117 LQR 521

The retreat from *Osman* will doubtless be welcomed by many, especially the higher courts. It is, however, hoped that the courts do not revert completely to a pre-*Osman* position. One commentator has argued that *Osman* has resulted in two benefits worthy of retention. First, one benefit of the 'courts' post-*Osman* approach is their readiness to scrutinize the various policy factors involved in the "fair, just and reasonable" test much more carefully than in the past'.[92] Second, the courts have been much more reluctant to strike out applications brought against public authorities. The benefit of this is that cases are decided based upon their specific facts, as opposed to a (potentially incorrect) presumption that a duty does, or does not, exist.[93]

---

88. Tom R Hickman, '"Uncertain Shadow": Throwing Light on the Right to a Court Under Art 6(1) ECHR' [2004] PL 122, 133 fn 65.

89. *Barrett v London Borough of Enfield* [2001] 2 AC 550 (HL) 558 (Lord Browne-Wilkinson).

90. *X v Bedfordshire County Council* [1995] 2 AC 633 (HL).   91. (2002) 34 EHRR 3, [100].

92. ACL Davies, 'The European Convention and Negligence Actions: "*Osman*" Reviewed' (2001) 117 LQR 521, 523.   93. ibid 524.

Breach of duty

Establishing a duty of care is only the first step in proving liability for negligence. The justification for the imposition of liability is that the duty has been breached. This will be determined by discussing the two questions that the court will ask once it has been established that a duty is owed.

1. What is the standard of care owed by the defendant?
2. Has he met that standard?

For the courts, these are questions of law and fact, and the test established to determine the existence of breach of duty is an objective, 'reasonable man' test.

The standard of care

The duties of care that we owe to others are not absolute: we are not required to guarantee the safety of others, nor are we required never to cause damage to others. The standard imposed is one of reasonableness, not perfection. This is derived from the often-quoted statement of Alderson B in *Blyth v Birmingham Waterworks Co*.[94]

> Negligence is the omission to do something which a reasonable man, guided upon those considerations which ordinarily regulate the conduct of human affairs, would do, or doing something which the prudent and reasonable man would not do.[95]

So, who is the 'reasonable man'? Put simply, he is an ordinary citizen or, according to Greer LJ: ' "the man in the street," or "the man in the Clapham omnibus," or "the man who takes the magazines at home, and in the evening pushes the lawn mower in his shirt sleeves".'[96] It is apparent, therefore, that the standard imposed is an objective one. Accordingly, it is not a defence for the defendant to claim that he did his best or that he honestly believed that his actions were not negligent. In this sense, it is 'an impersonal test. It eliminates the personal equation and is independent of the idiosyncrasies of the particular person whose conduct is in question.'[97] This is the case even where those idiosyncrasies contribute towards the alleged negligence, as the following case demonstrates.

 Nettleship v Weston [1971] 2 QB 691 (CA)[98]

FACTS: The claimant, an experienced driver (but not a driving instructor), agreed to provide driving lessons to the defendant. On her third lesson, the defendant panicked and hit a lamp-post. Although the car was moving at walking pace when it collided with the lamp-post, the claimant suffered a broken kneecap. A duty of care was easily established and the claimant had to show that this duty was breached.

---

94. (1856) 11 Ex 781 (Ex).   95. ibid 784.
96. *Hall v Brooklands Auto Racing Club* [1933] 1 KB 205 (CA) 224.
97. *Glasgow Corporation v Muir* [1943] AC 448 (HL) 457 (Lord Macmillan).
98. See also *Roberts v Ramsbottom* [1980] 1 WLR 823 (QB).

> **HELD:** The claimant succeeded. The Court of Appeal held that the fact that the defendant was a learner driver was irrelevant. Lord Denning MR stated: 'The learner driver may be doing his best, but his incompetent best is not good enough. He must drive in as good a manner as a driver of skill, experience and care.'[99]

The decision in *Nettleship* may appear harsh, but it can be justified. Oliver Wendell Holmes Jr, regarded by many as one of the finest justices ever to sit in the US Supreme Court, stated that:

> The standards of the law are standards of general application. The law takes no account of the infinite varieties of temperament, intellect, and education which make the internal character of a given act so different in different men…[W]hen men live in society, a certain average of conduct, a sacrifice of individual peculiarities going beyond a certain point, is necessary to the general welfare. If, for instance, a man is born hasty and awkward, is always having accidents and hurting himself or his neighbors, no doubt his congenital defects will be allowed for in the courts of Heaven, but his slips are no less troublesome to his neighbors than if they sprang from guilty neglect. His neighbors accordingly require him, at his proper peril, to come up to their standard, and the courts which they establish decline to take his personal equation into account.[100]

The courts have, however, acknowledged that, in certain circumstances, a completely objective approach may lead to injustice. Accordingly, in a number of specific instances, the courts will allow an element of subjectivity into their deliberations.

Children

It would clearly be unfair to apply an objective reasonable man test to the actions of a child, because children cannot be expected to meet the same standard of care as adults. The law still imposes an objective standard, but the standard in most cases is that of a reasonable and prudent child of the same age as the defendant.

 Orchard v Lee [2009] EWCA Civ 295

FACTS: The defendant (a 13-year-old child) was playing tag with another child in the courtyard of a school. Whilst playing the game, the defendant ran backwards and collided with the claimant (a lunchtime assistant who worked at the school). The back of the defendant's head collided with the claimant's cheek, causing quite serious injuries. The claimant commenced proceedings. At first instance, the claim failed and the claimant appealed.

HELD: The appeal was dismissed. Aikens LJ stated that:

> the question is whether a reasonable 13 year old boy, in the situation that [the defendant] was in, would have anticipated that some significant personal injury would result from his actions in playing tag as he did…A reasonable 13 year old boy in that position would not have regarded such an injury as being sufficiently probable to lead him to anticipate it. Therefore [the defendant] did not fall below the standard of care required of him.[101]

---

99. [1971] 2 QB 691 (CA) 699.
100. Oliver Wendell Holmes Jr, *The Common Law* (The Lawbook Exchange 2004) 108.
101. [2009] EWCA Civ 295, [2009] PIQR P16 [24].

Mental and physical disability or incapacity

The courts will take into account the physical and mental factors that may have contributed towards the defendant's negligence.

 Mansfield v Weetabix Ltd [1998] 1 WLR 1263 (CA)

FACTS: A lorry driver employed by the defendant was unaware that he was suffering from a malignant insulinoma. The effect of this was to starve his brain of glucose and oxygen, which resulted in a gradual loss of consciousness. In the course of a 40-mile journey, he was involved in a series of minor accidents. He failed to negotiate a bend in the road properly and crashed into the claimant's shop.

HELD: The Court of Appeal held that the applicable standard was that which was to be expected of 'a reasonably competent driver unaware that he is or may be suffering from a condition that impairs his ability to drive'.[102] Applying this, the Court held that the defendant was not negligent; the crash was not his fault and there was therefore no liability.

Skill or expertise

In relation to children and physical or mental disability, the introduction of an element of subjectivity serves to lower the standard of care. However, it may be the case that a characteristic of the defendant demands the raising of the standard of care, such as where the defendant has some special skill or expertise that 'the man in the Clapham Omnibus' would not normally possess.

 Bolam v Friern Hospital Management Committee [1957] 1 WLR 582 (QB)

FACTS: The claimant was a voluntary patient at the defendant's mental hospital. The claimant was undergoing electroconvulsive therapy (ECT), which involved passing an electric current through the brain. If a muscle relaxant was not administered, the shocks could be accompanied by violent spasms. In accordance with normal practice, the ECT therapy was administered without a muscle relaxant. The claimant convulsed and fractured a bone in his hip. The claimant sued.

HELD: McNair J stated:

[W]here you get a situation which involves the use of some special skill or competence, then the test as to whether there has been negligence or not is not the test of the man on the top of a Clapham omnibus, because he has not got this special skill. The test is the standard of the ordinary skilled man exercising and professing to have that special skill. A man need not possess the highest expert skill; it is well established law that it is sufficient if he exercises the ordinary skill of an ordinary competent man exercising that particular art.[103]

Applying this, the defendant was not liable, because it was common practice to administer ECT without the use of a muscle relaxant.

---

102. [1998] 1 WLR 1263 (CA) 1268 (Legatt LJ).   103. [1957] 1 WLR 582 (QB) 586.

The application of the '*Bolam* test' can be problematic where the defendant is highly specialized. For example, if a patient is alleging negligence against an oncologist (a doctor who specializes in diagnosing and treating cancer), is the defendant to be judged by the standard of a reasonable doctor, or is he to be judged by the standard of a reasonable oncologist? The following case provided the answer.

Wilsher v Essex Area Health Authority [1988] AC 1074 (HL)

FACTS: The claimant was a baby, born at the defendant's hospital. He was born three months' premature and was placed in a special baby care unit. The most significant problem faced by premature babies is that their underdeveloped lungs cannot take in enough oxygen, making death through brain damage a serious threat. To combat this, the claimant's oxygen supply was increased—but due to a junior doctor inserting the catheter into the wrong vein, the claimant was given too much oxygen and he developed retrolental fibroplasia, which rendered him completely blind in one eye and seriously impaired the vision in his other eye. The claimant sued the defendant.

HELD: It was irrelevant that the doctor in question was a junior doctor. No allowance would be made for inexperience. The relevant standard of care is not based upon the individual defendant, but rather the post that he holds. This would indicate that the doctor was negligent, but the House held that there was no liability on causation grounds.

 See Andrew Grubb, 'Causation and Medical Negligence' (1988) 47 CLJ 329

Accordingly, where the defendant is a professional or has a special skill, the standard of care is that of the reasonably competent person occupying the same post, or carrying out the same function, as the defendant. However, are the courts qualified to determine the liability of such persons? The *Bolam* test stated that a defendant would not be negligent where his actions were considered appropriate by a body of competent persons exercising the same function as the defendant. Referring specifically to medical negligence cases, Lord Scarman has stated that 'the law imposes the duty of care; but the standard of care is a matter of medical judgment'.[104] This statement would seem to indicate that the courts have abdicated determination of the standard of care to the professionals—a sentiment echoed by several commentators who contend that the courts have 'elevated to the status of an unquestionable proposition of law…that professional practice will *not* be reviewed by the courts'.[105]

Thankfully, more recent decisions have indicated that professional practice will be reviewed by the courts.

Bolitho v City and Hackney Health Authority [1998] AC 232 (HL)

FACTS: A two-year-old child was admitted to the defendant's hospital suffering from breathing difficulties. The following day, he suffered two episodes of respiratory difficulty. On both occasions, a doctor was called to attend, but did not, and the child apparently

---

104. *Sidaway v Board of Governors of Bethlehem Royal Hospital* [1985] AC 871 (HL) 881.
105. Ian Kennedy and Andrew Grubb, *Medical Law: Text with Materials* (2nd edn, Butterworths 1994).

recovered after both attacks. Half an hour after the second attack, he suffered acute respiratory failure, which resulted in cardiac arrest. The child suffered brain damage and later died. The claimants (the child's parents) alleged that the doctor should have attended the child and that he should have been intubated (a procedure that opens the airways) following the second episode. Medical evidence submitted was inconclusive: five of the eight expert witnesses called thought that intubation was appropriate; three thought that it was inappropriate. Applying *Bolam*, the Court of Appeal upheld the trial judge's decision that, because a body of medical opinion thought that intubation was inappropriate, the defendant was not liable for the child's death. The claimants appealed.

HELD: The appeal was dismissed by the House of Lords. However, Lord Browne-Wilkinson stated:

> The court is not bound to hold that a defendant doctor escapes liability for negligent treatment or diagnosis just because he leads evidence from a number of medical experts who are genuinely of the opinion that the defendant's treatment or diagnosis accorded with sound medical practice...[T]he court has to be satisfied that the exponents of the body of opinion relied upon can demonstrate that such an opinion has a logical basis...in cases of diagnosis and treatment there are cases where, despite a body of professional opinion sanctioning the defendant's conduct, the defendant can properly be held liable for negligence...In the vast majority of cases the fact that distinguished experts in the field are of a particular opinion will demonstrate the reasonableness of that opinion...But if, in a rare case, it can be demonstrated that the professional opinion is not capable of withstanding logical analysis, a judge is entitled to hold that the body of opinion is not reasonable or responsible.[106]

As the following case demonstrates, the level of scientific or expert knowledge at the time of the alleged breach of duty can have a significant impact upon a case.

 ### *Roe v Minister of Health* [1954] 2 QB 66 (CA)

FACTS: Roe (the claimant) was admitted to hospital for a minor operation. An anaesthetist employed by the defendant would administer an anaesthetic that was contained in a glass ampoule that was, in turn, kept in a phenol solution. To ensure that no phenol leaked into the anaesthetic, the anaesthetist inspected the ampoule for cracks. Not finding any, he injected the anaesthetic into Roe's spine. After the operation, Roe developed spastic paraplegia, which rendered him permanently paralysed from the waist down. The paraplegia had been caused by phenol seeping through invisible cracks in the ampoule into the anaesthetic. Administering a coloured agent to the phenol could have revealed the presence of invisible cracks.

HELD: The Court of Appeal held that the anaesthetist had not acted negligently. The operation took place in 1947, yet the risk of 'invisible cracks' was not made known to the medical profession until 1951. Accordingly, a reasonable man in the anaesthetist's position would not have been aware of the danger and so could not be held to have breached his duty.

---

106. [1998] AC 232 (HL) 241, 243.

The defendant's circumstances

The courts have acknowledged that whilst the standard to be met is that of the reasonable man, what is reasonable may depend upon the circumstances facing the defendant. For example, conduct that normally would be regarded as unreasonable may be regarded as reasonable in an emergency situation.[107] Accordingly, the standard to be applied is that of the reasonable man in the defendant's position.

 Harris v Perry [2008] EWCA Civ 907

FACTS: Two parents (the defendants) hired a bouncy castle and a bungee run for their triplets' tenth birthday party. The mother was supervising a number of children on the bouncy castle. At one stage, she went to help at the bungee run and turned her back on the bouncy castle. One child (who was older and larger than the other children) performed a somersault and his foot struck another child (the claimant) on the head, causing his skull to fracture, and leaving him with permanent cognitive and behavioural difficulties. The claimant alleged that the defendants had breached their duty of care. In particular, he drew attention to the bouncy castle hire agreement, which stated that children of different sizes should not play on the bouncy castle and that it should be supervised at all times.

HELD: The defendants had not breached their duty of care. They were required to take such care as a reasonably careful parent would take for the safety of his child of the claimant's age playing on a bouncy castle. A reasonably careful parent could foresee that boisterous children playing on a bouncy castle would run the risk of injury, but a reasonable parent would not foresee the severity of such injury. The standard of care requires parents to protect children from foreseeable harm and the injuries suffered by the claimant were not foreseeable. In relation to the precautions stated in the hire agreement, the Court said that no significance should be attached to them. Instead, the Court should:

> identify the standard of care required in the circumstances of this case on the basis of the facts of which the defendant knew or ought to have known. These could not include the contents of documents that the defendant neither saw nor ought to have seen.[108]

Factors determining breach of duty

In the US case of *United States v Carroll Towing Co*,[109] Learned Hand J established a formula to determine the existence of breach of duty—namely, $B < PL$, where B represented the cost of the precautions needed to eliminate the risk of injury, P represented the probability of injury, and L represented the seriousness of the likely loss. Whilst English courts have not adopted the 'Learned Hand formula' itself, the factors identified within it have been adopted by the courts and added to, resulting in a number of factors that the court will take into account when determining whether the duty has been breached.

Likelihood of injury

The courts will attempt to determine the extent to which injury was likely as a result of the defendant's actions. It follows that the more foreseeable the injury, the more

---

107. *Jones v Boyce* (1816) 171 ER 540.
108. [2008] EWCA Civ 907, [2009] 1 WLR 19 [36] (Lord Phillips CJ).   109. 159 F 2d 169 (1947).

the law will expect of a defendant. Two contrasting cases with similar facts demonstrate this approach in practice.

 Bolton v Stone [1951] AC 850 (HL)

FACTS: The claimant was standing outside her house, which was adjacent to a cricket ground. A cricket ball cleared the 17-foot-high fence surrounding the ground and hit the claimant, causing her injury. Evidence indicated that on only six occasions in the previous thirty years had a ball left the cricket ground and that the claimant was the first person actually to be hit by a ball. The claimant contended that the defendant should have done more to guard against the possibility of a ball leaving the cricket ground.

HELD: The House of Lords held that the defendant was not liable. Although the risk of a ball leaving the ground was foreseeable, the risk was so small that a reasonable person would not have anticipated it.

 Miller v Jackson [1977] QB 966 (CA)

FACTS: As in *Bolton*, the claimants owned a house adjacent to a cricket ground. A ball did not hit the claimant, but balls did strike the claimants' property, causing damage. Further, the claimants alleged that the fear of a ball hitting their property or themselves caused them to become extremely apprehensive of danger, resulting in a loss of enjoyment of their property. Evidence indicated that, in the previous season alone, a ball had entered their garden five times.

HELD: As the risk was much greater and more foreseeable than in *Bolton*, the Court of Appeal held that the defendant was liable in negligence for damage caused by balls entering the claimants' property.

Seriousness of injury

If the court is of the opinion that injury is likely and foreseeable, it will then fall to it to determine how serious that injury is likely to be. The greater the potential injury, the greater the likelihood that the defendant was negligent, and the greater will be the steps required to prevent against such injury. As Singleton LJ stated: 'The law expects of a man a great deal more care in carrying a pound of dynamite than a pound of butter.'[110]

 Paris v Stepney Borough Council [1951] AC 367 (HL)

FACTS: The claimant was employed as a mechanic at the defendant's garage. The claimant only had one eye and the defendant was aware of this. Whilst striking a bolt with a hammer, a metal chip flew off and struck him in his good eye, blinding him completely. At the time of

110. *Beckett v Newalls Insulation Co Ltd* [1953] 1 WLR 8 (CA) 16.

the injury, he was not wearing goggles, and argued that his employer was negligent in failing to require him to wear, and to provide him with, a pair of goggles. The defendant argued that it was not normal practice to provide its mechanics with goggles.

HELD: The House of Lords held that the defendant was liable. Whilst failing to provide safety goggles to a normal employee might not constitute a breach of duty, it does constitute a breach of duty where the claimant has only one good eye and would accordingly suffer greater injury if his good eye were lost. This warranted an increase in the level of care owed to him and the defendant should have taken extra precautions—namely, to provide goggles.

COMMENT: Initially, this may appear to be an application of the 'eggshell skull' rule that is discussed later in this chapter. However it is not, because the application of the 'eggshell skull' rule is not determined by reasonable foreseeability, whereas in this case, reasonable foreseeability was clearly a determining factor. Further, because the 'eggshell skull' rule is a principle of remoteness, it only comes into effect once breach of duty has been established.

 The eggshell skull rule is discussed at p 413

Cost of prevention

The greater the risk of damage, the greater the precautions that the court will require the defendant to take, even if the cost of such precautions is considerable. However, where the cost of precautions is out of proportion to the magnitude of the risk, then the courts will not hold that the duty has been breached.

 Latimer v AEC Ltd [1953] AC 643 (HL)

FACTS: An unusually heavy rainstorm flooded the defendant's factory. The defendant did all that it could to eliminate the effects of the flooding, but some areas of the flooring were still flooded and slippery. The claimant (an employee of the defendant) slipped and injured his ankle. He sued the defendant, alleging that it should have shut the factory down until it was completely safe.

HELD: His claim failed. The House of Lords held that the defendant had done all that it could reasonably do. The majority of the factory floor was rendered safe, so the risk of injury was minimal. Accordingly, the cost of shutting the factory down would have been wholly out of proportion to the risk involved.

What, however, is the situation where the cost of prevention is not disproportionate, but the defendant lacks the resources to take the necessary precautions? In such a case, it is clear that the activity in question that is generating the risk of injury should not be engaged in (that is, that lack of resources will not be an excuse if injury ensues because the defendant lacked the resources to make an act reasonably safe).[111] It would appear, however, that this rule is relaxed in the case of public authorities.

Knight v Home Office [1990] 3 All ER 237 (QB)

FACTS: A patient in a prison mental hospital was placed on 'suicide watch' and observed every 15 minutes. Despite this, he still managed to kill himself. His widow claimed against the prison.

---

111. *Latimer v AEC Ltd* [1953] AC 643 (HL).

HELD: The High Court acknowledged that had the medical facility in question been a National Health Service facility, it is likely that the defendant's conduct would have amounted to a breach of duty. However, Pill J (as he then was) stated that 'the resources available for the public service are limited'.[112] Given this, it was held that checking on the patient every 15 minutes was a reasonable precaution.

Usefulness of the defendant's conduct

An act that causes injury to another might not be regarded as a breach of duty if the act is of significant benefit to the public, or even to the claimant. The court has to balance the risk of injury with the usefulness of the act in question, of which the following case provides a clear example.

 Watt v Hertfordshire County Council [1954] 1 WLR 835 (CA)

FACTS: The claimant was an on-duty fireman. An emergency arose whereby a woman was trapped under a car and heavy-lifting equipment would be needed to rescue her. Only one fire engine was equipped to carry heavy-lifting equipment, but it was on call at another emergency. Accordingly, the equipment was loaded onto a lorry, which lacked the means to secure the equipment adequately. On the way to the trapped woman, the driver was forced to brake suddenly. The lifting equipment slid along the lorry's floor and seriously injured the claimant's ankle. He sued his employer.

HELD: The employer was not liable. The fire brigade was under a duty to provide proper equipment and to take reasonable care not to expose its firemen to unreasonable risks. However the saving of life and limb justifies exposing its firemen to abnormal risk, and so there was no liability.

COMMENT: Initially, it would seem correct that firemen be required to expose themselves to risk—but is it fair that firemen (and others who work for the emergency services) are less likely to recover compensation for work-related injuries than those in other occupations? Such concerns have been raised. In *King v Sussex Ambulance Service Ltd*,[113] Buxton LJ argued that if the public interest compels those who work for the emergency services to offer aid, should it not also be regarded as in the public interest to compensate those who are foreseeably injured when protecting the public?[114] Despite these comments, the principle in *Watt* has now been given statutory force by s 1 of the Compensation Act 2006.

Proof of breach of duty

The factors discussed so far help the court to establish the standard of care owed by the defendant. It is for the claimant to prove, on the balance of probabilities, that the defendant breached his duty of care (that is, that he has fallen below the standard of care). In establishing this, the claimant is aided by:

- the application of the maxim *res ipsa loquitur*; and
- the Civil Evidence Act 1968.

---

112. [1990] 3 All ER 237 (QB) 243.   113. [2002] EWCA Civ 953, [2002] ICT 1413.
114. ibid [47].

Res ipsa loquitur

The claimant's task of establishing breach of duty may be rendered easier in cases in which the maxim *res ipsa loquitur* ('the thing speaks for itself') can be applied. In cases in which it applies, the defendant's breach of duty will be inferred. The classic example and exposition of the maxim can be seen in the following case.

Scott v London and St Katherine's Dock Co (1865) 3 H & C 596 (Ex)

FACTS: Six bags of sugar fell from the defendant's warehouse onto the claimant, causing him injury. The claimant could not explain how the sugar fell on him, so the trial judge directed the jury to dismiss his claim, which it did. The claimant appealed.

HELD: His appeal was allowed and a retrial was ordered. Erle CJ stated:

> There must be reasonable evidence of negligence. But where the thing is shown to be under the management of the defendant or his servants, and the accident is such as in the ordinary course of things does not happen if those who have the management use proper care, it affords reasonable evidence, in the absence of explanation by the defendants, that the accident arose from want of care.[115]

Accordingly, where the maxim applies, a presumption of negligence is inferred. However, *res ipsa loquitur* does not reverse the burden of proof. The burden of proof is still placed upon the claimant—*res ipsa loquitur* merely assists him in discharging that burden of proof.[116]

In order for *res ipsa loquitur* to apply, three requirements must be met. First, the incident causing the claimant's damage is one that would not normally occur if proper care were being taken. *Scott* (discussed above) is a clear example of this: if proper care is taken, bags of sugar do not normally fall from warehouses. Other examples of incidents that were held not to occur if proper care had been taken include:

- the damaging of teeth following the finding of a stone in a bun;[117]
- a hospital patient dying following an operation and the autopsy discovering a surgical swab inside the deceased's body.[118]

Second, there must be no complete explanation for the incident that causes the claimant's loss. If, based on the evidence, the court can discern how and why the incident occurred, there is no scope for inferring a breach of duty; the breach of duty will be established regardless. Thus, where a tyre on a bus bursts, causing the bus to career down an embankment, and it was proven that the tyre defect was the result of the defendant's negligent tyre inspection system, *res ipsa loquitur* will not be needed to establish the defendant's breach of duty.[119] Where only a partial explanation for the incident can be provided, *res ipsa loquitur* may still be used by the claimant to aid his case.

---

115. (1865) 3 H & C 596 (Ex) 601.   116. *Ng Chun Pui v Lee Chuen Tat* [1988] RTR 298 (PC).
117. *Chapronière v Mason* (1905) 21 TLR 633 (CA).   118. *Mahon v Osborne* [1939] 2 KB 14 (CA).
119. *Barkway v South Wales Transport Co Ltd* [1950] AC 185 (HL).

Third, the cause of the incident must have been under the defendant's control, or the control of those for whom the defendant is responsible. If it can be demonstrated that the cause of the incident could be attributable to someone else, *res ipsa loquitur* cannot be used, as the following contrasting examples demonstrate.

 Res ipsa loquitur and train doors

A four-year-old child falls through the door of a train, seven miles after the last station stop. *Res ipsa loquitur* will not apply, because the train could have been opened by any of the passengers in the intervening seven miles. Accordingly, the defendant lacks sufficient control of the door.[120]

Conversely, where a claimant falls through a train door moments after it leaves the train station, *res ipsa loquitur* could apply, because the door was very recently under the control of the defendant and was much more unlikely to have been interfered with.[121]

The Civil Evidence Act 1968

Whereas the maxim *res ipsa loquitur* will make proving negligence considerably easier for the claimant, s 11 of the Civil Evidence Act 1968 completely relieves the claimant of the burden of proof in certain cases. Section 11 provides that where a defendant has been convicted of a criminal offence and a civil action arises out of the same facts that led to the conviction, that conviction will be *prima facie* evidence of the defendant's civil liability. As it only constitutes *prima facie* proof, it is open for the defendant to adduce proof denying his civil liability. Put another way, s 11 creates a rebuttable presumption that a defendant who has been convicted of a criminal offence is also liable in civil proceedings in respect of any consequences that flow from that offence. Section 11 applies only to criminal convictions; acquittals cannot be adduced as evidence of innocence in subsequent civil proceedings.

Causation

In Chapter 12, it was noted that a claimant who had suffered damage due to the defendant's breach of contract would need to establish a causal link between the breach and the damage suffered. The same rule applies in tort: even when the duty of care has been breached, the claimant must still show that the defendant's breach of duty caused, in fact and in law, the damage in question.

The requirement of causation (unlike the rules relating to remoteness discussed later) applies to all torts, not only negligence. As virtually all of the principles of causation were laid down in negligence cases, it is appropriate to discuss the issue here.

---

120. *Easson v London & North Eastern Railway* [1944] 1 KB 421 (CA).
121. *Gee v Metropolitan Railway* (1873) LR 8 QB 161 (Ex).

The 'but for' test

A negligence case may involve a mass of facts, some relevant to determining causation, some irrelevant. The courts screen out the irrelevant facts by applying what is known as the 'but for' test. This test basically asks whether the claimant would have suffered the loss 'but for' the defendant's breach of duty. If the claimant is to succeed, the answer must be 'no'. If the answer is 'yes', this would mean that the loss would have happened anyway and the claim will fail. An application of the test can be seen in the following case.

McWilliams v Sir William Arrol & Co Ltd [1962] 1 All ER 623 (HL)[122]

FACTS: McWilliams was a steel erector, who fell 70 feet to his death. This would have been avoided if he had been wearing a safety harness, but his employer (the defendant) had not provided him with one. Witness testimony from his work colleagues indicated, however, that even if a harness had been provided, McWilliams would not have worn it.

HELD: The defendant had been negligent in failing to provide a harness, but the House of Lords held that McWilliams' widow could not recover damages, because the defendant's breach had not caused McWilliams' death: had it provided a harness, McWilliams probably would not have worn it and so he would have fallen anyway.

In *McWilliams*, the House could not be certain that McWilliams would not have worn the harness if provided—but the evidence clearly indicated that he would most likely not have worn a harness. So what is the situation if the evidence is not so helpful? What is the court to do if the actions of the claimant are much more uncertain? Such a situation faced the House of Lords in the following case.

Chester v Afshar [2004] UKHL 41

FACTS: The claimant complained of back pain and was advised by the defendant neurosurgeon to undergo a spinal surgical procedure. The defendant failed to inform the claimant that, even if the operation was performed perfectly, there was still a 1–2 per cent chance that she could develop cauda equina syndrome (a neurological condition affecting all motor ability below the spinal cord). The surgery was performed competently, but the claimant developed the syndrome. She alleged the defendant's failure to warn her of the risk amounted to negligence. Evidence indicated that had the claimant been warned of the risk, she would not have undertaken the surgery immediately, but would have sought further advice.

HELD: The claimant could obtain compensation. Lord Steyn stated that the 'but for' test had been satisfied: had she undergone the surgery at a later date, the risk would still only have been 1–2 per cent; had she not had the surgery at all, the risk would be 0 per cent. Either way, the defendant's breach could be argued to have caused the loss. However, this was not the reason behind the House's decision. The House based its decision on public policy—namely, that if the claimant could not recover damages in this case, the surgeon's duty to disclose material information would be rendered impotent.

★ See Jane Stapleton, 'Occam's Razor Reveals an Orthodox Basis for *Chester v Afshar*' (2006) 122 LQR 426

---

122. See also *Barnett v Chelsea and Kensington Management Committee* [1969] 1 QB 428 (QB).

In such uncertain cases, the standard of proof becomes important. The claimant will need to establish, on the balance of probabilities, that the defendant's negligence caused the claimant's loss.

Problematic applications of the 'but for' test

In many cases, the application of the 'but for' test will be unproblematic. In certain cases, however, the courts have struggled to apply the test in a consistent and accepted manner. In particular, the 'but for' test results in considerable problems where there are multiple causes for the defendant's loss, with such cases arising in one of three ways:

1. Concurrent multiple causes (several negligent causes occur at the same time).
2. Successive multiple causes (a negligent act causes loss and a second subsequent negligent act causes the same loss, or greater loss).
3. Cumulative multiple causes (where several negligent acts contribute over time to the claimant's loss, but it may be inconclusive which of the multiple negligent acts actually caused the loss).

Each will now be discussed.

Concurrent causes

Applying the 'but for' test is problematic where the claimant's loss was the result of concurrent (occurring at the same time) multiple acts of negligence. The problem is clearly demonstrated by the following Canadian case.

 Cook v Lewis [1952] 1 DLR 1 (Supreme Court of Canada)

FACTS: The two defendants were hunting. They both simultaneously fired their guns, but instead of hitting their intended target, one of them hit the claimant. As it was impossible to establish which of the two defendants had shot the claimant, the 'but for' test was useless.

HELD: The Canadian Supreme Court held that both defendants were liable. The onus of proof was on them to show that they had not been negligent. Neither of them was able to show this.

The following example demonstrates the problem with applying the 'but for' test to cases involving multiple concurrent causes.

 Causation and arson

Ricky negligently lights a fire. Half a mile away, Karl also negligently lights a fire. The two instances are unrelated. Both fires spread, merge, and burn down Steve's house. If we were to apply the 'but for' test, neither Ricky nor Karl would be liable. If we were to ask 'but for Ricky's negligence, would Steve have suffered loss?', the answer would be 'yes', because Karl's fire would still have probably caused the house to burn down, thereby rendering Ricky not liable. If we were to ask 'but for Karl's negligence, would Steve have suffered loss?', the answer would again be 'yes', rendering Karl not liable. Such a situation would clearly be unacceptable.

It has been argued that this is the major weakness of the 'but for' test—namely, that it assumes that only one negligent act brings about the claimant's loss.[123] Accordingly, where two unrelated acts of negligence cause the claimant's loss, the 'but for' test will not apply and instead the claimant is free to sue either one, or both, of the tortfeasors (therefore, liability is joint and several), but, obviously, will not be permitted to recover full damages twice. Therefore, in the above example, Steve could:

- sue Ricky for the full loss;
- sue Karl for the full loss; or
- sue Ricky for 50 per cent of the loss and Karl for 50 per cent of the loss (or a different percentage if the court were to think that Ricky or Karl was more to blame).[124]

It may be thought unfair that Steve could recover the full loss from one party only, given that both Ricky and Karl contributed to Steve's loss. To alleviate this, if Steve does claim the full loss from one party, that party may bring a claim against the other wrongdoer and seek a contribution from him.[125]

Successive causes

Where the negligent acts are successive (occurring one after the other), the application of the 'but for' test is more straightforward. If the negligent act of *B* causes *exactly the same loss* as the prior negligent act of *A*, then, applying the 'but for' test, *B* will not be liable because the rule is that the first cause in time is treated as the operative cause to the exclusion of others.

 Performance Cars Ltd v Abraham [1962] 1 QB 33 (CA)

FACTS: The first defendant negligently collided with the claimant's Rolls Royce, thereby requiring the front wing to be resprayed. Before the repairs could be performed, the second defendant also negligently collided with the Rolls Royce, also damaging the front wing, but caused no greater damage than the first collision.

HELD: 'But for' the second defendant's negligence, would the claimant have suffered loss? As the car already needed a respray, the answer is 'yes', and so the Court of Appeal held that the second defendant was not liable for the cost of the respray.

 See Alec Samuels, 'Scratching a Rolls: Consecutive Tortfeasors' Liability for Damages' (1962) 25 MLR 345

However, what would the situation be if the second act of negligence were to cause *greater* damage than the first? The following case demonstrates the courts' approach.

 Baker v Willoughby [1970] AC 467 (HL)

FACTS: In 1964, the claimant was crossing the road when the defendant negligently ran him over in his car, thereby causing injury to the claimant's left leg and reducing his earning capacity. The claimant sued the defendant but, in 1967, before the case reached court, the

---

123. HLA Hart and Tony Honoré, *Causation in the Law* (2nd edn, OUP 1985) 113.
124. *Holtby v Brigham & Cowan (Hull) Ltd* [2000] 3 All ER 421 (CA).
125. Civil Liability (Contribution) Act 1978, ss 1 and 2.

claimant was shot in his left leg during an armed robbery, and his leg had to be amputated. The defendant argued that his liability only extended up until the time of the robbery (that is, between 1964 and 1967). After that time, the original injury no longer existed, because the claimant's leg was removed, and so the defendant contended that he should not be liable for any loss of earnings following that date.

HELD: The second injury would not obliterate the effects of the first. Lord Reid treated the two torts as examples of concurrent causes (even though they were factually successive). Accordingly, the House awarded damages on the basis that the defendant's negligence ensured that the claimant had lost the use of his left leg for the rest of his life. This would include any loss of earning that occurred after the leg had been amputated.

COMMENT: The defendant's negligence only caused the claimant to lose the use of his left leg for three years. Even if the defendant had not been negligent, the claimant would still have lost his leg in 1967. Therefore, why did the House quantify damages based on the defendant losing the use of his leg for the rest of his life? It is clear that the House was concerned about under-compensating the claimant. Had it limited damages up to the date of the shooting, the claimant could not have recovered damages for the loss of earnings occurring after 1967. Even if the armed robbers were caught, the claimant could not sue them, because his leg was already useless at the time that he was shot. Further, the defendant suffered no extra loss due to the amputation. Had the shooting not occurred, he would still have been liable for any loss of earnings occurring after the date of the first injury.

In *Baker*, the House refused to recognize that the effects of the first tort were overtaken by the second tort. Shortly after the decision in *Baker*, a notable query amongst academics[126] was whether the court would take the same approach if the original loss were overtaken by a non-tortious act. The answer came in the following case.

 ***Jobling v Associated Dairies Ltd* [1982] AC 794 (HL)**

FACTS: In 1973, the claimant suffered an injury to his back due to the defendant's negligence. This injury reduced the claimant's earning capacity by 50 per cent—something that he intended to claim for in the upcoming litigation. However, in 1976, before the trial could take place, the claimant was found to be suffering from a spinal disease called myelapothy—a condition that would render him totally unfit for work by the end of 1976.

HELD: The House of Lords held that the defendant was only liable for the losses caused between 1973 and 1976.

COMMENT: In *Baker*, the House's decision was clearly intended to avoid the claimant being under-compensated for his loss. In *Jobling*, the House was keen to avoid over-compensating the claimant. So, where does this leave *Baker*? Although the House in *Jobling* was critical of the reasoning employed in *Baker*, it did appear to believe that the actual result was 'acceptable on its own facts'.[127] It would appear therefore that the courts do distinguish between cases involving successive torts and cases in which the original loss is overtaken by a neutral, non-tortious event.

Figure 14.1 explains the effect of the above two cases.

---

126. See e.g. H McGregor, 'Variations on an Enigma' (1970) 33 MLR 378, 382.
127. [1982] AC 794 (HL) 809 (Lord Edmund-Davies).

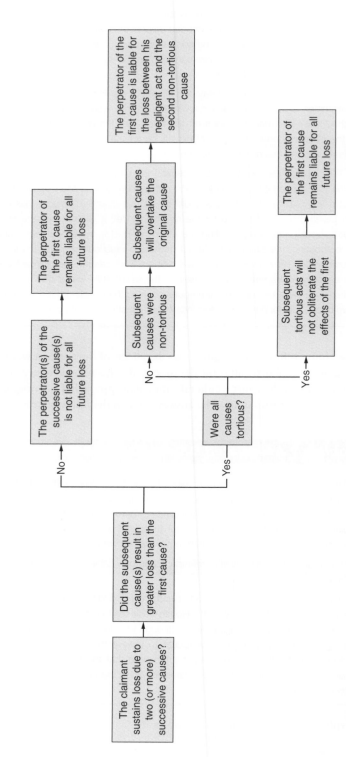

FIGURE 14.1 Successive causes

Acts that materially increase risk

The claimant's loss may have been caused by a number of cumulative causes. In some cases, all of the causes are tortious; in other cases, there is a mixture between tortious and non-tortious causes. A common thread amongst many of these cases is that it is impossible to state with certainty which one of the causes actually caused the loss in question. In such a case, the court has recognized that the 'but for' test is insufficient and will instead adopt a test based on which cause 'materially contributed' to the loss in question. Virtually all of the key cases in this area have occurred in relation to the claimant's ability to claim for negligent exposure to asbestos, but the case that established the 'material contribution' test did not concern an asbestos-related condition; rather, it related to the contraction of dermatitis.

 McGhee v National Coal Board [1973] 1 WLR 1 (HL)

FACTS: The claimant worked in the defendant's brick kilns. Conditions were extremely dusty, but the defendant failed to provide on-site facilities to wash away the brick dust. Accordingly, the claimant was unable to remove the dust until he got home, thereby prolonging his exposure. He contracted dermatitis and sued the defendant. The medical evidence could not, however, establish whether the dermatitis was caused by the prolonged exposure to brick dust (due to a lack of washing facilities), or whether it was caused by the innocent exposure to brick dust that was part of his everyday job.

HELD: The House of Lords found for the claimant. Whilst it could not be established that the prolonged exposure caused the dermatitis, it could be established that the defendant's negligence materially contributed to an increase in the risk of contracting dermatitis. The material contribution to the increased risk could be regarded as a material contribution towards the claimant's loss.

⭐ See GR Rubin, 'Employer's Breach of Duty and Cause of Accident' (1973) 2 ILJ 96

The evidential uncertainty in *McGhee* was considerable, in that the cause of the dermatitis could not be conclusively established. However, the evidential uncertainty in the following case was even more pronounced.

 Fairchild v Glenhaven Funeral Services Ltd [2002] UKHL 22

FACTS: The claimant contracted mesothelioma, an incurable form of cancer that is usually lethal within a year of diagnosis. It is caused by asbestos exposure. Unlike asbestosis, however, it is not caused by long-term exposure; it can be contracted through an encounter with a single fibre of asbestos and, once contracted, subsequent exposure will not exacerbate or accelerate the condition. The problem was that the claimant had been negligently exposed to asbestos whilst working for a number of different employers and it was impossible to determine which employer had negligently exposed him to the asbestos fibre that caused his cancer. Further, a number of his previous employers had since become insolvent and so could not be proceeded against.

HELD: The House of Lords held that the claimant could recover damages from any of the employers that were still solvent (the employers were jointly and severally liable).

COMMENT: In this case, injustice could not be avoided. Had the House ruled that the claimant could not recover damages, it would disadvantage persons who worked for multiple employers. By ruling in favour of the claimant, it ensures that an employer may be liable even if it did not cause the claimant's loss. This would be especially harsh on an employer that employed a claimant only briefly. Lord Nicholls freely admitted the House's dilemma and stated that its decision was a policy one aimed at securing justice:

> The unattractive consequence, that one of the [defendants] will be held liable for an injury he did not in fact inflict, is outweighed by the even less attractive alternative, that the innocent plaintiff should receive no recompense even though one of the negligent [defendants] injured him. It is this balance…which justifies a relaxation in the standard of causation required. Insistence on the normal standard of causation would work an injustice.[128]

The House in Fairchild stated that, in cases such as this, 'the court is applying a different and less stringent test'[129] than the 'but for' test, but the exact nature of this different test was never truly made clear. Further, the approach of the majority differed considerably. Lord Bingham laid down a specific six-part test. Lord Rodger also laid down a six-part test, but it was much more general and little more than an expanded account of the test established in McGhee. Lord Hoffmann's five-part test was different again. The House was clear in holding, however, that the decision in Fairchild was exceptional and, in many cases, the imposition of joint and several liability would not be suitable.

⭐ See Jonathan Morgan, 'Lost Causes in the House of Lords: *Fairchild v Glenhaven Funeral Services*' (2003) 66 MLR 277

The result of *Fairchild* is that, in relation to mesothelioma cases, the normal rules of causation do not apply and a more relaxed approach is taken. This relaxed approach to causation has become known as the '*Fairchild* exception' and was defined by Lord Phillips in a later case as:

> when a victim contracts mesothelioma each person who has, in breach of duty, been responsible for exposing the victim to a significant quantity of asbestos dust and thus creating a 'material increase in risk' of the victim contracting the disease will be held to be jointly and severally liable for causing the disease.[130]

It is clear that, in developing the *Fairchild* exception, the House of Lords was concerned about securing fairness and justice. Such concerns were also at the heart of the following case.

🔑 *Barker v Corus Group Ltd* [2006] UKHL 20

FACTS: Barker had died after contracting mesothelioma. He contracted it through being exposed to asbestos (i) while working for the defendant; (ii) while working for a company that had since become insolvent; and (iii) while self-employed. The claimant (Barker's widow) initiated a claim against the defendant. At first instance and in the Court of Appeal, it was held that the claimant could recover the full amount of damages from the defendant.

HELD: With one dissentient, the House of Lords reversed the decision of the Court of Appeal in part. Although the House upheld *Fairchild*, it stated that while each employer could be held liable for exposing the claimant to asbestos dust, even though it could not be proved to have caused the mesothelioma, the imposition of joint and several liability

---

128. [2002] UKHL 22, [2003] 1 AC 32 [39].   129. ibid [45] (Lord Nicholls).
130. *Sienkiewicz v Grief (UK) Ltd* [2011] UKSC 10, [2011] 2 AC 229 [1].

was unfair to defendants. Accordingly, it held that a person responsible for the exposure to asbestos could be liable only according to his relative degree of contribution to the cause of the claimant contracting mesothelioma. In other words, an individual defendant would only be liable for the extent that he contributed to the risk. Therefore, liability was several only and defendants would not be liable for the increase in risk contributed by other parties.

COMMENT: Whilst the House may have been of the opinion that several liability provided a fair compromise between the interests of the claimant and defendant, it was soon apparent that Parliament did not share its opinion. Shortly after the decision, s 3 of the Compensation Act 2006 reversed the decision of the House of Lords in *Barker* in relation to mesothelioma, by providing that the claimant can recover the full damages from any one defendant; ergo joint and several liability is restored. It must be emphasized, however, that s 3 applies only in relation to mesothelioma cases. In any other case, the principle in *Barker* will continue and the defendant will be liable only for the increase in the risk to which it contributed. Therefore, if *McGhee* were to be heard today, the owner of the brick kilns would be liable only for the increase in risk that his breach of duty caused.

See Adam Kramer, 'Smoothing the Rough Justice of the *Fairchild* Principle' (2006) 122 LQR 547

The scope of the *Fairchild* exception was discussed by the Supreme Court in the following case.

Sienkiewicz v Greif (UK) Ltd [2011] UKSC 10

FACTS: This case involved two consolidated appeals. The leading appeal concerned Mrs Costello, who had died of mesothelioma in 2006 (the case was brought by her daughter as administratrix of her Estate), after being exposed to asbestos whilst working in the defendant's factory. She had also been exposed to low levels of asbestos in the area around the defendant's factory. It was clear that the exposure in the factory was tortious, but the exposure in the area around the factory was not. Statistical evidence indicated that the exposure to asbestos that occurred in the factory increased her risk of contracting mesothelioma by only 18 per cent (in other words, the non–tortious exposure was much more likely to have caused the mesothelioma). The claimant sought compensation, seeking to rely on the *Fairchild* exception. The defendant argued that the *Fairchild* exception only applied in cases involving multiple employers, and therefore the 'but for' test should apply. The defendant went on to argue that the claimant would need to show that, on the balance of probabilities, the exposure from the factory caused Costello's mesothelioma, which would require the claimant to show that the tortious exposure doubled the risk.[131] As the tortious exposure only increased the risk by 18 per cent, the defendant argued the claimant could not establish this.

HELD: The seven-member Supreme Court unanimously rejected the defendant's argument and held that the claimant was entitled to compensation. The Court stated that the *Fairchild* exception was not limited to cases involving multiple employers and could, as was the case here, apply to cases involving a single employer. The Court also rejected the defendant's argument that the claimant needed to show that the tortious exposure doubled the risk. Lord Brown stated that 'any person who negligently or in breach of duty exposes another more than minimally to the inhalation of asbestos fibres will be liable.'[132] An 18 per cent risk is more than minimal and so liability was imposed.

---

131. This argument was taken from a ratio in *Novartis Grimsby Ltd v Cookson* [2007] EWCA Civ 1261, a case concerning a carcinoma and not mesothelioma.

132. [2011] UKSC 10, [2011] 2 AC 229 [175].

⭐ See Sandy Steel and David Ibbetson, 'More Grief on Uncertain Causation in Tort' (2011) 70 CLJ 451.

COMMENT: In some respects, the Court was careful to limit the scope of the case and to emphasize its exceptional nature. Several Justices noted that the *Fairchild* exception exists due to medical knowledge being unable to conclusively determine which asbestos fibre resulted in the mesothelioma (they referred this as the 'rock of uncertainty'), but that once medical knowledge removed this uncertainty, the *Fairchild* exception would not longer need to exist.[133] In other respects, the scope of the decision is unclear. For example, only one Justice (namely Lord Barker) stated that the principle in *Sienkiewicz* applied only to mesothelioma (although other Justices were wary of extending the principle to other cases).

The above cases concerned mesothelioma, which is a condition that can be contracted from exposure to one asbestos fibre. A more common condition is asbestosis, a serious lung disease that is caused by long-term exposure to asbestos. If the claimant suffering from asbestosis only worked for one employer, causation is unproblematic, but where he worked for several employers, all of whom negligently exposed the claimant to asbestos, it becomes extremely difficult to determine which employer 'caused' the asbestosis. In cases in which multiple negligent defendants successively and cumulatively contribute to the claimant's loss, the courts may be able to determine the extent that the defendant contributed towards the loss and apportion compensation accordingly.

Holtby v Brigham & Cowan (Hull) Ltd [2000] 3 All ER 421 (CA)

FACTS: Between 1942 and 1981, Holtby (the claimant) worked as a marine fitter—a job that exposed him to dangerous amounts of asbestos dust. He carried out work for the defendant and a number of other employers, none of which supplied him with any safety equipment. In 1996, he was diagnosed with asbestosis. He sued the defendant.

HELD: The Court of Appeal determined that had the defendant provided the claimant with breathing equipment, his asbestosis would have been 75 per cent less severe. As 75 per cent of his condition was due to the defendant, the Court required the defendant to pay compensation only for the damage caused by it. Accordingly, the Court ordered a 25 per cent reduction of the damages claimed by Holtby.

⭐ See Louise Gullifer, 'One Cause After Another' (2001) 117 LQR 403

Loss of a chance

If the claimant cannot establish that the defendant's tort materially contributed to his damage, there is an alternative argument. The claimant can argue that whilst the tort did not materially contribute to the damage itself, it did contribute to the loss of a chance to avoid that damage. Such an approach would avoid the 'all or nothing' outcome in which most of the cases discussed resulted, but the courts have been reluctant to take such an approach, as the following case demonstrates.[134]

---

133. See e.g. Lord Rodger at [142].
134. See also *Hotson v East Berkshire Area Health Authority* [1987] AC 750 (HL).

Gregg v Scott [2005] UKHL 2

FACTS: In 1994, the claimant discovered a lump under his arm and sought the advice of his GP (the defendant). The defendant diagnosed the lump as a benign lipoma and, accordingly, saw no need to refer the claimant to an oncologist. In 1995, the claimant moved home and registered with a new GP. Upon seeing the lump, the GP referred the claimant to an oncologist, who confirmed that the lump was a symptom of a malignant form of cancer known as non-Hodgkin's lymphoma. In 1996, it was discovered that the cancer had spread to his chest. Had the claimant been treated in 1994, he would have had a 42 per cent chance of surviving for ten years. The nine-month delay in diagnosing the cancer reduced this to 25 per cent and the claimant claimed for the loss of this chance.

HELD: The House of Lords dismissed the claimant's action. Immediate action would merely increase his chances of a cure (defined as living beyond ten years) to 42 per cent. It was therefore, more likely than not that even if treatment was received in 1994, the claimant would still have died within ten years. It therefore could not be established, on the balance of probabilities, that even if the claimant had received immediate treatment, he would have been cured.

COMMENT: The House was not completely dismissive to the possibility of awarding damages for the loss of a chance. Lord Phillips MR indicated that awarding damages for loss of a chance may be appropriate where the defendant's negligence leads to an 'adverse outcome'.[135] However, Lord Phillips was not convinced that the defendant's negligence had resulted in an adverse outcome. The fact that, when the case was heard in 2004, the claimant was still alive and had been in remission for six years could be taken as evidence that the defendant's negligence had not resulted in an adverse outcome for the claimant.

See Edwin Peel, 'Loss of a Chance Revisited: *Gregg v Scott*' (2003) 66 MLR 623

Despite the above case, the courts are willing to award compensation for loss of a chance in limited circumstances—namely, where the claimant's loss depends on the hypothetical action of a third party.

 Allied Maples Group Ltd v Simmons & Simmons [1995] 1 WLR 1602 (CA)

FACTS: The defendant firm of solicitors advised the claimant to purchase several businesses from a third party. The proposed contract effecting the purchase contained a term that provided that the businesses were not subject to any outstanding liabilities, but this term was absent from the final contract. The claimant purchased the businesses and, due to the term being absent, it became liable for the losses of one of the businesses. The claimant alleged that the defendant's negligence in omitting the term had deprived it of the chance to avoid the loss.

HELD: The Court of Appeal held that the claimant could recover compensation for the loss of the chance to avoid the loss.

COMMENT: Why the Court was willing to compensate the claimant for the loss of a chance is not strictly clear. The Court favoured the view that compensation for loss of a chance can be recovered where the claimant's loss depends upon the acts of a third party. However, the weight of academic opinion appears to favour the view that the courts are more open to recovery for loss of a chance in cases involving economic loss. Certainly all of the cases in

See Thomas Church, 'Where Causation Ends and Quantification Begins' (1996) 55 CLJ 187

which compensation for loss of a chance has been recovered concern economic loss[136]— but this would appear to be out of line with the general view that physical injury is more deserving of compensation than economic loss.

Intervening acts or events

The discussion thus far has focused on whether the defendant's breach of duty was the factual cause of the claimant's loss. The claimant will also need to establish that the defendant's breach of duty was the cause in law of the claimant's loss. The defendant may commit a tortious act, but before the claimant suffers loss, an event may occur that affects—or even exacerbates—the loss that the claimant subsequently suffers. The question for the court is whether the defendant is still liable for the loss, or whether the intervening act breaks the chain of causation, thereby relieving the defendant of liability.

➡ *novus actus interveniens*: 'new intervening act'

An act that breaks the chain of causation is known as a *novus actus interveniens*. Such acts fall into one of three well-established categories. The first category of *novus* concerns natural events (for example, storms, lightning, earthquakes, etc). In relation to such events, the courts have to strike a delicate balance. On the one hand, it would seem unfair to require a defendant to compensate the claimant for damage the immediate cause of which is a natural event; on the other hand, if the courts regard such events as breaking the chain of causation, it will leave the claimant without any source of redress.

 Carslogie Steamship Co v Royal Norwegian Government [1952] AC 292 (HL)

FACTS: The claimant's ship was damaged in a collision with the defendant's ship that was caused by the defendant's negligence. The claimant's ship altered course towards a port where it could obtain repairs—but on the way to port, it encountered a violent storm, which rendered the ship unseaworthy. When it arrived at port, it took thirty days to repair the collision and storm damage. Had the ship not been damaged in the storm, the collision damage alone could have been repaired in ten days. The claimant alleged that it should be able to claim thirty days' lost profits on the ground that it would not have been caught in the storm had it not sustained the damage due to the collision with the defendant.

HELD: The House of Lords held that the storm damage was not the result of the collision. The storm broke the chain of causation between the defendant's negligence and the storm damage. Accordingly, the defendant was liable only for the damage caused by the original collision.

The second category of *novus* concerns intervening acts of third parties. This usually arises where the defendant's negligence provides an opportunity for a third party to act. The third party's acts may be beneficial (for example, a rescue), or they may be detrimental (for example, the commission of a crime). Whether a third-party act will constitute a *novus* will very much depend on the facts of the case, but it is relatively well established that if the third-party act constitutes a tort, it will be

---

136. For example, *Kitchen v Royal Air Force Association* [1958] 1 WLR 563 (CA) (failure of a solicitor to bring a claim within the limitation period); *Spring v Guardian Assurance plc* [1995] 2 AC 296 (HL) (inaccuracies in an employment reference).

regarded as an intervening cause (especially if the act was unreasonable or deliberate).[137] The following two cases demonstrate the courts' approach.

 The Oropesa [1943] 1 All ER 211 (CA)

FACTS: A ship, *The Manchester Regiment,* collided with the defendant's ship, *The Oropesa.* The collision was caused partly by the negligence of the defendant. *The Manchester Regiment* was badly damaged, but its master thought that it could be saved. Accordingly, he and sixteen other men set out in a lifeboat towards *The Oropesa* to discuss how to save *The Manchester Regiment.* Unfortunately, before they could reach *The Oropesa,* the weather became worse and the lifeboat capsized, drowning nine of the crew (including the claimant's son). *The Manchester Regiment* subsequently sank. The issue was whether the defendant was liable for the deaths of the crewmen, or whether the master's decision to sail to *The Oropesa* in a lifeboat constituted a *novus.*

HELD: The master's actions were reasonable. Therefore, the Court of Appeal held that the deaths were not caused by the master's actions, but by the collision. Accordingly, the defendant was liable for the death of the claimant's son.

⭐ See W Freidman, 'The Manchester Regiment: Chain of Causation—Alternative Danger' (1943) 6 MLR 237

 Knightley v Johns [1982] 1 WLR 349 (CA)

FACTS: The defendant negligently overturned his car in a one-way tunnel. The police inspector in charge forgot to close the tunnel and so a police motorcyclist (the claimant) was ordered to close the tunnel. The claimant drove back to the tunnel against the flow of traffic, believing this to be the quickest way to close the tunnel and avoid a further incident. Whilst driving around a blind bend, the claimant (who was found by the Court not to have been negligent) collided with another motorist and was injured. The issue before the Court was whether the defendant was liable for the claimant's injuries, or whether the inspector's acts were negligent and, if so, whether his negligence constituted a *novus.*

HELD: Stephenson LJ stated: 'Negligent conduct is more likely to break the chain of causation than conduct which is not.'[138] The Court of Appeal held that the actions of the police inspector were negligent and therefore constituted an intervening act that broke the chain of causation. Accordingly, the defendant was not liable for the claimant's injuries. The Court of Appeal further stated that an act of a third party would not break the chain of causation if it were a reasonably foreseeable consequence of the defendant's negligence. The inspector's negligence could not be regarded as reasonably foreseeable.

The third category of *novus* concerns acts of the claimant. Normally, cases in which the claimant contributes to his loss will concern contributory negligence, not causation. In some cases, however, it may be argued that the claimant's actions were such that they broke the chain of causation. The advantage of such a claim is that it would provide a complete defence, whereas contributory negligence only provides

---

137. *Lamb v Camden London Borough Council* [1981] QB 625 (CA).
138. [1982] 1 WLR 349 (CA) 366.

a partial defence. The general rule seems to be that the court will be more likely to regard the claimant's own conduct as a *novus* if it can be shown to be so unreasonable as to wipe out the defendant's original wrongdoing.

McKew v Holland & Hannen & Cubitts (Scotland) Ltd [1969] 3 All ER 1621 (HL)

FACTS: The claimant's leg was injured due to the negligence of the defendant, his employer. As a result, without warning, he occasionally lost control of his leg and it would give way. Three weeks later, he was inspecting a house that he was considering renting. He attempted to walk down some steep stairs, while holding a small child by the hand. The stairs had no handrail for him to hold onto with the other hand. His leg gave way and, to avoid falling, he jumped to the bottom of the stairs, breaking his ankle in the process. The claimant alleged that the defendant was also responsible for this injury.

HELD: The House of Lords held that the defendant was not responsible for the second injury. The claimant's unreasonable conduct had broken the chain of causation. Note that it was not the act of jumping down the stairs that was deemed unreasonable: it was his decision to walk down a steep staircase without assistance that was held to constitute the *novus*.

Remoteness

 The contractual rules of remoteness are discussed at p 328

Having established that the defendant's negligence was the factual and legal cause of the claimant's loss, it needs to be determined whether that loss was too remote—a concept that we have already examined in relation to contract law. The rules relating to remoteness serve to limit the liability of a defendant for his acts of negligence. Such limitations may be justified on policy reasons; other limitations may be simply practicable. As Winfield stated: 'The line must be drawn somewhere…not on the grounds of pure logic, but simply for practical reasons.'[139] The need to 'draw a line' can be seen in the following example.

 The need for rules on remoteness

On 5 September, Charlotte is walking along the pavement, when Joe, a drunk driver, negligently mounts the pavement and collides with her. Charlotte is seriously injured. She has to spend a month in hospital and her mobility will be impaired for the rest of her life. She was due to get married on 9 September, but the wedding and honeymoon had to be cancelled. Due to the short notice of cancellation, refunds of monies paid were unavailable. Further, she had applied for a promotion within her firm and was shortlisted for an interview to take place on 23 September. As she was unable to attend, the promotion was awarded to someone else. The above events have resulted in Charlotte becoming depressed and she is receiving private psychiatric treatment.

In this relatively simple example, a substantial number of losses occur:

1. **Physical injury** Obviously, Charlotte sustained injury in the initial collision, but her mobility will also be impaired for the rest of her life.

---

139. WVH Rogers, *Winfield & Jolowicz on Tort* (18th edn, Sweet & Maxwell 2010) 334.

2. **Property damage** The collision may also have caused damage to property on her person (for example, clothes, mobile phone, etc).

3. **Loss of earnings** Charlotte was off work for a period of time. Her lack of mobility may affect her ability to do her job or to gain future employment.

4. **Economic loss** Cancelling the wedding and honeymoon has resulted in significant economic loss. Further, she has lost out on a chance of gaining a promotion. She is also paying for private psychiatric treatment.

5. **Distress** The injuries sustained would have caused significant distress, as would the occurrence of the subsequent events.

Should Joe have to compensate Charlotte for all of the above losses, or should a 'line be drawn'? Should damages be limited to the direct consequences of Joe's negligence? Should it matter that Joe could not have known the consequences of his actions would cause so much loss? The law relating to remoteness aims to answer these questions.

Reasonable foreseeability

It used to be the case that a claimant could recover all direct losses resulting from the tort, even if such losses were unforeseeable.[140] In 1961, this changed and the courts held that the defendant would only be liable for those types of loss that were a reasonably foreseeable consequence of his negligence.

Overseas Tankship (UK) Ltd v Morts Dock & Engineering Co (The Wagon Mound) (No 1) [1961] AC 388 (PC)

FACTS: The defendant's ship, *The Wagon Mound*, was taking on oil whilst moored in Sydney Harbour. The defendant's negligence resulted in a large quantity of oil being discharged into the harbour, which spread to a wharf owned by the claimant, where it contaminated the slipways (known as 'fouling'). The claimant was a shipbuilder and repairer, and was concerned that its welding could ignite the oil. The wharf manager, after consulting the manager of an oil company, informed the defendant that it could carry on welding. A piece of molten metal dripped onto a floating cloth, which caught fire and ignited the oil. There was no way that the defendant could have known that this could happen. The fire damaged the claimant's wharf and several ships being repaired there.

HELD: The defendant was not liable for the fire damage. In overturning *Re Polemis*, the Privy Council held that the defendant would only be liable if the type of damage suffered by the claimant was reasonably foreseeable. The fire damage was not reasonably foreseeable, so the claim failed. The damage caused to the wharf by fouling was foreseeable, however, and was therefore recoverable.

★ See RWM Dias, Negligence: Remoteness—The *Polemis* Rule' [1961] CLJ 23

Type of harm

As established earlier, a claimant can only recover loss due to the negligence of another if the type of harm suffered was reasonably foreseeable. The issue for the

---

140. *Re Polemis and Furness, Withy & Co* [1921] 3 KB 560 (CA).

courts to determine is how wide or narrow should be the interpretation of the phrase 'type of harm'. Unfortunately, the following two cases demonstrate that the courts' approach has been somewhat inconsistent, with the first case adopting a narrow approach, and the second case adopting a wider approach.[141]

Tremain v Pike [1969] 1 WLR 1556 (CA)

FACTS: The defendant farmer employed the claimant as a herdsman. The defendant negligently allowed rats to infest a number of the farm buildings. The claimant contracted leptospirosis (better known as 'Weil's disease')—a disease caused by exposure to rat's urine.

HELD: The claimant could not recover damages. The Court of Appeal stated that whilst it was reasonably foreseeable that the claimant could suffer injury due to the rat infestation (for example, rat bites, food contamination), the contraction of Weil's disease was not regarded as reasonably foreseeable and was therefore too remote.

 See RWM Dias, 'Kind and Extent of Damage in Negligence' (1970) 28 CLJ 28

Jolley v Sutton London Borough Council [2000] 1 WLR 1082 (HL)

FACTS: For two years, a boat had been left abandoned on a piece of land owned by the defendant, beside which stood a block of flats. The defendant knew of the boat and planned to remove it, but never did. The claimant, a 14-year-old boy, and his friend jacked up the boat in order to repair it. The jack gave way and the boat fell on the claimant, causing serious spinal injuries that rendered him a paraplegic. The Court of Appeal held that the damage was too remote. It held that the only reasonably foreseeable risk resulting from the council's failure to remove the boat was that children might climb on it and fall through the rotten deck. Accordingly, injury caused by a jack giving way was not reasonably foreseeable. The claimant appealed.

HELD: The House of Lords allowed the appeal. The House held that the foreseeable risk was a mere general one of children meddling with the boat and being injured in the process. The harm to the claimant was therefore recoverable.

 See Robert Williams, 'Remoteness: Some Unexpected Mischief' (2001) 117 LQR 30

It would appear that, currently, the more accepted view is the claimant-friendly approach evidenced in *Jolley*, as indicated by the following decision of the House of Lords.

Corr v IBC Vehicles Ltd [2008] UKHL 13

FACTS: The defendant employed Corr as an engineer. Due to a malfunctioning machine of the defendant, Corr suffered severe injuries that left him disfigured. He developed post-traumatic stress disorder and, following a suicide attempt, he was admitted to a psychiatric hospital where he underwent electroconvulsive shock therapy (ECT), which failed

141. See also *Doughty v Turner Manufacturing Co Ltd* [1964] 1 QB 518 (CA).

to remedy his depression. Six years after the original incident, he committed suicide. Prior to his death, he had commenced proceedings against the defendant for the injuries sustained. His widow was substituted as claimant and continued the proceedings. The defendant admitted that the accident was caused by its negligence, but argued that it was not liable for Corr's suicide, because the suicide constituted a *novus*.

HELD: The House of Lords held that the defendant was liable for Corr's suicide and that the claimant could therefore recover compensation under the Fatal Accidents Act 1976. Lord Bingham stated that 'the inescapable fact is that depression, possibly severe, possibly very severe, was a foreseeable consequence of this breach'[142] and that 'it was not incumbent on [the claimant] to show that suicide itself was foreseeable'.[143] He went on to state:

> The rationale of the principle that a novus actus interveniens breaks the chain of causation is fairness...It is in no way unfair to hold the employer responsible for this dire consequence of its breach of duty, although it could well be thought unfair to the victim not to do so.[144]

⭐ See Janet O'Sullivan, 'Employer's Liability for Injured Employee's Suicide' (2008) 67 CLJ 241

The 'eggshell skull' rule

The 'eggshell skull' rule constitutes a major exception to the reasonable foreseeability rule. Currently, the 'eggshell skull' rule arises where *A* commits a tort that causes *B* injury but, due to *B* having some form of weakness or pre-existing condition, the harm suffered by *B* is much greater than could foreseeably be expected. The question arising is whether *A* should be liable for the damage caused, or only for that damage which could be foreseen. The rule was established in the following case.

 Dulieu v White & Sons [1901] 2 KB 669 (DC)

FACTS: The claimant was a pregnant woman, who worked behind the bar in a pub. An employee of the defendant negligently drove a horse-drawn van through the doors of the pub. The shock of witnessing this caused the claimant to become ill and she gave birth prematurely. As a result, the child was born with learning difficulties (although the statement of the claim worded it less delicately, stating 'the said child was born an idiot').[145] The claimant sought damages for her illness and for the premature birth of her child. The defendant argued that, because there was no immediate physical injury, but only psychiatric illness resulting from shock, the illness was too remote and could not be recovered.

HELD: The court rejected the defendant's argument, and awarded the claimant damages for her illness and the premature birth of her child. Kennedy J stated:

> If a man is negligently run over or otherwise negligently injured in his body, it is no answer to the sufferer's claim for damages that he would have suffered less injury, or no injury at all, if he had not had an unusually thin skull or an unusually weak heart.[146]

Accordingly, a defendant is fully liable to a claimant whose injuries are aggravated by an inherent defect, even though the defendant could not reasonably have foreseen this. The eggshell skull rule also extends to cases in which the secondary injury due to the inherent defect is of a different type to the original injury, as the following case demonstrates.

---

142. [2008] UKHL 13, [2008] 1 AC 884 [13].   143. ibid.
144. ibid [15] and [16].   145. [1901] 2 KB 669 (DC) 670.   146. ibid 679.

Smith v Leech Brain & Co [1962] 2 QB 405 (QB)

FACTS: The negligence of Smith's employer (the defendant) caused Smith (the claimant) to be burnt on the lip by a piece of molten metal. Unknown to both Smith and the defendant, the tissue in Smith's lips was pre-cancerous. The burn triggered the cancer and he died three years later. Had the burn not occurred, his cancer might never have arisen, although it was likely that it would. Smith's widow claimed damages for his death from the defendant. The defendant argued that it could not reasonably have foreseen that Smith would contract cancer due to the burn.

HELD: The High Court stated that the correct test was not whether the defendant could foresee the cancer, but whether it could foresee the type of injury that was suffered—namely, the burn. The answer to this was 'yes'. Once that was established, the eggshell skull rule meant that the defendant was also liable for the results of the burn. Accordingly, the claimant was awarded damages for her husband's death.

★ See Gerald Dworkin, 'A Negligent Tortfeasor Still Takes His Victim as He Finds Him' (1962) 25 MLR 471

To date, the vast majority of cases have involved physical injury. Whether some form of the eggshell skull rule could apply universally to non-physical injury (for example, property damage) has yet to be decided. The closest that the courts have come to applying the eggshell skull rule to property damage has been in cases involving the claimant's **impecuniosity**. It appears to be the case that, if the defendant's tort causes the claimant to suffer loss, but this loss is then increased by the claimant's financial inability to minimize the loss, the defendant will be liable for the increased loss.[147]

➡ **impecuniosity:** the state of having little, or no, money

Chapter conclusion

There is little doubt that negligence is the most important tort and is central in allowing victims of accidents to obtain compensation for injuries that they suffer. Given the breadth of the tort and the potential for liability under it, it is therefore important that businesses understand to what extent they can be liable for their negligent acts (and, as discussed in Chapter 16, for the negligent acts of their employees). At the very least, this involves a sound understanding of the duties of care that businesses potentially owe. Indeed, given the scope of a business' activities, the duty of care that it owes will be considerably wider than that owed by an individual and the potential for liability that much greater.

However important negligence might be, it is not the only tort that can affect businesses. In Chapter 15, a number of other business-related torts are examined, including torts that aim to protect businesses from the interference of others.

Key points summary

- The current test to establish a duty of care requires (i) foreseeability of damage; (ii) proximity; and (iii) that the imposition of a duty must be just, fair, and reasonable.

- Generally, liability is not imposed for omissions—but a duty of care may arise depending upon the relationship between the parties, or between the parties and a third party.

---

147. *Lagden v O'Connor* [2003] UKHL 64, [2004] 1 AC 1067.

- A claimant may recover damages for psychiatric damage that is consequential upon physical injury.

- Generally, a claimant cannot recover damages for 'pure' economic loss (that is, financial loss unassociated with physical injury or property damage), but there are exceptions.

- Once the claimant has established that a duty of care exists, he will need to establish that the defendant breached that duty.

- The standard of care owed is that of the reasonable man. If the defendant is a child, the standard is that of a reasonable and prudent child of the defendant's age.

- Four factors are relevant when determining breach of duty: (i) the likelihood of injury; (ii) the seriousness of the injury; (iii) the cost of precautions; and (iv) the usefulness of the defendant's conduct.

- The claimant will need to establish that the defendant's negligence was the factual and legal cause of his loss.

- The court will ask whether the claimant would have suffered the loss 'but for' the defendant's negligence. An affirmative answer means that the loss would have occurred anyway and the defendant will not be liable.

- The claimant will need to establish that the harm suffered was not too remote from the defendant's negligent act. The defendant is only liable for those types of harm that are a reasonably foreseeable consequence of his negligence.

Self-test questions

1. What are the requirements for establishing negligence?

2. Gabriel is considering purchasing shares in Digisoft plc, a software company. He acquires a copy of the company's annual accounts, which show the company to be extremely profitable. He therefore purchases a thousand shares in Digisoft at a price of £6 per share. A week later, it is announced that Digisoft have entered voluntary liquidation. It transpires that the company was not actually profitable, but was running at a loss, and that the directors had been siphoning away company funds for personal use. The company's auditors, who signed off on the company's accounts, discovered none of this. Advise Gabriel. Would your answer differ if Gabriel had not relied on the company's accounts, but on a report that Gabriel commissioned a firm of accountants to prepare for his use alone?

3. Explain the difference between a 'primary' victim and a 'secondary' victim in cases of psychiatric injury. Why does the law distinguish between the two?

4. Are damages recoverable in the following situations?
   (a) Peter works as a porter at an airport. A plane crashes into the runway, due to the malfunction of a component negligently manufactured by AviaTech plc. Peter witnessed the crash, but was safely inside the terminal when it happened. The next day, he discovers that his girlfriend Joanne, an air hostess, was on board the plane when it crashed and was killed. Peter becomes clinically depressed.
   (b) BioMed plc (a pharmaceutical company) and MedCare Ltd (a company running a number of private hospitals) agree that BioMed will provide drugs and medical equipment to MedCare for the next five years. Both parties instruct Evans & Grimwood LLP (a firm of solicitors) to draft a contract based on what has been

agreed, emphasizing that the contract needs to be drawn up and signed one month before the opening of a new private hospital in London. Evans & Grimwood fails to draft the contract on time and the hospital is opened, but cannot take any patients, because it lacks the equipment that would have been obtained from BioMed.

5. Why, historically, has the law of negligence been reluctant to allow recovery for 'pure' economic loss?

Further reading

Kit Barker, 'Wielding Occam's Razor: Pruning Strategies for Economic Loss' (2006) 26 OJLS 289
Discusses the three main approaches to the recovery of pure economic loss, and examines the combination approach evidenced in Customs and Excise Commissioners v Barclays Bank

John Cartwright, 'Remoteness of Damage in Contract and Tort: A Reconsideration' (1966) 55 CLJ 488
Analyses the rules relating to remoteness, focusing on the differences between the rules in contract and tort

John Murphy and Christian Witting, *Street on Torts* (13th edn, OUP 2012) ch 5
An excellent discussion of the rules relating to causation and remoteness

Donal Nolan, 'Psychiatric Injury at the Crossroads' (2004) 1 JPI Law 1
Provides a clear and comprehensive analytical overview of the law relating to psychiatric injury

WVH Rogers, *Winfield & Jolowicz on Tort* (18th edn, Sweet & Maxwell 2010) chs 5 and 6
A detailed, but clear and well-written, discussion of the law relating to the duty of care and breach of duty

Remember to visit the **Online Resource Centre** at <http://www.oxfordtextbooks.co.uk/orc/roach3e> to access the following resources on Chapter 14, 'The tort of negligence': more **practice questions** and answers; a **glossary** of key terms; **multiple-choice questions**; **revision summaries**; and **diagrams** in pdf. Updates to the law can be found on Twitter by following **@UKBusinessLaw**.

15 Business-related torts

- Product liability
- Wrongful interference with goods
- Employers' liability
- Occupiers' liability

- Nuisance and *Rylands v Fletcher*
- Defamation
- Breach of statutory duty

INTRODUCTION

Whilst, from a business perspective, negligence is probably the most important tort, there are many other torts that can be committed by and against businesses. Some of these are not torts in their own right, but rather specific forms of broader torts (for example, product liability at common law is a specific form of negligence). Others are applications of existing torts that have developed their own rules due to the tortfeasor's identity (for example, employers' liability). A detailed examination of the numerous torts that can arise in a business context is beyond the scope of this text. Here, the principal torts that can affect businesses will be discussed, beginning with one of the most important—namely, liability for defective products.

Product liability

The primary remedy for a person who has purchased a defective product will be a claim for breach of contract, especially where the implied terms found in the Sale of Goods Act 1979 apply. Privity will, however, ensure that such an action can only be brought by the person who purchased the goods, unless the Contracts (Rights of Third Parties) Act 1999 is applicable. A claimant third party who has sustained loss due to a defective product might be able to succeed in tort, where he will have a choice between an action against the manufacturer under the common law and/or an action under the Consumer Protection Act 1987. The availability of these actions becomes more important where the seller is insolvent.

Visit the **Online Resource Centre** for more on terms implied under the Sale of Goods Act 1979 in the chapter entitled 'The sale of goods'

Privity of contract and the 1999 Act are discussed at p 118

Common law

 The 'neighbour test' is discussed at p 364

Chapter 14 discussed how Lord Atkin, in the case of *Donoghue v Stevenson*,[1] laid down the 'neighbour test' that was to form the basis of the modern tort of negligence. However, the neighbour test was a mere *dictum*; the *ratio* of the case related specifically to defective products and is known as the 'narrow rule'. The narrow rule, which was also laid down by Lord Atkin, provides that:

> a manufacturer of products, which he sells in such a form as to show that he intends them to reach the ultimate consumer in the form in which they left him with no reasonable possibility of intermediate examination, and with the knowledge that the absence of reasonable care in the preparation…of the products will result in an injury to the consumer's life or property, owes a duty to the consumer to take reasonable care.[2]

The narrow rule still forms the basis of a claim for product liability at common law, and contains a number of phrases and terms that require further discussion.

Who is a 'manufacturer'?

Lord Atkin's narrow rule imposed a duty of care upon 'manufacturers' of products, but subsequent cases have expanded the scope of potential defendants to include virtually anyone who is involved in the supply chain (for example, erectors,[3] fitters,[4] repairers,[5] and assemblers).[6] A supplier or distributor of goods will not normally owe a duty of care, unless the circumstances are such that he ought reasonably to have checked the goods. A second-hand car dealer, for example, can reasonably be expected to check the brakes of a used car or, at least, to warn a prospective buyer that he has not done so.[7]

What are 'products'?

The word 'products' originally applied only to food and drink, but has since has been interpreted to include virtually any product (for example, motor vehicles,[8] lifts,[9] hair dye,[10] computer software,[11] chemicals,[12] and tombstones).[13] As Lord Atkin mentioned the 'preparation' of products, it follows that negligent packaging, labelling, or instructions of use can also result in liability.[14]

'Sells'

Lord Atkin's test refers to a manufacturer who 'sells' a product and while it is probable that liability under the narrow rule would not be imposed on a gratuitous

---

1. [1932] AC 562 (HL).   2. ibid 599.   3. *Brown v Cotterill* (1934) 51 TLR 21 (KB).
4. *Malfroot v Noxal Ltd* (1935) 51 TLR 551 (KB).
5. *Haseldine v CA Daw & Son Ltd* [1941] 2 KB 343 (CA).
6. *Howard v Furness-Houlder Argentine Lines Ltd* [1936] 2 All ER 296 (KB).
7. *Andrews v Hopkinson* [1957] 1 QB 229 (QB).
8. *Herschtal v Stewart and Ardern Ltd* [1940] 1 KB 155 (KB).
9. *Haseldine v CA Daw & Son Ltd* [1941] 2 KB 343 (CA).
10. *Watson v Buckley, Osborne, Garrett & Co Ltd* [1940] 1 All ER 174.
11. *St Albans City and District Council v International Computers Ltd* [1996] 4 All ER 481 (CA).
12. *Vacwell Engineering Co Ltd v BDH Chemicals Ltd* [1971] 1 QB 88 (QB).
13. *Brown v Cotterill* (1934) 51 TLR 21 (KB).
14. *Distillers Co (Biochemicals) Ltd v Thompson* [1971] AC 458 (PC).

provider of goods,[15] it is likely that liability could be imposed where goods are given away in the course of a business (for example, free samples[16] or promotional gifts).

Who is the 'ultimate consumer'?

The courts permit a wide array of persons to bring a claim under the narrow rule. This will obviously include users of the product,[17] but will also include anyone who could be foreseeably injured by the product[18] and anyone within physical proximity to the product.[19]

The effect of an 'intermediate examination'

According to Lord Atkin's test, a manufacturer will only owe a duty if the consumer could not reasonably be expected to carry out an intermediate examination. The mere possibility of an examination is not enough to deny the existence of a duty,[20] nor is the opportunity to examine the goods. In order for a duty of care to be denied, the manufacturer will need to show that an examination was a reasonable expectation (for example, where the seller specifically warned or recommended that the buyer examine the product).[21]

Breach of duty and causation

Once it is established that the manufacturer owes a duty of care to the ultimate consumer, it must be established that this duty was breached. The burden of proof is placed upon the claimant, who will need to establish that the manufacturer failed to take reasonable care. Establishing this under *Donoghue v Stevenson* was extremely difficult because Lord Macmillan stated that the claimant must prove that the defect that caused the loss was present when the product left the defendant's control and that the defect was not caused by the defendant's carelessness. He added that there was no presumption of negligence, nor any justification for applying the maxim *res ipsa loquitur*. This harshness has now been mitigated by the apparent application of *res ipsa loquitur* to product liability cases.[22]

Res ipsa loquitur is discussed at p 396

Establishing breach of duty will still prove a most formidable task, because the claimant will need to establish that it was the defendant's breach of duty that caused his loss and not the intervening act of an intermediate person. This will require the claimant to adduce sufficient evidence indicating that the defect existed when it left the control of the defendant and did not subsequently arise. The following case demonstrates how difficult this can be to establish.

---

15. John Murphy & Christian Witting *Street on Torts* (13th edn, OUP 2012) 420.
16. *Hawkins v Coulsdon and Purley Urban District Council* [1954] 1 QB 319 (CA) 333 (Denning LJ).
17. *Grant v Australian Knitting Mills* [1936] AC 85 (PC).
18. *Stennett v Hancock and Peters* [1939] 2 All ER 578 (KB).
19. *Brown v Cotterill* (1934) 51 TLR 21 (KB).
20. *Driver v William Willett (Contractors) Ltd* [1969] 1 All ER 665.
21. *Kubach v Hollands* [1937] 3 All ER 907 (KB).
22. *Grant v Australian Knitting Mills Ltd* [1936] AC 85 (PC). Although the Privy Council never actually used the phrase '*res ipsa loquitur*' itself, the language used makes it virtually certain that *res ipsa loquitur* will apply.

Evans v Triplex Safety Glass Co Ltd [1936] 1 All ER 283 (KB)

FACTS: The claimant purchased a car, the windscreen of which was made of 'Triplex Toughened Safety Glass', which was manufactured by the defendant. A year later, with no warning and with no apparent cause, the windscreen shattered whilst the claimant was driving, injuring him, his wife, and his son. The claimant sued.

HELD: The claim failed. The claimant could not establish that the windscreen was defective when it left the defendant's control. The High Court stated that it was possible that the glass could have been weakened when it was being attached to the car, or that the glass could have broken due to some other non-manufacturing defect.

Where the claimant uses the product in an unforeseeable or materially different purpose from that for which it was designed, then it is likely that causation will not be established. In such a case, the injury may not be caused by the product's defect, but by the claimant's misuse of the product. Where both a defect in the product and misuse are present, causation is likely to be proven, but the defendant will be likely to be able to successfully plead contributory negligence.[23]

⟋ The defence of contributory negligence is discussed at p 484

Injury

In order to recover damages, the manufacturer's negligence must result in 'injury to the consumer's life or property'. Accordingly, product liability at common law is concerned with physical loss caused by dangerous goods. It would appear that loss caused by defective goods is not covered: as Winfield and Jolowicz note, if Mrs Donoghue's bottle of ginger beer were to have contained pure water, her claim would be likely to have failed.[24] Where goods that are not dangerous, but merely unsatisfactory, have been sold, the appropriate source of redress is via an action under the Sale of Goods Act 1979.

Whilst damage to property is recoverable, this does not include damage to the product itself, because such loss amounts to pure economic loss (reduction in value of the product), which, as we have seen, is generally not recoverable. This is a problematic limitation, because it is not always easy to determine whether a product is itself a product or is merely part of a larger, more complex product, as the following example demonstrates.

Eg Damage to the product itself

Eddie purchases a brand new Ferrari F458. After he has driven the car a mere five miles, one of the tyres bursts, causing Eddie to drive into a wall. The car is a write-off, but Eddie sustains no injuries. Would the tyre itself count as a product, which caused property damage to the rest of the car, or would the car be regarded as the product and the tyre a mere component? The former interpretation would allow Eddie to claim for the damage to the car. The latter interpretation would bar Eddie's claim in tort, because damage to the product itself is not recoverable.

---

23. *Griffiths v Arch Engineering Co Ltd* [1968] 3 All ER 217.
24. WVH Rogers, *Winfield & Jolowicz on Tort* (18th edn, Sweet & Maxwell 2010) 497.

> The issue is divisive. Lord Lloyd stated *obiter*, in *Aswan Engineering Establishment Co v Lupdine Ltd*,[25] that his 'provisional view'[26] would be that the tyre would be a product in its own right (that is, separate from the car) and the damage to the car would constitute recoverable property damage. However, several commentators[27] contend that the tyre would merely be part of an overall defective product (the car), thereby rendering the damage irrecoverable in tort.
>
> Imagine that, instead of the new tyres bursting, they function perfectly. Two years later, as part of routine maintenance, TyreChange Ltd replaces all four tyres. If one of these tyres were to burst, causing the car to crash, it is much more likely that the replacement tyre would be regarded as a product in its own right, thereby allowing Eddie to claim for the damage sustained to his car.

The line between property damage and economic loss is a difficult one to draw, and there is little concrete authority on the subject—and what authority does exist is relatively superficial, with a notable number of split decisions.

The Consumer Protection Act 1987

In the 1950s and 1960s, thousands of pregnant women were prescribed a drug called Thalidomide to help alleviate their morning sickness. An unforeseen side effect of the drug resulted in thousands of these women giving birth to babies with severe deformities. The Thalidomide tragedy created a wave of public concern leading to the Law Commission[28] recommending the introduction of a strict liability regime in relation to product liability, whereby manufacturers would be liable merely because a product was defective: there would be no need to establish fault, as is required under the common law discussed earlier. Around the same time, the European Commission presented a draft directive on product liability to the Council of Ministers, but there were deep divisions within the Member States, which could not agree on the appropriate extent of manufacturer's liability. As a result, it was not until 1985 that Council Directive 85/374/EEC was passed, which required that each EU Member State introduce a system of strict liability in relation to defective products. In the UK, this Directive was implemented by Pt I of the Consumer Protection Act 1987 (CPA 1987).

It is important to note that the provisions of the CPA 1987 operate alongside existing measures. Where the injured party has a contract with the manufacturer of the defective product, the CPA 1987 will be largely redundant, because the Sale of Goods Act 1979 will be considerably more useful. Where no contract exists, however, the strict liability regime of the 1987 Act was expected to be of more use than the negligence-based approach of the common law. To date, however, there has been little litigation under Pt I of the Act.

In order to understand the regime introduced by the 1987 Act, it is essential to answer a series of questions, beginning with who can be liable under the Act.

---

25. [1987] 1 WLR 1 (CA).   26. ibid 21.

27. For example, John Murphy & Christian Witting, *Street on Torts* (13th edn, OUP 2012) 422.

28. Law Commission, *Liability for Defective Products: Report of the Two Commissions* (Law Com No 82, Cmnd 6831, HMSO 1977).

Who is liable?

The 1987 Act imposes liability upon four classes of persons. First, under s 2(2)(a), liability may be imposed upon the 'producer' of the product. Section 1(2) defines a producer as one of the following.

1. **The person who manufactured it** The Directive expressly included manufacturers of component parts within the definition of 'producer', but this was not included in the 1987 Act. The manufacturer of a component is a producer, however, because components are within the Act's definition of 'product'.

2. **In the case of a substance that has not been manufactured, but has been won or abstracted, the person who won or abstracted it** 'Abstract', in this sense, means 'to extract or remove' and therefore usually refers to substances that have been mined or quarried (for example, stone or metals).

3. **In the case of a product that has not been manufactured, won, or abstracted (for example, agricultural products), but which has essential characteristics that are the result of some process (for example, a sausage), the person who carried out this process** Unfortunately, the Act does not provide definitions of 'process' and 'essential characteristics', leading to a degree of uncertainty in this area.

By s 2(2)(b), the second class of persons liable are those persons who hold themselves out as the product's producer by putting their name on the product or some other distinguishing mark. This is a common business practice whereby companies will purchase goods manufactured by a third party and then affix their name or logo onto the product. It should be noted that liability would only be imposed on such persons if they were to hold themselves out as the producer. Fixing a name or logo to the product is unlikely to suffice in itself.

By s 2(2)(c), the third class of persons liable are importers within the EU who have imported products from outside the EU. The following example demonstrates the rationale behind imposing liability on such persons.

Eg Importers and product liability

Rachel purchases a new SamSharp television from TV-Mart Ltd, a company based in London. The televisions are manufactured in China, before being sent to Japan, where SamSharp affixes its logo onto the televisions and packages them. TV-Mart then imports the televisions from Japan and sells them. The television that Rachel purchases is defective and electrocutes her.

Both the manufacturer and the own-brander are outside Rachel's jurisdiction. Litigating in either Japan or China is likely to be an extremely expensive and time-consuming affair. Thankfully, she will not have to resort to this: she can proceed against TV-Mart, because it imported the goods into the EU.

Section 2(3) details the fourth and final class of persons who may be liable. It may be the case that the consumer obtained the product from a supplier who is a retailer or intermediary distributor not falling within the previous three classes. In such a case, a supplier will be liable unless he informs the claimant of the identity of the person who comes within the previous three classes.[29] This is important because

---

29. CPA 1987, s 2(3).

someone who buys from a retailer or intermediary distributor may well not know the name of the manufacturer, etc.

Who can recover damages?

The Act itself does not specifically identify who may sue; it merely refers to 'the person who suffered the damage'. This means that anyone who has suffered damage due to a defective product may initiate a claim. The claimant does not need to be the purchaser of the product, nor does he need to be a consumer of the product, and it is irrelevant that the damage caused was not reasonably foreseeable.[30]

What is a 'product'?

The defective product must be a 'product' within the meaning of the Act. Section 1(2) provides that a product 'means any goods or electricity and…includes a product which is comprised in another product, whether by virtue of being a component part or raw material or otherwise'. Section 45(1) expands the definition by defining 'goods' as including 'substances, growing crops and things comprised in land by virtue of being attached to it and any ship, aircraft or vehicle'. In turn, the words used in s 45(1) have often required further definition by the courts (for example, whether blood constitutes a substance).[31] Land clearly falls outside the definition of a 'product'. Buildings are excluded from the operation of the Act,[32] although products that are incorporated into buildings (for example, boilers and washbasins) are within the scope of the Act.

When will a product be 'defective'?

The claimant will need to establish that the product is 'defective'. Section 3(1) provides that 'there is a defect in a product…if the safety of the product is not such as persons are generally entitled to expect'. As with the common law, the 1987 Act is not concerned with unsatisfactory goods, but with unsafe goods. Further, the definition of 'defective' focuses entirely on users of the product; the conduct of the producer is not mentioned. It follows that even if the producer has not acted negligently and has done all that could reasonably be done, he will still be liable if the product did not meet the objective standard of expectation.

When determining the safety of a product, s 3(2) provides that the court should take into account all of the circumstances of the case, including:

- **The way in which, and the purposes for which, the product was marketed** As the test of safety is based upon what persons can expect, it follows that what they were led to believe by the product's marketing is of considerable importance.

- **The product's instructions and any warnings with respect to it** A suitably worded warning may make an inherently unsafe product safe. For example, many medicines can be harmful, but a warning not to exceed the stated dosage would ensure that the product was not defective.

- **What might reasonably be expected to be done with, or in relation to, the product** Where reasonable or normal usage of a product causes damage, liability will be imposed. Misuse of a product might still result in liability, however, provided that such misuse was reasonably foreseeable.

---

30. This is evidenced in s 6(3), which provides that if a product causes damage to a foetus, the child, once born, may sue for any disabilities caused.
31. In *A v National Blood Authority* [2001] 3 All ER 289 (QB), the High Court held that blood did constitute a substance and is therefore covered under the Act.   32. CPA 1987, s 45(1).

- **The time at which the producer (or another) supplied the product** The time at which a product was put into circulation is extremely relevant for two reasons. First, the defect may have been caused by 'wear and tear', in which case the producer would not be liable. Second, it would be unfair to judge older products in the same way as newer products (for example, a vintage car would not be judged unsafe simply because it did not have airbags fitted). The safety of the product will be based on the knowledge and safety standards at the time that the product was supplied. The true importance of this factor will be seen later, when the 'development risks' defence is discussed.

As Pt 1 of the CPA 1987 imposes strict liability, it is irrelevant that the producer has not acted in a negligent or careless manner.

What damage is required?

The claimant can only recover damages if the defect in a product, wholly or partly, causes 'damage', as defined by the Act. Section 5(1) provides that 'damage' means 'death or personal injury or any loss of or damage to any property (including land)'. Where the damage is to property, there are several further limitations, namely:

1. Damage to the product itself cannot be recovered.[33]
2. The Act does not apply to damage caused to business property. The property must be 'ordinarily intended for private use, occupation or consumption'.[34]
3. Damages are not recoverable where the property damage is less than £275.[35] In cases concerning such small amounts, most lawyers would advise their clients not to initiate proceedings.

What defences are available?

Section 4 provides for a number of relatively straightforward defences including:

- the defect is attributable to compliance with a legal obligation;
- the defect arose after the product was supplied;
- the defective product was not supplied by the defendant (for example, where it is stolen);
- the defective product was not supplied to another by the supplier in the course of a business.

One defence has proven to be extremely controversial. This is the 'development risks' defence (sometimes known as the 'state of the art' defence), which states that a producer of a defective product can escape liability where 'the state of scientific and technical knowledge at the relevant time was not such that a producer of products of the same description as the product in question might be expected to have discovered the defect.'[36] The following example demonstrates when this defence might be relevant.

 The development risks defence

In January 2011, BioTech plc released a new drug onto the market, which it claims will cure the common cold. The drug appears to work as claimed. In January 2014, however, a small proportion of those who took the drug start to develop colds again. Further, the

---

33. ibid s 5(2).   34. ibid s 5(3).   35. ibid s 5(4).   36. ibid s 4(1)(e).

symptoms are more severe and occur more often. It is discovered that around 2 per cent of those who took the drug suffered a side effect that caused their immune system to become compromised, making them more susceptible to colds and infections.

BioTech may be able to avoid liability if it can establish that the state of scientific and technical knowledge in January 2011 was such that it could not be expected to have discovered the side effect.

The controversy surrounding the defence arose due to the UK's implementation. The defence in the Directive was wholly objective, whereas the defence is s 4(1)(e) is based on when the producer 'might be expected to have discovered the defect'. It was argued that this made the defence wider, more subjective, and more pro-producer than the defence under the Directive, but both the European Court of Justice[37] and the High Court[38] disagreed. This is backed up by the fact that, to date, the development risks defence has yet to be successfully pleaded.

Whilst the correctness of the UK's implementation may have been determined, the defence itself is still highly problematic for three reasons. First, the court will have to determine the level of scientific and technical knowledge at the date that the product was supplied. This will not be easy to determine and the court may have to rely heavily on expert witnesses. Second, the defence is based on the discoverability of the defect—but it could be argued that, with enough testing, any defect is discoverable. The key issue will be how much testing is required and, on this, the Act provides no guidance. Third, it could be argued that the defence does not fit well within a statute that imposes strict liability, and its inclusion has turned a strict liability regime into a quasi-negligence-based regime.

Limitation periods

The limitation period for actions under Pt 1 of the of the CPA 1987 is three years from the date on which the damage was caused, or the date on which the claimant knew of the relevant facts, whichever is the later.[39] Either way, no action may be brought after the expiration of the period of ten years from 'the relevant time'.[40] Where the action is brought against a person who falls within s 2(2) of the CPA 1987, then the relevant time is the time at which the product was supplied to another. Where an action is brought against someone who is outside the scope of s 2(2), then the relevant time is the time at which the product was last supplied by a person to whom s 2(2) does apply in relation to the product.

Wrongful interference with goods

Product liability under Pt I of the CPA 1987 is not the only tort in relation to goods. Other torts exist that do not relate to the condition of goods, but relate to persons who interfere with goods belonging to others. Historically, a number of such torts existed and these torts were partially amalgamated by the Torts (Interference with

---

37. *Commission of the EC v United Kingdom* [1997] All ER (EC) 481.
38. *A v National Blood Authority* [2001] 3 All ER 289 (QB).   39. Limitation Act 1980, s 11A(4).
40. ibid s 11A(3).

Goods) Act 1977, which places them under the collective term 'wrongful interference with goods'.[41] For our purposes, the two principal torts to be discussed are:

1. trespass to goods; and
2. conversion.

Trespass to goods

Trespass to goods comprises any direct physical interference with goods that are in the possession of another person, without the consent of the person in possession, unless there is lawful justification for the interference. Several aspects of this definition require further discussion.

Interference

The first question to ask is what type of action constitutes direct physical interference with the goods. Interference can take many forms, including:

- taking[42] or moving[43] goods in the lawful possession of another;
- scratching the panel of a vehicle;[44]
- unlawfully clamping a wheel of a car;[45]
- beating[46] or killing[47] an animal.

The interference must be direct. Accordingly, placing out poison for an animal to eat would probably not constitute trespass to goods,[48] nor would locking a room containing the claimant's goods.[49] The defendant's actions must be intentional or negligent and, if they are, liability is strict, and it is irrelevant that the defendant did not realize that his actions constituted a trespass. Thus, if a person genuinely, but mistakenly, believes that goods belong to him and removes them from the possession of another, this will constitute trespass to goods because the interference was intentional.[50]

Although not definitively established, the weight of opinion favours the view that trespass to goods is actionable per se (that is, proof of damage to the goods is not required). However, if no damage is suffered, then the claimant will usually only be able to recover nominal damages.[51]

Possession

Unlike conversion, trespass to goods will only be established if the claimant was in possession of the goods at the time of the alleged interference. Ownership of the goods is irrelevant and, in fact, an owner of goods may be liable if he interferes with those goods whilst they are in the lawful possession of another.

Consent

No trespass will occur if the person in possession of the goods consented to the interference. In recent years, the issue of consent has arisen regularly in relation to the wheel-clamping of motor vehicles.

---

41. Torts (Interference with Goods) Act 1977, s 1.   42. *Brewer v Dew* (1843) 11 M & W 625 (Ex).
43. *Kirk v Gregory* (1876) 1 Ex D 55.   44. *Fouldes v Willoughby* (1841) 8 M & W 540.
45. *Vine v Waltham Forest London Borough Council* [2000] 1 WLR 2383 (CA).
46. *Wright v Ramscot* (1667) 1 Saund 84.   47. *Sheldrick v Abery* (1793) 1 Esp 55.
48. WVH Rogers, *Winfield & Jolowicz on Tort* (18th edn, Sweet & Maxwell 2010) 820.
49. *Hartley v Moxham* (1842) 3 QB 701.   50. *Wilson v Lombank Ltd* [1963] 1 WLR 1294.
51. *Kirk v Gregory* (1876) 1 Ex D 55.

Arthur v Anke [1997] QB 564 (CA)

FACTS: The owners of a piece of land engaged the defendant to prevent unauthorized parking on the land. The defendant displayed a number of prominent notices on the land indicating that the land was private and that vehicles parked without authority would be clamped. The claimant parked his car on the land and the defendant clamped it. The claimant alleged that the clamping constituted a trespass to goods.

HELD: No trespass to goods had occurred. By parking where he did, the claimant voluntarily accepted the risk that his car might be clamped and this amounted to implied consent to the interference.

COMMENT: It is now a criminal offence to wheel-clamp, without lawful authority, cars that are parked on private land.[52] However, landowners are given stronger remedies in relation to obtaining damages from those who park unlawfully on their land.

★ See Tony Weir, 'Clamping' (1996) 55 CLJ 423

Conversion

Conversion is an intentional act[53] of dealing with goods in a manner that is inconsistent with another's possession, or in a way that serves to deny another's right to immediate possession. An action for conversion can be brought by anyone who has possession of goods, or a right to immediate possession of goods,[54] irrespective of whether such a person is the owner of the goods. There are numerous situations in which a person has possession or a right to immediate possession of goods, including:

- **Ownership** Note, however, that a person who owns goods may lawfully lose the right to possession (for example, if he hires them to another, without providing for the right to repossession before the term of hire).
- **Sale** A purchaser of goods can sue if ownership of the goods has passed to him, even though he does not yet have possession of the goods.[55]
- **Lien** A person who has possession of goods under a lien can sue if those goods are converted, provided that title to those goods has not passed to a third party.[56]

lien: the right to hold the property of another until an obligation is satisfied

Only material, tangible goods can be converted; a **thing in action** is usually incapable of conversion.[57]

thing in action: an asset (other than land) that cannot be possessed or which has no physical existence (e.g. a share in a company)

What acts amount to conversion?

Many different types of act can amount to conversion, including:

- the theft or intentional destruction of goods;
- taking possession of goods via some legal process without appropriate justification;[58]

52. Protection of Freedoms Act 2012, s 54(1).
53. Conversion cannot be committed by omission (*Ashby v Tolhurst* [1937] 2 KB 242 (CA)).
54. *The Future Express* [1993] 2 Lloyd's Rep 542 (CA).
55. *North West Securities Ltd v Alexander Breckon Ltd* [1981] RTR 518 (CA).
56. *Pendragon plc v Walon Ltd* [2005] EWHC 1082 (QB).
57. *OBG Ltd v Allan* [2005] EWCA Civ 106, [2005] QB 762.   58. *Tinkler v Poole* (1770) 5 Burr 2657.

- possessing goods belonging to another, but refusing to allow the owner to collect them;[59]
- purchasing goods from a person who has no title to them;
- dealing with goods in a manner that is inconsistent with the rights of another;[60]
- using goods belonging to another as if they were one's own.[61]

Intention

Like trespass to goods, liability in conversion is strict. All that is required is that the defendant intended to carry out the act in question. It is irrelevant (i) whether or not the defendant realized that the act interfered with the rights of the claimant;[62] (ii) whether or not the defendant was acting in good faith;[63] or (iii) whether or not the defendant was ignorant or mistaken.

Remedies

A person whose goods have been wrongly interfered with may have access to several remedies, including:

- The principal remedy is an award of damages, the amount awarded being assessed so as to compensate the claimant for the destruction, damage, or deprivation of the goods, and for any consequential loss.
- Where the defendant is in possession of the goods, the court can (i) order the return of the goods; (ii) order the return of the goods, but give the defendant the alternative of paying damages by reference to the value of the goods; or (iii) order the payment of damages.[64]
- In some cases, a claimant may simply be able to retake the goods wrongly taken from his possession. Like all self-help remedies, however, this remedy must be carefully exercised.

In *BBMB Finance (Hong Kong) Ltd v Eda Holdings Ltd*,[65] the Privy Council held that, generally, where the claimant's property has been irreversibly converted, he has a right to damages measured by the value of the property at the date of conversion. It also held that, where the claimant has got his property back, damages should be assessed as the difference between the value of the property when the wrongful interference occurred and its value on its return.

If the defendant improves the converted goods, thereby increasing their value, the claimant normally cannot recover the increased value. Damages will be assessed based on the market value of the goods minus the amount spent on improving them.[66]

---

59. *Howard E Perry & Co Ltd v British Railways Board* [1986] 1 WLR 1375 (Ch).
60. *RH Willis & Son v British Car Auctions Ltd* [1978] 1 WLR 438 (CA).
61. *Lancashire and Yorkshire Rly Co v MacNicoll* (1918) 88 LJ KB 601.
62. *Caxton Publishing Co Ltd v Sutherland Publishing Co* [1939] AC 178 (HL).
63. *Fowler v Hollins* (1872) 7 QB 616.
64. Torts (Interference with Goods) Act 1977, s 3(2). Along with (i) and (ii), the court can also order the payment of consequential damages.
65. [1990] 1 WLR 409 (PC).   66. *Reid v Fairbanks* (1853) 13 CB 692.

Employers' liability

The Pearson Commission[67] of 1978 estimated that 1,300 employees were killed and that over 700,000 were injured in the course of employment. With the increased focus on safety and the enactment of health and safety legislation, these figures have been reduced considerably, but they could be lower. In 2012/13, 148 workers were killed whilst at work and 175,000 suffered injuries that resulted in over seven days of absence, while 1.8 million employees were at that time suffering from an illness that they believed was caused, or exacerbated, by their current, or previous, employment.[68] In total, 27 million working days were lost, which cost society around £13.8 billion.

Health and safety legislation is discussed at p 725

Employees harmed in the course of their employment will normally become entitled to a range of social security benefits if their injuries affect their ability to work. Such payments will not, however, compensate the employee fully for injuries sustained and will generally be considerably lower than the employee's wage. The employee may therefore decide to obtain additional compensation by suing his employer.

Employers may be liable to pay their employees compensation on a number of grounds, all of which are discussed elsewhere in this text:

- breach of an express or implied contractual term;
- breach of statutory duty (discussed later in this chapter);
- the employer might be vicariously liable for the acts of employees that injure other employees (discussed in Chapter 16);
- the employer might have breached the duty of care owed to his employees (discussed in Chapter 26).

Occupiers' liability

Occupiers of premises owe a statutory duty of care towards persons on those premises, whether they are there lawfully (for example, visitors) or unlawfully (for example, trespassers), in respect of the *state* of the premises. In relation to *activities* carried out on the premises, the occupier owes both a statutory and common law duty to lawful visitors, and a common law duty to non-lawful visitors. The common law duties are owed under the tort of negligence discussed in Chapter 14. Here, the statutory duties of care imposed are discussed, with this area of the law being largely dominated by two different Acts:

1. The Occupiers' Liability Act 1957 (OLA 1957), which governs liability in relation to lawful visitors.
2. The Occupiers' Liability Act 1984 (OLA 1984), which governs liability in relation to non-lawful visitors.

---

67. *Report of the Royal Commission on Civil Liability and Compensation for Personal Injury* (Cmnd 7054, HMSO 1978).
68. Health and Safety Executive, *Health and Safety Executive: Annual Statistics Report for Great Britain 2012/13* (HSE 2013) 1.

Scope

Occupier

Neither Act provides a definition of 'occupier', each preferring to state that the common law definition should be used,[69] as provided in the following case.

 Wheat v E Lacon & Co Ltd [1966] AC 552 (HL)

FACTS: The defendant's public house was run by a manager and his wife, both of whom were employed by the defendant. The agreement provided that the manager would sell drinks in the licensed ground-floor portion of the building and could live rent-free in living accommodation on the first floor of the building. The defendant allowed the manager's wife to take in paying guests, who would stay in the living accommodation. There was no direct access between the ground floor and the first floor, but there was a separate emergency staircase leading to the first floor, which was barred by a door marked 'private'. A paying guest fell down this staircase and was killed. The deceased's widow commenced proceedings and the House of Lords had to determine who was the occupier.

HELD: Lord Denning stated that anyone with a 'sufficient degree of control over [the] premises'[70] could be an occupier. Based on this definition, both the defendant and manager were held to be occupiers (although, on the facts, neither was liable). Lord Denning stated that other persons who could constitute occupiers include landlords, tenants, and independent contractors.

★ See Robert C Gardner, 'Vicarious Occupation?' (1965) 28 MLR 721

Both Acts impose duties on occupiers of premises, and also on occupiers of any fixed or moveable structure.[71] This expands the definition of occupier considerably and has been held to include scaffolding,[72] a ship in dry dock,[73] a lift,[74] and a 'splat wall.'[75]

Lawful visitors and non-lawful visitors

As is discussed later, the duty of care owed to lawful visitors is different from that owed to non-lawful visitors. It is therefore important to distinguish between the two. A person is a lawful visitor if:

- he has been invited by the occupier on to the occupier's premises; or
- he has a contractual right to be on the premises; or
- he is on the premises as of right (for example, under a statutory power of entry, such as that possessed by the police or firemen);[76] or
- he is on the premises because he has been expressly or impliedly permitted by the occupier to be on them. Implied permission (or the granting of an 'implied licence' as it is known) can be difficult to recognize. Certain implied licences are

---

69. OLA 1957, s 1(2); OLA 1984, s 1(2).
70. [1966] AC 552 (HL) 577. Accordingly, ownership or physical possession of the land is not necessary.
71. OLA 1957, s 1(3); OLA 1984, s 1(2).   72. *Kearney v Eric Waller Ltd* [1967] 1 QB 29 (QB).
73. *London Graving Dock Co Ltd v Horton* [1951] AC 737 (HL). This case was decided at common law, but is still applicable.
74. *Haseldine v Daw & Son Ltd* [1941] 2 KB 343 (CA). This case was decided at common law, but is still applicable.
75. *Gwilliam v West Hertfordshire Hospital NHS Trust* [2002] EWCA Civ 1041, [2003] QB 443 (a 'splat wall' is a velcro wall, which people attempt to stick onto by jumping onto it via a trampoline).
76. OLA 1957, s 2(6).

well established (for example, the right to visit a public library to borrow books). In all other cases, the existence of an implied licence is one of fact and it will be for the claimant to prove that he had an implied licence to be on the premises.[77] The mere toleration of non-lawful visitors incurring on premises is not normally enough to grant an implied licence, but if the occupier acts in such a way as to indicate assent to such incursions, then an implied licence might result.[78]

A lawful visitor may become a non-lawful visitor if he visits parts of the premises of the occupier to which he has not been invited or allowed to enter, or if he stays beyond a specified time.

It is often stated (incorrectly) that the OLA 1984 imposes duties on occupiers only in relation to trespassers. This is incorrect because the OLA 1984 imposes a duty on occupiers in relation to persons other than lawful visitors. This will obviously include trespassers, but can also include persons who are not trespassing (for example, those using a private right of way).

Liability to lawful visitors

The common duty that the occupier of premises owes towards the person and property of his lawful visitors is defined, under s 2(2) of the OLA 1957 as:

> a duty to take such care as, in all the circumstances of the case, is reasonable to see that the visitor will be reasonably safe in using the premises for the purposes for which he is invited or permitted by the occupier to be there.

The common duty of care imposed by the statute closely resembles the standard and duty of care that are the bases of the common law tort of negligence. It should be noted that s 2(2) requires occupiers to look after the reasonable safety of the visitor—the duty is not to make the premises reasonably safe. The operation of the duty imposed by s 2(2) can be seen in the following cases. In the first case, the duty was not breached, whereas in the second case, the duty was breached.

Bowen and Others v National Trust [2011] EWHC 1992 (QB)

FACTS: A group of schoolchildren were visiting a woodland trail in a wood managed by the defendant. It began to rain so the children and their teacher took shelter under a tree. Without warning, a large branch fell from the tree and landed on some of the children. One child was killed and three others were injured. The parents of the deceased child and the injured children commenced proceedings against the defendant. The claimants contended that the defendant's tree inspectors had not exercised reasonable care when examining the trees and tagging those trees that required attention.

HELD: The claimants' action failed. Mackay J stated that the 'inspectors used all the care to be expected of reasonably competent persons doing their job'[79] and that the incident was caused by 'the cruellest coincidence of the failure occurring at the very moment when this small group was standing under the branch...'[80]

---

77. *Edwards v Railway Executive* [1952] AC 737 (HL).   78. *Lowery v Walker* [1911] AC 10 (HL).
79. [2011] EWHC 1992 (QB) [43].   80. ibid.

Murphy v Bradford Metropolitan Council [1992] PIQR P68 (CA)

FACTS: The defendant occupied and managed a school, at which the claimant worked as a teacher. Snow fell several inches deep and the defendant initiated clearance work at around 6.30 a.m. A sloping path leading to the school was cleared and salt was placed down. At around 8.40 a.m., whilst walking on the path, the claimant slipped and was injured. A handrail was subsequently built along the path. The claimant sued.

HELD: Although the work to clear the snow began early, the actual steps taken were insufficient given the prevailing conditions. The sloping path was a likely source of an accident and was therefore 'a candidate for special attention'.[81] The subsequent building of the handrail, although not evidence of an omission on the defendant's behalf, was evidence that the path was deserving of special measures.

The OLA 1957 elaborates upon the duty in several ways. Section 2(3)(a) provides that the occupier must be prepared for children to be less careful than adults. Accordingly, the duty will require the premises to be safe for a child of that age but, in cases involving very young children, primary responsibility for the safety of such children rests with their parents,[82] and it would be socially undesirable to allow parents to shift the burden of looking after their children to those who have accessible premises. Provided that it is reasonably foreseeable that children will play on premises and be injured, it is irrelevant that their actual behaviour was unforeseeable.[83]

Section 2(3)(b) provides that 'an occupier may expect that a person, in the exercise of his calling, will appreciate and guard against any special risks ordinarily incident to it, so far as the occupier leaves him free to do so'. Should this person fail to guard against such risks and be injured, the occupier will not be liable.

Roles v Nathan [1963] 1 WLR 1117 (CA)

FACTS: Premises occupied by the defendant contained two chimney flues that required sealing. This was to be carried out by two chimney sweeps, who were warned about the danger of carbon monoxide poisoning. The work was partially completed, but the flues could not be fully sealed because the sweeps ran out of concrete. It was agreed that the work would be completed the following day, but the sweeps, without informing the defendant, decided to complete the work late that same night. The following day, both sweeps were found dead near the flues and carbon monoxide poisoning was established as the cause of death. The sweeps' widows alleged that the defendant had breached the duty imposed by the OLA 1957.

HELD: The Court of Appeal held that the duty had not been breached. The sweeps should have been aware of the risk of carbon monoxide poisoning and should have guarded against it.

---

81. [1992] PIQR P68 (CA) 72 (Stocker LJ).
82. *Phipps v Rochester Corporation* [1955] 1 QB 450 (CA). In this case, the children were five and seven years old.   83. *Jolley v Sutton LBC* [2000] 1 WLR 1082 (HL). This case is discussed at p 412.

Section 2(4)(b) provides that:

> where damage is caused to a visitor by a danger due to the faulty execution of any work of construction, maintenance or repair by an independent contractor employed by the occupier, the occupier is not to be treated without more as answerable for the danger if in all the circumstances he had acted reasonably in entrusting the work to an independent contractor and had taken such steps (if any) as he reasonably ought in order to satisfy himself that the contractor was competent and that the work had been properly done.

Even if the occupier has taken reasonable steps to ensure that the independent contractor is competent, he still needs to take steps to ensure that the contractor's work has been properly completed. If, however, the nature of the contractor's work is technical or specialized, the occupier will usually not be required to check the contractor's work.

Warnings

If an occupier warns his lawful visitors of a danger, he discharges his duty of care, provided that the notice in itself is enough to render a visitor reasonably safe.[84] Whether a notice is sufficient is a question of fact. It is generally thought that a notice must specify the nature and location of the danger, so that a prudent visitor can take steps to avoid it. Hence a notice that simply says 'Danger' would not discharge the occupier's duty unless the danger were obvious. However, if the danger is obvious, there may be no need to warn at all, because any visitor exercising reasonable care for his own safety should recognize and avoid the hazard.

 Darby v National Trust [2001] EWCA Civ 189

FACTS: The defendant occupied a piece of National Trust property that contained numerous ponds. There was a (somewhat inconspicuous) sign in the car park forbidding visitors from bathing and boating. The claimant's husband drowned whilst swimming in one of the ponds. She contended that the ponds should have 'No Swimming' signs displayed around them and that the lack of such signs amounted to a breach of duty.

HELD: The duty had not been breached. The water in the pond was murky and the risks posed by bathing in the pond were obvious. Accordingly, the defendant was not under a duty to warn against them.

Exclusion of the duty of care

An occupier may seek to exclude or restrict the duty that he would otherwise owe under the OLA 1957, either by a term in a contract with his visitor, or by means of a notice indicating that those who enter do so at their own risk. Whilst such terms and notices are permitted by s 2(1), there are limitations upon such terms and notices, including:

- An occupier cannot contractually exclude/restrict the common duty of care owed to those lawful visitors who enter by virtue of a contract, but who are not parties to that contract.[85]

---

84. OLA 1957, s 2(4)(a).   85. ibid ss 2(1) and 3(1).

- Any exclusion/restriction of liability by an exclusion clause must satisfy the common law rules relating to the exclusion/restriction of liability.
- An occupier of business premises cannot, by an exclusion clause or notice, exclude or restrict the duty of care imposed by s 2(2) of the OLA 1957 in respect of death or personal injury to visitors, and he can only exclude or restrict liability for causing other types of injury (for example, damage to property) if such exclusion or restriction is reasonable.[86]

> 🔗 The requirement of reasonableness under the Unfair Contract Terms Act 1977 is discussed at p 228

Defences

A defendant has access to two principal defences. First, s 2(5) provides that the duty imposed by s 2(2) does not impose on an occupier 'any obligation to a visitor in respect of risks willingly accepted as his by the visitor'. In other words, the defence of *volenti non fit injuria* is available. Second, s 2(3) provides that, in determining whether the s 2(2) duty has been breached, the court should take into account 'the degree of care, and of want of care, which would ordinarily be looked for in…a visitor'. Therefore, a want of care will entitle the defendant to raise the defence of contributory negligence.

> ➡️ *volenti non fit injuria*: 'to a willing person, no harm is done' (see 'Consent and voluntary assumption of risk' at p 477)

> 🔗 The defence of contributory negligence is discussed at p 484

Liability to non-lawful visitors

The OLA 1984 provides that occupiers owe a duty to all persons other than lawful visitors (for example, trespassers), but s 1(3) provides that this duty only arises if:

(a) he is aware of the danger or has reasonable grounds to believe that it exists;

(b) he knows or has reasonable grounds to believe that the other is in the vicinity of the danger concerned or that he may come into the vicinity of the danger (in either case, whether he has lawful authority for being in that vicinity or not); and

(c) the risk is one against which, in all the circumstances of the case, he may reasonably be expected to offer the other some protection.

In relation to (a) and (b), 'reasonable grounds to believe' require that the occupier should actually know the relevant facts, or know facts that provide grounds for a relevant belief established by evidence; it is not enough simply that he ought to have known.[87] Basically, the occupier is not in breach of duty if a non-lawful visitor is injured by a danger of which the occupier was reasonably unaware, but the occupier must protect a non-lawful visitor adequately from those dangers of which he is aware or ought reasonably to have been aware. Even when the occupier is aware of some danger to non-lawful visitors, his duty is not to render them safe, but to take reasonable care to see that the danger does not cause injury to that non-lawful visitor.[88] Moreover, even if the occupier is in breach of his duty under the OLA 1984, a non-lawful visitor can recover damages only for certain injuries—namely, death and personal injury—and not for damage to his property.[89]

The standard of care

Section 1(4) provides that the occupier is to take such care as is reasonable in all of the circumstances to see that the non-lawful visitor does not suffer injury on the

---

86. Unfair Contract Terms Act 1977, s 2.
87. *Swain v Natui Ram Puri* [1996] PIQR P442 (CA).   88. OLA 1984, s 1(4).
89. ibid s 1(8) and (9).

premises by reason of the danger concerned. The following two cases demonstrate the scope of this duty.

Platt v Liverpool City Council [1997] CLY 4864 (CA)

FACTS: The defendant engaged in a rehousing programme, involving the emptying, repairing, and, in some cases, the demolition of properties. The defendant secured one such property against intruders by fixing metal sheets over the doors and windows. Additionally, an employee of the defendant routinely checked the property. Following one such check, it was discovered that the property was so badly vandalized that it would need to be demolished. The defendant arranged for an eight-foot fence to be placed around the building. A group of boys entered the property, which then collapsed, killing one of the boys. The boy's father commenced proceedings.

HELD: The duty imposed by s 1(4) was to take such care as was reasonable in all of the circumstances. There was no evidence that, prior to the boys entering the property, anyone else had overcome the fence. Accordingly, the defendant had done what was reasonable to prevent injury and so was not liable.

Ratcliff v McConnell [1999] 1 WLR 670 (CA)

FACTS: The claimant, a 19-year-old college student, had been drinking with friends, but he was not drunk. They agreed to go swimming in the college's open-air swimming pool, which was surrounded by walls and fences, and secured by a locked gate. The claimant climbed over these and dived into the shallow end of the pool. As the pool was closed for the winter, however, it contained very little water and the claimant hit his head on the bottom, causing him to sustain severe injuries that rendered him tetraplegic. He sued the college governors.

HELD: The danger in question (that is, hitting one's head when diving into the shallow end of a swimming pool) was common to all swimming pools and was obvious to any adult (indeed, the claimant admitted knowing of this danger). The duty imposed by s 1(4) did not require occupiers to protect non-lawful visitors from dangers of which they should have been fully aware, and so the claim failed.

Warnings

Section 1(5) of the OLA 1984 states:

> Any duty owed by virtue of this section in respect of a risk may, in an appropriate case, be discharged by taking such steps as are reasonable in all the circumstances of the case to give warning of the danger concerned or to discourage persons from incurring the risk.

Under the OLA 1957, a warning will discharge the duty only if it enables the visitor to be reasonably safe. There is no such requirement in the case of the OLA 1984 and therefore warnings are more likely to discharge a duty owed to a non-lawful visitor than to a visitor, as the following example demonstrates.

Warnings under the OLA 1957 and OLA 1984

Dewi owns a disused factory surrounded by a large fence. On the fence and around the factory are signs stating 'Warning! Factory floor unsafe'. Dewi asks John, a structural engineer, to visit the factory and assess what renovations need to be completed to make the factory safe. Whilst at the factory, the floor gives way and John is injured. The presence of the warning will not discharge Dewi's liability, because the signs have not enabled John to be reasonably safe.

A day after John's accident, Owen climbs the fence and forces his way into the factory. Another portion of the floor gives way and Owen is injured. The warning will discharge Dewi's duty, because the signs warn of the danger and discourage persons from incurring the risk.

Exclusion of the duty of care

An occupier may seek to exclude or restrict the duty that he would otherwise owe under the OLA 1984 by means of a notice indicating that those who enter do so at their own risk. The 1984 Act does not indicate whether such exclusion of liability is permissible, but it might be thought odd if liability to lawful visitors could be excluded, but not liability to non-lawful visitors. The Unfair Contract Terms Act 1977 does not apply to the duty imposed by s 1(4) of the OLA 1984. Consequently, it appears that any occupier can exclude or restrict the duty owed to non-lawful visitors, unless any breach of duty also constitutes common law negligence.

Defences

As under the OLA 1957, the defences of *volenti* and contributory negligence are available.

Nuisance and *Rylands v Fletcher*

The ownership/occupation of land imposes an obligation on the owner and/or the occupier to take due care to ensure that the state of the land or activities carried out on it do not cause injury to others. If injury is caused to others, the owner/occupier of the land may be liable in negligence. Additionally, there are two other torts (which overlap with negligence) that impose obligations on those who own/occupy land—namely, nuisance and the rule in *Rylands v Fletcher*. Nuisance can be further subdivided into private nuisance and public nuisance, with Table 15.1 highlighting the differences between the two.

It should be noted that the two forms of nuisance are not mutually exclusive, and that an act can amount to both a public and private nuisance.

Private nuisance

Every occupier of property must expect his property and his enjoyment of it to be affected to some degree by the activities of his neighbours or the physical state of adjoining land. However, if this interference exceeds what one can reasonably be expected to endure, it is an actionable private nuisance.

TABLE 15.1 Private and public nuisance

	Private nuisance	Public nuisance
Legal status?	A tort only	Both a crime and a tort
Interest in land?	The claimant will require an interest in the land	No interest in the land is required to bring a claim
Damages recoverable?	Property damage and loss of enjoyment of rights over property	Property damage, loss of enjoyment of rights over property, personal injury, and economic loss
Defences	*Volenti*; contributory negligence; prescription; statutory authority	*Volenti*; contributory negligence

The classic definition of a private nuisance is provided by Winfield and Jolowicz, who define it as 'an unlawful interference with a person's use or enjoyment of land, or some right over, or in connection with it'.[90] This interference can take a number of different forms, including:

- **Physical interference** Physical damage to property can constitute a private nuisance. This could include damage to crops caused by fumes from a neighbouring copper-smelting works,[91] the collapse of the defendant's property onto the claimant's land,[92] and damage resulting from vibrations caused by neighbouring machinery.[93]

- **Encroachment** If some feature of a person's land encroaches on the land of another and causes damage (for example, damage caused to the foundations of the claimant's property by roots encroaching from a tree on the defendant's land),[94] this can constitute a private nuisance.

- **Interference with the enjoyment of land (known as 'amenity nuisance')** This is by far the widest category of private nuisance, and can include acts as diverse as the crowing of cockerels,[95] the opening of a sex shop in a residential area,[96] and the opening of a fish-and-chip shop in a fashionable street.[97]

The point to be drawn is that private nuisance requires the claimant to show proof of damage. The damage need not be physical, but it must be present.

When is interference unlawful?

It can be very difficult to distinguish between an act that amounts to the lawful use of land and an act that amounts to private nuisance. The courts are required to engage in a fine balancing act. As Lord Wright stated: 'A balance has to be maintained

---

90. WVH Rogers, *Winfield & Jolowicz on Tort* (18th edn, Sweet & Maxwell 2010) 712. The courts have adopted this definition on numerous occasions (e.g. *Read v Lyons & Co Ltd* [1945] KB 216 (CA) 236 (Scott LJ)).
91. *St Helen's Smelting Co v Tipping* (1865) 11 HL Cas 642 (HL).
92. *Wringe v Cohen* [1940] 1 KB 229 (CA).   93. *Grosvenor Hotel Co v Hamilton* [1894] 2 KB 836 (CA).
94. *Masters v Brent London Borough Council* [1978] QB 841 (QB).
95. *Leeman v Montagu* [1936] 2 All ER 1677.
96. *Laws v Florinplace Ltd* [1981] 1 All ER 659 (Ch). See also *Thompson-Schwab v Costaki* [1956] 1 WLR 335 (CA) (use of residential premises as for the purposes of prostitution).
97. *Adams v Ursell* [1913] 1 Ch 269 (Ch).

between the right of the occupier to do what he likes with his own [land], and the right of his neighbour not to be interfered with.'[98] This balance is reflected in the fact that the interference must be substantial: 'The law does not regard trifling inconveniences: everything is to be looked at from a reasonable point of view.'[99] An obvious example is noise pollution. One must expect a certain amount of noise from one's neighbours, but it is only when that noise becomes excessive that an actionable nuisance might have been committed.

Given the breadth of activities that could potentially amount to a private nuisance, the courts have adopted a broad approach, determining unlawfulness by reference to a reasonableness test. In determining whether an interference is reasonable or not, the court will take into account a number of factors. The first factor is the extent of the damage suffered by the claimant as a result of the interference, which will be highly dependent upon the facts of the case. The playing of loud music in the middle of the day might be a minor inconvenience, whereas playing loud music at 2 a.m. will constitute a more substantial interference. No action would arise if the person bringing the claim was deaf, because there would be no damage caused.

The second factor is the duration of the interference: the more persistent the interference, the more likely it is to constitute an actionable private nuisance. Isolated or infrequent acts are highly unlikely to constitute a private nuisance. Students who host one noisy party are highly unlikely to commit an actionable private nuisance—but students who host such parties every night almost certainly will have committed a private nuisance. Isolated or infrequent acts can, however, be actionable if they are extremely disruptive.[100]

Related to the duration and extent of the interference is the third factor—namely, the issue of locality. The submission of fumes or the making of noise by a factory in a heavy industrial area would be much less likely to amount to a nuisance than if the factory were close to a residential area. As Thesiger LJ famously stated: 'What would be a nuisance in Belgrave Square would not necessarily be so in Bermondsey.'[101] Where property damage is caused, the issue of locality is less relevant, because no one should expect to have his property damaged by the acts of another.

The fourth factor is the sensitivity of the claimant or his property. If the damage is attributable to the claimant's sensitivity to a greater degree than to the conduct of the defendant, no nuisance will be committed.

 ## Robinson v Kilvert (1889) 41 Ch D 88 (CA)

FACTS: The defendant landlord manufactured cardboard boxes in the cellar of his building. This required the cellar to be hot and dry, so he purchased a heating apparatus for that purpose. The claimant rented the floor above the cellar and used it, *inter alia*, to store delicate brown paper. The defendant's heaters caused the temperature to rise in the floor occupied by the claimant and, while the people who worked there were in no way inconvenienced by the rise in temperature, the heat caused the brown paper to dry and decrease in value. The claimant alleged that the defendant's actions amounted to a private nuisance.

98. *Sedley-Denfield v O'Callaghan* [1940] AC 880 (HL) 903.
99. *St Helen's Smelting Co v Tipping* (1865) 11 HL Cas 642 (HL) 653 (Lord Westbury).
100. *Spicer v Smee* [1946] 1 All ER 489 (KB) (an isolated incident of defective wiring that caused a neighbour's house to burn down).   101. *Sturges v Bridgman* (1879) 11 Ch D 852 (CA) 865.

HELD: The claimant's action was dismissed. The heat did not cause discomfort to the claimant's workforce, nor would it have affected normal paper. The damage was caused more by the paper's delicacy than by the defendant's actions.

The fifth factor is motive. An act that would normally be lawful and reasonable might become an actionable nuisance if it were to be motivated by malice.

Hollywood Silver Fox Farm Ltd v Emmett [1936] 2 KB 468 (KB)

FACTS: The claimant bred silver foxes. During the breeding season, the vixens were very nervous and, if disturbed, they would refuse to breed or would miscarry, or might even kill their young. The defendant occupied land adjoining that of the claimant and was concerned that the presence of the fox farm might affect the value of his property. He therefore caused his son to discharge guns near the claimant's land with the express purpose of disturbing the claimant's business.

HELD: As the defendant discharged the guns on his own land, this would not normally amount to a nuisance. However, as the defendant's actions were motivated by malice, an actionable nuisance was committed, and the claimant was granted an injunction and damages.

The final factor to be discussed is fault. Nuisance is not a strict liability tort, but neither does the claimant need to establish negligence. In *The Wagon Mound (No 2)*, Lord Reid stated that 'fault of some kind is almost always necessary and fault generally involves foreseeability'.[102] However, given that negligence is fault-based, how can it be said that negligence is not required? The answer lies in that Lord Reid stated that 'negligence in the narrow sense is not essential'.[103] What this means is that the claimant need not show that the defendant breached his duty or care; all that need be established is that the defendant failed to meet the standard of a reasonable man. In 1994, the House of Lords revisited the requirement of fault and stated that:

> [T]he fact that the defendant has taken all reasonable care will not of itself exonerate him…But it by no means follows that the defendant should be held liable for damage of a type which he could not reasonably foresee.[104]

Accordingly, no nuisance will be committed if the damage is not reasonably foreseeable, but if it is foreseeable, the fact that the defendant took reasonable steps to avoid the damage will not exonerate him.

Who can sue?

The occupier of property affected by the nuisance is the usual claimant, and he can recover damages for injury to, and for injury to enjoyment of, the property. Alternatively, or additionally, he may seek an injunction to prevent the nuisance

---

102. *Overseas Tankship (UK) Ltd v Miller Steamship Co Pty Ltd (The Wagon Mound)* [1967] 1 AC 617 (PC) 639.
103. ibid.
104. *Cambridge Water Co Ltd v Eastern Counties Leather plc* [1994] 2 AC 264 (HL) 300 (Lord Goff).

continuing. An owner of property who is not in occupation can also sue in nuisance, but only for damage to the property.

The claimant must have a proprietary interest in the land affected. Despite the criticism levelled against this requirement and a brief departure from it by the Court of Appeal,[105] the House of Lords has reaffirmed the requirement.[106] This requirement may not survive for long. Article 8(1) of the European Convention on Human Rights (ECHR) provides that '[e]veryone has the right to respect for his private and family life, his home and his correspondence'. This right is granted irrespective of propri-etary rights, so limiting nuisance actions to those persons who have a proprietary interest could be viewed as contrary to Art 8 and the retention of the requirement could be viewed as a breach of s 6 of the Human Rights Act 1998.

Section 6 of the 1998 Act is discussed at 'Acts of public authorities' on p 100

Who can be sued?

The person in occupation of the property from which the nuisance emanates is liable if either:

- he created the nuisance and was 'at fault' in so doing.[107] 'Fault' in nuisance means that the creator of the nuisance deliberately engaged in conduct that caused the nuisance (whether or not he intended to cause a nuisance) and the injury suffered by the claimant was either reasonably foreseeable or was a 'real risk'. A 'real risk' seems to mean that the injury to the claimant could have been foreseen, even if it was not *reasonably* foreseeable, and that the injury, if it occurred, was likely to be serious;[108] or

- the nuisance was created by a third party (for example, a trespasser),[109] or arose naturally (for example, a tree struck by lightning), and the person in occupation cannot prove that he was not negligent in failing to prevent the nuisance affect-ing the claimant. In deciding whether the defendant has done enough to prevent the injury to the claimant, the courts have regard to the defendant's personal circumstances, such as his age, financial circumstances, etc. Thus, unusually, the standard of care imposed on the defendant is that of a reasonable person in the *defendant's* circumstances.

If a person other than the occupier of the property from which it emanates cre-ated the nuisance, the person creating the nuisance is also liable. A landlord is not, however, responsible for nuisances committed by his tenants unless the nuisance is in some way connected with their occupation of the property and the landlord has authorized or adopted it.[110]

Defences

A defendant has access to several defences, namely:

- **Prescription** The defence of prescription arises where the defendant has com-mitted an actionable nuisance for twenty years and action has not been taken

---

105. *Khorasandjian v Bush* [1993] QB 727 (CA).

106. *Hunter v Canary Wharf Ltd* [1997] AC 655 (HL).

107. *Overseas Tankship (UK) Ltd v Miller Steamship Co Pty Ltd (The Wagon Mound (No 2))* [1967] 1 AC 617 (PC).

108. ibid.

109. *Sedleigh-Denfield v O'Callaghan* [1940] AC 880 (HL). The third party who created the nuisance was also liable.

110. *Hussain v Lancaster City Council* [2000] QB 1 (CA) (council not liable for harassment and racist abuse committed by tenants of its property).

during that period. Note that if there were periods during which the act was not actionable, the defence of prescription will not succeed.[111]

- *Volenti non fit injuria* Where the claimant voluntarily consents to the act that amounts to an actionable nuisance, the defendant may be able successfully to raise the defence of *volenti*.

🔗 *Volenti* is discussed at 'Consent and voluntary assumption of risk' on p 477

- **Contributory negligence** If the defendant contributes in some way to the act that amounts to an actionable nuisance, his damages may be reduced on the ground of his contributory negligence.

🔗 Contributory negligence is discussed on p 484

- **Statutory authority** The defendant may have the defence of statutory authority if the act in question is authorized by statute.

🔗 The defence of statutory authority is discussed on p 481

Remedies

Several remedies may be available to the victim of an actionable private nuisance, as follows.

- **Injunction** The primary remedy is the granting of an injunction to stop the nuisance. The injunction may be granted wholly or in part.[112]

- **Damages** Damages can be sought instead of, or in addition to, an injunction. Damages will compensate the claimant only for the loss in the value of the land and/or the loss of the ability to use or enjoy the land. Damages for other losses (for example, personal injury or economic loss) are not recoverable under the tort of nuisance. Only foreseeable losses can be claimed and the test of remoteness in nuisance is the same as in negligence.

🔗 The rules relating to remoteness in negligence are discussed at p 410

- **Abatement** Abatement involves the claimant taking steps to prevent or stop the nuisance himself (for example, by cutting off overhanging branches).[113] Abatement, like all self-help remedies, needs to be exercised cautiously and its exercise is usually advised against. It is usually only appropriate in clear and simple cases, or in an emergency.[114]

Public nuisance

A private nuisance is a tort only and is concerned with protecting a person's right in land. Conversely, a public nuisance is both a crime and a tort, and, as its name suggests, is concerned with protecting a wider group of persons. A public nuisance has been defined as one that 'materially affects the reasonable comfort and convenience of life of a class of the public who come within the sphere or neighbourhood of its operation'.[115] What constitutes a class of the public will depend upon the facts of the case. Examples of public nuisances include obstruction of the highway, selling food unfit for human consumption, the carrying on of an offensive trade, or the expulsion of noxious fumes over a wide area.

There are three significant limitations on the scope of what constitutes a public nuisance: (i) the claimant must prove the existence of widespread harm; (ii) the act must cause a common injury to the class of persons concerned;[116] and (iii) the claimant

---

111. *Sturges v Bridgman* (1879) 11 Ch D 852 (CA).

112. *Kennaway v Thompson* [1981] QB 88 (CA) (the Court held that nearby powerboats could not create a noise of over 75 decibels and no more than six boats could be on the water at any one time).

113. *Lemmon v Webb* [1895] AC 1 (CA).   114. *Burton v Winters* [1993] 1 WLR 1077 (CA).

115. WVH Rogers, *Winfield & Jolowicz on Tort* (18th edn, Sweet & Maxwell 2010) 709.

116. *R v Rimmington and Goldstein* [2005] UKHL 63, [2006] 1 AC 459 (HL).

must prove that he suffered special damage (that is, damage greater than that suffered by the class of persons affected by the act). This requirement does not apply in relation to actions brought by local authorities or the Attorney General.

Who can sue and be sued?

It would appear that proceedings may be commenced by the following.

- **Local authorities** A local authority may commence proceedings for an injunction in its own name for the purposes of 'promotion or protection of the interests of the inhabitants of their area'.[117]

> **relator action:** an action brought by the Attorney General upon application from a private person, inviting him to join in bringing proceedings

- **The Attorney General** As public nuisance is a crime, the Attorney General can bring a **relator action** seeking an injunction to prevent the nuisance. The Attorney General will only consider such an action if the applicant has suffered special harm.

- **Private citizens** A private citizen can commence proceedings for an injunction or for damages in two situations:

  - where the nuisance in question appears to be a private nuisance, but affects a much larger group of persons (the requisite number of persons will vary, depending on the facts);

  - even where the nuisance does not affect the claimant's land, he can still bring a claim if it affects the public, but it affects him to a greater degree (that is, he suffers special damage).

Persons who can be liable for public nuisance are the same as those who can be liable for private nuisance.

Defences

The available defences for a public nuisance are broadly the same as those for a private nuisance—but (i) because a public nuisance constitutes a crime, the defence of prescription is not available; and (ii) the Law Reform (Contributory Negligence) Act 1945 does not apply to criminal liability.

Remedies

Two remedies are available. First, as with private nuisance, an injunction may be available requiring the defendant to stop the nuisance. This may be sought by a local authority, the Attorney General, or a private citizen. Second, like private nuisance, damages are recoverable by a private person for damage to property, but, unlike private nuisance, damages are also recoverable for personal injury[118] and economic loss.[119]

Rylands v Fletcher

The rule in *Rylands v Fletcher* is a distinct tort in its own right, although it bears an extremely close resemblance to private nuisance. Where it differs is that a person with neither an interest in land nor exclusive possession of it could also have a cause of action. The rule was created in response to the infliction of harm caused to land by increased industrialization brought about by the Industrial Revolution. The courts'

---

117. Local Government Act 1972, s 222(1).

118. See e.g. *Castle v St Augustine's Links* (1922) 38 TLR 615 (KB) (taxi driver hit by golf ball).

119. See e.g. *Fritz v Hobson* (1880) 14 Ch D 542 (Ch) (loss of profits caused by obstruction of highway).

reputation. Defamation seeks to protect a person's reputation and occurs where the defendant publishes a statement referring to the claimant that lowers the claimant in the estimation of right-thinking members of society generally, or which would tend to make them shun or avoid him. Today, the majority of defamation cases tend to relate to statements made on television or in newspapers about celebrities or other persons in the public eye,[142] but defamation can have a strong commercial aspect too. For example, an auditor who states in his report that the directors are untrustworthy and engaged in suspect commercial transactions may be liable for defamation if such statements are untrue.

In March 2011, the coalition government published a consultation document in which the Secretary of State for Justice stated that 'our defamation laws are not striking the right balance, but rather are having a chilling effect on freedom of speech'.[143] The consultation was followed by a Defamation Bill, which has since been enacted as the Defamation Act 2013. The Act (which came into force on the 1 January 2014) does not seek to completely replace the common law rules relating to defamation, but instead reforms the law in a piecemeal manner. Accordingly, the Act's provisions will be referred to as and when relevant.

Before the law relating to defamation is discussed, one notable reform introduced by the Defamation Act 2013 should be noted. For a considerable period of time, there had been significant concern about the extent to which the English courts were a forum for 'libel tourism'. Libel tourism occurs where parties seek to take advantage of English law's claimant-friendly defamation laws by commencing defamation proceedings in a court in England and Wales, even though the reputational damage they may have suffered occurred largely outside of England and Wales (and, in many cases, neither of the parties are domiciled in the UK). Section 9(2) of the 2013 Act aims to curtail libel tourism by providing that:

> A court does not have jurisdiction to hear and determine an action to which this section applies unless the court is satisfied that, of all the places in which the statement complained of has been published, England and Wales is clearly the most appropriate place in which to bring an action in respect of the statement.

Libel and slander

Defamation is a collective term for two torts, namely libel and slander, and the distinction between them relates to the medium of publication:

- **libel** is a defamatory statement published in a permanent form (for example, a film, newspaper, or book);
- **slander** is a defamatory statement published in a non-permanent form (for example, through spoken words or gestures).

It is important to be able to distinguish between slander and libel for two reasons. First, slander per se is only ever a tort,[144] whereas libel is both a tort and a crime. Second, libel is actionable even if the libel has not caused any damage to

---

142. Although, in 2011, the number of such cases decreased considerably, as such persons instead sought to protect their reputations via the use of anonymized injunctions and superinjunctions.

143. Ministry of Justice, *Draft Defamation Bill: Consultation* (TSO 2011) 3.

144. Slanderous words accompanied by other more serious wrongs (e.g. blasphemy) may constitute a crime.

the claimant. Conversely, slander is generally not actionable unless damage has been caused to the claimant, but there are exceptions to this (for example, where the slander imputes that the claimant is dishonest or unfit for his office, trade, or profession.)[145]

Who can sue?

In Chapter 13, it was noted that the death of the claimant will not normally cause the right of action to lapse. Defamation is the sole exception to this: it is impossible to defame the dead and the death of the claimant will extinguish an existing cause of action. Accordingly, any living person (natural or legal) can sue for defamation. Local authorities and other organs of the state cannot sue for defamation, however, on the ground that '[i]t is of the highest public importance that a democratically elected governmental body, or indeed any governmental body, should be open to uninhibited public criticism'.[146]

The requirements for defamation

A statement[147] will only be defamatory if the party alleging defamation can satisfy three requirements, namely that:

1. the statement must be defamatory;
2. the statement must refer to the claimant; and
3. the statement must be published.

Each of these requirements will now be discussed.

The statement must be defamatory

The first requirement is that the statement was defamatory, with a defamatory statement defined as one that tends 'to lower the claimant in the estimation of right-thinking members of society generally'.[148] The use of the word 'generally' indicates that a statement that lowers the claimant in the estimation of a specific group of persons will not therefore amount to defamation.[149] However, a statement that is not, in itself, generally defamatory, but when coupled with facts known only to specific persons, may become defamatory.[150] Such a statement is known as an 'innuendo' and can be defamatory if the claimant can establish that the words have this hidden meaning known only to certain persons. In the following case, the judge found that a statement was defamatory based on its natural meaning, but went on to state that, if this opinion were wrong, the statement would be defamatory through its innuendo meaning.

---

145. Defamation Act 1952, s 2.
146. *Derbyshire County Council v Times Newspapers Ltd* [1993] AC 534 (HL) 547 (Lord Keith).
147. Section 15 of the Defamation Act 2013 defines a statement as 'words, pictures, visual images, gestures or any other method of signifying meaning'.
148. *Sim v Stretch* [1936] 2 All ER 1237 (HL) 1240 (Lord Atkin).
149. *Tolley v Fry & Sons Ltd* [1931] AC 333 (HL).
150. For example, *Cassidy v Daily Mirror Newspapers Ltd* [1929] 2 KB 331 (CA).

Lord McAlpine of West Green v Bercow
[2013] EWHC 1342 (QB)

FACTS: The claimant had been a high-profile politician in the Conservative Party. On the 2nd November 2012, the television programme *Newsnight* aired a story stating that 'a leading Conservative politician from the Thatcher years' had been implicated in a series of child abuse allegations. *Newsnight* did not name the politician who had been implicated and the individual who alleged the abuse later revealed that he had implicated the wrong person. The story was picked up by print newspapers and Internet websites, and several politicians, including the claimant, were named as potentially being the politician in question. On 4 November 2012, Mrs Bercow, the wife of the Speaker of the House of Commons, published a tweet that stated 'Why is Lord McAlpine trending? *Innocent face*'. Lord McAlpine commenced proceedings against Mrs Bercow.

HELD: At a preliminary hearing to determine whether the tweet was defamatory, Tugendhat J held that it would be reasonable to assume that readers of the tweet would link Lord McApline with the allegations that were aired on *Newsnight*. Such readers would also likely interpret the phrase 'innocent face' as being insincere and ironic. Readers reading the tweet would thereby infer, based on the ordinary and natural meaning of the words, that the tweet meant that Lord McAlpine was a paedophile. Tugendhat J went on to state that, even if this opinion were wrong, the tweet would bear an innuendo meaning to the same effect. Following this case, Bercow agreed with Lord McAlpine's lawyers to pay an undisclosed amount of damages.

When determining whether a statement is defamatory, the court will look at the context in which the statement is being made. This is important, as a statement that would not normally be defamatory can, based on the context in which it was made, become defamatory, as occurred in the following case.

Church v MGN Ltd [2012] EWHC 693 (QB)

FACTS: *The People* newspaper (which was owned by the defendant) published a story in which at alleged that Charlotte Church drunkenly proposed to her boyfriend during a 'boozy pub karaoke night'. The story was accompanied by the headline 'Marryoke'. It transpired that the couple in question was not Church and her boyfriend (indeed Church was performing elsewhere at the time of the incident). Church commenced proceedings against the defendant.

HELD: Tugendhat J stated that it was not defamatory to state that one person had proposed to another. However, he went on to state that:

> Whether or not words complained of are defamatory depends on the context in which they appear. The behaviour described might not be defamatory if attributed to some other people, but to attribute such drunken behaviour to a star such as the Claimant is in my judgment clearly capable of defaming her.[151]

---

151. [2012] EWHC 693 (QB), [2013] 1 WLR 284 [16].

The case was later settled when the defendant paid Church an undisclosed sum.

Section 1(1) of the Defamation Act 2013 introduced a notable limitation on what types of statement can be defamatory. Section 1(1) provides that a statement will not be defamatory 'unless its publication has caused or is likely to cause serious harm to the reputation of the claimant'. Section 1(2) goes on to state that 'harm to the reputation of a body that trades for profit is not "serious harm" unless it has caused or is likely to cause the body serious financial loss'.

The statement referred to the claimant

The second requirement is that the statement must refer to the claimant. This does not require that the statement refer to the claimant by name or that the defendant intended to refer to the claimant;[152] all that is required is that a reasonable person would believe that the statement referred to the claimant.[153] So, for example, a statement may refer to the occupier of a particular office, or to a group of persons that includes the claimant. However, where the group is large, the claimant will need to demonstrate that the statement in some way points specifically to him.[154]

The statement must be published

The final requirement is that the statement was published, but the word 'publication' does not bear its ordinary meaning; rather, it refers to the communication of the statement to at least one person other than the claimant. It follows that if the statement is sent only to the claimant, then no defamation has occurred.[155] This reinforces the notion that defamation is concerned with protecting the claimant's reputation in the eyes of others and not with protecting the claimant's own sense of self-esteem.

Under the common law, every republication of a defamatory statement would result in a new cause of action against the publisher of that statement[156] (usually, the original maker of the statement is not liable for its republication). Significantly, with each republication, the limitation period would, as against the publisher, begin anew. This multiple publication rule was strongly criticized by publishers, especially in the online age where a statement can be distributed to, and read by, millions in a matter of seconds. Accordingly, s 8 of the Defamation Act 2013 introduces a single publication rule, which provides that the date on which the limitation period commences will run from the date of first publication 'to the public' of the statement. Subsequent republication will not cause the limitation period to begin anew, unless the republication is materially different from the first publication.[157]

Defences

A number of defences are available to a person who is alleged to have made a defamatory statement. The Defamation Act 2013 has abolished and replaced certain common law defences, but other common law defences remain. The defences are:

- **Truth** It will be a complete defence for the defendant to demonstrate that 'the imputation conveyed in the statement complained of is substantially true'.[158]

---

152. *Houlton & Co v Jones* [1910] AC 20 (HL).   153. *Hayward v Thompson* [1982] QB 47 (CA).
154. *Knupffer v London Express Newspaper Ltd* [1944] AC 16 (HL).
155. *Pullman v W Hill & Co Ltd* [1891] 1 QB 524 (CA).
156. *M'Pherson v Daniels* (1829) 10 B & C 263.   157. Defamation Act 2013, s 8(4).
158. ibid s 2(1). This defence replaces the common law defence of justification.

- **Honest opinion** This defence arises where three conditions are satisfied, namely (i) the statement complained of must be a statement of opinion; (ii) the statement complained of must indicate, whether in general or specific terms, the basis of the opinion; and (iii) an honest person could have held the opinion on the basis of any fact which existed at the time the statement was published, or anything asserted to be a fact in a privileged statement published before the statement complained of.[159] Note that the defence will not succeed if the claimant can show that the defendant did not hold the opinion.[160]

- **Publication on matter of public interest** It will be a defence for the defendant to show that (i) the statement complained of was, or formed part of, a statement on a matter of public interest; and (ii) the defendant reasonably believed that publishing the statement complained of was in the public interest.[161]

- **Consent** A person who consents to publication of a defamatory statement cannot subsequently sue for defamation in relation to that statement.[162]

- **Responsibility for publication** A person who is not the author, editor, or publisher of the statement (for example, a printer or distributor) has a defence if he can show that he took reasonable care in relation to its publication and that he did not know, and had no reason to believe, that what he did caused or contributed to the publication of a defamatory statement.[163] The Defamation Act 2013 improves the protection of defendants in this area by providing that a court will not have jurisdiction to hear a defamation action brought against a person who was not the author, editor, or publisher of the statement complained of unless the court is satisfied that it is not reasonably practicable for an action to be brought against the author, editor, or publisher.[164]

- **Operators of websites** The Defamation Act 2013 provides a new defence for website operators that publish potentially defamatory statements on their websites. This provides that it will be a defence for the operator to show that it was not the operator who posted the statement on the website.[165] However, s 5(3) and (11) provides for instances in which the defence can be defeated (e.g. the defence will be defeated if it is not possible for the claimant to identify the person who posted the statement). If a statement on a website is found to be defamatory, then the court can order the operator of the website to remove the statement.[166]

- **Offer to make amends** A person who has published a statement that is allegedly defamatory can offer to make amends by issuing a suitable correction of the statement complained of, making a sufficient apology, and paying the aggrieved party such compensation (if any) and such costs as are agreed or determined to be payable.[167] If the offer is accepted, the party accepting the offer cannot continue proceedings, but can enforce the offer to make amends.[168] If the offer is rejected, the offer is a complete defence unless the claimant can show that, when publishing the defamatory material, the defendant knew, or had reason to believe, that it referred to the claimant, and was both false and defamatory.

- **Absolute privilege** A limited number of statements are absolutely privileged and cannot, normally, form the basis of an action for defamation. Examples of such statements include statements made in Parliament[169] and fair and accurate contemporaneous reports of court proceedings in (i) any court in the UK; (ii)

---

159. ibid s 8(1)–(4). This defence replaces the common law defence of fair comment.
160. ibid s 8(5).   161. ibid s 4(1).   162. *Monson v Tussauds Ltd* [1894] 1 QB 671 (CA).
163. Defamation Act 1996, s 1.   164. Defamation Act 2013, s 10(1).   165. ibid s 5(2).
166. ibid s 13(1).   167. Defamation Act 1996, s 2.   168. ibid s 3(2).
169. Bill of Rights 1688, art 9. Note, however, that the Defamation Act 1996, s 13, allows a Member of Parliament to waive parliamentary privilege.

any court established under the law of a country or territory outside the UK; or (iii) any international court or tribunal established by the Security Council of the United Nations or by an international agreement.[170]

- **Qualified privilege** A statement subject to a qualified privilege loses such privilege if it is made maliciously. Schedule 1 of the Defamation Act 1996 provides a non-exhaustive list of statements to which qualified privilege attaches. In addition, s 6 of the Defamation Act 2013 bestows qualified privilege upon peer-reviewed statements in scientific or academic journals.

Remedies

Damages

Defamation is an extremely unusual tort, in that it is a civil action that was, until the passing of the Defamation Act 2013, usually tried by jury[171] and it was the jury that therefore determined the quantum of damages. It has long been believed that juries award defendants damages in excess of their actual loss. Accordingly, three steps have been taken to ensure that the damages awarded by juries better reflect the claimant's loss:

- a judge may direct the jury regarding the quantum of damages in defamation cases;[172]
- juries can be referred to conventional compensation awards in personal injury cases by way of comparison;[173]
- where the Court of Appeal considers a jury's award of damages to be excessive, it can set aside the award of damages and either order damages to be reassessed by a new jury,[174] or substitute the award of the jury for 'such sums as appears to the court to be proper'.[175]

🔗 Exemplary damages are discussed at p 490

Exemplary damages may be awarded in libel cases in which the defendant publishes a libel believing that the revenue generated by the published item will exceed the likely award of damages payable.[176]

Injunction

A person who believes that he has been defamed may apply for an interim injunction to restrain publication of the allegedly defamatory statement until the jury can determine whether the statement is defamatory or not. Again, competing interests are involved, but it is clear that the law favours the freedom of expression and that an interim injunction restraining publication will not be granted unless the court is satisfied that 'the applicant is likely to establish that publication should not be allowed'.[177]

---

170. Defamation Act 1996, s 14.
171. Senior Courts Act 1981, s 69(1)(b) (now repealed) provided that there was a presumption that defamation cases would be tried by jury. The Defamation Act 2013 has abolished this presumption.
172. *Rantzen v Mirror Group Newspapers* [1994] QB 670 (CA).
173. *John v Mirror Group Newspapers Ltd* [1997] QB 586 (CA).
174. *Sutcliffe v Pressdram Ltd* [1991] 1 QB 153 (CA).
175. Courts and Legal Services Act 1990, s 8(2).
176. *Cassell & Co Ltd v Broome* [1972] AC 1136 (HL).   177. Human Rights Act 1998, s 12(3).

The effect of the Human Rights Act 1998

In relation to defamation, the law has always had to strike a fine balance between two conflicting legitimate principles—namely, the protection of a person's reputation and the preservation of freedom of expression. With the passing of the Human Rights Act 1998 and the consequent ability to domestically enforce the ECHR, striking the correct balance has become even more important. The two competing principles are both enshrined in the ECHR.

- Article 8 provides: 'Everyone has the right to respect for his private and family life, his home and his correspondence.' Accordingly, a person has a right not to have private information revealed that could damage his reputation.
- Article 10 provides: 'Everyone has the right to freedom of expression. This right shall include freedom to hold opinions and to receive and impart information and ideas without interference by public authority and regardless of frontiers.' However, this right is not absolute and signatory states may restrict freedom of expression to the extent that it is necessary in a democratic society to protect the reputation of others.

Even where issues of privacy are not involved, Art 10 can still conflict with the protection of a person's reputation. Defendants in defamation cases frequently invoke Art 10 and the courts will have to determine in each case which of the competing, but legitimate, rights is more deserving of protection. It is generally believed that the courts tend to protect freedom of expression to a greater degree than a person's reputation. The following case provides an example.

O'Shea v Mirror Group Newspapers Ltd [2001] EMLR 40 (QB)

FACTS: The first defendant published the *Sunday Mirror*. The second defendant ran a pornographic website, which was advertised in the *Sunday Mirror*. The advertisement contained a picture of a glamour model, who closely resembled the claimant. The claimant had stated that several people had believed that she was the woman in the advertisement. She commenced libel proceedings.

HELD: The High Court dismissed her claim. Morland J stated that, under the common law, her claim would have succeeded (because unintentional defamation is based on strict liability).[178] Such a result, however, could not stand with Art 10 and it would 'impose an impossible burden on a publisher if he were required to check if the true picture of someone resembled someone else who because of the context of the picture was defamed'.[179]

See Jonathan Coad, ' "Pressing Social Need" and Strict Liability in Libel' (2001) 12 Ent LR 199

However, this belief should be reassessed in light of the recent spate of cases involving anonymized injunctions and superinjunctions.

---

178. *Houlton & Co v Jones* [1910] AC 20 (HL).   179. [2001] EMLR 40 (QB) [43].

Breach of statutory duty

Statute may impose duties on persons, breach of which will result in sanctions set out in statute. Alternatively, the statute may not provide for any sanctions at all. Increasingly, aspects of business life are being regulated by statute. Much of this legislation imposes criminal liability if the duty is breached. The question that arises is whether a person who has suffered loss due to another's breach of statutory duty can commence a private action in tort to recover damages for that loss. Where such an action is permissible, the defendant may have committed a tort known as 'breach of statutory duty'. An action for breach of statutory duty can be advantageous, especially where the duty imposed is strict. In such a case, the claimant will not need to establish negligence or fault. In order for such a claim to succeed, a number of issues need to be addressed, beginning with whether the breach of the statutory duty gives rise to an action in tort.

Does the breach give rise to an action in tort?

Not every breach of a statutory duty results in the right to bring an action in tort for breach of statutory duty. The reason is that statutory provisions imposing a duty on organizations or people normally have a public purpose to achieve and provide sanctions for breach of the duty. Hence, the courts may think it inappropriate to hold that such a statute should also create private rights allowing individuals to sue for its breach. Thus, the first task of the court is to determine whether breach of the particular statutory duty that has caused injury is actionable in tort. In determining this, the court will seek to ascertain the intention of Parliament. In some cases, the statute itself may expressly indicate Parliament's intention by providing that breach of a statutory duty does not give rise to civil proceedings,[180] or breach of a statutory duty can specifically give rise to a private civil action by any person who suffers loss due to the breach.[181] In the majority of cases, however, the statute will be silent on this issue and the court will need to seek Parliament's implied intention. The following case demonstrates how an implied intention can manifest.

 Atkinson v Newcastle and Gateshead Waterworks Co (1877) 2 Ex D 441 (CA)

FACTS: The Waterworks Clauses Act 1847 placed a duty on the defendant to maintain a level of pressure in water pipes used to supply water to Newcastle. Breach of this duty resulted in a £10 fine, which would go to the overseers of the parish. Breaches of other duties in the 1847 Act were punishable with fines, part of which could be paid to those who suffered injury. The claimant's premises caught fire, but there was insufficient pressure in the pipes to expel water at a fast enough rate and so the premises burnt down. The defendant paid the £10 fine to the parish and the claimant brought a claim in damages for his loss.

---

180. For example, Health and Safety at Work etc. Act 1974, s 47(1)(a); Medicines Act 1968, s 133(2)(a); and Guard Dogs Act 1975, s 5(2)(a).

181. For example, Financial Services and Markets Act 2000, s 150(1); Consumer Protection Act 1987, s 41(1); and Mineral Workings (Offshore Installations) Act 1971, s 11.

HELD: No action in tort could arise for breach of the statutory duty. The Court was heavily influenced by the fact that the statute did not provide for payment to persons who suffered loss due to insufficient water pressure, but did provide payment to those who suffered loss as regards other breaches. The implied intention of Parliament was therefore that persons who suffer loss due to insufficient water pressure should not be able to recover compensation.

The courts take a restrictive view of when a statutory duty is actionable in tort. The courts will require that (i) the duty imposed protects a limited class of the public[182] (as opposed to the public generally); and (ii) Parliament intended to confer on members of that class a private right of action for breach of the duty. In determining this, a number of factors may be relevant, including:

- If there exists a common law duty in respect of particular activities, the courts may be inclined to find that breach of a statute dealing with similar activities is also tortious (and vice versa)[183] in so far as the civil action for breach of statutory duty complements the common law.

- If a statute is designed to prevent a particular type of injury and it is that type of injury that the claimant has suffered, an action in tort is more likely to exist.[184] However, if the loss suffered is pure economic loss, it is unlikely that the courts will impose civil liability on the party bearing the statutory duty.[185]

- If a statute provides no sanction for its breach, a civil action in tort may lie, because, unless such an action were available, breach of that statute would escape all punishment.[186]

- The fact that some part of a fine levied for breach of statutory duty can be used to compensate the victim of that breach militates against, but does not preclude, a right to sue in tort.[187]

- The fact that a statute, although designed to benefit a section of the public, has a community or social welfare remit (for example, the provision of education or housing) has tended to militate against the imposition of civil liability.[188] In such cases, it has been suggested that a remedy under the judicial review jurisdiction, rather than an action in tort, should be sought.

To whom is the duty owed?

Once it is determined that a statutory duty can give rise to an action in tort, the claimant will need to establish that the duty was owed to him.[189] Accordingly, a duty imposed upon railway authorities to fasten level-crossing gates securely was not owed to a train driver who was injured when an unfastened gate swung across the line.[190] However, if a statute imposes a duty, but does not define the class that the statute is designed to protect, the courts will tend to hold that the duty is owed to anyone adversely affected by the breach.[191]

---

182. *X v Bedfordshire County Council* [1995] 2 AC 633 (HL).
183. *Cutler v Wandsworth Stadium Ltd* [1949] AC 398 (HL).
184. *Monk v Warbey* [1935] 1 KB 75 (CA).
185. *Murphy v Brentwood District Council* [1991] 1 AC 398 (HL).
186. *Thornton v Kirklees Metropolitan Borough Council* [1979] QB 626 (CA).
187. *Groves v Lord Wimborne* [1898] 2 QB 402 (CA).
188. *O'Rourke v Camden London Borough Council* [1998] AC 188 (HL).
189. *Hartley v Mayoh & Co Ltd* [1954] 1 QB 383 (CA).
190. *Knapp v Railway Executive* [1949] 2 All ER 508 (CA).
191. *Westwood v Post Office* [1974] AC 1 (HL).

In addition, the injury sustained by the claimant must have been of the kind that the statute sought to prevent.

 Gorris v Scott (1874) 9 LR Exch 125

FACTS: Section 75 of the Contagious Diseases (Animals) Act 1869 placed a duty on the defendant to provide pens for any livestock being transported on his ship. He failed to do this and the claimant's sheep were washed overboard. The claimant sued.

HELD: The court held that the purpose of the duty contained in s 75 was to prevent the spread of disease amongst livestock and not to prevent them being washed overboard. Accordingly, the injury sustained by the claimant was not of the type the statute sought to protect and his claim failed.

Breach of duty

As with negligence, once a duty is established, the claimant will need to demonstrate that the duty was breached. The standard that a person must reach in order to avoid liability is determined by reference to the statute in question. In addition to defining the scope of the duty, a court must also, by reference to the statute, consider the degree of fault that the defendant must have displayed if he is to incur liability. For example, if a statute provides that an employer must do something, it must be done, and any failure to comply with the Act in question, however innocent, will constitute a breach of statutory duty.[192]

Causation

The claimant must establish that the breach caused his injuries. If the breach caused his injuries (at least partially), the claimant can recover damages even if he is also in breach of a statutory duty. Thus, if an employer fails to encourage his employees to wear safety goggles that he has provided and this failure is a breach of a statutory duty, an employee who suffers eye injuries while not using his goggles can recover damages. This is the case even if the employee was in breach of a statutory duty owed by him to wear the goggles.[193] On the other hand, if the claimant's breach of statutory duty is the sole cause of his injuries, he cannot recover damages even though the defendant was also in breach of a statutory duty.[194]

Defences

An employer can raise the defence of contributory negligence when sued by his employees for breach of statutory duty. However, it is the policy of the courts, in deciding whether an employee has contributed to his injuries:

to give due regard to the actual conditions under which men work in a factory or mine, to the long hours and the fatigue, to the slackening of attention which

192. *John Summers and Sons Ltd v Frost* [1955] AC 740 (HL).
193. *Bux v Slough Metals Ltd* [1973] 1 WLR 1358 (CA). In this case, the employee's damages were reduced by 40 per cent to reflect his partial responsibility for his injuries.
194. *Ginty v Belmont Building Supplies Ltd* [1959] 1 All ER 414 (QB).

naturally comes from constant repetition of the same operation, to the noise and confusion in which the man works, to his preoccupation in what he is actually doing at the cost perhaps of some inattention to his own safety.[195]

To do otherwise would be to deprive employees of the protection of much of the safety legislation that is designed to protect them.

The defence of *volenti* is also available, but in relation to employment cases involving breach of statutory duty, the courts adopt a paternalistic approach. It is settled law that an employer who is personally in breach of a statutory duty cannot rely on this defence at all.[196] An employer who is in breach of statutory duty because he is held vicariously responsible for the actions of another one of his employees can, however, raise this defence.[197]

Chapter conclusion

This chapter has discussed a number of torts that can be committed by, and against, businesses. They range from torts committed in relation to goods (for example, product liability and trespass to goods), to torts committed in relation to land (for example, nuisance and occupiers' liability). Some of the torts discussed are based on a party taking reasonable care (for example, occupiers' liability), whereas others are based on strict liability (for example, product liability under the Consumer Protection Act 1987). Some are designed to regulate the activities of businesses (for example, product liability), whereas others actually seek to protect businesses from interference from others (for example, the economic torts). The point to note is that the variety of business-related torts is substantial and, whilst negligence is undoubtedly the principal tort, businesses must be aware of the full scope of tortious liability in which their actions can result.

In many cases, the party liable for the commission of a tort is not actually the party who committed it. In Chapter 16, we discuss when one party can be liable for the tortious acts of another.

 Key points summary

Product liability

- Product liability at common law is based upon Lord Atkin's narrow rule from *Donoghue v Stevenson*. It is therefore a species of negligence.

- The Consumer Protection Act 1987 introduces a system whereby manufacturers of defective products can be liable even though they are not at fault.

- Any person who suffered damage due to a defective product may commence an action under the 1987 Act. The Act applies only to defective products that cause death, personal injury, or loss of, or damage to, non-business property.

---

195. *Caswell v Powell Duffryn Associated Collieries Ltd* [1940] AC 152 (HL) 178 (Lord Wright).
196. *Baddeley v Earl Granville* (1887) 19 QBD 423 (DC).
197. *ICI Ltd v Shatwell* [1965] AC 656 (HL).

Trespass to goods

- Trespass to goods comprises any direct physical interference with goods that are in the possession of another person, without the consent of the person in possession, unless there is lawful justification for the interference.

- Conversion is an intentional act dealing with goods in a manner that is inconsistent with another's possession, or which serves to deny another's right to immediate possession.

Occupiers' liability

- Occupiers of premises owe a statutory duty towards persons on those premises, whether they are there lawfully or unlawfully.

- The Occupiers' Liability Act 1957 provides that an occupier is under a duty to take such care as is reasonable, in all of the circumstances of the case, to see that the visitor will be reasonably safe in using the premises for the purposes for which he is invited or permitted by the occupier to be there.

- The Occupiers' Liability Act 1984 provides that an occupier is under a duty to take such care as is reasonable, in all of the circumstances, to see that the non-lawful visitor does not suffer injury on the premises by reason of the danger concerned.

Nuisance and *Rylands v Fletcher*

- An unlawful interference with a person's use or enjoyment of land or some right over, or in connection with, it may constitute a private nuisance. A private nuisance is a tort only.

- A public nuisance is one that materially affects the reasonable comfort and convenience of life of a class of the public that comes within the sphere or neighbourhood of its operation. A public nuisance is both a tort and a crime.

- The tort of *Rylands v Fletcher* occurs where a person brings a thing onto his land, or allows a thing to accumulate on his land, that, if it were to escape, would be likely to do mischief.

Defamation

- Defamation occurs where the defendant publishes a statement referring to the claimant that lowers the claimant in the estimation of right-thinking members of society generally, or which would tend to make them shun or avoid him.

- A defamatory statement published in permanent form constitutes libel, whereas a defamatory statement published in a non-permanent form constitutes slander. Slander per se is only a tort, whereas libel can be both a tort and a crime.

Breach of statutory duty

- Not all breaches of statutory duty will give rise to liability in tort. Whether an action in tort can be founded will be ascertained by reference to Parliament's intention. This intention can be express or implied.

Self-test questions

1. Define the following:
   (a) strict liability;
   (b) own-brander;
   (c) trespass to goods;
   (d) conversion;
   (e) prescription.

2. In the following scenarios, can liability be imposed under the Consumer Protection Act 1987, Pt I? Explain the reasons behind your answer.
   (a) John purchases a new flat-screen television from his local branch of Asteroid Ltd, a countrywide chain of electrical retailers. A circuit board in John's television is defective causing sparks to be omitted from the rear of the television. John removes the rear casing of the television to try to fix the problem himself. John is electrocuted in the attempt and sustains severe burns to his hand. Can John sue Asteroid Ltd?
   (b) Perdita is employed as a test driver for ALV plc, a car manufacturer. She is test-driving a new prototype car with an electric engine on the company's test track. The brakes are defective and Perdita crashes, sustaining severe injuries.

3. lsquo;The existence of the tort of nuisance means that the rule in *Rylands v Fletcher* is now of no practical importance and should be abolished.' Do you agree with this statement? Provide reasons for your answer.

4. Discuss whether or not the following acts constitute a nuisance.
   (a) A neighbour keeps chickens that crow noisily at around 1 p.m.
   (b) A factory emits fumes. The fumes would not normally damage flowers and plants, but a nearby resident grows rare and delicate roses that are damaged by the fumes.
   (c) An errant golf ball struck from a golf course leaves the course and strikes a person walking along a pavement.
   (d) Discuss whether or not the reforms contained in the government's draft Defamation Bill will improve the law relating to defamation.

Further reading

Kirsty Horsey and Erika Rackley, *Tort Law* (3rd edn, OUP 2013) ch 13
A clear and well-structured discussion of product liability at common law and under the Consumer Protection Act 1987

Mark Lunney and Ken Oliphant, *Tort Law: Text and Materials* (5th edn, OUP 2013) chs 12 and 13
Chapter 12 provides an excellent account of the torts of nuisance and Rylands v Fletcher and provides useful commentary on many key cases. Chapter 13 provides an up-to-date discussion of the tort of defamation, which incorporates the amendments made by the Defamation Act 2013

Christopher Newdick, 'The Development Risks Defence of the Consumer Protection Act 1987' (1988) 47 CLJ 455
Discusses the background to, and offers an analysis of, the development risks defence

WVH Rogers, *Winfield & Jolowicz on Tort* (18th edn, OUP 2010) chs 7 and 9
Provides an in-depth discussion of breach of statutory duty and occupiers' liability

Remember to visit the **Online Resource Centre** at **<http://www. oxfordtextbooks.co.uk/orc/roach3e>** to access the following resources on Chapter 15, 'Business-related torts': more **practice questions** and answers; a **glossary** of key terms; **multiple-choice questions**; and **revision summaries**. Updates to the law can be found on Twitter by following **@UKBusinessLaw**.

16 Vicarious liability

- The fundamental principles
- The employer–employee relationship
- The commission of a tort
- In the course of employment
- Defences and obtaining a contribution

INTRODUCTION

A pedestrian is negligently knocked over by a lorry driver who was not insured by his employer to drive company vehicles. A cleaner in a hospital fails to indicate that a patch of flooring is wet, causing a patient to slip and injure himself. A trainee journalist writes a defamatory article in a local newspaper. A junior accountant fails to notice that the directors of a company he audits are engaged in fraud.

In all of these cases, the ability of the tortfeasor to compensate the victims fully for any loss is doubtful. It is here that the doctrine of vicarious liability is of crucial importance, because it allows the victim to claim compensation from the tortfeasor's employer for acts of his employees. Accordingly, it is crucial that businesses understand the extent of their liability for acts of their employees.

The fundamental principles

In August 2000, Mr Hawley visited a nightclub in Essex. Upon leaving the nightclub, he was, without apparent cause, assaulted by a doorman, who thereby committed the tort of **battery**. Mr Hawley commenced legal proceedings for battery against the company that owned the nightclub and employed the doorman. His claim succeeded and the owner of the nightclub was required to pay damages to Mr Hawley. The case of *Hawley v Luminar Leisure Ltd*[1] clearly demonstrates the fundamental principles behind the doctrine of vicarious liability that had been established in previous decisions, as outlined in Table 16.1.

➡ **battery:** the direct application of unlawful violence to another

Distinguishing vicarious liability from personal liability is vital. In *Hawley*, the doorman was personally liable because he committed the tort and caused Mr Hawley to suffer loss. The nightclub owner's liability was vicarious, because it did not actually

---

1. [2005] EWHC 5 (QB), [2005] Lloyd's Rep IR 275.

TABLE 16.1 *Hawley* and the fundamental principles of vicarious liability

Principle	Application in *Hawley*
A person (usually an employer) may be liable in tort for the wrongful acts of another (usually the employer's employee)	In *Hawley*, the employer was vicariously liable for the wrongful acts of the doorman
Liability in tort is usually imposed on a party who has displayed some degree of fault or blameworthiness. Vicarious liability is an exception to this principle and a person (usually an employer) may be vicariously liable even though he is not, in any way, at fault	In *Hawley*, the fault lay with the doorman, yet his blameless employer was held liable
Vicarious liability is not a tort in itself and does not create a cause of action; rather, it enables the claimant to sue on an existing cause of action against a party other than the tortfeasor, provided that the other party has a particular relationship with the tortfeasor and the tort committed was referable to that relationship	In *Hawley*, the claimant had an existing cause of action in battery against the doorman. The doctrine of vicarious liability simply allowed the claimant to pursue this cause of action against the doorman's employer
The word 'vicarious' is somewhat misleading, because it derives from the Latin *vicarius* meaning 'substitute'. This would seem to indicate that the tortfeasor's liability is substituted onto another party, thus extinguishing the liability of the tortfeasor. This is not the case, because *both* the tortfeasor and the other party are jointly liable to compensate the claimant and the claimant is free to proceed against whoever he wishes	In *Hawley*, the claimant had already received compensation from the doorman before he commenced proceedings against the doorman's employer. Vicarious liability provides an additional defendant, not an alternative one

commit the tort, but was held liable as if it had. Why should an employer (who, in many cases, will be blameless) be liable for the acts of its employees? Several justifications have been advanced, including:

- The employer is likely to have access to greater funds than the employee and is therefore a more reliable source of compensation. Further, it is more sensible that the employer bears the loss, because the employer will be better able to absorb any losses, either by passing the cost on to customers in the form of a price increase, or by providing insurance for the workforce.[2]
- As employers derive an economic benefit from the acts of their employees, they should also bear any loss deriving from such acts. As Fleming stated: '[A] person who employs others to advance his own economic interest should in fairness be placed under a corresponding liability for losses incurred in the course of the enterprise.'[3]

Vicarious liability encourages employers to monitor their employees to ensure that they act in a proper manner. If this were a valid justification, however, the law would limit the employer's liability to those instances in which it could have prevented the employee's commission of the tort.[4] The law has never imposed such a limitation.

It is worth mentioning at the outset that the concept of vicarious liability does not only apply to common law torts, but can also apply to a breach of any statutory obligation (where the breach can result in damages) imposed upon the employee. As Lord Nicholls stated: 'Unless the statute expressly or impliedly indicates otherwise, the

---

2. Under the Employers' Liability (Compulsory Insurance) Act 1969, s 1, every employer must insure his employees against 'liability for bodily injury or disease'.
3. John G Fleming, *The Law of Torts* (9th edn, LBC 1998) 410.
4. Nicholas J McBride and Roderick Bagshaw, *Tort Law* (3rd edn, Pearson 2008) 653.

principle of vicarious liability is applicable where an employee commits a breach of a statutory obligation sounding in damages while acting in the course of his employment.[5] This broadens the scope of the concept of vicarious liability significantly.

Most vicarious liability cases occur within a relationship of employment. However, other relationships can give rise to the imposition of vicarious liability, including the following:

- Partners in a partnership are vicariously liable for the acts of each other provided that they are 'acting in the ordinary course of the business of the firm';[6]
- A principal will be vicariously liable for torts committed by his agent provided that the agent is acting within the scope of his authority[7]—but personal liability is likely to be imposed upon the agent if he assumes a personal responsibility towards the third party[8] or if he knowingly makes a false statement.[9]

    The law of agency is discussed in Chapter 8

- In *JGE v Portsmouth Roman Catholic Diocesan Trust*,[10] the Court of Appeal held that vicarious liability could be imposed in cases of relationships that were 'akin to employment'. In that case, the Court held that a bishop could be liable for the abuse committed by a parish priest.

However, as the vast majority of vicarious liability cases concern the employer–employee relationship, this chapter will focus on the three requirements needed to impose vicarious liability upon an employer for the acts of an employee:

1. there must be an employer–employee relationship;
2. the employee must have committed a tort; and
3. the tort must have been committed in the course of the employee's employment.

The employer–employee relationship

The imposition of vicarious liability is generally dependent upon there being an employer–employee relationship between the tortfeasor and his purported employer. It follows that if the employer can establish that the tortfeasor is, in fact, not an employee, vicarious liability cannot normally be imposed. It is therefore necessary to determine exactly who is an employee. In particular, it is crucial that we draw a distinction between employees and independent contractors, because employers are not vicariously liable for torts committed by their independent contractors. The justification behind this is that an employer will have less control over the actions of an independent contractor and so should not be liable for his actions. It is worth noting that the distinction between employees and independent contractors is not only relevant in relation to tort, but is also crucial in a number of other areas, notably employment law.

The importance of the distinction for employment law purposes is discussed at p 690

5. *Majrowski v Guy's and St Thomas' NHS Trust* [2006] UKHL 34, [2007] 1 AC 224 [17].

6. Partnership Act 1890, s 10. This provision is discussed in 'Liability for tortious and other wrongful acts' at p 521.

7. *Lloyd v Grace, Smith & Co* [1912] AC 716 (HL).

8. *Williams v Natural Life Health Foods Ltd* [1998] 2 All ER 577 (HL).

9. *Standard Chartered Bank v Pakistan National Shipping Corporation (Nos 2 and 4)* [2002] UKHL 43, [2003] 1 AC 959.

10. [2012] EWCA Civ 938, [2013] QB 722.

The starting point is to define what an 'employee' is. Section 230(1) of the Employment Rights Act 1996 defines an employee as an 'individual who has entered into or works under…a contract of employment' and s 230(2) defines 'a contract of employment' as 'a contract of service or apprenticeship, whether express or implied, and (if it is express) whether oral or in writing'. An employee therefore is someone who operates under a contract *of* service, as opposed to an independent contractor who operates under a contract *for* services. However, this distinction provides little aid, and so the responsibility of determining how to distinguish between employees and independent contractors has been left to the courts and employment tribunals.

 These tests are discussed in 'Distinguishing between employees and independent contractors' at p 692

The courts have been unable to devise a single test that can differentiate between an employee and an independent contractor. Instead, a number of differing tests have been used. As these tests are crucial to numerous employment law issues, the various tests are discussed in the employment law section of this text.

Identifying the employer

The majority of cases in this area have focused on attempting to identify whether or not the tortfeasor was an employee or not. In certain situations, however, there may be doubt as to the identity of the employer. This arises most commonly when an employer (known as the 'permanent employer') lends or hires an employee to another employer (known as the 'temporary employer'). If the employee commits a tort, which employer is vicariously liable? Guidance came in the following case.

Mersey Docks and Harbour Board v Coggins & Griffith (Liverpool) Ltd [1947] AC 1 (HL)

FACTS: The Harbour Board (the permanent employer) employed a crane driver named Newall. It hired Newall and a crane to Coggins (the temporary employer) under a contract that provided that Newall would be an employee of Coggins, although he would continue to be paid by the Harbour Board. Coggins instructed Newall as to what goods needed unloading, but did not instruct him on how to unload them. While unloading the goods, Newall negligently injured the claimant. The question was whether the Harbour Board or Coggins was vicariously liable for Newall's negligence.

HELD: The House of Lords held that the Harbour Board was vicariously liable. The House made the following statements.

- The permanent employer would be presumed to be the employer unless he could clearly establish otherwise.
- A term in the contract providing that the employee is to be an employee of the temporary employer will not avoid the imposition of vicarious liability on the permanent employer.[11]
- The most important factor is who controlled the way in which the employee was to work. Coggins (the temporary employer) could only tell Newall what to load and unload; it could not tell him how to do it.

---

11. Although it may be construed by the courts as an indemnity clause entitling the permanent employer to seek an indemnity from the temporary employer if the permanent employer is held vicariously liable for the employee's tort (*Thompson v T Lohan (Plant Hire) Ltd* [1987] 2 All ER 631 (CA)).

The result of *Mersey Docks* was that, in cases involving multiple employers, the permanent employer would be liable unless he could prove that employment had transferred to the temporary employer (which was extremely difficult in practice). This principle, however, has been disturbed somewhat by the following case, in which the Court of Appeal held that the permanent and temporary employers could both be vicariously liable.

 Viasystems (Tyneside) Ltd v Thermal Transfer (Northern) Ltd [2005] EWCA Civ 1151

FACTS: The claimant engaged the first defendant to install air conditioning in one of its factories. The first defendant subcontracted the fitting of air ducts to the second defendant. The ducting work itself would be carried out by a fitter and his mate (the tortfeasors), supplied to the second defendant (the temporary employer) by the third defendant (the permanent employer). Whilst carrying out the ducting work, the fitter and his mate negligently fractured the fire protection sprinkler system, causing the factory to flood. The issue was who was the fitter's employer for the purposes of establishing vicarious liability?

HELD: Whilst there was a long-standing assumption that dual vicarious liability was not possible, it provided a coherent solution to cases involving borrowed employees. Accordingly, both the second and third defendants were held vicariously liable for the acts of the fitter and his mate.

COMMENT: Two comments can be made. First, the Court held the fitter and his mate to be employees, even though there was no contract of employment. Second, whilst both judges involved agreed as to the result, their reasoning differed. For May LJ, 'the core question is who was entitled, and in theory obliged, to control the employee's relevant negligent act so as to prevent it',[12] and if the answer was that both employers had control of the employee, then dual vicarious liability should be imposed. However, Rix LJ stated:

> I am a little sceptical that the doctrine of dual vicarious liability is to be wholly equated with the question of control...[W]hat one is looking for is a situation where the employee in question...is so much a part of the work, business or organisation of both employers that it is just to make both employers answer for his negligence.[13]

★ See Douglas Brodie, 'The Enterprise and the Borrowed Worker' (2006) 35 ILJ 87

Hawley v Luminar Leisure Ltd,[14] discussed at the beginning of this chapter, affirmed the view that dual vicarious liability was permissible, but failed to clarify whether the 'control' test of May LJ or the 'integration' test of Rix LJ was to be preferred. Subsequent cases[15] appeared to favour the control test but, in many of these cases, the possibility of imposing dual vicarious liability was not discussed and the traditional position established in *Mersey Docks* was applied (that is, the permanent employer was found liable). However, in the following case, the Supreme Court held that Rix LJ's approach is to be preferred.

---

12. [2005] EWCA Civ 1151, [2006] QB 510 [49].   13. ibid [79].

14. [2005] EWHC 5 (QB), [2005] Lloyd's Rep IR 275.

15. See e.g. *Biffa Waste Services Ltd v Maschinenfabrik Ernst Hese GmbH* [2008] EWCA Civ 1257, [2009] QB 725; *Colour Quest Ltd v Total Downstream UK plc* [2009] EWHC 540 (Comm), [2009] 2 Lloyd's Rep 1.

> ## Various Claimants v Institute of the Brothers of the Christian Schools [2012] UKSC 56[16]
>
> **FACTS:** The 170 claimants had been pupils of St William's school over a forty-year period until its closure in 1994. The headmaster of the school and many of its teaching staff were drawn from an unincorporated association called the Institute of the Brothers of Christian Schools ('the Institute'). The brothers of the Institute took lifelong vows of chastity. It was discovered that the headmaster and some of the brothers who taught at the School had, for many years, been physically and sexually abusing the pupils. The brothers involved were found guilty of multiple offences and sentenced to significant terms of imprisonment. The issue to be determined in this case was who was vicariously liable for the acts of the brothers. The Court of Appeal held that, as the brothers were employed by the school, it was the school, and not the Institute, that was vicariously liable. The claimants appealed, arguing that the Institute should also be vicariously liable.
>
> **HELD:** In relation to the two approaches established in *Viasystems*, Lord Phillips stated that 'the approach of Rix LJ is to be preferred to that of May LJ'.[17] In applying Rix LJ's approach, Lord Phillips stated that there was a 'very close connection between the relationship between the brothers and the Institute and the employment of the brothers as teachers in the school'.[18] Accordingly, the appeal was allowed and the Court held that both the school and the Institute were vicariously liable for the acts of the brothers.

⭐ See Phillip Morgan, 'Vicarious Liability On the Move' (2013) 129 LQR 139

Personal liability

Having discussed the difference between employees and independent contractors, it is worth noting that whilst employers are not *vicariously* liable for the acts of independent contractors, they may be *personally* liable for the acts of their independent contractors in certain situations, including:

- Where the employer fails to take adequate care in the selection or instruction of that contractor.[19]

- Where the contractor is undertaking a 'non-delegable duty'. A non-delegable duty is not a duty that cannot be delegated by an employer; rather, it simply means that if the employer does delegate the duty to another, the employer cannot escape liability if the duty is improperly performed by that other person. For example, the duty placed upon an employer to take reasonable steps to provide and maintain a safe system of work has been classified as non-delegable.[20]

- An employer can be personally liable if he authorizes or ratifies the commission of a tort by his independent contractor.[21]

- An employer can be personally liable for the acts of an independent contractor if that contractor is engaged in particularly hazardous activities.[22]

---

16. This case is also known as *Catholic Care Welfare Society v Institute of the Brothers of the Christian Schools*.
17. [2012] UKSC 56, [2013] 2 AC 1 [45].   18. ibid [91].
19. *Pinn v Rew* (1916) 32 TLR 451 (DC).
20. *McDermid v Nash Dredging and Reclamation Co* [1987] AC 906 (HL).
21. *Ellis v Sheffield Gas Consumers Co* (1853) 2 E & B 767.
22. *Biffa Waste Services Ltd v Maschinenfabrik Ernst Hese GmbH* [2008] EWCA Civ 1257, [2009] PNLR 12.

In the following Court of Appeal decision, the close connection test was reviewed and the Court attempted to provide some much-needed clarification.

 Gravil v Carroll [2008] EWCA Civ 689

FACTS: The claimant and first defendant were semi-professional rugby players. The first defendant's contract of employment with his rugby club (the second defendant) provided that he would not assault opposing players and that the second defendant might be liable for acts of the first defendant committed in the course of employment. Following a scrum, an altercation developed in which the first defendant punched the claimant, causing the claimant to sustain an orbital fracture near his right eye. The trial judge found the first defendant liable, but refused to impose vicarious liability on the second defendant. The claimant appealed.

HELD: The appeal was allowed. When the battery occurred, it was during the type of altercation that frequently occurs during rugby matches. The punch was regarded by the Court as an ordinary incident of a rugby match and was therefore so closely connected with his employment as to be in the course of employment, thereby rendering the second defendant vicariously liable.

COMMENT: Sir Anthony Clarke MR reviewed the relevant authorities and laid down a number of propositions, as follows.

- The essential question is 'whether the tort is so closely connected with the employment, that is with what was authorised or expected of the employee, that it would be fair and just to hold the employer vicariously responsible'.[38] In answering this question, the court must take into account all of the circumstances of the case.
- 'It will ordinarily be fair and just to hold the employer liable where the wrongful conduct may fairly and properly be regarded as done while acting in the ordinary course of the employee's employment...This is because an employer ought to be liable for a tort which can fairly be regarded as a reasonably incidental risk to the type of business being carried on.'[39]
- 'It is not appropriate to ask...whether in all the circumstances of the case it would be fair and just to hold the club liable. The critical factor is the nature of the employment and the closeness (or otherwise) of the connection between the employment and the tort. The question what is fair and reasonable must be answered in the context of the closeness or otherwise of that connection.'[40]

Defences and obtaining a contribution

If the requirements discussed here have been satisfied, vicarious liability can be imposed on an employer. At this point, the employer has two options to avoid or limit liability—namely, to rely on a defence, or to obtain a contribution from the tortfeasor.

---

38. [2008] EWCA Civ 689, [2008] ICR 1222 [21].   39. ibid.   40. ibid [22].

Defences

🔗 Defences are examined in more depth in Chapter 17.

Those persons found vicariously liable for the acts of others may rely on the defences of *volenti non fit injuria* and contributory negligence.

Obtaining a contribution

As vicarious liability imposes joint and several liability upon the employer and employee, the claimant may elect to sue either party for the full amount. Given that the employer will be insured against such loss and will have 'deeper pockets' than the employee, it is almost always the employer that is sued and which ends up paying damages. As the employee is a joint tortfeasor, however, statute permits the employer to obtain a contribution from the employee[41] that is 'just and equitable having regard to the extent of that person's responsibility for the damage in question'.[42]

Lister v Romford Ice & Cold Storage Ltd [1957] AC 55 (HL)

FACTS: The claimant employed Lister (Lister Jr) as a lorry driver. On one journey, Lister Jr was accompanied by his father (Lister Sr), who was also a fellow employee. Lister Sr got out of the lorry whilst his son parked it. While parking the lorry, Lister Jr negligently drove into his father, injuring him. Lister Sr commenced proceedings against his son's employer, alleging that it was vicariously liable for his son's negligence. His claim succeeded and his son's employer's insurance company paid Lister Sr £1,600. Exercising its right to **subrogation**, the insurance company sued Lister Jr for a contribution.

subrogation: the ability to enforce the legal rights of others

HELD: The insurance company's claim succeeded. The House of Lords held that the insurance company could recover the full £1,600 from Lister Jr.

COMMENT: The *ratio* in *Lister* strongly favours insurance companies. It allows them to continue to receive insurance premiums from employers and to obtain a full contribution from their client's joint tortfeasors. In other words, it allows them to compensate themselves fully for the risk that their clients are paying them to bear.

⭐ See JA Jolowicz, 'The Right to Indemnity Between Master and Servant' (1956) CLJ 101

The controversy surrounding the pro-insurance company stance evident in *Lister* was such that, following a committee of inquiry, all members of the British Insurance Association entered into a gentleman's agreement, which stated:

> Employers' Liability Insurers agree that they will not institute a claim against the employee of an insured employer in respect of the death of or injury to a fellow-employee unless the weight of evidence clearly indicates (i) collusion or (ii) wilful misconduct on the part of the employee against whom a claim is made.[43]

The scope of *Lister* has been qualified further by the case of *Morris v Ford Motor Co*,[44] in which the Court of Appeal prevented a subrogated claim from proceeding on the ground that it was not 'just and equitable',[45] even though such a requirement had never been imposed before.

---

41. Civil Liability (Contribution) Act 1978, s 1.   42. ibid s 2.
43. Reproduced in *Morris v Ford Motor Co* [1973] QB 792 (CA) 799.   44. [1973] QB 792 (CA).
45. ibid 801 (Lord Denning MR).

It has been argued that, in the context of subrogation, such a vague and subjective standard is 'unworkable'.[46] Now that the right to subrogate is contained in statute, the courts' ability to impose such limitations is curtailed. As the quantum of the contribution is limited to what is 'just and equitable', however, the court can limit the contribution to nil if it wishes to deny the insurer's right to subrogation.

Chapter conclusion

Vicarious liability is not a tort in its own right, but is a means whereby one party can be liable for the tortious acts of another. Vicarious liability can arise through a number of relationships, but by far the most common is that of employer and employee. Vicarious liability therefore greatly increases the legal exposure faced by the business community, especially given that liability can be imposed even where the employer is in no way to blame for the loss sustained. Given the level of exposure that vicarious liability can place upon employers, it is vital that businesses with employees have measures in place to minimize the opportunities that its employees have to commit negligent acts (for example, adequate supervision and the prohibition of certain acts). Where an employer is sued for the tortious acts of an employee, the employer may be able to obtain a contribution from the employee, but, given the employee's comparative lack of funds, any such contribution might not offset the damages that the employer was required to pay to the claimant. Further, unless the employer dismisses the employee in question, obtaining a contribution would be likely to sour the employer–employee relationship—although it would certainly send a signal to other employees not to engage in tortious acts.

 Key points summary

- Vicarious liability generally involves the imposition of liability on employers for the tortious acts of their employees. The imposition of vicarious liability does not depend upon the employer being at fault.

- Vicarious liability does not create a cause of action; rather, it allows an existing cause of action to be relied on against the tortfeasor's employer.

- Employers cannot be vicariously liable for the acts of their independent contractors, but in certain circumstances, they may be personally liable.

- The employee's tortious act must have been committed in the course of his employment.

- The close connection test asks whether there was so close a connection between that task and the tort committed by the employee that it would be fair and just to impose vicarious liability on the employer.

- An employer deemed vicariously liable still has access to certain tortious defences (for example, *volenti non fit injuria* and contributory negligence).

- As vicarious liability is joint and several, the claimant can sue either the employer or the employee.

- An employer deemed vicariously liable can seek a contribution from the employee who committed the tort.

---

46. Reuben Hasson, 'Subrogation in Insurance Law: A Critical Evaluation' (1985) 5 OJLS 416, 435.

Self-test questions

1. Why may the word 'vicarious' provide a misleading understanding of the nature of vicarious liability?

2. What are the requirements for the imposition of vicarious liability?

3. Can vicarious liability be imposed in the following cases?
   (a) Charlotte is employed as a courier for Regal Mail plc. On a Sunday, she uses a company van to give her friend a lift to the airport. On the return trip home, she decides to make a number of deliveries to locations between the airport and her house. After making one such delivery, she negligently crashes into a car being driven by Pat.
   (b) Charles is employed as a doorman by Lion Lion plc, a company that owns a chain of nightclubs throughout the UK. One night, whilst working at one of Lion Lion's clubs, he is alerted to a drunken customer who has been kicking the toilet doors and has caused substantial property damage. Charles ejects the customer, but in doing so, he breaks the customer's arm. Would your answer differ if Charles had been expressly prohibited from manhandling troublesome customers?

4. What rights does an employer have against an employee who has committed a tort that results in the employer having to pay compensation?

Further reading

Simon Deakin, ' "Enterprise Risk": The Juridical Nature of the Firm Revisited' (2003) 32 ILJ 97
Discusses the 'enterprise risk' analysis of vicarious liability used in Canadian cases and argues it is preferable to the 'close connection' test established in Lister

Kirsty Horsey and Erika Rackley, *Tort Law* (3rd edn, OUP 2013) 326–38
Provides a clear, well-structured, and up-to-date discussion of vicarious liability

Richard Kidner, 'Vicarious Liability: For Whom Should the Employer Be Liable?' (1995) 15 LS 47
An excellent article that discusses how the emergence of new forms of employment has affected the definition of 'employee'

Claire McIvor, 'The Use and Abuse of the Doctrine of Vicarious Liability' (2006) 35 CLWR 268
Examines recent vicarious liability cases and provides clear criticism; argues that these decisions have been based on a mistaken understanding of the doctrine's theoretical foundations

Ewan McKendrick, 'Vicarious Liability and Independent Contractors: A Re-examination' (1990) 53 MLR 770
Examines the legal relationship between employers and independent contractors; argues that the test for the existence of employment should be context-specific, and that one test should not cover tort and employment law

Robert Weekes, 'Vicarious Liability for Violent Employees' (2004) 63 CLJ 53
Analyses various rationales for imposing vicarious liability and uses them to criticize the court's decision in Mattis v Pollock

Remember to visit the **Online Resource Centre** at **<http://www. oxfordtextbooks.co.uk/orc/roach3e>** to access the following resources on Chapter 16, 'Vicarious liability': more **practice questions** and answers; a **glossary** of key terms; **multiple-choice questions**; and **revision summaries**. Updates to the law can be found on Twitter by following **@UKBusinessLaw**.

17 Tortious defences and remedies

- Defences
- Remedies

INTRODUCTION

The commission of a tort does not guarantee the claimant a remedy, as the defendant may be able to fully excuse or lessen the impact of his tort by successfully raising a defence. It may be the case that a business may need to engage in an act that, in the absence of a defence, would constitute a tort. In such a case, knowing the nature and extent of a defence is extremely important if liability and the payment of compensation are to be avoided. A business that suffers loss due to another's tort will also need to be aware, before it commences legal proceedings, of whether or not the tortfeasor has a potential defence.

If the defendant cannot successfully raise a defence, the claimant will usually be entitled to a remedy. From the perspective of a party that has suffered harm, the overriding concern is what remedy can be obtained and, ultimately, the principal purpose of tort law is to compensate those who have suffered harm due to the tortious acts of another. The scope and purpose of tortious remedies is therefore of immense importance. However, damages will not always be sufficient and the claimant may instead seek an injunction, or may even be able to exercise a remedy himself without the courts' involvement.

In this final chapter on the law of torts, the defences available to a defendant and the remedies sought by a claimant are discussed.

Defences

Even if the claimant can establish that the defendant's actions fulfil the requirements of the tort alleged, it may still be the case that the claim will fail (or damages will be reduced) because the defendant can successfully raise a defence. Certain defences (for example, voluntary assumption or risk, and illegality) are classified as general defences and can be pleaded in relation to any tort. However, the majority of defences either apply only to certain torts (for example, the defence of contributory negligence applies to most torts, but does not apply to actions in deceit or some other actions),[1] or will be specific to a certain tort (for example, self-defence can only be pleaded in cases involving **trespass to the person**).

→ **trespass to the person:** a group of torts relating to the intentional and direct application of force to a person, including assault, battery, and false imprisonment

---

1. *Standard Chartered Bank v Pakistan National Shipping Corporation* [2002] UKHL 43, [2003] 1 AC 599.

Consent and voluntary assumption of risk

A person may have been caused harm by the breach of duty of another, but may be denied a legal remedy on the ground that he in some way consented to the act that caused him harm. In such a case, the tortfeasor can raise the defence of *volenti non fit injuria*. *Volenti* operates as complete defence, fully exonerating the tortfeasor for the harm that he has caused. *Volenti* can arise in two situations:

→ *volenti non fit injuria*: 'to a willing person, no harm is done'

1. A party may decide voluntarily to assume the risk of being injured without having any subsequent legal redress (for example, by accepting a lift in a plane with a drunk pilot).[2] This is more likely to arise in torts involving negligence and strict liability.

2. A party may consent to the act that causes his injury. This is more likely to arise in the case of intentional torts such as trespass to the person. An obvious example of this would be consenting to a medical procedure (performing a medical procedure on a person who has not consented amounts to assault). Consent can act as a defence to such trespasses within the limits of public policy (for example, a patient cannot lawfully consent to a medical act that is designed to kill him in order to relieve suffering, known as 'euthanasia').[3] In such cases, the claimant may consent to the act that causes injury, but does not consent to having no legal redress if the person to whom consent is given performs some other act of wrongdoing (for example, the medical procedure is performed negligently).

As torts involving negligence and strict liability occur much more frequently than intentional torts, it is in relation to the voluntary assumption of risk (that is, the first type of *volenti*) that much of the case law has arisen. Therefore, this chapter will focus on *volenti* as a defence to negligence.

In *Nettleship v Weston*,[4] Lord Denning MR stated:

> Now that contributory negligence is not a complete defence…the defence of *volenti*…has been closely considered and, in consequence, it has been severely limited. Knowledge of the risk of injury is not good enough. Nor is a willingness to take the risk of injury. Nothing will suffice short of an agreement to waive any claim for negligence. The [claimant] must agree, expressly or impliedly, to waive any claim for any injury that may befall him due to the lack of reasonable care by the defendant.[5]

This passage indicates that *volenti* requires three conditions to be fulfilled:

1. the claimant must have known of the risk;
2. the claimant must have voluntarily assumed the risk of having no legal redress; and
3. the claimant must have agreed to waive the right to claim in negligence if the risk results in injury.

Knowledge of the risk

A claimant cannot voluntarily consent to a risk he was not aware of.[6] It follows that the defendant must show that the claimant actually and subjectively knew of the risk—claiming that he ought to know of the risk, but did not, will cause *volenti* to

---

2. *Morris v Murray* [1991] 2 QB 6 (CA).   3. *Airedale NHS Trust v Bland* [1993] AC 789 (HL).
4. [1971] 2 QB 691 (CA).   5. ibid 701.
6. *Harrison v Vincent* [1982] RTR 8 (CA).

fail.[7] However, simply because a claimant knows of the risk, it does not follow that he automatically consents to it.

 Smith v Charles Baker & Sons [1891] AC 325 (HL)

FACTS: The defendant railway contractors employed the claimant to drill holes in a rock cutting. The claimant worked near a crane, which, from time to time, would pass over his position carrying crates of heavy stones. He was aware of this and had worked under these conditions for several months, although he had complained about the danger of falling stones. A stone fell from the crane, seriously injuring the claimant. He sued and his employer raised *volenti* as a defence.

HELD: The defence of *volenti* was rejected. Although the claimant knew of the danger, mere knowledge was insufficient. The defendant would need to show that the claimant had voluntarily consented to the risk. On the evidence, this was not established.

If knowledge were to result in consent, those who willingly engaged in dangerous activities designed to benefit others (the obvious example being rescuers) would never be able to recover damages for losses suffered and would be deterred from engaging in such socially beneficial conduct. Thankfully, knowledge of the risk will not bar such persons from claiming damages, due to the requirement of voluntary assumption of risk.

Voluntary assumption of risk

It is widely believed that all that the defendant need establish is that the claimant voluntarily assumed the risk of injury, but this is not the case. *Volenti* requires more than this. What is required is that the claimant also voluntarily assumed the risk of having no legal redress, as the following case demonstrates.

 Nettleship v Weston [1971] 2 QB 691 (CA)

FACTS: The claimant, an experienced driver (but not a driving instructor), agreed to provide driving lessons to the defendant. Before agreeing to provide the lessons, the claimant checked that the defendant was suitably insured. On her third lesson, the defendant panicked and drove into a lamp-post, resulting in the claimant breaking his kneecap. The defendant was convicted of driving without due care and attention, but the claimant also initiated a claim for damages, alleging negligence. The defendant pleaded *volenti*.

HELD: The defence of *volenti* failed and the Court ordered that the claimant be compensated. In teaching a learner driver, the claimant had accepted that there was a risk of injury. However, he had not accepted the risk of having no legal redress, which was evidenced by him ensuring that, in the event of him being injured, he would be adequately compensated by the defendant's insurance company.

COMMENT: Today, the defence of *volenti* is statute-barred in cases involving drivers of road vehicles and their passengers.[8]

★ See WVH Rogers, 'Trouble with Learners' (1972) 30 CLJ 24

7. *Smith v Austin Lifts Ltd* [1959] 1 WLR 100 (HL).
8. Road Traffic Act 1988, s 149.

The defendant will need to demonstrate that the claimant voluntarily consented. If the claimant's consent is forced in any way, the defence of *volenti* will fail. Accordingly, consent procured by fraud or duress will not establish *volenti*. With one exception,[9] the defence of *volenti* has failed in all cases involving injured rescuers, because it cannot be said that rescuers freely volunteer to run the risk of having no legal redress.

The defence of *volenti* will be extremely difficult to establish in the context of an employment relationship. In the early nineteenth century, employees were assumed to consent voluntarily to any risk involved in the course of their employment.[10] As time progressed, the courts began to accept that, given the inequality of power between employer and employee, an employee will, in many cases, continue to work in dangerous conditions not because he has accepted the risk, but because he does not wish to lose his job. This was doubtless why the claimant in *Smith v Charles Baker & Sons* (discussed earlier) continued to work in such dangerous circumstances. It is now accepted that 'it must be shown that a servant who is asked or required to use dangerous plant is a volunteer in the fullest sense; that, knowing of the danger, he expressly or impliedly said he would do the job at his own risk, and not that of his master'.[11] As this requirement is extremely difficult to meet, the defence of *volenti* plays almost no part in cases involving employer and employee, but where an employee chooses an especially dangerous method of performing an act that requires no such danger, or where an employee is injured through the tortious act of a fellow employee, the defence of *volenti* may succeed.

 ICI Ltd v Shatwell [1965] AC 656 (HL)

FACTS: The claimant was one of a team of three shot-firers employed by the defendant. They were required to test detonators and were instructed to carry out such tests from a properly constructed shelter (indeed, statutory regulations passed at the time required as much). The wire was not long enough to reach the shelter and one of the shot-firers went to obtain a longer wire. The claimant and the remaining shot-firer decided not to wait for their colleague to return, and tested the detonators whilst in the open. Both men were injured, with the claimant sustaining severe injuries. The claimant sued the defendant and the defendant pleaded *volenti*.

HELD: The defence of *volenti* succeeded. The claimant had voluntarily undertaken to act in a needlessly dangerous, not to mention unlawful, manner and had therefore voluntarily assumed the risk of having no legal redress. The defendant had not pressured the claimant to take such a risk and had, in fact, expressly prohibited the claimant from acting in such a way.

★ See Paul Brodetsky, 'Employers' Joint Breach of Statutory Duty' (1964) 27 MLR 705

Agreement

The final requirement stated by Lord Denning MR is that the claimant has expressly or impliedly agreed to waive any claim for the injury that may befall him. This requirement has been strongly criticized and is undoubtedly a severe restriction on the ability

---

9. *Cutler v United Dairies (London) Ltd* [1933] 2 KB 297 (CA). *Volenti* was permitted in this case, because the defendant's negligence posed no real danger and it was not reasonably necessary for the claimant to attempt a rescue.　　10. See e.g. *Woodley v Metropolitan District Railway Co* (1877) 2 Ex D 384 (CA).
11. *Bowater v Mayor, Aldermen and Burgesses of the Borough of Rowley Regis* [1944] KB 476 (CA) 481 (Goddard LJ).

to establish *volenti*. Where an express and effective agreement exists (for example, via an effective exclusion clause), *volenti* can be successfully pleaded. An agreement to waive liability might also be implied by the courts, although they are extremely reluctant to do this. The following case provides an instance in which an agreement was implied.

 Morris v Murray [1990] 2 QB 6 (CA)

FACTS: The claimant and a friend had been drinking in a number of bars. The friend, who held a pilot's licence, suggested that they go for a fly in his private plane. Both parties were drunk, but the friend was exceptionally drunk (the subsequent autopsy revealed that he had drunk the equivalent of seventeen whiskies). The claimant knew that his friend was drunk, but agreed to the flight anyway. The plane crashed, killing the friend and severely injuring the claimant. The claimant alleged negligence against the deceased's estate. The defendant pleaded *volenti*.

HELD: The defence of *volenti* succeeded. Knowingly accepting a plane ride from a drunken pilot was so dangerous that it created an implied waiver of any liability that resulted.

★ See Kevin Williams, 'Defences for Drunken Drivers: Public Policy on the Roads and in the Air' (1991) 54 MLR 745

It has been argued that the requirement for agreement 'is very difficult to reconcile with the case law without resort to fiction, because the parties typically give no thought to the matter'.[12] In *Morris*, the implication of an agreement was clearly fictitious, because both parties had not given the matter a moment's thought.

Consent and the standard of care

🔗 The law relating to the standard of care and breach of duty is discussed in Chapter 14

Establishing *volenti* is not easy and many defendants will be unable to meet the three requirements discussed. However, provided that the claimant had knowledge of the risk, the standard of care expected of the defendant may be lowered to such an extent that breach of duty cannot be established. If this occurs, the defendant will not need to rely on a defence, because negligence will not be established, as the following case demonstrates.

Wooldridge v Sumner [1963] 2 QB 43 (CA)

FACTS: The defendant was competing at a horse show. He lost control of the horse after taking a corner too quickly. The claimant was struck by the horse and was seriously injured. At first instance, the defendant's actions were held to be negligent and the claimant recovered damages. The defendant appealed pleading, *inter alia*, *volenti*.

HELD: The appeal was allowed. The defence of *volenti* did not apply in this case, because the defence presupposes the existence of a tort. The actions of the defendant were not negligent and that, accordingly, *volenti* was inapplicable. Diplock LJ (as he then was) indicated that where the claimant has knowledge of a risk, this will affect the standard of care owed by the defendant:

> A person attending a game or competition takes the risk of any damage caused to him by any act of a participant done in the course of and for the purposes of the game or competition notwithstanding that such act may involve an error of judgment or a lapse of skill, unless the participant's conduct is such as to evince a reckless disregard of the spectator's safety.[13]

12. WVH Rogers, *Winfield & Jolowicz on Tort* (18th edn, Sweet & Maxwell 2010) 1042–43.
13. [1963] 2 QB 43 (CA) 68.

Exclusion of liability

Businesses may attempt to exclude or limit their liability via a contractual exclusion clause or notice (although, as discussed in Chapter 9, such clauses are paternalistically regulated). As signing a contract that contains an exclusion clause is tantamount to agreeing to waive the right to legal redress, contractual exclusions of liability are often regarded as forming part of the defence of *volenti*. In fact, the express exclusion of liability is a separate and distinct defence, as is indicated by s 2(3) of the Unfair Contract Terms Act 1977 (UCTA 1977), which states that a person's agreement to, or knowledge of, an exclusion clause is not of itself to be taken as indicating his voluntary assumption of any risk.

Statutory authority

Statute may specifically authorize an act that would, in the absence of the statute, constitute a tort. A claimant who sustains loss due to such an authorized act has no remedy other than that provided for by the relevant Act. The majority of cases in this area concern actions in nuisance, such as the following leading case.

 Nuisance is discussed at p 436

 Allen v Gulf Oil Refining Ltd [1981] AC 1001 (HL)

FACTS: The defendant operated an oil refinery. The claimant alleged that the operation of the refinery was a nuisance, in so much as it expelled gases that produced a noxious smell, generated offensive levels of noise, and caused vibrations on the claimant's property.

HELD: The Gulf Oil Refining Act 1965 gave the defendant the power to operate a refinery in the area. Once this was established, the defendant needed to demonstrate that it was impossible to construct and operate a refinery that conformed to Parliament's intentions, without causing the nuisance alleged, or any nuisance. The defendant could establish this, so there was no nuisance.

★ See RA Buckley, 'Nuisance, Negligence and Statutory Authorisation' (1980) 43 MLR 219

As can be seen from the decision in *Allen*, the existence of a statutory authorization does not provide a blanket immunity. Before holding that the acts did not constitute a tort, the courts will consider numerous factors including:

- Was the commission of the tort expressly or impliedly authorized by statute?
- Is the authorization total, or does it operate only in the absence of negligence?
- Could the tort have been avoided (for example, by engaging in the activity elsewhere, or by doing it in a different manner)?

Illegality

In *Gray v Thames Trains Ltd*,[14] Lord Hoffmann stated that the illegality defence operates in two forms. The narrow form of the defence provides that 'you cannot recover for damage which flows from loss of liberty, a fine or other punishment lawfully

---

14. [2009] UKHL 33, [2009] 1 AC 1339.

imposed upon you in consequence of your own unlawful act'.[15] The case of *Gray* itself demonstrates this in practice.

Gray v Thames Trains Ltd [2009] UKHL 33

FACTS: The defendant's negligence was the cause of the Ladbroke Grove rail crash, in which 31 people were killed and over 520 were injured. The claimant sustained minor physical injuries as a result of the crash and subsequently developed Post-Traumatic Stress Disorder. Two years later, under the effects of the condition, he stabbed to death a pedestrian who walked out in front of his car. The claimant was convicted of manslaughter and sentenced to indefinite detention in a mental hospital. He sued the defendant for, *inter alia*, (i) general damages for his conviction, detention, and feelings of guilt and remorse, and for damage to his reputation; and (ii) special damages in relation to loss of earnings occurring before and during his detention. He also sought an indemnity against any claims that might be brought by the dependants of the pedestrian.

HELD: The claim was rejected. The House quoted with approval the following passage of Samuels JA:

> If the plaintiff has been convicted and sentenced for a crime, it means that the criminal law has taken him to be responsible for his actions and has imposed an appropriate penalty. He or she should therefore bear the consequences of the punishment, both direct and indirect. If the law of negligence were to say, in effect, that the offender was not responsible for his actions and should be compensated by the tortfeasor, it would set the determination of the criminal court at nought. It would generate the sort of clash between civil and criminal law that is apt to bring the law into disrepute.[16]

⭐ See Paul S Davies, 'The Illegality Defence and Public Policy' (2009) 125 LQR 556

The wider form of the defence provides that 'you cannot recover compensation for loss which you have suffered in consequence of your own criminal act'.[17] In such a case, the courts will apply the maxim *ex turpi causa non oritur actio* to hold that the defendant did not owe the claimant a duty of care. The following case demonstrates this form of the defence in practice.

➡️ *Ex turpi causa non oritur actio*: 'an action does not arise from a base cause'

Clunis v Camden and Islington Health Authority [1998] QB 978 (CA)

FACTS: Mr Clunis (the claimant) was a patient at the defendant's mental hospital. He failed to attend aftercare appointments when released from the hospital. Three months later, without any provocation, he stabbed a man to death and was later convicted of manslaughter. He alleged that the loss that he suffered (deprivation of liberty) was caused by the defendant's failure to provide him with adequate treatment, which resulted in his mental state, which, in turn, resulted in the unprovoked attack. The defendant pleaded *ex turpi causa*.

HELD: The defence succeeded. The loss that the claimant sustained was not due to the acts of the defendant, but due to his own criminal act.

⭐ See CA Hopkins, '*Ex Turpi Causa* and Mental Disorder' [1998] 57 CLJ 444

---

15. ibid [29].
16. *State Rail Authority of New South Wales v Wiegold* (1991) 25 NSWLR 500, 514, quoted by Lord Hoffmann (at [40]) and Lord Rodger (at [67]).
17. [2009] UKHL 33, [2009] 1 AC 1339 [29].

courts take a case-by-case approach and there is no general test used to determine the extent of the reduction. This can cause uncertainty which, in turn, may encourage a claimant to accept a low settlement. The adoption of a system of fixed reductions (as suggested by Lord Denning MR in *Froom v Butcher*, discussed earlier) would alleviate this to an extent.

As each case is dependent upon its facts, appeal courts are reluctant to interfere with a trial judge's decision and will only do so if they consider it plainly wrong.[43] Whilst there is no single test, it does appear that the courts will take into account two significant factors: (i) the extent to which the claimant's act caused the damage; and (ii) the blameworthiness of the claimant's conduct.

It would appear that the court's discretion is limited, insomuch as it has been stated *obiter* that the court cannot reduce damages by 100 per cent.[44] As the 1945 Act presupposes fault by both the claimant and defendant, it follows that a claimant cannot be 100 per cent contributorily negligent. Futher, a 100 per cent reduction would permit contributory negligence to act as a complete defence in a manner similar to *volenti*.

Limitation of actions

As with contractual claims, tortious actions must be brought within a specified period, and, as in contract, claims brought outside this period are not barred from being initiated and will be allowed to proceed if the defendant fails to raise the passing of the limitation period as a defence. The limitation rules for claims in tort are more generous than for claims in contract because, in breach of contract cases, the loss sustained by the claimant usually arises during the lifetime of the contract, or shortly afterwards. Conversely, in tort cases, the harm might not arise for many years after the conduct in question.

Perhaps the most significant benefit is the date on which the limitation period commences. Section 2 of the Limitation Act 1980 provides that time begins running 'from the date on which the cause of action accrued'. This date will depend upon the tort in question. Where a tortious claim can be brought without establishing that damage occurred (for example, trespass), the limitation period will commence on the date of the defendant's act. However, where proof of damage is required (for example, negligence), the limitation period will commence when the first damage is sustained, thereby allowing for the situations in which damage occurs many years after the conduct in question. It can be seen that this rule is more generous than in contract, in which the limitation period generally starts running on the date of breach.

The general limitation period in tort is six years[45] from the date on which the period begins to run. Statute has, however, created a number of exceptions to this general rule, including:

- Where the claim includes damages for personal injury, the limitation period is reduced to three years.[46] The court does, however, have an unfettered power to extend this period if it appears equitable to do so.[47]

---

43. *Hannam v Mann* [1984] RTR 252 (CA).
44. *Pitts v Hunt* [1990] 1 QB 24 (CA) 48 (Beldam LJ), cf *Reeves v Commissioner of Police of the Metropolis* [1999] QB 169 (CA) 195 (Morritt LJ).
45. Limitation Act 1980, s 2.   46. ibid s 11(4).
47. Limitation Act 1980, s 33(1).

- In cases involving libel, slander, and malicious falsehood, the limitation period is reduced to one year.[48]
- Claims brought under the Consumer Protection Act 1987 must be brought within three years of the date on which the damage was first sustained or the date of knowledge of the defect (whichever is later).[49]

If the claimant is subject to a legal disability (for example, he is a minor or mentally disabled) when the cause of action accrues, then the action may be brought at any time within the period of six years (three years in personal injury cases) after he ceases to be disabled, or he dies, whichever occurs first.[50]

Where the tortious act is one that continually causes *recurring* damage (for example, the continuous commission of a nuisance),[51] then, as long as the damage continues, a fresh cause of action accrues every day. Once the damage ceases, the claimant has the right to claim for any harm that was caused within the previous six years (three if the harm involved personal injury).

Latent damage

The commission of a tort may result in existing damage that is hidden or damage that does not manifest itself until many years after the tort was committed (this is known as 'latent' damage). In such cases, the rules relating to limitation periods are modified, depending upon the type of loss sustained.

In cases involving personal injury or death caused by negligence, nuisance, or breach of duty, the three-year limitation period will commence only once the claimant acquires certain 'knowledge'. This includes the knowledge that an injury has been suffered; the injury is significant; the injury was caused by negligence, nuisance, or breach of duty; and the injury can be attributed to an identified defendant.[52]

In cases involving negligence resulting in damage other than personal injury or death (for example, property damage or economic loss), the claimant can elect either the standard six-year limitation period, or a three-year period commencing on the date on which the claimant had both the right to bring an action and knowledge of the material facts.[53] However, no action may lie fifteen years after the commission of the breach that caused the damage[54] (this is known as the 'longstop' provision).

Remedies

If the claimant has established that a tort has been committed and the defendant has failed successfully to raise a defence, or has only managed to raise a partial defence (for example, contributory negligence), the final issue to be determined is what remedy should the claimant be awarded. As in contract, the principal remedy will be an award of damages, although tortious damages can operate in a very different manner from contractual damages. In certain cases, where financial compensation will not

---

48. ibid s 4A. However, s 32A(1) allows the court to disregard this period where it would inequitably prejudice the claimant.
49. ibid s 11A(4).
50. ibid s 28(1).   51. *Earl of Harrington v Corporation of Derby* [1905] 1 Ch 205 (Ch).
52. Limitation Act 1980, s 14(1).   53. ibid s 14A(4)(b) and (5).   54. ibid s 14B(1).

adequately compensate the claimant, the court may be willing to grant an injunction. Finally, it may be that the claimant need not involve the court at all, because certain torts can be remedied by the claimant taking matters into his own hands.

Damages

The basic aim of an award of damages is to compensate the claimant for any injury or loss caused by the defendant's tort. The rules relating to the calculation of tortious damages are extremely complex and a detailed examination is beyond the scope of this text. Readers who wish to learn more on the calculation of damages are advised to read a more specialist text.

Traditionally, damages are awarded only once for each tort in the form of a single lump sum, assessed at the date of trial. The rationale behind this approach is that it provides the defendant with 'closure'. However, the problem with a lump-sum award is that damages will frequently need to compensate the claimant for future losses (especially in personal injury cases), which will result in the judge having to esti-mate the extent of the future loss. If the judge underestimates the loss, the lump sum cannot be subsequently corrected and the claimant will be under-compensated. To combat this, the courts have established a number of devices, including postponed or split trials, interim or provisional damages, structured settlements, and periodic or reviewable payments. These are all beyond the scope of this text and will not be discussed further.[55]

Although damages for breach of contract are always compensatory and damages in tort are usually compensatory, their measure is different. Damages for breach of contract normally will aim to put the claimant in the position in which he would have been had the contract been performed properly. In tort, the aim of damages is to put the claimant in the position in which he would have been before the tort was committed (this is known as *restitutio in integrum* and would equate with the aim of reliance loss in contract). However, unlike damages for breach of contract, which are always compensatory, there are several types of damages for tort that are non-compensatory in nature, namely contemptuous damages, nominal damages, and exemplary damages.

🔗 Reliance loss is discussed at p 322

Contemptuous damages

Contemptuous damages constitute probably the lowest award of damages that the court can make and traditionally consist of an amount equal to the lowest value coin of the realm (currently 1 pence). Contemptuous damages are awarded where the claimant's legal rights have technically been infringed, but where the action is frivo-lous, or where the claimant has acted in a manner that the court deems entirely lack-ing in merit. Claimants who receive contemptuous damages will almost always have to pay their own costs (which will certainly result in them being out of pocket) and may also be ordered to pay the costs of the other party. Today, contemptuous dam-ages are almost only ever awarded in defamation cases.[56]

---

55. Students who wish to explore these alternatives to a lump-sum payment are advised to read Simon Deakin, Angus Johnston, and Basil Markesinis, *Markesinis & Deakin's Tort Law* (7th edn, OUP 2013) 816–26.

56. See e.g. *Reynolds v Times Newspapers Ltd* [1998] 2 WLR 862 (HL).

Nominal damages

Nominal damages are awarded in both contract and tort where the claimant's legal rights have been infringed, but no actual loss has occurred. In tort, they are awarded in relation to torts that do not require proof of damage and will constitute a minimal sum only (typically around £5). For example, in *Grobbelaar v News Group Newspapers Ltd*,[57] the claimant (a goalkeeper for Liverpool Football Club) was libelled by *The Sun*, which stated that he had fixed football matches. He had not fixed any matches, but he had agreed to concede goals deliberately in return for payment. The jury awarded him £85,000 damages. On appeal, this was reduced to £1. Given that he was a proven cheat, the libel had not caused him any further loss and so nominal damages were appropriate. Grobbelaar was also ordered to pay two-thirds of the defendant's legal costs (around £1 million).

Aggravated damages

Although there is debate on the issue, aggravated damages tend to be regarded as a special form of compensatory damages. They are awarded to compensate the claimant for hurt feelings or injured pride, usually in situations in which the defendant's actions have been improperly motivated, or are spiteful, malicious, or oppressive. As such, traditionally, they have not been awarded in negligence cases,[58] and tend to be limited to cases involving deceit, defamation, malicious falsehood and prosecution, false imprisonment, and trespass.

Examples of cases in which aggravated damages have been awarded include:

- A dentist who carried out expensive and unnecessary treatment on patients was ordered to pay an extra 15 per cent in aggravated damages for the distress and annoyance that he had caused.[59]

- Victims of false imprisonment or malicious prosecution should be awarded aggravated damages, which will rarely be less than £1,000, but will normally not exceed twice the normal compensatory damages.[60]

- *Private Eye* accused the wife of Peter Sutcliffe (a serial killer known as the 'Yorkshire Ripper') of agreeing to sell her story to a national newspaper for £250,000. After the wife initiated proceedings against *Private Eye* for defamation (which she subsequently won), it continued to publish further allegations about her. She was awarded aggravated damages.[61]

Although aggravated damages take into account the conduct of the defendant, they are not awarded in order to punish the defendant. If the courts wish to punish the defendant for his behaviour, they will award exemplary damages.

Exemplary damages

As was noted in Chapter 13, the law of torts is not only compensatory; it is also meant to act as a deterrent. Contract law does not have this function, which is why exemplary damages are not available. Exemplary damages (also known as 'punitive' damages) are not compensatory; rather, they are awarded in order to punish the defendant for his unacceptable, outrageous, or reprehensible conduct.

---

57. [2002] UKHL 40, [2002] 1 WLR 3024.
58. *AB v South West Water Services Ltd* [1993] QB 507 (CA).
59. *Appleton v Garrett* [1996] PIQR P1 (QB).
60. *Thompson v Commissioner of Police of the Metropolis* [1998] QB 498 (CA).
61. *Sutcliffe v Pressdram Ltd* [1991] 1 QB 153 (CA).

Self-test questions

1. Define the following legal words and phrases:
   (a) *volenti non fit injuria*;
   (b) *ex turpi causa non oritur actio*;
   (c) contributory negligence;
   (d) latent damage;
   (e) multiplicand;
   (f) multiplier;
   (g) *quia timet* injunction.

2. Matthew is the getaway driver for an armed robbery. Whilst driving away from the bank, Matthew's car is involved in an accident with another vehicle, being driven by Katie. Although Matthew was driving quickly, the accident was the result of Katie's negligent driving. Matthew and his fellow criminals sustain severe injuries. Discuss the imposition of liability and the availability of any defences.

3. Explain the differences between the defences of contributory negligence and the voluntary assumption of risk.

4. Define and explain the differences between the following types of damages. Which types are compensatory and which are not?
   (a) Contemptuous.
   (b) Nominal.
   (c) Aggravated.
   (d) Exemplary.
   (e) General.
   (f) Special.

5. How do damages in tort differ from damages in contract?

6. Les is injured due to the negligence of his employer. Based on the following facts, calculate the amount of damages to which Les would be entitled. Where damages cannot be quantified precisely (because you do not have all of the facts), indicate what additional heads of damages can be recovered.
   (a) One of Les' arms has to be amputated and he loses the sight in one eye. The injury that caused him to lose the use of the eye also caused visible scarring on Les' face. This results in Les' wife leaving him.
   (b) Les is unable to work for two years. He worked as a barrister and earned around £65,000 per year. When he returns to work, his injuries mean that he is only able to work part-time (he works around a third of the hours he used to). Les plans to retire in eight years' time.
   (c) As a result of the accident, Les will require medical care for the next ten years. This medical treatment can be extremely painful. The cost of this treatment is estimated at £6,000 per year.
   (d) At the time of the accident, Les was holding his laptop. The accident caused the laptop to become damaged beyond repair. At the time of the accident, the laptop cost around £1,500, but, at the date of the trial, the same model laptop could be purchased for £700.

Further reading

Andrew Bartlett, 'Attribution of Contributory Negligence: Agents, Company Directors and Fraudsters' (1998) 114 LQR 460
Discusses the extent to which contributorily negligent acts of directors, agents, or other professionals can be attributed to the companies for which they work

Allan Beever, 'The Structure of Aggravated and Exemplary Damages' (2003) 23 OJLS 87
Discusses the distinctions between aggravated and exemplary damages; argues that exemplary damages are inconsistent with the goals of civil liability and should be abolished

Kirsty Horsey and Erika Rackley, *Tort Law* (3rd edn, OUP 2013) ch 10
Provides a clear, yet detailed, discussion of the defences discussed in this chapter

AJE Jaffey, '*Volenti non fit injuria*' (1985) 44 CLJ 87
Provides an in-depth discussion of whether or not an agreement is needed in order to establish volenti; argues that such an agreement is necessary, and provides several methods of establishing such an agreement

Judicial College, *Guidelines for the Assessment of General Damages in Personal Injury Cases* (12th edn, OUP 2013)
Sets out the tariffs for the quantification of general damages in personal injury cases

Law Commission, *The Illegality Defence in Tort: A Consultation Paper* (Law Com CP No 160, HMSO 2001)
Examines the defence of illegality and provides suggestions for possible reform; like all Law Commission papers, the discussion of the law is very clear and readable

WVH Rogers, *Winfield & Jolowicz on Tort* (18th edn, Sweet & Maxwell 2010) ch 22
Examines the various remedies available; provides an accessible account of the complex principles relating to the quantification of damages

Remember to visit the **Online Resource Centre** at **<http://www.oxfordtextbooks.co.uk/orc/roach3e>** to access the following resources on Chapter 17, 'Tortious defences and remedies': more **practice questions** and answers; a **glossary** of key terms; **multiple-choice questions**; and **revision summaries**. Updates to the law can be found on Twitter by following **@UKBusinessLaw**.

PART IV
partnership law and company law

18 Unincorporated business structures

- Sole proprietorship
- Partnership

INTRODUCTION

A person who wishes to engage in some form of business activity will need to do so via some form of business structure. Such structures can provide the proposed business with a number of significant advantages. Whereas some countries allow for the creation of dozens of forms of business structure, businesses in England and Wales primarily operate through one (or more) of four business structures:

1. the sole proprietorship;
2. the partnership;
3. the limited liability partnership (LLP); and
4. the company.

Two of these structures (the LLP and the company) are created via a process called 'incorporation', which is discussed in detail in Chapter 19. This chapter will focus only on the two unincorporated structures—namely, the sole proprietorship and the partnership.

Sole proprietorship

The simplest method of carrying on business is through a sole proprietorship. In 2012/13, 454,895 sole proprietors were engaged in business in the UK.[1] A sole proprietor is normally defined as a single person carrying on some form of business activity, but this definition can be slightly misleading in that, whilst a sole proprietorship will be run largely for the benefit of the sole proprietor, sole proprietors are free to take on employees.[2] The key point to note is that the business is not incorporated, nor does the sole proprietor undertake business activity in partnership with anyone else.

---

1. Office for National Statistics, *UK Business: Activity, Size and Location—2013* (ONS 2013) Table A5.4A
2. Although the vast majority do not, and those that do take on few (87% of sole proprietorships have 0–4 employees—Office for National Statistics, *UK Business: Activity, Size and Location—2013* (ONS 2013) Table A5.4A).

Sole proprietorships come in two forms:

1. Where the sole proprietor is a professional (for example, a solicitor or accountant, etc), then he will be known as a 'sole practitioner'.

2. Where the sole proprietor is not a professional, then he will be known as a 'sole trader'. Although it is common to refer to all single person businesses as sole traders, sole practitioners are not actually sole traders.

Unlike companies and limited liability partnerships, there is no separation between a sole proprietor and his business, and sole proprietorships are not legal persons. Therefore, the sole proprietor owns all of the assets of the business and is also entitled to all of the profits that the business generates.

Formation

Setting up business as a sole proprietor is extremely simple and involves much less formality than incorporating a business. All that an individual need do to commence business as a sole proprietor is register himself with HM Revenue and Customs (HMRC) as self-employed. Failure to register within three months of commencing business is punishable by a £100 fine. Once the sole proprietorship's turnover reaches a certain amount,[3] the sole proprietor will need to register for Value Added Tax (VAT). Sole proprietors are required to complete their own tax returns, and should therefore ensure that they keep clear and accurate records of all sales and purchases, so that the process of self-assessment can be completed quickly and easily.

The name of the business

One of the few areas in which a sole proprietorship is subject to stringent regulation is in relation to its name. The Companies Act 2006 imposes a number of restrictions on what names can and cannot be used,[4] and these restrictions apply to sole proprietorships that have a 'business name'.[5] A business name is a name other than the surname (including forenames or initials) of the sole proprietor.[6] Accordingly, the Act will not apply where the sole proprietorship's name is simply the name of the sole proprietor (for example, 'Smith', or 'J Smith', or 'John Smith'). However, if the sole proprietorship were to be called 'Smith's Construction' or 'John Smith & Co', then the name would be a business name and the Act would apply.

Finance

In terms of raising enough finance to commence trading, sole proprietorships are at a disadvantage compared with other business structures. A partnership can raise finance by admitting new partners; a company (especially public companies) can raise finance by selling shares. Neither of these options is available to a sole proprietor who wishes to remain a sole proprietor. A sole proprietor will either need to invest his own money into the business, or obtain a loan. Given that many sole proprietorships are small affairs, banks are cautious when lending to them and obtaining large sums of **debt capital** is usually impossible.

➡ **debt capital:** capital raised through borrowing

---

3. For 2014/15 the figure is £81,000. It is likely that this figure will rise in subsequent Budgets.

4. Most of these restrictions relate to the use of sensitive words or expressions, or the use of misleading names—see the Companies Act 2006, ss 1193–1198.

5. The restrictions also apply to partnerships, limited liability partnerships, and companies (Companies Act 2006, s 1192(1)).   6. Companies Act 2006, s 1192(2)(a).

Liability

The principal disadvantage of carrying on business as a sole proprietorship is that the liability of the sole proprietor is personal and unlimited. Whereas partnerships and companies can be limited, it is impossible to create a limited sole proprietorship. All of the sole proprietor's assets (including private assets, such as the sole proprietor's house, car, and bank accounts) can be seized and sold in order to satisfy the debts of the sole proprietorship. Further, if the sole proprietor attempts to prevent assets from being seized by transferring them to another person, the court can set aside the transfer and order that the assets be returned to the sole proprietor.

Dissolution

The dissolution of a sole proprietorship may be imposed upon the sole proprietor via a court order. Should a sole proprietor voluntarily decide to bring the sole proprietorship to an end, this can be achieved very easily. The first step is to cease acquiring any new business. The sole proprietor can then tie up any loose ends, such as collecting any debts owed, paying the businesses' creditors, laying off employees, etc. Any money left over belongs to the sole proprietor. Unless the sole proprietor is intending to form another sole proprietorship, he should inform HMRC that he is no longer self-employed. Of course, the sole proprietor is perfectly free to sell the business as a going concern to another person instead of dissolving it.

➡ **going concern:** a business that those who run it believe will continue in operational existence for the foreseeable future

Partnership

A group of persons who wish to carry on business together clearly cannot do so as a sole proprietorship. For such persons, a partnership may be a more appropriate business structure. As of 2012/13, there were 255,410 partnerships operating in the UK.[7] Partnerships come in one of three forms:

- **Ordinary partnerships** The vast majority of partnerships are ordinary partnerships or 'partnerships' as they are usually known
- **Limited partnerships** Created under the Limited Partnerships Act 1907, these permit the partners to limit their liability to the amount contributed. Limited Partnerships are discussed later in this chapter at p 509.
- **Limited liability partnerships (LLPs)** Although LLPs are technically partnerships, they are formed through incorporation and have more in common with companies than with standard partnerships. Accordingly, they are discussed in Chapter 19.

What is a 'partnership?'

Section 1(1) of the Partnership Act 1890 (PA 1890) defines a partnership as 'the relation which subsists between persons carrying on a business in common with a view of profit'. Although this short definition appears straightforward, it contains a

---

7. Office for National Statistics, *UK Business: Activity, Size and Location—2013* (ONS 2013) Table A5.4b.

number of words and phrases that have proven deceptively complicated to define in practice.

'The relation which subsists'

Section 1(1) makes clear that a partnership is based upon the relationship between the partners. Whereas the creation of a LLP or company requires permission from the state (usually through acceptance of registration), a partnership is created simply by the agreement between the partners. This agreement need not take any particular form: it may be written, oral, or implied through conduct (although, to avoid disputes, it is common for it to be in writing). The basis of the partnership agreement is in contract, and the majority of partnership agreements are usually executed by deed and will contain written terms setting out the terms under which the partnership is to be run, with the 1890 Act providing a number of implied terms that can be varied or excluded by the partnership agreement.

The terms implied by the Partnership Act 1890 are discussed in 'Implied terms' at p 511

Defining a partnership as a form of contractual relationship makes clear that a partnership does not enjoy legal personality[8] and therefore cannot acquire rights or incur obligations in its own name, nor can it own assets. Further, a partner cannot be an agent for his firm, because this would require the firm to act as principal and this would also require separate personality. However, the language used by partnerships and the 1890 Act does not reinforce this. It is common for the name of a partnership to end with the suffix '& Co', but use of this phrase has no legal significance. Further, the 1890 Act provides that persons who have entered into a partnership are collectively called a 'firm'.[9] The Law Commission has argued that defining a partnership as a 'relation' is 'out of touch with ordinary usage'[10] and that the phrase 'voluntary association'[11] is more appropriate, but this recommendation has not been acted upon.

'Between persons'

A partnership is a relationship that exists 'between persons'. The use of the word 'persons' is important because it indicates that (i) a single person cannot establish a partnership; and (ii) a partnership can consist of both natural and legal persons. Therefore, a natural person is free to enter into partnership with a legal person, such as a company.

The only limitation on the ability of natural and legal persons to enter into a partnership is their capacity to contract. As the partnership relationship is contractual, all partners must have the requisite contractual capacity. Contractual capacity is discussed in Chapter 5, where it is noted that special rules apply to minors and mentally unsound persons. A partnership agreement entered into with a minor is voidable at the minor's instance during his minority, or for a reasonable time after attaining the age of majority.[12] A mentally unsound person who enters into a partnership and subsequently seeks to avoid the agreement, can do so only if he can show that his partners knew, at the time that he entered into the partnership, that he was of such unsound mind as not to be capable of understanding what he was doing. As long as a person of unsound mind is a partner, he incurs liability on the

---

8. Unlike in Scotland, where a partnership is 'a legal person distinct from the partners of whom it is composed' (PA 1890, s 4(2)).   9. PA 1890, s 4(1).
10. Law Commission, *Partnership Law: A Joint Consultation Paper* (Law Com CP No 159, HMSO 2000) [5.14].
11. ibid [5.16].
12. *Goode v Harrison* (1821) 5 B & Ald 147.

partnership's contracts and for its debts, unless the person seeking to enforce a contract or debt knew of his incapacity at the time of its creation.

'Carrying on'

Section 1(1) requires the persons to be 'carrying on a business'. The phrase 'carrying on' would appear to imply some form of continuous activity, thereby prohibiting the creation of a partnership for a one-off transaction. The courts, however, have not limited the creation of partnerships in this manner and have held that a partnership may be formed for a one-off transaction.[13]

Provided that some form of business activity is being undertaken, a partnership can be created, even though it has yet to start trading. The court will, however, require a certain level of activity to exist and this will be a question of fact in each case.

 Khan v Miah [2000] 1 WLR 1232 (HL)

FACTS: The claimant agreed to finance the opening of a restaurant that would be run by the defendant. A joint bank account was opened and a bank loan was obtained (in both transactions, the parties were described as 'partners'). Premises were leased, building work was undertaken, and equipment was purchased. Finally, an advertisement was placed in the local press. Before the restaurant opened, the parties argued and their agreement ended. In order to determine the dispersal of assets and capital, it was necessary to determine whether or not a partnership had been formed.

HELD: The House of Lords held that a partnership had existed. Lord Millett stated:

> There is no rule of law that the parties to a joint venture do not become partners until actual trading commences...The question is not whether the restaurant had commenced trading, but whether the parties had done enough to be found to have commenced the joint enterprise in which they had agreed to engage.[14]

However, Lord Millett did make clear that a mere agreement to become a partner would be insufficient, as is merely describing oneself as a partner to a third party. There must be clear evidence that the parties have 'embarked upon the venture' and this will be a question of fact in each case.

★ See Tim Vollans, 'Partnership Defined?' (2001) 6 Cov LJ 93

Accordingly, parties who wish to form a partnership may do so before it actually starts trading. In contrast, where the parties intend to form a company, their activities as promoters prior to the company's formation will not result in the creation of a partnership.[15]

'A business'

Section 1(1) requires that the partnership must be carrying on 'a business' and the 1890 Act defines 'business' to include 'every trade, occupation or profession'.[16] This

---

13. *George Hall & Sons v Platt* [1954] TR 331. In such a case, the partnership will end once the transaction has been completed (*Mann v D'Arcy* [1968] 1 WLR 893 (Ch)).

14. [2000] 1 WLR 1232 (HL) 2127, 2128.

15. *Keith Spicer Ltd v Mansell* [1970] 1 WLR 333 (CA).   16. PA 1890, s 45.

does not, however, prevent the rules of a particular profession or trade prohibiting its members to practise or operate in a partnership.

'In common'

In order for persons to be carrying on business as a partnership, they must be carrying on business 'in common'. Factors relevant in determining whether persons are carrying on business 'in common' include:

- that any profits of the business earned, or any of its losses, accrue to them. Thus, executors carrying on the business of a testator in accordance with his will were held not to be acting 'in common', because any benefits passed to the testator's estate;[17]
- that the concern is being carried on by, or on behalf of, all of them. A person may be carrying on a business in common despite taking no active role in running the business (for example, a sleeping partner)—but this is not always the case (for example, a supplier of goods who is paid with a share in the firm's profits will not be acting 'in common' with the firm's partners);[18]
- a person who does not participate in or have any control over the business is unlikely to be acting 'in common'.

Several of these factors were evidenced in the following case.

 Saywell v Pope [1979] STC 824 (Ch)

FACTS: From 1960 to 1972, Mr Saywell and Mr Prentice were partners in a firm. Their wives were employed by the firm and carried out minor roles, for which they received a small salary. In 1973, the firm acquired a lucrative contract and, in April 1973, a new partnership agreement was drawn up, which stated that Mr and Mrs Saywell, and Mr and Mrs Prentice, had gone into partnership. The wives never contributed any capital to the firm and never received a share of the firm's profits. Although their role increased, they played no role in its management. The partnership agreement was not, however, signed until 1975. The question was whether between 1973 and 1975, the wives should be taxed as employees of the firm or as partners.

HELD: Although the agreement provided that the wives were partners from April 1973 onwards, the reality of the situation did not reflect this. Before 1975, the wives did not exercise any managerial powers, nor did they share in the firm's profits (although profits were credited to them, they did not draw upon them). Accordingly, they had not acted 'in common' with their husbands, and so were not partners until 1975.

'With a view to profit'

The final requirement is that the business be carried on 'with a view to profit'. A business in which no financial return is anticipated will not constitute a partnership: unlike companies, partnerships cannot be formed for altruistic or benevolent purposes. Historically, the entitlement to a share in the firm's profits was enough to

---

17. *Re Fisher & Sons* [1912] 2 KB 491 (KB).
18. *Strathearn Gordon Associates Ltd v Commissioners of Customs and Excise* [1985] VATTR 79.

establish the existence of a partnership.[19] This is no longer the case and the receipt of a share in the profits is merely *prima facie* evidence that a person is a partner.[20]

The fact that a profit is not actually made does not mean that the business is not a partnership; rather, what is required is that the parties *intended* to make a profit. The wording of the 1890 Act does not require persons actually to receive a share in the profits to be partners, provided that they intended that a profit be made. Historically, the courts did not favour this argument,[21] but, in the following case, the Court held that a person may be a partner even though he does not receive a share of the profits.

M Young Legal Associates Ltd v Zahid (A Firm) [2006] EWCA Civ 613

FACTS: Bashir wished to establish a firm of solicitors. He had, however, only been qualified for two years and the Solicitors' Practice Rules required that every firm have a supervisory solicitor who has been qualified for three years or more.[22] He therefore asked an experienced solicitor, Lees, to act as the supervisory solicitor. Lees would not receive a share of the profits, but would instead be paid a fixed annual salary. The firm of solicitors began practising as 'Zahid Solicitors' in 2002. The claimant claims-handling company alleged that it was owed money by Zahid Solicitors, but in 2004, Zahid Solicitors was dissolved. The claimant sought to recover the money owed from Bashir and Lees. Lees argued that, because he did not share in the firm's profits, he was not a partner and so not liable for the firm's debts.

HELD: Lees was a partner. There was nothing in s 1(1) that indicated that partners should share in the profits of the firm, and the partners could therefore remunerate themselves in any way they deemed fit.

COMMENT: As is discussed later, there has been doubt as to whether salaried partners are actually partners at all. This case confirms that they are and states clearly that such partners will be exposed to the same liability as general partners.

⭐ See Peter Breakey, 'Fair Share' (2006) 156 NLJ 1195

Types of partner

A partnership may have several different types of partner, with each type having different rights and responsibilities. The rights and responsibilities of each type of partner will be discussed shortly, but, first, it is important that the distinction between partners and employees is understood.

Partnerships can take on employees (although many do not), but the distinction between a partner and an employee is not always straightforward. Partnership and employment are mutually exclusive: it is impossible to be a partner of the firm and its employee. It is vital to distinguish between the partners of the firm and its employees because:

- the partners are usually entitled to the profits of the firm, whereas the employees are not—but the employees are not liable for the firm's debts in the way that the partners are;

---

19. *Waugh v Carver* (1793) B BI 235.   20. PA 1890, s 2(3).
21. *Pooley v Driver* (1877) 5 Ch D 458 (CA).
22. Solicitors Practice Rules 1990, r 13.2 (now the Solicitor's Code of Conduct 2007, r 5.02(2)(b)).

- employees are granted a substantial number of rights by statute (for example, the right not to be unfairly dismissed), which are not granted to partners.

There is no standard test to determine whether a person is a partner or an employee, although certain factors (for example, the right to share in the firm's profits)[23] may constitute *prima facie* evidence that a person is a partner; rather, each case must be decided on its facts. The following case provides an example of the thin dividing line between a partner and an employee.

E Rennison & Son v Minister of Social Security (1970) 10 KIR 65 (QB)

FACTS: A firm (*A*) terminated the employment contracts of a group of employees and formed new contracts, whereby the dismissed persons were regarded as self-employed and could work for other firms if they so chose. The dismissed employees entered into an agreement, which was described as a 'deed of partnership' (*B*). The agreement provided that the business of *B* would be carried on at *A*'s offices, and that the profits and losses would be divided among *B*'s partners. Subsequently, *A* agreed to pay *B* a weekly sum based on the same hourly rate of work as their previous contracts of employment. The issue arose as to whether *A* had to pay National Insurance contributions—that is, whether the dismissed persons were partners of *B* or employees of *A*.

HELD: They were employees of *A*. Each person had an individual contract of service that was identical to the previous contract. That they were described as partners in the deed of partnership was irrelevant, because they were, in reality, still employees.

Having established the importance of the distinction between partners and employees, the different forms of partner can be discussed. It is perfectly permissible and increasingly common for a single firm to have several different types of partner.

General partners

Those partners who do not fall within the specialist types of partner discussed in subsequent sections (and few do) are known simply as 'partners', or 'general partners'. The default rights of general partners are set out in ss 24 and 25 of the PA 1890, which provides for, *inter alia*, a right to be involved in the management of the firm and the right to an equal share in the profits of the firm. These rights, however, are subject to the partnership agreement, so it is perfectly permissible, for example, for a partner's right to manage the firm to be limited in some way, or even excluded.

General partners are not required to contribute capital to the firm, but are required to contribute equally to the debts and liabilities of the firm.[24] A partner will not be liable for debts that arose before he became a partner,[25] however, unless he chooses to accept responsibility for them.

Sleeping partners

'Sleeping' or 'dormant' partners are not mentioned in the 1890 Act. The term has arisen to describe those partners who contribute capital to the firm (although this

---

23. PA 1890, s 2(3).   24. ibid s 24(1).   25. ibid s 17(1).

may not be the case), but currently play no part in the firm's management. As the Act does not overtly recognize sleeping partners, they have the same liabilities as general partners.

Limited partners

The Limited Partnerships Act 1907 provides for the ability to form limited partnerships, the partners of which are not subject to the unlimited levels of liability to which general and sleeping partners are subject. Limited partnerships are extremely rare, largely because limited liability is more readily obtainable by incorporating the business. In 2012/13, there were only 23,828 limited partnerships registered in the UK.[26]

Limited partnerships can consist of any number of limited partners, but there must be at least one general partner, whose liability will be unlimited.[27] Unlike ordinary partnerships, limited partnerships are not formed via the partnership agreement, but, like companies, are formed (but not incorporated) by applying for registration to the Registrar of Companies.[28] Until the application is accepted, the firm will remain an ordinary partnership and its partners will be general partners.[29] Upon successful registration, a limited partnership will be formed and the limited partners will be liable only for the capital that they have already contributed. Failure to comply with the Act will result in the limited partner becoming a general partner with unlimited liability. In practice, failure to comply occurs in two ways:

1. Limited partners are not permitted to take part in the management of the firm, nor do they have the power to bind the firm.[30] A limited partner who does take part in management will be liable for the debts and liabilities of the firm as if he were a general partner.

2. The registration documents will state how much capital each limited partner must contribute.[31] A limited partner who has not yet contributed this amount (for example, by guaranteeing to pay this amount in the future) will be regarded as a general partner.[32]

Salaried partners

The growth of professional partnerships, such as solicitors and accountancy firms, has been accompanied by an increase in the number of salaried partners. The typical salaried partner is a relatively young person who does not wish, or cannot afford, to contribute capital to the firm in the way that a general partner does. Instead, he will be represented as a partner (for example, his name will appear on the list of partners) and he may have some of the normal powers of a partner (for example, the power to bind the firm), but he will be paid a salary instead of receiving a share of the firm's profits (although salaried partners may receive a bonus based on the amount of profit).

The law has struggled to articulate clearly the legal position of salaried partners, especially in relation to their level of liability. As salaried partners do not contribute capital to the firm or receive a share of the profits, are they actually partners, or are they more accurately described as employees? The distinction is crucial, because

---

26. Companies House, *Statistical Tables on Companies Registration Activities 2012/13* (Companies House, 2013) 28, Table E2.   27. Limited Partnerships Act 1907, s 4(2).
28. The information required in the application is specified by the PA 1890, s 8A.
29. Limited Partnerships Act 1907, s 5.   30. ibid s 6(1).   31. ibid s 8A(2)(d).
32. *Rayner & Co v Rhodes* (1926) 24 Ll L Rep 25 (KB).

partners have unlimited liability, whereas employees are in no way liable for the debts of the firm. The courts' approach to determining the liability of a salaried partner was laid down in the following case.

 Stekel v Ellice [1973] 1 WLR 191 (Ch)

FACTS: The defendant was a partner in a firm of two partners. The other partner died and the defendant therefore took on the claimant as a salaried partner in 1968. A temporary agreement was entered into, which was to last until April 1969, at which point, a new agreement would be made wherein the claimant would become a general partner. The temporary agreement also provided that the defendant would provide all of the capital and would be entitled to the profits of the firm. The claimant's name appeared on the list of partners on the firm's stationery and he acted as a partner. In April 1969, the claimant had not been made into a general partner and no new agreement was made. The temporary agreement continued, but by August 1970, the two parties had fallen out. The claimant sought to dissolve the firm and contended that he was merely an employee. The defendant argued that the claimant was a partner and that the partnership agreement only provided him with the right of dissolution in specified events, none of which had occurred.

HELD: Megarry J stated that: 'It seems to me impossible to say that as a matter of law a salaried partner is or is not necessarily a partner in the true sense. He may or may not be a partner, depending on the facts.'[33] This would depend upon the substance of the relationship, as opposed to the label that the parties attached to it. On the facts, the claimant was held to be a partner. Aside from the capital requirements, the claimant acted and appeared to outsiders as a partner. Therefore, he could not dissolve the company, because he was bound by the original partnership agreement.

Stekel, along with *M Young Legal Associates*, discussed earlier, places salaried partners in a somewhat precarious position. Both cases indicate that the fact that a person does not share in the profits does not prevent him being classified as a partner. In such a case, the salaried partner does not reap the full benefits of being a partner, but may be liable to the full extent of the law for the debts and liabilities of the partnership. Perhaps for this reason, more recent cases have tended to lean towards salaried partners being classified as employees.[34] Even so, salaried partners wishing to avoid unlimited liability should take steps to indicate that they are not general partners (for example, omitting their name from the firm's letterhead and describing themselves as a 'salaried partner').

The relationship between the partners

The partnership agreement may impose express duties and obligations upon the partners. In addition, the PA 1890 implies additional rights and duties into the partnership agreement that aim to regulate the relationship between the partners.

---

33. [1973] 1 WLR 191 (Ch) 199.
34. See e.g. *Nationwide Building Society v Lewis* [1998] Ch 482 (CA); *Cobetts LLP v Hodge* [2009] EWHC 786 (Ch), [2010] 1 BCLC 30.

Implied terms

Most partners would do well to have in place, before the partnership commences business, a written and comprehensive partnership agreement that clearly sets out the partners' rights and obligations. Where such an agreement does not exist, the 1890 Act implies a number of fundamental rights and obligations into whatever agreement does exist. Further, even where a written agreement does exist, the implied terms will continue to apply, except where they are inconsistent with the agreement. Sections 24 and 25 imply ten terms into the partnership agreement, which can broadly be divided into implied terms relating to (i) the financial affairs of the firm; and (ii) the management and composition of the firm. Table 18.1 sets out the implied terms.

TABLE 18.1 Terms implied into the partnership agreement

Implied terms relating to the financial affairs of the firm	• Right to equal share in the profits and capital of the firm • Right to an indemnity • Right to interest payments for advances made • No right to interest on capital prior to ascertainment of profits • Right to inspect and copy the firm's books
Implied terms relating to management and the composition of the firm	• Right to take part in management • No right to remuneration • No person may be introduced as a partner without the consent of all of the other partners • Differences relating to ordinary matters may be decided by majority • The majority cannot expel a partner unless an express power to do so has been agreed on by all of the partners

Only the principal implied terms will be discussed here.[35] Section 24(1) provides that all of the partners will share equally in the capital and profits of the firm, and will also share equally in the losses of the firm. This applies even where the partners have not contributed equal amounts of capital. If a partner is to receive less/more capital or profit than his fellow partners, or if he is to bear less/more of the firm's losses, the partnership agreement must provide for this.[36] It is common for partnership agreements to provide that partners who contribute less capital will contribute less to the firm's losses, or the capital or profits received by the partners will be proportional to the capital that they contribute. For this reason, the Law Commission recommended that the presumption regarding equal return of capital be abolished,[37] but this recommendation has not been acted upon.

Section 24(2) implies a term providing that partners are to be indemnified by the firm for any payments made or personal liabilities incurred (i) in the ordinary conduct of the business; or (ii) in or about anything necessarily done for the preservation of the business or property of the firm. This is a consequence of the partners' joint and several liability for the firm's debts. Where one partner pays out money in the ordinary conduct of the firm, or pays off a debt of the firm, it is only proper that

---

35. For a detailed discussion of all the implied terms, see Geoffrey Morse, *Partnership Law* (7th edn, OUP 2010) 175–95.

36. *Popat v Schonchhatra* [1997] 1 WLR 1367 (CA).

37. Law Commission, *Partnership Law* (Law Com No 283, HMSO 2003) [10.23].

the firm indemnify him. The same is true in relation to payments made, or liabilities incurred, in preserving the firm's survival.

Perhaps the most crucial implied term is found in s 24(5), which provides that every partner may[38] take part in the management of the firm. As noted earlier, partners are persons carrying on business 'in common', and so all partners should have a right to manage the firm, because they all have a common interest in it. A partner who is denied the right to participate in the management of the firm may be able to dissolve the firm on 'just and equitable grounds'. Whilst the partners may have a right to manage the firm, s 24(6) states that the partners do not have a right to be remunerated (receive a salary) for acting in the partnership business. This is because the partners will usually be rewarded via the distribution of profits. The increasing prevalence of salaried partners in recent years demonstrates that these implied terms are default rules only and can be ousted by an express contrary provision in the agreement.

Section 24(7) provides that no new partners may be admitted to the firm without the consent of all of the other partners. This is a sensible requirement. The admission of a new general partner will dilute the share of the profits received by the other partners. Further, because the partners are liable for each other's acts, they will be keen to ensure that new partners are not going to impose severe financial burdens in the future. Given the potential liabilities, it would be unfair to permit the majority of partners to impose a new partner on the minority.

Section 24(8) provides that where the partners are in disagreement in relation to *ordinary* matters connected with the firm's business, the view of the majority will prevail. Where the disagreement concerns the nature of the firm's business (for example, alteration of the agreement), unanimity will be required. In practice, distinguishing between ordinary matters and matters that change the nature of the firm's business is not always easy.

There is one additional implied term that is not contained in s 24, but is found in s 25. The implied terms in s 24 can be excluded or modified expressly or impliedly; conversely, the term contained in s 25 can only be excluded by an express agreement between the partners. Section 25 provides that '[n]o majority of the partners can expel any partner unless a power to do so has been conferred by express agreement between the partners'. Where a partnership agreement does contain an expulsion clause, this will not necessarily validate the expulsion, and the court will consider three factors:

1. Was the expulsion covered by the clause? If the answer is 'no', the expulsion will be invalid. Thus, where an expulsion clause provided for expulsion upon the commission of fraud, the expulsion of a partner for repeated acts of adultery was invalid.[39]

2. Has the expelled partner been informed of the reason for the expulsion and had the opportunity to defend himself? The extent of this requirement is unclear. In one case, the court held that failure to inform the expelled partner of the reason for his expulsion would render the expulsion unlawful.[40] However, in a later case, in which a partner was expelled for flagrant and repeated breaches of the partnership agreement, the court held that failure to inform him of the reason

---

38. Note that s 24(5) states 'may', and not 'should' or 'must'. Partners are not required to take part in management and, as has been discussed, sleeping partners have long been recognized.

39. *Snow v Milford* (1868) 18 LT 142.

40. *Barnes v Young* [1898] 1 Ch 414 (Ch).

for expulsion did not invalidate the expulsion.[41] It has been argued that the latter case was not a true expulsion case, but a dissolution case (as we shall see, repeated breaches of the partnership agreement constitute grounds for dissolution), and that the general principle is that an expulsion will be unlawful where reasons for expulsion are not provided.[42]

3. Did the partners conducting the expulsion act in good faith? If not, the expulsion will be invalid. Thus, where the partners used an expulsion clause to obtain a partner's share in the firm at a discount, the expulsion was deemed invalid.[43]

Alteration of the partnership agreement

The partners may wish to exclude or modify the implied terms by express provision, or to alter the original agreement. The ability to alter the partnership agreement is contained in s 19, which provides that the agreement may be altered by the consent of all of the partners and that such consent can be express or inferred from the partner's conduct. An example of such inferred consent is provided below.

 Inferred alteration of the partnership agreement

Johnson & Sons is a partnership consisting of twenty-five partners. The agreement provides that only one of the partners, Louis, may enter into negotiations with outside parties and bind the firm contractually. The firm becomes profitable and Louis cannot meet with all of the parties who wish to transact with the firm. Accordingly, it becomes common practice for Bill, another partner, also to take part in negotiations and to enter into contracts on the firm's behalf. The other partners accept this practice and the firm thrives. In such a case, the court is likely to hold that it can be inferred from the actions of the partners that they wished the agreement to be altered to allow Bill to bind the firm in the same manner as Louis. Therefore, unanimous acquiescence to an alteration may operate as inferred consent to that alteration.

Utmost good faith

In Chapter 10, it is noted that certain types of contract are branded of the utmost good faith (*uberrimae fidei*). Partnership agreements constitute a contract of the utmost good faith, the result of which is to impose a number of fiduciary duties upon the partners, irrespective of whether such duties are contained in the partnership agreement or not. The 1890 Act itself provides for three such duties.

The first duty is contained in s 28 and states that partners are 'bound to render true accounts and full information of all things affecting the partnership to any partner or his legal representatives'. The duty imposed is a strict one, which means that an innocent failure to disclose will suffice; breach of duty is not dependent upon the presence of fraud or negligence. The following case demonstrates the potential consequences of breaching the duty.

---

41. *Green v Howell* [1910] 1 Ch 495 (CA).
42. B Davies, 'The Good Faith Principle and the Expulsion Clause in Partnership Law' (1969) 33 Conv NS 32.
43. *Blisset v Daniel* (1853) 10 Hare 493.

Law v Law [1905] 1 Ch 140 (CA)

FACTS: The four Law brothers carried on business as a partnership, based in Halifax. Two of the brothers died. One of the remaining brothers (the claimant) lived in London and took little part in the running of the business. The other brother (the defendant) offered to purchase the claimant's share in the business for £21,000, to which the claimant agreed. The claimant subsequently discovered that the firm had assets worth around £80,000 that the defendant had failed to disclose. The claimant initiated an action, contending that the purchase for £21,000 was voidable on the ground of non-disclosure.

HELD: The contract between the claimant and defendant was voidable at the claimant's instance. The defendant was under a duty to disclose the true value of the firm and had breached that duty in concealing the full value of the firm's assets.

The second duty imposed by the Act could be regarded as a mere extension of the duty to account. Section 29(1) states that 'every partner must account to the firm for any benefit derived by him without the consent of the other partners from any transaction concerning the partnership, or from any use by him of the partnership property name or business connexion'. The obvious example of a breach of s 29(1) would be where a partner acts on behalf of a partnership, and in doing so, obtains some form of secret profit.

Bentley v Craven (1853) 18 Beav 75

FACTS: Four individuals had formed a partnership refining sugar. The defendant acted as the firm's buyer and was able to obtain sugar at a discounted price. Instead of purchasing the sugar on behalf of the firm at the discounted rate, on several occasions and unbeknownst to the other partners, he personally purchased the sugar at the discounted rate and then sold it to the firm at wholesale price, making a profit on each occasion. When the partners discovered this, one of them brought a claim against the defendant for the profit made.

HELD: The defendant was ordered to account to the firm for the profit made. It was irrelevant that, without the defendant, the firm would have to pay the wholesale price. All that mattered was the defendant had made a personal and secret profit from a transaction involving the partnership.

Where, as in *Bentley*, a partner uses a partnership asset to make a personal profit, the requirement to account for that profit is uncontroversial. However, where the asset in question is information, the issue is more complex. The question is whether a partner is liable to account for a profit made whilst engaged in an activity that has no connection to his firm, but which arose due to information obtained whilst acting as a partner. In the following case, the Court stated that the partner did not need to account for such profit.

Aas v Benham [1891] 2 Ch 244 (CA)

FACTS: The defendant was a partner in a firm of shipbrokers. He was involved in setting up a shipbuilding company, and used information and experience gained whilst acting as a partner for his firm of shipbrokers. He was paid a fee for his assistance and was made a director of the board of the new company. The partners of his firm sought to recover the fee paid and the salary paid for acting as director.

HELD: The defendant could keep the profit made. The information used by the partner was employed in a venture outside the scope of the firm. The key determinant was the use of the information, not from where it derived.

COMMENT: The decision in *Aas* was doubted (but not overruled) in cases involving other types of fiduciary—namely, solicitors[44] and company directors.[45] In these cases, the House of Lords held that the defendant had to account for the profit obtained by use of information derived as a fiduciary even though the acts of the defendant had not, in any way, deprived the other party of a benefit. These cases have been criticized for being unduly harsh, but they cast significant doubt upon the extent to which *Aas* can be relied upon as a general principle.

The third and final duty contained in the 1890 Act can be found in s 30, which states that '[i]f a partner, without the consent of the other partners, carries on any business of the same nature as and competing with that of the firm, he must account for and pay over to the firm all profits made by him in that business.' Clearly, a partner engaged in competition with his firm will not be acting in good faith and there would be a substantial conflict of interest. There is a considerable overlap between ss 29(1) and 30 and cases may often involve an alleged breach of both duties. There is, however, a clear distinction between the two duties. Breach of the duty in s 29(1) is dependent upon a profit being made through use of an asset belonging to the partnership, but there is no need to establish that the profit was made whilst in competition with the firm. Conversely, s 30 is not dependent upon use of a partnership asset, but does require that the profit be made whilst engaged in competition with the firm.[46]

Partnership property

As partnerships do not have separate personality, it follows that they cannot own property in the way that incorporated bodies can. The 1890 Act does refer to 'partnership property',[47] but this does not refer to property belonging to the partnership. An express agreement may exist stating what amounts to partnership property, but where such an agreement does not exist, s 20(1) of the PA 1890 provides three ways in which property becomes partnership property:

1. Where property is originally brought into the partnership stock, by purchase or otherwise, on account of the firm (that is, using the firm's money),[48] it shall be called partnership property.

2. Where property is acquired, by purchase or otherwise, on account of the firm, it shall be called partnership property.

---

44. *Boardman v Phipps* [1967] 2 AC 46 (HL).
45. *Regal (Hastings) Ltd v Gulliver* [1967] 2 AC 134 (HL).
46. *Rochwerg v Truster* (2002) 212 DLR (4th) 498 (Ontario Court of Appeal). 47. PA 1890, s 20.
48. ibid s 21.

3. Property acquired for the purposes and in the course of partnership business shall be called partnership property. It is not enough that property is merely used by the firm; it must be essential to the viability of the firm, as the following case demonstrates.

 Miles v Clarke [1953] 1 WLR 537 (Ch)

FACTS: The defendant wished to establish a firm of photographers. He leased premises for such a purpose, and purchased furniture and photographic equipment. As the defendant was not a photographer, he entered into partnership with the claimant, an experienced freelance photographer. It was agreed that the two partners were entitled to an equal share of the profits and that the claimant could draw £125 per month as his share of the profits. The claimant was able to attract a considerable amount of custom to the firm and it prospered, but the two partners fell out and the firm was wound up. The claimant brought an action claiming a share in all of the assets of the firm. The defendant alleged that certain items of property were not partnership property.

HELD: The lease of the premises, the furniture, and the equipment purchased were the property of the defendant. Accordingly, the claimant was not entitled to a share of these assets. Items merely used by the firm should not be regarded as partnership property, unless regarding them as such is essential to the business efficacy of the firm.

In practice, it can be difficult to distinguish between partnership property and property that belongs to individual partners, but the distinction must be made for several reasons. Table 18.2 clarifies the practical importance of the distinction.

TABLE 18.2 Distinguishing between partnership property and the property of individual partners

	Partnership property	Property belonging to a partner
Use of property	Must be used exclusively for the purposes of the firm and in accordance with the partnership agreement	Can be used for whatever lawful purposes the partner deems fit
Change in value of the property	The change in value belongs to the partnership (i.e. all of the partners)	The change in value belongs to the individual partner
Availability of property to creditors	Available to the partnership's creditors upon insolvency	Not available to the partnership's creditors, but is available to the individual partner's creditors
Sale upon dissolution	Upon dissolution, partners can insist on sale of partnership property and are entitled to the proceeds of sale	Can only be sold by the individual partner, who is entitled to the proceeds of sale

In interpreting s 20(1), the courts will not be bound by a literal interpretation that serves to defeat the commercial intentions of the parties. Instead, the courts have adopted a more purposive approach that emphasizes the commercial realities of a situation, as the following case demonstrates.

> ### 🔑 *Don King Productions Inc v Warren* [2000] Ch 291 (CA)
>
> **FACTS:** The defendant was a boxing manager and promoter, focusing primarily on UK-based boxers. The claimant was a boxing promoter, focusing on US-based boxers. Their respective companies formed a partnership, and the defendant purported to assign to the partnership his management and promotion agreements with boxers. However, the agreements could not be assigned, because they were contracts of personal service and/or contained non-assignment clauses. A second agreement was therefore entered into, which provided that the partners should hold all promotion agreements for the benefit of the partnership. The defendant entered into a multi-fight deal that would benefit only himself, which caused the parties to fall out and the partnership to be dissolved. The claimant sought a share in the property of the partnership. The defendant contended that the management and promotion agreements did not constitute partnership property, because they were not validly assigned to the firm. As such, the claimant was not entitled to a share in them.
>
> **HELD**: The Court rejected the defendant's argument and held that the non-assignable contracts constituted partnership property. The Court affirmed Lightman J's first-instance judgment, in which he stated that the task of the court is to determine 'the commercial purpose which the businessman and entities…must as a matter of business common sense have intended to achieve'[49] and that 'the Court may have to require what may appear to be errors or inadequacies in the choice of language to yield to that intention'.[50]

⭐ See Raji Azim-Khan, 'Contract: Boxing' (1999) 10 Ent LR N66

Duty of care

As the liability of the partners is joint, the acts of one partner can result in liability being imposed upon all of the partners.[51] Where one partner causes the other partners to become liable to a third party through some act of wrongdoing, can that partner be liable to the other partners? In other words, do partners owe a duty of care to each other? There is little doubt that the answer is 'yes', but the exact nature of this duty is unclear and there is little English law on the subject. What authority does exist leans towards the standard of the duty of care being an objective one (that is, the standard is that of a 'reasonable businessmen in the situation',[52] or that the partner must exercise 'reasonable care in all the relevant circumstances').[53] There is, however, no definitive higher court judgment indicating the exact scope of the duty of care and, until there is, the position will remain unclear. Placing the duties of care owed by partners on a statutory footing (as has happened in the case of company directors) would have provided much clarity in this area, but the Law Commission rejected this.[54]

Dissolution

Later in the chapter, the situations in which a partnership can be dissolved will be discussed. Here, the effects of dissolution amongst the partners themselves will be examined. Certain events capable of causing the firm's dissolution (for example, the death or bankruptcy of a partner) may not, in fact, cause the business to end. Where

---

49. [1998] 2 Lloyd's Rep 176 (Ch) 176, 177.   50. ibid 177.   51. PA 1890, s 12.
52. *Winsor v Schroeder* (1979) 129 NLJ 103.
53. *Ross Harper & Murphy v Banks* 2000 SC 500 (OT) 510 (Lord Hamilton).
54. Law Commission, *Partnership Law* (Law Com No 283, Cm 6015, HMSO 2003) [11.56].

this is the case, the firm will need to account for the departing partner. This will normally involve valuing the partner's assets and paying the appropriate sum to the departing partner or his estate.

Where the firm is dissolved, the debts of the partnership must be paid. The partners are entitled to sell the partnership property and to use the proceeds to pay off the firm's debts.[55] Valuing and selling the physical assets of the firm is straightforward, but other assets of the firm are more complex—notably, the firm's 'goodwill'.

Goodwill is likely to be one of the firm's major assets, although it will never show up in the firm's accounts. The concept of goodwill was defined by Lord Macnaghten as 'the reputation and connection of the firm, which may have been built up by years of honest work or gained by lavish expenditure of money'.[56] In more modern terms, it is usually defined as 'the difference between the value of the business as a going concern and the value of its assets'.[57] These definitions indicate that valuing the goodwill of a firm is a highly complex and specialized issue. In summary, the effect of a sale of goodwill is that:

- only the buyer may represent himself as continuing or succeeding to the seller's business;[58]
- the buyer has the exclusive right to use the former partnership's name, although the seller is free to set up a similar business in competition with the rival[59] (unless the seller covenanted not to do so in the contract of sale);
- the seller may advertise his new business, but he may not solicit or canvass the customers of the former partnership.[60]

When goodwill is sold, covenants are usually entered into that set out the rights of the seller and buyer after the sale. This is a wise precaution, especially from the point of view of the buyer, because the seller may be tempted to usurp or recover the goodwill that he has sold.

Once the assets of the partnership have been realized, there must occur a final account, which will consist of a record of all transactions from the date of the last account up to the date of the dissolution. Once this final account has been made, the proceeds realized by the sale of the firm's assets can be distributed. The partnership agreement may state how the proceeds are to be distributed, but in the absence of such an agreement, s 44 (and decided case law) provides as follows.

1. The losses of the partnership must be paid, first, out of the firm's profits and, once the profits are gone, out of the firm's capital. If this fails to meet the firm's losses, the remainder is borne by the partners in proportion to their profit-share entitlement. If a partner is unable to pay his contribution towards to the partnership's losses, the other partners must pay his contribution between them in the same proportion as profits were divided.[61]

2. The assets of the partnership (including any contributions by partners to make up losses or deficiencies of capital) must be applied to the following persons in the following order:

   (a) Outside creditors.

   (b) Any partners who made loans to the firm.

55. PA 1890, s 39.   56. *Trego v Hunt* [1896] AC 7 (HL) 24.
57. Geoffrey Morse, *Partnership Law* (7th edn, OUP 2010) 220.
58. *Churton v Douglas* (1859) 28 LJ Ch 841.   59. *Trego v Hunt* [1896] AC 7 (HL).
60. *Curl Bros Ltd v Webster* [1904] 1 Ch 685 (Ch).
61. *Garner v Murray* [1904] 1 Ch 57 (Ch).

(c) The costs of the dissolution.[62]

(d) Each partner is repaid the capital contribution that he made.

(e) Any remaining assets are divided amongst the partners in proportion to the division of profits.

Once the firm is dissolved, the authority of each partner to bind the firm continues, but only in so far as to complete transactions begun, but unfinished, at the time of the dissolution.[63]

The relationship between partners and third parties

Sections 5–18 of the PA 1890 regulate the relationship between the partners and third parties. This will most obviously include the extent to which the partners can contractually bind the firm and the other partners to a third party, but it also lays down rules to establish when the firm and the partners can be liable for the unlawful acts of a single partner that have caused loss to a third party.

Agency

Regarding a partner's ability to bind the partnership and his co-partners, the key provision is s 5, which provides that:

> Every partner is an agent of the firm and his other partners for the purpose of the business of the partnership; and the acts of every partner who does any act for carrying on in the usual way business of the kind carried on by the firm of which he is a member bind the firm and his partners...

Accordingly, each partner is an agent of the firm and of his co-partners. The concept of agency is discussed in detail in Chapter 8, but a brief summary will be helpful here. An agency relationship is simply a relationship between two parties, whereby one party (known as the 'agent') carries out some task on behalf of another party (known as the 'principal'). The ability of the agent to act on the principal's behalf will be limited by the authority that his principal grants him. The important point to note is that the agent can contractually bind the principal to a third party, provided that the agent acts within his authority, as the following example demonstrates.

 An agency relationship

Anna (the principal) instructs Jo (the agent) to purchase an item at an upcoming auction. Jo must not bid any more than £10,000 (this constitutes her authority). Jo goes to the auction and obtains the item with a bid of £9,000. As Jo has acted within her authority, a binding contract exists between Anna and the auction house. If Jo were to have obtained the item for £11,000, however, she would have breached her authority, and the contract would most likely have been between her and the auction house.

---

62. *Potter v Jackson* (1880) LR 13 Ch D 845 (Ch).
63. PA 1890, s 38.

🔗 The authority of an agent is discussed at p 193

Provided that a partner acts within his authority, he is able to bind his firm and his co-partners to a third party. Clearly, the central factor is the partner's authority. An agent's authority is a complex affair and it will not be discussed here.

Section 5 provides that a partner cannot bind his firm and his co-partners where 'the partner so acting has in fact no authority to act for the firm in the particular matter, and the person with whom he is dealing either knows that he has no authority, or does not know or believe him to be a partner'. What this is saying is that a partner who has no authority to carry out an act can nevertheless bind the firm and his co-partners provided that (i) the third party is not aware that the partner lacks authority; or (ii) the third party believed the partner to be a partner of the firm. Where a third party is aware of the partner's lack of authority, or believes that the partner is not, in fact, a partner, the firm and the co-partners will not be bound.

It should be remembered that a partner's ability to bind his firm and co-partners only applies to 'an act for carrying on in the usual way business of the kind carried on by the firm'. This requires us to define:

- an 'act for carrying on in the usual way'; and
- 'business of the kind carried on by the firm'.

In determining whether an act arose 'in the usual way', the courts distinguish between trading and non-trading firms. A trading firm is one the business of which involves the buying and selling of goods.[64] Table 18.3 sets out what acts are within and beyond the scope of the usual authority of trading and non-trading firms.

TABLE 18.3 The usual authority of trading and non-trading firms

	Usual authority	No usual authority
Non-trading firm	• To sell partnership property • To purchase goods necessary for the firm's business • To employ and dismiss employees • To accept or indorse cheques • To instigate proceedings on the firm's behalf • To employ an agent	• To borrow money • To pledge partnership property as security • To accept or indorse negotiable instruments (except cheques) • To give a guarantee in the firm's name • To submit a dispute to arbitration • To make an outsider a partner, or to put co-partners into partnership with others
Trading firm	• To sell and pledge partnership property • To purchase goods necessary for the firm's business • To borrow money and pay debts • To employ and dismiss employees • To accept or indorse negotiable instruments • To instigate proceedings on the firm's behalf • To employ an agent	• To give a guarantee in the firm's name • To submit a dispute to arbitration • To make an outsider a partner, or to put co-partners into partnership with others

---

64. *Wheatley v Smithers* [1906] 2 KB 321 (CA).

The courts have held that the phrase 'business of the kind carried on by the firm' should be interpreted in exactly the same way as the phrase 'ordinary course of business', as found in s 10.[65] The interpretation of this phrase is discussed later.

As each partner has the power to bind his co-partners contractually, it follows that every partner is liable jointly (but not severally) for all debts and obligations of the firm incurred while he is a partner. Partners, however, differ from other joint debtors in that the estate of a deceased partner is severally liable for any of the firm's debts incurred while the deceased was a partner.[66] These rules have been supplemented by the Civil Liability (Contribution) Act 1978, which provides that the mere fact that one partner has been sued (successfully or not) on a contract does not preclude an action on that contract against another partner.[67] A partner successfully sued on a contract can seek a contribution from his co-partners.[68]

Liability for tortious and other wrongful acts

The above provisions deal with a partner's liability in contract, although the rules of agency are wide enough to cover non-contractual liability. Partners may also be liable in tort or even held guilty of a criminal offence. Section 10 of the PA 1890 provides that:

> Where, by any wrongful act or omission of any partner acting in the ordinary course of the business of the firm, or with the authority of his co-partners, loss or injury is caused to any person not being a partner in the firm, or any penalty is incurred, the firm is liable therefor to the same extent as the partner so acting or omitting to act.

What s 10 basically states is that the partnership and each partner is vicariously liable in tort for the wrongful acts or omissions of another partner, provided that the partner was acting within his authority, or that the act was done whilst in the ordinary course of the firm's business. The following example demonstrates s 10 in operation.

 vicariously liable: liability imposed on a person for the acts of another (see Chapter 16)

 Eg **The operation of s 10 of the PA 1890**

Price & Young is a firm of accountants consisting of fifty partners. One of the firm's partners, Greg, is conducting a financial audit of KP Coopers Ltd—but he conducts the audit negligently. Under s 10, Price & Young and the other forty-nine partners face liability for Greg's act of negligence.

What constitutes the ordinary course of the firm's business was discussed in detail in the following case.

O **_Dubai Aluminium Co Ltd v Salaam_ [2002] UKHL 48**

FACTS: Salaam defrauded the claimant company out of US$50 million. Salaam was the client of a law firm, whose senior partner assisted Salaam in defrauding the claimant by drafting certain documents. However, neither the senior partner, nor any other partners of the firm, received any of the fraudulent proceeds. Were the co-partners liable for the acts of the senior partner? The Court of Appeal said 'no', on the ground that drafting documents in order to assist the commission of a fraud was not in the course of the firm's business.

---

65. *JJ Coughlan Ltd v Ruparelia* [2003] EWCA Civ 1057, [2004] PNLR 4.   66. PA 1890, s 9.
67. Civil Liability (Contribution) Act 1978, s 3.   68. ibid s 1.

HELD: The House of Lords reversed the decision and held the co-partners liable. Providing that the act itself was within the firm's business, it did not matter that it was carried out in an unauthorized or unlawful way. As drafting documents was within the firm's business, the fact the documents were drafted for an unlawful purpose did not take the acts outside the scope of the firm's business. Lord Nicholls stated:

> Drafting these particular agreements is to be regarded as an act done within the ordinary course of the firm's business even though they were drafted for a dishonest purpose. These acts were so closely connected with the acts [the senior partner] was authorised to do that for the purpose of the liability of the [law] firm they may fairly and properly be regarded as done by him while acting in the ordinary course of the firm's business.[69]

COMMENT: Accordingly, whether an act is within the course of the firm's business will depend on the closeness of the connection between the act of wrongdoing and what the partner is authorized to do. This will be a question of fact in each case. Lord Millett stated clearly that s 10 does not apply only to actions in tort, but can also apply to any fault-based common law or statutory wrong.

 See Charles Mitchell, 'Partners in Wrongdoing?' (2003) 119 LQR 364

An act will not be within the ordinary course of the firm's business if the partner committed the act in a personal capacity and not as a member of the firm, even if the act itself is one that he is authorized to perform.

 Chittick v Maxwell (1993) 118 ALR 728

FACTS: The claimant built a house on land belonging to his daughter and son-in-law (the defendant). The parties agreed that the claimant would be permitted to live in the house until he died, whereupon it would pass to the defendant and his wife. The defendant, being a solicitor, drew up the agreement, but omitted to protect the claimant's right to possession. The defendant repeatedly mortgaged the land, and, when he failed to repay, the mortgagees obtained a possession order and evicted the claimant. The claimant sued the defendant and his firm for the negligent drafting of the agreement.

HELD: The defendant's firm and his co-partners were not liable. Although drafting agreements of this nature was within the ordinary business of the firm, it was clear that the defendant was engaged in this activity in a personal capacity, not in his capacity as a member of the firm.

An act that is not within the ordinary course of the firm's business may still result in liability under s 10 if it is within the partner's authority.

Hamlyn v John Houston & Co [1903] 1 KB 81 (CA)

FACTS: The defendant was a firm of grain merchants consisting of two partners. One of the partners obtained confidential information on the claimant (a rival firm) by bribing one of the

69. [2002] UKHL 48, [2003] 2 AC 366 [36].

claimant's employees. The claimant lost money due to the information being divulged and it sued the defendant.

HELD: Obtaining information on rival businesses was a legitimate business aim and within the authority of the partner. The fact that he obtained this information illegitimately was not enough to place it outside the partner's authority.

Liability imposed under s 10 is joint and several, meaning that the claimant can sue each partner in turn, or all of the partners at the same time, until he has recovered the full amount of his loss. This differs from liability under s 9, which is joint only, meaning that the claimant has only one cause of action against all of the partners, who are jointly liable for his loss.

Holding out

Section 14(1) of the PA 1890, which overlaps with s 5 and with normal agency rules, provides that any person who, by words or conduct, represents himself, or knowingly suffers himself to be represented, as a partner in a partnership is liable as if he were a partner to any third party who has 'given credit' (that is, incurred any liability) to the partnership on the faith of that representation. The effect of s 14(1) is that the person held out as being a partner is estopped from denying that he was a partner if that was the impression created, by a representation to that effect, in the mind of the person who relied on that representation in his dealing with the partnership. In order for a third party to rely on s 14(1) and obtain a remedy against the person holding himself out as a partner (*X*), he will need to establish that:

- a representation was made, indicating that *X* was a partner. The representation can be made by *X* or by another person, provided that *X* is aware that the other person is holding him out as a partner;
- the representation was made to the third party directly, or to another who subsequently repeated it to the third party; and
- the third party acted on the representation by giving credit to the partnership. All that he need establish is that he believed the representation and acted on it; he does not need to show that he would not have given credit had he known the truth.

Liability following a change in the partnership's composition

The composition of a partnership will alter over time: new partners will be admitted to the firm and old partners may leave or retire. How do these changes affect the liability of the partners? Are new partners liable for acts committed before they joined the firm? Are existing partners liable for acts committed prior to their leaving the firm?

The liability of new partners

Determining the liability of new partners appears straightforward. Section 17(1) of the PA 1890 provides that '[a] person who is admitted as a partner into an existing firm does not thereby become liable to the creditors of the firm for anything done before he became a partner'. However, the situation can be more complex than it appears, as the following example demonstrates.

The liability of new partners

In November 2013, a firm enters into a contract. In January 2014, Ron becomes a partner of the firm. In March 2014, the firm breaches the contract. The contract was entered into before Ron became a partner, but the breach occurred while he was a partner. Can Ron be liable?

Section 17(1) does not appear to provide an answer to this question, so the issue has been left to the courts. The issue revolves around the phrase 'anything done before he became a partner'. In Ron's case, does 'anything done' refer to the entering into of the contract or the breach of contract? Where the contract requires the firm to perform a single continuous act, it would appear that 'anything done' would refer to the contract being entered into[70] and that, accordingly, the new partner will not be liable. Where the contract involves a number of repeated acts, if liability arises following the new partner joining the firm, the phrase 'anything done' would appear to relate to the act of wrongdoing[71] and so the new partner would be liable. The following example clarifies the distinction.

 Single and repeated acts

Single continuous act

In January 2014, a firm enters into a contract with a Jo (a solicitor) to recover a debt owed to it. In February 2014, Marc becomes a partner in the firm. In March 2014, the firm indicates that it is not happy with Jo's progress in recovering the debt and terminates the contract without paying her. Jo sues the firm for breach of contract. As the contract provides for a single continuous act (recovery of the debt), the entering into the contract will constitute 'anything done' under s 17(1). Accordingly, Marc is not liable for the firm's breach of contract.

Repeated acts

In January 2014, a firm enters into a contract to supply consignments of goods to a company based in the USA. The contract provides that the consignments shall be supplied 'as and when the US company requests them'. In February 2014, several consignments are delivered. In March 2014, Paul becomes a partner of the firm and several more consignments are delivered. In April 2014, more consignments are delivered, but one of them fails to meet the standard specified in the contract. As the contract provides for repeated acts (supplying goods on request), the delivery of the unsatisfactory goods will constitute 'anything done' under s 17(1). Accordingly, Paul will be liable for the firm's breach.

Liabilities existing on retirement

Consider the following example.

 Liabilities existing on retirement

In January 2014, a firm enters into a contract to purchase goods. The firm will pay for the goods in twelve monthly instalments. In March 2014, one of the partners retires from the firm. Is the retiring partner liable for the remaining payments?

---

70. *Court v Berlin* [1897] 2 QB 396 (CA).   71. *Bagel v Miller* [1903] 2 KB 212 (KB).

Section 17(2) of the PA 1890 provides that '[a] partner who retires from a firm does not thereby cease to be liable for partnership debts or obligations incurred before his retirement'. However, this is a *prima facie* rule only and the court will apply the same rule as applies to new partners. If the contract requires a single continuous act by the firm, the retiring partner will remain liable. If the contract requires a series of repeated acts by the firm, the partner is only liable for those acts that arose before his retirement. The partner will not, however, be liable to a third party for debts occurring after he retires if the partnership agreement provides that he shall not be liable, or if he enters into an agreement with the other partners and the third party that provides that he shall not be liable.[72]

Liabilities incurred after retirement

Section 36(1) of the PA 1890 provides that '[w]here a person deals with a firm after a change in its constitution he is entitled to treat all apparent members of the old firm as still being members of the firm until he has notice of the change'. Accordingly, if a retired partner appears to be a partner and a third party has no notice that the partner has retired, the partner will remain liable to that third party. To avoid liability to the third party for any debts that are incurred after retirement, the partner should make the fact of his retirement known to the third party (although an advertisement placed in the *Gazette* will provide notice to persons who have not had dealings with the firm prior to the dissolution or the date of the advertisement).[73] If the third party did not know that the retiring partner was a partner in the first place, the partner will not be liable to the third party for any debts that accrue after his retirement.[74] This will also be the case where the partner leaves the firm through death or bankruptcy.[75]

→ *Gazette*: the official newspaper of record for the UK

Dissolution

A partnership can be brought to an end in numerous ways, but whereas the creation of a partnership is a straightforward affair, the dissolution of a partnership can be a lengthy and complex matter. Here, the principal methods and causes of dissolution will be discussed (see Table 18.4 for the various categories of dissolution), but, before that, it is worth categorizing the various methods. A partnership can be dissolved:

- as a result of a term in the partnership agreement;
- as a result of some rule of law; or
- by an order of the court.

Express and implied terms, and dissolution by agreement

As a partnership agreement is merely a form of contract, many of the rules relating to the termination of contract will apply here. For example, in Chapter 11, it is noted that a contract may be simply brought to an end upon the agreement of the parties. This agreement may be express, but it can also be implied through the acts of the partners.

Alternatively, the partnership agreement itself may contain a number of terms specifying when the partnership will be dissolved (for example, if a partner is

---

72. PA 1890, s 17(3).   73. ibid s 36(2).   74. ibid s 36(3).   75. ibid.

TABLE 18.4 Categories of dissolution

Contractual dissolution	Dissolution by operation of law	Dissolution by court order
• Express terms • Implied terms (could include rules relating to death and bankruptcy) • Mutual agreement of the parties • Rescission • Repudiation	• Illegality • Death or bankruptcy of a partner (could be regarded as implied terms)	• Mental or permanent incapacity • Prejudicial conduct • Wilful or persistent breaches of the partnership agreement • Carrying on the business at a loss • Just and equitable

convicted of a serious criminal offence,[76] or is found to be committing professional misconduct).[77] The PA 1890 also implies six terms into the agreement that provide for dissolving events:

1. If the partnership is entered into for a fixed term, it will be dissolved at the end of that term, subject to any agreement otherwise by the parties.[78]

2. If the partnership is for a single adventure or undertaking, it will dissolve once the adventure or undertaking is completed or terminated, subject to any agreement otherwise between the partners.[79]

3. If a partnership agreement is entered into for an undefined period, it can be dissolved by a partner by giving notice to the other partners of his intention to dissolve, subject to any agreement otherwise between the partners[80] (for example, by providing that termination may only occur by mutual agreement).

4. The death of a partner (except a limited partner) will dissolve the partnership, unless the partners agree otherwise.[81] If the partner is a body corporate, its dissolution will be treated as death. Due to the inconvenience caused by the death of a partner, most partnership agreements will provide that, upon the death of a partner, the firm will continue (although, technically, the firm is still dissolved, but is immediately replaced by a new firm).

5. The bankruptcy of a partner will dissolve the partnership, unless the partners agree otherwise.[82]

6. Where a partner, in order to satisfy his private debt, grants a charge over his share of the firm's assets, then the firm can be dissolved at the option of the other partners.[83]

Illegality

The six events discussed above will, by default, result in the dissolution of the partnership. Dissolution can, however, be avoided by excluding the implied terms via an agreement between the partners. What cannot be excluded is that the partnership will be dissolved where it becomes tainted by illegality.[84] Note that this applies to partnerships that are untainted by illegality, but subsequently become tainted: a

---

76. *Essel v Hayward* (1860) 30 Beav 158.   77. *Clifford v Timms* [1908] AC 112 (HL).

78. PA 1890, s 32(a).   79. ibid s 32(b).

80. ibid s 32(c). Section 26(1) provides an identical right in cases in which a partnership has no fixed term of duration.

81. ibid s 33(1).   82. ibid.   83. ibid s 33(2).   84. ibid s 34.

partnership formed for an illegal purpose will be regarded as void *ab initio* on the ground of illegality.

The taint of illegality need not affect all of the partners, as the following case demonstrates.

 Hudgell Yeates & Co v Watson [1978] QB 451 (CA)

FACTS: A solicitors' firm consisted of three solicitors, all of whom were partners. One of the partners forgot to renew his practising certificate. Without a certificate, the solicitor was not legally entitled to practise.[85]

HELD: The partnership had become tainted with illegality and was automatically dissolved, even though all three partners were unaware of the illegality.

Rescission

A partnership agreement can be rescinded just like any other contract. For example, if a person is induced to become a partner based upon another person's misrepresentation, this will provide grounds for the rescission of the partnership agreement. In addition to the right to rescind, the representee also has access to other remedies, including:

- If the misrepresentation is fraudulent or negligent, damages can be recovered.
- Once the partnership's liabilities have been met, the representee will acquire a lien over any remaining assets in relation to any capital paid by him.[86]

  → **lien:** the right to hold the property of another until an obligation is satisfied

- The creditors' rights will be **subrogated** to the representee (that is, the representee will be able to stand in the place of the partnership's creditors for payments made by him in respect of the partnership's liabilities).[87]
- The representee is entitled to be indemnified by the person who committed the fraud or misrepresentation against all of the debts and liabilities of the firm.[88]

  → **subrogation:** the ability to take on the legal rights of others

Repudiation

One of the partners may breach the partnership agreement to such an extent that the other partners are entitled to terminate it (that is, the breach is repudiatory). Where the innocent party accepts the breach, the partnership agreement will be rescinded, but the effect of rescission here is more complex. Whilst repudiation may terminate the partnership agreement, it does not follow that it terminates the partnership itself.

 Hurst v Bryk [2002] 1 AC 185 (HL)

FACTS: A solicitors firm consisted of twenty partners, of which the claimant was one. Eighteen of the partners served retirement notices and gave nine months' notice, as required by the partnership agreement. However, before the nine months had expired, all of the partners, except the claimant, entered into an agreement terminating the partnership. The actions of the nineteen other partners (the defendants) amounted to a repudiatory breach

---

85. Solicitors Act 1974, s 1(c).   86. PA 1890, s 41(a).   87. ibid s 41(b).
88. ibid s 41(c).

of the partnership agreement. The claimant accepted the breach and sought a declaration from the court stating that he was not liable for the liabilities of the partnership that accrued after the date of repudiation.

HELD: The House of Lords refused to make such a declaration. Although the acceptance by the claimant of the repudiatory breach of the other partners discharged all of the partners from further performance of their obligations, it did not operate to divest rights already unconditionally acquired. Therefore, the claimant remained liable for the debts of the partnership and remained liable to contribute upon its winding up.

COMMENT: Whilst this decision might appear odd at first, it does have a powerful justification. As shall be seen, wilful or persistent breaches of the partnership agreement can result in the court dissolving the partnership. If, in *Hurst*, the claimant's repudiation were automatically to result in the dissolution of the firm, it would strongly undermine the courts' discretion to grant dissolution orders.

Accordingly, repudiation of the partnership agreement does not automatically dissolve the partnership itself. This does, however, result in one significant criticism—namely, that upon termination of the partnership agreement, the partnership will become a 'partnership at will'. A partnership at will is simply a partnership that has no fixed duration (which, by definition, a partnership without a partnership agreement must be). The point to note is that one partner serving notice on another may terminate such partnerships immediately.[89] Therefore, following the dissolution of the agreement, the partnership itself can be dissolved by mere notice.

Mental or permanent incapacity

Where a partner lacks mental capacity, the partnership is not automatically dissolved; instead, the other partners can petition the court for an order dissolving the partnership.[90] Such an order is granted entirely at the discretion of the court. The same applies where the partner is rendered in any other way 'permanently incapable of performing his part in the partnership contract'.[91] The incapacity must be permanent—if the possibility exists that the partner's condition will improve (for example, where medical evidence indicates an improvement in the medical condition of a partner who suffered a stroke),[92] the court is unlikely to grant a dissolution order. For this reason, it is common for partnership agreements to contain a term permitting dissolution once a partner has been incapacitated for a specified period.[93]

Prejudicial conduct and wilful, or persistent, breaches of the partnership agreement

Where a partner engages in activity that is 'calculated to prejudicially affect the carrying on of the business', any of the other partners may petition the court for a dissolution order.[94] This could include adverse activities occurring within the firm (for example, a partner misappropriating of the firm's assets),[95] but can also include

---

89. ibid s 26(1).
90. Mental Incapacity Act 2005, ss 16 and 18(1)(e).
91. PA 1890, s 35(b).   92. *Whitwell Arthur* (1863) 35 Beav 140.
93. In *Peyton v Mindham* [1972] 1 WLR 8 (Ch), the partnership agreement provided that the partnership would be dissolved if any partner were to be incapacitated for more than nine consecutive months.
94. PA 1890, s 35(c).   95. *Essel v Hayward* (1860) 30 Beav 158.

activity outside the firm (for example, a partner committing a crime).[96] Lawful, but immoral, conduct is unlikely to suffice unless it adversely affects the partnership.[97]

Innocent partners may also petition the court where one partner 'wilfully or persistently commits a breach of the partnership agreement, or otherwise so conducts himself in matters relating to the partnership business that it is not reasonably practicable for the other partner or partners to carry on the business in partnership with him'.[98] Note that the conduct required will normally need to be of sufficient seriousness, so minor squabbles amongst the partners will not suffice. Minor breaches may, however, warrant dissolution where they are persistent. Thus, in *Cheesman v Price*,[99] one partner had, on seventeen occasions, failed to document properly in the firm's books monies received. Although the amounts of money were small, the persistent nature of the breach warranted dissolution.

Loss-making

As noted, a partnership must be carried on with 'a view to a profit'. It follows that where the making of a profit becomes impossible (that is, where the business of the partnership can only be carried on at a loss), the partners may apply to the court for a dissolution order.[100] The partners will, however, need to demonstrate the impossibility of making a profit. Thus, where a firm failed to make a profit because its senior partner was ill, a dissolution order was not granted, because the other partners could still operate the firm at a profit.[101]

Just and equitable

The final ground for a dissolution order is where the court feels that it is 'just and equitable that the partnership be dissolved'.[102] Many of the cases in this area do not concern partnerships, but so-called 'quasi-partnerships'—small, private companies that bear all of the hallmarks of a partnership.[103]

The rules relating to the dissolution of companies on just and equitable grounds are discussed in more detail in 'The petition for winding up' at p 655

Reform

In November 1997, the Department of Trade and Industry (now the Department for Business Innovation & Skills (BIS)) requested the Law Commission and the Scottish Law Commission to undertake a joint review of partnership law. A report was published in November 2003,[104] in which the two Commissions recommended that a number of changes be made to the PA 1890 and to the Limited Partnerships Act 1907. In July 2006, the government announced that the reforms of the 1890 Act would not be considered at this time, but that the reforms of the 1907 Act would be implemented. In August 2008, the government published a consultation document[105]

---

96. *Carmichael v Evans* [1904] 1 Ch 486 (Ch) (travelling on the railway whilst intending to avoid paying the fare).

97. *Snow v Milford* (1868) 16 WTR 554 (persistent adultery).

98. PA 1890, s 35(d).   99. (1865) 35 Beav 142.   100. PA 1890, s 35(e).

101. *Handyside v Campbell* (1901) 17 TLR 623 (Ch).

102. PA 1890, s 35(f). This is also a ground for winding up a company: see Insolvency Act 1986, s 122(1)(g).

103. In *Re Yenidje Tobacco Co Ltd* [1916] 2 Ch 426 (CA) 432, Cozens-Hardy MR described a quasi-partnership as 'a partnership in the form or the guise of a private company'.

104. Law Commission, *Partnership Law* (Law Com No 283, Cm 6015, HMSO 2003).

105. Department for Business, Enterprise and Regulatory Reform, *Legislative Reform Order to Repeal and Replace the Limited Partnerships Act 1907* (BERR 2008).

indicating the government's intention to pass a legislative reform order that would repeal the Limited Partnerships Act 1907 and replace its provisions with additions to the Partnership Act 1890. Ultimately, this did not occur, but an order was passed that introduced several notable reforms into the 1907 Act (for example, limited partnerships are now required to end their name with the suffix 'limited partnership' or 'LP').[106]

Chapter conclusion

An individual who wishes to commence business, but wishes to avoid complex formation procedures and extensive regulation, will be well served by conducting business as a sole proprietor. He will retain full control over the activities of the business and will be entitled to all of the profits. But he will also be solely liable for the business' debts to an unlimited amount. Similar benefits are available to those who conduct business through a partnership. Partnerships are easy to set up and subject to much less regulation than companies or limited liability partnerships—but the liability of the partners is joint and unlimited, and ending a partnership is much more complex than ending a sole proprietorship. For those persons who wish to avoid unlimited liability, it is possible to set up business as a limited partnership, but limited partners are not permitted to manage the firm. Accordingly, for many persons wishing to set up business, the disadvantages of unincorporated structures outweigh the advantages. For such persons, setting up business through a body corporate will be a much more advantageous proposition.

Key points summary

- A sole proprietorship is a non-incorporated business created by a single person.

- A sole proprietor may keep the profits generated by the sole proprietorship, but he is also personally liable for the business' debts and this liability is unlimited.

- A partnership is 'the relation which subsists between persons carrying on a business in common with a view of profit'.

- There are three types of partnership: (i) ordinary partnerships; (ii) limited partnerships; and (iii) limited liability partnerships (discussed in Chapter 19).

- General partnerships do not have separate personality and their partners do not have limited liability. Their liability is unlimited.

- The Partnership Act 1890 implies a number of terms into the partnership contract, but these terms can be varied or excluded by the agreement itself.

- The partners are agents of the firm and of each other, meaning that each partner can bind the firm and his co-partners, provided that he acts within his authority. Partners can also be vicariously liable for the wrongful acts of their co-partners.

---

106. Limited Partnerships Act 1907, s 8B(2).

Self-test questions

1. Define the following:
   (a) sole proprietorship;
   (b) sole practitioner;
   (c) sole trader;
   (d) partnership;
   (e) *uberrimae fidei*;
   (f) partnership property;
   (g) holding out.

2. Jeff has an idea for a new business. His friend, Ryan, offers to help Jeff set up business. Jeff is unsure whether to commence business on his own, or to enter into partnership with Ryan. Advise Jeff on the advantages and disadvantages of conducting business as a sole proprietor and through a partnership.

3. Explain the distinction between: (i) a general partner; (ii) a sleeping partner; (iii) a limited partner; and (iv) a salaried partner.

4. Discuss the following.
   (a) In May 2013, Card & Co, a firm of solicitors, undertakes to recover a debt for Vincent. In July 2013, Shane becomes a partner of the firm. In November 2013, Vincent informs Card & Co that it will be impossible to recover the debt, because the debtor has become insolvent. Had the firm acted more quickly, Vincent might have been able to recover the money owed. Vincent alleges that the firm has been negligent and commences proceedings. Does Shane face any liability?
   (b) Tom and Dave are partners in a firm that has a number of female employees. Tom sexually harasses one of these females and she commences legal proceedings. To what extent is Dave liable for Tom's act?
   (c) Helen is a partner in a firm of accountants. Her sister, Emma, asks her if she would audit her company's accounts as a personal favour. Helen conducts the audit using her firm's premises and staff, but does not charge Emma a fee. The audit is negligently conducted and Emma sues Helen's firm. Are the firm and Helen's co-partners liable?

5. Richard has been a partner in a trading firm for over forty years. He is due to retire next month and is keen to ensure that, upon his retirement, he does not share in the liabilities of the firm. Advise him of his legal position and what steps should be taken to ensure that his liability as a partner will end upon his retirement.

6. Explain the three broad categories by which a firm can be dissolved and give examples from each category.

Further reading

Department for Business, Enterprise and Regulatory Reform, *Legislative Reform Order to Repeal and Replace the Limited Partnerships Act 1907* (BERR 2008)
A consultation document proposing that the Limited Partnerships Act 1907 be repealed and the provisions relating to limited partnerships be inserted into the Partnership Act 1890

Law Commission, *Partnership Law* (Law Com No 283, Cm 6015, HMSO 2003)
As with all Law Commission reports, the current law is stated clearly and with impressive
depth; good criticism of current law and suggestions for reform

Geoffrey Morse, *Partnership Law* (7th edn, OUP 2010)
A popular, accessible, and well-structured account of the law and practicalities relating to
partnerships

Websites

<**https://www.gov.uk/government/organisations/
department-for-business-innovation-skills/about/statistics**>
*Provides extensive statistics on the number of sole proprietors and partnerships in the UK;
also provides data on their composition*

<**http://www.companieshouse.gov.uk**>
*The official website of Companies House; provides useful statistical data relating to the
number of limited partnerships*

Remember to visit the **Online Resource Centre** at <**http://www.
oxfordtextbooks.co.uk/orc/roach3e**> to access the following resources
on Chapter 18, 'Unincorporated business structures': more **practice
questions** and answers; a **glossary** of key terms; **multiple-choice
questions;** and **revision summaries.** Updates to the law can be found on
Twitter by following **@UKBusinessLaw** and **@UKCompanyLaw**.

19 Incorporation and bodies corporate

- Companies
- Types of registered company
- The advantages and disadvantages of incorporation
- Corporate personality and 'lifting the veil'
- The constitution of the company
- Limited liability partnerships

INTRODUCTION

In Chapter 18, the advantages and disadvantages of conducting business through an unincorporated structure are discussed. Unincorporated structures, whilst suitable for certain forms of business, contain several inherent disadvantages that will render them unsuitable or undesirable in certain circumstances. Where this is the case, conducting business through a body corporate will be more suitable. Bodies corporate come in two principal forms:

1. companies;[1] and
2. limited liability partnerships (LLPs).[2]

Such business entities are known as 'bodies corporate' because they are bodies created via the process of incorporation and have corporate personality. This chapter will examine the two forms of bodies corporate, and the various advantages and disadvantages that incorporation can bring. Our discussion begins with the principal body corporate—namely, the registered company.

Companies

There are three principal methods by which a company can be created:

1. incorporation by Act of Parliament;
2. incorporation by royal charter; and
3. incorporation by registration.

---

1. Companies Act 2006, s 16(2), provides that a registered company is a 'body corporate'.
2. Limited Liability Partnerships Act 2000, s 1(2), provides that a LLP is a 'body corporate'.

It is important to note that the provisions of the Companies Act 2006 (CA 2006) apply only to companies incorporated by registration,[3] but the Secretary of State does have the power to extend specified provisions of the CA 2006 to unregistered companies.[4] As registered companies vastly outnumber unregistered companies, this book will concentrate on the law that applies to registered companies, but an understanding of the two methods of creating an unregistered company is still helpful.

Incorporation by Act of Parliament

The distinction between public and private Acts of Parliament is discussed in 'Creating legislation' at p 49

Parliament may create companies by passing a public or private Act of Parliament. Companies created as the result of a public Act are usually created to serve some public need (for example, the Post Office,[5] and the National Assembly of Wales).[6] The organization of the 2012 London Olympics was the responsibility of the Olympic Delivery Authority—a company created by a public Act of Parliament.[7]

Companies may also be created by a private Act and such companies are known as 'statutory companies'. These companies are normally created to facilitate the petitioner's commercial dealings (for example, many former public utilities became statutory companies,[8] although many of them have since become standard registered public companies).

Incorporation by Royal Charter

A company may be created by Royal Charter. Historically, the monarch granted these Charters to further some aim that was beneficial to the country. As of March 2014, there were 999 Chartered bodies (although only around 400 are still active),[9] the first of which was the University of Cambridge, which was granted its Charter in 1231. Between the sixteenth and nineteenth centuries, Royal Charters were granted to trading companies engaged in activities that the monarch or government wished to encourage (for example, exploration, colonization, and overseas trade). Virtually all of the early joint-stock companies (for example, the East India Company and the South Sea Company) were created by Royal Charter. Today, Royal Charters tend to be fewer in number (in 2013, only eight companies were created by Royal Charter) and are exclusively granted, upon advice from the Privy Council, to bodies engaged in charitable, educational, or non-profit-making activities. Examples of such Chartered companies include the Bank of England (1694), the Law Society (1845), the Royal College of Music (1883), the Institute of Chartered Accountants of England and Wales (1880), the British Broadcasting Corporation (1926), and the Chartered Institute of Management Accountants (1975). The Recognition Panel

---

3. CA 2006, s 1.   4. ibid s 1043.

5. Created by the Post Office Act 1969, s 6 (repealed by the Postal Services Act 2000).

6. Created by the Government of Wales Act 1998, s 1.

7. The Olympic Delivery Authority was created by the London Olympic Games and Paralympic Games Act 2006, s 3(1).

8. Examples include British Telecom (Telecommunications Act 1984; repealed by the Communications Act 2000), British Gas (Gas Act 1972; repealed by the Gas Act 1986), and the regional water authorities (Water Act 1973; repealed by the Water Act 1989).

9. A full list of chartered companies is available from the website of the Privy Council Office <http://privycouncil.independent.gov.uk>.

(namely, the approved regulator of the media recommended by the Leveson Report) is also a body corporate created by Royal Charter.

Incorporation by registration

Petitioning for a Royal Charter or the creation of an Act of Parliament is not the most accessible or efficient way to create a company. In 2012/13, 483,000 new companies were incorporated.[10] This many companies could never be created by the mechanisms just discussed. Accordingly, to meet demand, a simple, quick, and efficient method of incorporation was required; with the passing of the Joint Stock Companies Act 1844, such a method was created—namely, incorporation by registration. Today, the vast majority of new companies are created by registration in accordance with the CA 2006. Any persons who wish to create a company (such persons are known as promoters) need only register certain documents with their respective Registrar of Companies to bring a company into existence.

The registration process

Incorporation by registration is so called because it is based upon the registration of certain documents. These documents, once registered and authorized, bring a registered company into existence. However, before these documents can be drafted and registered, the promoters have some important decisions to make, including:

- Will the proposed company be public or private?
- Will the proposed company have a share capital or not?
- Will the proposed company be unlimited or limited (if limited, will it be limited by shares or guarantee)?

Once the relevant decisions have been made, the promoters can prepare the registration documents. A number of documents are required, but, historically, the most important were the memorandum and articles of association (historically, these documents were known as the 'constitution' of the company and are discussed later in this chapter). In addition to the memorandum and articles, other documents need to be registered:

The constitution of the company is discussed at p 55

- a registration application detailing the proposed company name; the location of the company's registered office; whether the members will have limited liability and, if so, whether will it be limited by shares or guarantee; and whether the company will be public or private;[11]
- if the company is to have a share capital, a statement of capital and initial shareholdings. If the company is limited by guarantee, a statement of guarantee will be required instead;[12]
- a statement identifying the company's proposed officers,[13] including the first directors and, if applicable, the first company secretary;[14]
- a statement of compliance, indicating that the requirements of the CA 2006 have been met.[15]

---

10. Companies House, *Annual Report & Accounts 2012/13* (TSO 2013) 28.
11. CA 2006, s 9(2).
12. ibid s 9(4)(a) and (b).
13. ibid s 9(4)(c).
14. ibid s 12(1).
15. ibid ss 9(1) and 13.

These documents must then be delivered to the appropriate Registrar of Companies,[16] who will, if satisfied that the documents are complete and accurate, issue a certificate of incorporation upon payment of the registration fee.[17] This certificate constitutes conclusive proof that a company is registered under the relevant Act. From the date of registration, the company has all of the powers and obligations of a registered company, and the promoters will formally become the company's directors.

Off-the-shelf companies

Registration of the required documents is not an unduly burdensome process—but it does require a relatively serious layperson's knowledge of the procedures by which a company is run. Further, preparation of the documents can be time-consuming, especially if the promoters require bespoke articles that cater for the particular needs of the proposed company. Persons who lack such knowledge or wish to gain access to the benefits of incorporation quickly may therefore prefer to purchase an 'off-the-shelf' company.

There are businesses and individuals (known as 'incorporation agents', or 'company formation agents') that specialize in creating and selling companies. They will register the necessary documents with the Registrar and then leave the company 'on the shelf' until such time as it is purchased. When this occurs, the incorporation agent will notify the Registrar of the relevant changes (for example, change of directors, registered office, etc). It has been estimated that incorporation agents are responsible for around 60 per cent of all new company formations.[18]

The use of an incorporation agent brings several benefits, chief amongst them being speed and lack of expense. Many incorporation agents operate online only and can provide purchasers with an off-the-shelf company for under £20 (although this is likely not to include hard copies of the relevant documentation). There is, however, one major drawback to purchasing an off-the-shelf company: because the company was created months, or even years, before it was purchased, it will not be tailored to meet the needs of the new business. If the promoters are willing to spend more money and wait a little longer, however, incorporation agents will create a bespoke company that meets the promoter's needs.

Pre-incorporation contracts

Prior to obtaining the certificate of incorporation, the promoters may need to enter into contractual agreements with third parties in order to cater for the needs of the company to be incorporated (for example, the incorporators may enter into contracts for premises, supplies, etc). As discussed later, a company has contractual capacity upon incorporation but, until the company is incorporated, it will not exist as a separate entity and so will have no capacity. Are such pre-incorporation contracts void or, because they are clearly for the benefit of the company-to-be, are they regarded

---

16. The UK has three such Registrars: (i) the Registrar of England and Wales, based in Cardiff; (ii) the Registrar of Scotland, based in Edinburgh; and (iii) the Registrar of Northern Ireland, based in Belfast.
17. Companies House has stated that, eventually, all incorporations will be completed electronically, and this encouragement to go paperless is reflected in the registration fee. It currently costs £40 for a paper registration, compared to £13 for software registration. Promoters who wish to incorporate quickly can pay £100 for same-day paper incorporation (reduced to £30 in the case of same-day software registration).
18. Company Law Review Steering Group, *Modern Law for a Competitive Economy: Developing the Framework* (DTI 2000) [11.32].

as valid? Historically, the common law provided the answer, but it was based on determining the intent of the parties, as revealed in the contract[19]—a process which provided to be notoriously difficult and which resulted in significant confusion in the law and a perception that cases in this area could turn based on complex and technical distinctions. For an example, contrast the cases of *Kelner v Baxter*[20] and *Newborne v Sensolid (Great Britain) Ltd.*[21] In *Kelner*, the promoter signed the contract 'on behalf of' the unformed company, and it was held that a binding contract existed between the promoter and the third party. In *Newborne*, the promoter signed the contract using the company's name and added his own signature underneath. It was held that the contract was between the promoter and the unformed company and, as the company had no contractual capacity, no contract existed.

As a consequence of the entry of the UK into the EU, it was obliged to implement Art 7 of the First EU Company Law Directive,[22] which states:

> If, before a company has acquired legal personality (that is, before being formed) action has been carried out in its name and the company does not assume the obligations arising from such action, the persons who acted shall, without limit, be jointly and severally liable therefore, unless otherwise agreed.

This has been implemented by s 51(1) of the CA 2006, which states:

> A contract that purports to be made by or on behalf of a company at a time when the company has not been formed has effect, subject to any agreement to the contrary, as one made with the person purporting to act for the company or as agent for it, and he is personally liable on the contract accordingly.

Accordingly, where s 51(1) applies, the common law distinction no longer exists and a promoter will be personally liable for a pre-incorporation contract, irrespective of whether he signed the contract in the company's name or on behalf of the company. This obviously benefits third parties who contract with promoters, because they will now be able to sue the promoter—but can the promoter enforce the contract against the third party? The Court of Appeal has stated that the promoter can enforce the contract,[23] but the fact that clarification was required from the courts is an indication of a flaw in the drafting of s 51.

Once incorporated, the company cannot ratify or adopt the contract made on its behalf.[24] The only way in which the company can take benefit from the pre-incorporation contract is to discharge the pre-incorporation contract and enter into a new contract with the third party in respect of the same subject matter.[25] This discharge and re-creation of the contract can occur expressly or impliedly, but it will not arise merely by virtue of the company acting on the pre-incorporation contract.[26] It will be noted that Art 7 permitted a company to 'assume the obligations' of the pre-incorporation contract, but that s 51 confers no such power on the company. One could therefore argue that s 51 only partially implements Art 7.

---

19. *Phonogram Ltd v Lane* [1982] QB 938 (CA).
20. (1866) LR 2 CP 174.   21. [1954] 1 QB 45 (CA).
22. Council Directive 68/151/EEC.
23. *Braymist Ltd v Wise Finance Co Ltd* [2002] EWCA Civ 127, [2002] Ch 273.
24. *Re Northumberland Avenue Hotel Co Ltd* (1886) 33 Ch D 16 (CA).
25. *Howard v Patent Ivory Manufacturing Co* (1888) 38 Ch D 156 (Ch).
26. *Re Northumberland Avenue Hotel Co Ltd* (1886) 33 Ch D 16 (CA).

Where the promoters enter into a contract before purchasing an off-the-shelf company, s 51 will not apply, provided that the company was in existence at the time that the contract was entered into.

Types of registered company

The CA 2006 provides for a number of different forms of registered company that are classifiable by reference to certain characteristics, as follows.

1. Is the company public or private?
2. Is the liability of its members to be limited or unlimited? If liability is to be unlimited, the company must be private.
3. Does the company have a share capital or not? A public company must have a share capital.

The vast majority of companies incorporated by registration are created with a share capital. In 2012/13, 482,800 new companies were registered in the UK, only 16,400 of which did not have a share capital.[27] A limited company that does not have a share capital will be known as a 'company limited by guarantee'[28] and will have no shareholders, but will instead have 'members'. In a company limited by shares, however, shareholders will also normally qualify as members.[29] As companies limited by shares vastly outnumber companies limited by guarantee, this book will focus almost entirely on companies with a share capital and therefore the term 'shareholder' should be regarded as synonymous with the term 'member', unless otherwise stated.

As the focus is on companies limited by shares, it is the first two characteristics mentioned above that are of crucial importance, beginning with the difference between public and private companies.

Public and private companies

When creating a company, its promoters are required to state whether the company is to be registered as a public company or a private company. A public company is a company limited by shares, or limited by guarantee and having a share capital, the certificate of incorporation of which states that it is a public company.[30] A private company is defined simply as any company that is not a public company.[31]

Public and private companies differ in a number of ways, including:

1. A public company is so called because it can offer to sell its shares to the public at large and, to facilitate this, it may list its shares on a stock market (such companies are known as **listed, or quoted, companies**), with the principal market in the UK being the London Stock Exchange. Doing this allows public companies to raise massive amounts of capital very quickly. Private companies may not

➜ **listed, or quoted, companies:** a public company, the shares of which are listed on a stock exchange

27. Companies House, *Statistical Tables on Companies Registration Activities 2012/13* (Companies House 2013) 15.

28. Although certain guarantee companies registered prior to December 1980 can have a share capital.

29. Providing that they consent to be members and their names are entered onto the register of members (CA 2006, s 112).   30. CA 2006, s 4(2).   31. ibid s 4(1).

It is important to be able to determine which property belongs to the company for two reasons:

1. any capital borrowed by the company will be secured against the company's assets, not the assets of the members; and

2. if the company fails to repay the loan, the creditors can bring claims against the assets of the company, not the assets of the members.

The ability to commence legal proceedings

Determining who can sue in cases involving unincorporated businesses has historically proven to be an extremely troublesome issue. No such problems exist in relation to companies, because it is clear that where a company is wronged, the company, as an entity, is the proper claimant.

Transferable shares

In a partnership, the transfer of a partner's interest can be a complex exercise and is dependent upon the existence of an express agreement. Conversely, the transfer of interests in a company is relatively straightforward—a shareholder who wishes to transfer his interest to another need only sell his shares for his interest in the company to come to an end.

Floating charges

A company has access to a specific form of security known as a 'floating charge' (currently sole proprietors and partnerships are not permitted to grant floating charges). The detailed operation of these charges is discussed in Chapter 20. All that need be noted here is that access to this form of security makes it easier for companies to acquire **debt capital** than it is for sole proprietorships and partnerships, which, despite their unlimited liability, can face difficulties when attempting to do so.

> 🔗 Floating charges are discussed at p 599

> ➡ **debt capital:** capital borrowed from another

Disadvantages

Whilst incorporation carries some notable benefits, a promoter considering incorporation should also be aware of several disadvantages.

Increased formality, regulation, and publicity

Companies are subject to substantially more formality and regulation than unincorporated businesses. The formalities involved in creating and running a company are considerably more complex than those for an unincorporated structure. There are lengthy and complex rules relating to the conduct of meetings and the passing of resolutions. Company directors are subject to a raft of statutory duties that do not apply to partners and sole proprietors. Incorporation also results in a loss of privacy, because companies are required to make certain information available to the public throughout their existence.

Civil liability

Just as the company can commence legal proceedings where it has been wronged, so too can it be subject to proceedings where it has committed a wrong. In certain cases (for example, breach of contract), imposing liability on the company poses no problems, but in other cases, the fact that the company acts through natural persons

Vicarious liability is discussed in Chapter 16

(namely, its directors and employees) can cause problems. Establishing the vicarious liability of the company is one method of solving this problem, but certain civil wrongs require defendants to have a certain level of knowledge that the company will lack, for obvious reasons. In such a case, vicarious liability cannot be imposed.

The courts' answer is, in certain cases, to attribute the knowledge of certain persons (usually its directors, but not always) to the company. This is known as 'identification theory', and the courts will usually attribute the knowledge of a person to a company where that person is the 'directing mind and will' of the company.

Lennard's Carrying Co Ltd v Asiatic Petroleum Co Ltd [1915] AC 705 (HL)

FACTS: Section 502 of the Merchant Shipping Act 1894 provided that the owner of a British seagoing ship was not liable for 'any loss or damage happening without his actual fault or privity' in relation to goods on board the ship that were lost or damaged by fire. The defendant company owned a ship, the cargo hold of which contained a cargo of benzine that belonged to the claimant. The ship's boilers were in a poor state of disrepair and failed en route, grounding the ship upon a reef which, in turn, damaged the cargo hold. The benzine escaped, came into contact with the boiler's combustion chambers and exploded, completely destroying the ship and its cargo. The claimant sued. It transpired that one of the defendant's directors knew that the ship was unseaworthy. The defendant argued that the company had no knowledge and could not be held liable.

HELD: The defendant was liable. Viscount Haldane LC stated that:

> a corporation is an abstraction. It has no mind of its own any more than it has a body of its own; its active and directing will must consequently be sought in the person of somebody who...is really the directing mind and will of the corporation, the very ego and centre of the personality of the corporation...[I]f [the director] was the directing mind of the company, then his action must, unless a corporation is not to be liable at all, have been an action which was the action of the company itself within the meaning of s. 502.[50]

The question that arises is who can constitute the 'directing mind and will' of the company? The position has been best stated by Lord Reid:

> Normally the board of directors, the managing director and perhaps other superior officers of a company carry out the functions of management and speak and act as the company. Their subordinates do not. They carry out orders from above and it can make no difference that they are given some measure of discretion. But the board of directors may delegate some part of their functions of management giving to their delegate full discretion to act independently of instructions from them. I see no difficulty in holding that they have thereby put such a delegate in their place so that within the scope of the delegation he can act as the company. It may not always be easy to draw the line but there are cases in which the line must be drawn.[51]

---

50. [1915] AC 705 (HL) 713, 714.   51. *Tesco Supermarkets Ltd v Nattrass* [1972] AC 153 (HL) 171.

Criminal liability

A company can be convicted of a crime in just the same way as can a natural person—but there are limits to this. A company cannot be imprisoned, so a company cannot be convicted of a crime for which the only offence is imprisonment (e.g. murder).[52] It used to be thought that a company could not be convicted of a crime that had a *mens rea* requirement. However, this is no longer the case and, applying identification theory (discussed earlier), the courts will attribute *mens rea* to those who are the 'directing mind and will' of the company.

➜ *mens rea*: 'guilty mind;' the mental element required for the commission of certain crimes

Public disquiet over the lack of successful prosecutions of companies following high-profile incidents causing death resulted in repeated calls for the introduction of a statutory crime of corporate manslaughter. Although companies could be convicted for manslaughter,[53] such convictions were rare, because the court would convict only if it could be established that the death was the result of the actions and gross negligence of an identifiable member of the directing mind and will within the company.[54] The difficulty of securing a conviction was a source of significant criticism and so Parliament passed the Corporate Manslaughter and Corporate Homicide Act 2007. Under this Act, corporate manslaughter is committed by an organization[55] if the way in which its activities are managed or organized causes a person's death, and amounts to a gross breach of the relevant duty of care owed by the organization to that person.[56] However, liability will be imposed only if the way in which the organization is managed or organized by its senior management is a substantial element in that breach. These rules constitute a notable relaxation of the common law requirement that an individual's actions need to be identified as the cause of the death.

Corporate personality and 'lifting the veil'

Upon incorporation, a company becomes a legal person in its own right. In company law terms, this is known as 'corporate personality' (or 'separate personality', or 'legal personality'). The practical consequences of the company having its own personality have already been examined. Here, the true significance of corporate personality and to what extent this separate personality can be disregarded will be discussed.

Students often mistakenly believe that the following case established the concept of corporate personality, but this is not true. The existence of corporate personality was available to unregistered companies long before *Salomon* and, in 1844, became much more generally available with the introduction of incorporation by registration. It was, however, only in the following case that the courts finally appreciated

---

52. *R v ICR Haulage Ltd* [1944] KB 551.

53. The notable example being *R v P and O European Ferries (Dover) Ltd* (1990) 3 Cr App R 72, in which the company was convicted of manslaughter following the sinking of the *Herald of Free Enterprise*, resulting in the loss of 193 lives.

54. *Attorney General's Reference (No 2 of 1999)* [2000] QB 796 (CA).

55. For the purposes of the Act, an 'organization' will include both a partnership and a company (Corporate Manslaughter and Homicide Act 2007, s 1(2)).

56. ibid s 1(1).

the true significance of corporate personality—namely, that promoters, directors, and shareholders could legitimately use a company's separate personality to shield themselves from certain liabilities.

Salomon v A Salomon and Co Ltd [1897] AC 22 (HL)

FACTS: Salomon was a sole trader engaged in the business of bootmaking. He decided to incorporate and, to that end, he created a company and sold the bootmaking business to this newly created company in return for £39,000. This payment came in a number of forms:

- 20,000 £1 shares;
- £10,000 worth of **debentures**, secured by a floating charge over all of the assets of the company; and
- the balance in cash.

Legislation at the time[57] required that a company have a minimum of seven members. Accordingly, the company's 20,007 shares were divided up, with Salomon holding 20,001[58] shares, and his wife and five children each holding one share. Shortly thereafter, the business failed and went into liquidation. The company owed money to several creditors, including Salomon (the £10,000 in debentures). As Salomon had secured his loan (via a floating charge), he enforced this and claimed the £10,000 that he was owed. Unfortunately, this meant that there were no more assets to pay the other creditors. The company liquidator, arguing on behalf of the other creditors, stated that, instead of taking money from the company, Salomon should be personally liable for its debts. At first instance, the judge held that the company was Salomon's agent and that he was therefore liable for its debts. In the Court of Appeal, it was held that, by appointing six 'dummy' shareholders, the company was not incorporated within the spirit and intent of the legislation. Accordingly, the Court held that the company acted as a trustee for Salomon and he should be liable for its debts. Salomon appealed to the House of Lords.

HELD: The appeal was allowed. Whilst it could be said that the company does carry on business for the benefit of its shareholders, it does not follow that this creates a principal–agent relationship, or a trustee–beneficiary relationship. Further, the relevant legislation did not require the seven members all to be active members. Accordingly, Salomon had complied fully with the requirements for incorporation and was therefore not liable to pay the company's debts.

COMMENT: Many regard *Salomon* as the most important case in company law, for three reasons:

1. It recognized that an incorporated company could legitimately be used to shield its members from liability.
2. It implicitly recognized the validity of the 'one-man company' (that is, a company run only by one person, with a number of dormant nominee shareholders).
3. The fact that an individual holds shares in a company (even all of the shares) is not enough to establish a relationship of agency or trusteeship.

debenture: a document evidencing a loan to a company

---

57. Namely, the Companies Act 1862, s 6.
58. The 20,000 £1 shares plus the one share to which he subscribed when he registered the company.

Salomon is regarded by many as an 'unyielding rock'[59] and 'a cornerstone of English company law'.[60] However, the ability to shield oneself from liability by incorporating a company is clearly open to abuse. Therefore, both statute and the courts have the ability to ignore corporate personality and impose personal liability on the directors or members (this is known as 'piercing', or 'lifting', the 'veil'—referring to the 'corporate veil' that hides the directors and members from view). There is no single principle or test used to determine when the veil will be pierced and, traditionally, instances in which the veil is pierced are discussed in relation to whether it is statute or the courts that have pierced the veil.

Statute

As corporate personality is bestowed upon a registered company by statute,[61] it follows that statute can brush aside corporate personality and impose liability on those behind the veil. For example, s 213 of the Insolvency Act 1986 provides that where, in the course of a winding up, it appears that the company has been run with intent to defraud the creditors, the courts will lift the veil and impose personal liability to contribute to the assets of the company upon the directors (or any other persons) who were knowingly parties to carrying on the business in such a way.

Common law

As corporate personality is granted to registered companies by statute, it is understandable that the courts are reluctant to pierce the veil and impose liability on the directors or members, as the following case demonstrates.

 Adams v Cape Industries plc [1990] Ch 433 (CA)

FACTS: A large multinational group of companies was engaged in the mining, marketing, and selling of asbestos. The parent company (Cape) was based in England. The asbestos was mined by a subsidiary company based in South Africa, and was marketed and sold by two companies: (i) NAAC (based in Illinois, US); and (ii) Capasco (based in England). The asbestos was sold to a factory in Texas, the employees of which subsequently developed medical conditions caused by exposure to asbestos. A number of actions were initiated against Cape, Capasco, and NAAC, and were settled out of court for around US$20 million. Cape then decided to place NAAC in liquidation and a new company (CPC) was set up to continue NAAC's work. This new company was not a subsidiary of Cape, but did receive financial support from Cape. A further 206 claimants from the Texas factory initiated proceedings against Cape and Capasco, and a US court ordered that damages of just over US$15 million be paid. The claimants therefore sought to enforce the judgment in the UK against Cape and Capasco. The only way in which this could be achieved was if these companies were held to be present in the US. The claimants argued that Cape and Capasco were present in the US through their subsidiaries, NAAC and CPC. For this

---

59. Lord Templeman, 'Forty Years On' (1990) 11 Co Law 10, 10.
60. Derek French, Stephen Mayson, and Christopher Ryan, *Mayson, French & Ryan on Company Law* (30th edn, OUP 2013) 127.
61. CA 2006, s 16(2).

argument to succeed, the separate corporate personalities of each company would need to be disregarded, and Cape, Capasco, and NAAC/CPC treated as one entity.

HELD: The US subsidiaries were separate and distinct from their English parent. Accordingly, Cape and Capasco were not present in the US, and so the US judgment could not be enforced against them. The reason why Cape had created subsidiaries in the US was so that liability would fall on those subsidiaries. *Salomon* recognized that this was a valid use of the company and nothing in the case convinced the Court that the principle in *Salomon* should not be followed.

 See Stephen Griffin, 'Holding Companies and Subsidiaries: The Corporate Veil' (1991) 12 Co Law 16

In *Adams*, the claimants put forward a number of arguments in favour of lifting the veil:

1. the subsidiary was a fraud or a sham;
2. the group of companies was, in fact, one 'single economic unit';
3. the subsidiary was an agent of Cape; and
4. lifting the veil was fair and just given the circumstances of the case.

These arguments are discussed in more detail later. In *Adams*, they all failed (the first three failed on the facts, and the fourth argument was not deemed a sufficient reason to lift the veil), and the Court of Appeal strongly reaffirmed the principle in *Salomon* and indicated that a company's corporate personality will not be lightly cast aside. It should be noted at the outset that the extent to which three of the above instances can be regarded as genuine examples of piercing the veil has been doubted by the Supreme Court in what is now the leading case, namely *Petrodel Resources Ltd v Prest*.[62] In order to fully understand the significance of *Prest*, it is important to look at the common law position before the Supreme Court decision in *Prest*, beginning with the courts' ability to pierce the veil in cases where the company was being used to perpetrate a fraud, or where it as being used to evade a legal obligation.

Fraud, sham, or cloak

In *Adams*, the Court stated that 'there is one well recognised exception to the rule prohibiting the piercing of the "corporate veil"'.[63] This is where the company is used to perpetrate a fraud, or where the company is a façade or a sham. A common theme amongst these cases is that the company is used to evade a contractual obligation, such as a restrictive covenant, or even to avoid the sole purpose of a contract entirely.

Gilford Motor Co Ltd v Horne [1933] Ch 935 (CA)[64]

FACTS: The defendant was the managing director of the claimant company. His employment contract contained a restrictive covenant that provided that, upon leaving the claimant's employment, he would not attempt to solicit any of its customers. The defendant's contract was terminated, but he convinced his wife to set up a company in her name, which was nonetheless under the defendant's control. This new company competed directly with the

---

62. [2013] UKSC 34, [2013] 3 WLR 1.
63. *Adams v Cape Industries plc* [1990] Ch 433 (CA) 539 (Slade LJ).
64. See also *Jones v Lipman* [1962] 1 WLR 832 (Ch).

claimant. The claimant sought an injunction to enforce the restrictive covenant and prevent the new company from soliciting the claimant's customers. The defendant argued that the covenant was binding on him only, not on the new company.

HELD: An injunction preventing the defendant and the new company from soliciting the claimant's customers was granted. Lord Hanworth MR stated that the new company was 'formed as a device, a stratagem, in order to mask the effective carrying on of a business of [the defendant]'.[65]

The question that arises is, in cases where a person uses a company to evade a contractual obligation, will a contract exist between that person and the claimant. In *Antonio Gramsci Shipping Corp v Stepanovs*,[66] Burton J stated that a contract entered into by a 'puppet company' could be enforced against the company and the puppeteer (i.e. the wrongdoer(s) in control of the company). However, in the following case, the Supreme Court overruled *Antonio Gramsci* on this point and held that the puppeteer would not be bound.

VTB Capital plc v Nutritek International Corp [2013] UKSC 5

FACTS: VTB Capital plc (VTB, an English company) lent US$225 million to Russagroprom LLC (RAP), which RAP intended to use to purchase a number of Russian companies from Nutritek. RAP defaulted on the loan. VTB alleged that it was induced into entering into the loan agreement with RAP based on fraudulent misrepresentations made by Nutritek. VTB alleged that representations were made indicating that RAP and Nutritek were not under common control, whereas the truth of the matter was that both companies were controlled by Mr Malofeev, a Russian entrepreneur. VTB commenced proceedings against Nutritek, Malofeev, and several other companies that were involved, alleging that they were liable for RAP's breach of contract. In order for this claim to succeed, the corporate personality of RAP would need to be pierced and VTB argued that the veil should be pierced on the ground that Malofeev and his associated companies were using RAP as a puppet company to orchestrate a fraud against VTB. VTB claimed that once the veil was pierced, the defendants would become party to the original loan agreement between VTB and RAP, and so would be liable on it.

HELD: The Supreme Court refused to pierce the corporate veil. Lord Neuberger stated that, to find the defendants liable on the loan agreement would involve an extension of the circumstances in which the veil could be pierced. It would, in effect, result in Malofeev becoming a co-contracting party with RAP under the loan agreement. He refused to do this on the ground that:

> where B and C are the contracting parties and A is not, there is simply no justification for holding A responsible for B's contractual liabilities to C simply because A controls B and has made misrepresentations about B to induce C to enter into the contract. This could not be said to result in unfairness to C: the law provides redress for C against A, in the form of a cause of action in negligent or fraudulent misrepresentation.[67]

⭐ See Christopher Hare, 'From Salomon to Spiliada: Orthodoxy and Uncertainty in the Supreme Court' (2013) 72 CLJ 280.

---

65. [1933] Ch 935 (CA) 956.
66. [2011] EWHC 333 (Comm), [2012] 1 All ER (Comm) 293.
67. [2013] UKSC 5, [2013] 2 WLR 398 [139].

'Single economic unit'

As was seen in *Adams*, it is common for larger companies to carry out their various functions via a number of smaller subsidiary companies. Are the various companies to be regarded as having separate corporate personalities or are they to be treated as one 'single economic unit'? The answer was provided by Roskill LJ, who stated that it was 'long established and now unchallengeable by judicial decision…that each company in a group of companies…is a separate legal entity possessed of separate legal rights and liabilities'.[68] This statement was designed to affirm the principles established in *Salomon* and to ensure that the law in this area remained certain. Unfortunately, the following case has introduced a measure of unwelcome uncertainty into the law.

DHN Food Distributors Ltd v Tower Hamlets London Borough Council [1976] 1 WLR 852 (CA)

> **holding company:** a company that controls a subsidiary company (or companies)

> **bare licensee:** someone who is permitted to be present on another's land, but is required to leave if the owner withdraws permission

FACTS: DHN was a **holding company** that included two other wholly owned subsidiaries. One of the subsidiaries (Bronze Investments Ltd) did not carry on any business activity, but it did own the land upon which DHN carried out business (DHN occupied the land as a **bare licensee**). The local authority compulsorily purchased this land and £360,000 was paid to Bronze, as the owner of the land. DHN could not find alternative premises, so all three companies went into liquidation, thereby entitling the holder of a legal or equitable interest in the land to receive compensation for disturbance to the business. The claimant (DHN) argued that it was entitled to such compensation. The defendant (the local authority) argued that Bronze Investments owned the land, that Bronze Investments had not been disturbed, and that DHN was not entitled to any compensation for disturbance because it had no legal or equitable interest in the land (a bare licence not conferring such an interest).

HELD: DHN was entitled to compensation for the disturbance to the business that the compulsory purchase caused. In a much-criticized passage, Lord Denning MR stated:

> The subsidiaries are bound hand and foot to the parent company and must do just what the parent company says…This group is virtually the same as a partnership where all the three companies are partners…The three companies should, for present purposes, be treated as one, and the parent company, DHN, should be treated as that one.[69]

COMMENT: Although the judges involved were unanimous that the three companies should be treated as one, there was no clear test established to determine when groups of companies should be regarded as one single economic unit. The statement of Denning MR quoted above indicates the lack of clarity, because he described the subsidiaries as 'bound hand and foot' before going on to describe them as 'partners'. A subsidiary that 'must do just what the parent company says' cannot realistically be regarded as a 'partner'.

> ★ See David Hayton, 'Contractual Licenses and Corporate Veils' (1977) 36 CLJ 12

The validity of *DHN* has been questioned by subsequent courts, but not overruled. In *Adams*, Slade LJ stated:

> The relevant parts of the judgment in the *DHN* case must…be regarded as decisions on the relevant statutory provisions for compensation, even though these

---

68. *The Albazero* [1977] AC 774 (HL) 807.   69. [1976] 1 WLR 852 (CA) 860.

parts were somewhat broadly expressed, and the correctness of the decision was doubted by the House of Lords in *Woolfson v Strathclyde Regional Council*.[70]

More recently, however, there are slight indications that the courts are more willing to regard groups of companies as one 'business enterprise'. In *Beckett Investment Management Group Ltd v Hall*,[71] the Court of Appeal approved the words of Lord Denning MR in a previous case in which he stated that 'the law today has regard to the realities of big business. It takes the group as being one concern under one supreme control'.[72] Whether such views become more prominent remains to be seen.

Agency

As discussed in Chapter 8, where two parties are involved in an agency relationship, the principal is responsible for the acts of the agent, provided that the agent acts within his authority. In the corporate context, this means that if two companies are in an agency relationship, the principal (normally the parent company) could be liable for the acts of its agent (normally a subsidiary company). In effect, the corporate personality of the agent is ignored and the principal made liable, as demonstrated in the following case.

 The authority of an agent is discussed at p 193

Smith, Stone and Knight Ltd v Birmingham Corporation [1939] 4 All ER 116 (QB)

FACTS: The claimant company manufactured paper. It acquired a partnership that was involved in the waste paper business. The claimant set up a subsidiary company to run this waste paper business, but never transferred ownership of the business to the subsidiary and retained ownership of the land upon which the subsidiary operated. The land upon which the subsidiary conducted business was compulsorily purchased by the defendant, who planned to pay the subsidiary compensation for the loss of the land and the disturbance caused to the business. The claimant contended that it was entitled to the compensation. The defendant argued that, because the subsidiary was a separate entity, it should receive the compensation.

HELD: The subsidiary was the agent of the claimant and, as such, the claimant recovered the compensation. The crucial factor was that the waste paper business and the land upon which it operated still belonged to the claimant.

It should be noted that cases such as *Smith, Stone & Knight* are rare. In *Adams*, the Court stressed that, in the absence of an express agreement of agency,[73] it is highly unlikely that a relationship of agency will exist between a parent and subsidiary.[74] In *Smith, Stone & Knight*, the level of domination that the parent exhibited over the subsidiary was a crucial factor in the court's decision. The parent owned the subsidiary's business and the land upon which it conducted business. The parent also owned 497 of the subsidiary's 502 shares and nominees of the parent held the remaining five

---

70. *Adams v Cape Industries plc* [1990] Ch 433 (CA) 536.
71. [2007] EWCA Civ 613, [2007] ICR 1539.
72. *Littlewoods Organisation Ltd v Harris* [1977] 1 WLR 1472 (CA) 1482.
73. For a case in which an express agreement existed, see *Southern v Watson* [1940] 3 All ER 439 (CA).
74. *Adams v Cape Industries plc* [1990] Ch 433 (CA) 545–9 (Slade LJ).

shares. This is important, because the actual relationship of agency was deemed to be between the subsidiary and its principal shareholder (that is, its parent).

Justice or convenience

Several judges have contended that the court should have a general power to ignore a company's corporate personality where justice demands. In *Re a Company*,[75] the Court of Appeal stated that 'the court will use its powers to pierce the corporate veil if it is necessary to achieve justice'.[76] However, the Court in *Adams* firmly rejected this, stating that 'the court is not free to disregard the principle of *Salomon*...merely because it considers that justice so requires'.[77]

Whilst this has been upheld in a number of cases,[78] there are still those who advocate a more wide-ranging ability to pierce the veil. In *Conway v Ratiu*,[79] Auld LJ (with whom Laws LJ expressed his 'emphatic agreement'[80] and Sedley LJ agreed) referred to 'the readiness of the courts, regardless of the precise issue involved, to draw back the corporate veil to do justice when common-sense and reality demand it'.[81] As these judges did not refer to *Adams* or any other similar cases, however, it is likely that their comments are to be regarded as **per incuriam**. Whilst the view in *Adams* is doubtless currently the authoritative view, a substantial body of the judiciary clearly believes that the courts should be free to disregard corporate personality where they feel that it is just to do so.

➡ *per incuriam:* 'through want of care'; where the court did not discuss relevant authority

Whilst the courts lack a general power to pierce the veil in the interests of justice, in a number of cases, the courts have indicated that they are willing to do so as a matter of convenience and to minimize legal costs, as can be seen in the following case.

🔓 Re H (Restraint Order: Realizable Property) [1996] 2 All ER 391 (CA)

FACTS: The three defendants owned 100 per cent of the shares in two family-run companies. The Commissioners of Customs and Excise alleged that the defendants had, through the two companies, evaded excise duty to the amount of £100 million. Accordingly, the Commissioners had obtained an order restraining the use of certain properties belonging to the companies. The defendants argued that the companies' property could not be restrained, because it was they who had been charged with tax evasion, not the companies.

HELD: Had the companies' corporate personality been stringently observed, the Court of Appeal would have lacked the jurisdiction to grant the restraining orders. The two companies could have been charged with tax evasion, but Rose LJ stated that 'it seems to me that no useful purpose would have been served by introducing into criminal proceedings the additional complexities as to the corporate mind and will which charging the companies would have involved'.[82] Accordingly, the Court treated the restrained property as if it belonged to the defendants and the order was upheld.

---

75. [1985] BCLC 333 (CA).   76. ibid 337–8.
77. *Adams v Cape Industries plc* [1990] Ch 433 (CA) 536 (Slade LJ).
78. See e.g. *Re Polly Peck International plc (No 3)* [1996] 2 All ER 433 (Ch).
79. [2005] EWCA Civ 1302, [2006] 1 All ER 571.   80. ibid [186].   81. ibid [75].
82. [1996] 2 All ER 391 (CA) 402.

The new approach

The decision of the Court of Appeal in *Adams v Cape Industries plc* clearly indicates that the courts are not quick to pierce the veil and the number of grounds upon which the veil can be pierced are limited. The Supreme Court case of *Petrodel Resources Ltd v Prest*[83] has further limited the grounds on which the veil can be pierced by stating that there is only one instance in which the veil can be pierced and, even in that instance, the veil will only be pierced if it is necessary to do so. *Prest* must now be regarded as the leading case in this area.

 Petrodel Resources Ltd v Prest [2013] UKSC 34

FACTS: The case involved a divorce settlement between Mr and Mrs Prest. The High Court had awarded Mrs Prest a divorce settlement totalling £17.5 million,[84] but much of Mr Prest's assets were tied up in companies that were solely owned and controlled by him. Section 24(1)(a) of the Matrimonial Causes Act 1973 grants the court the power to 'order that a party to the marriage shall transfer to the other party . . . property to which the first mentioned party is entitled . . .' The High Court utilized this power to pierce the corporate veils of these companies and order the relevant properties to be transferred to Mrs Prest. Mr Prest appealed, questioning whether the court had the power to do this given that the properties did not belong to Mr Prest, but to his companies. The Court of Appeal, in allowing Mr Prest's appeal, held that the veil could not be pierced in these circumstances and so the High Court had no jurisdiction to make the order under s 24(1)(a). Mrs Prest appealed.

HELD: The appeal was unanimously allowed, but not on the ground that the veil could be pierced. The Supreme Court held that the properties were held on trust by the companies for the benefit of Mr Prest and, as such, they could form part of the divorce settlement. More importantly for present purposes, the Court unanimously refused to pierce the corporate veil and significantly limited the instances in which the veil could be pierced. The leading judgment of Lord Sumption began by looking at what piercing the corporate veil actually means.

> Properly speaking, it means disregarding the separate personality of the company. There is a range of situations in which the law attributes the acts or property of a company to those who control it, without disregarding its separate legal personality. The controller may be personally liable, generally in addition to the company, for something that he has done as its agent or as a joint actor. Property legally vested in a company may belong beneficially to the controller, if the arrangements in relation to the property are such as to make the company its controller's nominee or trustee for that purpose . . . But when we speak of piercing the corporate veil, we are not (or should not be) speaking of any of these situations, but only of those cases which are true exceptions to the rule in *Salomon* . . . i.e. where a person who owns and controls a company is said in certain circumstances to be identified with it in law by virtue of that ownership and control.[85]

Accordingly, it is clear that Lord Sumption does not regard many of the cases discussed as true situations in which the veil was pierced. Accordingly, the question is when can the courts pierce the veil. Lord Sumption stated that there was only one instance in which the courts could pierce the veil, namely where 'a person is under an existing legal obligation or liability

---

83. [2013] UKSC 34, [2013] 3 WLR 1.   84. *Prest v Prest* [2011] EWHC 2956 (Fam).
85. [2013] UKSC 34, [2013] 3 WLR 1 [16].

⭐ See Ernest Lim, 'Salomon Reigns' (2013) 129 LQR 480

or subject to an existing legal restriction which he deliberately evades or whose enforcement he deliberately frustrates by interposing a company under his control'.[86] Further, a court could only pierce the veil in this instance if 'all other, more conventional, remedies have proved to be no assistance'.[87]

The result of *Prest* is that many cases that were previously thought to be instances of piercing the veil must no longer be regarded as such. The limitations established by the Supreme Court could mean that 'it is unlikely that there will in the future be a case in which the two conditions imposed by the Supreme Court will be met and it will be correct to pierce the corporate veil'.[88] Whether this statement proves correct depends on whether the courts are willing to provide new grounds for piercing the veil. Clearly, Lords Sumption and Neuberger were of the opinion that the courts should not create new grounds on which to pierce the veil, but other Justices (namely Lords Mance and Clarke) were open to the idea, albeit with Lord Mance stating that such instances would be 'novel and very rare'.[89]

A direct duty of care

Clearly, Lords Sumption and Neuberger were of the opinion that many of the cases that are traditionally regarded as examples of piercing the veil did not in fact involve a piercing of the veil, and that liability was imposed in some other way. Lord Neuberger even went so far as to say that there has never been 'a single instance in this jurisdiction in which the doctrine [of piercing the veil] has been invoked properly and successfully'.[90] The result is that, in certain cases, the courts can, by alternative means, achieve the same result as if they pierced the veil without actually having to pierce the veil. The following case provides a good example of a case where the Court was able to impose liability on a parent company for the acts of a subsidiary without piercing the corporate veil.

Chandler v Cape plc [2012] EWCa Civ 525

FACTS: Mr Chandler (the claimant) was, for periods between April 1959 to February 1962, an employee of Cape Building Products Ltd (CBP), a subsidiary of Cape plc. In 2007, Chandler discovered that he had contracted asbestosis as a result of being exposed to asbestos whilst working for CBP. He sought to obtain compensation, but CBP had been dissolved many years before and, during Chandler's period of employment, CBP had no insurance policy in place which would indemnify Chandler for his loss. Accordingly, Chandler commenced proceedings against the parent, Cape plc.

HELD: The Court held that Cape plc assumed responsibility towards Chandler and so owed him a duty of care, which it had breached. Accordingly, Cape plc was ordered to pay damages to Chandler.

⭐ See Andrew Sanger, 'Crossing the Corporate Veil: The Duty of Care Owed by a Parent Company to the Employees of its Subsidiary' (2012) 71 CLJ 478.

---

86. ibid [35].   87. ibid [62].

88. Derek French, Stephen Mayson, and Christopher Ryan, *Mayson, French & Ryan on Company Law* (30th edn, OUP 2013) xxix.   89. [2013] UKSC 34, [2013] 3 WLR 1 [100].   90. ibid [64].

Chandler is an important case, but it is important to understand its current impact. The Court emphatically rejected any suggestion that the imposition of liability on Cape plc involved a piercing of the corporate veil. The Court stated clearly that the duty was based on Cape assuming a responsibility towards Chandler, which it had breached. The Court was also keen to stress that the duty of care owed by a parent company to the employees of its subsidiaries did not arise automatically, and would only occur where the three-stage test in *Caparo Industries plc v Dickman* was met. Accordingly, whilst *Chandler* is not an example of the courts piercing the veil, it does demonstrate that liability can be imposed on a parent for the actions of its subsidiary without having to pierce the corporate veil. It will be interesting to see how the law develops following *Chandler*, and whether subsequent courts will seek to limit its impact, or widen its application.

The three-stage test in *Caparo* is discussed in 'The modern duty of care' at p 366

The constitution of the company

As noted, historically, the two most important documents requiring registration with the Registrar of Companies were the memorandum and articles. Collectively, these two documents formed the constitution of the company. However, with the passing of the CA 2006, the role of these documents has changed substantially.

- **Memorandum of Association** Under the Companies Act 1985 (CA 1985), the memorandum was of immense importance. It would contain key information, including the name of every corporate officer, the location of its registered office, the aims of the company (known as its 'objects'), whether the company was public or private, whether the liability of its members was limited or unlimited, and the company's authorized share capital. Under the CA 2006, the memorandum, whilst still a necessary document, has lost much of its importance. Under the 2006 Act, the memorandum will simply contain a statement indicating that the subscribers wish to form a company under the 2006 Act and agree to become members of the company.[91] Most of the information that was contained in memorandum under the 1985 Act can now be found in other registration documents. Accordingly, the memorandum is now simply an 'historical snapshot', indicating the state of affairs at the time that the company was set up.

- **Articles of Association** Under the CA 1985, the articles would set out the internal rules of the company, such as the appointment and powers of the directors, how general meetings should be conducted, and rules relating to share capital. Under the 2006 Act, the articles are now the principal document of importance. Whilst they still contain the internal rules mentioned, they can also contain, if a company wishes, a statement setting out the objects of the company.[92] These objects were formerly contained in the memorandum. The reason for the change of location is that, under the 1985 Act, the limitations on the company's power were found in two documents. Placing all of the limitations in one document is much simpler and clearer.

---

91. CA 2006, s 8(1). Where the company is to have a share capital, the memorandum must also state that the subscribers have agreed to take at least one share each.
92. By default, a company's objects are unrestricted (CA 2006, s 31(1)).

The articles now form the company's most important constitutional document and every company must have a set of articles.[93] The articles form the principal rules by which the company is to be run, focusing on the internal rules that bind the company and its shareholders. Promoters are free to draft their own articles and submit them upon registration, but drafting articles can be a complex and time-consuming business, and many small business owners will lack the knowledge required to draft appropriate articles. Therefore, for many years, statutory instruments have provided a set of model articles that limited companies may adopt if they choose. The Companies (Model Articles) Regulations 2008[94] provide model articles for public companies[95] and private limited companies.[96] Unlimited companies, being relatively rare, are not provided with model articles and will therefore need to register their own articles. Where promoters of a limited company do not register their own set of articles, these model articles will form the articles of their proposed company.[97] Even if the promoters do register their own articles, the model articles will still form part of the company's articles unless the registered articles exclude or modify them.[98] Companies formed under pre-2006 companies legislation (which are usually governed by the old Table A model articles)[99] will not be governed by the new model articles, but can adopt them if they so choose.

It is important to note that, under s 17 of the CA 2006, the company's constitution is not only its articles, but also includes any resolution or agreement that would need to be notified to the Registrar.[100] Section 32 identifies several other 'constitutional documents', such as the certificate of incorporation. In addition, references to the company's constitution in the part of the CA 2006 dealing with the company's directors include:

- any decision agreed by the shareholders, or a class of the shareholders, which is treated in law as equivalent to a decision of the company;[101]
- any resolution or other decision arrived at in accordance with the constitution.[102]

Extent of a registered company's contractual capacity

Previously, it was noted that, because the company is a legal person with its own distinct personality, it can enter into contracts in much the same way as can a natural person. The contractual capacity of the company is, however, subject to a major limitation to which natural persons are not: a natural person may enter into any contract that he chooses, but a company can only enter into contracts that fall within its objects. The objects of a company basically set out the purposes for which the powers of the company may be exercised. Under the CA 1985, the company's objects clause would be located in its memorandum, but the 2006 Act provides that the objects will now become part of the articles.[103] Accordingly, the articles can act as an important limitation upon the company's ability to enter into contracts.

---

93. CA 2006, s 18(1).   94. SI 2008/3229.   95. ibid Sch 3.
96. ibid Schs 1 (model articles for private companies limited by shares) and 2 (model articles for private companies limited by guarantee).   97. CA 2006, s 20(1).   98. ibid s 20(1)(b).
99. Companies (Tables A to F) Regulations 1985, SI 1985/805.   100. CA 2006, ss 17, 29, and 30.
101. ibid s 257.   102. ibid.   103. ibid s 28.

Any act that is beyond the objects of the company will be *ultra vires*. Historically, the *ultra vires* doctrine has been regarded as overly technical and complex, and numerous ad hoc reforms did little to improve matters. Accordingly, the CA 2006 provides that, unless the company chooses to restrict its objects, the objects will be unrestricted,[104] with the result that the contractual capacity of the company will also be unrestricted. For such companies, the *ultra vires* doctrine has been effectively abolished. Further, whereas the 1985 Act provided that all public companies must have an objects clause at all times, the 2006 Act has abolished this requirement. Companies may still restrict their objects if they so choose, however, and, for such companies, the *ultra vires* doctrine will still be relevant.

Today, the effect of the *ultra vires* doctrine has been largely nullified. This is because s 39(1) of the CA 2006 provides that the validity of an act may not be called into question on the ground of lack of capacity because of anything in a company's constitution. This means that if the company enters into a contract that is *ultra vires*, the contract will still be binding and enforceable. As the directors are subject to a statutory duty to act in accordance with the company's constitution,[105] however, causing the company to enter into an *ultra vires* transaction will result in them being in breach of duty.

> *ultra vires*:
> 'beyond one's powers'

> The duty to act within the company's powers is discussed at p 624

Alteration of the articles

It may become necessary or beneficial for a company to alter its articles, and s 21(1) provides that the company may amend its articles by passing a **special resolution**. It is noteworthy that this power is vested in the company, because it means that the contract between the members and the company can only be altered by the company (albeit acting through the shareholders). It also means that the minority may be bound by article provisions to which they object. The ability to alter the articles is not boundless, and statute imposes restrictions upon a company's ability to alter its articles.[106] However, the most important limitation on the company's ability to alter its articles is not found in statute, but was introduced by Lindley MR in *Allen v Gold Reefs of West Africa Ltd*,[107] who stated that the power to alter the articles must:

> **special resolution:** a vote requiring no less than a 75 per cent majority

> like all other powers, be exercised subject to those general principles of law and equity which are applicable to all powers conferred on majorities and enabling them to bind minorities. It must be exercised, not only in the manner required by law, but also bona fide for the benefit of the company as a whole…[108]

The test is subjective, meaning that, provided that the majority believed the alteration to be for the benefit of the company as a whole, the court will not invalidate it simply because it disagrees with the members' assessment.[109]

A minority shareholder who wishes to challenge an article alteration on this ground will face a difficult task. Given that the principle of majority rule is fundamental to the operation of the company, the courts are extremely reluctant to strike down alterations to the articles, as the following case demonstrates.

---

104. ibid s 31(1).   105. ibid s 171(1)(a).

106. For example, s 98(6) of the CA 2006 provides that, where the members of a public company object to its being re-registered as a private one, the court can prevent a company from altering its articles without the court's leave.   107. [1900] 1 Ch 656 (CA).   108. ibid 671.

109. *Shuttleworth v Cox Brothers & Co (Maidenhead) Ltd* [1927] 2 KB 9 (CA).

Greenhalgh v Arderne Cinemas Ltd [1951] Ch 286 (CA)

FACTS: The claimant was a minority shareholder in a company, the articles of which provided that a shareholder should not sell his shares to an outsider if an existing shareholder was willing to purchase them. The managing director, who was also the company's majority shareholder, wished to sell his shares to an outsider. He therefore (in his capacity as a shareholder) altered the articles to permit the selling of shares to an outsider, provided that it was approved by an ordinary resolution (which would be a certainty, given that he owned the majority of the company's shares). The claimant challenged the alteration, on the ground that it was not for the benefit of the company as a whole. The majority shareholder admitted that he had not acted in the interests of the company, but argued that the company had no interest in who its shareholders were.

HELD: Evershed MR stated:

> the phrase, 'the company as a whole' does not...mean the company as a commercial entity, distinct from the corporators: it means the corporators as a general body. That is to say, the case may be taken of an individual hypothetical member and it may be asked whether what is proposed is, in the honest opinion of those who voted in its favour, for that person's benefit.[110]

Applying this 'hypothetical member' test, the Court held that the alteration was valid. If an outsider offers to purchase the shares of a hypothetical member for a fair price, the ability to sell to the outsider might very well be of benefit and the hypothetical member would be justified in acting in a manner that benefits himself as an individual. Further, the alteration of the articles was not discriminatory, in that the advantage obtained by the majority (the ability to sell shares to outsiders) was also obtained by the minority.

COMMENT: As can be seen, Lord Evershed MR established two tests in this case, namely (i) the hypothetical member test; and (ii) the discrimination test. The discrimination test has, however, been somewhat ignored and it is the hypothetical member test that has become prominent. The problem is that the courts have never fully articulated who the hypothetical member actually is. To what extent does the hypothetical member differ from the real member in question? Are the hypothetical member's interests purely financial? Evershed MR's test fails to answer these questions.

Entrenched article provisions

It is a long-held principle of company law that a company cannot make its own article provisions unalterable.[111] For the first time, however, the 2006 Act does allow companies to entrench article provisions in their articles. Such entrenchment cannot make the articles unalterable, but it does make it more difficult to alter them, by requiring that additional conditions be met (for example, by requiring unanimity instead of the normal special resolution), or that more restrictive procedures be adhered to (for example, certain identified shareholders must approve the alteration in order for it to be valid).[112]

---

110. [1951] Ch 286 (CA) 291.   111. *Walker v London Tramways Co* (1879) 12 Ch D 705 (Ch).
112. CA 2006, s 22(1).

To combat possible abuse, several safeguards are imposed, including:

- Entrenchment will not prevent alteration of the articles where (i) all of the members of a company agree to the alteration; or (ii) the court, or some other authority having power to alter the articles, makes an order altering the articles.[113]
- Therefore, the company must notify the Registrar of Companies if its article provisions permit entrenchment.[114]
- If a company wishes to entrench an article provision after it has been formed, it can only do so with the agreement of *all* of the members of the company.[115]

The constitution as a contract

The courts have long held that a company's articles of association constitute a contract between the company and its members, and between the members *inter se*.[116] Section 33(1) of the CA 2006 expands the scope of this contract to include not only the articles, but also those resolutions and agreements that, by virtue of s 17, together with the articles, make up the constitution of the company. Section 33(1) provides that '[t]he provisions of a company's constitution bind the company and its members to the same extent as if there were covenants on the part of the company and of each member to observe those provisions'. The company's constitution therefore forms what is known as a 'statutory contract', which imposes obligations upon:

➜ *inter se:* 'between, or amongst, themselves'

- the company when dealing with its members;
- the members when dealing with the company; and
- the members when dealing with each other.

Breach of certain obligations contained in the constitution will therefore constitute breach of contract, thereby allowing the innocent party to obtain a remedy. Before discussing the ability of the parties to enforce the statutory contract, it is important to note that the statutory contract is a highly unusual one and differs from a standard contract in several notable ways, as Table 19.2 indicates.

It can therefore be seen that several standard rules of contract law do not apply to the statutory contract. One rule that does apply, however, is the doctrine of privity. The statutory contract is formed between a company and its members, and outsiders are therefore not permitted to enforce the constitution, as the following case demonstrates.

🔗 The doctrine of privity is discussed at p 118

Eley v Positive Government Security Life Assurance Co (1876) LR 1 Ex D 88 (CA)

FACTS: The claimant solicitor drafted the defendant company's articles, which were then duly registered. The articles provided that the claimant would act as the defendant's solicitor and would not be removed from office unless he were to engage in some form of misconduct. The claimant acted as the company's solicitor for a period, but the company then ceased to employ him and employed other solicitors. The claimant brought an action alleging that the defendant had breached the contract formed by the articles.

---

113. ibid s 22(3).   114. ibid s 23(1).   115. ibid s 22(2).
116. *Re Tavarone Mining Co (Pritchard's Case)* (1873) LR 8 Ch App 956 (CA).

HELD: The Court of Appeal dismissed the claimant's action. He was not a party to the statutory contract and so could not sue for its breach.

COMMENT: It might be thought that, because the defendant had obtained a valuable benefit from the acts of the claimant, s 1 of the Contracts (Rights of Third Parties) Act 1999 would apply, thereby allowing the doctrine of privity to be avoided. However, s 6(2) of the 1999 Act provides that the s 33 contract is not subject to s 1 of the 1999 Act.

TABLE 19.2 Differences between a standard contract and the statutory contract

	Standard contract	Contract created by s 33 of the CA 2006
Derives binding force from?	Derives its binding force from the agreement between the parties	Derives its binding force from s 33 of the CA 2006
Alteration of terms against a party's wishes?	The terms of a standard contract cannot usually be altered against the wishes of the parties	As the articles can be altered by passing a special resolution, the majority can alter the terms against the wishes of the minority
Action for breach of contract?	If any term of a standard contract is breached, it can give rise to an action for breach of contract	Only those terms of the constitution that relate to membership rights can form the basis for an action for breach of contract
Rectification of contract?	The courts may be willing to rectify a standard contract if it fails to give effect to the parties' intentions, or if it contains a mistake	The courts will not rectify the contract created by s 33 if it fails to give effect to the parties' intentions, or if it contains a mistake[1]
Defeasible on certain grounds?	Standard contracts can be defeated on the grounds of mistake, misrepresentation, duress or undue influence	The contract created by s 33 cannot be defeated on the grounds of mistake, misrepresentation, duress or undue influence

[1]*Scott v Frank F Scott (London) Ltd* [1940] Ch 794 (CA).

The contract between the company and its members

As the constitution of the company forms a contract between the company and its members, both parties can enforce compliance with the terms of the constitution. In the following case, the company enforced the constitution against one of its members.

 Hickman v Kent or Romney Marsh Sheepbreeders' Association [1915] 1 Ch 881 (Ch)

FACTS: The articles of the defendant company provided that any dispute between it and a member should be referred to arbitration. The defendant purported to expel one of its members (the claimant), but instead of referring the dispute to arbitration, the claimant petitioned the High Court for an injunction restraining his expulsion.

HELD: The articles formed a contract between the company and its members. The company was therefore permitted to enforce the provisions and require disputes to be referred to arbitration. The High Court therefore stayed the legal proceedings and the claimant was subsequently expelled.

The opposite is also true, so a member can enforce compliance of a term of the constitution against the company.

 Pender v Lushington (1877) 6 Ch D 70 (Ch)

FACTS: The company's articles provided that its members would have one vote for every ten shares held, up to a maximum of 100 votes. Consequently, shareholders with over 1,000 shares would not have voting power commensurate with their shareholdings. To remedy this, members with over 1,000 shares transferred some of their excess shares to several nominees (including the claimant), thereby unlocking the votes within them. The chairman of the company (the defendant) refused to accept the votes of the nominees. The claimant alleged that his votes were improperly rejected.

HELD: The High Court upheld the claim. The shares were properly transferred and registered, so refusing to accept the nominees' votes constituted a breach of the articles. The court therefore issued an injunction restraining the rejection of the nominees' votes.

It is important to note, however, that not all of the terms of the constitution will form a contract between the company and its members. As Buckley LJ stated: 'The purpose of the [constitution] is to define the position of the shareholder as shareholder, not to bind him in his capacity as an individual.'[117] Therefore, only the terms of the constitution that relate to the members in their capacity as members (that is, those that relate to membership rights) will form part of the statutory contract. The following case provides an example of a claim that failed because the member was not seeking to enforce a membership right.

 Beattie v E and F Beattie Ltd [1938] Ch 708 (CA)

FACTS: The claimant company's articles contained a provision providing that any disputes between the company and its members would be referred to arbitration. It was alleged that one of the defendants (a director and shareholder of the company) had been improperly drawing a salary without the authorization of the company or the general meeting. The claimant therefore initiated legal proceedings to recover the unauthorized payments. The defendant alleged that, because he was a member, the matter should be referred to arbitration.

HELD: Lord Greene MR stated that 'the contractual force given to the [constitution] by [s 33] is limited to such provisions...as apply to the relationship of the members in their capacity as members'.[118] As the defendant was relying on the articles in his capacity as a director and not as a member, the Court of Appeal held that the defendant could not enforce the arbitration agreement.

Accordingly, provisions of the constitution that relate to the rights of directors will not normally form part of the statutory contract. However, in certain types of company,

---

117. *Bisgood v Henderson's Transvaal Estates Ltd* [1908] 1 Ch 743 (CA) 759.
118. [1938] Ch 708 (CA) 721.

Quasi-partnerships are discussed at p 656

classified as 'quasi-partnerships', the dividing line between member and director is blurred, because the members may have an expectation of being involved in management. In such companies, provisions conferring rights upon directors will be regarded as membership rights in relation to those members who have such an expectation.[119]

The contract between the members inter se

Just as the constitution forms a contract between the company and its members, so too does it form a contract between the members themselves. Accordingly, a breach of the statutory contract by a member can be enforced by another member, provided that the provision breached concerns a membership right.

 Rayfield v Hands [1960] Ch 1 (Ch)

FACTS: The company's articles provided that if a member were to wish to sell his shares, he should inform the directors of this and they would then 'take the said shares equally between them at a fair value'. The claimant wished to sell his shares and notified the directors (the defendants) of this, but the directors refused to purchase his shares. The directors were all members of the company (in fact, the articles required that the directors be members). The claimant sought a court order requiring the directors to purchase his shares.

HELD: The High Court made such an order and the defendants were required to purchase the claimant's shares at fair value. Vaisey J stated that the provision in question affected the directors in their capacity as members and that therefore the claimant could enforce it.

COMMENT: Vaisey J's assertion that the provision affected the directors in their capacity as members is not wholly convincing and it is submitted that the decision should be confined to the facts. In the context of the company in question (which was akin to a quasi-partnership), blurring the line between director and member might be justified, but in many companies, there will be a clear demarcation between the rights of the directors and the rights of the members.

⭐ See LCB Gower, 'The Contractual Effect of Articles of Association' (1958) 21 MLR 401

Limited liability partnerships

With the passing of the Limited Liability Partnerships Act 2000 (LLPA 2000), it is now possible for two or more persons to conduct business through an entity called a 'limited liability partnership' (LLP).[120] Initially, one might wonder why this discussion is not taking place in Chapter 18, in which partnerships were discussed—but it is more appropriate to discuss LLPs alongside registered companies for four reasons:

1. Like a registered company, a LLP is incorporated through registration of certain documents with Companies House.
2. Like a registered company, a LLP is a 'body corporate' and therefore has corporate personality.

---

119. *Rayfield v Hands* [1960] Ch 1 (Ch).
120. LLPs should not be confused with limited partnerships, which are discussed at p 509. As will be seen, LLPs bear virtually no similarities to limited partnerships.

3. Like most registered companies, a LLP has limited liability.
4. Generally, LLPs are regulated by company law, although there are notable areas in which they are regulated by partnership law.

LLPs are often described as a 'hybrid' business structure, because they combine the characteristics of a company and a partnership. Whilst this is true, there is little doubt that LLPs have more in common with registered companies than with partnerships. In fact, their resemblance to companies is so apparent that it has been argued that describing LLPs as partnerships is 'misleading'.[121] Table 19.3 demonstrates the numerous differences between LLPs and ordinary partnerships.

TABLE 19.3 The differences between an ordinary partnership and a LLP

	Ordinary partnership	LLP
Formation?	Can be formed informally by two or more persons agreeing to carry on business in partnership	Formally incorporated by registering certain documents with the Registrar of Companies
Has corporate personality?	No	Yes
Regulated by?	Regulated by partnership law, notably the PA 1890	Regulated by company law, unless the LLPA 2000 states otherwise
Partners known as?	The partners of an ordinary partnership are simply known as 'partners'	The partners of a LLP are known as 'members'
Liability of partners?	The partners of an ordinary partnership are jointly liable for the debts of the partnership and are jointly and severally liable for its liabilities	The members of a LLP are not generally liable for the debts and liabilities of a LLP—the LLP itself will be liable
Disqualification?	The partners of an ordinary partnership cannot be disqualified from acting as a partner of an ordinary partnership	The members of a LLP can be disqualified from acting as a member of a LLP

In order to understand the true function and purpose of LLPs, it is necessary to discuss briefly the reasons behind the passing of the LLPA 2000. For many years, the partnership and the provisions of the Partnership Act 1890 (PA 1890) provided businesses with a flexible method of conducting business for firms that wished to avoid the regulation and inflexibility that comes with conducting business through a registered company. As time progressed and the size of partnerships (especially professional firms) grew, certain firms came more to resemble companies and the partnership was no longer entirely suitable for their needs, with the principal weakness being the imposition of unlimited joint and several liability upon the partners. Additionally, certain professions (notably, auditors) were prohibited from contractually excluding or limiting their liability.[122] Accordingly, large accountancy firms began lobbying for a partnership structure that provided for limited liability. In 1996, Jersey enacted legislation allowing firms to register as LLPs. Fearing that large firms would register in Jersey, the UK government capitulated and the LLPA 2000 was eventually passed.

---

121. PL Davies, *Gower & Davies' Principles of Modern Company Law* (8th edn, Sweet & Maxwell 2008) 6.
122. Today, limitation is possible through 'liability limitation agreements', which are discussed at p 596.

The above discussion indicates that the LLP was never designed to be a business structure of mass appeal and, certainly, it was not intended to be a vehicle for small businesses, as some at the time argued that it could be. It was created largely to cater for the needs of those who lobbied for it—namely, large professional firms. This is indicated by the fact that, as of March 2014, there were only 59,327 LLPs registered in the United Kingdom.[123] Virtually all large accountancy and solicitors firms have adopted LLP status.

Section 1(2) of the LLPA 2000 provides that a LLP shall be a body corporate, meaning that, like a company, it will have a legal personality separate from that of its members. Accordingly, the consequences of having separate personality discussed earlier in relation to companies will also apply to LLPs. The LLP itself will be liable for its debts and will be vicariously liable for the acts of its agents. Where a member of a LLP is liable to any person (other than another member of the LLP) as a result of a wrongful act or omission of his in the course of the business of the limited LLP or with its authority, the LLP is liable to the same extent as the member.[124] All LLPs have unlimited capacity,[125] so a LLP cannot act *ultra vires*.

The LLPA 2000 and the regulation of LLPs

The LLPA 2000 itself is a short Act, comprising only nineteen sections and one Schedule. The reasons for the shortness of the Act are twofold: first, unless otherwise stated in the Act, LLPs are not subject to partnership law;[126] second, detailed regulation of LLPs is contained in a series of statutory instruments (the principal one being the Limited Liability Partnership Regulations 2001),[127] which were passed subsequent to the LLPA 2000. In addition, regulations have been passed that provide that large parts of the CA 2006 and Insolvency Act 1986 will also apply to LLPs.

Formation

Like a registered company, a LLP is formed through incorporation by registration with the Registrar of Companies. Section 2(1) of the LLPA 2000 provides three basic requirements for registration:

1. two or more persons[128] associated for carrying on a lawful business with a view to profit must have subscribed their names to an incorporation document;
2. there must have been delivered to the Registrar either the incorporation document or a copy authenticated in a manner approved by him; and
3. there must be delivered to the Registrar a statement of compliance indicating that two or more persons associated for carrying on a lawful business with a view to profit must have subscribed their names to an incorporation document.

The incorporation document is the LLP equivalent of a company's pre-2006 memorandum. Section 2(2) of the LLPA 2000 states that the incorporation document must state:

- the name of the LLP, the address of its registered office, and the name and address of each of the persons who are to be members of the LLP on incorporation; and

---

123. Statistics derived from the Companies House website <http://www.companieshouse.gov.uk>.
124. LLPA 2000, s 6(4).   125. ibid s 1(3).   126. ibid s 1(5).   127. SI 2001/1090.
128. These persons need not be natural persons—they can be companies or other LLPs.

- which of those persons are to be designated members, or that every person who, from time to time, is a member of the LLP is a designated member. This requirement has no parallel in company law. The designated members are the members of the LLP charged by the legislation with ensuring that the requirements of the legislation as to disclosure and notification to the Registrar have been satisfied. A LLP must always have at least two designated members.

If the Registrar is satisfied that these requirements have been complied with, he must register the incorporation and issue a certificate of incorporation.[129] The certificate provides conclusive evidence that the LLP has been incorporated.[130]

Management of a LLP

A LLP, unlike a company, can adopt whatever structure for managing the entity the members choose. The LLP agreement is likely to specify the decision-making arrangements within the LLP. Where no agreement exists, the default rules provide that every member may participate in management.

Particularly in larger LLPs, it is likely that management functions will be delegated to a management committee, and the LLP agreement should make plain how the relationship of the members and the managing members (or managers who are not members) is to be structured.

Membership of a LLP

Unlike in an ordinary partnership, those who form LLPs are not known as partners, but as 'members' (another indication of how closely LLPs resemble companies). The term 'member' is used loosely throughout the various pieces of LLP legislation to refer to roles that, in companies legislation, would apply more specifically to directors, officers, or shareholders. Indeed, there is a presumption that, in companies legislation that also applies to LLPs, the terms 'director' and 'officer' apply also to members of a LLP.

There are two ways in which to become a member of a LLP:

1. by subscribing to the incorporation document;
2. by subsequently joining with the agreement of all of the existing members.[131]

Rights and duties

Section 5(1) of the LLPA 2000 provides that the rights and duties of the members (towards the LLP and each other) are set out and governed by:

1. The agreement between the members, or between a LLP and its members. There is no requirement for a LLP to have some form of partnership agreement in place, although the frequent reference to such an agreement in the LLPA 2000 indicates that such an agreement is envisaged and encouraged.
2. The relevant regulations, namely the Limited Liability Partnership Regulations 2001. These regulations impose a number of default rights and obligations on the members,[132] which apply where no partnership agreement exists, or where an agreement does exist, but its provisions are not inconsistent with the default provisions.

---

129. LLPA 2000, s 3(1).   130. ibid s 3(4).   131. ibid, s 4(1) and (2).
132. Limited Liability Partnership Regulations 2001, regs 7 and 8. These default provisions are virtually identical to the terms implied by the PA 1890, ss 24 and 25 (discussed at p 511).

Whether members are subject to any additional duties is unclear. It has been contended that the members will owe a duty of care to the LLP itself (although the standard of that duty is unclear) and, in limited circumstances, may owe fiduciary obligations towards each other.[133]

The members as agents

As noted, a LLP has unlimited capacity and thus has the same capacity to enter into any transaction as a legal person. Like other bodies corporate, however, the LLP can act only through others and it is important to determine to what extent the actions of others can bind the LLP.

Under normal principles of agency, any authorized agent can bind the LLP. In addition, s 6(1) of the LLPA 2000 provides that every member of a LLP is the agent of the LLP. The LLP will not, however, be bound by a member's actions where (i) the member had no authority to perform the act in question; or (ii) the person with whom the member dealt knows that he has no authority, or does not know or believe him to be a member of the LLP.[134]

Minority protection

🔗 Minority shareholder protection is discussed in Chapter 23.

The law provides a substantial amount of protection for minority shareholders of companies. Such protection is also available to members of a LLP under the following circumstances.

- At common law, the members of a LLP are entitled to bring a derivative action for wrongs committed against the LLP.[135] The provisions relating to the statutory derivative claim found within the CA 2006 do not, however, apply to LLPs.
- A member of a LLP may petition the court where he feels that the LLP's affairs are being conducted in a manner that is unfairly prejudicial to his interests.[136] However, this right can be excluded by agreement, provided that all of the members of the LLP agree and that the agreement is set out in writing.
- A member of a LLP can petition to court to have the LLP wound up on just and equitable grounds.[137]

Cessation of membership

Section 4(3) of the LLPA 2000 provides that a person who wishes to cease his membership of a LLP can do so in accordance with an agreement with the other members (presumably, this agreement can be in the LLP agreement or agreed from time to time) and, in the absence of such a provision or agreement, on the giving of reasonable notice. What constitutes reasonable notice will be a question of fact.

Where a member ceases to be a member for other reasons, including his death or bankruptcy, or where he assigns his share in the LLP to another, then neither he, nor his personal representative, trustee in bankruptcy, or assignee, can interfere in the management or business affairs of the LLP.[138]

---

133. Geoffrey Morse, *Partnership Law* (7th edn, OUP 2010) 328–9.   134. LLPA 2000, s 6(2).
135. *Feetum v Levy* [2005] EWCA Civ 1601, [2006] Ch 585.
136. This remedy is provided to company shareholders by virtue of the CA 2006, s 994. Regulation 48 of the Limited Liability Partnerships (Application of Companies Act 2006) Regulations 2009, SI 2009/1804 provides that s 994 will also apply to members of LLPs.
137. Limited Liability Partnerships Regulations 2001, Sch 3.   138. LLPA 2000, s 7.

Liability of the members to contribute

In the event of an ordinary partnership being dissolved, the partners are liable for the debts of the firm, with such liability being unlimited; conversely, the members of a LLP need contribute nothing when it is wound up. There are, however, three notable exceptions to this. First, the members of a LLP can be found liable for fraudulent and wrongful trading in exactly the same way as company directors can, and may therefore be required to contribute upon a winding up.[139]

Second, s 1(4) of the LLPA 2000 provides that the members of a LLP have such liability to contribute to its assets in the event of its being wound up 'as is provided for in the Act'. Regulations created under the Act have imposed additional liability on the members by virtue of modifying s 74 of the Insolvency Act 1986, which provides that a member is liable to contribute on the winding up of the LLP such sum as has been agreed between the members of the LLP. Where such an agreement exists, the liability of the members is similar to the liability of the members of a company limited by guarantee (that is, to pay what they have agreed to pay), except that the members of a LLP are not obliged to make such an agreement.

Third, s 214A of the Insolvency Act 1986 (known as the 'clawback' provision) allows the court to order the member to contribute an additional sum where:

- within a two-year period ending on the date of the winding up, the member withdrew any property of the LLP (including a share of the profits, drawing a salary, or taking a repayment);
- it is proved by the liquidator that, at the time of the withdrawal, the member knew, or had reasonable ground for believing, that the LLP (i) was unable to pay its debts; or (ii) would become unable to pay its debts as a result of the withdrawal, and any other withdrawals made by the members contemporaneously;
- that, at the time of the withdrawal, the member knew, or ought to have known, that there was no reasonable prospect that the LLP would avoid insolvent liquidation.

Disqualification

A member of a LLP can be disqualified from being a LLP member or company director under the Company Directors Disqualification Act 1986.[140] The maximum period of disqualification is fifteen years. Breaching a disqualification order constitutes a criminal offence.

The disqualification of directors is discussed at p 586

Termination

Virtually all of the provisions of the Insolvency Act 1986 apply to LLPs as well as companies.[141] Therefore, its members can wind up a LLP; alternatively, it can be struck off by the Registrar of Companies (for example, where it appears to have ceased to carry on a business, is put into administration or receivership, or is wound up by a creditor).

---

139. Limited Liability Partnerships Regulations 2001, reg 5.
140. ibid reg 4(2).   141. ibid reg 5.

Chapter conclusion

Incorporation and its consequent benefits—notably, corporate personality and limited liability—have contributed hugely to the social, financial, and technological developments of the last century. In 1911, Nicholas Murray Butler, then President of Colombia University, in a much-quoted passage stated:

> [T]he limited liability corporation is the single greatest discovery of modern times…Even steam and electricity are far less important than the limited liability corporation, and would be reduced to comparative impotence without it.[142]

There is little doubt that the proliferation of companies (in both size and number) is due to a massive increase in the number of persons (natural and legal) willing to invest in companies. Investment on such scope would not have occurred if a company's members were liable for the debts of the company, or if the members' liability were unlimited.

Carrying on business through a company has a significant number of fundamental benefits. In fact, it has been argued that incorporation is too easily obtainable,[143] and that the consequent regulation, publicity, and formality are too low a price for the key benefits of corporate personality and limited liability. Such a contention is debatable. What is not debatable is that easy access to the corporate form has altered the global business landscape in a way that could never have been predicted when incorporation by registration was first introduced in 1844.

Having discussed the advantages and disadvantages of conducting business through a registered company, Chapter 20 will move on to discuss the role played by the various constituents that contribute to the running of the company.

Key points summary

- A company can be incorporated by Act of Parliament, Royal Charter, or registration. The vast majority of companies are incorporated by registration.

- Promoters of a company will be personally liable for any contracts entered into prior to the company being fully incorporated.

- Public companies may offer shares to the public, are subject to minimum capital requirements, must have at least two directors, and are legally required to appoint a company secretary.

- Private companies cannot offer shares to the public, have no minimum capital requirements, can be formed with one director, and do not need to appoint a company secretary.

- All companies have corporate personality, which means that a company is a legal person, with many of the same rights and abilities as a natural person.

- In a company limited by shares, a shareholder's liability is limited to the amount unpaid on their shares. Where the company is limited by guarantee, a guarantor's liability is limited to a specified amount.

---

142. Nicholas Murray Butler, *Why Should We Change Our Form of Government?* (Girvin Press 2007) 82.
143. See e.g. Jacob S Ziegel, 'Is Incorporation (With Limited Liability) Too Easily Available?' (1990) 31 Cahiers de Droit 1075.

- A company's corporate personality can be set aside, or pierced, by statute or the courts (although the courts will only do so in one instance and only then if it is necessary to do so).

- A company's constitution is found principally in its articles of association, which provide the internal rules of the company.

- The purpose of a company may be limited by placing a restrictive objects clause in the company's articles. In the absence of such objects, the company has unrestricted contractual capacity.

- A company may alter its articles by passing a special resolution, but statute may limit the company's ability to alter its articles and any alterations must be exercised bona fide for the benefit of the company as a whole.

- The constitution of a company forms a statutory contract between (i) the company and its members; and (ii) the members themselves. Only those provisions relating to membership rights will form part of the statutory contract.

- Two or more persons who wish to carry on a lawful business with a view to profit can create a body corporate known as a 'limited liability partnership' (LLP).

Self-test questions

1. Define the following words and phrases:
   (a) corporate personality;
   (b) limited liability;
   (c) perpetual succession;
   (d) promoters;
   (e) single economic unit;
   (f) *ultra vires*.

2. Explain the difference between the following.
   (a) A public company and a private company.
   (b) A limited company and an unlimited company.
   (c) A company limited by shares and a company limited by guarantee.

3. Sam is the chief executive officer of AeroFlight plc, a large airline. He owns 99 per cent of the company's shares. The company owns a fleet of private airplanes, one of which is only ever used by Sam. In his will, Sam bequeaths this private plane to his son. Sam is killed in a car crash and the company refuses to let the executors of Sam's will give the plane to Sam's son. Advise the executors.

4. The characteristics of public or private, limited or unlimited, and limited by shares or guarantee can be combined to produce five possible forms of company. Bearing in mind the restrictions that exist (for example, that a public company cannot be unlimited), what are these five possible types of company?

5. Cathryn is the sole director and shareholder of Shoes in the City Ltd, a company that sells ladies' designer shoes. Cathryn runs the business in an inefficient manner and the company is liquidated, owing a number of creditors substantial amounts of money. Two months later, Cathryn starts up a new company, also called Shoes in the City Ltd. She acquires the stock of the previous company at a considerable discount and carries on business much as before. Do the creditors have a claim against Cathryn? Will the courts pierce the veil?

6. Explain how the contract created by the company's constitution differs from a normal contract. What limits are placed upon one party's ability to force the other to observe the provisions of the constitution?

7. 'The Limited Liability Partnerships Act 2000 was passed to create a business structure that was suitable for small businesses.' Do you agree with this quote? Provide reasons for your answer.

Further reading

Stuart R Cross, 'Limited Liability Partnerships Act 2000: Problems Ahead?' (2003) JBL 268
Discusses the background and operation of the Limited Liability Partnerships Act 2000, and highlights a number of problem areas that are likely to impede the general usefulness of limited liability partnerships

Paul L Davies and Sarah Worthington *Gower & Davies' Principles of Modern Company Law* (9th edn, Sweet & Maxwell 2012) ch 2
An excellent discussion of the advantages and disadvantages of incorporation

Derek French, Stephen Mayson, and Christopher Ryan, *Mayson, French, & Ryan on Company Law* (30th edn, OUP 2013) xxvi and ch 5.
An in-depth examination of the concept of corporate personality and the instances in which the court will pierce the corporate veil; also provides an extremely useful account of corporate law theory

Geoffrey Morse, *Partnership Law* (7th edn, OUP 2010) ch 10
Provides a detailed, yet accessible, account of the law relating to limited liability partnerships

S Ottolenghi, 'From Peeping Behind the Corporate Veil to Ignoring It Completely' (1990) 53 MLR 338
Examines the way in which judicial piercing of the corporate veil can be classified; provides an alternative classification based on the extent to which the veil is set aside

Murray A Pickering, 'The Company as a Separate Entity' *(1968) 31 MLR 481*
Provides a detailed analysis of the nature and extent of corporate personality

FG Rixon, 'Competing Interests and Conflicting Principles: An Examination of the Power of Alteration of Articles of Association' (1986) 49 MLR 446
Provides an in-depth analysis of the power to alter the articles and examines the limitations upon this power; also discusses what remedies are available to those who wish to challenge an alteration to the articles

Remember to visit the **Online Resource Centre** at <**http://www. oxfordtextbooks.co.uk/orc/roach3e**> to access the following resources on Chapter 19, 'Incorporation and bodies corporate': more **practice questions** and answers; a **glossary** of key terms; **multiple-choice questions**; and **revision summaries**. Updates to the law can be found on Twitter by following **@UKBusinessLaw** and **@UKCompanyLaw**.

20 The constituents of a company

- The members
- The directors
- The company secretary
- The auditor
- Creditors

INTRODUCTION

Although a company is a legal person, it is highly dependent upon other legal persons and natural persons to operate it, and to provide it with the resources that it needs to continue. Certain persons are required by all companies (for example, all companies must have at least one director (with public companies needing at least two)) and there are other persons who will be required by most companies (for example, most companies will need to appoint an auditor and most companies will have members). Finally, certain persons are required by some companies (for example, public companies are required to appoint a company secretary). Without these various constituents, companies could not function. Accordingly, this chapter will discuss the principal constituents who make up, and contribute to, the success of the company, beginning with the most numerous constituent—namely, the members.

The members

Members play two vital roles. Firstly, through the purchase of shares, they contribute capital to the company. The nature of shares and share capital is discussed in detail in Chapter 21. This chapter will focus instead on the second vital role of the members—namely, their ability to make decisions. As will be seen, a significant amount of power is placed in the hands of the members and numerous key decisions are reserved for them alone. However, before the members' ability to exercise this power is discussed, it is important to understand the difference between a company's shareholders and its members.

Shareholders and members

Chapter 19 briefly noted that the terms 'shareholder' and 'member' are used interchangeably and, in the vast majority of cases, a shareholder will also be a member and vice versa. There is, however, a difference and it is important that this difference is understood. The most obvious difference occurs in a company that does not have a share capital: such companies have members, but they do not have shareholders.

However, the distinction exists even in companies that have a share capital. Purchasing shares might make a person a shareholder, but it does not automatically make him a member. What constitutes membership of the company is stated in s 112 of the Companies Act 2006 (CA 2006), which provides that:

- the subscribers of a company's memorandum are deemed to have agreed to become members of the company, and, on its registration, become members and must be entered as such in the register of members;
- every other person who agrees to become a member of the company and whose name is entered in its register of members is a member of the company.

Therefore a person may purchase shares in a company (thereby making him a shareholder), but he will not become a member until he has agreed to become a member and his name has been entered in the register of members.

Resolutions

As is discussed later, the general power to manage the company is usually vested in the directors by the company's articles. Despite this, there are still a number of extremely important powers that may be exercised by the members, including:

- only the members can amend the company's articles;[1]
- approval of the members is required if the company wishes to (i) convert from a private company to a public company,[2] or vice versa;[3] or (ii) convert from an unlimited company to a limited company;[4]
- the members have the power to remove a director (or directors) from office;[5]
- numerous loans and other transactions involving directors require the approval of the members;
- the members may ratify conduct of the directors that amounts to negligence, default, breach of duty, or breach of trust;[6]
- the members may petition the court to have the company wound up.[7]

⊘ Transactions involving the directors that require approval of the members are discussed at p 635

The company's members exercise these powers via the passing of resolutions. A resolution is simply a more formal word for a vote, whereby the members resolve themselves to a particular decision or course of action.

Types of resolution

The CA 2006 provides for two different types of resolution, namely:

1. **Ordinary resolution** An ordinary resolution is one passed by a simple majority[8] (that is, over 50 per cent—remembering that an exact 50 per cent split means that the resolution is lost).

2. **Special resolution** A special resolution is one passed by a majority of not less than 75 per cent.[9] Special resolutions tend to be reserved for more important decisions and constitutional changes.

---

1. CA 2006, s 21(1).   2. ibid s 90(1).   3. ibid s 97(1).   4. ibid s 105(1).
5. ibid s 168(1).   6. ibid s 239.   7. Insolvency Act 1986, s 122(1)(a).
8. CA 2006, s 282(1).
9. ibid s 283(1).

Where the resolution is tabled at a meeting, the above majorities refer to those persons present at the meeting, not to the total members of the company. Often, the CA 2006 will simply state that a 'resolution' is required, without specifying its type. In such cases, the resolution required will be an ordinary resolution, but the company is free to require a higher majority (or unanimity) by inserting a provision in its articles to that effect.[10] Where the CA 2006 specifies that an ordinary or special resolution is required, the articles cannot alter the majority required.

Regarding public companies, resolutions can only be passed at a meeting of the members.[11] The members of private companies can pass resolutions at a meeting, or they can take advantage of what is known as a 'written resolution'.[12]

Written resolutions

The convening and running of a meeting involves compliance with a substantial body of procedures that can prove onerous and potentially costly, especially for smaller companies. Further, where the number of members is small or where the directors are the members, convening a meeting in order to pass resolutions seems a somewhat redundant exercise. Accordingly, the CA 2006 allows private companies to pass a written resolution in substitute for a resolution passed at a meeting and the ability to substitute a written resolution cannot be excluded by the articles.[13]

The written resolution procedure can be used for any resolution, except a resolution to remove a director or auditor before the expiry of their term of office.[14] Written resolutions require the same majorities, and have the same force, as resolutions passed at meetings.[15] Where the company has a share capital, each shareholder has one vote per share. As regards companies without a share capital, each member has one vote.[16]

A written resolution can be proposed by (i) the directors;[17] or (ii) members holding 5 per cent of the total voting rights in the company, or some other lower percentage specified in the articles.[18] In both cases a copy of the resolution must be sent to every member eligible to vote,[19] along with instructions on how to signify agreement and the date by which the resolution must be passed.[20] Failure to comply with these requirements constitutes an either way offence,[21] but the validity of the resolution, if passed, will not be affected.[22]

Irrespective of who proposed the written resolution, it must be passed within a certain period or it will lapse. This period can be specified in the company's articles, but if it is not, the resolution will lapse twenty-eight days after the copy of the resolution was first circulated to the company's members.[23]

General meetings

The resolutions of public companies must be passed at meetings; resolutions of private companies must be passed by meeting unless the written resolution procedure is used. It is perfectly possible for a private company to go its entire existence without

10. ibid s 281(3).   11. ibid s 281(2).   12. ibid s 281(1).   13. ibid s 300.
14. ibid s 288(2).
15. ibid s 288(5). Under the CA 1985, all written resolutions required unanimity.   16. ibid s 284(1).
17. ibid s 291(1).   18. ibid s 292(1) and (5).   19. ibid ss 291(2) and 293(2)(a)
20. ibid ss 291(4) and 293(4).   21. ibid ss 291(5) and 293(5).
22. ibid ss 291(7) and 293(7).   23. ibid s 297(1).

ever having to call a meeting. Conversely, public companies must have at least one meeting every financial year that will constitute an annual general meeting (AGM).[24] Resolutions passed at general meetings are only valid if the procedural requirements laid down in the CA 2006 are complied with,[25] and these procedures cannot usually be excluded or modified by the articles.

These procedural requirements are extensive and, after their discussion, it will be easier to appreciate why the written resolution procedure is so valued by private companies.

The calling of meetings

The general power to call a general meeting is vested in the directors,[26] but the members can require that the directors call a general meeting of the company, providing that the members requiring the meeting represent 5 per cent of the company's paid-up share capital or, if the company does not have a share capital, 5 per cent of the voting rights of all the members.[27] The members' request must state the general nature of the business to be dealt with at the requested meeting and may also include any resolutions proposed to be voted on at the meeting.[28]

Once a valid request has been received, the directors must, within twenty-one days, call a general meeting, which must be held within twenty-eight days of the date of the notice convening the meeting.[29] If the request proposes a resolution intended to be voted on at the meeting, the notice of the meeting must also include notice of the resolution.[30]

If the directors fail to comply with a valid request from the members to call a meeting, then the members who requested the meeting, or any of them representing over half of the total voting rights of the company, may call a meeting themselves at the company's expense, provided that such expenses are reasonable.[31] This meeting must take place within three months of the date on which the directors became subject to the requirement to call a meeting.[32]

Where it is not practicable to call a meeting in accordance with these provisions, then the court may, of its own volition or upon the application of a director or member, order a meeting to be called, held, and conducted in any manner that it deems fit.[33] The purpose of this is to prevent members or directors from frustrating meetings through their own conduct (for example, by refusing to attend, so that the meeting is inquorate).

Notice of meetings

Resolutions passed at general meetings are only valid if adequate notice of the meeting and of the resolution is provided to those entitled to such notice.[34] The members (irrespective of whether or not they are entitled to vote), the directors, and the auditor are entitled to notice of a meeting.[35] Except in relation to the company's auditor, the entitlements of notice may be modified by the company's articles.[36]

Notice of a meeting must state the time, date, and place of the meeting, and, subject to the articles, the general nature of the business to be dealt with at the meeting.[37]

24. ibid s 336(1).   25. ibid s 301.   26. ibid s 302.   27. ibid s 303(2).
28. ibid s 303(4).   29. ibid s 304(1).   30. ibid s 304(2).   31. ibid s 305(1) and (6).
32. ibid s 305(3).   33. ibid s 306.   34. ibid s 301.
35. ibid ss 310(1) and 502(2)(a).   36. ibid s 310(4)(b).   37. ibid s 311.

It is usual for this information to be sent to all members in the form of a 'circular', which is also likely to contain a brief agenda setting out the business of the meeting.

Notice must also be provided within a sufficient period prior to the meeting. Notice of a meeting must generally be provided at least fourteen days prior to the meeting, rising to twenty-one days in the case of the AGM of a public company.[38] The company's articles are free to specify a longer notice period,[39] but they cannot specify a shorter notice period. It is possible to shorten the notice period of a meeting, but only with the agreement of the majority of the shareholders having the right to attend and vote at the meeting, who, together, hold not less than the requisite percentage in nominal value of the shares.[40] In the case of a private company, the requisite percentage is 90 per cent of the nominal value of the shares, or, if the company does not have a share capital, of the total voting rights at that meeting. In the case of a public company, the requisite percentage is 95 per cent.[41] The notice period of a public company's AGM can only be shortened if all of the members entitled to attend and vote agree to the shorter notice period.[42]

Special notice (twenty-eight days) will be required where, at a meeting, a resolution is proposed that purports to (i) remove a director under s 168 of the CA 2006; (ii) appoint a person to fill the vacancy caused by the removal of a director under s 168; or (iii) remove or replace an auditor under ss 510 or 515 of the CA 2006.[43]

Procedure at meetings

In addition to the procedures relating to the calling of general meetings and the provision of notice, the actual meeting itself is also subject to a raft of procedural requirements. A meeting (and any decisions made at it) will only be valid if a quorum is present. In relation to general meetings, a quorum is the minimum number of 'qualifying persons' required in order validly to conduct business. A qualifying person is:

- a member of the company;
- a representative of a corporate member; or
- a **proxy** of the member.[44]

> **proxy:** someone appointed by a member to vote on his behalf

Where a limited company has only one qualifying member, that member constitutes a quorum.[45] In all other cases, two qualifying persons constitute a quorum, unless the articles provide otherwise.[46] If a quorum is not present, the meeting is said to be 'inquorate' and no business may be conducted at the meeting, except the appointment of a chair for the meeting.[47]

Regarding the passing of resolutions at the meeting, there are two methods of voting: (i) on a show of hands; or (ii) by poll. The general rule is that resolutions are taken on a show of hands and so each member will have one vote. The model articles for both private and public companies provide that a resolution at a meeting will be decided on a show of hands unless a poll is demanded in accordance

---

38. ibid s 307(1) and (2).   39. ibid s 307(3).   40. ibid s 307(4) and (5)(a).
41. ibid s 307(6).   42. ibid s 337(2).   43. ibid s 312(1).
44. ibid s 318(3). In all cases, the member in question must be entitled to vote (*Henderson v James Loutitt and Co Ltd* (1894) 21 R 674).   45. ibid s 318(1).   46. ibid s 318(2).
47. Model articles for private companies limited by shares, art 38; model articles for public companies, art 30.

with the articles.[48] Unless the articles provide otherwise, where a vote is taken on a poll, each member will have one vote per share (unless the company has no share capital, in which case, each member has one vote).[49] The members have the right to demand that a vote be taken on a poll and any provision in the articles that purports to exclude this right is void, unless it relates to the election of a chair or the adjournment of the meeting.[50]

Members need not attend the meeting to exercise their voting rights. Section 324 of the CA 2006 grants members the right to appoint another person (who may or may not be a member) to exercise their rights to attend, speak, and vote at general meetings, and this person is known as a 'proxy'. In large public companies, the appointment of proxies is especially important, because only a small minority of the company's members will actually attend the meeting. When public companies send out notice of a meeting, it is common for the notice to contain a document allowing the member to appoint a proxy who can exercise the member's vote. Unsurprisingly, the person nominated by the company to act as proxy is usually one of the directors.

The annual general meeting

Under the CA 1985, both public and private companies were required to hold an annual general meeting (AGM), although private companies could opt out of this requirement. The CA 2006 does not require private companies to hold an AGM, although they may do so. Public companies must hold an AGM every year within a six-month period ending on the date of the company's financial year.[51] Failure to hold an AGM in the required period constitutes an either way offence on the part of every officer of the company who is in default.[52]

The AGM is subject to its own procedures, which must be complied with by any company that holds an AGM. As noted earlier, the normal notice period for a meeting is fourteen days, but where the meeting is an AGM of a public company, this is extended to twenty-one days.[53] The notice of any AGM must state that the meeting is an AGM.[54]

The CA 2006 does not prescribe what business must be dealt with at the AGM, but it is customary that certain matters be dealt with there—namely, the laying out of the accounts and the directors' report, and the reappointment of the directors and/or auditor. The UK Corporate Governance Code recommends that, the 'board should use the AGM to communicate with investors and to encourage their participation'.[55] In listed companies especially, the AGM is likely to constitute the only opportunity that the members will have to question the board.

Unanimous consent

Convening meetings and passing resolutions can be a complex issue and failing to comply with the numerous procedural requirements could invalidate any decisions made. To mitigate this stringency, the common law has long provided that if all of the members entitled to vote on a matter agree on the matter, then that agreement is valid, even if no meeting was convened and no resolution took place.[56] This rule

---

48. Model articles for private companies limited by shares, art 42; model articles for public companies, art 34.   49. CA 2006, s 284(3).   50. ibid s 321(1).   51. ibid s 336(1).
52. ibid s 336(3).   53. ibid s 307(2)(a).   54. ibid s 337(1).
55. Financial Reporting Council, *The UK Corporate Governance Code* (FRC 2012) [E.2].
56. *Baroness Wenlock v The River Dee Co* (1883) 36 Ch D 675 (CA).

tends to be known as the *Duomatic* principle, named after the case of *Re Duomatic Ltd*,[57] in which Buckley J stated:

> where it can be shown that all shareholders who have a right to attend and vote at a general meeting of the company assent to some matter which a general meeting of the company could carry into effect, that assent is as binding as a resolution in general meeting would be.[58]

As the procedural rules relating to the passing of resolutions and the convening of meetings are put in place to protect the members as a whole, it is unsurprising that the ability of the members to make a decision through unanimous consent is closely watched. Restrictions on the rule include:

- Nothing less than unanimity will suffice. Thus a member who held 99 per cent of a company's shares could not take advantage of the *Duomatic* principle by himself.[59]
- Unanimous consent will not suffice where the decision in question could not have been taken at a meeting.[60]
- It is likely that decisions that cannot be taken by written resolution (namely, the removal of a director or auditor) also cannot be taken by unanimous consent.

The directors

A company may be a legal person possessing its own rights and powers, but it requires human intermediaries in order to exercise the powers granted to it. As discussed, certain powers of the company are exercisable only by the members, but the power to run the company generally is vested in the directors. The CA 2006 provides that every private company must have at least one director and that every public company must have at least two directors.[61] A director can be a natural person or a body corporate, but every company must have at least one director who is a natural person.[62]

The definition of 'director'

A company may be run by persons who are described by the articles, or describe themselves, as 'governors' or 'managers'. Conversely, the practice is growing whereby persons who are not involved in management at board level are called 'directors'. Are such persons actually directors? Answering this question is crucial, because many provisions in the CA 2006 are aimed squarely at directors of the company.

The CA 2006 does not define specifically what a director is; rather, it provides that a director 'includes any person occupying the position of director, by whatever name called'.[63] This encompasses those who have been validly appointed to the office of director (who are known as *de jure* directors), but also encompasses persons who ➡ **de jure:** 'in law'

---

57. [1969] 2 Ch 365 (Ch).
58. ibid 373.   59. *Re D'Jan of London* [1994] 1 BCLC 561 (Ch).
60. *Re New Cedos Engineering Co Ltd* [1994] 1 BCLC 797 (Ch).   61. CA 2006, s 154.
62. ibid s 155(1).   63. ibid s 250.

have not been validly appointed, but who act as directors (such persons are known as *de facto* directors). *De facto* directors, although not validly appointed, are directors, and are subject to the obligations and duties of that office.[64]

de facto: 'in fact'

Shadow directors

A person who has neither been appointed a director, nor acted as director, may be treated as a director if he is 'a person in accordance with whose directions or instructions the directors of the company are accustomed to act',[65] other than where that advice is given in a professional capacity.[66] Such a person is termed a 'shadow director' and it is vital that shadow directors can be identified because the CA 2006 often expressly states that a particular duty or obligation is also imposed upon shadow directors (for example, regarding the rules relating to directorial transactions that require shareholder approval, a shadow director is to be treated as a director).[67] In practice, however, determining who constitutes a shadow director is not always straightforward. That the courts often give inconsistent guidance does not help the issue.[68]

Two cases provide the principal guidance. In *Secretary of State for Trade and Industry v Deverell*,[69] Morritt LJ established five propositions, namely:

1. The definition of a shadow director should not be strictly construed.
2. It is not necessary for a shadow director to give directions or instructions over the whole field of the company's activities.
3. Whether a communication by a shadow director constitutes a direction or instruction is to be assessed objectively.
4. Non-professional advice can constitute a direction or instruction.
5. It is not necessary to show that the *de jure* directors acted in a subservient manner or surrendered their respective discretions.

Lewison J provided additional guidance in the case of *Ultraframe (UK) Ltd v Fielding*.[70]

- It is insufficient that some of the *de jure* directors follow the directions or instructions of the purported shadow director. In order for a person to be a shadow director, a governing majority of the board must be accustomed to acting on his directions and instructions.
- The *de jure* directors must be 'accustomed' to a person's directions and instructions for that person to be a shadow director. Accordingly, there may be an initial period during which a person who gives directions and instructions is not a shadow director. Further, transactions entered into before the *de jure* directors become accustomed cannot be retrospectively invalidated.
- A person will not become a shadow director until the directors actually act in accordance with his directions and instructions. The mere giving of directions and instructions is insufficient.

---

64. *Re Canadian Land Reclaiming and Colonizing Co* (1880) 14 Ch D 660 (CA).
65. CA 2006, s 251(1).   66. ibid s 251(2).   67. ibid s 223(1).
68. For example, in *Secretary of State for Trade and Industry v Hollier* [2006] EWHC 1804 (Ch), [2007] Bus LR 352, the court stated that shadow directorships and *de facto* directorships were alternatives, but in *Secretary of State for Trade and Industry v Aviss* [2006] EWHC 1846 (Ch), [2007] BCC 288 (Ch), the court held that a person could simultaneously be a shadow director and *de facto* director.
69. [2001] Ch 340 (CA) 354.   70. [2005] EWHC 1638 (Ch), [2006] FSR 17.

- Shadow directors are not subject to the same duties as *de jure* and *de facto* directors. Lewison J went on to state that in many cases, the relationship that a shadow director has with the company would not be enough to impose upon a shadow director fiduciary duties (e.g. a duty of loyalty). However, this comment has been doubted in the recent case of *Vivendi SA v Richards*,[71] where Newey J stated that 'my own view is that Ultraframe understates the extent to which shadow directors owe fiduciary duties. It seems to me that a shadow director will typically owe such duties in relation at least to the directions or instructions that he gives to the de jure directors.'[72]

Chairman and managing director

Senior members of the board may undertake additional services for the company, which could include being appointed to positions of seniority over their fellow directors. Two positions are of importance:

1. A director may be appointed as the 'managing director' (also known as the 'chief executive officer', or CEO), the exact role of whom will depend upon the company in question.
2. A director may be appointed as the 'chairman', whose role is to chair board meetings and, in the event of deadlock, usually to have the casting vote.

Historically, it was common for one person to act as both managing director and chairman. But fearing that this concentrated too much power in one person, the UK Corporate Governance Code now provides that companies should split the roles of chairman and managing director,[73] and that, upon appointment, the chairman should meet the Code's independence criteria.[74]

Executive and non-executive directors

It is important that students understand the distinction between executive and non-executive directors, especially given the recent prominence of non-executive directors as a governance mechanism. It is worth stressing at the outset that the CA 2006 does not recognize the distinction, and that it treats executive and non-executives alike (the phrase 'non-executive director' does not appear anywhere in the CA 2006).

Executive directors work for the company full-time and are responsible for the company's day-to-day management. Conversely, non-executive directors are part-time directors, devoting around one or two days a month to the company, and tend to be paid considerably less than their executive counterparts (around £30,000 per year). Although non-executive directors will be involved in management, from a governance standpoint, their key role is monitoring (from a theoretically neutral standpoint) the activities of the executives. The UK Corporate Governance Code provides that, except for smaller companies, at least half of the board should consist of independent non-executive directors.[75]

*⌗ Visit the **Online Resource Centre** for more on non-executive directors as a mechanism for improving standards of corporate governance in the chapter entitled 'Corporate governance'*

---

71. [2013] EWHC 3006 (Ch), [2013] BCC 771.   72. ibid [143].
73. Financial Reporting Council, *The UK Corporate Governance Code* (FRC 2012) [A.2.1].
74. ibid [A.3.1].   75. ibid [B.1.2].

Eligibility and appointment

Eligibility

Generally, anyone can be appointed to the office of director, but statute does impose certain restrictions.

- An individual under the age of 16 cannot be appointed as a director,[76] unless the appointment is not to take effect until the individual's sixteenth birthday,[77] or the appointment is within an exception specified by the Secretary of State.[78]
- A company's auditor is disqualified from acting as its director.[79]
- An undischarged bankrupt who acts as a director commits an either way offence, unless leave has been obtained from the court.[80]

Appointment

Chapter 19 noted that the registration documents submitted to the Registrar of Companies must include details of the company's proposed officers.[81] Accordingly, a company's first directors are nominated when the company is first registered and such persons will be appointed to the office of director upon the company's registration.[82] Following incorporation, directors may vacate office or the board may wish to expand its number. The power to appoint directors post-incorporation is usually a matter for the company's articles, but where the articles are silent on this, the power to appoint directors is vested in the members[83] and is usually exercised by passing an ordinary resolution.

The model articles provide that directors may be appointed by an ordinary resolution of the members, or by a decision of the directors.[84] When appointing directors, the members must exercise their power of appointment for the benefit of the company as a whole.[85] The UK Corporate Governance Code recommends that the appointment of directors should be led by a nomination committee, which should consist predominantly of independent non-executive directors.[86] This rule was introduced to combat the perception of the 'old boys' network' that many believe operated amongst larger public companies. This nomination committee will make recommendations to the board regarding appointments.

Any appointment will only become effective once the person in question has agreed to act as director.[87] Lack of capacity or understanding may vitiate such agreement.

The board

Board meetings

Collectively, the directors are referred to as the 'board' and, as will be discussed, much of a company's power is concentrated in its board. The board exercises its power via board meetings (not to be confused with general meetings of the company) and the

76. CA 2006, s 157(1).   77. ibid s 157(2).   78. ibid s 158.

79. ibid s 1214(1) and (2).   80. ibid s 11(1).   81. ibid s 9(4)(c).   82. ibid s 16(6).

83. *Worcester Corsetry Ltd v Witting* [1936] Ch 640 (CA).

84. Model articles for private companies limited by shares, art 17(1); model articles for public companies, art 20.

85. *Re HR Harmer Ltd* [1959] 1 WLR 62 (CA).

86. Financial Reporting Council, *The UK Corporate Governance Code* (FRC 2012) [B.2.1].

87. *Re British Empire Match Co Ltd* (1888) 59 LT 291.

procedures relating to the function of board meetings are found in the company's articles. Decisions of the directors are only valid if made at a board meeting, unless all of the directors agree with, or acquiesce to, a decision.[88] The general rule is that decisions at board meetings are made by majority vote,[89] but a decision can be made via a written resolution if all of the directors agree to the decision in writing. Where the number of votes is equal, the chairman or other director chairing the meeting will have the casting vote.

The model articles allow any director to call a board meeting by giving notice to the other directors.[90] It is not necessary that all of the directors are present at the meeting, but decisions at board meetings are only valid if a quorum can be obtained. The model articles set the quorum at two,[91] but companies are free to increase (but not decrease) this number. Decisions taken at a meeting that lacks a quorum are invalid.[92]

Powers of management

A company, while a legal person, can only operate and be operated through human intermediaries, thereby raising the issue of who has the power to run the company. The power to run the company is initially vested in the members of the company, but in all but the smallest companies (in which the directors and members are normally the same persons), it is impractical for the members to exercise day-to-day control over the company's affairs and their powers are therefore delegated to surrogates. Since all companies must have at least one director, the directors are usually the members' appointees. The issue then arises as to who has the right to determine what the company will do: the members or the directors?

The directors have only such power as is delegated to them by the members. Most companies have in their articles a provision vesting day-to-day control of the company in the directors as a body, or in a managing director. Where power has been vested in the directors, the members have no right to interfere in management, unless that power has been reserved to the members in the articles or by statute.

 Automatic Self-Cleansing Filter Syndicate Co Ltd v Cuninghame [1906] 2 Ch 34 (CA)

FACTS: The articles of the claimant company conferred general powers of management on the directors and provided that they could sell any property of the company on such terms as they deemed fit. The company's members passed an ordinary resolution resolving to sell the assets and undertakings of the claimant, but the directors did not believe such a sale to be in the interests of the company and so refused.

---

88. *Charterhouse Investment Trust Ltd v Tempest Diesels Ltd* [1986] BCLC 1 (Ch).

89. Model articles for private companies limited by shares, art 7(1); model articles for public companies, art 13(1).

90. Model articles for private companies limited by shares, art 9(1); model articles for public companies, art 8(3).

91. Model articles for private companies limited by shares, art 11(2); model articles for public companies, art 10(2). Where the company is private and has only one director, then the quorum shall be one (model articles for private companies limited by shares, art 7(2).

92. *Re Greymouth Point Elizabeth Railway and Coal Co Ltd* [1904] 1 Ch 32 (Ch).

> **HELD:** The right to manage the company and the right to determine which property to sell was vested in the directors. Accordingly, the directors were not compelled to comply with the resolution unless the articles so provided.

As the division of power between the members and directors is a matter for the articles, the provisions of the model articles are of considerable importance. Article 3 of the model articles provides that, '[s]ubject to the articles, the directors are responsible for the management of the company's business, for which purpose they may exercise all the powers of the company'. Clearly, this places a significant amount of power in the hands of the directors, but, because it is subject to the articles, provisions can be inserted that alter this balance of power, as the following case demonstrates.

Salmon v Quin & Axtens Ltd [1909] 1 Ch 311 (CA); aff'd [1909] AC 442 (HL)

FACTS: The articles of the defendant company conferred general powers of management upon the directors, but such powers were subject to the articles. Article 80 provided that resolutions of the directors relating to the acquisition or letting of certain premises would not be valid if two named members (who were also the company's managing directors) were to dissent. The directors passed a resolution resolving to acquire certain property, but one of the named members (the claimant) vetoed the resolution. An extraordinary meeting was called and the members passed an ordinary resolution similar to the one the directors attempted to pass. The claimant commenced proceedings, seeking an injunction to restrain the property acquisitions.

HELD: Whilst the directors had a general power of management, it was subject to the articles. Accordingly, the claimant's veto was valid and the company could not override it by passing an ordinary resolution.

In both *Automatic Self-Cleansing* and *Salmon*, ordinary resolutions passed by the members could not affect the powers conferred in the articles, because this would permit the members to alter the articles indirectly by ordinary resolution. It follows from this that a direction from the members passed by special resolution should be valid and this is reflected in art 4(1) of the model articles, which states that the members may, by special resolution, direct the directors to take, or refrain from taking, specified action. Accordingly, whilst power is vested in the directors, the members retain a specific supervisory power exercisable by passing a special resolution. This supervisory power is not retrospective, however, and cannot be used to invalidate anything that the directors have done prior to the resolution. In practice, this power is rarely used on the ground that there is little need to pass a special resolution compelling the directors to act a certain way, when it is easier to pass an ordinary resolution removing them from office.

Article 4 confers a specific power upon the members, but the general power to run the company is still vested in the directors by art 3. However, where the directors are unwilling or unable to exercise the powers conferred by art 3, then the general

🔗 The members' ability to remove the directors from office is discussed in 'Termination of office' at p 583

power to manage reverts to the members.[93] It should be noted that the default powers of the general meeting operate only where the board is completely incapable of making decisions and not when a minority of directors use any power that they may have been given by the articles to block the implementation of a decision by the majority of the board (as in *Salmon v Quin & Axtens Ltd*, discussed earlier). In the latter case, the board is precluded from acting by the operation of the articles, not by any incapacity to act.

Unitary and two-tier boards

Mention should briefly be made of board structures. Although the UK system of corporate governance has several different types of director, they all sit on a single board (although this board may have several satellite committees devoted to determining remuneration, nominating directorial candidates, etc). The UK therefore has what is known as a 'unitary' board structure. Conversely, other countries segregate their directors into multiple boards, or multiple tiers of a single board. The dual-board system found in Germany provides the classic example. German companies will have a management board (the *Vorstand*), which is responsible for managing the company and in whom much of the company's power is concentrated. There will also be a supervisory board (the *Aufsichtsrat*) consisting of non-executives and employee representatives, which will play a role in management, but will also supervise and approve many decisions of the management board.

Remuneration

Generally, directors are office holders, rather than employees (although a director can be an employee if he has an employment contract). A consequence of this is that they are not generally entitled to be remunerated for acting as a director.[94] This general rule is, in practice, however, normally excluded either by providing for remuneration in a director's service contract, or by including a provision in the articles entitling the directors to remuneration for their services. The model articles provide that directors are to be paid for their services as directors, and for any other services that they undertake for the company.[95]

The UK Corporate Governance Code recommends that companies establish a remuneration committee consisting entirely of non-executive directors, the function of which will be to determine the remuneration of the executives.[96]

*Visit the **Online Resource Centre** for more on the effectiveness of remuneration committees in the chapter entitled 'Corporate governance'*

Termination of office

A director's term of office may be terminated in one of several different ways.

Termination in accordance with the articles

A company's articles may lay down a number of events that will cause a director to cease to hold office. For example, the model articles state that a person will cease to

---

93. *Barron v Potter* [1914] 1 Ch 895 (Ch).
94. *Hutton v West Cork Railway Co* (1883) 23 Ch D 654 (CA).
95. Model articles for private companies limited by shares, art 19; model articles for public companies, art 23.
96. Financial Reporting Council, *The UK Corporate Governance Code* (FRC 2010) [D.2.1–D.2.2].

be a director if he is prohibited from being a director by law[97] (for example, where he has been disqualified from acting as a director), or if a bankruptcy order is made against him.[98] A director may be reappointed as a director once the event has passed, but whilst the event is current, he cannot hold office as a director and the other directors cannot waive the effects of any article provision causing a director to cease to hold office.[99]

Resignation

A director may, at any time, relinquish office by giving notice to the company and the company must accept his resignation. The articles or the director's service contract may provide restrictions on the director's ability to resign, but in the absence of such restrictions, resignation is effective as soon as it is given and cannot be retracted without the consent of the company.[100] Where the articles or service contract do not provide for a notice period, the courts will imply a term into the service contract requiring a reasonable period of notice.[101]

Retirement by rotation

A company's articles may provide for the retirement of the directors by rotation. In practice, it is only public companies that tend to require retirement by rotation and art 21 of the model articles for public companies requires that the directors of a public company retire at its first general meeting. At every subsequent general meeting, any directors appointed by the directors since the last general meeting, or any directors who were not appointed or reappointed at one of the preceding two general meetings, must retire from office and may offer themselves for reappointment. In practice, this means that directors of public companies must be re-elected every three years. The UK Corporate Governance Code goes further and recommends, controversially, that the directors of FTSE 350 companies should be subject to annual election.[102]

Removal

Section 168(1) of the CA 2006 provides that '[a] company may by ordinary resolution at a meeting[103] remove a director before the expiration of his period of office, notwithstanding anything in any agreement between it and him'. Despite the wording of s 168, the resolution can seek the removal of multiple directors. Special notice (twenty-eight days) is required for the resolution and the company must send a copy of the resolution to the director(s) concerned.[104]

The director(s) whose removal is sought has a right to be heard at the meeting where the resolution is to take place.[105] The director(s) may make written

---

97. Model articles for private companies limited by shares, art 18(a); model articles for public companies, art 22(a).

98. Model articles for private companies limited by shares, art 18(b); model articles for public companies, art 22(b). Company Directors Disqualification Act 1986, s 11(1), provides that it is a criminal offence for an undischarged bankrupt to act as a director, except with leave of the court.

99. *Re Bodega Co Ltd* [1904] 1 Ch 276 (Ch).   100. *Glossop v Glossop* [1907] 2 Ch 370 (Ch).

101. *CMS Dolphin Ltd v Simonet* [2002] BCC 600 (Ch).

102. Financial Reporting Council, *The UK Corporate Governance Code* (FRC 2012) [B.7.1].

103. As the resolution must be at a meeting, the written resolution procedure cannot be used to effect a removal under s 168.

104. CA 2006, ss 168(1) and (2), 169(1), and 312(1).

105. ibid s 169(2).

representations to the company and, if such representations are received in time, the company must send them to every member to whom notice of the meeting has been sent.[106]

Section 168(5)(b) provides that s 168 should not be construed as derogating from any power to remove a director that exists outside s 168. Accordingly, the power to remove a director under s 168 exists alongside any other power. This can allow a removal to be effected more easily, as the following example demonstrates.

> ### Eg Removal of a director other than through s 168
>
> Computech Ltd has a provision in its articles that states that 'a director of the company may be removed by passing an ordinary resolution'. As this provision makes no mention of the resolution requiring special notice, such notice is not required. As the provision does not require the resolution to be passed at a meeting, it can be passed using the written resolution procedure. Finally, the provision does not provide the directors with a right to make representations, so none may be made. Where a company has such an article provision, the members have a choice between removing the director via the s 168 procedure or the procedure under the articles. The articles can even provide for a method of removal that does not involve the members (for example, removal upon a vote of the directors).

Once a director has been removed, the only remaining remedies available to him are to petition the court for a winding-up order, or (if he is also a member) to bring a claim alleging that the removal was unfairly prejudicial to his interests as a member. This latter remedy is only likely to have a chance of success if the company is a quasi-partnership.

These remedies and the concept of the quasi-partnership are discussed in Chapter 23

Initially, the power granted to members under s 168 appears extremely substantial, but, in practice, its effectiveness is emasculated in two ways. First, a removal under s 168 does not deprive the director of any compensation payable as a result of the removal.[107] For example, a director removed under s 168 who still has a period of his service contract left to run will be able to obtain damages for breach of contract. If the director's remuneration is high and/or the period remaining on his service contract is lengthy, removing him may be extremely costly to the company.

Second, s 168 does not prohibit the company from including in its articles a weighted voting clause. Such a clause usually provides that, in the event of a vote to remove a director from office, the voting power of the director shall be increased (usually to such an extent as to enable him to defeat any resolution seeking his removal). The following case demonstrates how a weighted voting clause operates in practice and how it can severely emasculate the power granted to the members by s 168.

---

106. ibid s 169(3). If the representations are sent too late, the director(s) can require that the representations be read out at the meeting (s 169(4)).
107. ibid s 168(5)(a).

Bushell v Faith [1970] AC 1099 (HL)

FACTS: A company had 300 shares, equally divided between three siblings. Two of the siblings (the claimant and defendant) were the company's only directors. The articles contained a weighted voting clause that provided that, in relation to resolutions to remove a director, the director involved would have his voting power trebled (that is, each share would carry three votes). Two of the siblings (one of whom was the claimant) sought to remove the third sibling director (the defendant), but the weighted voting clause meant that the defendant's shares were worth 300 votes, whereas the claimant and the other sibling could only muster 200 votes between them. Accordingly, the defendant argued that the resolution was defeated. The claimant contended that the resolution was passed by 200 votes, compared to the defendant's 100 votes, and she sought an injunction preventing the defendant from acting as a director.

HELD: The claim failed. The weighted voting clause was effective and the resolution was therefore validly defeated. The Companies Acts did not expressly state that such clauses were invalid and there was therefore no reason to imply such an intention.

COMMENT: Unsurprisingly, the decision in *Bushell* has proved controversial on the ground that a weighted voting clause could serve to entrench a director and make him irremovable. In practice, the effect of *Bushell* may be more limited than many realize. First, it has been argued that the decision was justified on the ground that the company in question was a quasi-partnership, in which all of the members will expect to be involved in management. It may therefore be the case that such clauses are effective only in relation to such companies (although there are no *obiter dicta* or *rationes* to this effect). Second, such clauses probably breach the Listing Rules and so will not be adopted by public companies. Third, a weighted voting clause could be removed by passing a special resolution (although admittedly, members with 75 per cent of the company's votes could probably defeat even a director with weighted voting rights).

★ See Dan Prentice, 'Removal of Directors from Office' (1969) 32 MLR 693

Finally, it should be noted that the members are not the only party granted the power to remove a director. Schedule B1, para 61 of the Insolvency Act 1986 provides that where a company is in administration, the administrator has the power to remove a director.

Disqualification

The shareholders can decide to dismiss a director, but the Company Directors Disqualification Act 1986 (CDDA 1986) grants a court the power to make a disqualification order disqualifying a person from promoting, forming, or taking part in the management of a company (or LLP) without the leave of the court. Alternatively, since 2000, instead of obtaining a disqualification order from a court, the Secretary of State may, if it is in the public interest, accept from a person a disqualification undertaking, whereby that person undertakes not to do anything prohibited by a disqualification order.[108] The majority of disqualifications are now made this way.

The CDDA 1986 provides numerous grounds for disqualification, including:

- Section 2 provides for disqualification upon conviction of an indictable offence in connection with the promotion, formation, or management of a company.

---

108. CDDA 1986, s 1A.

- Section 3 provides for disqualification for persistent[109] breaches of companies legislation requiring returns, accounts, or other documents to be filed, delivered, or sent to the Registrar.

- Section 5 provides for disqualification where the director has, within a five-year period, been convicted of three or more summary offences in relation to requiring a return, account, or other document to be filed with, delivered, or sent, or notice of any matter to be given, to the Registrar of Companies.

- Section 9A provides for disqualification where the director commits a breach of competition law and that breach renders him unfit to be concerned in the management of a company.

- Section 10 provides for disqualification where a person has been required to contribute to the company's assets under ss 213 or 214 of the Insolvency Act 1986.

🔗 Visit the **Online Resource Centre** for more on competition law in the chapter entitled 'Unfair and unlawful commercial practices'

🔗 Sections 213 and 214 are discussed in 'Fraudulent trading' at p 674

The most wide-ranging ground for disqualification (and the ground that most disqualification cases concern) can be found in s 6, which provides for disqualification where a person is a director of a company that has become insolvent (whether while he was a director or subsequently), and his conduct as a director makes him unfit to be concerned in the management of the company. Conduct need not be unlawful or dishonest in order to be unfit.[110]

In *Re Sevenoaks Stationers (Retail) Ltd*,[111] Dillon LJ stated that it was 'beyond dispute'[112] that the purpose of s 6 was to protect the public and creditors from losing money through companies becoming insolvent. The words of s 6 should be treated as ordinary English words and what amounts to unfitness will turn on the facts of each case. Incompetence or negligence will not normally result in disqualification, but they may do where they are to 'a very marked degree'.[113]

The maximum length of disqualification depends upon the ground of disqualification. Breaches of ss 3 or 5 can result in a maximum disqualification period of five years. Breaches of ss 2, 4, 6, 9A, or 10 can result in a maximum disqualification period of fifteen years. Breach of s 6 is also subject to a minimum disqualification period—namely, two years. In *Re Sevenoaks Stationers*, Dillon LJ divided s 6 cases into three brackets.

1. Disqualification periods of ten years or more should be reserved for particularly serious cases. This may include a case in which a director already has one period of disqualification imposed upon him and is disqualified a second time.

2. Disqualification periods of between six and ten years should be reserved for serious cases that do not fall into (1) above.

3. Disqualification periods of two to five years should apply where disqualification is mandatory, but the case is, relatively, not very serious.[114]

Breach of a disqualification order constitutes an either way offence.[115] Further, a director who contravenes a disqualification order by taking part in the management of a company can be personally liable for the debts and liabilities of the company incurred during the duration of the contravention.[116] A director subject to a disqualification order can become involved again in corporate management if he obtains

---

109. CDDA 1986, s 3(2) provides that three or more defaults in a five-year period will be regarded as persistent.   110. *Re Deaduck Ltd* [2000] 1 BCLC 148 (Ch).   111. [1991] Ch 164 (CA).
112. ibid 176.   113. ibid 184.   114. ibid 174.
115. CDDA 1986, s 13.   116. ibid s 15.

leave from the court. Leave will only be granted where the company has need of the director's services and the public is adequately protected.[117]

The company secretary

The company secretary is an officer of the company,[118] whose function is to carry out the administrative tasks imposed on companies by the Companies Acts (although the CA 2006 itself does not specifically require these tasks to be carried out by the secretary). Common administrative tasks include:

- ensuring the timely filing of accurate documents with the Registrar of Companies;
- maintaining the statutory registers (for example, the register of members that is kept at the company's registered office);
- preparing the agenda for, and minuting, board meetings; and
- ensuring that general meetings are conducted according to the procedures laid down in the CA 2006 (for example, providing members with adequate notice).

 Apparent authority is discussed at p 195

In relation to these sorts of administrative tasks, the secretary has apparent authority to bind the company, as the following case demonstrates.

> ### Panorama Developments (Guildford) Ltd v Fidelis Furnishing Fabrics Ltd [1971] 2 QB 711 (CA)
>
> **FACTS:** The defendant's company secretary was a man named Bayne. Using the defendant's notepaper, Bayne hired a number of cars from the claimant, telling the claimant that they would be used to transport important customers of the defendant. The agreement of hire stated that Bayne was the hirer and he was described as 'Company Secretary'. Bayne used the cars for personal purposes and not for the company's business. The hire charges were not paid and the claimant sued the defendant for the outstanding charges. The defendant, unsurprisingly, denied liability.
>
> **HELD:** The defendant was liable to pay the hire charge. Lord Denning MR stated that a company secretary is not:
>
> > a mere clerk. He regularly makes representations on behalf of the company and enters into contracts on its behalf which come within the day-to-day running of the company's business. So much so that he may be regarded as held out as having authority to do such things on behalf of the company.[119]

The company secretary must also obey the lawful orders of the directors, but he is not normally to be regarded as being involved in the company's management. His ability to bind the company will not therefore extend to commercial matters, unless he has been expressly authorized to engage in such matters.

---

117. *Re Gibson Davies Ltd* [1995] BCC 11 (Ch).
118. CA 2006, s 1121(2).   119. [1971] 2 QB 711 (CA) 716–17.

Appointment and dismissal

Every public company must appoint a company secretary,[120] and the Secretary of State may direct a public company that has failed to appoint a company secretary to do so.[121] Failure to comply with this direction will constitute a summary offence on the part of the company and every officer of the company who is in default.[122] Not only must a public company appoint a company secretary, but its directors are also under a duty to take all reasonable steps to ensure that the secretary has the requisite knowledge and experience, and also the appropriate qualifications.[123] Appropriate qualifications include:

- holding the office of secretary of a public company for at least three of the five years preceding the appointment;
- being a member of certain professional bodies (for example, the Institute of Chartered Accountants, the Institute of Chartered Secretaries and Administrators, or the Chartered Institute of Management Accountants);
- being a barrister, advocate, or solicitor.[124]

A private company may appoint a company secretary, but is not required to do so[125] unless its articles provide that a company secretary must be appointed. It is anticipated that larger private companies will retain a company secretary. Where a private company does not appoint a company secretary, anything authorized or required to be given or sent to, or served on, the company by being sent to its company secretary is satisfied if it is sent to or served on the company.[126] A director, or a person authorized on behalf of the directors, can undertake anything that must be authorized or done by the company secretary.[127]

Article 99 of the Companies (Tables A to F) Regulations 1985[128] (Table A) provided that a company secretary may be appointed and dismissed by the directors. Curiously, the current model articles contain no references whatsoever to the appointment or dismissal of company secretaries.

Legal duties and liabilities

Company secretaries are subject to a number of duties, and liability can be imposed upon them in a number of ways. In one, notable, Canadian case, the Canadian Supreme Court held that the duties placed upon directors can also apply to those in senior management positions[129] (this would presumably include company secretaries, because they are officers of the company). English courts have not yet adopted this view and there is little doubt that the general duties of directors are not imposed on company secretaries. It is settled, however, that company secretaries owe fiduciary duties to the company that are similar to those owed by directors (for example, not to compete and not to make a secret profit).

In addition, the CA 2006 imposes numerous obligations upon the company, breach of which can result in liability being imposed upon the company and its officers, which would include the company secretary. In fact, breach of many of these

🔗 The general duties of directors are discussed in Chapter 22

---

120. CA 2006, s 271. Although not stated by the Act, one of the company's directors may act as company secretary.   121. ibid s 272(1).   122. ibid s 272(6) and (7).   123. ibid s 273(1).
124. ibid s 273(2) and (3).   125. ibid s 270(1).   126. ibid s 270(3)(a).
127. ibid s 270(3)(b).   128. SI 1985/805.
129. *Canadian Aero Service v O'Malley* [1973] 40 DLR 3d 371 (Canadian Supreme Court).

🔗 The duties imposed upon employees are discussed in 'Implied terms relating to the conduct of the employee' at p 703

🔗 The duties imposed upon agents are discussed at p 203

obligations constitutes a criminal offence punishable by a fine, which, in certain cases, may be payable by the company secretary.

If the company secretary is an employee of the company, he will be subject to the normal duties imposed upon employees (for example, the duty of mutual trust, confidence, and respect, and the duty of fidelity). Should a company secretary place himself in an agency relationship with the company, he will be subject to the fiduciary duties imposed on an agent.

The auditor

For each financial year, the directors are under a duty to prepare 'individual accounts' providing information relating to the company's financial position.[130] Although the directors must not approve such accounts unless they give a true and fair view of the company's financial position,[131] the directors may nevertheless be tempted to present these accounts in an overly favourable way (or simply to lie) in order to encourage investment. To discourage such behaviour, the law requires that these accounts be subject to an independent third-party verification by a statutory auditor.

Appointment, eligibility, and remuneration

As a general rule, all companies must appoint (or reappoint) an auditor each financial year[132] and such persons are known as 'statutory auditors'. Where the law requires that an auditor be appointed, but one is not, the company in question must notify the Secretary of State, who has the power to appoint an auditor on the company's behalf.[133] Failure to notify the Secretary of State constitutes a summary offence by the company and every officer of the company who is in default.[134]

As the effectiveness of the audit rests on the skill and independence of the auditor, the CA 2006 imposes several eligibility requirements, including:

- A person is ineligible for appointment as a statutory auditor if he is an officer or employee of the company, or he is the partner, or in partnership with such a person.[135]

- An individual or firm may only act as statutory auditor if he or it is a member of a recognized supervisory body (for example, the Institute of Chartered Accountants in England and Wales), and he is eligible for appointment under the rules of that body.[136]

- An individual may only act as a statutory auditor if he holds an 'appropriate qualification', with such qualifications being defined in s 1219 of the CA 2006.

Any ineligible person who acts as a statutory auditor commits an either way offence,[137] but it is a defence for him to show that he did not know and had no reason to believe that he was ineligible for appointment.[138]

---

130. CA 2006, s 394.   131. ibid s 393(1).   132. ibid ss 485 and 489.
133. ibid ss 486(1) and 490(2).   134. ibid ss 486 and 490.   135. ibid s 1214(1).
136. ibid s 1212(1).   137. ibid ss 1213(3) and 1215(2).
138. ibid ss 1213(8) and 1215(7).

Private companies

A private company must appoint an auditor each financial year, unless the directors reasonably resolve otherwise on the ground that audited accounts are unlikely to be required.[139] The directors can make the appointment of an auditor for the first financial year, but, to encourage independence, subsequent appointments must be made by the members passing an ordinary resolution.[140] The UK Corporate Governance Code recommends that an audit committee consisting of non-executive directors be established to make recommendations to the board regarding the appointment and re-appointment of auditors.[141]

Other than in the company's first financial year, the appointment must be made within twenty-eight days of the date by which the company's accounts must be sent out to the members, or, if earlier, the date on which the accounts actually are sent out.[142] Unless reappointed, an auditor loses office at the end of his term of appointment, but s 487(2) provides that reappointment is automatic unless:

- he was appointed by the directors;
- the company's articles require actual reappointment;
- 5 per cent (or some other percentage as specified in the articles) of the company's members present a notice to the company stating that the auditor should not be reappointed;
- the members have resolved that he should not be reappointed; or
- the directors have resolved that no auditor(s) should be appointed for the financial year in question.

Public companies

A public company must appoint an auditor each financial year, unless the directors reasonably resolve otherwise on the ground that audited accounts are unlikely to be required.[143] The rules relating to the appointment of a statutory auditor for a public company are exactly the same as those for a private company, except that:

- as public companies are required to lay their accounts out to the general meeting, the appointment of the auditor must take place before the end of the meeting in which the accounts are laid out;[144]
- there is no provision for the automatic reappointment of a public company's statutory auditor.

The audit market for large public companies (especially listed companies) is dominated by four firms (known as the 'Big Four')[145], namely PriceWaterhouseCoopers, Ernst & Young, KPMG, and Deloitte. The domination of the Big Four coupled with the fact that large companies rarely change their auditors has led to concerns that the audits for such companies may not be as independent as they could be.

139. ibid s 485(1).

140. ibid s 485(3) and (4).

141. Financial Reporting Council, *The UK Corporate Governance Code* (FRC 2012) [C.3.1–C.3.2].

142. CA 2006, s 485(2).   143. ibid s 489(1).   144. ibid s 489(2).

145. These firms are segregated from the rest due to the significant size gap between them and other firms. For example, in 2013, the fourth largest auditor, Ernst & Young, had a UK fee income of £1.63 billion, whereas the fifth largest firm, Grant Thornton, had a UK income of only £460 million.

Several measures have been introduced, or are being considered, in an attempt to remedy this:

- The UK Corporate Governance Code recommends that FTSE 350 companies should put their audit contract out to tender at least every ten years.[146]
- In October 2011, the Office of Fair Trading referred the statutory audit market to the Competition Commission. Following a lengthy investigation, the Competition Commission published a report in October 2013 in which it stated that it intends to require FTSE 350 companies to put their statutory engagement out to tender at least every ten years.[147]
- The European Union has expressed support[148] for a system of mandatory rotation on large companies, which would require such companies to change their auditor within certain periods. The details of the system are, at the time of writing, being negotiated.

Exemptions

Three types of company are exempt from the requirement to appoint an auditor. First, a company that has been dormant since its formation, or which has been dormant since the end of the previous financial year, is exempt from the requirement to appoint an auditor.[149] Second, companies deemed 'small companies' under the CA 2006 are exempt from the requirement to appoint an auditor in relation to the financial year in which they qualify as a small company. The CA 2006 defines a small company as one that meets two of the following three criteria:

1. it has a turnover of no more than £6.5 million;
2. it has a balance sheet total of not more than £3.26 million; and
3. it has no more than fifty employees.[150]

Third, a subsidiary company will be exempt from having its individual accounts audited if it meets the following criteria:

(a) its parent company is established in an EEA state;[151]

(b) all the members of the subsidiary agree to the exemption from audit in respect of the financial year in question, and written notice of this agreement must be provided to the Registrar of Companies;[152]

(c) the parent company must provide a declaration of guarantee in relation to that financial year, and must deliver this declaration to the Registrar of Companies;[153]

(d) the subsidiary company must be included in the consolidated accounts drawn up for that year,[154] and the notes to the consolidated accounts must state that the subsidiary is exempt from audited accounts under s 479A;[155]

(e) the directors must deliver to the registrar certain specified documents.[156]

---

146. Financial Reporting Council, *The UK Corporate Governance Code* (FRC 2012) [C.3.7].

147. Competition Commission, *Statutory Audit Services for Large Companies Market Investigation (Competition Commission* 2013) [16.3].

148. It is worth noting that the UK argued against mandatory rotation, but was defeated.

149. CA 2006, s 480(1).

150. ibid ss 382(3) and 477. Additionally, s 478 provides that a public company cannot qualify as a small company.

151. ibid s 479A(1)(b).   152. ibid s 479A(2)(a) and 479A(2)(e)(i).

153. ibid s 479A(2)(b) and 479A(2)(e)(ii). The information required under the declaration of guarantee is set out in s 479C.   154. ibid s 479A(2)(c).   155. ibid s 479A(2)(d).

156. ibid s 479A(2)(e). These documents include a copy of the consolidated accounts, a copy of the auditor's report on these accounts, and a copy of the consolidated annual report drawn up by the parent company.

Remuneration

Once appointed, the auditor will need to be paid. Section 492(2) provides that the remuneration of an auditor appointed by the directors can be fixed by the directors. In all other cases, the auditor's remuneration must be fixed by either the members passing an ordinary resolution, or some other method, as determined by the members by passing an ordinary resolution.[157] In practice, the auditor's remuneration is usually determined by the directors, because the members pass a resolution allowing them to do so.

Powers of investigation

The principal function of an auditor is to examine the annual accounts prepared by the directors and to prepare an auditor's report, which is then sent out to the members (in the case of a private company), or laid before the general meeting (in the case of a public company).[158] The auditor's report must state whether, in the auditor's opinion, the annual accounts give a true and fair view of the company's financial position, and whether they have been prepared in accordance with the CA 2006. If the auditor is of the opinion that the company has kept inadequate records, or that the records are inconsistent with the annual accounts, then this must be stated in his report.[159] An auditor commits an either way offence if he knowingly or recklessly causes an auditor's report to include any matter that is misleading, false, or deceptive, or if he knowingly or recklessly omits a required statement.[160]

Preparing an auditor's report will therefore involve a substantial amount of investigative work and, indeed, auditors are under a duty to carry out such investigations.[161] To aid auditors in complying with this duty, the Act grants auditors significant investigative powers, including:

- the right of access, at all times, to the company's books and accounts;[162]
- the right to require certain persons (for example, officers and employees of the company) to provide him with such information and explanations as he thinks necessary;[163]
- the right to view all notes and communications relating to any general meeting, and also to attend and be heard at any general meetings.[164]

A person who fails to comply with the auditor's right to information without delay commits a summary offence,[165] but no offence will be committed where it was not reasonably practicable for him to provide the information or explanations.[166] A person who knowingly or recklessly provides to the auditor any information or explanation that is misleading, false, or deceptive commits an either way offence.[167]

Liability of an auditor

Contractual liability

A contractual relationship exists between the company and its auditor. As with any provider of a service, there will be an implied contractual term placing a duty upon

---

157. ibid s 492(1).   158. ibid s 495(1).   159. ibid s 498(2).   160. ibid s 507(1) and (2).
161. ibid s 498(1).   162. ibid s 499(1)(a).   163. ibid s 499(1)(b).   164. ibid s 502.
165. ibid s 501(3) and (5).   166. ibid s 501(3).   167. ibid s 501(1).

the auditor to carry out his functions with reasonable care and skill.[168] Accordingly, an auditor may be liable to pay damages to a company if his audit is conducted in a negligent manner.

It is clear from established cases that, historically, the contractual duty placed upon auditors was not an onerous one. This is evident from the following statement of Lopes LJ:

> It is the duty of an auditor to bring to bear on the work he has to perform that skill, care, and caution which a reasonably competent, careful, and cautious auditor would use…An auditor is not bound to be a detective, or…to approach his work with suspicion or with a foregone conclusion that there is something wrong. He is a watch-dog, but not a bloodhound. He is justified in believing tried servants of the company in whom confidence is placed by the company. He is entitled to assume that they are honest, and to rely upon their representations, provided he takes reasonable care. If there is anything calculated to excite suspicion he should probe it to the bottom; but in the absence of anything of that kind he is only bound to be reasonably cautious and careful.[169]

This statement indicates that, in the absence of suspicious circumstances, the auditors are free to rely on information provided by the directors. It is debatable whether this is still the case. In *Fomento (Sterling Area) Ltd v Selsdon Fountain Pen Co Ltd*,[170] Lord Denning stated that the auditors should carry out their functions 'with an inquiring mind—not suspicious of dishonesty…but suspecting that someone may have made a mistake somewhere and that a check must be made to ensure that there has been none'.[171]

The Auditing Practices Board's International Standards on Auditing state that the auditor should 'plan and perform an audit with an attitude of professional skepticism recognizing that circumstances may exist that cause the financial statements to be materially misstated'.[172] They go on to state that an attitude of 'professional skepticism' includes 'a questioning mind, being alert to conditions which may indicate possible misstatement due to error or fraud, and a critical assessment of audit evidence'.[173]

Given that such professional standards constitute 'very strong evidence as to what is the proper standard which should be adopted',[174] it is almost certainly the case that auditors cannot rely blindly on information provided to them by the directors and will need to engage in a certain amount of independent research.

Tortious liability for negligent misstatement

➡ **proper claimant principle:** the principle that, where the company is wronged, only the company can sue on that wrong (see 'The rule in *Foss v Harbottle*' at p 645)

The doctrine of privity of contract, alongside the **proper claimant principle**, ensures that, if the auditor breaches his contractual duty of care and skill, only the company may initiate a claim for loss. The same is not true in relation to the auditor's liability

---

168. Supply of Goods and Services Act 1982, s 13.
169. *Re Kingston Cotton Mill Co (No 2)* [1896] 2 Ch 279 (CA) 288–9.
170. [1958] 1 WLR 45 (HL).
171. ibid 61.
172. Audit Practices Board, *International Standards on Auditing: Overall Objectives of the Independent Auditor and the Conduct of an Audit in Accordance With International Standards on Accounting* (APB 2009) [15].
173. ibid [13(l)].
174. *Lloyd Cheyham and Co Ltd v Littlejohn and Co* [1987] BCLC 303 (QB) 313 (Woolf J).

in tort, under which the auditor may owe a duty of care to third parties as well as to the company.

The requirements for the imposition of a duty of care to third parties were set down in the case of *Caparo Industries plc v Dickman*,[175] a case previously discussed. The House of Lords examined the existing authorities and reformulated the requirements to establish negligent misstatement in a way that was much more acceptable to auditors than to third parties. The House reiterated that the auditors owe a duty of care to the company the accounts of which are being audited, but the company is not the only party who may rely on the audited accounts: potential investors will also examine the accounts before deciding whether or not to invest. The House made clear that, as a general rule, the auditor's duty of care will not extend to potential investors who rely on the audited accounts. However, the House acknowledged that there may be situations in which auditors do owe a duty of care to third parties.

⚭ The facts and decision in *Caparo* are discussed at p 382

In order for a third party to establish that the auditor owed him a duty of care, he will need to prove the existence of a 'special relationship' between himself and the auditor. In relation to claims against auditors, this would require the claimant to show that the following four factors were present:

1. that the audited accounts were required for a purpose, which was made known to the auditor;
2. that the auditor knew that the audited accounts would be communicated to the claimant, either specifically or as part of a ascertainable class, for the purpose made known;
3. that the auditor knew that, upon publication of the audited accounts, the claimant was likely to act upon the audited accounts; and
4. that the claimant acted on the audited accounts to his detriment.

These four factors establish that there will need to be a sufficient degree of proximity between the claimant and the auditor. In the absence of even one of the four factors, the relationship will not be sufficiently proximate and will almost certainly result in the claimant's action failing, but even if the claimant can establish that these four factors are present, this will merely establish that sufficient proximity exists. The court may still hold that a duty should not be imposed on the ground of fairness and reasonableness.

Assuming that a claimant can establish that the auditor owed him a duty of care, he will then need to establish that the auditor breached the standard of care. The standard that an auditor is required to meet is not a particularly high one. In *Saif Ali v Sydney Mitchell & Co*,[176] Lord Diplock stated:

> No matter what profession it may be, the common law does not impose…any liability for damage resulting from what in the result turn out to have been errors of judgment, unless the error was such as no reasonably well-informed and competent member of that profession could have made.[177]

Further, auditors are unlikely to have breached their duty of care where they acted in accordance with a practice that a body of skilled and professional persons would regard as proper.[178]

---

175. [1990] 2 AC 605 (HL).   176. [1980] AC 198 (HL).   177. ibid 220.
178. *Lloyd Cheyham and Co Ltd v Littlejohn and Co* [1987] BCLC 303 (QB).

Limitation and relief of liability

From a legal point of view, auditors have historically occupied a vulnerable position due to their joint and several liability. The following example demonstrates this vulnerability in practice.

 The joint and several liability of auditors

> Fearne & Conway LLP is engaged to audit the accounts of Hammond plc. The directors of Hammond have been defrauding the company, but Fearne & Conway negligently fails to discover the fraud, which eventually leads to the company's insolvency. Thousands of shareholders and a number of creditors sustain significant losses, and are looking for legal redress.
>
> Fearne & Conway and the directors of Hammond plc are jointly and severally liable for the losses sustained, meaning that a claimant may elect to sue either of them for the full extent of his loss (even if one party is significantly less blameworthy). As Fearne & Conway is likely to have greater access to funds and more comprehensive insurance cover than the directors of Hammond plc, it will almost always be the auditor who is sued. The auditor can obtain a contribution from the directors, but by this time, the directors may be financially wiped out.

The auditors' vulnerability was exacerbated in that, historically, they were prohibited absolutely from contractually restricting their liability via an exclusion clause.[179] Generally, the prohibition still exists, with s 532 of the CA 2006 declaring void any provision that seeks to exempt or restrict an auditor's liability for negligence, default, breach of duty, or breach of trust. Concerted lobbying from the Big Four accounting firms resulted in the government relenting, and auditors can now limit their liability through the use of 'liability limitation agreements' (LLAs). LLAs are closely regulated in several ways:

- An LLA must not last for longer than one financial year.[180]
- An LLA is only effective if authorized by a resolution of the members.[181]
- An LLA can only limit an auditor's liability to an amount that is 'fair and reasonable in all the circumstances of the case'.[182]

Finally, it should be mentioned that the courts have a general power to relieve, wholly or partly, the liability of any auditor for negligence where they consider the auditor to have acted honestly and reasonably, and, given the circumstances of the case, that he ought fairly to be excused.[183]

Leaving office

An auditor may cease to hold office in three ways:

1. resignation;
2. removal; or
3. replacement (that is, he is not reappointed).

---

179. CA 1985, s 310 (now repealed).   180. CA 2006, s 535(1)(a).   181. ibid s 536.
182. ibid s 537(1).   183. ibid s 1157(1).

It may be the case that the auditor has ceased to hold office because he has conducted a thorough investigation of the company's affairs and has discovered inconsistencies in the reports, and the directors have removed him in an attempt to silence him. To avoid this, where an auditor ceases to hold office, he must deposit at the company's registered office a statement setting out the circumstances surrounding his cessation of office, unless he considers that there are no circumstances in connection with his ceasing to hold office that need to be brought to the attention of members or creditors of the company.[184] Failure to deposit the statement constitutes an either way offence,[185] but it will be a defence for the auditor to show that he took all reasonable steps to avoid the commission of the offence.[186]

Resignation

Section 516 provides that an auditor of a company may resign his office by depositing a notice in writing to that effect at the company's registered office, but the resignation will not be effective unless it is accompanied by the statement discussed above.

Removal

Section 510(1) and (2) provides that the members of a company may remove an auditor at any time by passing an ordinary resolution at a meeting (therefore the written resolution procedure cannot be used). Special notice (twenty-eight days) must be given of the resolution.[187] Notice of the meeting must also be provided to the auditor whose removal is sought.[188] The auditor has the right to make written representations to the company and (unless the representations are received too late) the company must send a copy of the representations to all of the members to whom notice of the resolution has been sent.[189]

An auditor removed under s 510 is not deprived of any compensation payable to him in respect of the removal.[190]

Replacement

Finally, an auditor may lose office by not being reappointed. This may happen in one of two ways:

1. a private company may pass a written resolution, the effect of which is to replace the existing auditor with a new auditor once the existing auditor's term of office has expired;[191] or

2. any company may pass an ordinary resolution, the effect of which is to replace the existing auditor with a new auditor once the existing auditor's term of office has expired.[192] Special notice (twenty-eight days) is required.[193]

In both cases, the outgoing auditor is entitled to make representations, copies of which must be circulated to the members (unless they are received too late, or an application is made alleging that the auditor has made the representations in order to secure needless publicity for defamatory matter).[194]

---

184. ibid s 519(1).   185. ibid s 519(7).   186. ibid s 519(6).   187. ibid s 511(1).
188. ibid s 511(2).   189. ibid s 511(3) and (4).   190. ibid s 510(3).
191. ibid s 514(1) and (2).   192. ibid s 515(1).   193. ibid s 515(2).
194. ibid ss 514(4), (5), and (7), and 515(4), (5), and (7).

Creditors

A company needs capital in order to function and most companies have two principal sources of capital:

🔗 Share capital is discussed in Chapter 21

- Capital obtained through the selling of shares is known as 'share capital', or 'equity capital'.
- Capital obtained through borrowing is known as 'loan capital', or 'debt capital'.

It may be the case that a company can obtain all of the capital that it needs through selling shares, but in most companies, this is not the case and extra capital will need to be obtained by borrowing it from others. Those who lend money to the company are known as its 'creditors' and they form an important class of persons. Accordingly, in this section, the company's ability to borrow and grant security for such borrowing is discussed.

A company can obtain loan capital in a number of different ways, including: (i) making use of an overdraft facility; (ii) obtaining a loan from a bank; or (iii) by mortgaging the property of the company. Virtually all companies will have a power to obtain loan capital in these various forms,[195] but some forms of loan (especially loans involving directors) may require the passing of a resolution.

The document by which a company creates or acknowledges a debt is known as a 'debenture'.[196] One popular method of raising substantial amounts of loan capital is for a company to issue debenture stocks or bonds, which are similar to shares, except that the holder is a creditor of the company and not a member.

A creditor of a company has such rights as are given by the contract creating the loan. Typically, the contract will include provisions for repayment of the loan, the payment of interest (if any), and the ability of the creditor to attend company meetings or otherwise influence company policy (generally, none). A debenture holder should be sent a copy of the company's annual accounts and reports,[197] and is entitled to ask for the company's accounts. A debenture is transferable (unless the contract creating it prohibits transfer), and a transfer may be affected by simple delivery from the current holder to the new holder (a bearer debenture), or by delivery and the completion of a transfer document.

It is not a legal requirement, but a prudent lender may insist on having some claim upon the assets of the company, so that if the company defaults on the loan, he will have some security that he can sell to repay his debt. Where the contract of loan, or a linked contract, provides that if the company fails to meet its obligations the creditor can have recourse to the company's assets and can obtain the sums outstanding by selling the assets or receiving income generated by those assets, the loan is said to be 'secured'. Should the company be wound up, the secured creditors will have the right to be paid before the unsecured creditors. The assets of the company covered by this security are said to be 'charged' and the creditor who obtained the charge is called the 'chargee'. The person (the company) that granted the charge is known as the 'surety', or 'chargor'.

---

195. *General Auction Estate and Monetary Co v Smith* [1891] 3 Ch 432 (Ch).
196. CA 2006, s 738, states that a debenture includes 'debenture stock, bonds and any other securities of a company, whether or not constituting a charge on the assets of the company'.
197. CA 2006, s 423(1)(b).

Charges

The two principal types of charge are fixed charges and floating charges. Table 20.1 highlights the principal differences between them.

TABLE 20.1 The differences between a fixed charge and a floating charge

	Fixed charge	Floating charge
Legal or equitable?	Can be legal or equitable	Equitable only
Subject matter of charge?	Usually taken over a specific, identifiable asset or assets	Usually taken over a class of assets, or the entire undertaking
Effect on the charged asset(s)?	The ability of the chargor to deal with the charged asset will usually be limited	The chargor will usually be free to deal with the charged assets
Better suited for which assets?	Better suited for assets that the company does not need to deal with	Suitable for all types of assets
Priority?	Ranks ahead of all other debts	Ranks behind fixed chargeholders, liquidation expenses and preferential creditors
Reliant on liquidator?	Not reliant on the liquidator. Fixed chargeholders can obtain the charged asset and sell it to satisfy the debt	Floating chargeholders are reliant on the liquidator to obtain satisfaction of their debt
Set aside by liquidator?	A liquidator has no power to set aside a fixed charge	A liquidator has the power to set aside certain floating charges (see p 678)

Fixed charges

A fixed charge is the simplest form of charge and is simply a charge over a fixed, identifiable asset of the company (for example, a building, vehicle, or machine). Should the company default on the loan, the creditor may look to the charged asset to satisfy the debt (usually by selling it and recovering the proceeds). A classic example of a fixed charge is a mortgage: should the mortgagor (the company) fail to keep up with the mortgage repayments, the mortgagee (the creditor) can seize possession of the mortgaged asset and sell it.

Fixed charges are very useful from the creditor's point of view because they allow it to secure its loan over an identifiable and quantifiable asset. Further, the company can only deal with the charged asset to the extent permitted by the charge contract, which will normally prohibit the company from disposing of the charged asset. Unless the charge contract provides otherwise, the company may create multiple fixed charges over one specific asset, with prior charges having priority over subsequent ones (unless the terms of the first charge provide that subsequent fixed charges can be made that take priority).

Floating charges

Whilst fixed charges provide certainty, they are also highly inflexible, in that the company's ability to deal with the charged assets is highly limited. As a result, certain assets that fluctuate (for example, raw materials) are not appropriate subjects of a fixed charge. A more flexible form of charge was therefore required and the floating charge provides this flexibility.

In *Re Yorkshire Woolcombers' Association Ltd*,[198] Romer LJ identified three factors that point to a charge being a floating charge, which also indicate the flexible nature of the charge.

1. A floating charge is normally taken over a class of assets (for example, plant, machinery, raw materials, or even the entire undertaking), as opposed to a specific asset.
2. The class of asset charged is normally constantly changing (for example, raw materials will be used and replenished).
3. A floating charge leaves the company free to use and deal with those assets.

The third factor is what makes the floating charge so flexible. A floating charge 'floats' over the class of assets charged, but is not fixed on them, and so the company is free to deal with those assets. The company may also grant subsequent fixed charges over the assets that the charge floats over, which may (depending on the terms of the floating charge) rank ahead of the floating charge.[199] However, the company cannot create a subsequent floating charge over the exact same class of assets as a prior floating charge that has priority over the first charge, unless the first chargee agrees.[200] The company may create subsequent floating charges over *part* of the assets charged by a prior floating charge and the general rule is that later floating charges rank behind earlier ones (although the terms of the first charge may provide that later charges can take priority).[201]

Upon the occurrence of certain events, the charge will cease to float and will become a fixed charge over the charged assets, and the company's ability to deal freely with the charged assets will disappear (this process is known as 'crystallization'). Certain events will always cause a floating charge automatically to crystallize:

- the appointment of an administrator or receiver by the court or the chargee;
- the company going into liquidation;[202]
- the company ceasing to carry on business as a going concern;[203]
- an event that a clause (known as an 'automatic crystallization' clause) in the security contract specifies as causing automatic crystallization.[204]

Additionally, it is common for the security contract to provide that the chargee (the creditor) can bring about crystallization by giving notice to that effect. In cases in which the chargee seeks to crystallize the charge by notice, strict compliance with the security contract is necessary for crystallization to occur.[205]

Despite their flexibility, floating charges do suffer from two notable disadvantages. First, upon winding up, a floating charge ranks behind preferential debts. Second, a floating charge attaches only to assets of the relevant class that belong to the company. The floating chargeholder may discover that the company has disposed of much, or all, of the class of charged assets when the charge crystallizes.

🔗 Winding up and preferential debts are discussed in Chapter 24

---

198. [1903] 2 Ch 284 (CA).
199. *Wheatley v Silkstone and Haigh Moor Coal Co* (1885) 29 Ch D 715 (Ch).
200. *Re Benjamin Cope and Sons Ltd* [1914] 1 Ch 800 (Ch).
201. *Re Automatic Bottle Makers Ltd* [1926] Ch 415 (CA).
202. *Wallace v Universal Automatic Machines Co* [1894] 2 Ch 547 (CA).
203. *Re Woodroffes (Musical Instruments) Ltd* [1986] Ch 366 (Ch).   204. ibid.
205. *Re Brightlife Ltd* [1987] Ch 200 (Ch).

Registration

For obvious reasons, prior to providing a company with capital, a potential creditor will want to know of any charges over the company's assets. Accordingly, successive Companies Acts have long provided for a system of registration of charges. It should be noted that the law in this area has changed significantly following Pt 25, Ch A1 of the CA 2006 coming into force in April 2013. Prior to that date, the law relating to registration was deemed to be overly complex and the new rules simplify notably the registration system.

Prior to April 2013, the parties to a charge were required to register it and limited companies were under a legal obligation to maintain, at the registered offices, a register of charges.[206] Failure to comply with these rules constituted a criminal offence. The new system does not require mandatory registration of charges by the parties, nor does it require the company to maintain a register of charges. Instead, s 859A provides that if any person interested in a charge registers at Companies House, within the period allowed for delivery, a statement of particulars[207] relating to the charge, then the Registrar of Companies must register the charge. Either party (i.e. the company or the chargeholder) or any other party interested in the charge may register the charge, but the registration will only be effective if it is made within the 'period allowed for delivery', which is 21 days beginning on the date of the creation of the charge.[208] Upon successful registration, the Registrar will issue a certificate which will provide 'conclusive evidence that the documents required…were delivered to the registrar before the end of the relevant period allowed for delivery'.[209]

As noted, prior to April 2013, companies were under an obligation to maintain a register of charges. However, the failure to maintain a register did not affect the validity of the charge concerned and criminal prosecutions were rarely sought. Accordingly, the requirement to maintain a register has been abolished, but ss 859P and 859Q do require companies to keep copies of the charge instruments and to make such documents available for inspection.

At first, it may be thought that the abolition of the requirement to register and the introduction of a discretion to register would be a significant step. However, the consequences of non-registration are so severe that, in practice, it is likely to be the case that the vast majority of registrable charges will be registered. If the statement of particulars relating to the charge is not registered at Companies House within the twenty-one-day period (or such longer period as allowed by the courts), then the security afforded to the creditor by the charge will be void against a liquidator, administrator, or creditor of the company.[210] In other words, the creditor will still be owed the sum in question, but the secured status afforded by the charge will be lost.

---

206. CA 2006, ss 861 and 876 (now repealed).
207. The content of this statement of particulars can be found in s 859D.
208. CA 2006, s 859A(4). Under s 859F, the court does have the power to extend this period in certain cases (e.g. where the court thinks it is just and equitable to do so).
209. ibid s 859I(6).
210. ibid s 859H.

Chapter conclusion

For centuries, academics have been attempting to conceptualize what a company is. A prominent theory (known as the 'new economic theory of the firm', or the 'nexus of contracts' theory) contends that a company is simply a collection of contracts and inputs deriving from various persons. Whether we regard this theory as accurate or not, it emphasizes the importance of the persons who contribute to the company's well-being. In this chapter, we have discussed five groups of person who, in differing ways, are essential to the effective running of the company. Certain groups (for example, the directors) are essential from a legal point of view, whereas others (for example, creditors) may be essential from a financial point of view.

There is one important advantage of conducting business through a company on which we only touched in this chapter—namely, the ability to raise money through investment and borrowing. How a company raises capital and—more importantly, from the perspective of the company's creditors—how the law requires levels of capital to be maintained are the focus of Chapter 21.

Key points summary

- Members make important decisions regarding the company's activities via the passing of resolutions.

- An ordinary resolution requires a simple majority (that is, over 50 per cent) to pass. A special resolution requires not less than 75 per cent to pass.

- Resolutions of public companies must be passed at general meetings, but private companies can pass most resolutions via a written resolution without the need for a meeting.

- Every private company must have at least one director and every public company must have at least two directors. The company's articles normally vest day-to-day control of the company in the board of directors.

- The company secretary is an officer of the company responsible for carrying out the administrative tasks imposed by the Companies Acts.

- A company's auditor verifies that the annual accounts provide a true and fair view of the company's financial position.

- All companies (except dormant companies and companies classified as 'small' under the Companies Act 2006) are required to appoint an auditor each financial year and the law imposes restrictions on who can act as a company's statutory auditor.

- Creditors provide a company with capital, known as 'debt capital', or 'loan capital'.

- A prudent creditor will secure the loan, usually through the creation of a charge.

- A fixed charge is taken over a tangible, identifiable asset, and allows the creditor to seize the asset and sell it should the company default. The company may not deal with the charged asset.

- A floating charge is usually taken over a class of assets that is constantly changing. Companies are free to deal with the charged assets.

Self-test questions

1. Define the following:
   (a) resolution;
   (b) annual general meeting (AGM);
   (c) shadow director;
   (d) non-executive director;
   (e) charge;
   (f) crystallization.

2. Explain the distinction between a shareholder and a member.

3. Explain the division of power between the board of directors and the members.

4. Do you agree with the position taken by the Companies Act 2006 regarding the appointment of company secretaries in private companies? Provide arguments both for and against.

5. 'The law affords auditors too much protection.' Do you agree with this statement? Provide arguments both for and against.

6. Explain the differences between a fixed and a floating charge. What are the advantages and disadvantages of each?

Further reading

Paul L Davies and Sarah Worthington, *Gower & Davies' Principles of Modern Company Law* (9th edn, Sweet & Maxwell 2012) chs 14 and 32
Chapter 14 discusses the role, structure, appointment, and removal of the board of directors; ch 32 provides a detailed, but readable, account of the benefits of taking security and the rules relating to company charges

Derek French, Stephen Mayson, and Christopher Ryan, *Mayson, French, & Ryan on Company Law* (30th edn, OUP 2013) ch 15 and pp 529–47
Chapter 15 provides a very thorough account of the role, appointment, and remuneration of the directors, and how their office may be terminated; pp 529–47 discuss the company secretary and the statutory auditor

Andrew Hicks, *'Director Disqualification: Can It Deliver?'* [2001] JBL 433
Discusses the general effectiveness of the Company Directors Disqualification Act 1986 and highlights a number of notable weaknesses

Len Sealy and Sarah Worthington, *Sealy & Worthington's Cases and Materials in Company Law* (10th edn, OUP 2013) ch 4
Provides a very readable account on the role of the members.

 Remember to visit the **Online Resource Centre** at <http://www.oxfordtextbooks.co.uk/orc/roach3e> to access the following resources on Chapter 20, 'The constituents of a company': more **practice questions** and answers; a **glossary** of key terms; **multiple-choice questions**; and **revision summaries**. Updates to the law can be found on Twitter by following **@UKBusinessLaw** or **@UKCompanyLaw**.

21 Shares and capital maintenance

- Shares and share capital
- Capital maintenance

INTRODUCTION

The vast majority of companies can function only if they can obtain enough capital. The *Oxford English Dictionary* defines 'capital' as 'of or pertaining to the original funds of a trader, company or corporation'.[1] Whilst the word 'capital' may have a broad meaning, in company law terms, it is used to refer to a very specific form of capital—namely, the capital received by the company in payment for shares. Although share capital is only one form of capital (and, in many companies, it may not even be a major source of capital), the law has always made special provision for the raising and maintaining of share capital. In many cases, breach of the provisions relating to share capital can result in significant civil and criminal liability. It is therefore of substantial importance that companies with a share capital are fully aware of the complex procedures relating to raising and maintaining share capital. This chapter will therefore examine the nature of shares and share capital, and the provisions for the maintenance of capital as they apply to companies with a share capital.

Shares and share capital

Section 540(1) of the Companies Act 2006 (CA 2006) defines a 'share' as a 'share in the company's share capital', but this definition grossly undervalues the full nature of a share. A share is an item of property,[2] known as a 'thing in action'. A 'thing' (formerly known as a 'chose') is simply an asset other than land and a 'thing in action' is simply an intangible thing,[3] which, being intangible, can only be claimed or enforced by legal action, as opposed to by taking possession of it.[4] A share has no physical existence, but rather confers a number of rights and liabilities upon its holder, including providing evidence of the existence of a contract between the shareholder and the company. As shares are items of property, they

---

1. See the Oxford English Dictionary Online <http://www.oed.com>.
2. CA 2006, s 541.
3. Tangible things are known as 'things in possession'.
4. *Torkington v Magee* [1902] 2 KB 427 (KB) 430 (Channell J).

can be transferred from person to person, with the process of transfer subject to the rules specified in the company's articles, which may, in the case of a private company, restrict transferability.[5] A share does not give a shareholder a proprietary right over the assets of the company.[6] A shareholder may own 50 per cent of the shares in a company, but he is not entitled to 50 per cent of the assets, nor can he demand 50 per cent of the profits. Shares in quoted companies are used principally as an investment: the investor is looking for income or capital growth, and may not expect to exercise any significant control over the actions of the directors. Shareholders in private companies, many of which are small and/or family-run, may well be involved in management or may otherwise work for the company. For such companies, the shares are more significant as a measure of the degree of control that an individual has over the company.

Classifications of share capital

The law relating to share capital and capital maintenance abounds with terminology, which can render the subject complex. Before we can discuss the legal nature of shares and the capital maintenance regime, it is essential to explain the various classifications of share capital.

Nominal value

All shares in a limited company with a share capital are required to have a fixed 'nominal' value,[7] (also known as 'par' value) and failure to attach a nominal value to an allotment of shares will render the allotment void.[8] The nominal value represents a notional value of the shares' worth, but, in reality, the nominal value may bear no resemblance whatsoever to the share's actual value. The nominal value of a share represents the minimum price for which the share can be allotted and also sets the level of liability of a shareholder if the company is wound up. In other words, once the shareholder had paid the nominal value, he cannot usually be required to contribute more.

Whilst shares cannot be allotted for less than their nominal value, it is common for shares to be sold for more than their nominal value and the excess is known as the 'share premium'. Where the company in question is a public company, the premium must be fully paid at the time of allotment.[9]

The prohibition on allotting shares at a discount is discussed at p 609

Authorized share capital

Prior to the CA 2006, companies were required to state in their memoranda the total nominal value of shares that may be issued by the company and this value would represent the company's authorized share capital.

---

5. For example, art 26(5) of the model articles for private companies limited by shares allows the directors to refuse to register a share transfer.
6. *Borland's Trustee v Steel Bros & Co Ltd* [1901] 1 Ch 279 (Ch).
7. CA 2006, s 542(1). It follows that unlimited companies can issue shares with no nominal value.
8. ibid s 542(2).
9. ibid s 586(1). One quarter of the nominal value of the shares must also be paid at the time of allotment.

Authorized share capital

MicroTech plc has an authorized share capital of £1 million. Thus, the maximum number of shares that it could allot could not have a combined nominal value of over £1 million. So, for example, it could allot:

1. a million shares with a nominal value of £1; or

2. 500,000 shares with a nominal value of £2, etc.

In practice, the requirement to state the authorized share capital was largely pointless. Companies would choose an arbitrary and inflated figure, confident that it would never be reached. Even if it were, passing an ordinary resolution could increase the authorized share capital. Accordingly, companies incorporated under the CA 2006 are not required to state the authorized share capital, and such companies can simply create and allot as many shares as they wish. However, companies that were incorporated under prior Companies Acts and have retained their authorized share capital provisions, and companies incorporated under the CA 2006 that have chosen to include an authorized share capital clause in their constitution, will be bound by the amount stated.

Issued and unissued share capital

The authorized share capital used to represent the maximum nominal value of shares that could be allotted. The nominal value of the shares that actually has been allotted is known as the 'issued' share capital.

 Issued share capital

BioCom plc has issued 3 million shares with a nominal value of £3 each. Accordingly, its issued share capital is £9 million. Prior to the CA 2006, a company's issued share capital could never exceed its authorized share capital.

'Unissued' share capital represented the difference between the authorized share capital and the issued share capital (i.e. the nominal value of shares that could still be allotted). With the abolition of authorized share capital, the concept of unissued share capital has also been abolished for those companies that have no authorized share capital.

Paid-up, called-up, and uncalled share capital

Shareholders may not be required to pay fully for their shares upon allotment (for example, as noted, the shares in public companies need only have a quarter of their nominal value paid at the time of allotment). Shares may be partly paid for at allotment (that is, the payment made is less than the nominal value), with the remainder to be paid at a later date. The combined total of the nominal share capital that has actually been paid is known as the 'paid-up' share capital.

Paid-up share capital

TechSoft Ltd has allotted and issued a million shares with a nominal value of £1 each (its issued share capital is therefore £1 million). The company allows allottees to pay 50 pence on allotment and the remainder at a later date to be specified by the company. All of the million shares are allotted and purchased, and every shareholder pays the required 50 pence per share only. No shareholder pays more than 50 pence at allotment. The paid-up capital is therefore £500,000.

If shares are not fully paid for, the company may call for any outstanding amounts to be paid, or the company may require payment in instalments and an instalment may have become due. The paid-up share capital plus the amount called for or the instalment due is known as the 'called-up' share capital.

Eg **Called-up share capital**

Following on from the TechSoft example, the company then calls for an additional 25 pence per share to be paid. The called-up share capital is therefore £750,000 — that is:

$$£500,000 + (1,000,000 \times £0.25)$$

Paid-up share capital x (number of shares issued x amount called for)

Note that the amount called for forms part of the called-up capital irrespective of whether it is actually paid or not.

The difference between the company's issued capital and its called-up capital is known as the 'uncalled' share capital.

The issuing and allotment of shares

There are two principal ways in which a person can become a shareholder in a company:

- as shares are freely transferable (subject to any limitations contained in the articles),[10] he can become a shareholder by purchasing shares from an existing shareholder; or
- he can become a shareholder by purchasing from the company new shares that it has created.

The latter process is considerably more complex, and the remainder of this section will examine the various rules relating to the allotment and issuing of shares. The terms 'allotment' and 'issue' are often used interchangeably, but there is a distinction:

- Shares are allotted 'when a person acquires the unconditional right to be included in the company's register of members in respect of the shares'.[11]

---

10. ibid s 544(1).   11. ibid s 558.

- Shares are issued when the person's name is actually entered into the register of members.[12] From this, it follows that the issuing of shares takes place after they have been allotted.

The power to allot shares

The directors must not allot shares except in accordance with the procedures set out in the CA 2006, and any director who knowingly contravenes, permits, or authorizes an unlawful allotment commits an offence triable either way,[13] although the allotment itself will remain valid.[14] Where a private company has only one class of share, the power to allot shares is vested in the directors, subject to any limitations contained in the company's articles.[15] Regarding any other form of company, whether public or private, the directors may only allot shares if they are authorized to do so by the company's articles or by a resolution of the company.[16] This authority can be general or for the purposes of a particular allotment, and can be subject to conditions or unconditional.[17] All forms of authority are, however, subject to the following limitations and requirements:

- The authorization must state the maximum number of shares that can be allotted under it.[18]
- The authorization must specify a date on which it is to expire and this date cannot be longer than five years after authorization is granted. Authorization can be renewed, but the renewal is also subject to the five-year maximum.[19]
- The authorization can be revoked or varied at any time by passing an ordinary resolution.[20]
- Any resolution granting, varying, or revoking authority must be sent to the Registrar of Companies within fifteen days of its passing.[21] Failure to do so constitutes a summary offence.[22]

Once the allotment has taken place, the company must, within two months, complete and have ready for delivery share certificates for all of the shares allotted,[23] unless the conditions of allotment provide that no certificate will be issued, or the shares are to be allotted in uncertificated form through a central securities depository such as Euroclear. The share certificate provides *prima facie* evidence that the person named in the certificate has title to the shares specified in the certificate,[24] but this can be rebutted if evidence can be adduced establishing that the bearer's title is defective. For example, the company might seek to disclaim all liability for a share certificate on the basis that the person who had issued it on behalf of the company was not authorized so to do,[25] or that the share certificate was forged.

When exercising the power to allot shares, directors are under a statutory duty to exercise this power for the purpose for which it was conferred.[26] As will be seen, many cases involving improper uses of directors' powers relate to the allotment of shares.

The 'proper purpose' doctrine is discussed at p 624

---

12. *National Westminster Bank v IRC* [1995] 1 AC 119 (HL).
13. CA 2006, s 549(4) and (5).   14. ibid s 549(6).
15. ibid s 550. The model articles contain no such limitations.   16. ibid s 551(1).
17. ibid s 551(2).   18. ibid s 551(3)(a).   19. ibid s 551(3)(b) and (4)(a).
20. ibid s 551(4)(b).   21. ibid ss 30(1) and 551(9).   22. ibid s 30(2) and (3).
23. ibid s 769.   24. ibid s 768(1).   25. *Ruben v Great Fingall Consolidated* [1906] AC 439 (HL).
26. CA 2006, s 171(b).

Pre-emption rights

An inevitable consequence of a new allotment of shares is the dilution of the share-holdings of existing shareholders, or the possibility of control being transferred to a new shareholder. To combat these consequences, existing shareholders are given a right of pre-emption, whereby any new allotment of shares must be offered first to the existing shareholders in proportion with their existing shareholdings. The share-holders' pre-emption rights are, however, limited in three ways. First, pre-emption rights only apply to the allotment of equity securities, defined as ordinary shares, or the right to subscribe to, or convert securities into, ordinary shares.[27] Second, pre-emption rights do not apply to an allotment of **bonus shares**,[28] or shares to be held under an employees' share scheme.[29] Third, pre-emption rights do not apply where shares are to be paid up, wholly or partly, otherwise than in cash.[30]

➡️ **bonus shares:** shares allotted to existing shareholders and paid for out of the company's distributable profits

Pre-emption rights can be completely excluded or disapplied in certain situations, including:

- private companies may include a provision in their articles excluding pre-emption rights;[31]
- the directors of a private company with only one class of shares may allot shares ignoring the pre-emption rights of the members if they have been so authorized by the articles or by special resolution;[32]
- a general power of disapplication is given to directors of any company if they are generally authorized by s 551 to allot shares and the power of disapplication is contained in the articles, or is granted to the directors by passing a special resolution.[33]

An allotment that contravenes the pre-emption rights of existing shareholders is still valid, but the company and every officer who knowingly authorized or permitted the contravention are jointly and severally liable to compensate the shareholders who would have benefited from the pre-emptive offer.[34]

Prohibition on allotting shares at a discount

The common law has long held that shares cannot be allotted at a discount (that is, below their nominal value)[35] and this general prohibition can now be found in s 580 of the CA 2006, which provides that a contract that purports to allot shares at a discount is void. Where discounted shares actually are allotted, the allottee is liable to pay to the company an amount equal to the discount including interest.[36] In addition, the company and every officer in default commit an either way offence.[37]

In relation to private companies, however, the effectiveness of the prohibition in s 580 is seriously weakened by the fact that shares do not have to be paid for in cash. Section 582(1) provides that shares can be paid for in 'money or money's worth (including goodwill and know-how)', and it is reasonably common to pay for shares with goods, property, services, or even by transferring an existing business to a company in return for shares (as Mr Salomon did). By overvaluing the non-cash payment, the shares can effectively be issued at a discount. This problem could be

🔗 The *Salomon* case is discussed at p 546

---

27. ibid s 560(1).   28. ibid s 564.   29. ibid s 566.   30. ibid s 565.
31. ibid s 567(1). The model articles contain no such provision.   32. ibid s 569(1).
33. ibid s 570(1).   34. ibid s 563(2).
35. *Ooregum Gold Mining Co of India Ltd v Roper* [1892] AC 125 (HL).
36. CA 2006, s 580(2).
37. ibid s 590.

remedied if the courts were willing to query the value of the non-cash consideration, but the courts have stated that, as regards private companies, they will only inquire where the consideration is illusory or manifestly inadequate.[38] As a result, it is likely to be rather easy for a private company to issue shares at a discount if it so chooses.

Regarding public companies, the rules are much more stringent. First, public companies cannot accept payment for shares in the form of services.[39] Second, where a public company allots shares for non-cash consideration, that consideration must have been independently valued[40] as being equivalent to the value of the amount paid up on the shares. An independent person eligible for appointment as the company's auditor must have made the valuation.[41]

Classes of share

Most companies will only have one class of shareholder, who will hold 'ordinary shares', with the usual rights attributable to a shareholder. However, provided that the articles so authorize, companies are free to have different classes of share, conferring different rights upon the holder,[42] examples of which could include:

- differing nominal values for different classes of share;[43]
- shares with increased or decreased voting rights (shares that entitled the holder to receive a dividend if declared and to surplus assets on winding up, but do not entitle the holder to vote at meetings, are known as 'non-voting ordinary shares');
- shares that provide that the holder will only receive a dividend once the ordinary shareholders have received a certain amount (these are known as 'deferred shares').

A common form of share class is the preference share. The precise rights granted to preference shareholders will change from company to company, but preference shares normally provide the holder with preferential claims on any surplus assets on winding up and/or entitle the holder to a predetermined percentage dividend before anything is payable to the ordinary shareholders.

The rights attached to a particular class of shares are known as 'class rights' and shareholders of one class may attempt to deprive shareholders of another class of some beneficial class right (especially if the right grants some form of benefit upon the latter class of shareholders). Accordingly, the variation of class rights will only be effective if it complies with the requirements laid down in the CA 2006.

The variation of class rights

Before looking at the procedures for varying class rights, it is important to define what constitutes a 'variation'. It is clear that **abrogation** of a right constitutes variation. Section 630(5) provides that '[a]ny amendment of a provision contained in a company's articles for the variation of the rights attached to a class of shares, or the insertion of any such provision into the articles, is itself to be treated as a variation of

➡ abrogation: abolishing, or putting an end to

---

38. *Re Wragg Ltd* [1897] 1 Ch 796 (CA).
39. CA 2006, s 585(1).   40. ibid s 593(1).   41. ibid s 1150(1).
42. Differing classes of shares are permissible under the model articles for private companies limited by shares (art 22) and the model articles for public companies (art 43). In both cases, an ordinary resolution is required.
43. *Re Scandinavian Bank Group plc* [1988] Ch 87 (Ch).

those rights'. Whether or not an alteration constitutes a variation is a matter for the courts, and the courts are generally reluctant to hold that an alteration is a variation, as the following case demonstrates.

 Re Mackenzie and Co Ltd [1916] 2 Ch 450 (Ch)

FACTS: The company had issued preference shares, each with a nominal value of £20. Owners of these preference shares were entitled to a 4 per cent dividend on the amount paid up and, because the preference shares were fully paid up, this worked out at 80 pence per share. The articles were amended to reduce the nominal value of the preference shares to £12, thereby reducing the dividend to 48 pence per share.

HELD: The alteration of the articles did not constitute a variation of the class right, because the right had remained the same (that is, 4 per cent of the amount paid up).

COMMENT: This case demonstrates that, provided that the right remains the same, an alteration will not be classified as a variation if its effect is to render the right less valuable or even to render the right worthless.[44]

There are only two ways in which class rights can be varied. First, where the company's articles contain a class rights variation clause, a variation is valid if it complies with that clause.[45] Second, where the articles contain no variation clause, a variation will be valid if it is:

- approved by the written consent of the holders of three-quarters in nominal value of the issued shares of the relevant class (not merely three-quarters of those voting);[46] or
- approved by the passing of a special resolution at a meeting of holders of that class.

Where class rights are varied, the holders of not less than 15 per cent of the class of shares in question may apply to the court to have the variation cancelled, provided that they did not consent in writing to the variation, or vote in favour of the resolution approving the variation.[47] The variation will have no effect until it has been confirmed by the court.[48] The court must refuse to confirm a variation if it would unfairly prejudice the shareholders of the relevant class.[49] The court's decision is final and once a variation has been made, the company must, within one month of the variation, inform the Registrar of Companies of the variation.[50] Failure to do so constitutes a summary offence.

Minimum capital requirements imposed on public companies

Private companies with a share capital are not subject to a minimum share capital requirement and can accordingly be set up by issuing a single 1 pence share to a single member. Conversely, a public company cannot conduct business until it has

---

44. *Dimbula Valley (Ceylon) Tea Co Ltd v Laurie* [1961] Ch 353 (Ch).
45. CA 2006, s 630(2)(a). The model articles contain no such clauses.   46. ibid s 630(4).
47. ibid s 633(2).   48. ibid s 633(3).   49. ibid s 633(5).   50. ibid s 637(1).

been issued with a trading certificate,[51] and the Registrar will not issue a trading certificate unless he is satisfied that the nominal value of the company's allotted share capital is not less than the authorized minimum, which is currently set at £50,000.[52] A company that conducts business or exercises borrowing powers without a trading certificate commits an offence triable either way, and so does every officer in default.

The rationale behind the imposition of minimum capital requirements upon public companies is to attempt to ensure that there is always a minimum level of capital available to satisfy the company's debts. However, it is widely acknowledged that, in practice, the minimum capital requirement does little to aid creditors for three reasons:

1. The authorized minimum is simply too low to offer creditors any real security, and has been described as 'derisory'[53] and 'miniscule compared to the size of the debts of most public companies'.[54]

2. The shares do not even need to be fully paid up. Only one quarter of the nominal value and the whole of the premium need be paid up at the time of allotment.[55]

3. The authorized minimum is measured at the time that the company wishes to commence trading, but little account is taken of the possibility that it will be reduced once trading commences. Once the company has commenced trading, the only safeguard imposed is that should the company's assets fall to half or less than its called-up share capital, then the directors must call a general meeting to consider what steps, if any, should be taken.[56] By the time that the assets reach this level, it is highly likely that some form of insolvency procedure is already in place, thereby rendering the general meeting largely useless.

🔗 The various insolvency procedures are discussed in Chapter 24

Capital maintenance

Having obtained share capital via the allotment of shares, the law requires that the company 'maintain' that capital by not distributing it in unauthorized ways. The principal reason for this is that it is the company's capital to which the creditors look for payment in the event of a winding up, and any depreciation in the company's capital could increase the risk of the company defaulting. Of course, creditors appreciate that the company's capital will increase and decrease in the normal course of business based on the company's fortunes, but the creditors will not expect the company to return share capital to the shareholders. Accordingly, the law generally prohibits companies from returning capital to their shareholders, thereby providing protection to the creditors and helping to ensure that certain assets remain inviolate for the payment of the company's creditors. These rules are known collectively as the 'capital maintenance regime' and the principal rules are explained below.

---

51. ibid s 761(1).   52. ibid s 763(1).
53. Paul L Davies and Sarah Worthington, *Gower & Davies' Principles of Modern Company Law* (9th edn, Sweet & Maxwell 2012) 280.
54. Louise Gullifer and Jennifer Payne, *Corporate Finance Law: Principles and Policy* (Hart Publishing 2011) 127.   55. CA 2006, s 586(1).   56. ibid s 656.

The restructuring of share capital

A company may seek to restructure its issued share capital in a number of ways, including:

- increasing its share capital by allotting new shares;
- subdivision (that is, taking existing shares and subdividing them into shares of a smaller nominal value than the existing shares, thereby creating an overall increase in the number of shares);[57]
- consolidation (that is, consolidating existing shares into shares with a larger nominal value than the existing shares, thereby producing an overall decrease in the number of shares).[58]

None of these restructurings of capital adversely affect the level of share capital and therefore pose no danger to the creditors' interests. Accordingly, these are matters to be decided on by the shareholders alone. A reduction of issued share capital does, however, have the potential to affect the creditors' interests adversely and is therefore regulated by statute. The general position is that a reduction of issued share capital is unlawful unless authorized by ss 641–53 of the CA 2006.[59] That statute permits a company to reduce its share capital in recognition of the fact that a reduction can be beneficial in certain circumstances and, whilst the CA 2006 does not limit the ways in which a company can reduce its capital, s 641(4) provides a non-exhaustive list of examples of ways it can do so.[60]

Under s 135 of the now-repealed Companies Act 1985 (CA 1985), a company could only reduce its share capital if (i) the articles permitted a reduction; (ii) a special resolution was obtained authorizing the reduction; and (iii) the court approved the reduction. However, requiring private companies to obtain court approval imposed substantial regulatory burdens on private companies, as well as the courts. Accordingly, the CA 2006 no longer requires private companies to obtain court approval and provides for two methods of effecting a reduction.

Special resolution and court confirmation

The first method of effecting a reduction of capital is available to all types of company, and provides that a reduction is valid where the members authorize the reduction by passing a special resolution and the company then applies to the court for an order confirming the reduction.[61] Where a public company wishes to reduce its share capital below the authorized minimum discussed earlier (£50,000), then an expedited procedure is provided, allowing the public company to re-register as a private company without the usually required special resolution.[62]

The requirement of court approval is the source of creditor protection, because the courts' principal concern is to protect the interest of the company's creditors. In addition to the interests of creditors, the court will also take into account the interests of existing shareholders, with two factors being of particular importance:

1. The reduction should be fair and equitable between the different classes of shareholder,[63] and between shareholders of the same class,[64] unless such shareholders consent to be treated differently.

---

57. ibid s 618.   58. ibid.   59. ibid s 617(2)(b).
60. ibid s 641(3) provides that, subject to s 641(2), a company may reduce its share capital in any way.
61. ibid s 641(1)(b).
62. ibid s 651. Unless the public company re-registers as private, the Registrar must not register the reduction unless the court so directs (s 650(2)).
63. *Poole v National Bank of China Ltd* [1907] AC 229 (HL).
64. *British and American Trustee and Finance Corporation Ltd v Couper* [1894] AC 399 (HL).

2. The company should ensure that, when explaining to the shareholders why a reduction is desired, any information presented is accurate and enables the shareholders to make an informed choice.[65]

Special resolution supported by a solvency statement

The second method of effecting a reduction of capital is available to private companies only and does not require court approval. A private company can effect a reduction of capital by passing a special resolution authorizing the reduction, supported by a statement of solvency from the directors.[66] This statement must be made no more than fifteen days before the special resolution is passed[67] and will provide that each of the directors has formed the opinion that:

- there is no ground on which the company could then be found to be unable to pay (or otherwise discharge) its debts; and
- the company will be able to pay (or otherwise discharge) its debts as they fall due during the year immediately following the date of the statement. If it is intended to commence the winding up of the company within twelve months of the date of the statement, each director must be of the opinion that the company will be able to pay (or otherwise discharge) its debts in full within twelve months of the commencement of the winding up.[68]

Within fifteen days of the resolution being passed, a copy of the statement, along with a statement of capital (which will indicate the share capital of the company following the reduction) and a copy of the resolution must be delivered to the Registrar of Companies.[69] The resolution will not take effect until the Registrar registers these documents.[70]

If the directors make a solvency statement without reasonable grounds for the opinions expressed within it and the statement is delivered to the Registrar of Companies for registration, every director who is in default commits an offence triable either way,[71] although this will not affect the validity of the resolution.

The acquisition of own shares

The common law absolutely prohibited companies from purchasing their own existing shares, on the ground that such a purchase would result in a return of capital to the shareholders and a consequent reduction in the capital available to pay creditors.[72] Section 658 of the CA 2006 continues to take a strict approach and provides that a company cannot purchase its own shares, except in accordance with the methods set down in the CA 2006. Where s 658 is contravened, the purported acquisition is void, and the company and every officer of the company who is in default commits a criminal offence triable either way.

The CA 2006 provides for several exceptions to the general prohibition, including the following.

Redeemable shares

A limited company has the power to issue redeemable shares (that is, shares that are issued, but which can be redeemed by the company at the insistence of either

65. *Re Jupiter House Investments (Cambridge) Ltd* [1985] 1 WLR 975 (Ch).   66. CA 2006, s 641(1)(a).
67. ibid s 642(1)(a).   68. ibid s 643(1).   69. ibid s 644(1).   70. ibid s 644(4).
71. ibid s 643(4).   72. *Trevor v Whitworth* (1887) 12 App Cas 409 (HL).

the company or the shareholder),[73] but a public company can only issue redeemable shares if its articles so provide.[74] Private companies require no authorization by the articles,[75] but the articles may exclude or restrict redeemable shares being issued.[76]

The issuing and redemption of redeemable shares is subject to a number of restrictions:

- Redeemable shares can only be issued at a time when the company has issued shares that are not redeemable.[77]
- Redeemable shares can only be redeemed if they are fully paid up[78]—the company cannot purchase unissued or partly paid-up redeemable shares.
- When redeeming shares, the company must pay fully for them at the time of redemption, unless the terms of redemption provide for a later date.[79]
- The redeemable shares of public companies must be paid for out of distributable profits of the company, or out of the proceeds of a fresh issue of shares made for the purposes of redemption.[80] This will ensure that the company's share capital is not reduced by the redemption.

Shares that are redeemed are treated as cancelled.[81] Within one month of the redemption, the company must inform the Registrar of Companies of the redemption. Failure to notify the Registrar constitutes a criminal offence by the company and every officer in default.

Purchase by a company of its own shares

Whilst issuing redeemable shares does provide the company with the ability to acquire its own shares, its flexibility is limited in two ways: first, the company will need to decide, prior to issue, that the shares are to be redeemable; second, the company can only then purchase those additional shares. What companies wanted was a general power to purchase any shares; such a power was introduced by the Companies Act 1981 and can now be found in s 690 of the CA 2006. However, a number of general restrictions are imposed, including:

- Only limited companies may purchase their own shares.
- The company may not purchase its own shares if to do so would result in there being no member holding any shares other than redeemable shares or **treasury shares**.[82]
- The shares purchased must be fully paid and where the company purchases its own shares, the shares must be fully paid for on purchase.[83]
- Authorization in the articles for the purchase is not required (as was required under the CA 1985), but the articles can restrict or exclude the company's ability to purchase its own shares.[84]
- Purchase of the shares must be paid for out of distributable profits, or out of the proceeds of a fresh issue of shares made for the purpose of financing the purchase.[85] As is discussed later, however, there is a procedure whereby private companies can purchase their own shares out of capital.

➡ **treasury shares:** shares held in the company's own treasury

---

73. CA 2006, s 684(1).

74. ibid s 684(3). Article 43(2) of the model articles for public companies permits public companies to issue redeemable shares.

75. Article 22(2) of the model articles for private companies limited by shares provides such authorization.

76. CA 2006, s 684(2).   77. ibid s 684(4).   78. ibid s 686(1).   79. ibid s 686(2) and (3).

80. ibid s 687(2).   81. ibid s 688.   82. ibid s 690(2).   83. ibid s 691.

84. ibid s 690(1)(b).   85. ibid s 692(2).

Additional requirements are imposed that depend on whether the purchase is to be a market purchase or an off-market purchase. As market purchases are conducted through a recognized investment exchange with its own safeguards, they are less regulated by the CA 2006 than are off-market purchases.

Irrespective of whether the purchase is market or off-market, once the purchase has been made, the company must, within twenty-eight days beginning on the date on which the shares were delivered, deliver to the Registrar a return indicating the number and nominal value of the shares sold. Where the company is public, it must also indicate the aggregate amount paid by the company for the shares, and the maximum and minimum prices paid.[86] Failure to deliver the return to the Registrar constitutes an either way offence by the company and every officer in default.[87]

Redeeming or purchasing shares out of capital

Normally, a company that wishes to purchase its own shares must, in order to avoid returning capital to the shareholders, pay for such shares out of distributable profits or via a fresh issue of shares. Private companies may, however, often lack distributable profits and may not wish to issue new shares. The only other option formerly was to reduce share capital, but, prior to the 2006 Act, court approval was required, thereby making the process potentially expensive. Given that, in many private companies, the capital maintenance regime is of limited practical usefulness, it was decided to permit private limited companies to redeem or purchase their own shares out of capital, and such a power is now provided for by s 709, but such a payment will only be valid if a number of stringent requirements are complied with.[88]

Financial assistance to acquire shares

Under the CA 1985, all companies were generally prohibited from providing financial assistance to another to purchase it shares. Exceptions existed, but they were narrow and strictly regulated. The problem that arose was that the prohibition served to prevent perfectly innocent and beneficial transactions, especially as regards private companies. Accordingly, for private companies, the prohibition on providing financial assistance has been abolished. Sections 678 and 679 preserves the prohibition for public companies, and provides that a public company may not provide financial assistance for the acquisition of its own shares, or for the acquisition of the shares in a private company of which the public company is a subsidiary. Contravention of the prohibition constitutes an either way offence by the company and any director in default.[89] Any agreement to provide financial assistance unlawfully will be unenforceable[90] and any assistance received may also be held on trust for the company where the recipient knew or ought to have known of the illegality.[91] Additionally, any directors involved may be found to have breached their duties and could be subject to a disqualification order.[92]

The prohibition, however, is not absolute and there are instances in which a public company can provide financial assistance, including:

- Financial assistance given in good faith in the interests of the company is permitted where (i) the principal purpose of the assistance is not for the acquisition of

86. ibid s 707(4).   87. ibid s 707(7).   88. ibid ss 709–723.   89. ibid s 680(1).
90. *Brady v Brady* [1989] AC 755 (HL).
91. *Belmont Finance Corporation v Williams Furniture Ltd* [1980] 1 All ER 393 (CA).
92. See e.g. *Re Continental Assurance Co of London plc* [1997] 1 BCLC 48 (Ch).

shares; or (ii) where the purpose of the assistance is to acquire shares, but it is part of some larger purpose of the company.[93]

- Certain transactions are excluded from the prohibition, including (i) the distribution of the company's assets by way of dividend lawfully made, or by way of a distribution in the course of the company's winding up; (ii) a reduction in capital; and (iii) a redemption or purchase of shares.[94]

- Certain transactions are excluded from the prohibition, providing that the assistance does not reduce its net assets, or is paid out of distributable profits. These transactions include (i) the provision of financial assistance where the lending of money is part of the ordinary business of the company; and (ii) employees' share schemes.[95]

Distributions

As is discussed at p XXX, a director is under a duty to promote the success of the company for the benefit of its members.[96] The imposition of such a duty is recognition of the fact that the principal purpose of most commercial companies is to make a profit. In turn, the shareholders will expect to receive a share in the profits, usually via the distribution of a payment known as a 'dividend'. Dividends are simply the distribution, usually in cash,[97] of profits to the shareholders, usually at a fixed amount per share. Accordingly, the more shares held, the greater the dividend payment. Normally, companies will retain a portion of the profits to reinvest in the company and will distribute the remainder in the form of dividends, but it is important to note that, until the company is wound up, companies are not under a legal obligation to distribute profits to their shareholders[98] and that therefore shareholders have no 'right' to a dividend. A failure to pay a dividend could, however, constitute unfairly prejudicial conduct,[99] or possibly justify winding up on just and equitable grounds.[100]

A dividend can only be paid if it is properly declared and authorized, with the applicable procedures being found in the company's articles. The normal procedure contained in the model articles[101] is as follows.

These remedies are discussed in Chapter 23

1. The directors must first recommend the amount of profits to be distributed by way of dividend.

2. The company will then 'declare' a dividend by passing an ordinary resolution. This resolution cannot be passed until the directors have made their recommendation and the shareholders cannot declare an amount greater than that recommended by the directors (although they can declare a lesser amount). Once the dividend has been declared, it becomes a debt of the company owed to the shareholders.

3. The responsibility for paying out the dividend in accordance with the rights of the shareholders is placed upon the directors.

---

93. CA 2006, s 678(2).   94. ibid s 681.   95. ibid s 682.   96. ibid s 172.

97. Non-cash payments may only be made if the articles permit (*Wood v Odessa Waterworks Co* (1889) 42 ChD 636 (Ch)). The model articles allow for non-cash distributions.

98. *Burland v Earle* [1902] AC 83 (PC).   99. *Re Sam Weller & Sons Ltd* [1990] Ch 682 (Ch).

100. *Re a Company, ex p Glossop* [1988] BCLC 570 (Ch).

101. See article 30 of the model articles for companies limited by shares, and art 70 of the model articles for public companies.

Profits available for distribution

From a capital maintenance perspective, the key restriction is established in s 830(1), which provides that a 'company may only make a distribution out of profits available for the purpose', with such profits defined as 'its accumulated, realised profits, so far as not previously utilised by distribution or capitalisation, less its accumulated, realised losses, so far as not previously written off in a reduction or reorganisation of capital duly made'.[102] Two words used in this definition deserve elaboration.

- **Accumulated** This indicates that when determining 'profits available for the purpose' of paying a dividend, the company cannot ignore previous years' trading performance and must include any losses sustained in previous years. This is to prevent a situation in which a company has several years' poor performance, but then has a profitable year and pays out dividends, even though the profitable year has not replaced the losses sustained in previous years.

- **Realised** The inclusion of the word 'realised' is to prevent the company paying a dividend based on estimated profits. Companies used to be able to pay out dividends based on estimated profits;[103] if those profits were never to materialize, the payment would have come out of capital. Companies are now required to determine profits based on gains and losses realized. 'Realised' is to be defined in accordance with generally accepted accounting principles,[104] and realized profits are therefore defined as profits 'in the form of either cash or of other assets, the ultimate cash realisation of which can be assessed with reasonable certainty'.[105]

Payment by the company of an unlawful distribution, or part of one, to one of its shareholders can result in several consequences, although the CA 2006 itself only provides for one—namely, that if the shareholder, at the time of the distribution, knew or had reasonable grounds to believe that the distribution was unlawful, he is required to repay it, or part of it, to the company.[106] The directors who authorized the payment are liable under the common law to repay the money to the company if they knew, or ought to have known, that the distribution was illegal.[107] This is a substantial deterrent. For example, in *Bairstow v Queens Moat Houses plc*,[108] the directors of the company were required to pay back an unlawful distribution of £26.7 million plus an additional £15.2 million in interest. If an unlawful distribution is made based on erroneous accounts, the company's auditor, if negligent in failing to identify the error, is also liable under the common law to the company for such negligence and is liable to repay the amount of the unlawful distribution.[109]

It is clear that these rules are primarily designed to protect creditors by prohibiting a distribution out of capital. The creditors have no right to commence an action to restrain a wrongful distribution,[110] however, although they can seek to have the company wound up.

---

102. CA 2006, s 830(2).   103. *Dimbula Valley (Ceylon) Tea Co Ltd v Laurie* [1961] Ch 353 (Ch).
104. CA 2006, s 853(4).
105. Accounting Standards Board, *Financial Reporting Standard 18: Accounting Policies* (ASB 2000) [28].
106. CA 2006, s 847(1) and (2).   107. *Re National Funds Assurance Co* (1878) 10 Ch D 118 (Ch).
108. [2001] EWCA Civ 712, [2002] BCC 91.
109. *Leeds Estate Building and Investment Co v Shepherd* (1887) 36 Ch D 787 (Ch).
110. *Mills v Northern Rly of Buenos Ayres* (1870) 5 Ch App 621 (CA).

Chapter conclusion

There is little doubt that the rules relating to the raising and maintenance of share capital have been simplified by the CA 2006, but the rules are still complex and highly technical. Such complexity may be justified if the rules were to provide effective protection for creditors, but it has been doubted that the rules offer much protection in practice. The concept of the nominal value of a share has been heavily criticized and might well have been abolished were it not a requirement of the Second Company Law Directive.[111] The minimum capital requirement imposed on public companies is of little practical use and private companies easily sidestep the rules prohibiting the allotment of shares at a discount. For public companies, effecting a reduction in capital, even for a wholly sensible and beneficial reason, is still an onerous undertaking. A company wishing to acquire its own shares will need to ensure that a raft of procedures is complied with and the law relating to distributions requires a serious layperson's knowledge of accounting principles. Whilst it cannot be doubted that creditor protection is an essential feature of any system of company law, the extent to which the capital maintenance regime actually protects the interests of creditors is open to discussion.

 Key points summary

- Shares are items of personal property that provide their holders with certain rights, but provide no proprietary rights over the company's assets.

- All shares have a fixed nominal value, and this can be used to calculate the company's issued capital, paid-up capital, called-up capital, and uncalled capital.

- Generally, when a company allots shares, it must first offer them to existing shareholders (this is known as a 'pre-emption right').

- A public company will not be issued with a trading certificate unless the nominal value of its allotted share capital is not less than £50,000.

- All companies may reduce their capital by passing a special resolution, which is then confirmed by the court. Private companies need not obtain court approval provided that a statement of solvency supports the special resolution.

- Companies are generally prohibited from purchasing their own shares, but may do so where the shares are redeemable shares, or where the procedures relating to market and off-market purchases are complied with.

- Subject to certain exceptions, public companies are normally prohibited from providing financial assistance for the acquisition of their shares. Private companies are free to provide such financial assistance.

- Distributions (for example, dividends) must be made only out of profits available for the purpose.

---

111. Council Directive (EC) 77/91/EEC.

Self-test questions

1. Define the following:
   (a) thing in action;
   (b) nominal value;
   (c) pre-emption rights;
   (d) preference shares;
   (e) redeemable shares;
   (f) dividend.

2. Explain the distinction between:
   (a) called-up and uncalled share capital;
   (b) the allotment and issue of shares;
   (c) the subdivision and consolidation of shares.

3. MultiSoft plc was incorporated in 2006. Its memorandum states that it has an authorized share capital of £2 million. Since then, it has issued 1.2 million shares, all with a nominal value of £1.50. The terms of all allotments to date have provided that shares can be partly paid for with a minimum 90 pence payable at allotment and the remainder due when called for. Of the 1.2 million shares, 500,000 have 90 pence paid up, 400,000 have £1.20 paid up, and the remainder are fully paid up. The company calls for 10 pence per share on all unpaid shares. Based on the information provided, calculate Multisoft's:
   (a) issued share capital;
   (b) unissued share capital;
   (c) paid-up capital;
   (d) called-up capital;
   (e) uncalled capital.

4. 'The rules relating to capital maintenance are overly complex and too technical and the Companies Act 2006 has done little to improve the protection afforded to creditors.' Do you agree with this statement? Provide reasons for your answers.

Further reading

John H Armour, 'Share Capital and Creditor Protection: Efficient Rules for a Modern Company Law' (2000) 63 MLR 355
Discusses the rationale behind the capital maintenance provisions from an economic viewpoint

Derek French, Stephen Mayson, and Christopher Ryan, *Mayson, French, & Ryan on Company Law* (30th edn, OUP 2013) chs 6 and 10
A comprehensive and detailed account of the nature of shares and the rules relating to capital maintenance

Louise Gullifer and Jennifer Payne, *Corporate Finance Law: Principles and Policy* (Hart Publishing 2011)
An excellent text that provides an extremely comprehensive and analytical discussion of the law in this area.

Paul Myners, *Pre-Emption Rights: Final Report* (DTI 2005)
Analyses the law relating to pre-emption rights and discusses why such rights are needed

Robert R Pennington, 'Can Shares in Companies Be Defined?' (1989) 10 Co Law 140
Discusses the nature of the share since the first chartered companies up to the proliferation
  of the registered company

 Remember to visit the **Online Resource Centre** at **<http://www.
oxfordtextbooks.co.uk/orc/roach3e>** to access the following resources
on Chapter 21, 'Shares and capital maintenance': more **practice
questions** and answers; a **glossary** of key terms; **multiple-choice
questions**; and **revision summaries**. Updates to the law can be found on
Twitter by following **@UKBusinessLaw** and **@UKCompanyLaw**.

22 Directors' duties

- Codification
- The general duties
- Transactions requiring member approval

- Limitation periods
- Relief from liability

INTRODUCTION

Chapter 20 noted that the directors of the company are vested with a substantial amount of discretionary power. The problem with such a concentration of power is that the directors may be tempted to engage in self-benefiting acts, acts for an improper purpose, or other acts that are not in the company's interests. This chapter will discuss the principal method by which such acts are discouraged and remedied—namely, the imposition of duties upon directors.

By and large, the duties of directors were not radically amended by the Companies Act 2006, but this Act did introduce a major alteration in that, after over a century of discussion on the topic, the duties of directors have finally been codified.

Codification

Historically, the duties of directors were derived from a mass of case law based on the common law of negligence and equitable duties analogous to those imposed on trustees. The result was that the law was unclear, inaccessible, and out of date. Accordingly, as far back as 1895,[1] it had been suggested that directors' duties should be **codified** in some manner, but it was only following a 1999 Law Commission report[2] and a review of company law[3] that it was finally decided to enact a statutory statement of directors' duties. The result can be found in ss 170–181 of the Companies Act 2006 (CA 2006), which codify the common law and equitable duties,

→ codified: the process whereby law is collected and restated in statute

---

1. Davey Committee, *Report of the Departmental Committee to Inquire what Amendments are Necessary in the Acts Relating to Joint Stock Companies Incorporated with Limited Liability* (C 7779, HMSO 1895).
2. Law Commission, *Company Directors: Regulating Conflicts of Interest and Formulating a Statement of Duties* (Law Com No 261, Cm 4436, HMSO 1999).
3. Company Law Review Steering Group, *Modern Company Law for a Competitive Economy: Final Report, Vol 1* (DTI 2001).

and set them out in a more accessible and up-to-date manner. In addition, ss 188–226 restate the law relating to directorial transactions requiring shareholder approval.

The general duties

The restated duties are referred to in the Act as the 'general duties' and are 'based on certain common law rules and equitable principles as they apply in relation to directors'.[4] It is clear therefore that codification has not radically altered the duties in any way, but has rather restated them in a more appropriate manner (although, as is discussed later, several notable reforms have been made). Doubtless, this is to ensure that the authoritative and extremely useful body of case law that has developed should remain highly relevant—an assertion that is backed up by s 170(4), which provides that 'regard shall be had to the corresponding common law rules and equitable principles in interpreting and applying the general duties'. These duties are in addition to any duties that the director might have in his capacity as an agent or employee. These duties apply to shadow directors to the same extent as did the corresponding common law rules.[5]

Before examining these duties, it is important to understand to whom these duties are owed, because, generally, only that person can sue the directors for breach of duty. Statute preserves the common law position[6] by providing that the general duties 'are owed by a director of a company to the company'.[7] Generally therefore, directors do not owe their duties to members,[8] creditors,[9] employees, or anyone else, and only the company (and those who can act on its behalf) can sue for breach of such a duty. However, exceptions do exist and in two limited circumstances, the directors may owe a duty directly to the members:

1. Where a director undertakes to act as agent for one or more members, he will owe a duty directly to those members,[10] but such a duty derives from his position as an agent and not by virtue of him being a director.
2. Where the company is the target of a takeover bid, the directors may owe a direct duty to the members to provide honest advice regarding the bid and not to prevent the members from obtaining the best price for their shares.[11]

In addition, in limited circumstances, a member might be able to sue for breach of duty via a derivative claim.

Derivative claims are considered at p 644

Although the general duties themselves are set out in statute, the specific remedies for their breach are not. Instead, s 178(1) provides that the consequences of breaching the general duties are the same as those that would apply if the corresponding common law or equitable principle were to have been breached. These remedies are discussed alongside the corresponding general duty.

---

4. CA 2006, s 170(3).   5. ibid s 170(5).   6. *Percival v Wright* [1902] 2 Ch 421 (Ch).
7. CA 2006, s 170(1).
8. *Multinational Gas and Petrochemical Co v Multinational Gas and Petrochemical Services Ltd* [1983] Ch 258 (CA).
9. ibid.   10. *Allen v Hyatt* (1914) 30 TLR 444 (PC).
11. *Heron International Ltd v Lord Grade* [1983] BCLC 244 (CA).

Duty to act within the company's powers

The first general duty is contained in s 171 and is an amalgam of two prior common law duties:

1. the duty to act in accordance with the company's constitution; and
2. the duty to exercise powers only for the purposes for which they are conferred.

Duty to act in accordance with the constitution

As discussed in Chapter 19, the powers of the company will predominantly be set out in the company's articles, and the default position is that companies created under the 2006 Act will have unrestricted articles. It is common, however, for companies to impose some form of limitation on the power of the directors, and directors who breach such limitations will breach the general duty contained in s 171.

Where the directors cause the company to enter into a transaction with a third party that is outside the scope of its constitution, the transaction cannot be set aside and will bind the company.[12] Where such a transaction is due to occur, but has not yet been entered into, however, a members can apply to the court for an injunction restraining the proposed act.[13] Where the company enters into such a transaction with a director, or someone connected to a director, the transaction is voidable by legal proceedings brought at the company's instance.[14] Irrespective of whether the transaction is avoided or not, the director will be required to account for any gains made and to indemnify the company for any losses resulting from the transaction. It would appear that the members cannot ratify this element of the duty, especially where the directors act outside the scope of the articles. To permit ratification would, in effect, allow the members to alter the articles indirectly by ordinary resolution, whereas, a special resolution is required to alter the articles.

Duty to exercise powers for a proper purpose

The second strand of the s 171 duty is based on the common law 'proper purpose' doctrine and requires that directors exercise their powers for the purposes for which they are conferred. A purpose outside this scope is usually known as an 'improper purpose' and many cases involving improper purposes relate to directors using their powers to benefit themselves financially or to retain control of the company. Determining whether an exercise of power breaches this duty can be difficult, because the directors will often exercise their powers for several purposes, some of which are proper and others improper. The courts' approach to ascertaining the propriety of the exercise of a power was established in the following case.

 Howard Smith Ltd v Ampol Petroleum Ltd [1974] AC 821 (PC)

FACTS: The claimant controlled 55 per cent of the shares in company X and wished to take it over. A rival bid was made by the defendant, but was rejected by X's majority shareholder—namely, the claimant. The directors of X favoured the defendant's bid because it was higher than that offered by the claimant but, given that the claimant was X's majority shareholder, the

---

12. CA 2006, s 39.   13. ibid s 40(4).   14. ibid s 41(2).

defendant's bid could never succeed. The directors of X therefore issued $10 million worth of new shares to the defendant, the purpose of which was twofold: first, it would allow X to raise much-needed finance for the building of two oil tankers; and second, it would relegate the claimant's holdings to 37 per cent, thereby making it a minority shareholder. The claimant alleged that the issuing of the shares was for an improper purpose.

HELD: The court should consider first the nature of the power in question (that is, why this power was conferred on the directors). The court should then objectively determine the substantial or dominant purpose for which the power was exercised. If the dominant purpose is proper, no breach will occur. Conversely, if the dominant purpose is improper, a breach will occur irrespective of the fact that other subservient proper purposes exist. Here, the dominant purpose was to reduce the shareholding of the claimant, thereby manipulating the voting power of one shareholder over another. This was deemed to be an improper purpose.

COMMENT: The majority of cases relating to the proper purpose doctrine relate to the directors' power to issue shares and the courts have categorically stated that where the dominant purpose of an issue of shares is to manipulate shareholder voting power, or to enable the directors to maintain themselves in office, then the exercise of power will be for an improper purpose.

⭐ See JH Farrar, 'Abuse of Power by Directors' (1974) 33 CLJ 221

Where the directors act for an improper purpose, such acts are voidable at the company's instance and the director in breach may be required to compensate the company for any loss sustained. However, these consequences are avoided where the members ratify the breach of duty.[15]

Duty to promote the success of the company

Of the seven general duties, the duty contained in s 172 is perhaps the most fundamental and contains a reformulation of the common law duty to act bona fide in the interests of the company.[16] Section 172(1) requires the director to 'act in the way he considers, in good faith, would be most likely to promote the success of the company for the benefit of its members as a whole'. It is immediately clear that this duty is subjective, meaning that what matters is what the directors honestly believed would promote the success of the company.[17] It is not the courts' place to substitute their beliefs for those of the directors. As Lord Wilberforce famously stated: 'There is no appeal on merits from management decisions to courts of law: nor will courts of law assume to act as a kind of supervisory board over decisions within the powers of management honestly arrived at.'[18] It follows that, provided that the decision of the directors was honest, it does not matter that it was unreasonable.[19]

However, there are limits on the subjectivity of the duty. In *Hutton v West Cork Rly Co*,[20] Bowen LJ stated that if the duty were entirely subjective then 'you might have a lunatic conducting the affairs of the company, and paying away its money with both hands in a manner perfectly bona fide yet perfectly irrational.'[21] Accordingly, the courts will closely examine the evidence and try to determine whether or not the

---

15. *Hogg v Cramphorn* [1967] Ch 254 (Ch).   16. *Re Smith and Fawcett Ltd* [1942] Ch 304 (CA).
17. *Regentcrest plc v Cohen* [2001] 2 BCLC 80 (Ch) 105 (Jonathan Parker J).
18. *Howard Smith Ltd v Ampol Petroleum Ltd* [1974] AC 821 (PC) 832.
19. *Extrasure Travel Insurance Ltd v Scattergood* [2003] 1 BCLC 598 (Ch).
20. (1883) LR 23 ChD 654 (CA).   21. ibid 671.

directors honestly believed that their actions were designed to promote the success of the company for the benefit of its members. Where a director's act or omission causes the company harm, the court will not be easily persuaded that the director honestly believed his actions to be in the company's interest.[22] There is little doubt that where the evidence does not provide a conclusive answer, the courts will temper the subjective test with an objective examination, but the test still remains primarily subjective.[23]

The duty imposed by s 172 is a broad one and can impact upon other duties. In *Item Software (UK) Ltd v Fassihi*,[24] the Court held that a director who breaches a fiduciary duty will be required to disclose that breach of duty to the company if the duty to act in the interests of the company requires such disclosure. The court in *British Midland Tool Ltd v Midland International Tooling Ltd*[25] held that this obligation extends to disclosing the breaches of fellow directors. In keeping with the subjective nature of this duty, the key factor is whether the director honestly considers that it is in the company's interest to know about the breach.[26] Clearly, disclosure of a breach of duty will usually be in the company's interests and a failure to do so might result in a breach of s 172, in addition to a breach of the original duty. A failure to disclose can result in a loss of employment benefits (for example, share options, or certain employment rights) and may provide a justification for summary dismissal.[27] In *GHLM Trading Ltd v Maroo*,[28] Newey J went further and stated, *obiter*, that this duty of disclosure could extend to disclosing matters other than wrongdoing and that disclosure might be justified to a person other than a board member.

'Success of the company for the benefit of its members'

The phrase 'promote the success of the company for the benefit of its members' is interesting, but the Act does not indicate how the success of the company is to be measured. In many cases, the interests of the company and its members will align, so no problem arises. However, this will not always be the case and, in some cases, the interests of the company and its members may conflict. The following case indicates that where the interests of the company and part of its membership conflict, preference should be given to the interests of the company. Whether the directors can favour the company over the members as a whole is unclear.

 Mutual Life Insurance Co of New York v Rank Organisation Ltd [1985] BCLC 11 (Ch)

FACTS: The defendant company issued twenty million shares, half of which were made available, on preferential terms, to existing shareholders. However, existing shareholders in the US and Canada were excluded from this offer on the ground that to include them would require the company to comply with complex legislation in those countries which would prove

---

22. *Regentcrest plc v Cohen* [2001] 2 BCLC 80 (Ch).

23. Unless of course, the director has not at all considered whether his actions would promote the success of the company for the benefit of its members. In such a case, the test becomes entirely objective (*Charterbridge Corporation Ltd v Lloyds Bank Ltd* [1970] Ch 62 (Ch)).

24. [2004] EWCA Civ 1244, [2004] BCC 994.   25. [2003] EWHC 466 (Ch), [2003] 2 BCLC 523.

26. *Fulham Football Club (1987) Ltd v Tigana* [2004] EWHC 2585 (QB).

27. *Tesco Stores Ltd v Pook* [2003] EWHC 823 (Ch), [2004] IRLR 618.

28. [2012] EWHC 61 (Ch), [2012] 2 BCLC 369.

these rules are reformulated in s 175, with s 175(1) providing that '[a] director of a company[33] must avoid a situation in which he has, or can have, a direct or indirect interest that conflicts, or possibly may conflict, with the interests of the company'. Section 175(2) provides that this duty arises in particular to 'the exploitation of any property, information or opportunity (and it is immaterial whether the company could take advantage of the property, information or opportunity)'. Focusing on these specific forms of conflict indicates that the statutory duty is based on what is known as the 'corporate opportunity' doctrine.

The corporate opportunity doctrine

The corporate opportunity doctrine is based upon the premise that the director breaches his duty if he personally takes advantage of an opportunity that rightly belongs to the company. Where the director does this, he will be liable to account for any profit that he makes. The strictness of the courts' approach can be seen in the following case.

 Bhullar v Bhullar [2003] EWCA Civ 424[34]

FACTS: For over fifty years, the families of two brothers (M and S) had run a company that, *inter alia*, let commercial property. The families fell out and it was decided that they would go their separate ways. M's family (the claimants) decided that the company would not acquire any further properties and S's family (the defendants) agreed. A director of the company who was part of the defendant's family discovered, by chance and not whilst acting in the course of the company's business, a piece of property adjacent to property owned by the company. Through another company that they owned, the defendants acquired this property without informing the claimants. The claimants discovered the acquisition and alleged that the defendants had breached their fiduciary duties.

HELD: The defendants had breached their fiduciary duties. Despite the fact that the defendants had acquired knowledge of the property in a 'private' capacity, the Court held that the opportunity to purchase the property was one that belonged to the company. There was doubt as to whether it was 'worthwhile' for the company to acquire the property, given that it was in the process of being wound up. The Court stated that whether or not the company could, or would, have acquired the property was irrelevant.

COMMENT: Understandably, this case has been criticized—notably, because the company agreed (at the claimants' behest) not to acquire any more properties. The Court, in effect, allowed the claimants to change their minds opportunistically at the moment that an attractive commercial opportunity arose.

★ See Dan D Prentice and Jennifer Payne, 'The Corporate Opportunity Doctrine' (2004) 120 LQR 198

There is little doubt that s 175 preserves the strict and inflexible position evidenced in *Bhullar*, but pre-CA 2006 law did contain an important exception to the above rules—namely, where the conflict was authorized.

---

33. The duty also applies to former directors in relation to any property, information, or opportunities of which they may have become aware in their former directorship (CA 2006, s 170(2)(a)).
34. See also *Regal (Hastings) Ltd v Gulliver* [1967] 2 AC 134 (HL).

Authorization

The harshness of the rule was mitigated in one important respect—namely, that a director who engaged in a conflict could keep any profit made where the act in question was disclosed and authorized. In effect, disclosure and authorization would exclude the operation of the no-conflict and no-profit rules.

Section 175 preserves this, but the requirement of authorization is different. Under pre-CA 2006 law, authorization would occur where the director disclosed the conflict and obtained consent from the company in general meeting,[35] but it was common for companies to provide in their articles that disclosure to the board was sufficient.[36] Under the 2006 Act, where the company is a private company, the directors alone can give authorization, provided that there is nothing to the contrary in the company's constitution.[37] The directors of public companies can only give authorization if the articles so provide.[38] For obvious reasons, the vote(s) of the director(s) in conflict will not count in determining authorization.[39]

Remedies for breach

Where a director fails to disclose a conflict or fails to obtain valid authorization, any resulting contract is voidable at the company's instance, provided that the third party involved has notice of the director's breach.[40] In addition, the company can require the director to account for any profit made as a result of the conflict.[41] Where the directors refuse to authorize a conflict, the director engaging in the conflict can avoid the above consequences by obtaining ratification from the members in general meeting.[42]

Duty not to accept benefits from third parties

The second general duty relating to conflicts of interest is found in s 176(1), which places a duty on a director not to accept from a third party a benefit conferred by reason of his being a director, or by doing (or not doing) anything as a director. As with the s 175 duty, *mala fides* is not a requirement and it will therefore be no defence for the director to argue that he acted in good faith. The duty extends to a former director in relation to acts or omissions prior to his ceasing to be a director.[43]

➡ *mala fides:* 'bad faith'

Initially, the inclusion of this duty appears odd, because s 176(4) provides that this duty is not breached 'if the acceptance of the benefit cannot reasonably be regarded as likely to give rise to a conflict of interest'. As this duty covers only benefits that are likely to give rise to a conflict, it would be thought that such benefits would be adequately covered by the duty to avoid conflicts of interest contained in s 175. Indeed, there is considerable overlap between the two duties, but there is a notable difference—namely, that a conflict under s 175 can be authorized by the directors, but the receipt of a third-party benefit under s 176 can only be authorized by the members in general meeting.[44] This clearly indicates that the receipt of third-party benefits

---

35. *Aberdeen Rly Co v Blaikie Bros* (1854) 2 Eq Rep 1281 (HL).

36. Companies (Tables A to F) Regulations 1985, Table A, art 85.

37. CA 2006, s 175(4)(b) and (5)(a).   38. ibid s 175(4)(b) and (5)(b).   39. ibid s 175(6).

40. *Hely-Hutchinson & Co Ltd v Brayhead Ltd* [1968] 1 QB 549 (CA).

41. *Aberdeen Rly Co v Blaikie Bros* (1854) 2 Eq Rep 1281 (HL).   42. CA 2006, s 180(4)(a).

43. ibid s 170(2)(b).

44. Authorization by the members is not expressly stated, but is a consequence of s 180(4)(a).

constitutes a much greater danger to board impartiality than the conflicts covered by s 175 (indeed, as is discussed in Chapter 8, under the rules of agency, such benefits would be classed as 'bribes'). It has been argued that the requirement of member authorization amounts to a 'near-ban on the receipt of third party benefits'.[45]

Remedies for breach

Where a director accepts an unauthorized third-party benefit, the company can rescind the contract[46] and the benefit can be recovered. Instead of recovering the benefit, the company may claim damages in fraud from either the director in breach or the third party.[47] In addition, the company can summarily terminate the director's service contract and dismiss him.[48]

Duty to declare interest in proposed transactions or arrangements

The third general duty relating to conflicts of interest is found in s 177(1), which provides that '[i]f a director of a company is in any way, directly or indirectly, inter-ested in a proposed transaction or arrangement with the company, he must declare the nature and extent of that interest to the other directors'. The declaration must be made before the company enters into the transaction or arrangement.[49] Under the pre-CA 2006 common law, disclosure and authorization by the company in general meeting was required, although the articles could modify this to require mere dis-closure. Several points should be noted:

- The duty imposed by s 177 relates to *proposed* transactions or arrangements only. *Existing* transactions or arrangements are covered by s 182, which is dis-cussed later.

- The duty relates only to transactions or arrangements between the director and his company. Transactions between directors and outsiders are covered by the duties relating to conflict of interests and third-party benefits, discussed earlier.

- The duty relates only to transactions or arrangements that could reasonably be regarded as giving rise to a conflict of interest.[50]

- As the duty covers indirect transactions or arrangements, a director need not be party to the transaction or arrangement in order for the duty to arise.

- A declaration is not required where the director in question is not aware of the interest, or of the transaction or arrangement as the case may be,[51] or where the other directors are aware of it.[52]

- Where a company only has one director, a declaration is not required.[53] Where the company has only one member, who is also a director, the transaction or arrangement must either be in writing, or be set out in a written memorandum and recorded in the company's minutes.[54] Failure to comply with these require-ments constitutes a criminal offence.

---

45. Paul L Davies and Sarah Worthington, *Gower & Davies' Principles of Modern Company Law* (9th edn, Sweet & Maxwell 2012) 611.   46. *Shipway v Broadwood* [1899] 1 QB 369 (CA).
47. *Mahesan v Malaysia Government Officers' Co-operative Housing Society Ltd* [1979] AC 374 (PC).
48. *Boston Deep Sea Fishing Co v Ansell* (1888) 39 Ch D 39 (CA).   49. CA 2006, s 177(4).
50. ibid s 177(6)(a).   51. ibid s 177(5).
52. ibid s 177(6)(b). In this context, the directors are treated as being aware of anything of which they ought reasonably be aware.
53. ibid Explanatory Notes [352].   54. ibid s 231(2).

TABLE 22.1 Disclosure and authorization of conflicts of interest

Duty	Disclosure required?	When is disclosure required?	Is authorization required?
Section 175—To avoid conflicts of interest Section 176—Not to accept benefits from third parties	The CA 2006 does not expressly require the director to disclose the conflict/benefit. However, as authorization is required, the director will, in practice, need to disclose the existence of the conflict/benefit prior to obtaining authorization. Further, the courts have made clear that a director should disclose the existence of a conflict/benefit in order to comply with the duty to act in the interests of the company[1] and it is likely that this will continue to apply in relation to the duty imposed by s 172		Yes. In private companies, the directors can authorize the interest, providing that the constitution does not preclude such authorization. In public companies, the directors can authorize the interest only if the constitution so provides Yes. The benefit can be authorized by the members in general meeting
Section 177—To declare interest in proposed transactions or arrangements with the company	Yes. The director must disclose the nature and extent of the interest to the other directors	Disclosure must be made prior to the company entering into the transaction or arrangement	No, but if the directors do not approve of the transaction/arrangement, they will likely prevent the company from entering into it
Section 182—To declare interest in existing transactions or arrangements entered into by the company	Yes. The director must disclose the nature and extent of the interest to the other directors	Disclosure must be made as soon as is reasonably practicable	No

[1] *Industrial Development Consultants Ltd v Cooley* [1972] 1 WLR 443.

- The requirement of disclosure to the directors constitutes the minimum requirement. A company, if it so chooses, can impose more exacting requirements in its constitution[55] (for example, by inserting a provision in the articles requiring authorization by the general meeting).

The declaration can take any form, but it is not enough for a director merely to state that he has an interest in a proposed transaction or arrangement; he must also declare the nature and extent of the interest.[56] If a declaration proves to be, or becomes, inaccurate or incomplete, then if the company has not yet entered into the transaction or arrangement, the director must make a further declaration correcting the previous one before the company enters into the transaction or arrangement.[57]

Existing transactions or arrangements

The s 177 duty relates to *proposed* transactions or arrangements, whereas s 182 contains separate rules relating to *existing* transactions or arrangements.[58] Section 182(1)

---

55. ibid s 180(1). 56. ibid s 177(1). 57. ibid s 177(3).

58. It should be noted that s 182 does not come under the umbrella of the 'general duties', but is so closely related to the duty contained in s 177 (which is one of the general duties) that it makes sense to discuss it alongside s 177.

provides that '[w]here a director of a company is in any way, directly or indirectly, interested in a transaction or arrangement that has been entered into by the company, he must declare the nature and extent of the interest to the other directors'. Whether this is a distinct general duty or simply a duty supplementary to s 177 is unclear (although its location in ch 3 of Pt 10 would indicate that it is a supplementary duty), but it is clear that if a declaration under s 177 takes place, a subsequent declaration under s 182 is not required once the transaction comes into effect.[59]

The declaration requirements in s 182 largely mirror those of s 177, except that a declaration under s 182 must be made 'as soon as is reasonably practicable',[60] whereas, as already stated, under s 177, a declaration need only occur at a time prior to the transaction or arrangement being entered into.[61]

Remedies for breach

Where the director enters into a proposed transaction or arrangement with the company in contravention of s 177, the transaction or arrangement is voidable at the company's instance. Where the director enters into an existing transaction or arrangement with the company in contravention of s 182, he commits an either way offence.[62]

Table 22.1 clarifies the differences between the various conflict of interest duties in relation to disclosure and authorization.

Transactions requiring member approval

The law imposes 'specific statutory duties'[63] on directors in relation to certain transactions and arrangements into which they enter with the company. In relation to such transactions or arrangements, compliance with the general duties discussed earlier is insufficient[64] and member approval is generally required.

Service contracts

Historically, directors would attempt to negotiate lengthy service contracts in order to entrench their position, as the following example demonstrates.

 Entrenchment through lengthy service contracts

Danny is appointed as CEO of BioTech plc. He has negotiated a ten-year service contract and is to be paid £4 million per year. After one year, it is apparent that he is incompetent. The company wishes to remove him from office, but to do so would breach Danny's service contract, enabling him to recover £36 million in damages (£4 million × the number of years left on his contract). Danny's position is entrenched by making it prohibitively expensive to remove him.

---

59. CA 2006, s 182(1).   60. ibid s 182(4).
61. ibid s 177(4).   62. ibid s 183.
63. Alistair Alcock, John Birds, and Steve Gale, *Companies Act 2006: The New Law* (Jordans 2007) [12.30].
64. CA 2006, s 180(3).

In order to curtail this practice, s 188 provides that a director cannot have a guaranteed term of employment of over two years[65] in length unless it has been approved by resolution of the company's members. As a result of s 188, directors now tend to have rolling contracts, whereby, once their service contract ends, they are reappointed on similar terms—and where the contract specifies, such reappointment can be automatic.

Remedies for breach

A provision in a service contract that provides a director with guaranteed employment for over two years is void if shareholder approval has not been obtained.[66] Further, the contract will also be deemed to contain a term allowing the company to terminate it at any time by giving reasonable notice.[67]

Substantial property transactions

Where a director has a conflict or an interest in a proposed or existing transaction or arrangement, the general duties require him to declare that conflict or interest to the other directors. Where, however, an arrangement[68] amounts to a 'substantial property transaction', disclosure to the directors is insufficient and a company may not enter into such an arrangement unless it has been approved in advance by a resolution of the members or is conditional on such approval being obtained.[69]

Two types of arrangement require member approval:

1. Where a director of the company or of its holding company, or a person connected with such a director, acquires, or is to acquire, from the company (directly or indirectly) a substantial non-cash asset.

2. Where the company acquires, or is to acquire, a substantial non-cash asset (directly or indirectly) from such a director or a person so connected.

A 'non-cash asset' is 'any property or interest in property, other than cash'[70] and a non-cash asset is substantial if it (i) is over £100,000; or (ii) exceeds 10 per cent of the company's asset value and is more than £5,000.[71]

Remedies for breach

A substantial property transaction entered into without member approval is voidable at the company's instance, unless restitution is impossible, the company has been indemnified, or avoidance would affect the rights of a person who had acquired those rights bona fide for value and without actual notice of the contravention.[72] In addition, irrespective of whether the arrangement was avoided, any director or connected person who was involved in the arrangement (including any directors who authorized the arrangement) will be liable to account for any direct or indirect gains made, and is also required to indemnify the company for any losses sustained as a result of the arrangement.[73] However, a connected person or director who authorized the arrangement can escape liability if he shows that, at the time that the arrangement

---

65. Financial Reporting Council, *The UK Corporate Governance Code* (FRC 2012) [D.1.5] recommends that directors' service contracts should be no longer than one year in length.   66. CA 2006, s 189(a).
67. ibid s 189(b).
68. The use of the word 'arrangement' in s 190 includes an agreement or understanding that does not have contractual effect (*Re Duckwari plc* [1999] Ch 253 (CA)).   69. CA 2006, s 190.
70. ibid s 1163(1).   71. ibid s 191(2).   72. ibid s 195(2)   73. ibid s 195(3).

was entered into, he was unaware of the relevant circumstances constituting the contravention.[74]

Loans, quasi-loans, and credit transactions

Under the CA 1985, a company was prohibited from making any form of loan to one of its directors (subject to several exceptions) and breach of this prohibition constituted a criminal offence. The CA 2006 adopts a very different approach that is dependent upon the type of loan and the type of company in question, as follows.

- No company can make a loan to its directors unless the transaction has been approved by a resolution of the members.[75]

- A public company cannot make a quasi-loan to its directors unless the transaction has been approved by a resolution of the members.[76] Section 199(1) provides that a quasi-loan occurs where the company agrees to pay a sum on behalf of the director, or where it reimburses expenses incurred by another party due to actions of the director.

- A public company cannot enter into a credit transaction with a director of the company unless the transaction has been approved by a resolution of the members.[77] Examples of credit transactions include hire purchase or conditional sales agreements, the leasing or hiring of goods, and the disposition of land, goods, or services on the understanding that payment is to be deferred.[78]

In the case of quasi-loans and credit transactions, the requirement of member approval also applies to any company 'associated with' a public company[79]—the obvious example being a private subsidiary of a public holding company.[80]

The requirements for approval of loans, quasi-loans, and credit transactions do not apply in a number of situations, including:

- loans, quasi-loans, or credit transactions of up to £50,000 to meet the director's expenditure on company business;[81]

- loans or quasi-loans that do not exceed £10,000;[82]

- credit transactions that do not exceed £15,000.[83]

Remedies for breach

Any transaction or arrangement that contravenes ss 197, 198, or 201 is voidable at the company's instance, unless restitution is impossible, the company has been indemnified, or avoidance would affect the rights of a person who had acquired those rights bona fide for value and without actual notice of the contravention.[84] Irrespective of whether the transaction or arrangement has been avoided, any director, or person connected with the director involved, is liable to account to the company for any gains made and is also liable to indemnify the company for any losses sustained as a result of the transaction or arrangement.[85] The company's right to rescind the transaction or arrangement will be lost if the members ratify the transaction or arrangement.[86]

74. ibid s 195(7).   75. ibid s 197(1).   76. ibid s 198(2).   77. ibid s 201(2).
78. ibid s 202(1).   79. ibid ss 200(1)(b) and 201(1)(b).   80. ibid s 256.   81. ibid s 204.
82. ibid s 207(1).
83. ibid s 207(2).   84. ibid s 213(2).   85. ibid s 213(3).   86. ibid s 214.

Payments for loss of office

The law requires that the members approve certain voluntary payments made by the company to directors losing office. 'Payment for loss of office' is generally defined as a payment made to a director or past director:

- by way of compensation for loss of office;
- by way of compensation for loss, while a director, of any other office or employment in connection with the management affairs of the company (or of a subsidiary undertaking of the company); or
- as consideration for, or in connection with, his retirement as director or an officer or employee involved in the management of the affairs of the company (or of a subsidiary undertaking of the company).[87]

A company may not make a payment for loss of office to a director unless the payment has been approved by a resolution of the members. However, the requirement of shareholder approval does not apply to (i) a payment made in good faith to discharge a legal obligation, or to compensate another for breach of such obligation, or to settle a claim arising from termination of a person's office or employment, or by way of a pension in respect of past services,[88] or (ii) a payment that does not exceed £200.[89]

Remedies for breach

Where member approval is not obtained for payment for a general loss of office, the recipient will hold the payment on trust for the company, and any director who authorized the payment is jointly and severally liable to indemnify the company for any loss resulting from the payment.[90] Where the unapproved payment for loss of office is in connection with a transfer of the undertaking, the recipient will hold the payment on trust for the company the undertaking or property of which is being, or is proposed to be, transferred.[91] Where the payment for loss of office is in connection with a share transfer, the recipient will hold the payment on trust for the persons who have sold their shares.[92]

Limitation periods

Section 21(3) of the Limitation Act 1980 provides that an action alleging breach of duty must normally be brought within six years of the date on which the action accrued, unless any other provision in the Act applies that provides for a different limitation period. However, s 21(1) provides that, in two cases, there will be no limitation period and an action can be brought at any time:

1. where the director was party to a fraud or fraudulent breach of trust; or
2. where the director is in possession of the company's property or proceeds of the company, or where the director has received company property and converted it to his use.

---

87. ibid s 215(1).   88. ibid s 220(1).   89. ibid s 221(1).   90. ibid s 222(1).
91. ibid s 222(2).   92. ibid s 222(3).

Relief from liability

A director who is liable for breaching the duties discussed earlier may be able to obtain relief from such liability in several ways.

Exclusion and indemnity clauses

A director may attempt to obtain relief from liability for negligence, default, breach of duty, or breach of trust via a provision (either in the articles or in his service contract) excluding such liability. Section 232(1) of the CA 2006 provides that such a provision is void. The director may try to obtain relief via a provision requiring the company to indemnify the director for any loss or liability sustained by him due to his breach of duty. Again, such a provision will be void,[93] except:

- where the company purchases and maintains insurance for a director in relation to liability for breach of duty;[94]
- where the company indemnifies directors in respect to proceedings brought by third parties;[95] and
- where the company, which is a trustee of an occupational pension scheme, indemnifies the director for liability incurred in connection with the company's activities as a trustee for an occupational pension scheme.[96]

Ratification

Section 239 of the CA 2006 puts in place, for the first time, a statutory scheme concerning the ratification of acts committed by directors (including former directors and shadow directors) that amount to negligence, default, breach of duty, or breach of trust. Where effective ratification occurs, any cause of action that the company had in respect of the breach is extinguished, but this new scheme does not affect any previous rules of law denying the ability to ratify. Accordingly, an act that could not be ratified under the pre-2006 law cannot be ratified under the CA 2006. Unratifiable acts would therefore include illegal acts,[97] acts not bona fide in the interests of the company, and acts that involved a 'fraud on the minority'.[98]

Ratification requires a resolution of the company's members. Where the director is also a member of the company, his votes will be disregarded, although he may attend the meeting.[99] This is in contrast to the pre-2006 position, which permitted a director's votes to count, provided that they were made in good faith.[100] In order for ratification to be valid:

- the directors must have fully disclosed their interest in the transaction in breach;[101]
- the ratification by the members must be informed,[102] and the decision to ratify must be 'honest, bona fide and in the best interest of the company';[103]

---

93. ibid s 232(2).   94. ibid s 233.   95. ibid s 234.   96. ibid s 235.
97. *Re Exchange Banking Co (Flitcroft's Case)* (1882) 21 Ch D 519 (CA).
98. *Burland v Earle* [1902] AC 83 (PC).   99. CA 2006, s 239(4).
100. *North-West Transportation Co Ltd v Beatty* (1887) 12 App Cas 589 (PC).
101. *Kaye v Croydon Tramways Co* [1898] 1 Ch 358 (CA).   102. *Knight v Frost* [1999] 1 BCLC 364 (Ch).
103. *Madoff Securities International Ltd v Raven* [2011] EWHC 3102 (Comm), [2012] 2 All ER (Comm) 634 [123] (Flaux J).

- the ratification 'must not be brought about by unfair or improper means, and is not illegal or oppressive towards the shareholders who oppose it'.[104]

Relief from the court

A director who is unable to obtain authorization or ratification from the directors or the members has one last option for avoiding liability—namely, the ability of the court to grant relief. Section 1157(1) allows a court that has found an officer or auditor of the company liable for negligence, default, breach of duty, or breach of trust to grant that officer, either wholly or partly, relief from liability[105] on such terms as it sees fit. Section 1157(2) allows an officer or auditor to petition the court for such relief where he has reason to believe that such a claim for negligence, etc will be made against him.

In both cases, relief will only be granted where the court is of the opinion that the officer:

- has acted honestly—a test that is subjective, meaning that the crucial factor is whether the officer actually believed that he acted honestly;[106]
- has acted reasonably, which, unlike honesty, must be assessed objectively;[107]
- given all of the circumstances of the case, ought fairly to be excused. Given that *all* of the circumstances of the case need to be examined, it is very rare that a case involving the granting of relief under s 1157 will be **struck out** and, usually, a full trial should occur.[108]

 striking out: the dismissal by the court of all or part of a statement of a case

The following case provides a classic example of the courts' discretion to grant relief from liability.

Re Duomatic Ltd [1969] 2 Ch 365 (Ch)

FACTS: A company had three directors, E, H, and T, who owned all of the company's ordinary shares. E and T were critical of H's performance, and wished to remove him. H threatened to sue if they tried to dismiss him so, instead, E and T paid H £4,000 to leave the company. H did so and transferred his shares to E. The company's articles provided that the directors' remuneration had to be authorized by the company's members, but no such resolution was ever passed. Instead, the directors drew sums from the company as needed and, at the end of the year, the sums drawn were totalled and entered into the company's accounts as 'directors' salaries'. These sums were drawn with the knowledge and approval of all of the members who were entitled to vote at the company's meetings. This practice continued until the year prior to the company's liquidation, when E, who by now was the majority shareholder, drew £9,000 before the company's final accounts had been prepared. The company entered voluntary liquidation and the liquidator sought to claim:

1. sums drawn by E and T as salary;

---

104. *North-West Transportation Co Ltd v Beatty* (1887) 12 App Cas 589 (PC) 593, 594 (Sir Richard Baggallay), affirmed by *Franbar Holdings Ltd v Patel* [2008] EWHC 1534 (Ch), [2008] BCC 885.

105. This will include liability to account for profits gained as well as liability to pay damages (*Coleman Taymar Ltd v Oakes* [2001] 2 BCLC 749 (Ch)).

106. ibid.

107. *Re MDA Investment Management Ltd* [2004] EWHC 42 (Ch), [2005] BCC 783.

108. *Equitable Life Assurance Society v Bowley* [2003] EWHC 2263 (Comm), [2004] 1 BCLC 180.

2. the £9,000 drawn by E in the final year; and

3. the £4,000 loss-of-office payment paid to H.

HELD: Buckley J held that there was little doubt that all three payments were in breach of duty; the question arising was whether relief could be obtained. Regarding (1), the court held that relief should be granted and the payments remained valid. Buckley J stated that:

> where it can be shown that all shareholders who have a right to attend and vote at a general meeting of the company assent to some matter which a general meeting of the company could carry into effect, that assent is as binding as a resolution in general meeting would be.[109]

The court also granted relief for (2), stating that E was merely following a practice that had been followed in preceding years. However, Buckley J refused to grant relief for (3), and held that E and T were jointly liable to pay back the £4,000. There was no disclosure or authorization under what, today, would be s 217 of the CA 2006, and it was therefore a misapplication of the company's funds.

Chapter conclusion

The codification of directors' duties is arguably the most significant reform contained in the Companies Act 2006, and has clarified the content and scope of the duties owed. Prior to the CA 2006, an analysis of this area would have involved a discussion of a mass of common law rules and equitable principles. The general duties set out in the Act are, however, broad indicators, at best, of how the directors should manage the company. Recourse to the substantial body of prior case law will still be essential in order for directors to understand fully the duties to which they are subject and how best to comply with them. Still, there can be little doubt that the restatement of the duties in the CA 2006 is an improvement in terms of accessibility and clarity. It remains to be seen, however, whether the codification is clear enough for directors to understand sufficiently. It has been argued, quite correctly, that the codification contained in the CA 2006 is not as clear as that recommended by the Law Commission. Only time will tell whether or not the codification of directors' duties will have a notable impact.

 Key points summary

- Directors are under a duty to act in accordance with the company's constitution and to exercise their powers for the purposes for which they are conferred.

- Directors are under a duty to promote the success of the company for the benefit of its members, but in doing so, they must also have regard to the wider interests, such as those of the employees, suppliers, consumers, and the environment.

- Directors are under a duty to exercise independent judgment, but they can enter into an agreement binding themselves to a certain course of action where they believe it to be in the interests of the company.

- Directors are under a duty to exercise reasonable care, skill, and diligence when performing their functions.

---

109. [1969] 2 Ch 365 (Ch) 373.

- Directors are under a duty to avoid conflicts of interest, but a conflicting act will not constitute a breach of duty where the other directors authorize it.

- Directors must not accept unauthorized benefits from third parties. Receipt of such a benefit cannot be authorized by the directors, but it can be authorized by the members.

- Directors are under a duty to declare an interest in any proposed or existing transaction or arrangement. Failure to declare an interest in an existing transaction or arrangement will constitute a criminal offence.

- A director cannot have a guaranteed term of employment for over two years, unless it has first been approved by a resolution of the members.

- Where a director wishes to enter into a substantial property transaction with the company, the transaction will first need to be approved by a resolution of the members.

- No company can make a loan to one of its directors without first obtaining approval by a resolution from the members. Public companies cannot make a quasi-loan to, or enter into a credit transaction with, a director without first obtaining approval by a resolution from the members.

- Generally, a company cannot provide a payment for loss of office to a departing director for loss of office unless the members first approve that payment by a resolution.

Self-test questions

1. Define the following:
   (a) improper purpose;
   (b) substantial property transaction;
   (c) quasi-loan;
   (d) credit transaction.

2. Discuss the advantages and disadvantages of codifying the duties of directors.

3. AssetStrip Ltd launches a takeover bid for MicroCorp plc. The directors of MicroCorp are aware that if the takeover is successful, AssetStrip will break up MicroCorp and sell its assets off to various interested parties. The directors of MicroCorp believe that the takeover will be highly detrimental to the company's shareholders. The directors therefore issue a large batch of shares, thereby making the takeover prohibitively expensive. AssetStrip retracts its takeover bid. Has a breach of duty occurred?

4. 'The duty to promote the success of the company for the benefit of its members preserves the view that UK company law is based on a narrow, shareholder-centred approach. Instead the law should allow the courts to balance equally the interests of shareholders and non-shareholder constituents.' Do you agree with this statement? Provide reasons for your answer.

5. Read the following cases and discuss whether or not each would be decided differently today under the CA 2006.
   (a) *Re Brazilian Rubber Plantations and Estates Ltd*.[110]
   (b) *Regal (Hastings) Ltd v Gulliver*.[111]
   (c) *West Mercia Safetywear Ltd v Dodd*.[112]

---

110. [1911] 1 Ch 425 (Ch).   111. [1967] 2 AC 134 (HL).   112. (1988) 4 BCC 30 (CA).

Further reading

Bryan Clark, 'UK Company Law Reform and the Directors' Exploitation of 'Corporate Opportunities' (2006) 17 ICCLR 231
Discusses the corporate opportunity doctrine and argues that the retention by the Companies Act 2006 of a strict approach is the correct approach

Rod Edmunds and John Lowry, 'The Continuing Value of Relief for Directors' Breach of Duty' (2003) 66 MLR 195
Discusses the court's ability to grant relief for breach of duty and argues that a more radical approach is required than that contained in s 1157

Deryn Fisher, 'The Enlightened Shareholder: Leaving Stakeholders in the Dark—Will Section 172(1) of the Companies Act 2006 Make Directors Consider the Impact of Their Decisions on Third Parties?' (2009) 20 ICCLR 10
Discusses the likely impact of the duty imposed by s 172 and argues that, in practice, it will not make directors consider the interests of stakeholders; contends that the pluralist approach could provide a more inclusive approach

Derek French, Stephen Mayson, and Christopher Ryan, *Mayson, French, & Ryan on Company Law* (30th edn, OUP 2013) ch 16
A highly detailed and analytical discussion of the general duties and those transactions requiring shareholder approval

Andrew Keay, 'The Duty of Directors to Exercise Independent Judgment' (2008) 29 Co Law 290
Discusses the common law background to the duty to exercise independent judgment and explores to what extent, if any, the duty contained in the Companies Act 2006 will adopt a different approach

Law Commission, *Company Directors: Regulating Conflicts of Interest and Formulating a Statement of Duties—Consultation Paper* (Law Com CP No 153, HMSO 1998)
Discusses all of the duties and requirements examined in this chapter; provides a clear, yet detailed, analysis of the law and recommends a number of options for reform

 Remember to visit the **Online Resource Centre** at <http://www.oxfordtextbooks.co.uk/orc/roach3e> to access the following resources on Chapter 22, 'Directors' duties:' more **practice questions** and answers; a **glossary** of key terms; **multiple-choice questions**; and **revision summaries**. Updates to the law can be found on Twitter by following @ **UKBusinessLaw** and **@UKCompanyLaw**.

23 Members' remedies

- Derivative claims
- Unfairly prejudicial conduct
- The petition for winding up

INTRODUCTION

Where the company, its directors, or its members have committed some form of maladministration or breach of duty, or some other act that has caused loss, how can redress be obtained? The problem that arises is that, very often, the parties who have **standing** to commence proceedings to obtain redress are the very parties who have caused the harm. Members, especially minority shareholders, who sustain loss due to the wrongdoer's acts or omissions would, without the law's aid, be left without a remedy. Accordingly, several remedies[1] are provided for by statute, of which the principal three are:

1. the statutory derivative claim;
2. the unfair prejudice remedy; and
3. a petition to wind up the company.

⟶ standing: the right to be heard in a court

Derivative claims

A particular problem arises where a director breaches his general duties, or commits some other act that causes the company loss. As the company has suffered the loss, only the company as a separate entity can generally commence proceedings to remedy it. However, because a company can only function through human actors and the power to commence proceedings on the company's behalf is usually vested in the board of directors,[2] a problem arises where the directors or majority shareholders themselves have committed the wrong and they are reluctant to sue a member of their board. Can the members commence litigation on the company's behalf where the directors are unwilling to do so?

---

1. These remedies are traditionally known as 'shareholder's remedies' (indeed, virtually all current texts use this term). However, given that they are available to members and not just shareholders (indeed, the relevant legislative provisions use the word 'member'), they will be referred to here as members' or member remedies.
2. Article 3 of the model articles provides that the directors may 'exercise all the powers of the company', which would include the right to litigate on behalf of the company. Where an insolvency procedure has been initiated, the liquidator also acquires the right to commence proceedings on the company's behalf.

The rule in *Foss v Harbottle*

In the case of *Foss v Harbottle*,[3] the Court of Chancery established three principles, which have come to be known as 'the rule in *Foss v Harbottle*':

1. **The 'proper claimant' principle** This principle, which is a natural corollary of corporate personality, provides that only the company can commence proceedings for wrongs committed against it. Accordingly, members cannot normally sue on the company's behalf.

2. **The 'internal management' principle** This provides that where a company is acting within its powers, the courts will not interfere in matters of internal management unless the company itself commences proceedings.

3. **The 'irregularity' principle** This principle, which is a corollary of the principle of majority rule, provides that where some procedural irregularity is committed, an aggrieved member cannot commence proceedings where the irregularity is one that can be ratified by a simple majority of the members. This principle applies both to rights vested in the company and to personal rights of the members. Accordingly, even where the right to commence proceedings is vested personally in a member, proceedings cannot be commenced if the irregularity in question can be ratified by the members.

Each principle has its own justifications, but there is an additional rationale behind all three principles—namely, the often-cited 'floodgates' argument, which contends that if members were to have the right to commence litigation on the company's behalf, then every minor irregularity would be litigated, thereby flooding the court with claims.[4]

'Exceptions' to the rule

The rule in *Foss v Harbottle* is not absolute; were it to be so, wrongs committed by the directors or majority shareholders would rarely be subject to litigation. Accordingly, there are instances where the members are permitted to bring an action on the company's behalf. Such actions were known as 'derivative' actions, because the members were bringing an action based on rights derived from the company. This derivation is reinforced by the fact that, if the derivative action succeeded, the remedy was granted to the company, not to the member who brought the action. With the creation of the statutory derivative claim and the consequent abolition of the common law derivative action, the common law exceptions to *Foss* have lost a measure of their relevance, but parallels do exist between these exceptions and the scope of the statutory derivative claim, so a basic knowledge of the common law exceptions will be of aid.

Historically, it has been stated that there were four exceptions to the rule in *Foss v Harbottle*.[5]

1. where the act complained of was illegal[6] or *ultra vires*;[7]

2. where the act complained of infringed the personal rights of a member (for example, the failure to provide sufficient notice of meetings,[8] the failure to

➡️ *ultra vires:* 'beyond one's powers'

---

3. (1843) 2 Hare 461.
4. See the classic statement of Mellish LJ in *MacDougall v Gardiner* (1875) 1 Ch D 13 (CA) 25.
5. See the judgment of Jenkins LJ in *Edwards v Halliwell* [1950] 2 All ER 1064 (CA).
6. See e.g. *Taylor v National Union of Mineworkers (Derbyshire Area)* [1985] BCLC 237 (unlawful strike action).
7. See e.g. *Simpson v Westminster Palace Hotel Co* (1860) 8 HL Cas 712 (HL).
8. *Baillie v Oriental Telephone and Electric Co Ltd* [1915] 1 Ch 503 (CA).

provide dividends in the manner provided for by the articles,[9] or the improper rejection of votes);[10]

3. where the act complained of could only be done or sanctioned by the passing of a special resolution;[11] and

4. where the act complained of constituted a 'fraud on the minority'.

Today, it is generally acknowledged that the only 'true' exception to *Foss* was the fraud on the minority exception. The reason for this is the first three so-called exceptions did not concern rights vested in the company, but concerned personal rights belonging to the member. Accordingly, they were not 'exceptions' to *Foss*, but rather areas in which *Foss* had no application.

The fraud on the minority exception was created specifically for those instances in which those who control the company (including those having the right to commence litigation on the company's behalf) have committed some form of fraud. 'Fraud' is defined widely to include actual fraud (such as a breach of the Theft Act 1968, or the Fraud Act 2006) and equitable fraud (such as conduct tainted with impropriety—for example, although the courts have maintained that negligence, however gross, is not a fraud on the minority,[12] where an act of negligence benefits those who control the company (thereby tainting it with impropriety), this can constitute a fraud on the minority).[13]

A court would, however, deny a member a right to sue on behalf of the company, even though there was fraud on the minority, if it did not serve the interests of justice. Examples of cases in which a member has been denied the chance to bring a derivative action include where the conduct of the member seeking to sue is itself tainted by impropriety,[14] or where the independent members (that is, not the wrongdoer nor the applicant) have already indicated that they do not wish there to be litigation on behalf of the company.[15]

The statutory derivative claim

Whilst the Law Commission agreed with the underlying approach of the rule in *Foss v Harbottle* (that is, that members should rarely be able to commence actions for wrongs done to the company), it was also of the opinion that the rules relating to derivative actions had become 'complicated and unwieldy'.[16] As a result of the Law Commission's recommendations (which were largely adopted by the Company Law Review Steering Group), Pt 11 of the CA 2006 now allows for the making of a statutory derivative claim. The provisions contained in Pt 11 do not actually affect the rule in *Foss v Harbottle* itself, which retains much of its forcefulness (especially in relation to personal claims); rather, the provisions of Pt 11 now replace the common law rules relating to when a derivative action may be brought. Accordingly, the common law derivative action is abolished.

9. *Wood v Odessa Waterworks Co* (1889) 42 Ch D 636 (Ch).

10. *Pender v Lushington* (1877) 6 Ch D 70 (Ch)

11. *Edwards v Halliwell* [1950] 2 All ER 1064 (CA).

12. *Pavlides v Jensen* [1956] Ch 565 (Ch).   13. *Daniels v Daniels* [1978] Ch 406 (Ch).

14. *Nurcombe v Nurcombe* [1985] 1 WLR 370 (CA).   15. *Smith v Croft (No 2)* [1988] Ch 114 (Ch).

16. Law Commission, *Shareholder Remedies* (Law Com No 246, 1997) [6.4].

Scope

Section 260(1) defines a derivative claim as one brought by a member in respect of a cause of action vested in the company, seeking relief on behalf of the company. This reiterates that any benefits obtained as a result of the claim accrue to the company and not to the derivative claimant. Section 260(2) provides that a derivative claim can only be brought under Pt 11 of the Act, or in pursuance of a court order under s 994. Section 260(3) provides that a claim can only arise from an actual or proposed act or omission involving one of the following.

🔗 The unfair prejudice remedy found in s 994 is discussed at p 651

- **Negligence** It will be remembered that negligence could not found a common law derivative action unless the wrongdoer gained some form of benefit from the negligent act. This limitation is not preserved by the Act, leading to a concern from directors that the number of derivative claims will substantially increase (to date, this has not occurred).
- **Default** 'Default' is a general term used in many pieces of legislation that refers to a failure to perform a legally obligated act (for example, to appear in court when required).
- **Breach of duty** Accordingly, a member will have standing to commence a derivative claim for breach of the general duties discussed in Chapter 22.
- **Breach of trust**.

The act or omission must be by a director.[17] Under the common law, the actions of members could found a derivative action,[18] but this is no longer the case. However, even though the act or omission must be by a director, the derivative claim may be brought against a director or another person (or both).[19] This would allow a claim to be brought against members or other persons who are somehow involved in the director's act or omission.

Section 260(4) provides that it is immaterial whether the cause of action arose before or after the person seeking to bring or continue the derivative claim became a member of the company. The timing of membership is irrelevant, because the claim belongs to the company and not the member.

Permission from the court

Section 261(1) provides that a member who brings a derivative claim must apply to the court for permission to continue it. If the member cannot establish a *prima facie* case for permission, the court must either dismiss the application or make any consequential order that it considers appropriate.[20] If a *prima facie* case is established, the court will direct the company to provide evidence. After hearing the application, the court may (i) give permission to continue the claim on such terms as it deems fit; (ii) refuse permission and dismiss the claim; or (iii) adjourn proceedings and give such directions as it sees fit.[21] The rationale behind this procedure is to screen out unmeritorious claims before the defendant becomes involved.

Key to the exercise of the court's discretion is s 263, which provides the court with guidance on the granting of permission under s 261 or 262. Section 263(2) provides

---

17. For the purposes of Pt 11, 'director' also includes former directors and shadow directors (CA 2006, s 260(5)(a) and (b)).

18. See e.g. *Estmanco (Kilner House) Ltd v Greater London Council* [1982] 1 WLR (QB).

19. CA 2006, s 260(3).

20. ibid s 261(2).   21. ibid s 261(4).

that the court *must* refuse permission if it is satisfied that any one of three conditions is satisfied. First, the court must refuse permission if a person acting in accordance with s 172 (director's duty to promote the success of the company) would not seek to continue the claim. This reinforces the fact that a derivative claim should be for the benefit of the company. Permission must be refused where a claim does not benefit the company and, in relation to derivative claims, this will be judged by reference to whether a hypothetical director would not seek to continue the claim.

Second, the court must refuse permission where the cause of action arises from an act or omission that is yet to occur, and the act or omission has been authorized by the company. An act or omission that has been authorized is no longer a wrong done to the company, so no claim should arise.

Third, the court must refuse permission where the cause of action arises from an act or omission that has already occurred, and the act or omission was authorized by the company before it occurred, or has been ratified by the company since it occurred. Authorization or ratification will prevent the act or omission from constituting a wrong done to the company.

Section 263(3) provides that when considering whether or not to grant permission, the court must take into account a number of factors (several of which are highly relevant to the refusal of permission under s 263(2)), including:

- whether the member is acting in good faith in continuing the claim;
- the importance that a person acting in accordance with s 172 (director's duty to promote the success of the company) would attach to continuing with the claim;
- where the cause of action arises from an act or omission that is yet to occur, whether the act or omission could be, and in the circumstances would be likely to be authorized before it occurs, or ratified after it occurs;
- where the cause of action arises from an act or omission that has already occurred, whether the act or omission could be, and in the circumstances would be likely to be, ratified;
- whether the company has decided not to pursue the claim; and
- whether the act or omission in respect of which the claim is brought gives rise to a cause of action that the member could pursue in his own right rather than on behalf of the company.

An additional factor was added late in the Bill's passage through the House of Lords and can be found in s 263(4), which provides that '[i]n considering whether to give permission…the court shall have particular regard to any evidence before it as to the views of members of the company who have no personal interest, direct or indirect, in the matter'. This resembles the 'majority of the minority' test that existed under the common law and is of particular relevance where the company has decided not to pursue the claim. The company may have perfectly legitimate reasons for not pursuing a claim (for example, waste of time and expense), and seeking the views of members with no interest in the matter may aid the court in determining whether to allow the action to go ahead even though the company does not wish it to.

Figure 23.1 clarifies the two-stage procedure for granting permission.

The 'no reflective loss' principle

An act or omission of a director may cause loss to both the company and, in turn, to its members. Such an act/omission might provide both the company and its members with a cause of action against the director. The company and the members

🔗 The duty to promote the success of the company, imposed by s 172, is discussed at p 625

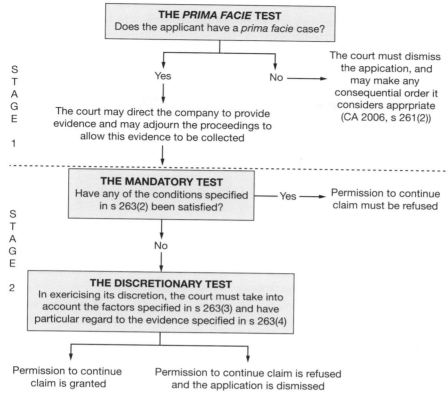

FIGURE 23.1 The two-stage procedure to determine whether permission is granted

might have a personal claim against the director, and/or the members might be able to bring a derivative claim against the director on behalf of the company. In such cases, the ability of the members to recover certain personal losses is limited by what is known as the 'no reflective loss' principle. This basically states that, where the loss sustained by the members is reflective of the loss sustained by the company, then the members will not be permitted to recover those losses that are reflective of the company's loss, which could be recovered by the company. The following example demonstrates this.

Eg The 'no reflective loss' principle

The directors of Undercard Ltd commit an act of negligence that causes a substantial reduction in the company's profits. This, in turn, reduces significantly the dividends paid to the members and the value of the company's shares decreases. Marc, a member of Undercard, wishes to commence a derivative claim against the directors involved. He will be unable to do so, because the loss sustained by the members is merely a reflection of the loss sustained by the company. The members' loss is embodied in the loss of the company.

In such cases, the company will be the proper claimant (which is the first principle of the rule in *Foss v Harbottle*) and its claim will generally trump that of the members, as the following case demonstrates.

Prudential Assurance Co Ltd v Newman Industries Ltd (No 2) [1982] Ch 204 (CA)

FACTS: The directors breached their duty by selling an asset of the company to a third party for less than it was worth, thereby causing the company loss. In order for the sale to be valid, the Listing Rules required the consent of the members, which the directors obtained by providing the members with misleading information regarding the sale. The transaction at an undervalue caused a reduction in the value of the company's shares. The members commenced a personal action against the directors.

HELD: The personal claims were 'misconceived'.[22] The loss suffered by the members was reflective of the loss suffered by the company, which could be recovered by the company by bringing a claim against the directors. In such a case, the company should bring the action and the members would not be permitted to recover the reflective loss.

COMMENT: Whilst the no reflective loss principle may prevent personal claims from succeeding, it will not prevent a member from succeeding in a derivative claim. As the benefits of a derivative claim go to the company, no issue of double recovery arises and the company's creditors are not adversely affected. The no reflective loss principle would not have prevented the members in *Prudential* from bringing a derivative claim although, in such cases, the courts still regard it as preferable for the company to recover its loss.

The rationale behind the no reflective loss principle is to prevent double recovery. If both the company and the members could recover the loss, then the defendant would be forced to pay compensation twice. If the members were to be allowed to recover their losses at the exclusion of the company, then the company and its creditors would be harmed. Accordingly, as Lord Millett stated in *Johnson v Gore Wood & Co (No 1)*,[23] '[j]ustice to the defendant requires the exclusion of one claim or the other; protection of the interests of the company's creditors requires that it is the company which is allowed to recover to the exclusion of the shareholders'.[24]

The no reflective loss principle applies to any situation where the company and members have a cause of action deriving from the same facts, and not just where the members have a derivative cause of action. It can therefore apply in cases where the wrongdoer was not a director. For example, in *Johnson v Gore Wood & Co*, the wrongdoer was the company's firm of solicitors. The rule also applies where the company has decided not to commence proceedings. However, the principle will not apply where the defendant's actions leave the company unable to commence proceedings, such as where the defendant's actions cause the company such loss that it cannot afford to commence proceedings.[25]

---

22. [1982] Ch 204 (CA) 222.
23. [2002] AC 1 (HL).   24. ibid 62 (Lord Millett).
25. *Giles v Rhind* [2002] EWCA Civ 1428, [2003] Ch 618.

Unfairly prejudicial conduct

Part 30 of the CA 2006 consists of a mere six sections, yet it provides what is perhaps the most important member remedy. Section 994 allows a member to petition the court for a remedy on the ground that the company's affairs will be, are being, or have been conducted in a manner that is unfairly prejudicial to the interests of members generally, or of some part of its members (including at least himself).

Section 994 re-enacts almost identically s 459 of the Companies Act 1985 (CA 1985), so case law decided under s 459 is still highly relevant. Section 459 was regarded as an extremely useful and popular member remedy, largely because of the courts' willingness to interpret it in a liberal manner. Key to the effectiveness of s 994 has been the courts' interpretation of the phrases 'unfairly prejudicial' and 'the interests of members'.

'Unfairly prejudicial'

The conduct complained of must be 'unfairly prejudicial'. The courts take an objective approach when determining whether conduct is unfairly prejudicial.[26] Accordingly, there is no requirement for the petitioner to 'come with clean hands', but unmeritorious behaviour on the part of the petitioner might lead the court to conclude that the conduct complained of was not unfair, or that the remedy granted should be reduced.[27]

The starting point in determining what constitutes unfairly prejudicial conduct is the much-quoted passage from Neill LJ, who stated that:

> The words 'unfairly prejudicial' are general words and they should be applied flexibly to meet the circumstances of the particular case…The conduct must be both prejudicial (in the sense of causing prejudice or harm to the relevant interest) and also unfairly so: conduct may be unfair without being prejudicial or prejudicial without being unfair, and it is not sufficient if the conduct only satisfies one of these tests.[28]

As the words 'unfairly prejudicial' are general words, the courts have not sought to impose a general standard or test, but it has been emphasized that the courts' discretion must be judiciously exercised. In *O'Neill v Phillips*,[29] Lord Hoffmann (who was involved in many of the major cases concerning the unfair prejudice remedy) stated that Parliament chose the concept of fairness to:

> free the court from technical considerations of legal right and to confer a wide power to do what appeared just and equitable. But this does not mean that the court can do whatever the individual judge happens to think fair. The concept of fairness must be applied judicially and the content which it is given by the courts must be based upon rational principles…Although fairness is a notion which can be applied to all kinds of activities its content will depend upon the context in which it is being used. Conduct which is perfectly fair between competing businessmen may not be fair between members of a family.[30]

26. *Re Guidezone Ltd* [2000] 2 BCLC 321 (Ch).
27. *Re London School of Electronics Ltd* [1986] Ch 211 (Ch).
28. *Re Saul D Harrison and Sons plc* [1995] 1 BCLC 14 (CA) 30, 31.
29. [1999] 1 WLR 1092 (HL).   30. ibid 1098.

Accordingly, whether conduct is unfairly prejudicial or not is a matter for each case. Examples of conduct that the courts have held capable of being unfairly prejudicial include:

- non-payment of dividends,[31] or payment of low dividends;[32]
- exclusion from the management of a quasi-partnership company;[33]
- serious mismanagement[34]—the requirement of serious mismanagement being crucial (mismanagement will not normally constitute unfairly prejudicial conduct);[35]
- preventing the members from obtaining the best price for their shares;[36]
- the payment of excessive remuneration;[37]
- the improper transfer of assets.[38]

'Interests of members'

The conduct must unfairly prejudice the 'interests of members'. Defining the extent of the members' interests has proven to be a complex issue that has generated a substantial body of case law. Historically, the courts imposed a member *qua* member requirement similar to that imposed upon members when attempting to enforce the constitution. As time progressed, however, the courts have eroded this requirement more and more, with the following case indicating how far away from the member *qua* member rule the court is prepared to go in order to achieve a just result.

 qua: 'in the capacity of'

Gamlestaden Fastigheter AB v Baltic Partners Ltd [2007] UKPC 26

FACTS: The claimant company entered into a joint venture with a man named Karlsten. The venture operated through a company (the first defendant). The claimant held 22 per cent of the shares in the first defendant and, in order to finance the joint venture, it had also made substantial loans to the first defendant over a two-year period. The claimant alleged that Karlsten and others had withdrawn substantial funds from the venture with the approval of the first defendant's directors (who were also defendants), but that no consideration had been provided for the withdrawals. The claimant alleged that this constituted unfairly prejudicial conduct and argued that the first defendant's directors should compensate the first defendant (not the claimant) for the withdrawals that they authorized. At the time of the hearing, the first defendant had become insolvent and its directors therefore argued that the payment of compensation to the first defendant would benefit the claimant company *qua* creditor, but would not benefit it *qua* member and, as such, the conduct did not affect its interests as a member.

HELD: The Privy Council rejected the directors' arguments and found for the claimant company. Lord Scott stated:

---

31. *Re a Company (No 00370 of 1987)* [1988] 1 WLR 1068 (Ch).
32. *Re Sam Weller & Sons Ltd* [1990] Ch 682 (Ch).
33. *Re RA Noble & Sons (Clothing) Ltd* [1983] BCLC 273 (Ch).
34. *Re Macro (Ipswich) Ltd* [1994] BCC 781 (Ch).   35. *Re Elgindata Ltd* [1991] 1 BCLC 959 (Ch).
36. *Re a Company (No 008699 of 1985)* [1986] BCLC 382 (Ch).
37. *Re Cumana Ltd* [1986] BCLC 430 (CA).
38. *Re London School of Electronics Ltd* [1986] Ch 211 (Ch).

in a case where an investor in a joint venture company has, in pursuance of the joint venture agreement, invested not only in subscribing for shares but also in advancing loan capital, the investor ought not...to be precluded from the grant of relief...on the ground that the relief would benefit the investor only as loan creditor and not as member.[39]

COMMENT: This case is significant for two reasons: first, the claimant company succeeded, even though the case was brought in its capacity as a creditor and not as a member of the first defendant; second, the claimant company did not seek compensation for itself, but on behalf of the first defendant. The claimant therefore enforced a right on behalf of the defendant company, which would normally be prohibited by the rule in *Foss v Harbottle*. A prior derivative claim had failed on the ground that the case did not come within any of the common law exceptions to *Foss*. To allow the claimant to use the unfair prejudice remedy to obtain relief for the first defendant confirms that a principal reason for the remedy's creation was to outflank the rule in *Foss v Harbottle* where fairness requires.

 See Tony Singla, 'Unfair Prejudice in the Privy Council' (2007) 123 LQR 542

The courts have, however, only been prepared to go so far and the member *qua* member requirement has not been fully abandoned. The court will still require the petitioner's interest to be sufficiently related to his membership. Thus, the courts have rejected claims where the petitioner has brought a claim in his capacity as an employee of the company,[40] or where a claim is brought in the capacity of a freeholder of land upon which a business was run, as opposed to a member of the company that runs the business.[41]

Equitable considerations

Section 994 focuses on the members' interests, as opposed to their rights. The members' rights are found in the company's constitution, but their interests are wider than this.[42] In particular, in certain types of company, the members may agree that the company is to be run in a certain way, but that agreement may never be formalized or inserted into the constitution. The courts have indicated that the majority may not be permitted to rely on the articles if reliance unfairly prejudices the interests of the members by defeating the 'legitimate expectations'[43] to which such agreements may give rise.

The courts' approach was stated in the only case involving unfair prejudice to reach the House of Lords.

O'Neill v Phillips [1999] 1 WLR 1092 (HL)

FACTS: The defendant owned all of the shares (a hundred) in a company but, in 1985, he gave twenty-five shares to the claimant (who was an employee) and made him a

---

39. [2007] UKPC 26, [2007] BCC 272, [37].

40. *Re John Reid & Sons (Strucsteel) Ltd* [2003] EWHC 2329 (Ch), [2003] 2 BCLC 319.

41. *Re JE Cade & Son Ltd* [1992] BCLC 213 (Ch).

42. *Re a Company (No 00477 of 1986)* [1986] BCLC 376 (Ch).

43. This phrase was first used by Lord Hoffmann in *Re Saul D Harrison and Sons plc* [1995] 1 BCLC 14 (CA). He has since indicated in *O'Neill v Phillips* [1999] 1 WLR 1092 (HL) that the term should not be used and that the term 'equitable considerations' is preferable.

director. The defendant also retired from the board, leaving the claimant as *de facto* managing director. The company's profits were split between the defendant (75 per cent) and the claimant (25 per cent), but the defendant voluntarily gave up 25 per cent of his profits, so that their share of the profits was equal. It was also discussed between them that the claimant's shareholding might be increased to 50 per cent. In 1991, the business experienced difficulties and the defendant returned to oversee management. He offered the claimant the opportunity to manage, under the defendant's direction, either the English or German branch of the business—the claimant choosing the German branch. Later in the year, the defendant claimed to be entitled once again to receive 75 per cent of the profits and the claimant left the company, claiming unfair prejudice. The Court of Appeal held that the claimant had a legitimate expectation that he would receive 50 per cent of the profits and would receive 50 per cent of the shares. The defendant appealed.

HELD: The House of Lords allowed the defendant's appeal. Lord Hoffmann stressed that:

> a member of a company will not ordinarily be entitled to complain of unfairness unless there has been some breach of the terms on which he agreed that the affairs of the company should be conducted. But...there will be cases in which equitable considerations make it unfair for those conducting the affairs of the company to rely upon their strict legal powers. Thus unfairness may consist in a breach of the rules or in using the rules in a manner which equity would regard as contrary to good faith.[44]

On the facts, the House held that the claimant had not been excluded from management, nor had the defendant promised to transfer any shares to the claimant (even if the claimant had hopes of such a transfer). Further, the defendant had not promised that the claimant would always receive 50 per cent of the profits; rather, the claimant had, at most, been promised 50 per cent of the profits whilst he remained *de facto* managing director. The defendant had not breached the articles or memorandum, nor was there anything giving rise to the equitable considerations of which Lord Hoffmann spoke.

★ See Dan D Prentice and Jennifer Payne, 'Section 459 of the Companies Act 1985: The House of Lords' View' (1999) 115 LQR 587

🔗 Quasi-partnerships are discussed in more detail at p 656

Although the category of equitable considerations is open-ended, the majority of cases in this area have involved members being excluded from management. The exclusion from management is an excellent example of when equitable considerations will be relevant. In public companies and most private companies, the members will have no expectations beyond those found in the company's constitution[45] and they will certainly not expect to manage. Conversely, in quasi-partnerships, the members are likely to have an expectation that they will participate in management and such an expectation may derive from an informal agreement, as opposed to the constitution. Exclusion from management in such companies is likely to amount to unfairly prejudicial conduct, but it must be noted that the expectation must be legitimate: a mere hope that the company's affairs will be run in a certain way will be insufficient and the court will only seek to enforce what was actually agreed. As Lord Hoffmann stated, the unfair prejudice remedy 'enables the court to give full effect to the terms and understandings on which the members of the company become associated but not to rewrite them'.[46]

---

44. [1999] 1 WLR 1092 (HL) 1098–99.
45. *Re Blue Arrow plc* [1987] BCLC 585 (Ch).
46. *Re Postgate and Denby (Agencies) Ltd* [1987] BCLC 8 (Ch) 14.

Remedies

Where a s 994 petition is successful, the court has significant remedial flexibility, being able to make 'such order as it thinks fit for giving relief in respect of the matters complained of'.[47] Section 996(2) provides examples of orders that the court could make, including:

- an order regulating the conduct of the company's affairs in the future (in *Re HR Harmer Ltd*,[48] the Court of Appeal allowed an elderly director, who snooped on staff, ignored board decisions, and insulted customers, to remain as chairman of the company, but deprived him of any executive role);
- an order requiring the company to refrain from doing an act complained of, or to perform an act that it has failed to perform;
- an order requiring the company not to make any, or any specified, alterations in its articles without the leave of the court;
- an order providing for the purchase of the shares of any members of the company by other members or by the company itself and, in the case of a purchase by the company itself, a reduction of the company's capital accordingly. This is by far the most common remedy ordered under s 996 and it is usually the majority shareholders who are ordered to purchase the petitioner's shares.[49]

A petition under s 994 is not subject to a limitation period, but because the granting of relief is discretionary, the court may refuse to grant a remedy where a substantial period has elapsed between the unfairly prejudicial conduct and the petition being brought.[50] The lack of a limitation period has been criticized on the ground that it encourages counsel to trawl through the company's history and adduce excessive amounts of evidence to back up any claims. This has resulted in s 994 claims gaining a reputation for being lengthy and expensive. For example, in one case concerning shares worth around £24,600, the legal costs amounted to £320,000.[51] The case of *Re Freudiana Music Co Ltd*[52] took over 165 days of court time, with the successful respondent awarded costs of £2 million.

The petition for winding up

Perhaps the most extreme remedy available to an aggrieved member is to petition the court for an order winding up the company. Despite the remedial flexibility afforded to the court in cases involving unfairly prejudicial conduct, winding up is not available under s 996 of the CA 2006. A member desiring the winding up of the company will need to petition the court under s 122(1) of the Insolvency Act 1986 (IA 1986), which lists eight circumstances in which a winding up may be ordered.

---

47. CA 2006, s 996(1).

48. [1959] 1 WLR 62 (CA).

49. In rare cases, however, the majority may be ordered to sell their shares to the petitioner (*Re Brenfield Squash Racquets Club Ltd* [1996] 2 BCLC 184 (Ch)).

50. For example, *Re Grandactual Ltd* [2005] EWHC 1415 (Ch), [2006] BCC 73 (nine-year delay between conduct and petition).

51. *Re Elgindata Ltd* [1991] 1 BCLC 959 (Ch).

52. *The Times* (London, 4 December 1995) (CA).

For our purposes, two of these are of importance. A company may be wound up where the company passes a special resolution resolving that the company should be wound up.[53] This will, however, clearly be of no use to an aggrieved minority shareholder, for whom the key provision is s 122(1)(g), which allows the court to wind up a company where it is 'of the opinion that it is just and equitable that the company should be wound up'. A single member may petition the court[54] under s 122(1)(g), thereby making it an extremely significant remedy.

Since the introduction of the unfair prejudicial remedy, the number of s 122(1)(g) petitions has decreased, but the precise relationship between the two remedies has never been truly clear. There is no doubt that the remedies overlap and that unfairly prejudicial conduct might also justify winding up under s 122(1)(g). Indeed, it is common for a winding-up order to be pleaded alongside a petition under s 994, but s 125(2) of the IA 1986 provides that the court will not order a winding up where an alternative remedy is available and the petitioner is acting unreasonably in seeking winding up as opposed to the alternative remedy. This indicates that the remedies are complementary, as opposed to mutually exclusive, but also recognizes that winding up is a much more drastic remedy that will be ordered only rarely.[55] Despite this, a number of instances can be identified in which the court is more likely to order a winding up, including:

- where the company is fraudulently promoted[56] or set up for a fraudulent purpose;[57]
- where the company is deadlocked[58] (that is, where management or the members are divided and refuse to be reconciled), meaning that it is unable to make any decisions, and the court will therefore order its winding up;
- where a company's objects clause indicates that it has been formed for a particular purpose (this purpose is known as the company's 'substratum'), a winding-up order will be appropriate if that purpose can no longer fulfilled. Thus, where a company was set up to manufacture goods based on a patent application, the fact that the patent was never granted constituted a loss of substratum sufficient to justify the company's winding up.[59] Cases involving a loss of substratum are likely to disappear over time, because companies created under the CA 2006 have unrestricted objects by default;[60]
- where the directors displays a lack of probity[61] (that is, honesty or decency). Note that inefficiency or negligence will not be enough.[62]

Quasi-partnerships

Section 122(1)(g) acquires an increased importance where the company in question is a 'quasi-partnership'. Indeed, as has been discussed, other member remedies also acquire increased importance in relation to such companies. What constitutes a

---

53. IA 1986, s 122(1)(a).

54. Petitions may also be brought by the company itself, a director, a creditor, or a liquidator.

55. This is backed up by a Practice Direction ([1990] 1 WLR 490), which provides that petitioners should not apply under both ss 994 and 122(1)(g), unless a winding-up order is genuinely preferred.

56. *Re London and County Coal Co* (1866) LR 3 Eq 355.

57. *Re Walter Jacob Ltd* [1989] BCLC 345 (CA).   58. *Re Yenidje Tobacco Co Ltd* [1916] 2 Ch 426 (CA).

59. *Re German Date Coffee Co* (1882) 20 Ch D 169 (CA).   60. CA 2006, s 31(1).

61. *Loch v John Blackwood Ltd* [1924] AC 783 (PC).

62. *Re Five Minute Car Wash Service Ltd* [1966] 1 WLR 745 (Ch).

quasi-partnership and the importance of s 122(1)(g) to such companies was the subject of the following case.

Ebrahimi v Westbourne Galleries Ltd [1973] AC 360 (HL)

FACTS: In 1945, E (the claimant) and N formed a partnership that sold rugs and carpets. In 1958, they incorporated the business, and E and N became its first directors, but shortly afterwards, G (N's son) also became a director. Between them, N and G held the majority of the company's shares. In 1969, a dispute arose, and N and G used their majority shareholding to vote E out of office. At the time, the unfair prejudice remedy did not exist, so E petitioned the court for a winding-up order.

HELD: In many companies, the rights of the members would be exhaustively stated in the company's constitution. However, certain companies, known as 'quasi-partnerships', also conducted business based on legitimate expectations and agreements made between the members and, in such companies, effect should be given to such expectations and agreements.

Although the characteristics of quasi-partnerships cannot be exhaustively stated, the House stated that, typically, quasi-partnerships would display all, or some, of the following characteristics:

- the company will be an association formed on the basis of mutual trust and confidence;
- there will be an agreement that some, or all, of the shareholders will be involved in management; and
- the shares of the company will not be freely marketable, thereby locking an aggrieved shareholder into the company.

The defendant company was clearly a quasi-partnership and had been formed on the understanding that all of the shareholders would participate in management. As this understanding had been breached, the House ordered the company to be wound up.

COMMENT: This case demonstrates that where a company is a quasi-partnership, the conduct of the majority should not be judged purely based on the rights of the parties, but also by the legitimate expectations of the parties and any informal agreements that existed between them. The courts have confirmed on multiple occasions that, in most quasi-partnerships, there will be an expectation that all of the members will participate in management and that exclusion of a member from management will be likely to justify the winding up of the company.[63]

⭐ See Dan D Prentice, 'Winding Up on the Just and Equitable Ground: The Partnership Analogy' (1973) 89 LQR 107

Chapter conclusion

The law relating to member remedies can be complex and there is considerable overlap between the three remedies discussed. The instances in which a member can commence an action on behalf of the company have been slightly extended and clarified by the introduction of the statutory derivative claim, but whether it encourages derivative claimants

---

63. See e.g. *Re Davis and Collett Ltd* [1935] Ch 693 (Ch); *Tay Bok Choon v Tahansan Sdn Bhd* [1987] 1 WLR 413 (PC).

to commence proceedings remains to be seen. The unfair prejudice remedy remains the same as it was under the CA 1985, and is likely to remain the most popular and broad shareholder remedy, but the CA 2006 has done nothing to remedy the practical problems associated with unfair prejudice claims—namely, excessive length and cost. Finally, a member has the option of petitioning the court for a winding-up order. Such a remedy will almost always be a remedy of last resort and certain decisions of the courts have further narrowed its scope in practice. The introduction of the unfair prejudice remedy has had a marked impact upon the other remedies. One could argue that the time may be approaching for the consolidation of member remedies but, at the moment, such a reform is unlikely. The Law Commission recommended that the courts should be able to make a winding-up order in cases of unfair prejudice,[64] thereby effectively consolidating s 994 and s 122(1)(g) into one remedy, but it was felt by the Company Law Review Steering Group that this remedy would be open to abuse and so the recommendation was never adopted.

 Key points summary

Derivative claims

- The rule in *Foss v Harbottle* consists of three principles:

  1. The 'proper claimant' principle provides that only a company can sue in respect of wrongs committed against it.
  2. The 'internal management' principle provides that the courts will not interfere in the internal management of a company.
  3. The 'irregularity' principle provides that a member cannot bring an action for an irregularity that could be ratified by a simple majority of the members.

- Today, the only form of derivative action available is known as a 'statutory derivative claim' and may be brought where a director commits an act or omission involving negligence, default, breach of duty, or breach of trust.

- A derivative claimant will require the permission of the court in order to continue with the claim and the claim will be dismissed if the claimant cannot establish a *prima facie* case.

- The courts will not allow a personal claim to proceed where the member's loss is merely reflective of the loss of the company.

Unfair prejudice remedy

- Section 994 allows a member to petition the court where the conduct of the company's affairs has unfairly prejudiced his interests as a member.

- The conduct complained of must be both unfair and prejudicial to the interests of the members.

- In most companies, the members' interests will not extend beyond the rights found in the company's constitution, but in certain cases, the members may have legitimate expectations not found in the constitution that are deserving of protection.

---

64. Law Commission, *Shareholder Remedies* (Law Com No 246, 1997) [4.35].

The winding up petition

- Section 122(1)(g) of the Insolvency Act 1986 allows the court to wind up a company where it considers it just and equitable to do so.

- The court will not wind up a company where an alternative remedy is available and the petitioner is acting unreasonably in seeking the winding up.

- Winding up may be appropriate where (i) the company is fraudulently promoted or set up for a fraudulent purpose; (ii) the company is deadlocked; (iii) it becomes impossible for the company to fulfil its objects; or (iv) the directors display a lack of probity.

Self-test questions

1. Define the following:
   - (a) *qua*;
   - (b) derivative claim;
   - (c) reflective loss;
   - (d) legitimate expectations;
   - (e) quasi-partnership.

2. Discuss the extent to which the statutory derivative claim provides a more effective remedy than the common law derivative action.

3. Helen, Tom, and Joseph have, for ten years, run a small but successful partnership. They decide to incorporate the business and a new company (JME Ltd) is created and the business is transferred to the new company. Helen, Tom, and Joseph become directors and each take 300 shares in the company. A further 200 shares are issued and allotted to Dave, a local businessman. The articles of JME Ltd provide that (i) no director can be removed without his or her prior consent; (ii) each director is to receive a salary of £150,000 per year; and (iii) any shareholder who wishes to sell his shares must first offer them to the directors.

   After incorporation the company was successful but no dividends were paid as all the profits were ploughed back into the company, the directors drawing only their salaries of £150,000 each year.

   In 2006 Joseph had an argument with Tom and Helen over matters of business policy. After this argument, Tom and Helen made all the business decisions in advance and outvoted Joseph at all the directors' meetings. Joseph initially complained but has now lost interest and ceased attending meetings. Recently, Tom and Helen have voted to remove Joseph as a director at a general meeting and also have voted to distribute the profits by increasing the directors' salaries to £300,000 per annum.

   Discuss whether or not JME Ltd has been run in a manner that is unfairly prejudicial, or whether any conduct has taken place that would justify winding up the company.

4. 'The unfair prejudice remedy is the principal source of redress for an aggrieved shareholder. In fact the remedy under s 994 of the CA 2006 is so useful that the derivative claim and the winding-up remedy are no longer required.' Do you agree with this statement? Provide reasons for your answer.

Further reading

MR Chesterman, 'The "Just and Equitable" Winding Up of Small Private Companies' (1973) 36 MLR 129
Discusses the winding-up remedy found in the Insolvency Act 1986, s 122(1)(g), focusing on its use in relation to quasi-partnerships

Paul L Davies and Sarah Worthington, *Gower & Davies' Principles of Modern Company Law* (9th edn, Sweet & Maxwell 2012) ch 20
A detailed, yet lucid, account of the unfair prejudice remedy and the ability to petition the court for a winding-up order on just and equitable grounds

Law Commission, *Shareholder Remedies: Consultation Paper* (Law Com CP No 142, 1996)
A Consultation Paper that discusses the rule in Foss v Harbottle, the unfair prejudicial remedy, and the winding-up remedy

Charles Mitchell, 'Shareholders' Claims for Reflective Loss' (2004) 120 LQR 457
Provides a readable and analytical account of the 'no reflective loss' principle

Jill Poole and Pauline Roberts, 'Shareholder Remedies: Efficient Litigation and the Unfair Prejudice Remedy' [1999] JBL 38
Discusses the Law Commission's proposed reforms of the unfair prejudice remedy, focusing on those measures designed to make s 994 cases less lengthy and costly

Paul Von Nessen, SH Goo, and Chee Keong Low, *'The Statutory Derivative Action: Now Showing Near You'* (2008) 7 JBL 627
Discusses the worldwide proliferation of the statutory derivative claim and examines how such derivative claims operate in the UK, Commonwealth countries, the US, and Hong Kong

KW Wedderburn, 'Shareholders' Rights and the Rule in *Foss v Harbottle*' [1957] CLJ 194
Despite its age, this remains a seminal article on the ability of a member to enforce the constitution and how this ability relates to the rule in Foss v Harbottle

 Remember to visit the **Online Resource Centre** at <**http://www. oxfordtextbooks.co.uk/orc/roach3e**> to access the following resources on Chapter 23, 'Members' remedies': more **practice questions** and answers; a **glossary** of key terms; **multiple-choice questions; and revision summaries**. Updates to the law can be found on Twitter by following **@UKBusinessLaw** and **@UKCompanyLaw**.

Corporate rescue, insolvency, and dissolution

- Fostering a 'rescue culture'
- Administration
- Company voluntary arrangements
- Receivership
- Liquidation
- Dissolution

INTRODUCTION

This final company law chapter discusses the various procedures available to companies that are experiencing financial difficulties that could jeopardize their survival. A company need not utilize any of these procedures and may simply attempt to trade its way out of difficulty but, in many cases, such a strategy will not prove successful, and the company will either need the aid of the law in order to become profitable again, or it will decide that there is no prospect of avoiding insolvency and enter into a process whereby it is brought to an end. This chapter discusses those procedures that:

- aim to help struggling companies;
- allow creditors of the company to recover monies owed; and
- bring about the death of a company and provide for the distribution of its remaining assets.

Fostering a 'rescue culture'

The failure of a company and its subsequent liquidation can have a substantial effect on a significant number of persons:

- the company's employees will lose their jobs;
- the company's creditors are unlikely to recover the full extent of the debt owed to them;
- the company's members will lose the value of their investment and their shares are likely to become worthless;
- suppliers that relied on the company may be forced into liquidation;
- retailers that sold the company's goods may be adversely affected;
- if the company is a large national or multinational company, it can even adversely affect the national economy in which it is based.

One would therefore assume that the law would be keen to establish mechanisms designed to help companies in a financially precarious position. However, prior to the passing of the Insolvency Act 1985 and its replacement by the Insolvency Act 1986 (IA 1986), the law did little to help struggling companies, who were basically 'left to die'. The problem is one of balancing interests. The pre-1985 law protected creditors by seeking to ensure that the creditors received as much of the money owed to them as possible, but the result of this was invariably that the company was liquidated and dissolved, even where it could have been saved. Alternatively, one can contend that the law should seek to aid financially vulnerable companies by creating a 'rescue culture', whereby such companies are encouraged to attempt to return to profitability. Of course, if the attempt fails, the company's assets may be depleted further and the creditors will receive even less than they would have done had the company been promptly liquidated.

The Cork Report[1] firmly favoured the fostering of a rescue culture, and this was reflected in the Insolvency Acts of 1985 and 1986, which established a number of mechanisms primarily aimed at providing a means 'for the preservation of viable commercial enterprises capable of making a useful contribution to the economic life of the country',[2] the principal one of which being administration. Whilst it is still the case that most insolvent companies are liquidated, administration has been used successfully either to rescue a company, or to result in a more advantageous winding up.

Administration

In January 2009, the UK officially entered a recession for the first time since 1991. The preceding few months were notable for the unprecedented number of prominent high-street companies (e.g. The Pier, Woolworths, Zavvi, USC, Whittard of Chelsea, and MFI) that went into administration. Even once the recession was over, the sustained difficult economic conditions resulted in many more high-street companies entering administration (e.g. HMV, Blockbuster, Comet, JJB Sports, Peacocks). In such difficult economic times, the value of the administration procedure is greater than ever. Administration was introduced by the IA 1986 and is a clear example of the law's desire to foster an increased rescue culture, as is evidenced by Figure 24.1, which sets out the hierarchy of objectives that the administrator is appointed to realize.

Certainly, when compared with liquidation, administration can have a number of beneficial effects:

- it is likely to be cheaper than liquidation;
- it may allow the sale of a going concern, rather than a 'fire sale' on liquidation, during which the assets are sold off for whatever price the liquidator can get;
- it allows a company currently trading profitably, but burdened by debt from past unsuccessful enterprises, to trade on with some form of debt moratorium or restructuring operating; and
- it means that creditors (including directors and employees) may have better prospects of payment than they do in a liquidation.

---

1. *Report of the Review Committee on Insolvency Law and Practice* (Cmnd 8558, HMSO 1982).
2. ibid [198].

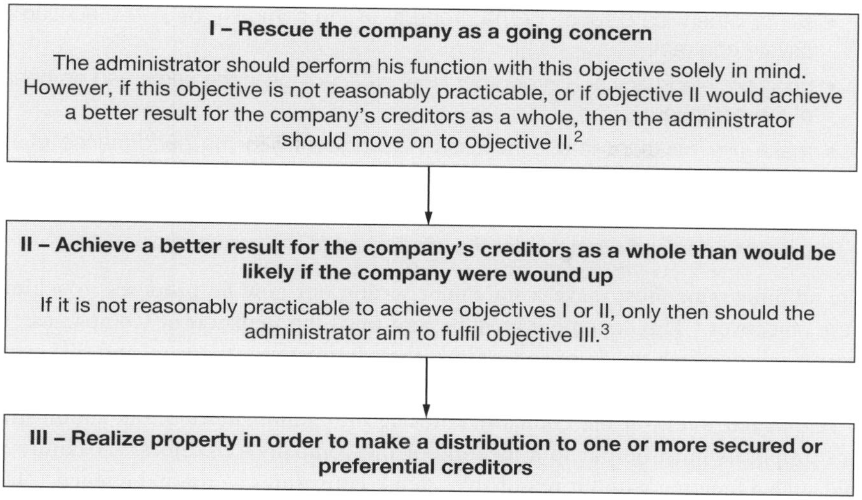

> **I – Rescue the company as a going concern**
>
> The administrator should perform his function with this objective solely in mind. However, if this objective is not reasonably practicable, or if objective II would achieve a better result for the company's creditors as a whole, then the administrator should move on to objective II.[2]

> **II – Achieve a better result for the company's creditors as a whole than would be likely if the company were wound up**
>
> If it is not reasonably practicable to achieve objectives I or II, only then should the administrator aim to fulfil objective III.[3]

> **III – Realize property in order to make a distribution to one or more secured or preferential creditors**

FIGURE 24.1 The purposes of administration[1]

[1] IA 1986, Sch 3(1), para 3(1).   [2] ibid para 3(3).   [3] ibid para 4(4).

The appointment of an administrator

The appointment of an administrator places the company 'in administration'. An administrator may be appointed in one of several ways, as follows.

- Upon an application from the company, its directors, or one or more of the company's creditors, a court may make an administrative order appointing a person as the administrator of a company.[3] The court may only make an administration order if it is satisfied that the company is likely to become unable to pay its debts, or that the administration order is reasonably likely to achieve the purpose of administration.[4]

- An administrator may be appointed out of court by the holder of a qualifying floating charge.[5]

- An administrator may be appointed out of court by either the company or its directors.[6]

Floating charges are discussed at p 559

The powers of an administrator

The effect of an administrator's appointment is substantial. The administrator will manage the company's affairs and the directors can no longer exercise any managerial powers without the administrator's consent.[7] As the administrator becomes, in effect, the board, he is given the power to 'do anything necessary or expedient for the management of the affairs, business and property of the company'.[8] Schedule 1 then provides an extensive list of specific powers afforded to the administrator, including the power to:

- take possession of, collect, and get in the property of the company, and, for that purpose, to take such proceedings as may seem to him expedient;

3. IA 1986, Sch B1, paras 10 and 12(1).
4. ibid Sch B1, para 11.   5. ibid Sch B1, para 14.   6. ibid Sch B1, para 22.
7. ibid Sch B1, para 64(1).   8. ibid Sch B1, para 59(1).

- sell or otherwise dispose of the property of the company by public auction or private contract;
- bring or defend any action or other legal proceedings in the name and on behalf of the company;
- make any payment that is necessary or incidental to the performance of his functions;
- carry on the business of the company and establish subsidiaries of the company;
- present or defend a petition for the winding up of the company.

The administrator must make a statement setting out how he proposes to achieve these objectives.[9] This statement must be sent to (i) the Registrar of Companies; (ii) every creditor of whose claim and address the administrator is aware; and (iii) every member of whose address the administrator is aware.[10]

Within ten weeks of the company entering into administration, the administrator's proposals must be put to a meeting of the company's creditors.[11] A failure to hold such a meeting without reasonable excuse constitutes a criminal offence.[12] The meeting may approve, modify, or reject the proposals, but whatever the outcome, the result of the meeting must be reported to the court. If the creditors approve the proposals, the administrator is under a duty to exercise his powers in accordance with the approved proposals.[13] If, however, the proposals are rejected, the court may:

- terminate the administrator's appointment;
- adjourn the hearing conditionally or unconditionally;
- make an interim order;
- make an order on a petition for winding up; or
- make any other order that it thinks appropriate.[14]

The statutory moratorium

Perhaps the most beneficial aspect of administration is the imposition of the statutory moratorium. The principal objective of administration (that is, to rescue the company as a going concern) would be frustrated if the company's creditors were then able to enforce their security. Accordingly, unless permission has been obtained from the administrator or the court, no creditor may, during the period of the administration:

- take steps to enforce security over the company's property;
- take steps to repossess goods in the company's possession under a hire-purchase agreement;
- institute or continue any legal process (including legal proceedings, execution, and distress) against the company or property of the company.[15]

In addition, during the period of administration, an administrative receiver cannot be appointed[16] and a winding-up order cannot be made (except a public interest winding-up order made on application by the Secretary of State).[17] The purpose of the moratorium is clear: it grants the company vital breathing space, and allows the

9. ibid Sch B1, para 49(1). 10. ibid Sch B1, para 49(4).
11. ibid Sch B1, para 51(2). 12. ibid Sch B1, para 51(5). 13. ibid Sch B1, para 53(1).
14. ibid Sch B1, para 55(2). 15. ibid Sch B1, para 43. 16. ibid Sch B1, para 43(6A).
17. ibid Sch B1, para 42.

administrator to put his proposals into effect and enter into arrangements with the creditors, with the aim of rescuing the company.

The termination of administration

A company can exit administration in a number of different ways, including:

- A creditor or member may apply to the court for an order terminating the administration on the grounds that (i) the administrator's actions are unfairly harming, or his proposed actions will unfairly harm, the applicant's interests; or (ii) the administrator is not performing his functions as quickly or as efficiently as is reasonably practicable.[18]

- The appointment of an administrator will automatically end after one year from the date of appointment, but this can be extended by the court, or with the consent of the creditors.[19]

- Upon an application from the administrator, the court can terminate an administrator's appointment.[20]

- An administrator's appointment will be terminated where he files a notice with the court and the Registrar of Companies stating that the purpose of the administration has been sufficiently achieved.[21]

- The administrator's appointment must be terminated where the court orders a winding up on public interest grounds.[22]

- The administrator's appointment will cease if he sends notice to the Registrar of Companies indicating that he intends to place the company into a creditors' voluntary liquidation,[23] or that he intends to dissolve it.[24]

Company voluntary arrangements

The company voluntary arrangement (CVA) is an important, but much underused,[25] rescue procedure that basically allows a company to enter into a binding scheme or arrangement with its creditors. There are two types of CVA:

1. the standard CVA, which does not provide a moratorium; and
2. a CVA available to 'eligible companies', which does provide a moratorium.

Commencement of a CVA

The first step in entering into a CVA is the proposal of a scheme or arrangement. If the company is in administration, the administrator will propose the arrangement.[26] If the company is in liquidation, the liquidator will propose the

---

18. ibid Sch B1, para 74(1), (2), and (4)(d).
19. ibid Sch B1, para 76. 20. ibid Sch B1, para 79. 21. ibid Sch B1, para 80.
22. ibid Sch B1, para 82. 23. ibid Sch B1, para 83. 24. ibid Sch B1, para 84.
25. Companies House, *Statistical Tables on Companies Registration Activities 2012–13* (Companies House 2013) 22, Table C2 states that, in the UK in 2012–13, there were 22,715 liquidations and 2,557 administrators appointed, compared with only 879 CVAs. 26. IA 1986, s 1(3)(a).

arrangement.[27] If the company is in neither administration nor liquidation, the directors will make the proposal.[28] Neither the company's members nor its creditors can propose a CVA. An arrangement proposed by an administrator or liquidator can be supervised by that administrator or liquidator, but if it is not, or if the arrangement is proposed by the directors, it will need to be supervised by a qualified insolvency practitioner or by some other authorized person,[29] who is known as the 'nominee'.

Within twenty-eight days of receiving notice of the directors' proposal (or such longer period as the court may allow), the nominee must submit a report to the court stating:

- whether, in his opinion, the proposed voluntary arrangement has a reasonable prospect of being approved and implemented;
- whether, in his opinion, meetings of the company and of its creditors should be summoned to consider the proposal; and
- if in his opinion such meetings should be summoned, the date on which, and time and place at which, he proposes that the meetings should be held.[30]

Where the nominee's report states that meetings of the company (that is, a meeting of the members) and creditors should be convened, the nominee should convene such meetings, unless the court directs otherwise.[31] These meetings, which are normally chaired by the nominee, must decide whether to approve, modify, or reject the proposal, but no proposal or modification can be approved if it:

- affects the right of a secured creditor of the company to enforce his security, except with the concurrence of the creditor concerned;[32]
- affects the priority of any preferential debt, unless the preferential creditor concerned concurs.[33]

Approval is granted if (i) at the creditors' meeting, a majority in excess of three-quarters in value of the creditors present in person or by proxy vote on the resolution;[34] and (ii) at the meeting of the company, a majority in excess of half in value of the members present in person or by proxy vote on the resolution.[35] If the decisions of the two meetings conflict, the decision of the creditors' meeting prevails,[36] but a member may, within twenty-eight days, apply to the court, which may order that the decision of the members' meeting shall have effect, or make any other order that it sees fit.[37] If the proposal is approved, it binds every person who was entitled to vote at, or who would have been entitled to vote at had they had notice of, the creditors' meeting,[38] but within twenty-eight days of the relevant report of the meeting being given to the court, an application to the court may be made on the grounds that the CVA unfairly prejudices the interests of a creditor, member, or contributory of the company, or that there has been some material irregularity at or in relation to either of the meetings.[39] Such an application can be made by the nominee, the liquidator, or administrator (if the company is in liquidation or administration, respectively), or anyone who had the right to vote at any of the meetings.[40] If the court agrees with the applicant, it can revoke or suspend any decision approving the

27. ibid s 1(3)(b).   28. ibid s 1(1).   29. ibid s 1(2).
30. ibid s 2(2).   31. ibid s 3(1).   32. ibid s 4(3).   33. ibid s 4(4).
34. Insolvency Rules 1986, SI 1986/1925, r 1.19.1.   35. ibid r 1.20.1.   36. IA 1986, s 4A(2).
37. ibid s 4A(3)–(6).   38. ibid s 5(2).   39. ibid s 6(1) and (3)(a).   40. ibid s 6(2).

CVA, or give directions for a further meeting to be convened to consider a revised proposal.[41]

'Eligible companies' and the moratorium

As noted, CVAs are useful, but underused. One significant reason for this is that it is relatively easy for an aggrieved creditor to derail a CVA proposed by the directors by appointing an administrator or receiver, or by petitioning the court for a winding-up order. To combat this, a new form of CVA was introduced that is identical to the one above, but which provides for a 28-day moratorium (which may be extended by a further two months) whilst the proposal is being considered. During this moratorium:

- no petition may be presented, or resolution passed, that orders the winding up of the company;
- an administrator or administrative receiver may not be appointed;
- no other steps may be taken to enforce any security over the company's property, or to repossess goods in the company's possession under any hire-purchase agreement, except with the leave of the court and subject to such terms as the court may impose.[42]

A CVA with a moratorium is, however, only available to 'eligible companies'—namely, companies that satisfy any two of three criteria for being a small company:

1. a turnover of no more than £6.5 million;
2. a balance sheet total of no more than £3.26 million; and
3. employees numbering no more than fifty.[43]

The moratorium is certainly useful, but it could be argued that its usefulness is outweighed by the complex nature of the procedures for obtaining it and the fact that administration appears to be a much more effective (and certainly much more popular) procedure. From the point of view of the directors, however, the obvious advantage of a CVA over administration is that they remain in control of the company.

Receivership

Receivership is a mechanism by which a secured creditor can recover payment owed. The usual procedure is that the secured creditor appoints a receiver, who then takes control of the charged assets and uses them to satisfy the debt of the creditor who appointed him.

A receiver can be appointed in one of two ways. First, the court can appoint a receiver upon an application from a creditor. If the application is successful, the Official Receiver attached to the court will act on behalf of the applicants.[44] Second, the instrument creating the charge may confer upon the chargeholder the power to appoint a receiver without the need to apply to the court. The majority of receivers are appointed this way.

---

41. ibid s 6(4).

42. ibid Sch A1, para 12.   43. ibid Sch A1, para 3; CA 2006, s 382(3).   44. IA 1986, s 32.

There are restrictions on who can be appointed as a receiver. A body corporate (that is, a company or limited liability partnership) cannot act as a receiver, and if one does so, it will commit an either way offence.[45] Similarly, an undischarged bankrupt commits an either way offence if he acts as a receiver, unless the court has appointed him.[46]

The role of a receiver

The role of the receiver and the obligations that he owes depend upon the nature of his appointment. Where a person is appointed solely to act as a receiver, his principal duty will be to realize the charged assets and to satisfy the debt of the creditor who appointed him. He will have power only to deal with the charged assets and will have no general powers of management (in turn, the directors will lose the power to deal with the charged assets if they had such a power). However, it is usual for the instrument creating the security to provide that the receiver will be an agent of the company, and he will therefore be able to enter into contracts and engage in other acts on the company's behalf. The receiver's principal duty is to the creditor who appointed him[47] and he is free to subordinate the interests of the company, or the other creditors, to those of his client. This can be contrasted with an administrator, whose principal function is to rescue the company, or, if that is not reasonably practicable, to secure a result that is beneficial to the creditors as a whole.

It is increasingly common for a person to be appointed as both receiver and manager. In such a case, the person will have the normal powers of a receiver discussed earlier, but will also have a general power to manage the company (and this power displaces that of the directors, although the directors still retain office). As the receiver's powers are limited to the charged assets, however, a general power of management arises only in relation to a floating charge taken over the whole of the undertaking.

Administrative receivership

A special form of receiver must be mentioned—namely, an administrative receiver. The office of administrative receiver was created by the Insolvency Act 1985 and has been largely abolished by the Enterprise Act 2002. The right to appoint an administrative receiver is granted only to floating charge holders who registered their charges before 15 September 2003 and whose charge covers the whole, or substantially the whole, of the company's property.[48] Floating charge holders whose charges were registered after this date cannot appoint an administrative receiver, but, as noted earlier, can appoint an administrator.[49] This is a significant reform and a clear indication of the law's desire to foster a rescue culture.

The administrative receiver has the sole right to deal with the charged assets. Given the breadth of the charges that permitted the appointment of an administrative receiver, this usually means that the directors cease to manage the company, although they remain in office. Administrative receivers are agents of the company[50]

---

45. ibid s 30 and Sch 10.   46. ibid s 31.

47. Where a receiver is appointed by the court, he is accountable to the court and so need not obey the instruction of the creditor who applied for his appointment.

48. IA 1986, s 29(2).

49. ibid Sch B1, para 14(1). Floating charge holders with the right to appoint an administrative receiver also have the right to appoint an administrator.

50. ibid s 44(1)(a). The agency ends if the company goes into liquidation.

and so can engage in acts on the company's behalf, but, unlike other agents, administrative receivers are personally liable for any contracts entered into by them in the carrying out of their functions (except in so far as the contract of appointment provides otherwise).[51] Like a normal receiver, an administrative receiver is tasked with realizing the charged assets and satisfying the debt of the floating charge holder who appointed him. However, certain debts rank ahead of those of floating charge holders (for example, preferential debts) and these debts must be paid out of the proceeds of the charged assets before the floating charge holder can be paid.

Once his task is complete, the administrative receiver's relationship with that company ends and the directors regain their powers (although, by this time, the company usually has few assets left to manage and its liquidation is likely).

Liquidation

In many cases, corporate rescue is not possible and a company that cannot trade out of its difficulties will usually be liquidated (also known as 'winding up'). Liquidation is the final step before a company is dissolved. It is the process whereby the assets of the company are collected and realized, its debts and liabilities paid, and the surplus distributed to the members. Liquidations come in two forms (i) compulsory; and (ii) voluntary.

Compulsory winding up

A compulsory winding up occurs where a specified party petitions the court to have a company wound up on specified grounds. The court then has the discretion whether or not to order the company's winding up. In 2012–13, there were 4,796 compulsory winding-up orders made by the courts in the UK.[52] The court has no ability to wind up a company on its own initiative: a compulsory winding-up order can only be made following a petition, with the IA 1986 stating that the following may petition the court for a compulsory winding-up order, including:

- the company itself,[53] or its directors;[54]
- any creditor(s) of the company (including contingent or prospective creditors);[55]
- a contributory of the company[56] (that is, any person who is liable to contribute to the assets of the company in the event of it being wound up,[57] an obvious example being a member of the company);
- the Secretary of State[58] (providing that certain conditions have been satisfied);
- an official receiver, but only if the company is in the process of being voluntarily wound up;[59]
- an administrator.[60]

The court will only consider a petition from the above parties on specified grounds.

---

51. ibid s 44(1)(b). An administrative receiver can obtain an indemnity from the company in respect of such liability (s 44(1)(c)).
52. Companies House, *Statistical Tables on Companies Registration Activities 2012–13* (Companies House 2013) 22, Table C2.   53. IA 1986, s 124(1).   54. ibid.   55. ibid.   56. ibid.
57. ibid s 79(1).   58. ibid ss 124(a), 124(b) and 124A.   59. ibid s 124(5).
60. ibid Sch B1, para 60, and Sch 1, para 21.

Grounds for winding up

The court will only consider a petition on specified grounds, with s 122(1) specifying the grounds upon which a compulsory winding-up order may be made, including:

- where the company has, by special resolution, resolved that the company be wound up by the court;
- where a public company has not been issued with a trading certificate and more than a year has expired since its registration;
- where the company does not commence its business within a year from its incorporation, or suspends its business for a whole year;
- where the company is unable to pay its debts;
- where a moratorium attached to a CVA ends and there is no approved voluntary arrangement in effect;
- where the court is of the opinion that it is just and equitable that the company should be wound up.

🔗 Winding up on just and equitable grounds is discussed in 'The petition for winding up' at p 655

The vast majority of compulsory winding-up orders made are made on the ground that the company is unable to pay its debts and, of orders sought under this ground, the vast majority of the petitions made are by a creditor (usually the one whose debt the company has been unable to meet). Despite the wording used, a creditor will not need to establish that the company cannot pay any of its debts; rather, failure to pay one debt will suffice. This is reinforced by s 123(1), which states that a company will be unable to pay its debts if:

- a creditor who is owed a sum exceeding £750 makes a written demand for payment and, three weeks later, the sum has not been paid, or security acceptable to the creditor has not been given; or
- execution or other process issued on a judgment, decree, or order of any court in favour of a creditor of the company is returned unsatisfied in whole or in part; or
- it is proved to the satisfaction of the court that the company is unable to pay its debts as they fall due.

Again, however, it should be stressed that the court is not bound to make a winding-up order if any of the above requirements are met. For example, a creditor may decide to petition the court for a winding-up order on the ground that petitioning for a winding-up order may, in terms of recovering monies owed, be less troublesome than commencing a direct action to recover the debt. The court may regard this as an abuse of the system and refuse to make such an order.[61] In any case, the court may want to determine the wishes of the creditors or contributories and, to this end, s 195(1) of the IA 1986 allows the court to call meetings of the creditors or contributories to determine whether or not such parties would wish for the company to be wound up.

Consequences of a compulsory winding up

If the court orders that a company should be wound up, the Official Receiver attached to the court will become the company's liquidator until such time as another is appointed.[62] The role and powers of a liquidator are discussed later, but his basic function is to gather in the assets of the company and distribute them to persons

---

61. *London Wharfing Co* (1866) 35 Beav 37.   62. IA 1986, s 136(2).

entitled to such assets. It may be the case that the company's assets are insufficient even to cover the liquidator's fees. In such a case, the liquidator will usually apply to the Registrar of Companies for early dissolution of the company.[63] The creditors and contributories also have the power to appoint a liquidation committee,[64] and this committee, as will be seen, is granted various powers under the IA 1986.

If a court decides to order a winding up, depending on the facts, a number of consequences may follow.

- In all cases, the company must forward a copy of the winding-up order to the Registrar of Companies,[65] who will then publish notice of the winding up in the *Gazette*.
- The court may stay any proceedings currently outstanding against the company.[66]
- Once a winding up has been commenced, any disposition of the company's property, and any transfer of shares, or alteration in the status of the company's members, are void unless authorized by the court.[67]
- Although not expressly stated in the IA 1986, the powers of the directors will cease upon the appointment of a liquidator[68] and, whilst it is not settled, the weight of authority would appear to indicate that the directors cease to hold office upon the appointment of a compulsory liquidator.[69] Given this, the directors have the right to appeal the winding-up order, because the cessation of their powers derives from the order, which they may wish to contest.[70]
- The company's employees are dismissed, although the liquidator may reappoint them.
- The business of the company will normally cease, although the liquidator may, upon obtaining permission from the court, carry on the business of the company in order to realize the most beneficial distribution of assets.[71]
- Any floating charges taken over the company's assets will crystallize.

Voluntary winding up

The majority of windings up do not occur due to an order from the court, but occur voluntarily. In 2012–13, of the 22,715 company liquidations in the UK, 16,848 were voluntary.[72] A company can be voluntarily wound up in one of two ways:

1. a members' voluntary winding up; or
2. a creditors' voluntary winding up.

In both cases, the winding up is commenced by the members passing a special resolution stating that the company is to be wound up voluntarily.[73] The distinction lies in whether or not a declaration of solvency is made. Where a majority of the company's directors make such a declaration, the winding up will be a members' winding up and the creditors will likely be paid in full. Where no such declaration is made, the winding up will be a creditors' winding up[74] and the creditors may not be paid in full.

---

63. ibid s 202.
64. ibid s 141(1).   65. ibid s 130(1).   66. ibid s 126.   67. ibid s 127.
68. *Re Farrow's Bank Ltd* [1921] 2 Ch 164 (CA).
69. *Measures Brothers Ltd v Measures* [1910] 2 Ch 248 (CA); cf *Madrid Bank Ltd* (1866) 2 QB 37.
70. *Re Diamond Fuel Co* (1879) 13 Ch D 400 (CA).   71. IA 1986, s 167(1)(a).
72. Companies House, *Statistical Tables on Companies Registration Activities 2012–13* (Companies House 2013) 22, Table C2.   73. IA 1986, s 84(1)(b).   74. ibid s 90.

The declaration of solvency

In order for a winding up to be a members' winding up, a majority of the directors must, within the five weeks preceding the passing of the resolution,[75] make a declaration of solvency. This declaration must state that the directors have made a full inquiry into the company's affairs and that, having done so, they have formed the opinion that the company will be able to pay its debts in full, together with interest at the official rate, within such period, not exceeding twelve months from the commencement of the winding up, as may be specified in the declaration.[76] The declaration must be delivered to the Registrar of Companies within fifteen days of the resolution being passed.[77] Failure to do so constitutes a summary offence by every officer in default.[78] Any director who makes a declaration of solvency without reasonable grounds for the opinion expressed in it commits an either way offence.[79]

The appointment of a liquidator

In the case of a members' voluntary winding up, it is the members in general meeting who will appoint a liquidator[80] and this will normally take place at the meeting at which the general meeting resolved to wind up the company.

In the case of a creditors' winding up, the members may also resolve to appoint a liquidator but, no more than fourteen days after the resolution was passed, the company must summon a meeting of its creditors.[81] If, at this meeting, the creditors do not approve of the members' choice of liquidator, they may nominate a person to replace the member's choice and this person will become the liquidator.[82] The creditors also have the power to appoint a liquidation committee of not more than five persons.[83] Where such a committee is appointed, the company may also nominate five persons to sit on the committee, but the creditors may veto any or all of the company's nominations, whereupon they will not form part of the liquidation committee unless the court directs otherwise. The court can also appoint other persons to act in place of the company's nominees.[84]

Consequences of a voluntary winding up

Once the resolution has been passed, the voluntary winding up is deemed to commence,[85] and several consequences follow.

- The company ceases to carry on business, except so far as may be required for its beneficial winding up.[86]
- Any transfer of shares is void, unless authorized by the liquidator.[87]
- Any alteration in the status of the company's members is void.[88]
- Upon the appointment of a liquidator, the powers of the directors cease. If the winding up is a members' voluntary winding up, the directors may continue to exercise such powers as may be determined by the general meeting or the liquidator.[89] If the winding up is a creditors' voluntary winding up, the directors may continue to exercise such powers as may be determined by the liquidation committee or, if no such committee exists, the creditors.[90]

75. ibid s 89(1) and (2).   76. ibid s 89(1).   77. ibid s 89(3).   78. ibid s 89(6).
79. ibid s 89(4).   80. ibid s 91(1).   81. ibid s 98(1).   82. ibid s 100(1) and (2).
83. ibid s 101(1).   84. ibid s 101(2) and (3).   85. ibid s 86.   86. ibid s 87(1).
87. ibid s 88.   88. ibid.   89. ibid s 91(2).   90. ibid s 103.

- The company's employees are dismissed, although the liquidator may reappoint them.
- Any floating charges taken over the company's assets will crystallize.

The crystallization of floating charges is discussed in 'Floating charges' at p 599

The role and powers of a liquidator

As can be seen, the liquidator occupies an extremely important position. The liquidator's role is basically to gather in all of the assets of the company, to pay off the company's debts and liabilities, and to distribute any remaining assets to persons entitled to them in the correct order. To this end, the liquidator is granted a wide array of general powers, including:

The distribution of assets is discussed at p 678

1. The ability to pay any creditors in full, or to enter into compromises or arrangements with the creditors.
2. The power to compromise in relation to any claims or debts (and liabilities capable of resulting in debts) owed to the company.
3. The power to bring legal proceedings under certain sections of the IA 1986, and a general power to bring or defend legal proceedings on behalf of the company.
4. The power to carry on the business in order to obtain a beneficial winding up, and to sell any of the company's property by public auction or private contract.
5. The power to appoint an agent to conduct business that the liquidator himself cannot conduct.
6. The power to do all such other things as may be necessary for winding up the company's affairs and distributing its assets.

Additionally, the liquidator can maximize the size of the pool of assets by requiring certain persons to make contributions, or by preventing assets from being removed. In the case of the summary remedy, the liquidator himself may be required to make a contribution.

Summary remedy against delinquent directors etc

Section 212 of the IA 1986 applies where, during the course of a winding up, it appears that an officer of the company, a liquidator, an administrative receiver, or other person involved in the promotion, formation, or management of the company has misapplied or retained, or become accountable for, any money or other property of the company, or has been guilty of any **misfeasance** or breach of any fiduciary or other duty in relation to the company. In such a case, the court may examine the conduct of the above persons, but only upon an application from the liquidator, the official receiver, a creditor, or a contributory.[91]

➡ **misfeasance:** the improper or unlawful performance of a lawful act

If the court is of the opinion that s 212 has been breached, it may order the defendant to:

- repay, restore, or account for the money or property, or any part of it, with interest at such rate as the court thinks just; or
- contribute such sum to the company's assets by way of compensation in respect of the misfeasance or breach of fiduciary or other duty as the court thinks just.[92]

---

91. ibid s 212(3). A liquidator and a contributory may only make an application with the leave of the court (s 212(4) and (5)).
92. ibid s 212(3).

Fraudulent trading

Section 213 provides that if, in the course of the winding up[93] of a company, it appears that any business of the company has been carried on with intent to defraud creditors of the company or creditors of any other person, or for any fraudulent purpose, then the court, on the application of the liquidator,[94] may declare that any persons who were knowingly parties to the carrying on of the business in such a manner are liable to make such contributions to the company's assets as the court thinks proper.

In an often-quoted passage, Maugham J defined 'fraudulent activity' as 'actual dishonesty involving, according to current notions of fair trading among commercial men, real moral blame'.[95] Whether or not a person has an 'intent to defraud' is heavily dependent upon the facts of the case, but the courts have indicated that certain conduct is highly likely to involve an intent to defraud (for example, inducing a person to provide a company with credit, when it is known that the company will be unable to repay).[96] Finally, it must be shown that the parties involved were knowing parties to the fraud. What the liquidator will need to show to establish this was stated by Patten J in *Morris v Bank of India; Re BCCI Ltd*:[97]

- a liquidator will need to show that the defendant knew that the relevant transactions were being entered into to defraud, or for a fraudulent purpose;
- the liquidator will not need to know every detail of the fraud, or how it was carried out, but he will have to know, either through observation or through being told, that the company was intent on a fraud;
- the liquidator must have actual contemporaneous knowledge of the fraud (a failure to realize that a fraud is being committed is not enough to breach s 213, no matter how obvious the fraud might be with hindsight);
- a defendant will have knowledge where it 'shuts its eyes to the obvious because of a conscious fear that to enquire further will confirm a suspicion of wrongdoing which already exists'.[98]

Where a director is found to have engaged in fraudulent trading, the court may also make a disqualification order against the director, for a maximum period of fifteen years.[99]

Wrongful trading

As fraud must be proved beyond reasonable doubt and the liquidator must prove subjective knowledge of the fraud, actions under s 213 rarely succeed. The Jenkins Committee[100] and the Cork Committee[101] (the recommendations of which led to the IA 1986) therefore recommended that a lesser form of civil liability be introduced, and this was implemented by s 214, which allows the court to require current and

---

93. Fraudulent trading under s 213 only applies in the course of a winding up. It should not be confused with the offence of fraudulent trading found in the CA 2006, s 993, which can apply at any time. It is, however, possible for one fraudulent transaction to breach both provisions, and civil and criminal liability to be imposed.

94. If fraudulent trading has occurred, but the liquidator fails to take action, the victims of the fraud may have the right to bring an action under the tort of deceit (*Contex Drouzhba Ltd v Wiseman* [2007] EWCA Civ 1201, [2008] BCC 301).   95. *Re Patrick and Lyon Ltd* [1933] Ch 786 (Ch) 790.

96. *R v Grantham* [1984] QB 675 (CA).   97. [2004] EWHC 528 (Ch), [2004] BCC 404.

98. ibid [13].   99. Company Directors Disqualification Act 1986, s 10.

100. *Report of the Company Law Committee* (Cmnd 1749, HMSO 1962).

101. *Report of the Review Committee on Insolvency Law and Practice* (Cmnd 8558, HMSO 1982).

former directors of a company to contribute to the company's assets where they have engaged in 'wrongful trading'. A person will have engaged in wrongful trading where, during the course of a winding up, it appears that:

- the company has gone into insolvent liquidation;
- at some time before the commencement of the winding up of the company, that person knew, or ought to have concluded, that there was no reasonable prospect that the company would avoid going into insolvent liquidation; and
- that person was a director of the company at that time.[102]

Trading whilst insolvent does not, in itself, constitute wrongful trading. As Chadwick J stated:

> The companies legislation does not impose on directors a statutory duty to ensure that their company does not trade while insolvent; nor does that legislation impose an obligation to ensure that the company does not trade at a loss...Directors may properly take the view that it is in the interests of the company and of its creditors that, although insolvent, the company should continue to trade out of its difficulties. They may properly take the view that it is in the interests of the company and its creditors that some loss-making trade should be accepted in anticipation of future profitability. They are not to be criticised if they give effect to such views, properly held.[103]

Liability will be imposed only if a person knew, or ought to have known, that there was no reasonable prospect of avoiding insolvent liquidation. However, no liability under s 214 will lie if, after the person concerned first knew, or ought to have concluded, that there was no reasonable prospect of the company avoiding insolvent liquidation, he took every step to minimize the potential loss to the company's creditors that he ought to have taken.[104]

For the purposes of s 214, the facts that a director of a company ought to know or ascertain, the conclusions that he ought to reach, and the steps that he ought to take are those that would be known or ascertained, or reached or taken, by a reasonably diligent person having both:

(a) the general knowledge, skill, and experience that may reasonably be expected of a person carrying out the same functions as are carried out by that director in relation to the company; and

(b) the general knowledge, skill, and experience that that director has.[105]

It will be remembered that this dual objective–subjective test is identical to the test used to determine whether or not a director has breached the duty of care, skill, and diligence under s 174 of the CA 2006. The objective test in s 214(4)(a) applies to all directors, irrespective of their skills and qualifications, and therefore represents the minimum level expected. The subjective test in s 214(4)(b) applies to those directors whose subjective abilities raise them above the standard expected in s 214(4)(a) (for example, those who are highly qualified or highly experienced). Therefore, all directors are judged by the standard of a reasonably competent hypothetical director, except directors who are better qualified than this hypothetical director—such directors are judged by reference to their own qualifications.

The duty of care, skill, and diligence is discussed at p 629

---

102. IA 1986, s 214(2). 103. *Secretary for State and Industry v Taylor* [1997] 1 WLR 407 (Ch) 414.
104. IA 1986, s 214(3). 105. ibid s 214(4).

The first ever reported case regarding s 214 is still one of the most important and illuminating regarding its operation.

Re Produce Marketing Consortium Ltd [1989] BCLC 520 (Ch)

FACTS: A company (that was incorporated in 1964) imported fruit, and was profitable until 1980. Between 1980 and 1984, its profitability and turnover decreased, it built up a large overdraft, its liabilities exceeded its assets, and it was trading at a loss. Between 1984 and the company's liquidation in October 1987, these losses continued. By February 1987, one of the directors realized that liquidation was inevitable, but the company continued to trade until October 1987. The rationale behind the decision to continue trading was to dispose of the fruit that had been stored in the company's cold storage. Upon the company's liquidation, the liquidator sought a contribution from the two directors under s 214.

HELD: The directors should have concluded by July 1986 that liquidation was inevitable. Over a period of seven years, the company went from being profitable, having excess assets, and no overdraft, to trading at a loss, having liabilities that exceeded its assets, and regularly exceeding the overdraft limit. Further, the directors had failed to take all steps to minimize loss. The Court estimated that prompt liquidation could have saved the company £75,000, so it ordered the directors to contribute this amount.

★ See Len S Sealy, 'Insolvent Company: Wrongful Trading' (1989) 48 CLJ 375

Transactions at an undervalue

Clearly, companies that are nearing insolvency should be engaged in acts designed to increase the assets of the company. The directors of such companies may, however, cause their companies to sell off their assets cheaply (usually to the directors or other connected persons) in order to place them out of the control of a future liquidator. To combat this, s 238 provides that where, at a 'relevant time', a company has gone into liquidation (or administration), the liquidator (or administrator) may apply to the court for a remedy on the ground that the company has entered into a transaction at an undervalue. If the application is successful, the court will make such order as it thinks fit for restoring the position to that which it would have been had the company not entered into that transaction.[106]

A company enters into a transaction at an undervalue with a person if:

- the company makes a gift to that person, or otherwise enters into a transaction with that person on terms that provide for the company to receive no consideration; or
- the company enters into a transaction with that person for a consideration the value of which, in money or money's worth, is significantly less than the value, in money or money's worth, of the consideration provided by the company.[107]

An application for an order can, however, only be made in relation to transactions at an undervalue that occurred at the 'relevant time', this time being two years ending on the date of insolvency.[108] However, a transaction will only fall within the relevant

---

106. ibid s 238(3).   107. ibid s 238(4).
108. ibid s 240(1)(a).

time if, at the time the transaction was made, the company was unable to pay its debts, or became unable to pay its debts due to the transaction.[109]

Even if a company does enter into a transaction at an undervalue at the relevant time, no order shall be made if the company entered into the transaction in good faith and for the purposes of carrying on the business, and, at the time, there were reasonable grounds to believe that the transaction would benefit the company.[110]

Preferences

As noted, a principal role of the liquidator is to distribute surplus assets to persons entitled to them in the event of a company being wound up. As is discussed later, this distribution of assets is hierarchical, with certain types of creditor ranking ahead of others. A company may attempt to avoid this hierarchy by paying off certain low-ranking creditors prior to insolvency, with the result that there may be insufficient assets to pay higher-ranking creditors. This is known as a 'preference' and where a company has provided a creditor with a preference, the liquidator may apply to the court, which may make such order as it thinks fit for restoring the position to that which it would have been had the company not given that preference.[111]

A company provides a person with a preference if:

- that person is one of the company's creditors, or a surety or guarantor for any of the company's debts or other liabilities; and
- the company does anything or suffers anything to be done that has the effect of putting that person into a position that, in the event of the company going into insolvent liquidation, will be better than the position in which he would have been had that thing not been done.[112]

Like transactions at an undervalue, a preference must be given at the 'relevant time' in order to obtain a remedy, with the relevant time depending on the identity of the person to whom the alleged preference was granted:

- If the company granted the alleged preference to someone connected with the company (for example, directors, or the spouses, relatives, business partners or employees of directors), then the relevant time is two years ending on the date of insolvency.[113]
- In all other cases, the period is six months ending on the date of insolvency.[114]

The decision to make a preference must have been influenced by the desire to place a person in the advantageous position described above.[115] There is no need for such a desire to be the sole, or even the dominant, influence, provided that it is present to some degree.[116] Where a preference is given by a company to a connected person other than an employee, this influence is presumed to exist unless the contrary can be shown.[117] In all other cases, the liquidator will need to establish such influence.

Extortionate credit transactions

Section 244 allows a liquidator (or administrator) to petition the court for a remedial order where, within a three-year period ending on the date of insolvency (or the granting of the administration order), the company entered into an 'extortionate

---

109. ibid s 240(2).
110. ibid s 238(5).   111. ibid s 239(3).   112. ibid s 239(4).
113. ibid ss 240(1)(a), 249, and 435.   114. ibid s 240(1)(b).   115. ibid s 239(5).
116. *Re MC Bacon Ltd* [1990] BCC 78 (Ch).   117. IA 1986, s 239(6).

credit transaction'. Unless the contrary is proven, a credit transaction will be presumed to be extortionate if:

- the terms of it are, or were, such as to require grossly exorbitant payments to be made (whether unconditionally or in certain contingencies) in respect of the provision of the credit; or
- it otherwise grossly contravened ordinary principles of fair dealing.[118]

If the court is of the opinion that a credit transaction is extortionate, it may make an order containing one or more of several provisions including:

- a provision setting aside all, or part, of the transaction;
- a provision varying the terms of the transaction, or varying the terms on which any security for the purposes of the transaction is held;
- a provision requiring any person who is, or was, a party to the transaction to pay to the liquidator (or administrator) any sums paid to that person, by virtue of the transaction, by the company;
- a provision requiring any person to surrender to the office holder any property held by him as security for the purposes of the transaction.[119]

Avoidance of floating charges

The directors of a company may cause the company to grant them a floating charge over the assets of the company, thereby prioritizing themselves over other creditors in the event of the company's liquidation. To prevent this, s 245 invalidates floating charges created within the relevant time prior to insolvency.[120] The relevant time is:

- two years, where the charge was granted to a person connected with the company;[121]
- twelve months for an unconnected person[122]—but a floating charge to an unconnected person will not be invalidated, even if created within the relevant time, if the company was able to pay its debts at the time that the charge was granted and did not become unable to pay its debts due to the granting of the charge.[123]

Distribution of assets

In relation to a voluntary winding up, s 107 states that:

> the company's property in a voluntary winding up shall on the winding up be applied in satisfaction of the company's liabilities pari passu and, subject to that application, shall...be distributed among the members according to their rights and interests in the company.

In relation to compulsory windings up, a similar provision can be found in s 143(1). The use of the words *pari passu* generally means that creditors receive an equal share of the company's assets—but it is subject to a number of important qualifications:

pari passu: 'with equal step'

- Creditors who have taken security over the company's assets (for example, fixed or floating charges) can usually recover monies owed without relying on the

---

118. ibid s 244(3).   119. ibid s 244(4).   120. ibid s 245(2).   121. ibid s 245(3)(a).
122. ibid s 245(3)(b).   123. ibid s 245(4).

liquidator by taking the charged assets and selling them. As we shall see, whilst this is true regarding fixed charges, the issue is more complex regarding floating charges.

- The expenses of liquidation are paid out of the assets realized by the liquidator.[124]
- Certain creditors are classified by statute as 'preferential creditors' whose claims rank above those of others.

Charge holders

The principal reason for taking a charge over the company's assets is to acquire a means by which to recover monies owed without having to rely on the liquidation process. Where a person has secured a debt of the company by way of fixed charge, upon the company's liquidation, he may take the charged asset, sell it, and use the proceeds to satisfy the debt owed to him. Of course, if the proceeds exceed the sum owed, the remainder must be returned to the company and will be added to the pool of assets to be distributed by the liquidator.

Regarding floating charges, the position is slightly more complex, in that charges created after 15 September 2003 are subject to new rules introduced by the Enterprise Act 2002. Regarding such charges, once the liquidator has determined the assets that would go to the floating charge holders, he must then set aside a percentage of those assets to pay off the unsecured creditors.[125] The prescribed percentage is:

- 50 per cent of the first £10,000;
- 20 per cent of the remainder, up to a limit of £600,000.[126]

This rule, however, will not apply where the company's net property is worth less than £10,000,[127] or where the liquidator, administrator, or receiver thinks that the cost of making a distribution to unsecured creditors would be disproportionate to the benefits.[128]

Preferential debts

Statute classifies certain debts as preferential debts, meaning that they rank ahead of all other debts (except debts secured by fixed change, and liquidation expenses). The categories of preferential debts can be found in Sch 6 of the IA 1986, but it is worth noting that Crown debts (for example, debts owed to HM Revenue and Customs) are, following the passing of the Enterprise Act 2002, no longer classified as preferential.

Preferential debts include:

- pension scheme contributions;
- remuneration owed to employees (but only remuneration earned in the four months prior to the relevant date,[129] up to a maximum of £800,[130] will rank as preferential—the remainder will rank as unsecured);
- any amount owed by way of accrued holiday pay.

---

124. ibid ss 115 and 175(2)(a).   125. ibid s 176A.
126. Insolvency Act 1986 (Prescribed Part) Order 2003, SI 2003/2097, art 3.
127. IA 1986, s 176A(3)(a); Insolvency Act 1986 (Prescribed Part) Order 2003, art 2.
128. IA 1986, s 176A(3)(b).
129. What constitutes the relevant date will depend upon the type of administration procedure. The IA 1986, s 387, provides a list of the relevant dates.
130. Insolvency Proceedings (Monetary Limits) Order 1986, SI 1986/1996, art 4.

Preferential debts rank equally among themselves, meaning that if there are insufficient assets to pay all of the preferential debts, the preferential creditors will all receive an equal proportion.[131] Of course, this means that creditors who rank below the preferential creditors will receive nothing.

The order of distribution

The order of distribution of assets is given in Figure 24.2.

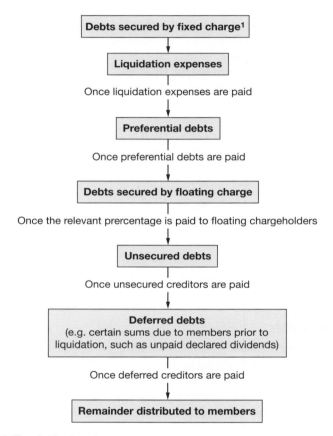

FIGURE 24.2 The distribution of assets

[1] It should be noted that fixed chargeholders do not need to rely on the liquidator to recover monies owed. They can simply seize the charged asset and sell it.

The groups are paid off one by one, so the higher a debt ranks, the more chance it has of being paid. Once a group is paid in full, the remaining assets are used to pay the next group. If there are insufficient assets to pay a group fully, each creditor amongst that group will receive the same percentage of their debt (that is, the *pari passu* rule operates amongst members of each group).

---

131. IA 1986, s 175(2).

Dissolution

None of the procedures discussed so far actually brings about the death of a company (although liquidation is certainly the final step in bringing about a company's demise). In order for a company to cease to exist, it must be removed from the register of companies, via a process known as 'dissolution'. Dissolution ends a company's separate personality, and terminates the relationship between a company and its members.

A company may be dissolved in a number of different ways, including:

- The Registrar of Companies may strike a company from the register if he believes it to be 'defunct' (that is, if it is not carrying on business).[132] Before doing this, he must send a letter to the company's registered address enquiring whether it is still carrying on business. The majority of companies that are dissolved are defunct.

- The decision of the Registrar to register a company is subject to judicial review, provided that the application for judicial review is brought by the Attorney General. The court may order the Registrar to cancel the registration and remove the company from the register.[133]

- Three months after the Registrar has been notified that a winding up has been completed, the company will be automatically struck off the register.[134]

- If an administrator of a company thinks that the company has no property that can be distributed to its creditors, he must send a notice to that effect to the Registrar. The Registrar will register the notice and, three months later, the company will be deemed to be dissolved.[135]

- An Act of Parliament may dissolve a company (for example, the HSBC Investment Banking Act 2002).

Restoration

It may be necessary to restore to the register of companies a company that has been dissolved (for example, where further assets of the dissolved company are discovered). A company may be restored by:

- applying to the Registrar on the ground that a company has been incorrectly struck off as defunct.[136] Only a former member or director may make such an application,[137] and it must be made within six years of the date of dissolution;[138]

- applying to the court for restoration. Such an application can be made where (i) the company was struck off by the Registrar for being defunct, but at the time of the striking off, it was actually carrying on business; or (ii) the company was voluntarily struck off, but the relevant requirements for such a striking off were not complied with; or (iii) in any other case the court considers it just to do so.[139]

An application must normally be made within six years of the date of dissolution,[140] but there is no time limit where the application is made for the purpose of bringing proceedings against the company for damages for personal injury.[141]

---

132. CA 2006, s 1000(1).
133. See e.g. *R v Registrar of Companies, ex p Attorney General* [1991] BCLC 476 (DC).
134. IA 1986, ss 201 and 205.   135. ibid Sch B1, para 84.
136. CA 2006, ss 1024 and 1025.   137. ibid s 1024(3).   138. ibid s 1024(4).
139. ibid s 1031(1).   140. ibid s 1030(4).   141. ibid s 1030(1).

Chapter conclusion

Liquidation still lies at the heart of our insolvency law regime. In fact, it is worth remembering that, in many cases, liquidation occurs even though a company is solvent or even financially healthy. In all cases, it is vital that there is a clear procedure in place regarding who can wind up a company and how the assets of the company are distributed. Despite the importance of liquidation, the growth of the UK's rescue culture should not be underestimated. Administration and, to a lesser extent, CVAs have radically affected the underlying philosophy behind our insolvency law regime. The result is that companies facing serious financial difficulties now have a number of options available to them, ranging from attempting to trade back into profitability, to liquidating and distributing the assets of the company.

 Key points summary

- The principal aim of administration is to rescue the company as a going concern. If this is not reasonably practicable, the administrator should aim to achieve a better result for the company's creditors than would be available if the company were to be wound up.

- A company in administration is subject to a statutory moratorium, which prevents creditors from enforcing security, repossessing goods, or continuing any legal process against the company or its property.

- A company voluntary arrangement (CVA) allows the company to enter into a binding scheme or arrangement with its creditors.

- Receivership is a mechanism whereby a secured creditor can recover payment owed.

- Liquidation is the process whereby the assets of the company are collected and realized, its debts and liabilities paid, and the surplus distributed to the members. The company is then usually dissolved.

- A winding up can be ordered by the court (known as a 'compulsory winding up') upon a petition from certain persons. This petition must be made based on defined grounds, the most common of which is that the company is unable to pay its debts.

- A company may voluntarily wind itself up (known as a 'voluntary winding up'). If the winding up is accompanied by a statement of solvency, it will be a members' voluntary winding up. If no statement is made, it will be a creditors' voluntary winding up.

- A liquidator will be appointed, whose task it is to realize the company's assets, pay off the company's debts and liabilities, and distribute any remaining assets to those entitled to them.

- Fixed charge holders can normally recover the charged assets without the liquidator's involvement.

- The liquidator will distribute assets in the following order:
  - liquidation expenses;
  - preferential debts;
  - debts secured by floating charge;
  - unsecured debts;
  - deferred debts; and
  - surplus to the members.

Self-test questions

1. Define the following:
   (a) rescue culture;
   (b) administration;
   (c) moratorium;
   (d) receivership;
   (e) liquidation;
   (f) misfeasance;
   (g) preference;
   (h) *pari passu*.

2. What procedures are designed to help companies survive as going concerns? To what extent has the Insolvency Act 1986 introduced a rescue culture into English law?

3. Other than through selling the assets of the company, how else can a liquidator maximize the pool of assets to be distributed?

4. In April 2014, Ethos plc enters insolvent liquidation. Below is a list of Ethos' creditors.
   (a) Around fifty of Ethos' employees have not been paid in the last six months. Each is owed around £9,000.
   (b) Ethos owes around £5,000 in tax to HM Revenue and Customs.
   (c) Your fee for conducting the liquidation is around £3,000.
   (d) Andrew, who is owed £60,000, has taken out a fixed charge over Ethos' fleet of company cars. The cars have a market value of £90,000. He also took out, in December 2013, a floating charge over all of the company's assets.
   (e) Ceri, the wife of one of Ethos' directors, lent the company £3,000. One month before Ethos entered liquidation, Ethos paid Ceri back the full £1,000.

   Skene & Jordan Ltd is Ethos's auditor and it transpires that it advised the directors of Ethos in January 2014 that the company's insolvency was inevitable. The assets of Ethos have been collected in and amount to around £75,000. You have been appointed as Ethos' liquidator. Explain what your role is and how you would go about performing it in relation to Ethos plc.

5. In what ways can a company be dissolved?

Further reading

Carol Cook, 'Wrongful Trading: Is It a Real Threat to Directors or Is It a Paper Tiger?' (1999) 3 Insolv L 99
Discusses the effectiveness of s 214 and examines a number of cases concerning the provision; argues that several decisions of the courts prevent s 214 from reaching its full potential

Roy Goode, *Principles of Corporate Insolvency Law* (4th edn, Sweet & Maxwell 2011)
A detailed, but highly readable, account of insolvency law in England and Wales; examines in depth all of the insolvency procedures discussed in this chapter

Muir Hunter, 'The Nature and Functions of a Rescue Culture' [1999] JBL 491
Discusses in depth what constitutes a rescue culture and whether such a culture is justified

Websites

<http://www.companieshouse.gov.uk>
The official website of Companies House; provides information and guidance booklets on liquidation and company charges

<http://www.bis.gov.uk/insolvency>
The official website of the Insolvency Service; provides a substantial amount of information on the various insolvency procedures

 Remember to visit the **Online Resource Centre** at <**http://www.oxfordtextbooks.co.uk/orc/roach3e**> to access the following resources on Chapter 24, 'Corporate rescue, insolvency, and dissolution': more **practice questions** and answers; a **glossary** of key terms; **multiple-choice questions; and revision summaries**. Updates to the law can be found on Twitter by following **@UKBusinessLaw** and **@UKCompanyLaw**.

PART V

employment law

25 The contract of employment

- Employment tribunals and the Employment Appeal Tribunal

- Employees and independent contractors

- The terms of the employment contract

INTRODUCTION

One of the most long-standing debates in employment law concerns the issue of how to determine whether an individual is an employee or not. Recent years have witnessed an increase in the debate's intensity and complexity as new forms of worker have emerged. Arguably, the historical distinction between employees and the self-employed is becoming less important due to the increasing trend of employment law statutes offering protection to 'workers', but it can be argued that the addition of this new class has served to make the issue even more complex. Even if it can be established that an individual has a contract of employment, the terms of that contract can derive from a number of vastly differing sources. This chapter aims to clarify these complex issues.

Employment tribunals and the Employment Appeal Tribunal

Before the contract of employment is discussed, it is worth discussing how disputes in employment law are resolved. The majority of employment disputes are resolved not in courts of law, but in the various employment tribunals. It is therefore important that students understand how these various tribunals work and how they fit into the administrative structure of the English legal system.

Employment tribunals

Employment tribunals are classified as First-tier Tribunals under the Tribunals, Courts and Enforcement Act 2007. They were originally called 'industrial tribunals' when established by the Industrial Training Act 1964, but were renamed as employment tribunals in 1998.[1] The majority of employment litigation is handled by

---

1. Employment Rights (Dispute Resolution) Act 1998, s 1(1).

employment tribunals and, in recent years, their jurisdiction has increased dramatically, to encompass hearings on a wide array of employment issues (all of which are discussed in subsequent chapters), including:

- allegations of unfair dismissal;
- contraventions of legislation relation to discrimination;
- equal pay claims;
- breaches of the Working Time Regulations 1998;[2]
- breaches of the National Minimum Wage Act 1998;
- cases involving breaches of the contract of employment.

This increase in jurisdiction has been accompanied by an increased caseload. In 2004–05, employment tribunals accepted 86,181 cases. In 2012–13, this had increased to 191,541 cases.[3] In an effort to reduce the workload faced by employment tribunals, the Enterprise and Regulatory Reform Act 2013 adds a new ss 18A and 18B to the Employment Tribunals Act 1996, which will compel claimants to seek conciliation from ACAS before a claim can be made to an employment tribunal. These provisions are not yet fully in force, but are expected to come into force in the spring of 2014.

Employment tribunals are not courts and the parties are not required to have legal representation. This results in a number of advantages—namely, that employment tribunals tend to hear cases more quickly than the courts, and that cases tend to be decided more quickly and with less formality (although formalities are increasing and the rapidly rising caseload has increased delays). Lacking the status of a court means, however, that employment tribunal decisions are not binding on any other court or tribunal, and that they cannot enforce their decisions. Research conducted by the Citizens Advice Bureau indicates that 10 per cent of those whose case succeeds at an employment tribunal do not obtain the compensation ordered.[4] If a court order is breached, it will constitute contempt of court, but if an order of the employment tribunal is breached, it will not constitute contempt and the aggrieved party may need to initiate a claim in a county court to have the employment tribunal's decision enforced—and such proceedings may be lengthy and expensive.

Whilst employment tribunals are not courts, they are, however, bound by the decisions of certain courts—namely, the Court of Appeal and the Supreme Court/House of Lords. Employment tribunals are also bound by decisions of the Employment Appeal Tribunal, which is discussed later.

Composition

A typical employment tribunal will consist of three persons:[5] a legally qualified chairman (who is also known as an 'employment judge') and two lay members (known as 'wing members'). In order to obtain a balanced bench, one of the lay members will be drawn from a list of persons representing employers (for example, the Confederation of British Industry); the other, from a list representing workers (for example, the Trades Union Congress). Decisions of employment tribunals are based on a majority and the votes are equal, meaning that the two lay members may outvote the chairman—although this is extremely rare and 96 per cent of employment tribunal decisions are

---

2. SI 1998/1833.

3. Statistics derived from <https://www.gov.uk/government/collections/tribunals-statistics>.

4. Citizens Advice Bureau, *Justice Denied: The Deliberate Non-Payment of Employment Tribunal Awards By Rogue Employers* (CAB 2008) 1.   5. Employment Tribunals Act 1996, s 4(1).

unanimous.[6] To combat the rise in the employment tribunals' caseload, a significant range of cases[7] can be heard by a chairman alone. In 2012, the coalition government passed subordinate legislation that now permits unfair dismissal cases to be heard by the chairman (or employment judge) alone.[8] This is a controversial development, as many contend that unfair dismissal cases are the very types of cases that benefit most from having lay members present, as they can bring their practical experience to bear.

Fees

Historically, in employment tribunal cases, each party usually paid his own costs. However, in 2013, the coalition government introduced controversial and far-reaching reforms in relation to fees via the Employment Tribunals and Employment Appeal Tribunal Fees Order 2013.[9] The effect of the 2013 Order is that a fee is now payable by the claimant upon making a claim (known as the issue fee) and a further fee (known as the hearing fee) will be payable if the case proceeds to a full hearing.[10] The fees charged will depend upon the type of case, with certain cases (usually the less complex cases) being classified as Type A cases[11] and all other cases being classified under Type B. Table 25.1 sets out the fees for Type A and Type B cases.

TABLE 25.1 Employment tribunal fees

Type of case	Issue fee	Hearing fee	Examples of cases
Type A cases	£160	£230	• Complaint of unauthorized deduction from wages • Claims that employer has failed to pay maternity pay/minimum wage/payment for annual leave • Claims in relation to redundancy payments
Type B cases	£230	£950	• Claims for unfair dismissal • Complaints in relation to discrimination under the Equality Act 2010 • Whistleblowing cases

It can be seen why the introduction of these fees has proven controversial. An employee who claims for unfair dismissal may be required to pay out £1,180 in tribunal fees if his case proceeds to a full hearing. Two measures should be noted that can mitigate against the fees shown in Table 25.1. First, certain persons (notably those on lower incomes or those claiming certain benefits) can apply for remission, which will allow them to avoid paying the fees, or to pay a reduced fee.[12] Second, if the employee's claim succeeds, the tribunal can order the employer to reimburse the employee's costs, but this is entirely at the tribunal's discretion. Although it is too early to categorically state the effect the imposition of fees will have upon the

---

6. Astra Emir, *Selwyn's Law of Employment* (17th edn, OUP 2012) 9.

7. The full list of such case can be found in s 4(3) of the Employment Tribunals Act 1996.

8. Employment Tribunals Act 1996, s 4(3)(c), as amended by the Employment Tribunals Act 1996 (Tribunal Composition) Order 2012, SI 2012/988.

9. SI 2013/1893. These fees only apply to claims presented, or appeals lodged, on or after the 29 July 2013.

10. Employment Tribunals and Employment Appeal Tribunal Fees Order 2013, art 4(1).

11. The full list of Type A cases can be found in Sch 2, Table 2 of the 2013 Order.

12. Employment Tribunals and Employment Appeal Tribunal Fees Order 2013, arts 17 and 18, and Sch 3.

employment tribunals' caseload, statistics for the third quarter of 2013 do reveal a marked decrease (17 per cent) in the number of cases heard by employment tribunals when compared to the same quarter in 2012.[13]

The Employment Appeal Tribunal

Decisions of employment tribunals can be appealed to an Upper Tribunal known as the 'Employment Appeal Tribunal' (EAT), which was set up by the Employment Protection Act 1975. The jurisdiction of the EAT is exclusively appellate and, in 2012–13, it disposed of 2,155 appeals.[14] As the EAT will generally only hear appeals on points of law (a policy introduced to minimize the number of appeals), legal representation is highly recommended, although it is not compulsory. As with employment tribunals, fees have now been introduced into the EAT, with a fee of £400 to lodge an appeal and a further fee of £1,200 if the appeal proceeds to a full hearing.[15]

Historically, EAT cases were heard by three persons, two of whom were lay members (rising to four lay members in certain exceptional cases). The Enterprise and Regulatory Reform Act 2013 amended the Employment Tribunals Act 1996, so that the general rule is that EAT cases will now be heard by a single judge alone.[16] However, the judge may direct that proceedings may be heard by a judge and either two or four appointed members, or, with the consent of the parties, the judge may direct that proceedings may be heard by a judge and either one or three appointed members.[17]

Although the EAT is not technically a court, it is a superior 'court of record', meaning that its decisions are reported and form precedents that must be followed by employment tribunals. The EAT is not bound by its own decisions,[18] but is bound by decisions of the Court of Appeal and the Supreme Court/House of Lords. Decisions of the EAT can be appealed to the Court of Appeal, and leave to appeal is required, either from the EAT or from the Court of Appeal. From the Court of Appeal, an appeal would lie to the Supreme Court in the normal way.

Employees and independent contractors

→ **vicarious liability:** liability imposed on an employer for torts committed by his employee

It was noted in Chapter 16 that establishing vicarious liability is largely dependent upon the existence of an employer–employee relationship. Courts and tribunals must therefore determine who qualifies as an employee and who does not. The significant distinction to be made is between employees and independent contractors (also known as 'self-employed persons'), and distinguishing between the two is crucial, not only for the purposes of establishing liability in tort, but also because the

---

13. Ministry of Justice, *Tribunals Statistics Quarterly: July to September 2013* (Ministry of Justice 2013) 8.
14. Ministry of Justice, *Tribunal Statistics Quarterly (Including Employment Tribunals and EAT): April to June 2013* (Ministry of Justice 2013) 18.
15. Employment Tribunals and Employment Appeal Tribunal Fees Order 2013, arts 13 and 14.
16. Employment Tribunals Act 1996, s 28(2).   17. ibid s 28(3) and (4).
18. *Secretary of State for Trade and Industry v Cook* [1997] ICR 288 (EAT).

distinction is of immense practical significance in relation to employment law, for several reasons:

- Employees pay tax under Schedule E, whereas independent contractors are taxed under Schedule D.[19] This allows independent contractors to set off business expenses for tax purposes and to pay tax off in arrears. Employees pay Class 1 National Insurance contributions, whereas independent contractors pay their own contributions under Class 2 (and Class 4 if profits are high enough).[20]
- Many statutory and common law employment rights are reserved solely for 'employees' (for example, only employees have the right to claim for unfair dismissal).
- In relation to health and safety issues, the duty owed to employees is stronger than that owed to independent contractors.

It is therefore of immense practical importance that the law can distinguish between an employee and an independent contractor. However, these are not the only classes of persons that need to be defined, with legislation increasingly serving to protect 'workers'. It may be the case that the parties attempt to gain the above benefits by defining their status themselves and labelling themselves as employees, workers, or independent contractors. To what extent is such self-classification valid?

 Autoclenz Ltd v Belcher [2011] UKSC 41

FACTS: The defendant provided car-cleaning services to motor retailers and auctioneers at several depots around the country. The twenty claimants worked as valeters at one such depot. Their contracts provided that the claimants would be self-employed and, as such, that they would pay their own NI contributions, and that they were not, and would not, become employees of the defendant. In 2007, the defendant required the claimants to sign new contracts, which provided that (i) the relationship between the claimants and defendant was one of client and independent contractor; (ii) the claimants could engage other persons to work on their behalf; (iii) they were free to refuse any work provided by the defendant and; (iv) the defendant was not bound to provide work. However, the defendant told the claimants how to carry out work, it provided the cleaning materials, it determined the rate of pay, and required the claimants to provide prior notification if they were unable to work. The claimants alleged that they were in fact employees and sought a declaration from the court to this effect.

HELD: Lord Clarke stated that, where a party asserts that the contractual terms do not accurately reflect the reality of the agreement, the task of the court is to determine 'whether the terms of any written agreement in truth represent what was agreed and the true agreement will often have to be gleaned from all the circumstances of the case, of which the written agreement is only a part'.[21] Applying this, he was satisfied that 'the documents did not reflect the true agreement between the parties'[22] and so the claimants were held to be employees.

★ See Julie McClelland, 'A Purposive Approach to Employment Protection or a Missed Opportunity?' (2012) 75 MLR 427

---

19. As a strict matter of law, the terminology of 'Schedules D and E' was abolished by the Income Tax (Earnings and Pensions) Act 2003, but the terminology is still used and is likely to be for some time.
20. As NI contributions entitle the payer to Jobseeker's Allowance and statutory sick pay, it follows that self-employed persons are not entitled to these allowances.
21. [2011] UKSC 41, [2011] IRLR 820 [35].   22. ibid [38].

Clearly, Lord Clarke believed that it is for the courts to determine the employment relationship, not the parties themselves. This does not mean, however, that the intention of the parties is not relevant, as the courts will consider the parties' classification of the relationship, but it will only be one factor amongst several.

Distinguishing between employees and independent contractors

The starting point is to define what an 'employee' is. The Employment Rights Act 1996 (ERA 1996) defines an employee as an 'individual who has entered into or works under…a contract of employment'.[23] We therefore need to define what a 'contract of employment' is, and this is defined as 'a contract of service or apprenticeship, whether express or implied, and (if it is express) whether oral or in writing'.[24] An employee therefore is someone who operates under a contract *of* service, as opposed to an independent contractor who operates under a contract *for* services. Unfortunately, this distinction provides little aid, and so the responsibility of determining how to distinguish between employees and independent contractors has been left to the courts and employment tribunals. The courts and employment tribunals have, however, been unable to articulate a single test, and what tests have been devised tend to be vague and difficult to apply to marginal cases.

The control test

In the nineteenth century, the courts adopted the control test, which defined an employee as 'a person subject to the command of his master as to the manner in which he shall do his work'.[25] At this time, when the workforce was largely based on agrarian and manual work, this test was perfectly acceptable, but, as technology and industry progressed, skilled workers were increasingly employed whose actions were not under the direct control of their employers (for example, surgeons[26] or ships' captains).[27] In such cases, the control test lost much of its effectiveness[28] (although, in certain cases, it will still be relevant and even decisive) and new tests had to be created to supplement it. This led to the development of the 'integration' test.

The integration test

The integration test was developed by Denning LJ, who stated that an individual would be an employee if he 'is employed as part of the business and his work is done as an integral part of the business'.[29] Conversely, an individual would not be an employee if 'his work, although done for the business, is not integrated into it but only accessory to it'.[30] Whilst the integration test better catered for skilled workers than the control test, it was rarely used, largely due to the vagueness of the terms used (for example, what does it mean to be 'an integral part of the business'). The

---

23. ERA 1996, s 230(1).
24. ibid s 230(2).   25. *Yewens v Noakes* (1880–81) LR 6 QBD 530 (CA) 532–33 (Bramwell LJ).
26. *Cassidy v Ministry of Health* [1951] 2 KB 343 (CA).
27. *Gold v Essex County Council* [1942] 2 KB 293 (CA).
28. In *Nora Beloff v Pressdram Ltd* [1973] FSR 33 (Ch) 42, Ungoed-Thomas J stated 'the greater the skill required for an employee's work, the less significant is control in determining whether the employee is under a contract of service'.
29. *Stevenson, Jordan & Harrison Ltd v Macdonald and Evans* (1952) 69 RPC 10 (CA) 22.   30. ibid.

problems were best laid out by MacKenna J, who stated that the integration test 'raises more questions than I know how to answer'.[31]

The multiple test

The inadequacies of the control and integration tests led the courts to conclude that no single test could categorically determine whether an individual was an employee or self-employed. The courts will therefore now look at all of the facts of a case and weigh up all of the relevant factors.

Ready Mixed Concrete (South East) Ltd v Minister of Pensions & National Insurance [1968] 2 QB 497 (QB)

FACTS: Ready Mixed Concrete introduced an 'owner-driver' scheme, whereby the company's lorry drivers were dismissed and re-employed after they had purchased their lorries. Certain terms in the contract indicated the drivers were employees (they had to wear uniforms and could only use the lorries for company business), whereas other terms indicated that they were self-employed (they had no set hours of work and, if they were unable to work, they could substitute others to work in their place). A tax dispute arose and the court had to determine if the drivers were employees or independent contractors.

HELD: The drivers were independent contractors. The High Court was heavily influenced by the fact that, in the event of sickness or unavailability, the drivers could substitute another to take their place. Further, the risk of the venture was placed upon the drivers, not the company.

⭐ See BA Hepple, 'Servants and Independent Contractors' (1968) 26 CLJ 227

In *Ready Mixed Concrete*, the court listed three factors that might be relevant in determining the case. In *O'Kelly v Trust House Forte plc*,[32] it has been argued that the court listed *seventeen* possible factors that might be relevant.[33] Whilst the multiple test grants the courts the flexibility to take into account a wide variety of factors, it also increases uncertainty, because it allows judges to weigh the relevant considerations subjectively. One judge may regard a certain factor as crucial, whereas, in another case, it may be regarded as trivial. The scope for inconsistent decisions is considerable.

In more recent years, the courts have attempted to introduce a measure of certainty by referring to the 'irreducible minimum' required for a person to be contract of employment to exist. Several such irreducible minimum requirements have been stated by the courts, including:

- the need for personal service by the employee;[34]
- that the employee should be subject to the control of the employer;[35] and
- a mutuality of obligation between the employer and employee.[36]

---

31. *Ready Mixed Concrete (South East) Ltd v Minister of Pensions and National Insurance* [1968] 2 QB 497 (QB) 524.
32. [1984] QB 90 (CA).
33. Malcolm Sargeant and David Lewis, *Employment Law* (6th edn, Pearson 2012) 22.
34. *Express & Echo Publications Ltd v Tanton* [1999] ICR 693 (CA).
35. *Montgomery v Johnson Underwood Ltd* [2001] EWCA Civ 318, [2001] ICR 819.
36. *Carmichael v National Power plc* [1999] 1 WLR 2042 (HL).

In relation to the requirement of a mutuality of obligations (i.e. the idea that each party owes obligations to the other), mention should be made of the recent growth of zero hour contracts. These contracts typically provide that the employer does not guarantee to offer work to the worker, with the result that the worker is placed in a rather insecure position. The question arises whether a worker operating under a zero hours contract is an employee or not. In the majority of cases, the worker will be a worker only and will not acquire employee status. If, however, the substance of the relationship indicates that a employment relationship exists, then the courts/tribunals will rule that the worker is an employee, irrespective of what the contract states.

Pulse Healthcare Ltd v Carewatch Care Services Ltd (EAT, 6 August 2012)

FACTS: Carewatch Care Services Ltd entered into a contract with a local primary care trust under which Carewatch would provide care to a severely disabled lady. Carewatch entered into contracts with the five claimants. These contracts were entitled 'Zero Hours Contract Agreement', but they made repeated reference to 'employment' and provided the claimants with numerous benefits that were common to employment contracts (e.g. the right to sick pay). The claimants produced evidence indicating that they had worked fixed hours on a regular basis over several years. The contract to care for the disabled lady was taken over by Pulse Healthcare Ltd and the claimants contended that Pulse also took over their contracts of employment under the relevant legislation relating to transfers of undertakings. The relevant legislation only applied to contract of employment and Pulse argued, *inter alia*, that as the contracts were zero hour contracts, they were not contracts of employment and so it was not obliged to take the contracts on.

HELD: The EAT stated that the zero hours agreement 'did not reflect the true agreement between the parties' and that, given the round-the-clock nature of the care package provided to the disabled lady, it was 'fanciful to suppose that Carewatch relied on ad hoc arrangements in the provision of such a package'. Accordingly, the EAT held that the contracts were indeed contracts of employment and so they were transferred to Pulse.

COMMENT: In many cases, a zero hours contract will not amount to an employment contract. However, the decision in *Pulse* tells us that the courts will look at the substance of the agreement and employers who do not wish for workers on such contract to become employees should ensure that such zero hours contracts are drafted carefully.

Atypical workers

The use of the multiple test has proven effective in dealing with what have been termed 'atypical' workers. These are workers who may work outside the normal working hours of many employees and who are likely to work from home, of which the two principal examples are homeworkers and agency workers.

Homeworkers

A significant number of cases involving homeworkers relate to those working in the clothing industry but, in recent years, with the advent of modern communications, a new form of homeworker known as a 'teleworker' has emerged. Homeworkers do have certain specific rights under statute,[37] but to qualify for more general rights, they need to be classified as employees.

 Nethermere (St Neots) Ltd v Taverna [1984] ICR 612 (CA)[38]

FACTS: The claimant was a homeworker sewing pockets onto trousers using a machine provided by the defendant. She had no set hours, was paid according to how much work she did, and was not obliged to carry out a minimum amount of work. She was dismissed and initiated an unfair dismissal claim. The defendant alleged that she was not an employee and that she therefore could not claim for unfair dismissal.

HELD: She was an employee. The Court focused on the mutuality of obligations between the parties. These obligations were never written down, but, during the course of a number of years, they gave rise to sufficient obligations on both sides to justify the existence of a contract of employment.

⭐ See J Warburton, 'The Employment of Home Workers' (1984) 13 ILJ 251

Agency workers

Over 8,000 recruitment agencies (and 6,000 recruitment professionals) in the UK assign work to nearly 1.4 million temporary workers every week in an industry worth over £26 billion.[39] Historically, there was limited statutory protection for agency workers but, with the passing of the Agency Worker Directive[40] and its implementation via the Agency Workers Regulations 2010,[41] agency workers covered by the Regulations will be entitled to many of the same working and employment conditions as persons who are directly recruited by the hirer.[42]

Consequently, determining whether an agency worker is an employee will not be required in many cases, as the agency worker will have the same basic rights as an employee. However, there will still be instances (notably where the Regulations do not apply) when the employment tribunal/court will need to determine whether or not an agency worker is an employee and, on this issue, the 2010 Regulations are silent, and so the issue has been left to the courts. The courts have emphasized that there is no single test or factor that could point towards the legal status of an agency worker. Instead, they take into account the individual facts of the case to determine one of a possible number of outcomes:

- the agency worker is employed by the recruitment agency;[43]
- the agency worker is employed by the client of the agency (known as the 'end-user');[44]

---

37. Notably, the right to a minimum wage under the National Minimum Wage Act 1998, s 35.
38. See also *Airfix Footwear Ltd v Cope* [1978] ICR 1210 (CA).
39. Figures derived from the website of the Recruitment and Employment Confederation <http://www.rec.uk.com>.
40. Directive 2008/104/EC of the European Parliament and of the Council of 19 November 2008 on temporary agency work [2008] OJ L327/9. 41. SI 2010/93.
42. Agency Workers Regulations 2010, regs 5–13.
43. *McMeechan v Secretary of State for Employment* [1997] ICR 549 (CA).
44. *Dacas v Brook Street Bureau (UK) Ltd* [2004] EWCA Civ 217, [2004] ICR 1437.

- the agency worker is employed by both the recruitment agency and the end-user, and the duties of an employer are shared between them;
- the agency worker is not employed by either the recruitment agency or the end-user.[45]

The following two cases demonstrate how important the particular facts of the case can be.

Dacas v Brook Street Bureau (UK) Ltd [2004] EWCA Civ 217

FACTS: The defendant recruitment agency had assigned Dacas (the claimant) to clean a hostel owned and run by Wandsworth Council (the end-user). Although Wandsworth Council exercised day-to-day control over her activities, the recruitment agency paid her wages, deducted tax and NI, and had the power to discipline and terminate her contract. After six years, the local authority asked the agency not to assign her to it, following an allegation that she had been rude to a visitor of the hostel. The agency informed Dacas that it would not assign her any further work. She alleged unfair dismissal against both the recruitment agency and Wandsworth Council—but only an employee can allege unfair dismissal.

HELD: Dacas was an employee of Wandsworth Council, but not of the recruitment agency. The recruitment agency was not required to provide her with work, nor was she under an obligation to accept work from it. It did not exercise day-to-day control over Dacas— that was the role of Wandsworth Council. The Court agreed that no express contract of employment existed, but that did not preclude the Court from finding the existence of an implied employment contract between Dacas and the end-user.

★ See Frederic Reynold, 'Negligent Agency Workers: Can There Be Vicarious Liability?' (2005) 34 ILJ 270

James v London Borough of Greenwich [2008] EWCA Civ 35

FACTS: James (the claimant) had worked for the end-user for three years, having been assigned to it by two successive recruitment agencies. A contract existed between James and the agency, which contained clauses denying her employee status with the agency and provided that either party could terminate the agreement. A second contract existed between the agency and the end-user, which stated that James was under the full control of the end-user. Following a period of illness, the end-user decided that it no longer required her services and the agency terminated her agreement. She could not allege unfair dismissal against the agency, because it lacked the requisite control over her and had an express term stating that she was not an employee. She therefore alleged that there was an implied contract between her and the end-user and that, as such, she was the end-user's employee.

HELD: James was not an employee of the end-user. It would be rare to imply a contract between a worker and an end-user where no pre-existing contract existed. Further, working for one end-user for a significant period is not enough per se to justify the implication of a contract.

★ See Michael Wynn, 'End of the Line for Temps?' (2008) 158 NLJ 352

---

45. *Wickens v Champion Employment* [1984] ICR 365 (EAT).

The consequence of the above decisions is that many agency workers are unable to demonstrate the existence of a contract of employment, either due to a lack of mutuality or control, or because the court is unwilling to imply a contract of employment. It may be the case, however, that, in certain fields of employment law, such agency workers can gain protection by bringing themselves within the definition of a 'worker'.

Distinguishing 'workers' and 'employees'

The divide between employees and independent contractors can be significant and, arguably, 'the legal dichotomy between "employee" and "independent contractor" is now too simplistic to fit our diverse workforce, and leaves too many people potentially in a hole in the middle'.[46] What is required is an intermediate category for those who do not fit neatly into the definition of 'employee' or 'self-employed'. It can be argued that such a category has existed for some time—namely, the concept of the 'worker'.

The definition of 'worker' is important on both a European and domestic level. From a European perspective, English translations of directives have used the term inconsistently, with certain directives applying to workers,[47] whilst others apply to employees.[48] The Court of Justice (CoJ) stated that how these terms are defined is a matter for the individual Member States, unless the CoJ (or the General Court) considers that a Community meaning of the term is required in order to create uniform harmonization.[49] The lack of uniformity is apparent in domestic law, too, but there is little doubt that the term 'worker' is gradually replacing the term 'employee' in employment legislation.[50] It is therefore of vital importance to define what a worker is. Section 230(2) of the ERA 1996 defines a worker as:

- someone who has entered into a contract of employment; or
- someone who has not entered into a contract of employment, but who undertakes to perform personally work or services for another, provided that these services are not being provided for a professional client.

The leading judicial discussion of the term 'worker' can be found in the case of *Byrne Bros v Baird*.[51] In this case, which concerned the Working Time Regulations 1998, the EAT articulated why these Regulations apply to workers and not only employees, stating:

> The reason why employees are thought to need such protection is that they are in a subordinate and dependent position vis-à-vis their employers: the purpose of the Regulations is to extend protection to workers who are, substantively and economically, in the same position.[52]

The EAT also indicated that, in determining whether an individual was a worker or not, it would use the same considerations used when determining whether an individual is an employee or self-employed, 'but with the boundary pushed further in the [assumed] worker's favour'.[53]

---

46. Ian Smith and Aaron Baker, *Smith & Wood's Employment Law* (11th edn, OUP 2013) 67.
47. For example, the Health and Safety Directive (Council Directive No 89/391/EC) and the Working Time Directive (Council Directive No 93/104/EC).
48. For example, the European Works Council Directive (Council Directive No 94/45/EC) and the Insolvency Directive (Council Directive No 80/987/EC).
49. Case C-53/81 *DM Levin v Staatssecretaris van Justitie* [1982] ECR 1035.
50. For example, the National Minimum Wage Act 1998, ss 1 and 54, and the Working Time Regulations 1998, reg 2(1).
51. [2002] ICR 667 (EAT).   52. ibid 677.   53. ibid.

It is argued that the increasing use of the term 'worker' is a welcome one. Too often, employers are able to avoid their obligations by convincing a court or tribunal that an individual is not an employee under the relevant legislation. There is little doubt that the wider notion of the 'worker' will result in an extension of protection to previously unprotected individuals. Further, it will avoid the need for the court to force the individual into one of two polarized possibilities: employee or self-employed.

The terms of the employment contract

Historically, the existence of an employer–employee relationship derived from the status of master and servant. Today, it is clear that the basis of the employment relationship is to be found in the contract of employment. Judges and academics have stated repeatedly that an employment contract 'is but an example of contracts in general, so that the general law of contract will be applicable'.[54] Certainly, it is true that contracts of employment are subject to the normal rules of contract, but it is also true that the contract of employment is subject to so much statutory regulation and implied terms that 'it is certainly open to doubt whether we should still accept that contract law alone provides the underlying structure of employment law'.[55]

The sources and content of the terms of the contract of employment will now be considered.

Express terms

Subject to limitations imposed by statute, the parties may (either orally or in writing) specify terms to be included in the contract. Since 1963, employees have been entitled to receive a copy of the written particulars of the contract following the commencement of employment.[56] Today, the right is found in s 1 of the ERA 1996, which provides that employees have a general right to receive a written statement of the particulars of employment no later than two months following the commencement of employment. The Act also prescribes exactly what particulars must be included:

- the names of the employer and employee, the date on which employment began, and the date on which the contract of employment commences (known as the 'date of continuous employment');
- the employee's scale or rate of remuneration, or its method of calculation, and the frequency of payment;
- the employee's hours of work;
- information concerning holiday entitlements and pay, sick pay, and pension schemes;
- notice requirements;
- the job title and/or description;
- the length of employment if the contract is not permanent;

---

54. *Laws v London Chronicle* [1959] 2 All ER 285 (CA) 287 (Evershed MR).
55. Ian Smith and Aaron Baker, *Smith & Wood's Employment Law* (11th edn, OUP 2012) 71.
56. Contracts of Employment Act 1963, s 4.

- the place of work or, where the employee is required or permitted to work at various places, an indication of that, and the address of the employer;
- collective agreements that directly affect the terms and conditions of employment (discussed later); and
- where the employee is required to work outside the UK for a period of more than one month, the period for which he is to work outside the UK and any additional payment that he is to receive for working outside the UK.

Under s 11, if the statement is not provided within two months, or if the statement is incomplete, the employee has the right to refer the issue to an employment tribunal, which can determine what should be included in the statement (although it cannot invent terms).[57] The tribunal will also award the employee a minimum of two weeks' pay,[58] unless the failure to receive a statement is connected to unfair dismissal or discrimination, in which case the minimum award is increased to four weeks' pay.

These particulars are straightforward, but one does require further explanation—namely, collective agreements. Collective agreements are agreements (usually relating to working conditions, holiday entitlements, etc) made between employers and trade unions,[59] and, unless expressly stated otherwise in writing, they are not presumed to be legally enforceable.[60] However, if the parties expressly incorporate them into the contract, they will become enforceable as express terms and will be required to form part of the written statement discussed earlier. It is also possible for collective agreements to be implied into a contract, but simply belonging to the union or association that negotiated the collective agreement is insufficient to justify its implication.[61] If, however, it can be demonstrated that, during bargaining, it was the intention of the parties that the final agreement would be binding, the court may imply the agreement into the contract.[62] The terms of a collective agreement may also be implied into a contract if it can be demonstrated that there is a reasonable, certain, and notorious custom to that effect.[63]

Implied terms relating to the conduct of the employer

The concept of implying terms into a contract has already been examined in relation to contract law. In relation to employment law issues, terms may be implied from a number of sources:

🔗 The implication of terms is discussed at p 173

- by the courts, as a matter of fact based upon the intentions of the parties;
- by the courts as a matter of law;
- by statute;
- by custom and practice.

The principal duties placed upon employers will now be discussed.

---

57. *Eagland v British Telecommunications plc* [1993] ICR 644 (CA).
58. Employment Act 2002, s 38(4)(a).
59. The precise definition and scope of collective agreements can be found in the Trade Union and Labour Relations (Consolidation) Act 1992, s 178.   60. ibid s 179(1).
61. *Hamilton v Futura Floors Ltd* [1990] IRLR 478.
62. *Rookes v Barnard* [1964] AC 1129 (HL).
63. *Henry v London General Transport Services Ltd* [2002] EWCA Civ 488, [2002] ICR 910.

Duty to provide work

In *Collier v Sunday Referee Publishing Co Ltd*,[64] a newspaper sub-editor was hired, but not given any work to do. He initiated a claim for breach of contract against his employer. In a much-quoted passage, Asquith J stated: 'It is true that a contract of employment does not necessarily, or perhaps normally, oblige the master to provide the servant with work. Provided I pay my cook her wages regularly she cannot complain if I choose to take any or all of my meals out.'[65] However, whilst no general duty to provide work exists, specific duties will arise in certain circumstances:

- where the employee is paid by commission,[66] because refusal to provide work will mean that the employee will earn no money;
- where the job in question requires regular practice in order to maintain skills;[67]
- where the lack of a job would lead to loss of publicity or reputation (for example, that of an actor/actress).[68]

Duty to pay the employee

In *Beveridge v KLM (UK) Ltd*,[69] Beveridge, after a long-term period of illness and having exhausted her right to sick pay, announced that she was fit to return to work. Her employer would not, however, let her return to work until its own doctor deemed her fit to return—a process that took six weeks, during which time Beveridge was not being paid, even though she was willing to work. The EAT held that, in the absence of a contractual provision, employees who offer work to their employers are entitled to be paid. This duty to pay the employee will not apply, however, where the lack of work is due to circumstances outside the control of the employer (for example, a strike,[70] or the closure of a workplace due to a natural disaster).[71]

Duty to indemnify the employee

The employer is under a duty to indemnify the employee for any expenses reasonably incurred during the course of his employment. This would not only include obvious examples such as travelling expenses, but may also include indemnifying the employee for any costs incurred in defending a legal action.[72] This duty will not apply, however, where the employee has incurred costs defending his own negligence.

Duty of mutual trust, confidence, and respect

As the employment relationship is based upon confidence and trust, it follows that employers are under a duty not to act in a manner that would jeopardize this relationship. Examples of breach of this duty include requiring an employee to relocate at short notice[73] and referring to an employee as an 'intolerable bitch'.[74] Virtually all

---

64. [1940] 2 KB 647 (KB).   65. ibid 650.   66. *Turner v Goldsmith* [1891] 1 QB 544 (CA).
67. *William Hill Organisation Ltd v Tucker* [1999] ICR 291 (CA).
68. *Marbé v George Edwardes (Daly's Theatre) Ltd* [1928] 1 KB 269 (CA).
69. [2000] IRLR 765 (EAT).
70. *Miles v Wakefield MDC* [1987] AC 539 (HL).
71. *Browning v Crumlin Valley Collieries Ltd* [1926] 1 KB 522 (KB) (flooding in a mineshaft).
72. *Re Famatina Development Corporation Ltd* [1914] 2 Ch 271 (CA).
73. *United Bank v Akhtar* [1989] IRLR 507 (EAT).
74. *Isle of Wight Tourist Board v JJ Coombes* [1976] IRLR 413 (EAT).

cases in this area are constructive dismissal cases, but the first case not involving constructive dismissal provided the duty with a renewed prominence.

Malik v Bank of Credit and Commerce International SA (in liq) [1998] AC 20 (HL)

FACTS: In 1991, BCCI entered insolvent liquidation amidst allegations of fraud, corruption, and criminal activity. The liquidator dismissed two employees named Malik and Mahmud. Both men claimed that, due to the stigma surrounding the collapse of BCCI, their reputations had been damaged to such an extent that they could not obtain alternative employment. This, they argued, amounted to a breach of the implied duty of mutual trust and confidence.

HELD: The claimants succeeded and they were awarded 'stigma damages'. The House of Lords held that, by acting in a dishonest and corrupt manner, BCCI had damaged the claimant's employment prospects. This, in turn, had damaged the relationship of trust and confidence, entitling the claimants to compensation.

> → **constructive dismissal:** an employee's termination of his employment as a result of the negative actions of the employer (discussed at p 790)

> ★ See Michael Jefferson, 'Stigma Damages Against Corrupt Companies' (1998) 19 Co Law 21

Duty to take reasonable care of employees' health and safety

As discussed in Chapter 26, employers are under both a common law and statutory duty to take reasonable care of the health and safety of their employees. What is important to note here is that this implied term may actually override any express terms of the contract (for example, if an employee's contract requires him to work a number of hours that can be damaging to health).[75]

Duty to deal with grievances

Employers are under a duty to put into place measures to deal effectively and promptly with the grievances of their employees. In *WA Goold (Pearmak) v McConnel*,[76] a change in sales methods resulted in the reduction of commission due to two salesmen. The company had no grievance procedure, so they tried to raise the matter informally with their manager, the managing director, and, ultimately, the chairman. When this failed, they resigned, alleging constructive dismissal. The EAT held that their employer had breached an implied term to provide a reasonable opportunity to obtain redress for any grievances.

Duty of confidentiality

As discussed later, it is well established that an employee owes a duty of confidentiality to his employer, but it has only recently been accepted that the employer may owe a similar duty to his employees. Thus, in *Dalgleish v Lothian and Borders Police Board*,[77] an injunction was granted to stop the defendant disclosing to a local council details of its employees to ascertain if they had paid their community charge.

Statute (notably the Data Protection Act 1998) also provides employees with rights relating to the use of their personal information. It is a criminal offence to intercept employee communications in the course of transmission[78] (for example,

---

75. See the judgment of Stuart-Smith LJ in *Johnstone v Bloomsbury Area Health Authority* [1992] QB 333 (CA).
76. [1995] IRLR 516 (EAT).
77. 1992 SLT 721. It should be noted that, because this is a Scottish case, it provides only persuasive authority.
78. Regulation of Investigatory Powers Act 2000, s 1.

monitoring telephone calls). Employers are, however, able to access, without consent, the employee's email account and other forms of communication in a number of circumstances (for example, to protect national security, to aid in the detection of a crime, or to discover whether the communications are being used for business purposes).[79]

Duty to provide accurate references

Employers may be reluctant to provide references, largely because of the potential imposition of liability for defamation or negligent misstatement.[80] In *Spring v Guardian Assurance plc*,[81] the House of Lords held that employers have both a tortious and contractual duty not to produce a negligent reference. Note that this does not prevent the employer from writing an unflattering reference; rather, it simply places a duty on the employer not to write a negligent reference.

 Cox v Sun Alliance Life Ltd [2001] EWCA Civ 649

FACTS: Cox (the claimant) was promoted to office manager but, following an altercation with several members of staff who, according to Rix LJ, had 'mutinied against him',[82] he was suspended. During his suspension, allegations were made that Cox had received a number of improper payments totalling £1,250. The employer's own investigation was not particularly thorough and an audit investigation found no evidence of dishonesty. Cox resigned, upon the agreement that his employers would provide him with an agreed reference making no mention of the alleged and unproven dishonesty. Subsequently, however, Cox's former employer spoke to two employers who had agreed to employ Cox, informing them of the allegations of dishonesty. Both employers dismissed Cox.

HELD: Cox's ex-employer had breached its duty of care to provide Cox with an accurate and fair reference. His ex-employer had acted without objectivity and its conduct was 'wholly unfair'.

★ See Jonathan Gidney, 'Walking the Reference Tightrope' (2001) 151 NLJ 1274

The question that arises is whether the employer is now under a positive duty to provide a reference if one is requested. The existence of a general duty is unlikely,[83] but specific duties may exist. In *Spring*, Lords Hadley and Woolf indicated that a duty would exist where the current occupation of the employee is of the type that normally requires a reference. Lord Woolf even stated that the duty could continue to exist for a reasonable time after the employee's contract has ended. It is also likely that a failure to provide a reference on discriminatory grounds (such as sex, race, etc) will constitute a breach of the Equality Act 2010.

🔗 The Equality Act 2010 is discussed in Chapter 27

Duties in relation to trade unions

Statute imposes a number of duties upon the employer in relation to trade unions. It is unlawful to refuse to employ a person on the ground that he belongs to, or refuses

---

79. Telecommunications (Lawful Business Practice) (Interception of Communications) Regulations 2000, SI 2000/2699, reg 3. 80. *Hedley Byrne & Co Ltd v Heller & Partners Ltd* [1964] AC 465 (HL).
81. [1994] ICR 596 (HL). 82. [2001] EWCA Civ 649, [2001] IRLR 448, [26].
83. *Gallear v JF Watson & Son Ltd* [1979] IRLR 306 (EAT).

to join a union,[84] and dismissal of an employee on the ground that he belongs to, or refuses to join or to take part in the activities of, a trade union is automatically regarded as unfair dismissal.[85]

Implied terms relating to the conduct of the employee

Duty of obedience

An employee is under a duty to obey any reasonable instructions from the employer and failure to do so will constitute a breach of contract, which will usually allow the employer to dismiss the employee without notice. Thus, in *Pepper v Webb*,[86] a gardener who refused who put plants into a garden was validly dismissed. The duty of obedience will also include reasonable requests to relocate[87] and the adaptation to new working methods.[88] This duty is, however, subject to a number of qualifications, including:

- The instructions must be lawful. Therefore, an employee will not breach this duty if he refuses to drive an uninsured vehicle,[89] or refuses to falsify records.[90]
- The instructions must not place the employee in danger. In *Ottoman Bank v Chakarian*,[91] an employee who was under a death sentence in Turkey disobeyed his employer, which had ordered him to remain in Constantinople (now Istanbul). The employee had not breached his duty of obedience. The belief in the danger must be reasonable and personal. Thus an employee was validly dismissed for refusing to go to Wexford, Ireland, based upon an unsubstantiated belief that it was a seat of terrorist activity.[92]
- The instructions must not relate to activities outside the scope of the employee's contract.

Duty of fidelity

The duty of fidelity (or of good faith, as it is often called) is an extremely wide-ranging duty that encompasses a number of activities that could validly be regarded as duties in their own right. Here, several key aspects of the duty will be discussed.

The employee will breach the duty of fidelity if he acts in a manner that disrupts the employer's business. Thus, in *British Telecommunications plc v Ticehurst*,[93] Ticehurst (a BT manager) organized and took part in a strike and a withdrawal of goodwill. The company informed its employees that further strike action would be regarded as a breach of their employment contracts. Ticehurst continued to strike and BT refused to pay her for the duration of the strike, leading Ticehurst to claim for the deducted pay. Her claim failed: by refusing to work in a normal manner, her

---

84. Trade Union and Labour Relations (Consolidation) Act 1992, s 137(1).
85. ibid s 152(1).   86. [1969] 1 WLR 514 (CA).
87. *United Kingdom Atomic Energy Authority v Claydon* [1974] ICR 128 (NIRC).
88. *Cresswell v Inland Revenue Commissioners* [1984] ICR 508 (Ch) (employees refused to adapt to computer-based tax system).   89. *Gregory v Ford* [1951] 1 All ER 121.
90. *Morrish v Henlys (Folkestone)* [1973] ICR 482 (NIRC).   91. [1930] AC 277 (PC).
92. *FG Walmsley v UCED Refrigeration Ltd* [1972] IRLR 80.   93. [1992] ICR 383 (CA).

actions had disrupted and inconvenienced her employer, and breached her duty of fidelity.

The duty of fidelity can also be breached if an employee has an interest that conflicts with those of his employer. Such conflicts can arise in a number of ways. For example, an employee may make a profit by virtue of his employment and not disclose it to his employer. In such a case, the employee will be in breach of duty and the employer will be able to recover the profit made.[94] The principal conflict of interest arises where the employee's activities compete with the interests of his employer. The courts are normally reluctant to impose limits on what the employee does in his spare time, but if the employee is engaged in an activity in his spare time that causes harm to his employer, it is likely to constitute a breach of duty. In *Hivac Ltd v Park Royal Scientific Instruments Ltd*,[95] employees of the claimants made hearing aids. In their spare time, they did exactly the same work for a rival firm. The Court found them in breach of duty and granted an injunction preventing them from working for the rival firm. Note, however, the existence of a breach of duty will depend on the nature of the work (for example, it is likely that the result in *Hivac* would have differed if the employees were to have been engaged in manual or non-skilled work).

Does this duty extend beyond the employee's employment? Can an employee be prevented from resigning and setting up a rival business or joining a rival firm? Employers may try to achieve this via a restrictive covenant or a 'garden leave' clause.

The validity of restrictive covenants that restrain trade is discussed at p 283

- **Restrictive covenants** are simply contractual undertakings requiring a party to refrain from something (for example, competition with the other party). They are, however, strictly regulated, and such a covenant will be void unless it is reasonably in the interests of the parties and the public.[96]

- **Garden leave clauses** simply impose lengthy notice periods on employees, during which time they receive full pay, but are unable to work for anyone. Therefore, an employee with skills that could be useful to a rival may have such a clause imposed upon him, requiring a lengthy notice period (for example, a year), during which time he will be unable to work for a rival firm. Such clauses are, however, enforced via the granting of an injunction,[97] which is a discretionary remedy. The courts may, therefore, deny a garden leave clause by refusing to enforce it if they feel that it is unreasonable (for example, where allowing an employee to leave would not harm the business interests of the employer).[98]

Duty to use reasonable skill and care

It is a long-established principle that, when an individual is employed, 'there is on his part an implied warranty that he is of skill reasonably competent to the task he undertakes'.[99] Breach of this duty allows the employer to dismiss the employee and to claim damages for any loss. Thus, in *Janata Bank v Ahmed (Qutubuddin)*,[100] a bank

---

94. *Reading v Attorney General* [1951] AC 507 (HL).   95. [1946] Ch 169 (CA).

96. *Thorsten Nordenfelt v The Maxim Nordenfelt Guns and Ammunition Company* [1894] AC 535 (HL).

97. As occurred in *Evening Standard Co Ltd v Henderson* [1987] ICR 588 (CA), in which the Court enforced a year-long garden leave clause and prevented a newspaper production manager from taking up employment with a rival newspaper.   98. *Provident Financial Group plc v Hayward* [1989] ICR 160 (CA).

99. *Harmer v Cornelius* [1843–60] All ER Rep 624, 625 (Willes J).   100. [1981] ICR 791 (CA).

manager who lent substantial sums to individuals without checking their credit-worthiness was held to have breached this duty and was required to compensate his employer.

The significance of this duty arises where an employee commits a tort that causes loss to a third party and the third party commences proceedings against the employer via the doctrine of vicarious liability. It has already been noted that an employer can obtain a contribution from the employee under the Civil Liability (Contribution) Act 1978, but it is also open for the employer to claim damages for breach of the implied term to exercise reasonable skill and care.[101]

The ability to obtain a contribution under the 1978 Act is discussed in 'Obtaining a contribution' at p 472

Duty of confidentiality

Some regard the duty of confidentiality as an aspect of the duty of fidelity discussed earlier, but, given its recent prominence, it is beneficial to discuss it separately. Issues of confidentiality can arise in a number of ways. An employee might pass on trade secrets belonging to his employer in return for payment or a job offer. This would clearly constitute a breach of duty, but what if an employee were to leave his employer and set up a new business using information acquired in his previous occupation? In other words, does the duty of confidentiality owed to an employer end once the employee leaves its employment? The answer is clearly 'no'. In *Roger Bullivant Ltd v Ellis*,[102] an employer who set up a new firm after acquiring techni-cal data and customer lists from his previous employer was held to have breached his duty to his former employer. The courts have, however, distinguished genuinely confidential information from commercial 'know-how', with usage or disclosure of the latter not constituting a breach of duty.[103]

So what is the position if an employee wishes to disclose confidential *unlawful* acts of an employer? The employee is not legally obliged to disclose, but if he does, will he breach his duties of confidentiality? The 1980s and 1990s witnessed a number of instances of fatal accidents (for example, the Zeebrugge ferry dis-aster,[104] and the Clapham rail crash[105]) and instances of corporate corruption (for example, BCCI), which could have been prevented had certain employees been free to disclose what they knew without fear of retribution. In response to such instances, the Public Interest Disclosure Act 1988 was passed, to allow so-called 'whistleblowers' to disclose freely instances of employer wrongdoing that are deemed 'protected'. This includes disclosure of criminal offences, fail-ures to comply with a legal obligation, the endangerment of health and safety, or instances of miscarriages of justice.[106] Disclosure may be made to the employer, or, where it relates to the employer's conduct, it may be made to an outside party (for example, a regulator).

Figure 25.1 sets out examples of the terms of the employment contract.

---

101. See *Lister v Romford Ice and Cold Storage Co Ltd* [1957] AC 555 (HL).
102. [1987] ICR 464 (CA).   103. *Faccenda Chicken v Fowler* [1987] Ch 117 (CA).
104. In 1987, the ferry *Herald of Free Enterprise* sank, killing 193 passengers.
105. In 1988, two trains collided near Clapham Junction, killing 35 people and injuring another 500.
106. Employment Rights Act 1996, s 43B.

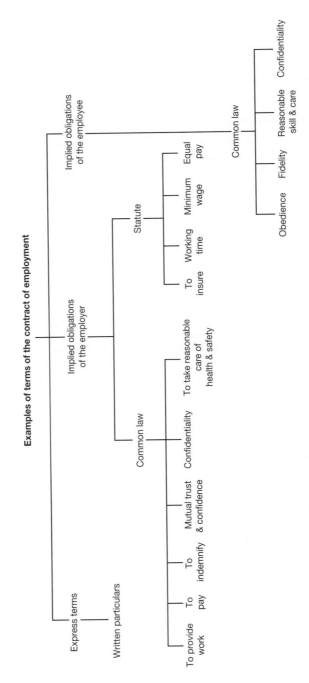

FIGURE 25.1 Terms of the employment contract

Chapter conclusion

There is a gradual move towards increasing the scope of employment law protection by providing it to 'workers', as opposed to the narrower category of 'employees'. When such a practice is universal, determining the scope of the protection offered by employment law legislation should become considerably easier, but that day has yet to arrive, and businesses and employers still need to be aware of the distinction between 'employees', 'independent contractors', and 'workers'.

Whilst employers will doubtless be aware of the express obligations imposed upon them in the contract of employment, they should also ensure they are fully aware of the considerable number of implied obligations that employment contracts contain. These implied terms impose a substantial number of duties upon employers and breach of these duties will also constitute breach of the employment contract, entitling the employee to a remedy. Employers should also be aware of the express and implied obligations placed upon employees, because breach of such obligations might allow the employer to remove an employee whose actions could cause harm to the business.

 Key points summary

- Employment tribunals deal with the majority of employment law disputes.

- Decisions of employment tribunals do not constitute precedent and can be appealed to the Employment Appeal Tribunal (EAT).

- Decisions of the EAT are binding upon employment tribunals. EAT decisions can be appealed to the Court of Appeal.

- Self-labelling of an employment relationship is not conclusive and the courts will only take such labels into account if the issue is ambiguous.

- Historically, the courts developed several tests to distinguish employees and independent contractors. But the modern view is that this distinction now depends upon the individual facts of the case.

- Increasingly, statutes are expanding the scope of the protection offered by providing rights to 'workers' instead of 'employees'.

- Employees have a statutory right to receive written particulars of the contract within two months of commencing employment.

- Terms of the contract may be express or implied.

- Express terms may derive from the parties themselves or from a collective agreement (an agreement between an employer and a trade union).

- Implied terms may derive from the intentions of the parties, the courts, statute, and through trade and custom.

- Employers are, *inter alia*, subject to duties to provide work, to pay the employee, to indemnify the employee, to treat the employee with trust and confidence, to take reasonable care of the employees' health and safety, to deal with grievances, to provide a fair and accurate reference, to preserve confidentiality, and various duties in relation to trade unions.

- Employees are, *inter alia*, subject to duties of obedience, fidelity, to perform their jobs with reasonable skill and care, and not to breach confidentiality in relation to information belonging to their employer.

Self-test questions

1. Define the following:
   (a) Employment Appeal Tribunal;
   (b) garden leave;
   (c) whistleblower;
   (d) protected disclosure.

2. Explain the practical significance of the distinction between employees and independent contractors.

3. Explain the operation of the various tests used by the courts to determine the distinction between employees and independent contractors, and to what extent these tests have survived.

4. Christian is a marketing consultant. He contracts with MicroMart plc to carry out a review of the company's marketing strategy. The contract is based on standard terms drawn up by Christian. The contract provides that Christian is to be an employee of MicroMart for the duration of the review, and that he is not required to take orders from MicroMart's management and can cancel the contract without notice at any time. Christian's work proves to be unsatisfactory and MicroMart terminates the contract. Christian alleges that he has been unfairly dismissed, but the right not to be unfairly dismissed only extends to employees. MicroMart argue that Christian was never its employee. How would you advise Christian?

5. What is required to be included in the written statement of particulars provided to employees and when must this statement be provided?

6. Has a breach of the employment contract occurred in the following cases?
   (a) Dylan works in a factory. Due to the negligence of another employee, the factory catches fire and severe damage is caused. The factory will be closed for a week and, during this week, all employees (including Dylan) will not be paid.
   (b) John is employed as an area manager for CostMart Ltd. A rival company offers John a better job and more money, but only if John provides it with a reference from his current employer. CostMart wishes to keep John and so refuses to provide a reference.

Further reading

Nigel Baker, 'Employee Status: Ongoing Saga' (2006) 29 CSR 177
Discusses recent cases concerning the statutory definition of 'employee'

Douglas Brodie, 'Legal Coherence and the Employment Revolution' (2001) 117 LQR 604
Examines the employer's duty of mutual trust and confidence, and how it has been affected by statute

Guy Davidov, 'Who is a Worker?' (2005) 34 ILJ 57
Discusses the philosophy behind, and the importance of the increased use of, the term 'worker' in UK legislation

Department of Trade and Industry, *Better Dispute Resolution: A Review of Employment Dispute Resolution in Great Britain* (DTI 2004)
Examines the effectiveness of employment tribunals and the Employment Appeal Tribunal, and suggests a number of reforms aimed at improving dispute resolution in employment cases

Robert Flannigan, 'The (Fiduciary) Duty of Fidelity' (2008) 124 LQR 274
Examines the origins and evolution of the employee's duty of fidelity

Sandra S Fredman, 'Labour Law in Flux: The Changing Composition of the Workforce' (1997) 26 ILJ 337
Examines the response of the law to non-standard forms of work—especially casual, part-time, and temporary workers

Patricia Leighton and Michael Wynn, 'Temporary Agency Working: Is the Law on the Turn?' (2008) 29 Co Law 7
Detailed, but highly readable, examination of current developments relating to the employment law protection offered to agency workers

Sam Middlemiss, 'The Truth and Nothing but the Truth? The Legal Liability of Employers for Employee References' (2004) 33 ILJ 59
Examines a number of recent cases concerning the employer's duty to provide a reference, and also looks at the human rights aspects and the role of exclusion clauses

Ian Smith and Aaron Baker, A, *Smith & Wood's Employment Law* (11th edn, OUP 2013) chs 2 and 3
Provides a detailed, but readable, account of the differing forms of worker and the contents of the contract of employment

Websites

<https://www.gov.uk/browse/working/contract-working-hours>
Accessible and up-to-date information on the contract of employment collated from a number of online governmental sources

<http://www.justice.gov.uk/tribunals/employment-appeals>
The official website of the Employment Appeal Tribunal; contains up-to-date information on the work of the EAT, as well as access to all judgments of the EAT since 1999

<http://www.justice.gov.uk/tribunals/employment>
The official website of employment tribunals; contains a significant amount of up-to-date information and links to relevant legislation

Remember to visit the **Online Resource Centre at <http://www.oxfordtextbooks.co.uk/orc/roach3e>** to access the following resources on Chapter 25, 'The contract of employment': more **practice questions** and answers; a **glossary** of key terms; **multiple-choice questions; revision summaries**; and **diagrams** in pdf. Updates to the law can be found on Twitter by following **@UKBusinessLaw**.

26 Employment rights, and health and safety

- Employment rights
- Health and safety

INTRODUCTION

Chapter 25 discussed the contract of employment and the rights within it. This chapter will move on to examine what employment rights are provided by law to employees. Employees are granted numerous rights to which employers are required to adhere, including the right to equal pay and working conditions, and a raft of rights relating to the family. Additionally, employers are also subject to substantial obligations in terms of protecting the health and safety of their employees. For both employers and their employees, the losses caused by inadequate health and safety measures can be substantial. In 2012–13, 1.1 million employees suffered from an illness that they believed to be work-related, 148 employees were killed due to work-related accidents, and 175,000 suffered work-related injuries. The combined result is that UK businesses lost 27 million working days due to work-related illnesses and injuries in 2012–13.[1] The cost of such losses to society has been estimated at £13.8 billion[2] and the actual cost will be even greater once the cost of settling or contesting any resultant litigation is included. Clearly, it is therefore vital that we have an effective system of regulation for health and safety at work in place in order to minimize such losses.

Employment rights

In addition to any rights contained in the employment contract, the law provides employees with a number of free-standing rights. It should be noted at the outset that certain employment rights have been significantly affected by the Growth and Infrastructure Act 2013, which inserts a new s 205A into the Employment Rights Act 1996 (ERA 996). Section 205A establishes a specific class of employee known as an 'employee shareholder'. An individual will be an employee shareholder if:

(a) the company and the individual agree that the individual is to be an employee shareholder;

(b) in consideration of that agreement, the company issues or allots to the individual shares which have a value of no less than £2,000;

---

1. Health and Safety Executive, *Annual Statistics Report 2012/13* (HSE 2013) 1.   2. ibid.

(c) the company provides the individual with a written statement of the particulars of the status of an employee shareholder and the rights which attach to the shares given to the individual as a result of (b); and

(d) the individual gives no other consideration other than entering into the agreement.[3]

The basic effect of s 205A is to provide employee shareholders with shares in the company in return for which the employee shareholder consents to forego a number of key employment rights, or agrees to some rights being reduced in scope. The effect that s 205A has on the rights will be discussed as they arise.

The national minimum wage

The concept of a national minimum wage is widespread around the world. Twenty-one of the EU's twenty-eight Member States have in place some form of statutory minimum wage. Forty-five of the US' fifty states have enacted minimum wage laws, with sixteen of those states enacting higher minimum wage rates than the federal minimum. In the UK, the introduction of a national minimum wage was comparatively recent. The introduction of a national minimum wage had been proposed by the Labour Party for a number of years and, following its election victory in 1997, one of its first acts in government was to pass the National Minimum Wage Act 1998 (NMWA 1998). Much of the detail, however, including the actual minimum rates of pay, are set out in the National Minimum Wage Regulations 1999.[4] Any attempt to contract out of the protection offered by the minimum wage legislation is void.[5]

Entitlement

Section 1(1) of the NMWA 1998 provides that '[a] person who qualifies for the national minimum wage shall be remunerated by his employer in respect of his work in any pay reference period at a rate which is not less than the national minimum wage'. From this, two issues arise.

1. Who is entitled to the minimum wage?
2. How much is the minimum wage?

Turning to the first issue, the Act takes a very broad approach to entitlement, stating that a person will qualify for the minimum wage provided that he is a worker, is working (or ordinarily works) in the UK, and has ceased to be of compulsory school age.[6] As the word 'worker' is used as opposed to 'employee', it follows that a contract of employment is not essential in order to claim the minimum wage. Agency workers,[7] home workers,[8] casual workers, workers paid on commission, and part-time workers are therefore all entitled to the minimum wage. However, certain workers are not entitled to the minimum wage, including (i) self-employed persons; (ii) company directors (unless their contracts classify them as workers);[9] (iii) voluntary

---

3. ERA 1996, s 205A(1).   4. SI 1999/584.   5. NMWA 1998, s 49(1).   6. ibid s 1(2).
7. ibid s 34.   8. ibid s 35.
9. The majority of executive directors will have a contract of service and so will be classed as employees, and ergo, will also be classed as workers.

workers (for example, workers employed by a charity);[10] and (iv) students undertaking work placements not exceeding one year.[11]

Having determined whether or not a worker is entitled to the minimum wage, the second issue is to determine how much the minimum wage is. The 1998 Act established the Low Pay Commission,[12] an independent body, the sole function of which is to advise the government regarding the national minimum wage. The Low Pay Commission advises the Secretary of State for Employment who, in turn, sets the minimum wage by amending the 1999 Regulations. The initial minimum wage (£3.60 per hour) was set well below what the trade unions were recommending, but it has increased every October (although the NMWA 1998 requires no such increase), as Table 26.1 indicates.

Enforcement

The provisions of the NMWA 1998 can be enforced in several different ways. As the right to the minimum wage is a contractual one,[13] the worker can claim arrears via an ordinary claim for breach of contract. Alternatively, the worker can bring a claim under Pt II of the Employment Rights Act 1996 (ERA 1996), on the ground that the underpayment constitutes an unlawful deduction in wages. In both cases, the burden of proof is reversed, so the worker will be presumed to qualify for the minimum wage and it will also be presumed that he has been paid less than the minimum wage.[14]

TABLE 26.1 The national minimum wage

	Adult rate (workers aged 21 and over)	Development rate (workers aged 18–20)	16–17 year olds rate	Apprentice rate (apprentices under the age of 19, or aged 19 and over and in the first 12 months of their apprenticeship)
Oct 2014	£6.50	£5.13	£3.79	£2.73
Oct 2013	£6.31	£5.03	£3.72	£2.68
Oct 2012	£6.19	£4.98	£3.68	£2.65
Oct 2011	£6.08	£4.98	£3.68	£2.60
Oct 2010	£5.93	£4.92	£3.64	£2.50
Oct 2009	£5.80	£4.83	£3.57	-
Oct 2008	£5.73	£4.77	£3.53	-
Oct 2007	£5.52	£4.60	£3.40	-
Oct 2006	£5.35	£4.45	£3.30	-
Oct 2005	£5.05	£4.25	£3.00	-
Oct 2004	£4.85	£4.10	£3.00	-
Oct 2003	£4.50	£3.80	-	-
Oct 2002	£4.20	£3.60	-	-
Oct 2001	£4.10	£3.50	-	-
Oct 2000	£3.70	£3.20	-	-
April 1999	£3.60	£3.00	-	-

10. NMWA 1998, s 44.
11. National Minimum Wage Regulations 1999, SI 1999/584, reg 12(9A).
12. NMWA 1998, s 8(9); see <https://www.gov.uk/government/organisations/low-pay-commission>.
13. ibid s 17(1).   14. ibid s 28.

In addition, HM Revenue and Customs (HMRC) enforcement officers can serve a 'notice of underpayment' to any employer who is paying his employees less than the minimum wage, requiring the employer to pay the arrears in pay within twenty-eight days of the notice being served.[15] Failure to pay within this period will result in a financial penalty.[16] If the notice is not complied with, the officer can also bring a claim on the worker's behalf under Pt II of the ERA 1996, as described earlier.[17]

In addition to these civil remedies, the NMWA 1998 also provides for a number of summary criminal offences. For example, an employer who refuses, or wilfully neglects, to pay a worker the minimum wage will commit an either way offence.[18]

If a worker is dismissed for any reasons relating to the entitlement to receive the minimum wage, or following an employer being convicted of a criminal offence under the 1998 Act, then that dismissal shall be regarded as unfair, irrespective of whether or not the worker's right to the minimum wage has been infringed.[19]

Transfer of undertakings

It is common for the ownership structure of a business to change during its life-time: a business may be sold to another party; it may be subject to a takeover bid; or it may merge with another business to create a new commercial enterprise. The issue with which we are concerned here is, where such a change in ownership occurs, what effect this has on the employees' contracts of employment. Historically, such employees were placed in an extremely vulnerable position. At common law, where the ownership of a business changed, the employment contracts of the business were not transferred to the new owner,[20] thereby allowing the new owner to choose which employees to retain. This placed the employees in an extremely vulnerable position, in so much as if the new owner were to decide not to take their contracts on, the employees would lose their jobs, with no legal redress.

The unfairness of this situation was remedied by the passing of the Acquired Rights Directive,[21] which protected the employees' contracts of employment by automatically transferring them to the new owner upon a transfer of ownership of the business. The Directive was belatedly implemented into national law by the Transfer of Undertakings (Protection of Employment) Regulations 1981,[22] but both the Directive and the Regulations were notoriously complex. Accordingly, the Directive was amended in 1998[23] and consolidated into a new Directive in 2001.[24] The Regulations themselves have been amended four times, with the most recent version being the Transfer of Undertakings (Protection of Employment) Regulations 2006 (TUPE 2006).[25]

In January 2013, the government published a consultation document in which it expressed concerns that the TUPE 2006 were perceived by businesses as overly

---

15. ibid s 19(2).

16. ibid s 19A. This penalty, payable to HMRC, currently amounts to 50 per cent of the underpayment, subject to a minimum penalty of £100 and a maximum penalty of £5,000. However, the government has stated that it plans to increase the penalty to 100 per cent of the underpayment, subject to a maximum of £20,000. The government hopes to have these increases in force sometime in 2014.

17. ibid s 19D(1)(a).   18. ibid s 31(1) and (9).   19. ERA 1996, s 104A.

20. *Nokes v Doncaster Amalgamated Collieries Ltd* [1940] AC 1014 (HL).

21. Council Directive No 77/187/EC.   22. SI 1981/1794.

23. Council Directive No 98/50/EC.   24. Council Directive No 2001/23/EC.

25. SI 2006/246.

bureaucratic.[26] In September 2013, the government announced that it intended to introduce reforms that would 'remove excessive parts of the TUPE regulations and reduce the bureaucracy of a transfer'.[27] These changes were introduced via the Collective Redundancies and Transfer of Undertakings (Protection of Employment) (Amendment) Regulations 2014.[28]

Relevant transfer

The TUPE 2006 only apply where the change in ownership amounts to a 'relevant transfer', of which there are two types. The first is where there is a 'transfer of an undertaking, business or part of an undertaking or business situated immediately before the transfer in the United Kingdom to another person where there is a transfer of an economic entity which retains its identity'.[29] Several of the words and phrases within this provision require elaboration:

- **Undertaking** An 'undertaking' is simply another word for a trade or business. Originally, non-commercial ventures (for example, charities) were not classified as 'undertakings', but, following the holding of the European Court of Justice that this was contrary to the Directive,[30] the TUPE 2006 now specifically applies to 'public and private undertakings engaged in economic activities whether or not they are operated for gain'.[31]

- **Economic entity** An 'economic entity' is defined as 'an organized grouping of resources which has the objective of pursuing an economic activity, whether or not that activity is central or ancillary'.[32]

- **Retention of identity** In order to qualify, the undertaking must retain its identity following the transfer. This will require a measure of continuance post-transfer, so where a business was closed down upon transfer, or where the nature of its activity changes, it will not fall within the TUPE 2006. The new entity does not need to be identical to the prior one, but merely identifiable with it.[33]

The second 'relevant transfer' occurs where there is a 'service provision change'. This will occur in one of three situations set out in reg 3(1)(b). First, reg 3(1)(b)(i) provides that a service provision change will occur where activities cease to be carried out by a person (a client) on his own behalf and are carried out instead by another person on the client's behalf (a contractor).

 A service provision change under reg 3(1)(b)(i)

MicroTech plc (the client) owns a number of warehouses. At night, security guards employed by MicroTech guard the warehouses. MicroTech decides to contract out its security services to GuardCorp Ltd (the contractor). The security guards employed by MicroTech will have their contracts taken over by GuardCorp.

---

26. Department of Business, Innovation & Skills, *Transfer of Undertakings (Protection of Employment) Regulations 2006: Consultation on the Proposed Changes to the Regulations* (BIS 2013).

27. Department of Business, Innovation & Skills, *Transfer of Undertakings (Protection of Employment) Regulations 2006: Government Response to Consultation* (BIS 2013) 3.

28. SI 2014/16.   29. TUPE 2006, reg 3(1)(a).

30. Case C-29/91 *Dr Sophie Redmond Stichting v Bartol* [1992] IRLR 366.

31. TUPE 2006, reg 3(4)(a).   32. ibid reg 3(2).

33. *Securicor Guarding Ltd v Fraser Security Services Ltd* [1996] IRLR 552 (EAT).

Second, reg 3(1)(b)(ii) provides that a service provision change will occur where activities cease to be carried out by a contractor on a client's behalf (whether or not those activities had previously been carried out by the client on his own behalf) and are carried out instead by another person (a subsequent contractor) on the client's behalf.

> ### Eg   A service provision change under reg 3(1)(b)(ii)
>
> MicroTech (the client), not happy with the price charged by GuardCorp (the contractor), puts its security needs out to tender. The tender is obtained by KeepSafe Ltd (the subsequent contractor). The contracts of the security guards who worked for MicroTech, but now work for GuardCorp, will now be transferred to KeepSafe.

Third, reg 3(1)(b)(iii) provides that a service provision change will occur where activities cease to be carried out by a contractor or a subsequent contractor on a client's behalf (whether or not those activities had previously been carried out by the client on his own behalf) and are carried out instead by the client on his own behalf.

> ### Eg   A service provision change under reg 3(1)(b)(iii)
>
> Not happy with the service provided by KeepSafe (the subsequent contractor), MicroTech (the client) decides not to contract out its security needs and will once again arrange its own security. The security guards who originally worked for MicroTech will once again become employees of MicroTech.

The 2014 Regulations inserted a new reg 3(2A) into the TUPE 2006, which provides that a service provision change under reg 3(1)(b) will only occur where the activities carried on after the change are 'fundamentally the same as the activities carried out previously'. This amendment has doubtless had the effect of narrowing the scope of a service provision change.

The effect of a transfer

The key provision is reg 4(1), which provides that, except where an objection is made under reg 4(7) (discussed later):

> a relevant transfer shall not operate so as to terminate the contract of employment of any person employed by the transferor…[and]…any such contract shall have effect after the transfer as if originally made between the person so employed and the transferee.[34]

Accordingly, where a relevant transfer takes place, the employees of the original owner become the employees of the new owner. Accordingly, the effect of reg 4(1) is to **novate** the employees' contracts. This novation is automatic: the views of the parties are irrelevant[35] (subject to reg 4(7), discussed later) and the contract will be

 novate: substitute (one contract) for another

---

34. TUPE 2006, reg 4(1).

35. Case C-144/87 *Berg and Busschers v Besselsen* [1989] IRLR 447.

transferred even where the employee is unaware of the undertaking being trans-ferred.[36] All of the rights, powers, duties, and non-criminal liabilities[37] of the original owner under, or in respect of, the employment contract are transferred to the new owner,[38] and any act or omission of the original owner in respect of that contract prior to the transfer are deemed to be an act or omission of the new owner.[39]

The protection afforded to employees by reg 4(1) applies not only to those employees employed 'immediately before the transfer', but also to employees who would have been so employed had they not been unfairly dismissed because of the transfer.[40] Such a dismissal occurs where an employee is dismissed before or after a relevant transfer and the dismissal is solely or principally due to the transfer itself.[41] However, where the reason for the dismissal is solely or principally an economic, technical, or organizational reason, the dismissal may be valid. The onus of proof is placed upon the employer to demonstrate that such a reason exists and that it was why the employee was dismissed.[42] The aim of these provisions is to prevent an employer from avoiding reg 4(1) by dismissing his employees shortly before a transfer.[43]

Upon transfer, the new owner may seek adversely to alter the terms and condition of the novated employment contracts. This could occur for unmeritorious reasons (for example, the new owner is disgruntled at having to take on the prior owner's employees and wishes to force them to resign), or for valid reasons (for example, to avoid potential equal pay claims, especially where the novated contracts provide for a higher rate of pay than that received by the new owner's existing employees). The ability to vary the terms of the novated contracts is limited by reg 4(4), which provides that any purported variation of the novated contract is void if the reason for the variation is the transfer itself. A variation is permitted, however, where (a) the reason for the variation is an economic, technical, or organizational reason entailing changes in the workforce;[44] or (b) the reason for the variation is the transfer, provided that the terms of that contract permit the employer to make such a variation.[45]

Objecting to a transfer

Although the transfer of the contract of employment is normally automatic, the employee can prevent the transfer from taking place by informing the new owner that he objects to being employed by the new owner.[46] Where this occurs, the con-tract of employment will be terminated, but the employee will not be regarded as dismissed,[47] thereby leaving him without any form of legal redress against either the original owner or the new owner. The harshness of this is partially mitigated by reg 4(9), which provides that, where the employee does not wish to transfer his employ-ment because it would involve a substantial and detrimental change in his working conditions, he may elect to treat the employment contract as terminated and will also be regarded as being dismissed, thereby entitling him to compensation.

---

36. *Secretary of State for Trade and Industry v Cook* [1997] IRLR 150 (EAT).
37. TUPE 2006, reg 4(6).   38. ibid 4(2)(a).   39. ibid 4(2)(b).   40. ibid reg 4(3).
41. ibid reg 7(1).   42. ibid reg 7(2) and (3).
43. Even before the passing of the TUPE 2006, the House of Lords had curtailed this activity in *Litster v Forth Dry Dock and Engineering Co Ltd* [1990] 1 AC 546 (HL).
44. A newly inserted reg 3(5A) provides that a 'change in the workforce' will include a change to the place where employees are employed to carry on the business of the employer.
45. TUPE 2006, reg 4(5).   46. ibid reg 4(7).   47. ibid reg 4(8).

Parental rights

When the Labour Party came to power in 1997, it promised to increase the maternity and paternity rights of employees substantially and to introduce new rights. This promise was kept and, in the last fifteen years, the length of maternity leave has increased substantially, as has the amount of maternity pay. Paternity leave and paternity pay have been introduced. An additional right to parental leave has supplemented paternity and maternity leave, and a right to take time off for antenatal care has been introduced. Parents of young children have also acquired the right to request flexible working hours. The reforms are not yet complete but, as will be seen, certain proposed extensions to existing rights have been postponed indefinitely.

In this section, the principal parental rights available will be discussed, beginning with maternity leave. It should be noted that several of the rights discussed are due to change when the Children and Families Act 2014 comes fully into force, and these changes are noted where relevant. The Act also provides for the introduction of a new parental right, namely shared parental leave.

Maternity leave and maternity pay

All pregnant employees are entitled to maternity leave. The law in this area used to be extremely complex, but a raft of recent legislation has greatly simplified the determination of maternity leave. The various pieces of legislation establish three different periods of maternity leave.

1. **Compulsory maternity leave (CML)** The period of CML begins on the day of childbirth and lasts for two weeks.[48] Any employer who permits an employee to work during her period of CML commits a criminal offence.[49]

2. **Ordinary maternity leave (OML)** All pregnant employees are entitled to OML, irrespective of how long they have worked for their employer. The length of OML is currently set at twenty-six weeks,[50] but can only be claimed if, by the end of the fifteenth week before the expected week of childbirth (EWC), the employee informs her employer of her pregnancy, the EWC, and when she intends the period of OML to start.[51] During this period, the employee is entitled to all of the benefits of the terms and conditions of her contract of employment[52] (for example, holiday entitlements, insurance, etc), except in relation to remuneration.[53] Instead of her contractual rate of pay, she will receive maternity pay, which is discussed later.

3. **Additional maternity leave (AML)** All employees entitled to OML are also entitled to an additional twenty-six weeks' AML,[54] which will run immediately after the OML period has finished. As with OML, the employee is entitled to all of the benefits of her contract of employment,[55] except in relation to remuneration.[56] Instead of her contractual rate of pay, she will receive maternity pay, which is discussed later. The combined fifty-two weeks (OML + AML) is known as Statutory Maternity Leave.

---

48. Maternity and Parental Leave etc Regulations 1999, SI 1999/3312, reg 8(b).
49. ERA 1996, s 72. Where the employee works in a factory, an offence is committed if she is allowed to return to work within a four-week period following childbirth (Factories Act 1961, s 61).
50. Maternity and Parental Leave etc Regulations 1999, reg 7(1).   51. ibid reg 4(1)(a).
52. ERA 1996, s 71(4)(a).   53. ibid s 71(5)(b).
54. Maternity and Parental Leave etc Regulations 1999, reg 7(4).   55. ERA 1996, s 73(4)(a).
56. ibid s 73(5)(b).

Therefore, an employee is entitled to up to fifty-two weeks of Statutory Maternity Leave (CML, being mandatory, is not an entitlement and so is not counted towards this period). The government wished to encourage employees on maternity leave and employers to keep in touch during the maternity period. Accordingly, the employee is permitted to work for up to ten days during her Statutory Maternity Leave period, and such work will not cause her maternity leave to end,[57] nor will it extend the period of leave.[58]

During the period of maternity leave, an employee will not receive her contractual rate of pay, but will instead receive Statutory Maternity Pay (SMP). Whereas all pregnant employees will qualify for maternity leave (subject to the requirements of notice), the entitlement for SMP is dependent upon meeting the following requirements:

- prior to the fifteenth week before the EWC, the employee must have worked for the employer for a minimum period of twenty-six weeks;[59]
- the employee must be earning enough to require her to make National Insurance (NI) contributions[60] (as of April 2014, this amount is £111 per week, although it is likely to change in April 2015);[61]
- the employee must notify the employer of her pregnancy, the EWC, and the date on which she intends her OML to commence. The employer can require the employee to produce medical evidence stating the EWC;[62]
- the employee must have reached the eleventh week before the EWC.[63]

Currently, employees meeting these requirements will receive SMP for up to thirty-nine weeks. Section 1 of the Work and Families Act 2006 provides that this will be increased to 52 weeks, but the government has stated that implementation of this increase has been postponed indefinitely.

The rate of maternity pay is fixed by statute. For the first six weeks of maternity leave, the employee will receive 90 per cent of her normal weekly earnings.[64] For the remaining weeks, the employee will receive either a flat rate of £138.18 per week[65] (as of April 2014), or 90 per cent of her standard pay, whichever is the lesser amount.[66] The employer, in turn, is able to recover from the government most of the money paid in maternity pay by deducting it from PAYE and NI contributions.

Those employees not entitled to statutory maternity pay (for example, because they do not earn enough to make NI contributions) may be entitled to a maternity allowance. In order to qualify, the following conditions must be met:

- the employee must have reached the eleventh week before her EWC;[67]
- the employee must have been employed for at least twenty-six out of the sixty-six weeks prior to her EWC;[68]
- the employee's average weekly earnings must not be less than the maternity allowance threshold[69] (currently, £30 per week).

57. Maternity and Parental Leave etc Regulations 1999, reg 12A(1).
58. ibid reg 12A(7).　　59. Social Security Contributions and Benefits Act 1992, s 164(2)(a).
60. ibid s 164(2)(b).　　61. See <http://www.hmrc.gov.uk/rates/nic.htm>.
62. Maternity and Parental Leave etc Regulations 1999, reg 4(1).
63. Social Security Contributions and Benefits Act 1992, s 164(2)(c).　　64. ibid s 166(1)(a) and (2).
65. Statutory Maternity Pay (General) Regulations 1986, SI 1986/1960, reg 6. This figure tends to rise every April.
66. Social Security Contributions and Benefits Act 1992, s 166(1)(b).
67. ibid s 35(1)(a).　　68. ibid s 35(1)(b).　　69. ibid s 35(1)(c).

Maternity allowance is paid for the same period as SMP (currently thirty-nine weeks)[70] and is paid at the same rate as SMP, or 90 per cent of her standard pay, whichever is the lesser amount.[71]

Within twenty-eight days of maternity leave commencing, the employee must provide her employer with the date on which her maternity leave will end. If the employee wishes to return to work early from AML, she will need to provide her employer with at least eight weeks' notice of her return.[72] An employee returning from OML is entitled to return to the same job in which she was employed prior to her maternity leave.[73] An employee returning from AML is entitled to return to the same job or, where this is not reasonably practicable, to return to a suitable and appropriate job[74] on terms no less favourable than those to which she was subject prior to taking leave.[75]

The right to return to work also includes protection from redundancy and dismissal. It may be the case that, during an employee's period of maternity leave, her employer may need to make her redundant. In such a case, the employer is bound to offer the employee any suitable alternative vacancy under a new contract of employment.[76] Where the employee is dismissed and the principal reason for the dismissal is related to, *inter alia*, pregnancy, childbirth, or the taking of maternity leave, the employee shall be regarded as unfairly dismissed.[77] It is also likely that such a dismissal will constitute discriminatory conduct.

& Discrimination on the grounds of pregnancy or maternity is discussed at p 761

Antenatal care

Antenatal care refers to care and treatment administered during pregnancy. The right to time off to receive antenatal care was introduced in 1980 to combat the UK's alarmingly high perinatal mortality rate (PMR).[78] Today, the right to time off for antenatal care can be found in s 55 of the ERA 1996 and is available to all women, irrespective of their length of service. The Children and Families Bill also allows an employee who is in a qualifying relationship (e.g. husband, civil partner etc) with a pregnant woman to take time off to accompany the expectant mother to two antenatal care appointments.

The right to time off for antenatal care is dependent upon the pregnant employee making an appointment for antenatal care upon the advice of a registered medical practitioner, midwife, or nurse.[79] Where the employee obtains time off to receive antenatal care, she is entitled to be paid at her normal rate of pay.[80] Should the employer refuse to provide the employee with time off, the employee may take her case to an employment tribunal, but it should be noted that the right to time off is not absolute and that an employer may be entitled to refuse time off for reasonable reasons (for example, where the employee could have obtained antenatal care outside working hours, but chose not to do so).[81]

---

70. ibid s 35(2). As with SMP, the right to maternity allowance was due to increase to 52 weeks, but this increase has been suspended indefinitely.

71. ibid s 35A(1).

72. Maternity and Parental Leave etc Regulations 1999, reg 11(1). Where the employee is an employee shareholder, then she will need to provide sixteen weeks' notice (ERA 1996, s 205A(3)(A)).

73. ibid reg 18(1).   74. ibid reg 18(2).   75. ibid reg 18A(1)(b).

76. ibid reg 10(2).   77. ibid reg 20.

78. The PMR represents the number of stillbirths and neonatal deaths per thousand births. In 1973, the UK's PMR stood at 21 per 1,000—one of the highest in Europe. Today, the PMR stands at 4.4 per 1,000.

79. ERA 1996, s 55(1)(b).   80. ibid s 56(1).   81. *Gregory v Tudsbury* [1982] IRLR 267 (IT) [8].

Paternity leave and paternity pay

Pregnant employees have long had the right to maternity leave, but only recently has a similar right been extended to expectant fathers. Prior to this, unless the employer had a voluntary scheme for paternity leave, fathers wishing to take time off were forced to use their holiday entitlement or to ask their employer for a period of unpaid leave. The Employment Act 2002 introduced the concept of 'paternity leave' by inserting new provisions into the ERA 1996. Paternity leave is obtainable upon satisfaction of several requirements:[82]

- the employee must have been employed for at least twenty-six continuous weeks prior to the fourteenth week of the EWC;
- the employee must be (i) the biological father of the child; or (ii) married to, or the partner (including civil partners) of, the child's mother, but not the child's father;
- the employee must have, or must expect to have, responsibility for the child's upbringing.

There are two forms of paternity leave. Employees meeting the above requirements can take ordinary paternity leave (OPL) of one week's leave or two weeks' consecutive leave.[83] New rules have been introduced by the Additional Paternity Leave Regulations 2010, which basically allow the mother to return to work early and transfer up to twenty-six weeks of her remaining maternity leave to the father (this transferred leave is known as additional paternity leave (APL)). APL can be taken at any time within a period that begins twenty weeks after the birth of the child and ends twelve months after that date. It should be noted that when the right to shared parental leave (discussed later) comes into operation, the provisions relating to APL will be repealed.

During the period of paternity leave, a man is entitled to the benefit of all of the terms and conditions of employment that would have applied had he not been absent, except those terms relating to remuneration.[84] Providing that the father is earning enough to make NI contributions (£111 per week, as of April 2014), he will receive ordinary statutory paternity pay (during the period of OPL) and, providing that the mother was entitled to statutory maternity pay, additional statutory paternity pay (during the period of APL). In both cases, the amount will received will be £138.18 per week (as of April 2014), or 90 per cent of his average weekly earnings, whichever is the lesser amount.

Many employers will have their own scheme of paternity leave. If these are less advantageous to the employee than the statutory scheme, the employee may choose the statutory scheme.

Shared parental leave

The Children and Families Act 2014 will, when the relevant provisions are in force, amend the ERA 1996 to introduce a new system of shared parental leave and statutory parental pay. The exact details of the system (including eligibility requirements) will be contained in regulations that will be enacted following the passing of the Children and

---

82. These are found in the Paternity and Adoption Leave Regulations 2002, SI 2002/2788, reg 4(2), and the Additional Paternity Leave Regulations 2010, SI 2010/1055, reg 4(2).
83. Paternity and Adoption Leave Regulations 2002, reg 5(1).
84. Paternity and Adoption Leave Regulations 2002, reg 12; Additional Paternity Leave Regulations 2010, reg 27.

Families Act 2014. Under a system of shared parental leave, an employed mother will continue to be eligible for 52 weeks' maternity leave as a day one right. However, she can then choose to end her maternity leave and pay after the two-week compulsory maternity leave period has expired, and to share her remaining leave and pay with her spouse or partner. This leave can be taken concurrently (i.e. mother and father take leave at the same time) or consecutively (i.e. mother and father take leave in turn). The government has stated that the system of shared parental leave will be in operation by April 2015.

Parental leave

The right to parental leave (not to be confused with shared parental leave discussed earlier) is in addition to the right to maternity or paternity leave. It was introduced by the Maternity and Parental Leave etc Regulations 1999,[85] which were enacted in order to comply with the Parental Leave Directive.[86] An employee can only obtain parental leave if he has been continuously employed for not less than one year,[87] and has, or expects to have, responsibility for a child.[88] 'Parental responsibility' is defined as 'all the rights, duties, powers, responsibilities and authority which by law a parent of a child has in relation to the child and his property'.[89]

Employees who meet these requirements are entitled to eighteen weeks' unpaid parental leave per child.[90] This leave must be taken before the child's fifth birthday,[91] except where the child is disabled, when it must be taken before his eighteenth birthday.[92]

Upon returning from parental leave, the employee is entitled to return to the same job in which he was employed before his absence,[93] except where leave is taken for over four weeks, or where parental leave is taken immediately following AML, in which case, the employee is entitled to return to the same job or, where this is not reasonably practicable, to return to a suitable and appropriate job.[94]

Adoption leave

The basic right to Statutory Adoption Leave is similar to maternity leave—namely, a period of paid ordinary adoption leave of twenty-six weeks,[95] followed by a period of unpaid additional adoption leave for a further twenty-six weeks.[96] However, whereas all employees are entitled to maternity leave, entitlement to adoption leave is different in the following ways:

- where a couple adopt a child, only one of the adoptive parents is entitled to adoption leave;
- adoption leave is only available where the employee has twenty-six weeks' continuous service, ending with the week in which the employee is informed that he has been matched with a child.[97]

During ordinary adoption leave, the employee will be entitled to the benefit of all of the terms and conditions of employment that would have applied had he not been absent, except those terms relating to remuneration.[98] Providing that the employee

---

85. SI 1999/3312.   86. Council Directive No 96/34/EC.
87. Maternity and Parental Leave etc Regulations 1999, reg 13(1)(a).   88. ibid reg 13(1)(b).
89. Children Act 1989, s 3(1).   90. Maternity and Parental Leave etc Regulations 1999, reg 14(1).
91. ibid reg 15(1).
92. ibid reg 15(3).   93. ibid reg 18(1).   94. ibid reg 18(2).
95. Paternity and Adoption Leave Regulations 2002, reg 18(1).   96. ibid reg 20(2).
97. ibid reg 15(2)(b).   98. ibid reg 19.

is earning enough to make NI contributions (£111 per week, as of April 2014), he will receive, for thirty-nine weeks, Statutory Adoption Pay of £138.18 per week (as of April 2014), or 90 per cent of his average weekly earnings, whichever is the lesser amount. As with maternity pay, employers can recover from the government the majority of adoption pay paid out. The rights upon return from work and protection from dismissal are the same as those for maternity leave.

When the relevant provisions of the Children and Families Act 2014 come into effect, then adoptive parents will be entitled to shared parental leave (discussed earlier), thereby acquiring the same rights as birth parents.

Flexible working conditions

Once maternity, paternity, parental, or adoption leave has ended, employees will often find it difficult to return to work and raise their new child. To ease this difficulty, the Employment Act 2002 provided workers with increased flexible working rights. The rights conferred are, however, somewhat weak. At the time of writing, flexible working rights apply only to employees who meet the conditions of entitlement:[99]

(a) the employee must have been continuously employed for at least twenty-six weeks;

(b) the employee must be a mother, father, adopter, guardian, special guardian, foster parent, or private foster carer. Partners, civil partners, and spouses of such persons also qualify;

(c) the employee must have, or expect to have, responsibility for the upbringing of a child who is under the age of 17 (or 18, if the child is disabled).

However, the Children and Families Act 2014 will extend the scope of the right to claim for flexible working conditions by removing the entitlement conditions found in (b) and (c), but the twenty-six week qualifying period will remain.

Employees meeting these requirements may apply to their employer for a change in their terms of employment in relation to hours, times, and places of work,[100] except for employee shareholders who do not have the right to request flexible working conditions.[101] The employee does not have a right to flexible working conditions, but only the right to apply to his employer for more flexible conditions, with the Children and Families Act 2014 establishing a duty upon the employer to 'deal with the application in a reasonable manner' and to notify the employee of the decision regarding the application within the decision period. The application must be in writing[102] and, within twenty-eight days of receipt of the application, the employer must either accept the employee's request or hold a meeting with the employee to discuss the application.[103] Within fourteen days of this meeting, the employer must notify the employee of the decision made.[104] Under the Children and Families Act 2014, this will be amended so that the employer has three months in which to notify

---

99. ERA 1996, s 80F(1)(b); Flexible Working (Eligibility, Complaints and Remedies) Regulations 2002, SI 2002/3236, regs 3(1) and 3A.

100. ERA 1996, s 80F(1)(a). Such an application may only be made once per year (s 80F(4)).

101. Ibid s 205A(2)(b).

102. Flexible Working (Eligibility, Complaints and Remedies) Regulations 2002, reg 4(a).

103. Flexible Working (Procedural Requirements) Regulations 2002, SI 2002/3207, reg 3.

104. ibid reg 4.

the employee of the decision following the submission of the application, or a longer period as may be agreed by the employer and employee.

Where the application is granted, the change will be permanent, unless the parties agree otherwise. Accordingly, if the employee finds the new arrangements to be disadvantageous, there is no automatic right to revert to the prior terms and conditions. Where the application is rejected, the notice must state why the application was rejected, with the ERA 1996 providing an exhaustive list of valid grounds for refusal (for example, the burden of additional costs, the inability to reorganize work among existing staff, etc).[105] The rejection notice must also inform the employee that he has a right to appeal within fourteen days of notice of the decision.[106] The employer must notify the employee of the result of the appeal within fourteen days.[107] Failure of the employer to adhere to these procedures can result in a complaint to an employment tribunal, which can award the employee compensation not exceeding eight weeks' pay.[108]

Time off

In addition to maternity, paternity, shared parental, parental, and adoption leave, an employee is entitled to time off in several situations, including the following.

Dependant care

Employees have a right to reasonable time off to care for dependants. A dependant is defined as a spouse (or civil partner), child, parent, or someone who lives in the same household as the employee, but is not his employee, lodger, or tenant.[109] Examples of instances in which reasonable time off should be granted include where a dependant falls ill, dies, gives birth, or is injured or assaulted.

Unlike other forms of leave, no period of leave is stated, because the leave required will depend upon the circumstances. The period of leave must be reasonable, but this will be very difficult to define in practice. Unlike maternity and paternity leave, there is no requirement to pay an employee who takes time off to care for a dependant. An employee who is refused time off may complain to an employment tribunal, provided that the complaint is brought within three months of the date of the refusal.[110]

Public duties

A substantial number of public bodies can only continue to operate through part-time contributors. As the performance of such public duties is in the collective interests of the country, s 50 of the ERA 1996 provides that employers must permit their employees to take reasonable time off if they wish to perform certain public duties including:

- acting as a Justice of the Peace (magistrate);
- working for a local authority or statutory tribunal;
- working for a health body or education body.

---

105. ERA 1996, s 80G(1)(b).
106. Flexible Working (Procedural Requirements) Regulations 2002, reg 6.   107. ibid reg 9.
108. ERA 1996, s 80I.
109. ibid s 57A(3).
110. ibid s 57B.

The right contained in s 50 is not dependent upon a minimum length of service, but employers are not required to pay employees for the time that they take off to perform public duties. An employee who is refused time off under s 50 may present a complaint to an employment tribunal, provided that the complaint is brought within three months beginning on the date on which the refusal occurred, or within whatever period the tribunal considers reasonable if the three-month period is not reasonably practicable.[111]

Although not covered by s 50, another public duty for which the employee is entitled to time off is jury service. Further, an employee who is dismissed due to absence caused by attending jury service is to be regarded as being unfairly dismissed.[112]

Study or training

Certain employees are entitled to paid time off in order to undertake study or training leading to a relevant qualification. Section 63A(1) of the ERA 1996 provides that, in order to obtain this entitlement, the employee:

- must be aged 16 or 17;
- must not be receiving full-time secondary or further education; and
- must not have attained such minimum standards of education as prescribed by reg 3 of the Right to Time Off for Study and Training Regulations 2001[113] (for example, grades A* to C in five subjects at GCSE level).

Employees satisfying these requirements are entitled to a period of paid time off that is reasonable in all of the circumstances, having regard, in particular, to (i) the requirements of the employee's study or training; and (ii) the circumstances of the business of the employer or the principal and the effect of the employee's time off on the running of that business. Employee shareholders are not entitled to apply for time off under s 63A.[114]

An employee entitled to such time off may make a complaint to an employment tribunal if his employer unreasonably refuses to allow him to take time off under s 63A, or refuses to pay him if he does take such time off.[115]

Health and safety

In addition to the employment rights just described, employees also have the right to have their health and safety protected. Employers who fail to protect the health and safety of their employees adequately may find themselves facing liability in three different ways.

1. **Tort** Employees who suffer illness or injury due to acts of their employers may be able to recover compensation under the tort of negligence.
2. **Contract** It is an implied term of the employment contract that employers will take reasonable care of the health and safety of their employees. Failure to do so can result in damages being awarded for breach of contract.

---

111. ibid s 51(2).   112. ibid s 98B(1).   113. SI 2001/2801.   114. ERA 1996, s 205A(2)(a).
115. ibid s 63C(1).

3. **Criminal liability** The Health and Safety at Work etc Act 1974 places a duty on employers to take reasonable care, so far as is reasonably practicable, of their employee's health and safety. Employers who breach this duty commit a criminal offence.

These forms of liability are not mutually exclusive, and an employer who fails to protect the health and safety of his employees may be both civilly liable to pay compensation and guilty of a criminal offence.

Negligence

An employee who suffers some form of injury whilst at work may be able to recover damages if he can demonstrate that the injury was caused by his employer's negligence. The usual requirements of negligence apply. Issues of breach of duty, causation, and remoteness are the same as for general negligence. Here, the focus will be on the scope of the duty of care owed by the employer and the available defences.

🔗 The requirements of negligence are discussed in Chapter 14

It is well established that the employer owes a duty of care to his employees, but what does this duty entail? The classic formulation of the employer's duty of care was laid down by Lord Wright in *Wilsons and Clyde Co Ltd v English*,[116] in which he stated that the duty of care was met by 'the provision of a competent staff of men, adequate material, and a proper system and effective supervision'.[117] Each of these three elements will be examined, along with a fourth element (namely, the duty to protect employees from psychiatric harm) that has been subsequently added.

However, before the scope of the duty is discussed, two points need to be made. First, the duty is non-delegable, meaning that employers cannot avoid liability by arguing that they delegated responsibility for the employees' health and safety to someone else. Second, the duty is not owed to the employees collectively, but to each individual employee. This means that if an employer is aware that an employee is more susceptible to health risks whilst at work, the employer should take special precautions to ensure the employee's protection.[118]

'The provision of a competent staff of men'

The first element of Lord Wright's duty of care provides that employers are under a duty to provide competent fellow employees. Where an employee is injured due to the actions of an incompetent colleague, the employer may have breached his duty of care to the injured employee. Employers should ensure that their employees receive adequate training and should also curtail any undesirable practices of which they become aware.

> ### 🔑 *Hudson v Ridge Manufacturing Co* [1957] 2 QB 348
>
> **FACTS**: An employee of the defendant had a reputation as a practical joker, and frequently made a nuisance of himself to the claimant and fellow employees. For over four years, the defendant was aware of the employee's activities, but beyond several formal reprimands, no further action was taken to curtail the employee's behaviour. On one occasion, the employee

---

116. [1938] AC 57 (HL).   117. ibid 78.
118. *Paris v Stepney Borough Council* [1951] AC 367 (HL).

tripped up the claimant (who was disabled). The claimant sustained a broken wrist and claimed damages from the defendant.

HELD: The defendant was aware of the employee's disruptive and potentially dangerous conduct and, in failing to prevent it, it had breached the duty of care that it owed to the claimant. The claimant recovered damages for the injury sustained.

'Adequate material'

The second element of the duty states that employers should provide safe work equipment (for example, machinery, vehicles, protective clothing, etc) and also safe premises (for example, effective lighting and ventilation, clear and unobstructed fire exits, etc).

 Bradford v Robinson Rentals Ltd [1967] 1 WLR 337

FACTS: The defendant employed the claimant, a 57-year-old man. During the winter of 1963, the claimant was required to exchange a van for another, which would involve a twenty-hour journey of around 450 miles (the motorway system at the time was much less extensive than it is today). The defendant knew that both vans were unheated (the heater in the first van was broken and the second van had no heater), but still required the claimant to engage in the journey. During the journey, the claimant contracted frostbite, causing permanent damage to his hands and feet.

HELD: The defendant knew that the claimant would be exposed to prolonged periods of extreme cold and that, by failing to provide him with a heated vehicle, it had breached the duty of care owed. Although contracting frostbite was unusual in England, the actions of the defendant had made it reasonably foreseeable.

The law relating to the provision of safe work equipment has been made substantially more stringent with the passing of the Employer's Liability (Defective Equipment) Act 1969. Section 1(1) of this Act provides that where an employee suffers personal injury in the course of his employment from a defect in equipment provided by his employer for the purposes of the business, and the defect is attributable wholly or in part to the negligence or other tort of a third party (for example, the manufacturer or supplier of the equipment), the injury shall be deemed also to be attributable to the negligence of the employer. Thus, the employee may sue his employer, rather than the manufacturer or other third party who was at fault; the employer, in turn, may then seek a contribution from the third party. The effect of s 1(1) can be seen in the following case.

 Knowles v Liverpool City Council [1993] 1 WLR 1428 (HL)

FACTS: The claimant was employed by the defendant to lay flagstones. One of the flagstones was defective and broke, crushing the claimant's right index finger. The flagstones were not manufactured by the defendant, but purchased from a third party.

HELD: The flagstones constituted 'equipment' and, although the defect was not due to the defendant's negligence, the 1969 Act deemed the defendant negligent for equipment that was defective due to the actions of a third party. Accordingly, the defendant was ordered to pay the claimant £3,092 in damages.

COMMENT: This case is notable for the width of the House's interpretation of the term 'equipment'. Lord Jauncey (with whom the other judges agreed) stated that the term 'equipment' could apply to any article provided by the employer for the purposes of the business, irrespective of whether the employee was required to, or had in fact, used the article.

 See Geoffrey H Holgate, 'Employers' Liability and the Provision of Defective "Equipment"' (1993) 22 ILJ 214

The courts will not impose liability on an employer who has taken all reasonable precautions in avoiding the act that led to the claimant's injury. Where the employer would need to take precautions wholly out of proportion to the risk involved, the courts will not hold that failure to take such precautions constitutes a breach of the duty of care.

Eg ***Latimer v AEC Ltd* [1953] AC 643 (HL)**

FACTS: An unusually heavy rainstorm flooded the defendant's factory. The defendant did all that it could to eliminate the effects of the flooding, but some areas of the flooring were still flooded and slippery. The claimant (an employee of the defendant) slipped and injured his ankle. He sued the defendant, alleging that it should have shut the factory down until it was completely safe.

HELD: His claim failed because the defendant had done all that it could reasonably do. The majority of the factory floor was rendered safe, so the risk of injury was minimal. The only other option was to shut the factory down and the cost of such action would have been wholly out of proportion to the risk involved.

'A proper system and effective supervision'

The third element of the duty states that employers should provide a safe system of work. This duty is extremely wide and can overlap with the other duties. A safe system of work could include ensuring that the workplace is safe, ensuring that effective supervision is in place, ensuring that employees are trained to deal with work-related hazards and risks, and ensuring that proper safety equipment is available, etc. The provision of safety equipment has proven to be a troublesome issue—notably, where safety equipment is available, but the employee decides not to use it. Historically, in such cases, employers were not liable for injuries caused due to an employee's failure to use available safety equipment,[119] but more recent cases have moved away from this position and will impose liability where the employer acquiesces to the employee's decision not to use the available equipment.

---

119. *McWilliams v Sir William Arrol & Co Ltd* [1962] 1 WLR 295 (HL).

Bux v Slough Metals Ltd [1973] 1 WLR 1358 (CA)

FACTS: The defendant employed the claimant as a die-caster. His work involved the pouring of molten metal into a die. Safety goggles were supplied to the claimant, but he did not wear them. When his superintendant questioned him on this, the claimant stated that the goggles were useless, because they misted up. The superintendant did not attempt to convince the employee to wear the goggles. Whilst pouring molten metal into a die, the metal splashed on the claimant's face, causing him to lose the sight fully in one eye and suffer partial blindness in the other. He claimed damages from the defendant.

HELD: The defendant should have instructed the claimant to wear the goggles 'in a reasonable and firm manner'[120] and then followed up the instruction to check that the goggles were being worn. The defendant's failure to do this was a breach of its duty of care. The claimant was awarded damages of just over £19,400.

COMMENT: Section 7 of the Health and Safety at Work Act 1974 (discussed later), places a duty on employees to take reasonable care for their own safety. Had this claim been brought under the 1974 Act, it is likely that it would have failed.

⭐ See Brenda Barrett, 'Another Look at the Contribution to Occupational Safety of the "Safe System"' (1974) 37 MLR 577

Where the safety equipment becomes ineffective (not due to being defective) and the employee fails to take steps to obtain new equipment, however, the employer will not be liable.

 Smith v Scot Bowyers [1986] IRLR 315 (CA)

FACTS: The claimant's job required him to walk on floors covered in oil. To prevent him from slipping, he was provided with a pair of boots with ridged soles designed to grip slippery surfaces. Through use, however, the soles had become worn and failed to grip adequately, but the claimant failed to request a new pair from his employer. The claimant slipped and was injured.

HELD: The employer was not liable for the claimant's injuries, as it had acted reasonably in providing boots and informing employees that replacement boots were available on request. The claimant should have taken responsibility for his own safety by requesting a replacement pair of boots.

⭐ See Brenda Barrett, 'The Employers' Duty to Ensure that Safety Measures are Taken by Employees' (1987) 52 ILJ 57

A final point to note is that this duty still applies even where the employee's activities take place away from the employer's premises. Thus, an employee who worked for a firm of window cleaners could claim damages for injuries caused by a defective safety belt, even though his work was not carried out on the defendant's premises.[121]

Duty to protect employees from psychiatric illness

The duty to protect employees from psychiatric illness was not part of Lord Wright's original threefold formation of the employer's duty of care; rather, it was established in the following case.

---

120. [1973] 1 WLR 1358 (CA) 1372 (Stephenson LJ).
121. *General Cleaning Contractors Ltd v Christmas* [1953] AC 180 (HL).

Walker v Northumberland County Council [1995] ICR 702 (QB)

FACTS: The claimant had worked for the defendant for seventeen years. In 1986, he suffered a nervous breakdown due to stress caused from overwork. Several months later, he returned to work and informed the defendant that his workload would need to be reduced. The defendant agreed to provide extra assistance to the claimant for as long as the claimant required it. However, after only one month, the assistance was withdrawn and, by September 1987, the claimant suffered from a stress-related condition. Shortly after, he suffered a second nervous breakdown and was dismissed on the ground of permanent ill health.

HELD: In withdrawing the extra assistance, the defendant had breached the duty of care owed (in relation to the second nervous breakdown) to the claimant and was ordered to pay damages. The possibility of a stress-related condition was foreseeable, given the claimant's level of work, and psychiatric illness became even more foreseeable following his first nervous breakdown.

★ See Lesley Dolding and Richard Mullender, 'Law, Labour and Mental Harm' (1996) 59 MLR 297

This area of the law is still developing, as is evidenced by the substantial number of recent cases on the topic, of which the most important is *Sutherland v Hatton*.[122] In this case, Hale LJ took the available case law and summarized it into sixteen propositions,[123] of which the principal ones include:

- The key question is whether the kind of harm to the particular employee was reasonably foreseeable.

- Foreseeability depends on what the employer knows about the individual employee. Mental disorders are more difficult to foresee than physical injury.

- The test of foreseeability is the same, irrespective of the type of employment—there are no occupations that should be regarded as intrinsically dangerous to mental health.

- Factors relevant in determining foreseeability include the nature and extent of the work undertaken by the employee, and whether the employee has displayed signs of impending ill health.

- The employer is entitled to take what he is told by his employee at face value.

- The employer will only be liable if he failed to take those steps which were reasonable in the circumstances.

- The claimant must establish that the employer's breach of duty caused, or materially contributed to, the harm suffered—it is not enough to show that occupational stress caused the harm.

- Where the harm was only partly caused by the employer, the employer will only be liable for the proportion of harm that it caused.

The onus on foreseeability will doubtless make it more difficult for claimants to succeed, especially as Hale LJ stated that mental disorders are more difficult to foresee than physical injuries. Despite this, however, the case has been largely welcomed as 'providing a significant contribution to the ongoing debate'[124] and constituting 'a balanced and highly desirable settlement of the law'.[125]

---

122. [2002] EWCA Civ 76, [2002] All ER 1.   123. ibid [43].

124. Nicholas J Mullany, 'Containing Claims for Workplace Mental Illness' (2002) 118 LQR 373, 374.

125. Ian Smith and Aaron Baker, *Smith & Wood's Employment Law* (11th edn, OUP 2013) 147.

Defences

An employee who has suffered injury due to his employer's negligence may be denied a remedy if the employer can successfully raise a defence. As tortious defences are examined in detail in Chapter 17, only the principal defences available will be briefly highlighted here.

Where the employer's negligence has caused the employee injury, but the employee's own conduct also contributed to that injury occurring, then the employer can plead the defence of contributory negligence. Contributory negligence is a partial defence only and will serve to reduce the damages recoverable, based on the extent to which the employee's actions contributed to his injury. For example, in the case of *Bux v Slough Metals Ltd*[126] (discussed earlier), the Court held that the employee, in refusing to wear the provided safety goggles, was 40 per cent to blame for his injuries and therefore his damages were reduced by 40 per cent.

If the employer can demonstrate that the employee consented to the actions that caused his injury, then he will be able to raise the defence of *volenti non fit injuria*. As discussed, *volenti* is a complete defence, serving to exonerate the defendant completely.[127]

→ *volenti non fit injuria:* 'to a willing person, no harm is done' (see p 477)

Breach of contract

In addition to a claim in negligence, an employee injured at work might also have a claim for breach of contract. There is an implied term in the contract of employment that imposes a duty on the employer to take reasonable care of his employees' safety.[128] The scope of this duty is largely similar to the tortious duty discussed earlier, and whether it is preferable to bring a claim in contract or tort depends on a number of factors, including:

- As has been noted, the courts are reluctant to award damages for pure economic loss in tort. Contractual damages for pure economic loss, however, are freely recoverable.

 The law relating to pure economic loss is discussed at p 379

- The construction of the employment contract may, in some way, preclude a contractual claim. A claim in tort may not be limited by the terms of the contract.
- The limitation periods in tort are generally more generous than those in contract.
- The claimant may choose to bring a claim in contract to deny the employer access to certain tortious defences.
- Damages in contract and tort are calculated differently. Depending on the facts, choosing the correct claim might result in a higher award of damages.

The Health and Safety at Work etc Act 1974

Prior to the passing of the Health and Safety at Work etc Act 1974 (HSWA 1974), the law relating to the health and safety of employees was spread across a mass of legislation: over thirty Acts and 500 statutory instruments. The 1972 Robens Report[129]

---

126. [1973] 1 WLR 1358 (CA).
127. *ICI Ltd v Shatwell* [1965] AC 656 (HL). This case is discussed at p 479.
128. *Lister v Romford Ice and Cold Storage Co* [1957] AC 555 (HL).
129. Lord Robens, *Report of the Committee on Safety and Health at Work* (Cmnd 5034, HMSO 1972).

was highly critical of the state of the law relating to the health and safety of employees, branding it a 'haphazard mass of law which is intricate in detail, unprogressive, often too difficult to comprehend and difficult to amend and keep up to date'. The report recommended that the mass of legislation be swept away and replaced by a 'comprehensive and orderly set of revised provisions under a new enabling Act'. This Act would cover only the general duties of employers, with more detailed regulation coming in the form of subordinate legislation and non-statutory codes of practice. The rationale behind this reliance on subordinate legislation was the desire to ensure that the law was flexible and could be amended easily, thereby ensuring that it would remain up to date. The recommendations of the Robens Report were almost universally adopted, resulting in the passing of the HSWA 1974.

As envisaged by Robens, the Act is an enabling one, stating only the general duties of employers and other relevant parties (for example, manufacturers and suppliers). Unlike previous piecemeal legislation, however, it applies to all types of workplace and all types of employer. The Act does not provide employees with civil remedies for injuries caused in the workplace[130]—to obtain such remedies, the employee should bring a claim in tort or contract, as discussed earlier. Instead, the Act imposes criminal liability upon employers that breach the duties owed to employees.

Duties owed by employers to employees

The overriding duty owed by employers to their employees can be found in s 2(1) which provides that '[i]t shall be the duty of every employer to ensure, so far as is reasonably practicable, the health, safety and welfare at work of all his employees'. Section 2(2) then provides a non-exhaustive list of matters that come within the s 2(1) duty:

- the provision and maintenance of plant and systems of work that are, so far as is reasonably practicable, safe and without risks to health;
- arrangements for ensuring, so far as is reasonably practicable, the safety of, and absence of risks to health in connection with, the use, handling, storage, and transport of articles and substances;
- the provision of such information, instruction, training, and supervision as is necessary to ensure, so far as is reasonably practicable, the health and safety at work of employees;
- so far as is reasonably practicable as regards any place of work under the employer's control, the maintenance of that place of work in a condition that is safe and free from risks to health, and the provision and maintenance of means of access to and egress from that place of work that are safe and free from such risks;
- the provision and maintenance of a working environment for employees that is, so far as is reasonably practicable, safe, free from risks to health, and adequate as regards facilities and arrangements for the employees' welfare at work.

It will be noted that each of these matters is subject to a limitation—namely, that the employer need only comply with the duty 'so far as is reasonably practicable'. The meaning of this phrase was considered in the following case.

---

130. HSWA 1974, s 47(1). It should be noted that the Enterprise and Regulatory Reform Act 2013 has amended s 47 to provide that an employee has no right to bring a civil claim for breach of statutory duty under health and safety legislation, unless the legislation itself provides for such a right (see s 47(2) and (2A)).

Edwards v National Coal Board [1949] 1 KB 704 (CA)

FACTS: A miner walking along a travelling road that led to a coal mine was killed by a fall of material from the side of the mine, caused by a latent defect in the side of the road. His widow claimed damages from the defendant, on the ground it had breached the now repealed Coal Mines Act 1911, s 49 of which placed a duty on employers to make secure 'every travelling road and working place'. The Act provided that liability would not be imposed where it was 'not reasonably practicable to avoid a breach' of s 49. The defendant argued that, given that it was impossible to know when and where a fall could occur, it would have to prop and support every travelling road, the cost of which was not reasonably practicable.

HELD: The risk of an accident had to be measured against the costs (in terms of money, time, or trouble) of precautions. Where the risk of injury is great, the issue of cost is given less weight. Asquith LJ stated:

'Reasonably practicable' is a narrower term than 'physically possible' and seems to me to imply that a computation must be made by the owner, in which the quantum of risk is placed on one scale and the sacrifice involved in the measures necessary for averting the risk (whether in money, time or trouble) is placed in the other; and that if it be shown that there is a gross disproportion between them—the risk being insignificant in relation to the sacrifice—the defendants discharge the onus on them.[131]

Here, the risk was considerable and, because the employer had presented little evidence to support its assertion, the Court found in the claimant's favour.

Like the common law, the HSWA 1974 does not expect the impossible, nor does it impose strict liability. The Act permits employers to balance the need to comply with the s 2 duty with the costs required for compliance. However, the normal burden of proof is reversed, so that the employer will need to demonstrate that compliance with the duty was not reasonably practicable.[132] As the following case demonstrates, establishing this does not appear to be overly difficult.

 West Bromwich Building Society Ltd v Townsend [1983] ICR 257 (QB)

FACTS: An environmental health inspector served an improvement notice on the defendant building society, alleging that it had contravened s 2(1) of the HSWA 1974 by not installing anti-bandit screens to protect employees from attack. The defendant challenged the improvement notice. An industrial tribunal held that, because installing screens was well within the financial means of the defendant, the improvement notice was valid. The defendant appealed.

HELD: The tribunal had erred and the correct question was not whether the installation of screens was financially viable, but whether the installation of screens was reasonably practicable, given the risk of a robbery occurring. As the tribunal had erred in law, the Court allowed the appeal and quashed the improvement notice.

★ See R Howells, 'Criminal Attacks Upon Employees' (1983) 12 ILJ 182

---

131. [1949] 1 KB 704 (CA) 712.   132. HSWA 1974, s 40.

Complying with the duty contained in s 2(1) might involve the provision of safety equipment, training, etc. In relation to this, s 9 imposes a further duty on employees not to charge their employees for any health and safety provision, but this duty extends only to provision provided to meet the statutory duties, and employers may charge for provision if it goes beyond what is required by statute.

Duties owed by employers to persons who are not their employees

Employers also owe duties to persons who are not their employees (for example, employees of others, independent contractors, or members of the public). Section 3(1) provides that:

> It shall be the duty of every employer to conduct his undertaking in such a way as to ensure, so far as is reasonably practicable, that persons not in his employment who may be affected thereby are not thereby exposed to risks to their health or safety.

In the following case, it was noted that injury to health is not required to establish a breach of s 3(1), but only a breach that *exposes* persons who are not their employees to injury.

R v Board of Trustees of the Science Museum [1993] 1 WLR 1171 (CA)

FACTS: The defendant's air conditioning system was found to contain legionella pneumophila, the bacterium that causes legionnaires' disease. It was charged under s 3(1) of the HSWA 1974 on the ground that members of the public could be exposed to the bacterium. The defendant argued that no harm had actually been caused and that there was no evidence to indicate that members of the public had inhaled the bacterium.

HELD: The Court of Appeal upheld the conviction. Actual damage to health was not required to be proven; only that the defendant's conduct had exposed persons other than its employees to the possibility of danger.

COMMENT: This case demonstrates the difference in approach between the common law and the HSWA 1974. In order to succeed, a claim in contract or tort would require a claimant who had suffered loss. As regards the HSWA 1974, no loss need occur. This more stringent approach fits in with the Act's aim of preventing injury.

See Brenda Barrett, 'Trends in Occupational Health and Safety' (1994) 23 ILJ 60

Duties owed by other persons

Although the principal duties contained in the HSWA 1974 are imposed on employers, the Act does impose duties on a number of other parties, including:

- A self-employed person is under a duty under s 3(2) to conduct his undertaking in such a way so as to ensure, as far as is reasonably practicable, that he and other persons (who are not his employees) who may be affected by the undertaking, are not exposed to risks to their health and safety.

- A duty is imposed by s 4 upon occupiers and controllers of premises (except domestic premises) to take care for the safety of persons who are not their employees on their premises.

KEY POINTS SUMMARY

- The majority of workers over school age are entitled to receive the national minimum wage.
- The provisions of the NMWA 1998 can be enforced by an action for breach of contract, in an action for an unlawful deduction of wages, and via an enforcement notice issues by HM Revenue and Customs. Failure to pay the national minimum wage can also result in the commission of a criminal offence.
- The Transfer of Undertakings (Protection of Employment) Regulations 2006 provide that, if the transfer is a relevant transfer, the employees' contracts of employment are transferred to the new owner.
- All pregnant employees are entitled to twenty-six weeks' ordinary maternity leave and another twenty-six weeks' additional maternity leave. For thirty-nine of these weeks, they are also entitled to receive statutory maternity pay.
- Ordinary paternity leave of up to two weeks, and additional paternity leave of up to twenty-six weeks, is currently available to fathers, provided that they have served at least twenty-six weeks' continuous service.
- The employer owes a duty of care to all of his employees to (i) provide competent fellow employees; (ii) provide safe equipment and premises; (iii) provide a safe system of work; and (iv) protect the employees from psychiatric illness.
- Breach of the duties contained in the Health and Safety at Work etc Act 1974 constitutes a criminal offence. The Act provides no civil remedies.
- The Working Time Regulations 1998 provide that a worker's working week should not exceed an average of forty-eight hours per week across the reference period (which is normally seventeen weeks).

Self-test questions

1. Define the following:
   (a) undertaking;
   (b) maternity allowance;
   (c) dependant;
   (d) young worker;
   (e) night worker.

2. Explain the distinction between: (i) compulsory maternity leave; (ii) ordinary maternity leave; and (iii) additional maternity leave.

3. 'The recent increase in the scope and number of employment rights places intolerable burdens upon employers and businesses and therefore employers should be permitted to exclude these employment rights where it is reasonable to do so.' Discuss.

4. Has there been a breach of health and safety legislation in the following cases?
   (a) David has been employed by BuildCo Ltd as a labourer for the previous six months. He normally works a forty-hour week, but for five weeks, he was required to work an extra fifteen hours per week of overtime.
   (b) Olivia is employed as a trainee solicitor. The firm is engaged in a high-profile merger and, with the deadline for the merger approaching, the partners require the trainees to work longer hours than normal. In the period leading up to the merger deadline, Olivia is required to work for eight consecutive days.

Further reading

Astra Emir *Selwyn's Law of Employment* (17th edn, OUP 2012) chs 6–9 and 11
An excellent and up-to-date discussion of all the employment law rights and health and safety provisions discussed in this chapter

Health and Safety Executive, *Health and Safety Statistics 2012/13* (HSE 2013)
Provides detailed statistics of all work-related injuries and illnesses; also provides statistics relating to the issuing of improvement and prohibition notices

Grace James, 'The Work and Families Act 2006: Legislation to Improve Choice and Flexibility?' (2006) 35 ILJ 272
Examines the reforms introduced by the 2006 Act and contends that such piecemeal reforms have little to offer interested parties

John McMullen, 'An Analysis of the Transfer of Undertakings (Protection of Employment) Regulations 2006' (2006) 35 ILJ 113
Examines in depth the TUPE and argues that the aims set out in the Acquired Rights Directive have been met only in part

Bob Simpson, 'The National Minimum Wage Five Years on: Reflections on Some General Issues' (2004) 33 ILJ 22
Discusses the early operation of the National Minimum Wage Act 1998 and argues that it plays a valuable, if limited, role

Websites

<http://www.hse.gov.uk>
The official website of the Health and Safety Executive; provides useful guidance of all health and safety legislation, as well as links to more detailed research publications

<https://www.gov.uk/government/organisations/low-pay-commission>
The official website of the Low Pay Commission; contains useful guidance on the national minimum wage, and links to various reports and publications

Remember to visit the **Online Resource Centre** at <http://www.oxfordtextbooks.co.uk/orc/roach3e> to access the following resources on Chapter 26, 'Employment rights, and health and safety': more **practice questions** and answers; a **glossary** of key terms; **multiple-choice questions; and revision summaries**. Updates to the law can be found on Twitter by following **@UKBusinessLaw**.

27 Discrimination law

- The Equality Act 2010
- Prohibited conduct
- Protected characteristics
- Positive action
- Enforcement and remedies

- Equality of contractual terms between men and women
- Discrimination against part-time workers and fixed-term employees

INTRODUCTION

As one commentator has correctly noted '[e]quality as an ideal is a relatively modern construct'.[1] In the early nineteenth century, employees were not protected from the discriminatory acts of their employers and an employer was free to refuse a person employment 'for the most mistaken, capricious, malicious or morally reprehensible motives that can be conceived'.[2] The situation today is very different and the last forty years have witnessed the enactment of a staggering amount of anti-discrimination legislation. The problem that arose was that each form of discrimination was governed by its own piece of legislation, with each piece of legislation operating in subtly different ways and using different terms and concepts. The lack of harmony ensured that certain forms of discriminatory conduct remained (the most notable perhaps being the significant pay gap between men and women). The government's response was to pass the Equality Act 2010, which aims to harmonize most (but not all) of the various grounds for discrimination under a single piece of legislation.

The Equality Act 2010

Prior to the enactment of the Equality Act 2010, the law relating to discrimination was spread across a mass of primary, subordinate, and EU legislation. In 2000, it was calculated that, in order to obtain a full understanding of the law relating to the various forms of discrimination, a person would need to consult over thirty Acts of Parliament, thirty-eight statutory instruments, eleven codes of practice, and

---

1. Sandra Fredman, *Discrimination Law* (2nd edn, OUP 2011) 4.
2. *Allen v Flood* [1898] AC 1 (HL) 172 (Lord Davey).

twelve EU directives and recommendations.[3] By 2008, that number had increased significantly and it was estimated that the number of statutory instruments alone was around 100.[4] Whilst much of the legislation followed a similar format and used similar definitions, there were notable differences that rendered the law confusing at best and inconsistent at worst, with two commentators stating that the 'chaotic state of British anti-discrimination legislation…arguably brought the law into disrepute'.[5] Accordingly, for a considerable period, there were growing calls for a Single Equality Act that would unify all of the anti-discrimination legislation in one single statute— an approach that has been adopted in Australia, Canada, the US, and Ireland.

Initially, the government did not seem interested in unifying the various Acts and statutory instruments, and even when it was persuaded that a single Act was the best way forward, the announcement of a Bill was delayed on several occasions. A Consultation Paper was finally published in June 2007,[6] and the Bill itself was introduced into Parliament in April 2009 and was passed in April 2010.

As a result of the Act's passing, many pre-2010 pieces of legislation were fully or largely repealed or revoked, including:

- the Equal Pay Act 1970;
- the Sex Discrimination Act 1975;
- the Race Relations Act 1976;
- the Disability Discrimination Act 1995;
- the Employment Equality (Religion or Belief) Regulations 2003;[7]
- the Employment Equality (Sexual Orientation) Regulations 2003;[8]
- the Employment Equality (Age) Regulations 2006.[9]

However, it is worth noting that, in relation to most grounds of discrimination, the 2010 Act does not radically alter the law and so much pre-2010 case law will remain relevant.

The provisions of the Act relating to employment apply only to those who are in 'employment', which is defined as working 'under a contract of employment, a contract of apprenticeship or a contract personally to do work'.[10] This definition of employment is wider than the definition found in other legislation (notably, the definition of employment found in the ERA 1996) and will include persons not normally protected in other pieces of legislation (such as self-employed persons).[11]

Prohibited conduct

Prior to the enactment of the 2010 Act, each ground of discrimination had its own forms of prohibited conduct, which operated differently in subtle and complex ways. The 2010 Act harmonizes the various forms of prohibited conduct across the various grounds of discrimination (these grounds are known as 'protected characteristics'

---

3. Bob Hepple, *Equality: A New Framework* (Hart Publishing 2011) 21.
4. Government Equalities Office, *Framework for a Fairer Future: The Equality Bill* (HMSO 2008) 6.
5. Ian Smith and Aaron Baker, *Smith & Wood's Employment Law* (11th edn, OUP 2013) 307.
6. Department for Communities and Local Government, *A Framework for Fairness: Proposals for a Single Equality Act for Great Britain* (HMSO 2007).   7. SI 2003/1660.   8. SI 2003/1661.
9. SI 2006/1031.   10. Equality Act 2010, s 83(2)(a).
11. Case C-256/01 *Allonby v Accrington and Rossendale College* [2004] ECR I-873.

and include sex, race, disability, etc) by providing for five principal forms of prohibited conduct, namely (i) direct discrimination; (ii) combined discrimination; (iii) indirect discrimination; (iv) harassment; and (v) victimization. Certain protected characteristics also have their own additional unique forms of prohibited conduct, which are discussed alongside the relevant protected characteristic.

 Protected
characteristics are
discussed at p 752

Direct discrimination

Direct discrimination occurs where, because of a protected characteristic, a person (*A*) treats another person (*B*) less favourably than *A* treats or would treat others.[12]

> **Eg** **Direct discrimination**
>
> Helen is applying for a job as a PA to the managing director of a large bank. She is shortlisted for an interview, along with two other candidates, Tom and Dave. The bank's managing director instructs the personnel department not to invite Tom and Dave for an interview, because he would prefer his PA to be a woman, and to offer Helen the job. Tom and Dave have been treated less favourably than Helen because of their sex, and so have been directly discriminated against.

In order for direct discrimination to arise, the unfavourable treatment must occur 'because of a protected characteristic'. From this phrase, two consequences follow. First, the claimant need not fall within the scope of the protected characteristic for direct discrimination to arise. Direct discrimination can arise where a person is treated less favourably due to their association with a third party who has a particular protected characteristic,[13] as occurred in the following case.

> **Showboat Entertainment Centre Ltd v Owens**
> **[1984] 1 WLR 384 (EAT)**
>
> **FACTS:** The claimant, a white man, was employed as the manager of an entertainment centre owned by the defendant. The defendant instructed the claimant to exclude all black customers from the centre. The claimant refused and was dismissed.
>
> **HELD:** Direct racial discrimination usually occurs due to the race of the claimant, but it can also occur where the claimant was treated less favourably due to the race of a third party. Accordingly, the claimant had been directly discriminated against on the ground of race.

Second, the definition would appear to be wide enough to cover those instances where the victim does not have a protected characteristic, but the employer wrongfully believes that he does (for example, where an employer rejects a job application

---

12. Equality Act 2010, s 13(1).

13. As is discussed at p 761, this will not be the case where the protected characteristic is marriage or civil partnership.

from a white man who, due to his exotic-sounding name, the employer mistakenly believes to be black).

In cases involving direct discrimination, the key factor is the employer's actual treatment of the person alleging discrimination, not how he intended to treat that person, or the reasons behind that treatment (in other words, the test is objective, not subjective). The reasons for a discriminatory act are irrelevant, no matter how laudable they may be.

🔑 James v Eastleigh Borough Council [1990] 2 AC 751 (HL)

FACTS: The defendant council provided free swimming facilities to persons of pensionable age. Mr and Mrs James, who were both aged 61, visited a swimming pool run by the defendant. At the time, the pensionable age for women was 60 and 65 for men, meaning that Mrs James was admitted for free, whereas Mr James had to pay. Mr James brought an action against the defendant alleging that he had been treated less favourably because he was a man. The Court of Appeal rejected his claim on the ground that the reason for the policy was to encourage pensioners to swim, not to discriminate against men. Mr James appealed.

HELD: It was clear that the defendant did not intend to discriminate, but the House of Lords, by a majority of three to two, held that this was irrelevant and allowed the appeal. It was irrelevant whether the motive for the discriminatory act was benign or not. The question to ask was 'would the complainant have received the same treatment but for his or her sex?'[14] But for Mr James' sex, he would have received the same treatment, and so direct discrimination was proven.

COMMENT: Lord Griffiths gave a powerful, if short, dissenting speech. He applauded the defendant's 'wholly admirable practice of treating old age pensioners with generosity'[15] and stated that he could not believe 'that it was the intention of Parliament that this benevolent practice should be declared to be unlawful'.[16] Lord Lowry agreed, stating that the free swimming facilities were provided to persons because they were of pensionable age, not because they were men or women. Ultimately, Lords Griffiths and Lowry were in the minority, and the principal result of *James* was to make it easier for a claimant to establish direct discrimination by preventing the defendant from using motive as a defence.

⭐ See Geoffrey H Mead, 'The Role of Intention in Direct Discrimination' (1990) 19 ILJ 250

Section 13(2) to (7) provides that, in relation to certain protected characteristics, the rules relating to direct discrimination may be clarified, qualified, or excluded. These clarifications, qualifications, and exclusions are discussed alongside their corresponding protected characteristic later in the chapter.

The comparator

Section 23(1) provides that, in relation to direct discrimination, combined discrimination, and indirect discrimination, on a comparison of cases, there must be no material difference between the circumstances relating to each case. What this means is that the treatment of the claimant must be compared to a person (known as the comparator) who does not share the protected characteristic of the claimant (or either of

---

14. [1990] 2 AC 751 (HL) 774 (Lord Goff).   15. ibid 767.   16. ibid.

the characteristics in relation to combined discrimination), but whose circumstances are not otherwise materially different. The following example demonstrates this.

 The comparator

Shannon, who is blind, has applied to MegaCorp plc for a secretarial position. Although her qualifications are excellent, she is not invited for an interview because the personnel officer at MegaCorp wrongly assumes the blind persons cannot use computers. In determining whether discrimination has taken place, MegaCorp's treatment of Shannon would be compared to that of a person who is not blind, but who has the same ability to undertake the job as Shannon.

If no actual comparator exists or if one cannot be located, then a hypothetical comparator must be used.[17] Irrespective of whether the comparator is actual or hypothetical, the comparator's circumstances must not materially different from those of the claimant. If they are, the claim will fail, as occurred in the following case.

 ***Bullock v Alice Ottley School* [1993] ICR 138 (CA)**

FACTS: The defendant operated a policy whereby teaching and domestic staff were forced to retire at the age of 60, whereas gardeners and maintenance staff retired at the age of 65. As the majority of domestic staff were female, one of them brought an action alleging that being forced to retire earlier than gardeners and maintenance staff (who were predominantly male) constituted direct sex discrimination. The defendant argued that the disparity in retirement age was not due to sex, but to the fact that gardeners and maintenance staff were more difficult to recruit.

HELD: The Court of Appeal rejected the claim. As gardeners and maintenance staff were more difficult to recruit, the circumstances between the two comparators were materially different and did not provide a proper basis for comparison.

In relation to direct discrimination, it does not matter whether the alleged discriminator has the same protected characteristic as the person alleging discrimination.[18]

Combined discrimination; dual characteristics

Combined discrimination occurs where, because of two relevant protected characteristics, a person (*A*) treats another person (*B*) less favourably than *A* treats or would treat a person who does not share either of those characteristics.[19] The following example demonstrates how combined discrimination might arise.

---

17. *Balamoody v United Kingdom Central Council for Nursing, Midwifery and Health Visiting* [2001] EWCA Civ 2097, [2002] IRLR 288.   18. Equality Act 2010, s 24(1).
19. ibid s 14(1). Section 14(2) provides that the relevant protected characteristics are (i) age; (ii) disability; (iii) gender reassignment; (iv) race; (v) religion or belief; (vi) sex; or (vii) sexual orientation.

Combined discrimination

> An employer refuses to employ a Muslim man on the ground that Muslim men are likely to be terrorists. In this case, the discrimination is not because he is a man (so a claim based on direct sex discrimination would fail), nor is it necessarily because he is a Muslim (so a claim based on direct religious discrimination might fail). The discrimination is based on the combination of the protected characteristics of sex and religion or belief, and so would likely amount to combined discrimination.

A few points should be noted:

- a claimant can simultaneously bring separate claims for direct discrimination and combined discrimination in the same proceedings;[20]
- the claimant must show that the less favourable treatment was due to the combination alleged, as compared with how a person who does not share either characteristic is or would be treated;[21]
- the claimant does not need to demonstrate that a claim of direct discrimination in respect of each protected characteristic would have been successful if brought separately;[22]
- a combined discrimination claim will not succeed where an exception or justification applies to the treatment in respect of either or both of the relevant protected characteristics.[23]

Section 14 did not come into force alongside the rest of the Act's provisions, due to the potential costs of its implementation. The 2010 Act's Impact Assessment estimated that implementing the combined discrimination provision would cost businesses £3 million per year.[24] The government's 2011 *Plan for Growth* sought to reduce the cost of regulation on all businesses and, as part of this reduction, the government announced that it would not be bringing s 14 into force.[25]

Indirect discrimination

Indirect discrimination occurs where a person (*A*) applies to another person (*B*) a provision, criterion, or practice (PCP) which is discriminatory in relation to the relevant protected characteristic of *A*.[26] This will occur if:

- *A* applies, or would apply, the PCP to persons who do not share that characteristic;
- it puts, or would put, persons with whom *B* shares the characteristic at a particular disadvantage when compared with persons who do not share that characteristic;
- it puts, or would put, *B* at a disadvantage; and
- *A* cannot show it to be a proportionate means of achieving a legitimate aim.[27]

Basically, indirect discrimination occurs where a PCP is applied in the same way to everybody, but it has a particularly disadvantageous effect on persons with a protected characteristic, as the following example demonstrates.

---

20. Equality Act 2010, Explanatory Notes [66].   21. ibid [65].
22. Equality Act 2010, s 14(3).   23. ibid s 14(4).
24. Government Equalities Office, *Equality Act Impact Assessment* (TSO 2010) 21–2.
25. HM Treasury and Department for Business Innovation and Skills, *The Plan for Growth* (HM Treasury 2011) [2.51].   26. Equality Act 2010, s 19(1).   27. ibid s 19(2).

Indirect discrimination

EngineCorp plc is looking to promote a number of its Grade 2 engineers to Grade 1 status. The company's promotion policy states that, in order to be promoted to Grade 1 status, Grade 2 engineers must attend a number of training courses that only take place on weekends. Toby, an orthodox Jew, who is a Grade 2 engineer, decides not to apply for the promotion because this would require him to engage in work on a Saturday, which is prohibited by Jewish law. Although the promotion policy affects all employees, it is particularly disadvantageous to Jewish employees, and so might constitute indirect discrimination.

Indirect discrimination will not occur if the PCP can be shown to be a proportionate means of achieving a legitimate aim. Guidance on this proportionality test was provided in the following case.

 ***R (on the Application of Elias) v Secretary of State for Defence* [2006] EWCA Civ 1293**

FACTS: Mrs Elias was a British subject, born in Hong Kong. Throughout the Japanese occupation of Hong Kong that occurred during the Second World War, she was interned at a Japanese prisoner-of-war camp, where she suffered extremely traumatic events that caused long-term psychological damage. Despite being a British citizen, who had lived full-time in the UK since 1976 (and part-time between 1945 and 1976), she was denied compensation under a British government scheme which only paid out if she, or her parents or grandparents, had been born in the UK (which was not the case). She alleged that the scheme was indirectly discriminatory on the ground of race, specifically national origin.

HELD: The Court held that the birth criteria aimed to control the public expenses of the state, and was therefore a legitimate aim. However, Mummery LJ stated that '[t]he real question is not about the end to be achieved but the means by which it was to be achieved and, in particular, whether the birth link criteria were a reasonably necessary and proportionate way of achieving the aim.'[28] The Court concluded that the birth link criterion was not a proportionate way of achieving the aim, and so the scheme was held to be indirectly discriminatory.

During the course of his judgment, Mummery LJ provided guidance on the proportionality test:

- It is the alleged discriminator who must justify the PCP,[29] and the courts will adopt 'a rigorous standard in scrutinising the reasons advanced'.[30]
- The objective of the PCP must 'correspond to a real need and the means used must be appropriate with a view to achieving the objective and be necessary to that end. So it is necessary to weigh the need against the seriousness of the detriment to the disadvantaged group.'[31]
- In determining whether the PCP is proportionate, a three-stage test should be applied. 'First, is the objective sufficiently important to justify limiting a fundamental right? Secondly, is the measure rationally connected to the objective? Thirdly, are the means chosen no more than is necessary to accomplish the objective?'[32]

---

28. [2006] EWCA Civ 1293, [2006] 1 WLR 3213 [144].   29. ibid [133].   30. ibid [158].
31. ibid [151].   32. ibid [164].

Previous anti-discrimination legislation provided that indirect justification would not be unlawful if it was 'justified'. It has been contended that '[t]he proportionality test means that the lax earlier decisions on justification should be considered unreliable.'[33]

Harassment

Section 26 provides for three different types of harassment (with s 40 (discussed later) providing for a fourth type). The first type occurs where a person (*A*) engages in unwanted conduct related to a relevant protected characteristic[34] that has the effect of violating the dignity of another person (*B*), or creating an intimidating, hostile, degrading, humiliating, or offensive environment for *B*.[35]

 Unwanted conduct related to a relevant protected characteristic

Imran, a Pakistani man, is employed by TechnoBuild Ltd. His line manager mocks Imran in front of his fellow employees by engaging in an offensive stereotypical Pakistani accent and referring to Imran as a 'Paki'.

The second type occurs where *A* or another person engages in unwanted conduct of a sexual nature and that conduct creates an intimidating, hostile, degrading, humiliating, or offensive environment for *B*.[36]

 Unwanted conduct of a sexual nature

Joanne works as a firefighter. A number of her male colleagues place on a wall of the station canteen a calendar featuring a number of topless women, onto whose bodies Joanne's head has been digitally added.

The third type occurs where *A* or another person engages in unwanted conduct of a sexual nature that is related to gender reassignment or sex, and (i) that conduct creates an intimidating, hostile, degrading, humiliating, or offensive environment for *B*; and (ii) because of *B*'s rejection of, or submission to, the conduct, *A* treats *B* less favourably than *A* would treat *B* if *B* had not rejected, or submitted to, the conduct.[37]

 Unwanted conduct of a sexual nature related to gender reassignment or sex

Sylvie is told by her line manager, Scott, that she is next in line for promotion. Later that day, Scott sexually propositions Sylvie, but she refuses his advances. A few weeks later, the promotion is awarded to someone else. Sylvie is sure that she would have been promoted had she not spurned Scott.

---

33. Bob Hepple, *Equality: The New Legal Framework* (Hart Publishing 2011) 69.
34. The Equality Act 2010, s 26(5) provides that the relevant characteristics are age, disability, gender reassignment, race, religion or belief, sex, and sexual orientation.   35. ibid s 26(1).
36. ibid s 26(2).   37. ibid s 26(3).

All three forms of harassment have several features in common:

- A single incident can constitute harassment if sufficiently serious.[38]
- The conduct must be 'unwanted', which has been defined as 'unwelcome' or 'uninvited'.[39]
- The conduct must create an intimidating, hostile, degrading, humiliating, or offensive environment for B. In determining this, account must be taken of the perception of B, the other circumstances of the case, and whether it is reasonable for the conduct to have that effect.[40] In relation to this, the Employment Appeal Tribunal (EAT) has stated that it is 'important not to encourage a culture of hypersensitivity or the imposition of legal liability in respect of every unfortunate phrase'.[41]

Victimization

Victimization occurs where a person (*A*) subjects another person[42] (*B*) to a detriment because (i) *B* does a protected act; or (ii) *A* believes that *B* has done, or may do, a protected act.[43] A 'protected act' is defined as:

- bringing proceedings under the Equality Act 2010 (for example, making a direct discrimination claim against an employer);
- giving evidence or information under the Act (for example, supporting a colleague's claim for direct discrimination);
- doing any other thing for the purposes of, or in connection with, the Act;
- making an allegation that *A* or another person has contravened the Act (for example, alleging that the employer refuses to make reasonable adjustments in relation to disabled employees).[44]

The Explanatory Notes to the Act make clear that victimization only occurs where the protected act is done 'in good faith'[45] and s 27(3) provides that giving false evidence or information, or making a false allegation, is not a protected act if the evidence or information is given, or the allegation is made, in bad faith.

Discrimination in employment

Discrimination and victimization in employment

The previous sections serve to define the various forms of prohibited conduct, but s 39 makes clear that these forms of conduct are prohibited in relation to employment by providing that:

- An employer (*A*) must not discriminate against, or victimize, a person (*B*) (i) in the arrangements *A* makes for deciding to whom to offer employment; (ii) as to the terms on which *A* offers *B* employment; and (iii) by not offering *B* employment.[46]

---

38. *Insitu Cleaning Co Ltd v Heads* [1995] IRLR 4 (EAT).   39. ibid.
40. Equality Act 2010, s 26(4).
41. *Richmond Pharmacology v Dhaliwal* [2009] ICR 724 (EAT) 733 (Underhill J).
42. Although the Act uses the word 'person' to describe the victim, s 27(4) states that the protection against victimization only applies to individuals (that is, it will not apply to bodies corporate).
43. Equality Act 2010, s 27(1).   44. ibid s 27(2).
45. Equality Act 2010, Explanatory Notes [100].   46. Equality Act 2010, s 39(1) and (3).

- An employer (*A*) must not discriminate against, or victimize, an employee of *A*'s (*B*) (i) as to *B*'s terms of employment; (ii) in the way *A* affords *B* access, or by not affording *B* access, to opportunities for promotion, transfer or training, or for receiving any other benefit, facility, or service; (iii) by dismissing *B*; and (iv) by subjecting *B* to any other detriment.[47]

Certain provisions of the Act relating to discrimination and victimization in employment (namely s 39(1)(a) or (c), or 39(2)(b) or (c)) will not be contravened where the employer establishes a requirement in relation to a protected characteristic, and the employer can demonstrate that the requirement is (i) an occupational requirement; (ii) a proportionate means of achieving a legitimate aim; and (iii) the person in question does not meet the requirement.[48]

Harassment of employees and applicants

Section 40(1) provides that an employer (*A*) must not, in relation to employment by *A*, harass a person (*B*) who is an employee of *A*'s, or who has applied to *A* for employment. Originally, s 40(2) went on to provide that such harassment would include the situation where a third party harassed *B* in the course of employment, and *A* failed to take such steps as would have been reasonably practicable to prevent the third party from doing so. Section 40(2) has now been repealed on the ground that it added nothing to pre-existing law (although this argument has not been universally accepted and many believe that the repeal of s 40(2) has significantly affected the effectiveness of s 40).

Protected characteristics

The forms of prohibited conduct discussed so far apply in relation to what are termed 'protected characteristics',[49] namely:

1. age;
2. disability;
3. gender reassignment;
4. marriage and civil partnership;
5. pregnancy and maternity;
6. race;
7. religion or belief;
8. sex; and
9. sexual orientation.

In line with the Act's aim of harmonizing the law, most forms of prohibited conduct are common to all nine protected characteristics, but there are exceptions. For example, there is no concept of indirect discrimination in relation to the protected characteristic of marriage and civil partnership. Table 27.1 clarifies which forms of prohibited conduct apply to which protected characteristics.

---

47. ibid s 39(2) and (4).   48. ibid Sch 9, para 1.   49. ibid s 4.

TABLE 27.1 Prohibited conduct and protected characteristics

	Direct discrimination	Combined discrimination (not in force)	Indirect discrimination	Harassment	Victimization	Other
Age	✓	✓	✓	✓	✓	✗
Disability	✓	✓	✓	✓	✓	• Discrimination arising from disability • Duty to make adjustments
Gender reassignment	✓	✓	✓	✓	✓	• Cases involving absence from work because of gender realignment
Marriage and civil partnership	✓	✗	✓	✓ (note that s 26(1) will not apply)	✓	✗
Pregnancy and maternity	✓	✗	✓	✓ (note that s 26(1) will not apply)	✓	• Discrimination due to pregnancy or due to pregnancy-related illness • Discrimination due to maternity leave
Race	✓	✓	✓	✓	✓	✗
Religion and belief	✓	✓	✓	✓	✓	✗
Sex	✓	✓	✓	✓	✓	✗
Sexual orientation	✓	✓	✓	✓	✓	✗

Each protected characteristic will now be discussed.

Age

The UK has an increasingly ageing population. By mid-2012, there were just over 10.8 million persons of state pensionable age or over (that is, 65 years of age).[50] The number of persons under the age of 16 is now lower than the number of persons over state pensionable age, and the fastest-growing age group in the UK is those who are aged 85 and over.[51] By 2033, there will be more people over the age of 40 than under it.[52] The ageing population has had a marked impact on the UK's workforce, with persons staying in work and applying for jobs at a much later age than in previous decades. Age discrimination has consequently become an increasingly significant problem and, in 2012–13, employment tribunals accepted 2,818 cases involving age discrimination.[53]

Prior to the 1997 election, the Labour Party indicated that it intended to legislate in this area, but initial efforts were lacklustre at best. Impetus for more effective legislation came in the form of the Equal Treatment Directive[54] in 2000. The controversial nature of age discrimination is evidenced in that the provisions of the Directive relating to age were given a six-year implementation period. The Directive was

---

50. Office for National Statistics, *Annual Mid-Year Population Estimates, 2011 and 2012* (ONS, 2013) 1.
51. Karen Dunnell, *Ageing and Mortality in the UK: National Statistician's Annual Article on the Population* (ONS 2008) 10.
52. Office for National Statistics, *National Population Projections 2008-Based* (ONS 2010) 2.
53. Statistics derived from <https://www.gov.uk/government/collections/tribunals-statistics>.
54. Council Directive No 2000/78/EC.

implemented by the Employment Equality (Age) Regulations 2006,[55] which have since been largely revoked and replaced by the Equality Act 2010.

Prohibited conduct

Direct discrimination, indirect discrimination, harassment, and victimization are all prohibited on the ground of age. However, in relation to direct discrimination, s 13(2) establishes a notable exception that does not apply to any other protected characteristic, namely that if *A* directly discriminates against *B* on the ground of age, it will not amount to direct discrimination if *A* can demonstrate that his treatment of *B* was a proportionate means of achieving a legitimate aim.

Rolls-Royce plc v Unite the Union [2009] EWCA Civ 387

FACTS: The claimant employer and the defendant trade union entered into two collective agreements, which included agreements on how employees would be selected for redundancy. Length of service was a factor, meaning that employees who worked for the claimant for longer periods were less likely to be made redundant than employees who worked for the claimant for a shorter period. The claimant sought a declaration that this discriminated against younger employees.

HELD: The Court held that the length of service criterion was a proportionate means of achieving a legitimate aim, and so the length of service criterion was not discriminatory. Wall LJ stated:

> The legitimate aim is the reward of loyalty, and the overall desirability of achieving a stable workforce in the context of a fair process of redundancy selection. The proportionate means is in my judgment amply demonstrated by the fact that the length of service criterion is only one of a substantial number of criteria for measuring employee suitability for redundancy, and that it is by no means determinative.[56]

Several other exceptions exist, including:

The national minimum wage is discussed at p 712

- The different age bands for the national minimum wage, which pay older workers more than younger workers, do not amount to age discrimination.[57]
- It is common for many employers to provide additional benefits to workers who have worked for the employer for a certain period (for example, length of service increments, increase in holiday entitlements, etc). The problem is that such benefits can indirectly discriminate against younger workers. The Act therefore provides that awarding benefits based on length of service will not amount to age discrimination.[58]

Retirement

The Equality Act 2010, when first enacted, permitted employers to impose compulsory retirement on employees aged 65 or over, and it further provided that dismissing a worker aged 65 or over would not amount to prohibited conduct on the ground of age if the reason for the dismissal was retirement.[59] This is no longer the

---

55. SI 2006/1031.
56. [2010] EWCA Civ 387, [2010] 1 WLR 318, [100].
57. Equality Act 2010, Sch 9, paras 11 and 12.   58. ibid Sch 9, para 10.
59. ibid Sch 9, para 8 (now repealed).

case. The Employment Equality (Repeal of Retirement Age Provisions) Regulations 2011[60] have abolished the default retirement age of 65, meaning that employers who impose compulsory retirement upon employees reaching a certain age will have engaged in prohibited conduct on the ground of age, unless they can demonstrate that it constitutes a proportionate means of achieving a legitimate aim. The abolition of the default retirement age also applies to selection processes, so employers cannot discriminate against applicants aged 65 or over, unless such conduct constitutes a proportionate means of achieving a legitimate aim.

Disability

According to the 2012 Labour Force Survey, 46.3 per cent of disabled persons were in employment, whereas 76.4 per cent of non-disabled persons were in employment. Whilst the significant employment gap can be explained to an extent by the impairments that disabled persons face, it is also likely that the presence of disability discrimination is a notable factor. Despite the scale of the problem, the UK was tardy in dealing with it and only passed legislation prohibiting disability discrimination in 1995, namely the Disability Discrimination Act 1995. The 1995 Act has now been repealed and replaced by the relevant provisions of the Equality Act 2010. In 2012–13, employment tribunals accepted 7,492 cases involving disability discrimination.[61]

What constitutes a 'disability?'

Section 6(1) of the Equality Act 2010 Act provides that a person has a disability if he has a physical or mental impairment, which has a substantial and long-term adverse effect on his ability to carry out normal day-to-day activities. In *Goodwin v Patent Office*,[62] the EAT stated that this definition established four conditions that would need to be satisfied, namely:

1. Does the claimant have an impairment that is physical or mental?
2. Is this impairment adverse and does it affect the claimant's ability to carry out day-to-day activities?
3. Is the adverse effect substantial?
4. Is the adverse effect long-term?

The first requirement that the claimant must demonstrate is that he has a physical or mental impairment.[63] The phrase 'physical or mental impairment' is not defined in the 2010 Act, doubtless to allow the courts and tribunals a measure of flexibility given the number of existing and newly discovered medical conditions. The Court of Appeal has stated that the word 'impairment' should bear its 'ordinary and natural meaning',[64] and, in many cases, there will be no dispute as to whether a claimant has an impairment or not. Whether the cause of the impairment is physical or mental is irrelevant; what matters is how the impairment affects the claimant. This approach can be useful in cases in which an impairment exists, but there is no discernible cause.[65]

---

60. SI 2011/1069.
61. Statistics derived from <https://www.gov.uk/government/collections/tribunals-statistics>.
62. [1999] ICR 302 (EAT).
63. *McNicol v Balfour Beatty Rail Maintenance Ltd* [2002] EWCA Civ 1074, [2002] IRLR 711.
64. ibid [17] (Mummery LJ).
65. See e.g. *College of Ripon and York St John v Hobbs* [2002] IRLR 185 (EAT).

Prior to 2005, it was a requirement that any mental impairment be 'clinically well recognized' in order to qualify, but this requirement no longer exists. The scope of mental impairment is, however, still watched closely. The EAT has stated that whether the claimant's mental condition constitutes mental impairment 'is very much a matter for qualified and informed medical opinion'.[66] It also stated that the claimant should obtain a written diagnosis from a suitably qualified medical practitioner of an illness specified in the World Health Organization's International Classification of Diseases, or some other proof that a body of respectable medical opinion recognizes the impairment.[67] Examples of mental conditions deemed to qualify include:

- Asperger's syndrome;[68]
- depression (provided that it is not short term);[69]
- dyslexia;[70]
- myalgic encephalomyelitis, or ME (also known as 'chronic fatigue syndrome');[71]
- paranoid schizophrenia.[72]

The 2010 Act itself specifically states that certain medical conditions will always qualify as disabilities, namely cancer, HIV, AIDS, and multiple sclerosis.[73] The Act also provides that Regulations may be made which specify which medical conditions will, or will not, qualify as impairments under the 2010 Act.[74] The Equality Act 2010 (Disability) Regulations 2010[75] provide such guidance, including:

- addiction to alcohol, nicotine, or any other substance will not be regarded as an impairment;[76]
- pyromania (a tendency to start fires), kleptomania (the tendency to steal), the tendency to commit physical or sexual abuse, exhibitionism, voyeurism, and seasonal allergic rhinitis (that is, hay fever) will not be regarded as impairments;[77]
- persons who are certified as blind, severely sight impaired, sight impaired, or partially sighted by a consultant ophthalmologist will be regarded as having an impairment.[78]

It is likely that future Regulations will be passed that better define what conditions will and will not amount to impairments under the 2010 Act.

The second requirement that the claimant must establish is that the impairment adversely affects his ability to carry out normal day-to-day activities. Note that as all the impairment need do is adversely *affect* the claimant's ability to carry out day-to-day tasks, it follows that even if the claimant can still carry out these tasks, he may still qualify as disabled, provided that the impairment makes these tasks more difficult in some way.

---

66. *Morgan v Staffordshire University* [2002] ICR 475 (EAT) 485 (Lindsay J).   67. ibid 479.
68. *Hewett v Motorola Ltd* [2004] IRLR 545 (EAT).
69. *Kapadia v Lambeth London Borough Council* [2000] IRLR 699 (CA).
70. *Whitbread Hotel Ltd v Bayley* [2006] WL 1078905 (EAT).
71. *O'Neill v Symm & Co Ltd* [1998] IRLR 233 (EAT).
72. *Goodwin v Patent Office* [1999] ICR 302 (EAT).   73. Equality Act 2010, Sch 1, para 6.
74. ibid Sch 1, para 1.   75. SI 2010/2128.
76. Equality Act 2010 (Disability) Regulations 2010, reg 3(1).
77. ibid reg 4. In *Power v Panasonic UK Ltd* [2003] IRLR 151 (EAT), the EAT stated that impairments caused by these conditions may suffice.
78. ibid reg 7.

The courts and tribunals take a broad view of what constitutes a normal day-to-day activity, defining it as an activity 'which most people do on a frequent or fairly regular basis',[79] or 'anything which is not abnormal or unusual'.[80] The previous government stated that activities undertaken whilst at work, however, will not normally qualify 'because no particular form of work is "normal" for most people'.[81] Whether this limitation remains under the 2010 Act is not yet clear.

The third requirement is that the claimant must establish is that the impairment has a 'substantial' effect on the claimant's ability to carry out normal day-to-day activities. The Act itself rather unhelpfully defines 'substantial' as 'more than minor or trivial',[82] but it does provide limited specific guidance (for example, an impairment which consists of a severe disfigurement will normally be treated as having a substantial adverse effect).[83]

When determining whether an impairment has a substantial effect, the tribunal should focus on those things that the claimant cannot do, or those that he can do only with difficulty, rather than focusing on what he can do, as the following case demonstrates.

 Goodwin v Patent Office [1999] ICR 302 (EAT)

FACTS: The claimant was a paranoid schizophrenic, who was dismissed by the defendant following complaints about his behaviour from fellow workers. He believed that other people could read his mind and he suffered from auditory hallucinations whilst at work. His condition, however, had little effect on his domestic life, in which he was able to cook, clean, and go shopping without help. On this basis, an employment tribunal dismissed his claim of disability discrimination, because his impairment was not substantial. The claimant appealed.

HELD: The appeal was allowed. The employment tribunal had focused on what the claimant could do, whereas the focus should have been on what he could *not* do, or what he could do only with difficulty. Given that his impairment had most effect at work, this was the focus of the case, and his impairment clearly had a substantial adverse effect on his ability to work.

⭐ See Simon Taylor and Robin Allen, 'The Meaning of "Disability"' (1999) 149 NLJ 10

The Act provides that Regulations may be made which specify which impairments will, or will not, qualify as having a substantial adverse effect under the 2010 Act.[84]

The fourth and final requirement is that the impairment's effects are long term. An impairment will have a long-term effect if it has lasted, or is likely to last, at least twelve months, or if is likely to last for the rest of the person's life.[85] Where an impairment has ceased to have a substantial adverse effect (for example, because it is intermittent, such as epilepsy), it will be regarded as continuing if it is likely to recur.[86]

The Act provides that Regulations may be made which specify which impairments will, or will not, be regarded as long term under the 2010 Act.[87]

---

79. *Vicary v British Telecommunications plc* [1999] IRLR 680 (EAT) 682 (Morison P).

80. *Ekpe v Commissioner of the Police of the Metropolis* [2001] ICR 1084 (EAT) 1092 (Langstaff QC).

81. Department for Work and Pensions, *Disability Discrimination Act: Guidance on Matters to be Taken Into Account in Determining Questions Relating to the Definition of Disability* (HMSO, 2006) [D7].

82. Equality Act 2010, s 212(1).   83. ibid Sch 1, para 3(1).   84. ibid Sch 1, para 4.

85. ibid Sch 1, para 2(1).   86. ibid Sch 1, para 2(2).   87. ibid Sch 1, para 2(4).

Prohibited conduct

Direct discrimination, indirect discrimination, harassment, and victimization are all prohibited on the ground of disability. In relation to direct discrimination, s 13(3) provides that, where the protected characteristic is disability, no discrimination will occur if the person alleging discrimination is not disabled, and is alleging that the employer treats or would treat disabled persons more favourably (in other words, favourable treatment of disabled persons is permitted).

In addition, persons regarded as disabled under the 2010 Act are afforded two specific measures of protection available only in cases involving disability discrimination. The first is found in s 15(1), which provides that a person (*A*) discriminates against a disabled person (*B*) if *A* treats *B* unfavourably because of something arising in consequence of *B*'s disability, and *A* cannot show that the treatment is a proportionate means of achieving a legitimate aim. The following example demonstrates a possible breach of s 15(1).

 Discrimination arising from disability

Matt, a blind man who is dependent upon his guide dog, Winston, applies for a job at TechnoCorp, but is rejected because he would be required to bring Winston to work in contravention of the company's 'no dogs at work' policy. The rejection clearly arises in consequence of Matt's disability and so could constitute discrimination arising from disability.

However, s 15(1) will not be breached if *A* can establish that he did not know, and could not reasonably have been expected to know, of *B*'s disability.[88] Section 15(1) will also not be breached if *A* can establish that the alleged discrimination arising from disability was a proportionate means of achieving a legitimate aim, such as looking after the health and safety of *B*.

 ***Lane Group plc v Farmiloe* [2002] PIQR P22 (EAT)**

FACTS: The claimant suffered from psoriasis, which meant that he was unable to wear the protective boots provided by his employer (the defendant). The defendant accordingly stated that the claimant did not need to wear the boots, but the local authority's Senior Health and Safety Officer stated that this was unacceptable and that the Personal Protective Equipment at Work Regulations 1992[89] required that the claimant wear protective boots. Accordingly, the claimant was suspended on full pay, whilst the defendant determined what boots the claimant could wear. It soon became obvious that no manufacturers could provide suitable footwear that would not worsen the claimant's condition. The defendant could not find a position for the claimant that did not require protective boots, and so the claimant was dismissed. An employment tribunal held that the claimant was the victim of disability discrimination. The defendant appealed.

HELD: The appeal was allowed. The defendant was subject to an absolute legal duty to ensure that its employees wore protective footwear. The health and safety of employees

---

88. ibid s 15(2).   89. SI 1992/2966.

took priority over discrimination issues and so the defendant was obliged to dismiss the claimant.

COMMENT: Schedule 1, para 1 of the 2010 Act now provides that discrimination on certain grounds (namely age, disability, religion or belief, sex, or sexual orientation) is permissible in order to comply with some other legal requirement.

The second specific measure of protection is found in s 20, which imposes a duty on employers to make reasonable adjustments. This duty comprises of three requirements:

1. Where a provision, criterion, or practice of the employer puts a disabled person at a substantial disadvantage in comparison with persons who are not disabled, the employer must take such steps as it is reasonable to have to take to avoid the disadvantage (for example, by providing materials in large print format to employees with sight impairments).

2. Where a physical feature puts a disabled person at a substantial disadvantage in comparison with persons who are not disabled, the employer must take such steps as it is reasonable to have to take to avoid the disadvantage (for example, by installing ramps to aid wheelchair users).

3. Where a disabled person would, but for the provision of an auxiliary aid, be put at a substantial disadvantage in comparison with persons who are not disabled, the employer must take such steps as it is reasonable to have to take to provide the auxiliary aid (for example, by installing an induction loop system to aid employees with hearing impairments).

Failure to comply with any of these requirements will amount to disability discrimination,[90] and s 20(7) prohibits the employer from passing the costs of the adjustments onto the employee (unless an express provision to the contrary exists).

Whether the employer does not know, or could not reasonably have been expected to know, of the disability or the effects that the disability might have, then the duty will not be imposed.[91] Where the employer knows of the disability, he will be required to make reasonable enquiries in order to determine what reasonable adjustments should be made. However, as the following case demonstrates, only reasonable enquiries need be made.

 Ridout v TC Group [1998] IRLR 628

FACTS: The claimant applied to the defendant for a job. The claimant disclosed that she suffered from photosensitive epilepsy, and that the condition had been controlled with medication for twenty years. She was invited for an interview, which took place in a room lit only by fluorescent lighting, which she knew could trigger an attack. The claimant brought sunglasses, but did not wear them during the interview, nor did she exhibit any symptoms or indicate that she felt disadvantaged. She was not offered the job and claimed that she was put at a disadvantage by the defendant's failure to make reasonable adjustments.

HELD: Her claim failed. The EAT concluded that no reasonable employer would have been expected to know, without further explanation from the claimant, that the lighting

---

90. Equality Act 2010, s 21(2).
91. *Secretary of State for Work and Pensions v Alam* [2010] ICR 665 (EAT).

See Shantanu Majumdar, 'Guilty Knowledge' (2000) 150 NLJ 497

arrangements could be disadvantageous. The defendant was not required to make every possible enquiry regarding the claimant's disability.

COMMENT: This case also demonstrates that the duty to make reasonable adjustments applies in relation to applicants as well as employees.[92]

Whereas other forms of discrimination are about less favourable treatment, in order to comply with the duty to make reasonable adjustments, the employer might actually have to give preferential treatment to a disabled employee, as the following case demonstrates.

Archibald v Fife Council [2004] UKHL 32

FACTS: The defendant employed the claimant as a road sweeper. Due to a complication following surgery, it became almost impossible for her to walk, which rendered her unable to continue sweeping roads. She asked the defendant if she could perform a more sedentary role and, being aware of the duty to make reasonable adjustments, the defendant sent her on several training courses. But despite applying for over a hundred jobs, she failed to impress the various interview panels (it was council policy that all candidates attend an interview). The defendant dismissed her, arguing that it had exhausted all options. The claimant brought an action alleging breach of the duty to make reasonable adjustments.

HELD: The House of Lords found in favour of the claimant. Baroness Hale stated that the 1995 Act does not require able-bodied persons and disabled persons to be treated the same way; instead, it 'necessarily entails an element of more favourable treatment'.[93]

See Pauline Hughes, 'Disability Discrimination and the Duty to Make Reasonable Adjustments: Recent Developments' (2004) 33 ILJ 358

Gender reassignment

This protected characteristic arises where a person is proposing to undergo, is undergoing, or has undergone a process (or part of a process) for the purpose of reassigning that person's sex by changing physiological or other attributes of sex.[94] Transsexuals are also included within this definition.[95] It should be noted that a person need not be under medical supervision in order for this protected characteristic to arise. Accordingly, persons who choose to live as the opposite sex without undergoing any medical treatment are as protected as those who undergo hormone treatment or gender realignment surgery.

Prohibited conduct

Direct discrimination, indirect discrimination, harassment, and victimization are all prohibited on the ground of gender reassignment. In addition, s 16 provides that a person (*A*) discriminates against a transsexual person (*B*) if, in relation to an absence of *B*'s that is because of gender reassignment, *A* treats *B* less favourably than *A* would treat *B* if (i) *B*'s absence was because of sickness of injury; or (ii) *B*'s absence was for some other reason and it is not reasonable for *B* to be treated less favourably.

---

92. This point is made clear in the Equality Act 2010, Sch 8, para 5.
93. [2004] UKHL 32, [2004] 4 All ER 303 [47].   94. Equality Act 2010, s 7(1).
95. ibid s 7(2).

Marriage and civil partnership

As this protected characteristic arises only in relation to persons who are married or civil partners,[96] it follows that engaged couples, couples whose marriage/civil partnership has been dissolved, and unmarried couples who merely live together are not covered. Accordingly, employers can discriminate against single persons, but cannot discriminate in favour of such persons. Given the number of single people in society, and the number of couples who are delaying getting married or entering into a civil partnership, it can be argued that this limitation is not justifiable.

Prohibited conduct

Direct discrimination, indirect discrimination, and victimization are all prohibited on the ground of marriage and civil partnership. As noted earlier, the Act's definition of direct discrimination covers not only discriminatory acts against the person with the protected characteristic, but also persons who associate with someone who has that characteristic. This breadth does not extend to the protected characteristic of marriage and civil partnership as s 13(4) provides that the victim must be the one who is married or a civil partner.

Harassment in relation to unwanted conduct under s 26(1) does not apply to the protected characteristic of marriage and civil partnership as it is not a 'relevant protected characteristic' under s 26(1) and (5). It would appear that the other two forms of harassment (found in s 26(2) and (3)) do apply as they make no reference to a 'relevant protected characteristic'.

Pregnancy and maternity

For many years, there has been agreement that pregnant women should be protected from discrimination, but there was disagreement as to the method of protection. The European Court of Justice took the view that, as only women could get pregnant, discrimination on the ground of pregnancy amounted to direct sex discrimination.[97] The view that ultimately prevailed was that discrimination on the ground of pregnancy and maternity was a form of discrimination in its own right.

A woman will first fall within the protected characteristic of pregnancy and maternity when she becomes pregnant, but the precise starting point of pregnancy is still a matter of debate. The leading authority is the case of *Mayr v Backerei und Konditorei Gerhard Flocker OHG*,[98] where the European Court of Justice stated that pregnancy begins, not at conception, but when the embryo adheres to the uterus lining (this is known as nidation and typically occurs around the sixth day following the fertilization of the ovum). For women who become pregnant as a result of *in vitro fertilization*, pregnancy begins when the fertilized ova are implanted into the woman's uterus.

Prohibited conduct

Direct discrimination and victimization are both prohibited on the ground of pregnancy and maternity. The provisions relating to indirect discrimination do not apply.

---

96. ibid s 8(1).
97. Case C-177/88 *Dekker v Stichting Vormingscentrum voor Jonge Volwassenen Plus* [1990] ECR I-3941.
98. Case C-506/06 [2008] ECR I-1017.

Harassment in relation to unwanted conduct under s 26(1) does not apply to the protected characteristic of pregnancy and maternity as it is not a 'relevant protected characteristic' under s 26(1) and (5). It would appear that the other two forms of harassment (found in s 26(2) and (3)) do apply as they make no reference to a 'relevant protected characteristic'.

In addition, s 18(2) provides that a person (*A*) discriminates against a woman if, in the protected period of pregnancy, *A* treats her unfavourably because of the pregnancy, or because of an illness suffered by her as a result of the pregnancy. The protected period of pregnancy begins when the pregnancy begins and ends:

⬦ Compulsory, ordinary, and additional maternity leave are discussed at p 718

- if she has the right to ordinary and additional maternity leave, at the end of the additional maternity leave period or (if earlier) when she returns to work after the pregnancy;
- if she does not have that right, at the end of the period of two weeks beginning with the end of the pregnancy.[99]

Discrimination will also occur where *A* discriminates against the woman because (i) she is on compulsory maternity leave; or (ii) because she is exercising, or seeking to exercise, or has exercised, the right to ordinary or additional maternity leave.[100]

Race

The first piece of legislation prohibiting discrimination related to race discrimination (namely the Race Relations Act 1965), and great advances have been made in combatting racial discrimination since. However, more work needs to be done, and empirical evidence indicates that racial disparities in employment still exist, as the following statement indicates:

> White British men are more likely to be in full-time employment than other ethnic groups. While 60.2% of White British men, 57.5% of Indian, and 52.7% of Black African men are in full-time employment, only 34.4% of Bangladeshi and 36.2% of Chinese men are…The proportion of men in some form of employment is highest for White British men (78.6%), followed very closely by Indian men (76.2%), but falls dramatically for the other ethnic groups. Similarly, unemployment and inactivity are lowest amongst White British.[101]

Similar trends also exist in relation to pay. The pay of white British men is 22.9 per cent and 17.8 per cent higher than that earned by Pakistani men and black African men respectively.[102] White British women also typically earn more than women from certain other ethnic backgrounds. Whilst the pay gap cannot be attributed solely to discrimination, it is clear that racial discrimination in the workplace still occurs, as evidenced by the fact that, in 2012–13, employment tribunals accepted 4,818 cases involving racial discrimination.[103]

Defining 'race'

Section 9(1) provides that 'race' includes colour, nationality, and ethnic or national origins. A group of persons defined by reference to these characteristics is known

99. Equality Act 2010, s 18(6).   100. ibid s 18(3) and (4).

101. Simonetta Longhi and Lucinda Platt, *Pay Gaps Across Equality Areas* (EHRC 2008) [2.2].

102. ibid [3.5], Table 3.1.

103. Statistics derived from <https://www.gov.uk/government/collections/tribunals-statistics>.

as a 'racial group', and the fact that a racial group comprises two or more distinct racial groups (for example, black and British) shall not prevent it from constituting a racial group.[104] Although these definitions are relatively straightforward, clarification from the courts has still been required, especially as regards the relationship between race and religion. For example, do Jews fall within the protected characteristic of race? They have no country of origin, but many would include them within the definition, due to their 'ethnic origins'. Clarity was provided in the following case.

 Mandla v Dowell Lee [1983] 2 AC 548 (HL)

FACTS: The claimants were a Sikh father and son who, in accordance with their religion, wore turbans over uncut hair. A school owned by the defendant refused to admit the son because he would not cut his hair and cease to wear a turban. The claimants alleged that this amounted to race discrimination. At first instance and in the Court of Appeal, the action was dismissed, because the discrimination was not on 'racial grounds'. The claimants appealed.

HELD: The House of Lords allowed the appeal on the ground that Sikhs could be regarded as a group who were defined by their ethnic origins. To determine whether a group would qualify, two requirements were essential, namely (i) a long-shared history; and (ii) a cultural tradition of its own. Other relevant factors would include whether the group had a common geographical origin, common language (but not necessarily peculiar to the group), common literature peculiar to the group, or a common religion different from that of neighbouring groups or from the general community surrounding it. Being a minority, or an oppressed or dominant group, within a larger community would also be a relevant factor.

COMMENT: Since _Mandla_, it has been held that both Jews[105] and gypsies[106] fall within the definition of 'race', but Rastafarians are not protected, because they lack a 'long-shared history'.[107]

⭐ See GT Pagone, 'The Lawyer's Hunt for Snarks, Religion and Races' (1984) 43 CLJ 218

Prohibited conduct

Direct discrimination, indirect discrimination, harassment, and victimization are all prohibited on the ground of race. In relation to direct discrimination, segregating the claimant from others will constitute less favourable treatment.[108]

Certain provisions of the Act (notably those relating to discrimination in employment) will not apply where being a particular race is an occupational requirement. For example, a casting director could insist on employing a black man to play Othello.

---

104. Equality Act 2010, s 9(3) and (4).   105. _Seide v Gilette Industries_ [1980] IRLR 427 (EAT).
106. _Commission for Racial Equality v Dutton_ [1989] QB 783 (CA).
107. _Dawkins v Department of the Environment_ [1993] IRLR 284 (CA). Rastafarians will, however, fall within the protected characteristic of religion or belief (_Harris v NLK Automotive Ltd and Matrix Consultancy Ltd_ [2007] UKEAT 01 34 07 DM).
108. Equality Act 2010, s 13(5).

Religion or belief

As has been discussed, discrimination against certain religions (for example, Sikhs and Jews) may be classified as race discrimination, but not all religions were able to obtain protection on this ground and, until relatively recently, legislation did not prohibit religious discrimination in employment. Empirical research indicates that employment and pay inequalities between persons of different religions are not as pronounced as between other groups, and this is borne out in that, in 2012–13, employment tribunals accepted only 979 cases involving religious discrimination.[109]

What constitutes a 'religion or belief?'

The rationale behind the inclusion of the word 'belief' was doubtless to avoid the need to have to specifically define what 'religion' meant and thereby limit the protection offered. Section 10(1) of the Act provides that 'religion' means 'any religion and a reference to a religion includes a reference to a lack of religion'. Accordingly, discriminating against a person because he is an atheist would amount to religious discrimination.

Section 10(2) provides that 'belief' means 'any religious or philosophical belief and a reference to belief includes a reference to a lack of belief'. Determining whether a belief is religious or not is unlikely to be problematic in most cases, but determining what amounts to a philosophical belief is likely to be more difficult and is likely to involve cross-examining the person alleging discrimination. In the following case, the EAT sought to better delineate what amounted to a philosophical belief.

 Grainger plc v Nicholson [2010] ICR 360 (EAT)

FACTS: The claimant was employed by the defendant as a surveyor and head of sustainability. His employment was terminated, and the defendant claimed this was on the ground of redundancy. The claimant contended that his employment was terminated due to his opinions relating to climate change, which he stated amounted to a 'strongly held philosophical belief'. Accordingly, the claimant contended that he was the victim of discrimination on the ground of religion or belief. The defendant contended that opinions regarding climate change did not amount to a philosophical belief.

HELD: The claimant's belief concerning climate change could amount to a philosophical belief. Burton J stated that, in order for a belief to amount to a philosophical belief, it (i) must be genuinely held; (ii) must be a belief and not merely an opinion or viewpoint based on presently available information; (iii) must be a belief as to a weighty and substantial aspect of human life and behaviour; (iv) must attain a certain level of cogency, seriousness, cohesion, and importance; and (v) must be worthy of respect in a democratic society, not be incompatible with human dignity, and not conflict with the fundamental rights of others.[110] He went on to state that support of a political party would not amount to a philosophical belief, but belief in a certain political philosophy or doctrine (such as Capitalism, Marxism, or Communism) might.

Lucy Vickers, 'Religious Discrimination in the Workplace: An Emerging Hierarchy?' [2010] 12 Ecc LJ 280

---

109. Statistics derived from <https://www.gov.uk/government/collections/tribunals-statistics>.
110. [2010] ICR 360 (EAT) 370.

Clearly, the Act's definitions of 'religion' and 'belief' are very wide, thereby providing tribunals and courts with flexibility to determine the appropriate scope of this protected characteristic. The disadvantage of such an approach is that it does increase the likelihood of tribunals and courts reaching inconsistent decisions.

Prohibited conduct

Direct discrimination, indirect discrimination, harassment, and victimization are all prohibited on the ground of religion or belief. It should be noted that in order for discrimination based on religion or belief to arise, the employer must be aware of the claimant's religion or belief.[111] When determining whether any of these forms of prohibited conduct has occurred, the tribunal will examine why the employer/employee acted as he did, in order to determine if the motives were truly due to religion or belief.

 McFarlane v Relate Avon Ltd [2010] EWCA Civ 880

FACTS: The defendant employed the claimant as a relationship counsellor. The defendant was a member of the British Association for Sexual and Relationship Therapy, whose Code of Ethics required all members to avoid discrimination on grounds of sexual orientation. The claimant's employment contract expressly stated that he would adhere to the Code of Ethics. The claimant, a Christian, refused to offer counselling to homosexuals on the ground that 'same sex sexual activity is sinful'. He was dismissed, and he claimed, *inter alia*, that he was discriminated against on the ground of religion or belief.

HELD: His claim failed. He was dismissed, not due to his religious beliefs, but because of his failure to comply with the Code of Ethics that he had contractually agreed to adhere to.

COMMENT: McFarlane took his case to the European Court of Human Rights (ECtHR),[112] alleging that his rights under Art 9 of the ECHR (the right to freedom of thought, conscience, and religion) had been breached. His claim failed.

★ See Russell Sandberg, 'Laws and Religion: Unravelling McFarlane v Relate Avon Limited' (2010) 12 Ecc LJ 361

Many of the cases relating to alleged discrimination on the ground of religion or belief have concerned the issue of whether or not a person has a right to manifest their religion or belief through certain items of clothing, symbols etc. In the following highly-publicized case, the ECtHR rejected the approach taken by the domestic authorities and held that the applicant did indeed, based on the facts, have the right to wear a religious symbol.

 Eweida and Others v United Kingdom (2013) 57 EHRR 8

FACTS: Eweida was a devout Christian who worked as a member of the check-in staff for British Airways plc. As her job was customer facing, she was required to wear a uniform that, until 2004, included a high-necked blouse, under which she wore a cross around her neck. In 2004, a new open-necked blouse was introduced and the company's uniform

---

111. *McClintock v Department of Constitutional Affairs* [2008] IRLR 29 (EAT).
112. *Eweida and Others v United Kingdom* (2013) 57 EHRR 8.

policy provided that any accessories or clothing worn for religion reasons should be covered up by the uniform. Initially, she complied with this but, eventually, she started wearing the cross openly. She was asked to conceal the cross but refused to do so, and so, in September 2006, her employer sent her home without pay until such time as she complied with the uniform policy. Following adverse press reaction to the decision, British Airways relented and allowed certain religious symbols (including the cross wore by Eweida) to be worn openly and, in February 2007, Eweida returned to work. However, British Airways refused to pay her for the period between September and February in which she was not working. She commenced proceedings against her employer, but her claim was rejected by an employment tribunal, the EAT,[113] and the Court of Appeal.[114] She took her claim to the ECtHR, alleging that her Art 9 rights had been breached.

HELD: The ECtHR stated that a balance had to be struck between the interests of the employer and employee. Eweida wished to manifest her religious beliefs, whereas British Airways wished to protect its corporate image. The ECtHR stated that, whilst the company's desire to protect its image was legitimate, the various tribunals and the Court of Appeal had accorded it too much weight, and there was no evidence that Eweida's wearing of the cross negatively impacted upon British Airways' image or reputation. Accordingly, the ECtHR held that the domestic authorities had failed to sufficiently protect Eweida's right to manifest her religion and so her claim succeeded.

See David H McIlroy, 'A Marginal Victory for Freedom of Religion' (2013) 2 OJLS 210.

Occupational requirements

The need to avoid discrimination must be balanced with certain religious beliefs, especially given that a person's religion or beliefs can conflict with other protected characteristics (notably that of sexual orientation, discussed later). Accordingly, certain provisions relating to discrimination in employment will not be contravened if the employer imposes a requirement based on religion or belief and:

- the employment is for the purposes of an organized religion;
- the requirement is applied in order to avoid conflicting with the strongly held religious convictions of a significant number of the religion's followers; and
- the person to whom the requirement is applied does not meet it.[115]

The requirement can involve (i) specifying a person be of a particular sex; (ii) requiring a person not to be a transsexual; (iii) requiring the person not to be married or a civil partner; (iv) requiring a person not to be married to, or the civil partner of, a person who has a former living spouse or civil partner; (v) a requirement relating to circumstances in which a marriage or civil partnership came to an end; and (vi) a requirement relating to sexual orientation.[116]

The above exception applies only to cases involving an organized religion. A less specific exception exists which provides that a person (*A*) with an ethos based on religion and belief does not contravene certain provisions of the Act by applying, in relation to work, a requirement to be of particular religion or belief, if *A* shows that, having regard to the ethos and to the nature and context of the work (i) it is an occupational requirement; (ii) the application of the requirement is a proportionate

---

113. *Eweida v British Airways plc* [2009] ICR 303 (EAT).
114. *Eweida v British Airways plc* [2010] EWCA Civ 80, [2010] ICR 890.
115. Equality Act 2010, Sch 9, para 2.   116. ibid Sch 9, para 2(4).

means of achieving a legitimate aim; and (iii) the person to whom *A* applies the requirement does not meet it.[117]

Sex

Section 11 provides that the protected characteristic of sex refers to being a man or a woman. This makes clear that it is the biological differences between a man and a woman that are important and not issues of gender or sexuality. Accordingly, discriminating against a person because she is a lesbian would not amount to sex discrimination[118] (although it would amount to discrimination due to sexual orientation, discussed later).

Of all the protected characteristics, sex discrimination accounts for the most claims, with employment tribunals accepting 18,814 claims involving sex discrimination in 2012–13.[119]

Prohibited conduct

Direct discrimination, indirect discrimination, harassment, and victimization are all prohibited on the ground of sex. In cases involving direct discrimination (i) less favourable treatment of a woman will include less favourable treatment because she is breast-feeding; and (ii) where the person discriminated against is a man, no account is to be taken of special treatment afforded to a woman in connection with pregnancy or childbirth.[120]

Sexual orientation

Until the passing of the Sexual Offences Act 1967, homosexuality was a criminal offence, and as both the European Court of Justice[121] and the House of Lords[122] had steadfastly refused to grant homosexuals protection under sex discrimination legislation, employers were free to discriminate on the ground of sexual orientation. This lacuna has now been filled with s 12(1) of the Equality Act 2010 providing that the protected characteristic of sexual orientation refers to a person's sexual orientation towards persons of the same sex, persons of the opposite sex, and persons of either sex. Accordingly, discriminating against a person on the grounds that the person is homosexual, heterosexual, or bisexual is prohibited.[123] In 2012–13, employment tribunals accepted 639 cases involving discrimination due to sexual orientation.[124]

Prohibited conduct

Direct discrimination, indirect discrimination, harassment, victimization, and discrimination in employment are all prohibited on the ground of sexual orientation. As discussed earlier, the protected characteristic of sexual orientation can often clash with other protected characteristics, notably that of religion or belief. The following case indicates that, outside the specific exemptions involving religion provided for

---

117. ibid Sch 9, para 3.
118. *Pearce v Governing Body of Mayfield School* [2003] UKHL 34, [2004] 1 All ER 339.
119. Statistics derived from <https://www.gov.uk/government/collections/tribunals-statistics>.
120. Equality Act 2010, s 13(6).   121. Case C-249/96 *Grant v South-West Trains* [1998] ECR I-621.
122. *AG for Scotland v Macdonald* [2003] UKHL 34, [2004] 1 All ER 339.
123. It would appear that asexuals (i.e., persons with no sexual orientation) are not covered.
124. Statistics derived from <https://www.gov.uk/government/collections/tribunals-statistics>.

by the 2010 Act where a particular sexual orientation is an occupational requirement, where the protected characteristics of sexual orientation and religion or belief clash, the characteristic of sexual orientation will usually be upheld.

Ladele v Islington London Borough Council [2009] EWCA Civ 1357[125]

FACTS: The defendant council employed the claimant as a registrar of births, marriages, and deaths. When the Civil Partnership Act 2004 came into force, all the defendant's registrars were designated as civil partnership registrars, but the claimant refused to perform civil partnership duties on the ground that same-sex unions were 'contrary to God's instructions'. She was told that, unless she agreed to perform civil partnership duties, she would be subject to formal disciplinary proceedings. She claimed that she was discriminated against due to her religious beliefs.

HELD: Her claim was dismissed. Lord Neuberger MR stated that Art 9(1) of the European Convention on Human Rights provided that everyone has the 'right to freedom of thought, conscience, and religion' but that Art 9(2) provides that the right to manifest such beliefs shall only be subject to such limitations 'as are prescribed by law and are necessary in a democratic society' for, *inter alia*, 'the protection of the rights and freedoms of others'. This led him to conclude that the claimant's 'proper and genuine desire to have her religious views relating to marriage respected should not be permitted to override [the defendant's] concern to ensure that all its registrars manifest equal respect for the homosexual community as for the heterosexual community'.[126]

COMMENT: This case also demonstrates the strong overlap that can exist between a person's right not to be discriminated against and that person's human rights. Indeed, following the dismissal of her claim, Ladele took her case to the ECtHR,[127] but her claim was rejected.

See Tracey Reeves, 'Ladele v Islington LBC: Employment Discrimination' (2010) 15 Cov LJ 45

Positive action

As discrimination is based on treating a person less favourably than another, it follows that positive discrimination has generally been prohibited in the UK. Pre-Equality Act legislation did contain some limited exceptions to this in relation to encouraging women and ethnic minorities to apply for jobs and obtain training, but these exceptions were rarely used. Further, they were out of date, as EU law had since provided that positive discrimination in relation to sex, race, religion or belief, disability, age, and sexual orientation was permitted in certain circumstances.

Accordingly, s 158 of the Equality Act 2010 now permits positive action to occur in a much wider set of circumstances. It will apply where a person (such as an employer) reasonably thinks that:

---

125. See also *McFarlane v Relate Avon Ltd* [2010] EWCA Civ 880, [2010] IRLR 872 (discussed on p 765).

126. [2009] EWCA Civ 1357, [2010] 1 WLR 955 [55].

127. *Eweida and Others v United Kingdom* (2013) 57 EHRR 8.

- persons who share a protected characteristic suffer a disadvantage connected to that characteristic.[128] In such a case, the Act will not prohibit an employer from taking action, which is a proportionate means of achieving the aim of enabling or encouraging persons who share the protected characteristic to overcome or minimize that disadvantage;[129]

- persons who share a protected characteristic may have needs that are different from the needs of persons who do not share it.[130] In such a case, the Act will not prohibit an employer from taking action, which is a proportionate means of achieving the aim of meeting those needs;[131]

- participation in an activity by persons who share a protected characteristic is disproportionately low.[132] In such a case, the Act will not prohibit an employer from taking action, which is a proportionate means of enabling or encouraging persons who share the protected characteristic to participate in the activity.[133]

Section 159 contains similar provisions in relation to the recruitment and promotion of persons with a protected characteristic.

Enforcement and remedies

An employee (or applicant) who believes that he has been the victim of prohibited conduct may make a complaint to an employment tribunal,[134] providing that the claim is brought within three months starting on the date on which the act to which the complaint relates, or such other period as the employment tribunal thinks just and equitable.[135] If the tribunal finds that a contravention of the Act has occurred, it can make one or more of the following remedies:

- **Declaration** A declaration is an order that sets out the rights of the parties involved in relation to the matters to which the proceedings relate.[136] Basically, it amounts to the tribunal stating that discrimination has taken place, and a declaration will accordingly be made wherever a complaint is upheld.

- **Compensation** The tribunal may order the employer to pay compensation to the employee (or applicant).[137] Damages are calculated based on the amount that would be ordered by a county court in tort proceedings, and can include an amount for injured feelings.[138]

- **Recommendation** A recommendation is an order requiring the employer to take a specified step for the purpose of obviating (removing) or reducing the adverse effects of any matter to which the proceedings relate.[139] If the employer, without reasonable excuse, fails to comply with the recommendation, the tribunal can require the employer to pay compensation or, if the employer was already required to pay compensation, the amount can be increased.[140]

The tribunal should not make an award of compensation, unless it first considers whether to make a declaration or recommendation.[141]

---

128. Equality Act 2010, s 158(1)(a).   129. ibid s 158(2)(a).   130. ibid s 158(1)(b).
131. ibid s 158(2)(b).   132. ibid s 158(1)(c).   133. ibid s 158(2)(c).   134. ibid s 120(1).
135. ibid s 123(1).   136. ibid s 124(2)(a).   137. ibid s 124(2)(b).
138. ibid ss 124(6) and 119.   139. ibid s 124(2)(c) and (3).   140. ibid s 124(7).
141. ibid s 124(5).

Equality of contractual terms between men and women

The provisions relating to the protected characteristic of sex do not apply in relation to contractual terms of employment.[142] This is because the Equality Act 2010 contains specific provisions designed to ensure equality of contractual terms between men and women. Although such provisions have existed since the enactment of the Equal Pay Act 1970 (EPA 1970), equality of terms (especially in relation to pay) has not been achieved. As of April 2013, the median gross annual earnings for men were £28,912; for women, the figure was £23,868.[143] This pay gap is considerable and it has been estimated that, at the current rate of progress, the pay gap will not close until 2085.[144] In 2012–13, employment tribunals accepted 23,638 equal pay claims.[145]

With the passing of the Equality Act 2010, the 1970 Act has been repealed, but many of its provisions were simply transplanted into ss 64–83 of the 2010 Act, so pre-2010 case law will remain relevant.

The sex equality clause

Section 66(1) of the Equality Act 2010 provides that '[i]f the terms of *A*'s work do not (by whatever means) include a sex equality clause, they are to be treated as including one'. Section 66(2) provides that the effects of the sex equality clause are:

- if *A*'s employment contract contains a term that is less favourable to *A* than a corresponding term in *B*'s contract, then the term in *A*'s contract shall be modified so that it is not less favourable; and
- if *B*'s employment contract contains a term benefiting him, but such a term is not found in *A*'s employment contract, then the beneficial term shall also be included in *A*'s contract.

It is important to note that the sex equality clause refers to the equality of individual terms. Therefore, provided that a single term is deemed unfavourable to *A*, it does not matter that the contract overall is equally favourable to *A* and *B*, as the following case demonstrates.

Hayward v Cammell Laird Shipbuilders Ltd [1988] AC 894 (HL)

FACTS: The claimant worked in a shipyard as a cook and was classified by the defendant as unskilled. She claimed that she was undertaking work of equal value compared to male shipyard workers (namely, a painter, a joiner, and an engineer), who were classified as skilled and so received higher pay. The defendant argued that whilst the men received better pay, the claimant received better sickness benefits and holiday pay, resulting in her overall contract being equally favourable.

---

142. ibid s 70.
143. Statistics derived from the Office of National Statistics' *Annual Survey of Hours and Earnings.*
144. Government Equalities Office, *Framework for a Fairer Future: The Equality Bill* (HMSO 2008) 7.
145. Statistics derived from <https://www.gov.uk/government/collections/tribunals-statistics>.

HELD: The House of Lords allowed her claim. Section 1(2)(c) of the EPA 1970 (now s 65(2) of the Equality Act 2010) referred to a specific term being unfavourable, not to the entire contract. As the specific term regarding pay was unfavourable, it did not matter that the contract overall was equally favourable. The House accepted that the claimant performed equal work and so the equality clause became operational. The claimant's contract was improved so that her rate of pay was equal to that of the men.

COMMENT: As a result of this, the men, in turn, became entitled to the improved sickness benefits and holiday pay that the claimant received.

⭐ See Evelyn Ellis, 'A Welcome Victory for Equality' (1988) 51 MLR 781

In order for *A* to rely on the sex equality clause, she[146] will need to demonstrate that she is employed on work that is equal to the work that a comparator of the opposite sex (*B*) does.[147] This will require *A* to establish that her work is:

- like *B*'s work; or
- rated as equivalent to *B*'s work; or
- of equal value to *B*'s work.[148]

Note that *A* only needs to satisfy one of these three tests. Each test will now be discussed.

Like work

The first test provides that *A* will need to establish that her work is 'like *B*'s work'. *A* will be employed in like work with that of *B* if *A*'s work and *B*'s work are the same or broadly similar, and such differences as there are between their work are not of practical importance in relation to the terms of their work.[149] The wording used indicates that the courts should not focus too heavily on minute and technical differences, and that the words used in s 65(2) should be interpreted broadly. Therefore, it will not be necessary for *A* to demonstrate that she performs an identical job to *B* in order to satisfy the 'like work' test.

 Capper Pass Ltd v Lawton [1977] ICR 83 (EAT)

FACTS: The defendant employed the claimant as a cook and catering manager. She worked a forty-hour week in a kitchen, during which she prepared daily lunches for between ten and twenty of the defendant's directors. In a different kitchen, two male assistant chefs provided lunches for the defendant's employees. The male chefs prepared around 350 meals (including breakfast, lunch, and tea) every day and they worked a forty-hour week, in addition to five-and-a-half hours' overtime and one Saturday in three. The male chefs' hourly rate of pay was higher than that of the claimant and their staff conditions were better. The claimant argued that she was entitled to a sex equality clause in her contract.

HELD: The claimant was entitled to a sex equality clause. Although the job she performed was not identical to that of the male chefs, the type of work was broadly similar and both parties required similar skills in order to perform their functions.

---

146. In the majority of equal pay cases, the person seeking enforcement of the sex equality clause is a woman, so 'she' will be used to refer to *A*, and 'he' will be used to refer to *B*.
147. Equality Act 2010, s 64(1).   148. ibid s 65(1).   149. ibid s 65(2).

Where *A* and *B* perform identical tasks, the 'like work' test will normally be satisfied, but the following controversial decision of the European Court of Justice indicates that this will not always be the case.

Case C-309/97 Angestelltenbetriebsrat der Wiener Gebietskrankenkasse v Wiener Gebietskrankenkasse [1999] ECR I-2865

FACTS: A health fund based in Vienna employed trainee physiotherapists (the majority of whom were female) and a number of qualified doctors (the majority of whom were male). Both parties performed identical functions, but the doctors received a higher salary. The trainees sought a declaration from the European Court of Justice that they were entitled to the same pay as the doctors.

HELD: The Court refused to make such a declaration. Whilst the trainees and doctors might have performed identical tasks, the doctors could draw upon superior training and experience when performing their functions. Further, although not required by their contracts, the doctors could perform a much wider range of functions if needed.

COMMENT: This case should not be considered to impose a general rule that a difference in qualifications will cause the 'like work' test to fail. In fact, a difference in qualifications should be regarded as irrelevant, unless it results in a 'genuine material difference' between the work carried out by the men and the women.

In relation to any differences that exist, s 65(3) states that, in comparing *A*'s work with that of *B*, it is necessary to have regard to the frequency with which differences between their work occur in practice, and the nature and extent of the differences. A key phrase here is 'in practice', because this indicates that the courts should focus on what *A* and *B* *actually* do, as opposed to what they *may* have to do or what their contract *requires* them to do. The following case demonstrates the distinction.

Shields v E Coomes Holdings Ltd [1978] ICR 1159 (CA)

FACTS: The claimant was employed as a counterhand in a betting shop owned by the defendant. She was paid 92 pence per hour, whereas a male counterhand in the same betting shop was paid £1.06 per hour. Both employees performed identical tasks, except that the male employee was required to provide physical assistance should any customers cause trouble or attempt to steal from the betting shop. There had, however, never been any trouble of this kind. The claimant commenced proceedings, alleging that she was entitled to equal pay.

HELD: The claimant's action succeeded. The Court of Appeal stated that the claimant performed 'like work' to that of the male employee, and that the differences between the employment were not of practical importance, because the man had not been called upon to exercise his additional duties.

This focus on the practical realities of employment means that, even if *A* and *B* perform similar or identical functions, a disparity in pay may be justified where *B*'s level of responsibility is greater than that of *A*, or the consequences of his failure more severe. Thus, in *Eaton Ltd v Nuttall*,[150] a man and a woman were both employed as production schedulers, but the man earned £51.88 per week, whereas the woman earned £45.38 a week. The EAT held that the disparity in pay was justified, because the man handled packages worth between £5 and £1,000, whereas the woman handled packages worth a maximum of £2.50.

Work rated as equivalent

The second test is satisfied where *A*'s work is 'rated as equivalent to *B*'s work'. This will occur where a job evaluation study has been carried out and that study either:

- gives an equal value to *A*'s job and *B*'s job in terms of the demands made on the worker; or
- would give an equal value to *A*'s job and *B*'s job in those terms were the evaluation not made on a sex-specific system.[151]

The functions performed by *A* and *B* may be very different (so the 'like work' test would not be satisfied), but if the job evaluation study grades them equally, *A* will be able to pass the test and the sex equality clause will likely come into operation. Whilst the Equality Act 2010 does not lay down any requirements for such an evaluation scheme, it has been held that it must be valid, meaning that it must be 'thorough in analysis and capable of impartial application'.[152] It follows that even where a study has been carried out, it can be challenged.

It is worth pointing out a flaw with this second test, namely, that it is satisfied where the work is rated as 'equivalent'. On a literal interpretation on this test, the equality clause will not operate where *A*'s work is rated more highly than *B*'s, because the rating is not equivalent. Fortunately, the Court of Appeal has rectified this and stated that a greater rating will qualify as equivalent,[153] but the fact that it required a decision of the Court demonstrates a flaw in the Act's drafting.

Work of equal value

The third test is satisfied where *A*'s work is of equal value to *B*'s work. This test applies where *A* cannot satisfy the first two tests (that is, she does not provide 'like work' or 'work rated as equivalent') but her work is 'nevertheless equal to *B*'s work in terms of the demands made on *A* by reference to factors such as effort, skill and decision-making'.[154]

'Like work' and 'work rated as equivalent' are both concepts that can be determined without undue complexity. 'Equal work' is much more ambiguous, involving an examination of 'the almost religious mysteries of job evaluation'.[155] Consequently, of the three tests, equal value claims are by far the most complex, and initial cases took several years to resolve. In 1989, the then president of the EAT stated that

---

150. [1977] ICR 272 (EAT).

151. Equality Act 2010, s 65(4). Section 65(5) provides that a system is sex-specific if, for the purposes of one or more of the demands of a worker, it sets values for men different from those it sets for woman.

152. *Eaton Ltd v Nuttall* [1977] ICR 272 (EAT) 277 (Phillips J).

153. *Redcar and Cleveland Borough Council v Bainbridge* [2007] EWCA Civ 929, [2008] ICR 238.

154. Equality Act 2010, s 65(6).

155. Ian Smith and Aaron Baker, *Smith & Wood's Employment Law* (11th edn, OUP 2013) 362.

the procedures resulted in 'delays which are properly described as scandalous and amount to a denial of justice to women seeking remedy through the judicial process'.[156] A series of regulations passed in 2004 aimed to streamline the procedures involved, and the procedure can now be found in s 131 of the Equality Act 2010:

1. The tribunal can either immediately determine, based on the evidence, whether A's work is of equal value to B's, or it can require an independent expert to prepare a report on the issue. The tribunal may withdraw the requirement of a report, but if it does not do so, it must not determine the case until it has received the report.

2. If A's work and B's work have been graded differently by a job evaluation study, the tribunal must conclude that A's work is not of equal value to B's, unless the study was based on a system that discriminates because of sex, or is otherwise unreliable.

3. The tribunal will determine, on the facts, whether or not the work carried out by A is, in fact, equal to that of B.

The comparator

In order for A to rely on the sex equality clause, she will need to demonstrate that she is employed in work that is equal to the work that a comparator of the opposite sex (B) does.[157] The claimant will therefore, in addition to satisfying one of the three tests above, also have to locate an employee of the opposite sex (known as the 'comparator') against whom the claimant's terms of employment can be compared.[158] If A is employed, then B will be a comparator if either:

- B is employed by A's employer or by an associate of A's employer, and A and B work at the same establishment; or

- B is employed by A's employer or by an associate of A's employer; B works at an establishment other than the one A works at; and common terms apply at the establishments (either generally or as between A and B).[159]

Finding a suitable comparator can be difficult. Certain businesses (for example, textiles and secretarial services) may be dominated by women to such an extent that a female claimant may find it impossible to locate a comparator. Accordingly, many female claimants contended that they should be able to choose a male comparator who used to be 'in the same employment', but was not at the time of the case. The Court of Appeal referred this issue[160] to the European Court of Justice, which held that a woman has the right to compare her pay to that of a male predecessor in the same job.[161] The Court of Appeal applied the decision of the European Court of Justice[162] and the EAT has since extended the principle to include a comparison with a successor.[163] Despite this, the claimant might still be unable to locate a comparator and, accordingly, the sex equality clause will not apply. Fortunately, s 70

---

156. *Aldridge v British Telecommunications plc* [1989] ICR 790 (EAT) 799 (Wood J).

157. Equality Act 2010, s 64(1).

158. A court or tribunal cannot select the comparator; he must be selected by the claimant (*Ainsworth v Glass Tubes and Components Ltd* [1977] IRLR 74 (EAT)).

159. Equality Act 2010, s 79(1), (2), (3), and (4).

160. *Macarthys Ltd v Smith* [1979] 1 WLR 1189 (CA).

161. Case C-129/79 *Macarthys Ltd v Smith* [1980] ECR 1275.

162. *Macarthys Ltd v Smith* [1981] QB 180 (CA).

163. *Diocese of Hallam Trustee v Connaughton* [1996] ICR 860 (EAT).

has remedied this lacuna by allowing a claim for direct discrimination or combined discrimination to be brought in cases where the sex equality clause would not apply (for example, where the claimant cannot locate a comparator).

Defence of material factor

If *A* has satisfied one of the three tests described and has located a suitable comparator, then a presumption is raised that the disparity in the terms of employment is due to sex discrimination and the sex equality clause will come into effect. The employer may, however, be able to rebut the presumption by raising the defence that the difference in *A*'s terms and *B*'s terms is due to a 'material factor' other than sex.[164] The existence of this defence recognizes that there are reasons unrelated to sex that may justify a employee having different terms than an employee of the opposite sex, including:

- **Qualifications** A highly qualified employee may be entitled to more favourable terms than a less-qualified employee of the opposite sex.
- **Length of service** An employee who has worked for a company for a long period of time may be entitled to more preferable terms than an employee of the opposite sex who has worked for the company for a shorter period of time.[165]
- **Geographical location** An employee based in a part of the country with a higher cost of living (for example, London) may be entitled to more favourable terms than an employee of the opposite sex based in another part of the country, where the cost of living is much less.[166]

These material factors are easy to justify, but a number of cases have proven more problematic—namely, cases involving (i) part-time workers;[167] (ii) 'red-circling'; (iii) collective bargaining; and (iv) market forces.

Providing part-time workers with less favourable terms than full-time workers could be viewed as indirectly discriminatory on the ground that women constitute a high proportion of the part-time labour market. Early cases regarded part-time work as a material factor, thereby entitling a full-time male employee to more favourable terms (usually a higher hourly rate of pay) than a part-time female.[168] However, more recent cases indicate that the tribunals and courts will not regard part-time work as a material factor unless the favourable terms of full-time workers are objectively justified by some reason other than sex,[169] as occurred in the following case.

 ***Barry v Midland Bank plc* [1999] ICR 859 (HL)**

FACTS: The claimant was, between 1979 and 1990, a full-time employee of the defendant. After giving birth in 1990, she continued to work part-time until 1993, when she accepted voluntary redundancy. The severance payment was calculated based on her salary at the date of redundancy (accordingly, her eleven years' full-time service was irrelevant). She

---

164. Equality Act 2010, s 69(1)(a).   165. *Capper Pass Ltd v Lawton* [1977] ICR 83 (EAT).
166. *NAAFI v Varley, The Times* (London, 1 January 1976) (EAT).
167. Part-time workers are protected by the Part-Time Workers (Prevention of Less Favourable Treatment) Regulations 2000, so recourse to the Equality Act 2010 will not be required in many cases. The 2000 Regulations are discussed at p 779.   168. *Handley v H Mono Ltd* [1979] ICR 147 (EAT).
169. *Jenkins v Kingsgate (Clothing Productions) Ltd (No 2)* [1981] ICR 715 (EAT).

contended that, in failing to take into account the fact that, for eleven years, her salary was that of a full-time worker, the defendant had indirectly discriminated against her on the ground of sex.

HELD: Her claim was dismissed. As the severance payment was calculated based on pay at the time of redundancy, all employees were treated the same. Further, the defendant's actions were objectively justified, in that it sought to cushion the impact of the redundancies, which was a legitimate justification that was not based on sex.

The second problematic area relates to 'red-circling'. This usually occurs where an employee's job is downgraded, but to avoid breaching the employment contract, the employer protects (or 'red-circles') the pay of the downgraded employee. The following example demonstrates the problem that has arisen.

 The problem of 'red-circling'

John is employed as a 'Grade 1' engineer. His employment contract entitles him to £25,000. He is downgraded to a 'Grade 2' engineer. Such engineers are only paid £20,000 per year, but to pay John this amount would constitute a breach of his employment contract. Accordingly, his employer protects (red-circles) John's salary and he continues to receive £25,000 per year. Kelly is employed as a 'Grade 2' engineer and receives £20,000 per year, even though she is performing exactly the same work as John, who is receiving £5,000 more.

The courts have stated that red-circling can constitute a material factor, provided that the red-circling occurs for a reason not (directly or indirectly) related to sex,[170] as occurred in the following case.

 Methven v Cow Industrial Polymers Ltd **[1980] ICR 463 (CA)**

FACTS: The defendant company employed three clerks (one each for the mill, the press shop, and the trimming shop). The clerk of the press shop (a man) was paid more than the clerks of the mill and the trimming shop (both women), even though they all did the same work (in effect, the post of clerk of the press shop was red-circled). The reason for this was that, for the previous twenty-five years, the clerk of the press shop was a long-standing employee who had been moved to the press shop due to age or ill health. The female clerks alleged that their lower pay was discriminatory.

HELD: The red-circling constituted a material factor and so was not discriminatory. The post of clerk of the press shop was not red-circled due to reasons of sex, but due to reasons of age and ill health.

---

170. *Snoxell v Vauxhall Motors Ltd* [1978] QB 11 (EAT).

The third problematic area relates to collective bargaining, which is a process under which employers will negotiate with relevant parties (e.g. employees, trade unions etc) on numerous employment issues, including the terms and conditions of employment. The problem that arises is that a collective bargaining agreement may not affect all of the employees of the company, resulting in some employees obtaining better terms of employment than others, even though their work would be similar or identical. Historically, it was held that collective bargaining that resulted in different employment terms between employees was a valid material factor other than sex.[171] However, in the following case, the ECJ rejected this view and held that collective bargaining was not a material factor.

Case C-127/92 *Enderby v Frenchay Health Authority* [1993] ECR I-5535

FACTS: Enderby was a speech therapist, who commenced proceedings against her employer for breach of the sex equality clause. The comparators were a male pharmacist and a male clinical psychologist. Although Enderby was engaged in work of equal value to the comparators, she was paid less than them. The majority of speech therapists employed by her employer were women, whereas the majority of pharmacists and clinical psychologists were men. Enderby's employer stated that the disparity in pay was due to a collective bargaining agreement and therefore the disparity was due to a material factor other than sex. The EAT rejected Enderby's claim on the ground that the collective bargaining agreement was not sexually discriminatory.[172] Enderby appealed to the Court of Appeal and the Court decided to refer the case to the ECJ.[173]

HELD: The ECJ held that the fact that different rates of pay of two jobs (one carried out by women and the other carried out by men) were arrived at by collective bargaining processes which were distinct and not in themselves discriminatory, was not a sufficient objective justification for the difference in pay between the two jobs.

★ See Michael Wynn, 'Equal Pay and Gender Segregation' (1994) 110 LQR 556.

The fourth and final problematic issue relates to market forces. This tends to occur where market forces dictate that an employer, in order to attract employees of sufficient calibre, will need to provide new employees with more favourable terms than existing employees. Where a new employee has more favourable terms than an existing employee of the opposite sex, the existing employee is likely to feel aggrieved. The question is whether the market forces that forced the employer to offer the more favourable terms can constitute a genuine material factor.

In the following case, the House of Lords established that where a difference in terms exists for some sound economic reason, this will constitute a material factor.

---

171. *Reed Packaging Ltd v Boozer* [1988] ICR 391 (EAT).
172. *Enderby v Frenchay Health Authority (No 1)* [1991] 1 CMLR 626 (EAT).
173. *Enderby v Frenchay (No 1)* [1992] IRLR 15 (CA).

> ### 🔑 *Rainey v Greater Glasgow Health Board* [1987] AC 224 (HL)
>
> **FACTS**: The defendant Health Board set up a prosthetic fitting service. In order to attract sufficient numbers of qualified prosthetists from the private sector, the Health Board stated that it would pay such prosthetists the same pay as they were earning in the private sector. Twenty new prosthetists were taken on, all of whom happened to be men. A female prosthetist was taken on a year later, but because she was not previously employed in the private sector, she received £2,790 less than the men, even though she was doing the same work. She initiated proceedings, alleging that she was entitled to the same pay as the new male prosthetists.
>
> **HELD:** The House of Lords rejected her claim and held that the material factor defence was not limited to personal characteristics, but can also apply to other objective grounds. Here, the increased pay paid to the new prosthetists was based on a sound objective justification—namely, to expand the prosthetics fitting service. The fact that all of the new prosthetists employed were male was simply coincidental.

⭐ See Peter Schofield, 'Equal Pay: What's the Difference?' (1987) 50 MLR 379

In addition to establishing that the material factor was for a reason other than sex, the employer will also need to demonstrate that the material factor was 'a proportionate means of achieving a legitimate aim'.[174] Such a requirement was not part of the defence when it was part of the EPA 1970, and was introduced by the 2010 Act. To date, there have been no cases involving this new requirement, so it is too early to predict its effect. The Act itself provides limited guidance by stating that the long-term objective of reducing inequality between men's and women's terms of work will always be regarded as a legitimate aim.[175]

Enforcement and remedies

A claim for equal pay may be brought before an employment tribunal,[176] provided that the claim is brought within three months of the date of the act to which the complaint relates, or some other period as the employment tribunal thinks just and equitable.[177] If the employment tribunal believes that the provisions relating to equal pay have been contravened, it can:

- make a declaration as to the rights of the complainant and respondent in relation to the matters to which the proceedings relate;
- order the respondent to pay compensation to the complainant;
- make an appropriate recommendation, namely that within a specified period the respondent takes specified steps for the purposes of obviating or reducing the adverse effects of the matter complained of.[178] If the respondent fails, without reasonable excuse, to comply with this recommendation, the Tribunal may increase the amount of compensation to be paid.[179]

---

174. Equality Act 2010, s 69(1)(b).   175. ibid s 69(3).

176. ibid s 120(1)(a). Under the EPA 1970, such cases could also be heard by a county court.

177. ibid s 123(1).   178. ibid s 124(1), (2), and (3).   179. ibid s 124(7)(a).

Maternity equality clause

In addition to the sex equality clause, the 2010 Act also provides for a maternity equality clause. Section 73(1) of the Act provides that '[i]f the terms of the woman's work do not (by whatever means) include a maternity equality clause, they are to be treated as including one.' The basis effect of the maternity equality clause is that if, during the protected period (which is defined in the same manner as in s 18(6) discussed in 'Pregnancy and maternity' at p 761) the woman's pay increases, or would have increased had she not been on maternity leave, then this increase must be taken into account when calculating her maternity pay.[180] In addition, any bonuses that she would have received had she not been on maternity leave must be paid[181] and, upon returning to work, her rate of pay must take into account any pay increase she would have received had she not been on maternity leave.[182]

Maternity pay is discussed at p 719

Discrimination against part-time workers and fixed-term employees

Not all forms of discrimination fall within the remit of the Equality Act 2010, and specialist legislation remains in relation to discrimination against part-time workers and fixed-term workers.

Part-time workers

The Part-Time Workers (Prevention of Less Favourable Treatment) Regulations 2000 (PTWR 2000)[183] provide that a part-time worker has the right not to be treated less favourably than a full-time worker.[184] This will only apply, however, where the part-time worker is treated less favourably on the ground that he works part-time[185] and the employer cannot objectively justify his actions.[186] As the following example demonstrates, whether a part-time employee is treated less favourably than a full-time employee will be determined on a pro rata basis, unless it is inappropriate to do so.[187]

Eg **The pro rata principle**

Steve works full-time, and his contract provides that he shall work forty hours per week and shall receive thirty days' holiday leave per year. Karl works part-time, and his contract provides that he shall work twenty hours per week and shall receive ten days' holiday leave per year. As Karl works half the number of hours that Steve does, on a pro rata basis, he is entitled to half the benefits to which Steve is entitled. This would entitle Karl to fifteen days' holiday leave per year and, because he only has ten days' leave, he has a claim under the PTWR 2000.

---

180. ibid s 74(1)–(5).   181. ibid s 74(6) and (7).   182. ibid s 74(8).
183. SI 2000/1551.   184. PTWR 2000, reg 5(1).   185. ibid reg 5(2)(a).
186. ibid reg 5(2)(b).   187. ibid reg 5(3).

In order to make a pro rata comparison, an actual full-time comparator will be required. The comparator must be:

- employed under the same type of contract as the part-time employee;
- engaged in identical or broadly similar work; and
- based in the same establishment, unless there is no full-time worker based in the same establishment, in which case a full-time worker from a different establishment will suffice.[188]

Fixed-term employees

The Fixed-Term Employees (Prevention of Less Favourable Treatment) Regulations 2002 (FTER 2002)[189] aim to protect employees[190] on fixed-term contracts who receive less favourable treatment than those on permanent contracts. These Regulations provide employees on fixed-term contracts with an identical level of protection to that provided to part-time workers under the PTWR 2000. Accordingly, the right not to be treated less favourably is largely the same and less favourable treatment is determined in the same pro rata manner.

Chapter conclusion

The prevention of discrimination is a comparatively recent development and we are still struggling to discover the best method of preventing it. It could be argued that the pre-2010 pieces of discrimination legislation were based around a core structure. It is clear that the core structure found in the SDA 1975 and RRA 1976 provided a template for future legislation—but there were enough subtle, but nonetheless important, differences between the various forms of discrimination to cause confusion to businesses, employers, employees, and applicants. For example, disability discrimination occured in a very different manner from the other forms of discrimination. It is hoped that the Equality Act 2010 will provide a unified framework that greatly simplifies and minimizes the amount of legislation in this complex area of the law. But more is needed. It could be argued that the law is not clear regarding the underlying purpose of anti-discrimination legislation. Should the law aim to prevent discrimination or promote equality? In many cases, the two aims will coincide, but in relation to topics such as positive action, the two aims may be contradictory. To promote equality, discrimination may have to occur. It will be interesting to see which of the two aims is favoured.

 Key points summary

- The Equality Act 2010 aims to harmonize the laws relating to the various grounds of discrimination.

- The Act provides for five forms of prohibited conduct, namely (i) direct discrimination; (ii) combined discrimination; (iii) indirect discrimination; (iv) harassment; and (v) victimization. The provisions relating to combined discrimination will not be brought into force.

---

188. ibid reg 2(4).   189. SI 2002/2034.

190. Whereas many other pieces of anti-discrimination legislation apply to workers, the FTER 2000 apply specifically to employees only.

- The Equality Act 2010 prohibits discrimination on nine grounds (known as 'protected characteristics'), namely (i) age; (ii) disability; (iii) gender reassignment; (iv) marriage and civil partnership; (v) pregnancy and maternity; (vi) race; (vii) religion or belief; (viii) sex; and (ix) sexual orientation.

- Some forms of prohibited conduct are not applicable to all nine protected characteristics. Certain protected characteristics have their own specific forms of prohibited conduct.

- A person who believes that he has been the victim of prohibited conduct can make a claim to an employment tribunal. If established, the tribunal can (i) make a declaration; (ii) award compensation; and/or (iii) make a recommendation.

- The Equality Act 2010 implies a sex equality clause into a contract where A carries out 'like work', 'work rated as equivalent', or 'work equal in value' to that of an employee of the opposite sex.

- The Equality Act 2010 does not offer protection to persons discriminated against on the grounds of working part-time or being employed on a fixed-term contract, but such persons are protected by specific subordinate legislation.

Self-test questions

1. Define the following:
   (a) direct discrimination;
   (b) indirect discrimination;
   (c) victimization;
   (d) harassment;
   (e) positive action;
   (f) disability;
   (g) race.

2. Has discrimination occurred in the following cases? If so, identify the form of prohibited conduct and the relevant protected characteristic.
   (a) A firm of solicitors advertises a job opening. The advertisement states that the successful applicant will have between five and seven years' post-qualifying experience and will be under the age of 30.
   (b) Mohinder emigrated from India to the UK when he was 28 years old. He is now aged 35 and in employment. He applies for a job, but is rejected, because the job requires the applicant to have ten years' experience working in the UK.
   (c) Sharon is employed to cover for another employee who is taking maternity leave. A few days into the job, Sharon discovers that she is pregnant. Sharon informs her employer, who promptly dismisses her.

3. 'The Equality Act 2010 is based on standard terms that applied throughout the various grounds of discrimination in previous anti-discrimination legislation, and therefore does not alter the law in a meaningful way.' Discuss.

Additional reading

Astra Emir, *Selwyn's Law of Employment* (17th edn, OUP 2012) ch 4

Provides a detailed, yet engaging, discussion of all of the protected characteristics and forms of prohibited conduct operating under the Equality Act 2010

Sandra Fredman, *Discrimination Law* (2nd edn, OUP 2011)

Discusses discrimination law in general and provides an analytical account of the evolution of this area of the law

Bob Hepple, *Equality: The New Framework* (Hart Publishing 2011)

An excellent and highly readable discussion of the Equality Act 2010

Simonetta Longhi and Lucinda Platt, *Pay Gaps Across Equality Areas* (ECHR 2008)

Discusses employment disparities and pay gaps in relation to a number of equality areas (for example, gender, religion, ethnicity etc)

Russell Sandberg, 'The Right to Discriminate' (2011) 13 Ecc LJ 157

Discusses the tensions that exist between religion and sexual orientation and examines how the Equality Act 2010 allows religious persons and bodies to follow their own beliefs regarding sexuality

Websites

<https://www.gov.uk/government/organisations/government-equalities-office>
The official website of the government Equalities Office

<http://www.equalityhumanrights.com>
The official website of the Equality and Human Rights Commission

 Remember to visit the **Online Resource Centre** at <**http://www.oxfordtextbooks.co.uk/orc/roach3e**> to access the following resources on Chapter 27, 'Discrimination law': more **practice questions** and answers; a **glossary** of key terms; **multiple-choice questions**; and **expanded revision summaries**. Updates to the law can be found on Twitter by following **@UKBusinessLaw**.

28 The termination of employment

- What is dismissal?
- Termination upon notice
- Termination upon expiry of a limited-term contract
- Summary dismissal
- Constructive dismissal
- Wrongful dismissal
- Unfair dismissal
- Redundancy

INTRODUCTION

The termination of employment constitutes an extremely litigious area of the law. Over half of the cases heard by employment tribunals concern the termination of employment, and owners and controllers of businesses are required to pay out millions of pounds each year in compensation to employees who have been wrongfully or unfairly dismissed. A termination of employment may also place an obligation upon the employer to provide dismissed employees with redundancy pay. Clearly, therefore, the termination of employment is an issue that businesses need to take extremely seriously. Both statute and the common law impose a raft of obligations upon employers when considering terminating contracts of employment, and detailed and complex procedures are in place to ensure that employees are treated fairly. In this chapter, these obligations and procedures will be discussed in detail. It will be seen that the protection provided is primarily aimed at employees who have been dismissed and it is therefore important that businesses are aware of what forms of termination constitute dismissal.

What is dismissal?

Dismissal is the second most common form of termination, next to resignation. For two reasons, it is vital to determine whether or not the termination of employment constitutes a dismissal or not: first, a claim for wrongful or unfair dismissal can only be brought if an employee is dismissed; second, only dismissed employees are entitled to redundancy pay.

Sections 95(1)[1] and 136(1)[2] of the Employment Rights Act 1996 (ERA 1996) provide that an employee is dismissed where:

- the employment contract is terminated by the employer (whether with or without notice);
- he is employed under a limited-term contract and that contract terminates by virtue of the limiting event, without being renewed under the same contract; or
- the employee terminates the contract (with or without notice) in circumstances under which he is entitled to terminate it without notice by reason of the employer's conduct (known as 'constructive dismissal').

As is discussed later, other forms of termination may constitute a dismissal for the purposes of a redundancy claim, but not another claim (for example, termination of employment due to a frustrating event that affects the employer constitutes dismissal for the purposes of a redundancy pay claim, but not for the purposes of unfair dismissal).

As a result of ss 95 and 136, when the contract of employment is terminated due to resignation, frustration, or agreement, it will not normally constitute dismissal.

Resignation

An employee can terminate the contract of employment by resigning. As resignation is the voluntary termination of the employment contract by the employee, it follows that it does not constitute a dismissal and the employee will not be entitled to redundancy pay, or to claim he was wrongfully or unfairly dismissed. However, if the resignation is not voluntary, it will constitute a dismissal.

 Essex County Council v Walker (1972) 7 ITR 280 (NIRC)

FACTS: The claimant had a disagreement with her employer. Subsequently, her employer stated that if she did not resign, she would be dismissed and that resigning was in her best interests. Accordingly, she resigned. She later claimed redundancy pay, but was refused, on the ground that she had not been dismissed. She appealed.

HELD: The claimant had been dismissed and was entitled to redundancy pay. Brightman J stated that 'if an employee is told that she is no longer required in her employment and is expressly invited to resign, a court of law is entitled to come to the conclusion that, as a matter of common sense, the employee was dismissed'.[3]

Frustration

An employment contract will be frustrated if it becomes impossible to perform or illegal, or where performance will produce a result that is radically different from that envisaged by the parties when the contract was made. Examples of events that

---

1. Section 95(1) defines what constitutes a dismissal for the purposes of an unfair dismissal claim.
2. Section 136(1) defines what constitutes a dismissal for the purposes of determining entitlement to redundancy pay.
3. (1972) 7 ITR 280 (NIRC) 281.

could frustrate an employment contract include the employee being imprisoned,[4] or the employee being called up for military service.[5]

The frustration of an employment contract has two principal effects. First, the contract of employment is automatically terminated. The wishes of the parties are irrelevant and neither party need take any steps in order for their contractual relationship to end. Second, as the contract is terminated by the operation of law, it follows that the employee has not been dismissed. However, if the frustrating event is an event affecting the employer, then the employee will be regarded as dismissed[6] and entitled to redundancy pay (but not entitled to bring a claim for unfair dismissal).

Three types of frustrating event are slightly more complex and warrant further discussion—namely (i) the death of an employer or employee; (ii) the dissolution of a business; and (iii) illness or injury of the employee.

Death

At common law, the death of the employee automatically frustrates the employment contract.[7] The same is true if the business ceases on the employer's death. It follows that the employee has not been dismissed and cannot claim unfair dismissal, but the employee is regarded as dismissed for the purposes of the redundancy provisions and is entitled to redundancy payment.[8] Where the employer's **personal representatives** or trustees continue the business and the employee continues to work for the business, however, there is deemed to be no termination and the employment continues unbroken.[9] If, following the employer's death, the business ceases, then, for the purposes of claiming redundancy pay, the employee is regarded as being dismissed.[10]

> ➡ **personal representatives:** an administrator or executor, whose function it is to settle the affairs of deceased persons

Dissolution

In many cases, the employer will be a company and so cannot 'die' in the literal sense of the word. Where the employer is a company, the method of the company's dissolution is an important factor. Certain events, such as the appointment of a receiver, will cause the employees' contracts to be terminated.[11] Commencement of a compulsory winding up will constitute notice to dismiss,[12] as will commencement of a voluntary winding up where there is no intention to carry on the business in any form.[13] Where a company is voluntarily wound up, but is to continue in some form (for example, where it is taken over), there will be no dismissal.[14]

Illness or injury

That illness or injury can result in the frustration of the employment contract is undisputed. The problem is that it is not clear what length or type of illness or injury is required in order for an employer to regard the contract as frustrated. Further, where the illness or injury amounts to a disability, any negative action taken by the employer could amount to disability discrimination. Mere absence from work is unlikely in itself to frustrate a contract. Thus, where a cabinetmaker was absent from work for two years, but continued to submit sick notes during that period, an

> 🔗 Disability discrimination is discussed at p 755

---

4. *FC Shepherd & Co Ltd v Jerrom* [1987] QB 301 (CA).   5. *Morgan v Manser* [1948] 1 KB 184 (KB).
6. ERA 1996, ss 136(5) and 139(4).   7. *Stubbs v Holywell Rly Co* (1867) LR 2 Exch 311.
8. ERA 1996, ss 136(5) and 139(4).   9. ibid s 218(4).   10. ibid s 139(1).
11. *Reid v Explosives Co* (1887) 19 QBD 264 (CA).
12. *Re General Rolling Stock Co (Chapman's Case)* (1866) LR 1 Eq 346.
13. *Reigate v Union Manufacturing Co (Ramsbottom) Ltd* [1918] 1 KB 592 (CA).
14. *Midland Counties District Bank Ltd v Attwood* [1905] 1 Ch 357 (Ch).

industrial tribunal held that the contract was not frustrated, because his job was not the type that required filling by a permanent replacement.[15]

The Employment Appeal Tribunal (EAT) sought to establish guidance in the following case.

 ### Egg Stores (Stamford Hill) Ltd v Leibovici [1977] ICR 260 (EAT)

FACTS: The claimant was injured in a car accident in November 1974 and was off work for five months. His employer paid his wages until January 1975 and another employee completed his work. In April 1975, the claimant felt able to return to work, but was informed that his position had been filled. The claimant sought redundancy pay or compensation for unfair dismissal. The employer argued that it was entitled to terminate his contract on the ground of frustration.

HELD: The contract had been frustrated. Phillips J stated that there may be illnesses or injuries that are so dramatic (for example, a crippling accident) that everyone is aware that the employment contract must be regarded as coming to an end. In most cases, however, the illness or injury will be less severe and its effects more uncertain. In such cases, a contract will become frustrated at that point at which 'the prospects for the future were so poor, that it was no longer practical to regard the contract as still subsisting'.[16]

When determining whether this point has arrived, the following should be taken into account:

- the length of the employment;
- how long the employment would have been likely to continue;
- the nature of the job;
- the nature, length, and effect of the illness or injury;
- the need of the employer for the work to be done, and the need for a replacement to do it;
- the risk to the employer of acquiring obligations in respect of redundancy payments or compensation for unfair dismissal to the replacement employee;
- whether wages have continued to be paid;
- the acts and the statements of the employer in relation to the employment, including the dismissal of, or failure to dismiss, the employee; and
- whether, in all of the circumstances, a reasonable employer could be expected to wait any longer.

★ See HG Collins, 'Frustration of the Contract of Employment' (1977) 6 ILJ 185

Two further factors have since been added to the list outlined in the above case, namely (i) the terms of the employment contract in relation to sick pay; and (ii) the employee's prospects of recovery.[17]

Agreement

🔗 The law relating to discharge by agreement is discussed at p 294

Like any other contract, an employment contract may be discharged if both parties agree to the discharge. As the employment contract is discharged by the consent of both parties, it follows that the employee is not dismissed,[18] but in order for the

---

15. *Maxwell v Walter Howard Designs* [1975] IRLR 77 (IT).   16. [1977] ICR 260 (EAT) 265.
17. *Williams v Watson Luxury Coaches Ltd* [1990] ICR 536 (EAT).
18. *Strange Ltd v Mann* [1965] 1 WLR 629 (Ch).

discharge to be valid, the employee must agree freely and there must be no coercion. This is a crucial requirement, because, without it, employers would pressure their employees into agreeing to a discharge to avoid the consequences that can result following a dismissal. A finding of discharge by agreement avoids the need to pay redundancy pay and will prevent a claim for unfair dismissal from being made. Accordingly, employers may try to argue that an agreement to discharge was present when it was clearly not, as the following case demonstrates.

 McAlwane v Boughton Estates [1973] ICR 470 (NIRC)

FACTS: The defendant employer informed the claimant employee that his employment would be terminated on 19 April. The claimant asked the defendant if the employment could be terminated on 12 April, so that he could start a new job. The defendant agreed. The defendant refused to pay the claimant redundancy pay on the ground that, in agreeing to terminate the employment on 12 April, the employment had been terminated by agreement. Consequently, the claimant was not dismissed and so was not entitled to redundancy pay.

HELD: The claimant's request to bring forward the date of termination did not constitute a discharge by agreement; rather, it merely altered the terms of the dismissal. Accordingly, the claimant had been dismissed and was entitled to redundancy pay.

COMMENT: Section 95(2) of the ERA 1996 now expressly states that a request to terminate the employment on a date earlier than that stated by the employer will constitute a dismissal.

Termination upon notice

Either party can normally terminate an employment contract upon giving notice. If the employer gives notice of termination, this will constitute dismissal. Normally, where the employee gives notice, this will constitute resignation, which, as discussed earlier, does not normally constitute dismissal. However, as is discussed later, it is possible for an employee to give notice and still be regarded as dismissed.

The minimum notice period is normally stated in the employment contract. In the absence of such a period, the requisite notice period is subject to common law and statutory rules.

Common law

Where the notice period is not provided for by the contract and there is no minimum period established by custom or trade usage, the parties will need to provide 'reasonable notice' of termination.[19] What is reasonable will depend upon the facts in question, but it is common for a reasonable period to correspond with the period of payment (that is, weekly or monthly). The problem with this approach is that

---

19. *Richardson v Koefod* [1969] 1 WLR 1812 (CA).

an employee paid monthly would be entitled to a month's notice irrespective of whether he had worked for the employer for a week or for thirty years. Long-serving employees should be entitled to longer periods of notice and this was eventually provided for by statute.

Statute

An employee who has been continuously employed by his employer for one month or more must provide a minimum of one week's notice.[20] This applies even if the contract provides for a shorter notice period, but it does not prevent a party from waiving the right to notice or accepting payment in lieu of notice.[21] It follows that an employee who fails to provide the requisite notice will be in breach of contract.

Section 86(1) of the ERA 1996 lays down the minimum period of notice that an employer must provide. These periods are the minimum and the courts may very well hold that the common law requirement for 'reasonable notice' requires a longer period. Under s 86(1), the minimum notice period depends upon the length of service:

- Employees employed for less than one month are not entitled to notice under the ERA 1996, but will be entitled to reasonable notice under the common law.
- Employees employed for one month or more, but less than two years, are entitled to no less than one week's notice.
- Employees employed for over two years, but less than twelve years, are entitled to an additional week's notice for every additional year of their employment (for example, an employee with nine years' service would be entitled to nine weeks' notice).
- Employees employed for over twelve years are entitled to no less than twelve weeks' notice.

As these constitute the minimum notice periods, the parties are free to provide for a longer period if they so wish. If they do so, the minimum notice period will be the longer period contained in the employment contract. Either party may waive the right to notice or can accept payment in lieu of notice.[22]

Termination upon expiry of a limited-term contract

Employment contracts are usually deemed to continue indefinitely, but can be discharged by reasonable notice.[23] Parties are free to enter into limited-term contracts, however, with such limitations tending to occur in one of two ways.

---

20. ERA 1996, s 86(2).   21. ibid s 86(3).
22. ibid s 86(3). It was held in *Trotter v Forth Ports Authority* [1991] IRLR 419 (CA) that where a party waives the right to notice, he loses the right to be paid in lieu of notice.
23. *Richardson v Koefod* [1969] 1 WLR 1812 (CA).

1. The parties may provide that the employment contract will continue for a fixed period of time. As soon as this period expires, the contract terminates automatically.[24]
2. If an employee is employed solely to complete a single specific task, then once that task is complete, the contract will automatically terminate.

In both cases, the employee is not technically dismissed, because his contract simply reaches its end. The termination of the contract could be regarded as a form of discharge by agreement or performance, but in order to prevent employers from avoiding the rules relating to redundancy payments and unfair dismissal, terminations due to expiry of a limited term are regarded as dismissals.[25]

Summary dismissal

Summary dismissal (also known as 'dismissal for cause') occurs where the employer dismisses the employee without notice.[26] Summary dismissal is permitted (that is, will not amount to wrongful or unfair dismissal) where the employee has committed an act that amounts to a **repudiatory breach** of the contract (that is, the employee has 'caused' his dismissal). The employer is entitled to accept the repudiatory act and treat the contract as immediately terminated.

➡️ **repudiatory breach:** a breach of contract that gives rise to the right to terminate

What amounts to a repudiatory act was set out by Lord Evershed MR when he stated that 'the question must be—if summary dismissal is claimed to be justifiable—whether the conduct complained of is such as to show the servant to have disregarded the essential conditions of the contract of service'.[27] Based upon this, the following have been held to constitute repudiatory breaches that justify summary dismissal:

- disclosure of confidential information;[28]
- taking part in strike action;[29]
- disobeying the employer's lawful orders;[30]
- Internet or email abuse;[31]
- acts of dishonesty;[32]
- gross negligence.[33]

It should be noted that the courts have indicated that summary dismissal will be justified only in exceptional circumstances.[34] So, for example, mere negligence will normally not justify summary dismissal.[35] The courts have also indicated that summary dismissal will rarely be justified for a single act.

---

24. *R v Secretary of State for Social Services, ex p Khan* [1973] 2 All ER 104 (CA).

25. ERA 1996, ss 95(1)(b) and 136(1)(b).

26. The introduction of minimum notice periods by the ERA 1996 does not deprive the employer of the right to dismiss summarily (ERA 1996, s 86(6)).

27. *Laws v London Chronicle (Indicator Newspapers) Ltd* [1959] 1 WLR 698 (CA) 700.

28. *Denco Ltd v Joinson* [1991] IRLR 63 (EAT).   29. *Simmons v Hoover Ltd* [1977] QB 284 (EAT).

30. *Pepper v Webb* [1969] 1 WLR 514 (CA).

31. *Thomas v Hillingdon London Borough Council, The Times* (London, 4 October 2002) (EAT) (downloading pornography).   32. *Sinclair v Neighbour* [1967] 2 QB 279 (CA).

33. *Jupiter General Insurance Co Ltd v Shroff* [1937] 3 All ER 67 (PC).   34. ibid.

35. *Gould v Webb* (1855) 4 E & B 933.

Where an employer acquires the right to dismiss an employee summarily, it must do so within a reasonable period. Failure to do so will be regarded as a waiver of the right, entitling the employer to damages only.

Constructive dismissal

As noted, where the employee terminates the employment contract, this will usually constitute resignation and not dismissal. However, ss 95(1)(c) and 136(1)(c) of the ERA 1996 provides that, for the purposes of unfair dismissal and redundancy pay respectively, an employee will be regarded as dismissed where:

> the employee terminates the contract under which he is employed (with or without notice) in circumstances in which he is entitled to terminate it without notice by reason of the employer's conduct.

In other words, where the employer's conduct is such that it entitles the employee to terminate the contract without giving notice, the employee is regarded as if he was dismissed. This is known as 'constructive dismissal' and is, in many respects, similar to summary dismissal, except that we are concerned with the employer's conduct. The question therefore is what conduct will entitle the employee to terminate without notice. Initially, the courts took a reasonably wide view and stated that an employee would be entitled to terminate without notice where the employer's conduct was 'of a kind which in accordance with good industrial relations practice no employee could reasonably be expected to accept'.[36] However, this reasonable expectations test was firmly rejected and a narrower test introduced in the following case.

Western Excavations (ECC) Ltd v Sharp [1978] QB 761 (CA)

FACTS: The claimant asked his employer if he could have an afternoon off (in order to play cards). His request was refused, but he took the afternoon off anyway and was subsequently suspended from work without pay. As a result, his financial situation deteriorated and so he asked his employer if he could have an advance of his accrued holiday pay. The employer refused, and, in order to obtain this holiday pay, the claimant resigned and claimed that he was unfairly dismissed.

HELD: Lord Denning MR stated:

> If the employer is guilty of conduct which is a significant breach going to the root of the contract of employment, or which shows that the employer no longer intends to be bound by one or more of the essential terms of the contract, then the employee is entitled to treat himself as discharged from any further performance. If he does so, then he terminates the contract by reason of the employer's conduct. He is constructively dismissed. The employee is entitled in those circumstances to leave at the instant without giving any notice at all or, alternatively, he may give notice and say he is leaving

---

36. *George Wimpey & Co Ltd v Cooper* [1977] IRLR 205 (EAT) 224 (Phillips J).

at the end of the notice. But the conduct must in either case be sufficiently serious to entitle him to leave at once.[37]

Applying this test, the claimant had not been constructively dismissed, because the employer had not breached or repudiated the contract.

COMMENT: Although Lord Denning MR's test is a narrow one, it should not be applied too rigidly. In applying the test, Lawton LJ stated that 'what is required for the application of this provision is a large measure of common sense'.[38] Subsequent decisions have further expanded the scope of the test by implying a term of mutual respect into the employment contract, so that unreasonable conduct by the employer can be regarded as a breach of this implied term.

An employee will only be regarded as constructively dismissed where the employer has breached a term of the contract and the breach is so substantial that it constitutes a repudiatory breach. In applying Lord Denning MR's test, the tribunals and courts have held that the types of conduct by the employer that could justify the employee being regarded as constructively dismissed include:

- instruction to discriminate against ethnic customers;[39]
- refusal to pay the employee's wages;[40]
- failure to follow grievance procedures,[41] or the imposition of disproportionate punishment;[42]
- failure to provide a safe system of work;[43]
- breach of the implied term of mutual trust and confidence;[44]
- unjustifiable demotion or suspension of an employee.[45]

 The implied term of mutual trust and confidence is discussed at p 700

An employee who has been the victim of such conduct has two options. First, he can continue to work for the employer, thereby affirming the employer's breach. Second, he can resign and claim that he was constructively dismissed, but he must resign quickly. A failure to act quickly will lead an employment tribunal to infer that the employee has acquiesced to the employer's conduct and affirmed the breach, with the result that a subsequent resignation will not amount to a dismissal.[46]

A constructive dismissal is not necessarily an unfair dismissal. A constructive dismissal merely demonstrates that the employee was dismissed, and if the employer can justify his actions, then the constructive dismissal will be fair.

Savoia v Chiltern Herb Farms Ltd [1982] IRLR 166 (CA)

FACTS: The claimant was absent from work due to illness, and so another employee took over his work. The defendant employer found this employee to be more cooperative than the claimant. Accordingly, when the production foreman died, the defendant offered the

---

37. [1978] QB 761 (CA) 769.   38. ibid 772–3.
39. *Weathersfield Ltd v Sargent* [1999] ICR 425 (CA).
40. *Cantor Fitzgerald International v Callaghan* [1999] ICR 639 (CA).
41. *Post Office v Strange* [1981] IRLR 515 (EAT).   42. *BBC v Beckett* [1983] IRLR 43 (EAT).
43. *Keys v Shoefayre* [1978] IRLR 476 (IT).
44. *Courtaulds Northern Textiles v Andrew* [1979] IRLR 84 (EAT).
45. *McNeill v Charles Crimm (Electrical Construction) Ltd* [1984] IRLR 179 (EAT).
46. *Jeffrey v Laurence Scott Electromotors Ltd* [1978] IRLR 466 (EAT).

claimant this job, and offered the claimant's job to the other employee. Although it was a promotion, the claimant refused, because he believed that the job would expose him to the risk of contracting conjunctivitis. The defendant wished to test this claim by having the claimant undergo a medical examination, but the claimant refused. The defendant refused to let the claimant return to his old job and the claimant resigned, alleging that he had been constructively dismissed.

HELD: The claimant had been constructively dismissed, but it was held that the dismissal was fair. The reorganization of the business was justified and the employer had offered the claimant a promotion, thereby taking reasonable steps to ease the transition.

Accordingly, a constructive dismissal will not always amount to an unfair dismissal. However, as a constructive dismissal will amount to a breach of contract on the part of the employer, it is likely to amount to a wrongful dismissal, which is discussed next.

Wrongful dismissal

Wrongful dismissal occurs where the employer, in breach of contract, dismisses the employee. Examples of such breaches could include:

- terminating the employee's contract without providing sufficient notice;
- terminating a fixed-term contract before the expiry of the contract; and
- summarily dismissing an employee without sufficient justification.

Wrongful dismissal is a common law claim and should not be confused with unfair dismissal, which is a claim under the ERA 1996. Unfair dismissal requires the dismissal to be unfair, whereas wrongful dismissal does not; all that need be established is that the dismissal was in breach of contract. The claims are not mutually exclusive, and it is common for an employee to allege that he was both unfairly and wrongfully dismissed.

An employee who believes that he has been wrongfully dismissed may either initiate a claim in a civil court, or in an employment tribunal. The usual limitation periods apply (that is, three months where the case is brought before an employment tribunal, and six years where the claim is brought before a court).

Damages

As a wrongful dismissal claim is an action for breach of contract, it follows that damages will be the principal remedy and will be assessed on a contractual basis (that is, to put the claimant in the position in which he would have been had the breach not occurred, in so far as money is able to do this).[47] This strongly limits the amount of damages that can be claimed, as the following example demonstrates.

The quantification of damages in contract claims is discussed in 'Damages' at p XXX

---

47. *Robinson v Harman* (1848) 1 Ex 855 (Ex).

Eg Damages for wrongful dismissal

Hywel is employed by DataTech plc. His employment contract is to last five years and can be terminated by either party at any time by providing four weeks' notice. After two years, DataTech terminates Hywel's contract, but only provides him with two weeks' notice. Hywel makes a claim for wrongful dismissal.

There is no doubt that Hywel has been wrongfully dismissed—but what damages can he claim? He cannot claim for the remaining three years left on his contract, because DataTech was entitled to terminate the contract at any time upon providing four weeks' notice. Had the breach not occurred, Hywel would have received four weeks' notice. It follows that all that Hywel is entitled to is the wages and other benefits that he would have received had he been given sufficient notice (that is, two weeks' worth).

Accordingly, in cases in which inadequate notice is given, the damages recoverable are limited to what the employee would have obtained during the period of notice to which he was entitled or which he was denied. This would include pay and any benefits that the employee would have received had he worked the full notice period.[48] Several other limitations apply, as follows.

- Damages cannot be recovered for injured feelings or where the nature of the dismissal was humiliating.[49]

- Damages cannot be recovered for discretionary payments that could have been made by the employer (for example, bonuses), even where the employee expected to receive such payments.[50] The employer cannot, however, simply refuse to pay the discretionary payment: the exercise of the decision to pay or not to pay must be rational and bona fide.[51]

- Where the wrongful dismissal causes the employee to lose the right to bring an unfair dismissal claim (for example, because the employee is dismissed before he has acquired two years' continuous service), damages cannot be recovered for this loss.[52]

- The normal rules regarding mitigation apply, so the employee's damages may be reduced if he failed to take reasonable steps to mitigate his loss (for example, by looking for another job). The burden of proof is placed upon the employer to demonstrate this.

  🔗 The rules relating to mitigation are discussed at p 331

- Where a claim is brought before a tribunal, the maximum damages that can be awarded are £25,000.[53] Many have argued that this limit is too low, especially given that tribunals can award much higher sums in unfair dismissal cases. Employees seeking damages in excess of £25,000 are therefore advised to commence proceedings in a county court or the High Court.

- Where damages are over £30,000, the excess is taxable.[54] This is not the case regarding damages for unfair dismissal.

---

48. *Silvey v Pendragon plc* [2001] EWCA Civ 789, [2001] IRLR 685.
49. *Addis v Gramophone Co Ltd* [1909] AC 488 (HL).
50. *Lavarack v Woods of Colchester Ltd* [1967] 1 QB 278 (CA).
51. *Horkulak v Cantor Fitzgerald International* [2004] EWCA Civ 1287, [2005] ICR 402.
52. *Harper v Virgin Net Ltd* [2004] EWCA Civ 271, [2005] ICR 921.
53. Employment Tribunals Extension of Jurisdiction (England and Wales) Order 1994, SI 1994/1623, art 10.
54. Income Tax (Earning and Pensions) Act 2003, ss 401, 403, and 404.

Accordingly, it can be seen that the courts take a restrictive approach to the recovery of damages in wrongful dismissal cases. There are, however, several notable exceptions to this approach. First, where the dismissal is wrongful because an employee on a fixed-term contract that is not terminable by notice is dismissed before the expiry of the contract, the damages awarded will reflect what the employee would have earned had the contract run its stated length. Second, whilst damages are not normally recoverable for loss of reputation caused by being dismissed,[55] where an employment is undertaken and it is envisaged that the employee will receive a greater benefit than a simple wage (such as an increase in reputation),[56] damages may be recoverable for the loss of this benefit upon dismissal.

Enforcing the contract

 Injunctions and specific performance are discussed in Chapter 12

Given the limited ability to recover damages, a wrongfully dismissed employee may instead wish to have the employment contract enforced via an injunction or an order for specific performance. Such remedies will, in effect, compel both parties to continue working together (at least until the contractual notice period has been served, or the fixed term of the contract expires). The general rule is that the courts will not allow either party to enforce the contract. Statute prohibits the court from making any form of order that compels an employee to do any work or attend a place to do any work.[57] The courts have clearly indicated that, because employment contracts are personal contracts, they should not be enforced against any party who does not wish enforcement. As Fry LJ stated:

> I should be very unwilling to extend decisions the effect of which is to compel persons who are not desirous of maintaining continuous personal relations with one another to continue those personal relations. I have a strong impression and a strong feeling that it is not in the interest of mankind that the rule of specific performance should be extended to such cases.[58]

Employment contracts are based on mutual trust and confidence, and it would be wrong to enforce a contract where this trust and confidence was not present. Accordingly, it would appear to be the case that an order of specific performance will never be granted in cases of wrongful dismissal. In a number of rare instances, however, the courts have been willing to grant an injunction to restrain the employer from committing the breach that caused the wrongful dismissal.

Hill v CA Parsons & Co [1972] Ch 305 (CA)

FACTS: The defendant agreed with a trade union that, after one year, it should be a condition of service that all technical staff join the trade union. The claimant was an engineer who had worked for the defendant for thirty-five years. He refused to join the trade union and was dismissed. He was due to retire in two years' time and, because his pension was calculated based on his wages in the three years leading up to retirement, the dismissal had

---

55. *Johnson v Unisys Ltd* [2001] ICR 480 (HL).
56. *Marbé v George Edwardes (Daly's Theatres) Ltd* [1929] 1 KB 536 (CA).
57. Trade Union and Labour Relations (Consolidation) Act 1992, s 236.
58. *De Francesco v Barnum* [1890] LR 45 Ch D 430 (Ch) 438.

a substantial effect upon his pension rights. The claimant brought an action for wrongful dismissal and sought an interim injunction preventing the dismissal.

HELD: An interim injunction was granted preventing the defendant from terminating the claimant's employment for six months. Lord Denning MR stated that the rule against enforcement of an employment contract was not inflexible and that exceptions could be made. He said: 'It may be said that, by granting an injunction in such a case, the court is indirectly enforcing specifically a contract for personal services. So be it.'[59]

COMMENT: There were three reasons why the Court departed from the normal rule and enforced the contract. First, there was no breakdown of trust and confidence between the parties; rather, the dismissal was due to pressure from the trade union. Second, damages were an inadequate remedy, because they would not have compensated the claimant for the effect to his pension rights. Third, the Industrial Relations Act 1971 was due to come into force shortly after the case. This Act created the concept of unfair dismissal and the claimant's dismissal would certainly be regarded as unfair. By delaying the termination, the Court ensured that the claimant was an employee when the Act came into force and could bring an action for unfair dismissal.

The facts of *Hill* are unique and subsequent courts have restricted it by branding it as decided on its facts. It has not been overruled, however, and it has been applied in a small number of cases, resulting in injunctions being granted effectively to enforce a contract of employment.[60]

Unfair dismissal

The concept of 'unfair dismissal' was first introduced by the Industrial Relations Act 1971 and can now be found in s 94(1) of the ERA 1996, which provides that '[a]n employee has the right not to be unfairly dismissed by his employer'. Today, claims for unfair dismissal form the third most common form of complaint made to employment tribunals, with 49,036 unfair dismissal claims being accepted in 2012–13.[61] Unfair dismissal claims far outnumber claims for wrongful dismissal for a simple reason: unlike wrongful dismissal, a claim for unfair dismissal does not depend upon the employment contract being breached. However, whereas any employee who has been wrongfully dismissed may bring a claim for wrongful dismissal, the right not to be unfairly dismissed only extends to employees who meet the eligibility requirements.

Eligibility

Before an individual can claim that he has been unfairly dismissed, he will need to meet three eligibility requirements:

1. he must have been an 'employee' of the employer;
2. he must have been continuously employed by the employer for no less than two years; and
3. he must have been dismissed.

---

59. [1972] Ch 305 (CA) 315.

60. For example, *Irani v Southampton and South-West Hampshire Health Authority* [1985] ICR 590 (Ch); *Powell v Brent London Borough Council* [1988] ICR 176 (CA).

61. Statistics derived from <https://www.gov.uk/government/collections/tribunals-statistics>.

In addition, it should be noted that employee shareholders (discussed on p 711) do not have the right to claim for unfair dismissal,[62] unless the reason for the dismissal is one that (i) is regarded as automatically unfair; or (ii) amounts to a breach of the Equality Act 2010.[63]

Employee

🔗 The distinction between workers and employees is discussed at p 697

Previous chapters noted that there is an increasing trend for employment legislation to provide rights to a wider category of persons known as 'workers'. Indeed, many rights under the ERA 1996 itself apply to workers, but the right to bring an unfair dismissal claim is not one of them and the individual concerned will be unable to bring a claim unless he is an 'employee'. Accordingly, an independent contractor will be unable to bring a claim and will have to resort to a claim for breach of contract or wrongful dismissal.

Two years' continuous service[64]

Normally, an employee will only be permitted to bring a claim if he has been 'continuously employed for a period of not less than two years ending with the effective date of termination'.[65] This qualifying period has fluctuated over the years. Initially, it was six months and was then raised to a year in 1979 and to two years in 1985. It was reduced to one year in 1999, but increased back to two years in 2012.[66] This recent increase to two years has understandably, provoked controversy on the ground that it reduces the number of employees who are able to claim that their dismissal was unfair.

The period of continuous employment usually begins on the day on which the employee starts work for the employer.[67] The employee's employment will be continuous for '[a]ny week during the whole or part of which an employee's relations with his employer are governed by a contract of employment'.[68] In other words, if the employee does not work for the employer for a period of at least one week, then the period of service will be broken and will begin to run again when the employee does work. Time off work due to sickness, injury, family leave, or annual leave will not break the period of service, and will count toward the qualifying period. Provided that the employee works for the employer under a contract of employment, continuous service will not be broken by the employee changing roles or working in a different location within the UK. Continuous service will also not be broken by the undertaking being transferred to another employer.[69]

The employee must have two years' continuous employment ending on the 'effective date of termination'. Determining the exact date on which the employment ended is important for three reasons. First, it allows the court to calculate exactly

---

62. ERA 1996, s 205A(2)(C).   63. ibid s 205A(9).

64. It should be noted that the requirement of a minimum period of continuous service applies in relation to many statutory employment rights. The rules discussed here apply to all of these rights, not merely the right to claim for unfair dismissal.

65. ERA 1996, s 108(1). As is discussed later, where the dismissal is automatically regarded as unfair, this requirement does not apply. The requirement will also not apply where the reason for the dismissal is, or relates to, the employee's political opinions or affiliations (ERA 1996, s 108(4)).

66. This change came into force on the 6 April 2012. Employees who were employed by their employer before this date will be able to claim once they have attained one year's continuous service.

67. ERA 1996, s 211(1)(a).   68. ibid s 212(1).   69. ibid s 218(2)(b).

whether the employee has two years' continuous employment. Second, it allows the court to calculate whether the claim has been brought within the limitation period (an unfair dismissal claim must be brought within three months beginning on the effective date of termination, unless the court believes that it is just and equitable to extend this period).[70] Third, it is used to calculate the amount of compensation that the employee will receive if his claim succeeds.

Section 97 of the ERA 1996 defines what constitutes the effective date of termination:

1. Where the contract is terminated by notice (either by the employer or employee), the effective date of termination is the date on which the notice expires (irrespective of whether the notice was the proper length).
2. Where the termination is without notice (for example, summary dismissal), the effective date of termination will be the date on which the termination takes effect. This will normally be the date on which the employer tells the employee that he has been dismissed.
3. Where the employee is employed under a fixed-term contract, the effective date of termination will be the date on which the fixed-term expires.

It could be argued that the requirement of a minimum period of two years' continuous service is a harsh one. In effect, the requirement provides that employers may dismiss newer employees for any reason (provided that it is not a reason deemed automatically unfair) and the employee will be unable to sue for unfair dismissal. Further, provided that the employer provides the requisite period of notice, the employee will also be unable to bring a claim for wrongful dismissal. The initial reasons behind the rule (namely, to prevent part-timers from making a claim, and to allow employers to freedom to subject employees to lengthy probation periods and then dismiss them without fear of reprisal) were attacked by the EU and the qualifying period had to be lowered. It could be argued that the time has come to remove the qualifying period requirement completely. However, given the coalition government's recent increase in the qualifying period, it is highly unlikely that this will occur.

Dismissal

An employee who has served the qualifying period must then prove that he was actually dismissed. The forms of dismissal that will qualify for the purposes of making an unfair dismissal claim are:

- where the employer terminates the employment, with or without notice;[71]
- where a fixed-term employment contract expires and is not renewed;[72]
- where an employee resigns due to the conduct of the employer (that is, constructive dismissal);[73]
- where an employee resigns, but the resignation is not voluntary.[74]

Once the employee has established that a dismissal took place, the eligibility requirements will be met. Figure 28.1 helps to clarify the steps that the employee will need to establish in order to meet the eligibility requirements.

---

70. ibid s 111(2)(a).
71. ibid s 95(1)(a).   72. ibid s 95(1)(b).   73. ibid s 95(1)(c).
74. *Essex County Council v Walker* (1972) 7 ITR 280 (NIRC).

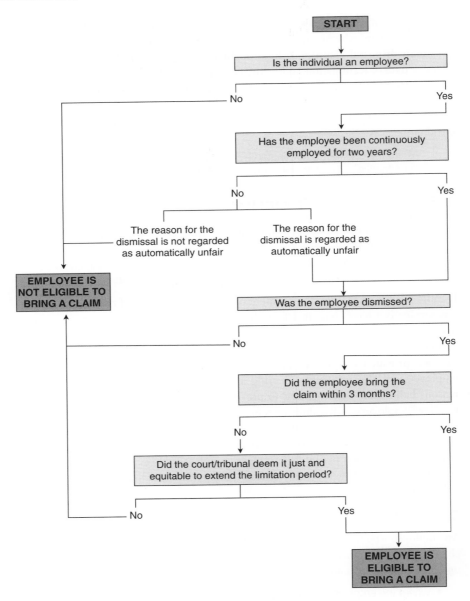

FIGURE 28.1 Eligibility requirements for bringing an unfair dismissal claim

Once an employee has established that he is eligible to bring a claim, the burden of proof is transferred to the employer, who must establish the reason (or, if more than one, the principal reason) for the dismissal.[75] If the employer cannot produce a reason for the dismissal, it will be regarded as unfair. An employee who wishes to discover the reason for his dismissal is aided by s 92(1) of the ERA 1996, which entitles a dismissed employee to request a written statement from the employer, providing details regarding why the dismissal took place, provided that the employee has at least one year's continuous service.[76] Once the employer has provided a reason for

---

75. ERA 1996, s 98(1)(a).　　76. ibid s 92(3).

the dismissal, the task of the employment tribunal is to determine if this was the real reason behind the dismissal. If the tribunal does not believe the employer, or holds that its reasons were inadequate, it may attempt to determine what the real reason for the dismissal was.

Once the employee has established that a dismissal took place and the reason for the dismissal has been determined, the next stage is to determine whether or not the dismissal was unfair. The burden of proof is placed upon the employer to establish that the dismissal was fair, but there are a number of cases in which the employer will be unable to argue that the dismissal was fair, because the law deems certain dismissals to be automatically unfair.

Automatically unfair reasons

A dismissal for certain reasons will automatically be regarded as unfair and cannot be justified by the employer. Further, where such a dismissal occurs, the requirement of two years' continuous service does not apply.[77] Automatically unfair reasons include where the sole or principal reason for the dismissal was:

- that the employee took some form of family leave (for example, maternity or parental leave);[78]
- that the employee carried out activities designed to prevent or reduce risks to health and safety, and had been designated to carry out such activities;[79]
- that the employee refused to work hours that contravened the Working Time Regulations 1998, or that he refused to forego the rights granted by those Regulations;[80]
- that the employee brought proceedings against the employer to enforce a statutory right (for example, the right to the minimum wage);[81]
- that the employee did not disclose the existence of a spent conviction;[82]
- that the employee was dismissed before or after a relevant transfer under the TUPE 2006, and the reason for the dismissal was the transfer;[83]
- that the employee made a 'protected disclosure' (that is, **whistleblowing**).[84]

The Working Time Regulations 1998 are discussed at p 737

The rights of an employee upon the transfer of an undertaking are discussed at p 714

➡ **whistleblowing:** the reporting of alleged misconduct to a person or body inside or outside of the whistleblower's employment

Reasons that are *prima facie* fair

If the reason for the dismissal is not regarded as automatically unfair, then the employer will be given the opportunity to establish that the dismissal was *prima facie* fair. This will require the employer to show that the dismissal fell within one of five reasons set down by s 98 of the ERA 1996. If the employer cannot establish this, the dismissal will be unfair. These reasons will now be discussed, but it should be noted

---

77. ibid s 108(3).
78. ibid s 99.   79. ibid s 100(1)(a).   80. ibid s 101A(1).
81. ibid s 104(1). Section 104(2) provides that it is irrelevant whether or not the employee actually had the right in question.
82. Rehabilitation of Offenders Act 1974, s 4(3)(b). It should be noted that certain professions, such as medical practitioners, barristers, and police officers, are excluded from the operation of the 1974 Act.
83. TUPE 2006, reg 7(1). Regulation 7(2) provides that reg 7(1) does not apply to dismissals that take place for economic, technical, or organizational reasons entailing changes in the workforce.
84. ERA 1996, s 103A.

that they merely establish that a dismissal was *prima facie* fair. Once this is established, the tribunal will then determine the *actual* fairness of the dismissal.

Capability or qualifications

Dismissal due to incapability to perform the job, or a lack of qualifications, is deemed *prima facie* fair.[85] 'Capability' is determined by reference to 'skill, aptitude, health or any other physical or mental quality'.[86] The test employed is a subjective one—namely, that, provided that the employer had reasonable grounds to believe that the employee lacked capability, it will not be necessary to show that the employee actually was objectively incapable.[87] Where an employee lacks capability due to insufficient skill or aptitude, the tribunal must strike a balance between allowing the employer to protect its business by removing an incompetent employee and the need to treat the employee fairly. In practice, this means that the employer should investigate fully the facts that have led to the possibility of dismissal before dismissing the employee. It may be the case that the employee's incompetence is due to a lack of training or supervision, in which case, the tribunal may feel that immediate dismissal is inappropriate and that the employer should instead provide the requisite training.

 Davison v Kent Meters [1975] IRLR 145 (IT)

FACTS: The claimant was employed by the defendant to assemble components. The supervisor demonstrated to the claimant how to assemble the components and then left her to get on with her work. Of the 500 components she assembled, 471 were faulty. She was dismissed.

HELD: The dismissal was unfair. The supervisor should have instructed her more fully and then checked her work after she had assembled a small number of the components.

What should an employer do when faced with an incompetent employee? The Advisory, Conciliation and Arbitration Service (ACAS) provides a Code of Practice on Disciplinary and Grievance Procedures, which provides that:

> Where misconduct is confirmed or the employee is found to be performing unsatisfactorily, it is usual to give the employee a written warning. A further act of misconduct or failure to improve performance would normally result in a final written warning…If an employee's first misconduct or unsatisfactory performance is sufficiently serious, it might be appropriate to move directly to a final written warning. This might occur where the employee's actions have had, or are liable to have, a serious or harmful impact on the organisation…Some acts, termed gross misconduct, are so serious in themselves or have such serious consequences that they may call for dismissal without notice for a first offence.[88]

The courts have expressed similar sentiments, by indicating that the employer should be slow to dismiss an employee, and that a warning and the chance to improve

---

85. ibid s 98(2)(a).   86. ibid s 98(3)(a).
87. *Taylor v Alidair Ltd* [1978] IRLR 82 (CA).
88. ACAS, *Disciplinary and Grievance Procedures* (ACAS 2009) [18]–[22]. The Trade Union and Labour Relations (Consolidation) Act 1992, s 207, provides that, where relevant, employment tribunals must take this Code of Practice into account.

should usually be given. Where, however, the incompetence is sufficiently severe, or where the job is one that requires a high degree of care, immediate dismissal may be justified. Thus, when an airline pilot performed a poor landing that damaged the aircraft, immediate dismissal was justified.[89]

Dismissals of employees deemed incapable due to prolonged or regular illness has proven to be a troublesome area. A particularly severe illness could serve to frustrate the contract,[90] thereby remedying the employer's problem. Conversely, such an illness might also constitute a disability, so that if the employer dismisses the employee, the dismissal might be automatically regarded as unfair on discriminatory grounds. It is reasonably settled that, in determining whether or not a dismissal due to illness was fair, the question that the tribunal should ask is whether it was reasonable for the employer to wait any longer before dismissing the employee.[91] The tribunals and courts have also indicated that usually a full review of the employee's case should be undertaken, which could include obtaining medical evidence. The employee should then be issued with an appropriate warning. Where this warning is not heeded, dismissal will usually be justified.[92]

The extent to which illness can frustrate an employment contract is discussed in 'Illness or injury' at p 785

'Qualifications' is defined as any degree, diploma, or other academic, technical, or professional qualification relevant to the position that the employee held.[93] In practice, very few cases arise in relation to a lack of qualifications, because unqualified applicants tend not to be offered the job in the first place.

Conduct

Dismissal may be justified due to the employee's conduct.[94] Clearly, the facts of the case are all important and examples of misconduct deemed sufficient to justify dismissal include:

- a refusal to obey reasonable and lawful orders (although, usually, the employee will need to be warned of the possibility of dismissal should he continue to disobey orders, unless the misconduct is so serious as to justify summary dismissal, and if the employee refuses to carry out acts that are not within his contractual duties, a dismissal on such grounds is likely to be unfair);[95]
- breach of confidentiality;[96]
- acts of dishonesty;[97]
- failure to disclose unspent convictions;[98] and
- inflicting violence upon another employee.[99]

Criminal conduct is likely to cause the employer to consider dismissal. Crimes committed whilst at work (for example, theft of company property) will almost always provide sufficient grounds for dismissal.[100] Crimes committed outside of work are

---

89. *Taylor v Alidair Ltd* [1978] IRLR 82 (CA).
90. *Notcutt v Universal Equipment Co (London) Ltd* [1986] 1 WLR 641 (CA).
91. *East Lindsey District Council v Daubney* [1977] ICR 566 (EAT).
92. *International Sports Co Ltd v Thomson* [1980] IRLR 340 (EAT).   93. ERA 1996, s 98(3)(b).
94. ibid s 98(2)(b).   95. *Redbridge London Borough Council v Fishman* [1978] ICR 569 (EAT).
96. *Denco Ltd v Joinson* [1991] 1 WLR 330 (EAT).
97. *British Railways Board v Jackson* [1994] IRLR 235 (CA).
98. *Torr v British Railways Board* [1977] ICR 785 (EAT).
99. *Fuller v Lloyds Bank plc* [1991] IRLR 336 (EAT).
100. *Trust House Forte Hotels Ltd v Murphy* [1977] IRLR 186 (EAT).

not per se grounds for dismissal,[101] unless the commission of the crime renders the employee unsuitable to perform his job.

P v Nottinghamshire County Council [1992] ICR 706 (CA)

FACTS: The claimant was employed as a groundsman at a school run by the defendant. The claimant's daughter, who was a pupil at the school, complained to a teacher that the claimant had indecently assaulted her. The defendant, upon discovering that the claimant intended to plead guilty to the offence, suspended him and then dismissed him. The claimant alleged that he was unfairly dismissed.

HELD: Even though the defendant had not investigated whether or not the claimant had committed the alleged crime, the dismissal was deemed fair. Where a defendant pleads guilty or is found guilty, the employer is entitled to believe that the offence was committed. As the offence clearly rendered the claimant unsuitable for a job at a school, the Court held that the dismissal was wholly justified.

 See RA Watt, 'Unfair Dismissal: A Duty to Redeploy in Misconduct Cases?' (1993) 22 ILJ 44

🔗 Redundancy is discussed in detail at p 810

Redundancy

Dismissal due to redundancy is deemed *prima facie* fair.[102] In order to demonstrate that the dismissal is *actually* fair, the EAT has established[103] a number of principles that employers should follow:

- The employer will seek to give as much warning as possible of impending redundancies.
- The employer will consult the union as to the best means by which the desired management result can be achieved fairly and will seek to agree the criteria to be applied in selecting the employees to be made redundant.
- The employer will seek to establish criteria for selection that, so far as possible, do not depend solely upon the opinion of the person making the selection, but can be objectively checked against such things as attendance record, efficiency at the job, experience, or length of service.
- The employer will seek to ensure that the selection is made fairly in accordance with these criteria.
- The employer will seek to see whether, instead of dismissing an employee, he could offer him alternative employment.

Where the employer fails to consult with either the trade union or the employee, the dismissal will normally be unfair, unless the employment tribunal is of the opinion that a reasonable employer would have believed consultation to be utterly futile.[104]

Illegality

A dismissal will be *prima facie* fair where continuing to employ the dismissed employee would breach a statutory provision[105] (for example, continuing to employ

---

101. ACAS, *Disciplinary and Grievance Procedures* (ACAS 2009) [30].   102. ERA 1996, s 98(2)(c).
103. *Williams v Compair Maxam Ltd* [1982] ICR 156 (EAT) 162 (Browne-Wilkinson J).
104. *Mugford v Midland Bank plc* [1997] ICR 399 (EAT).   105. ERA 1996, s 98(2)(d).

a company director who had been disqualified under the Company Directors Disqualification Act 1986).

Some other substantial reason

The previous four categories of *prima facie* fair dismissals operate within relatively narrow confines. Conversely, the final category provides a 'catch-all' provision, which states that a dismissal will be *prima facie* fair if it is for 'some other substantial reason of a kind such as to justify the dismissal of an employee holding the position which the employee held'.[106] The reason for the breadth of this category is that Parliament 'can hardly have hoped to produce an exhaustive catalogue of all the circumstances in which an employer would be justified in terminating the services of an employee'.[107] The tribunals must strike a balance between permitting employees to dismiss employees for justifiable reasons whilst protecting employees from dismissal for trivial reasons. There is little doubt that, in striking this balance, the tribunals have leaned in favour of the employers and the majority of reasons advanced by employers have been accepted as sufficiently substantial.

Examples of dismissals deemed *prima facie* fair by legislation or case law under this category include:

- where an employee is employed in order to cover for another employee who is taking leave on medical grounds, or who is on maternity leave or adoption leave, and, upon that employee's return, the new employee is dismissed;[108]
- where an employee is dismissed following the transfer of an undertaking, and the reason for the dismissal is economic, technical, or organizational;[109]
- where an employee is dismissed because his personality clashes with others to such an extent that it causes the working atmosphere to become intolerable;[110]
- where an employee is dismissed due to his refusal to accept a pay cut that is necessary to avoid the company suffering severe financial difficulties.[111]

Fairness and reasonableness

Once the employer has established that the reason for the dismissal falls within one of the five *prima facie* fair categories discussed, the tribunal will then decide whether or not the employer acted reasonably in dismissing the employee for this reason (that is, whether the dismissal was *actually* fair). Section 98(4)(a) provides that this will depend on 'whether in the circumstances (including the size and administrative resources of the employer's undertaking) the employer acted reasonably or unreasonably in treating the reason as a sufficient reason for dismissing the employee', and s 98(4)(b) provides that the determination of fairness 'shall be determined in accordance with equity and the substantial merits of the case'.

Determining reasonableness

The focus on 'reasonableness' in s 98(4)(a) would appear to indicate that tribunals should take an objective approach when determining the fairness of a dismissal, and

---

106. ibid s 98(1)(b).
107. *RS Components Ltd v Irwin* [1973] ICR 535 (NIRC) 540 (Sir John Brightman).
108. ERA 1996, s 106.   109. TUPE 2006, reg 7(3)(b).
110. *Treganowan v Robert Knee & Co Ltd* [1975] ICR 405 (QB).
111. *St John of God (Care Services) Ltd v Brooks* [1992] IRLR 546 (EAT).

early cases did indeed take such an approach.[112] There has, however, been a move away from a purely objective test, towards a much more subjective test, as the following case demonstrates.

 ***Iceland Frozen Foods Ltd v Jones* [1983] ICR 17 (EAT)**

FACTS: The claimant, a night-shift foreman, was dismissed by the defendant for forgetting to lock up the premises at the end of the night and for allegedly attempting to deceive the defendant into paying extra overtime payments. An industrial tribunal held that the dismissal was unfair, because, in its opinion, the claimant's conduct was not sufficiently serious to warrant dismissal. The defendant appealed.

HELD: The relevant test was not whether, in the tribunal's opinion, the dismissal was reasonable; the tribunal should consider the reasonableness of the employer's conduct, not simply whether it considers his actions to be fair or not. The tribunal should not substitute its decision as to the right course of action for that of the employer. In many cases, the employee's conduct could result in a band of reasonable responses, within which one employer might take one response, whereas another employer might take another. The function of the tribunal is to determine, based on the facts of the case, whether the decision to dismiss comes within this band of reasonable responses. If it does, the dismissal will be fair. If it does not, it will be unfair. As the industrial tribunal had applied the wrong test, the case was remitted to a new tribunal.

★ See Andy Freer, 'The Range of Reasonable Responses Test—From Guidelines to Statute' (1997) 27 ILJ 335

Subsequent cases were critical of this 'band of reasonable responses' test, including one case in which the EAT stated that '[t]here is, in reality, no range or band to be considered, only whether the employer acted reasonably in invoking that sanction'.[113] The chief criticism of the band of reasonable responses test was that it could result in a decision to dismiss being reasonable, and a decision not to dismiss also being deemed reasonable, provided that both reasons were within the band of reasonable responses. Polarized decisions could come within the band of reasonable responses, leading to a test that strongly favours the employer, because only extreme conduct would fall outside the band. The Court of Appeal, however, has strongly disagreed with this criticism and reaffirmed that the band of reasonable responses test was correct.[114]

Procedural fairness

What should an employment tribunal or court do where an employee has acted in a manner that is deserving of dismissal but, when dismissing him, the employer has failed to comply with the correct procedures? When the concept of unfair dismissal was first introduced, a significant number of unfair dismissal cases involved this very question. Initially, the EAT established the 'no difference rule', under which a dismissal would be fair if compliance with the correct procedures would have made no difference to the outcome.[115] In the following case, however, the House of Lords moved away from this rule.

---

112. *Bessenden Properties Ltd v Corness* [1977] ICR 821 (CA).
113. *Haddon v Van Den Bergh Foods Ltd* [1999] ICR 1150 (EAT) 1160 (Morison J).
114. *Post Office v Foley; HSBC Bank plc v Madden* [2000] ICR 1283 (CA).
115. *British Labour Pump v Byrne* [1979] ICR 347 (EAT).

Polkey v AE Dayton Services Ltd [1988] AC 344 (HL)

FACTS: The claimant was one of four van drivers employed by the defendant. The defendant decided to make three of the van drivers redundant. Without any warning, the claimant was called into the manager's office, was informed that he was being made redundant and was sent home. The claimant alleged that, as he had been made redundant without any consultation (consultation was required by the defendant's code of practice), he had been unfairly dismissed. The defendant stated that it would have made the claimant redundant, even if a consultation had taken place. Due to this, an employment tribunal, the EAT and the Court of Appeal held that the dismissal was fair. The claimant appealed.

HELD: The question that should be considered was whether the employer had been reasonable or unreasonable in deciding that his reason for dismissing the employee was a sufficient reason. Whether the decision not to comply with the relevant procedures would render the dismissal unfair was for the tribunal to consider, in light of the circumstances known to the employer at the time the dismissal occurred. Accordingly, the 'no difference rule' was overruled, the appeal was allowed, and the case was remitted to a differently constituted tribunal.

In 2002, in an attempt to reduce the number of procedural cases reaching tribunals, statutory disciplinary and dismissal procedures were introduced,[116] with s 98A(1) of the ERA 1996 providing that where these procedures apply and where, due to a failure wholly or partly attributable to the employer, these procedures are not complied with, the dismissal is automatically unfair, unless following these procedures would have made no difference to the decision whether or not to dismiss the employee (in other words, the 'no difference rule' was resurrected and *Polkey* was reversed). These statutory procedures and s 98A have now been repealed and *Polkey* once again provides the leading authority on the failure to follow correct procedures.

Figure 28.2 helps to clarify the process by which the tribunal determines whether a dismissal is fair or unfair.

Remedies

The ERA 1996 specifies three remedies for unfair dismissal—namely, reinstatement, re-engagement, and compensation. Once a dismissal is deemed unfair, the tribunal will explain to the claimant that it has the power to order his reinstatement or re-engagement and will ask whether or not the claimant would want such a remedy. Should a tribunal fail to do this, it will not render a decision as to compensation a nullity, but if, as a result, unfairness or injustice is caused, then the case should be sent back to an employment tribunal.[117]

Reinstatement and re-engagement

The ERA 1996 provides that a tribunal or court may make an order for reinstatement or an order for re-engagement (collectively referred to as 're-employment orders'). Where the court makes an order for reinstatement, 'the employer shall treat the complainant in all respects as if he had not been dismissed'.[118] In other words, the claimant

---

116. Employment Act 2002, Sch 2, Pt 1 (now repealed).
117. *Cowley v Manson Timber Ltd* [1995] ICR 367 (CA).   118. ERA 1996, s 114(1).

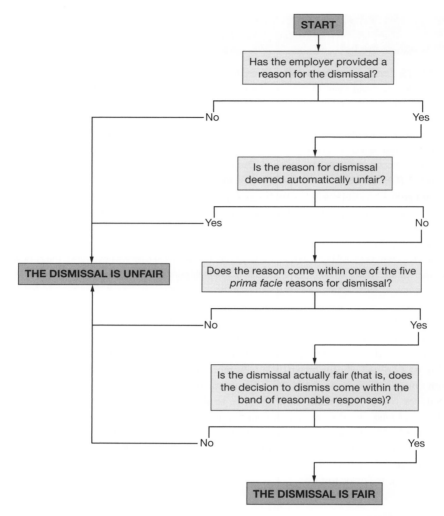

FIGURE 28.2 Is the dismissal unfair?

should be given his old job back on the same terms and conditions as before. He will be entitled to any benefits that he should have received whilst he was dismissed—notably, back pay.[119] The tribunal will specify a date on which the reinstatement is to occur.

A tribunal will be unlikely to order reinstatement where the claimant does not wish to be reinstated, where it would be unjust to order reinstatement (for example, because the claimant contributed in some way to his dismissal), or where it is not practicable for the employer to reinstate the claimant.[120] If the tribunal considers that reinstatement is not appropriate, it should consider making an order for re-engagement (re-engagement should not be considered until reinstatement is ruled out).[121] Where an order for re-engagement is made, the employee will not get his old job back, but must be given 'employment comparable to that from which he

119. ibid s 114(2)(a).   120. ibid s 116(1).
121. *Pirelli General Cable Works Ltd v Murray* [1979] IRLR 190 (EAT).

was dismissed or other suitable employment'.[122] As with reinstatement, the claimant is entitled to any benefits that he would have received whilst he was dismissed.[123]

In practice, orders for reinstatement and re-engagement are not made very often for the same reasons that discourage the courts from enforcing the contract in wrongful dismissal cases—namely, that the relationship of mutual trust and confidence will usually have broken down to such an extent that forcing the two parties to work together would be inappropriate.

As noted in Chapter 25, a recurring problem faced by tribunals is the inability to enforce their decisions. If an employer refuses to re-employ the claimant or does not fully comply with a re-employment order, the tribunal cannot hold the employer in contempt of court or impose a fine. All that the tribunal can do is, upon an application from the claimant, increase the compensation ordered via an 'additional award', which will amount to between twenty-six and fifty-two weeks' pay.[124]

Compensation

Compensation awards for unfair dismissal consist of two parts:

1. the basic award, which aims to reward service (and discourage unfair dismissals); and
2. the compensatory award, which aims to compensate the claimant's actual loss.

The basic award is calculated via a set formula, and is heavily dependent upon the length of the employee's service and his age. The basic award is calculated by multiplying the employee's weekly pay by the number of years' continuous service. Three points should be noted. First, the weekly pay is subject to a maximum limit and this is usually increased every year (as of April 2014, the maximum is £464).[125] Second, his weekly pay is multiplied by the number of years' continuous service accrued at the effective date of termination. This, too, is subject to a maximum limit—namely, twenty years.[126] Where an employee has over twenty years' continuous service, only those twenty years preceding the effective date of termination will count. Third, older employees receive more basic compensation than younger employees, based on the following formula:[127]

- for each year served during which the employee was under the age of 22, he shall receive half a week's pay;
- for each year served during which the employee was aged 22 or over, but under the age of 41, he shall receive one week's pay;
- for each year served during which the employee was aged 41 or over, he shall receive one-and-a-half weeks' pay.

For each age range that applies, the following formula should be used:

Weekly wage × number of years continuous service × weeks' pay = basic award

The following examples demonstrate how the basic award is calculated.

---

122. ERA 1996, s 115(1).
123. ibid s 115(2)(d).
124. ibid s 117(3). As of April 2014, a week's pay is limited to £464 (ERA 1996, s 186(1)), but it is likely that this figure will rise in 2015.
125. ibid s 186(1).   126. ibid s 119(3).   127. ibid s 119(2).

Calculating the basic award (based on figures as of April 2014)

Arthur

Arthur is unfairly dismissed at the age of 64, after working for his employer for thirty-five years. At the time of dismissal, he earned £550 per week. Arthur can claim for a maximum of twenty years, ending on the date of termination. He will therefore claim for the twenty years during which he was aged between 44 and 64. As he was over the age of 41 during this period, he will receive one-and-a-half weeks' pay for each of the twenty years. As he earns over the maximum weekly limit, the week's pay will be limited to £464 per week. Accordingly:

$$£\ 464\ (\text{weekly wage}) \times 20\ (\text{number of year's service})$$
$$\times 1.5\ (\text{one-and-a-half weeks' pay} =)\ £13,920$$

Therefore, Arthur's basic award of compensation is £13,920

Gwen

Gwen is unfairly dismissed at the age of 43, after working for her employer for fifteen years. Her weekly wage is £300. Of these fifteen years, two were served after the age of 41, and the remaining thirteen were served over the age of 22, but under the age of 41. Accordingly:

$$£300\ (\text{weekly wage}) \times 2\ (\text{number of years served whilst over the age of 41}) \times 1.5$$
$$(\text{one-and-a-half weeks' pay}) = £300$$
$$\text{plus}$$
$$£300\ (\text{weekly wage}) \times 13\ (\text{number of years served whilst over the}$$
$$\text{age of 22, but under the age of 41}) \times 1\ (\text{one week's pay}) = £3,900$$

$$= £4,800$$

Therefore, Gwen's basic award of compensation is £4,800.

Whilst the basic award is subject to a maximum (currently £13,920),[128] it is generally not subject to a minimum amount. In certain situations (for example, where the employee is dismissed due to redundancy), however, a minimum award is applicable.[129] At the time of writing, this minimum is £5,676.

In several cases, a tribunal has the power to reduce the basic award:[130]

- where the employer has offered to reinstate the employee and the employee has unreasonably refused the offer;
- where the tribunal considers that any conduct of the claimant before the dismissal was such that it would be just and equitable to reduce, or to reduce further, the amount of the basic award;
- where the employee has already received a redundancy payment, this must be deducted from the basic award.

---

128. This figure is based on a person claiming the maximum weekly pay for the maximum number of years at one-and-a-half weeks' pay (as Arthur in our example did).

129. ERA 1996, s 120.

130. ibid s 122.

The rules regarding mitigation of loss do not apply to the basic award (as opposed to the compensatory award, to which the rules relating to mitigation of loss do apply).

Whereas the basic award compensates the claimant for his years of service, the compensatory award aims to provide the claimant with an amount that is 'just and equitable in all the circumstances having regard to the loss sustained by the complainant in consequence of the dismissal'.[131] At the time of writing, the maximum compensatory award that can be awarded is £76,574 or one year's annual gross salary (whichever is the lower).[132]

The compensatory award is in addition to the basic award and, as it is calculated based on what is just and equitable, the tribunal has considerable discretion. In order to avoid this discretion becoming overly vague, a number of heads of damage have been established and tribunals should set out in their judgments the amount of compensation under each head.[133] The principal heads of damage are:

- **Immediate loss of earnings** This would be the loss of pay that the employee has sustained from the date of dismissal up to the date of the hearing.

- **Manner of dismissal** This would relate to the loss that the employee could sustain in the future due to being dismissed (for example, if the dismissal will make it more difficult for him to obtain employment). If the dismissal does not make the employee less likely to obtain work, no compensation should be awarded under this head.

- **Future loss of earnings** The aim of this head of damage is to compensate the claimant for the period following the hearing during which he is likely to remain unemployed. The burden of proof in establishing this will be placed on the claimant. If the employee has already gained employment, no compensation should be awarded under this head, unless the salary being paid is less than that paid under the original employment. In that case, the tribunal should determine how long it will take to reach the salary that would have been paid had the employee not been dismissed.

- **Loss of rights** Certain statutory rights (such as the right to claim unfair dismissal or the right to redundancy pay) are based on a minimum period of continuous service. Unfair dismissal breaks the period of continuous service and affects the availability of these rights. The claimant should be compensated for any rights lost due to the dismissal.

- **Loss of pension rights** The claimant should be compensated for any loss caused to his pension entitlements due to the dismissal. Such losses can be significant, especially if the employee cannot transfer his existing pension rights to a new employer.

- **Loss of other benefits** In addition to loss of earnings, the claimant is entitled to be compensated for the loss of any benefit that he would have expected to obtain but for the dismissal[134] (for example, company car, health insurance, etc).

The claimant should take reasonable steps to mitigate the above losses, and failure to do so may result in the compensatory award being reduced.[135] It follows that any reasonable expenses incurred in mitigating the loss (for example, travel expenses incurred in attending interviews) can also be recovered.

---

131. ibid s 123(1).
132. ibid s 124(1). Section 124(1A) does provide that, in certain cases, this maximum will not apply (e.g. health and safety cases).   133. *Norton Tool Co Ltd v Tewson* [1973] 1 WLR 45 (NIRC).
134. ERA 1996, s 123(2)(b).   135. ibid s 123(4).

Redundancy

The entitlement to redundancy pay was first introduced by the Redundancy Payments Act 1965 and can now be found in s 135 of the ERA 1996. The majority of redundancies are negotiated in advance, following consultation with trade unions and employees. In such cases, little dispute arises, and this is evidenced by the available statistics. In 2012–13, around 563,000 people were made redundant,[136] yet employment tribunals heard only 12,748 claims involving redundancy pay and an additional 11,075 claims in relation to the failure to consult.[137] Just like the right not to be unfairly dismissed, the right to receive redundancy pay is conditional upon eligibility requirements being satisfied.

Eligibility

A person wishing to claim redundancy pay must meet three eligibility requirements. The first requirement is that the employee has at least three years' continuous service.[138] The second requirement is that the employee was dismissed, with the following constituting dismissal for the purposes of claiming redundancy pay:

- where the employer terminates the employment, with or without notice;[139]
- where a fixed-term employment contract expires and is not renewed;[140]
- where an employee resigns due to the conduct of the employer (that is, constructive dismissal);[141]
- where an act of the employer or an event occurring to the employer causes the contract to be terminated by the operation of law (for example, frustration).[142]

The third requirement is that the employee is not an employee shareholder, as such employees do not have the right to claim redundancy pay.[143]

What constitutes redundancy?

Redundancy pay is only payable to persons dismissed 'by reason of redundancy'.[144] Accordingly, it is fundamental that employers are aware of what constitutes redundancy. Section 139(1) of the ERA 1996 provides that redundancy occurs where the dismissal is wholly or mainly attributable to:

- the fact that the employer has ceased, or intends to cease to carry on the business for the purposes of which the employee was employed by him; or has ceased to carry on that business in the place where the employee was so employed; or
- the fact that the requirements of the business for the following have ceased or diminished, or are expected to cease or diminish:
  (a) for employees to carry out work of that particular kind; or
  (b) for employees to carry out work of a particular kind in the place where the employer employed the employee.

---

136. Statistics extrapolated from the Office of National Statistics' *Labour Market Statistics.*
137. Statistics derived from <https://www.gov.uk/government/collections/tribunals-statistics>.
138. ERA 1996, s 155.   139. ibid s 136(1)(a).   140. ibid s 136(1)(b).
141. ibid s 136(1)(c).   142. ibid s 136(5).   143. Ibid s 205A(2)(d).   144. ibid s 135.

This definition indicates that a dismissal will amount to redundancy in three situations, which will now be examined.

Cessation of the business

Where the employer completely ceases the business in which the employees are employed, the resulting dismissals will constitute redundancies. Where the business is taken over by another, however, its employment contracts will also usually be taken on by the new owner, and there will be no dismissals and no redundancies.

 The rules relating to employment contracts upon the transfer of a business are discussed at p 714

Cessation of the business at a particular location

Businesses will often operate in numerous locations. Where an employer ceases business in one location, any resulting dismissals will constitute redundancies even though the employer continues business elsewhere. In many cases, there will be no dispute, but where the employee's contract of employment contains a mobility clause, this issue is more complex.

A mobility clause is a term of the contract that can require the employee to work at a different location from that at which he normally works. Where such employees work in several different locations, and one of these locations is closed down and the employee is dismissed for refusing to move to another location, does the dismissal constitute a redundancy? The courts used to take a strict contractual approach to answering this question, as the following case demonstrates.

 Rank Xerox Ltd v Churchill [1988] IRLR 280 (EAT)

FACTS: The defendant employed the six claimants in its London headquarters. The claimants' contracts of employment provided that they would be based in London, but added that they might be required to transfer to another location. The defendant decided to move its headquarters to Marlow, but the claimants refused to move. They left the employment and claimed redundancy.

HELD: The phrase 'the place where the employee was so employed' contained in s 139(1) referred not to the actual place of work, but to where they could be required to work under their contract. Accordingly, the claimant's place of work still existed, meaning that they had not been made redundant. They had resigned.

In *Rank Xerox*, the EAT focused on the contract of employment to determine 'the place where the employee was so employed'. Recent cases have, however, moved away from a contractual test and held that a geographical test is more appropriate.

Bass Leisure Ltd v Thomas [1994] IRLR 104 (EAT)[145]

FACTS: The claimant was employed by the defendant at a depot in Coventry, which was about 10 minutes' drive from her home. Her employment contract provided that she could be transferred to a suitable alternative place of work. The defendant closed the Coventry

---

145. Affirmed by *High Table Ltd v Horst* [1998] ICR 409 (CA).

depot and the claimant was offered employment at another depot around 20 miles away. She refused to move, terminated her employment, and claimed redundancy pay.

HELD: She had been made redundant. The place of work could not be extended to anywhere she might be contractually required to work; instead, the place of work should be determined geographically by asking where the claimant actually works. Based on this test, she worked in the Coventry depot, and, because it had closed, her dismissal was due to the closure and so had been made redundant.

 On how this case affects mobility clauses, see Andrew Williamson, '*High Table v Horst:* Are Mobility Clauses Redundant?' (1998) 142 SJ 394

Diminution in the need for labour

The demand for a business' products or services may lessen to such an extent that the employer does not need, or cannot afford, to employ the current number of employees. Alternatively, certain employees may not be required for other reasons (for example, where certain processes become automated). Where employees are no longer required to carry out 'work of that particular kind', are such employees made redundant or not? The question revolves around defining what 'work of that particular kind' means. Initially, two tests were developed:

1. **The 'functional' test** This test focused on the work that the employee actually did and asked whether or not this type of work was still required. If it were not, the employee's dismissal would constitute redundancy.

2. **The 'contract' test** This test focused not on the work that the employee actually did, but on what work the employee could be required to do under the contract. Only where this contractual work was no longer required could the dismissal be said to amount to redundancy.

For a time, the contract test was the more favoured, but, in the following case, the EAT held that both tests were incorrect and a new, three-stage, 'statutory' test was introduced.

🔑 *Safeway Stores plc v Burrell* [1997] ICR 523 (EAT)

FACTS: The defendant employed the claimant as the manager of a petrol station. The defendant reorganized the management structure. Under the new structure, the post of petrol station manager would disappear and be replaced by petrol station controller. This new post paid around £2,000 less than the post of manager. Accordingly, the claimant refused to apply for the post and terminated his employment. The claimant accepted the redundancy pay that he was offered, but subsequently alleged that he had not been made redundant and had been unfairly dismissed. The two lay members of an industrial tribunal applied the functional test and held that there was no redundancy, whereas the chairman applied the contract test and argued that the claimant had been made redundant. The defendant appealed.

HELD: The EAT held that both the functional test and the contract test were flawed. The correct approach was to adopt a three-stage 'statutory' test, as follows.

1. Was the employee dismissed?
2. If so, had the requirements of the employer's business for employees to carry out work of a particular kind ceased or diminished, or were they expected to cease or diminish?
3. If so, was the dismissal of the employee caused wholly or mainly by the cessation or diminution?

As the industrial tribunal had applied the wrong test, the appeal was allowed, and the EAT held that a fresh industrial tribunal should hear the case and determine whether or not the dismissal was due to redundancy.

COMMENT: The House of Lords[146] has approved the three-stage statutory test established by the EAT in *Safeway Stores* and it must therefore be regarded as the correct test.

⭐ See Catherine Barnard, 'Redundant Approaches to Redundancy' (2000) 59 CLJ 36

Redundancy selection procedures and consultation

The EAT has established[147] a number of principles that employers should follow when making redundancies. These were discussed when those instances in which a redundancy can constitute an unfair dismissal were examined. Here, the procedure relating to consultation will be discussed in slightly more detail.

🔗 The principles that should be followed when making redundancies are discussed at p 802

Where redundancies are to be made, the employer should consult the trade union as to the best means by which the desired management result can be achieved fairly and will seek to agree the criteria to be applied in selecting the employees to be made redundant. Statute has gone further and provided that, where an employer is to make redundant twenty or more employees at one establishment within a period of ninety days or less, the employer is under a statutory duty to consult with the appropriate trade union representatives.[148] This consultation must take place at least thirty days before any redundancies are made, except where the employer proposes to make a hundred or more redundancies, in which case, this period increases to at least forty-five days.[149] In both cases, the employer must notify the Secretary of State of the redundancy proposal and failure to do so constitutes a criminal offence.[150] The consultation must include discussions on avoiding the dismissals, reducing the number of dismissals, and mitigating the consequences of those dismissals that do have to be made.[151]

Where the employer or the trade union fails to comply with any of the above requirements, the claimant may make a complaint to an employment tribunal. If the complaint is upheld, the employment tribunal may make a declaration, or it may make a protective award, which requires the employer to pay the claimant remuneration during the protected period. This period begins on either the date on which the first of the redundancies are made or the date on which the award is made, whichever is the earlier.[152] The award will continue for such length as the tribunal thinks just and equitable, up to a maximum of ninety days.

Calculating and recovering redundancy pay

Redundancy pay is calculated in exactly the same way as the basic award of compensation for unfair dismissal,[153] except that there is no discretion to reduce the pay where the employee contributed to the dismissal. An employee who has been made

🔗 The calculation of the basic award is discussed in 'Compensation' at p 807

---

146. *Murray v Foyle Meats Ltd* [2000] 1 AC 51 (HL).

147. *Williams v Compair Maxam Ltd* [1982] ICR 156 (EAT) 162 (Browne-Wilkinson J).

148. Trade Union and Labour Relations (Consolidation) Act 1992, s 188(1). However, it should be noted that in *USDAW v Ethel Austin Ltd and Others* [2013] IRLR 686 (EAT), the EAT held that s 188(1) should be read so as to omit the words 'at one establishment', as this limitation was not found in the Directive that led to the enactment of s 188.   149. ibid s 188(1A).   150. ibid s 194(1).

151. ibid s 188(2).   152. ibid s 189(4)(a).   153. ERA 1996, s 162.

redundant has no right to compensatory pay (for example, along the lines of the compensatory award to which an unfairly dismissed employee is entitled). For this reason, given the choice, a claim for unfair dismissal can be preferable. An employer should provide the employee with a written statement indicating how the redundancy pay was calculated. An employer who fails to do this commits a criminal offence.[154] If, following this failure, the employee requests a written statement and the employer, without reasonable excuse, fails to provide one, a further offence is committed.[155]

One of the principal reasons for making an employee redundant is because the employer lacks the financial means to continue to employ him. It is likely that such an employer also lacks the ability to pay the requisite redundancy pay. Where the employer has refused or failed to pay the requisite redundancy pay, and either the employee has taken all reasonable steps (other than legal proceedings) to recover payment or the employer is insolvent, the employee can apply to the Secretary of State for payment.[156] This payment will come from the National Insurance Fund and the employer will be required to pay the money back to the Secretary of State, who will pay any money received into the Fund.[157]

Loss of the right to redundancy pay

An employee who is entitled to redundancy pay may engage in acts that cause him to lose this entitlement, including:

- Where the employee commits an act that entitles his employer to terminate his employment contract without notice, he loses the right to redundancy pay, provided that the dismissal is (i) without notice; or (ii) with a period of notice that is shorter than would be required but for the conduct; or (iii) by giving notice that includes, or is accompanied by, a statement in writing that the employer would, by reason of the employee's conduct, be entitled to terminate the contract without notice.[158]

- Where an employee, upon being made redundant, is offered suitable alternative employment or a renewal of the contract by his employer, and the employee unreasonably refuses, he loses his entitlement to redundancy pay.[159]

- Where an employer has given notice of termination and the employee, having then taken part in strike action during the period of notice, fails to comply with a notice extending the notice period for a number of days equivalent to those lost through strike action, he will lose his entitlement to redundancy pay.[160]

Chapter conclusion

With the exception of a claim for wrongful dismissal, the rights and obligations relating to the termination of employment derive almost exclusively from statute. In many cases, the obligations are absolute and cannot be avoided or excluded. Breach of these obligations will, in many cases, provide the claimant with the opportunity to obtain compensation from an employment tribunal. It is therefore crucial that any business or employer that is

---

154. ibid s 165(2). 155. ibid s 165(4). 156. ibid s 166. 157. ibid s 167.
158. ibid s 140(1). 159. ibid s 141(2). 160. ibid s 143.

considering terminating a contract of employment has a thorough understanding of the obligations placed upon them and the accompanying rights of the dismissed employee. Failure to do so could cost the employer dear and may even constitute a criminal offence.

Key points summary

- An employee whose employment contract is terminated in a manner that does not constitute dismissal cannot claim that he was wrongfully or unfairly dismissed and is not entitled to redundancy pay.

- Where the employee voluntarily resigns, there will be no dismissal.

- Where the employment contract becomes frustrated, this will not constitute a dismissal for the purposes of unfair dismissal, but will constitute a dismissal for the purposes of redundancy payment.

- The death of the employer may constitute dismissal, depending on the circumstances.

- Where both parties agree freely to the discharge of the employment contract, this will not amount to a dismissal.

- Either party can terminate a contract by giving notice. Where the employer gives notice, the termination will amount to dismissal. Where the employee gives notice, the termination will usually not amount to dismissal.

- Where a limited-term contract expires without renewal, the employee will be regarded as dismissed.

- Summary dismissal without notice occurs due to the conduct of the employee. Constructive dismissal occurs where the employee resigns due to the conduct of the employer.

- Where, in breach of contract, the employer terminates the contract of employment, the termination may constitute a wrongful dismissal.

- The primary remedy for wrongful dismissal is damages, but in exceptional cases, the tribunal may be willing to enforce the contract by granting an injunction. A declaration can also be made.

- Employees have the right not to be unfairly dismissed, provided that they have at least two years' continuous service. Where a dismissal is automatically unfair, this requirement does not apply.

- The employer must provide a reason for the dismissal. Failure to do so will make the dismissal unfair. The employer must then establish that the dismissal was for one of five *prima facie* fair reasons. If the dismissal was not for one of these reasons, it will be unfair.

- A *prima facie* fair dismissal can still be unfair if the decision to dismiss was not within the band of reasonable responses.

- A tribunal may also order that the unfairly dismissed employee be reinstated to his old job or re-engaged to a similar job.

- The principal remedy for unfair dismissal is an award of compensation, which consists of a basic award that is based on length of service, and a compensatory award that is based on the employee's actual loss.

- Redundancy occurs where an employee is dismissed because (i) the business ceases; (ii) the place of business at which the employee carries on work ceases to exist; or (iii) the need for labour diminishes.

- Employees made redundant are entitled to redundancy pay provided that they have two years' continuous service.

- Redundancy pay is calculated in the same way as the basic award of compensation for unfair dismissal. Redundant employees are not entitled to an additional element of compensatory pay.

Self-test questions

1. Define the following:
   (a) resignation;
   (b) notice;
   (c) limited-term contract;
   (d) constructive dismissal;
   (e) summary dismissal;
   (f) redundancy.

2. Claire is a compensation consultant. She is employed by OmniCorp plc to review the remuneration packages of the directors. The contract of employment provides that the contract will last six months and that she will complete her review within that time. She will be paid £2,000 per month. She completes the review after only two months and hands it to the board of OmniCorp. Because OmniCorp no longer needs Claire's services, it terminates the contract of employment. Advise Claire of her legal position.

3. Explain the distinction between wrongful dismissal and unfair dismissal. When is it preferable to claim for one as opposed to the other?

4. What is the distinction between reinstatement and re-engagement? How does the calculation of redundancy pay differ from the calculation of compensation for unfair dismissal?

5. Food-Mart plc decides to make 150 employees redundant. The management selects the 150 employees and the employees are given six weeks' notice (the contracts of employment entitle them to eight weeks' notice) and are told that they will receive redundancy pay. Has Food-Mart complied with the law and should the employees accept the redundancy pay?

Further reading

Hugh Collins, *Nine Proposals for the Reform of the Law on Unfair Dismissal* (Institute of Employment Rights 2004)
Examines the strengths and weaknesses of the law relating to unfair dismissal, and suggests options for reform aimed at increasing the right not to be unfairly dismissed

Andy Freer, 'The Range of Reasonable Responses Test—From Guidelines to Statute' (1997) 27 ILJ 335

Discusses the 'reasonable responses' test used to determine whether a dismissal was fair and contends that the test heavily favours employers

Sinom Honeyball, *Honeyball & Bowers' Textbook on Employment Law* (12th edn, OUP 2012) ch 9

Analyses in depth the law relating to statutory redundancy payments and the accompanying procedures

Gillian S Morris and Bob Hepple, 'The Employment Act 2002 and the Crisis of Individual Employment Rights' (2002) 31 ILJ 245

Discusses the reforms and procedures introduced by the Employment Act 2002, and argues that the Act downgrades the importance of procedural fairness

Ian Smith and Aaron Baker, *Smith & Wood's Employment Law* (11th edn, OUP 2013) chs 6, 7, and 8

Provides a detailed account of the law relating to the termination of employment, unfair dismissal and redundancy

Websites

<http://www.acas.org.uk>

The official website of the Advisory, Conciliation and Arbitration Service; provides access to numerous useful reports and research publications

 Remember to visit the **Online Resource Centre** at **<http://www.oxfordtextbooks.co.uk/orc/roach3e>** to access the following resources on Chapter 28, 'The termination of employment': more **practice questions** and answers; a **glossary** of key terms; **multiple-choice questions**; **revision summaries**; and **diagrams** in pdf. Updates to the law can be found on Twitter by following **@UKBusinessLaw**.

Appendix 1: Additional chapters

Seven bonus chapters will be available through our Online Resource Centre on topics including business ethics, corporate governance, consumer credit transactions, sales of goods, and unfair commercial practices. These bonus chapters will help you gain a more holistic appreciation of the law, especially for those studying for CIMA or ACCA.

These chapters are available free of charge to all readers of the book. To access them please follow the instructions below:

1. Go to: www.oxfordtextbooks.co.uk/orc/roach3e/
2. Click on the 'Bonus chapters' link
3. Enter the login details (case sensitive)
   - **Username:** Roach3e
   - **Password:** businesslaw

Business ethics

Throughout *Card & James' Business Law* we discussed how the law regulates conduct that, whilst lawful, can be used for unlawful purposes, or in an unlawful way. For example, exclusion clauses are not per se unlawful, but the law provides that certain clauses will be regarded as unlawful and therefore unenforceable. The law does not only seek to ensure that businesses act in a lawful manner, but also aims to ensure that businesses act in an ethical manner too. In this chapter, we examine the prohibitions on four significant areas of unethical conduct. In some cases, the conduct will result in civil liability, but the majority of the forms of conduct discussed in this chapter are deemed so unethical that criminal liability can be imposed. The four areas of unethical conduct examined are:

1. The offence of fraudulent trading
2. Market abuse
3. The offence of insider dealing, and
4. Money laundering.

Consumer credit

Understanding the laws relating to the provision of credit is vital for both businesses and consumers alike. Most of us will at some point in our lives purchase goods, or obtain a service, through the use of credit, be it through a simple bank loan, the use of an overdraft facility, or the granting of a mortgage to purchase a house. In the vast majority of cases, the credit that we obtain will be provided by a business, whose bargaining power may dwarf that of their customers. Accordingly, the person obtaining the credit needs to be protected from unscrupulous businesses, who might seek to impose unfair terms of vulnerable debtors (e.g. extortionate rates of interest). Therefore, the law puts in place numerous safeguards to protect debtors from those persons that provide credit to others. Creditors must be aware of and adhere to the safeguards and procedures put in place, and failure to do so could result in the credit agreement being unenforceable, or the creditor committing a criminal offence. In this chapter, the law relating to the provision of consumer credit will be examined, including a discussion of the most common forms of credit agreement.

Corporate governance

In recent years, largely due to corporate scandals such as Enron, Parmalat, and BCCI, there has been an explosion of interest in corporate governance. One could be forgiven for thinking that corporate governance is therefore a relatively new topic, but this is most certainly not the case. The term 'corporate governance' may be of relatively recent origin, but the theoretical foundations of the topic were being debated before the registered company even existed. However, whilst the topic itself is not new, it is only in the last two decades that the topic has started to receive the attention it has always deserved.

Historically, it could be argued that corporate governance formed an arcane and largely theoretical branch of company law. Today, it could legitimately be argued that company law is now a branch of corporate governance and, whilst the topic may have originated in a legal area, it has since spilled over to become a topic that also encompasses finance, accounting, economics, marketing and many other business disciplines.

Corporate governance is too large a topic to cover comprehensively in a single book, let alone a single chapter. Accordingly, our discussion will focus on a few key areas and developments. First, we will discuss what corporate governance actually is. Second, we will examine the evolution of the UK's corporate governance regime, noting especially the heavy reliance on non-legal reports and codes. Finally, we will analyse a number of corporate governance mechanisms that have risen to prominence in recent years.

The economic torts

This chapter discusses a group of torts that were established to protect the interests of businesses from unlawful interference by others. Unfortunately, in recent years, many books and law courses have neglected these so called 'economic torts' but, from the point of view of businesses, they can be extremely important. The torts discussed in this chapter include:

- Inducing breach of contract
- Conspiracy

- Passing off, and
- Unlawful interference with trade

The sale of goods

The Sale of Goods Act 1979 (SGA 1979) is one of the most important Acts on the statute book. Its importance to both businesses and consumers cannot be overestimated and the Act dominates the law in relation to the sale of goods. Virtually all businesses will, in some form or another, buy or sell goods. It is therefore crucial that business persons have a thorough understanding of the SGA 1979 and the rights, duties, obligations and remedies it provides for. In chapter 7, we discussed terms of the contract and noted that a contract can consist of much more than its express terms, and that businesses must be aware of any terms that can be implied into the contract. The SGA 1979 contains perhaps the most important implied terms found in English law and these will be discussed in detail. Equally important is knowledge of the duties that parties to a sale of goods contract are subject to. Businesses purchasing goods are subject to duties regarding payment and businesses that sell goods are subject to duties regarding the delivery of goods. Finally, if a party to a sale of goods contract breaches a term implied by the SGA 1979 or a duty imposed by the Act, it will be fundamental for the other party to appreciate what remedies are available and what limits are placed upon those remedies.

Unfair commercial practices

The chapters on the law of contract noted that many businesses, when contracting with others, will contract on pre-drafted standard terms designed to facilitate the business' aims. In consumer contracts, given the inequality of bargaining power between the consumer and the business, the business, if left unchecked, could impose all manner of onerous or unfair terms on the consumer. Businesses may engage in unfair practices in order to encourage persons to enter into contract for its goods or services. The latter half of the twentieth century has witnessed an explosion in legislation designed to combat the use of unfair business practices. In some cases, the practice is prohibited and any contracts resulting from it are deemed unenforceable. In other cases, the law goes further and deems such practices to be criminal offences warranting substantial punishments. In this chapter, we shall examine a selection of the principal unfair and criminal commercial and consumer practices and discuss how the law has attempted to curtail such practices.

Environmental law

Laws that protect the environment are mentioned throughout the text. When directors' duties were discussed in Chapter 22, it was noted that directors, when acting in a manner that promotes the success of the company, must have regard to 'the impact of the company's operations on the community and the environment.'[1] A business that engages in activity that damages the environment may be found liable for committing the torts of negligence, nuisance or *Rylands v Fletcher*. These established areas of law, however, are not concerned per se with protecting the environment. That goal is left to a more recently established area of the law called environmental law.

As businesses are increasingly being required to consider the environmental impacts of their activities, the field of environmental law has become more important. Compliance with environmental law can impose substantial costs upon businesses but, as will be seen, if businesses fail to fully appreciate the need to protect the environment, the costs will not only be greater, they will be borne by us all.

Environmental law is an extremely broad topic and a detailed analysis is beyond the scope of this text. This chapter will instead focus on how the law seeks to address two principal environmental issues, namely (i) air pollution and climate change, and (ii) water pollution. In addition, the chapter will discuss the various sources of environmental law.

---

1. CA 2006, s 172(1)(d).

table of cases

table of legislation

Statutory Instruments

European Union Legal Acts

Treaties and Conventions

index

M